W9-CEJ-255

A LANIER GUIDE

THE COMPLETE GUIDE TO

Bed & Breakfasts

THE ORIGINAL:
Often Imitated,
Never Equaled!

INNS & GUESTHOUSES / INTERNATIONAL

Pamela Lanier

The best loved, best selling guide to over 4,000 inns – Over 2.5 million copies in print!

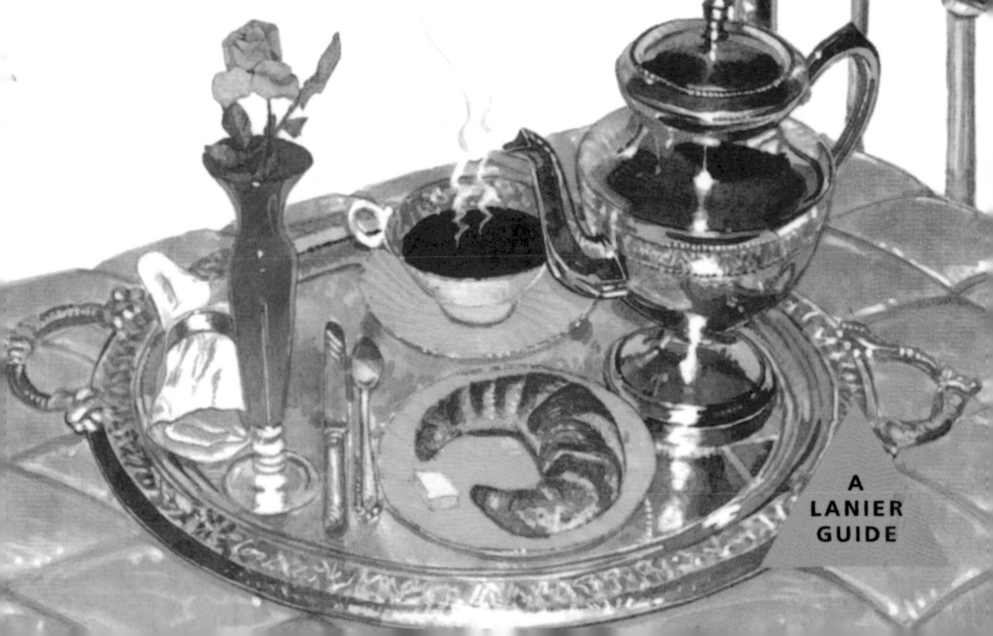

A LANIER GUIDE

What they're saying about

The Complete Guide to Bed & Breakfasts, Inns & Guesthouses . . .

. . . all necessary information about facilities, prices, pets, children, amenities, credit cards and the like. Like France's Michelin . . .

— New York Times

Definitive and worth the room in your reference library.

— Los Angeles Times

. . . innovative and useful . . .

—Washington Post

A must for the adventurous . . . who still like the Hobbity creature comforts.

— St. Louis Post-Dispatch

What has long been overdue: a list of the basic information of where, how much and what facilities are offered at the inns and guesthouses.

— San Francisco Examiner

Standing out from the crowd for its thoroughness and helpful cross-indexing . . .

—Chicago Sun Times

A quaint, charming and economical way to travel—all in one book.

— Waldenbooks (as seen in USA Today)

Little descriptions provide all the essentials: romance, historical landmarks, golf/fishing, gourmet food, or, just as important, low prices. Take your pick!

— National Motorist

For those travelling by car, lodging is always a main concern . . . The Complete Guide to Bed & Breakfasts, Inns & Guesthouses provides listings and descriptions of more than 2,500 inns.

— Minneapolis Star & Tribune

. . . the most complete compilation of bed and breakfast data ever published.

—Denver Post

Unique and delightful inns . . .

— Detroit Free Press

THE COMPLETE GUIDE TO BED & BREAKFASTS, INNS & GUESTHOUSES IN THE UNITED STATES, CANADA, & WORLDWIDE

PAMELA LANIER

YAHOO!® Internet Life's Gold Star Sites: **BEST** BED & BREAKFAST GUIDE

PAMELA LANIER'S TRAVEL GUIDES ONLINE

"Cozy and charming, a bed-and-breakfast inn can be a refreshing change of pace from staying in a hotel. Whatever your destination, Pamela Lanier's site covers small inns around the world with a personal touch. Besides searching by geography, you can specify whether you're looking for a family place or a romantic getaway, select such amenities as histoic locale or vegetarian food, and even limit your choice to B&Bs that you can book online. Most inn pages feature a photo and links to a map. Some even tell you which room is the best in the house, so you know what to ask for."

Visit our websites: www.LanierBB.com
www.TravelGuideS.com

Email: lanier@TravelGuideS.com

A *Lanier* Guide

Other Books By Pamela Lanier

Bed and Breakfast, Australia's Best
All-Suite Hotel Guide
Elegant Small Hotels
Elegant Hotels—Pacific Rim
Condo Vacations: The Complete Guide
Family Travel & Resorts
Golf Resorts: The Complete Guide
22 Days in Alaska
Cinnamon Mornings & Raspberry Teas
Sweets & Treats

The information in this book was supplied in large part by the inns themselves and is subject to change without notice. We strongly recommend that you call ahead to verify the information presented here before making final plans or reservations. The author and publisher make no representation that this book is absolutely accurate or complete. Errors and omissions, whether typographical, clerical, or otherwise, may sometimes occur herein. Some of the inns in this directory have been charged a listing fee by the author to help defray the costs of compilation.

The information about the properties in this publication is intended for personal use only. Any and all commercial use of the information in this publication is strictly prohibited.

For further information, please contact:
The Complete Guide to Bed & Breakfasts,
Inns and Guesthouses
Drawer D
Petaluma, CA 94953

2003 edition. First printing - 1982

ISBN 1-58008-448-6

Distributed to the book trade by:
Ten Speed Press
P.O. Box 7123
Berkeley, CA 94707
website: www.tenspeed.com tel. 1-800-841-2665

Cover by Jim Wood, Laura Lamar

Design & Production by J.C. Wright

Typeset by John Richards

Printed in Canada on recycled paper

In a nationwide survey of innkeepers conducted by *Innsider Magazine*

For J.C. Dolphin Valdés

Acknowledgements

Corrine Rednour and George Lanier for your help, love, and support–thank you.

Edited by: The Editorial Staff at LanierBB: Ruth Wilson, Mariposa Valdes, Karen Aaronson, Sally Carpenter, Chelsea Patocchi.

To my friends who were so generous with their time and skills:

Venetia Young, Carol McBride, Marianne Barth, Vincent Yu, Madelyn Furze, Rus Quon, Terry Lacey, John Garrett, Chris Manley, Mary Kreuger, Mr. Wiley, Adele Novelli, Ruth Young, Mrs. Gieselman (the best English teacher ever), Mary Institute, Ingrid Head, Sumi Timberlake, Marvin Downey, Marguerite Tafoya, Peggy Dennis, Judy Jacobs, Derek Ng, Katherine Bertolucci, Margaret Callahan, Mary Ellen Callahan, Mariposa Valdés, Hal Hershey, Leslie Chan, Jane Foster, Carolyn Strange, Carrie Johnson, Sally Carpenter, Mary Flynn, Karen Aaronson, Fara Richardson, Shannon Holl, Cliff Burdick, Gillian Pelham, Rachel Cullen, Byron Whitlock, Troy Arnold, Cliff Burdick, Chelsea Patocchi.

Special thanks to Richard Paoli

To the great folks in the Chambers of Commerce, State and Regional Departments of Tourism, I am most grateful.

To the innkeepers themselves who are so busy, yet found the time to fill out our forms and provide us with all sorts of wonderful information, I wish you all the greatest success.

Lanier Publishing facilitates the planting of 9 trees for every tree used in the production of our guides.

Contents

2003 INN OF THE YEAR

THE BOOTHBY INN
ERIE, PENNSYLVANIA

Walk through the front door of this Victorian era home and expect to say "wow" when you see the rich oak paneled hallway with its impressive stairway. The luxury and style is very apparent as you open the door to any of the four guestrooms. The rooms, named after Scotland, France, Japan, and Africa, each have 310 thread count sheets, fluffy and generous towels, goose down pillows, down comforters, and terry cloth robes. Business travelers have also found a home at the inn with data ports, desks, phones and early breakfasts when needed.

Innkeepers Wally and Gloria Knox have thought of everything. Down the hall is the guest galley. Help yourself to refreshments and snacks in the refrigerator; fill your ice bucket; try some fruit or homemade cookies. An hour before breakfast, the coffeemaker will have freshly brewed coffee. In the morning, enjoy a sumptuous breakfast that might feature Lemon Soufflé Pancakes or Blueberry Croissant French Toast served to you on the garden patio accompanied by a fountain's quiet, soothing sounds or in the spacious dining room. Or, stroll through the perennial garden and sit on the comfortable front porch in the late afternoon with a glass of lemonade and watch the world go by.

This home has been lovingly restored to its former glory. Imagine being pampered in a gracious home while you transact your business or enjoy your vacation.

INNS OF THE YEAR — HONOR ROLL

- 2002 Rosewood Inn, Bradford, NH
- 2001 Candlelite Inn, Bradford, NH
- 2000 Albergo Allegria, Windham, NY
- 1999 Black Friar Inn, Bar Harbor, ME
- 1998 Calico Inn, Sevierville, TN
- 1997 Legacy, Williamsburg, VA
- 1996 Chicago Pike Inn, Coldwater, MI
- 1995 Williamsburg Sampler, Williamsburg, VA
- 1994 Captain Freeman, Brewster, Cape Cod, MA
- 1993 Whalewalk Inn, Eastham, MA
- 1992 Lamplight Inn, Lake Luzerne, NY
- 1991 Kedron Valley Inn, S. Woodstock, VT
- 1990 The Veranda, Senoia, GA
- 1989 Wedgwood, New Hope, PA
- 1988 Seacrest Manor, Rockport, MA
- 1987 Governor's Inn, Ludlow, VT
- 1986 Carter House, Eureka, CA
- 1985 Joshua Grindle, Mendocino, CA

Introduction

There was a time, and it wasn't so long ago, when bed and breakfast inns were a rarity in the United States. Travelers made do at a hotel or motel; there was no alternative. The few bed and breakfast inns were scattered across the rural areas of New England and California. They were little known to most travelers; often their only advertisement was by word of mouth.

But in a few short years that has changed, and changed in a way that could only be called dramatic. There has been an explosion in the number of bed and breakfast inns. Today, inns can be found in every state, and often in cities; they have become true alternatives to a chain motel room or the city hotel with its hundreds of cubicles.

This sudden increase in bed and breakfast inns started less than two decades ago when Americans, faced with higher costs for foreign travel, began to explore the backroads and hidden communities of their own country.

Other factors have influenced the growth and popularity of bed and breakfast inns. Among them, the desire to get away from the daily routine and sameness of city life; the desire to be pampered for a few days; and also the desire to stay in a place with time to make new friends among the other guests.

The restored older homes that have become bed and breakfast inns answer those desires. The setting most often is rural; the innkeepers provide the service–not a staff with name tags–and the parlor is a gathering place for the handful of guests. They are a home away from home.

The proliferation of these inns as an alternative lodging has created some confusion. It's been difficult to find–in one place–up-to-date and thorough information about the great variety of inns.

Some books published in the past five or six years have tried to provide this information. But those books focused on one region of the country or named too few inns. While some earlier books gave detailed descriptions of the inns, few bothered to provide information about the type of breakfast served, whether there are rooms for non-smokers, and such things as whether the inn offered free use of bicycles or whether it had a hot tub.

An effort to collect as much information about as many inns as possible in one book has been overdue. Now that has been remedied. You hold a copy of the result in your hands.

Richard Paoli,
Travel Editor
San Francisco Examiner

How to Use This Guide

Organization

This book is organized with the United States first, alphabetically by state, and within a state, alphabetically by city or town that the inn wants to be listed in. Within the feature listings, each property's actual city will show if it is different from the List City. The US Territories of Puerto Rico and US Virgin Islands are listed next. After the United States, Canada is listed next alphabetically by province and then identical to the US listings. Then the Worldwide listings follow, organized by country and within the country by city. At the back of the guide are listings of the reservation service organizations serving each state, and inns with special characteristics.

Three Types of Accommodations

Inn: Webster's defines an inn as a "house built for the lodging and entertainment of travelers." All the inns in this book fulfill this description. Many also provide meals, at least breakfast, although a few do not. Most of these inns have under 30 guest rooms.

Bed and Breakfast: Can be anything from a home with three or more rooms to, more typically, a large house or mansion with eight or nine guest accommodations where breakfast is served in the morning.

Guest House: Private homes welcoming travelers, some of which may be contacted directly but most of which are reserved through a reservation service organization. A list of RSOs appears toward the back of this guide.

Breakfasts

We define a **full breakfast** as one being along English lines, including eggs and/or meat as well as the usual breads, toast, juice, and coffee.

Continental plus is a breakfast of coffee, juice, and choice of several breads and pastry and possibly more.

Continental means coffee, juice, bread or pastry.

If there is a charge for breakfast, then we note it as (fee).

Meals

Bear in mind that inns that do not serve meals are usually located near a variety of restaurants.

Can We Get a Drink?

Those inns without a license will generally chill your bottles and provide you with set-ups upon request.

Prices

Price range at the top of the second column is for double room, double occupancy in U.S. dollars, Canadian dollars, or international currency symbol (¤).

Appearing to the right of the price is a code indicating the type of food services available:

BB: Breakfast included in quoted rate

EP (European Plan): No meals

MAP (Modified American Plan): Includes breakfast and dinner

AP (American Plan): Includes all three meals

All prices are subject to change. Please be sure to confirm rates and services when you make your reservations.

Credit Cards and Checks

If an establishment accepts credit cards, it will be listed as VISA, MC, AmEx, Disc or Most CC. Most inns will accept your personal check with proper identification, but be sure to confirm when you book.

Ratings

One of the beauties of bed & breakfast travel is the individual nature of each inn. And innkeepers thrive on their independence! Some inns are members of their local, state or national inn association (most of which have membership requirements), and/or are members of or are rated by AAA, Mobil and others. Each of these rating systems relies upon different inspection protocol, membership and evaluative criteria. We use *Rated* in the listings to designate inns which have informed us that they have been rated by or are affiliated with any of these groups. If ratings are important to you, we suggest that you call and inquire of the specific inn for details. We continue to find, however, that some very good inns remain unrated, simply because of their size or idiosyncratic nature.

Reservations

Reservations are essential at most inns, particularly during busy seasons, and are appreciated at other times. Be sure to reserve, even if only a few hours in advance, to avoid disappointment. When you book, feel free to discuss your requirements and confirm prices, services and other details. We have found innkeepers to be delightfully helpful. Please tell your hosts that Pamela Lanier sent you!

Visit our web site – http://www.lanierbb.com

Most inns will hold your reservation until 6 p.m. If you plan to arrive later, please phone ahead to let them know.

A deposit or advance payment is required at some inns.

Children, Pets, Smoking, and Handicap Equipped

Children, pets, smoking and physical handicaps present special considerations for many inns. Whether or not they can be accommodated is generally noted as follows:

	Yes	Limited	No
Children	C-yes	C-ltd	
Pets	P-yes	P-ltd	P-no
Smoking	S-yes	S-ltd	S-no
Handicap Equipped	H-yes	H-ltd	H-no

However, many inns with limited facilities for children will often have one or two rooms set aside for families. Be sure to inquire when you book your room.

Because many inns are housed in old buildings, access for handicapped persons in many cases is limited. Where this information is available, we have noted it as above. Be sure to confirm your exact requirements when you book.

Big Cities

In many big cities there are very few small, intimate accommodations. We have searched out as many as possible. We strongly advise you to investigate the guest house alternative, which can provide you with anything from a penthouse in New York to your own quiet quarters with a private entrance in the suburbs. See our RSO listings at the back of the book.

Bathrooms

Though shared baths are the norm in Europe, this is sometimes a touchy subject in the U.S.A. We list the number of private baths available directly next to the number of rooms. Bear in mind that those inns with shared baths generally have more than one.

Manners

Please keep in mind when you go to an inn that innkeeping is a very hard job. It is amazing that innkeepers manage to maintain such a thoroughly cheerful and delightful presence despite long hours. Do feel free to ask your innkeepers for help or suggestions, but please don't expect them to be your personal servant. You may have to carry your own bags.

When in accommodations with shared baths, be sure to straighten the bathroom as a courtesy to your fellow guests. If you come in late, please do so on tiptoe, mindful of the other patrons visiting the inn for a little R&R.

Sample Bed & Breakfast Listing

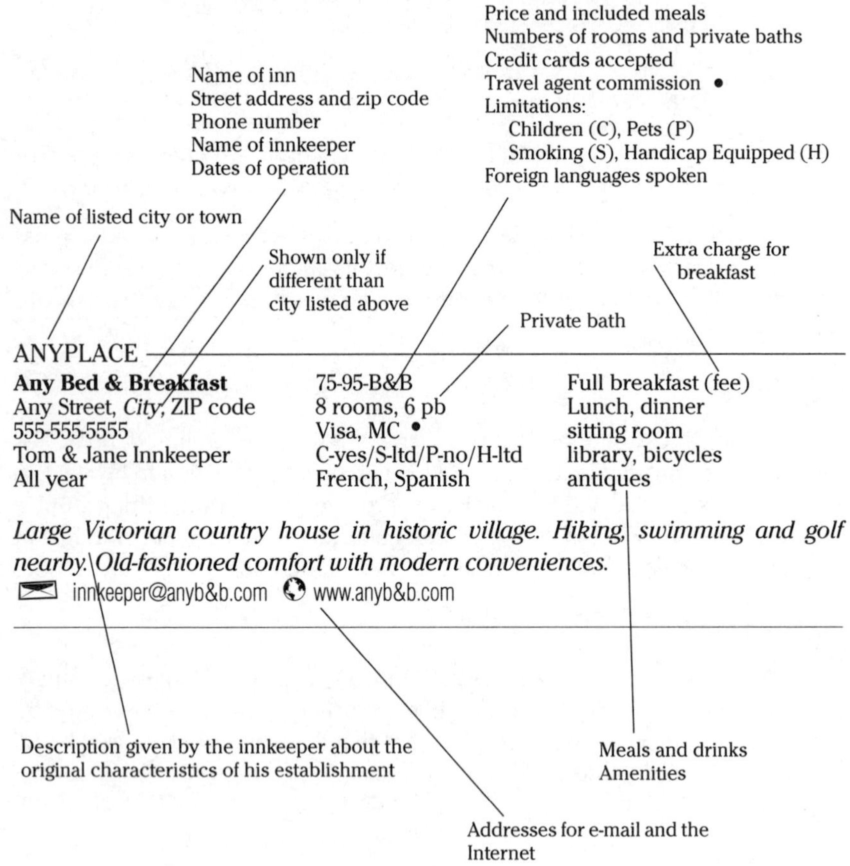

Price and included meals
Numbers of rooms and private baths
Credit cards accepted
Travel agent commission •
Limitations:
Children (C), Pets (P)
Smoking (S), Handicap Equipped (H)
Foreign languages spoken

Name of inn
Street address and zip code
Phone number
Name of innkeeper
Dates of operation

Name of listed city or town

Shown only if different than city listed above

Extra charge for breakfast

Private bath

ANYPLACE

Any Bed & Breakfast	75-95-B&B	Full breakfast (fee)
Any Street, *City*, ZIP code	8 rooms, 6 pb	Lunch, dinner
555-555-5555	Visa, MC •	sitting room
Tom & Jane Innkeeper	C-yes/S-ltd/P-no/H-ltd	library, bicycles
All year	French, Spanish	antiques

Large Victorian country house in historic village. Hiking, swimming and golf nearby. Old-fashioned comfort with modern conveniences.

innkeeper@anyb&b.com www.anyb&b.com

Description given by the innkeeper about the original characteristics of his establishment

Meals and drinks
Amenities

Addresses for e-mail and the Internet

Alabama

ANNISTON

Victoria, A Country Inn & Rest.
PO Box 2213
1604 Quintard, 36201 36202
256-236-0503 Fax: 256-236-1138
800-260-8781
Fain & Beth Casey
All year

79-319-BB
60 rooms, 60 pb
Most CC, *Rated*, •
C-yes/S-ltd/P-no/H-yes

Continental breakfast
Restaurant, bar service
Swimming pool, family friendly facility, gardens, gazebo

This Southern estate is located midway between Atlanta & Birmingham & offers Victorian amenities from the antiques within the main house to the reproductions in the annex.
thevic@mindspring.com http://www.thevictoria.com

FAIRHOPE

Bay Breeze Guest House
PO Box 526
742 S Mobile St 36533
251-928-8976 Fax: 251-929-2389
866-928-8976
Bill & Becky Jones
All year

115-145-BB
5 rooms, 5 pb
Most CC
C-ltd/S-no/P-ltd/H-ltd

Full breakfast
Snacks, complimentary wine
Sitting room, library, bikes, suites, cable TV, accom. bus. travel

Located on the shores of historic Mobile Bay—private pier, beach. Swimming, sailing, fishing. http://www.bbonline.com/al/baybreeze

---

Church Street Inn
PO Box 526
51 S Church St 36532
334-928-5144 Fax: 251-929-2389
866-928-8976
Bill & Becky Jones
All year

100-BB
3 rooms, 3 pb
Most CC
C-ltd/S-no/P-no/H-no

Continental breakfast
Snacks
Sitting room, bikes, fireplaces, cable TV

Listed on National Register. Five generations of antiques. Within walking distance to shops, restaurants, municipal pier with park and rose garden.
http://www.bbonline.com/al/churchstreet

Fellers Cove
19195 Scenic Hwy 98 36532
251-928-1929
Flor Fellers
All year

125-150-BB
3 rooms, 3 pb
Most CC, *Rated*, •
C-no/S-ltd/P-no/H-ltd
Spanish, Kiswahili, Pigsen

Full breakfast
Soft drinks, wine
Bikes, croquet lawn, ping pong, private wharf

On Mobile Bay. Sunsets, hammocks, croquet lawn, bikes, ping pong. Private wharf. All unique and special. In quaint village of Fairhope. Specialty shops, restaurants. A must destination. fellerscove@aol.com http://fellerscove.com

FLORENCE

Wood Avenue Inn
658 N Wood Ave 35630
256-766-8441
Gene & Alvern Greeley
All year

75-115-BB
4 rooms, 4 pb
Most CC, *Rated*, •
C-ltd/S-ltd/P-no/H-no

Full breakfast
Dinner available only by reservation, tea, snacks
Sitting room, library, cable TV, accommodate business travelers

Elegant Victorian Mansion in the heart of historic Florence, the sister city of Florence, Italy. Romantic garden for small weddings.
woodaveinn@aol.com http://www.woodavenueinn.com

Wood Avenue Inn, Florence, AL

GREENVILLE

The Martin House	65-85-BB	Full breakfast
212 E Commerce St 36307	4 rooms, 4 pb	Afternoon tea, snacks, comp. wine, dinner avail.
334-382-2011 Fax: 334-382-0728	Most CC, *Rated*, •	Sitting room, cable TV, accommodate business travelers
877-627-8465	C-ltd/S-ltd/P-ltd/H-ltd	
M. Jo Weitman		
All year		

Restored Queen Ann Victorian on the Register of Historic Places; offers a full breakfast; dinner is available with reservation, close to Cambrian Ridge Golf Trail.
themartinhouse@greenlynk.com *http://www.martinbb.com*

GULF SHORES (REGION)

The Original Romar House	77-199-BB	Full breakfast
23500 Perdido Beach Blvd, *Orange Beach* 36561	7 rooms, 6 pb	Complimentary wine and cheese
251-974-1625 Fax: 251-974-1163	Visa, MC, *Rated*	Bar service, library, sitting room, hot tubs, bicycles, private beach
800-487-6627	C-ltd/S-ltd/P-no/H-no	
Darrell Finley All year		

Quiet ambience, comfort, quaint surroundings, friendly service & white sandy beaches for romantic weekends. original@gulftel.com http://www.bbonline.com/al/romarhouse/

LOGAN MARTIN LAKE (REGION)

Treasure Island	85-150-BB	Full breakfast
230 Treasure Island Circle, *Cropwell* 35054	4 rooms, 4 pb	Snacks & cold drinks
205-525-5172	C-yes/S-no/P-no/H-no	Fireplaces, satellite TVs, gym, pool table, Internet access, pontoon boat
Earl & Lillie Hardy	Russian	
All year		

Lake house on main channel of Coosa River at Logan Martin Lake. "Plantation style" breakfast served overlooking main channel of river. Pontoon river boat cruise for guests in late afternoon. treasureislandbb@aol.com
http://www.treasureislandbedandbreakfast.com

MENTONE

Mountain Laurel Inn	80-140-BB	Full breakfast
PO Box 443	5 rooms, 5 pb	Snacks
624 Road 948 35984	Visa, MC, Disc, *Rated*	Sitting room, library, suite, hiking trails, guest refrigerator
256-634-4673 800-889-4244	C-yes/S-ltd/P-no/H-no	
Sarah Wilcox All year		

Country hideaway, seven acres on a bluff overlooking Little River. Hike to DeSoto Falls, relax on the porches. sawilcox@mindspring.com http://www.bbonline.com/al/mli

MENTONE

Raven Haven
651 Country Rd 644 35984
256-634-4310
Anthony & Eleanor Teverino
All year

75-105-BB
4 rooms, 4 pb
C-ltd/S-no/P-no/H-yes

Full breakfast
Sitting room, fireplaces

When you need to get away, you don't have to go as far as you think. Ten acres of nature outside the back door, and 1/4 mile trail to soothe your spirits.
teverinor@aol.com

MONTGOMERY

Red Bluff Cottage
551 Clay St 36104
334-264-0056 Fax: 334-263-3054
888-551-2529
Barry & Bonnie Ponstein
All year

90-BB
4 rooms, 4 pb
Most CC, *Rated*, •
C-yes/S-no/P-no/H-no

Full breakfast
Plush towels/robes,flowers,iron, lighted parking,porches,gardens,gazebo

Award winning Bed and Breakfast in oldest historic neighborhood in Montgomery, AL. Two-story raised cottage offers panoramic view of river plain and state capitol. Family antiques, gardens and gazebo. redblufbnb@aol.com http://www.redbluffcottage.com

Alaska

ANCHORAGE

Alaska's Natural Wonders
5320 O'Malley 99507
907-562-3311 Fax: 907-336-3710
866-537-3646
Mike & Kathryn O'Connor
All year

70-120-BB
4 rooms, 4 pb
Visa, MC, •
C-yes/S-no/P-no/H-ltd

Alaska style complete or cont.
Drinks, snacks, latte, mocha cappucino machine
Outdoor Jacuzzi (8 person) dry sauna, decks, huge living room with fireplace

Come to the city, but stay in the country. 1.35 beautifully landscaped acres, surrounded by woods. Just 12 minutes from the airport and downtown Anchorage, just minutes from shopping and restaurants.
info@aknaturalwonders.com http://www.aknaturalwonders.com

Alaska's North Country Castle
PO Box 111876
14600 Joanne 99511
907-345-7296
Cindy and Wray Kinard

109-159-BB
3 rooms, 3 pb
Most CC, *Rated*, •
C-ltd/S-ltd/P-no/H-no
Spanish, German
May 15–Sep 30

Full breakfast
Sitting room, Jacuzzi, Alaskan library, 4 decks, piano

Luxuriate! Sunny Victorian home on forested acreage. Sparkling mountain and ocean views from 4 decks. Bounteous gourmet breakfast watching for munching moose from "gazebo" nook. Romantic Suite.
nccbnb@customcpu.com http://www.customcpu.com/commercial/nccbnb

---

Alaskan Frontier Gardens
PO Box 24-1881
Corner Hillside & Alatna 99524
907-345-6556 Fax: 907-562-2923
Rita Gittins
All year

75-195-BB
3 rooms, 2 pb
Visa, MC, AmEx, *Rated*, •
C-yes/S-no/P-no/H-no

Full gourmet breakfast
Sitting room, library, sauna, laundry, Jacuzzi, fireplace, 6 person hot tub

Elegant Alaskan hillside estate, on peaceful scenic acres by Chugach State Park. Spacious luxury suites. Gourmet breakfast.
afg@alaska.net http://www.alaskafrontiergardens.com

ANCHORAGE

Anchorage Jewel Lake
8125 Jewel Lake Rd 99502
907-245-7321 Fax: 907-245-2313
Troy Roberts
All year

75-125-BB
5 rooms
Most CC, •
C-yes/S-ltd/P-no/H-no

Continental plus breakfast
Teas, wines, snacks and other munchies
Large deck, fireplace, sitting room, guest kitchen

Jewel Lake Bed and Breakfast is a year round, wonderful alternative to a busy hotel. We will work to make your stay as comfortable as possible.
info@jewellakebandb.com http://www.jewellakebandb.com

Anchorage Mahogany Manor
204 E 15th Ave 99501
907-278-1111 Fax: 907-258-7877
888-777-0346
Mary Ernst & Russ Campbell
All year

129-199-BB
4 rooms, 4 pb
Most CC, *Rated*, •
C-ltd/S-no/P-no/H-ltd
German, Spanish

Hearty Continental plus breakfast
Aft. tea, evening snacks/dessert
Sitting room, library, Jacuzzis, pool, suites, fireplaces, cable TV/VCR

Experience Alaska at Mahogany Manor. Enjoy warm hospitality in a lodge atmosphere, in the midst of indoor waterfalls and gardens and crackling fireplaces.
innkeeper@mmanor.com http://www.mmanor.com

Anchorage Walkabout Town
1610 E St 99501
907-279-7808 Fax: 907-258-3657
Sandra J. Stimson
April-October

70-115-BB
3 rooms
Rated, •
C-yes/S-no/P-no/H-no

Full breakfast
Deck, cable TV, freezer, free laundry, parking, 4 in a room

Downtown convenience with beautiful park and coastal trail. Hearty Alaskan breakfast of sourdough waffles, reindeer sausage.
tstimson@compuserve.com http://www.alaskaone.com/walkabout/

Camai
3838 Westminster Way 99508
907-333-2219
Fax: 907-337-3959
800-659-8763
Craig & Caroline Valentine
All year

40-110-BB
3 rooms, 3 pb
Rated, •
C-yes/S-no/P-no/H-yes

Full or continental breakfast
Suites kitchenette, suites have private phone lines & dataports

Anchorage's premier B&B offers three large suites with private baths and many amenities. Ideal for families or travelers wanting spaciousness. Glorious flower gardens.
camai@alaska.net http://www.camaibnb.com

Chugach
3901 Laron Ln 99504
907-333-4615
Fax: 907-337-6095
Betty Husted
All year

85-105-BB
3 rooms, 3 pb
Most CC, •
C-ltd/S-no/P-no/H-no

Full or continental plus
Complimentary snacks, sodas, bottled water

A stay at Chugach B&B, at the foot of the beautiful Chugach mountains, will be one of your most memorable Alaskan experiences. 15 minutes to airport & downtown. Walking distance to many sites. info@chugachbbalaska.com http://www.chugachbbalaska.com

---

Glacier Bear
4814 Malibu Rd 99517
907-243-8818
Fax: 907-248-4532
Cleveland & Belinda Zackery
All year

70-120-BB
3 rooms, 3 pb
Visa, MC, *Rated*, •
C-ltd/S-ltd/P-no/H-no

Continental plus breakfast
Snacks
Hiking & biking trails, restaurants nearby, sitting room, 8 person spa

First-class accommodations at reasonable rates. Our location: 1.2 mi. from airport, 3 miles to downtown. gbear@alaska.net http://www.touristguide.com/b&b/alaska/glacierbear

Lynn's Pine Point, Anchorage, AK

ANCHORAGE

Lake View 9256 Campbell Terrace 99502 907-243-4624 Fax: 907-243-4624 Tanya & Patrick Kowach All year	75-125-BB 3 rooms, 3 pb Visa, MC, AmEx C-yes/S-no/P-no/H-yes Ukrainian, Russian, German, Spanish	Full or continental breakfast Sitting room, Jacuzzis, fireplaces, accommodate business travelers

Enjoy a quiet setting overlooking scenic Campbell Lake. Unwind with a leisure tour of our quaint garden setting. lakeview@alaska.net http://reservations.lodging.com/servlet/PropertyInformation/IP_1717/n1h

The Lilac House 950 P Street 99501 907-278-2939 Fax: 907-278-4939 Debi Shinn All year	75-135-BB 3 rooms, 1 pb Visa, MC, AmEx, *Rated*, • C-ltd/S-no/P-no/H-no	Continental plus breakfast Sunny Breakfast Room

An exceptional B&B, The Lilac House was designed for the convenience and comfort of all guests and is perfect for both the business and pleasure traveler. lilac@pobox.alaska.net http://www.alaska.net/~tango

Lynn's Pine Point 3333 Creekside Dr 99504 907-333-2244 Fax: 907-333-1043 Lynn & Rich Stouff All year	105-130-BB 3 rooms, 3 pb Visa, MC, Disc, *Rated*, • C-ltd/S-no/P-no/H-no	Continental plus breakfast Tea, wine Sitting room, robes, family bedroom, two decks

Lovely cedar retreat with all the comforts of home. Queen beds, private baths, phones, and cable TV. richs@gci.net http://www.lynnspinepoint.com

Ruby's Vintage PO Box 220855 4011 Marquis Way 99502 907-243-7000 Fax: 907-243-7046 Babette Brewer All year	55-95-BB 3 rooms, 1 pb Most CC, *Rated*, • C-yes/S-no/P-no/H-no	Hearty Alaskan style breakfast Fresh fruit & Alaska wildberry specialties Relax in the living room or view the lake from the outdoor deck

Ruby's offers casual elegance in bed and breakfast accommodations. Featured in the Anchorage Alaska Holiday Tour of Homes. Located near the airport and minutes from downtown. info@alaskarubys.com http://www.alaskarubys.com

Gwin's Lodge, Cooper Landing, AR

ANCHORAGE

Rural Alaska Connection
5224 Emmanuel Ave 99508
907-332-3332 Fax: 907-929-7821
888-862-3332
All year

85-115-BB
2 rooms, 2 pb
Visa, MC
C-ltd/S-no/P-no/H-no

Full breakfast
Coffee, tea, desert, fresh fruit, breads & jellies
Sitting room, library, TV/VCR, laptop computer, internet access

A premier, affordable B&B offering scrumptious breakfasts, comfortable rooms, lovely garden, beautiful art, delicious desserts, Internet access, and gracious hospitality on the banks of Chester Creek. menegats@gci.net http://www.ruralalaskaconnection.com

COOPER LANDING

Alaskan Sourdough B&B
PO Box 812
18360 Bean Creek Rd 99572
907-595-1541 Fax: 907-595-1541
Willie & Lovie Johnson
All year

105-115-BB
6 rooms, 6 pb
Visa, MC, AmEx, *Rated*, •
C-yes/S-ltd/P-no/H-yes
Eskimo, French

Full breakfast
In-room tea, coffee, popcorn & breakfast
Library, TV in rooms, sitting room, bicycle

We recommend only the best eating places, trails for hiking nearby, wildlife often on grounds. sourdoughbb@arctic.net http://www.alaskansourdoughbb.com

Gwin's Lodge
14865 Sterling Hwy
Milepost 52 Sterling Hwy 99572
907-595-1266 Fax: 907-595-1681
800-GWINS-44
Robert Siter All year

109-159-EP
16 rooms, 14 pb
Visa, MC, Disc, *Rated*, •
C-yes/S-yes/P-ltd/H-yes

Restaurant, bar
Fishing tackle shop, parking, embroidered clothing store

Historic Alaskan log roadhouse. Fully appointed log chalet units. Closest to Kenai & Russian Rivers, world's best sockeye salmon fishery.
gwins@arctic.net http://www.ool.com/gwins

DENALI NATIONAL PARK (REGION)

Denali EarthSong Lodge
PO Box 89
Mile 4 Stampede Rd, *Healy* 99743
907-683-2863 Fax: 907-683-2868
Karin Nierenberg All year

115-135-EP
10 rooms, 10 pb
Visa, MC, *Rated*, •
C-yes/S-no/P-no/H-no

Tea, snacks for sale at cafe
Sitting room, library, gift shop, evening slideshow by staff

Denali's secluded alternative to the commercial park experience. Lovely lodge with ten charming log cabins, each with own private baths, amenities, country charm. Come and share the dream. karin@earthsonglodge.com http://www.earthsonglodge.com

DENALI NATIONAL PARK (REGION)

Valley Vista
PO Box 395, *Healy* 99743
907-683-2842 Fax: 907-683-2841
877-683-2841
Keith Family All year

115-BB
3 rooms, 3 pb
Most CC, •
C-yes/S-ltd/P-ltd/H-no

Continental plus breakfast
Full guest kitchen
Sitting room, Jacuzzis, cable TV, in-room phones, private entrance.

One of Denali's finest B&Bs. Newly remodeled with private baths, all with Jacuzzi tubs. Full guest kitchen, private entrances, and beautiful landscaping.
info@valleyvistabb.com http://www.valleyvistabb.com

FAIRBANKS

Country Comforts B&B
174 Crest Dr 99712
907-457-6867 Fax: 907-479-6867
Ken & Audrey Dunshie
All year

85-95-BB
3 rooms, 1 pb
Most CC, *Rated*, •
C-yes/S-no/P-no/H-ltd

Full breakfast
Snacks
Sitting room, Jacuzzis, suites, cable TV, exercise sauna, acc. bus. trav.

Country Comfort with Alaskan Art collectibles; wild animals visit, gold panning, Alaskan full breakfast, large rooms, comfortable beds, and hospitality at its best.
ctycomf@ptialaska.net http://www.countrycomfortsbb.com

Fox Creek
2498 Elliott Hwy 99712
907-457-5494 Fax: 907-457-5464
Arna King-Fay & Jeff Fay
All year

68-98-BB
2 rooms, 1 pb
Rated, •
C-yes/S-ltd/P-yes/H-no

Full breakfast
Sitting room, library, spacious rooms, family friendly facility

Quiet, secluded setting in historic Fox, Alaska. Frequent aurora/wildlife sightings. Modern Alaskan-style home. Lifelong Alaskan proprietors.
foxcreek@ptialaska.net http://www.ptialaska.net/~foxcreek

Seven Gables Inn & Suites
PO Box 80488
4312 Birch Ln 99708
907-479-0751 Fax: 907-479-2229
P & L Welton All year

50-180-BB
24 rooms, 24 pb
Visa, MC, *Rated*, •
C-yes/S-ltd/P-ltd/H-yes
Spanish, German

Full gourmet breakfast
Compl. refreshments
Sitting room, library, cable TV/VCR, phones, bikes, Jacuzzis, canoes

Luxury accommodations at affordable rates. Our rooms and suites have private baths, with Jacuzzi tubs, cable TV/VCRs. A full gourmet breakfast is included in room rates.
gables7@alaska.net http://www.7gablesinn.com

GLACIER BAY (REGION)

Annie Mae Lodge
PO Box 55
#2 Grandpa's Farm Rd, *Gustavus* 99826
907-697-2346 Fax: 907-697-2211
800-478-2346
Rachel & Jason Parks All year

215-260-BB
11 rooms, 9 pb
Most CC, *Rated*, •
C-yes/S-ltd/P-no/H-yes

Full breakfast
Lunch, dinner, snacks
Sitting room, library, bikes, activities, accom. bus. travelers

Country Inn boasting comfort and hospitality combined with cozy rooms and gourmet meals. Located in meadows next to beautiful river and near small community.
anniemae@cheerful.com http://www.anniemae.com

Glacier Bay Country Inn
PO Box 5
Mile 1, Tong Rd., *Gustavus* 99826
907-697-2288 Fax: 907-697-2289
800-628-0912
P & S Marchbanks All year

370-AP
8 rooms, 7 pb
Rated

Full breakfast

For fifteen years the Glacier Bay Country Inn has served as both guide and gateway to the adventure, wildlife and unique natural landscapes found only in southeast Alaska.
gbci@thor.he.net http://www.glacierbayalaska.com/

HAINES

The Summer Inn
PO Box 1198
117 Second Ave 99827
907-766-2970 Fax: 907-766-2970
Mary & Bob Summer All year

80-100-BB
5 rooms
•

Full breakfast

Charming historic house overlooking Lynn Canal. Celebrating our 15th year of innkeeping! summerinnB&B@wytbear.com http://www.summerinn.wytbear.com/

HEALY

Denali Dome Home
PO Box 262
12 miles north of Denali National Park 99743
907-683-1239 Fax: 907-683-2322
1-800-683-1239
Ann & Terry Miller All year

75-115-BB
7 rooms, 7 pb
Most CC, *Rated*, •
C-yes/S-no/P-no/H-yes
Alaskan, Spanish, Russian

Amazing, full, Alaskan breakfasts
Coffees, teas, juices, and homemade snacks
Huge, rock fireplace; book and video library; decks; paved parking, 5 acres.

Located 12 miles north of Denali National Park, Denali Dome Home is the longest running B&B in the Healy area. The Miller Family is keenly aware of area's best attractions and scenic locations. info@denalidomehome.com http://www.denalidomehome.com

HOMER

Shorebird Guest House
PO Box 204
4774 Kachemak Drive 99603
907-235-2107 Fax: 907-235-5435
Claudia Ehli & Rose Beck
May 1–Labor Day

120-EP
1 rooms, 1 pb
Visa, MC, *Rated*, •
C-yes/S-ltd/P-no/H-ltd

Snacks
Bicycles, cable TV

Sits on a cliff overlooking spectacular Kachemak Bay with stairs to beach; beautiful gardens; private and clean; views of glaciers, seals, otters, shorebirds.
peeps@alaska.net http://shorebirdcabin.com

Spruce Acres Private Cabins
910 Sterling Hwy 99603
907-235-8388 Fax: 907-235-0636
877-500-7404
John & Joyce Williams
All year

65-105-BB
4 rooms, 4 pb
Visa, MC, Disc, *Rated*, •
C-yes/S-no/P-ltd/H-ltd

Continual breakfast
Suites, movies, cable TV, coffee/tea/mocha in your own cabin

Private cabins established 1987—cozy, comfortable, Country Victorian decor, squeaky clean, private baths, kitchenettes, satellite TV/VCR, phones, laundry facilities.
sprucea@ptialaska.net http://www.spruceacrecabins.com

HYDER

Kathy's Korner
PO Box 21
505 Main St 99923
250-636-2393 Fax: 250-636-2343
Kathy & Ron Tschakert
All year

65-75-BB
3 rooms
Visa, MC
C-ltd/S-ltd/P-no/H-no

Continental plus
Fresh fruits in season, cheeses, fresh breads
Internet, fax, copier, scanner, satellite TV, laundry, kitchen option

Our sunny deck is ideal for relaxing after a long day observing and photographing the wildlife which abounds in our valley. You may see both Black and Grizzly Bear strolling up and down the road. kathys_korner@hotmail.com

JUNEAU

A Pearson's Pond Luxury Inn
4541 Sawa Circle 99801
907-789-3772 Fax: 907-789-6722
888-6-JUNEAU
Steve & Diane Mayer Pearson
All year

99-269-BB
5 rooms, 5 pb
Most CC, *Rated*, •
C-ltd/S-no/P-ltd/H-ltd

Continental plus breakfast
Afternoon tea, wine, cheese, snacks
Hot tubs, fireplaces, bikes, boats, views, BBQ, massage, fitness, concierge

B&B resort #4 World's Most Romantic Destination, Best B&B of Alaska/America. Waterview Spa-Fireplace suites, 4-poster bed, kitchen. I-Net, bike, massage, fitness. Wedding, Ski, adventure, spa pkg. book@pearsonspond.com http://www.pearsonspond.com

KETCHIKAN

Almost Home
412 D-1 Loop Rd 99901
907-247-5337 Fax: 907-247-5337
800-987-5337
Wanda & Darrell Vandergriff
All year

150-250-BB
3 rooms, 3 pb
Visa, MC, AmEx,
Rated, •
C-yes/S-ltd/P-ltd/H-ltd

Continental breakfast
Outfitted kitchen, BBQ
Sitting room, suites, cable TV, deck, family friendly facility, conference

Privacy and comfort in your own outfitted one, two or three-bedroom apartment. Full kitchen stocked with all you need including staple foods and breakfast makings to feel "almost home."
info@ketchikan-lodging.com http://www.ketchikan-lodging.com/bb15.html

---

Blueberry Hill
PO Box 9508
500 Front St 99901
907-247-2583 Fax: 907-247-2584
877-449-2583
Vicki & John Zahler All year

90-135-BB
4 rooms, 4 pb
Visa, MC, Disc, *Rated*, •
C-yes/S-no/P-no/H-no

Full Breakfast changes daily
Common parlor, excellent library, cable TV

Elegant, unique, historic home allows restful stay in downtown Ketchikan. Grand common parlor, excellent library. Light, spacious guestrooms invite relaxation. Easy walk to all downtown attractions. stay@blueberryhillbb.com http://www.blueberryhillbb.com

---

Corner
PO Box 5023
3870 Evergreen Ave 99901
907-225-2655 Fax: 907-247-2655
Carolyn & Win Wilsie All year

85-130-BB
1 rooms, 1 pb
Visa, MC, *Rated*, •
C-yes/S-ltd/P-no/H-ltd

Continental breakfast
Sitting room, cable TV, conference facilities

Clean, comfortable & private with queen beds, ground level and off street parking. Private bath and phone. Fully equipped kitchen, cable TV/VCR, convenient location and friendly accommodating hosts. cjwilsie@ptialaska.net http://www.cornerbnb.com

NORTH POLE

Gram's Cabin B&B
1402 Michael Ln 99705
907-488-6513

80
2 rooms, 2 pb
C-yes/H-no

Continental self-serve fixings
Kitchen, TV/VCR, videos, phone

Nestled among gorgeous spruce & birch trees on beautiful three-acre parcel bordering Chena River, Gram's Cabin is a generously sized, one-room cabin located halfway between Fairbanks and North Pole. info@gramscabin.com http://www.gramscabin.com

PALMER

Alaska Gold Rush
HC05 Box 6914P
7850 Lucky Shot Ln 99645
907-745-5312 Fax: 907-746-5312
877-745-5312
Ken & Mary Littlefair
All year

80-95-BB
7 rooms, 7 pb
Visa, MC, Disc, •
C-yes/S-no/P-no/H-no

Full, hot, delicious & Alaskan
Snacks, coffee, tea, ice cold pure Alaskan water
Sitting room, library, suites, conference, cabins

Choose a spacious suite, comfortable room, or incredible Cabin! Full breakfasts in the sun-drenched Solarium. True Alaskan hospitality awaits you! A delightful setting of Gold Rush and Alaskana! stay@alaskagoldrush.com http://www.alaskagoldrush.com

---

Hatcher Pass
HC 5 Box 6797-D
Mile 6.6 Palmer Fishhook
99645
907-745-6788 Fax: 907-745-6787
Dan & Liz Hejl All year

60-145-BB
5 rooms, 5 pb
Visa, MC, •
C-yes/S-ltd/P-ltd/H-no

Full breakfast

Authentic Alaskan log cabins with modern conveniences; bath, kitchenette, phone, TV/VCR. Nestled at the base of beautiful Hatcher Pass–home to year round activities, only 8 miles from Palmer. cabins@hatcherpassbb.com http://www.hatcherpassbb.com

PALMER

Iditarod House
PO Box 3096
12100 Woodstock Dr 99645
907-745-4348 Fax: 907-745-4346
Donna & Glenn Massay
All year

55-70-BB
3 rooms, 3 pb
Visa, MC, Disc, *Rated*, •
C-yes/S-no/P-ltd/H-yes

Continental plus breakfast
Afternoon tea, snacks
Sitting room

Comfy rooms with mountain views. Located on 7 scenic acres, only one mile from Palmer in the heart of Matanuska Valley. Genuine Alaskan hospitality.
stay@iditarodhouse.com http://www.iditarodhouse.com

SELDOVIA

Swan House South
6840 Crooked Tree Dr
175 Augustine Ave N 99507
907-346-3033 Fax: 907-346-3535
800-921-1900
Judy Swanson May–Sept

129-259-BB
5 rooms, 5 pb
Visa, MC, Disc, *Rated*, •
C-ltd/S-no/P-no/H-no

Full gourmet breakfast
Afternoon tea
Library, bikes, hiking, halibut & salmon fishing charters, suites available

Waterfront hideaway with never-ending views! Walking distance from airport, marina, & town. Seldovia is a remote island-like getaway.
swan1@alaska.net http://www.alaskaswanhouse.com

SEWARD

Angels Rest on Resurrection Bay
PO Box 1741
13730 Beach Dr, Lowell Point 99664
907-224-7378 Fax: 907-224-7379
866-904-7378
Lynda M. Paquette All year

EP
1 pb
Visa, MC, •
C-ltd/S-no/P-no/H-ltd

A very special getaway with incredible scenery and wildlife.
reservations@angelsrest.com http://www.angelsrest.com

Bell-in-the-Woods
PO Box 345
13881 Bruno Rd 99664
907-224-7271 Fax: 907-224-7271
Jerry & Peggy Woods All year

109-170-BB
7 rooms, 7 pb
Visa, MC, Disc, •
C-yes/S-no/P-no/H-yes

Full breakfast
Sitting room, library, suites, cable TV

Country, wooded setting with panoramic mountain views; full, hot breakfast; concierge table with area attractions.
bellwoodbnb@juno.com http://www.bellinthewoodsbnb.com

Harborview
PO Box 1305
804 Third Avenue 99664
907-224-3217 Fax: 907-224-3218
888-324-3217
Jolene & Jerry King

59-189
37 rooms, 37 pb
Visa, MC, AmEx
C-yes/S-no/P-no/H-ltd
All year

Coffee pots in all rooms, places to eat nearby
All rooms—non-smoking, exceptionally clean and beautifully decorated

Harborview Inn, owned and operated by a native Alaskan, offers you fantastic views, personal touches and friendly service.
info@sewardhotel.com http://www.sewardhotel.com

SITKA

Alaska Ocean View Inn
1101 Edgecumbe Dr 99835
907-747-8310 Fax: 907-747-3440
888-811-6870
Carole Denkinger
All year

89-189-BB
3 rooms, 3 pb
Most CC, *Rated*, •
C-ltd/S-no/P-ltd/H-no

Full or continental plus
Coffee, tea, hot chocolate, snacks, artesian water
Concierge service, ocean view, library, luxurious robes, hot tub, fireplaces.

Western red cedar executive home in scenic setting. Walk to beach, wilderness trails, shopping, attractions and historic sites. Luxurious amenities in casual, relaxed setting, king/queen size beds. alaskaoceanview@gci.net http://www.sitka-alaska-lodging.com

SOLDOTNA

Longmere Lake Lodge
PO Box 1707
35955 Ryan Lane 99669
907-262-9799 Fax: 907-262-5937
Tom & Pat Dwinnell
All year

95-135-BB
5 rooms, 5 pb
Visa, MC, *Rated*, •
C-ltd/S-no/P-no/H-no

Hearty breakfast
Beautiful lakeside setting, fishing, seminar/business groups welcome

Picturesque lake setting, immaculate facilities, and warm service by longtime Alaskan hosts have given our lodge a strong reputation.
bblodge@ptialaska.net http://www.longmerelakelodge.com

Sprucewood Lodge
PO Box 2946
99669
907-260-5420 Fax: 907-260-5419
888-844-9737
John King All year

100-210-BB
8 rooms, 8 pb
Visa, MC, AmEx, •
C-yes/S-no/P-no/H-no

Full breakfast
Afternoon tea, snacks
Sitting room, accommodate business travelers

Sprucewood Lodge is a handcrafted log lodge on the banks of the Kenai River. We offer 8 spacious rooms each with its own private bath and large comfortable common areas for gathering. info@sprucewood.net http://www.sprucewood.net

WASILLA

Alaska Lake Lucille
235 West Lakeview Avenue
99654
907-357-0352 Fax: 907-357-0353
888-353-0352
Carol Smith All year

79-135-BB
4 rooms, 2 pb
Visa, MC, *Rated*, •
C-yes/S-no/P-no/H-no
German

Varied menu . . . great food!
Evening pie, cake, or snack, & coffee
Sitting room, meeting room for 12, lake and mountain views

Wasilla, Alaska affordable 1st Class lakeside accommodations with mountain views less than 1 mile from downtown Wasilla. On the way to everything. Ask about "7 days in the valley tours." Stay@alaskaslakelucillebnb.com http://www.alaskaslakelucillebnb.com

---

Shady Acres Inn
1000 Easy St 99654
907-376-3113 Fax: 907-376-3113
800-360-3113
Fred & Marie Lambing
All year

BB
2 rooms

Located in Wasilla near Parks Highway and Downtown. Surrounded by quiet, serene forest. Warm, cheerful home atmosphere with indoor and outdoor entertainment space.
lambing@gci.net http://home.gci.net/~sabnb

Arizona

BISBEE

Bisbee Grand Hotel
PO Box 825
61 Main St 85603
520-432-5900 Fax: 520-432-5900
800-421-1909
Bill Thomas
All year

75-150-BB
11 rooms, 7 pb
Most CC, *Rated*, •
C-ltd/S-ltd/P-no/H-no

Full breakfast
Bar service
Sitting room, library, coin laundry, gift shop

An elegant and romantic step back to the turn-of-the-century. Each room has a private bath. BisbeeGrandHotel@msn.com http://www.bisbeegrandhotel.com

BISBEE

Inn at Castle Rock
PO Box 1161
112 Tombstone Canyon Rd
85603
520-432-4449 Fax: 520-432-7868
800-566-4449
Jeanenne Babcock

59-77-BB
16 rooms, 16 pb
S-no/P-yes/H-no
All year

Full breakfast

Give a special treat to your sweet . . . bring your true love to the Inn at Castle Rock this spring. mail@theinn.org http://www.theinn.org

CAVE CREEK (REGION)

Full Circle Ranch
PO Box 5521
40205 N 26th St, *Carefree* 85377
623-465-7570 Fax: 623-465-7575
Jim Langan
All year

160-BB
3 rooms, 3 pb
Visa, MC, AmEx
C-ltd/S-ltd/P-no/H-ltd

Full breakfast
Dinner avail., comp. wine, bar service
Jacuzzis, swimming pool, accomodate business travelers

Located in one of the most scenic areas of the beautiful Sonoran Desert. Tucked into a valley surrounded by desert mountains, away from congestion and noise of the city.
jlangan@fullcircleranch.com http://www.fullcircleranch.com

DRAGOON

And the Horse You Rode In On
PO Box 158
2400 W Dragoon Rd 85609
520-826-5410 Fax: 520-826-1078
Deborah and Will Scott
All year

70-95-BB
4 rooms, 1 pb
C-ltd/S-no/P-ltd/H-yes
Spanish, French

Full breakfast
Snacks
Sitting room, library, Jacuzzis, 10 guest horse stalls

Furnished in Southwestern style, with amenities in each room including many items of Western art from the owners' personal collection.
info@horseyourodeinon.com http://www.horseyourodeinon.com

FLAGSTAFF

Birch Tree Inn
824 W Birch Ave 86001
928-774-1042 Fax: 928-774-8462
888-774-1042
The Pettingers, The Znetkos
All year

69-119-BB
5 rooms, 3 pb
Most CC, *Rated*, •
C-ltd/S-no/P-no/H-no

Full breakfast
Afternoon tea, snacks
Sitting room, piano, pool table, tennis court nearby

Comfortable, country charm; savory, down-home, hearty breakfasts. A four season retreat in the magnificent beauty of Northern Arizona.
info@birchtreeinn.com http://www.birchtreeinn.com

Comfi Cottages
1612 N Aztec St 86001
928-774-0731 Fax: 928-773-7286
888-774-0731
Pat & Ed Wiebe All year

120-260-BB
6 rooms, 6 pb
Most CC, *Rated*, •
C-yes/S-no/P-no/H-ltd
French

Full breakfast
Afternoon tea, snacks, complimentary wine
Sitting room, library, bikes, fireplaces, cable TV

Arizona Republic's choice "Best Weekend Getaway." 6 charming cottages, all located near the heart of downtown. pat@comficottages.com http://www.comficottages.com

---

Fall Inn to Nature
8080 N Colt Dr 86004
928-714-0237 Fax: 928-714-0237
888-920-0237
Annette & Ron Fallaha
All year

80-95-BB
3 rooms, 2 pb
Visa, MC, AmEx, *Rated*, •
C-ltd/S-ltd/P-no/H-no

Full breakfast
Cider & cookies upon arrival!
Sitting room, fireplaces, cable TV, horseback riding/trails, outdoor hot tub

The place with the personal touch! Sits on 2.5 acres with views, in a country setting with the sounds of nature. Exquisite breakfast! In-house massage therapists.
fallinn@infomagic.net http://www.bbonline.com/az/fallinn

Inn at 410
410 N Leroux St 86001
928-774-0088 Fax: 928-774-6354
800-774-2008
Howard & Sally Krueger
All year

135-190-BB
9 rooms, 9 pb
Visa, MC, *Rated*, •
C-yes/S-no/P-no/H-no

Full breakfast
Homemade cookies and iced tea in the afternoon.
Sunny sitting room, quiet garden gazebo, some rooms with fireplace/Jacuzzi.

A top 10 ranked Arizona bed and breakfast. Your choice for luxurious, romantic accommodations. In historic downtown Flagstaff, walk to restaurants and shops, and just 85 miles to the Grand Canyon. info@inn410.com http://www.inn410.com

---

Jeanette's
3380 E Lockett Rd 86004
520-527-1912 Fax: 520-527-1713
800-752-1912
Jeanette & Ray West
All year

99-130-BB
4 rooms, 4 pb
Visa, MC, AmEx, *Rated*, •
S-ltd/P-no/H-no

Full breakfast
Snacks
Sitting room, fireplaces, accom. bus. travelers, porch w/view

Flagstaff's most romantic inn. This Victorian style B&B boasts antique-filled rooms, fresh flowers, private baths w/ clawfoot tubs, & a full gourmet breakfast.
romance@jeanettesbb.com http://www.jeanettesbb.com

Lake Mary
5470 S "J" Diamond Rd 86001
520-779-7054 Fax: 520-779-7054
888-244-9550
Frank & Christine McCollum
All year

80-110-BB
4 rooms, 4 pb
Visa, MC, *Rated*, •
C-yes/S-ltd/P-no/H-no

Full breakfast
Afternoon tea, snacks
Sitting room, library, family friendly facility

Small country style B&B with a big heart. Lots of antique furnishings, large guestrooms with private baths, gourmet breakfast.

The Tree House
615 W Cherry Ave 86001
520-214-8664 Fax: 520-214-7219
888-251-9390
Jenean & Scott Perelstein
All year

95-115-BB
2 rooms, 2 pb
Visa, MC, AmEx, *Rated*
C-ltd/S-no/P-no/H-no
German

Full breakfast
Snacks
Suites, cable TV, accomodates business travelers

Spacious suites decorated w/ comfort & privacy in mind. Enjoy breakfast under a canopy of our Cottonwood trees, or in privacy of your room.
http://www.bbonline.com/az/treehouse

GLOBE

Cedar Hill
175 E Cedar St 85501
520-425-7530 Fax: 520-425-2888
Helen Elizabeth Gross
All year

50-BB
2 rooms
Rated
C-yes/S-ltd/P-yes/H-no

Full breakfast
Snacks
Sitting room, library, cable TV, accommodate business travelers

Located in small, active mining town surrounded by mountains—antique furnishings, full breakfast-your choice, cities, lakes, casino in area. cedarhill175@theriver.com

GOLD CANYON

Sinelli's
5605 S Sage Way 85218
480-983-3650 Fax: 480-983-3650
Carl & Patricia Sinelli
All year

75-BB
3 rooms, 1 pb
•
C-ltd/S-yes/P-no/H-no

Continental breakfast
Full breakfast avail. by request, snacks
Lunch & dinner avail., comp. wine, sitting room

Two bedroom. apt., completely furnished, short or long stay. Casual Southwest living in foothills of the Superstition Mtns. sisu1941@juno.com

GRAND CANYON (REGION)

Mountain Country Lodge 437 W Rte 66, *Williams* 86046 520-635-4341 Fax: 520-635-1450 800-973-6210 The Barnes All year	54-99-BB 9 rooms, 9 pb Visa, MC, • C-yes/S-no/P-ltd/H-no Spanish	Continental plus breakfast Snacks Bicycles, cable TV, one family suite, bikes, suites, fireplace

Built as a mansion in 1909, the lodge boasts 9 uniquely decorated rooms. Located on Old Rte 66 & only 60 miles from the Grand Canyon, it's the ideal place for visiting the Southwest. DanD1245@aol.com http://www.thegrandcanyon.com/mclodge

Red Garter Bed & Bakery PO Box 95 137 W Railroad Ave, *Williams* 86046 928-635-1484 800-328-1484 John Holst	85-125-BB 4 rooms, 4 pb Visa, MC, Disc, *Rated*, • C-ltd/S-no/P-no/H-no Valentine's–Thanksgiving	Continental plus breakfast Afternoon tea, snacks Bakery, coffee shop, bikes, suites, fireplace

Offering lodging in a beautiful 1897 saloon & bordello with antique furnishings and breakfast in the bakery. Located on old Rt 66 across from Grand Canyon Railway, an hour south of the Grand Canyon. reservation@redgarter.com http://www.redgarter.com

Terry Ranch 701 Quarterhorse, *Williams* 86046 520-635-4171 Fax: 520-635-2488 800-210-5908 Glenn & Leisa Watkins	115-155-BB 4 rooms, 4 pb Most CC, *Rated*, • C-ltd/S-no/P-no/H-yes Spanish & Dutch All year	Full breakfast Snacks Sitting room, library, fireplaces, cable TV, 2 person jetted tub, gazebo

Our large log home offers country Victorian decor, spacious guestrooms w/private baths & sitting areas, beautiful mountain scenery from a wraparound verandah and full family style country breakfasts.
terryranch@workmail.com http://www.grand-canyon-lodging.net

GREER

Red Setter Inn & Cottages PO Box 133 8 Main St 85927 928-735-7441 Fax: 928-735-7425 888-994-7337 Jim Sankey, Ken Conant	135-220-BB Visa, MC, AmEx, *Rated* S-no/P-no/H-yes All year	Full breakfast Lunch, afternoon tea, snacks Sitting room, library, Jacuzzis, suites, fireplace, accommodate bus. trav.

Log lodge on the river, gourmet breakfasts, complimentary lunch with two nights stay–4 season getaway–8500 feet–romantic getaway–some brand new luxury log cabins available. jsankey@redsetterinn.com http://www.redsetterinn.com

White Mountain Lodge PO Box 143 140 Main St 85927 928-735-7568 Fax: 928-735-7498 888-493-7568 Charlie and Mary Bast	85-145-BB 7 rooms, 7 pb Most CC C-ltd/S-no/P-no/H-ltd All year	Full breakfast Snacks (bottomless cookie jar) and assorted drinks sitting room, porches, spa, library, fireplaces and whirlpool tubs in suites

Country home on the bank of the Little Colorado River in the heart of the National Forest. Exceptional accommodations and breakfasts. Rooms and cabins with fireplaces and whirlpool tubs. bast@cybertrails.com http://www.wmlodge.com

JEROME

Ghost City Inn PO Box T 541 Main St 86331 928-634-4678 888-634-4678 Allen & Jackie Muma All year	85-125-BB 6 rooms, 2 pb Most CC, *Rated*, • C-ltd/S-no/P-no/H-no	Full American breakfast Afternoon tea, snacks Hot tubs, sitting room, family friendly facility

Romantic get-a-way/pampered atmosphere. Experience the elegance of days gone by. Magnificent views that rival the Grand Canyon-unforgettable memories.
innkeeper@ghostcityinn.com http://www.ghostcityinn.com

JEROME

Inn at Jerome
PO Box 901
309 Main St 86331
928-634-5094 800-634-5094
Juanita Schuyler
All year

55-85-BB
8 rooms, 2 pb
Most CC, •
C-yes/S-no/P-no/H-ltd

Full breakfast
Coffee & tea are served in the parlor mornings.
Our quaint Victorian parlor is available for reading or quiet conversation.

Our Inn has been restored to its Victorian splendor. The eight guest rooms brim with detail as everything has been hand selected with the utmost care–even our down pillows get compliments! innatjerome@sedona.net http://www.innatjerome.com

PHOENIX

The Honey House
5150 N 36th St 85018
602-956-5646 Fax: 602-224-9765
Jeanette Irwin
All year

79-99-BB
3 rooms, 3 pb
Most CC, *Rated*, •
C-yes/S-no/P-yes/H-no

Full breakfast
Sitting room, library, bikes, hot tub, conference facility

Historic homesteaded property (1895). Lush acre has citrus grove, antique roses, and arbored gardens. Centrally located near museums, shopping, and golfer's paradise.
honeyhous@aol.com http://www.travelguides.com/home/honeyhouse

---

Maricopa Manor
15 W Pasadena Ave 85013
602-274-6302 Fax: 602-266-3904
800-292-6403
Jeff Vadheim
All year

99-219-BB
5 rooms, 5 pb
Rated
C-yes/S-yes/H-yes

Continental plus breakfast
Complimentary wine
Sitting room, library, pool with fountains, hot tubs

Old World charm, elegant urban setting. Central and Camelback, close to everything. Luxury suites, secluded, gardens, patios, and palm trees.
res@maricopamanor.com http://www.maricopamanor.com

Spanish Moss
844 E Spanish Moss Ln 85022
602-494-8896 Fax: 602-795-9632
Ruth Isenberg
All year

55-75-BB
2 rooms
•
C-ltd/S-ltd/P-no/H-no

Full breakfast
Iced Tea, wine and beer
Family room, sitting room, pool, Jacuzzi

Spanish Moss B&B is located in North Phoenix. Only a twenty minute drive from Sky Harbor Airport, Downtown Phoenix and Scottsdale. I-17 to Sedona, Flagstaff and the Grand Canyon is only 3 miles away.
spanishmossbnb@hotmail.com http://www.bbonline.com/az/spanishmoss

PHOENIX (REGION)

Bedlam
15253 N Skylark Circle, *Fountain Hills* 85268
480-837-9695 Fax: 480-836-1447
Pam Carlson
In Season Oct 1–Apr 30,

75-135-BB
3 rooms, 3 pb
Most CC, *Rated*, •
C-ltd/S-no/P-ltd/H-ltd
Spanish

Full breakfast
Sitting porch, Jacuzzis, swimming pool, cable TV, porch swings

Our home is newly built next to desert wilderness. A 5,000-ft. custom home on cul-de-sac acre. Designed for mountain views.
pam.carlson@cox.net http://www.stayatbedlam.com

Old Town
8276 W Monroe St, *Peoria* 85345
623-412-7797
Tom & Vicki Hunt All year

75-95-BB
4 rooms, 2 pb
Most CC, •
C-ltd/S-ltd/P-no/H-no

Full breakfast
Afternoon tea, snacks
sitting room, cable TV, accommodate business travelers

1940's red brick home in historic old town Peoria. Outdoor gardens, patios, fountains, gazebo. Beautifully appointed rooms, parlor, complete with antiques.
innkeeper@oldtownbb.com http://www.oldtownbb.com

PINETOP (REGION)

Oakwood Inn
6558 Wagon Wheel Lane,
Pinetop-Lakeside 85929
928-537-3030 Fax: 928-537-8661
800-959-8098
Ron & Shawn Monette
All year

85-125-BB
4 rooms, 4 pb
Most CC, •
C-yes/S-ltd/P-no/H-no

Full Country Breakfast
Tasty afternoon snack
Spacious rooms, fireplace, horses welcome, turndown service

Welcome to Oakwood Inn, located in the beautiful White Mountains of Eastern Arizona under towering pines and great oak trees in the resort town of Pinetop-Lakeside, near Show Low. monettes@citlink.net http://www.oakwoodinnbandb.com

PINETOP-LAKESIDE

Mountain Haven Inn
1120 E White Mountain Blvd
85935
928-367-2101 888-854-9815
Donna Spillman
All year

49-175-EP
13 rooms, 13 pb
Visa, MC, *Rated*, •
C-yes/S-no/P-no/H-no
French

Coffee & tea service offered in all rooms
Suites, outdoor fireplace, color cable TV, accommodate business travelers

Clean mountain hideaway in a quaint, small town setting. All rooms and kitchenette suites are decorated like those found in a B&B...but without breakfast. Affordable and unique: you'll love us! mtnhaven@juno.com http://www.mountainhaveninn.com

---

Pinetop Country
2444 Jan Lane 85935
928-367-0479 Fax: 928-367-0479
888-521-5044
Karen & Steve Kraxberger
All year

115-130-BB
4 rooms, 4 pb
Visa, MC, *Rated*, •
C-ltd/S-ltd/P-no/H-no

Full breakfast, choice of 10 items
Snacks, complimentary wine
Sitting room, library, bicycles, Jacuzzis, suites, fireplace

5500 sq. ft. Inn nestled in the cool mountains of Arizona. We offer too many amenities to mention. Ten items to choose from for your breakfast pleasure.
innkeepers@pinetopcountry.com http://www.pinetopcountry.com

PRESCOTT

Briar Wreath Inn
232 S Arizona Ave 86303
928-778-6048
Terry F. Fowler and Fred R. Munch All year

100-150-BB
4 rooms, 4 pb
Most CC, *Rated*, •
C-ltd/S-no/P-no/H-no

Full breakfast
Snacks, Complimentary wine
Sitting room, library, Jacuzzi, fireplace, cable TV, business travelers

1904 Craftsman style inn with wood embellished floors, walls and ceilings. Cozy great room with fireplace, library, and piano. Walking distance to town.
office@briarwreath.com http://www.briarwreath.com

Hassayampa Inn
122 E Gurley St 86301
520-778-9434 Fax: 520-445-8590
800-322-1927
Bill & Georgia Teich
All year

120-175-BB
68 rooms, 68 pb
Visa, MC, AmEx, *Rated*, •
C-yes/S-ltd/P-no/H-yes
Limited Spanish

Full breakfast
Lunch/dinner available (fee)
Restaurant, Bar service, tennis, suites, AAA 3 diamond, patio with Gazebo.

68-room, 3 diamond, historic hotel in mile-high Prescott; yesterday's charm gracefully restored, modern amenities; renowned 3-diamond restaurant.
inn@primenet.com http://www.hassayampainn.com

Lynx Creek Farm
PO Box 4301
Call for directions 86302
928-778-9573 888-778-9573
Greg & Wendy Temple
All year

85-200-BB
6 rooms, 6 pb
Most CC, *Rated*, •
C-yes/S-ltd/P-yes/H-ltd
Spanish

Full gourmet breakfast
Complimentary drinks, appetizers
Private decks & hot tubs, kitchenettes, BBQ, pool, wood stoves, croquet

Secluded, country setting on picturesque apple farm minutes from town. Coffee in rooms, quilts. lcf@vacation-lodging.com http://www.vacation-lodging.com

PRESCOTT

The Pleasant Street Inn
142 S Pleasant St 86303
928-445-4774 877-226-7128
D. and B. Chadderdon
All year

99-135-BB
4 rooms, 4 pb
Most CC, *Rated*
C-ltd/S-no/P-no/H-ltd

Full breakfast
Soft drinks
One suite with fireplace, another with private deck

Lovely Victorian three blocks from Court House Plaza. Four guestrooms all with private baths. Featured in the July 2001 issue of Phoenix Magazine as one of "Arizona's 23 Best B&Bs." info@pleasantbandb.com http://www.pleasantstreetinn-bb.com

---

Prescott Pines Inn
901 White Spar Rd 86303
928-445-7270 Fax: 928-778-3665
800-541-5374
Jean, Mike, & Sue
All year

65-269-EP
14 rooms, 12 pb
Visa, MC, *Rated*
C-ltd/S-no/P-no/H-ltd

Full breakfast available, coffee & teas
BBQ, kitchenettes, lib., sitt. rm., ceiling fan, games, gardens, porches

11 guestrooms in 3 guesthouses, 1-3 bedroom chalet for 4 couples, all on an acre w/ponderosa pines & gardens. Some rooms w/frpl., kitchenettes.
info@prescottpinesinn.com http://www.prescottpinesinn.com

PRESCOTT (REGION)

The Oasis Ranch
PO Box 256
13495 W Cottonwood Ln, *Skull Valley* 86338
520-442-9559 Fax: 520-442-9557
Bonnie & Bruce Jackson
All year

100-125-EP
2 rooms, 2 pb
Rated
C-ltd/S-yes/P-no/H-no

Sitting room, Jacuzzis, swimming pool, suites, fireplaces, cable TV, stables

Luxurious waterfront cottages located just outside Prescott, AZ. Grounds include a private hot tub room and a waterfront barbecue area. Escape to the country this season!
oasisaz@primenet.com http://www.oasisranch.net

SCOTTSDALE

Inn at the Citadel
8700 E. Pinnacle Pk 108 85255
480-585-6133 Fax: 480-585-3436
800-927-8367
Lisa DeLeo All year

79-335
11 rooms, 11 pb
Rated

SCOTTSDALE (REGION)

Southwest Inn at Eagle Mtn.
9800 N Summer Hill Blvd, *Fountain Hills* 85268
480-816-3000 Fax: 480-816-3090
800-992-8083
Conna ray
Season inquire

99-399-BB
42 rooms, 42 pb
Rated, •

Continental breakfast
Private decks and patios, great views, pool, spa, meeting rooms, golf

Pampered is what you will be in this beautiful brand new Santa Fe style property on the Eagle Mountain Golf Course. info@southwestinn.com http://www.southwestinn.com

---

Valley O' the Sun
PO Box 2214, *Tempe* 85252
480-941-1281 Fax: 480-941-1281
866-941-1281
Kathleen Kennedy Curtis
All year

45-60-BB
3 rooms, 1 pb
Most CC, •
C-ltd/S-ltd/P-no/H-no

Continental plus breakfast
Full breakfast on weekends
Sitting room, close to nearby attractions, cable TV, fax available

Valley O' the Sun B&B located in Tempe, near ASU. We are Arizona's only Irish Bed & Breakfast! valleyothesunbnb@owol.net http://www.valleyothesunbnb.com

SEDONA

4 Diamond Adobe Village Graham Inn
150 Canyon Circle Dr 86351
928-284-1425 Fax: 928-284-0767
800-228-1425
Steward & Ilene Berman
All year

169-499-BB
11 rooms, 11 pb
Most CC, *Rated*, •
C-yes/S-ltd/P-no/H-yes

Full breakfast
Afternoon hot hors d'oeuvres
Pool, private balconies & patios, Jacuzzis, fireplaces, red rock views

Five star award–9 year four diamond AAA award. Romantic setting, private balconies, red rock views info@sedonasfinest.com http://www.sedonasfinest.com

---

A Southwest Inn at Sedona
3250 W Hwy 89A 86336
928-282-3344 Fax: 928-282-0267
800-483-7422
Joel & Sheila Gilgoff
All year

99-239-BB
28 rooms, 28 pb
Most CC, *Rated*, •
C-yes/S-no/P-no/H-yes
Spanish

Continental plus breakfast
Refreshments
Hot tubs, swimming, phones/TVs, hiking, fireplaces, biking, Internet cafe

AAA Diamond rated for over 7 years. Award-winning southwest architecture and decor combined with great views make our combination B&B-small luxury inn unique.
info@swinn.com http://www.swinn.com

A Sunset Chateau B&B
665 Sunset Dr 86336
928-282-2644 Fax: 928-282-9121
877-655-BEDS
Rosemary Corneto
All year

110-220-BB
22 rooms, 22 pb
Visa, MC, AmEx, *Rated*
C-no/S-no/P-no/H-yes
Spanish

Full breakfast
Sitting room, library, Jacuzzis, suites, fireplace, cable TV, conference

Our Inn sits on top of a hill and has a view of the town and a most awesome panoramic view of the Red Rock that Sedona is so well known for.
info@asunsetchateau.com http://www.asunsetchateau.com

A Territorial House
65 Piki Dr 86336
928-204-2737 Fax: 928-204-2230
800-801-2737
Larry & Suzie Galisky
All year

115-185-BB
4 rooms, 4 pb
Most CC, *Rated*, •
C-yes/S-ltd/P-no/H-no

Full breakfast
Afternoon tea, snacks
Sitting room, whirlpool tub, fireplace, deck, outdoor hot tub

A ranch style home built of Red Rock and Cedar located in a canopy of Cottonwood trees in the heart of Red Rock Country. Friendly and Peaceful with Old West Decor and Old West Hospitality. info@territorialhousebb.com http://www.territorialhouse.com

---

A Country Gardens
PO Box 2603
170 Country Ln 86339
928-282-1343 Fax: 928-204-2246
800-570-0102
Sue & Dan Neimy All year

165-225-BB
4 rooms, 4 pb
Most CC, •
C-ltd/S-ltd/P-no/H-no

Full breakfast
Library, sitting room, outdoor hammocks

A Country Gardens Bed & Breakfast is a private, secluded, romantic country inn bordering thousands of acres of national forest, yet only minutes from specialty shops, restaurants and art galleries. grtbandb@sedona.net http://www.SedonaCountryInn.com

---

A Touch of Sedona
595 Jordan Rd 86336
928-282-6462 Fax: 928-282-1534
800-600-6462
Joanne Leone
All year

119-169-BB
5 rooms, 5 pb
Most CC, *Rated*, •
C-yes/S-no/P-no/H-yes

Full gourmet breakfast
Cookies/homemade breads; special diets welcome
Redrock views, walk uptown to restaurants, shopping, galleries

Panoramic red rock views in uptown Sedona. Walk to nearby shops, art galleries, hiking/biking trails, great restaurants and sandwich shops. No parking hassles.
touch@touchsedona.com http://www.touchsedona.com

A Touch of Sedona, Sedona, AZ

SEDONA

Alma de Sedona Inn
50 Hozoni Dr 86336
928-282-2737 Fax: 928-203-4141
800-923-2282
Ron & Lynn McCarroll
All year

169-285-BB
12 rooms, 12 pb
Visa, MC, AmEx,
Rated, •
C-ltd/S-no/P-no/H-yes
French, Spanish

Full breakfast
Afternoon appetizers, luscious cookies
Sitting room, fireplaces, swimming pool, cable TV, conference facilities

Fodor's recommends and AAA awarded 4-Diamond status because guests receive luxury, privacy, romance and impeccable service in the warm folds of Alma de Sedona Inn.
innkeeper@almadesedona.com http://www.almadesedona.com/

Apple Orchard Inn
656 Jordan Rd 86336
928-282-5328 Fax: 928-204-0044
800-663-6968
Jean McDonald, Stephanie & Philip Sherwin
All year

135-230-BB
7 rooms, 7 pb
Visa, MC, AmEx,
Rated, •
C-ltd/S-no/P-no/H-yes
German

Full breakfast
Snacks
Sitting room, cable TV/VCRs, Jacuzzis, fridge, fireplaces, pool & spa

Sedona's newest AAA 4-Diamond. Romantic getaway in the heart of Sedona. Red rock, views, hiking, pool & spa. Theme rooms with all amenities.
appleorc@sedona.net http://www.appleorchardbb.com

B&B at Saddle Rock Ranch
255 Rock Ridge Dr 86336
928-282-7640 Fax: 928-282-6829
Fran & Dan Bruno
All year

149-179-BB
3 rooms, 3 pb

Fall in love with the spell of Sedona. Capturing the romantic spirit of a former era, Saddlerock Ranch invites you to be our guest.
saddlerock@sedona.net http://www.saddlerockranch.com

Boots & Saddles
PO Box 1950
2900 Hopi Dr 86339
928-282-1944 Fax: 928-204-2230
800-201-1944
John & Linda Steele
All year

165-245-BB
4 rooms, 4 pb
Most CC, *Rated*, •
C-ltd/S-ltd/P-no/H-ltd

Full breakfast
Snacks
Sitting room, bikes, jetted tubs, gas fireplaces, refrigerators, cable TV

Rooms are decorated for casual western themes. Sidekick packages, horseback, jeep tours, & golf avail. Unique western cowboy headboards in each bedroom.
oldwest@sedona.net http://www.oldwestbb.com/bs1.html

SEDONA

Briar Patch Inn
3190 N Highway 89 A 86336
928-282-2342 Fax: 928-282-2399
888-809-3030
Rob Olson
All year

169-325-BB
17 rooms, 17 pb
Visa, MC, AmEx,
Rated, •
C-yes/S-ltd/P-no/H-ltd
Spanish

Continental plus breakfast
Homemade cookies, tea, coffee
Sitting room, library, fireplaces, kitchenettes, massage, swimming hole

One of the most beautiful spots in Arizona. Cottages nestled on 9 spectacular acres on sparkling Oak Creek. Warm, generous hospitality. A real gem!
briarpatch@sedona.net http://www.briarpatchinn.com

Canyon Villa Inn
125 Canyon Circle Dr 86351
928-284-1226 Fax: 928-284-2114
800-453-1166
Les & Peg Belch
All year

189-279-BB
11 rooms, 11 pb
Most CC, *Rated*, •
C-ltd/S-no/P-no/H-yes

Full breakfast
Hors d'ouevres, 24 hr sodas, juices, coffee, teas
Sitting room, library, swimming pool, golf & tennis, hiking & biking nearby

Southwest-style inn faces the highlands desert with unmatched bed-side views of Sedona's red rocks. A luxury B&B providing exceptional guest service. All rooms have private patios or balconies. canvilla@sedona.net http://www.canyonvilla.com

---

Canyon Wren - Cabins For Two
6425 N Hwy 89A 86336
928-282-6900 Fax: 928-282-6978
800-437-9736
Mike & Milena Pfeifer-Smith
All year

135-150-BB
4 rooms, 4 pb
Most CC, *Rated*, •
C-no/S-no/P-no/H-ltd
Slovenian

Continental plus breakfast
Coffee, tea, hot chocolate always available
Easy access to the creek, hosts pleased to advise, patios, hiking

Fodor's "best value in Oak Creek Canyon"! In spectacular canyon with red rock views. Cozy cabins have queen bed, full kitchen, fireplace, whirlpool bathtub, decks, patio with gas grill. cnynwren@sedona.net http://canyonwrencabins.com

---

Casa Sedona Inn
55 Hozoni Dr 86336
928-282-2938 Fax: 928-282-2259
800-525-3756
Bob & Donna Marriott
All year

180-260-BB
16 rooms, 16 pb
Visa, MC, *Rated*, •
C-ltd/S-no/P-no/H-yes

Full breakfast
Tea or hot cider, cookies, afternoon appetizers
Spa tubs, fireplaces, hairdryers, robes, TV/VCR, iron, ironing board

AAA 4-Diamond Inn to be featured on the Travel Channel's "Best of the Best Hotels & Inns" series, Fall 2002. Panoramic Red Rock views. Designed by Frank Lloyd Wright protege. Quiet, romantic and relaxing. casa@sedona.net http://www.casasedona.com

---

The Cozy Cactus
80 Canyon Circle Dr 86351
928-284-0082 Fax: 928-284-4210
800-788-2082
Linda Caldwell
All year

100-135-BB
5 rooms, 5 pb
Most CC, *Rated*, •
C-yes/S-ltd/P-no/H-ltd
French

Full breakfast
Hiking, mountain biking and golf nearby,TV/VCR, movie collection, fireplaces

Fantastic views from a ranch-style house on the edge of the forest. Five comfortable rooms with private baths, fireplaces, patios, birding and hiking trails right outside the door.
info@cozycactus.com http://www.cozycactus.com

Don Hoel's Cabins
9440 North Hwy 89A 86336
928-282-3560 Fax: 928-282-3654
800-292-4635
David Watters
2/15-11/30

100-115-BB
18 rooms, 18 pb
Most CC, •
C-yes/S-no/P-no/H-no

Continental breakfast
Parlor with books & TV, Country store

Located in the tall pines of Oak Creek Canyon you will find 18 cottages that are Don Hoel's Cabins. Each unique & quaint in its own way. A perfect getaway for a relaxing weekend with someone special. cabins@hoels.com http://www.hoels.com

SEDONA

The Inn on Oak Creek
556 Hwy 179 86336
928-282-7896 Fax: 928-282-0696
800-499-7896
Rick & Pam Morris
All year

190-285-BB
11 rooms, 11 pb
Most CC, *Rated*, •
C-ltd/S-no/P-no/H-yes

Full breakfast
Snacks
Spa tubs, suites, fireplaces, TV/VCR, hair dryers, robes, waterfront & views

Sedona's only AAA 4 diamond B&B on Oak Creek. Luxury, romance and culinary delights await you. Select Registry Member. theinn@sedona.net http://www.sedona-inn.com

---

Lantern Light Inn
3085 W. Hwy 89A 86336
928-282-3419 Fax: 928-203-9380
877-275-4973
Edward & Kris Varjean
All year

125-295-BB
5 rooms, 5 pb
Rated, •
C-ltd/S-ltd/P-no/H-no

Full breakfast
Snacks
Sitting room, library, suites, fireplaces, cable TV, large video library

Rated by Phoenix Magazine (July 2001) as one of 23 best "Homey Hideaways" in Arizona. lanternlightinn@earthlink.net

---

Lodge at Sedona
125 Kallof Place 86336
928-204-1942 Fax: 928-204-2128
800-619-4467
Shelley Wachal
All year

150-285-BB
14 rooms, 14 pb
Visa, MC, Disc, *Rated*, •
C-ltd/S-ltd/P-ltd/H-yes
Spanish, German

Five course gourmet breakfast
Sunset beverages & snacks, Sedona Gold coffee
Fireside lounge, health club and swimming pool privileges, massage therapy,

"Romance and Intrigue, comfort and luxury, beauty and character, escape and adventure– The Lodge at Sedona has it all." Arizona Daily News.
Info@LODGEatSEDONA.com http://www.LODGEatSEDONA.com

Rose Tree Inn
376 Cedar St 86336
928-282-2065 Fax: 928-282-0083
888-282-2065
Gary Dawson
All year

89-135-EP
5 rooms, 5 pb
Visa, MC, *Rated*, •
C-ltd/S-yes/P-no/H-no

In-room coffee & tea
Patios, library, Jacuzzi, phones & TV/VCR in rms., bicycles, kitchenettes

A quiet, cozy inn with five rooms, private baths, TV and VCR, kitchens. Two rooms with fireplaces. info@rosetreeinn.com http://www.rosetreeinn.com

---

Wishing Well
995 N Hwy 89A 86336
928-282-4914 Fax: 928-204-9766
800-728-9474
Valda Esau
All year

170-195-BB
5 rooms, 5 pb
Most CC, *Rated*, •
C-ltd/S-no/P-no/H-no

Continental plus breakfast
Sitting room, library, Jacuzzis, fireplaces, cable TV

5 room luxury B&B atop a hill nestled at forest edge, guests enjoy private baths, fireplaces, & hot tubs. Linger over breakfast served in your room or on your private deck.
wishwell@sedona.net http://www.sedonawishingwell.com

SONOITA

Rancho Milagro
PO Box 981
11 E Camino Del Corral 85637
520-455-0381
Michael & Karen
All year

125-BB
3 rooms, 3 pb
C-ltd/S-no/P-no/H-no

Continental breakfast
Spa tubs, wood burning fireplaces, serenity, majestic mountain vistas

Casitas-like suites with modern amenities. From your private porch, watch glorious sunsets over the Santa Ritas, or watch the sunrise over the Mustangs. Privacy, peace and serenity are highly prized. info@ranchomilagrobb.com http://www.ranchomilagrobb.com

TUCSON

Adobe Rose Inn
940 N Olsen Ave 85719
520-318-4644 Fax: 520-325-0055
800-328-4122
Joy Andrews
All year

95-150-BB
5 rooms, 5 pb
Rated

Full breakfast

Nestled in the Santa Catalina Mountains of Southern Arizona, Tucson offers enough diversions and appeal of the Southwestern lifestyle to tempt any vacationer or business group. aroseinn@mindspring.com http://www.aroseinn.com

---

Agave Grove Inn
800 W Panorama Rd 85704
520-797-3400 Fax: 520-797-0980
888-822-4283
John & Denise Kiber
All year

65-175-BB
5 rooms, 4 pb
Most CC, *Rated*, •
C-yes/S-ltd/P-no/H-yes

Full breakfast
Tea, snacks
Sitting room, library, Jacuzzis, swimming pool, suites, fireplace, cable TV

Romantic estate on 2.5 acres, majestic mountain views, private baths, gourmet breakfast, billiard table, courtyards with Ramada, fountain.
agavebb@earthlink.net http://www.bbonline.com/az/agave

Bienestar B&B
10490 E Escalante Rd 85730
520-290-1048 Fax: 520-290-1367
800-293-0004
R. Scanlin & D. Strausser
All year

90-150-BB
4 rooms, 4 pb
Most CC, *Rated*, •
C-ltd/S-no/P-no/H-ltd

Full breakfast
Evening refreshments
Sitting room, library, hot tub, swimming pool, TV/VCRs in each room

Lovely desert hacienda near national park featuring delicious breakfasts from whole natural foods.

Cactus Cove
10066 E Kleindale Rd 85749
520-760-7730 Fax: 520-749-3304
800-466-0083
Sally and Ivan Gunderman
All year

155-195-BB
3 rooms, 3 pb
Most CC, *Rated*
C-ltd/S-no/P-no/H-ltd

Full breakfast
Snacks
Sitting room, library, Jacuzzis, swimming pool, suites, cable TV

It is a peaceful oasis in the middle of the Sonoran Desert. Quiet is our most noticeable quality.
cactuscv@azstarnet.com http://azcactuscove.com

The Cactus Quail
14000 N Dust Devil Dr 85739
520-825-6767
Marty & Sue Higbee
Season Inquire

109-139-BB
Visa, MC
C-ltd/S-no/P-no

Full or continental breakfast

It's beyond the lights of the city. Close enough to the mountains so there is nothing between them and you. Far enough so you can grasp the full splendor of shadowy folds and dancing color changes. spectacularviews@cactusquail.com http://www.cactusquail.com

---

Car-Mar's Southwest
6766 W Oklahoma St 85735
520-578-1730 Fax: 520-578-7272
888-578-1730
Carole Martinez & Richard Quindry
All year

75-145-BB
4 rooms, 2 pb
Visa, MC, *Rated*
C-yes/S-ltd/P-ltd/H-ltd

Full breakfast
Snacks
Sitting room, Jacuzzis, pool, fireplaces, cable TV

Our huge territorial home has 4 guestrooms from nostalgic antique to casual southwestern design.
Carmarbb@aol.com http://members.aol.com/carmarbb

TUCSON

Casa Alegre 316 E Speedway Blvd 85705 520-628-1800 Fax: 520-792-1880 800-628-5654 Phyllis Florek All year	85-135-BB 4 rooms, 4 pb Visa, MC, Disc, *Rated*, • C-ltd/S-no/P-no/H-no	Full breakfast Afternoon tea, snacks Sitting room, library, swimming pool, Jacuzzi, public tennis courts

Beautiful 1915 Craftsman bungalow near U of AZ, metropolitan Tucson, golf, mountain and desert attractions.
alegre123@aol.com http://www.casaalegreinn.com

Casa Tierra Adobe Inn 11155 West Calle Pima 85743 520-578-3058 Fax: 520-578-8445 866-254-0006 Barb & Dave Malmquist August 15–June 15	135-325-BB 5 rooms, 5 pb Most CC, *Rated*, • C-yes/S-no/P-no/H-no	Full gourmet vegetarian breakfast Fruit and snack basket, 24 hr. yogurt, bagels Media room, gym, hot tub, telescope, private patios

Internationally acclaimed, rustic but elegant adobe hacienda. Five acres near Desert Museum. Courtyards, fountains, telescope, gym, hot tub, private baths, patios.
info@casatierratucson.com http://www.casatierratucson.com

Catalina Park Inn 309 E 1st St 85705 520-792-4541 800-792-4885 Mark Hall All year	84-154-BB 6 rooms, 6 pb Visa, MC, Disc, *Rated* C-ltd/S-no/P-no/H-no	Full breakfast Afternoon tea, snacks Sitting room, lush gardens, many amenities

Stylish inn featuring beautifully decorated guestrooms & full range of amenities. Enjoy our lush perennial garden.
innkeeper@catalinaparkinn.com http://www.catalinaparkinn.com

Crickethead Inn 9480 Picture Rocks Rd 85743 520-682-7126 Michael Lord Oct 1–May 31	70-80-BB 3 rooms, 3 pb *Rated* C-ltd/S-ltd/H-no Spanish	Full breakfast

Secluded and quiet, beamed ceiling, fired adobe brick, borders national park, lots of birds, flowers, plants, Mexican tile bathrooms, full breakfast, great coffee.

Desert Dove 11707 E Old Spanish Trail 85730 520-722-6879 877-722-6879 Harvey & Betty Ross All year	80-97-BB 2 rooms, 2 pb Most CC, *Rated* C-no/S-no/P-no	Full breakfast Soft drinks, tea & afternoon snacks Spa/bathrobes, phone, common area refrig & microwave

Our Inn is located in Tucson, Arizona on four acres, which are nestled in the foothills of the Rincon Mountains near Saguaro National Park East.
info@desertdovebb.com http://www.desertdovebb.com

Desert Oasis 3935 N Mt Pleasant Dr 85749 520-749-7095 Fax: 520-760-0336 888-799-4284 Dennis & Cynthia Bressler All year	120-125-BB 2 rooms, 2 pb Visa, MC, *Rated* C-ltd/S-ltd/P-no/H-no	Continental plus breakfast Fireplaces, suites, cable TV, accommodate business travelers

Peace, tranquility, and privacy are trademarks of our B&B. Spectacular sunsets, mountain views and night sky. Close to golfing, hiking, horseback riding and restaurants.
info@desertoasisbnb.com http://desertoasisbnb.com

TUCSON

Flying V Ranch
6810 Flying V Ranch Rd
6800 Flying V Ranch Rd 85750
520-299-0702 Fax: 520-299-0702
Nellia Shields-Young
Closed July & August

95-175-EP
6 rooms, 6 pb
C-yes/S-ltd/P-no/H-ltd

Herbal & regular teas, coffees & basic condiments
Swimming pool, cottages all have at least two rooms

Built in 1902, we have owned the ranch since 1946. We are small & hands on. All units are self contained w/fully-equipped kitchens or kitchenettes.
flyingvranch@worldnet.att.net http://home.att.net/~flyingvranch

---

Hacienda
5704 E Grant Rd 85712
520-290-2224 Fax: 520-721-9066
888-236-4421
Barbara & Fred Shamseldin
All year

95-145-BB
4 rooms, 4 pb
Visa, MC, AmEx,
Rated, •
C-yes/S-ltd/P-no/H-yes

Full gourmet breakfast
Afternoon tea
Solar pool, heated spa, exercise room, patio, dance floor, TV/VCR

Two rooms, 4 upstairs suites (2 w/jetted tub), gourmet breakfast. Quiet, convenient, central location for shopping, museums, meetings, sports & parks.
info@tucsonhacienda.com http://www.tucsonhacienda.com

Hacienda del Desierto
11770 E Rambling Trail 85747
520-298-1764 Fax: 520-722-4558
800-982-1795
David and Rosemary Brown
All year

100-175-BB
4 rooms, 4 pb
Most CC, •
C-yes/S-ltd/P-no/H-no

Continental plus breakfast
Kitchenettes
Sitting room, robes, TV/VCR, fireplace, hydrotherapy spas, Spanish courtyard

Old Spanish style Hacienda on 16 acres next to national park. Romantic hideaway. Mountain views. oasis@tucson-bed-breakfast.com http://www.tucson-bed-breakfast.com

---

Hacienda del Rey
7320 N Cortaro Rd 85743
520-579-0425 Fax: 520-579-3830
Bill & Polly Ritchie
All year

115-BB
3 rooms, 3 pb
Most CC, *Rated*
C-yes/S-ltd/P-no/H-yes

Full breakfast
Snacks
Sitting room, library, Jacuzzis, cable TV

Enjoy our large Mexican hacienda on 4 acres of lush, tranquil, saguaro studded Sonoran desert.
ritchie@pollyritchie.com http://www.bbhost.com/hacdelrey

June's
3212 W Holladay St 85746
520-578-0857
June Henderson
All year

45-55-BB
3 rooms
Rated
C-ltd/S-no/P-no/H-no

Continental breakfast
Sitting room, piano, heated swimming pool, art studio, exercise rm.

Mountainside home with pool. Majestic towering mountains. Hiking in the desert. Sparkling city lights. Beautiful backyard & patio.

Karrels' Double K Ranch
3930 N Smokey Topaz Ln
85749
520-749-5345 Fax: 520-760-5594
Ken & Mary Karrels
All year

95-125-BB
3 rooms, 3 pb
Rated, •
C-yes/S-ltd/P-ltd/H-ltd

Full breakfast
Snacks, complimentary wine
Sitting room, library, Jacuzzi, swimming pool, fireplace, acc. bus. trav.

Railroad theme B&B on 4 acres of stately saguaros. SP caboose restored with attention to detail and comfort. Full ranch breakfast on patio with garden railway.
karrels@doublekranch.com http://www.doublekranch.com

TUCSON

The Mesquite Tree
860 W Ina Rd 85704
520-297-9670 Fax: 520-326-6400
800-317-9670
Barbara & Jeffrey Minker
All year

200-375-BB
2 rooms, 2 pb
Rated
C-ltd/S-no/P-no/H-no

Full breakfast
Snacks, complimentary drinks and fruits
Library, Jacuzzi, swimming pool, fireplace

Seven acre secluded, luxurious, two-bedroom two-bath colonial-Mexican guesthouse.
minker@mesquitetree.com http://www.mesquitetree.com

Mountain Views
3160 N Bear Canyon Rd 85749
520-749-1387 Fax: 520-749-1516
Roy & Mim Kile
All year

75-90-BB
2 rooms, 2 pb
Visa, MC, AmEx, *Rated*, •
C-ltd/S-no/P-no/H-ltd

Full breakfast
Complimentary wine
Sitting room, swimming pool, cable TV, accommodate business travelers

Mountain Views B&B is nestled in vegetated desert setting, secluded 3.3 acres on Tucson's far eastside, w/beautiful panoramic mountain views.
Rkile85749@aol.com http://www.mtviewsbb.com

Peppertrees
724 E University Blvd 85719
520-622-7167 800-348-5763
Marjorie G. Martin
All year

88-135-BB
9 rooms, 3 pb
Rated, •
C-ltd/S-no/P-no/H-no

Full gourmet breakfast
Picnic lunch to go, afternoon tea
Library, TV, VCR, walk to restaurants

Warm, friendly territorial home. Great location for visiting Univ. of Arizona. Quiet, tranquil patio, comfortable rooms, excellent breakfast.
pepperinn@gci-net.com http://www.peppertreesinn.com

La Posada del Valle
1640 N Campbell Ave 85719
520-795-3840 Fax: 520-795-3840
888-404-7113
Karin Dennen
All year

75-159-BB
5 rooms, 5 pb
Rated, • 5
C-ltd/S-no/P-no/H-no
German

Full gourmet breakfast
Afternoon tea
TV/VCR

Elegant 1920's inn nestled in the heart of the city, offering gourmet breakfast, privileges at racquet and swim club. Enchanting courtyards.
laposadabandbinn@hotmail.com http://www.bbonline.com/az/laposada

---

Quail's Vista
826 E Palisades Rd 85737
520-297-5980
Fax: 520-297-5980
Barbara & Richard Bauer
Oct 1–May 1

65-85-BB
3 rooms, 1 pb
Rated, •
C-ltd/S-ltd/P-no/H-no

Continental plus breakfast
Snacks
Sitting room, Jacuzzis, fireplace, cable TV, swim stream spa outside

Passive solar rammed earth and adobe house has 27" thick walls and is located on two acres of desert, with views of the Catalina Mountains.
quails-vista@juno.com http://www.quails-vista-bb.com

Rancho Quieto
12051 W Fort Lowell Rd 85743
520-883-3300
Corinne Still
September 15–May

125-150-BB
4 rooms
•
C-ltd/S-no/P-ltd/H-no

Full breakfast
Sitting room, Jacuzzis, swimming pool, suites, fireplaces

Spacious suites and 2 guesthouses are available September 15–May. Grounds are rented for corporate parties and spring & fall weddings.

Quail's Vista, Tucson, AZ

TUCSON

Royal Elizabeth 204 S Scott Ave 85701 520-670-9022 Fax: 520-629-9710 877-670-9022 Robert Ogburn & Jack Nance	90-180-BB 6 rooms, 6 pb Most CC, *Rated* C-ltd/S-no/P-no/H-no All year	Full Gourmet Breakfast Afternoon tea, snacks Sitting room, library, Jacuzzis, pool, suites, cable TV

Gracious 1878 Victorian adobe mansion meticulously renovated for your comfort. Spacious suites with period antiques, private baths, gourmet breakfasts, pool & spa in downtown historic district. inn@royalelizabeth.com http://www.royalelizabeth.com

Sam Hughes Inn 2020 E Seventh St 85719 520-861-2191 Fax: 1-254541-1363 Susan Banner All year	75-125-BB 4 rooms, 4 pb Most CC, • C-no/S-no/P-no/H-ltd	Full breakfast Snacks on request high season, Dec.-April only Great room with library, game room, shaded garden

Lush vegetation surrounds this 1930's era California Mission styled house. In a National Historic District, Sam Hughes Inn is centrally located within steps of the University of Arizona. innkeeper@samhughesinn.com http://www.samhughesinn.com

WILLIAMS

Legacies B&B 450 S 11th St 86046 928-635-4880 Fax: 928-635-2509 866-370-2288 Linda Dixon All year	99-124-BB 3 rooms, 3 pb Most CC C-ltd/S-no/P-no/H-no	Full breakfast Champagne/sparkling cider, sodas Great room with wood burning fire, hot tub, patio, alcove area, wooded yard

Find romance near the south rim of the Grand Canyon in this lavishly appointed bed and breakfast nestled in a beautiful mountain town.
rosebud07@earthlink.net http://www.legaciesbb.com

Arkansas

BELLA VISTA

The Inn at Bella Vista 1 Chelsea Rd 72714 501-876-5645 Fax: 501-876-5662 877-876-5645 Bill & Beverly Williams	120-150-BB 5 rooms, 5 pb Most CC, *Rated*, • C-ltd/S-no/P-ltd/H-no All year	Full breakfast Snacks Sitting room, library, bikes, pool, cable TV, fireplaces, conference fac.

14 acres, 9,000 square feet, natural setting, breathtaking views, personal services, great good. Lots to do, or nothing at all.
innkeeper@iabv.com http://www.iabv.com

BRANSON (REGION)

Antiques & Lace/Evening Shade Inn
3079 E Van Buren
Highway 62 East, *Eureka Springs* 72632
479-253-6264
800-992-1224
Ed & Shirley Nussbaum

120-160-BB
7 rooms, 7 pb
Visa, MC, AmEx, *Rated*, •
C-no/S-no/P-no/H-no
All year

Continental breakfast plus
Snacks, wine
Jacuzzis, fireplace, cable TV, conference facility

Luxurious honeymoon cottages and bed and breakfast on ten wooded acres in Eureka Springs. Romantic, private, quiet. Relax in a swing, or in the Gazebo.
eveshade@ipa.net http://www.eveningshade.com

CADDO GAP

River's Edge
HC 65, Box 5
63 Hwy 240 W 71935
870-356-4864 800-756-4864
T & Judy Cone

95-125
7 rooms, 7 pb
All year

River's Edge Bed and Breakfast Inn: a haven of serenity in a natural wooded setting, providing an ideal location for romantic getaways and visitors seeking picturesque scenery & soothing relaxation. riversbb@ipa.net http://www.riversedgebnb.com

DEVALLS BLUFF

Palaver Place B&B
Rt 1 Box 29A 72041
870-998-7206
Charles Spellman
All year

65-BB
4 rooms, 4 pb
Visa, MC, *Rated*, •
C-yes/S-ltd/P-yes/H-yes

Full breakfast
Tea, snacks, wine, lunch & dinner available
Library, Jacuzzi, swimming pool, fireplaces, cable TV, accom. bus. travelers

Rustic and comfortable inn built from old houses and barns.
JWH@seark.net http://www.palaver-place.com

EUREKA SPRINGS

11 Singleton House
11 Singleton 72632
479-253-9111 800-833-3394
Barbara Gavron
All year

69-135-BB
5 rooms, 5 pb
Most CC, *Rated*, •
C-yes/S-no/P-no/H-no
Spanish

Full breakfast
Guest ice-box, microwave
Cottage, swing, rockers, INNternship program, Jacuzzi w/private balcony

1894 Victorian, antiques, folk art; breakfast balcony overlooks colorful garden & goldfish pond. Just one block walk to Eureka shops.
info@singletonhouse.com http://www.singletonhouse.com

1881 Crescent Cottage Inn
211 Spring St 72632
479-253-6022 Fax: 479-253-6234
800-223-3246
Ray & Elise Dilfield
All year

99-145-BB
4 rooms, 4 pb
Visa, MC, Disc, *Rated*, •
C-ltd/S-no/P-no/H-no

Full breakfast
Coffee, tea, juices
Historic district, all rooms have Jacuzzis, 2 rooms with fireplaces

Famous 1881 landmark Victorian home on Nat'l Register. Porches, gardens, and superb mountain views. Antiques throughout, 2 rooms with fireplaces.
raphael@ipa.net http://www.1881crescentcottageinn.com

1884 Bridgeford House
263 Spring St 72632
479-253-7853 Fax: 479-253-5497
888-567-2422
All year

95-150-BB
5 rooms, 5 pb
Most CC, *Rated*, •
C-ltd/S-ltd/P-no

Full breakfast

Southern hospitality combined with Victorian charm await you at our beautiful Queen Anne/Eastlake home! 1884 Bridgeford House is nestled in the very heart of Eureka Springs. innkeeper@bridgefordhouse.com http://www.bridgefordhouse.com

EUREKA SPRINGS

1908 Ridgeway House 28 Ridgeway St 72632 479-253-6618 877-741-4222 Gayla & Keith Hubbard All year	99-149-BB 5 rooms, 5 pb Visa, MC, Disc, • C-ltd/S-ltd/P-no/H-no	Homemade evening desserts, coffee, tea, sod

The Ridgeway House offers gracious Southern hospitality in Eureka Springs' quaint Historic District. rheureka@ipa.net http://www.ridgewayhouse.com

---

5 Ojo Inn 5 Ojo St 72632 479-253-6734 Fax: 479-253-8831 800-656-6734 Paula Kirby Adkins All year	89-149-BB 10 rooms, 10 pb Visa, MC, Disc, *Rated*, • C-yes/S-ltd/P-no/H-no	Full breakfast Dietary attention, snack Library, hot tub, gazebo, Jacuzzis, fireplaces, deck, weddings, parking

Award winning restoration of Victorian home says "stay here and revive." Historic District; 8-min. walk to shops and galleries. Fireplaces in 7 rooms and whirlpool tubs for 2 in all rooms. ojo@ipa.net http://www.5ojo.com

---

Arbour Glen 7 Lema 72632 479-253-9010 Fax: 479-253-1264 800-515-4536 The Roses' All year	85-135-BB 5 rooms, 5 pb Most CC, *Rated*, • C-ltd/S-ltd/P-ltd/H-no	Full breakfast Sitting room, Jacuzzis, suites, fireplaces, cable TV

The Arbour Glen Bed & Breakfast, Circa 1896, is nestled on a hillside within the Eureka Springs' Historic District. arbglen@ipa.net http://www.arbourglen.com

---

Arsenic & Old Lace 60 Hillside Ave 72632 479-253-5454 Fax: 479-253-2246 800-243-5223 Debbie & Jens Hansen All year	130-195-BB 5 rooms, 5 pb Visa, MC, Disc, *Rated*, • C-no/S-no/P-no/H-no German	Full gourmet breakfast Complimentary soft drinks & wine, homemade cookies TV/VCR's, large video library, Jacuzzi tubs, fireplaces, spa showers, bathro

The premier Bed & Breakfast in Eureka Springs. Queen Anne style Victorian mansion with large wrap-around verandah. Beautiful private hillside setting in the Historic District. Walk to downtown shopping, restaurants and galleries.
ArsenicOldLaceBB@aol.com http://www.arsenicoldlace.com

Beaver Lake Cottages 2865 Mundell Rd 72631 479-253-8439 Fax: 479-253-0067 888-701-8439 K. & J. Fleischmann, C. & D. Goodwin All year	145-165-EP 8 rooms, 8 pb Visa, MC, Disc, *Rated*, • C-no/S-ltd/P-no/H-no	Juice, pastries,snacks & coffee Jacuzzis, suites, fireplace, king beds, BBQ grills, nature trails

Glass Front cabins overlooking mountainous Beaver Lake, in Eureka Springs in the Ozark Mountains. beaverlake@ipa.net http://www.beaverlakecottages.com

---

Bonnybrooke Farm Atop Misty Mtn. Misty Mountain 72631 479-253-6903 Bonny & Joshua All year	125-EP 5 rooms, 5 pb *Rated*, • C-no/S-no/P-no/H-no	Bread & fruit at arrival Books & games, fireplace, Jacuzzi, glass showers, basketball court.

Sweet quiet & serenity atop Misty Mountain. Fireplace, Jacuzzi (for 2), shower under the stars in glass shower. bonnybrooke@estc.net http://bonnybrooke.apexhosting.com

EUREKA SPRINGS

Brownstone Inn
75 Hillside Ave 72632
479-253-7505 Fax: 479-253-2285
800-973-7505
Rosalie & Gary Andrews
All year

95-135-BB
4 rooms, 4 pb
Visa, MC, Disc
C-ltd/S-ltd/P-no/H-yes

Full breakfast
Soft drinks, coffee, tea and baked goods
TV w/cable, early coffee/tea basket at your doorstep, independant heat/ac.

The exterior of our 2-story limestone building retains its original look, and with the interior creates a luxurious retreat. Two suites and two large rooms, all with private baths/entrances. brownstone@mynewroads.com http://www.eureka-usa.com/brownstone/

Candlestick Cottage Inn
6 Douglas St 72632
479-253-6813 800-835-5184
Bill & Patsy Brooks
All year

65-120-BB
6 rooms, 6 pb
Most CC, *Rated*, •
C-ltd/S-no/P-no/H-no

Full breakfast
Reservations for local restaurants, attractions, Jacuzzi suites, queen beds.

Located in historic district one block from downtown shops. Authentic Victorian-country setting. candleci@ipa.net http://www.candlestickcottageinn.com

---

Cliff Cottage Inn Luxury Suites
42 Armstrong St
Heart of Historic Downtown 72632
479-253-7409 800-799-7409
Sandra CH Smith
All year

170-210-BB
6 rooms, 6 pb
Visa, MC, *Rated*, •
C-ltd/S-ltd/P-ltd/H-no
French, Spanish, German

Elf delivers full-gourmet bkfst.
Victorian picnics, sunset supper cruises
Refrigerator in room, pool, library, tennis, golf, boat, picnics, Jacuzzis

Only B fireplaces; full gourmet breakfast delivered by the elf.
cliffctg@aol.com http://www.cliffcottage.com

Elmwood House
110 Spring St 72632
479-253-5486 888-234-5486
Lavenya & Bill Schenck
All year

105-BB
2 rooms, 2 pb
Visa, MC, Disc
C-ltd/S-no/P-no/H-no

Continental breakfast
Complimentary soft drinks, juices and water
Library, Jacuzzi, suites, fireplace, cable TV, private parking

Historic 3 story structure originally built as a boarding house (1886) from local brick as a means to counter the many fires that plagued early Eureka Springs.
schenck@ipa.net http://www.virtualcities.com/ons/ar/e/are5706.htm

---

Eureka Sunset at Dogwood Ridge
10 Dogwood Ridge 72632
479-253-9565 Fax: 479-253-1265
888-253-9565
Jack & Ada Dozier
All year

95-125-BB
2 rooms, 2 pb
Visa, MC, Disc, *Rated*, •
S-no/P-ltd/H-no

Full breakfast
Snacks, complimentary wine
Jacuzzis, fireplaces, cable TV

For those too focused on the future to enjoy the present, we have the perfect remedy.
esunset@ipa.net http://www.eureka-usa.com/sunset

Heartstone Inn & Cottages
35 Kings Hwy 72632
479-253-8916 Fax: 479-253-5361
800-494-4921
Rick & Cheri Rojek
February-December

75-139-BB
12 rooms, 12 pb
Most CC, *Rated*, •
C-ltd/S-ltd/P-no/H-no

Full gourmet breakfast
Complimentary beverages
Sitting room, cable TVs, wedding gazebo, decks, Jacuzzi suite

Award-winning. Antique furniture, private baths & entrances, king/queen beds. Historic district by attractions. heartinn@ipa.net http://www.heartstoneinn.com

EUREKA SPRINGS

Morningstar Retreat on Kings River
370 Star Lane 72632
479-253-5995 800-298-5995
Janet & Michael Avenoso
All year

95-175-EP
6 rooms, 6 pb
Visa, MC, Disc, *Rated*
C-yes/S-no/P-no/H-no

Home baked, afternoon snacks, hot cocoa, lemonade.
Double Jacuzzi tubs, kitchenettes, private decks, hot tub, walking paths

Escape the Ordinary: The ultimate country experience at reasonable rates. Luxury cottages, nestled in secluded valley on the King's River, 9 mi. from Eureka Springs. New! Honeysuckle House, sleeps 8.
office@morningstarretreat.com http://www.morningstarretreat.com

---

Piedmont House
165 Spring St 72632
501-253-9258 Fax: 501-253-2204
800-253-9258
Vince & Kathy DiMayo
All year

80-135-BB
10 rooms, 9 pb
Visa, *Rated*
C-ltd/S-ltd/H-yes

Full breakfast
Dinner included on Friday
Wraparound porch, sitting room, library

Over 100 years old with orig. guest book also over 100 years old. "Homey" atmosphere; comfortable rooms & beautiful views of the mountain & Christ of the Ozark Statue.
piedmont@ipa.net http://www.eureka-usa.com/piedmont/

Pond Mountain Lodge & Resort
1218 Hwy 23 S 72632
479-253-5877 Fax: 479-253-9087
800-583-8043
Judy Jones
All year

100-150-BB
7 rooms, 7 pb
Visa, MC, Disc, *Rated*, •
C-ltd/S-no/P-ltd/H-ltd

Full breakfast
Picnic lunch available
Sitting room, library, hot tubs, pool, fishing ponds, horseback riding

Mountain-top breezes, panoramic views, casual elegance ... with fishing ponds, heated pool, riding stables, billiards, fireplace, and hearty breakfasts.
pondmtn@estc.net http://www.pondmountainlodge.com

Rock Cottage Gardens
10 Eugenia St 72632
479-253-8659 Fax: 479-253-8659
800-624-6646
Jim & Linda Little
All year

118-139-BB
5 rooms, 5 pb
Most CC
C-ltd/S-ltd/P-no/H-ltd

3 course gourmet breakfast
Tea, snacks, coffee, bottled water, soft drinks
Jacuzzi tubs for 2, gas log fireplaces (in season), feather beds, antiques

We offer private cottages for two. Each cottages includes a Jacuzzi tub for two, queen bed with feather mattress, complimentary beverages, off street parking and complete 3 course gourmet breakfast. rockbnb@mynewroads.com http://eureka-net.com/rockcottage

FORT SMITH

Beland Manor Inn
1320 S Albertpike 72903
501-782-3300 Fax: 501-782-7674
800-334-5052
Mike & Suzy Smith
All year

79-155-BB
8 rooms, 8 pb
Most CC, *Rated*, •
C-ltd/S-no/P-no/H-no
Spanish

Full breakfast
Weekend dinners
Snacks, bar service, sitting room, Jacuzzis, fireplace, cable TV

Comfortable beds, delectable breakfasts, memorable hospitality & superb location make Beland Manor 1st choice for the tourist as well as the business traveler.
innkeeper@fort-smith.net http://www.fort-smith.net

HARDY

Hideaway Inn
84 W Firetower Rd 72542
870-966-4770 888-966-4770
Julia Baldridge
All year

55-125-BB
5 rooms, 3 pb
•
C-yes/S-ltd/H-no

Full or continental breakfast
Snacks
Swimming pool, family friendly facility, fireplace, cable TV

Seeking solitude, this contemporary home or log cabin is an ideal place to hide away.
hideawayinn@centurytel.net http://www.bbonline.com/ar/hideaway

HARDY

Olde Stonehouse Inn
108 West Main St 72542
870-856-2983 800-514-2983
Greg & JaNoel Bess
All year

79-150-BB
9 rooms, 9 pb
Visa, MC, Disc, *Rated*, •
C-ltd/S-ltd/P-no/H-no

Full breakfast
Evening snacks
Sitting room, lib., A/C, ceiling fans, TV, VCR, Jacuzzi tubs in suites

Inn located in historic downtown district. All rooms with private baths, cable TV, & individual heat and air control.
info@hardy-stonehouse.com http://www.oldstonehouse.com

HEBER SPRINGS

Azalea Cottage Inn
320 W Sunny Meadow Rd 72543
501-362-1665 Fax: 501-362-2376
888-233-7931
Betty & Sam Hazel
All year

89-110-BB
4 rooms, 4 pb
Visa, MC, *Rated*
C-ltd/S-no/P-no/H-ltd

Full breakfast
Evening cookies, soft drinks, bottled water
Sitting room, movie library, Jacuzzis, fireplace, cable TV, VCRs

Beautiful Colonial Revival inn on a tree covered acre, near Greers Ferry Lake and the Little Red River. azalea@arkansas.net http://www.AzaleaCottageInn.com

HOT SPRINGS

1890 Williams House
420 Quapaw Ave 71901
501-624-4275 Fax: 501-321-9466
800-756-4635
David & Karen Wiseman
All year

99-165-BB
5 rooms, 5 pb
Most CC, *Rated*, •
C-ltd/S-ltd/P-no/H-no

Full breakfast
Spring water, iced tea, wine
Sitt. rm., frplc., piano, picnic tables, weddings, hiking trail maps

Williams House shows Victorian flair for convenience and elegance. Your home away from home, nestled in Oachita Mountains. Romantic atmosphere.
willmbnb@ipa.net http://www.1890WilliamsHouse.com

HOT SPRINGS NAT'L PARK (REGION)

The Historic Park Hotel
211 Fountain Street, *Hot Springs* 71901
501-624-5323 Fax: 501-623-0052
800-895-7275
Joe A. Powell, Gen Mgr

85-BB
50 rooms, 50 pb
Visa, MC, AmEx, *Rated*, •
C-yes/S-ltd/P-yes/H-yes
All year

Full breakfast
Restaurant, bar, lunch & dinner available
Suites, cable TV

The Historic Park Hotel was built in 1930 and has been maintained in its original elegance. ThePark Hotel@aol.com http://www.TheHistoricParkHotel.com

LITTLE ROCK

Empress of Little Rock
2120 Louisiana 72206
501-374-7966 Fax: 501-375-4537
Bob Blair & Sharon Welch-Blair
All year

125-195-BB
5 rooms, 5 pb
Visa, MC, AmEx, *Rated*, •
C-ltd/S-ltd/P-no/H-no

Full gourmet breakfast
Snacks, comp. decanters of liquor
Sitting room, fireplace, cable TV/VCR, dataports, featherbeds, his/her robes

Experience the opulence of the 1880s in AAA 4-diamond luxury! Majestic double stairwell, secret card room in the turret, sensual featherbeds, candlelit gourmet breakfast.
hostess@theempress.com http://www.TheEmpress.com

Rosemont
515 West 15th St 72202
501-374-7456 Fax: 501-374-2111
Susan Payne Maddox
All year

75-100-BB
5 rooms, 5 pb
Visa, MC, AmEx, *Rated*, •
C-ltd/S-no/P-no/H-no

Full gourmet breakfast
Snacks, complimentary wine
Sitting room, library, Jacuzzis, cable TV, accom. bus. trav.

Rosemont is a graciously restored Victorian built in 1880 as a gentleman's farmhouse. Five individually designed guestrooms & private baths have every necessity and luxury we could think of. rosemontbb@aol.com http://www.rosemontoflittlerock.com

OZARK

Spirit Mountain Lodge & Cabins
4117 Spirit Mountain Loop
Ozark Mountains 72949
479-667-1919
Gwen & Rex Benham

82-335-BB
20 rooms, 8 pb
Visa, MC, AmEx, •
C-yes/S-ltd/P-no/H-ltd
All year

Breakfast included in Lodge price
Catered meals by request
Full kitchens, master massage therapist on staff

250 acres of meadows and woods in the Ozark National Forest. Hiking, canoeing, fishing; waterfalls, winery, herb tours, ATV and horse trails. Arkansas Times Editors' Choice "Best Resort in Arkansas." spiritmtnlodge@aol.com http://www.spiritmountainlodge.com

SILOAM SPRINGS (REGION)

Apple Crest Inn
PO Box 1254
12758 S Hwy 59, *Gentry* 72734
479-736-8201 Fax: 479-736-8201
888-APPLE-US
Dianne & Gary Affolter
All year

85-155-BB
6 rooms, 6 pb
Most CC, *Rated*, •
C-ltd/S-no/P-ltd/H-ltd

Full breakfast
Snacks
Sitting room, library, Jacuzzis, fireplaces, cable TV, bus. travelers

Victorian manor home & carriage house located in rural historical "sleepy hollow." Furnished with antiques & stained glass accents, we have large rooms with private baths & sitting areas. Applecrestinn@tcainternet.com http://www.applecrestinn.com

California

ALAMEDA

Garratt Mansion
900 Union St 94501
510-521-4779 Fax: 510-521-6796
Royce & Betty Gladden
All year

95-175-BB
7 rooms, 5 pb
Visa, MC, AmEx, *Rated*
C-ltd/S-no/P-no/H-no

Full breakfast
Cookies, hot & cold drinks
Sitting room, phones and private baths in most rooms, TV available

An elegant Victorian nestled in the quiet island community of Alameda, just 20 minutes from downtown San Francisco or Berkeley, offering personalized attention.
garrattm@pacbell.net http://www.garrattmansion.com

ANGELS CAMP (REGION)

Angels Hacienda
4871 Hunt Rd, *Farmington* 95230
209-785-8533 Fax: 209-785-8535
800-827-8533
Pam & Steve Hatch All year

129-295-BB
8 rooms, 8 pb
Visa, MC, Disc, *Rated*, •
C-yes/S-no/P-ltd/H-yes
Spanish

Full breakfast
A 3 course Dinner is available upon request.
Sitting room, library, Jacuzzis, pool, suites, fireplcs, Cable TV, bus. trvl

Historic 8-room Spanish Hacienda located on a very restful ranch of 100 acres. Guests enjoy swimming, relaxing, games, walks, biking, and just enjoying nature.
pam@angelshacienda.com http://www.angelshacienda.com

ARCATA

Cats' Cradle
815 Park Pl 95521
707-822-2287 Fax: 707-822-5287
Duane & Barbara Holzer
All year

65-105-BB
4 rooms, 2 pb
Visa, MC, Disc, •
C-ltd/S-no/P-no/H-no
Spanish

Full breakfast
Library, suites, garden with gazebo & views

Mid-Century classic home set among the redwoods with ocean vistas. Back-soothing mattresses, spirit soothing surroundings. Books, antiques, collectibles, unique garden.
catcradl@humboldt1.com
http://www.travelhero.com/prophome.cfm/id/71217/hotels/reservations/

ATASCADERO

Oak Hill Manor 12345 Hampton Court 93422 805-462-9317 Fax: 805-462-0331 866-OAKMANOR Maurice & Rise Macare All year	155-235-BB 8 rooms, 8 pb Visa, MC, AmEx, *Rated* C-ltd/S-ltd/P-no/H-yes	Full breakfast Snack, complimentary wine Sitting rm, library, Jacuzzi, suites, fireplace, cable TV, acc. bus. trav.

Comfortable elegance on three acres of oak-studded hills, fantastic views and sunsets, gracious hospitality, full breakfast, appetizers, beverages.
macare@oakhillmanorbandb.com http://www.oakhillmanorbandb.com

AUBURN

Power's Mansion Inn PO Box 602076 164 Cleveland Ave 95860 530-885-1166 Fax: 530-885-1386 Arno & Jean Lejnieks All year	109-189-BB 13 rooms, 13 pb *Rated*, • C-ltd/S-no/P-no/H-yes German, Latin	Full breakfast Deluxe amenities, fireplaces, patios, decks, terry robes

1898 mansion built from gold-mining fortune. Has elegance of detailed restoration & antique furnishings. powerinn@westsierra.net http://www.vfr.net/~powerinn

BALLARD

The Ballard Inn 2436 Baseline Ave 93463 805-688-7770 Fax: 805-688-9560 800-638-2466 Christine Forsyth All year	195-275-BB 15 rooms, 15 pb *Rated*, •	Full breakfast

Located in the Santa Ynez Valley, about forty minutes from Santa Barbara, the Ballard Inn offers comfortably elegant accommodations in a peaceful and quiet setting.
innkeeper@ballardinn.com http://www.ballardinn.com

BENICIA

The Inn at Benicia Bay PO Box 1025 145 East D St 94510 707-746-1055 Fax: 707-745-8361 Michael & Patricia Lamb All year	129-229-BB 9 rooms, 9 pb Visa, MC, AmEx, • C-ltd/S-no/P-no/H-no	Continental plus breakfast Snacks & complimentary wine Sitting room, library, Jacuzzis, suites, fireplaces, cable TV

The warm atmosphere at The Inn at Benicia Bay makes this country inn a relaxing getaway. All rooms are decorated in period antiques, all with their own personalities.
theinnbb@aol.com http://www.theinnatbeniciabay.com

Jefferson Street Mansion 1063 Jefferson St 94510 707-747-5653 Reed Robbins All year	350-BB 4 rooms, 4 pb

1861 pre-Civil War officer's mansion. Guest has the use of the entire mansion, which is decorated in Empire period. Museum collections, gardens, lawns.
info@jeffersonstreetmansion.com http://www.jeffersonstreetmansion.com

BERKELEY

Rose Garden Inn 2740 Telegraph Ave 94705 510-549-2145 Fax: 510-549-1085 Kathy Kuhner All year	99-279-BB 40 rooms, 38 pb Most CC	Afternoon coffee, tea and cookies Free parking on a space-available basis, cable TV, phone w/dataport

Experience the charming comfort of our 40 guestrooms surrounded by flowering gardens, some with sweeping views and soothing fountains.
info@rosegardeninn.com http://www.rosegardeninn.com

BIG BEAR LAKE

Alpenhorn
PO Box 2912
601 Knight Ave 92315
909-866-5700 Fax: 909-878-3209
888-829-6600
Chuck & Robbie Slemaker

159-245-BB
8 rooms, 8 pb
Visa, MC, AmEx,
Rated, •
C-no/S-no/P-no/H-yes
All year

4-course gourmet breakfast
Wine, hors d' oeuvres, after-dinner liqueurs
In-room spas, fireplaces, TV/VCRs, private balconies, video library

Relish a glass of wine while watching a sunset in our exquisite gardens, or sit by the fire and watch snowfall magically blanket the landscape. Enjoy modern elegance amidst tranquility. innkeeper@alpenhorn.com http://www.alpenhorn.com

---

Carolyn's Cottage
PO Box 132015
42728 Cougar Rd 92315
909-584-2467
Julie Walsh

BB
Visa, MC
S-no/P-no
All year

When it's Time for a Break from the Ordinary! Relax and Enjoy a Romantic Stay. . . . Your hosts, Bob & Julie will arrange a weekend you will never forget.
carolynscottage@yahoo.com http://www.carolynscottage.com

Knickerbocker Mansion Country Inn
PO Box 1907
869 Knickerbocker Rd 92315
909-878-9190 Fax: 909-878-4248
800-388-4179
Stanley R. Miller & Thomas F. Bicanic
All year

110-225-BB
11 rooms, 11 pb
Most CC, •
C-ltd/S-no/P-no/H-yes
German

Full Gourmet Breakfast
Afternoon tea, snacks
Sitting Room, TV/VCR, phones, Internet, Conference Room

A magnificently restored unique historic log mansion and Carriage House built in 1920.
knickmail@aol.com http://www.knickerbockermansion.com

BIG BEAR LAKE (REGION)

Gold Mountain Manor
PO Box 2027
1117 Anita, *Big Bear City* 92314
909-585-6997 Fax: 909-585-0327
800-509-2604
Jim & Trish Gordon
All year

149-225-BB
7 rooms, 7 pb
Most CC, *Rated*, •
C-ltd/S-ltd/P-ltd/H-no

Full breakfast
Complimentary beverages, snacks
Billiard table, parlor with woodburning fireplace, wraparound porch, library

Historic log cabin B lots of special touches. Park-like setting, Wood-burning fireplaces, wraparound porch, candlelit breakfast.
info@goldmountainmanor.com http://www.goldmountainmanor.com

BODEGA BAY (REGION)

Sonoma Coast Villa Inn & Spa
PO Box 236
16702 Coast Hwy 1, *Bodega* 94922
707-876-9818 Fax: 707-876-9856
888-404-2255

225-325-BB
16 rooms, 16 pb
Visa, MC, AmEx, •
C-ltd/S-ltd/P-no/H-yes
Spanish
Cyrus Griffin
All year

Full breakfast
Wine hour
Courtyard Spa, Jacuzzi, pool, putting green, library, pool table, Ping-Pong

Enjoy a taste of Tuscany without your passport. An elegant country inn nestled amidst rolling hills. Secluded resort, one hour north of San Francisco. Close to the coast, redwoods, and wine country. reservations@scvilla.com http://www.scvilla.com

BOONVILLE

Anderson Creek Inn
12050 Anderson Valley Way 95415
707-895-3091 Fax: 707-895-9466
800-552-6202
Grace & Jim Minton

100-180-BB
5 rooms, 5 pb
Visa, MC, Disc, *Rated*
C-ltd/S-ltd/P-no/H-no
All year

Full breakfast
Afternoon tea
Sitting room, library, swimming pool, fireplaces

Gracious ranch-style inn located on 16 acres in the Anderson Valley wine country.
innkeeper@andersoncreekinn.com http://www.andersoncreekinn.com

BRIDGEPORT

The Cain House
PO Box 428
340 Main St 93517
760-932-7040 Fax: 760-932-7419
800-433-CAIN
Chris & Marachal Gohlich
May 1-Nov. 1

90-145-BB
7 rooms, 7 pb
AmEx, Most CC,
Rated, •
C-ltd/S-no/P-no/H-no

Full breakfast
Complimentary wine and cheese
Sitting room, tennis courts, 6 rooms A/C, 2 with private entrance, phones

The grandeur of the eastern Sierras is the perfect setting for evening wine and cheese.
cainhouse@qnet.com http://www.cainhouse.com

CALISTOGA

Calistoga Country Lodge
2883 Foothill Blvd 94515
707-942-5555 Fax: 707-942-5864
Rae Ellen
February-Dec.

120-195-BB
6 rooms, 4 pb
Most CC, *Rated*
C-ltd/S-no/P-no/H-no

Continental plus buffet
Snacks, complimentary wine
Sitting room, gardens, Jacuzzi & new pool in renovated patio area

1917 ranch house restored in Southwest style offering country solitude, spacious common area, views of valley & open land. bnbccl@napanet.net http://www.countrylodge.com

---

Christopher's Inn
1010 Foothill Blvd 94515
707-942-5755 Fax: 707-942-6895
Christopher & Adele Layton
All year

175-425-BB
19 rooms, 19 pb
Visa, AmEx, *Rated*, •
C-ltd/S-no/H-ltd

Continental plus breakfast

Elegant 19-room country inn and gardens. Laura Ashley interiors, cozy wood-burning fireplaces, romantic garden courtyards with fountains, Jacuzzi spas in the rooms.
christophersinn@earthlink.net http://www.christophersinn.com

Cottage Grove Inn
1711 Lincoln Ave 94515
707-942-8400 Fax: 707-942-2653
800-799-2284
Wendy
All year

235-295-BB
16 rooms, 16 pb
Most CC, *Rated*, •
C-ltd/S-no/P-no/H-yes

Continental plus breakfast
Complimentary wine
Library, bikes, hot tubs, fireplaces in each room

Romantic private cottages with fireplaces and two person deep Jacuzzi soaking tubs in the beautiful, quaint town of Calistoga.
innkeeper@cottagegrove.com http://cottagegrove.com

Culver Mansion
1805 Foothill Blvd 94515
707-942-4535 Fax: 707-942-4557
877-281-3671
Jaqueline LeVesque
All year

175-195-BB
6 rooms, 6 pb
Most CC, *Rated*
C-ltd/S-no/P-no/H-no
French

Full breakfast
Afternoon tea, snacks, cheese, wine
Jacuzzi, swimming pool, sauna

A comfortable, elegant Victorian home furnished in antiques; full breakfast; afternoon sherry and hors d'oeuvre. Come as a guest, leave as a friend.
jacrose@culvermansion.com http://www.culvermansion.com

The Elms
1300 Cedar St 94515
707-942-9476 Fax: 707-942-9479
800-235-4316
Alicia Syliva
All year

135-245-BB
7 rooms, 7 pb
Visa, MC, Disc, *Rated*,
• 8
C-ltd/S-ltd/P-yes/H-ltd
Spanish

Full gourmet breakfast
Complimentary afternoon wine & cheese
Port for after dinner, chocolates at bedtime, irons, blow dryers

The Elms B & B is a French Victorian Mansion built in 1871 and listed on the National Register of Historic Places. It is the last of the "Great Eight" homes that once graced Calistoga. info@theelms.com http://www.theelms.com

CALISTOGA

Foothill House 3037 Foothill Blvd 94515 707-942-6933 Fax: 707-942-6933 800-942-6933 Doris & Gus Beckert All year	175-325-BB 4 rooms, 4 pb Visa, MC, AmEx, *Rated*, • C-ltd/S-no/P-no/H-no	Full breakfast Complimentary wine & cheese Turndown service, sherry, 3 rooms with Jacuzzi tub, sitting room, A/C

In a country setting, Foothill House offers 3 spacious rooms individually decorated w/antiques, each w/private bath, entrance & fireplace. 1 cottage.
gus@calicom.net http://www.foothillhouse.com

Hideaway Cottages 1412 Fairway 94515 707-942-4108 Fax: 707-942-6110 M. Wilkinson All year	100-500-EP 17 rooms, 17 pb Visa, MC, AmEx, • S-no/P-no/H-yes Spanish	Jacuzzis, swimming pool, cable TV, conference facilities

Situated amongst three tree filled acres, Hideaway Cottages is a perfect setting for complete relaxation. Offering a variety of accommodations–some including full kitchens.
http://www.hideawaycottages.com

Hillcrest 3225 Lake Co Hwy 94515 707-942-6334 Fax: 707-942-3955 Debbie O'Gorman All year	69-175-BB 6 rooms, 4 pb *Rated*, • C-ltd/S-ltd/P-ltd/H-ltd	Continental bkfst–wknds, holidays Sitting room, library, Jacuzzis, pool, cable TV, fireplaces, conference

Secluded hilltop home with "million dollar view." Home is filled with antique silver, china, rugs, artwork, & furniture. http://www.bnbweb.com/hillcrest

---

Scarlett's Country Inn 3918 Silverado Trail 94515 707-942-6669 Fax: 707-942-6669 Scarlett Dwyer All year	135-205-BB 3 rooms, 3 pb *Rated*, • C-yes/S-no/P-no/H-no Spanish	Full breakfast Complimentary wine & cheese Sitting room, A/C, TVs, microwaves & refrig., coffee makers, pool

Secluded French country farmhouse overlooking vineyards in famed Napa Valley. Breakfast served by woodland swimming pool.
scarletts@aol.com http://members.aol.com/scarletts

Trailside Inn 4201 Silverado Trail 94515 707-942-4106 Fax: 707-942-4702 Lani Gray All year	165-185-BB 3 rooms, 3 pb Most CC, *Rated*, • C-ltd/S-ltd/P-no/H-no	Continental plus breakfast Complimentary wine Mineral water, fireplace, kitchens, library, A/C, spa, private deck, pool

1930s farmhouse comfortably decorated with quilts and antiques. Each suite has private entrance, 3 rooms plus bath. h.gray@worldnet.att.net http://www.trailsideinn.com

---

Zinfandel House 1253 Summit Dr 94515 707-942-0733 Fax: 707-942-4618 Bette & George Starke All year	120-145-BB 2 rooms, 2 pb Visa, MC, *Rated* C-ltd/S-no/P-no/H-no	Full breakfast Complimentary wine Library, sitting room, hot tub

Beautiful home situated on wooded hillside overlooking vineyards and mountains. Lovely breakfast served on outside deck or in dining room.
bette@zinfandelhouse.com http://www.zinfandelhouse.com

CALISTOGA (REGION)

Backyard Garden Oasis PO Box 1760 24019 Hilderbrand, *Middletown* 95461 707-987-0505 Fax: 707-987-3993 Greta Zeit All year	125-145-BB 3 rooms, 3 pb Most CC, *Rated*, • C-no/S-ltd/P-no/H-yes Spanish	Full breakfast Hot tub, fireplace, skylight, satellite TV/VCR, phone, modem access, AC

Located on the quiet side of wine country. Three rustic cottages...simple, yet elegant...Peace, serenity, privacy, king-sized beds, skylights, hot tub under the stars, great breakfasts!! bygoasis@jnb.com http://www.jnb.com/~bygoasis

CAMBRIA

The Blue Whale Inn 6736 Moonstone Beach Dr 93428 805-927-0244 800-753-9000 Jay & Karen Peavler All year	160-260-BB 6 rooms, 6 pb Visa, MC, *Rated* C-ltd/S-no/P-no/H-ltd	Full breakfast Snacks, afternoon tea, complimentary wine Sitting room, library, fireplaces, cable TV, romantic mini suites

Gracious hospitality. Luxurious and romantic ocean-view mini-suites. Gourmet breakfasts, wine, and hor d'oeuvres. innkeeper@bluewhaleinn.com http://www.bluewhaleinn.com

The J. Patrick House 2990 Burton Dr 93428 805-927-3812 Fax: 805-927-6759 800-341-5258 Ann & John All year	145-200-BB 8 rooms, 8 pb Visa, MC, Disc, *Rated* C-ltd/S-no/P-no/H-no	Full breakfast Comp. wine, hors d' oeuvres and milk and cookies Sitting room, library, in room massage,

Authentic log home in pines surrounded by country gardens. Woodburning fireplaces, private bath, country elegant decor and charm, in-room massage. Near Ocean, Hearst Castle, Wine Country. jph@jpatrickhouse.com http://www.jpatrickhouse.com

McCall Farm 6250 Santa Rosa Creek Rd 93428 805-927-3140 Teri McCall All year	125-135-BB 2 rooms, 2 pb Visa, MC C-ltd/S-ltd/P-ltd/H-no	Wine and appetizers Sitting room, gardens, walking paths, front porch, in-room refrigerators

Our restored farmhouse is nestled in the beautiful Santa Rosa Creek Valley, just ten minutes east of the village of Cambria. It sits among 20 acres of fruit trees and gardens on an operating farm. mccallfarm@earthlink.net http://www.mccallfarm.com

Olallieberry Inn 2476 Main St 93428 805-927-3222 Fax: 805-927-0202 888-927-3222 Marilyn & Larry Draper All year	95-190-BB 9 rooms, 9 pb Visa, MC, *Rated*, • C-ltd/S-no/P-no/H-yes	Full gourmet breakfast Complimentary wine & appetizers Parlor, gathering room, antiques, special diets, cookies and milk

1873 restored Greek Revival home features rooms decorated with fabrics, wall coverings and period antiques. olallieberry@olallieberry.com http://www.olallieberry.com

The Pickford House 2555 MacLeod Way 93428 805-927-8619 Fax: 805-927-8016 888-270-8470 Patricia Moore All year	145-195-BB 8 rooms, 8 pb Visa, MC, *Rated*, • C-ltd/S-ltd/P-no/H-yes	Full breakfast Cookies, wine after 5pm Homemade fruit breads, sitting room, fireplaces, TV in all rooms, antiques

8 beautiful guestrooms with bath and TV. Elegant, authentic antiques of 1900's, 20's, and 30's; named for Mary Pickford and friends of Hearst.
innkeeper@thepickfordhouse.com http://www.thepickfordhouse.com

CAPITOLA

Inn at Depot Hill
250 Monterey Ave 95010
831-462-3376 Fax: 831-462-3697
800-572-2632
Tom Cole
All year

195-325-BB
12 rooms, 12 pb
Most CC, *Rated*, •
C-ltd/S-no/P-no/H-yes
German, Spanish, Italian

Full gourmet breakfast
Wine, appetizers, dessert
Private patios with hot tubs, fireplace, TV/VCR, stereos, phones/modem

Santa Cruz County's only 4 star rated lodging. Voted one of top 10 Inns in the Country. Walk to beach, dining & shops.

lodging@innatdepothill.com http://www.innatdepothill.com/depot-frame.html

CARMEL

1929 Sandpiper Inn by the Sea
2408 Bay View Ave 93923
831-624-6433 Fax: 831-624-5964
800-633-6433
Audie Housman
All year

105-240-BB
17 rooms, 17 pb
Most CC, *Rated*, •
C-ltd/S-no/P-no/H-no
Spanish, German, French

Continental plus breakfast
Coffee, tea, sherry
Library, flowers, fireplace, lounge, close to tennis, golf, hiking

One-half block to Carmel Beach. European-style country inn, with some antiques & fresh flowers. Ocean views, fireplaces, garden.

sandpiper-inn@redshift.com http://www.sandpiper-inn.com

Candle Light Inn
PO Box 1900
San Carlos bet. 4th & 5th 93921
831-624-6451 Fax: 831-624-6732
800-433-4732
Jim Grieve All year

139-250-BB
20 rooms, 20 pb
Most CC, *Rated*, •
C-yes/S-no/P-no/H-ltd

Picnic Basket Breakfast
Fresh Baked Cookies
Spa

Tudor-style inn offers charm and warmth. Friendly staff provides good old-fashioned service. Centrally located in the heart of the village. Off-street parking. AAA rating—3 diamonds. janvan@innsbythesea.com http://www.innsbythesea.com

---

Carmel Country Inn
PO Box 3756
Dolores & 3rd 93921
831-625-3263 Fax: 831-625-2945
800-215-6343
Amy Johnson All year

135-225-BB
12 rooms, 12 pb
Most CC, *Rated*, •
C-ltd/S-no/P-ltd/H-ltd
Spanish

Expanded Continental Breakfast
In Room Refreshment Center, Coffee Maker, Sherry
Fireplaces, Sitting Rooms, Cable TV

Carmel Country Inn offers a great blend of convenience, comfort, and intimacy in a surrounding of natural beauty.

info@carmelcountryinn.com http://www.carmelcountryinn.com

Carmel River Inn
PO Box 221609
26600 Oliver Rd 93922
831-624-1575 Fax: 831-624-0290
800-882-8142
Matthew D'Attilio All year

60-205-EP
43 rooms, 43 pb
Visa, MC, *Rated*, •
C-yes/S-yes/P-yes/H-yes

Kitchens
Heated swimming pool, rooms & cottages, balconies, fireplaces

Wake up to the sound of birds singing and the smell of freshly ground coffee in one of our quaint, rustic, Carmel-style cottages. Enjoy the California sunshine at our large heated pool. info@carmelriverinn.com http://www.carmelriverinn.com

---

Carriage House Inn
PO Box 1900
Junipero btwn 7th & 8th 93921
831-625-2585 Fax: 831-624-0974
800-433-4732
Cathy Lewis All year

229-399-BB
13 rooms, 13 pb
Most CC, *Rated*, •
C-ltd/S-no/P-no/H-no

Expanded Continental Breakfast
Wine, hors d'oeuvres, cappucino bar, port & sherry
Sitting room, library

Intimate, romantic, luxurious. King-size beds, down comforters, fireplaces, whirlpool tub or Jacuzzi. Located in the heart of the village. AAA rating—4 diamonds.

concierge@innsbythesea.com http://www.innsbythesea.com/innres.htm#CH

CARMEL

Colonial Terrace Inn
PO Box 1375
San Antonio & 13th 93921
831-624-2741 Fax: 831-626-2715
800-345-8220
Joanna Wuelfing
All year

120-350-BB
25 rooms, 25 pb
Visa, MC, AmEx, •
C-yes/S-no/P-no/H-ltd

Continental breakfast
Most rooms have fireplaces

Colonial Terrace Inn, c. 1925, is one of Carmel's original inns. Completely refurbished in 2001. Just steps away from Carmel Beach, a long crescent of white sand edged with pine and cypress trees. info@colonialterraceinn.com http://www.colonialterraceinn.com

---

Cypress Inn
PO Box Y
Lincoln and 7th 93921
831-624-3871 Fax: 831-624-8216
800-443-7443
Hollace Thompson All year

125-395-BB
34 rooms, 34 pb
Most CC, *Rated*, •
C-ltd/S-ltd/P-yes/H-ltd

Continental breakfast
Afternoon tea, bar service
Fruit basket, sherry, daily paper, fresh flowers

Charming Spanish-Mediterranean style, built in 1929. In the heart of the village within walking distance to shops, restaurants and galleries.
info@cypress-inn.com http://www.cypress-inn.com

Dolphin Inn
PO Box 1900
San Carlos & 4th 93921
831-624-5356 800-433-4732
Bob & Lorraine Luce
All year

99-250-BB
27 rooms, 27 pb
Most CC, *Rated*, •
C-yes/S-no/P-no/H-no

Picnic Basket Breakfast
Fresh Baked Cookies
Heated pool, free off-street parking

California Colonial style inn located in the heart of the village, walking distance to shops, restaurants and the beach. janvan@innsbythesea.com http://www.innsbythesea.com

---

Edgemere Cottages
PO Box 2458
13th & Santa Lucia Sts 93921
831-624-4501 Fax: 831-624-6130
Kari JunKans
All year

120-160-BB
4 rooms, 4 pb
Visa, MC, AmEx, •
C-ltd/S-no/P-no/H-ltd

Continental plus breakfast
Snacks, Complimentary wine
Sitting room, fireplaces, cable TV, accommodations for business travelers

We are located one block from Carmel beach in a lovely garden setting.
info@edgemerecottages.com http://www.edgemerecottages.com

Happy Landing Inn
PO Box 2619
Monte Verde bet. 5th & 6th Ave 93921
831-624-7917 Fax: 831-624-4844
Robert Ballard & Dick Stewart
All year

95-185-BB
7 rooms, 7 pb
Visa, MC, *Rated*
C-ltd/S-no/P-no/H-yes

Continental plus breakfast
Complimentary sherry
Sitting room, gazebo, gardens, pond, Honeymoon cottage available

Hansel & Gretel cottages in the heart of Carmel, like something from a Beatrix Potter book. http://www.virtualcities.com/ons/ca/c/cac8501.htm

---

Sea View Inn
PO Box 4138
Camino Real @ 11th & 12th 93921
831-624-8778 Fax: 831-625-5901
Marshall & Diane Hydorn
All year

95-175-BB
8 rooms, 6 pb
Visa, MC, *Rated*, •
C-ltd/S-no/P-no/H-no

Continental plus breakfast
Afternoon tea & coffee
Comp. evening wine, sitting room, library, garden

Small, intimate, cozy Victorian near village and beach. Enjoy breakfast and evening wine served by the fireside, or relax in secluded garden.
seaviewinn@mymailstation.com http://www.seaviewinncarmel.com

CARMEL

Stonehouse Inn
PO Box 2517
8th below Monte Verde 93921
831-624-4569
Terri Navaille
All year

110-217-BB
6 rooms
Visa, MC, *Rated*, •
C-ltd/S-no/P-no/H-no

Full breakfast
Complimentary port & cookies
Sitting room, fireplace, bicycles

Historic Carmel house built in 1906, traditional Bed & Breakfast.
http://www.carmelstonehouse.com

Svendsgaards Inn
PO Box 1900
4th & San Carlos 93921
831-624-1511 Fax: 831-624-5661
800-433-4732
Samantha Thiel
All year

109-275-BB
35 rooms, 35 pb
Most CC, *Rated*, •
C-yes/S-ltd/P-no/H-ltd

Continental breakfast
Fresh baked cookies
Heated pool, garden area

The country decor and garden setting make Svendsgaard's Inn one of Carmel's most desirable destinations. Rooms with fireplace, kitchenette, or Jacuzzi available. Located in the heart of the village. janvan@innsbythesea.com http://www.innsbythesea.com

---

Tally Ho Inn
PO Box 3726
Monte Verde at 6th St 93921
831-624-2232 Fax: 831-624-2661
877-482-5594
John Wilson All year

115-250-BB
12 rooms, 12 pb
Most CC, *Rated*, •
C-yes/S-yes/P-no/H-no
French

Continental plus breakfast
Afternoon tea, brandy
Floral garden, sun deck, fireplaces, ocean views, close to beach

This English country inn has bountiful gardens with sweeping ocean views from individually appointed rooms and sun decks. info@tallyho-inn.com http://www.tallyho-inn.com/

Vagabond's House Inn
PO Box 2747
4th & Dolores 93921
831-624-7738 Fax: 831-626-1243
800-262-1262
Dawn Dull All year

125-195-BB
11 rooms, 11 pb
Visa, MC, *Rated*, •
C-ltd/S-yes/P-yes/H-no
French

Continental plus breakfast
Sitting room w/fireplace, library, courtyard, 2 blocks to downtown

Antique clocks and pictures, quilted bedspreads, fresh flowers, plants, shelves filled with old books. Sherry by the fireplace, breakfast served in your room.
innkeeper@vagabondshouseinn.com http://www.vagabondshouseinn.com

---

Wayside Inn
PO Box 1900
7th & Mission 93921
831-624-5336 Fax: 831-626-6974
800-433-4732
Cathy Lewis All year

109-280-BB
22 rooms, 22 pb
Most CC, *Rated*, •
C-yes/S-ltd/P-ltd/H-no

Continental breakfast
Fresh baked cookies
Sitting room

Ideal for families or extended stays. Mini-suites with full kitchen, Most rooms have fireplaces, some have Jacuzzis. Located in the heart of the village. Free off street parking.
janvan@innsbythesea.com http://www.innsbythesea.com

CHESTER

The Bidwell House
PO Box 1790
One Main St 96020
530-258-3338
Kim & Ian James All year

75-160-BB
14 rooms, 12 pb
Visa, MC, *Rated*, •
C-yes/S-ltd/P-no/H-yes

Full gourmet breakfast
Afternoon tea, snacks
Sitting room, library, hot tubs in rooms, Jacuzzis, fireplaces

Historic Inn on the edge of Lassen National Park, beautiful Lake Almanor and next to the Feather River; gourmet breakfast; hiking, biking and skiing paradise!
bidwellhouse@thegrid.net http://www.bidwellhouse.com

CHICO

L'abri
14350 Hwy 99 95973
530-893-0824 800-489-3319
Sharon & Jeff Bisaga All year

75-100-BB
3 rooms, 3 pb
Visa, MC, *Rated*
C-ltd/S-ltd/P-no/H-no

Full or continental plus breakfast
Snacks
Sitting room, library

Comfortable, country creek-side setting offers serene and peaceful haven from the pressure of modern life. labrichico@earthlink.net http://www.now2000.com/labri

---

Music Express Inn
1091 El Monte Ave 95928
530-345-8376 Fax: 530-893-8521
Barney & Irene Cobeen
All year

76-106-BB
9 rooms, 9 pb
Rated

Full breakfast

Wind down by laying back in your Jacuzzi tub while enjoying the peace and quiet. Tour the grounds, or go for a stroll through Bidwell Park, the second largest city park in the country. icobeen@aol.com http://www.now2000.com/musicexpress

CLOVERDALE

The Shelford House
29955 River Rd 95425
707-894-5956 Fax: 707-894-8621
800-833-6479
Stan & Anna Smith
All year

115-250-BB
7 rooms, 7 pb
Most CC, *Rated*
S-no

Full breakfast
Tennis nearby

A Wine Country Inn nestled in San Francisco's countryside; Alexander Valley wine country of Sonoma County. shelford@flash.netdex.com http://www.shelford.com

COLUMBIA

Blue Nile Inn
11250 Pacific St 95310
209-532-8041
Ray & Anita Miller
All year

105-135-BB
4 rooms, 4 pb
Most CC
C-ltd/S-ltd/P-no/H-no

Full breakfast
Afternoon snacks
Sitting room, library, Jacuzzis, fireplaces, phones, TV/VCR-great room

An elegant and luxurious bed & breakfast in historic Columbia, catering to adult romance and tranquility. Innkeeper@Blue-Nile-Inn.com http://www.Blue-Nile-Inn.com

---

Columbia City Hotel
PO Box 1870
22768 Main St 95310
209-532-1479 Fax: 209-532-7027
800-532-1479
Tom Bender All year

105-125-BB
10 rooms, 10 pb
Most CC, *Rated*, •
C-yes/S-no/P-no/H-no

Continental plus breakfast
California French restaurant
Sitting room, full service saloon, live theatre and ice cream parlour

Victorian Bed & Breakfast Inn located in Columbia State Historic Park in the heart of California's Gold Country info@cityhotel.com http://www.cityhotel.com

DAVENPORT

Davenport Inn
PO Box J
31 Davenport Ave 95017
831-425-1818 Fax: 831-423-1160
800-870-1817
Bruce & Marcia McDougal
All year

99-155-BB
12 rooms, 12 pb
Most CC, *Rated*, •
C-ltd/S-no/P-no/H-ltd

$14.00 coupon in restaurant
Continental plus breakfast on weekends
Restaurant, gift shop, picnic lunches, sitting room, gallery

Small coastal village half way between San Francisco and Carmel/Monterey. Ocean view rooms with antique and ethnic collections.
inn@swanton.com http://www.davenportinn.com

DAVIS

University Inn
340 A St 95616
530-756-8648 Fax: 530-756-8016
800-756-8648
Lynda & Ross Yancher
All year

73-BB
4 rooms, 4 pb
Most CC, *Rated*, •
C-yes/S-no/P-yes/H-yes

Continental plus breakfast
Complimentary beverages
Microwave, bicycles, airport shuttle

A great taste of Davis, ten steps from the University. Quiet location. Rooms with private phone, cable TV, refrigerator, microwave.
yancher@aol.com http://www.davis411.com

EUREKA

Carter House Inns
301 L St 95501
707-444-8062 Fax: 707-444-8067
800-404-1390
Mark & Christi Carter
All year

95-495-BB
32 rooms, 32 pb
Most CC, *Rated*, •
C-yes/S-no/P-no/H-yes

2 course breakfast
Wine, hors d'oeuvres, cookies, tea
Whirlpools, fireplaces, sitting rooms, Jacuzzis, TV/VCR, CD, stereo, gardens

4 Diamond Award Inn perched alongside Humboldt Bay in Victorian Eureka. Luxurious amenities, superior hospitality, spas, fireplaces, and antique furnishings. Wine Spectator award-winning restaurant.
reserve@carterhouse.com http://www.carterhouse.com

Cornelius Daly Inn
1125 H St 95501
707-445-3638 Fax: 707-444-3636
800-321-9656
Sue Clinesmith All year

90-160-BB
5 rooms, 3 pb
Most CC, *Rated*, •
C-yes/S-ltd/P-no/H-no

Full breakfast
Wine, hors d'oeuvres
Sitting room, library, Victorian gardens, pond, VCR/CD/stereo, gardens

A beautifully restored turn-of-the-century mansion, one of Eureka's finest. 1 room with twin beds, 4 rooms with queen beds. innkeeper@dalyinn.com http://www.dalyinn.com

---

Old Town
1521 Third St 95501
707-443-5235 Fax: 707-442-4390
888-508-5235
Steve & Karen Albright
All year

85-130-BB
5 rooms, 5 pb
Most CC
C-ltd/S-no/P-ltd/H-no

Full breakfast
TV/VCR in every room, large movie collection, Victorian parlor

The Inn is an 1871 restored Victorian home in the historic seaport village of Eureka. Each room has its own private bathroom, TV/VCR, quilts and period antiques. Senior and business rates. info@oldtownbnb.com http://www.oldtownbnb.com

---

A Weaver's Inn
1440 B St 95501
707-443-8119 Fax: 707-443-7923
800-992-8119
Robin, Bill, & Lea Montgomery All year

80-140-BB
4 rooms, 3 pb
Most CC, •
C-yes/S-ltd/P-yes/H-no

Full gourmet breakfast
Wine, beer or tea, coffee, juice in evening
Sitting room, hot tub in one room, Japanese garden

Stately Queen Anne Victorian (circa 1883). Quiet, genteel elegance, spacious lawn & flower gardens, gourmet breakfast.
info@aweaversinn.com http://www.aweaversinn.com

FAIRFAX

Fairfax Inn
15 Broadway 94930
415-455-8702 Fax: 415-485-5622
Jay Patel
All year

120-160-BB
12 rooms, 12 pb
Visa, MC, AmEx, *Rated*, •
C-yes/S-no/P-no/H-yes

Continental breakfast
Sitting room, Jacuzzi, suites, cable TV, fireplace, outside patio

Marin's newest B&B inn. Non-smoking facility with fireplaces, Jacuzzis. Golden Gate Bridge, Sausalito, Muir Woods. http://www.hotelfairfaxinn.com

Old Town B&B, Eureka, CA

FERNDALE

Collingwood Inn
PO Box 1134
831 Main St 95536
707-786-9219 Fax: 707-786-9869
800-469-1632
Chris & Peter
All year

119-203-BB
4 rooms, 4 pb
Most CC, •
C-ltd/S-ltd/P-yes/H-ltd
German, Italian

Full Country Breakfast Buffet
Afternoon wine, sherry, tea, snacks and sweets.
Parlor, Library, Gardens, Hot Tub, Bikes, Massage, Gift Shop, Art Gallery

Welcome to Collingwood Inn–Bed & Breakfast at The Hart House. Our historic inn is located on Main Street in beautiful Ferndale. We invite you to feel the elegance and splendor of the Victorian era.

innkeeper@collingwoodinn.com

Gingerbread Mansion Inn
PO Box 40
400 Berding St 95536
707-786-4000
Fax: 707-786-4381
800-952-4136
Tom Amato & Maggie Dowd
All year

150-385-BB
11 rooms, 11 pb
Visa, MC, AmEx, *Rated*, •
C-ltd/S-ltd/P-no/H-ltd

Full breakfast
Afternoon English Tea
4 guest parlors, 2 with fireplaces, English gardens

Gingerbread Mansion Inn, built in 1899, has everything; elegance, quietude, charm, warm hospitality, comfort, attention to detail, antiques, romance, beautifully lush English gardens.

innkeeper@gingerbread-mansion.com http://gingerbread-mansion.com

---

Queen of Harts
PO Box 1134
831 Main St 95536
707-786-9716
800-469-1632
Virginia & Keith Bettencourt
All year

115-185-BB
5 rooms, 4 pb
Most CC
C-ltd/S-no/P-no/H-ltd

Full breakfast
Evening dessert with coffee & tea
Sitting room, library, suites, fireplaces

1885 Italianate Victorian located in Historic Victorian Village. Antique furnishings, clawfoot tubs & showers in large room with featherbeds.

stay@ferndalebedandbreakfast.com http://www.ferndalebedandbreakfast.com

FERNDALE

Shaw House Inn
PO Box 1369
703 Main St 95536
707-786-9958 Fax: 707-786-9958
800-557-7429
Jan Culbert
All year

85-185-BB
8 rooms, 8 pb
Visa, MC
S-no

Full breakfast
Daily baked scones, afternoon tea
Intimate reading areas, free off-street parking, horseshoes

The Shaw House Inn is a beautiful Victorian Bed and Breakfast located in Ferndale, California, in Humboldt County. 8 guestrooms provide a private and comfortable getaway for those special occasions. stay@shawhouse.com http://www.shawhouse.com

---

Victorian Inn
PO Box 96
400 Ocean Ave 95536
707-786-4949 Fax: 707-786-4558
888-589-1808
Lowell & Jenny
All year

85-175-BB
12 rooms, 12 pb
Most CC, *Rated*
C-yes/S-no/P-no/H-ltd

Full breakfast
Lunch/dinner available, snacks
Restaurant, bar, sitting room, suites, fireplace, cable TV

The Victorian Inn stands as a monument to luxurious comfort & exquisite craftsmanship. It embodies the elegance and romance of the timber boom era on the North Coast.
innkeeper@a-victorian-inn.com http://www.a-victorian-inn.com

FORESTVILLE

Case Ranch Inn
7446 Poplar Dr 95436
707-887-8711 Fax: 707-887-8607
Diana Van Ry & Allan Tilton
All year

130-175-BB
3 rooms, 3 pb
Most CC
S-ltd/P-no

Full breakfast

A Sonoma County historical landmark, this circa 1894 Victorian farmhouse sits on 2 acres in a quiet residential neighborhood in the renowned Russian River Valley Wine Country.
info@caseranchinn.com http://www.caseranchinn.com

FORT BRAGG

Avalon House
561 Stewart St 95437
707-964-5555 Fax: 707-964-5555
800-964-5556
Anne Sorrells
All year

85-155-BB
6 rooms, 6 pb
Most CC, *Rated*, •
C-yes/S-no/P-no/H-no

Full breakfast
Complimentary sherry/port
Fireplaces in rooms, whirlpool tubs in rooms, fishing, spas

1905 Craftsman house in a quiet neighborhood close to ocean and Skunk Train Depot. Romantic Mendocino Coast retreat.
anne@theavalonhouse.com http://www.theavalonhouse.com

Grey Whale Inn
615 N Main St 95437
707-964-0640 Fax: 707-964-4408
800-382-7244
The Dawson Family
All year

100-210-BB
14 rooms, 14 pb
Most CC, *Rated*, •
C-ltd/S-no/P-no/H-yes

Full buffet breakfast
Tea, fresh fruit always
Parlor, TV-VCR, fireplace, upgrades, gift shop, art gallery

Mendocino coast landmark since 1915. Spacious rooms; ocean, town or garden views. Whale Watch with gas fireplace. Honeymoon suite with Jacuzzi & private sundeck.
stay@greywhaleinn.com http://www.greywhaleinn.com

The Weller House Inn
524 Stewart St 95437
707-964-4415 Fax: 707-964-4198
877-8-WELLER
Ted & Eva Kidwell
All year

95-185-BB
10 rooms, 10 pb
Most CC, *Rated*, •
C-ltd/S-no/P-no/H-ltd
Swedish

Full breakfast
Complimentary wine
Sitting room, library, cable, Jacuzzis, fireplaces, observation tower

Featured in New York Times and Sunset Magazine. Victorian beauty built in 1886. Lavish breakfast served in 900 square foot ballroom. 2 rooms in water tower topped by 40 foot high ocean view hot tub. innkeeper@wellerhouse.com http://www.wellerhouse.com

Avalon House, Fort Bragg, CA

FRESNO (REGION)

Wonder Valley Ranch Resort
6450 Elwood Rd, *Sanger* 93657
559-787-2551 Fax: 559-787-2556
800-821-2801
Larry & Myrna Oken
All year

93-168-BB
53 rooms, 53 pb
Visa, MC, *Rated*, •
C-yes/S-ltd/P-no/H-yes
Spanish

Continental plus breakfast
Lunch, dinner, snacks, restaurant, bar service
Sitting room, tennis, Jacuzzis, swimming, fireplaces, satellite TV

Nestled in the Sierra Nevada foothills, amid acres of shady oaks and sycamores and just minutes from Sequoia/Kings Canyon National Parks is a country hospitality at its best.
wondervalley@wondervalley.com http://www.wondervalley.com

GEORGETOWN

American River Inn
PO Box 43
6600 Orleans St 95634
916-333-4499 Fax: 530-333-9253
800-245-6566
Will & Maria Collin All year

85-115-BB
12 rooms, 9 pb
Rated, •

Full breakfast
Afternoon wine & hors d'oeuvres

Step back in time at our historic Queen Anne-style bed & breakfast inn, complete with old fashioned hospitality and turn-of-the-century antique furnishings.
ARiiNNkeeper@aol.com http://www.Americanriverinn.com

GEYSERVILLE

Hope-Merrill/Hope-Bosworth
PO Box 42
21253 Geyserville Ave 95441
707-857-3356 Fax: 707-857-4673
800-825-4233
C & R Scheiber All year

119-215-BB
12 rooms, 12 pb
Most CC, *Rated*, •
C-ltd/S-no/P-no/H-ltd

Full breakfast
Sitting room, library, Jacuzzis, suites, swimming pool, fireplace, cable TV

Facing each other are the Queen Anne Craftsman style Hope-Bosworth House and the strikingly restored Eastlake style Victorian Hope-Merrill House.
moreinfo@hope-inns.com http://www.hope-inns.com

GUERNEVILLE

Fern Grove Cottages
16650 Hwy 116 95446
707-869-8105 Fax: 707-869-1615
Mike & Margaret Kennett
All year

79-219-BB
21 rooms, 21 pb
Most CC, *Rated*, •
C-yes/S-no/P-yes/H-yes

Continental plus breakfast
Sitting room, library, spa tubs, suites, pool, cable TV, wine tours

Comfortable cottages in the redwoods–many with living rooms, fireplaces. Some with spa tubs. Relax among beautiful gardens. Pool. Easy walk to town, river beaches. Warm hospitality. Great breakfast. innkeepers@ferngrove.com http://www.ferngrove.com

GUERNEVILLE

Ridenhour Ranch House Inn 12850 River Rd 95446 707-887-1033 Fax: 707-869-2967 888-877-4466 Meilani Naranjo & Chris Bell All year	105-205-BB 8 rooms, 8 pb Most CC, *Rated*, • C-yes/S-ltd/P-ltd/H-ltd	Full gourmet breakfast Homemade cookies, complimentary port & sherry Outdoor hot tub, great room with fireplace, library, cable TV/VCR

Historic Bed and Breakfast nestled along the Russian River offers comfort and charm in the heart of Sonoma County's Wine Country.
ridenhourinn@earthlink.net http://www.ridenhourinn.com

River Village Resort & Spa PO Box 526 14880 River Road 95446 707-869-8139 Fax: 707-864-3096 800-529-3376 All year	90-195-BB 20 rooms, 20 pb Most CC, • C-yes/S-no/P-ltd/H-yes Spanish	Continental plus brkfst on weekends Snacks, wine tasting Sitting room, library, Jacuzzis, pool, suites, cable TV, full service spa

20 intimate cottages in lush gardens & towering redwoods in heart of Sonoma Cty Wine Country. Full service spa w/highest quality herbal products. Pool, outdoor Jacuzzi, cable TV/VCR, cont. breakfast. info@rivervillageresort.com http://www.rivervillageresort.com

HALF MOON BAY

The Cypress Inn on Miramar Beach 407 Mirada Rd 94019 650-726-6002 Fax: 650-712-0380 800-83-BEACH David Souza All year	180-365-BB 18 rooms, 18 pb Most CC, *Rated*, • C-ltd/S-no/P-no/H-yes	Full gourmet breakfast Afternoon tea, Evening dessert Unobstructed ocean views, frplcs., Jacuzzis, decks

Bay area's only oceanfront B&B located on 5 miles of sandy beach. 10 steps to the sand. Contemporary beach house with skylights, natural wicker & pine.
lodging@cypressinn.com http://www.innsbythesea.com

Landis Shores Oceanfront Inn 211 Mirada Rd 94019 650-726-6642 Fax: 650-726-6644 Ken Landis All year	275-345-BB 8 rooms, 8 pb Most CC, *Rated*, • C-ltd/S-no/P-no/H-yes	Full breakfast Snacks, complimentary wine Sitting room, Jacuzzis, fireplaces, cable TV, accom. bus. travelers

Elegant oceanfront accommodations, private balconies, fireplaces, whirlpool tubs, TV/VCRs and more. Enjoy a gourmet breakfast each morning and premium wines and appetizers every afternoon. luxury@landisshores.com http://www.landisshores.com

Old Thyme Inn 779 Main St 94019 650-726-1616 Fax: 650-726-6394 800-720-4277 Rick & Kathy Ellis All year	130-300-BB 7 rooms, 7 pb Most CC, *Rated*, • C-ltd/S-no/P-no/H-no French	Full breakfast Complimentary afternoon hors d'oeuvres Library of videos and recent magazines, peaceful herb and flower garden

"A world away . . . but ever so close" – tucked in the seaside village of Half Moon Bay. . .the ideal garden retreat in which to relax, renew, or simply slow down and gather your peace. rick@oldthymeinn.com http://www.oldthymeinn.com

HALF MOON BAY (REGION)

Goose & Turrets PO Box 370937 835 George St, *Montara* 94037 650-728-5451 Fax: 650-728-0141 Raymond & Emily Hoche-Mong All year	120-175-BB 5 rooms, 5 pb Most CC, *Rated*, • C-ltd/S-no/P-no French	Full breakfast Afternoon tea, snacks Sitting room w/woodstove, quiet garden, fireplaces, local airport pickup

An historic, classic B&B focusing on both B's: comfortable beds and four-course breakfasts. A slow-lane haven pampering fast-lane folks.
rhmgt@montara.com http://goose.montara.com

HEALDSBURG

Calderwood Inn
25 W Grant St 95448
707-431-1110 800-600-5444
Jennifer & Paul
All year

145-235-BB
6 rooms, 6 pb
MC, *Rated*, •
C-ltd/S-ltd/P-no/H-ltd

Full gourmet breakfast
Appetizers & wine, port & dessert
Fireplaces, whirlpools, luxurious towels & linens

Romantic 1902 Queen Anne Victorian surrounded by lush gardens, ancient redwood trees, fountains and koi ponds. Large porches for relaxation.
talktous@calderwoodinn.com http://www.calderwoodinn.com

Camellia Inn
211 North St 95448
707-433-8182 Fax: 707-433-8130
800-727-8182
Lucy Lewand
All year

99-209-BB
9 rooms, 9 pb
Visa, MC, *Rated*, •
C-ltd/S-ltd/P-no/H-ltd

Full breakfast
Complimentary beverage & snacks
Sitting room, swimming pool in summer, 4 rooms with whirlpool tubs

Elegant Italianate Victorian built in 1869, near Sonoma's finest wineries.
info@camelliainn.com http://www.camelliainn.com

The Grape Leaf Inn
539 Johnson St 95448
707-433-8140 Fax: 707-433-3140
866-732-9131
Richard & Kae Rosenberg
All year

165-325-BB
12 rooms, 12 pb
Visa, MC, *Rated*, •
C-ltd/S-no/P-no/H-yes

Full gourmet country breakfast
Complimentary wine & local cheese
Speakeasy, wine cellar, library, fireplace, suite

Victorian luxury amidst Sonoma County's finest wineries. Generous full breakfast, complimentary premium wines, all private baths. Walk to 6 excellent restaurants. 90 world class wineries within 10 minutes drive.
info@grapeleafinn.com http://www.grapeleafinn.com

Haydon Street Inn
321 Haydon St 95448
707-433-5228 Fax: 707-433-6637
800-528-3703
Dick & Pat Bertapelle
All year

110-260-BB
8 rooms, 8 pb
Visa, MC, *Rated*, •
C-ltd/S-no/P-no/H-no

Full breakfast
Afternoon tea, snacks
Sitting room, fireplaces, cable TV, Jacuzzis

Historic Wine Country Queen Anne home in quaint, friendly Sonoma County town. Walk to historic town plaza with great restaurants, antique stores & boutiques.
innkeeper@haydon.com http://www.haydon.com

Healdsburg Inn on the Plaza
110 Matheson St 95448
707-433-6991 Fax: 707-433-9513
800-431-8663
Genny Jenkins
All year

155-285-BB
10 rooms, 10 pb
Visa, MC, Disc, *Rated*
C-ltd/S-no/P-no/H-yes

Full healthy breakfast
Champagne brunch on weekends
Gallery, gift shops, A/C, fireplaces, open balconies

Individually appointed Victorian rooms with antiques, many with whirlpool tubs. Centrally located overlooking charming town square.
innpressions@earthlink.net http://www.healdsburginn.com

Madrona Manor, Wine Country Inn & Rest.
PO Box 818
1001 Westside Rd 95448
707-433-4231 Fax: 707-433-0703
800-258-4003
Bill & Trudi Konrad
All year

165-425-BB
21 rooms, 21 pb

Full breakfast

Nestled in the hills above the Dry Creek Valley of Sonoma County, Madrona Manor is an exceptionally lovely Victorian estate surrounded by eight acres of wooded and landscaped grounds. madronaman@aol.com http://www.madronamanor.com

HEALDSBURG

Raford House
10630 Wohler Rd 95448
707-887-9573 Fax: 707-887-9597
800-887-9503
Carole & Jack Vore
All year

130-200-BB
6 rooms, 6 pb
Most CC, *Rated*, •
C-ltd/S-ltd/P-no/H-ltd

Full breakfast
Complimentary wine
Porch, vineyards, patio, some fireplaces, roses

Victorian farmhouse overlooks vineyards of Sonoma County. Beautiful country setting is just 1½ hours from San Francisco. http://www.rafordhouse.com

HOLLYWOOD (REGION)

Elaine's Hollywood
1616 N Sierra Bonita Ave, *Los Angeles* 90046
323-850-0766 Fax: 323-851-6243
Elaine & Avik Gilboa
All year

60-85-BB
2 rooms, 2 pb
Rated, •
C-yes/S-no/P-yes/H-no
French, German, Spanish, Italian, Russian

Continental
Cable TV

Our B&B is a very warm and friendly home. Our guests become part of our family and enjoy the full facilities available at the house.
Avikg@aol.com http://people.we.mediaone.net/avielgilboa

HOPE VALLEY

Sorensen's Resort
14255 Hwy 88 96120
530-694-2203 800-423-9949
John & Patty Brissenden
All year

85-225-EP
30 rooms, 28 pb
Most CC, *Rated*, •
C-yes/S-no/P-ltd/H-ltd
Spanish

Full breakfast (fee)
Snacks, restaurant, wine & beer service
Library, hot springs nearby, bikes & skis nearby, wood-burning stoves

Cozy creek-side cabins nestled in Alps of California. Close to Tahoe & Kirkwood, Hope Valley Outdoor Center. sorensensresort@yahoo.com http://www.sorensensresort.com

IDYLLWILD

The Lodge at Pine Cove
PO Box 2157
24900 Marion Ridge Dr 92349
909-659-4463 Fax: 909-659-4531
866-LODGEPC
Geary Boedeker
All year

BB

The Lodge at Pine Cove is a 5-room B&B, just minutes from the beautiful alpine village of Idyllwild. Authentic lodge atmosphere w/parquet wood floor, vaulted ceiling, & fieldstone fireplace. innkeeper@thelogdeatpinecove.com http://www.thelodgeatpinecove.com

---

Strawberry Creek Inn
PO Box 1818
26370 State Hwy 243 92549
909-659-3202 800-262-8969
Diana Dugan & Jim Goff
All year

89-150-BB
9 rooms, 7 pb
Visa, MC, *Rated*
C-ltd/S-no/P-no/H-ltd

Full breakfast
Afternoon wine
Library, fireplaces, sitting room, refrigerators

Country inn located in the pines where comfort mixes with nostalgia in a uniquely decorated home. Cottage with spas. http://www.strawberrycreekinn.com

INVERNESS

Bayshore Cottage
PO Box 405
12372 Sir Francis Drake Blvd 94937
415-669-1148 Fax: 415-669-1148
Mare M. Hansen
All year

165-BB
1 rooms, 1 pb
Rated
C-ltd/S-no/P-no/H-no

Kitchen w/ provisions for breakfast
Snacks, complimentary wine
Sitting room, library, hot tub, cable TV, private deck, barbecue pit

A romantic, cozy cottage in a quiet secluded garden setting, looking toward Tomales Bay, located about ¾ of a mile south of the village of Inverness and 1 hour north of the Golden Gate Bridge. http://innformation.com/ca/bayshore

INVERNESS

Blackthorne Inn
PO Box 712
266 Vallejo Ave. 94937
415-663-8621 Fax: 415-663-8635
M. Bennett & S. Wigert

225-350-BB
5 rooms, 5 pb
Rated
C-ltd/P-no
All year

Blackthorne Inn provides intimate overnight accommodations in a beautiful rustic setting, just one hour north of San Francisco on the magnificent Point Reyes Peninsula.
susan@blackthorneinn.com http://www.blackthorneinn.com

Inverness Valley Inn
PO Box 429
13275 Sir Francis Drake Blvd,
Inverness 94937
415-669-7250 800-416-0405
Steve & Geertje Zamlich,
Bruce Graham All year

115-130-EP
11 rooms, 11 pb
Visa, MC
C-yes/S-ltd/P-no/H-no
Dutch, German, Italian,
French
Fax: 415-669-7868

Tennis, Jacuzzis, swimming,
fireplaces, cable,
kitchenettes, accom. bus. tra

Located on 15 acres of natural beauty, 1½ hours from San Francisco, our refurbished A-frame cottages each consist of four spacious units with high ceilings and plenty of light.
Invernessvalleyinn@earthlink.net http://www.invernessvalleyinn.com

---

Rosemary Cottages
PO Box 273
75 Balboa Ave 94937
415-663-9338 800-808-9338
Suzanne Storch All year

180-285-BB
2 rooms, 2 pb
Rated, •
C-yes/S-yes/P-yes/H-no

Continental plus breakfast
Complimentary tea, coffee
Kitchen, fireplace, decks,
secluded, hot tub in garden

Charming, romantic French country cottage nestled in secluded garden with dramatic forest views. rosemarybb@aol.com http://www.rosemarybb.com

---

Tree House
PO Box 1075
73 Drake Summit Rd 94937
415-663-8720
Lisa Patsel All year

125-155-BB
3 rooms, 3 pb
Visa, MC, AmEx
C-yes/S-no/P-yes/H-no
Italian

Continental plus breakfast
Suites, fireplaces

The Treehouse offers a secluded, peaceful getaway nestled among the trees atop Inverness Ridge. Overlooks Point Reyes Station, Black Mountain, and adjacent to the National Seashore's hiking trails. treehousebnb@juno.com http://www.treehousebnb.com

JACKSON

Gate House Inn
1330 Jackson Gate Rd 95642
209-223-3500 Fax: 209-223-1299
800-841-1072
Donna & Mark Macola
All year

130-205-BB
6 rooms, 6 pb
Most CC, *Rated*, •
C-ltd/S-no/P-no/H-no

Full gourmet candle light
breakfast
Beverages & fresh baked
snacks always available
Screened porch, Ping-Pong,
darts, horseshoes, outdr pool

Regal 1902 Country Victorian, on the National Register of Historic Places, 1 mile from downtown Jackson. Beautiful landscaped rose gardens, grape arbors, orchard and fountains. info@gatehouseinn.com http://www.gatehouseinn.com

---

Windrose Inn
1407 Jackson Gate Rd 95642
209-223-3650 Fax: 209-223-3793
888-568-5250
Paula & Bruce Stanbridge
All year

100-185-BB
4 rooms, 4 pb
Visa, MC, AmEx, •
C-ltd/S-ltd/P-no/H-ltd

Full breakfast
Complimentary wine
Sitting room, library, suites,
Jacuzzis, fireplaces, accom.
bus. travelers

An elegant 1897 Victorian nestled amid an acre of lush gardens, forested creek, expansive patio with koi pond, gazebo ... romantic country setting adjacent to downtown historic Jackson. info@windroseinn.com http://www.windroseinn.com

Gate House Inn, Jackson, CA

JAMESTOWN

The Jamestown Hotel
18153 Main St 95327
209-984-3902
Fax: 209-984-4149
800-205-4901
Annette & Norbert Mede
All year

80-175-BB
11 rooms, 11 pb
Most CC, *Rated*, •
C-yes/S-ltd/P-no/H-no
German

Continental plus breakfast
Business center and TV room with VCR, refrigerator for guests

Located on Main Street in Jamestown, the inn features eleven rooms with private baths, antiques, and some with whirlpool tubs. Fine dining restaurant and old time bar are open for lunch and dinner. info@jamestownhotel.com http://www.jamestownhotel.com

JENNER

Jenner Inn & Cottages
PO Box 69
10400 Coast Hwy 1 95450
707-865-2377 Fax: 707-865-0829
800-732-2300
Richard Murphy
All year

98-378-BB
20 rooms, 20 pb
Visa, MC, AmEx, *Rated*, •
C-yes/S-no/P-no/H-no

Full breakfast
Complimentary teas & aperitifs
Port & sherry available, sitting room, private cottages

A B&B Inn on the undiscovered Sonoma coast at the edge of California's premier Wine Country. Sweet dreams await you.
innkeeper@jennerinn.com http://www.jennerinn.com

JOSHUA TREE

Rosebud Ruby Star
PO Box 1116
92252
760-366-4676 877-887-7370
Sandy Rosen
All year

155-BB
2 rooms, 2 pb
Visa, MC, *Rated*, •
C-ltd/S-no/P-no/H-no

Full breakfast
Afternoon tea, snacks
Complimentary wine, evening food basket, beverages

Intimate pueblo-style hideaway with panoramic views overlooking surreal Joshua Tree National Park west gateway.
sandy@rosebudrubystar.com http://www.rosebudrubystar.com

The Jamestown Hotel, Jamestown, CA

JULIAN

Julian Gold Rush Hotel PO Box 1856 2032 Main Street 92036 760-765-0201 Fax: 760-765-0327 800-734-5854 Steve & Gig Ballinger All year	95-190-BB 16 rooms, 16 pb Visa, MC, AmEx, *Rated*, • C-yes/S-ltd/P-no/H-no	Full breakfast Afternoon tea Sitting room, library, piano, cottage, family rates

Surviving 1897 hotel in southern Mother Lode of CA, restored to full glory with American antiques. bnb@julianhotel.com http://www.julianhotel.com

KERNVILLE

Kern River Inn PO Box 1725 119 Kern River Dr 93238 760-376-6750 Fax: 760-376-6643 800-986-4382 Jack & Carita Prestwich All year	99-109-BB 6 rooms, 6 pb Most CC, *Rated*, • C-yes/S-no/P-no/H-yes	Afternoon refreshments with beverage. River view, fireplace, library, whirlpool tub, TV/VCR in living room.

Classic country inn across from the "wild and scenic" Kern River. Whitewater rafting, kayaking, fishing, golf, antique and collectibles shops, giant Sequoias, or just relax on the veranda! kernriverinn@lightspeed.net http://www.kernriverinn.com

Whispering Pines Lodge Rt 1, Box 41 13745 Sierra Way 93238 760-376-3733 Fax: 760-376-6513 877-241-4100 George & Darlene Randall All year	109-179-BB 17 rooms, 17 pb Most CC, *Rated*, • S-no/P-no/H-ltd	Full country breakfast Swimming pool, Jacuzzi, private patios, private decks, river views

Romantic country getaway, featuring Roman Jacuzzis, fireplaces, country breakfast on patio, w/ view of Sequoia Forest & wild, scenic Kern River.
thepines@kernvalley.com http://www.Kernvalley.com/inns

KLAMATH

Historic Requa Inn
451 Requa Rd 95548
707-482-1425
All year by reservation

69-105-BB
10 rooms, 10 pb
Most CC
C-ltd/S-no/P-ltd/H-no

Full breakfast
Dinner, tea, coffee, dessert
Lobby with river view

The Historic Requa Inn is a 10-room bed-and-breakfast inn located on the north California coast in the center of Redwood National Park on the Klamath River just one mile from the ocean.

innkeeper@requainn.com http://www.klamathinn.net

LAGUNA BEACH

Casa Laguna Inn
2510 South Coast Hwy 92651
949-494-2996
Fax: 949-494-7470
800-233-0449
Francois Leclair
All year

105-395-BB
20 rooms, 20 pb
Most CC, *Rated*, •
C-yes/S-ltd/P-yes/H-no
Spanish

Continental plus breakfast
Afternoon tea, snacks, comp. wine
Library, pool, suites, fireplaces, cable TV, accomm. bus. trav.

In the scenic seaside resort of Laguna Beach, nestled on a terraced hillside overlooking the Pacific Ocean. Queen palms & beautiful grounds frame the pool & sundeck. Offering sun, sand & sea.

francois@casalaguna.com http://www.casalaguna.com

LAKE TAHOE (REGION)

Black Bear Inn
1202 Ski Run Blvd, *South Lake Tahoe* 96150
530-544-4451 877-232-7466
Kevin Chandler & Jerry Birdwell   All year

205-475-BB
10 rooms, 8 pb
Visa, MC
C-ltd/S-no/P-no/H-yes

Full breakfast
Complimentary wine
Fireplaces, cable TV, accommodate business travelers

A small luxury lodge with five guest rooms plus three cabins on a wooded acre in a quiet mountain setting at South Lake Tahoe.

info@tahoeblackbear.com http://www.tahoeblackbear.com

LAKEPORT

Forbestown Inn
825 Forbes St 95453
707-263-7858 Fax: 707-263-7878
866-268-7858
Wally & Pat Kelley   All year

84-125-BB
4 rooms, 4 pb
Most CC, *Rated*, •
C-ltd/S-ltd/P-no/H-no

Full breakfast
Pool, corporate rates, roomy living room with wood-burning stove

Circa 1863 Victorian farmhouse style inn. Full breakfast in the garden by the pool when weather permits. Walk to Clear Lake and town center with shops and restaurants.

forbestowninn@zapcom.net http://www.forbestowninn.com

LONG BEACH

Lord Mayor's Inn
435 Cedar Ave 90802
562-436-0324 Fax: 562-436-0324
800-691-5166
Laura & Reuben Brasser
All year

85-140-BB
12 rooms, 5 pb
Visa, MC, AmEx, *Rated*, •
C-yes/S-no/P-no/H-no
Dutch, Danish

Full breakfast
Special luncheons/dinner
Library, sitting room, croquet, sundecks, IBM PC on request

Award-winning restored 1904 Edwardian home of Long Beach's first mayor. Spacious rooms with antiques, library, gardens, porches, parking. Guided walking tours, mystery nights. innkeepers@lordmayors.com http://www.lordmayors.com

---

The Turret House
556 Chestnut Ave 90802
562-983-9812 Fax: 562-437-4082
888-4-TURRET
Nina & Lee Agee
All year

100-140-BB
5 rooms, 5 pb
Most CC, *Rated*, •
C-ltd/S-no/P-no/H-no

Full breakfast
Afternoon tea, snacks
Fireplaces, cable TV, accommodate business travelers

Victorian hospitality and antique finery in elegantly restored 1906 home, in historic downtown residential district. innkeepers@turrethouse.com http://www.turrethouse.com

LOS ANGELES (REGION)

Casa Dulce Riding & Guest Ranch
8035 Clayvale Rd, *Agua Dulce* 91350
661-268-8946 Fax: 661-268-8947
Joyce Guenther All year

63-185-BB
3 rooms, 1 pb
•
C-yes/S-ltd/P-ltd/H-no

Continental breakfast
Lunch & dinner available, snacks
Sitting room, library, Jacuzzis, fireplaces, satellite TV, accom. bus. trav.

40 miles north of Los Angeles–country B&B guest ranch with mountain views. Includes horseback riding on extensive trails, arena & lessons. Rooms are beautifully decorated in country motif. horseranch@aol.com http://www.theguestranch.com

---

Sea Mountain Inn Resort & Spa
9510 Vassar St, *Malibu* 90265
877-928-2827 877-928-2827
Julie Dewey
All year

199-535-BB
5 rooms, 4 pb
Visa, MC, AmEx, *Rated*, •
C-no/S-ltd/P-no/H-ltd
10 languages by special request

Asian rices, eggs, local fruits
Complimentary cheeses and wines 4:00 -full menu
French spa,3 pools, ocean views,luxury tanning-massage-trails,waterfalls,vip

Sea Mountain Inn and spa is located 2800 ft above the sea, w/world class ocean views & luxury accommodations. The only Inn of its class–A hideaway for stress reduction & resort pleasures.3 pools- info@seamountaininn.com http://www.seamountaininn.com

MAMMOTH LAKES

Cinnamon Bear Inn
PO Box 3338
113 Center St 93546
760-934-2873 800-845-2873
R & M Harrison All year

99-179-BB
22 rooms, 22 pb
Most CC, *Rated*, •
C-yes/S-no/P-no/H-ltd
Fax: 760-934-2873

Full breakfast
Snacks, complimentary wine
Sitting room, Jacuzzis, suites, fireplaces, cable TV, ski packages

"Who needs the Ritz?" Friendly folks feature full breakfasts, free hors d'oeuvres and fabulous ski packages. Forested view rooms with private baths.
cinnabear1@aol.com http://www.cinnamonbearinn.com

MAMMOTH LAKES (REGION)

Rainbow Tarns at Crowley Lake
HCR 79, Box 55-C
505 Rainbow Tarns Rd, *Crowley Lake* 93546
760-935-4556 888-588-6269
Brock & Diane Thoman
Closed Dec 24/25,Apr/Nov

90-140-BB
3 rooms, 3 pb
Rated
C-ltd/S-ltd/P-no/H-yes

Full country breakfast
Afternoon wine, snacks
Sitting room, library, 2 rooms with Jacuzzis, vegy meals arranged

Secluded log cabin lodge in a beautiful, 7,000 foot high, three acre, Sierra mountain setting. info@rainbowtarns.com http://www.rainbowtarns.com

MANCHESTER

Victorian Gardens
14409 S Highway 1 95459
707-882-3606 Fax: 707-882-2718
Luciano & Pauline Zamboni
All year

180-250-BB
4 rooms, 3 pb
Visa, MC, AmEx, *Rated*, •
C-ltd/S-ltd/P-no/H-no
French, Italian

Full breakfast
Lunch/dinner available, restaurant
Aperitifs &, hors d'oeuvres 7-7:30pm, sitting room, library

An exquisitely appointed, fully restored gem of Victorian architecture offering total privacy & seclusion on 92 enchanted acres along the rugged Mendocino coast.
http://www.elkcoast.com/lodging.html

MARIPOSA

Restful Nest Resort
4274 Buckeye Creek Rd 95338
209-742-7127 Fax: 209-742-7127
800-664-7127
Lois Y. Moroni All year

95-125-BB
3 rooms, 3 pb
Most CC, *Rated*, •
C-ltd/S-ltd/H-no
French

Full gourmet breakfast
Hot tubs, swimming pool

We offer relaxation, old California hospitality, & the flavor of Provence in the beautiful foothills of the Sierra Nevada mountains.
restful@yosemite.net http://mariposa.yosemite.net/restful/

MENDOCINO

Agate Cove Inn
PO Box 1150
11201 N Lansing St 95460
707-937-0551 Fax: 707-937-0550
800-527-3111
D & N Freeze All year

119-269-BB
10 rooms, 10 pb
Visa, MC, AmEx, *Rated*
C-ltd/S-ltd/P-no/H-ltd

Full country breakfast
Complimentary sherry in rm
Ocean view, fireplace, TV/VCR/cable/HBO, CD player, down comforter

Agate Cove's romantic cottages and 1860's farmhouse boast unparalleled ocean views and spectacular gardens. Rooms feature king or queen beds.
info@agatecove.com http://www.agatecove.com

Alegria Oceanfront Inn
PO Box 803
44781 Main St 95460
707-937-5150 Fax: 707-937-5151
800-780-7905
Elaine Wing & Eric Hillesland
All year

129-259-BB
Most CC
C-ltd/S-ltd/P-no

Full breakfast

Alegria–the state of being joyful and happy...an inn that welcomes you by putting your cares to rest. inn@oceanfrontmagic.com http://www.oceanfrontmagic.com

---

Blackberry Inn
44951 Larkin Rd 95460
707-937-5281 800-950-7806
Ruth & Paul Tay
All year

90-195-BB
17 rooms, 17 pb
Visa, MC, *Rated*
C-yes/S-ltd/P-ltd/H-ltd
Spanish

Continental breakfast
Coffee, tea, cocoa, cookies, fruit, homemade bread
ocean views, fireplaces, whirlpool tubs

Blackberry Inn Motel Lodging in Mendocino, Calif. A most unique motel. TV, ocean views, fireplaces, decks, whirlpool tubs. Coffee, tea, fruit, homemade bread and cookies.
blackber@mcn.org http://www.blackberryinn.biz

Blue Heron Inn
PO Box 1142
390 Kasten 95460
707-937-4323 Fax: 707-937-3611
Linda Friedman All year

95-135-BB
3 rooms, 1 pb
Visa, MC
C-ltd/S-no/P-no/H-ltd

Continental plus breakfast

Country charm and simple elegance in the heart of Mendocino Village.
moosse@mcn.org http://www.theblueheron.com

Brewery Gulch Inn
9401 Coast Hwy 1 N 95460
707-937-4752 Fax: 707-937-1279
800-578-4454
Glenn Lutge
All year

150-280-BB
10 rooms, 10 pb
Visa, MC, AmEx, *Rated*, •
C-ltd/S-no/P-no/H-yes

Full gourmet breakfast
Wine hour with hors d'oeuvres; tea & coffee
Robes, toiletries, hair dryers, wine bar, concierge service, fine food

On a hillside overlooking Smuggler's Cove and the sea. Craftsman-style with ocean views, fireplaces, Jacuzzi tubs, private decks, spacious rooms, TVs, dataport telephones, wine bar, gourmet food. innkeeper@brewerygulchinn.com http://www.brewerygulchinn.com

---

Dennen's Victorian Farmhouse
PO Box 661
7001 N Hwy 1 Little River 95460
707-937-0697 Fax: 707-937-5238
800-264-4723
Fred Cox & Jo Bradley
All year

105-185-BB
10 rooms, 10 pb
Visa, MC, AmEx, *Rated*, •
C-ltd/S-no/P-no/H-ltd

Full breakfast delivered to room
Complimentary wine
Sitting room, Jacuzzis, fireplaces, parks, tennis nearby

Romantic Victorian home, inspired artist Thomas Kinkade. About 2 mi. to Mendocino. Feather beds, wood fireplaces, spa tubs, ocean access, breakfast in bed. AAA Three Diamond Rating. Affordable luxury.
frednjo@victorianfarmhouse.com http://www.victorianfarmhouse.com

Glendeven Inn, Mendocino, CA

MENDOCINO

Glendeven Inn PO Box 914 8205 North Hwy One 95460 707-937-0083 Fax: 707-937-6108 800-822-4536 Sharon & Higgins All year	135-245-BB 10 rooms, 10 pb Most CC, *Rated* C-no/S-no/P-no/H-ltd	Full breakfast Tea, wine Sitting room, suites, fireplace

Delightful 1867 country inn on the Mendocino coast with fireplaces, ocean views, and private baths. Breakfast delivered to your room.

innkeeper@glendeven.com http://www.glendeven.com

Inn at Schoolhouse Creek PO Box 1637 7501 N Hwy 1 95460 707-937-5527 Fax: 707-937-2012 800-731-5525 Al & Penny Greenwood All year	110-245-BB 15 rooms, 15 pb Most CC, *Rated*, • C-yes/S-ltd/P-ltd/H-ltd	Full breakfast Complimentary wine & hor d'ouvres Parlor, library, verandah, spa tubs, fireplaces, private beach access

On the quiet side of Mendocino, relaxed country inn with romantic ocean view cottages, surrounded by 8 1/2 acres of gardens & meadows. Beach access, hot tub with panoramic ocean view, fireplaces.

innkeeper@schoolhousecreek.com http://www.schoolhousecreek.com

John Dougherty House PO Box 817 571 Ukiah St 95460 707-937-5266 800-486-2104 David Wells All year	115-245-BB 8 rooms, 8 pb Visa, MC, Disc, *Rated*, • C-ltd/S-no/P-no/H-no	Full breakfast Complimentary wine Sitting room, verandas, ocean views, near tennis, antiques, English garden

Historic 1867 house in Village center. Large verandahs with ocean views; quiet peaceful nights; walk to shops & dining. Woodburning stoves in 5 rooms.

jdhbmw@mcn.org http://www.jdhouse.com

Joshua Grindle Inn PO Box 647 44800 Little Lake Rd 95460 707-937-4143 800-GRINDLE Charles & Cindy Reinhart All year	130-245-BB 10 rooms, 10 pb Visa, MC, *Rated* C-ltd/S-no/P-no/H-ltd	Full gourmet breakfast Aft./eve. sherry, tea & goodies in parlor Ocean views, fireplaces, whirlpool tubs, luxurious cotton robes

In the historic village. Park and forget your car. Stroll to fine dining, galleries, shops & Pacific Ocean headlands. cindy@joshgrin.com http://www.joshgrin.com

Dennen's Victorian Farmhouse, Mendocino, CA

MENDOCINO

MacCallum House Inn
PO Box 206
45020 Albion St 95460
707-937-0289 Fax: 707-937-3076
800-609-0492
Jed & Megan Ayres & Noah Sheppard All year

120-210-BB
19 rooms, 19 pb
Visa, MC, Disc, •
C-ltd/S-no/P-yes/H-yes
French, Spanish

Full breakfast
Fine dining and full bar
Gourmet Breakfast, Bar service, spa tubs, fireplaces, cottages, Ocean views

An 1882 vintage Victorian with charming garden cottages in the heart of Mendocino village. machouse@mcn.org http://www.maccallumhouse.com

---

Reed Manor
PO Box 127
10961 Palette Dr 95460
707-937-5446
Barbara & Monte Reed
All year

175-450-BB
5 rooms, 5 pb
Visa, MC, AmEx, *Rated*, •
C-ltd/S-no/P-no/H-no

Continental plus breakfast
Sitting room, Jacuzzis, fireplaces, cable TV

Romantic haven of luxury for guests looking to get away from it all–privacy.
mreed@mcn.org http://www.reedmanor.com

Sea Rock
PO Box 906
11101 Lansing St 95460
707-937-0926 800-906-0926
Susie & Andy Plocher
All year

149-279-BB
14 rooms, 14 pb
Most CC, *Rated*
C-ltd/S-no/P-no/H-no

Continental plus breakfast
Sitting room, gardens, lawns, ocean view, fireplace, king bed

With awe-inspiring views of the Mendocino coast from every guestroom, Sea Rock Inn consists of numerous cottages & newly constructed deluxe suites, all with TV/VCR, private bath, private deck & phone. searock@mcn.org http://www.searock.com

---

Stanford Inn by the Sea
PO Box 487
Hwy 1, Comptche-Ukiah Rd
95460
707-937-5615 Fax: 707-937-0305
800-331-8884
Joan & Jeff Stanford All year

215-365-BB
33 rooms, 33 pb
Most CC, *Rated*, •
C-yes/S-yes/P-yes/H-yes
French, Spanish

Full breakfast
Wine, organic vegetables
Indoor pool, hot tub, decks, nurseries, llamas, bicycles, canoe rentals

A truly elegant country inn in a pastoral setting. All accommodations with ocean views, fireplace, decks, antiques, four-posters and TVs.
j&j@stanfordinn.com http://www.stanfordinn.com

MENDOCINO

Whitegate Inn by the Sea
PO Box 150
499 Howard St 95460
707-937-4892 Fax: 707-937-1131
800-531-7282
Carol & George Bechtloff
All year

159-289-BB
6 rooms, 6 pb
Most CC, *Rated*, •
C-ltd/S-no/P-no/H-no

Full breakfast
Complimentary wine & hors d'oeuvres
Sitting rm w/antique piano, fireplaces, TVs, gardens, deck, gazebo, weddings

Historic Mendocino lacation. All rooms decorated in French and Victorian antiques, Ocean and garden views. English country & herb gardens. Featured in "Sunset Magazine, Country Inns, & Bon Appetit." staff@whitegateinn.com http://www.whitegateinn.com

MENDOCINO (REGION)

Albion River Inn
PO Box 100
3790 Hwy 1 N, *Albion* 95410
707-937-1919 Fax: 707-937-2604
800-479-7944 All year

200-310-BB
20 rooms, 20 pb
Visa, MC, AmEx, *Rated*
S-no/P-no/H-yes

Full breakfast
Din. (fee), comp. wine
Bar service, Jacuzzis, fireplaces, deck, priv., cottages, restaurant

The Albion River Inn: A spectacular ocean view inn on 10 magnificent headland acres. Small, romantic and private. ari@mcn.org http://www.albionriverinn.com

---

Fensalden Inn
PO Box 99
33810 Navarro Ridge Road, *Albion* 95410
707-937-4042 Fax: 707-937-2416
800-959-3850
Lyn Hamby All year

125-225-BB
8 rooms, 8 pb
Visa, MC, *Rated*, •
C-ltd/S-no/P-no/H-ltd

Full breakfast
Wine & hors d'oeuvres
Fireplaces in all rooms, bar refrigerators in all rooms, fax, pc hookup

An 1850's stage stop on 20 acres overlooking the ocean, Fensalden offers a quiet, romantic getaway, pampering, antique appointed rooms, gourmet breakfasts; friendly pigmy goats and flocks of birds. inn@fensalden.com http://www.fensalden.com

---

The Elk Cove Inn
PO Box 367
6300 S Hwy 1, *Elk* 95432
707-877-3321 Fax: 707-877-1808
800-275-2967
David Lieberman
All year

130-350-BB
15 rooms, 15 pb
Most CC, *Rated*, •
C-ltd/S-ltd/P-no/H-ltd
Spanish

Full gourmet breakfast
Cocktail Bar, complimentary port & hors d'ouevres
Kayaking, sitting room, deck, VCR, library, stereo, fishing, hot tub

1883 Victorian mansion on the Ocean. Dramatic views, private steps to beach, organic gardens, romantic gazebo. Luxury spa suites, cozy fireplace cottages and charming Victorian rooms. elkcove@mcn.org http://www.elkcoveinn.com

---

The Harbor House Inn
PO Box 369
5600 S Hwy 1, *Elk* 95432
707-877-3203 Fax: 707-877-3452
800-720-7474
Sam & Elle Haynes All year

250-475-MAP
10 rooms, 10 pb
Visa, MC, *Rated*
C-ltd/S-ltd/P-no/H-yes
French, Spanish

Full breakfast
4 course dinner included
Sitting room, piano, fireplace, parlor stove, new gardens, private beach

Spectacular north coast vistas of the sea. Renowned country gourmet cuisine. Wine lover's paradise. Rooms include original artwork, fireplaces or parlor stoves, and decks. innkeeper@theharborhouseinn.com http://www.theharborhouseinn.com

---

Sandpiper House Inn
PO Box 149
5520 S Hwy 1, *Elk* 95432
707-877-3587 800-894-9016
Ed & Atheon Haworth
All year

155-260-BB
5 rooms, 5 pb
Most CC, *Rated*
C-ltd/S-no/P-no/H-no

Full breakfast
Wine and hors d'oeuvres in the evening
Complimentary wine & sherry

Seaside country inn built in 1916. Rich redwood paneling in the living and dining rooms, lush perennial gardens that extend to the ocean bluff, stunning ocean views, fireplaces in all of the rooms. eclaire@mcn.org http://www.sandpiperhouse.com

MENDOCINO (REGION)

Annie's Jughandle Beach Inn
PO Box 228
32980 Gibney Ln, *Fort Bragg* 95460
707-964-1415 800-964-9957
Jean C. LaTorre All year

99-229-BB
7 rooms, 7 pb
Most CC, *Rated*, •
C-ltd/S-ltd/P-no/H-no
French, Cajun French, English

Full breakfast
hiking, beach access, tidepooling, whale watching (in season) spa tubs

Annie's Jughandle Beach Inn is an immaculately clean, affordable B&B on the fabulous Mendocino coastline, just 5 minutes from the village of Mendocino and the quaint fishing harbor at Fort Bragg. jean@ajinn.com http://www.ajinn.com

MILL VALLEY

Mill Valley Inn
165 Throckmorton Ave 94941
415-389-6608 Fax: 415-389-5051
800-595-2100
Karlene Holloman All year

160-399-BB
25 rooms, 25 pb
Most CC, *Rated*, •
C-yes/S-no/P-no/H-yes
French

Continental breakfast
Fireplaces, cable TV, free parking, voice mail

The Mill Valley Inn is tucked away in a redwood grove at the foot of Mt. Tamalpais in downtown Mill Valley. mgr@millvalleyinn.com http://www.millvalleyinn.com

MONTEREY

The Jabberwock
598 Laine St 93940
831-372-4777 Fax: 831-655-2946
888-428-7253
Joan & John Kiliany All year

120-265-BB
7 rooms, 7 pb
Visa, MC, *Rated*
C-ltd/S-ltd/P-no/H-no
Spanish

Full breakfast
Afternoon tea, bedtime milk & cookies
Sitting room, sun porch, two rooms with Jacuzzi, suite

Once a convent, this Craftsman style home sits 4 blocks above Cannery Row and the Aquarium. Guests enjoy Monterey Bay views, 3 rooms have double Jacuzzis & fireplaces, and late afternoon sherry hour.
innkeeper@jabberwockinn.com http://www.Jabberwockinn.com

The Monterey Hotel
406 Alvarado St 93940
831-375-3184 Fax: 831-373-2899
800-727-0960
Maureen Doran
All year

109-329-BB
45 rooms, 45 pb
Visa, MC, AmEx, *Rated*, •
C-yes/S-no/P-no/H-ltd
Spanish

Continental breakfast
Afternoon tea
Suites, fireplaces, cable TV, accommodate business travelers

The historic Monterey Hotel is located in the heart of downtown Monterey. Offering 45 lavishly restored guestrooms and suites with hand-carved furnishings.
gm@montereyhotel.com http://www.montereyhotel.com

MORRO BAY (REGION)

Baywood Inn
1370 Second St, *Baywood Park* 93402
805-528-8888 Fax: 805-528-8887
Suzanne McCollom
All year

90-340-BB
15 rooms, 15 pb
Visa, MC, *Rated*, •
C-yes/S-no/P-no/H-yes

Full breakfast
Cafe, complimentary wine
Conferences for up to 14, sitting room, fireplaces, 11 suites w/amenities

Bayfront Inn on South Morro Bay. Each room has its own personality. Near Hearst Castle, San Luis Obispo, Montano De Oro State Park.
innkeeper@baywoodinn.com http://www.baywoodinn.com

MOUNT SHASTA

Mount Shasta Ranch
1008 WA Barr Rd 96067
530-926-3870 Fax: 530-926-6882
Mary & Bill Larsen
All year

60-115-BB
10 rooms, 4 pb
Most CC, *Rated*, •
C-ltd/S-no/P-yes/H-no

Full breakfast
Afternoon tea, wine, snacks
Sitting room, library, Ping-Pong, TV & phone in room

Affordable elegance in historical setting; Main Lodge, Cottage and Carriage House.
alpinere@snowcrest.net http://www.stayinshasta.com

The Jabberwock, Monterey, CA

MUIR BEACH

Pelican Inn
10 Pacific Way 94965
415-383-6000 Fax: 415-383-3424
Katrinka McKay
Closed Christmas

201-239-BB
7 rooms, 7 pb
Visa, MC, *Rated*, •
C-yes/S-yes/P-no/H-ltd

Full English breakfast
Complimentary sherry
Sitting room, restaurant, British pub/bar, darts

A country inn capturing the spirit of 16th century England's West Country. 7 snug bedrooms, a cozy and hearty restaurant.

innkeeper@pelicaninn.com http://www.pelicaninn.com

MURPHYS

Dunbar House, 1880
271 Jones St 95247
209-728-2897 Fax: 209-728-1451
800-692-6006
Barbara & Bob Costa
All year

175-235-BB
5 rooms, 5 pb
Visa, MC, *Rated*, •
C-ltd/S-no/P-no/H-no

Full country breakfast
Complimentary bottle of wine
Sitting room, library, gas-burning stoves, clawfoot tubs, TVs, VCRs

Restored 1880 home with historical designation located in Murphys, Queen of the Sierra. 2-room suite with double Jacuzzi, champagne, towel warmer.

innkeep@dunbarhouse.com http://www.dunbarhouse.com

MYERS FLAT

Myers Country Inn
PO Box 173
12913 Ave of the Giants 95554
707-943-3259 Fax: 707-943-1800
800-500-6464
Rod Moschetti
All year

125-225-BB
10 rooms, 10 pb
Visa, MC, AmEx, *Rated*, •
C-yes/S-no/P-ltd/H-yes

Continental plus breakfast
Verandas

This historic stage stop inn is located along the scenic Avenue of the Giants, in the heart of Northern California's majestic redwood forests.

innkeeper@myersinn.com http://www.myersinn.com

NAPA

The 1801 Inn
1801 First St 94559
707-224-3739 Fax: 707-224-3932
800-518-0146
Darcy, Ramona and Brenna
All year

175-325-BB
8 rooms, 8 pb
Most CC, *Rated*, •
C-ltd/S-no/P-no/H-yes
Spanish

Full three course breakfast
Wine, hors d'oeuvres, 24 hr complimentary mini-bar
Concierge, in-room spa services, shade garden, complimentary gym/pool passes

An intimate urban retreat in the heart of downtown Napa. Luxurious Victorian featuring resort-style accommodations. The inn caters to savvy travelers who demand excellence in an intimate setting. innkeeper@the1801inn.com http://www.the1801inn.com

---

Beazley House
1910 First St 94559
707-257-1649 Fax: 707-257-1518
800-559-1649
Carol & Jim Beazley
All year

125-295-BB
11 rooms, 11 pb
Visa, MC, AmEx, *Rated*
C-ltd/S-ltd/P-ltd/H-yes
Spanish

Full gourmet breakfast
Complimentary sherry
Spas/frpls, garden, entertainment, sitt. rm, library, winery & rest. arrang.

The Beazley House is a Napa landmark. Relax in old-fashioned comfort. Personal wine tour orientation. Breakfast, complimentary sherry.
innkeeper@beazleyhouse.com http://www.beazleyhouse.com

La Belle Epoque
1386 Calistoga Ave 94559
707-257-2161 Fax: 707-226-6314
800-238-8070
Lynnette & Steve Sands
All year

215-350-BB
7 rooms, 7 pb
Most CC, *Rated*, •
C-ltd/S-no/P-no/H-no

Full gourmet breakfast
Complimentary wine, snacks
Sitting room, fireplace, fully A/C, TV/VCR

Historic Victorian bejeweled in stained glass, antique furnishings, gourmet breakfasts by the fireside. Walk to wine train depot, restaurant and shops.
innkeeper@labelleepoque.com http://www.labelleepoque.com

Blue Violet Mansion
443 Brown St 94559
707-253-2583 Fax: 707-257-8205
800-959-2583
Bob & Kathy Morris
All year

199-359-BB
17 rooms, 17 pb
Most CC, *Rated*, •
C-yes/S-no/P-no/H-yes
Spanish

Full gourmet breakfast
Dinner available, port in room, tea, eve sweets
Sitting room, spa tubs, pool, spa, porch, gazebo w/swing, rose garden

Gold Award winning Inn. Camelot Theme floor; hand painted rooms; 2 person whirlpool tubs, f/p, deluxe amenities. Fine cuisine nightly in Violette's at the Mansion; romantic in-room dinners/massage services.
bviolet@napanet.net http://www.bluevioletmansion.com

Castle in the Clouds
7400 St. Helena Hwy 94558
707-944-2785 Fax: 707 945-0882
Jean & Larry Grunewald
All year

235-325-BB
4 rooms, 4 pb
Visa, MC, AmEx, •
C-no/S-no/P-no/H-ltd

Full breakfast
Tea, coffee, soft drinks, snacks
Spa, library, large screen TV, digital satellite TV, patio, gardens, picnic

Luxurious accommodations, spectacular antiques, easy access to fine dining and wine tasting, hot tub, romantic patio and gardens, and "The Best Views in Napa Valley!"
jean@castleintheclouds.com http://www.castleintheclouds.com

Cedar Gables Inn
486 Coombs St 94559
707-224-7969 Fax: 707-224-4838
800-309-7969
Craig & Margaret Snasdell
All year

179-349-BB
8 rooms, 8 pb
Most CC, *Rated*, •
C-no/S-no/P-no/H-no

Full breakfast
Snacks, eve. wine/cheese hour. After dinner Port
Hot tubs, sitting room, located in wine country, romantic getaway

Built in 1892, this 10,000 sq. ft. mansion is styled after Shakespeare's time, which makes it different from any other residence in the state.
info@cedargablesinn.com http://www.cedargablesinn.com/

NAPA

Crossroads Inn
6380 Silverado Trail 94558
707-944-0646 Fax: 707-944-0650
Nancy & Sam Scott
All year

250-300-BB
3 rooms, 3 pb
Visa, MC, *Rated*, •
C-ltd/S-no/P-no/H-no

Full breakfast
Complimentary wine, host bar, afternoon tea,
Aftn. tea, brandy, library, game room, deck, hot tubs, bikes, gardens

Sweeping Napa Valley views. Custom 2-person spas, complete privacy. King-sized beds, wine bars, and full baths complement each suite.
info@crossroadsnv.com http://www.crossroadsnv.com

Hennessey House
1727 Main St 94559
707-226-3774 Fax: 707-226-2975
Gilda & Alex Feit
All year

105-295-BB
10 rooms, 10 pb
Most CC, *Rated*, •
C-ltd/S-no/P-no/H-no
Portuguese, Spanish, French

Full scrumptuous breakfast
Comp. wine & cheese, afternoon tea
Sitting room with TV, sauna, whirlpool tubs and fireplaces in some rooms

Napa's 1889 Queen Anne Victorian B&B. "A Great Place to Relax." Walk to restaurants and shops. Share wine and conversation by the garden fountain.
inn@hennesseyhouse.com http://www.hennesseyhouse.com

Inn of Imagination
472 Randolph St 94559
707-224-7772 Fax: 707-202-0187
Kim Thomas
All year

180-220-BB
3 rooms, 3 pb
Visa, MC, AmEx, •
C-no/S-ltd/P-no/H-no

Continental plus breakfast
Library Sculpture Garden
Expansive Grounds
Numerous Murals

Built in 1920 and on the National Historic Registry, our Inn celebrates imagineers who have created new & fanciful worlds. Come visit the worlds of Lewis Carroll, Dr. Seuss, and Jimmy Buffett. info@innofimagination.com http://www.innofimagination.com

---

Inn on Randolph
411 Randolph St 94559
707-257-2886 Fax: 707-257-8756
800-670-6886
Deborah Coffee
All year

144-289-BB
10 rooms, 10 pb
Most CC, *Rated*, •
H-yes

Full breakfast

Situated on one-half acre of landscaped grounds in historic "Old Town" Napa, you'll enjoy the serenity of a quiet residential neighborhood close to shops and restaurants.
innonrandolph@aol.com http://www.innonrandolph.com

John Muir Inn
1998 Trower Ave 94558
707-257-7220 Fax: 707-258-0943
800-522-8999
All year

BB
59 rooms, 59 pb
Most CC, *Rated*, •
C-yes/S-no/P-no/H-yes

Continental breakfast
Jacuzzis, swimming pool, suites, cable TV, accommodate business travelers

Our charming Inn has a Three Diamond AAA rating. We are conveniently located just off Highway 29 in North Napa at the gateway to the wine country with adjacent restaurants and nearby shopping centers. johnmuir@pacbell.net http://www.johnmuirnapa.com

---

The Napa Inn
1137 Warren St 94559
707-257-1444 Fax: 707-257-0251
800-435-1144
Brooke & Jim Boyer
All year

140-300-BB
8 rooms, 8 pb
Most CC, *Rated*, •
S-no
Spanish

Full breakfast

Built in 1899 as a wedding gift, The Napa Inn is located on a tree-lined street, walking distance to town. Relax in our garden and after breakfast, stroll to town for many shops & attractions. info@napainn.com http://www.napainn.com

NAPA

Oak Knoll Inn
2200 E Oak Knoll Ave 94558
707-255-2200 Fax: 707-255-2296
Barbara Passino
All year

250-450-BB
4 rooms, 4 pb
Visa, MC, *Rated*
C-ltd/S-no/P-no/H-no
Spanish

Full multi-course breakfast
Evening wine hour & hors d'oeuvres
Complimentary wine, spa, swimming pool, fireplaces in all rooms, featherbeds

Romantic, elegant stone country inn surrounded by vineyards and panoramic views. Spacious rooms with wood burning fireplaces. Sip wine watching the sunset over the mountains. napajohnk@aol.com http://www.oakknollinn.com

---

The Old World Inn
1301 Jefferson St 94559
707-257-0112 Fax: 707-257-0118
800-966-6624
Sam van Hoeve
All year

150-265-BB
8 rooms, 8 pb
Visa, MC, AmEx, *Rated*, •
C-ltd/S-no/P-no/H-no

Full gourmet breakfast
Complimentary wine & cheese
Afternoon tea, evening dessert buffet, sitting room, Jacuzzi

Run with Old World hospitality by its English innkeepers, this Victorian inn is uniquely decorated throughout in bright Scandinavian colors.
theoldworldinn@aol.com http://www.oldworldinn.com

La Residence
4066 St Helena Hwy 94558
707-253-0337 Fax: 707-253-0382
800-253-9203
David Jackson & Craig Claussen All year

225-350-BB
25 rooms, 25 pb
Most CC, *Rated*, •
C-yes/S-no/P-no

Full breakfast
Complimentary wine
CD players, hair dryers, new veranda, Jacuzzi spa, garden setting, pool

For the sophisticated traveler who enjoys elegant yet intimate style, La Residence is the only choice in Napa Valley. Two acres of landscaped grounds with ponds and fountains.
http://www.laresidence.com

Stahlecker House Country Inn/Gardens
1042 Easum Dr 94558
707-257-1588 Fax: 707-224-7429
800-799-1588
Ron & Ethel Stahlecker
All year

148-268-BB
4 rooms, 4 pb
Rated, •

Full Candlelight Breakfast

Stahlecker House is a AAA rated Inn (three diamonds). Secluded on one and a half acres of lush manicured lawns and flowering gardens, a nostalgic gem in Napa Valley.
stahlbnb@aol.com http://www.stahleckerhouse.com

NAPA VALLEY (REGION)

Adagio Inn
1417 Kearney St, *St. Helena* 94574
707-963-2238 Fax: 707-963-5598
888-8ADAGIO
John & Patti Valletta All year

200-275-BB
3 rooms, 3 pb
Visa, MC, *Rated*
C-no/S-no/P-no/H-no

Full breakfast
Wine and appetizers served in the afternoon.
Elegant parlor Grand Piano, TVs, refrigerators, concierge services

European elegance in the heart of Napa Valley.
innkeeper@adagioinn.com http://www.adagioinn.com

Ambrose Bierce House
1515 Main St, *St. Helena* 94574
707-963-3003 Fax: 707-963-9367
John & Lisa Wild-Runnells
All year

139-269-BB
3 rooms, 3 pb
Visa, MC, *Rated*, •
C-ltd/S-ltd/P-no/H-no

Full gourmet champagne breakfast
Premium wines and cheeses are served each evening
Hot tub, Jacuzzi tubs, canopy beds, antiques, A/C, warm hospitality

We offer "unequaled warm and enthusiastic hospitality," in a historic Victorian that is the former home of the author Ambrose Bierce. Famous full gourmet champagne breakfasts and wines/cheeses pm. ambrose@napanet.net http://www.ambrosebiercehouse.com

NAPA VALLEY (REGION)

Bartels Ranch & Country Inn
1200 Conn Valley Rd,
St. Helena 94574
707-963-4001 Fax: 707-963-5100
Jami Bartels
All year

199-455-BB
4 rooms, 4 pb
Most CC, *Rated*, •
C-ltd/S-yes/P-no/H-yes
Spanish, German

Full breakfast
In-room dinner service
Comp. wine/fruit/cheese, library, sauna, Jacuzzi, darts, horseshoes, BBQ

Elegant, secluded wine country estate; ideal for honeymoon. 10,000-acre view, fireplace, billiards, bicycles, TV/VCR & phones in all rooms.
bartelsranch@webtv.net http://www.bartelsranch.com

Bylund House
2000 Howell Mtn Rd,
St. Helena 94574
707-963-9073
Bill & Diane
All year

95-200-BB
2 rooms, 2 pb
Rated, •
S-ltd/P-no/H-no

Continental plus breakfast
Wine & hors d'oeuvres
Sitting room w/fireplace, pool, spa, golf, wineries, restaurant, tennis

Wine country villa designed by owner-architect in secluded valley with sweeping views.
bylundhouse@calicom.net http://www.bylundhouse.com

Deer Run Inn
PO Box 311
3995 Spring Mtn Rd, *St. Helena* 94574
707-963-3794 Fax: 707-963-9026
877-DEERRUN
Tom & Carol Wilson
All year

175-215-BB
3 rooms, 3 pb
Most CC, *Rated*, •
C-ltd/S-no/P-no/H-no

Full breakfast
Complimentary wine
Library, pool, Ping Pong, horseshoes, featherbeds, frplcs., priv. entrances

Tucked away in the forest on Spring Mountain above valley vineyards. Affords the quiet serenity of a private hideaway. A truly secluded, peaceful, cozy mountain retreat. Full breakfast in dining area. http://www.virtualcities.com/ons/ca/w/caw3602.htm

---

Elsie's Conn Valley Inn
726 Rossi Rd, *St. Helena* 94574
707-963-4614 Fax: 707-967-1160
Elsie Asplund Hudak
All year

165-250-BB
3 rooms, 2 pb

Full breakfast

In the heart of Napa Valley, Elsie's Conn Valley Inn is an authentic European-style Bed and Breakfast with personal hospitality and privacy in a warm, comfortable environment.
elsiesinn@earthlink.net http://www.elsiesinn.com

Hilltop House
PO Box 726
9550 St Helena Rd, *St. Helena* 94574
707-944-0880 Fax: 707-571-0263
Annette Gevarter Keefe
All year

145-225-BB
4 rooms, 4 pb
Visa, MC, *Rated*, •
C-yes/S-no/P-no/H-yes

Full breakfast
Complimentary sherry after dinner
Guest refrigerator, sitting room, hot tub, hiking trails

Secluded mountain hideaway in romantic setting on 135 acres of unspoiled wilderness. A hang glider's view of Mayacamas Mountains. Hot tub on deck. Extra person $35, cancellation fee $15 94925@aol.com

---

The Ink House
1575 St Helena Hwy, *St. Helena* 94574
707-963-3890 Fax: 707-968-0739
Diane DeFilipi
All year

110-215-BB
7 rooms, 5 pb
Rated, •
C-ltd/S-no/P-no/H-no

Full gourmet breakfast
Sherry, brandy available, wine & appetizer service
Parlor, 3 sitting rooms, concert grand piano, bicycles

Private, in beautiful St. Helena, antiques, fireplace, TV/VCRs. Rooftop observatory with views of vineyards and valley hills. inkhousebb@aol.com http://www.inkhouse.com

NAPA VALLEY (REGION)

Oleander House
7433 St Helena Hwy, *Yountville* 94599
707-944-8315 Fax: 707-944-4448
800-778-0357
Kathleen Matthews
All year

145-195-BB
4 rooms, 4 pb
Visa, MC, *Rated*, •
S-no/P-no/H-no
Spanish

Full breakfast
Complimentary soft drinks
Sitting room, spa, patio, near ballooning, tennis, golf, dining, shops

Country French charm. Antiques. Spacious rooms with brass beds, private decks, fireplaces, central A/C, and Laura Ashley fabrics and wallpapers.
Innkeeper@Oleander.com http://www.oleander.com/

NEVADA CITY

Red Castle Inn Historic Lodgings
109 Prospect St 95959
530-265-5135 800-761-4766
Conley and Mary Louise Weaver
All year

75-165
7 rooms, 7 pb

Buffet breakfast

As one of the first Bed and Breakfast inns in California, the incomparable Red Castle Inn has been acclaimed for its singular sense of time and place for more than four decades.
http://www.historic-lodgings.com

U.S. Hotel
233 B Broad St 95959
530-265-7999 Fax: 530-265-7990
Renee & Jim Salyards
All year

100-160-BB
7 rooms, 7 pb
Visa, MC, AmEx

Air-conditioning, balcony windows, canopy beds

A Unique Bed and Breakfast located in Nevada City California's downtown Historic District. katiebennet2001@yahoo.com http://www.ushotelbb.com/

NEWPORT BEACH

Portofino Beach Hotel
2306 W Oceanfront 92663
949-673-7030 Fax: 949-723-4370
800-571-8749
Ken & Betty Ricamore
All year

169-499-BB
12 rooms, 12 pb
Rated, •

Continental plus breakfast

Whether your stay is for business or pleasure, the Portofino Beach Hotel offers you an ocean front oasis of elegance and privacy.
info@portofinobeachhotel.com http://www.portofinobeachhotel.com

NICE

Featherbed Railroad Co.
PO Box 4016
2870 Lakeshore 95464
707-274-4434 Fax: 707-274-1415
800-966-6322
Lorraine Bassignani
All year

120-180-BB
9 rooms, 9 pb
Most CC, *Rated*, •
C-ltd/S-ltd/P-no/H-no

Full breakfast
Bikes, Jacuzzis, pool, suites, cable TV, accom. bus. travelers

Refurbished antique railroad cabooses, most with Jacuzzi tubs for 2. Full breakfast, private pier, bikes, park-like setting.
room@featherbedrailroad.com http://www.featherbedrailroad.com

---

Gingerbread Cottages
PO Box 4004
4057 E Highway 20 95464
707-274-0200
Buddy & Yvonne Lipscomb
Feb-Nov

95-170-BB
10 rooms, 10 pb
Most CC, *Rated*, •
C-ltd/S-ltd/P-yes/H-no

Continental breakfast
Snacks, beverages, & local wines for purchase
Enclosed spa, pool, dock, beach, kayaks, TV/VCR, kitchenettes, AC, phones

Romantic lakefront cottages on beautiful Clear Lake. Magnificent panoramic views of the lake, mountains, old oak trees and bird wildlife on a very unique park-like property.
mail@gingerbreadcottages.com http://www.gingerbreadcottages.com

NORTH LAKE TAHOE (REGION)

Royal George's Rainbow Lodge
PO Box 1100
9411 Hillside Dr, *Soda Springs* 95728
530-426-3871 Fax: 530-426-9221
800-666-3871
Alan Davis All year

99-165-BB
30 rooms, 16 pb
Visa, MC, *Rated*
C-yes/S-no/P-no/H-ltd

Full breakfast
Restaurant, lunch & dinner available, snacks
Bar service, library, sitting room, suites, fireplaces

Romantic getaway built in 1920 along a bend in the Yuba River that serves French country and California cuisine. marketing@royalgorge.com http://www.royalgorge.com

OAKHURST

Sierra Sky Ranch Country Lodge
50552 Rd 632 93644
559-683-8040 Fax: 559-658-7484
Kim Coles
March–December

69-169-EP
25 rooms, 25 pb
Visa, MC, AmEx, •
C-yes/S-no/P-yes/H-ltd

Dinner, restaurant, bar service
Sitting room, library, game room, swimming pool, suites, accom. bus. tvl.

Rustic mountain hideaway. Each room individually decorated. Family atmosphere. Great place to just getaway from the hustled bustle of everyday life.
skyranch@sierratel.com http://www.sierratel.com/skyranch/

OAKLAND

Washington Inn
495 10th St 94607
510-452-1776 Fax: 510-452-4436
510-452-1776
Sam Wilson All year

79-199-BB
47 rooms, 47 pb
Most CC, •
C-yes/S-no/P-no/H-yes

Full Weekdays / Continental Weekend
Coffee, tea, fruit
5 HBO's, 2 Sports, VCRs, in-room safes & irons

Old Oakland Landmark. Historic boutique hotel at Oakland Convention Center. Restaurant, Bar, meeting and banquet rooms. Breakfast incl. Smoke-Free.
rooms@thewashingtoninn.com http://www.thewashingtoninn.com

OJAI

Blue Iguana Inn
111 W Tapa Tapa St
11794 N Ventura Ave 93023
805-646-5277 Fax: 805-646-8078
Julia Whitman
All year

95-199-BB
11 rooms, 11 pb
Most CC, *Rated*, •
C-yes/S-ltd/P-ltd/H-ltd
Indonesian, Dutch, French, Spanish

Continental breakfast weekends only
Snacks
Jacuzzis, swimming pool, suites, cable TV, accommodate bus. travelers

Called "Hip & Stylish" by Sunset Magazine, the Blue Iguana is uniquely decorated by one-of-a-kind furnishings and art from throughout Mexico and the world.
info@blueiguanainn.com http://www.blueiguanainn.com

Emerald Iguana Inn
111 W Tapa Tapa St
End of N. Blanche St 93023
805-646-5277 Fax: 805-640-2866
Julia Whitman
All year

129-329-BB
13 rooms, 13 pb
Most CC, •
C-ltd/S-ltd/P-no/H-ltd
Spanish, Indonesian, French, Dutch

Continental Breakfast on weekends
Snacks
Bicycles, Jacuzzis, swimming pool, suites, clawfoot tub, fireplace, cable TV

Exquisitely designed and decorated cottages and rooms in an extraordinarily beautiful and serene setting. info@blueiguanainn.com http://www.emeraldiguana.com

---

Theodore Woolsey House
1484 E Ojai Ave 93023
805-646-9779 Fax: 805-646-4414
Ana Cross
All year

65-175-BB
5 rooms, 5 pb
Visa, MC
C-yes/S-no/P-no/H-no
Spanish

Continental plus breakfast
Library, Jacuzzis, swimming pool, fireplace, cable TV, accom. business trav.

This century old landmark sits on seven acres of flowering gardens and ornamental trees. Five rooms plus cottage with views.
twhouse@mindspring.com http://www.theodorewoolseyhouse.com

OROVILLE

Jean's Riverside PO Box 2334 1142 Middlehoff Ln 95965 530-533-1413 LARRY JENDRO All year	85-145-BB 9 rooms, 9 pb Visa, MC, *Rated* C-ltd/S-ltd/P-ltd/H-yes	Full breakfast River waterfront with dock, deck overlooking river, lawn games, golf, pool

Romantic waterfront hideaway with private Jacuzzis, fishing, gold-panning, bird watching, historical sites. Near hiking, Feather River Canyon, Oroville Dam.
jeansbandb@yahoo.com http://www.oroville-city.com/jeans/

OROVILLE (REGION)

Lake Oroville 240 Sunday Drive, *Berry Creek* 95916 530-589-0700 Fax: 530-589-3800 800-455-LAKE Cheryl & Ronald Damberger All year	75-155-BB 6 rooms, 6 pb Most CC, *Rated*, • C-yes/S-ltd/P-yes/H-yes French, Spanish	Full breakfast Lunch & dinner avail., snacks Sitting room, library, Jacuzzis, fireplaces, cable TV, accom. bus. travelers

Lakeviews, sunsets, star gazing. Secluded country setting, covered porches with private entrances. Enjoy the Wood-burning fireplace in the parlor, or a good book in the sunroom/library. bnb@rontimco.com http://www.lakeoroville.com/lakeoroville

PACIFIC GROVE

Centrella Inn 612 Central Ave 93950 831-372-3372 Fax: 831-372-2036 800-233-3372 Marian Taylor All year	119-250-BB 26 rooms, 26 pb Most CC, *Rated*, • C-ltd/S-no/P-no/H-yes Italian	Continental plus breakfast Tea, wine, hors d'oeuvres Parlor, Garden

Charming Victorian, designated as a Historical Landmark. Built in 1889. Traditional guestrooms w/private baths, parlor suites, attic suites, cottages w/fireplace. Garden Room w/Jacuzzi. Concierge@innsbythesea.com http://www.innsbythesea.com/innres.htm#ct

---

Gatehouse Inn 225 Central Ave 93950 831-649-8436 Fax: 831-648-8044 800-753-1881 Sue and Lew Shaefer Season Inquire	125-195-BB 8 rooms, 8 pb Visa, MC, AmEx, *Rated*, • C-ltd/S-no/P-no/H-yes Spanish	Full breakfast Afternoon tea Comp. wine & cheese, sitting room, binoculars, near ocean and downtown

Historic 1884 seaside Victorian home, distinctive rooms, stunning views, private baths, fireplaces, delicious breakfasts, afternoon wine and cheese. Centrally located.
lew@redshift.com http://www.sueandlewinns.com

Grand View Inn 557 Ocean View Blvd 93950 831-372-4341 Ed & Susan Flatley All year	175-375-BB 11 rooms, 11 pb Visa, MC, *Rated*, • C-ltd/S-no/P-no/H-ltd French, Spanish	Full breakfast Afternoon tea Welcome basket, evening turn-down service, afternoon tea, generous breakfast

Seaside Edwardian Mansion at the very edge of Monterey Bay overlooking Lovers' Point. Completely restored in 1995. All ocean view rooms with marble bathrooms.
http://www.pginns.com

Inn at 213 Seventeen Mile Drive 213 Seventeen Mile Dr 93950 831-642-9514 Fax: 831-642-9514 800-526-5666 Sally, Tony & Glynis All year	145-240-BB 14 rooms, 14 pb Visa, MC, AmEx, *Rated*, • S-no/P-no/H-yes	Full breakfast Snacks, complimentary wine Sitting room, bicycles, Jacuzzis, cable TV, accommodate business travelers

A heritage award winning craftsman house set amongst monarch butterfly trees. Walk or bike to Victorian Pacific Grove town. 213@innat17.com http://www.innat17.com

PACIFIC GROVE

Old St. Angela Inn | 110-210-BB | Full breakfast
321 Central Ave 93950 | 9 rooms, 9 pb | Complimentary wine/snacks, cookies
831-372-3246 Fax: 831-372-8560 | Visa, MC, Disc, *Rated*, • | Solarium, gardens, hot tub in garden, rooms with fireplaces & Jacuzzis
800-748-6306 | C-ltd/S-no/P-no/H-no
Susan Kuslis & Lewis Shaefer
All year

Intimate Cape Cod elegance overlooking Monterey Bay; walking distance to ocean & beaches, Monterey Bay Aquarium, Cannery Row, restaurants. Delicious breakfast.
lew@redshift.com http://www.sueandlewinns.com

The Martine Inn | 130-300-BB | Full breakfast
PO Box 330 | 23 rooms, 23 pb | Picnic lunches, wine, water, soda
255 Oceanview Blvd 93950 | Visa, MC, AmEx, *Rated*, • | Hors d'oeuvres, sitting room, game room, bicycles, conf. room
831-373-3388 Fax: 831-373-3896 | C-yes/S-yes/P-no/H-yes
800-852-5588 | Italian, Russian, Spanish
Don Martine & Lori Anderson
All year

12,000-sq ft mansion on Monterey Bay. Elegant, museum-quality American antiques. Breakfast served on Sheffield silver, crystal, Victorian china & lace. Rooms redecorated.
info@martineinn.com http://www.martineinn.com

Seven Gables Inn | 175-385-BB | Full breakfast
555 Ocean View Blvd 93950 | 14 rooms, 14 pb | High tea
831-372-4341 | Visa, MC, *Rated*, • | Welcome basket, evening turndown service, generous breakfast and tea.
Ed and Susan Flatley | C-ltd/S-no/P-no/H-no
All year | French, Spanish

Elegant Victorian mansion overlooking Monterey Bay. All rooms have ocean views, private baths & are elegantly furnished w/antiques. Guest comfort & service are our utmost concern. http://www.pginns.com

PALM DESERT

Inn at Deep Canyon | 59-209-BB | Continental breakfast
74470 Abronia Trail 92260 | 32 rooms, 32 pb | Jacuzzi, pool, suites, fireplace, cable TV, accom. bus. travel
760-346-8061 Fax: 760-341-9120 | Most CC, *Rated*, •
800-253-0004 | C-yes/S-ltd/P-ltd/H-ltd
Linda Carter
All year

Thirty-two newly refurbished rooms, all with refrigerator, coffee maker, color cable TV. Large heated pool, Jacuzzi, and BBQ grills. Centrally located.
reservations@inn-adc.com http://www.inn-adc.com

Tres Palmas | 90-200-BB | Continental plus breakfast
PO Box 2115 | 4 rooms, 4 pb | Snacks
73135 Tumbleweed Ln 92261 | Visa, MC, *Rated*, • | Library, sitting room, hot tub, swimming pool
760-773-9858 Fax: 760-776-9159 | C-ltd/S-no/P-no/H-no
800-770-9858
Karen & Terry Bennett
All year

Enjoy our casual, Southwest elegance indoors or our warm desert sun outdoors. Walk to fabulous shopping & dining on El Paseo. http://innformation.com/ca/trespalmas

PALM SPRINGS

Casa Cody Country Inn | 89-349-BB | Continental plus breakfast
175 S Cahuilla Rd 92262 | 23 rooms, 24 pb | Whirlpool spa, 2 swimming pools, cable TV
760-320-9346 Fax: 760-325-8610 | Most CC, *Rated*, •
800-231-2639 | C-ltd/S-ltd/P-ltd/H-yes
Therese Hayes & Elissa Goforth | French, Dutch, German
All year

A historic 1910 adobe two-bedroom house once owned by Metropolitan Opera star Lawrence Tibbett and frequented by Charlie Chaplin, is now open for our guests to stay.
casacody@aol.com http://www.palmsprings.com/hotels/casacody

PALM SPRINGS

Desert House
200 S Cahuilla Rd 92262
760-325-5281 Fax: 760-325-6736
800-549-9230
Doug & Donna Mannoff
All year

100-175-EP
6 rooms, 6 pb
Most CC, •
S-ltd/P-ltd/H-no

Snacks
Swimming pool, cable TV, kitchenettes

Desert House, an inn in the heart of the village of Palm Springs. Enjoy the best our "desert paradise" has to offer from its most charming and convenient location.
info@deserthouseinn.com http://www.deserthouseinn.com

Ingleside Inn
200 W Ramon Rd 92262
760-325-0046 Fax: 760-325-0710
800-772-6655
Armida Pedrin
All year

AP
30 rooms, 30 pb
Most CC, *Rated*, •
C-ltd/S-yes/P-no/H-yes
Spanish

Lunch, dinner, snacks, restaurant, bar service
Jacuzzis, swimming pool, suites, fireplaces, cable TV

Named one of the "Ten Best" by Lifestyles of the Rich & Famous. For the luxury of today with the fine hospitality of yesterday.
contact@inglesideinn.com http://www.inglesideinn.com

Orchid Tree Inn
261 S Belardo Rd 92262
760-325-2791 Fax: 760-325-3855
800-733-3435
Robert & Karen Weithorn
All year

79-180-BB
40 rooms, 40 pb
Rated, •

Continental plus breakfast
3 pools, 2 spas

Experience the comfort & romance of Old Palm Springs. 40 authentically restored rooms, studios, suites & bungalows (most w/kitchens)—no 2 alike! Beautifully landscaped, privately gated. info@orchidtree.com http://www.orchidtree.com

---

Villa Royale Inn
1620 Indian Trail 92264
760-327-2314 Fax: 760-322-3794
800-245-2314
Amy Aquino
All year

99-299-BB
31 rooms, 31 pb
Most CC, *Rated*, •
C-ltd/S-no/P-ltd/H-yes

Full breakfast
Restaurant, bar service, seasonal lunch
Full room service, 2 pools, Jacuzzi, in-room massage

Enchanting hideaway with Old World charm. 31 unique guestrooms & villas designed with relaxation & romance in mind. Private patios, kitchens & fireplaces. Exquisite dining at Europa Restaurant. info@villaroyale.com http://www.villaroyale.com

---

The Willows Historic Inn
PO Box 3340
412 W Tahquitz Canyon Way
92262
760-320-0771 Fax: 760-320-0780
800-966-9597
All year

295-575-BB
8 rooms, 8 pb
Most CC, *Rated*, •
S-no/P-no/H-ltd

Full breakfast
Restaurant, afternoon tea, snacks
Sitting room, library, pool, hot tubs, gardens, waterfall, Mt. views

The Willows offers exquisite accommodations for discriminating guests in an historic home restored to recreate the ambience of Palm Springs in the 1930s.
innkeeper@thewillowspalmsprings.com http://www.thewillowspalmsprings.com/

PALM SPRINGS (REGION)

Lake La Quinta Inn
78120 Caleo Bay, *La Quinta*
92553
760-564-7332 Fax: 760-564-6356
888-226-4546
Tim Ellis All year

99-399-BB
12 rooms, 12 pb
Most CC, •
C-ltd/S-no/P-no/H-yes
Spanish

Full breakfast
Snacks, complimentary wine
Sitting room, bikes, Jacuzzis, suites, fireplaces, cable, accom. bus. trav.

Wake up each morning to a sumptuous breakfast, in the evening join your Innkeeper and fellow guests for a glass of wine and hors d'oeuvres.
stay@lakelaquintainn.com http://www.lakelaquintainn.com

PALO ALTO

Victorian on Lytton	183-250-BB	Continental breakfast
555 Lytton Ave 94301	10 rooms, 10 pb	Complimentary appetizers,
650-322-8555 Fax: 650-322-7141	Visa, MC, AmEx, *Rated*	port
Susan & Maxwell Hall	C-ltd/S-no/P-no/H-yes	Complimentary sherry,
All year		occasional entertainment,
		computer modem ports, TV

A lovely Victorian built in 1895, offering a combination of forgotten elegance with a touch of European grace. VictorianLytton@aol.com http://www.victorianonlytton.com

PASADENA (REGION)

Artists' Inn	115-205-BB	Full breakfast
1038 Magnolia St, *South*	10 rooms, 10 pb	Picnic lunch, afternoon tea
Pasadena 91030	Visa, MC, AmEx, *Rated*	Snacks, sitting room, library,
626-799-5668 Fax: 626-799-3678	C-yes/S-no/P-no/H-no	Jacuzzis, suites, fireplaces,
888-799-5668		cable TV
Janet Marangi All year		

Like Grandma's House. White wicker on big front porch, English chintz, antiques, all cotton sheets, English towels, hair dryers, canopy & antique brass beds, fireplaces, Jacuzzis.
artistsinn@artistsinns.com http://www.artistsinns.com

PETALUMA

Cavanagh Inn	100-150-BB	Full gourmet breakfast
10 Keller St 94952	7 rooms, 5 pb	Afternoon wine
707-765-4657	Visa, MC, AmEx,	Sitting room, parlor, library,
Fax: 707-769-0466	*Rated*, •	within historic downtown
888-765-4658	C-ltd/S-no/P-no/H-no	
Ray & Jeanne Farris	Spanish	
All year		

Elegant 1902 Victorian & 1912 Craftsman cottage combine to form the Inn. Redwood paneling is used through out. Full breakfast is served. Located at the edge of historic downtown...
info@cavanaghinn.com http://www.cavanaghinn.com

Old Palms of Petaluma	145-200-BB	Full breakfast
2 Liberty St 94952	5 rooms, 5 pb	Afternoon tea,
707-658-2554	Visa, MC, *Rated*	complimentary wine, snacks
Patrick & Jurina Smida	C-ltd/S-ltd/P-no/H-yes	Sitting room, suites,
All year	Spanish, French,	accommodate business
	German, Slovak, Russian	travelers

Victorian B&B in the heart of historic Petaluma. Private bath with claw-foot tubs, crystal chandeliers, and antique furniture. info@oldpalms.com http://www.oldpalms.com

PLACERVILLE

Blair House Carousel Inn	110-140-BB	Full breakfast
2985 Clay St 95667	3 rooms, 3 pb	Evening refreshments
530-626-9006	Most CC, •	Book and video libraries
Fax: 530-295-9034	C-no/S-no/P-no/H-no	
Sandy & Ray Edmondson		
All year		

A unique turreted 1901 Queen Anne Victorian located in historic downtown Placerville, featuring, hillside gardens, original woodwork and a history of romance. Walk to shops, restaurants and more.
info@blairhousecarouselinn.com http://www.blairhousecarouselinn.com

Chichester-McKee House	100-140-BB	Special full gourmet
800 Spring St 95667	4 rooms, 4 pb	breakfast
530-626-1882 Fax: 530-626-7801	Most CC, *Rated*, •	Complimentary soft drinks
800-831-4008	C-ltd/S-no/P-no/H-no	""Doreen's brownies"",
Doreen & Bill Thornhill		queen-size beds, parlor,
All year		gardens, porches, library

Elegant 1892 grand Victorian home and gardens. Enjoy romance and relaxing hospitality. Find adventure in the Sierra foothills. info@innlover.com http://www.innlover.com

Blair House Carousel Inn, Placerville, CA

PLACERVILLE

River Rock Inn 1756 Georgetown Rd 95667 530-622-7640 Dorothy Irvin All year	85-110-BB 4 rooms, 2 pb *Rated*, • C-ltd/S-ltd/P-no/H-ltd	Continental breakfast Complimentary sherry Sitting room, hot tub, TV lounge, antiques

Relax on the 110-ft deck overlooking the American River, fish and pan for gold in the front yard.

http://www.sierraheritage.com/pages/ads/accommodations/rockinn.html

Shafsky House 2942 Coloma St 95667 530-642-2776 Fax: 530-642-2109 Rita Timewell & Stephanie Carlson All year	105-135-BB 3 rooms, 3 pb Most CC C-ltd/S-no/P-no/H-no	In-room coffee/tea Sitting room with library/games and satellite TV/VCR w/movies

Luxury in the Heart of Gold Country. Queen Anne-style Victorian built for department store owner Albert Shafsky.

shafsky@directcon.net http://www.shafsky.com

Walker House Lodge 3341 Oak Knoll Road 95667 530-621-4198 Stephanie Walker All year	125-150-BB 3 rooms, 3 pb Most CC, *Rated*, • C-no/S-ltd/P-no/H-ltd	Full breakfast On arrival bottle of wine, cheese, & fruit platter Hot tub, golfing green, table tennis, in-room TV movies, VCR, & more

Secluded, yet just 5 minutes from Old Town Placerville, the Walker's have created a retreat for your enjoyment set on three acres. Golfing Green, Hot Tub, Romantic Stone Fireplace, and more.

swalker@cwnet.com http://www.walkerhouseb-blodge.com

PLACERVILLE (REGION)

Camino Hotel-Seven Mile House
PO Box 1197
4103 Carson Road, *Camino* 95709
530-644-7740 Fax: 530-647-1416
800-200-7740
Paula Nobert All year

68-98-BB
9 rooms, 3 pb
Most CC, •
C-yes/S-no/P-no/H-no

Specially Prepared Full Breakfast
Homemade chocolate chip cookies
A/C, masseuse, wine tasting room, walk to cafes & pub, free local calls

C.1888, seven miles East of Placerville in Apple Hill. Jodar Wine Tasting Room. Massage Therapy. Along the old Carson Wagon Trail. Pony Express and Wagon Train still stop here each year. stay@caminohotel.com http://www.caminohotel.com

POINT REYES STATION

A Neon Rose
PO Box 632
76-1/2 Overlook Rd 94956
415-663-9143 Fax: 415-663-8060
800-358-8346
Sandy Fields All year

150-200-BB
1 rooms, 1 pb
C-ltd/S-no/P-no/H-no

Continental plus breakfast
Full kitchen
Jacuzzi, fireplace, cable TV, VCR, phone, full kitchen

Adjacent Point Reyes National Seashore, the Neon Rose is a fully equipped guest cottage. Expansive views of Tomales Bay and the sunset.
neon@neonrose.com http://www.neonrose.com

Ferrando's Hideaway Cottages
PO Box 688
31 Cypress Road 94956
415-663-1966 Fax: 415-663-1825
800-337-2636
Greg & Doris Ferrando
All year

250-300-BB
2 rooms, 2 pb
Visa, MC, *Rated*, •
C-ltd/S-no/P-no/H-no
German

Cottages are stocked with breakfast

Two luxurious and private cottages with private hot tubs, Wood-burning stoves and all amenities, just minutes from Point Reyes National Seashore.
doris@ferrando.com http://www.ferrando.com

Holly Tree Inn
PO Box 642
3 Silverhills Rd 94956
415-663-1554 Fax: 415-663-8566
800-286-HOLLY
Tom Balogh All year

130-285-BB
7 rooms, 7 pb
Visa, MC, AmEx
C-yes/S-no/P-no/H-no

Full breakfast
Outdoor hot tub, organic garden, creekside gazebo.

Located in a 19-acre private valley, the Holly Tree Inn offers guests a choice of four rooms or three cottages. In business for over 23 years, the Holly Tree Inn is a casually elegant retreat. info@hollytreeinn.com http://www.hollytreeinn.com

---

Knob Hill
PO Box 1108
94956
415-663-1784 888-663-1784
Janet Schlitt All year

70-160-EP
3 rooms, 3 pb
C-ltd/S-ltd/P-ltd/H-no

Coffee/Tea in Master Suite and Cottage

Abundant light, all-day sun. Exceptional views, fireplaces, Jacuzzi. Atop a small bluff, overlooking the Pt.Reyes Mesa, a 10 minute walk to the village. 3 (one a stand-alone cottage) private rooms. info@knobhill.com http://www.knobhill.com

---

Marsh Cottage
PO Box 1121
94956
415-669-7168
Wendy Schwartz All year

165-BB
1 rooms, 1 pb
Rated
C-yes/S-no/P-no/H-no

Full and continental plus
Complimentary coffee/tea/wine
Kitchen, library, sitting room, fireplace, porch, sun deck

Cheerful, carefully appointed private cottage along bay. Kitchen, fireplace, queen bed, desk. http://www.marshcottage.com

POINT REYES STATION

Old Point Reyes Schoolhouse
PO Box 56
11561 Coast Route #1 94956
415-663-1166 Fax: 415-663-1390
Karen Gray
All year

145-245-BB
1 rooms, 1 pb

Full and continental breakfasts

Choose charming Jasmine Cottage, elegant Gray's Family Retreat, or the beautiful Barn Loft. http://www.oldpointreyesschoolhouse.com

POINT RICHMOND

East Brother Light Station
117 Park Place 94801
510-233-2385
Captain Curt & Carolyn Henry
All year

290-410-MAP
5 rooms, 2 pb
Most CC, *Rated*
C-ltd/S-ltd/P-no/H-no

Full breakfast
Hors d'oeuvres & champagne, full dinner,lunch lmtd
Historical working lighthouse, parlor, library and bird & Bay watching.

Enjoy the panorama of San Francisco-Marin skylines from an island working lighthouse in San Francisco Bay. Experience the ultimate get-away and romantic sojourn.
info@ebls.org http://www.ebls.org

QUINCY

The Feather Bed
PO Box 3200
542 Jackson St 95971
530-283-0102 Fax: 530-283-0167
800-696-8624
Bob & Jan Janowski All year

90-150-BB
7 rooms, 7 pb
Visa, MC, AmEx, *Rated*, •
C-ltd/S-no/P-no/H-yes

Full breakfast
Afternoon tea & cookies
Sitting room, porch, Victorian garden, bikes, fountain, frplcs., A/C

Relax on the porch of our country Victorian. Enjoy the slower pace of our small mountain town. Walk to restaurants. Savor our berry smoothies served w/gourmet breakfasts.
info@featherbed-inn.com http://www.featherbed-inn.com

RED BLUFF

The Faulkner House Inn
1029 Jefferson St 96080
530-529-0520 Fax: 530-527-4970
800-549-6171
Mike & Kara Flynn All year

80-110-BB
4 rooms, 4 pb
Visa, MC, AmEx, *Rated*
C-ltd/S-no/P-no/H-no

Full breakfast
Complimentary beverage
Sitting room, bicycles, all rooms have private bath

1890s Queen Anne Victorian furnished in antiques. Screened porch on quiet street, hiking and skiing nearby. faulknerbb@snowcrest.net http://www.snowcrest.net/faulknerbb

REDDING

Tiffany House
1510 Barbara Rd 96003
530-244-3225
Susan & Brady Stewart
All year

90-140-BB
4 rooms, 4 pb
Visa, MC, AmEx, *Rated*, •
C-yes/S-ltd/P-no/H-ltd

Full breakfast
Complimentary refreshments
Sitting room, library, 1 rm w/ spa, gazebo, pool, parlor

Romantic Victorian within minutes of Sacramento River, beautiful lakes, water sports, championship golf. Elegant view of Lassen mountain range.
tiffanyhse@aol.com http://www.sylvia.com/tiffany.htm

RUTHERFORD

Rancho Caymus
PO Box 78
1140 Rutherford Rd 94573
707-963-1777 Fax: 707-963-5387
800-845-1777
Otto Komes All year

205-395-BB
26 rooms, 26 pb
Visa, MC, AmEx
C-ltd/S-no/P-no/H-ltd

Continental breakfast

We invite you stay at our family's "home away from home," the Rancho Caymus Inn.
http://www.florasprings.com/visit/rancho.html

Rancho Caymus, Rutherford, CA

SACRAMENTO

Amber House
1315 22nd St 95816
916-444-8085 Fax: 916-552-6529
800-755-6526
Michael Richardson
All year

149-289-BB
18 rooms, 11 pb
Most CC, *Rated*, •
C-ltd/S-ltd/P-no/H-no

Full breakfast
Complimentary wine, tea, coffee
Marble bathrooms, tandem bicycle, phones

Four historic homes, 18 rooms offer ultimate comfort for the business traveler and perfect setting for a romantic escape. Phones, cable TV, breakfast in room. New historic 1895 Colonial revival home. innkeeper@amberhouse.com http://www.amberhouse.com

---

Capitol Park
1300 T St 95814
916-414-1300 Fax: 916-414-1304
877-753-9982
Michael Spinato
All year

149-189-BB
4 rooms, 4 pb
Visa, MC, AmEx, •
C-no/S-no/P-no/H-no

Full breakfast

Off Capitol City Freeway and I-5. Federalist Home Built in 1910. Romantic Getaway. Queen Size and King Size bedding. Private Baths.
info@capitolparkbnbinn.com http://www.capitolparkbnbinn.com

Hartley House Inn
700 22nd St 95816
916-447-7829 Fax: 916-447-1820
800-831-5806
Randy Hartley
All year

159-199-BB
5 rooms, 5 pb
Rated, •
C-ltd/S-ltd/P-no/H-no
Spanish

Full breakfast cooked to order
Complimentary beverages, dinner available
Sitting room, in-room phones, modems, fax, A/C

A stunning turn-of-the-century mansion with the sophisticated elegance of a small European hotel in historic Boulevard Park in midtown.
randy@hartleyhouse.com http://www.hartleyhouse.com

On the Bluffs
9735 Mira Del Rio 95827
916-363-9933 866-807-9104
Penny Bingham
All year

110-165-BB
3 rooms, 3 pb
Most CC, *Rated*
S-no/P-no

Full breakfast
Refreshments
Sitting room, bicycles, swimming pool, garden courtyard, spa & decks, river

Close to freeways, shopping, gyms, restaurants & amenities. Offers a pool, spa, fireplace, comfortable rooms & homemade breakfast. Relaxing outdoor seating with a stunning view of the American River. relax@onthebluffs.com http://www.onthebluffs.com

SACRAMENTO (REGION)

The Holbrooke Hotel
212 W Main St, *Grass Valley*
95945
530-273-1353 Fax: 530-273-0434
Donna Weaver
All year

BB
27 rooms, 27 pb
Visa, MC, AmEx,
Rated, •
C-yes/S-no/P-no/H-yes

Continental breakfast
Lunch, dinner, restaurant, bar service
Sitting room, library, suites, fireplaces, cable TV, accom. bus. trav.

Located in the Heart of the Gold Country, the Holbrooke Hotel is reminiscent of California's glorious past. holbrooke@holbrooke.com http://www.holbrooke.com

SAN ANSELMO

San Anselmo Inn
339 San Anselmo Ave 94960
415-455-5366 Fax: 415-455-5380
800-598-9771
Jan & Jack Grimes
All year

99-159-BB
15 rooms, 13 pb
Visa, MC
C-ltd/S-no/P-no/H-yes
German

Continental plus breakfast
Suites, cable TV

San Anselmo Inn is located in the charming village of San Anselmo. This European style Inn provides privacy and comfort along with warm hospitality.
sainn@marinmail.com http://www.sananselmoinn.com

SAN DIEGO

A Victorian Heritage Park Inn
2470 Heritage Park Row 92110
619-299-6832 Fax: 619-299-9465
800-995-2470
Nancy & Charles Helsper
All year

120-250-BB
12 rooms, 12 pb
Most CC, *Rated*, •
C-yes/S-no/P-no/H-yes
Spanish

Full breakfast
Afternoon tea, picnics
Sitting room, library, bicycles, vintage films, discount tickets to Zoo

Grand 1889 Queen Anne mansion, secluded in a historic Victorian village, where guests are pampered with candlelit breakfasts, afternoon tea, Jacuzzis, turned-down beds with chocolates on your pillow.
innkeeper@heritageparkinn.com http://www.heritageparkinn.com

Beach Hut
3761 Riviera Drive 92109
858-272-6131 Fax: 858-483-3671
Billee J. York
All year

95-95-BB
1 rooms, 1 pb
Rated
C-no/S-no/P-no/H-no

Full breakfast
Private telephone & modem, 60 ch. TV, VCR, full kitchen, heated pool, patio

The Beach Hut is a small guest cottage for two at beautiful Mission Bay. A favorite choice for honeymoon and anniversary couples. Minutes from all San Diego area attractions.
BilleeJ@aol.com http://www.beachhutbb.com

California Cruisin'
1450 Harbor Island Dr 92101
619-296-8000 800-44-YACHT
Ken Cohen
All year

200-250-EP
Most CC, *Rated*, •
C-yes/S-ltd/P-ltd/H-ltd

Continental breakfast (fee)
Restaurant, bar service, snacks
Swimming pool, Jacuzzi, accomm. business travelers

Enjoy San Diego aboard your own luxurious private yacht. Rates start at $200.00.
http://www.californiacruisin.com

Carole's Inn
3227 Grim Ave 92104
619-280-5258 800-975-5521
C. Dugdale & M. O'Brien
All year

89-189-BB
8 rooms, 4 pb
Rated, •
C-ltd/S-no/P-no/H-no

Continental plus breakfast
Cheese
Sitt. rm., conf. for 10, swimming pool, spa, player piano, cable TV

Historical house built in 1904, tastefully redecorated/antiques. Centrally located near zoo, Balboa Park. Friendly, congenial atmosphere. http://www.bbonline.com/ca/caroles/

SAN DIEGO

The Cottage
PO Box 3292
3829 Albatross St 92103
619-299-1564 Fax: 619-299-6213
Carol & Robert Emerick
All year

75-125-BB
2 rooms, 2 pb
Visa, MC, *Rated*, •
C-yes/S-no/P-no/H-no

Continental breakfast
Herb garden, player piano, cable TV

Relaxation in a garden setting with turn-of-the-century ambiance is offered in a residential downtown San Diego neighborhood.
cemerick@sandiegobandb.com http://www.sandiegobandb.com/cottage.htm

---

Glory's Holiday House
3330 Ingelow St 92106
619-225-0784 Fax: 619-221-4420
Glory Giffin
All year

110-210-BB
3 rooms, 2 pb
Most CC, •
C-yes/S-ltd/P-yes/H-no

Full breakfast
Complimentary wine
Snacks, sitting room, swimming pool, hot tub

Incredible view of San Diego Bay, the city, Coronado, Mexico and ocean. Nautical decor. Queen-size Victorian bed, CATV/VCR, private phone line, private bathroom, full breakfast, pool, Jacuzzi. holidaybbb@yahoo.com

---

Harbor Hill Guest House
2330 Albatross St 92101
619-233-0638
Dorothy Milbourn
All year

75-110-BB
6 rooms, 6 pb
Visa, MC, *Rated*, •
C-yes/S-ltd/P-no/H-no

Continental breakfast
Kitchens on each level
Large sun deck & garden, barbecue, TV, phones, rooms with harbor views

Charming circa 1920 home; private entrances. Near Balboa Park, zoo, museums, Sea World, Old Town, harbor, shopping, theater. http://www.travelguides.com/home/harborhill/

Villa Serena
2164 Rosecrans St 92106
619-224-1451 Fax: 619-224-2103
888-416-7415
Kae & Alex Schreiber
All year

95-360-BB
3 rooms, 2 pb
Visa, MC, Disc, •
C-yes/S-no/P-no/H-no
Spanish

Choice of breakfast plans
Snacks
Sitting room, library, hot tubs, pool, children under 12-free

A wonderful Mediterranean paradise, 5 minutes to Sea World. Comfortable rooms, spa, abundant breakfasts, friendly hosts can help with suggestions.
kschrei468@aol.com http://www.villaserena.org

SAN DIEGO (REGION)

Cardiff-by-the-Sea Lodge
142 Chesterfield, *Cardiff by the Sea* 92007
760-944-6474 Fax: 760-944-6474
James & Jeanette Statser
All year

125-375-BB
17 rooms, 17 pb
Rated, •

Continental plus breakfast

Steps away from the blue Pacific and just minutes from all San Diego has to offer. There is a place where lush gardens bloom year round.
innkeeper@cardifflodge.com http://www.cardifflodge.com

Coronado Village Inn
1017 Park Pl, *Coronado* 92118
619-435-9318
Jauter & Ana Sianz
All year

80-100-BB
15 rooms, 15 pb
Visa, MC, AmEx
C-yes/H-yes

Continental breakfast
Kitchenette, laundry

Located off Coronado's main street, Coronado Village Inn is a historic bed and breakfast decorated in old Spanish style. http://www.tripadvisor.com/Hotel_Review-g32250-d112284-Reviews-The_Village_Inn-Coronado_California.html

SAN DIEGO (REGION)

Seabreeze Inn
121 N Vulcan Ave, *Encinitas* 92024
760-944-0318
Kirsten Richter
All year

79-160-BB
5 rooms, 5 pb
Rated, •
C-yes/S-yes/P-no/H-no

Continental plus breakfast
Complimentary wine & cheese
Wet bar, kitchenette, sitting room, near beach and tennis

Encinita, N. San Diego quiet beach town. Contemporary B&B w/oceanview. Penthouse Shangri-La with private 8' hot tub. http://www.seabreeze-inn.com

---

Zosa Ranch & Gardens Inn
9381 W Lilac Rd, *Escondido* 92026
760-723-9093 Fax: 760-731-7616
800-711-8361
Nena Zosa
All year

130-250-BB
15 rooms, 11 pb
Most CC, *Rated*, •
C-ltd/S-no/P-no/H-ltd
Spanish, Tagalog

Full breakfast
Afternoon tea, complimentary wine
Sitting room, bikes, tennis court, Jacuzzi, suites, accom. bus. travelers

This secluded hacienda sits on 22 beautifully landscaped acres. Located in the heart of Temecula's wine country. zosamd@aol.com http://www.zosagardens.com

---

Butterfield
PO Box 1115
2284 Sunset Dr, *Julian* 92036
760-765-2179 Fax: 760-765-1229
800-379-4262
Ed & Dawn Glass
All year

125-185-BB
5 rooms, 5 pb
Visa, MC, AmEx, *Rated*, •
C-ltd/S-ltd/P-no/H-ltd

Full breakfast
Coffees, tea, snacks
Sitting room, library, suites, fireplace, cable TV

Relax on our three-acre country garden setting in the quiet hills of Julian. Five unique rooms from country to formal decor.
butterfield@abac.com http://www.butterfieldbandb.com

Orchard Hill Country Inn
PO Box 2410
2502 Washington St, *Julian* 92036
760-765-1700 Fax: 760-765-0290
800-716-7242
Straube Family All year

185-310-BB
22 rooms, 22 pb
Visa, MC, *Rated*
C-ltd/S-no/P-no/H-yes

Full breakfast
Afternoon hors d'oeuvres included
A gourmet four-course dinner is served Wednesday and Saturday nights.

Four Diamond Country Inn, located in the heart of Julian's 1800's Historic District, offers accommodations of casual elegance.
information@orchardhill.com http://www.orchardhill.com

The B&B Inn at La Jolla
7753 Draper Ave, *La Jolla* 92037
858-456-2066 Fax: 858-456-1510
800-582-2466
Judy Robertson & Nabil Kabbani
All year

179-399-BB
15 rooms, 15 pb
Most CC, *Rated*, •
C-ltd/S-no/P-no/H-ltd
Spanish, French

Full breakfast
Complimentary wine, cheese, sweets, sherry, snacks
Library, sitting room, complimentary bicycle rentals, public tennis courts

Romantic getaway to historical and elegantly charming B&B Inn. One block from the beach and in the heart of the Renon La Jolla Village.
bedbreakfast@innlajolla.com http://www.innlajolla.com

Scripps Inn
555 Coast Blvd S, *La Jolla* 92037
858-454-3391 Fax: 858-456-0389
Mette Anderson All year

165-415-BB
14 rooms
Most CC

Continental breakfast

Just a shell toss away from the sandy white beaches of La Jolla, CA, rests the intimate Scripps Inn. As elegant as it is charming, the 14 room inn is the best kept secret of the California coast. scrippsinn@jcresorts.com http://www.scrippsinn.com

SAN FRANCISCO

Amsterdam Hotel
749 Taylor St 94108
415-673-3277 Fax: 415-673-0453
800-637-3444
Kenny Gopal
All year

99-149-BB
34 rooms, 34 pb
Visa, MC, AmEx,
Rated, •
C-yes/S-no/P-no/H-no

Continental breakfast
Sitting room, library, sunny patio, color TV & phones in rms

Located on Nob Hill. Quality accommodations and friendly service provided at modest rates. A little bit of Europe in America. Near Union Square, Financial District, cable car.
info@amsterdamhotel.com http://www.amsterdamhotel.com

The Andrews Hotel
624 Post St 94109
415-563-6877
Fax: 415-928-6919
800-926-3739
Barbara Vogler
All year

99-175-BB
48 rooms, 48 pb
Most CC, *Rated*, •
C-yes/S-no/P-no/H-no
Spanish, French

Continental breakfast
Restaurant, bar
Complimentary wine, coffee, tea, small meetings, color TV & phones in rooms

European-style charm in the heart of Union Square shopping and theater district. Features architectural bay windows. res@andrewshotel.com http://www.andrewshotel.com

---

Annie's Cottage
1255 Vallejo 94109
415-923-9990
Fax: 415-923-9911
Annie Bone
All year

140-BB
1 rooms, 1 pb
S-no/P-no/H-no

Continental breakfast
Near wharf & downtown, phone/answering machine, TV/VCR, queen bed

Guestroom with private entrance, private bath, sitting area, deck, refrigerator/microwave. Country hideaway in the middle of San Francisco. Furnished with antiques.
annie@anniescottage.com http://anniescottage.com

Artists Inn
2231 Pine St 94115
415-346-1919
Fax: 415-346-1904
800-854-5802
Denise & Bill Shields
All year

170-BB
3 rooms, 3 pb
Most CC
C-ltd/S-ltd/P-no/H-no
French

Continental breakfast
Complimentary wine
Sitting room, fireplace in main living room of house

Artists Inn is a charming 19th century farm house and an artist's studio building on either side of a secluded garden courtyard. Located in Pacific Heights in the heart of SF.
shields@artistsinn.com http://www.artistsinn.com

Castillo Inn
48 Henry St 94114
415-864-5111
Fax: 415-641-1321
800-865-5112
Mario Castillo
All year

60-80-BB
4 rooms
Visa, MC, AmEx, •
S-no/P-no/H-no
Spanish

Continental breakfast

Gay accommodations mostly. Centrally located close to Castro and Market Streets.
M4019C@yahoo.com

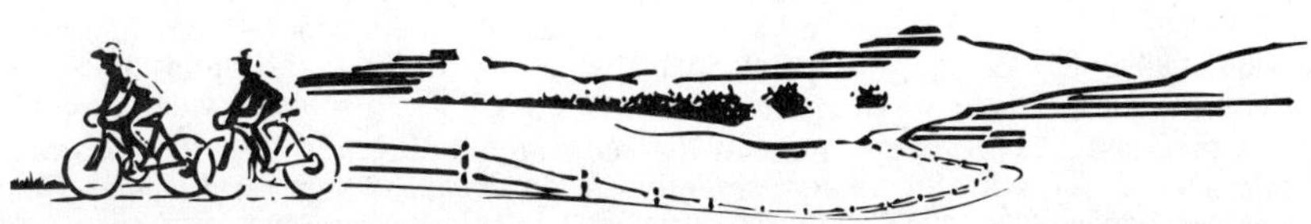

SAN FRANCISCO

Country Cottage PO Box 420009 5 Dolores Terrace 94110 415-899-0060 Fax: 415-899-9923 800-452-8249 Richard & Susan Kreibich Season Inquire	89-BB 4 rooms *Rated*, •	Full breakfast

The Country Cottage B&B is a cozy country-style B&B in the heart of San Francisco. The four guestrooms are comfortably furnished in American country antiques and brass beds.
reservations@bbsf.com http://www.bbsf.com/country.html

Edward II Inn & Suites 3155 Scott St 94123 415-922-3000 Fax: 415-931-5784 800-GREAT-INN Bob & Denise Holland All year	85-235-BB 32 rooms, 21 pb Visa, MC, AmEx, *Rated*, • C-yes/S-no/P-no/H-ltd	Continental breakfast Beer, wine, complimentary sherry Pub, Jacuzzis, Sitting Room, Limited Views

Edward II Inn is a three-story European-style inn situated only blocks from San Francisco's yacht harbor. The hotel was originally built to house guests who attended the 1915 Pan-Pacific Exposition. innkeeper@edwardii.com http://www.edwardii.com

The Garden Studio 1387 Sixth Ave 94122 415-753-3574 Fax: 415-753-5513 Alice & John Micklewright All year	110-EP 1 rooms, 1 pb *Rated* C-yes/S-no/P-no/H-no French	Coffee, Restaurants nearby Garden, private entrance, fully equipped kitchen, TV/VCR, telephone, radio

Studio apartment opens to garden, has private entrance, private bath, queen-sized bed. On lower level of charming Edwardian home; 2 blocks from Golden Gate Park.
gardenstudio@earthlink.net

The Golden Gate Hotel 775 Bush St 94108 415-392-3702 Fax: 415-392-6202 800-835-1118 John & Renate Kenaston All year	85-130-BB 23 rooms, 14 pb Most CC, *Rated*, • C-yes/S-ltd/P-no/H-no German, French	Continental breakfast Afternoon tea Sitting room, sightseeing tours, TV/VCR, telephone, radio

Charming turn-of-the-century hotel. Friendly atmosphere. Antique furnishings, fresh flowers. Ideal Nob Hill location, corner cable car stop.
info@goldengatehotel.com http://www.goldengatehotel.com

The Grove Inn 890 Grove St 94117 415-929-0780 Fax: 415-929-1037 800-829-0780 Rosetta Zimmermann All year	80-150-BB 16 rooms, 9 pb Visa, MC, AmEx, *Rated*, • C-yes/S-ltd/P-no/H-no Italian, German	Continental breakfast Sitting room, bicycles, laundry

Turn-of-the-century Victorian, fully restored, simply furnished with bay windows. Community kitchen, refrigerator. Part of Alamo Square Historic District.
grovinn@jps.net http://www.grovinn.com

The Inn at Union Square 440 Post St 94102 415-397-3510 Fax: 415-989-0529 800-288-4346 Susan D. Platt All year	195-375-BB 30 rooms, 30 pb Most CC, *Rated*, • C-ltd/S-no/P-no/H-yes French, Spanish	Extensive Continental Breakfast Wine and hors d'oeuvres Sitting room, complimentary massage and shoe shine, VCRs, room service

An elegant, cozy European-style hotel in the heart of San Francisco. A half-block from Union Square, & close to the finest restaurants, best shopping & wonderful theater. Our location in unbeatable! inn@unionsquare.com http://www.unionsquare.com

SAN FRANCISCO

The Inn San Francisco 943 South Van Ness Ave 94110 415-641-0188 Fax: 415-641-1701 800-359-0913 Marty Neely All year	95-265-BB 21 rooms, 19 pb Most CC, *Rated*, • C-yes/S-no/P-no/H-no Spanish, French, Cantonese, Mandarin	Full buffet breakfast Complimentary fruit, coffee, tea, sherry Sun deck, English garden, hot tub, phones, TVs, parking

Authentic 1872 Italianate Victorian Mansion. Rich Victorian decor. English Garden with Redwood Hot Tub. Sundeck with spectacular SF vistas. Excellent restaurants nearby. Be welcomed as a friend. innkeeper@innsf.com http://www.innsf.com

---

The Inn 4 Charlton Court 94123 415-921-9784 John & Beverlee All year	80-420-BB 11 rooms, 8 pb	

One of San Francisco's best kept secrets, we offer a variety of charming accommodations on a secluded courtyard, just a corner's turn from the excitement of Union Street.
bbia@1stb-bst.com http://www.thebandb.com

Moffatt House 1401 Seventh Ave 94122 415-661-6210 Fax: 415-564-2480 Ruth Moffatt All year	79-99-BB 4 rooms, 2 pb *Rated* C-yes/S-ltd/P-no/H-no Spanish, French, Italian	Continental plus breakfast Hot beverages Tennis, bicycles nearby, Japanese Tea Garden, runner's discount

Walk to Golden Gate Park's major attractions from our Arts & Crafts home. Safe location for active, independent guests. moffattbb@cs.com http://www.moffatthouse.com

---

The Monte Cristo 600 Presidio Ave 94115 415-931-1875 Fax: 415-931-6005 All year	83-118-BB 14 rooms, 12 pb Visa, MC, AmEx, *Rated*, • C-yes/S-yes/P-no/H-yes French, Spanish	Continental plus buffet Complimentary tea, wine Parlor with fireplace, phones, TV

1875 hotel-saloon-bordello furnished with antiques. Each room uniquely decorated: Georgian four-poster, Chinese wedding bed, spindle bed. Personal service.
http://www.virtualcities.com/ons/ca/b/cab3504.htm

Purple Door Inn 1724 Larkin St 94109 415-885-2778 800-881-4667 Lynn Smithers-Hubbard All year	65-120-BB 4 rooms Most CC, • C-no/S-no/P-no/H-no Spanish, Italian	Full continental self-serve bkfst. Upon request

100-year-old Victorian European-style guest house. In the middle of all San Francisco attractions, fine international dining. Very affordable prices. purpledoorinn@aol.com

---

Stanyan Park Hotel 750 Stanyan St 94117 415-751-1000 Fax: 415-668-5454 John K. Brocklehurst All year	130-315-BB 36 rooms, 36 pb AmEx, Most CC, *Rated*, • C-yes/S-no/P-no/H-yes Spanish, Tagalog	Continental plus breakfast Afternoon tea Sitting room, bikes, suites with kitchens, non-smoking hotel

The Stanyan Park Hotel is an elegant, thoroughly restored Victorian Hotel that will take you back to a bygone era of style, grace and comfort.
info@stanyanpark.com http://www.stanyanpark.com

SAN FRANCISCO (REGION)

Gerstle Park Inn
34 Grove St, *San Rafael* 94901
415-721-7611 Fax: 415-721-7600
800-726-7611
Jim Dowling
All year

179-245-BB
12 rooms, 12 pb
Visa, MC, AmEx,
Rated, •
C-yes/S-no/P-no/H-ltd

Full breakfast
Complimentary wine, snacks
Sitting room, fireplace, library, tennis court, hot tubs, gardens, bikes

All rooms have private baths, patio or decks. All are furnished with rich fabrics and beautiful antiques. King suites with Jacuzzi tub. innkeeper@gerstleparkinn.com http://www.gerstleparkinn.com

---

The Gables Inn-Sausalito
62 Princess St, *Sausalito* 94965
415-289-1100 Fax: 415-339-0536
800-966-1554
Alexandra Sainsbury
All year

135-325-BB
9 rooms, 9 pb
Visa, MC, AmEx, •
C-yes/S-no/P-no/H-yes
Spanish, French

Continental plus breakfast
Wine, bar
Sitting room, bicycles, tennis, Jacuzzis, fireplace, cable TV

Originally built in 1869, the inn has recently been completely renovated into a cozy B&B offering 9 distinctive suites artfully decorated. Just 5 minutes north of the Golden Gate Bridge. gablesinns@aol.com http://www.gablesinnsausalito.com

SAN JOSE

Briar Rose
897 E Jackson St 95112
408-279-5999 Fax: 408-279-4534
877-724-5999
The Worthy's, J. Wolkenhauer
All year

130-170-BB
6 rooms, 6 pb
Most CC, *Rated*, •
C-ltd/S-no/P-no/H-no

Full breakfast
Afternoon tea, sherry, freshly baked cookies
Porch, gardens, sitting room, library, period furnishings

An 1875 Victorian–once a flourishing walnut orchard–restored to its former grandeur. worthy@briar-rose.com http://www.briar-rose.com

SAN JOSE (REGION)

Country Rose Inn
PO Box 2500
455 Fitzgerald Ave #E, *Gilroy* 95021
408-842-0441 Fax: 408-842-6646
Rose Hernandez
All year

149-239-BB
5 rooms, 5 pb
Visa, MC, *Rated*, •
C-ltd/S-no/P-no/H-no
Spanish

Full breakfast
Snacks
Library, sitting room, suite with jet tub

A gracious farmhouse located in the heart of California's pastoral central coast. The coast is a scenic drive away. Unexpected. Serene. countryrosebnb@earthlink.net http://www.bbonline.com/ca/countryrose

SAN LUIS OBISPO

Petit Soleil
1473 Monterey St 93401
805-549-0321 Fax: 805-549-0383
800-676-1588
John & Dianne Conner
April 15–October 15

99-229-BB
15 rooms, 15 pb
Most CC, *Rated*
C-yes/S-ltd/P-no/H-ltd
Spanish

Full homemade breakfast
Wine & hor d'ouvres are available for purchase.
Outdoor patio, garden, getaway packages, include spa, kayak, wine

Opening Thanksgiving 2002 a cozy, comfortable, Provence-style Country Bed et Breakfast, in the heart of San Luis Obispo. petitsoleil@charter.net http://www.petitsoleilslo.com

SAN LUIS OBISPO (REGION)

Arroyo Village Inn
210 Oak St, *Arroyo Grande* 93420
805-489-5926 800-563-7762
John and Adriana
July, Aug. and Sept.

139-475-BB
7 rooms, 7 pb
Most CC, *Rated*, •
C-no/S-no/P-no/H-no
Spanish, Italian

Full gourmet breakfast mid-week
Weekend brunch
In-room spa & fireplace, feather bed, down comforter, VCR, robe,

15 minutes from San Luis Obispo. Luxury/Romance. In-room spa and fireplace. Laura Ashley prints/antiques. ginag@fix.net http://www.arroyovillageinn.com

SAN RAFAEL

Casa Soldavini
531 "C" St 94901
415-454-3140 Fax: 415-454-3140
Linda Soldavini & Dan Cassidy
All year

100-125-BB
3 rooms, 2 pb
S-no/P-yes

Quiet comfortable rooms in our home with private bath; walk to downtown San Rafael. Easy drive to Marin County attractions and San Francisco.
dnloasis@msn.com http://www.inn-guide.com/city/CASan-Rafael.html

---

Casa Soldavini
531 "C" St 94901
415-454-3140 Fax: 415-454-3140
Linda Soldavini & Dan Cassidy
All year

100-125-BB
3 rooms, 2 pb
S-no/P-yes

Quiet comfortable rooms in our home with private bath; walk to downtown San Rafael. Easy drive to Marin County attractions and San Francisco.
dnloasis@msn.com http://www.inn-guide.com/city/CASan-Rafael.html

SANTA BARBARA

Casa Del Mar Inn
18 Bath St 93101
805-963-4418 Fax: 805-966-4240
800-433-3097
Yun Kim
All year

99-299-BB
21 rooms, 21 pb
Most CC, *Rated*, •
C-yes/S-ltd/P-ltd/H-yes

Continental plus breakfast buffet
Evening wine/cheese buffet
Sitting room, hot tub, beach towels, umbrellas

Spanish-style villa, quiet, charming. One block from beach. Courtyard Jacuzzi. Several units with fireplaces and kitchens.
yunkim@casadelmar.com http://www.casadelmar.com

Cheshire Cat Inn
36 W Valerio St 93101
805-569-1610 Fax: 805-682-1876
Christine Dunstan, Amy Taylor,
All year

150-400-BB
21 rooms, 21 pb
Most CC, *Rated*, •
C-ltd/S-no/P-no/H-no

Continental breakfast
Wine & hors d'oeuvres
Hot tubs, balconies, fireplaces, spa treatments, outdoor Jacuzzi, gardens

Victorian elegance, uniquely decorated in Laura Ashley & English antiques. Spa treatments, Jacuzzis, fireplaces, cottages with outdoor hot tubs.
cheshire@cheshirecat.com http://www.cheshirecat.com

Country Inn By The Sea
128 Castillo 93101
805-963-4471 Fax: 805-962-2633
800-455-4647
John Devereaux All year

99-219-BB
47 rooms, 47 pb
Most CC, *Rated*, •
C-yes/S-no/P-no/H-ltd

Continental plus breakfast
Snacks
Sitting room, library, Jacuzzis, pool, sauna, cable TV, VCR, saunas, fridges

Luxurious, Old World decor, excellent breakfast, superb location–2 blocks to the beach. Walking distance to shops, restaurants, train station.
concierge@innsbythesea.com http://www.countryinnbythesea.com

The Eagle Inn
232 Natoma Ave 93101
805-965-3586 Fax: 805-966-1218
800-767-0030
Janet & Alan Bullock
All year

95-200-BB
27 rooms, 27 pb
Rated

Continental
Free on-site parking, cable, microwave, coffee maker, fridge, in-room safe

The Eagle Inn at the Beach provides comfortable lodging accommodations near the beach, pier, marina, and the main shopping street.
Info@theeagleinn.com http://www.theeagleinn.com

SANTA BARBARA

Old Yacht Club Inn
431 Corona Del Mar Dr 93103
805-962-1277 Fax: 805-962-3989
800-676-1676
Eilene Bruce & Vince Pettit
All year

110-230-BB
12 rooms, 12 pb
Most CC, *Rated*, •
C-ltd/S-no/P-ltd/H-ltd
Spanish

Full breakfast
Complimentary wine social, sherry, coffee & tea.
Complimentary bicycles, beach chairs and beach towels.

Located 1 block from famous East Beach! Santa Barbara's first and finest bed and breakfast. Our Mission Craftsman Inn served as the Santa Barbara Yacht Club in the roaring 1920's. info@oldyachtclubinn.com http://www.oldyachtclubinn.com

---

Prufrock's Garden Inn by the Beach
5004 6th St
600 Linden Ave 93013
805-566-9696 Fax: 805-566-9404
8PR-UFR-OCKS
Judy & Jim Halvorsen
All year

89-299-BB
7 rooms, 5 pb
Most CC, *Rated*, •
C-yes/S-no/P-no/H-yes
Spanish

Delicious home-cooked breakfast
'All the Time' drinks, desserts, fruit & snacks
'BestBeachinWest', beach amenities, mtns, Channel Islands, bicycles, gardens

Reader's Favorite-LA Times, Most Romantic Getaway-Santa Barbara Independent, Pictured Land's End catalog. innkeepers@prufrocks.com http://www.prufrocks.com

---

Secret Garden Inn &Cottages
1908 Bath St 93101
805-687-2300 Fax: 805-687-6576
800-676-1622
Dominique Hannaux
All year except Christmas

121-231-BB
11 rooms, 11 pb
Visa, MC, AmEx, *Rated*, •
C-ltd/S-ltd/P-no/H-no

Full gourmet breakfast
Wine & hors d'oeuvres at 5 PM
Evening sweets, sitting room, garden, brick patio, bicycles

Guestrooms, suites & private cottages filled with charm in a delightfully quiet and relaxing country setting. 4 rooms with private patio and outdoor hot tubs.
garden@secretgarden.com http://www.secretgarden.com

Simpson House Inn
121 E Arrellaga 93101
805-963-7067 Fax: 805-564-4811
800-676-1280
Glyn & Linda Davies & Dixie Adair Budke, Ph.D All year

215-650-BB
15 rooms, 15 pb
Most CC, *Rated*, •
C-ltd/S-ltd/P-no/H-yes
Spanish

Full California breakfast
Refreshments, hors d'oeuvres buffet, wine tasting
Sitt. room, lib., patio, veranda, garden, Jacuzzi, bikes, fireplaces, VCRs

Welcome to North Americas' only AAA FIVE-DIAMOND B&B. This beautiful Inn is located in a prestigious historic neighborhood of downtown Santa Barbara and secluded in an acre of English gardens.
reservations@simpsonhouseinn.com http://www.simpsonhouseinn.com

---

The Tiffany Country House
1323 De La Vina 93101
805-963-2283 Fax: 805-963-2825
800-999-5672
Jan Martin Winn
All year

155-350-BB
7 rooms, 7 pb
Visa, MC, AmEx, *Rated*, •
C-ltd/S-no/P-no/H-no

Full breakfast
Complimentary wine
Spa tub in 5 rooms, fireplaces in 5 rooms, VCRs

Classic antiques & period furnishings welcome you throughout this lovely restored 1898 Victorian. English Country-style decor.
upham.hotel@verizon.net http://www.tiffanycountryhouse.com

The Upham Hotel
1404 De La Vina St 93101
805-962-0058 Fax: 805-963-2825
800-727-0876
Jan Martin Winn
All year

160-425-BB
50 rooms, 50 pb
Most CC, *Rated*, •
C-yes/S-no/P-no/H-no
Spanish

Continental plus breakfast
Complimentary wine, coffee, tea
Restaurant, garden veranda, gardens, valet laundry, phones

California's oldest Victorian hotel. Cottage rooms with patios and fireplaces, lawn, flowers. Restaurant on property. upham.hotel@verizon.net http://www.uphamhotel.com

SANTA CLARA

Madison Street Inn 1390 Madison St 95050 408-249-5541 Fax: 408-249-6676 800-491-5541 Theresa Wigginton All year	80-150-BB 5 rooms, 3 pb Visa, MC, AmEx, *Rated*, • C-yes/S-ltd/P-no/H-no French	Full breakfast Lunch, dinner (upon request) Complimentary wine & beverages, library, sitting room, hot tub, bikes, pool

Santa Clara's only inn! A beautiful Victorian with landscaped gardens near Winchester Mystery House. Eggs Benedict is a breakfast favorite.
madstinn@aol.com http://www.madisonstreetinn.com

SANTA CRUZ

Babbling Brook Inn 1025 Laurel St 95060 831-427-2437 Fax: 831-427-2457 800-866-1131 Jennifer Stanger All year	130-250-BB 13 rooms, 13 pb Most CC, *Rated*, • C-ltd/S-no/P-no/H-ltd	Full buffet breakfast Complimentary wine, refreshments Romantic garden gazebo, cascading waterfall, meandering brook, water wheel

Secluded among waterfalls, gardens, Laurel Creek, pines all rooms w/ fireplaces.
lodging@babblingbrookinn.com http://www.babblingbrookinn.com

Chateau Victorian 118 First St 95060 831-458-9458 Alice June All year	120-150-BB 7 rooms, 7 pb Visa, MC, *Rated* C-ltd/S-no/P-no/H-no	Continental plus breakfast Complimentary wine & cheese Sitting room, deck, patio

One block from the beach and the boardwalk, in the heart of the Santa Cruz fun area. All rooms have queen-size beds with private bathrooms. http://www.chateauvictorian.com

Cliff Crest 407 Cliff St 95060 831-427-2609 Fax: 831-427-2710 831-252-1057 (Adriana Gehriger Gil & Constantin Gehriger All year	125-275-BB 5 rooms, 5 pb Most CC, • C-ltd/S-ltd/P-no/H-ltd Spanish, German, French, Swiss German	Tell us your dietary needs! Sitting room, large garden, free parking

1887 Queen Anne Victorian overlooking the Beach Boardwalk and the Santa Cruz Mountains. Five period guestrooms, all with private baths and some with fireplaces. Full breakfast included. Free parking. innkpr@CliffCrestInn.com http://www.CliffCrestInn.com

Compassion Flower Inn 216 Laurel St 95060 831-466-0420 Andrea Tischler All year	125-175-BB 4 rooms, 2 pb Most CC, *Rated*, • C-yes/S-ltd/P-no/H-no German	Full breakfast Afternoon tea Sitting Room, library, patio, Jacuzzi/spa, private parking.

Romantic Victorian Inn in downtown Santa Cruz and near the beach. Elegantly appointed guest rooms, sumptuous organic breakfasts, delicious coffee, spa in a friendly relaxed atmosphere.
reservations@compassionflowerinn.com http://www.compassionflowerinn.com

The Darling House 314 W Cliff Dr 95060 831-458-1958 Darrell & Karen Darling All year	95-260-BB 8 rooms, 2 pb Most CC, *Rated*, • C-ltd/S-ltd/P-no/H-ltd	Continental plus breakfast Complimentary beverages Library, fireplaces, double size bathtubs, fireplaces in rooms

1910 ocean side mansion with beveled glass, Tiffany lamps, Chippendale antiques, open hearths and hardwood interiors.
ddarling@darlinghouse.com http://www.darlinghouse.com

SANTA CRUZ

Pleasure Point Inn
2-3665 East Cliff Dr 95062
831-469-6161877-557-2567
Claire and Jonathan
All year

165-265-BB
4 rooms, 4 pb
Visa, MC, *Rated*, •
C-no/S-ltd/P-no/H-yes

Expanded continental breakfast
A welcome basket with fruits and goodies
Fireplaces, whirlpool tubs, 4 suites, TV/VCR, private phones, private baths

The Ocean Front Inn is located in front of the famous Pleasure Point Beach and offers spectacular full ocean views. The Inn has a large roof-top deck where you can soak in the hot tub. Inquiries@PleasurePointInn.com http://www.PleasurePointInn.com

---

Valley View Inn
PO Box 67438
600 Hacienda Dr 95067
650-321-5195 Fax: 650-325-5121
Tricia Young
All year

250-BB
2 rooms, 2 pb
Most CC, *Rated*, •
C-ltd/S-no/P-no/H-no
German, Spanish

Full breakfast
Sitting room, piano, bicycles, spa, BBQ
ENTIRE HOUSE TO YOURSELF for $250

ENTIRE HOME ALL TO YOURSELF! Overlooks 20,000 acres of redwood trees. 10 minutes to Santa Cruz beaches. 2 bedrooms, 2 baths, all amenities, granite kitchen, and a hot spa on the secluded deck. tricia@valleyviewinn.com http://www.valleyviewinn.com

SANTA CRUZ (REGION)

Apple Lane Inn
6265 Soquel Dr, *Aptos* 95003
831-475-6868 Fax: 831-464-5790
800-649-8988
Doug Groom
All year

100-200-BB
5 rooms, 5 pb
Most CC, *Rated*, •
C-yes/S-no/P-ltd/H-ltd

Full breakfast
Complimentary wine, tea, snacks
Sitting room, library, suites, fireplaces, accommodate business travelers

1870's Victorian Farmhouse on 2 country acres, just one mile from the beach. Five guestrooms decorated with museum quality antiques. Children and pets welcomed in the Wine Cellar Room. ali@cruzio.com http://www.applelaneinn.com

---

Chateau des Fleurs
7995 Hwy 9, *Ben Lomond* 95005
831-336-8943 800-291-9966
Laura Jonas
All year

115-155-BB
3 rooms, 3 pb
Most CC, *Rated*
C-yes/S-no/P-no/H-yes
German

Full breakfast
Complimentary wine
Sitting room, library, fireplaces, cable TV, A/C

A Victorian mansion once owned by the Barttlet (pear) family. This inn is special, spacious, sensational, historic, quiet, unforgettable.
laura@chateaudesfleurs.com http://www.chateaudesfleurs.com

Fairview Manor
245 Fairview Ave, *Ben Lomond* 95005
831-336-3355 800-553-8840
Nancy Glasson
Season Inquire

129-139-BB
5 rooms, 5 pb
Visa, MC, *Rated*, •
C-ltd/S-yes/P-no/H-yes

Full breakfast
Complimentary wine/hors d'oeuvres
Sitting room, bordered by river, weddings & meetings

Romantic country-style redwood home, majestic stone fireplace, 2 1/2 wooded acres of Santa Cruz Mountains. Total privacy. Walk to town.
fairviewbandb@aol.com http://www.fairviewmanor.com

Felton Crest Inn
780 El Solyo Heights Dr, *Felton* 95018
831-335-4011 Fax: 831-335-4011
800-474-4011
Hanna Peters All year

140-275-BB
4 rooms, 4 pb
Visa, MC, AmEx, •
C-ltd/S-ltd/P-no/H-yes

Continental breakfast
TV/VCR, in-room phones, Jacuzzis

Exclusive, romantic hideaway on one acre of sunny redwoods. Each room comes with a bottle of champagne, a cheese tray, a bowl of fruit, chocolate, and breakfast.
hannapeters@mymailstation.com http://www.feltoncrestinn.com

SANTA CRUZ (REGION)

Blue Spruce Inn | 135-240-BB | Full breakfast
2815 Main St, *Soquel* 95073 | 6 rooms, 6 pb | Snacks
831-464-1137 Fax: 831-475-0608 | Most CC, • | Sitting room, conference,
800-559-1137 | C-ltd/S-ltd/P-no/H-no | library, spa tubs, gas
Nancy, Carissa & Wayne | Spanish | fireplaces
Lussier All year

Award-winning inn as fresh as a sea breeze. Explore Monterey Bay! Enjoy Jacuzzis, fireplaces, original local art. Available for business meetings, retreats.
info@bluespruce.com http://www.bluespruce.com

SANTA ROSA

Pygmalion House | 79-99-BB | Full breakfast
331 Orange St 95401 | 6 rooms, 6 pb | Snacks
707-526-3407 Fax: 707-526-3407 | Visa, MC, *Rated* | Sitting room, fireplaces,
Caroline | C-ltd/S-no/P-no/H-no | cable TV, accom. bus.
All year | | travelers

Our Inn has many of Gypsy Rose Lee's antiques and also Sally Stanford's from her Valhalla restaurant in Sausalito (she was also mayor there).
http://www.travelhero.com/prophome.cfm/id/70782/hotels/reservations/index.html

SAUSALITO

Inn Above Tide | 235-600-BB | Continental plus breakfast
30 El Portal 94965 | 30 rooms, 30 pb | Wine & cheese reception at
415-332-9535 Fax: 415-332-6714 | Visa, MC, AmEx, | sunset
800-893-8433 | *Rated*, • | Most guestrooms have
Mark Davis Flaherty | C-yes/S-no/P-no/H-yes | fireplaces & private
All year | Spanish, French, | furnished decks over the
| Chinese, Portuguese | Bay.

The Inn Above Tide, an elegant and secluded waterfront hotel with exceptional bay views from every guestroom, is the only hotel on San Francisco Bay built over the water.
stay@innabovetide.com http://www.innabovetide.com

SEA RANCH

The Sea Ranch Lodge | 205-395-EP | Room serv. for breakfast
PO Box 44 | 20 rooms, 20 pb | All meals, bar (fee)
60 Sea Walk Dr, Hwy 1 95497 | Visa, MC, AmEx, • | Hot tub, sauna, swimming
707-785-2371 800-732-7262 | C-yes/S-yes/P-no/H-no | pool, tennis, fireside lounge,
Marianne Harder All year | | piano

On the Sonoma coast 3 hours from San Francisco, Sea Ranch is famed for architecture and natural beauty. Hiking, golfing, tennis.
info@searanchlodge.com http://www.searanchlodge.com

SEAL BEACH

The Seal Beach Inn & Gardens | 165-399-BB | Lavish full breakfast
212 5th St 90740 | 23 rooms, 23 pb | Complimentary wine &
562-493-2416 Fax: 562-799-0483 | Visa, MC, AmEx, | cheese
800-935-2422 | *Rated*, • | Fruit, tea, coffee, sitting
Marjorie & Harty Schmaehl | C-ltd/S-ltd/P-no/H-no | rooms, library, pool,
| All year | Jacuzzis, fireplaces

Elegant, historic, So. CA Inn, 1 block from ocean beach in charming prestigious seaside village. Inn has lush intimate gardens.
hideaway@sealbeachinn.com http://www.sealbeachinn.com

SEQUOIA NATIONAL PARK (REGION)

Montecito-Sequoia Mtn. Inn | 138-158-MAP | Full breakfast
8000 Generals Hwy Box 858, | 36 rooms, 36 pb | Dinner, restaurant, bar
Kings Canyon Nat'l Park 93633 | Most CC, *Rated*, • | Outdoor spa, volleyball,
650-967-8612 Fax: 650-967-0540 | C-yes/S-ltd/P-no/H-yes | tennis, hot tubs, pool, lake,
800-227-9900 | Italian | canoeing
Virginia C. Barnes All year

Charming alpine lodge at 7500 ft. on serene Lake Homavalo. Spectacular view of Sequoia National Park. info@mslodge.com http://www.mslodge.com

SHASTA LAKE (REGION)

O'Brien Mountain Inn
PO Box 27
18026 O'Brien Inlet Rd, *O'Brien* 96070
530-238-8026 Fax: 530-238-2027
888-799-8026
Greg & Teresa Ramsey
All year

105-245-BB
8 rooms, 6 pb
Most CC, *Rated*, •
C-yes/S-ltd/P-no/H-ltd

Full breakfast
Snacks
Sitting room, library, suites, fireplaces, accommodate business travelers

If you're looking for fresh flowers, chocolates, private baths, patios with lush forest views ... stay here. info@obrienmountain.com http://www.obrienmountain.com

SIERRA CITY

High Country Inn
HCR 2, Box 7
100 Greene Rd 96125
530-862-1530 Fax: 530-862-1000
800-862-1530
Bette & Bob Latta All year

85-150-BB
5 rooms, 3 pb
Most CC, *Rated*, •
C-ltd/S-no/P-no/H-no

Full breakfast
Snacks
Sitting room, library, suites, fireplaces

Come away from the noise, the traffic, the crowds ... Come to the High Country Inn.
blatta@sccn.net http://www.hicountryinn.com

SODA SPRINGS

Always Inn Tahoe
PO Box 861
10108 Soda Springs Road 95728
530-426-3010 Fax: 530-426-1100
877-56-TAHOE
Sheri & Greg Pasterick
All year

79-175-BB
4 rooms, 4 pb
Most CC, *Rated*
C-ltd/S-no/P-ltd/H-no

Full breakfast
Snacks
Sitting room, Jacuzzis, fireplaces, cable TV, accom. business travelers

Cozy B&B surrounded by the beautiful Yuba River, mountains, lakes and the Sierras. Nestled in an unspoiled enclave on Donner Summit, close to Lake Tahoe.
innkeeper@alwaysinn.net http://www.alwaysinn.com

SONOMA

Brick House Bungalows
313 First St East 95476
707-996-8091 Fax: 707-996-7301
Joe Gough & BJ Clarke
All year

125-275-BB
5 rooms, 5 pb
Most CC, *Rated*, •
C-ltd/S-ltd/P-no/H-ltd

Continental Plus
Snacks, wine
Sitting room, bicycles, tennis, suites, cable TV, conference

Located ½ block from Historic Sonoma Plaza, site of many fine restaurants, museums, galleries, shop & tasting rooms.
info@brickhousebungalows.com http://www.brickhousebungalows.com

---

Sonoma Chalet
18935 Fifth St W 95476
707-938-3129 800-938-3129
Joe Leese
All year

110-225-BB
7 rooms, 4 pb
Rated

Located in the Sonoma Wine Country, Sonoma Chalet offers private cottages and bed & breakfast accommodations on our very private three and one-half acre site.
sonomachalet@cs.com http://www.sonomachalet.com

Sonoma Hotel
110 W Spain St 95476
707-996-2996 Fax: 707-996-7014
800-468-6016
Tim Farfan & Craig Miller
All year

110-245-BB
16 rooms, 16 pb
Rated, •

Continental breakfast
Restaurant and Bar
A/C, TVs, phone with dataport

A wonderful vintage hotel (circa 1880) on Sonoma's Historic Plaza. Modern amenities were added, such as private baths, phones, TVs and A/C. Guests can walk to shops, historic sites and wineries. sonomahotel@aol.com http://www.sonomahotel.com

SONOMA

Thistle Dew Inn
171 W Spain St 95476
707-938-2909 Fax: 707-996-8413
800-382-7895
Larry Barnett
All year

135-275-BB
6 rooms, 6 pb
Most CC, *Rated*, •
C-ltd/S-ltd/P-no/H-ltd

Full breakfast
Comp. wine & appetizers
Sitting rm, spa, picnic baskets, bikes, rare plant/cactus collection

Two Victorian homes near Sonoma's historic plaza. Collector pieces of Stickley furniture; fresh-cut flowers; extensive collection of rare plants and cactus.
tdibandb@aol.com http://www.thistledew.com

Trojan Horse Inn
19455 Sonoma Hwy 95476
707-996-2430 Fax: 707-996-9185
800-899-1925
Joe & Sandy Miccio
All year

155-180-BB
6 rooms, 6 pb
Visa, MC, *Rated*, •
C-ltd/S-no/P-no/H-yes

Full breakfast
Complimentary wine
Hors d'oeuvres, outside Jacuzzi, bikes, 2 night minimum

Beautifully decorated 1887 Victorian, 6 rooms, private baths, full breakfast. Spa, bicycles, complimentary hors d'oeuvres w/wine and wine country hospitality.
trojaninn@aol.com http://www.trojanhorseinn.com

Victorian Garden Inn
316 E Napa St 95476
707-996-5339 Fax: 707-996-1689
800-543-5339
Donna Lewis
All year

125-230-BB
4 rooms, 4 pb
Visa, MC, AmEx, *Rated*, •
C-ltd/S-ltd/P-no/H-no
Spanish

Full breakfast
Tea, apple cider, hot chocolate, snacks, sherry
Therapeutic spa, swimming pool, gardens

Secluded 1870 Greek revival farmhouse. Antiques, private entrances, fireplaces, Victorian rose gardens, winding paths, near plaza.
vgardeninn@aol.com http://www.victoriangardeninn.com

SONOMA VALLEY (REGION)

Above the Clouds
3250 Trinity Rd, *Glen Ellen* 95442
707-996-7371 800-736-7894
Claude & Betty Ganaye
Feb 12-Oct. 30

175-175-BB
3 rooms, 3 pb
Most CC, *Rated*
C-no/S-no/P-no/H-ltd
French

Full breakfast
Complimentary wine
Outdoor Jacuzzi, swimming pool

Overlooking the Valley of the Moon above Sonoma Valley at 2000 ft elevation on 25 acres. In the middle of the wine country between Sonoma and Napa Valley.
abovetheclouds@vom.com http://www.abovethecloudsbb.com

Glenelly Inn–Sonoma
5131 Warm Springs Rd, *Glen Ellen* 95442
707-996-6720
Kristi Jeppesen
All year

150-175-BB
8 rooms, 8 pb
Most CC
C-yes/S-ltd/P-no/H-no
Norwegian

Full breakfast
Coffee, tea, iced tea, lemonade, homemade cookies
Common Room, flagstone patio, in-ground spa

Traditional bed most with queen beds, some with daybeds. Full breakfast, in-ground spa, family friendly, & reasonably priced. glenelly@glenelly.com http://www.glenelly.com

---

Rio Inn Historic Wine Country
4444 Wood Rd, *Guerneville* 95446
707-869-4444 Fax: 707-869-4443
800-344-7018
Dawson Church
Season Inquire

99-149-BB
12 rooms, 12 pb
Visa, MC, AmEx, •
C-yes/S-no/P-yes/H-yes

Continental breakfast plus
Sitting room, library, Jacuzzis, swimming pool

Epitomizing the grace, history and charm of the Russian River Wine Road, the 1890s vintage Rio Inn is nestled in the redwoods just 12 miles from Highway 101.
reservations@rioinn.com http://www.rioinn.com

SONORA

Lavender Hill
683 S Barretta St 95370
209-532-9024 800-446-1333 e
Gail S. Golding
All year

85-105-BB
4 rooms, 4 pb
Most CC, *Rated*, •
C-ltd/S-ltd/P-no/H-no

Full Country Breakfast
Complimentary afternoon refreshments
Sitting rm, porch swing, phone, TV & videos available, patio, library.

Restored Victorian in historic Gold Country. Antique furnishings, lovely grounds, wrap around porch and swing. Walk to town. Near Yosemite. Wine tasting, antiquing, outdoor recreation. lavender@sonnet.com http://www.lavenderhill.com

SOUTH LAKE TAHOE

Inn at Heavenly
PO Box 3066, Stateline, NV 89449
1261 Ski Run Blvd 96150
530-544-4244 Fax: 530-544-5213
800-MY-CABIN
Paul Gardner All year

89-195-BB
14 rooms, 14 pb
Most CC, •
C-ltd/S-no/P-yes/H-no
Spanish

Continental plus breakfast
Snacks, complimentary wine
Bikes, Jacuzzis, fireplaces, CTV/VCR, steam bath, sauna, fax

Welcome to the Inn at Heavenly Country Bed & Breakfast, where we specialize in comfortable, relaxing accommodations, custom-designed river rock fireplaces and of down-home Tahoe hospitality! mycabin@sierra.net http://www.innatheavenly.com

ST HELENA

Shady Oaks Country Inn
399 Zinfandel Ln 94574
707-963-1190 Fax: 707-963-9367
John & Lisa Wild-Runnells
All year

129-249-BB
5 rooms, 5 pb
Visa, MC, Disc, *Rated*, •
C-ltd/S-ltd/P-no/H-ltd

Full gourmet champagne breakfsts
Premium wines and cheeses are served each evening!
Fireplaces, Roman Pillared patio; innkeepers knowledgeable concierges

Romantic/secluded on 2 acres among finest wineries of Napa Valley. Elegant ambience, country comforts, antiques fireplaces, port and fine linens in guestrooms, "warm and gracious hospitality!" shdyoaks@napanet.net http://www.shadyoaksinn.com

SUSANVILLE

Roseberry House
609 North St 96130
Cleon & Ivan Walker
All year

BB

Roseberry House Bed & Breakfast is located in Historic Uptown Susanville, California. Susanville is the county seat and largest community in Lassen County, California. avolonte@c-zone.net http://www.roseberryhouse.com/

SUTTER CREEK

Sutter Creek Inn
PO Box 385
75 Main St 95685
209-267-5606 Fax: 209-267-9287
Jane Way All year

85-185-BB
17 rooms, 17 pb
Most CC, *Rated*, •
C-ltd/S-ltd/P-no/H-no

Full breakfast
Complimentary refreshments
Sitt. rm., library, A/C, fishing, gardens, massage

The inn has been opened and serving thousands of guests for over 35 years. Spacious grounds, patios, fireplaces, Jane Way's famous swinging beds. Eclectic style. Enjoy a related hospitality. info@suttercreekinn.com http://www.suttercreekinn.com/

TAHOE CITY

Chaney House
PO Box 7852
4725 W Lake Blvd 96145
530-525-7333 Fax: 530-525-4413
Gary & Lori Chaney
All year

140-220-BB
4 rooms, 4 pb
Most CC, *Rated*
C-ltd/S-no/P-no/H-no

Full breakfast
Evening Refreshments
Sitting room, private beach and pier

Unique stone lakefront home. Gourmet breakfast on patios overlooking the lake in season. Private beach and pier. gary@chaneyhouse.com http://www.chaneyhouse.com

TAHOE CITY

Cottage Inn at Lake Tahoe, Inc.
PO Box 66
1690 W Lake Blvd 96145
530-581-4073 Fax: 530-581-0226
800-581-4073
Susanne Muhr All year

150-255-BB
15 rooms, 15 pb
Visa, MC, *Rated*, •
C-ltd/S-no/P-no/H-ltd
German

Full breakfast

The Cottage Inn, 2 miles south of Tahoe City, features original knotty pine paneling throughout, w/unique themes and charming Tahoe appeal.
cottage@itol.com http://www.thecottageinn.com

TAHOE VISTA

Shore House at Lake Tahoe
PO Box 499
7170 North Lake Blvd 96148
530-546-7270 Fax: 530-546-7130
800-207-5160
Marty & Barb Cohen All year

175-270-BB
9 rooms, 9 pb
Visa, MC, Disc, *Rated*, •
C-ltd/S-no/P-no/H-no

Full gourmet breakfast
Afternoon tea, snacks, wine
All rooms with gas fireplaces, sitting room, skiing, hiking, biking

Romantic lakefront hideaway, custom log beds, down comforters, feather beds. Gourmet breakfast in lakefront dining room or at lakefront lawns & gardens.
innkeeper@shorehouselaketahoe.com http://www.tahoeinn.com

TIBURON

Waters Edge Hotel
25 Main St 94920
415-789-5999 Fax: 415-789-5888
877-789-5999
All year

195-399-BB
23 rooms, 23 pb
Most CC, •
C-yes/S-no/P-no/H-yes
French

Continental breakfast
Complimentary wine
Fireplaces, cable TV
CD player, spa robes, A/C, common viewing deck

Waters Edge brings an added ambience of global sophistication to this unique part of Northern California. mgr@watersedgehotel.com http://www.watersedgehotel.com

TRINIDAD

The Lost Whale Inn
3452 Patrick's Point Dr 95570
707-677-3425 Fax: 707-677-0284
800-677-7859
All year

140-210-BB
9 rooms, 9 pb
Most CC, *Rated*, •
C-yes/S-no/P-no/H-ltd

Full gourmet breakfast
Afternoon tea, snacks
Farmhouse available, sitting room, hot tubs, full playground, garden

The only B&B in CA with a private beach. Spectacular ocean view, sea lions, greenhouse, gardens, decks, Jacuzzi, and huge breakfast. Newly remodeled. Rebuilt farmhouse on 5 acres. lmiller@lostwhaleinn.com http://www.lostwhaleinn.com

TRUCKEE

Richardson House Inn
PO Box 2011
10154 High St 96160
530-587-5388 Fax: 530-587-0927
888-229-0365
Patty Zwers All year

100-175-BB
8 rooms, 8 pb
Most CC, *Rated*, •
C-ltd/S-no/P-no/H-yes

Full breakfast
24 hr refreshment, afternoon cookies
Parlor w/TV, VCR, CD player, player piano, feather beds

Overlooking historic Truckee, and just minutes to Lake Tahoe and surrounding Sierra, this restored Victorian offers all of the casual elegance that you would expect in a mountain retreat. innkeeper@richardsonhouse.com http://www.richardsonhouse.com

TWAIN HARTE

McCaffrey House
PO Box 67
23251 Highway 108 95383
209-586-0757 Fax: 209-586-3689
888-586-0757
M & S McCaffrey All year

125-175-BB
8 rooms, 8 pb
Visa, MC, AmEx, *Rated*, •
C-yes/S-no/P-no/H-no

Full breakfast
Complimentary wine & sparkling cider
Sitting room, library, outdoor hot tub and sun deck

Pure Elegance in a Wilderness Setting. Dedicated to creating a memorable experience of comfort blended with fresh adventure, culinary excellence, and a socially and invigorating environment. innkeeper@mccaffreyhouse.com http://www.mccaffreyhouse.com

TWENTY NINE PALMS

Homestead Inn, B&B & Spa
PO Box 609
74153 Two Mile Rd 92277
760-367-0030 Fax: 760-367-1108
877-367-0030
Jerry & Judy
Sep. 1-July 5

125-160-BB
7 rooms, 7 pb
Visa, MC, AmEx,
Rated, •
C-ltd/S-ltd/P-no/H-ltd

Full breakfast
Sack lunch, dinner w/reservation, snacks
Bar service, sitting room, library, Jacuzzis, fireplaces, cable TV

Wonderful cactus gardens surround this 1928 home, adjacent to Joshua Tree National Park; wildlife friendly. homestead@obtel.com http://www.joshuatreelodging.com

UKIAH

Vichy Hot Springs Resort
2605 Vichy Springs Rd 95482
707-462-9515 Fax: 707-462-9516
Gilbert & Marjorie Ashoff
All year

150-255-BB
27 rooms, 27 pb
Most CC, *Rated*, •
C-yes/S-ltd/P-no/H-yes
Spanish

Full breakfast
Warm carbonated mineral baths, hot pool, olympic size pool, massage

An historic hot springs country inn—quiet, elegant & charming. The warm and carbonated "Vichy" mineral baths are unique in North America.
vichy@vichysprings.com http://www.vichysprings.com

VALLEY SPRINGS

The 10th Green Inn
14 St Andrews Rd 95252
209-772-1084 Fax: 209-772-0267
888-727-8705
Jean & James Fox All year

69-99-BB
10 rooms, 10 pb
Most CC
C-ltd/S-ltd/P-no/H-yes

Continental plus breakfast
Fireplaces, located on golf course, next to club house

Beautiful English Tudor country inn nestled among majestic oak trees in heart of La Contenta, one of California's finest golf courses.
greeninn@goldrush.com http://www.10thgreeninn.com

VENTURA

La Mer
411 Poli St 93001
805-643-3600 Fax: 805-653-7329
Anthony Rhine & Dennis Lake
All year

90-185-BB
5 rooms, 5 pb
Most CC, *Rated*, •
C-ltd/S-ltd/P-ltd/H-no

Full Bavarian breakfast
Compl. wine or champagne.
Picnics, DVDs, bikes, we can arrange tours, massages, carriage rides.

La Mer Bed & Breakfast is a charming European-style guesthouse with all the modern amenities that the celebrities enjoy on their getaways.
Innkeeper@lamerbnb.com http://www.lamerbnb.com

VOLCANO

St. George Hotel
PO Box 9
16104 Main St 95689
209-296-4458 Fax: 209-296-4457
Mark & Tracey Berkner
Mid Jan–Dec

83-105-BB
20 rooms, 6 pb
Visa, MC, *Rated*
C-ltd/S-no/P-ltd/H-ltd

Continental breakfast
Bar, brunch & dinner available
Sitting room, pianos, porches & deck, fishing, conferences, walking tours

Elegant Mother Lode hotel built in 1862. Maintains a timeless quality. On National Registry of Historic Places. Back-to-1862 porches and balusters. Horseshoes, croquet, volleyball available. stgeorge@stgeorgehotel.com http://www.stgeorgehotel.com

WESTPORT

Howard Creek Ranch
PO Box 121
40501 N Hwy 1 95488
707-964-6725 Fax: 707-964-1603
Charles & Sally Grigg
All year

75-160-BB
14 rooms, 8 pb
Visa, MC, AmEx,
Rated, •
C-ltd/S-ltd/P-ltd/H-ltd
German, Italian, Dutch

Full ranch breakfast
Complimentary tea
Piano, hot tub, cabins, sauna, massage by res., heated swimming pool

Historic farmhouse filled with collectibles, antiques & memorabilia, unique health spa with privacy and dramatic views adjoining a wide beach.
howardcreekranch@mcn.org http://www.howardcreekranch.com

YOSEMITE NATIONAL PARK (REGION)

The Homestead 41110 Road 600, *Ahwahnee* 93601 559-683-0495 Fax: 559-683-8165 800-483-0495 Cindy Brooks & Larry Ends All year	135-225-BB 5 rooms, 5 pb Visa, MC, AmEx, *Rated*, • C-ltd/S-no/P-no/H-ltd Spanish	Continental breakfast Barbecue available Equine layover avail., near golf, antique shops, and Miwok village site

Romantic, private cottages with kitchens on 160 wooded acres close to Yosemite, Gold Country, golf and restaurants. Equine layover available.
homesteadcottages@sti.net http://www.homesteadcottages.com/

1859 Historic National Hotel PO Box 502 18183 Main St, *Jamestown* 95327 209-984-3446 Fax: 209-984-5620 800-894-3446 Stephen Willey All year	90-130-BB 9 rooms, 9 pb Most CC, *Rated*, • C-ltd/S-ltd/P-yes/H-no Spanish, French	Continental plus breakfast Full restaurant, espresso & historic saloon Sitting room, library, live entertainment, courtyard dining

Hotel c.1859 in heart of Gold Rush area. Rooms restored to casual elegance of a simpler/romantic era. Near Yosemite. Highly-acclaimed restaurant on premises. Lots of shopping, live theatre. info@national-hotel.com http://www.national-hotel.com

The Groveland Hotel PO Box 289 18767 Main St, *Groveland* 95321 209-962-4000 Fax: 209-962-6674 800-273-3314 Peggy A. Mosley All year	135-210-BB 17 rooms, 17 pb Visa, MC, AmEx, *Rated*, • C-yes/S-ltd/P-yes/H-yes French	Continental plus breakfast Dinner served nightly Conf. fac., comp. wine, bar service, sitting rm., lib., hot tubs, 3 suites

Beautiful, restored historic Gold Rush hotel. Gourmet dining in Victorian garden. Near Yosemite. Fly fishing and wilderness survival schools.
peggy@groveland.com http://www.groveland.com

Yosemite Boulder Creek 4572 Ben Hur Rd, *Mariposa* 95338 209-742-7729 Fax: 209-742-5885 800-768-4752 Michael & Nancy Haberman	99-BB 3 rooms, 3 pb Visa, MC, *Rated*, • C-ltd/S-ltd/P-no/H-no German All year	Full American Breakfast Afternoon tea, complimentary wine, beer etc. Hot tub under romantic gazebo

Chalet Style home in the Sierra foothills, open since 1988. Three acres frequently visited by deer and many hummingbirds. Full breakfast by German Gourmet Chef.
bcreekbb@yosemite.net http://mariposa.yosemite.net/bcreek/

Hounds Tooth Inn 42071 Hwy 41, *Oakhurst* 93644 559-642-6600 Fax: 559-658-2946 888-642-6610 B&A Williams, R&L Kiehlmeier All year	95-225-BB 13 rooms, 13 pb Most CC, *Rated*, • C-ltd/S-no/P-no/H-yes	Full breakfast Afternoon tea, snacks Library, Jacuzzis, suites, fireplaces, cable TV, sitting room

12 room Victorian style inn located 12 miles from Yosemite's Southern entrance in Oakhurst, 6 miles from Bass Lake. robray@sierratel.com http://www.houndstoothinn.com

Colorado

ALAMOSA

Cottonwood Inn & Gallery
123 San Juan 81101
719-589-3882 Fax: 719-589-6437
800-955-2623
Kevin & Deb Donaldson
All year

57-125-BB
10 rooms, 10 pb
Most CC, *Rated*, •
C-yes/S-ltd/P-ltd/H-no
Spanish

Full gourmet breakfast
Afternoon cookies & refreshments, catering avail.
Library, carriage house, Neutrogena soaps/creams, turn-down service

Lovely inn, rated as one of the best in Colorado, centrally located for exploring Southern Colorado and Northern New Mexico.

relax@cottonwoodinn.com http://www.cottonwoodinn.com

ANTONITO

Conejos River Guest Ranch
PO Box 175
25390 Hwy 17 81129
719-376-2464
Ms. Shorty Fry
May–Nov.

85-130-BB
8 rooms, 8 pb
Visa, MC, Disc, •
C-yes/S-ltd/P-yes/H-yes
Spanish

Full breakfast
Snacks, restaurant
Bar service, sitting room, library, bikes, fishing, suites, TV

The traveler's choice in south central Colorado; twelve park-like acres with mile of river frontage; fabulous food; hospitality extraordinaire.

info@conejosranch.com http://www.conejosranch.com

ASPEN

Hearthstone House
134 E. Hyman St 81611
970-925-7632 Fax: 970-920-4450
888-925-7632
Tracy Lofgren, Mark O'Brien, Tom Brinkmeyer
All year

95-310-BB
16 rooms, 16 pb
Most CC, *Rated*, •
C-yes/S-no/P-no/H-ltd

Continental plus breakfast
Wine, Cheese & Hors d'oeuvres
Sitting Room, Fireplace, Jacuzzi, Pool, Steam Room, Tennis, Cable TV

A uniquely romantic rendezvous in the heart of Aspen, Colorado, the Hearthstone House is the intimate and intensely personal resort you have been seeking.

hearthstone@aspeninfo.com http://www.hearthstonehouse.com

Hotel Lenado
200 S Aspen St 81611
970-925-6246
Fax: 970-925-3840
800-321-3457
Michelle Weaver
Late Nov–Apr & May–Oct

115-485-BB
19 rooms, 19 pb
Most CC, *Rated*, •
C-yes/S-ltd/P-no/H-no

Full breakfast
Appetizers, bar
Hot tub, library, screening room, meeting facilities

A new Aspen landmark–inventive architecture, romantic ambience, gracious service. Nineteen guest rooms furnished in applewood, ironwood, willow.

hotlsard@rof.net http://www.hotellenado.com

Innsbruck Inn
233 W Main St 81611
970-925-2980
Fax: 970-925-6960
Marie Marx
6/1–10/15, 11/23–4/15

80-169-BB
30 rooms, 30 pb
Most CC, *Rated*, •
C-yes/S-yes/P-no/H-no
German

Continental plus breakfast
Afternoon tea in the winter
Sitting room, hot tub, sauna

Warm hospitality and charm welcome you to this European style Inn. Offering a wonderful lobby, outdoor heated pool and Jacuzzi.

innsbruk@rof.net http://www.preferredlodging.com

ASPEN

Sardy House
128 E Main St 81611
970-920-2525 Fax: 970-920-4478
800-321-3457
Bob Bayless
Jun–Oct, Thksg–mid-Apr

125-850-BB
21 rooms, 21 pb
Most CC, *Rated*, •
C-yes/S-ltd/P-no/H-no

Full breakfast
Restaurant dinner (fee)
Bar, sitting room, library, hot tub, sauna, swimming pool

Beautifully restored 1892 Victorian with all the amenities of a small luxury hotel, on perfectly landscaped grounds in the heart of Aspen.
sardy@rof.net http://www.sardyhouse.com

Snow Queen Victorian
124 E Cooper St 81611
970-925-8455 Fax: 970-925-7391
Norma Dolle & David Ledingham
All year

89-239-BB
7 rooms, 7 pb
Visa, MC, *Rated*, •
C-yes/S-no/P-no/H-no
Spanish

Continental plus breakfast
Apres ski parties in winter
Parlor w/Fireplace, Hot Tub w/view of Aspen mtn., Rooms w/Kitchens & Decks

Historic 1886 Victorian B&B. Friendly, family run, affordable & just 2 blocks from downtown & Ski Lifts. Victorian rooms all have private baths, TV, phone & share Outdoor Hot Tub w/ view of Aspen Mt. sqlodge@rof.net http://www.snowqueenlodge.com

BOULDER

Alps Boulder Canyon Inn
38619 Boulder Canyon Rd 80302
303-444-5445 Fax: 303-444-5522
800-414-2577
Jeannine & John Vanderhart
All year

139-250-BB
12 rooms, 12 pb
Most CC, *Rated*, •
C-ltd/S-ltd/P-no/H-no
Spanish

Full breakfast
Afternoon tea, snacks
Lunch available, library, Jacuzzis, fireplaces

Historic luxury country inn in scenic Boulder Canyon. Amenities include Jacuzzi tubs, fireplaces and antiques. Winner of many awards.
info@alpsinn.com http://www.alpsinn.com

Briar Rose
2151 Arapahoe Ave 80302
303-442-3007 Fax: 303-786-8440
Bob & Margaret Weisenbach
All year

134-164-BB
9 rooms, 9 pb
Most CC, *Rated*, •
C-ltd/S-no/P-no/H-no
Spanish

Continental plus breakfast
Afternoon tea, cookies, sherry & lemonade
Bicycles, A/C, renovated, AAA rated 3 diamonds

Entering the Briar Rose is like entering another time, when hospitality was an art & the place for dreams was a feather bed. Three rooms with fireplaces.
brbbx@aol.com http://www.briarrosebb.com

Inn on Mapleton Hill
1001 Spruce St 80302
303-449-6528 Fax: 303-415-0470
800-276-6528
Ray & Judi Schultze
All year

88-167-BB
7 rooms, 5 pb
Visa, MC, AmEx, *Rated*, •
C-ltd/S-no/P-no/H-no

Full breakfast
Afternoon tea, snacks
Sitting room, library, fireplaces, A/C, phones

Basil the hound welcomes you to this 1899 inn, ideally set a block from the festive Pearl Street. Bountiful breakfast by resident owners.
maphillinn@aol.com http://www.innonmapletonhill.com

BRECKENRIDGE

Allaire Timbers Inn
PO Box 4653
9511 Hwy 9 80424
970-453-7530 Fax: 970-453-8699
800-624-4904
Jack & Kathy Gumph
All year

150-400-BB
10 rooms, 10 pb
Most CC, *Rated*, •
C-ltd/S-no/P-no/H-yes

Full breakfast
Snacks, complimentary wine
Great Room with fireplace, outdoor hot tub, sunroom, reading loft

Contemporary log lodge offering 1st class amenities in intimate setting. Rooms/suites offer TV, phone, priv. deck, robes, ceiling fans, king bed.
info@allairetimbers.com http://www.allairetimbers.com

Hunt Placer Inn, Breckenridge, CO

BRECKENRIDGE

B&B's on North Main St.
PO Box 2454
303 N Main St 80424
970-453-2975 Fax: 970-453-5258
800-795-2975
Fred Kinat & Diane Jaynes
All year

89-289-BB
11 rooms, 11 pb
Most CC, *Rated*, •
C-ltd/S-no/P-no/H-no

Full breakfast
Afternoon tea, snacks
Sitting room, Jacuzzis, fireplaces, cable TV, accommodate business travelers

On-river property is the 1885 Williams House, providing Victorian splendor, a private 1880 cottage inspiring romance, and a timber-frame country-style 1997 barn.
bnb@colorado.net http://www.breckenridge-inn.com

Evans House
PO Box 387
102 S French St 80424
970-453-5509
Pete and Georgette Contos
All year

68-150-BB
6 rooms, 6 pb
Most CC, *Rated*, •
C-yes/S-no/P-no/H-ltd
Greek, French

Full breakfast
Afternoon tea
Sitting room, library, meeting room, hot tub, TVs/phones in all rooms

Beautifully restored 1886 Victorian in heart of Breckenridge, all activities nearby. Known for our hospitality, service, and delicious breakfasts.
evans15@mindspring.com http://www.coloradoevanshouse.com

Fireside Inn
PO Box 2252
114 N French St 80424
970-453-6456 Fax: 970-453-9577
Niki & Andy Harris
All year

65-155-BB
9 rooms, 5 pb
Visa, MC
C-yes/S-no/P-no

Continental breakfast
Singles, couples and families welcome; suites, rooms and dorm-style

Conveniently located 2 blocks from Main St in the national historic district in Breckenridge, the Fireside Inn is a 10 minute walk or a free, short ride on the shuttle bus to Breckenridge Ski Area. info@firesideinn.com http://www.firesideinn.com

---

Hunt Placer Inn
PO Box 4898
275 Ski Hill Rd 80424
970-453-7573 Fax: 970-453-2335
800-472-1430
Trip & Kelly Butler All year

135-199-BB
8 rooms, 8 pb
Most CC, *Rated*, •
C-ltd/S-no/P-no/H-yes

Full breakfast
Afternoon tea
Sitting room, fireplaces, hot tub, game room, video library, hair dryers

Elegant Bavarian-style chalet surrounded by Aspen, Evergreens & beautiful wild flowers. Ideally located between the Breckenridge Ski Resort and historic Main Street.
info@huntplacerinn.com http://www.huntplacerinn.com

BRECKENRIDGE

Little Mountain Lodge
PO Box 2479
98 Sunbeam Dr 80424
970-453-1969 Fax: 970-453-1919
800-468-7707
Linda Buchanan All year

140-270-BB
10 rooms, 10 pb
Most CC, *Rated*, •
C-ltd/S-no/P-no/H-yes

Full breakfast
Afternoon refreshments
Sitting room, library, suites, fireplaces, cable TV, accom. bus. travelers

Luxury custom log lodge. 10 unique rooms with private decks and baths.
lml@colorado.net http://www.littlemountainlodge.com

Ridge Street Inn
PO Box 2854
212 N Ridge St 80424
970-453-4680 Fax: 970-547-1477
970-452-4680
Jane & Peter Shafroth
All year

70-175-BB
5 rooms, 3 pb
Visa, MC, *Rated*
C-yes/S-no/P-no/H-ltd
German, Spanish, French

Full breakfast
Tea, coffee, hot chocolate, afternoon snacks
Sitting room with gas fireplace, TVs with cable and HBO, lap top hook up

A charming 1890 Victorian Inn located in the heart of the Breckenridge Historic District. Easy access to ski slopes, bike path, hiking, etc. Your home away from home in Colorado's Rocky Mountains. ridge@colorado.net http://www.colorado.net/ridge

BUENA VISTA

Liar's Lodge
30000 CR 371 81211
719-395-3444 Fax: 719-395-4838
888-542-7756
Connie & Carl Bauer
All year

75-135-BB
5 rooms, 5 pb
Visa, MC, •
C-ltd/S-ltd/P-ltd/H-ltd
French, Spanish

Full breakfast
Snacks, complimentary wine
Sitting room, library, Jacuzzis, suites, fireplaces, cable TV

Modern log lodge right on the banks of the Arkansas River. Secluded on 23 acres, yet only a mile from town. Over 1/3 mile of virtually exclusive river frontage.
mail@liarslodge.com http://www.liarslodge.com

Sawatch Vistas
27627 Rancho Sawatch 81211
719-395-9199 866-395-9199
Dan & Nancy Bruce
All year

BB

Sawatch Vistas in historic, scenic Buena Vista, Colorado was built as a "bed and breakfast Rocky Mountains getaway."
sawatchvistas@amigo.net http://www.sawatchbedandbreakfast.com

CARBONDALE

Mt. Sopris Inn
PO Box 126
0165 Mt Sopris Ranch Road 81623
970-963-2209 Fax: 970-963-8975
800-437-8675
M. Thompson & D. Petechuk
All year

100-200-BB
13 rooms, 13 pb
Visa, MC, *Rated*, •
S-no/P-no/H-yes

Full breakfast
Sitting room, library, hot tubs, swimming pool, adults only, fireplaces, A/C

Treat yourself to the valley's best. If you value beauty, serenity and wish to renew yourselves, Mt. Sopris Inn is for you! mt.soprisinn@juno.com http://www.mtsoprisinn.com

CHIPITA PARK

Chipita Lodge Inn
9090 Chipita Park Rd 80809
719-684-8454 Fax: 719-684-8234
877-CHIPITA
Kevin & Martha Henry
All year

98-126-BB
3 rooms, 3 pb
Most CC, *Rated*, •
C-ltd/S-no/P-ltd/H-no

Full breakfast
Afternoon tea, snacks, complimentary wine
Sitting room, fireplaces, accommodate business travelers

Historic Log and Native Stone Lodge in the shadow of Pikes Peak, mountain and lake views, bountiful breakfast, fireplace, and hot tub.
chipitainn@aol.com http://www.chipitalodge.com

COLORADO SPRINGS

Black Forest
11170 Black Forest Rd 80908
719-495-4208 Fax: 719-495-0688
800-809-9901
Robert & Susan Putnam
All year

75-250-BB
5 rooms, 5 pb
Most CC, *Rated*, •
C-yes/S-no/P-no/H-yes
Survival Spanish

Continental plus breakfast
Snacks
Sitting room, library, weddings, retreats

Rustic Romantic Retreat in a massive log home on 20 acres of pines.
blackforestbb@msn.com http://www.blackforestbb.com

Chalice House
1116 N Wahsatch Avenue
80903
719-475-7505
888-475-7505
Laney & Joshua Duke

68-148-BB
3 rooms
All year

The Georgian Colonial takes its name and symbol from the Chalice Well–Glastonbury, England. Like that magical place, Chalice House, a bed & breakfast is a place of rest and renewal, serenity & well-being. inn@chalicehouse.com http://www.chalicehouse.com

---

Cheyenne Canon Inn
2030 W Cheyenne Blvd 80906
719-633-0625 Fax: 719-633-8826
800-633-0625
Keith & Alicia Hampton
All year

95-200-BB
10 rooms, 10 pb
Most CC, *Rated*, •
C-yes/S-ltd/P-no/H-no

Full buffet breakfast
Wines & appetizers, fresh baked cookies
Massage therapy services, hot tub, fireplaces, in-room modem hookup

An Invitation to Elegance . . . Welcome to Colorado's finest historic bed & breakfast. Beautiful views & access to hiking, biking, & driving tours. Mobil Four Stars.
info@cheyennecanoninn.com http://www.cheyennecanoninn.com

Crescent Lily Inn
6 Boulder Crescent St 80903
719-442-2331 Fax: 719-442-6947
800-869-2721
Mark Medicus, Lin Moeller
All year

95-140-BB
5 rooms, 5 pb
Visa, MC, AmEx, *Rated*, •
C-ltd/S-no/P-no/H-ltd

Full breakfast
Complimentary wine, snacks
Sitting room, suites, cable, fireplaces, jetted tubs, conference room

This 100-year-old inn has beveled glass windows, interior woodwork and a vanbriggle fireplace. info@crescentlilyinn.com http://www.crescentlilyinn.com

---

Holden House 1902
1102 W Pikes Peak Ave 80904
719-471-3980 Fax: 719-471-4740
888-565-3980
Sallie & Welling Clark
All year

130-145-BB
5 rooms, 5 pb
Most CC, *Rated*, •
S-no/P-no/H-yes

Full gourmet breakfast
Complimentary coffee, tea, snack
Parlor with TV, living room, suite with disabled access, veranda

Charming 1902 storybook Victorian home filled with antiques & family heirlooms near Historic District. Suites with fireplaces & phones.
mail@holdenhouse.com http://www.holdenhouse.com

Old Town Guest House
115 S 26th St 80904
719-632-9194 Fax: 719-632-9026
888-375-4210
Kaye & David Caster
All year

99-205-BB
8 rooms, 8 pb
Most CC, *Rated*, •
C-ltd/S-no/P-no/H-yes

Full breakfast
Afternoon wine & hors d'oeuvres
Sitting room, library, bicycles, hot tubs, adult environment, voice/dataport

Experience historic Old Town in urban luxury. Upscale amenities for adult leisure and business guests. Private conference facility.
luxury@oldtown-guesthouse.com http://www.oldtown-guesthouse.com

COLORADO SPRINGS

Room at the Inn
618 N Nevada Ave 80903
719-442-1896 Fax: 719-442-6802
800-579-4621
Dorian & Linda Ciolek
All year

99-160-BB
8 rooms, 8 pb
Most CC, *Rated*, •
C-ltd/S-no/P-no/H-yes

Full breakfast
Afternoon tea, snacks
Library, fireplaces, outdoor hot tub, phones, A/C, Jacuzzi tubs for 2

Experience the charm, elegance and hospitality of an 1896 Victorian home. A romantic retreat in the heart of the city. roomatinn@pcisys.net http://www.roomattheinn.com

COLORADO SPRINGS (REGION)

Rocky Mountain Lodge & Cabins
4680 Hagerman Rd, *Cascade* 80809
719-684-2521 Fax: 719-684-8348
888-298-0348
Brian & Debbie Reynolds

95-130-BB
5 rooms, 5 pb
Most CC, *Rated*
C-yes/S-no/P-no/H-ltd
All year

Full breakfast
Afternoon tea, snacks, evening dessert
Sitting room, hot tub, fireplace, cable TV/VCRs, modems, BBQ, gazebo, patio

Luxurious, rustic Colorado log lodge and cabins. Nestled in the Rocky Mountains, only minutes from all Pikes Peak attractions. A perfect spot for family reunions and vacations.
rockymountaincabins@msn.com http://www.rockymountainlodge.com

---

Outlook Lodge
PO Box 586
6975 Howard St, *Green Mountain Falls* 80819
719-684-2303 877-684-7800
Diane & Pat Drayton
All year

85-100-BB
5 rooms, 5 pb
Most CC, *Rated*, •
C-yes/S-no/P-no/H-ltd

Full gourmet breakfast
Piano, sitting room, fishing, tennis, hiking, horseback ride, library

1889 Victorian lodge set in an alpine village at 7800 feet of clear Colorado altitude. Great hiking out the back door. goofy7@worldnet.att.net http://www.outlooklodge.com

---

Blue Skies Inn
402 Manitou Ave, *Manitou Springs* 80829
719-685-3899 Fax: 719-685-3099
800-398-7949
Sally Thurston All year

135-235-BB
10 rooms, 10 pb
Most CC, *Rated*, •
C-yes/S-no/P-no/H-yes

Full breakfast
Chocolate-dipped strawberries & other treats
Sitting room, suites, fireplaces, cable TV, Jacuzzi

Hand-painted interiors, spacious private tiled baths and sitting rooms, Victorian architecture. Wooded setting, courtyard garden, gazebo, hot tub. Air conditioning, fireplaces, whirlpools, TV/VCR. sally@blueskiesbb.com http://www.blueskiesbb.com

---

Rockledge Country Inn
328 El Paso Blvd, *Manitou Springs* 80829
719-685-4515 Fax: 719-685-1031
888-685-4515
Hartman & Nancy Smith
All year

170-295-BB
4 rooms, 4 pb
Most CC, *Rated*, •
C-ltd/S-no/P-no/H-no

Full gourmet breakfast
Cocktails, hors d'oeuvres
Sitting room, library, swimming pool available

An elegant Bed & Breakfast on a 3½ acre wooded estate. Offerings include 2 room suites, gourmet breakfast, feather beds, and spectacular views.
rockinn@webcom.com http://www.rockledgeinn.com

CORTEZ

Kelly Place
14663 Road G 81321
970-565-3125 Fax: 970-565-3540
800-745-4885
Kristie & Rodney Carriker
All year

75-135-BB
10 rooms, 10 pb
Visa, MC, Disc, •
C-yes/S-ltd/P-no/H-ltd

Full breakfast
Lunch, dinner, afternoon tea, snacks
Sitting room, library, Jacuzzis, fireplaces, accom. bus. travelers

Archaeological preserve with adobe-style lodging near Mesa Verde National Park. Lodge rooms or cabins, courtyards, many Puebloan ruins onsite.
kellypl@fone.net http://www.kellyplace.com

CRESTED BUTTE

Cristiana Guesthaus
PO Box 427
621 Maroon Ave 81224
970-349-5326 Fax: 970-349-1962
800-824-7899
R & M Catmur All year

57-95-BB
21 rooms, 21 pb
Most CC, *Rated*, •
C-yes/S-no/P-no/H-no

Continental plus breakfast
Complimentary hot beverages
Sitting room, hot tub, sauna

Close to historic downtown. Relaxed, friendly atmosphere. Enjoy the hot tub, sauna, sun deck, and home-baked breakfast served in our cozy lobby.
cristian@rmi.net http://www.visitcrestedbutte.com/cristiana

Elk Mountain Lodge
PO Box 148
129 Gothic Ave 81224
970-349-7533 Fax: 970-349-5114
800-374-6521
Lee Tauck & Mike Nolan
Winter & Summer

75-133-BB
19 rooms, 19 pb
Most CC, *Rated*, •
C-ltd/S-no/P-no/H-no
Little Spanish

Continental plus breakfast
Afternoon tea, snacks, bar
Sitting room, library, Jacuzzis, suites, cable TV, conference facilities

Crested Butte's historic Inn. Turn of the century miners hotel beautifully renovated. Located in town, walking distance to everything.
info@elkmountainlodge.net http://www.elkmountainlodge.net

The Great Escape
PO Box 3305
329 Whiterock Ave 81224
970-349-1131 877-349-1131
Nita Kubricht All year

75-155-BB
4 rooms, 3 pb

As if majestic mountain views and pure, exhilarating air were not enough-there's The Great Escape! Our bed and breakfast is one of the best places in Crested Butte.
info@thegreatescapebnb.com http://www.thegreatescapebnb.com

DENVER

Adagio
1430 Race St 80206
303-370-6911 Fax: 303-377-5968
800-533-3241
Jim & Amy Cremmins All year

95-175-BB
6 rooms, 6 pb
Most CC, *Rated*, •
C-yes/S-no/P-no/H-no

Full breakfast
Afternoon tea, snacks
Sitting room, library, hot tubs, family friendly facility, suites, fireplace

Beautiful Victorian mansion on Capitol Hill. Close to downtown, shopping, museums, parks, fabulous dining. Delicious European style breakfast served daily.
Adagio@adagiobb.com http://www.adagiobb.com

Capitol Hill Mansion
1207 Pennsylvania St 80203
303-839-5221 Fax: 303-839-9046
800-839-9329
James R. Hadley & Carl S. Schmidt, II All year

85-175-BB
8 rooms, 8 pb
Most CC, *Rated*, •
C-yes/S-ltd/P-no/H-yes
Spanish

Full breakfast
Complimentary wine/snack, refrig.
Sitting room, hot tub, A/C, cable TV, phones, heirlooms, original art

Walk to convention center, museums & restaurants from this nationally listed 1891 ruby sandstone mansion. Features high turrets, balconies and soaring chimneys.
info@capitolhillmansion.com http://www.capitolhillmansion.com/

Castle Marne
1572 Race St 80206
303-331-0621 Fax: 303-331-0623
800-92-MARNE
The Peiker Family
All year

105-255-BB
9 rooms, 9 pb
Visa, MC, AmEx, *Rated*, •
C-ltd/S-no/P-no/H-no
Spanish, Hungarian

Full gourmet breakfast
Afternoon tea 4:30-6:00
Library, gift shop, game room with pool table, computer, Fax, copier

Luxury urban inn. Minutes from convention center, business district, shopping, fine dining. Nat'l Historic Structure. 3 rooms with private balconies, hot tubs for 2.
info@castlemarne.com http://www.castlemarne.com

Castle Marne, Denver, CO

DENVER

Holiday Chalet Victorian 1820 E Colfax Ave 80218 303-321-9975 Fax: 303-377-6556 800-626-4497 Margot & Lawson Crowe All year	94-160-BB 10 rooms, 10 pb Most CC, *Rated*, • C-yes/S-no/P-ltd/H-no Spanish, French, German	Full breakfast Library, fireplaces, beautiful courtyard, accommodates business travelers

We have offered warmth and comfort to travelers for over 47 years. Our luxury B&B is ideal for business travelers, vacationers and romantics.
holidaychalet@aol.com http://www.bbonline.com/co/holiday

Merritt House Inn 941 E 17th Ave 80218 303-861-5230 Fax: 303-861-9009 877-861-5230 Cathy Kuykendall All year	110-170-BB 10 rooms, 10 pb Most CC, *Rated*, • C-ltd/S-no/P-no/H-no	Full breakfast Lunch & dinner available Bar service, sitt. room, Jacuzzis, suites, cable, TV, conference facility

1889 Victorian Inn located in the heart of Denver. Extensive breakfast menu, cater to business and leisure traveler. info@merritthouse.com http://www.merritthouse.com

Queen Anne 2147 Tremont Pl 80205 303-296-6666 Fax: 303-296-2151 800-432-4667 The King Family All year	75-175-BB 14 rooms, 14 pb Most CC, *Rated*, • C-ltd/S-no/P-no/H-ltd	Full breakfast Afternoon wine Fresh flowers, phone, A/C, 7 rooms with special tubs, flower garden, patio

Award winning Victorian Inn. Facing downtown park. Walk to mall, shops, museums, convention center/business district.
travel@queenannebnb.com http://www.queenannebnb.com

DENVER (REGION)

Bears Inn 27425 Spruce Ln, *Evergreen* 80439 303-670-1205 Fax: 303-670-8542 800-863-1205 Darrell & Chris Jenkins All year	90-180-BB 11 rooms, 11 pb *Rated*, • S-no/P-no/H-no	Full breakfast Afternoon tea, snacks Sitting room, modem, fax, Use of executive office, Murder mystery weekend

Nestled in the pine trees at 8,000 feet. Great snow-cap mountain views, 11 rooms, private baths, TV, outdoor spa & firepit. Murder Mystery getaways in October through May.
innkeepers@bearsinn.com http://www.bearsinn.com

DENVER (REGION)

Alexander Jameson House 1704 Illinois St, *Golden* 80401 303-278-0200 Fax: 303-278-0200 888-880-4448 James & Carolyn Durgin All year	80-130-BB 4 rooms, 4 pb Visa, MC, AmEx, *Rated* C-ltd/S-ltd/P-no/H-ltd	Full breakfast Snacks, tea Sitting room, library, Jacuzzis, suites, fireplace, cable TV

Relax in a quiet comfort in the foothills of the Rockies. . .turn-of-the-century English country inn furnished in antiques. relax@jamesonhouse.com http://www.jamesonhouse.com

Blue Spruce PO Box 151210, *Lakewood* 80215 303-985-4012 Adella & Bob All year	55-65-BB 1 rooms, 1 pb C-no/S-no/P-no/H-no Czech	Full breakfast Lemonade, hot or ice tea, coffee Sitting room, hot tub, piano, TV, garden & patio, accom. bus. travel, A/C

Private, cozy guestroom in traditional suburban home. Squeaky clean. Tasteful decor. Scrumptious home cooking. Friendly hospitality. Patio swing beneath giant Blue Spruce overlooking flower garden. adellarobert@juno.com http://home.att.net./~adellarobert/

DOLORES

Lebanon Schoolhouse 24925 County Rd T 81323 970-882-4461 Ken & Laura Hahn All year	70-110-BB 5 rooms, 3 pb Most CC, • C-yes/S-no/P-ltd/H-no	Hearty gourmet fare Large patios, hot tub, TVs, massage available on site

Remodeled 1907 schoolhouse listed on the National Registry of Historic Places. Common areas feature high ceilings & huge windows. Turn-of-the-century antiques compliment the tasteful decor. VIEWS!!

info@lebanonschoolhouse.com http://www.lebanonschoolhouse.com

DURANGO

Elkstone Inn, Little House 34940 Hwy 550 North 81301 970-385-0488 Fax: 970-247-7890 888-753-3557 Debby & Greg Verheyden All year	89-130-BB 4 rooms, 4 pb Visa, MC, AmEx, *Rated*, • C-ltd/S-no/P-no/H-ltd	Full breakfast Tea, snacks, and dinner available Sitting room, library, fireplace, cable TV, spa, conference space

Located on the Animas River in the San Juan Mountains, the Elkstone boasts 1,700 square feet of redwood decks and award-winning desserts.

verheyden@frontier.net http://www.elkstoneinn.com

The Leland House/Rochester Hotel 721 E Second Ave 81301 970-385-1920 Fax: 970-385-1967 800-664-1920 Diane & Kirk Komick	109-320-BB 25 rooms, 25 pb Most CC, *Rated*, • C-ltd/S-no/P-ltd/H-yes Spanish All year	Full gourmet breakfast Afternoon tea, library Sitting room, conference space for 75, catering available

Historic downtown location-walk to unique shops, restaurants, Durango-Silverton RR Station. Cowboy Victorianna decor inspired by movies made in this area.

stay@rochesterhotel.com http://www.rochesterhotel.com

Lightner Creek Inn 999 CR 207 81301 970-259-1226 Fax: 970-259-9526 800-268-9804 Suzy & Stan Savage All year	75-205-BB 10 rooms, 10 pb Most CC, *Rated*, • C-yes/S-no/P-no/H-ltd Spanish, French, German	Full breakfast Afternoon tea, snacks Sitting room, cross-country skiing, hiking, mountain biking, Grand piano

Discover the romance of Lightner Creek Inn's country manor. Ten beautifully appointed guestrooms, some with whirlpool tubs & fireplaces.

lci@frontier.net http://www.lightnercreekinn.com

Elkstone Inn, Durango, CO

DURANGO (REGION)

Sundance Bear Lodge PO Box 1045 38890 Hwy 184, *Mancos* 81328 970-533-1504 Fax: 970-533-1507 866-529-2480 Susan & Bob Scott All year	80-160-BB 5 rooms, 3 pb Visa, MC, Disc, • C-yes/S-ltd/P-ltd/H-ltd	Full Breakfast Afternoon tea, soft drinks Snacks, sitting room, Jacuzzis, sauna, TV, office with computer

Enjoy Mesa Verde & mountain views from decks or hot tub. 80 plus acres to explore, plus Nat'l Forest nearby. Where the Old West still lives. Stay 1 day longer, it's worth it! Room for up to 20 guests. sue@sundancebear.com http://www.SundanceBear.com

Willowtail Springs PO Box 89, *Mancos* 81328 970-533-7592 Fax: 970-533-7641 800-698-0603 Peggy & Lee Cloy All year	145-185-EP 8 rooms, 5 pb Visa, MC, • C-yes/S-no/P-no/H-no	Coffee, tea, juices, bread, jam, granola, staples Comfort, kitchens, library, TV/VCR, gardens, antiques, fishing, boats

An enchanted 40 acres, log cabins, antiques, fireplaces and kitchens. Set amid gardens and streams, facing bass lake and mountains. Comfortable, romantic, creative atmosphere. Minutes to Mesa Verde. willowtl@fone.net http://www.willowtailsprings.com

ESTES PARK

Anniversary Inn 1060 Mary's Lake Rd 80517 970-586-6200 Walt & Trish Hebert All year	100-175-BB 4 rooms, 4 pb Most CC, *Rated* C-no/S-no/P-no/H-ltd	Full gourmet breakfast Homemade cookies, tea, sodas Great room with moss rock fireplace, library, 3 rooms with Jacuzzi tubs

Cozy, turn-of-the-20th-century log home one mile west of downtown Estes Park. Surrounded by Ponderosa pines and Spruce trees overlooking the Big Thompson River.
thebert@gte.net

The Baldpate Inn PO Box 4445 4900 S. Hwy 7 80517 970-586-6151 Lois, Jenny & MacKenzie Smith All year	95-150-BB 12 rooms, 5 pb Visa, MC, Disc S-no	Full gourmet breakfast 5-star restaurant

Located seven miles south of Estes Park, Colorado, Baldpate Inn is a classic mountain getaway offering lodging, a specialty restaurant, and spectacular views.
baldpatein@aol.com http://www.baldpateinn.com

ESTES PARK

Dripping Springs Inn
2551 Big Thompson Canyon
80517
970-586-3406 Fax: 970-586-3035
800-432-7145
Oliver & Janie Robertson
May–October

125-250-BB
13 rooms, 13 pb
Most CC, •
C-ltd/S-no/P-no/H-no
Spanish

Full breakfast
Breakfast is for B&B rooms, cabins have kitchens
Hot tubs, fireplaces, sauna, massage, weddings, Meditation Vision Quests

Let romance cast its spell on you in the serenity of this small country inn by the river. Cabins on the river have hot tubs, for families or couples, drop out of sight for a few days.
innestes@aol.com http://www.drippingsprings.com

Eagle Cliff House
PO Box 4312
2383 Hwy 66 80517
970-586-5425 Fax: 970-577-0132
800-414-0922
Nancy E. Conrin All year

95-150-BB
3 rooms, 3 pb
Visa, MC, *Rated*, •
C-yes/S-no/P-no/H-no
Spanish

Full breakfast
Complimentary wine, snacks
Hot tubs, golf, tennis, horseback riding, hiking, cross-country skiing, 2 fireplaces

Enjoy our cozy and quaint B&B and join us for one of our favorite hikes. Our backyard is the Rocky Mountain National Park!
eaglecliffhouse@hotmail.com http://www.eaglecliffhouse.com

Mountain Vista Acre
PO Box 3302
751 University Dr 80517
970-586-3547
Judy Speece April–October

90-100-BB
2 rooms, 2 pb
Visa, MC
C-yes/S-no/P-no/H-no

Full breakfast
Tea, coffee, hot chocolate
Sitting room with fireplace

The B&B is located on a ponderosa pine covered acre of land on Prospect Mountain. It offers spectacular views of Rocky Mountain National Park's Lumpy Ridge area. Very quiet and away from traffic. gmtnvista@aol.com

---

Quilt House
PO Box 339
310 Riverside Dr 80517
970-586-0427
Miriam & Hans Graetzer
All year

55-65-BB
4 rooms, 4 pb
Rated
C-ltd/S-no/P-no/H-ltd
German

Full breakfast
Sitting room, library, handmade quilts on each bed

Clean, comfortable rooms, hearty breakfast, free area maps, suggestions for hikes, scenic drives, restaurants, museums, shops, other activities. hgraetzer@aol.com

---

Taharaa Mountain Lodge, Inc.
PO Box 2586
3110 South St. Vrain 80517
970-577-0098 Fax: 970-577-0819
800-597-0098
Ken & Diane Harlan All year

130-279-BB
12 rooms, 12 pb
Visa, AmEx, Disc, Most CC, •
C-ltd/S-no/P-no/H-yes

Full gourmet breakfast
Happy hour of wine, beer & sodas daily
Great room, den, TV room, dining room, meeting room, dry sauna & hot tub

Taharaa Mountain Lodge is a luxury B&B offering unique accommodations of three suites & nine lodge rooms designed with the total comfort of our guests in mind.
info@taharaa.com http://www.taharaa.com/

EVERGREEN

Highland Haven Creekside Inn
4395 Independence Trail
80439
303-674-3577 Fax: 303-674-9088
800-459-2406
Gail Riley & Tom Statzell

95-270-BB
16 rooms, 16 pb
Most CC, *Rated*
C-yes/S-no/P-no/H-no
All year

Full breakfast
Afternoon tea, snacks
Sitting room, library, bicycles, tennis courts, hot tubs, sauna, pool

Mountain hideaway with exquisite views of mountains, streams, towering pines and gardens. Stroll to quaint shops and fine dining on Main Street Evergreen.
thehaven2@earthlink.net http://www.highlandhaven.com

FAIRPLAY

Hand Hotel
PO Box 1059
531 Front Street 80440
719-836-3595 Fax: 719-836-1799
Dale & Kathy Fitting All year

60-BB
11 rooms, 11 pb
Most CC, •
C-yes/S-no/P-yes/H-no

Continental plus breakfast
evening snacks
Evening tea & cookies,
Toiletries

Genuine western hospitality high in the heart of the Colorado Rocky Mountains. Each of our rooms is uniquely decorated. Our friendly staff will help you enjoy your stay at this comfortable old hotel. info@handhotel.com http://www.handhotel.com

FORT COLLINS

Elizabeth Street Guest House
202 E Elizabeth St 80524
970-493-2337 Fax: 970-493-6662
Sheryl & John Clark

70-90-BB
3 rooms, 1 pb
Rated
All year

Full breakfast

Only one block to Colorado State University.
sheryl.clark@juno.com http://www.bbonline.com/co/elizabeth

The Sheldon House
616 W Mulberry St 80521
970-221-1917 Fax: 970-490-2810
Jack & Maryann Blackerby
All year

110-150-BB
4 rooms, 4 pb
C-ltd/S-no/P-no

Beverages and snacks
Private phones, down comforters, bathrobes, central air conditioning

Welcome to the Sheldon House, a lovely Four Square Style home built just after the turn of the last century. sheldonhouse@aol.com http://www.bbonline.com/co/sheldonhouse

FORT COLLINS (REGION)

Porter House
530 Main St, *Windsor* 80550
970-686-5793 Fax: 970-686-7046
888-686-5793
Tom & Marni Schmittling
All year

95-155-BB
4 rooms, 4 pb
Visa, MC, AmEx, *Rated*, •
C-ltd/S-no/P-no/H-no

Full breakfast
Lunch/dinner available, afternoon tea
Library, bicycles, conference center for 30, outdoor hot tub

Exquisite 1898 Queen Anne Victorian inn offering relaxation, comfort, beautiful surroundings & impeccable service. phbbinn@aol.com

FRISCO

Creekside Inn
PO Box 4835
51 West Main St 80443
970-668-5607 Fax: 970-668-8635
800-668-7320 o
Vince & Jill Pierse
All year except May&Nov

125-200-BB
7 rooms, 7 pb
Visa, MC, Disc, *Rated*, •
C-ltd/S-no/P-no/H-yes

Full or continental breakfast
Afternoon tea, snacks
Sitting room, library, hot tubs, ski & bike storage, Large screen TV & VCR

In the heart of the Colorado Rockies, an adult retreat-contemporary, spacious, comfortable. Seven rooms with private bath, outdoor hot tub on the banks of Ten Mile Creek. Great breakfasts! creeksideinn@earthlink.net http://www.creeksideinn-frisco.com

---

Frisco Lodge
PO Box 1325
321 Main St 80443
970-668-0195 Fax: 970-668-0149
800-279-6000
Susan Wentworth
All year

40-260-BB
19 rooms, 13 pb
Most CC, *Rated*, •
C-yes/S-no/P-no/H-ltd
German, Swedish

Full Gourmet Breakfast
Afternoon snacks include bread & soup in season
Hot tub, internet, ski and bike room, phones, award winning gardens, outdoor

Historic bed and breakfast lodge built in 1885. A unique inn on Frisco's historic Main Street features 1800's ambience. A Distinctive Mountain Lodge with Victorian Flair.
info@friscolodge.com http://www.friscolodge.com

FRISCO

Galena Street Mountain Inn
PO Box 417
106 Galena St 80443
970-668-3224 Fax: 970-668-1569
800-248-9138
Tammy Henry-Smith
All year

75-170-BB
15 rooms, 15 pb
Most CC, *Rated*, •
C-yes/S-no/P-no/H-yes

Full breakfast
Afternoon snacks and tea
Sitting room, library, hot tubs, sauna, meeting rooms

Striking Neo-mission-style furnishings, down comforters, windowseats, mountain views. Located minutes from Breckenridge, Keystone, Copper Mountain.
galenast@aol.com http://www.colorado-bnb.com/galena

Lark Mountain Inn
PO Box 1646
109 Granite St 80443
970-668-5237 Fax: 970-668-1988
800-668-5275
Sheila Morgan
All year

90-180-BB
6 rooms, 4 pb
Visa, MC, *Rated*, •
C-ltd/S-no/P-no/H-no
English

Full breakfast
dinner on requ. low season
Snacks, sitting room, bicycles, hot tub in yard, libary, fireplace, cable TV

The Lark is a log and timber inn with a great view of Mount Royal.
smlark@oneimage.com http://www.toski.com/lark

GEORGETOWN (REGION)

The Peck House
PO Box 428
83 Sunny Ave, *Empire* 80438
303-569-9870 Fax: 303-569-2743
Gary & Sally St. Clair
All year

70-95-BB
11 rooms, 9 pb
Most CC, •
C-ltd/S-yes/P-no/H-ltd
French

Continental breakfast
Restaurant, dinner available
Bar service, sitting room, library, Jacuzzi

1862 Victorian inn furnished in antiques. Near ski areas and historic districts. In Empire, 5 miles from Georgetown, this historic landmark is known for excellent food and dramatic mountain scenery. info@thepeckhouse.com http://www.thepeckhouse.com

GLENWOOD SPRINGS

The B&B on Mitchell Creek
1686 Mitchell Creek Rd 81601
970-945-4002
Carole & Stan Rachesky
All year

125-BB
1 rooms, 1 pb
Visa, *Rated*
C-yes/S-no/P-ltd/H-no
Spanish

Full breakfast
Snacks
Hiking trails, golf, horseback riding, river rafting, massage

Located in mountain setting, one private, warm, romantic suite; full breakfast served on deck overlooking rushing creek. carole@rof.net http://www.bbinternet.com/mitchell

GOLDEN

Ashley House
30500 US Hwy 40 80401
303-526-2411 Fax: 303-526-2411
800-308-2411
Harv & Bonnie Hisgen
All year

95-110-BB
5 rooms, 5 pb
Rated

On a hillside, surrounded by the Rocky Mountains, you will enjoy the close-by convenience of the big city as well as serenity of mountain living.
bjatashley@aol.com http://www.ashleyhouse.com

The Dove Inn
711 14th St 80401
303-278-2209 Fax: 303-273-5272
888-278-2209
Connie & Tim Sheffield
All year

78-99-BB
7 rooms, 7 pb
Most CC, *Rated*, •
C-yes/S-no/P-no/H-no

Full breakfast
Rooms have A/C, desks, phones and TVs, Golden West Shuttle

Built in 1864, lots of country charm in the West Denver foothills. All Denver attractions and Rocky Mountains are nearby. innkeep@ix.netcom.com http://www.doveinn.com

GRAND LAKE

Spirit Mountain Ranch
PO Box 942
3863 County Road 41 80447
970-887-3551 Fax: 970-887-3551
Beth Wasmer & Sandy Wilson
All year

135-175-BB
4 rooms, 4 pb
Visa, MC, Disc, *Rated*, •
C-ltd/S-no/P-no/H-ltd

Full breakfast
Afternoon tea, snacks
Sitting room, library, hot tub, llama hikes

Luxurious accommodations: timber framed inn on 72 acres of aspens. Secluded & quiet, homemade, delicious full breakfasts–western hospitality.
spiritmtn@rkymtnhi.com http://www.spiritmtnranch.com

GUNNISON

The Inn at Rockhouse Ranch
13931 CR 730 81230
970-641-0601 Fax: 970-641-0669
888-641-0601
Sarah Phipps
All year

200-350-BB
3 rooms, 3 pb
Most CC
C-yes/S-no/P-yes/H-ltd

Full gourmet breakfast
Tea, coffee, cocoa, fresh baked cookies
Suite sitting rooms, hot tub, concierge, in-room massage, business services

The Inn at Rockhouse Ranch is a destination in its own right. The Inn is a beautifully renovated 1904 stone home set on 1000 private acres in one of the most scenic valleys in the Rocky Mountains. office@innatrockhouse.com http://www.innatrockhouse.com

---

The Mary Lawrence Inn
601 N Taylor 81230
970-641-3343 Fax: 970-641-6719
888-331-6863
Janette McKinny All year

69-135-BB
7 rooms, 7 pb
Visa, MC, AmEx, *Rated*, •
C-yes/S-no/P-no/H-no

Full breakfast
Sack lunch (fee)
Three suites, many books, sitting room, hot tub in gazebo, sunroom parlor

Our renovated home is inviting and comfortable; delectable breakfasts. Special diets accommodated. marylinn@gunnison.com http://commerceteam.com/mary.html

---

The Ranch House
233 County Rd 48 81230
(970)642-0210 Fax: 970-642-0211
1-866-895-0986
Steve & Tammy Shelafo
All year

75-100-BB
3 rooms, 2 pb
Visa, MC, AmEx
C-yes/S-no/P-yes/H-ltd

Choice of light or hearty breakfast
Beverages and snacks
Hot tub, picnic area and fire pit, library

The Ranch House is perfectly situated just minutes north of Gunnison, Colorado, at the entrance to the beautiful Ohio Creek Valley. Come join us!
ranchhouse@ranchhousebnb.com http://www.ranchhousebnb.com

HOT SULPHUR SPRINGS

Casa Milagro
13628 County Rd 3 80468
970-725-3640 Fax: 970-725-3617
888-632-8955
Lynn & Paul Schmaltz
All year

120-180-BB
4 rooms, 4 pb
Most CC, *Rated*, •
C-ltd/S-no/P-no/H-no

Full breakfast
Homecooked dinners available
Overnight horse fac., hiking, skiing, golf, fly fishing instruction

Mountain getaway on the river- snow-mobiling, snow shoeing, & only 18 mi. to hot springs! Vacation hemo-dialysis facilities nearby for kidney patients.
casamilagro@rkymtnhi.com http://www.casamilagro.com

KEYSTONE

Ski Tip Lodge
PO Box 38
764 Montezuma Rd 80435
970-496-4950 Fax: 970-496-4940
800-742-0905
David Wilcox
All year

70-210-BB
10 rooms, 9 pb
Most CC
C-yes/S-no/P-no/H-ltd
Spanish, German

Full breakfast
Afternoon tea, snacks, dinner available, restauran
Bar service, sitting room, bikes, tennis court, Jacuzzis, pool, fireplaces

Colorado's first ski lodge, gourmet breakfasts, world class four-course dinners, beautiful sitting areas complete with fireplaces, large patio overlooking lake and well tended gardens. dwilcox@vailresorts.com http://www.skitiplodge.com

LA VETA

Hunter House
PO Box 427
115 W Grand Ave 81055
719-742-5577
Bill & Wanda Hunter
All year

65-BB
3 rooms
C-yes/S-no/P-no/H-no

Full breakfast
Afternoon tea, snacks
Sitting room, library, fireplaces, satellite TV, hiking, fishing, Mt. climb

In the peaceful beauty of the mountains, our guests enjoy a relaxing visit surrounded by country charm and warm hospitality. http://www.flash.net/~hunterhs/

LEADVILLE

The Apple Blossom Inn
120 W 4th St 80461
719-486-2141 Fax: 719-486-0994
800-982-9279
Elizabeth Lang
All year

69-159-BB
5 rooms, 5 pb
Visa, MC, *Rated*, •
C-ltd/S-no/P-no/H-no

Full breakfast
Lunch & dinner available, snacks, afternoon tea
Homebaked brownies, games provided, sitting room, fireplace, hot tub

Elegant & comfortable 1879 renovated banker's home. Beautiful & charming guestrooms in historic Leadville. applebb@amigo.net http://theappleblossominn.com

---

The Ice Palace Inn
813 Spruce St 80461
719-486-8272 Fax: 719-486-0345
800-754-2840
Giles & Kami Kolakowski
All year

89-149-BB
8 rooms, 8 pb
Most CC, *Rated*, •
C-ltd/S-no/P-no/H-no

Full breakfast
Afternoon tea, snacks
Sitting room, library, biking, antiques, quilts, hiking, tennis, fishing

This gracious Victorian inn was built in 1899 using the lumber from Leadville's famous Ice Palace. All rooms have private baths, fireplaces, TV/VCR, and include a great gourmet breakfast. icepalace@bwn.net http://www.icepalaceinn.com

---

The Leadville Country Inn
127 East 8th St 80461
719-486-2354 Fax: 719-486-0300
800-748-2354
Maureen & Gretchen Scanlon
All year

70-158-BB
9 rooms, 8 pb
Most CC, *Rated*, •
C-ltd/S-no/P-no/H-no

Full breakfast
Afternoon tea, snacks
Hot tub, sitting room, Jacuzzi, suites, cable TV, coffee pot

A stay at this premier Victorian B&B is to take a journey back in time. A breakfast to remember greets you in the morning, while the garden hot tub is the perfect end to the day. lcinn@bemail.com http://www.leadvillebednbreakfast.com

LIMON

Midwest Country Inn
PO Box 550
795 Main St 80828
719-775-2373
Harold & Vivian Lowe
All year

50-60-EP
32 rooms, 32 pb
Most CC, *Rated*, •
C-yes/S-yes/P-no/H-no

Restaurant, 1 block
Sitting room, gift shop, listening waterfall, and watching fountain

Beautiful rooms, oak antiques, stained glass, elegant wallpapered bathrooms. Quilts & antiques in rooms.

LOVELAND

Cattail Creek Inn
2665 Abarr Dr 80538
970-667-7600 Fax: 970-667-8968
800-572-2466
Sue & Harold Buchman
All year

105-170-BB
8 rooms, 8 pb
Most CC, *Rated*, •
C-ltd/S-no/P-no/H-yes

Full breakfast
Sitting room, snacks, golf, trails, near art galleries

Come and Experience: gracious hospitality, gourmet breakfasts, golf course location, private decks, mountain views, serenity and romance!
info@cattailcreekinn.com http://www.cattailcreekinn.com

LOVELAND

The Lovelander
217 W 4th St 80537
970-669-0798 Fax: 970-669-0797
800-459-6694
Lauren & Gary Smith
All year

105-155-BB
11 rooms, 11 pb
Most CC, *Rated*, •
C-ltd/S-no/P-no/H-ltd

Full gourmet breakfast
Comp. bev, cookies, snacks
Sitting room, meeting & reception ctr., 3 whirlpool/deluxe rooms

Rekindle romance in a beautiful Victorian setting in Colorado's Sweetheart city. Enjoy the comforts of yesterday with the conveniences of today!
love@ezlink.com http://www.lovelander.com

MANITOU SPRINGS

Gray's Avenue Hotel
711 Manitou Ave 80829
719-685-1277 Fax: 719-685-1847
800-294-1277
Tom & Lee Gray
All year

65-85-BB
7 rooms, 7 pb
Most CC, •
C-ltd/S-no/P-no/H-no

Full breakfast
Snacks
Sitting room, library, suites, fireplaces, cable TV, accom. bus. travelers

The Inn was established in 1984, Manitou's first B&B. Some family suites, many antiques, large art collection, walk to shops and restaurants in downtown historic district.
Mackeson1@aol.com http://www.graysbandb.com

Red Crags Inn
302 El Paso Blvd 80829
719-685-1920 Fax: 719-685-1073
800-721-2248
H & L Lerner All year

85-185-BB
8 rooms, 8 pb
Most CC, *Rated*, •
C-ltd/S-no/P-no/H-no

Full breakfast
Afternoon tea, wine, dessert
Feather mattresses, down comforters, robes, outdoor Jacuzzi, some TV's

Historic, 1880 Victorian mansion—a romantic hideaway. Lose yourself somewhere in time. Antiques, large common rooms. Large herb/flower gardens. King beds & fireplaces. Favorite of Teddy Roosevelt. info@redcrags.com http://www.redcrags.com

---

Two Sisters Inn
Ten Otoe Place 80829
719-685-9684 800-274-7466
Sharon Smith & Wendy Goldstein
All year

69-125-BB
5 rooms, 4 pb
Visa, MC, Disc, *Rated*, •
C-ltd/S-no/P-no/H-no

Continental plus breakfast
Manitou sparkling lemonade, homemade treats
Itinerary planning, guided hikes, 1896 piano, dinner/theater reservations

Award-winning trad'l B&B & garden honeymoon cottage at Pikes Peak in Historic District. Creative 3-course breakfasts."Best Romantic Getaway." Caring, fun owners who know the area. Magical experience! twosistersinn@earthlink.net http://www.twosisinn.com

MOFFAT

Willow Spring
PO Box 500
223 Moffat Way 81143
719-256-4116 Fax: 719-256-4002
Jim & Harriet Campbell
All year

60-65-BB
9 rooms
Visa, MC, Disc, •
C-yes/S-no/P-ltd/H-no

Full breakfast
Sitting room, accommodate business travelers

Historic hotel furnished with antiques and spectacular views. After full gourmet breakfast, visit nearby hot spring spas, or explore the Great Sand Dunes and mountains.
willows@amigo.net http://willow-spring.com/

OURAY

Christmas House
PO Box 786
310 Main St 81427
970-325-4992 Fax: 970-325-4992
888-325-XMAS
George & Allyson Crosby
All year

88-160-BB
5 rooms, 5 pb
Visa, MC, Disc, *Rated*, •
C-ltd/S-no/P-no/H-ltd

Full breakfast from menu
Afternoon tea, snacks
Sitting room, library, Jacuzzis, suites, fireplace, cable TV

Christmas is year round in this 1889 Ouray Victorian located in the heart of the 14,000 ft. San Juan Mountains. Fireplaces in suites, DVD, Jacuzzis, saunas, satellite TV.
email@christmashousebandb.com http://www.christmashousebandb.com

OURAY

St. Elmo Hotel
PO Box 667
426 Main St 81427
970-325-4951 Fax: 970-325-0348
Dan & Sandy Lingenfelter
All year

85-135-BB
9 rooms, 9 pb
Visa, MC, *Rated*, •
C-ltd/S-ltd/P-no/H-no

Full breakfast
Restaurant
Comp. wine, coffee, tea, piano, outdoor hot tub, sauna, meeting room

Hotel & Bon Ton Restaurant surrounded by beautiful, rugged 14,000-ft. peaks. Furnished with antiques, stained glass & brass.
innkeeper@stelmohotel.com http://www.stelmohotel.com

PAONIA

Bross Hotel
PO Box 85
312 Onarga Ave 81428
970-527-6776 Fax: 970-527-7737
Linda Lentz & Susan Steinhardt All year

90-BB
10 rooms, 10 pb
Visa, MC, *Rated*
C-ltd/S-no/P-no/H-no
German, Italian

Full breakfast
Snacks
Sitting room, library, suites, cable TV, accom. bus. travelers

The Bross Hotel is a restored 1906 hotel furnished with antiques and handmade quilts. It provides easy access to Colorado's finest outdoor adventuring (biking, hiking, camping, fishing, hunting). brosshotel@paonia.com http://www.paonia-inn.com

PINE

Meadow Creek B&B Inn
13438 US Hwy 285 80470
303-838-4167 Fax: 303-838-0360
Loren & Ivan Fuentes
All year

110-225-BB
7 rooms, 7 pb

The historic stone lodge known as The Meadow Creek, built in 1929 was originally created as a summer hideaway for a well known Denver socialite and her husband, an Italian Prince. info@meadowcreekbb.com http://www.meadowcreekbb.com

PUEBLO

Abriendo Inn
300 W Abriendo Ave 81004
719-544-2703 Fax: 719-542-6544
Kerrelyn M. Trent
All year

69-140-BB
10 rooms, 10 pb
Most CC, *Rated*, •
C-ltd/S-no/P-no/H-no

Full breakfast
24 hr. snacks, beverages
All rooms have TV, phones, data ports, rooms with double whirlpool

Award winning distinctive lodging in a park like setting. On National Historic Register. Walk to shopping restaurants and local attractions.
info@abriendoinn.com http://www.abriendoinn.com

SALIDA

Gazebo Country Inn
507 E Third St 81201
719-539-7806 Fax: 719-539-6971
800-565-7806
Sharon & Jeff Rowe
All year

75-110-BB
4 rooms, 4 pb
Visa, MC, AmEx, •
C-ltd/S-no/P-no/H-no

Full gourmet breakfast
Snacks
Sitting room, library, backyard gazebo, 2nd floor deck, hot tub in garden

Quiet, relaxing Victorian home; views of 14,000 ft mountain peaks from deck and gazebo. Freshly baked afternoon treats. Walk to historic downtown Salida-art galleries, dining, shopping.
srowe1023@aol.com

River Run Inn
8495 Country Road 160 81201
719-539-3818 Fax: 801-659-1878
800-385-6925
Virginia Nemmers
All year

70-160-BB
7 rooms, 3 pb
Visa, MC, *Rated*, •
C-ltd/S-ltd/P-no/H-no

Full country breakfast
Complimentary tea, coffee, cider
Library, fishing, dorm room available, reunions, stocked trout pond, view

Secluded area on Arkansas River. Turn-of-the-century home, antiques. Special dinners for groups, meetings, events. riverrun@amigo.net http://www.riverruninn.com

Moving Mountains Chalet, Steamboat Springs, CO

SALIDA

Thomas House 307 East 1st St 81201 719-539-7104 Fax: 719-530-0491 888-228-1410 Tammy & Steve Office All year	65-120-BB 6 rooms, 6 pb Most CC, *Rated*, • C-yes/S-no/P-no/H-ltd	Continental plus breakfast Snacks Sitting room, library, Jacuzzis, suites, cable TV, kitchenettes

1880's railroad boarding-house decorated with family heirlooms, antiques & collectibles. Two blocks from Salida's Historic Downtown.

office@thomashouse.com http://www.thomashouse.com

SOUTH FORK

Arbor House Inn PO Box 995 31358 W US Hwy 160 81154 719-873-5012 888-830-4642 Keith & Laurie Bratton All year	89-149-BB 5 rooms, 5 pb Visa, MC, *Rated* C-ltd/S-ltd/P-no/H-ltd	Full breakfast Snacks, complimentary wine Sitting room, library, fireplaces, satellite TV

Relax by the river in rustic mountain elegance. Five themed guestrooms with river, cliff, mountain, or meadow views.

info@arborhouseinnco.com http://www.arborhouseinnco.com

STEAMBOAT SPRINGS

Moving Mountains Chalet 2774 Burgess Creek Rd 80487 970-870-9359 Fax: 970-870-9487 877-624-2538 Robin & Heather Craigen All year	135-225-BB 6 rooms, 6 pb Visa, MC, *Rated*, • C-yes/S-no/P-no/H-no Spanish, French	Full breakfast Afternoon tea, snacks, lunch & dinner available Sitting room, suites, fireplaces, cable TV, accommodate business travelers

Featured as "Inn of the Month" in Ski Magazine (9/99), offering full-service catered packages with full local area shuttle, airport pick-up, gourmet meals, luxury rooms on the mountain. info@movingmountains.com http://www.movingmountains.com

STEAMBOAT SPRINGS

Sky Valley Lodge
PO Box 3132
31490 E US Hwy 40 80477
970-879-7749 Fax: 970-879-7752
800-499-4759
Jerry LeSage All year

89-189-BB
12 rooms, 12 pb
Visa, MC, AmEx,
Rated, •
C-yes/S-no/P-no/H-no

Continental breakfast
Sitting room, library, hot tub, sauna

Nestled in the side of the mountains, this English country manor-style lodge affords a sweeping view of the valley below.
info@steamboat-lodging.com http://www.steamboat-lodging.com/prop-skyvalley.shtml

---

Steamboat
PO Box 775888
442 Pine St 80477
970-879-5724 Fax: 970-870-8787
877-335-4321
Gordon B. Hattersley III

109-189-BB
7 rooms, 7 pb
Most CC, *Rated*
C-ltd/S-no/P-no/H-no
Spanish
All year

Full breakfast
Afternoon tea seasonally
Sitting room, library, Jacuzzis, fireplaces, cable TV, accom. bus. travelers

Historic Victorian home uniquely furnished with antiques; private bedrooms with bath homemade breakfast; daily baked breads and pastries.
info@steamboatb-b.com http://www.steamboatb-b.com

STONEHAM

Elk Echo Ranch
47490 WCR 155 80754
970-735-2426 Fax: 970-735-2427
Bill & Cheryl Keelan
All year

99-139-BB
4 rooms, 4 pb
Visa, MC
S-ltd/P-no/H-yes

Full breakfast
Complimentary beverages and homemade treats
Whirlpool tubs, picnic lunches, gift shop, concierge

New log home especially designed for Bed and Breakfast. Homemade pie, overnight stay, full breakfast specialty, and your photo.
cheryl-keelan@juno.com http://www.elkecho.com

TELLURIDE

Bear Creek B&B
PO Box 2369
221 E Colorado Avenue 81435
970-728-6681 Fax: 970-728-3636
800-338-7064
T & C Whiteman All year

78-208-BB
9 rooms, 9 pb
Visa, MC, Disc, *Rated*, •
C-ltd/S-ltd/P-no/H-no

Full breakfast
Apres Ski during Ski Season, cookies
Rooftop Hot Tub, fireplace, cable TV, cedar-lined sauna, steam room

European ambiance coupled w/ Old West Hospitality. 9 lovely guest chambers located on 2nd & 3rd floors. Adjacent to Summer Festivals. Try our Deluxe & Premium rooms w/the famous 'Wall of Windows'. bearcreek@telluridecolorado.net
http://www.bearcreektelluride.com

Johnstone Inn
PO Box 546
403 W Colorado 81435
970-728-3316 Fax: 970-728-0724
800-752-1901
Bill Schiffbauer
Ski season & summer

90-130-BB
8 rooms, 8 pb
Visa, MC, AmEx,
Rated, •
C-ltd/S-no/P-no/H-no

Full breakfast
Ski season refreshments
Sitting room w/fireplace, games, outdoor hot tub, manicure on premises

Restored historic Victorian boarding house in center of Telluride. Walk to lifts, shops, and everything else. bschiff@rmii.com http://www.johnstoneinn.com

---

The San Sophia Inn
PO Box 1825
330 W Pacific 81435
970-728-3001 Fax: 970-728-6226
800-537-4781
Alicia Bixby & Keith Hampton
All year

99-300-BB
16 rooms, 16 pb
Visa, MC, AmEx,
Rated, •
C-yes/S-no/P-no/H-no

Full breakfast
Apres ski

Telluride's most luxurious inn. Nestled in the heart of the Historic District and only steps from the Gondola info@sansophia.com http://www.sansophia.com

VAIL

Intermountain
2754 Basingdale Blvd 81657
970-476-4935 Fax: 970-476-7926
Kay & Sepp Cheney
All year

89-200-BB
2 rooms, 2 pb
Rated, •
C-ltd/S-no/P-no/H-no

Continental plus breakfast
Snacks
Sitting room, cable TV

Contemporary home two miles from ski lifts on free bus route.
intermountainbb@cs.com http://www.vail.net/vailbb

WESTCLIFFE

Main Street Inn
501 Main Street 81252
719-783-4000 Fax: 719-783-4003
877-783-4006
Mark & Wanda Johnson
March 1–November 1

95-120-BB
5 rooms, 5 pb
Visa, MC
S-no/P-no/H-ltd

Full breakfast
Complimentary wine
Sitting room, library, Jacuzzis, fireplaces, cable TV, accom. bus. travlers

An 1890's Italianate in heart of rural Western town at base of Sangre de Christo Mountains. Features piped heat; push button lighting; private privy and direct dial phone.
mnstreetbb@aol.com http://www.mainstreetbnb.com

WINTER PARK

The Pines Inn of Winter Park
PO Box 15
115 County Rd 716 80482
970-726-5416 Fax: 970-726-1062
800-824-9127
Jan & Lee Reynolds
All year

95-140-BB
8 rooms, 6 pb
Most CC, *Rated*, •
C-yes/S-no/P-no/H-ltd

Full breakfast
Afternoon tea, snacks
Sitting room, fireplace, TV/game room, outdoor Jacuzzi

Comfortable, relaxed inn, close to slopes, but well-located for summer biking and golfing. We will recommend our favorite restaurants.
lee.reynolds@prodigy.net http://www.bestinns.net/usa/co/pine.html

Connecticut

BRISTOL

Chimney Crest Manor
5 Founders Dr 06010
860-582-4219 Fax: 860-589-8645
Dan & Cynthia Cimadamore
All year

105-175-BB
4 rooms, 4 pb
Visa, MC, *Rated*, •
C-ltd/S-no/P-no/H-no

Full breakfast
Sitting room, piano, 1 suite with fireplace, 1 suite with thermal spa

32-room Tudor mansion on National Historic Register. 20 minutes from Hartford & Litchfield. Walking distance to Carousel Museum. Mobil 3-star rating. chimnycrst@aol.com

CHESTER

123 Main
123 Main St 06412
860-526-3456 Fax: 860-526-1003
Chris & Randy Allinson
All year

95-145-BB
5 rooms, 3 pb
Most CC
C-ltd/S-no/P-no/H-no

Full or continental breakfast
Snacks

Chester has specialty shops and acclaimed restaurants for every taste, from funky bistro to French with four stars. chris@123main.net http://www.123main.com

Chimney Crest Manor, Bristol, CT

CHESTER

The Inn at Chester 318 W Main St 06412 860-526-9541 Fax: 860-526-4387 800-949-STAY Leonard Lieberman All year	105-215-BB 42 rooms, 42 pb Visa, MC, AmEx, *Rated*, • C-yes/S-ltd/P-ltd/H-yes	Continental breakfast Lunch/dinner available, tavern Bicycles, tennis, sauna, sitting room, library, piano, entertainment

The inn, on 12 wooded acres, centers around a 1776 farmhouse, with fireplaces and Eldred Wheeler antique reproductions.

innkeeper@innatchester.com http://innatchester.com/

EAST HADDAM

Bishopsgate Inn PO Box 290 7 Norwich Rd 06423 860-873-1677 Fax: 860-873-3898 The Kagel Family All year	105-165-BB 6 rooms, 6 pb Visa, MC, Disc, *Rated* C-ltd/S-no/P-ltd/H-no	Full breakfast Dinner available Sitting room, library, fireplaces

Circa 1818. This colonial house is furnished with period antiques and each floor of the Inn has a sitting area where guests often relax with a good book.

ctkagel@Bishopsgate.com http://www.bishopsgate.com

ESSEX (REGION)

Riverwind Inn 209 Main St, *Deep River* 06417 860-526-2014 Fax: 860-526-0875 Roger & Nicky Plante All year	95-175-BB 8 rooms, 8 pb Visa, MC, *Rated* C-ltd/S-ltd/P-no/H-no	Full breakfast Complimentary sherry, afternoon snacks 8 common rooms, piano, innkeeper is a justice of the peace

Decor is delightful & whimsical, furnished in country antiques. Candlelit country breakfast in fireplaced dining rooms begins each day.

innkeeper@riverwindinn.com http://www.riverwindinn.com

Butternut Farm, Glastonbury, CT

ESSEX (REGION)

The Copper Beech Inn
46 Main St, *Ivoryton* 06442
860-767-0330
Fax: 860-767-7840
888-809-2056
Ian & Barbara Phillips
All year

125-325-BB
13 rooms, 13 pb
Visa, MC, AmEx, *Rated*
C-ltd/S-no/P-no/H-ltd

Continental breakfast
Fine dining: French country & new American cuisine
TV, phones, A/C, Jacuzzi, gardens, Victorian conservatory

A gracious 13-room Victorian in Ivorytown, CT, one mile from Essex. AAA Four-Diamond restaurant, minutes from Connecticut River and beaches. 2 hours from NYC or Boston. Seasonal packages available.

info@copperbeechinn.com http://www.copperbeechinn.com

GLASTONBURY

Butternut Farm
1654 Main St 06033
860-633-7197
Fax: 860-659-1758
Don Reid
All year

90-110-BB
5 rooms, 5 pb
AmEx, *Rated*
C-yes/S-ltd/P-no/H-no

Full breakfast
Complimentary wine, chocolates
Piano, 8 fireplaces, sitting rooms, library, bicycle

An 18th-century jewel furnished with period antiques. Attractive grounds with herb gardens and ancient trees, dairy goats and prize chickens.

http://www.butternutfarmbandb.com

GRANBY

Dutch Iris Inn
239 Salmon Brook St 06035
860-844-0262 Fax: 860-844-0248
877-280-0743
Kevin & Belma Marshall
All year

89-119-BB
5 rooms, 4 pb
Most CC, •
C-yes/S-no/P-no/H-no
Some Spanish

Full breakfast
Fresh coffee, tea and cocoa available all day
Digital cable with 24 movie, 40 music channels, daily paper & USA Today

This 1812 Colonial home is a home away from home. We take pride in providing an atmosphere where comfort is the goal. Our "Romantic Touches" also make your stay one to remember.

dutchirisinn@cox.net http://www.dutchirisinn.com

KENT

Chaucer House
PO Box 826
88 N Main St 06757
860-927-4858 Fax: 860-927-5399
Mary Redrupp James
All year

110-150-BB
4 rooms, 4 pb
Visa, MC, AmEx, *Rated*
S-no/P-no/H-no
French, Spanish

Full or continental breakfast
complimentary sherry or port
Sitting room, bikes, cable TV, accommodate bus. travelers

Beautiful Colonial, short walk to center of town, gourmet breakfast served in dining room or in garden.
http://www.chaucerhouse.com

Fife 'n Drum Rest. & Inn
PO Box 188
53 N Main St 06757
860-927-3509 Fax: 860-927-4595
Elissa G.T. Potts
All year

95-125-EP
8 rooms, 8 pb
Visa, MC, AmEx, *Rated*
S-no/P-no/H-ltd
Spanish, Italiam, French, Croatian

Continental breakfast
Restaurant
Bar, lunch, dinner, telephones in rooms, newly redecorated

Family owned and operated for 22 years and located in the center of rural Kent. "Excellent restaurant and wine list"—Wine Spectator.
info@fifendrum.com http://www.fifendrum.com

KILLINGWORTH

Acorn B&B
628 Rt 148 06419
860-663-2214 Fax: 860-663-2214
877 978-7842
Carole & Richard Pleines
All year

110-125-BB
2 rooms, 2 pb
Most CC
C-no/S-no/P-no/H-no

Full breakfast
Complimentary bottle of our wine
Jacuzzis, swimming pool, fireplace in living room, newly redecorated

Offering a stress free, relaxing, private and comfortable home away from home. Country setting, full breakfast, private baths, pool, spa, antiques, A/C, fireplace, featuring old hickory furniture.
richard@acornbedandbreakfast.com http://www.acornbedandbreakfast.com/

LAKEVILLE

Wake Robin Inn
PO Box 660
Route 41 06039
860-435-2515 Fax: 860-435-2000
Michael Bryan Loftus
All year

149-259-BB
38 rooms, 38 pb
Visa, MC, AmEx, *Rated*
S-no/P-yes

Full Breakfast
Telephones, cable TV, lounge

Dramatic Georgian-Colonial Inn on 11 acres of rolling hills. 38 rooms, all with private baths, A/C, TV, multiple parlors, porches, and decks.
info@wakerobininn.com http://www.wakerobininn.com

MADISON

Tidewater Inn
949 Boston Post Rd 06443
203-245-8457 Fax: 203-318-0265
Jean Foy
All year

100-185-BB
9 rooms, 9 pb
Visa, MC, AmEx, *Rated*
C-ltd/S-no/P-no/H-no

Full breakfast
Cold drinks, snacks
Sitting room, fireplaces, Jacuzzi, Madison Beach passes, refrigerator

Explore coastal Connecticut in our elegant, cozy inn, near village and beaches. Antiques and estate furnishings. tidewaterinn@aol.com

MANCHESTER

The Mansion Inn
139 Hartford Rd 06040
860-646-0453
Marianne & Bruce Hamstra
All year

95-145-BB
5 rooms, 5 pb
Rated
C-ltd/S-no/P-no/H-no

Afternoon tea, wine, homebaked treats
Library, guest refrigerator stocked with soda and bottled spring water

Read in bed fireside, on pillows slipped in hand embroidered linens, the library's books all yours in a silk baron's mansion home. Historic District Award. Easy Interstate highway access. mansioninnkeeper@cox.net http://www.themansioninnct.com

MIDDLEBURY

Tucker Hill Inn	110-155-BB	Full breakfast
96 Tucker Hill Rd 06762	4 rooms, 2 pb	Tea & coffee served
203-758-8334 Fax: 203-598-0652	Visa, MC, *Rated*, •	Sitt. room, library, A/C,
Susan & Richard Cebelenski	C-yes/S-no/P-no/H-no	TV/VCR with free movies,
All year		small conf. facilities

Large Colonial-style inn near Village Green. Large, spacious period rooms. Hearty breakfast.

tuckerhill2@yahoo.com http://www.tuckerhillinn.com

MYSTIC

Adams House of Mystic	95-175-BB	Full breakfast
382 Cow Hill Rd 06355	7 rooms, 7 pb	Sitting room, fireplaces,
860-572-9551 Fax: 860-572-9552	Visa, MC, Disc, *Rated*	garden cottage
Gregory & Mary Lou Peck	C-ltd/S-no/P-no/H-no	
All year		

Historic 1750s home located 1½ miles from downtown Mystic; close to seaport and aquarium. Surrounded by lush greenery and flower beds.

adamshse@aol.com http://www.adamshouseofmystic.com

Comolli's Guest House	75-125-BB	Continental breakfast
36 Bruggeman Place 06355	2 rooms, 1 pb	Kitchen privileges
860-536-8723	C-ltd/S-no/P-no/H-no	TV in rooms, nearby many
Dorothy Comolli		activities, green on property
All year		

Immaculate home, situated on a quiet hill overlooking the Mystic Seaport complex; convenient to Olde Mystick Village & the Aquarium.

Harbour Inne & Cottage	55-300-BB	Continental breakfast
15 Edgemont St 06355	5 rooms, 5 pb	Kitchen privileges
860-572-9253	*Rated*, •	Sitting room, A/C, canoe &
Charles Lecouras, Jr.	C-yes/S-yes/P-yes/H-no	boats, cable TV, fireplaces,
All year	Greek	hot tub

Small inn, plus 3-room cottage on Mystic River. Walk to seaport & all attractions. Waterfront tables, canoeing, and boating.

harbourinne@earthlink.net http://www.harbourinne-cottage.com

Pequot Hotel	95-175-BB	Full country breakfast
711 Cow Hill Rd 06355	3 rooms, 3 pb	Complimentary beverages
860-572-0390 Fax: 860-536-3380	Visa, MC, *Rated*, •	Picnic lunch, 2 sitting rooms,
Nancy & Jim Mitchell	C-ltd/S-no/P-no/H-no	library, A/C, whirlpool tubs
All year		

Authentically restored 1840s stagecoach stop; friendly, casual elegance amongst period antiques. Relaxing parlors, romantic fireplaces.

pequothtl@aol.com http://www.pequothotelbandb.com

Steamboat Inn	125-300-BB	Continental breakfast
73 Steamboat Wharf 06355	10 rooms, 10 pb	Complimentary sherry, tea
860-536-8300 Fax: 860-536-9528	Most CC, *Rated*, •	Common Room, A/C,
All year	C-ltd/S-no/P-no/H-yes	whirlpool tubs, fireplaces,
		water views

Steamboat Inn is the perfect escape for romantics. Our individually decorated and spacious guestrooms offer charming sitting areas, fireplaces, Jacuzzis, and a spectacular river view.

sbwharf@aol.com http://www.visitmystic.com/steamboat

MYSTIC (REGION)

Homespun Farm
306 Preston Rd, *Griswold* 06351
860-376-5178 Fax: 860-376-5587
888-889-6673
Kate & Ron Bauer
All year

90-170-BB
2 rooms, 2 pb
Most CC
C-yes/S-ltd/P-ltd/H-ltd

Full breakfast
Snacks
Sitting room, library, suites, cable TV, conference, golf, hike, fireplaces

Homespun Farm bed and breakfast, a quintessential 1740 Colonial farmhouse, with beautifully kept grounds that include part of the 259 year-old farm's apple orchard.
relax@homespunfarm.com http://www.homespunfarm.com

The Mare's Inn
333 Col Ledyard Hwy, *Ledyard* 06339
860-572-7556 Fax: 860-572-2976
866-572-7556
Marilyn Richard
All year

95-175-BB
5 rooms, 5 pb
Most CC, *Rated*, •
C-ltd/S-ltd/P-ltd/H-ltd

Full breakfast
Pool, sauna, tennis courts, common Jacuzzi

7 miles to Foxwoods and 3 miles to Mystic. Home away from home, great breakfasts & hospitality. Private baths, very comfortable.
maresinn@aol.com http://www.maresinn.com

Lighthouse Inn Resort & Conf. Ctr.
6 Guthrie Pl, *New London* 06320
860-443-8411 Fax: 860-437-7027
888-443-8411
Jim & Marylis McGrath

115-339-BB
54 rooms, 54 pb
Most CC, •
C-yes/S-ltd/P-ltd/H-ltd
Spanish
All year

Continental breakfast
Lunch, dinner, snacks, restaurant, bar service
Sitting rm, library, suites, cable TV, high speed Internet, acc. bus. trav.

100 year-old Historic Inn located 1 block from Long Island Sound. Enjoy your time on our private beach, 4 star restaurant or on one of our 2 outdoor patios.
lrayburn@lighthouseinn-ct.com http://www.lighthouseinn-ct.com

---

The Queen Anne Inn
265 Williams St, *New London* 06320
800-347-8818 Fax: 860-443-0857
800-347-8818
Kasey Goss, Susan Ortaldo, Scott Danforth All year

95-175-BB
8 rooms, 8 pb
Most CC, •
C-ltd/S-no/P-no/H-no

Full breakfast
Tea and general catering services are available
General meeting room available

Queen Anne Inn Bed and Breakfast is a beautifully restored, 1903 Victorian home, offering the romance of an era long past, gracious hospitality, and a delicious full breakfast.
info@queen-anne.com http://www.queen-anne.com

Fourteen Lincoln Street
14 Lincoln St, *Niantic* 06357
860-739-6327 Fax: 860-739-6327
Cheryl M. Jean
Feb-Dec

155-175-BB
4 rooms, 4 pb
Visa, MC, AmEx, •
C-ltd/S-no/P-no/H-no
French

Bountiful chef-prepared breakfast
Afternoon tea
Elegant sitting room, garden terrace, library, Jacuzzi tubs.

Ever sleep in a choir loft? Built in the late 19th century as a Congregational church, this lovingly restored gem harbors a captivating bed & breakfast owned and operated by an award-winning chef. fourteenlincoln@aol.com http://www.14lincolnstreet.com

---

Inn at Harbor Hill Marina
60 Grand St, *Niantic* 06357
860-739-0331 Fax: 860-691-3078
Sally Keefe
All year

105-195-BB
8 rooms, 8 pb
Visa, MC, AmEx, *Rated*, •
C-yes/S-no/P-no/H-no
French, Italian, Spanish

Continental plus breakfast
Complimentary wine
Sitting room, fireplaces, cable TV, kayaks, beach passes, gardens

The only thing we overlook is the water! Panoramic views of the Niantic River and/or views of Long Island Sound from our rooms, or from wicker seating on wraparound porch or Adirondack chairs. info@innharborhill.com http://www.innharborhill.com

MYSTIC (REGION)

Antiques & Accommodations
32 Main St, *North Stonington* 06359
860-535-1736 Fax: 860-535-2613
800-554-7829
Ann & Tom Gray

129-249-BB
6 rooms, 6 pb
Visa, MC, *Rated*, •
C-ltd/S-no/P-no/H-no
German
All year

Full multi-course breakfast
Complimentary wine
Sitting room, library, garden, edible flowers, bicycles, gardens, lake

Two historic homes in a quiet village setting, all furnished with period antiques. Multi-course breakfast. anntomtovisit@aol.com http://www.antiquesandaccommodations.com

---

The Old Mystic Inn
PO Box 733
52 Main St, *Old Mystic* 06372
860-572-9422 Fax: 860-572-9954
Michael S. Cardillo, Jr.
All year

115-185-BB
8 rooms, 8 pb
Visa, MC, AmEx, *Rated*, •
C-ltd/S-no/P-no/H-no

Full country breakfast
Afternoon refreshments
Saturday evening wine and cheese in our Keeping Room

Located minutes from Mystic Seaport and Aquarium, this charming Inn, formerly The Old Mystic Book Shop, dates back to 1784, along with a Carriage House built in 1988.
omysticinn@aol.com http://www.oldmysticinn.com

Captain Grant's, 1754
109 Route 2A, *Poquetanuck* 06365
860-887-7589 Fax: 860-892-9151
800-982-1772
Ted & Carol
All year

79-149-BB
6 rooms, 6 pb
Most CC
S-no

Full breakfast

Come and experience New England ... with your lodging experience as enjoyable and memorable as the places you visit.
stay@captaingrants.com http://www.captaingrants.com

NEW HAVEN

Historic Mansion Inn
600 Chapel St 06511
203-865-8324 Fax: 203-752-1892
888-512-6278
Nick Mastrobuono
All year

139-159-BB
7 rooms, 7 pb
Most CC, •
C-yes/S-no/P-ltd/H-ltd
English, French, Italian

Full breakfast
Study/Living Room. Connected through 12' high archway. Mahogany double doors

Old Elegance and Style. Now an Inn/B&B. Downtown New Haven. Stately 12½' ceilings. Across from luscious Park. A block to famous restaurants. 4 blocks from Yale. Historic 1842 mansion restored 1999. innkeeper@thehistoricmansioninn.com
http://www.thehistoricmansioninn.com

The Inn at Oyster Point
104 Howard Ave 06519
203-773-3334 Fax: 203-777-4150
1-86-OYSTERPT
Vinny Cusenza & Steve Robles
All year

90-269-BB
6 rooms, 4 pb
Most CC, *Rated*, •
C-ltd/S-no/P-ltd/H-no
French, Spanish

Full breakfast
Snacks, beverages
Jacuzzis, fireplace, cable TV, voicemail, data ports, meeting rms, kitchens

A sumptuous B&B at a century-old oysterman's residence in a Victorian sea-faring village five minutes from Yale and New Haven—the cultural and dining capital of Connecticut.
innkeeper@oysterpointinn.com http://www.oysterpointinn.com

Three Chimneys Inn at Yale
1201 Chapel St 06511
203-789-1201 Fax: 203-776-7363
800-443-1554
Michael Marra
All year

180-BB
10 rooms, 10 pb
S-no

Continental breakfast
Snacks

Lovely 1870s "painted Lady with a past" is "dressed" in antiques, collectibles & American reproduction furnishings—her rich oak millwork dates from historic era of the Tall Ships.
chimneysnh@aol.com http://www.threechimneysinn.com/newhaven/index.htm

NEW MILFORD

Barton House 34 East St 06776 860-354-3535 Fax: 860-354-3535 Ray & Rachel Barton All year	99-125-BB 2 rooms, 2 pb Visa, MC, AmEx C-ltd/S-no/P-no/H-no	Full breakfast Snacks Sitting room, library, piano, fireplaces, cable TV, 3 acres with brook

Extra touches in room, fresh flowers, bottled water, fruits, romantic candlelight breakfast in formal/informal setting. Vegetable/cutting gardens. Each room tastefully decorated, A/C, ceiling fan, TV. Bartonhousebnb@aol.com

The Homestead Inn 5 Elm St 06776 860-354-4080 Fax: 860-354-7046 Rolf & Peggy Hammer All year	104-135-BB 15 rooms, 15 pb Visa, MC, AmEx, *Rated*, • C-ltd/S-ltd/P-no/H-no	Continental plus breakfast Sitting room, front porch, gardens, in village center

Small country inn in picturesque New England town next to village green, near shops, churches, restaurants, antiques, galleries, hiking, crafts. http://www.homesteadct.com

NEW PRESTON

Boulders Inn PO Box 2575 East Shore Rd (Rt 45) 06777 860-868-0541 Fax: 860-868-1925 800-552-6853 Kees & Ulla Adema All year	210-380-BB 17 rooms, 17 pb Visa, MC, AmEx, *Rated*, • C-ltd/S-yes/P-no/H-yes German, Dutch, French	Full breakfast Restaurant, bar, dinner Sitting room, bicycles, tennis, private beach, boats, hiking trail

Exquisitely furnished country inn in spectacular location, viewing Lake Waramaug. Lake-view dining inside or on terrace.
boulders@bouldersinn.com http://www.bouldersinn.com

NORFOLK

Angel Hill PO Box 504 54 Greenwoods Rd 06058 860-542-5920 Donna Bierbower All year	160-185-BB 5 rooms, 5 pb • C-ltd/S-no/P-no	Full breakfast Tea, sherry Sitting room, library

At Angel Hill our vision is a romantic one: to offer our guests a getaway with simple pleasures and quiet moments. http://www.angelhill.com

Blackberry River Inn 536 Greenwoods Rd W Rt 44 W 06058 860-542-5100 Fax: 860-542-1763 800-414-3636 Jose Lucas All year	85-215-BB 19 rooms, 9 pb Most CC, *Rated*, • C-yes/S-yes/P-no/H-ltd	Full country breakfast Restaurant, bar Sitt. rm., library, pool, Jacuzzi, 27 acres, lawns, 3 miles of hiking trails

A Colonial Inn, built in 1763, the Blackberry River Inn lies nestled in the foothills of the Berkshires on 27 scenic rural acres. Listed on the National Register of Historic Places.
blackberry.river.inn@snet.net http://www.blackberryriverinn.com

Manor House 69 Maple Ave 06058 860-542-5690 Fax: 860-542-5690 Hank & Diane Tremblay All year	125-275-BB 9 rooms, 9 pb Visa, MC, *Rated*, • C-ltd/S-ltd/P-no/H-ltd French	Full breakfast Complimentary tea, coffee, cocoa Weddings, massages, piano, sun porch, gazebo, bicycles, gardens, lake

Historic Victorian mansion furnished w/ genuine antiques, on 5 acres. Romantic, elegant rooms. Deluxe room w/ gas fireplace, 2 person Jacuzzi.
innkeeper@manorhouse-norfolk.com http://www.manorhouse-norfolk.com

NORFOLK

Mountain View Inn
PO Box 467
67 Litchfield Rd/Rt 272 06058
860-542-6991 Fax: 860-542-5689
Michele Sloane
All year

75-135-BB
10 rooms, 7 pb
Rated, •

Full breakfast

Lovingly restored, our 1880's Victorian Country-style Inn offers large, unique guestrooms, most with private baths–your choice of double, queen or two-bedded accommodations.
mvinn@snet.net http://www.mvinn.com

NORWALK

The Silvermine Tavern
194 Perry Ave 06850
203-847-4558 Fax: 203-847-9171
888-693-9967
Frank & Marsha Whitman
All year

110-185-BB
11 rooms, 11 pb
Most CC, *Rated*, •
C-yes/S-yes/P-no/H-no

Continental breakfast
Restaurant, bar
Lunch, dinner, live Jazz, sitting room, new suite, weddings and conferences

Charming 225-year-old country inn only an hour from New York City. Decorated with hundreds of antiques. Dixieland jazz on Thurs/Fri/Sat PM.
innkeeper@silverminetavern.com http://www.silverminetavern.com

OLD LYME

Bee & Thistle Inn
100 Lyme St 06371
860-434-1667 Fax: 860-434-3402
800-622-4946
Philip & Marie Abraham
All year

79-210-EP
11 rooms, 11 pb
Most CC, •
C-ltd/S-no/P-no/H-no

Full breakfast
Sunday Brunch, Lunch & Dinner

An inn on 5 1/2 acres in historic district. On the Lieutenant River set back amidst majestic trees. Creative American cuisine.
innkeeper@beeandthistleinn.com http://www.beeandthistleinn.com

---

Old Lyme Inn
85 Lyme St 06371
860-434-2600 Fax: 860-434-5352
800-434-5352
Keith and Candy Green
All year

135-235-BB
13 rooms, 13 pb
Most CC, *Rated*, •
C-yes/S-yes/P-ltd/H-yes

Continental breakfast
Lunch/dinner available, restaurant
Sitting room, TV, phones, clock radios, porch, teddy bear in the rooms

Elegant 1850 Victorian mansion located in Old Lyme's Historic District. 3-star restaurant (New York Times, 3 times). Empire and Victorian furnishings.
innkeeper@oldlymeinn.com http://oldlymeinn.com

OLD SAYBROOK

Deacon Timothy Pratt
325 Main St 06475
860-395-1229 Fax: 860-395-4748
Shelley Nobile
All year

100-225-BB
6 rooms, 6 pb
Visa, MC, AmEx, *Rated*, •
C-ltd/S-no/P-no/H-no
Spanish

Full breakfast wkends; cont. wkdys.
Sherry, tea, cookies, soft drinks avail. anytime
Beach passes, maps, massage therapy, picnic area

Magnificent National Historic Register Inn! Features elegant rooms w/ fireplaces, Jacuzzis. In historic district on pretty gas-lit Main St Walk to everything! 1mi to beaches, lighthouses, cruises, park. shelley.nobile@snet.net http://www.connecticut-bed-and-breakfast.com

PLYMOUTH VILLAGE (REGION)

Shelton House
663 Main St Rt 6, *Plymouth* 06782
860-283-4616 Fax: 860-283-4616
Pat & Bill Doherty All year

85-100-BB
4 rooms, 2 pb
Rated
S-no/P-no/H-no

Full breakfast
Afternoon tea
Large guest parlor with fireplace, perennial garden

Historic 1825 Greek Revival in scenic Litchfield Hills. Beautiful grounds; fountain; antiques. Listed on National Historic Register.
sheltonhbb@prodigy.net http://www.bnbsheltonhouse.com

Deacon Timothy Pratt, Old Saybrook, CT

RIDGEFIELD

The Elms Inn	150-210-BB	Continental breakfast
500 Main St 06877	20 rooms, 20 pb	Award Winning Elms
203-438-2541 Fax: 203-438-2541	Most CC, *Rated*	Restaurant & Tavern
The Scala Family	C-yes/S-ltd/P-no/H-no	Suites, cable TV, 4 poster
All year	Spanish, German	beds, 1799 Colonial Inn

A 1799 Inn for the discriminating traveler located in beautiful Ridgefield, CT. Beautiful, peaceful New England charm, fun antique shopping, restaurants, boutiques, library, parks at your doorstep. innkeeper@elmsinn.com http://www.elmsinn.com

Stone Ridge Manor	125-150-BB	Continental plus breakfast
24 Old Wagon Rd 06877	2 rooms, 2 pb	Complimentary snacks,
203-431-8426 Fax: 203-431-8538	Visa, MC, AmEx	soda, tea, coffee
Juliet & John Milo	C-yes/S-no/P-no/H-no	Sitting room, library, heated
All year		outdoor pool, exercise room

A "miniature stone castle," historic estate, renovated in the Arts and Crafts style, splashed with period antiques, solid oak arched doors, antique light fixtures, and period European wall coverings. inkeeper@stoneridgemanor.net http://www.stoneridgemanor.net

West Lane Inn	135-195-BB	Continental breakfast
22 West Ln 06877	17 rooms, 17 pb	Full breakfast (fee)
203-438-7323 Fax: 203-438-7325	Most CC, *Rated*, •	Golf, tennis nearby, cable TV,
Ms. Mayer & Debbie Prieger	C-yes/S-yes/P-no	voice mail
All year		

Colonial elegance framed by majestic old maples and flowering shrubs. Breakfast served on the verandah. Always a relaxing atmosphere. Newly decorated lobbies & rooms. westlanein@aol.com http://www.westlaneinn.com

RIVERTON

Old Riverton Inn	85-195-BB	Full breakfast
PO Box 6	12 rooms, 12 pb	Lunch/dinner available, bar
436 East River Rd 06065	Most CC, *Rated*	Sitting room, cable TV,
860-379-8678 Fax: 860-379-1006	C-ltd/S-no/P-no/H-ltd	outgoing phones and modem
800-EST-1796		hook-up
Mark & Pauline Telford		
All year		

Hospitality for the hungry, thirsty & sleepy since 1796. Overlooks wild & scenic West Branch of Farmington River & the Hitchcock Chair Factory Store. mark.telford@snet.net http://www.rivertoninn.com

SALISBURY

Earl Grey
PO Box 177
06068
860-435-1007 Fax: 860-435-1007
Patricia & Richard Boyle
All year

140-160-BB
2 rooms, 2 pb
C-ltd/S-no/P-no/H-ltd
French, German, Dutch, Japanese

Full breakfast
Afternoon tea, snacks, & complimentary wine
Fireplaces

On a quiet, private hill (with barn) in, and overlooking Salisbury village center.
rboyle@discovernet.net

SIMSBURY

Simsbury 1820 House
731 Hopmeadow St 06070
860-658-7658 Fax: 860-651-0724
800-879-1820
Diane Ropiak
All year

135-195-BB
34 rooms, 34 pb
Most CC, *Rated*, •
C-yes/S-yes/P-no/H-yes

Continental plus breakfast
Dinner available Monday-Thursday
Cafe (Mon-Thur), sitting room, 5 private dining rooms, weddings/meetings

A graciously restored 34-room, 19th-century mansion in period decor, with 20th-century amenities. visit@simsbury1820house.com http://www.simsbury1820house.com

SOUTH WINDSOR

The Watson House Inn
1876 Main St 06074
860-282-8888 Fax: 860-289-0530
Timothy Cameron
All year

95-125-BB
3 rooms, 3 pb
Visa, MC, AmEx, *Rated*
C-yes/S-no/P-no/H-yes

Full breakfast weekends
Continental breakfast weekdays
Comp. wine, sitting room, suites, all rms. w/cable, TV, phone, & fireplace

1788 Paladian mansion located on historic Old Main Street, less than a mile from the Connecticut River

SOUTHBURY

The Cornucopia at Oldfield
782 Main Street North 06488
203-267-6707 Fax: 203-267-6703
888-760-7947
Dave & Sue Andros
All year

140-200-BB
3 rooms, 3 pb
Most CC
C-yes/S-no/P-no/H-no

Full breakfast

Where gracious hospitality is the standard in an atmosphere of "down-home" elegance.
innkeeper@cornucopiabb.com http://cornucopiabb.com

THOMPSON

Lord Thompson Manor
PO Box 428
Rt 200 06277
860-923-3886 Fax: 860-923-9310
Jackie
All year

150-190-BB
6 rooms, 3 pb
Most CC
C-yes/S-no/P-no/H-yes

Full breakfast
Afternoon tea, snacks, bar service
Sitting room, suites, fireplaces, cable TV, accommodate business travelers

The elegance of the Manor, the serenity of the grounds, and our suites and outstanding service provide the ultimate get-away or Wedding Reception.
mail@lordthompsonmanor.com http://www.lordthompsonmanor.com

TOLLAND

The Tolland Inn
PO Box 717
63 Tolland Green 06084
860-872-0800 Fax: 860-870-7958
877-465-0800
Susan & Stephen Beeching
All year

95-179-BB
7 rooms, 7 pb
Visa, MC, AmEx, *Rated*, •
C-ltd/S-no/P-no/H-no

Full breakfast
Afternoon tea
Winter/summer sunporch, sitting room, bridal room, guest room with fireplace

Seven guestrooms, all with private baths. Two suites, one with hot tub, fireplace & the other with fireplace. All antique & handmade furnishings.
tollinn@ntplx.net http://www.tollandinn.com

WESTBROOK

Angel's Watch Inn B&B
902 Boston Post Rd 06498
860-399-8846 Fax: 860-399-2571
Bill & Peggy Millspaugh
All year

115-160-BB
5 rooms, 5 pb
Rated
Most CC
C-yes/S-no/P-ltd/H-ltd

Full breakfast
Beer, wine, champagne
Mind, body, spirit, wellness, sunset cruises, elopment, dinner, offseason

Stately Federal built in 1830, comfortable elegance, romantic, private. Please come . . . relax . . . and enjoy . . . Our sole purpose at Angel's Watch Inn is to give you your own private haven. info@angelswatchinn.com http://www.angelswatchinn.com

---

Captain Stannard House
138 S Main St 06498
860-399-4634 Fax: 860-3998549
Lee & Vern Mettin
Mid March to Dec.

105-165-BB
8 rooms, 8 pb
Visa, MC
C-ltd/S-ltd/P-no/H-no

Snacks, complimentary wine, beer and soft drinks
Billiards table, library,sitting room, bicycles, walk to the beach

Connecticut Shoreline Inn offers 8 guest rooms, all with private bath, individually decorated. Large common areas. Full breakfast served at your candlelight table for two. A perfect romantic getaway. vern@stannardhouse.com http://innsite.com/inns/A030424.html

---

Talcott House
161 Seaside Ave 06498
860-399-5020
Barbara Slusser
All year

150-175-BB
4 rooms, 4 pb
Visa, MC, AmEx
S-no/P-no/H-yes

Full or continental bkfst (wkdays)
Afternoon tea
Sitting room, fireplaces, cable TV

All rooms have a view of the sound. Private baths, fresh flowers, piano, elegance, sunset on the Atlantic, antiques, ambiance.
b.slusser19@hotmail.com http://www.ohwy.com/ct/t/talhoubb.htm

---

Welcome Inn
433 Essex Road (Rt 153) 06498
860-399-2500 Fax: 860-399-1840
Helen Spence
All year

79-145-BB
4 rooms, 3 pb
Visa, MC, AmEx,
Rated, •
C-ltd/S-no/P-no/H-no

Full or Continental Breakfast
Lunch or dinner upon request, tea, snacks, wine
Sitting room, library, bicycles, suite, fireplace, cable TV

A lovingly restored, romantic Victorian farmhouse. Furnished in cozy elegance with antiques & family heirlooms. Memorable breakfasts, complimentary refreshments. Unforgettable! HPSpence@aol.com http://www.welcomeinnbandb.com

WESTPORT

The Inn at National Hall
Two Post Rd W 06880
203-221-1351 Fax: 203-221-0276
800-NATHALL
Jim Cooper
All year

295-850-BB
15 rooms, 15 pb
Most CC, *Rated*, •
C-yes/S-no/P-no/H-no
Italian, French, Spanish

Continental breakfast
Miramar Restaurant, Tue.-Sun. 6pm to 10pm
TV/VCR, minibar, luxury turn down service, 2 line phone, data ports

Built in 1873 and transformed into a luxury hotel in 1993, The Inn at National Hall was selected for inclusion in The National Register of Historic places in 1994, just one year after its opening. info@innatnationalhall.com http://www.innatnationalhall.com

WETHERSFIELD

Chester Bulkley House
184 Main St 06109
860-563-4236 Fax: 860-257-8266
Tom Aufiero
All year

90-105-BB
5 rooms, 3 pb
Rated, •

Full breakfast

Nestled in the historic village of Old Wethersfield, Tom & Brad provide a warm and gracious New England welcome to the vacationer, traveler and business person.
chesterbulkley@aol.com

WOODSTOCK

Elias Child House 50 Perrin Rd 06281 860-974-9836 Fax: 860-974-1541 877-974-9836 Marybeth Gorke-Felice & Tony Felice All year	100-135-BB 3 rooms, 3 pb Most CC, • C-ltd/S-ltd/P-ltd/H-no Spanish	Full breakfast Sitting room, library, bicycles, pool, suites, fireplaces, cable TV

Described as the "mansion house" in the 1700's, Elias Child House is a historic treasure in northwestern Connecticut. tfelice@compuserve.com http://www.eliaschildhouse.com

Delaware

LEWES

The Kings Inn 151 Kings Hwy 19958 302-645-6438 Pat & Leon Rockett All year	65-85-BB 5 rooms, 5 pb Visa, MC, Disc, *Rated*, • C-yes/S-no/P-yes/H-no Spanish, French, German	Continental plus breakfast Complimentary wine Sitting room, bikes, Jacuzzis, cable TV, pool table

Victorian house with large rooms and high ceilings. AC and ceiling fans, colorful, full of art, 2 blocks from downtown–charming quiet 1631 town.

LEWES (REGION)

The Inn at Canal Square 122 Market St, *Milton* 19958 302-644-3377 Fax: 302-644-3565 888-644-1911 Joe Stewart & Ted Becker All year	150-350-BB 22 rooms, 22 pb Visa, MC, AmEx, *Rated*, • C-yes/S-no/P-ltd/H-ltd	Continental plus breakfast Snacks Sitting room, suites, fireplaces, cable TV, accommodate business travelers

All accommodations are generously sized, have private baths, and most feature a balcony overlooking the harbor. The Inn is open All year, offering an extensive continental breakfast every morning.
innatcanalsquare@ce.net http://www.beach-net.com/canalsquare.html

MILTON

The Governor's 327 Union St 19968 302-684-4649 Fax: 302-684-4609 William & Deborah Post All year	95-135-BB 2 rooms, 2 pb Most CC C-ltd/S-ltd/P-no/H-no	Full gourmet breakfast Snacks, complimentary wine Sitting room, library, fireplaces, cable TV, accom. bus. travelers

Built in 1790, the inn is situated on two landscaped acres in the Milton Historic District. It was built by Joln Hazzard who piloted Washington across the Delaware.
wdpost@aol.com http://www.bedandbreakfast.com/bbc/p600989.asp

NEW CASTLE

William Penn Guest House 206 Delaware St 19720 302-328-7736 Irma & Richard Burwell All year	70-89-BB 4 rooms Visa, MC, *Rated* C-ltd/S-no/P-no/H-no Italian	Continental breakfast Living room VCR with video library

This house was built about 1682, and William Penn stayed overnight!

The Governor's, Milton, DE

REHOBOTH BEACH

Bellmoor
PO Box 1
6 Christian St 19971
302-227-5800
Fax: 302-227-0323
800-425-2355
Chad & Todd Moore
All year

85-485-BB
78 rooms, 78 pb
Most CC, *Rated*, •
C-ltd/S-no/P-no/H-yes

Full gourmet breakfast provided
Afternoon tea, snacks
Concierge, 2 libraries, 2 swimming pools, whirlpools, fireplaces, Day Spa

Guests enjoy today's finest amenities amid yesterday's elegance in a warm, residential setting. "It's like visiting the seaside manor of a longtime friend."
info@bellmoor.com http://www.dinnerbellinn.com/

The Corner Cupboard Inn
50 Park Ave 19971
302-227-8553 Fax: 302-226-9113
Elizabeth G. Hooper
All year

80-BB
18 rooms, 18 pb

 ccinn@dmv.com

---

Lighthouse Inn
20 Delaware 19971
302-226-0407
Fax: 302-226-3385
800-600-9092
Jerry Sipes & Matt Turlinske
All year

50-185-BB
6 rooms, 6 pb
Visa, MC, Disc
C-ltd/S-ltd/P-ltd/H-no

Continental plus breakfast
Wine and Cheese
Sitting room, in-room refrigerators, TV/VCR, movies

The ideal Inn at the ideal location . . . only ½ block from the beautiful Atlantic Ocean and free off street parking. You will find a nautical relaxing beach atmosphere at our Inn.
skijo@erols.com http://www.lighthouseInn.net

Lord & Hamilton Seaside
20 Brooklyn Ave 19971
302-227-6960 Fax: N/A
877-227-6960
Grady Thompson
All year

75-175-BB
6 rooms, 6 pb
Visa, MC, *Rated*
C-ltd/S-ltd/P-no/H-no
German, French

Continental breakfast
Afternoon refreshments
Private baths, ocean views, priv. entrances, antiques

Vintage Victorian Inn (c. 1871). Wrap-around porch, private baths & ocean views. Steps to restaurants, shops, cafes, boardwalk and beach. Perfect spot for a romantic getaway or beach vacation! innkeeper@lordhamilton.com http://www.lordhamilton.com

REHOBOTH BEACH

Sea Voice Inn 14 Delaware Ave 19971 302-226-9435 800-637-2862 Susie & Jeff Bond May-September	75-200-BB 13 rooms, 9 pb Visa, MC, AmEx, • C-ltd/S-ltd/P-no/H-ltd	Full breakfast Snacks, complimentary wine Sitting room, bikes, cable TV, beach chairs & towels, coolers

A "Beach Victorian." Cheerful, comfortable, distinctively from a past era full of sweet memories. Large breakfast on porch. One minute walk to boardwalk and downtown.
relax@atbeach.com http://www.seavoice.com

Sea Witch Manor Inn 71 Lake Ave 19971 302-226-9482 866-732-9482 Inez Conover & Kathleen Bailey All year	155-275-BB 5 rooms, 5 pb Visa, MC, *Rated*, • S-ltd/P-no/H-ltd	Full gourmet breakfast Restaurant, lunch, dinner, PM tea, snacks, wine Sitting rm, library, bike, Jacuzzi, suite, fireplace, cable TV, bus. travele

The Sea Witch Manor Inn sits on a quiet tree-lined street that meets the sea, Victorian elegance & romance from the warmth of fireplaces in every room, to the delicious food.
InnKeeper@SeaWitchManor.com http://www.seawitchmanor.com

WILMINGTON

Darley Manor Inn 3701 Philadelphia Pike Claymont Community 19703 302-792-2127 800-824-4703 Ray & Judith Hester All year	85-139-BB 6 rooms, 6 pb Most CC, *Rated*, • C-ltd/S-ltd/P-no/H-no	Full Breakfast, with var. menu/time Afternoon tea, comp. wine, snacks Sitting room, TV/VCR, Jacuzzi, exercise room, phones

Historic register, c.1790 Colonial manor house, southern hospitality, first class amenities, & easy access to all Brandywine Valley attractions, Wilmington, DE, and Philadelphia, PA.
darley@dca.net http://www.darinn.com

District of Columbia

WASHINGTON

Aaron Shipman House PO Box 12011 20009 202-328-3510 Fax: 202-232-5693 877-893-3233 Charles & Jackie Reed All year	70-165-BB 6 rooms, 5 pb Visa, MC, AmEx, *Rated* C-yes/S-no/P-no/H-no French, Spanish	Full breakfast Snacks Sitting room, gardens, library, Victorian porch, piano, antiques

A beautifully restored Victorian featuring original wood work, stained glass, chandeliers, Victorian-style lattice porch, art nouveau and Victorian antiques.
bnbaccom@aol.com http://www.aaronshipmanhouse.com

Adams Inn 1744 Lanier Pl NW 20009 202-745-3600 Fax: 202-319-7958 800-578-6807 Anne Owens All year	65-75-BB 25 rooms, 15 pb Most CC C-yes/S-no/P-no/H-ltd Spanish	Continental breakfast Tea, coffee Internet access, sitting rooms, TV lounge, w/d, guest kitchen, patio

Only 1 block from the Adams Morgan's restaurant district & 7 blocks from the Woodley Park Red Line Metro, the newly-renovated Adam's Inn is convenient to everything. Limited parking is available. adamsinn@adamsinn.com http://adamsinn.com

WASHINGTON

Bull Moose on Capitol Hill
101 5th St NE 20002
202-547-1050 Fax: 202-548-9741
800-261-2768
Elizabeth Weber
All year

129-209-BB
10 rooms, 4 pb
Most CC
C-yes/S-no/P-no/H-no
Russian, Spanish

Continental plus breakfast
Imported Spanish sherry in parlor & evening treat

Nestled in the historic district of Capitol Hill, the Bull Moose Bed & Breakfast is a turreted brick Victorian tastefully restored in the year 2000.
reserve@BullMoose-B-and-B.com http://www.bullmoose-b-and-b.com/

Dupont at the Circle
1606 19th St NW
1604 19th St NW 20009
202-332-5251
Fax: 202-332-3244
888-412-0100
Alan & Anexora Skvirsky, Lydia Pena-Simone
All year

160-330-BB
8 rooms, 8 pb
Most CC, *Rated*, •
C-ltd/S-no/P-no/H-no
Spanish

Continental breakfast
Sitting room, suite, cable TV

Our charming Victorian inn with modern conveniences is in Washington DC's premier location. inn@dupontatthecircle.com http://www.dupontatthecircle.com

---

The Embassy Inn
1627 16th St NW 20009
202-234-7800
Fax: 202-234-3309
800-423-9111
Susan Stiles All year

99-179-BB
38 rooms, 38 pb
Most CC, *Rated*, •
C-yes/S-ltd/P-no/H-no
Spanish, French, Arabic

Continental plus breakfast
Complimentary sherry, snacks
Snacks, sitting room, cable TV & HBO, near Metro & White House

Near Metro, White House, restaurants and shops; knowledgeable and helpful staff. Colonial style, in renovated 1920s boarding house.

Jurys Normandy Inn
2118 Wyoming Ave NW 20008
202-483-1350 Fax: 202-387-8241
800-424-3729
Marina Hughes
All year

99-145-EP
75 rooms, 75 pb
Most CC, *Rated*, •
C-yes/S-yes/P-no/H-yes
Arabic, Spanish, German, French

Continental breakfast
Coffee, cookies; wine/cheese every Tuesday
Mini frig, data ports, coffee/coffeemaker, hairdryer, inroom safe, iron/brd

Charming boutique-style hotel located in the city's prestigious Embassy District, offering a gracious old-world retreat for visitors and a level of personalized service that is second to none. marina_hughes@jurysdoyle.com http://www.jurysdoyle.com

---

Kalorama Guest House
1854 Mintwood Place, NW 20009
202-667-6369 Fax: 202-319-1262
Michael, Karin & Katy
All year

60-120-BB
29 rooms, 15 pb
Most CC, *Rated*, •
C-ltd/S-no/P-no/H-no

Continental breakfast
Complimentary wine, lemonade
Parlor, sun room, fridge, 24-hour message service, free local phone calls

Victorian townhouse decorated in period furnishings. Antique-filled, spacious rooms. Beautiful sun room for your morning breakfast. Charming, unique & inexpensive.

WASHINGTON

Maison Orleans
414 5th St SE 20003
202-544-3694
Bill Rouchell
All year

95-135-BB
3 rooms, 3 pb
C-ltd/S-ltd/P-no/H-no

Continental plus breakfast
Sitting room, fireplaces, accommodate business traveler, off-street parking

This turn-of-the-century Federal row house is located five blocks SE of the Nation's Capitol, Library of Congress, and Supreme Court. Completely furnished with family pieces from the 30's and 40's. maisonorln@aol.com http://www.bbonline.com/dc/maisonorleans/

McMillan House
2417 First St, NW 20001
202-986-8989 Fax: 202-986-9747
800-240-9355
Albert Ceccone
All year

70-90-BB
10 rooms
Visa, MC, AmEx, *Rated*, •
C-yes/S-no/P-no/H-no
Italian & Spanish

Continental breakfast
Fireplace, cable TV, conference facilities, 800 number extension 09

The McMillan House is a newly renovated turn-of-the-century bed and breakfast with a fireplace, high ceilings and spacious rooms.
aceccone@aol.com http://www.mcmillanhouse.net

Swann House
1808 New Hampshire Ave NW 20009
202-265-4414 Fax: 202-265-6755
Mary Ross & Rick Verkler
All year

140-295-BB
9 rooms, 9 pb
Most CC, *Rated*
C-ltd/S-no/P-no/H-no

Continental plus breakfast
Tea, snacks
Parlour, Jacuzzis, swimming pool, suites, fireplace, cable TV, conference

Grand Richardson Romanesque mansion in Dupont Circle, D.C.'s most vibrant neighborhood. Eat at local outdoor cafes, walk to museums or relax by the pool or on our roof deck. stay@swannhouse.com http://www.swannhouse.com

---

The Windsor Inn
1842 16th St NW 20009
202-667-0300 Fax: 202-667-4503
800-423-9111
Susan Stiles
All year

99-179-BB
45 rooms, 45 pb
Most CC, *Rated*, •
C-yes/S-ltd/P-no/H-no
French, Spanish, Arabic

Continental plus breakfast
Complimentary sherry & snacks
Cable TV & HBO in rooms, renovated lobby, telephones

Relaxing and charming haven in heart of nation's capitol. Art deco flair. Close to Metro and restaurants. 11 blocks north of White House.

Windsor Park Hotel
2116 Kalorama Rd NW 20008
202-483-7700 Fax: 202-332-4547
800-247-3064
Sam Najjar
All year

BB
43 rooms, 43 pb
Most CC, *Rated*, •
C-yes/S-ltd/P-no/H-ltd

Continental breakfast
Snacks
Sitting room, suites, cable TV, small frig in rooms, acc. bus travelers

This boutique hotel, circa 1930, has all the modern conveniences built in. Our comfortable rooms and suites have private voice mail, hair dryers and mini refrigerators.
windsorparkhotel@erols.com http://www.windsorparkhotel.com

Woodley Park Guest House
2647 Woodley Rd NW 20008
202-667-0218 Fax: 202-667-1080
866-667-0218
Laura, Theirri, Hope
All year

70-140-BB
16 rooms, 11 pb
Visa, MC, AmEx
C-ltd/S-no/P-no
French, Arabic, Spanish

Continental plus breakfast
Housekeeping, concierge

Beautifully renovated bed and breakfast inn offering 16 guestrooms, steps from the Metro. This cozy urban guest house is a short walk from Dupont Circle and Georgetown.
info@woodleyparkguesthouse.com http://www.woodleyparkguesthouse.com

Florida

AMELIA ISLAND

1857 Florida House Inn
PO Box 688
20 South 3rd St 32034
904-261-3300 800-258-3301
Bob & Karen Warner
All year

79-189-BB
15 rooms, 15 pb
Most CC, *Rated*, •
C-yes/S-no/P-yes/H-yes
Spanish

Full breakfast
Restaurant serves lunch & dinner.
Sitting room, library, bicycles, near beaches, golf, tennis, fishing

Florida's oldest continually operating hotel, c.1857, in 50-block historic district. Antiques, quilts, shady porches, Jacuzzis, fireplaces, courtyard with fountain & gazebo.
innkeepers@floridahouseinn.com http://www.floridahouseinn.com

---

Bailey House
28 S 7th St 32034
904-261-5390 Fax: 904-321-0103
800-251-5390
Tom & Jenny Bishop
All year

129-199-BB
10 rooms, 10 pb
Most CC, *Rated*, •
C-ltd/S-no/P-no/H-yes

Full breakfast
Old pump organ, victrola, authentic antiques, A/C, heat, whirlpool tubs

Elegant 1895 Queen Anne Victorian on National Register, in historic district. Walk to shopping, restaurants, marina, dining.
baileyhs@bellsouth.net http://www.bailey-house.com

Elizabeth Pointe Lodge
98 S Fletcher Ave 32034
904-277-4851
Fax: 904-277-6500
800-772-3359
David & Susan Caples
All year

160-295-BB
25 rooms, 25 pb
Most CC, *Rated*, •
C-yes/S-yes/P-no/H-yes

Full breakfast
Complimentary wine/snack
Sitting room, library, bikes, oceanfront, kid friendly, 24 hr room service

Reminiscent of a turn-of-the-century lodge; oceanfront on a small Florida barrier island; bike to historic seaport village nearby.
info@elizabethpointelodge.com http://www.elizabethpointelodge.com

---

Fairbanks House
227 S 7th St 32034
904-277-0500 Fax: 904-277-3103
888-891-9897
Bill & Theresa Hamilton
All year

160-275-BB
12 rooms, 12 pb
Most CC, *Rated*, •
C-ltd/S-no/P-no/H-no

Full breakfast
Complimentary social hour
Sitting room, bicycles, pool, Jacuzzi, suites, conference facility

1885 Italianate villa & historic cottages, landscaped grounds and swimming pool. Within walking distance of many shops & restaurants.
email@fairbankshouse.com http://fairbankshouse.com

Hoyt House
804 Atlantic Ave 32034
904-277-4300
Fax: 904-277-9626
800-432-2085
Gayl Blount
All year

129-199-BB
10 rooms, 10 pb
Most CC, *Rated*
C-ltd/S-no/P-ltd/H-yes
Spanish

Full hot breakfast daily
Beverages, afternoon tea, snacks & wine
Music room,library & book exchange, bicycles, beach gear, VCR

Centerpiece of Historic Seaport of Fernandina. 1905 Queen Anne home surrounded by oaks, private gardens. Walk/bike to beach, harbor, restaurants, galleries and antiques.
innkeeper@hoythouse.com http://www.hoythouse.com

AMELIA ISLAND (REGION)

The Amelia Island Williams House
103 S 9th St, *Fernandina Beach* 32034
904-277-2328 Fax: 904-321-1325
800-414-9258
Nancy & Paul Barnes All year

165-245-BB
8 rooms, 8 pb
Visa, MC, *Rated*, •
C-ltd/S-no/P-no/H-yes

Full gourmet breakfast
Complimentary wine
Sitting room, bicycles, tennis courts, hot tubs, frequent flyer miles

"A top inn of the year," Country Inn magazine 1996. "One of the South's most exquisite B&B's." info@williamshouse.com http://www.williamshouse.com

ANNA MARIA ISLAND (REGION)

Angelinos Sea Lodge
103 29th Street
2818 Ave E, *Holmes Beach* 34217
941-778-9750 Fax: 941-779-9019
877-955-6343
Richard and Lynn Hazen
All year

95-160-EP
4 rooms, 4 pb
Most CC, •
C-yes/S-no/P-no/H-no

No breakfast, kitchen in lodge
Full kitchen, laundry room, beach chairs

Angelinos Sea Lodge beachfront cottages are on the Gulf Coast of beautiful Anna Maria island, Holmes Beach. Reserve your place in this little beach resort, a paradise on the Florida West Coast. lynnt@angel-sealodge.com http://www.angel-sealodge.com

APALACHICOLA

Bryant House
101 6th St 32320
850-653-3270 Fax: 850-653-9663
888-554-4376
Brigitte Schroeder All year

87-147-BB
3 rooms, 3 pb
Visa, MC, AmEx, *Rated*, •
C-ltd/S-no/P-no/H-no
German

Full German breakfast
Complimentary wine
Sitting room, classic, rose garden, fountain, fish pond

European hospitality in a quaint Victorian setting. Wrap-around porch, antique wicker to while away the hours and solve the world's problems.
ken@romantic-retreat.com http://www.romantic-retreat.com

BIG PINE KEY

Barnacle
1557 Long Beach Dr 33043
305-872-3298 Fax: 305-872-3863
800-465-9100
Tim & Jane Marquis All year

95-150-BB
4 rooms, 4 pb
S-yes/P-no/H-no

Full breakfast
Hot tub, bicycles, refrigerators, weddings & receptions

Barefoot living with panache. Secluded area on ocean in fabulous Florida Keys. Private cottage and efficiency unit barnacle@attglobal.net http://www.thebarnacle.net

---

Deer Run
PO Box 431
Long Beach Rd 33043
305-872-2015
Sue Abbott All year

110-185-BB
3 rooms, 3 pb
Rated, •
S-no/P-no/H-yes

Full southern breakfast
Comp. bottle of wine
Bicycles, beach, hot tubs, lib., hammocks, grill, king beds all rms

The house is 75 feet from the ocean- quiet, serene. Breakfast is served on the verandah overlooking the ocean. Veggie dining by request. Adults only. 33 miles to Key West.
deerrunbb@aol.com

BIG PINE KEY (REGION)

Ed & Ellens Lodgings
103365 Overseas Highway, *Key Largo* 33037
305-457-9949 888-333-5536
Ed & Ellen Handt

49-99-EP
6 rooms, 6 pb
Visa, MC
C-yes/S-no/P-no/H-no
Dec–Apr;June–Aug

Barbecues, picnic tables in Key Largo

Key Largo efficiencies sleep up to four. Big Pine Key duplexes sleep up to seven. Located close to state parks, diving, snorkeling, and fishing.
ehandte@yahoo.com http://ed-ellens-lodgings.com

CAPE CORAL (REGION)

Bayview
PO Box 35
12251 Shoreview Dr, *Cape Coral–Pine Island* 33993
239-283-7510
Diane & William LeRoy

79-149-BB
5 rooms, 5 pb
Rated, •
C-yes/S-ltd/H-ltd
All year

Continental plus breakfast

Tropical island waterfront B&B, view manatee/dolphins from your porch, fantastic sunsets, free use of canoe, 90' fishing pier. Near Sanibel-JN Ding Darling Preserve. Suites with private baths. cbirds@webtv.net http://www.webbwiz.com/bayviewbb

CAPTIVA (REGION)

Captiva Island Inn
PO Box 848
11509 Andy Rosse Ln, *Captiva Island* 33924
239-395-0882 Fax: 239-395-0862
800-454-9898
Sandra Stilwell
All year

99-280-BB
6 rooms, 6 pb
Most CC, *Rated*, •
C-yes/S-no/P-no/H-ltd

Full breakfast
Lunch & dinner avail, restaurant
Bicycles, suites, cable TV, beach chairs, accommodate business travelers

Visit our tropical island paradise in the heart of Olde Captiva Village. This charming Historic Inn has been tastefully restored with Island flair.
captivaislandinn@aol.com http://www.captivaislandinn.com

CEDAR KEY

Cedar Key
PO Box 700, 810 3rd St 32625
352-543-5050 Fax: 352-543-8070
877-543-5051
Lois Benninghoff & Bob Davenport
All year

80-130-BB
7 rooms, 7 pb
Most CC, *Rated*, •
C-ltd/S-ltd/P-ltd/H-yes

Full breakfast
Afternoon tea, snacks
Sitting room, library

Canopied by centuries old live oaks, this rambling 2-story house offers tastefully decorated rooms with high ceilings, paddle fans, private baths, porch access, and breakfast in a garden setting. bob@cedarkeybedbreakfast.com http://www.cedarkeybedbreakfast.com

COCOA

Indian River House
3113 Indian River Dr 32922
321-631-5660
Suzanne LaMee-Bender
All year

90-95-BB
4 rooms, 4 pb
Visa, MC, AmEx
C-ltd/S-ltd/P-no/H-no

Full breakfast
Afternoon refreshments at your leisure
Sitting room, library, bikes, fireplaces, cable TV, accom. bus. trav.

Lovely turn-of-the-century historic home located on the Indian River Lagoon. It's a good place to be, whether business or pleasure.
suzanne@indianriverhouse.com http://www.indianriverhouse.com

COCOA BEACH

The Inn at Cocoa Beach
4300 Ocean Beach Blvd 32931
321-799-3460
Fax: 321-784-8632
800-343-5307
Allen & Katherine Warren
All year

135-295-BB
50 rooms, 50 pb
Most CC, *Rated*, •
C-ltd/S-yes/P-no/H-no

Continental Plus Breakfast
Afternoon tea, snacks, comp. wine, bar service
Sitting room, library, bikes, Jacuzzis, pool, fireplaces, cable TV

An oceanfront property, quaint and romantic. We offer individually decorated rooms and beautifully landscaped grounds. Enjoy our fresh baked breakfast and wine & cheese social daily. awarren@theinnatcocoabeach.com http://www.theinnatcocoabeach.com

DAYTONA BEACH

The Coquina Inn 544 S Palmetto Ave 32114 386-254-4969 Fax: 386-254-1969 800-805-7533 Ann Christoffersen & Dennis Haight	80-110-BB 4 rooms, 4 pb Most CC C-ltd/S-no/P-no/H-no All year	Full breakfast Complimentary port, sherry, coffee Bikes, cable TV, guest phone, hot tub, off-street parking

Located in the Daytona Beach Historic District, this handsome circa 1912 house boasts an exterior of Coquina rock blended from shells.

coquinabnb@aol.com http://www.coquinainndaytonabeach.com

Live Oak Inn B&B and Rest. 444-448 South Beach St 32114 386-252-4667 Fax: 386-239-0098 800-881-4667 Lynn Smithers-Hubbard All year	80-165-BB 14 rooms, 14 pb Most CC, *Rated*, • C-ltd/S-no/P-ltd/H-yes Italian, Spanish	Full continental self-serve bkfst. High season wine & cheese or tea & cookies Jacuzzis, balcony, outdoor deck, gardens

Two carefully-restored homes (both on National Historic Register); charming setting by the Halifax River complete with period antiques and a historical garden.

FLORIDA KEYS (REGION)

Casa Morada Hotel 136 Madeira Rd, *Islamorada* 33036 305-664-0044 Fax: 305-664-0674 888-881-3030 Front Desk Manager All year	150-250-EP 16 rooms, 16 pb Visa, MC, AmEx, *Rated*, • C-ltd/S-ltd/P-ltd/H-ltd Italian, French, Spanish	Cont. Breakfast, Sat. & Sun. only Lunch, dinner, and complimentary wine Swimming pool, suites, fireplaces, cable TV, accom. bus. travelers, kayaks

Totally renovated, small hotel de charme; waterfront property with private island connected by pedestrian bridge; spectacular sunset views; walking distance to our club restaurant. info@casamorada.com http://www.casamorada.com

FORT LAUDERDALE

Caribbean Quarters Inn 3012 Granada St 33304 954-523-3226 Fax: 954-523-7541 888-414-3226 Bernd MetzAt All year	95-250-BB 12 rooms, 12 pb Most CC, *Rated*, • S-no/P-no/H-no	Continental plus breakfast Tropical courtyard, bikes, hot tubs, renovated in 1998

At Caribbean Quarters, today's traveler will enjoy the romance of the last century with the comforts of the new millennium.

cqbandb@aol.com http://www.caribbeanquarters.com

FORT LAUDERDALE (REGION)

A Little Inn by the Sea 4546 El Mar Dr, *Lauderdale by the Sea* 33308 954-772-2450 Fax: 954-938-9354 800-492-0311 Uli & Brigitte Brandt, Carole & Victor Lancry All year	79-318-BB 29 rooms, 29 pb Most CC, *Rated*, • C-yes/S-ltd/P-no/H-ltd German, French, Spanish	Continental plus breakfast Sitting room, library, pool, bicycles, tennis, family friendly facility

European Mediterranean B&B on the beach, very tropical setting, as if you are on an island, 3 natural reefs right in front of the beach.

alinn@gate.net http://www.alittleinn.com

FORT MYERS

The Best Western Springs Resort 18051 S Tamiami Tr 33908 941-267-7900 Fax: 941-267-9763 800-344-9794	BB All year

Great location providing guests easy access to all that Southwest Florida has to offer!

info@thespringsresort.com http://www.thespringsresort.com

FORT PIERCE

Villa Nina Island Inn
3851 North A 1 A 34949
561-467-8969
Glenn & Nina Rappaport
All year

125-240-BB
5 rooms, 5 pb
Visa, MC, *Rated*
C-no/S-no/P-no/H-no

Welcome basket with drinks and snacks in room
Beach access to the Atlantic Ocean, pool overlooking the Indian River

Romantic five-room beachside, riverfront inn on the Treasure Coast with private beach access to the Atlantic Ocean, plus pool on the Indian River.
villanina@villanina.com http://www.villanina.com

HOLMES BEACH

Harrington House Beachfront
5626 Gulf Dr 34217
941-778-5444 Fax: 941-778-0527
Jo & Frank Davis
All year

139-249-BB
8 rooms, 8 pb
Visa, MC, *Rated*, •
C-ltd/S-no/P-no

Full gourmet breakfast
Comp. iced tea, popcorn
Sitting room, bicycles, swimming pool

Charming restored 1920s home directly on Gulf of Mexico reflects "casual elegance."
harhousebb@mail.pcsonline.com http://www.harringtonhouse.com

HOMESTEAD

Redland Hotel an Historic Inn
5 S Flagler Ave 33030
305-246-1904 Fax: 305-246-9600
800-595-1904
Katy Oleson & Nancy Gust
All year

79-125-EP
Rated, •

Lunch, dinner, breakfast available in restaurant

The Redland Hotel promises to provide a uniquely flexible, full service hotel where you will be as comfortable planning a business conference, as you will just stopping by for a cup of coffee. info@redlandhotel.com http://www.redlandhotel.com

---

Room at the Inn
15830 SW 240 St 33031
305-246-0492 Fax: 305-246-0590
Sally C. Robinson
All year

85-110-BB
4 rooms, 3 pb
Rated
C-ltd/S-ltd/P-no/H-no

Full breakfast
Great room with fireplace, swimming pool with, heated spa, TV/VCR, flowers

Room at the Inn B&B is a charming, relaxing retreat on two acres in the agricultural/grove area five miles north of Homestead and two miles west of US1.
robinsonsfl@aol.com

INDIANTOWN

Seminole Country Inn
PO Box 1818
5885 SW Warfield Blvd 34956
772-597-3777 Fax: 772-597-2883
888-394-3777
Jonnie Flewelling
All year

65-95-AP
22 rooms, 22 pb
Most CC, *Rated*
C-yes/S-ltd/P-no/H-no

Continental breakfast
Lunch, dinner, snacks
Rest., sitting. rm., bikes, tennis, pool, conference, fireplaces, cable TV

Built in 1926, our Inn has the grandeur of an age gone by and outstanding Southern food & hospitality. Pool & garden area. seminole@aol.com http://www.seminoleinn.com

JACKSONVILLE

The Inn at Oak Street
2114 Oak St 32204
904-379-5525
Tina Musico & Bob Eagle
All year

145-165-BB
5 rooms, 5 pb
Most CC, •
C-ltd/S-no/P-no/H-no
English

Full breakfast
Evening wine hour and selection of treats
Plush robes, newspaper, flat screen TV's with DVD, whirlpool tubs.

The Inn at Oak Street is a grand 1902 five bedroom Bed & Breakfast located in the historic Riverside area of Jacksonville. We provide spacious accommodations in a luxurious and inviting atmosphere. tinamusico@yahoo.com http://www.innatoakstreet.com

Pelican Path by the Sea, Jacksonville Beach, FL

JACKSONVILLE

Plantation Manor Inn	150-180-BB	Full breakfast
1630 Copeland St 32204	9 rooms, 9 pb	Complimentary
904-384-4630 Fax: 904-387-0960	Visa, MC, AmEx, *Rated*	refreshments
Kathy Ray	C-ltd/S-no/P-no/H-no	Sitting room, spa, swimming
All year		pool

Restored 1905 Southern Mansion with antique furnishings and Oriental carpets. 2 blocks from river, restaurants, antique shops.

pmijaxfl@aol.com http://www.bbonline.com/fl/plantation

St. Johns House	85-110-BB	Full breakfast
1718 Osceola St 32204	3 rooms, 2 pb	Afternoon tea,
904-384-3724 Fax: 904-384-3724	C-yes/S-no/P-no/H-no	complimentary wine
Joan E. Moore		Sitting room square along
Closed July		river

A traditional B&B near downtown, the sports and convention centers and shopping. Just one block off the St. Johns River in a National Historic District.

JACKSONVILLE BEACH

Pelican Path by the Sea	80-175-BB	Full breakfast
11 N 19th Ave 32250	4 rooms, 4 pb	Sitt. rm., bikes, cable,
904-249-1177 Fax: 904-346-5412	*Rated*, •	Jacuzzis, phones, TV/VCR,
888-749-1177	S-no/P-no/H-no	refrigerators, spa tubs
Tom & Joan Hubbard	All year	

Pelican Path enjoys a superb location–an oceanfront, residential neighborhood with easy access to beach, stores, & restaurants. ppbandb@aol.com http://www.pelicanpath.com

KEY LARGO

Mullet Mansion	150-200-BB	Continental plus breakfast
97920 Overseas Hwy 33037	2 rooms, 1 pb	Snacks, complimentary
305-852-9383 Fax: 305-852-8078	•	wine, afternoon tea.
Suzy Barry	C-ltd/S-ltd/P-no/H-ltd	Bicycles, Jacuzzi, suites,
All year		fireplace, cable, swimming,
		paddle boat, sailboat

Like having your own mini-retreat, gorgeous seaside sunsets, personalized service with any special requests. Our surroundings are private, soothing, and ideal for couples.

mullet_mansion@yahoo.com http://www.vtraveler.com/vacations

KEY WEST

Ambrosia Key West
622 Fleming St
615, 618, 622 Fleming St 33040
305-296-9838 Fax: 305-296-2425
800-535-9838
Kate Miano & Toto the Wonderdog
All year

110-369-BB
19 rooms, 19 pb
Most CC, *Rated*, •
C-yes/S-ltd/P-yes/H-ltd

Continental plus breakfast
Bikes, Jacuzzis, pool, suites, cable TV, modems, accom. bus. travel

Romantic tropical oasis 1 block off Duval Street. Pool rooms, suites, townhomes & a cottage facing 3 pools on over an acre of lushly landscaped grounds.
ambrosia@bellsouth.net http://www.ambrosiakeywest.com

Andrews Inn
0 Whalton Lane 33040
305-294-7730 Fax: 305-294-0021
888-263-7393
Sally Garratt
All year

119-189-BB
6 rooms, 6 pb
Most CC, *Rated*, •
C-yes/S-ltd/P-no/H-no
Spanish

Continental plus breakfast
Evening cocktails
Swimming pool, tropical gardens, bikes, vaulted ceilings, private baths, A/C

Stroll down a shady lane off of Duval St. and you will find a lush tropical courtyard with a pool at its center and six charming rooms with private baths awaiting your arrival.
KWAndrews@aol.com http://www.andrewsinn.com

The Banyan Resort
323 Whitehead St 33040
305-296-7786 Fax: 305-294-1107
800-225-0639
Martin Bettencourt
All year

200-400-EP
38 rooms, 38 pb
Rated, •
C-ltd/P-no

The Banyan Resort is a lush, tranquil Caribbean estate tucked away in the heart of historic Old Town Key West. Private and secluded. Studio—1 bedroom and 2 bedroom.
martinmgr@aol.com http://www.banyanresort.com

Blue Parrot Inn
916 Elizabeth St 33040
305-296-0033 Fax: 305-296-5697
800-231-2473
Cleo, Frank & Larry
All year

79-487-BB
9 rooms, 9 pb
Most CC, *Rated*, •
S-yes/P-no/H-ltd

Continental plus breakfast
Refrigerator, most rooms
Ceiling fan, cable TV, heated pool, phones, A/C, private bath, bikes

Classic 1884 historic restoration, with charming gingerbread verandas. A quiet, secluded retreat in the heart of Old Town. We feature 7 rooms with private baths and 2 suites.
bluparotin@aol.com http://www.blueparrotinn.com

Casa Alante Guest Cottages
1435 S Roosevelt Blvd 33040
305-293-0702 800-688-3942
Sandy Erb & Katrina Birt
All year

85-260-BB
C-ltd/P-yes/H-yes
German

Continental breakfast

From the hammock swaying in the Mahogany trees, to the flower decorated breakfast tray delivered each morning to your private terrace—Casa Alante welcomes you to relax.
casa-alante@travelbase.com http://www.casaalante.com

Center Court Historic Inn
915 Center St 33040
305-296-9292 Fax: 305-294-4104
800-797-8787
Naomi Van Steelandt
All year

98-398-BB
25 rooms, 25 pb
Most CC, *Rated*, •
C-yes/S-ltd/P-yes/H-yes
Spanish, Hungarian, Polish

Continental plus breakfast
Complimentary afternoon Happy Hour
3 heated pools, private JACUZZIS, bikes delivered to your door

Romantic, affordable, luxurious ... steps from Duval Street. Rooms, suites (w/private Jacuzzis), villas, private homes, some w/private pools, in a tropically landscaped paradise. Pets welcome! info@centercourtkw.com http://www.centercourtkw.com

KEY WEST

Chelsea House & Red Rooster
707 Truman Ave 33040
305-296-2211 Fax: 305-296-4822
800-845-8859
Jim Durbin & Gary Williams
All year

75-235-BB
37 rooms, 37 pb
Most CC, *Rated*, •
C-no/S-ltd/P-yes/H-ltd

Continental plus breakfast
Coffee bar
Ceiling fans, cable TV, phones, refrigerators, room safes, bath amenities

Two Beautiful Restored Victorian Mansions in the Heat of Old Town Key West. Walking distance to everything. 37 unique rooms ranging from Cozy to Grand all with private bath. chelseahse@aol.com http://www.ChelseaHouseKW.com

---

Conch House Heritage Inn
625 Truman Ave 33040
305-293-0020 Fax: 305-293-8447
800-207-5806
Sam Holland & Hillary Lee
All year

98-228-BB
6 rooms, 6 pb
Most CC, *Rated*, •
C-ltd/S-yes/P-no/H-yes
Spanish

Continental plus breakfast
Swimming pool, phones, bikes, porches, garden

Victorian architecture with Bahaman influences. Family owned & operated over 100 years. Extremely large rooms, tropical cottages by pool/garden.
conchinn@aol.com http://www.conchhouse.com

Cypress House
601 Caroline St 33040
305-294-6969 Fax: 305-296-1174
800-525-2488
Dave Taylor
All year

99-350-BB
16 rooms, 8 pb
Most CC, *Rated*, •
C-ltd/S-yes/P-no/H-no

Continental plus breakfast
Complimentary wine
Sitting room, library, swimming pool, an adult only inn

1888 Bahamian Conch mansion. Private, tropical. Large rooms with A/C and ceiling fans. Walk to all historic sites, shopping, restaurants.
CypressKW@aol.com http://www.CypressHouseKW.com

Douglas House
419 Amelia St 33040
305-294-5269 Fax: 305-292-7665
800-833-0372
Robert Marrero
All year

99-269-BB
15 rooms, 15 pb
Visa, MC, AmEx, *Rated*, •
C-ltd/S-yes/P-yes/H-no
Spanish, French, German

Continental breakfast
Afternoon tea
Bikes, hot tub, swimming pool, an adult only inn

Choose from 15 deluxe rooms & large suites. Sit on your private porch as dusk turns to night & the warmth of the Caribbean Sea relaxes your body.
info@douglashouse.com http://www.DouglasHouse.com

Eden House
1015 Fleming St 33040
305-296-6868 Fax: 305-294-1221
800-533-KEYS
Michael Eden
All year

80-275-EP
40 rooms, 36 pb
Visa, MC
C-yes/S-no/P-no/H-no
Spanish, French, German

Cold drink at check-in
Swimming pool, Jacuzzi, snorkeling, scuba diving, sailing & jet ski nearby

In old Key West. Ceiling fans, white wicker. Sip a cool drink under a poolside gazebo, lounge on verandah, dine in garden cafe. Hammock area, elevated sundeck.
mike@edenhouse.com http://www.edenhouse.com

Frances Street Bottle Inn
535 Frances St 33040
305-294-8530 Fax: 305-294-1628
800-294-8530
MaryBeth McCulloch
All year

80-225-BB
8 rooms, 8 pb
Visa, MC, AmEx, *Rated*, •
C-yes/S-ltd/P-yes/H-yes

Continental Plus breakfast
Snacks, complimentary wine & soft drinks
Bicycles, Jacuzzis, cable TV, accom. bus. travelers, beach passes

Nestled under tropical Pounciana trees, this Historic Inn is steps from spectacular restaurants, intriguing galleries and the historic waterfront.
bottleinn@mindspring.com http://www.bottleinn.com

KEY WEST

The Grand Guest House
1116 Grinnell St 33040
305-294-0590 Fax: 305-294-0477
888-947-2630
Jeffrey Daubman, Jim Brown & Elizabeth Rose
Dec-May

108-268-BB
7 rooms, 7 pb
Most CC, *Rated*
C-ltd/S-ltd/P-ltd/H-no

Continental breakfast
A/C, cable, phone, fridge, suites, concierge, fans, off-street park.

Clean, crisp, affordable accommodations in the heart of Old Town Key West. Recipient of the Superior Florida Keys Lodging designation and a member of the Key West Innkeepers Association. thegrand@flakeysol.com http://www.thegrandguesthouse.com

---

Heron House
512 Simonton St 33040
305-294-9227 Fax: 305-294-5692
800-294-1644
Fred Geibelt/Robert Framarin
All year

119-369-BB
23 rooms, 23 pb
Visa, MC, AmEx, *Rated*, •
S-ltd/P-no/H-ltd

Continental plus breakfast
Breakfast bar
Orchid gardens, sun deck, in-room safes, pool, robes, concierge, phones

Old island charm situated in location central to all the main tourist attractions. Waterfall-rainforest theme on property. Pool, sun deck, gardens. Daily newspapers. Parking available. heronkyw@aol.com http://www.heronhouse.com

---

Key West B&B
415 William St 33040
305-296-7274 Fax: 305-293-0306
800-438-6155
Jody Carlson
All year

59-285-BB
8 rooms, 4 pb
Most CC, *Rated*, •
C-ltd/S-ltd

Continental plus breakfast
1 room with private deck, hot tubs, sauna, Jacuzzi, sun deck, sitting room

Comfortable, friendly, and filled with local art, The Popular House provides a memorable home for the Key West Bed and Breakfast.
relax@keywestbandb.com http://www.keywestbandb.com

Key West Hideaways
915 Eisenhower Drive 33040
305-296-9090 Fax: 305-292-2997
888-822-5840
Ken Schultz
15 Dec.-01 May

108-498-EP
22 rooms, 22 pb
Most CC, •
C-yes/S-no/P-yes/H-yes

Tropical Gardens, Bicycles, Jacuzzis, Swimming Pool, Suites, Cable TV.

Escape the "real world" while enjoying the perfect alternative to a luxury hotel with the added value of total privacy and the best locations in Key West.
reservations@keywesthideaways.com http://www.keywesthideaways.com

---

Knowles House
1004 Eaton St 33040
305-296-8132 Fax: 305-296-2093
800-352-4414
Les Vollmert & Paul Masse
All year

89-189-BB
8 rooms, 6 pb
Most CC, *Rated*, •
S-ltd/P-no/H-no

Continental plus breakfast
Complimentary wine
Jacuzzis, swimming pool, cable TV

Romantic historic inn in heart of Old Town Historic District, offering a relaxed, friendly atmosphere w/ elegant decor, tropical pool.
knowleshse@aol.com http://www.knowleshouse.com

The Mermaid & The Alligator
729 Truman Ave 33040
305-294-1894 Fax: 305-295-9925
800-773-1894
Dean Carlson, Paul Hayes
All year

88-248-BB
9 rooms, 7 pb
Visa, MC, AmEx, •
C-no/S-ltd/P-no/H-no

Full breakfast
Complimentary wine served each evening
Off-street parking, swimming pool, tropical gardens, free concierge services

An elegant circa 1904 Queen Anne house located in the center of Key West's Old Town, offering the warm hospitality of a traditional bed & breakfast.
mermaid@joy.net http://www.kwmermaid.com/

KEY WEST

The Paradise Inn
819 Simonton Street 33040
305-293-8007 Fax: 305-293-0807
800-888-9648
Shel Segel
All year

175-375-BB
18 rooms, 18 pb
Most CC, *Rated*, •
C-ltd/S-yes/P-no/H-yes
Spanish, Portuguese

Continental plus breakfast
Jacuzzis, swimming pool, suites, cable TV, accom. bus. trav., concierge

The Paradise Inn is uniquely an island within an island, a traditional Caribbean compound offering ideal accommodations-true "Conch" architectural diversity set in a secluded environment. ssegel@keysdigital.com http://www.theparadiseinn.com

---

La Pensione Inn
809 Truman Ave 33040
305-292-9923 Fax: 305-296-6509
800-893-1193
Monica Wemer
All year

108-168-BB
9 rooms, 9 pb
Most CC, *Rated*
C-ltd/S-yes/P-no/H-yes
Spanish, French, German

Continental breakfast
Swimming pool, A/C, off-street parking, rental bikes

Old Victorian completely renovated with spacious, clean rooms simply furnished with private baths, A/C, pool, parking available. Located in the heart of old town.
lapensione@aol.com http://www.lapensione.com/

Seascape Tropical Inn
420 Olivia St 33040
305-296-7776 Fax: 305-296-6283
800-765-6438
Tom & Nancy Coward
All year

89-269-BB
11 rooms, 11 pb
Visa, MC, AmEx, *Rated*, •
C-ltd/S-no/P-yes/H-no

Continental breakfast
Seasonal sunset wine hour
Heated pool-spa, sun decks, wicker, A/C, TVs, Bahaman fans

Recommended by NY Times, Seascape is ideally located in heart of old town Key West. Relax poolside on secluded sundecks & tropical gardens.
info@seascapetropicalinn.com http://www.seascapetropicalinn.com

---

Simonton Court Inn
320 Simonton St 33040
305-294-6386 Fax: 305-293-8446
800-944-2687
Terry Sullivan
All year

129-549-BB
23 rooms, 23 pb

Continental plus breakfast

Enter the serene setting of Simonton Court Historic Inn & Cottages and be greeted by fragrant tropical flowers blooming beneath gently swaying palms. One of the most beautiful properties in Key West. simontoncourt@aol.com http://www.simontoncourt.com

---

Travelers Palm
915 Center St
815 Catherine St 33040
305-294-9560 Fax: 305-294-4104
800-294-9560
Naomi Van Steelandt
All year

78-298-BB
19 rooms, 19 pb
Most CC, *Rated*, •
C-yes/S-ltd/P-yes/H-ltd
Spanish, Polish, Hungarian

Continental plus breakfast
Complimentary Friday happy hour.
Cable TV, A/C, ceiling fans, daily maid service, bicycles, heated pools.

Affordable, laid-back B&B and cottages in Old Town Key West, close to restaurants, galleries, shopping, beaches. Friendly & knowledgeable concierge staff to make your Key West vacation perfect! info@travelerspalm.com http://www.travelerspalm.com

---

Treetop Inn
806 Truman Ave 33040
305-293-0712 Fax: 305-294-3668
800-926-0712
Richard Rettig
All year

125-200-BB
3 rooms, 3 pb
Most CC, •
C-no/S-no/P-no/H-no

Continental breakfast
Refrigerator
Swimming pool, Cable TV

Conch Mansion completely restored, winner of Chamber of Commerce Business for Beauty Award, featured in Travel Holiday Magazine. Large elegant rooms, beautiful pool and deck. King bed, private bath. treetopinn@earthlink.net http://www.treetopinn.com

KEY WEST

Westwinds
914 Eaton St 33040
305-296-4440 Fax: 305-293-0931
800-788-4150
Robin Chippas
All year

70-170-BB
26 rooms, 26 pb
Visa, MC, Disc, *Rated*, •
C-ltd/S-no/P-no/H-yes

Continental breakfast
Vending machines for snacks and beverages
2 pools, guest lounge

Luxuriant tropical garden setting located in Old Town's Historic Seaport District. Tranquil neighborhood environment steps away from many activities.
frontdesk@westwindskeywest.com http://www.westwindskeywest.com

---

Whispers
409 William St 33040
305-294-5969 Fax: 305-294-3899
800-856-7444
John W. Marburg
All year

99-175-BB
7 rooms, 7 pb
Most CC, *Rated*, •
C-ltd/S-ltd/P-ltd/H-no

Full gourmet breakfast
Refrigerators in rooms
A/C, TV, health club, walk to all activities, sundeck, pool, fans, hot tub

Historic Register. Victorian old town inn. Gourmet breakfast in tropical garden. Antiques throughout. Jacuzzi on premise. Bbwhispers@aol.com http://www.whispersbb.com

LAKE WALES

Chalet Suzanne Inn
3800 Chalet Suzanne Dr 33859
863-676-6011 Fax: 863-676-1814
800-433-6011
Vita Hinshaw
All year

169-249-BB
30 rooms, 30 pb
Most CC, *Rated*, •
C-yes/S-yes/P-no/H-yes
German, French

Full country breakfast
Award-winning breakfast, lunch lounge
Comp. sherry in room, fresh fruit & flowers, pool, airstrip

Unique country inn centrally located for Florida attractions. Ranked one of 10 most romantic spots in Florida. info@chaletsuzanne.com http://www.chaletsuzanne.com

LAKE WORTH

The Mango Inn
128 N Lakeside Dr 33460
561-533-6900 Fax: 561-533-6992
888-626-4619
Erin & Bo Allen
All year

85-250-BB
8 rooms, 8 pb
Rated, •
C-ltd/H-no

Full breakfast
Complimentary wine and soda
Bikes, swimming pool

Lush, private pool with waterfall; walk to beach, golfing, parks, historic downtown "Arts & Antiques district" and fine restaurants.
info@mangoinn.com http://www.mangoinn.com

MELBOURNE (REGION)

Windemere Inn by the Sea
815 S Miramar Ave, *Indialantic* 32903
321-728-9334 Fax: 321-728-2741
800-224-6853
Tom & Vivien Hay
All year

95-205-BB
9 rooms, 9 pb
Most CC, *Rated*, •
C-ltd/S-no/P-no/H-ltd

Full breakfast
Afternoon tea, snacks
Sitting room, library, Jacuzzis, cable TV, accommodate bus. travel

When the warm sun beckons and the seashore calls, whether it is for romance, vacation, or respite, Windemere Inn By the Sea Bed and Breakfast can be your sanctuary.
bb@windemereinn.com http://www.windemereinn.com

MIAMI

Miami River Inn
118 SW South River Dr 33130
305-325-0045 Fax: 305-325-9227
800-HOTEL89
Sallye Jude & Jane Caporelli
All year

69-199-BB
40 rooms, 39 pb
Most CC, *Rated*, •
C-yes/P-yes

Continental breakfast
Cable TV, touch-tone phone, central air/heat, ceiling fan, private bath

Fresh squeezed paradise! Looking for something completely different? You'll find it at this restored turn-of-the-century hotel on the Miami River. About a 10 minute drive to the Art Deco District. miamihotel@aol.com http://www.miamiriverinn.com

MIAMI BEACH

Brigham Gardens
1411 Collins Ave 33139
305-531-1331 Fax: 305-538-9898
Erika Brigham
All year

70-145-EP
23 rooms, 23 pb
Visa, MC, AmEx, •
C-yes/S-yes/P-yes/H-no
Spanish, German, French

Coffee service in all rooms
Family friendly facility, close to beach, in heart of art Deco district

Historical south beach guest house. Over 100 special plants and many tropical birds. Half a block to the beach. info@brighamgardens.com http://brighamgardens.com

---

The Loft Hotel
952 Collins Ave 33139
305-534-2244 Fax: 305-538-1509
Pascal Nicol
All year

99-179-EP
20 rooms, 20 pb
Visa, MC, AmEx
C-yes/S-yes/P-yes/H-no
French, Spanish

Multilingual staff, valet parking, Cable TV/VCR, fully equipped kitchen

World-class boutique hotel. Recently renovated and featuring truly distinctive European styling, it is an upscale yet affordable address offering guests their choice of 20 junior suites.
thelofthotel@cs.com http://www.thelofthotel.com

MICANOPY

Herlong Mansion
PO Box 667
402 NE Cholokka Blvd 32667
352-466-3322 800-437-5664
Julie & Lon Boggs
All year

89-189-BB
11 rooms, 11 pb
Visa, MC, *Rated*
C-ltd/S-no/P-no/H-yes

Full breakfast
Non-alcoholic beverages complimentary
Sitting room, library, music room with piano, TV

The Herlong Mansion is a historic Greek Revival house, c.1845. It's listed on the National Register of Historic Places. info@herlong.com http://www.herlong.com

MOUNT DORA

Darst Victorian Manor
495 Old Hwy 441 32757
352-383-4050
Fax: 352-383-7653
888-53-DARST
Nanci & Jim Darst
All year

125-220-BB
6 rooms, 6 pb
Most CC, *Rated*, •
C-ltd/S-no/P-no/H-ltd

Full gourmet breakfast
Afternoon tea, snacks
Sitting room, Jacuzzis, suites, fireplaces, cable TV, game area

3 story Queen Anne Victorian on tree studded 2 acres overlooking Lake Dora, approximately 2 blocks west of historic downtown Mt. Dora.
darstb&b@mpinet.net http://www.bbonline.com/fl/darstmanor/

Mount Dora Historic Inn
221 E 4th Ave 32757
352-735-1212 Fax: 352-735-9743
800-927-6344
Lindsay & Nancy Richards
All year

75-125-BB
4 rooms, 4 pb
Most CC, *Rated*, •
C-ltd/S-ltd/P-no/H-no

Full breakfast
Afternoon tea, complimentary wine
Sitting room, accommodate business travelers

Relive the elegance of the past at the lovely Mount Dora Historic Inn. Only 25 minutes from Orlando. Escape to gracious hospitality, authentic period antiques & full gourmet breakfast. innkeeper@mountdorahistoricinn.com http://www.mountdorahistoricinn.com

NAPLES

Inn by the Sea
287 11th Ave South 34102
239-649-4124 Fax: 239-434-2842
800-584-1268
Maas & Connie Van Den Top
All year

94-189-BB
5 rooms, 5 pb
Rated, •

Continental plus breakfast
Sitting room, garden deck, bicycles, beach chairs & towels

Located just a short walk from the beaches of the Gulf of Mexico, in a quiet residential neighborhood of quaint "Old Florida" cottages.
cvdtop@aol.com http://www.innbythesea-bb.com

NEW SMYRNA BEACH

Night Swan Intracoastal
512 S Riverside Dr 32168
386-423-4940 Fax: 386-427-2814
800-465-4261
Chuck & Martha Nighswonger
All year

90-175-BB
15 rooms, 15 pb
Most CC, *Rated*, •
C-yes/S-no/P-no/H-yes

Full breakfast
Frozen yogurt
Sitting room, 4 suites, playground nearby, 140 foot dock fishing

Located in the Historic District on the Intracoastal Waterway, between Daytona Beach and Kennedy Space Center; just one mile from the beach.
info@nightswan.com http://www.NightSwan.com

ORLANDO

Courtyard at Lake Lucerne
211 N Lucerne Cr E 32801
407-648-5188 Fax: 407-246-1368
800-444-5289
Eleanor Meiner All year

89-225-BB
22 rooms, 22 pb
Rated

Expanded Continental breakfast
Complimentary wine, cocktail hour
Daily maid service

An award winning historic bed and breakfast getaway and restaurant for romantic couples and business travelers.
info@orlandohistoricinn.com http://www.orlandohistoricinn.com

---

Meadow Marsh
940 Tildenville School Rd 34787
407-656-2064 Fax: 407-654-0656
888-656-2064
C & J Pawlack All year

119-229-BB
5 rooms, 5 pb
Visa, MC, *Rated*, •
C-ltd/S-no/P-no/H-ltd

Full 3-course breakfast
Refreshments always available
Sitting room, piano, library, 3 suites with whirlpools, porches

Experience romantic ol' Florida as you stroll through gardens under majestic oaks, or cross the sunlit meadow at this beautiful 12-acre Victorian Estate.
cavelle5@aol.com http://www.meadowmarsh.net

PerriHouse Inn
10417 Vista Oaks Ct 32836
407-876-4830 Fax: 407-909-1294
800-780-4830
Mark & Becky Manganella
All year

89-145-BB
8 rooms, 8 pb
Most CC, *Rated*, •
C-yes/S-no/P-no/H-no

Continental plus breakfast
Coffee, tea, muffins, breads, cereals and fruit.
All rooms private entrances and baths, A/C & TV.

On 2 acres of voluntary bird sanctuary, these eight distinct rooms each feature a private outside entrance/private bath. 36-foot in-ground pool, gazebo-covered hot tub, and large sundeck. birds@perrihouse.com http://www.perrihouse.com/

ORLANDO (REGION)

Wonderland Inn
3601 S Orange Blossom Trail, *Kissimmee* 34746
407-847-2477 Fax: 407-847-4099
877-847-2477
Rosemarie O'Shaghnessy & Windy McClees All year

59-159-BB
11 rooms, 11 pb
Most CC, •
C-yes/S-no/P-no/H-ltd

Continental plus breakfast
Complimentary wine
Sitting room, suites, cable TV, accommodate business travelers

Only minutes from all Disney attractions. A charming country inn the moment you step inside you're surrounded by art, enveloped in beauty.
innkeeper@wonderlandinn.com http://www.wonderlandinn.com

Thurston House
851 Lake Ave, *Maitland* 32751
407-539-1911 Fax: 407-539-0365
800-843-2721
Carole Ballard
All year

140-160-BB
4 rooms, 4 pb
Visa, MC, AmEx, *Rated*, •
C-ltd/S-no/P-no/H-no

Continental plus wkdys, full wknds
Complimentary wine, snacks
Sitting room, screened porches, lake front

Newly renovated 1885 Queen Anne Victorian home. Hidden away in a country setting, but moments from downtown Orlando. Come experience the "old Florida."
thurstonbb@aol.com http://www.thurstonhouse.com

ORLANDO (REGION)

The Higgins House
420 S. Oak Ave, *Sanford* 32771
407-324-9238 Fax: 407-324-5060
800-584-0014
Roberta & Walter Padgett
All year

85-165-BB
3 rooms, 3 pb
Most CC, *Rated*, •
C-ltd/S-ltd/P-no/H-ltd

Full breakfast
Snacks, wine
Sitting room, bicycles, outdoor hot tub, deck, gardens, tennis nearby

Enjoy the romantic ambience this magnificent turn of the century "Queen Anne" residence has to offer, located close to the St. Johns River & Lake Monroe & a short walk to Sanford's Historic District. reservations@higginshouse.com http://www.higginshouse.com

PALATKA

The Azalea House
220 Madison St 32177
386-325-4547
Doug & Jill de Leeuw
All year

75-135-BB
6 rooms, 4 pb
Visa, MC, AmEx, *Rated*
C-ltd/S-no/P-no/H-no

Full breakfast
Swimming pool

124 year-old Queen Anne Victorian with encircling verandas, protruding bay windows and ornate gingerbread embellish. This 6 room inn has 150 pieces of needlework throughout.
AzaleaHouse@gbso.net http://www.theazaleahouse.com

PALATKA (REGION)

Ferncourt
150 Central Ave, *San Mateo* 32187
904-329-9755
Jack & Dee Dee Morgan

65-85-BB
Rated
All year

Full breakfast

Relax in the comfort of this 1889 'painted lady' known for her antique decor, and excellent food. Spacious rooms w/comfortable beds and private baths await your arrival. Country Victorian atmosphere. ferncourt@gbso.net

PALM BEACH

The Bradley House
280 Sunset Ave 33480
561-832-7050 Fax: 561-835-9666
800-822-4116
Allen Kronberg & Fernando Paredes All year

70-650-EP
34 rooms, 34 pb
Visa, MC, AmEx, •
C-yes/S-ltd/P-ltd/H-yes
Spanish

Complimentary wine

The historic yet beautifully rehabilitated Bradley House Hotel is located in downtown Palm Beach, only steps away from the beach.
info@bradleyhousehotel.com http://www.bradleyhousehotel.com

Palm Beach Historic Inn
365 S County Rd 33480
561-832-4009 Fax: 561-832-6255
800-528-6445
Sean and Jody Herbert
All year

85-325-BB
13 rooms, 13 pb
Most CC, *Rated*, •
C-yes/S-ltd/P-no

Continental breakfast
Suites, cable TV, accom. business travelers, beach chairs & umbrellas, robes

Nine rooms and four suites elegantly appointed with antiques and all the comforts of home! The Palm Beach Historic Inn is a historic landmark building, beautifully restored.
innkeeper@palmbeachbandb.com http://www.palmbeachbandb.com

PALMETTO

Palmetto House
1102 Riverside Dr 34221
941-723-1236 Fax: 941-723-1507
800-658-4167
Bob & Linda Gehring
All year

105-160-BB
8 rooms, 8 pb
Most CC, *Rated*, •
C-ltd/S-no/P-no/H-ltd

Full breakfast
Complimentary refreshments and snacks
Enclosed sun porch, heated pool, Jacuzzi style tub, nightly turndown service

Newly restored Historic 1912 Arts and Crafts Period home. Romantic Riverside Inn sits quietly secluded on the banks of the Manatee River, overlooking the Regatta Pointe Marina & skyline of Bradenton.
info@thepalmettohouse.com http://www.thepalmettohouse.com

PENSACOLA

Noble Manor
110 W Strong St 32501
850-434-9544 Fax: 850-433-0746
877-598-4634
Carol & John Briscoe
All year

75-100-BB
4 rooms, 4 pb
Visa, MC, AmEx,
Rated, •
C-ltd/S-no/P-yes/H-no

Continental plus
Evening cookies
Swimming pool, cable TV, HBO, fireplace, hot tubs, gas grill

Century-old Tudor Revival home lovingly restored to its original elegance. King or queen beds, private baths. Dramatic central staircase.
nmanor@bellsouth.net http://www.noblemanor.com

Springhill Guesthouse
903 N Spring St 32501
850-438-6887 Fax: 850-438-9075
800-475-1956
Michael and Rita Widler
All year

99-129-BB
2 rooms, 2 pb
Rated, •
C-yes/S-no/P-no/H-no

Full breakfast
Restaurant, or continental basket outside the door
Sitting room, suites, antique ornamental fireplace, cable TV, full kitchens

Charming and comfortable, this Queen Anne style home in Historic North Hill is the place to come home to. Conveniently located near downtown Pensacola and 10 minutes to the beaches. guesthouse@pcola.gulf.net http://www.springhillguesthouse.com

PORT ST. JOE

Cape San Blas Inn
4950 Cape San Blas Rd 32456
850-229-7070 800-315-1965
Britt & Jill Kuglar
All year

150-BB
5 rooms, 5 pb
Most CC
C-ltd/S-no/P-no/H-yes

Bicycles, canoes

America's #1 Beach for 2002 is the setting of this 5-bedroom, bayfront inn.
capesanblasinn@aol.com http://www.capesanblasinn.com

QUINCY

Millstone Farms
3895 Providence Rd 32351
850-627-9400 Fax: 850-627-9400
Pam & Ron Barnett
All year

85-BB
3 rooms, 3 pb
Visa, MC, AmEx, *Rated*
C-ltd/S-no/P-no/H-ltd

Full breakfast
Pool, wooded walking trails, working cattle farm

We offer rooms w/private baths, antique furnishings, landscaped yards, peaceful atmosphere. Stay w/us in our rustic farm house.
millstone@tds.net http://www.millstonefarms.com

SARASOTA (REGION)

Betts House
1523 1st Ave W, *Bradenton* 34205
941-747-3607 887-747-3607
Ms. Churchill Mallison
All year

65-70-BB
2 rooms
Most CC, *Rated*, •
C-ltd/S-ltd/P-no/H-no

Continental plus breakfast
Fruit
Sitting room, library, fireplaces, cable TV, accom. business travelers

In historic downtown Bradenton, 1913 home with open wrap-around porch at west end of the river-walk. Island beaches 20 minutes by car.
betts@tizart.com http://www.tizart.com

Turtle Beach Resort
9049 Midnight Pass Rd, *Siesta Key* 34242
941-349-4554 Fax: 941-312-9034
Gail & Dave Rubinfeld
All year

185-380-EP
10 rooms, 10 pb
Most CC, *Rated*, •
C-yes/S-no/P-ltd

Restaurant, sherry
Hot tubs, swimming pool, bicycles, honeymoons, romantic getaways

A "Caribbean" style waterfront inn, island paradise. Private cottages with private hot tubs! Gourmet waterfront dining next door. Four boat docks.
turtlebch1@aol.com http://www.turtlebeachresort.com

Bayfront Westcott House, St. Augustine, FL

SEASIDE

Josephine's
PO Box 4767
101 Seaside Avenue 32459
850-231-1940 Fax: 850-231-2446
800-848-1840
Bruce & Judy Albert All year

200-250-BB
11 rooms, 11 pb
Rated, •

Full breakfast

Josephine's embodies the spirit of elegance, intimacy, and charm in the number one beach community in America: Seaside, Florida.
judy@josephinesinn.com http://www.josephinesinn.com

ST. AUGUSTINE

Agustin Inn
29 Cuna St 32084
904-823-9559 Fax: 904-824-8685
800-248-7846
Sherri & Robert Brackett
All year

89-175-BB
12 rooms, 12 pb
Visa, MC, AmEx, •
C-yes/S-no/P-no/H-yes

Full breakfast
Weekend snacks & wine
Cable TV, Jacuzzis

Situated in St. Augustine's Historic walking district, our Victorian Inn captures the ambiance of old downtown St. Augustine. agustin@aug.com http://www.agustininn.com

---

Alexander Homestead
14 Sevilla St 32084
904-826-4147 Fax: 904-823-9503
888-292-4147
Bonnie Alexander All year

115-175-BB
4 rooms, 4 pb
Most CC, *Rated*, •
C-ltd/S-no/P-no/H-no

Full breakfast
Afternoon tea
Sitting room, bikes, Jacuzzis, fireplaces, cable TV

Elegant 1888 Victorian home, private baths, 1 with whirlpool Jacuzzi, Wood-burning fireplaces, private porches, authentic antique furnishings.
bonnie@aug.com http://www.alexanderhomestead.com

Bayfront Westcott House
146 Avenida Menendez 32084
904-824-4301 Fax: 904-824-1502
800-513-9814
Janice & Robert Graubard
All year

95-250-BB
9 rooms, 9 pb
Most CC, *Rated*, •
C-yes/S-ltd/P-no/H-no

Full breakfast
Compl. wine, chocolates, brandy, desserts
Sitting room, games, library, bicycles

Voted #1 bed and breakfast in St. Augustine! Elegant, romantic, historic district inn, walking distance to attractions; relax on porches with bay views of sailboats, dolphin, horses and carriages. westcott@aug.com http://www.westcotthouse.com

ST. AUGUSTINE

Carriage Way
70 Cuna St 32084
904-829-2467 Fax: 904-826-1461
800-908-9832
Bill & Larry Johnson
All year

89-190-BB
9 rooms, 9 pb
Most CC, •
C-ltd/S-no/P-no/H-no
French

Full breakfast
Snacks
Comp. wine & beverages, picnics, whirlpool tub

1883 Victorian home in heart of historic district; antiques & reproductions, clawfoot tubs, bicycles available. Casual, friendly atmosphere.
bjohnson@carriageway.com http://www.Carriageway.com

Castle Garden
15 Shenandoah St 32084
904-829-3839 Fax: 904-829-9049
Bruce & Brian Kloeckner
All year

65-199-BB
7 rooms, 7 pb
Most CC, *Rated*, •
C-ltd/S-ltd/P-no/H-no

Full breakfast
Complimentary wine & champagne
Picnic lunches, bicycles, fresh flowers, 3 bridal rooms with whirlpools

St. Augustine's only Moorish Revival dwelling, former Castle Warden Carriage House, built 1800s. Restored gardens. castleg@aug.com http://www.castlegarden.com

---

Cedar House Inn Victorian
79 Cedar St 32084
904-829-0079 Fax: 904-825-0916
800-233-2746
Russ & Nina Thomas
All year

119-210-BB
6 rooms, 6 pb
Visa, MC, Disc, *Rated*, •
C-ltd/S-no/P-no/H-no

Full breakfast
Dinner, afternoon tea, snacks
Sitting room, library, piano, porches, bikes, free walking tour guide

Capture romantic moments at our beautiful 1893 Victorian home, in the heart of historic St. Augustine. Enjoy hospitality at its finest.
travelguides@cedarhouseinn.com http://www.cedarhouseinn.com

Centennial House
26 Cordova St 32084
904-810-2218
Fax: 904-810-1930
800-611-2880
Geoff & Ellen Fugere
All year

110-250-BB
9 rooms, 9 pb
Most CC, *Rated*, •
C-ltd/S-no/P-no/H-yes

Full Elegant Breakfast
Wine and cheese social hour
Oversized whirlpools, fireplaces, luxury baths, individual climate controls

Luxury in the Historic District. Featuring private luxury baths, oversized whirlpools, fireplaces, cable TV/VCR, sound insulation. On the horse-drawn carriage route.
innkeeper@centennialhouse.com http://www.centennialhouse.com

Coquina Gables Oceanfront
1 F Street 32080
904-461-8727 Fax: 904-461-4346
Aubrey & Tracy Arnn
All year

129-219-BB
6 rooms, 6 pb
Visa, MC, AmEx, *Rated*, •
C-no/S-ltd/P-no/H-no

Full breakfast
Sangria happy hour
Pool, spa, bicycles, robes, beach towels, beach furniture

Coquina Gables, located on over an acre of property directly on St. Augustine Beach. Beautiful 1920's home with hardwood floors, cedar paneling and hand-hewn Honduran heart of pine beam ceilings. gables@aug.com http://www.coquinagables.com

---

The Kenwood Inn
38 Marine St 32084
904-824-2116 Fax: 904-824-1689
800-824-8151
Mark & Kerrianne Constant
All year

125-225-BB
15 rooms, 15 pb
Visa, MC, Disc, *Rated*
C-ltd/S-ltd/P-no/H-no

Continental plus breakfast
Sitting room, piano, swimming pool, walled-in courtyard

Lovely old 19th-century Victorian inn located in Historic District of our nation's oldest city. http://www.oldcity.com/kenwood/

ST. AUGUSTINE

The Old Powder House Inn
38 Cordova St 32084
904-824-4149 Fax: 904-825-0143
800-447-4149
Katie & Kal Kalieta
All year

85-205-BB
9 rooms, 9 pb
Most CC, •
C-ltd/S-no/P-no/H-ltd

Full gourmet breakfast
Hot/cold beverages, baked goods. Wine from 4-6PM.
Flowered courtyards & verandas. Bicycles.

Escape to a romantic getaway at our charming 1899 Victorian Inn, in the heart of the historic district. Old World charm, elegance, and hospitality. We'll help you plan that "perfect getaway." kalieta@aug.com http://www.oldpowderhouse.com

---

Southern Wind Inn
18 Cordova St 32084
904-825-3623 Fax: 904-810-5212
800-781-3338
Alana & Bob Indelicato
All year

99-225-BB
10 rooms, 10 pb
Visa, MC, AmEx, *Rated*, •
C-ltd/S-no/P-no/H-no

Full breakfast
Complimentary wine, lemonade
Spacious verandas, large, parlor, wraparound porch, cable TV, bicycles

On the Carriage Trail through historic district, Southern Wind offers an elegant 1916 columned masonry home with exceptional buffet breakfast.
swind@aug.com http://www.southernwindinn.com

St. Francis Inn
279 St George St 32084
904-824-6068 Fax: 904-810-5525
800-824-6062
Joe & Margaret Finnegan
All year

109-219-BB
14 rooms, 14 pb
Most CC, *Rated*, •
C-ltd/S-no/P-no/H-no

Full breakfast
Iced tea & lemonade
Sunday afternoon music, swimming pool, bicycles, private parking

Built in 1791, located in Historic District, one block west of the "Oldest House in USA." Several rooms with working fireplaces, telephones & Jacuzzi tubs.
innceasd@aug.com http://www.stfrancisinn.com

Victorian House
11 Cadiz St 32084
904-824-5214 Fax: 904-824-7990
877-703-0432
Ken & Marcia Cerotzke
All year

95-185-BB
8 rooms, 8 pb
Visa, MC, AmEx, *Rated*, •
C-ltd/S-no/P-no/H-no

Full breakfast
Wine
Sitting room, bicycles, suites, cable TV, hair dryers, ceiling fans

Our charming rooms have been lovingly restored and furnished in period antiques. The Victorian House, built in 1897, is located in the heart of the Historic District.
vhouse@victorianhousebnb.com http://www.victorianhouse-inn.com

ST. PETE BEACH

Island's End Resort
1 Pass-A-Grille Way 33706
727-360-5023 Fax: 727-367-7890
Jone & Millard Gamble
All year

82-235-BB
6 rooms, 6 pb
Visa, MC, *Rated*
C-ltd/S-ltd/P-no/H-ltd
Lithuanian, Latvian, Russian, Czech, Polish

Continental breakfast
Jacuzzis, suites, cable TV/VCR, beach towels, private parking

Island's End, an oasis of real peace & quiet, where the crystal blue waters of the Gulf of Mexico meet the Intracoastal Waterway. jzgpag@aol.com http://www.islandsend.com

ST. PETERSBURG

Bay Shore Manor
635 12th Ave NE 33701
727-822-3438 Fax: 727-822-3438
Tanja & Heiko Gross
All year

69-89-BB
7 rooms, 7 pb
Most CC, *Rated*, •
C-yes/S-ltd/P-no/H-no
German

Continental plus breakfast
Complimentary wine
Sitting room, library, bicycles, tennis court, cable TV

The Bay Shore Manor, built in 1928, is now hosted by the German Gross Family. Each suite is nicely furnished & has own bath, phone, TV, coffeemaker, microwave, & refrigerator.
reservations@bayshoremanor.com http://www.bayshoremanor.com

Island's End Resort, St. Pete's Beach, FL

ST. PETERSBURG

Bayboro House on Old Tampa Bay
1719 Beach Dr SE 33701
727-823-4955 Fax: 727-822-2341
877-823-4955
Sandy & Dave Kelly
All year

149-249-BB
8 rooms, 7 pb
Most CC, *Rated*
C-ltd/S-ltd/P-no

Expanded Continental Breakfast
Wine and cheese

Located on the beautiful shores of Tampa Bay, you will be awed by the peaceful serenity.
bayboro@tampabay.rr.com http://www.bayborohousebandb.com

Gulfside Resort
565 70th Ave 33706
727-360-7640 Fax: 727-367-6398
800-823-9552
Robert & Suzanne Teichert
All year

80-EP
10 rooms, 10 pb
Most CC, *Rated*, •
C-yes/S-ltd/P-no/H-no

Cable TV, swimming pool, suites, accommodate business travelers

Pristine, private complex 200 yds. to beach. Spacious one-bedroom suites, efficiencies, full kitchens, microwaves, cable TV. http://www.gulfsideresort.com

---

Inn at the Bay
126 4th Ave NE 33701
727-822-1700 Fax: 727-896-7412
888-873-2122
Dennis & Jewly Youschak
All year

119-250-BB
12 rooms, 12 pb
Most CC, •
C-ltd/S-no/P-no/H-yes

Full breakfast
Afternoon tea, snacks, complimentary wine
Sitting room, library, suites, fireplaces, cable TV, accom. bus. travelers

B&B restored in 2001, king and queen allergy-free feather beds, private baths, double whirlpool tubs, phones in rooms, hot full breakfast, romance, vacation, business.
info@innatthebay.com http://www.innatthebay.com

Mansion House & The Courtyard on Fifth
105 5th Ave NE
105 & 115 Fifth Ave NE 33701
727-821-9391 Fax: 727-821-6906
800-274-7520
Robert & Rose Marie Ray
Oct–May, June–Sept

99-220-BB
12 rooms, 12 pb
Most CC, *Rated*, •
C-ltd/S-ltd/P-ltd/H-ltd
Portuguese, French

Full American breakfast
Complimentary wine,coffee, tea, snacks
10 common areas, 2 libraries, garden, free local calls, robes, Jacuzzi, pool

12 Luxury rooms, cable TV, swimming pool, 10 common areas, courtyard garden, meeting/conference, phones/dataports; robes; ceiling fans, weddings/receptions; reunions.
mansion1@ix.netcom.com http://www.mansionbandb.com

Sunset Bay Inn, St. Petersburg, FL

ST. PETERSBURG

Sunset Bay Inn
635 Bay St NE 33701
727-896-6701 Fax: 727-898-5311
800-794-5133
Bob & Martha Bruce
All year

130-260-BB
8 rooms, 8 pb
Most CC, *Rated*, •
C-ltd/S-ltd/P-no/H-ltd

Full or continental plus breakfast
Complimentary wine, soda, baked goods
24 hour snack bar, video library, bicycles, cable TV/VCR, Jacuzzis

Exceptional guest accommodations, excellent service and an elegant atmosphere at this AAA-four diamond 1911 historic Colonial Revival home.
wrbcom@aol.com http://www.sunsetbayinn.com

La Veranda
111 5th Ave N 33701
727-824-9997 Fax: 727-827-1431
800-484-8423x8
Nancy Meuse
All year

89-249-BB
5 rooms, 5 pb
Most CC, *Rated*, •
C-yes/S-ltd/P-yes/H-ltd
Spanish, German

Full breakfast
Wine, soft drinks, snacks, afternoon tea, lunch
Sitting, bicycles, Jacuzzi, suites, fireplace, cable TV, business travelers

Elegant restored 1910 mansion with multi-room suites all opening directly on to large verandas. Canopy beds, antiques, Oriental rugs and art fill our rooms with ambience and comfort. info@laverandabb.com http://www.LaVerandabb.com

ST. PETERSBURG (REGION)

Pasa Tiempo
7141 Bay St, *St. Pete Beach* 33706
727-367-9907 Fax: 727-367-9906
Gordon & Ivone Meltzer
All year

125-200-BB
10 rooms, 10 pb
Visa, MC, AmEx, *Rated*, •
C-no/S-ltd/P-no/H-no
Portuguese

Continental plus breakfast
Afternoon tea, snacks, and complimentary wine
Cable TV, Internet access, and daily newspaper

Enjoy life's simply elegant pleasures in a relaxed Mediterranean style private resort on Boca Ciega Bay. Soak up some sun, cool off in our sparkling pool or relax in our elegant suites. info@pasa-tiempo.com http://www.pasa-tiempo.com

TALLAHASSEE (REGION)

McFarlin House
305 E King St, *Quincy* 32351
850-875-2526 Fax: 850-627-4703
877-370-4701
Richard & Tina Fauble
All year

85-175-BB
9 rooms, 9 pb
Rated
C-yes/S-no/P-no/H-ltd

Full breakfast
Snacks, dinner upon request/notice
Sitting room, Jacuzzis, fireplaces, cable TV, corporate rates

Tobacco farmer John McFarlin built this Queen Anne Victorian, notable for its left-handed turret and grand wraparound porch, in 1895. Listed in the National Register.
inquiries@mcfarlinhouse.com http://www.mcfarlinhouse.com/

The Banyan House, Venice, FL

TAMPA

Gram's Place GuestHouses
3109 N Ola Ave 33603
813-221-0596
Mark Holland
All year

15-95-BB
7 rooms, 4 pb
Visa, MC, AmEx, *Rated*, •
C-ltd/S-ltd/P-ltd/H-no

Self-serve continental breakfast
Courtyard w/BYOB bar
Sitting room, Jacuzzi, 2 waterfalls, sun deck, artists retreat, phone

Tampa Florida's Only Alternative Lodging with MUSIC THEMED rooms to Jazz, Blues, Folk, Country & Rock n Roll. Known as Little Amsterdam/Key West Located in the center of Tampa. AAA 2 diamond rated. gramspl@aol.com http://www.grams-inn-tampa.com/

TAMPA (REGION)

Ruskin House
120 Dickman Dr SW, *Ruskin* 33570
813-645-3842
Mr. & Mrs. Arthur M. Miller
All year

75-BB
3 rooms, 2 pb
Most CC, •
C-yes/S-ltd/P-no/H-ltd
French, Spanish

Continental plus breakfast
Full breakfast on weekends
Complimentary sherry and tea, sitting room, library, 3 acres, bicycles

Gracious 1910 waterfront home with period (1860–1920) antiques.
acantre@hotmail.com http://www.ruskinhousebandb.com

TARPON SPRINGS

Spring Bayou Inn
32 W Tarpon Ave 34689
727-938-9333 Fax: 727-938-9333
Sharon Birk, John & Linda Hall All year

80-125-BB
5 rooms, 5 pb
Rated, •
C-ltd/S-no/P-no/H-no

Full breakfast
Complimentary soft drinks
Parlor, library, fireplace, front porch, baby grand piano

Elegant Victorian Home with modern conveniences. Walk to Antique shops, Spring Bayou, restaurants, and the famous Sponge Docks, with its European Greek village atmosphere.
jshall2@gte.net http://www.springbayouinn.com

VENICE

The Banyan House
519 Harbor Dr South 34285
941-484-1385 Fax: 941-484-8032
Chuck and Susan McCormick
Closed in August

99-139-BB
10 rooms, 9 pb
Visa, MC, *Rated*
C-ltd/S-no/P-no

Continental plus breakfast
Sitting room, Jacuzzi, bicycles, hot tubs, swimming pool

Historic Mediterranean-style home. Enormous Banyan tree shades courtyard, pool and spa. relax@banyanhouse.com http://www.banyanhouse.com

1890 King-Keith House, Atlanta, GA

Georgia

AMERICUS

Americus Garden Inn	75-95-BB	Full breakfast buffet
504 Rees Park 31709	8 rooms, 8 pb	Snacks, soft drinks
229-931-0122	Most CC, •	Sitting room, library, cable
Fax: 229-924-3186	C-yes/S-ltd/P-yes/H-yes	TV, VCR, conferences
888-758-4749	Spanish	
Don & Jodi Miles All year		

We are a beautiful civil war era mansion with 8 huge, sunny guestrooms each with king or queen beds, large en-suite baths and furnished with all the guest amenities we could think of. reespark@bellsouth.net http://www.americusgardeninn.com

ATHENS

Nicholson House Inn	99-129-BB	Full breakfast
6295 Jefferson Rd 30607	9 rooms, 9 pb	Complimentary sherry
706-353-2200 Fax: 706-353-7799	Most CC, *Rated*	Two sitting parlours, library,
Celeste & Harry Neely	C-no/S-no/P-no/H-yes	cable TV, large verandah
All year		overlooking 6 acres

Slip back quietly in time to the grandeur of the Old South in this elegant Antebellum home. Originally built in 1820 as an inn, it is now a peaceful haven set on 34 natural acres.
1820@nicholsonhouseinn.com http://www.nicholsonhouseinn.com

ATLANTA

1890 King-Keith House	90-200-BB	Full breakfast
889 Edgewood Ave NE 30307	5 rooms, 5 pb	Snacks
404-688-7330 Fax: 404-584-8408	Visa, MC, AmEx,	Sitting rooms, porches,
800-728-3879	*Rated*, •	cottage w/Jacuzzi/frplc.,
Windell Keith All year	C-yes/S-no/P-no/H-no	suite

One of Atlanta's most photographed homes, this Victorian is loaded with period antiques, charm and romance. Close to downtown. Shops & restaurants nearby.
kingkeith@mindspring.com http://www.kingkeith.com

ATLANTA

Abbett Inn
1746 Virginia Ave 30337
404-767-3708 Fax: 404-767-1626
Donald Taylor-Farmer All year

79-149-BB
6 rooms, 4 pb
Most CC, *Rated*, •
C-ltd/S-ltd/P-no/H-no

Continental plus breakfast
Tea, snacks, wine
Sitting room, fireplace, cable TV/VCR

Built in 1887, six guestrooms each with private phone lines and cable TV. Close to Hartsfield International Airport, 10 minutes from downtown Atlanta.
abbettinn@bellsouth.net http://www.abbettinn.com

Ansley Inn
253 15th St NE 30309
404-872-9000 Fax: 404-892-2318
800-446-5416
Curt Levy All year

109-169-BB
22 rooms, 22 pb
Most CC, *Rated*, •
C-yes/S-ltd/P-no/H-yes
Spanish, Thai

Full breakfast
Afternoon refreshments, tea, coffee, juice
Sitting rm, jetted-tubs, health club membership, cable TV, terry cloth robes

Beautifully restored English Tudor Mansion built in 1907 by the famous clothier George Muse in the heart of Midtown Atlanta's Business and Arts District.
reservations@ansleyinn.com http://www.ansleyinn.com

Beverly Hills Inn
65 Sheridan Dr NE 30305
404-233-8520 Fax: 404-233-8659
800-331-8520
Mit Amin
All year

110-165-BB
18 rooms, 18 pb
Most CC, *Rated*, •
C-yes/S-yes/P-no/H-no

Continental plus breakfast
Sitting room, library, piano, health club, London taxi shuttle

Charming city retreat, fine residential neighborhood. Close to Lenox Square, Historical Society and many art galleries. http://www.beverlyhillsinn.com

---

Bonnie Castle
PO Box 359
2 Post Street 30220
770-583-3090 800-261-3090
Darwin & Patti Palmer
All year

80-95-BB
4 rooms, 2 pb
C-ltd/S-ltd/P-no/H-no

Sumptuous full breakfast
Tea or wine offered each evening
Victorian drawing room is open to the public as well as the spacious veranda

This two-story, 22 room mansion, listed on The National Register of Historic Places & The Heritage Highway, has 4 tastefully appointed guestrooms, offering gracious hospitality of a bygone era. bocastle@mindspring.com http://www.communitynow.com/bonniecastle

---

Gaslight Inn
1001 Saint Charles Ave NE 30306
404-875-1001 Fax: 404-876-1001
James E. Moss Jr.
All year

95-195-BB
7 rooms, 6 pb
Most CC, *Rated*, •
C-ltd/S-no/P-no/H-ltd

Continental plus breakfast
Snacks
Sitting room, library, grand piano, bike rental, walk to 35 restaurants

Featured in Better Homes & Gardens and Southern Homes magazines. Single rooms, suites, fireplaces, Jacuzzi tubs, whirlpool baths, sauna.
innkeeper@gaslightinn.com http://www.gaslightinn.com/

Highland Inn
644 N Highland 30306
404-874-5756 Fax: 404-874-5756
1-888-256-7221
Julie Barnette
All year

60-106-BB
104 rooms, 104 pb
Visa, MC, AmEx, •
C-yes/S-yes/P-no/H-no
Spanish, French

Continental breakfast
Hot Tea, Coffee, Fresh Fruit
Concierge service, cable TV, bicycle rentals, concierge room

The Highland Inn is Atlanta's Unique European Style Hotel. We offer comfortable, affordable, 'Old World' style accommodations in Virginia Highland, Atlanta's Most walkable Historic District. Thighlandi@aol.com http://www.thehighlandinn.com

ATLANTA

Inman Park/Woodruff Cottage
100 Waverly Way, NE 30307
404-688-9498 Fax: 404-524-9939
Eleanor Matthews
All year

100-110-BB
3 rooms
Visa, MC, AmEx, *Rated*, •
C-ltd/S-no/P-no/H-no

Continental plus breakfast
Private garden
Screened porch, fireplaces, secured parking

Totally restored Victorian located in historic Inman Park. 1 block to subway, close to restaurants. Eleanor@bellsouth.net

---

Stonehurst
923 Piedmont Ave NE 30309
404-881-0722 Fax: 404-881-5324
Saundra Altekruse
All year

90-100-BB
3 rooms, 3 pb
Visa, MC, *Rated*, •
C-ltd/S-no/P-no/H-no
French

Full breakfast
Snacks
Sitting room, cable TV

Built in 1896, this beautiful and historic B&B is located in historic midtown Atlanta.
innkeeper@stonehurstbandb.com http://www.stonehurstbandb.com

Sugar Magnolia
804 Edgewood Ave, NE 30307
404-222-0226 Fax: 404-681-1067
Debi Starnes & Jim Emshoff
All year

95-135-BB
3 rooms, 3 pb
Visa, MC, *Rated*, •
C-ltd/S-no/P-no/H-no

Continental plus breakfast
Afternoon tea, snacks
Bar service, sitting room, business center, roof deck, fireplaces, pool

Beautiful 1892 Queen Anne Victorian in historic, in-town neighborhood near Atlanta's attractions.
sugmagbb@aol.com http://www.sugarmagnoliabb.com

Virginia Highland B&B
630 Orme Circle, NE 30306
404-892-2735 Fax: 404-892-2735
877-870-4485
Adele Northrup
All year

125-BB
2 rooms, 2 pb
Visa, MC, AmEx, •
C-no/S-no/P-no/H-no

Full breakfast
Afternoon tea, snacks, complimentary wine
Suites, fireplace, cable TV/VCR, accom. bus. travelers, data port access

Beautiful urban retreat. Restored 1920 craftsman bungalow with elegant antiques and homey hospitality.
adelness@hotmail.com http://www.virginiahighlandbb.com

ATLANTA (REGION)

Serenbe
10950 Hutcheson Ferry Rd, *Palmetto* 30268
770-463-2610 Fax: 770-463-4472
Marie & Steve Nygren
All year

140-175-BB
8 rooms, 8 pb
Rated
C-yes/S-ltd/P-no/H-ltd

Full gourmet breakfast
Afternoon tea
Sitting room, library, Jacuzzis, pool, fireplaces, cable TV

Country setting, 800 acres, 100 farm animals, historic property, antiques, art, garden designed by world-famous Ryan Gainey, large pool and cabana with swings the size of twin beds.
steve@serenbe.com http://www.serenbe.com

Twin Oaks Country Inn
9565 E. Liberty Rd, *Villa Rica* 30180
770-459-4374
Earl & Carol Turner
All year

105-175-BB
4 rooms, 4 pb
Rated, •

Full breakfast
Candlelight Dinners ($40.00)

Located on 23 acres in the foothills of the NW GA mountains. Three exquisite guest cottages are ideal for honeymooners or celebrating an anniversary.
http://www.bbonline.com/ga/twinoaks/

AUGUSTA

The Partridge Inn
2110 Walton Way 30904
706-737-8888 Fax: 706-731-0826
800-476-6888
David E. Jones
All year

85-150-BB
156 rooms, 156 pb
Visa, MC, AmEx,
Rated, •
C-yes/S-ltd/P-ltd/H-ltd

Full breakfast
Snacks, lunch/dinner available
Restaurant, bar service, sitting room, library, pool, suites, cable TV

Historic 1890's Inn completely renovated and restored. Situated on the historic Summerville Hill. Easy access to downtown & area attractions. Award winning food & beverage.
info@partridgeinn.com http://www.partridgeinn.com

AUGUSTA (REGION)

1810 West Inn
254 N Seymour Dr, *Thomson* 30824
706-595-3156 Fax: 706-595-3155
800-515-1810
Virginia White
All year

65-105-BB
10 rooms, 10 pb
Most CC, *Rated*, •
C-ltd/S-no/P-no/H-no

Continental plus breakfast
Afternoon tea, snacks
Sitting room, library, jogging trail, pond, peacocks, 11 acres

Country charm, city amenities-restored historic plantation house c.1810 and adjoining folk houses on 14 landscaped acres.
DM1810westinn@aol.com http://www.bbonline.com/ga/1810west

PJ's Place
115 W Robert Toombs Ave, *Washington* 30673
706 678-5583
Paula Elliot
All year

BB
•

Continental breakfast

A new slant on an old favorite, the B&B is available for you to hide away and dream your dreams, bask in fond memories or create new ones. This grand old way of life is yours during your stay. de1483@aol.com

BRUNSWICK

Brunswick Manor
825 Egmont St 31520
912-265-6889 Fax: 912-265-7879
Claudia Tzucanow
All year

80-90-BB
9 rooms, 8 pb
Visa, MC, *Rated*, •
C-ltd/S-ltd/P-ltd/H-ltd
Spanish

Full gourmet breakfast
Complimentary wine, high tea
Sitting room, library, bicycles, tennis courts, hot tub, robes, veranda

Elegant historic 1886 inn near Golden Isles. Boat chartering avail. Gracious hospitality. All rooms with ceiling fans/refrigerators. cjrose11@bellsouth.net

CHATTANOOGA (REGION)

Captain's Quarters
13 Barnhardt Circle, *Fort Oglethorpe* 30742
706-858-0624 Fax: 706-861-4053
800-710-6816
Betty & Daniel McKenzie

99-159-BB
7 rooms, 7 pb
C-ltd
All year

3 course breakfast

This historic 1902 Inn on the outskirts of Chattanooga is a perfect spot for a romantic getaway or touring Chattanooga, middle Tennessee and Northwest Georgia.
Innkeeper@captains-qtrs-inn.com http://www.captains-qtrs-inn.com

---

Chanticleer Inn
1300 Mockingbird Ln, *Lookout Mountain* 30750
706-820-2002 Fax: 706-820-7976
Kirby & Judy Wahl All year

89-174-BB
17 rooms, 17 pb
Most CC, *Rated*, •
C-ltd/S-ltd/P-no/H-ltd

Continental plus breakfast
Common living room, outdoor pool, all rooms have own entrance

This historic charming Inn and stone cottages atop Lookout Mountain was recently renovated with English Country decor and antiques. King & Queen beds, some whirlpools, suites, fireplaces, Internet. info@stayatchanticleer.com
http://www.stayatchanticleer.com

CLARKESVILLE

Glen-Ella Springs Inn
1789 Bear Gap Rd 30523
706-754-7295 Fax: 706-754-1560
888-455-8893
Barrie & Bobby Aycock
All year

125-225-BB
16 rooms, 16 pb
Most CC, *Rated*, •
C-ltd/S-ltd/P-no/H-yes

Full breakfast
Restaurant, dinner only, BYOB
Conference room, pool, gardens, mountain creek, hiking trails

100-year-old inn on National Register, rustic rural setting near Tallulah Gorge, lovely views, genuine hospitality, outstanding food. info@glenella.com http://www.glenella.com

COLUMBUS

Gates House
PO Box 178
737 Broadway 31901
706-324-6464 Fax: 706-324-2070
800-891-3187
Carolyn & Tom Gates All year

95-175-BB
10 rooms, 10 pb
Visa, MC, AmEx, •
C-ltd/S-no/P-no/H-ltd

Full breakfast
Snacks, complimentary wine, tea
Library, Jacuzzis, fireplaces, cable TV, cable modem, bicycles,home theater

Two 1880's Colonial Revival houses furnished in Victorian antiques and spectacular window treatments. "Most comfortable beds in town." Read and relax in our library or our Charlestonian garden. info@gateshouse.com http://www.gateshouse.com

CUMBERLAND ISLAND

Greyfield Inn, A Historic Inn
PO Box 900
8 N 2nd St 32035
904-261-6408 Fax: 904-321-0666
Zachary Z. Zoul
All year

395-BB
17 rooms, 9 pb
C-ltd/S-no

Full southern-style breakfast
Hors d'oeuvres, snacks, non-alcoholic beverages
Library, living room with fireplace, bikes, kayaks, beach equipment, tours

Turn of the century mansion on pristine, tranquil Cumberland Island. Victorian antiques, Tiffany lamps and Chippendale furniture. Large verandah with porch swings and rockers. seashore@greyfieldinn.com http://www.greyfieldinn.com

DAHLONEGA

The Blueberry Inn & Gardens
400 Blueberry Hill 30533
706-219-4024 Fax: 706-219-4793
877-219-4024
Phyllis Charnley All year

75-105-BB
12 rooms, 12 pb
Visa, MC, •
C-ltd/S-ltd/P-no/H-yes

Full breakfast
Snacks, complimentary wine
Sitting room, library, fireplaces, business travelers, pleasure fishing

Country inn sits on top of a hill with wonderful views of the Blue Ridge Mountains, meadows large gourmet breakfast every morning; rooms furnished with antiques.
bluberrybb@aol.com http://www.blueberryinnandgardens.com

Lily Creek Lodge
2608 Auraria Rd 30533
706-864-6848 Fax: 706-864-6848
888-844-2694
Don & Sharon Bacek
All year

99-169-BB
12 rooms, 12 pb
Visa, MC, AmEx, *Rated*, •
C-yes/S-ltd/P-no/H-no
Spanish, French

Continental plus breakfast
Snacks, complimentary wine
Hot tub, pool, fireplace, suites, cable TV, fax, copier, laptop outlet

European chalet architecture, furnished with European antiques, art, feather duvets & pillows, fine linens! Your comfort & pleasure is our goal.
baceks@alltel.net http://www.lilycreeklodge.com

Mountain Top Lodge at Dahlonega
447 Mtn Top Lodge Rd 30533
706-864-5257 Fax: 706-864-8265
800-526-9754
Karen A. Lewan
All year

90-155-BB
13 rooms, 13 pb
Most CC
C-ltd/S-ltd/P-no/H-ltd

Full breakfast
Sitting room, library, hot tubs, horseshoe pit, suites, cable TV

Classic country hideaway in the foothills of the North Georgia mountains. Atmosphere is relaxed and casual. mountaintop@alltel.net http://www.mountaintoplodge.net

DAHLONEGA

Royal Guard Inn	95-125-BB	Full breakfast
65 S Park St 30533	4 rooms, 4 pb	Complimentary tea or
706-864-1713 877-659-0739	Visa, MC	wine & cheese
Suzanne & Steve Berninger	C-no/S-no/P-no/H-no	Library with fireplace, no
All year	Spanish, French, Italian	TVs or phones

Our home is on historic, residential Park Street and just one block from the town square. Enjoy afternoon tea or wine & cheese on the wrap-around porch shaded by enormous magnolia trees.

royalguardbnb@yahoo.com http://www.virtualcities.com/ons/ga/d/gad8703.htm

FOLKSTON

The Inn at Folkston	95-150-BB	Full breakfast
509 W Main St 31537	4 rooms, 4 pb	Afternoon tea, snacks,
912-496-6256 Fax: 912-496-6256	Most CC, *Rated*, •	complimentary wine
888-509-6246	C-yes/S-ltd/P-no/H-yes	Sitting room, library,
Genna & Roger Wangsness		Jacuzzis, suites, fireplaces,
closed July 15–Aug. 15		cable TV

Beautifully restored 1920's bungalow on two acres; located 10 minutes from Okefenokee Swamp, 45 minutes from Cumberland Island; Orientals and antiques provide elegant yet comfortable surrounding. info@innatfolkston.com http://www.innatfolkston.com

GAINESVILLE

The Dunlap House	85-155-BB	Full American breakfast
635 Green St 30501	10 rooms, 10 pb	Complimentary tea,
770-536-0200 Fax: 770-503-7857	Most CC, *Rated*, •	refreshments
800-276-2935	C-yes/S-no/P-no/H-yes	Wedding facilities, non-
David & Karen Peters		smoking inn, turndown
All year		service

Luxurious historic accommodations. Breakfast in common area, bed, or on verandah. Restaurant and lounge across the street.

innkeepers@dunlaphouse.com http://www.dunlaphouse.com

HARTWELL

The Skelton House	90-125-BB	Full breakfast
97 Benson St 30643	7 rooms, 7 pb	Afternoon snacks, tea, and
706-376-7969 Fax: 706-856-3139	Most CC, *Rated*	beverages
877-556-3790	C-yes/S-ltd/P-no/H-yes	Member "Select Registry"
Ruth & John Skelton		
All year		

Recently restored Victorian Village Breakfast Inn located in downtown area, only 2 miles from beautiful Lake Hartwell.

skeltonhouse@hartcom.net http://www.theskeltonhouse.com

HELEN

Alpine Hilltop Haus	89-125-BB	Full breakfast
362 Chattahoochee Strasse	4 rooms, 4 pb	Rooms with wood-burning
30545	*Rated*	fireplaces
706-878-2388 Fax: 706-878-0119	C-ltd/S-ltd/P-no/H-no	
Frankie Allen		
All year		

Tree-covered, secluded, hilltop location. Short walk to Alpine Village center. Deck overlooking Chattahoochee River. hilltop@hemc.net http://georgiamagazine.com/hilltop/

Ivy Ridge	BB	Full breakfast
114 Ridge Rd 30545	4 rooms, 4 pb	Afternoon wine and hors
706-878-3135 Fax: 706-892-1241	Visa, MC, *Rated*	d'oeuvres, evening snacks
Sally and Mel Whitehead	C-ltd/S-ltd/P-no/H-no	Common Room with F/P,
All year		porches, whirlpool, brook,
		waterfall, nature trails

The place for essential 3 Rs: Romance, Retreat, Recreation! 2+ acres of privacy, walk to Main St, nature trail, river, brook and waterfalls, delicious candlelight breakfast, wine/appetizers Fri/Sat. http://www.ivyridgeweb.com

HELEN (REGION)

Enota B&B Retreat Conf. Lodge
1000 Hwy 180, *Hiawassee* 30546
706-896-9966 Fax: 706-896-4737
800-990-8869
All year

25-260-BB
25 rooms, 16 pb
Visa, MC, *Rated*, •
C-yes/S-ltd/P-yes/H-ltd

Country Breakfast
Vegetarian, kosher, country
Jacuzzis, fireplaces, 3 in-ground trampolines, tipi village

Enota is nature in all its glory with 4 waterfalls, 5 streams, old lodge, cabins, camping, trout fishing, trampolines, game room, library. Come enjoy the deer, butterflies and happy friendly smiles!! enota@enota.com http://www.enota.com

HOGANSVILLE

The Grand Hotel Inc.
303 E Main St 30230
706-637-8828 Fax: 706-637-4522
800-324-7625
Glenda M. Gorden All year

100-150-BB
10 rooms, 10 pb
Visa, MC
C-ltd/S-ltd/P-ltd/H-ltd

Full breakfast
Lunch, afternoon tea, comp. wine
Bar service, sitting room, Jacuzzis, fireplaces, cable TV

Originally built in the late eighteen hundreds, the hotel has been completely remodeled and furnished throughout with period antiques.
info@thegrandhotel.net http://www.thegrandhotel.net

JASPER

The Woodbridge Inn
44 Chambers St 30143
706-692-6293 Fax: 706-692-9061
The Rueffert Family
All year

55-80-EP
18 rooms, 18 pb
Visa, MC, AmEx
C-yes/S-no/P-yes/H-yes
German, Spanish

Restaurant
Swimming pool, cable TV, accommodate business travelers

Family owned European style Inn and restaurant in the North Georgia mountains.
Wood@woodbridgeinn.net http://www.woodbridgeinn.net/

LAKEMONT

Lake Rabun Hotel
PO Box 10
Lake Rabun Rd 30552
706-782-4946 Fax: 706-782-4946
Roberta & Bill Pettys
April-Nov., weekends

55-165-BB
16 rooms, 2 pb
•
C-yes/S-ltd/P-no/H-ltd

Dinner weekends
Bar service, sitting room, library, bicycles, fireplaces

Unique, original mountain inn built in 1922, with homemade craftsman furniture, tasteful, comfortable rooms with the ambiance of yesteryear. http://www.lakerabunhotel.com

LITTLE ST. SIMONS ISLAND

The Lodge on Little St. Simons Island
PO Box 21078
31522
912-638-7472 Fax: 912-634-1811
888-733-5774
Maureen Ahern & Bo Taylor
All year

375-600-AP
13 rooms, 13 pb
Most CC, *Rated*, •
C-ltd/S-ltd/P-no/H-ltd

Full breakfast
All meals and snacks included in rate
Pool,boats,shelling,canoes,kayaks, wildlife, bikes, horses, hiking, birding

A 10,000-acre undeveloped island paradise with early 1900s lodge and guest cottages for up to 30 overnight guests. The Lodge serves regional southern cuisine. Meals & Activities included. LSSI@mindspring.com http://www.littlestsimonsisland.com

MARIETTA

The Stanley House, Inc.
236 Church St 30060
770-426-1881 Fax: 770-426-6821
Brenda Lawrence
All year

100-BB
5 rooms, 5 pb
Visa, MC, AmEx, *Rated*, •
C-ltd/S-no/P-no/H-no

Full breakfast
Sitting room, accommodate business travelers

Elegant and romantic 1895 Queen Anne Victorian within walking distance of historic Marietta square. Fully renovated while retaining the flavor of the times.
thestanleyhouse@msn.com http://www.thestanleyhouse.com

MILLEDGEVILLE

Antebellum Inn
115 Spruce Point, Eatonton, 31024
200 N Columbia St 31061
478-453-3993 Fax: 478-453-3993
Dianne Johnson All year

75-109-BB
5 rooms, 5 pb
Most CC, *Rated*
C-yes/S-ltd/P-no/H-ltd

Full breakfast
Snacks, complimentary wine
Sitting room, swim pool, fireplaces, cable TV/VCR, Internet, video library

Located in the Historic District, Dianne gives a personal touch with information on the city, tours, and restaurants. antebellum@alltel.net http://www.antebelluminn.com

PERRY

Henderson Village
125 S Langston Cr 31069
478-988-8696 Fax: 478-988-9009
888-615-9722
Stuart Macpherson
All year

165-325-BB
24 rooms, 24 pb
Most CC, *Rated*, •
C-yes/S-no/P-ltd/H-yes
German, Dutch

Full breakfast
Lunch, dinner, snacks, restaurant, bar service
Library, bikes, Jacuzzis, swimming, suites, fireplaces, cable, accom.bus.trv

Authentic southern hospitality awaits, with 12 historic homes beautifully restored and relocated to create a most charming country resort.
info@herdersonvillage.com http://www.hendersonvillage.com

PINE MOUNTAIN (REGION)

Georgian Inn
PO Box 1000
566 South Talbotton St, *Greenville* 30222
706-672-1600 Fax: 706-672-1666
Angela and John Hill
All year

100-125-BB
5 rooms, 5 pb
Visa, MC, AmEx
S-ltd/P-no

Full country breakfast

Please come experience true southern elegance and hospitality in this beautiful historic home. All rooms have private bath, queen bed, cable TV, and more.
georgianplace@hotmail.com http://www.georgianplace.com

Magnolia Hall
PO Box 326
127 Barnes Mill Rd, *Hamilton* 31811
706-628-4566 Fax: 706-628-5802
877-813-4394
Dale and Ken Smith All year

95-115-BB
5 rooms, 5 pb
Most CC, *Rated*, •
C-ltd/S-no/P-no/H-ltd

Full breakfast
Snacks, complimentary wine
Sitting room, library, suites, cable TV, horse shoe court

Completely renovated 1890's Victorian; inviting porch rockers and a wicker swing. Antique filled rooms; attention to detail; gourmet breakfast. We now accept major credit cards.
kgsmag@juno.com http://www.magnoliahallbb.com

SAUTEE

The Stovall House Country Inn
1526 Hwy 255 N 30571
706-878-3355
Hamilton Schwartz All year

84-92-BB
5 rooms, 5 pb
Rated
C-yes/S-no/P-no/H-ltd

Continental plus breakfast
Restaurant
Sitting room, A/C, central heating, Historic Register

Award-winning restoration of 1837 country farmhouse, on 28 serene acres with beautiful mountain views. One of the top 50 restaurants in Georgia.
info@stovallhouse.com http://www.stovallhouse.com

SAUTEE NACOOCHEE

Eagles' Brook
423 Chimney Mountain Rd 30571
706-878-4607
Marianne Griley
April-November

65-125-BB
4 rooms, 4 pb
•
C-yes/S-ltd/P-yes/H-no
French, Spanish

Continental plus breakfast
Outdoor Jacuzzi, Barbecue area

Discover the Magic of the Mountains, at Eagles' Brook Bed and Breakfast!
mgriley42@linkamerica.net http://www.eaglesbrookbnb.com

SAVANNAH

118 West 118 W Gaston St 31401 912-234-8557 Fax: 912-232-4706 Andrea D. Walker All year	125-BB 1 rooms, 1 pb *Rated* S-no/P-no/H-yes	Continental breakfast Fireplace, cable TV

One bedroom garden apartment with living room, fully equipped kitchen and full size bath, located in an 1850 townhouse in Savannah's historic district.
adwalker1@aol.com http://www.118west.com

Bed & Breakfast Inn 117 W Gordon St 31401 912-238-0518 Fax: 912-233-2537 Robert McAlister All year	89-169-BB 15 rooms, 15 pb Most CC C-yes/S-ltd/P-no/H-ltd	Full breakfast Afternoon tea Garden courtyards; walking distance to historic attractions & restaurants.

A warm welcome awaits you at the Bed & Breakfast Inn in Savannah.... Come on in and experience the charm of this wonderful city in our two restored 1853 Federal Row houses on Gordon Row. bnbinn@email.msn.com http://www.savannahbnb.com

Brie Manor Carriage House 401 Washington Ave 31405 912-786-5853 866-359-0297 John & Stacy McCarthy All year	95-100-EP 2 rooms, 1 pb Most CC C-yes/S-ltd/P-ltd/H-no	Self catering, Full Kitchen Complimentary bottle of wine Full kitchen, satellite TV, VCR, radio, air and heat (window unit)

Adorable little guest house, nicely furnished, located on beautiful oak-lined Washington Avenue in Savannah. Sleeps 2; 1 bedroom with Queen bed, a bath, and kitchen for your use. jrmccarthy@buckman.com http://www.briemanor.com

Comer House 2 East Taylor St 31401 912-234-2923 All year	125-175-BB 2 rooms, 2 pb *Rated* C-ltd/S-no/P-no/H-no	Continental breakfast stocked Self-catering Garden, Cable TV

A very large and historic Victorian residence located on Monterey square, offering two self-catering guest apartments within a walled courtyard and garden. Parking included in rear courtyard. comerhouse@bigfoot.com http://www.comerhouse.com

SAVANNAH

The Gastonian
220 E Gaston St 31401
912-232-2869
Fax: 912-232-0710
800-322-6603
Ann Landers
All year

200-375-BB
16 rooms, 16 pb
Rated, •

Full breakfast

The Gastonian is located in Savannah's beautiful Historic District. It is comprised of two adjacent mansions, which were built in 1868.
gastoniann@aol.com http://www.gastonian.com/inn/index.html

Hamilton-Turner Inn
330 Abercorn St 31401
912-233-1833
Fax: 219-233-0291
888-448-8849
Charlie & Sue Strickland
All year

149-358-BB
17 rooms, 17 pb
ost CC, *Rated*, •
C-yes/S-no/P-ltd/H-yes
Spanish, French

Full breakfast
Afternoon tea
Sitting room, bicycles, Jacuzzis, suites, fireplaces, cable TV

Located in the heart of the historic district overlooking Lafayette Square.
homemaid@worldnet.att.net http://www.hamilton-turnerinn.com

Joan's on Jones
17 West Jones St 31401
912-234-3863
Fax: 912-234-1455
888-989-9806
Joan & Gary Levy
All year

145-160-BB
2 rooms, 2 pb
Rated
C-yes/S-no/P-ltd/H-yes

Continental breakfast
Complimentary wine
Sitting room; tennis, golf, and fishing nearby

An exquisite "jewel" in the restored 1883 Victorian townhouse that has graced Jones Street, in the heart of Savannah's National Historic Landmark District, for generations.
joansonjones@aol.com http://www.bbonline.com/ga/savannah/joans/index.html

---

Magnolia Place Inn
503 Whitaker St 31401
912-236-7674
Fax: 912-236-1145
800-238-7674
R. & J. Sales
All year

165-325-BB
15 rooms, 15 pb
Most CC, *Rated*, •
C-ltd/S-no/P-no/H-no

Full breakfast
Afternoon tea & wine
Verandas, courtyard, Jacuzzis, 2 two-bedroom row houses

In the heart of Savannah's famed Historic District, circa 1878. Several rooms offer luxuries, Jacuzzi baths and fireplaces.
info@magnoliaplaceinn.com http://www.magnoliaplaceinn.com

Planters Inn
29 Abercorn St 31401
912-232-5678
Fax: 912-232-8893
800-554-1187
Natalie J. Miller
All year

115-195-BB
56 rooms, 56 pb
Visa, MC, AmEx,
Rated, •
C-yes/S-yes/P-no/H-yes

Continental breakfast
Complimentary wine
Athletic club, pool, parking garage, family friendly facility

This award-winning property blends the warmth and charm of a small inn with the services of a grand hotel.
plantinn@aol.com http://www.plantersinnsavannah.com

SAVANNAH

Sarah's Garden Inn
402 E Gaston St 31401
912-234-7716 Fax: 912-236-8297
866-266-2714
Jane & Rocky Reed
All year

150-205-BB
7 rooms, 7 pb
Visa, MC, *Rated*, •
C-yes/S-ltd/P-no/H-yes

Full breakfast
Snacks, complimentary wine
Sitting room, swimming pool, suites, fireplace, cable TV

Beautiful 1888 Victorian home, recently restored to perfection. We are in the Historic District with 3 beautiful suites and 3 luxurious bedrooms all with private baths.
sjrreed@aol.com http://www.sarahsgarden.com

The William Kehoe House
123 Habersham St 31401
912-232-1020 Fax: 912-231-0208
800-820-1020
Margaret Eden & Bonnie Sawyer   All year

205-295-BB
15 rooms, 15 pb
Most CC, *Rated*, •
C-yes/S-no/P-no/H-yes

Full breakfast
Afternoon tea, hors d'oeuvres
Snacks, concierge, fax, free off-street parking, newspaper, turndown

Offering a tradition of refined elegance and our dedication to Southern hospitality. Located on beautiful Columbia Square in Savannah's renowned historic district.
classmanagement@aol.com http://www.williamkehoehouse.com

SAVANNAH (REGION)

Palmyra Plantation Barn
2999 Islands Hwy
5836 Islands Hwy, *Midway* 31320
912-884-5779 Fax: 912-884-3046
888-246-8188
D., L., & M. Devendorf
All year

120-275-BB
9 rooms, 9 pb
Most CC, •
C-ltd/S-no/P-no/H-yes

Full breakfast
Lunch & dinner available, afternoon tea, snacks
Sitting room, library, bikes, pool, suites, kayaking

A restored 1930's coastal barn, set among cathedral oaks at river's edge, just south of Savannah. melonbluff@clds.net http://www.melonbluff.com

SENOIA

The Veranda
PO Box 177
252 Seavy St 30276
770-599-3905 Fax: 770-599-0806
877-525-3436
Jan & Bobby Boal   All year

125-175-EP
9 rooms, 9 pb
Most CC
C-ltd/P-no/H-yes

Complimentary snacks, coffee, tea, hot beverages
Breakfast available nearby

With wraparound porch and rocking chairs, this elegant turn-of-the-century National Register Inn offers a quiet, relaxed Southern lifestyle just 37 miles south of downtown Atlanta.
jbboal@aol.com http://www.selectregistry.com/inns/veranda

ST. MARYS

Spencer House Inn
101 E Bryant St
200 Osborne St 31558
912-882-1872 Fax: 912-882-9427
Mary & Mike Neff
All year

80-145-BB
14 rooms, 14 pb
Most CC, *Rated*
C-yes/S-no/P-no/H-ltd

Full breakfast
Afternoon tea, snacks
Sitting room, library, suites, cable TV, accom. bus. travel, elevator, ramp

Gateway to Cumberland Island National Seashore; large verandahs with rockers; spacious, sunny common areas; quiet, coastal, historic village; walk to restaurants, shops, museums and ferry. info@spencerhouseinn.com http://www.spencerhouseinn.com

SWAINSBORO

Edenfield House Inn
426 W Church St 30401
478-237-3007
Maxine Carter   All year

55-BB
9 rooms, 9 pb

This charming house, with its interior hallways bedecked with hand-painted murals, welcomes visitors with the warmth and hospitality that have always been associated with the refined south. mcarter1@pineland.net http://bbonline.com/ga/edenfield

1884 Paxton House Inn, Thomasville, GA

THOMASVILLE

1884 Paxton House Inn
445 Remington Ave 31792
229-226-5197
Susie Sherrod
All year

135-350-BB
9 rooms, 9 pb
Visa, MC, AmEx, *Rated*
C-ltd/S-no/P-no/H-no

Full gourmet breakfast
Afternoon and evening refreshments
Phone/data ports, Cable TV, robes, hair dryer, iron, pool/spa, computer

AAA Four Diamond Award 1884 Paxton House Inn in beautiful historic Thomasville, Georgia. Designed for adults, visited by royalty and the perfect retreat for leisure, romance or corporate traveler. 1884@rose.net http://www.1884paxtonhouseinn.com

---

Melhanna Plantation
301 Showboat Ln 31792
229-226-2290
Fax: 229-226-4585
888-920-3030
Charlie & Fran Lewis
All year

250-650-BB
38 rooms, 38 pb
Most CC, *Rated*, •
C-yes/S-ltd/P-no/H-yes

Full breakfast
Tea & treats, wine hour, turndown treats
Bathrobes, 24-hour room service, restaurant, pool,tennis, fitness center

Historic Southern Plantaion featuring 38 suites and fine dining nightly. Rated "Best of the top 10 Restaurants" by Georgia Trend 2001 and "Top Ten Most Romantic Inn's" by America Historic Inns 2001. info@melhana.com http://www.melhana.com

---

Serendipity Cottage
339 E Jefferson St 31792
229-226-8111
Fax: 229-226-2656
800-383-7377
Kathy & Ed Middleton
All year

95-135-BB
4 rooms, 4 pb
Most CC, *Rated*, •
C-ltd/S-no/P-no/H-no

Full breakfast
Snacks, complimentary wine
Sitting room, bikes, exercise equipment & golf, at private country club

A true Bed & Breakfast. Lovely circa 1906 restored and decorated house, welcoming porches, private relaxing accommodations, gourmet breakfasts. Like your home away from home without the worries.
goodnite@rose.net http://www.serendipitycottage.com

TIFTON

Sumner Carriage House
1604 Murray Ave 31794
229-388-1028 Fax: 229-386-8820
Daryl & Sherrie Sumner
All year

85-130-BB
2 rooms, 2 pb
Visa, MC
C-ltd/S-no/P-no/H-no

Full, gourmet breakfast
Cont. or no breakfast offered at reduced rate
Formal gardens, koi pond, walking paths

An elegantly rustic hide-away estate built in 1932, the Sumner Carriage House, although in town, is secluded on one and one half beautiful garden acres of pines, palms and Southern camellias. tds_sds@hotmail.com http://www.sumnercarriagehouse.com

VILLA RICA (REGION)

The Cabin at Sweetwater Farm
2565 Millertown Rd,
Temple 30179
770-459-5894
Robert & Shirley Meeks

100-BB
3 rooms, 3 pb
Rated, •
S-no/P-no/H-no
All year

Full breakfast
Homemade wine in cabin and pound cake upon arrival golf course discount available

30 acres of wooded land and trails cut through the woods, lake nearby, secluded cabin in the woods. Lots of privacy.

WARM SPRINGS

Hotel Warm Springs
PO Box 351
47 Broad St 31830
706-655-2114 Fax: 706-655-2406
800-366-7616
Geraldine Thompson
All year

70-125-BB
18 rooms, 18 pb
Rated, •

Full breakfast

Built in 1907, this hotel has hosted such guests as the King & Queen of Spain, the Queen of Mexico, President Sergio Osmena of the Philippines, and Bette Davis.
hotelwarmsprings@alltel.net

Hawaii

BIG ISLAND, CAPTAIN COOK

Areca Palms Estate
PO Box 489
81-1031 KeaPuka Mauka 96704
808-323-2276 Fax: 808-323-3749
800-545-4390
Janice & Steve Glass
All year

80-125-BB
4 rooms, 4 pb
Rated, •
C-yes/S-ltd/P-no/H-no

Full Hawaiian breakfast
Afternoon. tea, snacks
Jacuzzi, sunset viewing
Lanai, complimentary snorkel gear, game/reading room

Tropical country estate beautifully furnished and fresh flowers. Private grounds encased by palm trees and gardens. Minutes to best snorkeling/kayaking in Hawaii.
merryman@ilhawaii.net http://www.konabedandbreakfast.com

Cedar House and Coffee Farm
PO Box 823
B2-6119 Bamboo Rd 96704
808-328-8829 Fax: 808-328-8829
866-328-8829
Diana & Nik von der Luehe
All year

70-110-BB
5 rooms, 3 pb
Visa, MC, *Rated*, •
C-yes/S-no/P-no/H-no
German

Continental plus breakfast
Afternoon tea, snacks
Sitting room, cable TV, accommodate business travelers

Enchanting Bed wonderful breakfasts including our homegrown coffee; great panoramic ocean view. cedarhouse@hawaii.rr.com http://www.cedarhouse-hawaii.com

BIG ISLAND, CAPTAIN COOK

Hale Ho'ola
85-4577 Mamalahoa Hwy
96704
808-328-9117 877-628-9117
Betty Sherman
All year

75-95-BB
3 rooms, 3 pb
Rated, •
C-ltd/S-ltd/P-no/H-no

Full breakfast
Sitting room, library

Cool island plantation-style home nestled in a patchwork of tropical gardens and extensive ocean views. tlc@hale-hoola.com http://www.hale-hoola.com

---

Mara's Dive
PO Box 4
83-5389 Middle Ke'ei Rd 96704
808-328-8373 877-627-2348
Mara Hisiger & John Rees
All year

60-85-BB
2 rooms
Most CC
C-yes/S-ltd/P-ltd/H-ltd

Continental breakfast
Sitting room, cable TV, scuba tours & equip. rental, accom. bus. trav.

The place to stay and dive on the Big Island offering affordable lodging, complete PADI Scuba diving certifications, introductory scuba dives, snorkeling, kayak & dive tours, and a great view!!! mara@marasdive.com http://www.marasdive.com

BIG ISLAND, HILO

Na'ali'i Plantation
2939A Pulima Dr 96720
808-935-2109 Fax: 808-935-2109
Anne & Michael Maguire
All year

55-100-BB
2 rooms, 1 pb
Rated, •
C-yes/S-ltd/P-no/H-ltd
Spanish

Continental plus breakfast
Full kitchen, BBQ, Lanai
Croquet, badminton, VCR and videos

Very homey, country hideaway Hawaiian style—mauka—up the mountain.
naaliiplantation@prodigy.net http://www.naalii.net

Shipman House
131 Kaiulani St 96720
808-934-8002 Fax: 808-934-8002
800-627-8447
Barbara & Gary Andersen
All year

149-209-BB
5 rooms, 5 pb
Visa, MC, AmEx,
Rated, •
C-ltd/S-no/P-no/H-no
French

Continental plus breakfast
Snacks
Sitting room, library, 2 units-1910 house, 3 unit-big house, Grand piano

Hospitality so real you'll want to stay longer. Exotic flowers & fruits, garden-fresh. Hula classes twice a week. bighouse@bigisland.com http://hilo-hawaii.com

---

Wild Ginger Inn
100 Puueo St 96720
808-935-5556 Fax: 808-969-1225
800-882-1887
Richard Stancliff
All year

45-99-BB
20 rooms, 18 pb
Visa, MC, •
C-ltd/S-ltd/P-ltd/H-ltd

Continental breakfast
Fruit snacks available most of the time
Cable TV, lobby, lounge with social furniture groupings and hammock

Old plantation style bed & breakfast inn in the town that time forgot. Rain forest surroundings, yet 2 blocks from historic old downtown district.
gingerinn@aol.com http://www.wildgingerinn.com

BIG ISLAND, HILO (REGION)

Kai'i Kai B&B
HC 3 Box 10064
15-1825 Beach Rd, *Big Island, Keaau* 96749
808-982-9256 Fax: 808-982-9256
888-542-4524
John & Tory Mospens
All year

85-145-BB
3 rooms, 3 pb
Visa, MC, *Rated*, •
C-yes/S-no/P-no/H-ltd

Full breakfast
Sitting room, Jacuzzi, swimming pool, suites, cable TV

Ocean front retreat, each room with an ocean view. Whales seen in winter, dolphins and turtles seen all year. Full tropical breakfast with 100% Kona coffee.
innkeeper@hawaii-ocean-retreat.com http://www.hawaii-ocean-retreat.com

BIG ISLAND, HILO (REGION)

Rainforest Retreat
HCR-1 Box 5655
16-1874 36th Ave, *Big Island, Keaau* 96749
808-961-4410 Fax: 808-966-6898
888-244-8074
Lori & Mark Campbell All year

49-95-BB
4 rooms, 3 pb
Most CC, *Rated*, •
C-yes/S-ltd/P-no/H-ltd

Continental plus breakfast
Snacks
Bicycles, Jacuzzis, suites

Rejuvenate while enjoying the Hawaiian ambiance. Soak in the hot tub surrounded by wild orchids and tropical tradewinds.
retreat@bigisland.net http://www.rainforestretreat.com

Our Place Papaikou's
PO Box 469
3 Mamalahoa Highway, *Big Island, Papaikou* 96781
808-964-5250
Ouida Trahan & Sharon Miller

50-80-BB
3 rooms, 1 pb
Visa, MC, *Rated*, •
C-ltd/S-ltd/P-no/H-no
All year

Continental plus breakfast
Sitting room, library, cable TV

Located near Hilo on beautiful Hamakua Coast overlooking Kapua stream and tropical gardens. rplace@aloha.net http://www.ourplacebandb.com

BIG ISLAND, HONAUNAU

The Dragonfly Ranch
PO Box 675
Keala O Keawe Rd 96726
808-328-2159 Fax: 808-328-9570
800-487-2159
Barbara Moore
All year

85-200-BB
5 rooms, 3 pb

Kona, Hawaii eco-tourism treehouse spa hosts romantic honeymoons, B&B families, workshops–with dolphins, diving, labyrinth, birding, yoga studio, lomilomi massage and orchid flower essences. dfly@aloha.net http://www.dragonflyranch.com

BIG ISLAND, KAILUA-KONA

Hale Maluhia Country Inn
76-770 Hualalai Rd 96740
808-329-1123 Fax: 808-326-5487
800-559-6627
Ken & Sue Smith All year

90-150-BB
5 rooms, 5 pb
Most CC, *Rated*, •
C-ltd/S-ltd/P-no/H-yes

Full breakfast lovers buffet
Japanese spa, Tropical Gardens

Secluded, shaded up-country tropical Eden, world's best climate. Private baths. Stone/tile spa w/massage jets. Koi ponds, stream, waterfalls. Video library. Breakfast lovers buffet. Kailua-Kona 3 m. ken@hawaii-inns.com http://www.hawaii-inns.com/hi/kna/hmh

---

Kokoke Lani B&B
PO Box 2728
74-4969 Kealakaa St 96745
808-329-2226
Terry & Meredith Neumann

135-165-BB
5 rooms, 5 pb
Visa, MC, *Rated*, •
C-ltd/S-no/P-no/H-no
All year

Full island-style breakfast
A full service accommodation, daily maid and nightly turndown.

Private gated estate with breathtaking 180 degree views overlooking the Pacific. Sparkling 42' pool & hot tub. Full maid service and nightly turndown. Gracious hospitality and much Aloha. kokokelanibnb@hawaii.rr.com http://www.kokokelani.com

---

Pu' Ukala Lodge
PO Box 2867 96745
808-325-1729 Fax: 808-325-1729
1-888-325-1729
Tom Tripler & Ron Jackowitz

75-165-BB
4 rooms, 3 pb
Visa, MC, •
C-ltd/S-ltd/P-no/H-ltd
All year

Full breakfast

On the slopes of Mt. Hualalai, offering spectacular views comfort without air-conditioning. Breakfast served family-style. In the country & convenient to everything.
puukala1@aol.com http://www.puukala-lodge.com

BIG ISLAND, KEAAU

A Cottage in Paradise
HCR 1 Box 5212
12 Koali St, Hawaiian Paradise Park 96749
808-982-5369
Kim & Kahiki Hodson

65-98-BB
2 rooms, 2 pb
Visa, MC, •
C-yes/S-ltd/P-ltd/H-no
Hawaiian
All year

Continental plus breakfast
Jacuzzis, suites, large pavilion & picnic area

We are located on the east side of the Big Island of Hawaii, in the secluded beauty of Hawaiian Paradise Park.

hawaii@acottageinparadise.com http://www.acottageinparadise.com

BIG ISLAND, MOUNTAIN VIEW

Hale Nui
PO Box 127
18-7879 Leonaka Road 96771
808-968-6577 Fax: 808-968-8900
888-968-HALE
Kerry & Linda Greathouse

60-75-BB
4 rooms, 2 pb
Visa, MC, *Rated*, •
C-yes/S-ltd/P-no/H-no
All year

Continental Plus Breakfast
Cable TV, accommodate business travelers

This charming alpine style home is the perfect place to stay when visiting the Volcano or Hilo. Scrumptious breakfast buffet. Licensed massage therapist.

halenui@aol.com http://www.bbonline.com/hi/halenui

BIG ISLAND, OCEAN VIEW

Bougainvillea
PO Box 6045
Corner of Bougainvillea & Kahili, 96737
808-929-7089 Fax: 808-929-7089
800-688-1763
Martie Jean & Donald Nitsche

75-BB
4 rooms, 4 pb
Most CC, *Rated*, •
C-yes/S-yes/P-no/H-no
All year

Full breakfast
Library, Jacuzzis, swimming pool, satellite TV, BBQ, ping pong, horseshoes

Ideal location where you are treated like family. "Nights and breakfasts to remember," followed with secrets of where to shop, swim, snorkel, eat, tour, etc.

peaceful@interpac.net http://www.hi-inns.com/bouga/

BIG ISLAND, VOLCANO

Aloha Junction
PO Box 91
19-4037 Post Office Ln 96785
808-967-7289 Fax: 808-967-7289
888-967-7286 All year

75-99-BB
3 rooms, 2 pb
Visa, MC, *Rated*, •
C-ltd/S-ltd/P-ltd/H-no

Full breakfast
Sitting room, library, Jacuzzis, fireplaces, cable TV

Premier location, easy to find! One mile from Volcanoes National Park.

junction@aloha.net http://www.bbvolcano.com

The Chalet Kilauea Collection
PO Box 998
998 Wright Rd 96785
808-967-7786 Fax: 808-967-8660
800-937-7786
Brian & Lisha Crawford
All year

45-395-BB
6 rooms, 6 pb
Most CC, *Rated*, •
C-ltd/S-ltd/P-no/H-no
French, Dutch, Jap., Sp.

Full breakfast
Afternoon tea
Sitting room, library, hot tubs, 6 vacation homes–1 with Jacuzzi, massages

The collection offers a selection of fine accommodations set outside Hawaii's Volcanoes National Park. reservations@volcano-hawaii.com http://www.volcano-hawaii.com

---

The Guesthouse at Volcano
PO Box 6
11-3733 Ala Ohia 96785
808-967-7775 866-886-5226
Bonnie Goodell
All year

75-95-BB
4 rooms, 4 pb
Rated, •
C-yes/S-yes
English, Spanish

Continental breakfast
Breakfast & snack materials available anytime
TV/VCR, telephone, children toys, flashlights, binocs, umbrellas, library

Fully equipped apartments and cottages, on six acres of orchards and native rainforest, next to National Park. innkeeper@volcanoguesthouse.com
http://www.volcanoguesthouse.com

Kilauea Lodge, Volcano Village, Big Island, HI

BIG ISLAND, VOLCANO

Hale Sweet Hale PO Box 913 19-4104 Anuhea Circle Dr 96785 808-967-7271 Fax: 808-967-8598 800-709-0907	75-145-BB 5 rooms, 5 pb • C-yes/S-ltd/P-ltd/H-no Spanish Aurelia Gutierrez All year	Continental breakfast Parking ,TV/VCR, washer/dryer, full kitchens, mid-weekly maid service

We offer several cottages from one to five bedrooms, all featuring the finest in Hawaiian art and culture. Each cottage is completely private, spacious, less than 2 miles from the National Park. admin@halesweethale.com http://www.HaleSweetHale.com

Kilauea Lodge PO Box 116 19-3948 Old Volcano Rd 96785 808-967-7366 Fax: 808-967-7367 Lorna & Albert Jeyte All year	125-175-BB 13 rooms, 13 pb Visa, MC, *Rated* C-yes/S-ltd/P-no/H-ltd German, Spanish	Full breakfast Restaurant, bar, dinner available Sitt. rm., hot tub, garden gazebo, 2-bdrm cottage, hot towel racks, robes

Popular mountain lodge with full service restaurant. Six rooms with fireplace. One mile from spectacular Volcanoes National Park.
stay@kilauealodge.com http://www.kilauealodge.com

Volcano Country Cottages PO Box 545 96785 808-967-7960 Fax: 808-985-7104 800-967-7960 Kathleen Porter All year	85-125-BB 3 rooms, 3 pb Visa, MC, Disc, *Rated*, • C-yes/S-ltd/P-no/H-no	Continental breakfast

Adjacent to Hawaii Volcanoes National Park, lovely old family property in upland rainforest, 2-BR Artist's House & studio Ohelo Berry Cottage.
aloha@volcanocottages.com http://www.volcanocottages.com

Volcano Heart Chalet PO Box 404 11th Street left off Jade Ave 96785 808-248-7725 Fax: 808-248-7725 JoLoyce Kaia All year	75-100-BB 3 rooms, 3 pb *Rated*, • C-ltd/S-no/P-no/H-no	Continental breakfast Coffee and tea available Kitchenette, sitting room with gas fireplace, fee laundry facilities

Located in Volcano, Big Island, explore Volcano National Park, exotic gardens, Macadamia nut farms, Hilo's zoo & great restaurants! Then relax in the cool mountain air of Volcano. Romantic and fun.
volcanoheart@aol.com http://www.aol.com.hometown/joloyce/myhomepage/business.html

Volcano Inn PO Box 490 19-3820 Old Volcano Hwy 96785 808-967-7293 Fax: 808-985-7349 800-997-2292 Joan Prescott-Lighter All year	95-165-BB 9 rooms, 9 pb Most CC, *Rated*, • C-yes/S-no/P-ltd/H-ltd French	Full breakfast Afternoon tea, complimentary wine, lunch, dinner Sitting room, library, bikes, suites, fireplaces, cable TV

Spacious inn and fully equipped cedar cottages tucked into native giant tree ferns. Most unique accommodations adjacent to Hawaii Volcanoes National Park, offering true "Aloha" hospitality! AAA Rated volcano@volcanoinn.com http://www.volcanoinn.com

BIG ISLAND, WAIMEA (REGION)

Aah, the Views
PO Box 6593
66-1773 Alaweo St, *Big Island, Kamuela* 96743
808-885-3455 Fax: 808-885-4031
866-885-3455
Mare Grace All year

65-110-BB
4 rooms, 2 pb
Rated, •
C-yes/S-no/P-no/H-no

Continental plus breakfast
Sitting room, sauna, massage, yoga

On the slopes of Mauna Kea, our peaceful, beautiful B&B offers cool, quiet nights with starry skies, sumptuous breakfasts beside the stream, spectacular views, and a restful healing environment. tommare@aloha.net http://www.beingsintouch.com

KAUAI, HANALEI

B&B & Beach @ Hanalei Bay
PO Box 748
96714
808-826-6111
Carolyn Barnes All year

80-135-BB
4 rooms, 4 pb
Rated, •
C-ltd/S-no/P-no/H-no

Continental plus breakfast
Restaurant nearby
Sitting room, library, television, coolers, snorkel equipment available

Beach on famous Hanalei Bay is 125 yards away. View of 1000-foot waterfalls. Antiques & rattan. Hike Na Pali, snorkel, golf, kayak.
hanaleibay@aol.com http://www.bestofhawaii.com/hanalei

River Estates
PO Box 169
96714
808-826-4616 Fax: 808-826-4616
800 484-6030 All year

175-225
Most CC

Centrally located on Kauai's world famous North Shore, River Estate is considered a world class destination and vacation travelers delight.
markbar@aloha.net http://www.kauaifamilyvacation.com/

KAUAI, KALAHEO

Kalaheo Inn
PO Box 584
4444 Papalina 96756
808-332-6023 Fax: 808-332-5242
888-332-6023
Chet & Tish Hunt, Herb Brun

55-95-EP
C-yes/S-no/P-no
All year

Restaurant
Laundry facility, video store

The Kalaheo Inn offers comfortable and conveniently located Kauai accommodations. We have laundry, restaurant and video store on the site.
chet@aloha.net http://www.kalaheoinn.com

KAUAI, LAWAI

Hale Kua Guests
PO Box 649
4896 East Kua Road 96765
808-332-8570 Fax: 808-332-9825
800-440-4353
Bill & Cathy Cowern All year

95-120-EP
5 rooms, 5 pb
Rated, •
C-yes/S-ltd/H-no

Suites, cable TV, guest units with full kitchens, full baths, washer/dryer

Our secluded hillside retreat, located on Kauai's sunny south side, offers peace and serenity in one of our five choice accommodations.
halekua@aloha.net http://www.planet-hawaii.com/halekua

KAUAI, POIPU BEACH (REGION)

Gloria's Spouting Horn
4464 Lawai Beach Rd, *Kauai, Koloa* 96756
808-742-6995 Fax: 808-742-6995
Gloria & Bob Merkle
All year

250-300-BB
3 rooms, 3 pb
Rated
S-ltd/P-no/H-no

Full breakfast
Complimentary snacks, wine & selected beverages
Sitting room, pool, books/videos, telephone, TV/VCR, sunken tub, wetbar

Hawaii's only 4-star B&B, rated in top 25 in USA, this oceanfront B&B was featured on PBS-TV's "Country Inn Cooking. . . ." Sleep to the sound of the surf in a four-poster bed—just 40 ft from the water. glorbb@gte.net http://www.gloriasbedandbreakfast.com

KAUAI, POIPU BEACH (REGION)

Island Home
1707 Kelaukia St, *Kauai, Koloa* 96756
808-742-2839 Fax: 808-742-8668
800-555-3881
Kathleen M. Houser All year

90
2 rooms, 2 pb
Most CC
S-ltd

The Island Home is nestled in the Poipu Kai Resort.
info@kauaibedandbreakfast.com http://www.kauaibedandbreakfast.com

---

Poipu Plantation Resort
1792 Pe'e Rd, *Kauai, Koloa* 96756
808-742-6757 Fax: 808-742-8681
800-634-0263
Chris and Javed All year

95-175-BB
14 rooms, 14 pb
Visa, MC, *Rated*, •
C-ltd/S-ltd/P-no/H-ltd
Aloha!

Continental plus breakfast
Breakfast not offered for vacation rental guests
Bath, TV, A/C, ceiling fan, deck; cottages: wood floors, A/C, phone, etc.

Poipu Beach from $95. Honeymoons, Families and Romance abound. A 1938 Classic Hawaiian Plantation B&B House with our Honeymoon Ocean View Ali'i Suite and nine private Cottage Style Apartments.
plantation@poipubeach.com http://www.poipubeach.com

Sugar Mill Cottages
2391 Hoohu Rd, *Kauai, Koloa* 96756
808-742-9369 Fax: 808-742-6432
877-742-9369
Chet & Tish Hunt
All year

75-EP
12 rooms, 12 pb
Visa, MC, AmEx, •
C-yes/S-no/P-no/H-no

Tennis court, Jacuzzis, swimming pool, cable TV

12 luxury studio apartments within walking distance to Poipu Beach. Budget priced. Large pool and 8 tennis courts.
mail@suite-paradise.com http://www.accommodationspoipu.com

Poipu Inn
2720 Hoonani Rd, *Kauai, Poipu* 96756
808-742-0100 Fax: 808-742-6843
800-552-0095
Dotti Cichon All year

85-145-BB
9 rooms, 9 pb

Island style breakfast
Cable television, alarm radio

Treat yourself to a special Poipu vacation at our award-winning 1933 Historical Plantation Inn on Kauai's sunny south shore. info@poipu-inn.com http://www.poipu-inn.com

KAUAI, PRINCEVILLE

An Angel Abode
PO Box 223597
4064 Kaahumanu Place 96722
360-701-1455 Fax: 360-456-4040
Gail Spicuzza
All year

95-145-EP
3 rooms, 3 pb
Rated
C-yes/S-no/P-no/H-no

Snacks, many restaurants & grocery nearby
Library, bikes, boogie, boards, golf clubs, snorkel gear, suites, cable TV

A tastefully appointed and spacious custom home with views of majestic mountains, lush tropical vegetation and the splendor of the distant ocean. Only 5 minutes to the protected beach of Hanalei Bay. gail@travelkauai.com http://www.travelkauai.com

---

Hale 'Aha at Princeville
PO Box 223370
3875 Kamehameha 96722
808-826-6733 800-826-6733
Ruth Bockelman
All year

115-275-BB
4 rooms, 4 pb
Visa, MC, Disc
C-ltd/S-no/P-no/H-no

Continental breakfast
Many restaurants nearby
Hot tubs, on 480 ft of Princeville golf course, tennis/health spa nearby

Located on 480' of golf course, with distant ocean and mountain views. Panoramic Penthouse suite has BBQ on private balcony. kauai@pixi.com http://www.HaleAha.com

MAUI, HAIKU

Halfway to Hana House
PO Box 675
101 West Waipio Rd 96708
808-572-1176 Fax: 808-572-3609
Gail Pickholz
All year

85-EP
1 rooms, 1 pb
•
C-ltd/S-no/P-ltd/H-no
Spanish, French, Japanese

Continental Maui breakfast extra
Beer, wine, soft drinks, juices for purchase
Library, beach mats, coolers, CD player, color TV, hair dryer, razors

Conveniently located, this romantic, private studio on Maui's lush rural coast has spectacular panoramic ocean views, fragrant breezes and a hammock for two under the palms.
gailp@maui.net http://www.halfwaytohana.com

Maui Vacation Bungalow
100 Pii Alii Pl 96790
Dennis & Joan
All year

110-EP
1 rooms, 1 pb
•
C-ltd/S-no/P-no/H-no

Great views, peaceful, fully equipped

Enjoy our private, ocean view bungalow on 2 manicured acres, in the upcountry town of Haiku, on Maui's North Shore. windsurfing, waterfalls, golf and world famous restaurants are just minutes away. dandj@maui.net http://www.maui.net/~dandj

MAUI, HANA

Hana Maui Botanical Gardens
PO Box 404
470 Ulaino Road 96713
808-248-7725 Fax: 808-248-7725
Jo Loyce Kaia
All year

75-100-BB
2 rooms, 2 pb
•
C-ltd/S-no/P-no/H-no

Continental breakfast
Coffee, tea, cocoa, juice, muffins
Private kitchens, fresh fruit picking, queen-size beds

Located in a tropical botanical garden—the real Hawaii that few visitors see. Experience gardens, animals & friends you'll never forget. Hana is a unique experience!
joloyce@aol.com http://hometown.aol.com/joloyce/myhomepage/index.html

---

Hana Oceanfront Cottages
PO Box 843 96713
808-248-7558
Dan & Sandi Simoni
All year

190-225-EP
2 rooms, 2 pb
Visa, MC, •
C-no/S-no/P-no/H-no

Coffee and teas
Gourmet kitchens, gas BBQ grill, beach chairs, umbrellas and towels

Located in secluded and isolated Hana, Maui, Hawaii, these two oceanfront vacation homes offer the finest in luxury vacation rentals. Numerous beach activities and hiking are right outside your door! dansandi@maui.net http://www.hanaoceanfrontcottages.com

---

Heavenly Flora
PO Box 748
70 Maia Rd 96713
808-248-8680 Fax: 808-248-8059
Anthony Johnson
All year

115-175-BB
3 rooms, 1 pb
Visa, MC
C-no/S-ltd/P-no/H-no
French

Continental breakfast
Tea, Coffee available to guests
Sitting Room, Large Kitchen, Deck Seating & dining, Tropical Gardens

Heavenly Flora offers bed and breakfast accommodation in a beautiful private home set amid the splendor of a five-acre tropical flower farm and gardens, with gorgeous ocean and mountain views. info@heavenly-flora.com http://www.heavenly-flora.com

MAUI, KIHEI

Aloha Pualani
15 Wailana Place 96753
808-874-9265
Fax: 808-874-9127
800-782-5264
Keith & Marina Dinsmoor
All year

89-150-BB
5 rooms, 5 pb
Visa, MC, AmEx, •
C-yes/S-no/P-no/H-ltd

Continental plus breakfast
Sitting room, swimming pool, beach, snorkel, sailing trips

Five oceanview town homes with full kitchens and one B 100 ft from Maui's longest sandy beach. pualani@mauigateway.com http://www.alohapualani.com

MAUI, KIHEI

Eva Villa B&B
815 Kumulani Drive 96753
808-874-6407 Fax: 808-874-6407
800-884-1845
Rick & Dale Pounds
All year

105-150-BB
Rated, •
C-ltd/S-ltd/P-no/H-ltd

Continental plus breakfast
Jacuzzis, swimming pool, cable TV

Eva Villa is located at the base of Mt. Haleakala just above Wailea and Maui's best beaches. pounder@maui.net http://www.maui.net/~pounder/

Sunnyside of Maui B&B
2840 Umalu Pl 96753
808-874-8687 Fax: 808-875-1833
800-598-9550
David Morrell & Kim Insley-Morrell
All year

85-125-BB
2 rooms, 2 pb
Rated, •
C-yes/S-no/P-no/H-no

Continental breakfast
Jacuzzi, swimming pool, suites, cable TV, accomodate bus. travelers

Beautifully decorated suites in modern home, 1/2 mile from on of Maui's best beaches. sunnysidemaui@maui.net http://www.maui.net/nsidemaui/

MAUI, KULA

Silver Cloud Ranch
RR 2, Box 201 96790
808-878-6101 Fax: 808-878-2132
800-532-1111
Mike Gerry & Ana Lee Apple
All year

85-195
12 rooms, 12 pb
Most CC, *Rated*
C-yes

Full breakfast

Sit around the fireplace and have great conversations with people from around the world. slvrcld@maui.net http://www.silvercloudranch.com/index.html

MAUI, LAHAINA

Blue Horizons
3894 Mahinahina St 96761
808-669-1965 Fax: 808-665-1615
800-669-1948
Beverly Spence
All year

99-119-BB
4 rooms, 4 pb
Visa, MC, AmEx, •
C-yes/S-ltd/P-no/H-no

Full breakfast

Escape to this beautiful, upscale B&B with majestic ocean views, Lahaina Town and fabulous beaches just minutes away.
chips@maui.net http://www.bluehorizonsmaui.com

Garden Gate
67 Kaniau Rd 96761
808-661-8800 Fax: 808-661-0209
800-939-3217
Jaime & Bill Mosley
All year

65-95-BB
4 rooms, 4 pb
Visa, MC, AmEx,
Rated, •
C-yes/S-ltd/P-no/H-yes
Spanish, Japanese

Continental breakfast
Bicycles, cable TV, A/C, laundry facilities, beach w/in walking distance

We are a lovely Bed & Breakfast minutes from Lahaina and walking distance to Ka'anapali beaches. jaime@gardengatebb.com http://www.gardengatebb.com

---

Old Lahaina House
PO Box 10355
96761
808-667-4663 Fax: 808-667-5615
800-847-0761
John & Sherry Barbier
All year

60-160
4 rooms, 4 pb
Visa, MC, AmEx,
Rated, •
C-yes/S-no/P-no

Coffee and tea
Pool, TVs, phones, A/C, beach across street, laundry fac.

Air-conditioned privacy, tropical courtyard. Walk to historic Lahaina town with museums, shops, restaurants & harbor. olh@oldlahaina.com http://www.oldlahaina.com

MAUI, LAHAINA

Penny's Place Inn Paradise
1440 Front St 96761
808-661-1068 Fax: 808-667-7102
877-431-1235
Penny & Keith Weigel

88-125-BB
4 rooms, 4 pb
Visa, MC, •
C-yes/S-ltd/P-no/H-no
All year

Continental plus breakfast
Snacks
Cable TV

New-construction Hawaiian/Victorian guest home, across the street from the ocean. Four beautiful rooms with private baths, all on balcony level, separate entrance.
stay@pennysplace.net http://www.pennysplace.net

MAUI, MAKAWAO

Olinda Country Cottages & Inn
2660 Olinda Rd 96768
808-572-1453 Fax: 808-573-5326
800-932-3435
Ellen Unterman All year

120-195-BB
5 rooms, 5 pb
C-ltd/S-ltd/P-no/H-no

Continental breakfast
First mornings breakfast in cottages

Located in upcountry Maui, this beautiful Bed and Breakfast Estate, has been voted one of the BEST B & B's on Maui.
olinda@mauibnbcottages.com http://www.mauibnbcottages.com

MAUI, PAIA

The Spyglass House Oceanfront Inn
367 Hana Highway 96779
808-589-8608 Fax: 808-579-8608
800-475-6695
Poni Brendan & William McCormick All year

90-250-EP
6 rooms, 4 pb
Most CC, *Rated*, •
C-yes/S-no/P-ltd/H-ltd
English, Spanish

Tea, coffee, frozen waffles, and hot cereal
Full kitchen to use, living room, Jacuzzi, barbecue,

Oceanfront Vacation Rentals located 1/2 mi from surf town Paia. Three houses, 6 unique rooms, 30 ft. from the water's edge. info@spyglassmaui.com http://spyglassmaui.com

MAUI, PAIA (REGION)

Aloha Maui
PO Box 790210, *Maui, Haiku* 96779
808-572-0298
Ken Redstone All year

45-100-BB
4 rooms, 3 pb
Most CC, •
C-yes/S-ltd/P-no/H-no

Continental breakfast
Coffee & tea
Bicycles, sauna, complete kitchen, laundry room, private phone w/voicemail

Relax in your private cottage just walking distance from the island's most stunning waterfalls. Our B&B is nestled in a small valley on Maui's North shore close to the charming bohemian town of Paia. kenred101@yahoo.com

NAALEHU (REGION)

Macadamia Meadows Farm
PO Box 756
94-6263 Kamaoa Rd, *Big Island, Naalehu* 96772
808-929-8097 Fax: 808-929-8097
888-929-8118
Charlene & Cortney Cowan

75-125-BB
4 rooms, 3 pb
Most CC, *Rated*, •
C-yes/S-ltd/P-no/H-ltd
All year

Sumptuous tropical breakfast
Snacks
Tennis, swimming pool, suites, cable TV, conference, compl. orchard tours

For those seeking the "real" non-commercialized Hawaii. Located on an 8-acre working Macadamia nut farm estate in the historic Kau area; tennis court, pool, sumptuous tropical breakfasts. kaleena@aloha.net http://www.macadamiameadows.com

OAHU, HAWAII KAI (REGION)

Aloha
909 Kahauloa Place, *Oahu, Honolulu* 96825
808-395-6694
Phyllis Young All year

60-75-BB
3 rooms
C-yes/S-no/P-no/H-no

Full breakfast
Library, swimming pool, cable TV, large deck with patio table & chairs

Hawaii Kai non-smoking home, in executive community with partial ocean and marina view. Minutes from famed snorkeling beach, Hanauma Bay.
alohaphyllis@hawaii.rr.com http://home.hawaii.rr.com/alohaphyllis/

OAHU, HONOLULU

J & B's Haven
PO Box 25907
831 Kahena Street 96825
808-396-9462
Joan Webb & Barbara Abe
All year

65-75-BB
2 rooms, 2 pb
Rated
C-ltd/S-no/P-no/H-no
French

Continental plus breakfast
Sitting room, cable TV

Nestled in picturesque Hahaione Valley, just minutes from Hanauma Bay, a snorkelers' paradise. jnbshaven@hawaii.rr.com http://home.hawaii.rr.com/jnbshaven

---

Manoa Valley Inn
2001 Vancouver Dr 96822
808-947-6019
Fax: 808-946-6168
Theresa Wery
All year

99-140-BB
8 rooms, 5 pb
Visa, MC, *Rated*, •
C-ltd/S-no/P-no/H-no
German

Continental breakfast
Cable TV, large veranda for lounging

Beautiful historic mansion furnished with antiques. Breakfast served on the spacious verandah. Views of Waikiki skyline and Diamond Head.
manoavalleyinn@aloha.net http://www.manoavalleyinn.com

OAHU, KAILUA

Akamai
172 Kuumele Pl 96734
808-261-2227 Fax: 808-261-2227
800-642-5366
Diane and Joe Van Ryzin
All year

75-EP
2 rooms, 2 pb

Stocked refrigerators

Our B&B is in small and friendly Kailua, a beach town on the windward (NE) side of Oahu. Kailua is the perfect get-away location.
akamai@aloha.net http://www.planet-hawaii.com/akamaibnb/

Guesthouse Hawaii
585 Kawainui St 96734
808-262-2875
800-240-8640-0
Pam & Michael Aqui
All year

60-EP
1 rooms, 1 pb
Visa, MC, •
C-ltd/S-no/P-no/H-ltd

Cable TV

A charmingly furnished and, oh so clean, studio apartment within walking distance of Kailua Town, the beach, shopping and restaurants.
pamaqui@guesthousehi.com http://www.guesthousehi.com

Hawaii's Hidden Hideaway
1369 Mokolea Dr 96734
808-262-6560 Fax: 808-262-6561
877-443-3299
Janice Nielsen
All year

95-175-BB
3 rooms, 3 pb
•
C-yes/S-no/P-no/H-no

Continental plus breakfast
Snacks
Library, Jacuzzis, suites, cable TV, beach chair/towels, hair dryers, irons

Considered one of the best "Hideaways" on Oahu, the fabulous landscaping and Japanese garden will make you feel that you are in another world. Ideal for special occasions or business. hhhideaway@yahoo.com http://www.ahawaiibnb.com

---

Papaya Paradise
395 Auwinala Rd 96734
808-261-0316 Fax: 808-261-0316
Bob and Jeanette Martz
All year

85-BB
2 rooms, 2 pb
Rated, •
C-ltd/S-ltd/P-no/H-no

Continental breakfast
Swimming pool, cable TV

Private and quite getaway twenty miles from airport and Waikiki. Furnished in rattan and wicker. Enjoy a continental breakfast overlooking pool and garden with mountain views.
kailua@compuserve.com http://www.kailuaoahuhawaii.com

OAHU, KAILUA

Sheffield House
131 Kuulei Rd 96734
808-262-0721 Fax: 808-262-0721
Paul & Rachel Sheffield
All year

75-160
2 rooms, 2 pb
Rated, •

Continental breakfast

The Sheffield House is located in a residential neighborhood in Kailua away from the crowded hotels of Waikiki. sheffieldhouse@poi.net http://www.poi.net/~sheffieldhouse

OAHU, WAIMANALO

Nalo Winds
41-037B Hihimanu St
Beach Lots 96795
808-259-7792 866-625-6946
All year

65-145-BB
3 rooms, 3 pb
C-yes/S-ltd/P-ltd/H-ltd

Continental breakfast
Boogie Boards, snorkel gear, beach chairs, beach towels, etc.

Take a walk on the wild side.... come visit the town that time forgot.... Waimanalo. All private suites, steps to Waimanalo Beach.... 5 miles of white sand, islands off shore, no tourists to speak of. beachhousehawaii@aol.com http://www.nalowinds.com

Idaho

BOISE

A J.J. Shaw House Inn
1411 W Franklin St 83702
208-344-8899
Fax: 208-344-6677
877-344-8899
Junia Stephens
All year

79-119-BB
5 rooms, 5 pb
Most CC, *Rated*
C-ltd/S-no/P-no/H-no
German, Spanish

Full breakfast
Snacks
Sitting room, library, Jacuzzis, suites, cable TV, accom. bus. travelers

Masterfully built 1907 Queen Anne Victorian in historic, quiet North End-downtown; private baths and phone lines, clean, comfortable, vintage antiques.
jjshaw@earthlink.net http://www.jjshaw.com

BOISE (REGION)

The Maples
PO Box 1
10600 W State St, *Star* 83669
208-286-7419 877-286-7419
Mary & Don Wertman
All year

65-125-BB
4 rooms, 4 pb
Visa, MC, *Rated*
C-ltd/S-no/P-no/H-ltd

Full breakfast
Lunch/dinner available (fee)
Snacks, comp. wine, sitting room, cable TV, custom packages available, AC

The Maples is a beautifully restored and remodeled Victorian farm house, situated on 3/4 acre. maplesbb@mindspring.com http://www.mindspring.com/~maplesbb

CASCADE

Wapiti Meadow Ranch
HC 72
Milepost 16.63 Johnson Creek Rd, Valley Co. 83611
208-633-3217
Fax: 208-633-3219
Diana & Barry Bryant
June 1-October 31

100-200-AP
7 rooms, 7 pb
Rated
C-ltd/S-no/P-no/H-no

Full breakfast
Afternoon tea, snacks, complimentary wine & beer
Sitting room, library, bikes, Jacuzzis, suites, fireplaces

A remote, wilderness ranch and Orvis endorsed fly fishing lodge offering large, beautifully furnished cabins, hearty gourmet cuisine, horseback riding, superb fly fishing, wildlife viewing. wapitimr@aol.com http://www.wapitimeadowranch.com

COEUR D'ALENE

Baragar House
316 Military Dr 83814
208-664-9125 800-615-8422
Carolyn & Bernie Baragar
All year

99-149-BB
3 rooms, 1 pb
Visa, MC, AmEx
C-ltd/S-ltd/P-no/H-no

Gourmet full breakfast, Hot & cold beverages, many goodies
Hot tub, sauna, library, videos, park & lake

By beautiful Coeur d'Alene Lake, beach, park & downtown. Privately use indoor spa & sauna. Victorian Honeymoom Suite, Country Cabin & Garden Room have StellarVision ceilings (sleep under the stars).
stay@baragarhouse.com http://www.baragarhouse.com

Katie's Wild Rose Inn
7974 E Coeur'd Alene Lake Drive 83814
208-765-9474
Fax: 208-765-9474
800-371-4345
Karin & Gary Spence

85-150-BB
4 rooms, 2 pb
Visa, MC
C-yes/S-ltd/P-no/H-ltd
All year

Full breakfast
Sitting room, Jacuzzis, suites, fireplaces, cbl TV, Coeur d' Alene lake view

Surrounded by pine trees overlooking beautiful Coer d'Alene Lake. Warm, cozy atmosphere. Beautiful wedding gazebo on the Centennial Trail for hikers and bikers.
stay@katieswildroseinn.com http://www.katieswildroseinn.com

Kingston 5 Ranch
PO Box 2229
42,297 Silver Valley Rd 83816
208-682-4862
Fax: 208-682-9445
800-254-1852
Pat & Walt Gentry All year

125-190-BB
2 rooms, 2 pb
Visa, MC, *Rated*, •
C-ltd/S-ltd/P-ltd/H-ltd

Full gourmet breakfast
Bottomless cookie jar, fruit basket

This Country Inn offers a quiet, relaxing retreat or a wonderful romantic getaway. Guests enjoy "Award Winning Breakfasts" and our Jacuzzi/Fireplace Suites invite you to . . . Come, Relax & Be Pampered! info@k5ranch.com http://www.k5ranch.com

---

The Roosevelt Inn
105 E. Wallace Ave 83814
208-765-5200 Fax: 208-664-4142
800-290-3358
John & Tina Hough
All year

89-249-BB
15 rooms, 15 pb
Most CC, *Rated*, •
C-yes/S-no/P-yes/H-yes

Full breakfast
Afternoon tea, snacks
Sitting room, library, Jacuzzis, suites, cable TV, accom. business travelers

Historic red brick school house with bell tower, built in 1905. Completely remodeled and furnished in antiques. info@therooseveltinn.com http://www.therooseveltinn.com

---

Wolf Lodge Creek
515 S Wolf Lodge Creek Rd 83814
208-667-5902 Fax: 208-667-1133
800-919-9653
Terry Cavanaugh & Tricia Freeman

115-175-BB
5 rooms, 5 pb
All year

27 acres backing national forest provide the natural ambiance and beauty of this bed and breakfast. The secluded location guarantees you privacy, relaxation, and quiet.
wlcbb@wolflodge.com http://www.wolflodge.com

FISH HAVEN

Bear Lake
500 Loveland Lane 83287
208-945-2688
Esther Harrison
All year

60-BB
4 rooms, 1 pb

Full breakfast

http://www.bearlakebedandbreakfast.com

Greyhouse Inn, Salmon, ID

KAMIAH

Hearthstone Lodge PO Box 1492 Highway 12 Mile Post 64 83536 208-935-1492 Fax: 208-935-1873 877-LODGE-4U Harty & Marjorie Schmaehl All year	125-235-BB 5 rooms, 5 pb Most CC, *Rated*, • C-no/S-no/P-no/H-ltd German	Full breakfast Afternoon tea, lunch & dinner available Spacious suites, guest library, meeting space, quality amenities, data port

Elegant river lodge with fireplaces, Jacuzzis, river view balconies on historic Lewis Clark Trail. Twenty nine-acre pine forest setting. Extraordinary hideaway retreat.
visit@hearthstone-lodge.com http://www.hearthstone-lodge.com

KELLOGG

The Mansion on the Hill PO Box 456 105 S Division 83837 208-786-4455 Fax: 208-786-0157 877-943-4455 Dana Musick All year	115-140-BB 4 rooms, 4 pb Most CC C-ltd/S-no/P-no/H-no	Full breakfast Afternoon tea, restaurant Sitting room, Jacuzzis, suites, fireplaces, cable TV, accom. bus. travel

Affordable luxury. Beautiful historic home with country French decor. Enjoy a walk in our gardens, relax in the hot tub or just enjoy the quiet.
stay@mansionbnb.com http://www.mansionbnb.com

SALMON

Greyhouse Inn 1115 Hwy 93 South 83467 208-756-3968 800-348-8097 Sharon & David Osgood All year	70-90-BB 4 rooms, 2 pb Visa, MC, Disc, *Rated*, • C-ltd/S-ltd/H-no	Full gourmet breakfast Lunch, dinner, afternoon tea Snacks, sitting room, library, bikes, cable, hot tub, tours of Lewis & Clark

Lewis & Clark log cabins, queen log beds and private baths, large porch for viewing the beautiful mountains. osgoodd@salmoninternet.com http://www.greyhouseinn.com

SHOUP

Smith House 3175 Salmon River Rd 83469 208-394-2121 Fax: 850-927-3350 800-238-5915 Aubrey & Marsha Smith April 15th–October 15t	45-65-BB 5 rooms, 1 pb Visa, MC, • C-yes/S-ltd/P-yes/H-no	Full breakfast Hot tub (Summer only)

Since opening in 1987, this is the perfect place to stay for scenic beauty and stress-free holidays. Catering to small groups—birthdays, reunions, anniversaries and weddings.
aesmith49@yahoo.com

WARREN

Back Country
PO Box 77
Warren Wagon Rd 83671
208-636-6000 800-816-2848
Leland & Betty Cavner
All year

75-100-BB
4 rooms, 2 pb
C-ltd/S-no/P-no/H-no

Full breakfast
Night time dessert
Sitting room

Mountain getaway, rustic yet modern facility offering a relaxed family atmosphere and country breakfast.
backctry@ctcweb.net

WOODLAND (REGION)

Quilt House
HC11 Box 142, *Kamiah* 83536
208-935-7668 Fax: 208-935-7686
877-QUILTBB
Elaine Hutchison
All year

75-BB
5 rooms, 3 pb
Visa, MC, AmEx,
Rated, •
C-yes/S-no/P-no/H-no

Full breakfast
Lunch & dinner avail, aftn. tea, snacks, wine
Sitting room, suites, fireplaces, accom. bus. travelers

Down comforters and handmade quilts on every bed, fabulous views in quiet country mountain setting on the Lewis & Clark Trail.
quiltbb@camasnet.com http://www.quilthousebedandbreakfast.com

Illinois

ALTON

Beall Mansion
407 12th St 62002
618-474-9100 Fax: 618-474-9090 1-866-843-2325
Jim & Sandy Belote
All year

89-438-BB
6 rooms, 6 pb
Most CC, *Rated*, •
C-ltd/S-no/P-no/H-no

Gourmet, Continental or Room Only
Catering for showers, weddings, business mtgs.
2 Person whirlpools, Firepl., Imported chocolates, Plush robes, Cable TV

"Voted One of the Three Best Bed & Breakfasts in Illinois" –Illinois Magazine Readers Poll. Whirlpools for Two. Fireplaces. Chocolates. Plush Robes. Need we say more?
bepampered@beallmansion.com http://www.beallmansion.com

ARCOLA (REGION)

Breakfast in the Country
1750 E. St Rt #133, *Hindsboro* 61930
217-346-2739
Chloanne Greathouse
April–December

60-75-BB
3 rooms
Rated
C-yes/S-ltd/P-ltd/H-no

Full breakfast
Snacks
Sitting room, library, fireplaces, accommodate business travelers

Large country home on working farm. Llamas, sheep, dogs and kittens nearby.

BELLEVILLE

Victory Inn
712 S Jackson St 62220
618-277-1538 Fax: 618-277-1576
888-277-8586
Jo Brannan
All year

60-115-BB
3 rooms, 3 pb
Visa, MC, AmEx,
Rated, •
C-yes/S-ltd/P-no/H-no

Continental plus breakfast
Sitting room, Jacuzzis, suites, cable TV/VCR with movies

Victorian charm w/ modern comforts. Hosts welcome you w/ hospitality, offering comforts of home w/out the intrusions of the world.
jo@victoryinn.com http://www.victoryinn.com

BISHOP HILL

Colony Hospital
PO Box 97
110 N Olson St 61419
309-927-3506 Fax: 309-927-3506
George & Cheryl Dunivant
All year

80-120-BB
5 rooms, 5 pb
Visa, MC
C-ltd/S-ltd/P-ltd/H-no

Continental plus breakfast
Sitting room, library, Jacuzzis, fireplaces, accom. bus. travelers

Historic building in Swedish village founded in 1846. Peaceful, relaxing retreat in colony period surroundings with modern amenities.
colhosbb@winco.net http://www.bishophilllodging.com

BLOOMINGTON

Vrooman Mansion
701 E. Taylor St 61701
309-828-8816 Fax: 309-828-2596
Darcy Ackley
All year

80-125-BB
5 rooms, 3 pb
Rated
C-ltd/S-ltd/P-no/H-no

Full breakfast
Common sitting room w/cable TV/VCR, asst. video tapes, and DSL , library

Built in 1869, this B&B is nestled in a quiet neighborhood in Bloomington, 2 hours from Chicago. Beautifully appointed rooms w/antiques await you.
vroomanmansion@aol.com http://www.vroomanmansion.com

CARBONDALE

Sassafras Ridge
382 Fawn Trail 62901
618-529-5261 Fax: 618-529-1901
Frances & Myers Walker
All year

75-90-BB
3 rooms, 3 pb
Most CC, *Rated*, •
C-ltd/S-no/H-no

Full breakfast
Snacks
Sitting room, library, pet kennel nearby, cable TV, VCR with movies

Quiet, privacy, and informal hospitality, in a modern country home at the end of a lane near Shawnee National Forest. sassybb@go-illinois.com http://www.sassafrasbb.com

CARBONDALE (REGION)

Hidden Lake
PO Box 593
433 Cook Ave, *Jonesboro* 62952
618-833-5252 Fax: 618-833-5252
John & Mary Jo Smith
All year

80-125-BB
5 rooms, 5 pb
Visa, MC, AmEx, *Rated*
C-ltd/S-no/P-no/H-no

Full breakfast
Sitting room, bicycles, Jacuzzis, suites, fireplaces, conference facilities

Nestled amongst 12 acres of woods & gardens, Hidden Lake offers 5 finely appointed guestrooms and suites w/ private baths, robes & fluffy towels.
HiddenLk@aol.com http://www.hiddenlakebb.com

CHAMPAIGN

The Gold's
2065 County Rd 525 E 61822
217-586-4345
Rita & Bob Gold
All year

45-50-BB
3 rooms, 1 pb
Rated, •
C-yes/S-no/P-no/H-no

Continental plus breakfast
Cable TV, VCR w/movies

Country charm & hospitality in 1874 farmhouse. Handy to interstate & university attractions. Furnished with antiques.
reg@prairienet.org http://www.culocalbiz.com/goldsbandb

CHICAGO

City Scene
2101 North Clifton Ave 60614
773-549-1743 Fax: 773-529-4711
Mary A. Newman
All year

100-200-BB
2 rooms, 2 pb
Rated
C-ltd/S-no/P-no/H-no

Continental breakfast
Sitting room, each unit has TV

Comfortable suite on residential street in Sheffield historic District; close to dining, shopping, museums, parks, theatres, transportation.
cityscene@aol.com http://www.cityscenebb.com

CHICAGO

Flemish House of Chicago 68 E Cedar St 60611 312-664-9981 Mike Maczka & Tom Warnke All year	145-225-BB 6 rooms, 6 pb Visa, MC, AmEx, • C-ltd/S-no/P-no/H-no Spanish	Self-catered breakfast Coffee & tea all day

An apartment B&B in a Victorian rowhouse, located in the Gold Coast neighborhood of Chicago, steps from Michigan Avenue, Oak Street Beach and Lake Shore Drive.
info@chicagobandb.com http://www.chicagobandb.com

Gold Coast Guest House 113 West Elm St 60610 312-337-0361 Fax: 312-337-0362 Sally Baker All year	129-199-BB 4 rooms, 4 pb Most CC, *Rated*, • C-ltd/S-no/P-no/H-no	Continental breakfast Afternoon tea, snacks Comp. wine, sitting room, soaking tub, each unit has cable TV/CD/phone

This 1873 Victorian hides a contemporary secret inside ... a 20 foot high window-wall lets the garden in while you enjoy breakfast.
sally@bbchicago.com http://www.bbchicago.com

The House of Two Urns 1239 N Greenview Ave 60622 773-235-1408 Fax: 773-235-1410 877-Two-Urns Kapra & Miguel Fleming All year	82-150-BB 5 rooms, 1 pb Visa, MC, Disc, *Rated*, • C-yes/S-no/P-no/H-no German, Spanish, French	Continental plus breakfast Complimentary drinks Sitting room, cable TV, 3-night minimum, phone, answering machine

Charming urban inn complete with antiques & original art offer a quiet respite in an urban setting. twourns@earthlink.net http://www.twourns.com

---

Old Town Chicago 1442 N North Park Ave 60610 312-440-9268 Fax: 312-440-2378 Mike & Liz Serritella All year	139-199-BB 4 rooms, 4 pb Visa, MC, AmEx, *Rated* C-yes/S-ltd/P-no/H-no	Continental plus breakfast 24 hour breakfast & snacks Baldwin grand piano, marble fireplace, chef's kitchen, roof decks, laundry

Chicago's only Mobil 3-Star B&B, this sumptuously outfitted 1999 art deco mansion on a leafy residential street in downtown Chicago affords unmatched sleek, modern elegance in a neighborhood setting.
mail@oldtownchicago.com http://www.oldtownchicago.com

Rodgers Park House 2909 W Fargo Ave 60645 773-262-5757 Fax: 773-262-4018 Dr. Jerry Porzemsky All year	110-BB 2 rooms, 2 pb • C-ltd/S-no/P-ltd/H-yes German, Spanish	Continental breakfast Sitting room, fireplace.

Fantastic home – 1,000 house plants, gardens, exotic decor, patio, fireplace, kitchen facilities.
DrJerry4@hotmail.com

The Wicker Park Inn 1329 N Wicker Park Ave 60622 773-486-2743 Fax: 773-486-3228 David Parker & Stephen Taylor All year	100-135-BB 2 rooms, 2 pb Visa, MC, Disc, • C-ltd/S-ltd/P-no/H-no French, German	Continental Plus breakfast Afternoon tea Sitting room, library, bicycles, accom. bus. travelers

Enjoy relaxed, peaceful accommodations in a turn-of-the-century rowhouse just 7 minutes from downtown Chicago via subway and 35 minutes to O'Hare airport.
mail@wickerparkinn.com http://www.wickerparkinn.com

CHICAGO

Windy City Urban Inn
607 W Deming Place 60614
773-248-7091 Fax: 773-529-4183
877-897-7091
Mary & Andy Shaw
All year

125-325-BB
8 rooms, 8 pb
Most CC, *Rated*, •
C-ltd/S-no/P-no/H-no
Spanish, French

Continental plus breakfast
Complimentary snacks, soda, coffee, tea
Sitting area, Jacuzzi tub, air conditioning, fireplaces, cable TV, Internet

Quintessentially Chicago, our Victorian mansion, in the lively Lincoln Park neighborhood, offers a choice of guestrooms within the main house or apartments in the coach house.
stay@chicago-inn.com http://www.chicago-inn.com

Wooded Isle Suites
5750 S Stony Island Ave 60637
773-288-5578 Fax: 773-288-8972
800-290-6844
Charlie Havens & Sara Pitcher
All year

123-168-EP
13 rooms, 13 pb
Most CC, *Rated*, •
C-yes/S-no/P-no/H-no

Family friendly facility, equipped kitchens

Near Lake Michigan & Museum of Science & Industry. Guest flats in diverse, dynamic neighborhood south of McCormick Convention Center.
Reserve@woodedisle.com http://www.woodedisle.com/

CHICAGO (REGION)

The Homestead
1625 Hinman Ave, *Evanston* 60201
847-475-3300 Fax: 847-570-8100
Lynn Killinger
All year

130-140-BB
35 rooms, 35 pb
Visa, MC, AmEx, *Rated*
C-ltd/S-yes/P-no/H-ltd

Continental plus breakfast
French restaurant
Facilities for meetings of up to 15 people

Historic residential neighborhood; two blocks from Lake Michigan 30 minutes from downtown Chicago.

Margarita European Inn
1566 Oak Ave, *Evanston* 60201
847-869-2273
Barbara Gorham
All year

79-148-BB
32 rooms, 16 pb
Most CC, *Rated*, •
C-yes/S-yes/P-no/H-yes
Spanish, French

Continental breakfast (fee)
Restaurant serving lunch, dinner
Afternoon tea, sitting room, library, on Mississippi River

Relax to afternoon tea in our Georgian parlor room; snuggle up to a book in our wood-paneled English library. margaritainn@aol.com http://www.margaritainn.com

---

The Richmond Inn
10314 East St, *Richmond* 60071
815-678-2505
David & Randi DelGatto
All year

99-169-BB
4 rooms, 4 pb
Visa, MC, Disc, *Rated*, •
C-ltd/S-ltd/P-ltd/H-no
Spanish

Full breakfast
Lunch, dinner, afternoon tea, snacks
Sitting room, library, Jacuzzis, suites, fireplaces, cable TV, spa services

Relaxing retreat on 5 lush acres offers luxurious pampering at affordable prices, just an hour north of downtown Chicago.
rdelgatto@cobra.com http://www.TheRichmondInn.com

DU QUOIN

Francie's Inn On-Line
104 S Line St 62832
618-542-6686 Fax: 618-542-4834
877-877-2657
Cathy & Benny Trowbridge
All year

60-85-BB
5 rooms, 3 pb
Most CC, *Rated*, •
C-yes/S-ltd/P-ltd/H-no

Full breakfast
Snacks, complimentary beverages
Sitting room, bikes, suites, cable TV, accommodate business travelers

The place for a getaway vacation, romantic escape or business retreat. Walking distance to restaurants and shops, or relax on one of our big decks.
cathy@franciesinnonline.com http://www.franciesinnonline.com

Belle Aire Mansion Guest House, Galena, IL

DUNDEE (REGION)

Ironhedge Inn
305 Oregon Ave, *West Dundee*
60118
847-426-7777 Fax: 847-426-5777
Steve Fang & Eda Tomasone
All year

69-179-BB
8 rooms, 4 pb
Most CC
C-ltd/S-ltd/P-no/H-no

Full breakfast
Afternoon tea, snacks
Sitting room, library, bikes, Jacuzzis, suites, frplcs, cable, acm. bus. tvl

You will not believe your eyes when you step into this finely detailed architectural jewel.
EETomasone@aol.com http://www.ironhedge.net

GALENA

Aldrich Guest House
900 Third St 61036
815-777-3323
Sandra & Herb Larson
All year

95-195-BB
5 rooms, 3 pb
C-ltd/S-no/P-no

1843 Greek Revival visited by Lincoln, Twain and Grant. Totally restored to its 19th century opulence. larson6103@hotmail.com http://www.aldrichguesthouse.com

---

Belle Aire Mansion Guest House
11410 Route 20 West 61036
815-777-0893
Jan & Lorraine Svec
Closed Christmas Day/Eve

90-170-BB
5 rooms, 5 pb
Visa, MC, Disc, *Rated*, •
C-yes/S-no/P-no/H-no

Full breakfast
Snacks
Sitting room, Jacuzzis, suites, fireplaces

A warm home, with the friendliest Innkeepers you'll ever find. Located just minutes from Historic Galena. belleair@galenalink.com http://www.belleairemansion.com

---

Bernadine's Stillman Inn
513 Bouthillier St 61036
815-777-0557 Fax: 815-777-8097
866-777-0557
Dave & Bernadine Anderson
All year

104-265-BB
7 rooms, 7 pb
Visa, MC, Disc, *Rated*
C-ltd/S-ltd/P-no/H-no

Full breakfast
Bottomless cookie jar & ice cream treats
Whirlpool and fireplace rooms, cable and VCR with color TV in rooms

Romantic 1858 Victorian Mansion close to town and located in residential neighborhood. Tea room on site offering formal afternoon tea, lunch, breakfast and gift shop. Courtyards full of gardens. stillman@galenalink.com http://www.stillmaninn.com

GALENA

Captain Gear Guest House
PO Box 328
1000 South Bench St 61036
815-777-0222
Fax: 815-777-3210
800-794-5656
Susan Pettey
All year

155-195-BB
3 rooms, 3 pb
Visa, MC, Disc, *Rated*
S-no/P-no/H-no

Full formal breakfast
Historic house tour, garden patio, whirlpool, tub, VCR/TV in rooms

1855 Mansion, eight fireplaces, American antique furniture, on four secluded acres in the Galena National Register Historic District.
gearhouse@galenalink.com http://www.captaingearguesthouse.com

---

Captain Harris Guest House
713 S Bench St 61036
815-777-4713
Fax: 815-777-4713
800-996-4799
Judy Dixon and Ed Schmit
All year

90-190-BB
5 rooms, 5 pb
Visa, MC, Disc
S-no/P-no/H-no

Full breakfast
Sitting room, library, Jacuzzis, suites, fireplaces, cable TV

Historic home (c.1836) in the heart of Galena. Walk to all restaurants and attractions. Honeymoon cottage with whirlpool for that very special occasion.
inquiry@captainharris.com http://www.captainharris.com

Cloran Mansion
1237 Franklin St 61036
815-777-0583
Fax: 815-777-0580
866-234-0583
Carmine & Cheryl Farruggia
All year

85-195-BB
6 rooms, 6 pb
Most CC
C-ltd/S-ltd/P-ltd/H-yes

Full breakfast
Wine, snacks
Bicycles, landscaped front yard, library, comp. videotapes, games

1880 Mansion. Double whirlpools, fireplaces. One Suite, four rooms and a Cottage. King and Queen beds, all private baths. In-room stocked mini frig, cable TV-VCRs.
innkeeper@cloranmansion.com http://www.cloranmansion.com

Farmers' Guest House
334 Spring St 61036
815-777-3456 888-459-1847
Jess & Kathie Farlow
All year

110-195-BB
10 rooms, 10 pb
Most CC
C-ltd/S-no/P-no/H-ltd

Full breakfast
Snacks, beverages, wine at 6:00 PM
Sitting room, large common areas, hot tub

Farmers Guest House welcomes you with the delight and charm of a by-gone era plus the conveniences of today. We attend to the little things... so you can enjoy your stay and make our house your home. farmersgh@galenalink.net http://www.farmersguesthouse.com

---

Park Avenue Guest House
208 Park Ave 61036
815-777-1075 Fax: 815-777-1097
800-359-0743
Sharon & John Fallbacher
All year

95-125-BB
4 rooms, 4 pb
Visa, MC, Disc, *Rated*
C-ltd/S-no/P-no/H-no

Full breakfast
Afternoon tea, snacks
Sitting room with TV, 2 parlours, gazebo, A/C, fireplaces in rooms

Elegant yet comfortable, in quiet residential area. Short walk to beautiful Grant Park, Galena River and Main St. parkave@galenalink.com http://www.galena.com/parkave

---

Pine Hollow Inn
4700 N Council Hill Rd 61036
815-777-1071
Larry & Sally Priske
All year

95-135-BB
5 rooms, 5 pb
Visa, MC, Disc, *Rated*, •
C-ltd/S-no/P-no/H-no

Full breakfast
Hiking, streams, whirlpool bath

A secluded country inn located on 120-acres, just 1½ miles from downtown Galena. Nestle in front of your own cozy fireplace, or just relax on the porch.
pinehollowinn@pinehollowinn.com http://www.pinehollowinn.com

GURNEE

Sweet Basil Hill B&B Inn
15937 W. Washington St 60031
847-244-3333 Fax: 847-263-6693
Bob & Teri Jones
Summer/high season

95-150-BB
4 rooms, 4 pb
Most CC, *Rated*, •
C-yes/S-no/P-ltd/H-ltd
French

Full breakfast
cider, lemonade, cookies, popcorn
Fax service, copies, private phone lines with modem access, tv/vcr's

Sweet Basil Hill is a cozy New England style Bed and Breakfast on seven wooded acres midway between Chicago and Milwaukee. Sheep and llamas decorate the nearby pastures. basilhill@aol.com http://www.sweetbasilhill.com

KEWANEE

Aunt Daisy's
223 W Central Blvd 61443
309-853-3300 Fax: 309-853-4148
888-422-4148
Glen & Michele Schwarm
All year

95-BB
4 rooms, 4 pb
Most CC, *Rated*, •
C-ltd/S-no/P-no/H-no

Full breakfast
Snacks, comp. dessert in evenings
Library, suites

Gothic Victorian 1890 home. Many stained glass windows await the opportunity to charm you. Music parlor with a 1929 Aeolian player piano & a baby grand.
auntdaisy@juno.com http://www.auntdaisy.net

MORRISON

Hillendale
600 W Lincolnway 61270
815-772-3454 Fax: 815-772-7023
Barb & Mike Winandy
All year

70-200-BB
10 rooms, 10 pb
Visa, MC, *Rated*, •
C-ltd/S-no/P-no/H-no

Full breakfast
Sitting room, fireplaces, billiard & fitness rooms, whirlpools for two

Travel the world from rural America in our international theme rooms. Relax in the Japanese Teahouse & enjoy fish in the water gardens.
hillend@clinton.net http://www.hillend.com

PEORIA (REGION)

Glory Hill
18427 N Old Galena Rd, *Chillicothe* 61523
309-274-4228 Fax: 309-274-3266
Bonnie Russell
All year

75-95-BB
2 rooms, 2 pb
Visa, MC, Disc, *Rated*
C-ltd/S-ltd/P-no/H-no

Full breakfast
Afternoon tea, snacks
Sitting room, library, swimming pool, color TV, 1 room has whirlpool

1841 country estate, antique furnishings, verandah, porch, fireplace, gourmet breakfasts.
gloryhil@mtco.com

PLANO

Millhurst Inn
15426 Millhurst Rd 60545
630-552-8117 Fax: 630-552-8117
Arlene & Ken Koehler
All year

150-220-BB
S-no/P-no

Complimentary breakfast

Millhurst Inn has been completely restored to grandeur. The main floor with it's large open concept, adorns a 40 foot atrium. Beautiful woodwork throughout is reminiscent of a bygone age. aleash9@msn.com http://www.bestinns.net/usa/il/millhurst.html

PLYMOUTH

Plymouth Rock Roost
201 W Summer 62367
309-458-6444 877-458-6444
Joyce Steiner
All year

59-BB
3 rooms
Visa, MC, Disc, *Rated*
C-ltd/S-no/P-ltd/H-no

Full breakfast
Snacks
Sitting room, library, bicycles, Jacuzzi, fireplaces, cable TV

Queen Anne Victorian filled with orchids, light, and hospitality. Located in historic Hancock County, IL. plymouthrock@adams.net http://www.plymouthil.com

PRINCETON (REGION)

Chestnut Street Inn
PO Box 25
301 E Chestnut St, *Sheffield*
61361
815-454-2419 800-537-1304
Gail Bruntjen
All year

85-175-BB
4 rooms, 4 pb
Most CC, *Rated*, •
C-ltd/S-no/P-no/H-no

Full breakfast
Afternoon tea, snacks
Morning wake up tray

Historic landmark offering gracious accommodations in the English tradition-inviting, serene, sophisticated, lavishly elegant. Exquisite candlelight breakfasts.
gail@chestnut-inn.com http://www.chestnut-inn.com

RED BUD

Magnolia Place
317 S Main 62278
618-282-4141
Janice Krallman
All year

65-140-BB
4 rooms, 2 pb
Visa, MC, AmEx

Continental buffet

We at Magnolia Place welcome you and extend an invitation to stay awhile. We offer elegant accommodations and gracious hospitality.
magnoliaplacebb@hotmail.com http://www.magnolia-place.com

ROCK ISLAND

Top O' The Morning
1505 19th Ave 61201
309-786-3513
Sam & Peggy Doak
All year

60-100-BB
3 rooms, 3 pb
Visa, MC, *Rated*
C-yes/S-ltd/P-no

Full breakfast

Prairie-style brick mansion built by Hiram S. Cable, President of the Rock Island Railroad, circa 1912. http://www.bbonline.com/il/morning

ROCKFORD

River House Inn & Tepee
11052 Ventura Blvd 61115
815-636-1884 Fax: 775-242-3493
Patty Rinehart
All year

95-185-BB
4 rooms, 3 pb
Most CC, *Rated*
C-ltd/S-ltd/P-no/H-ltd

Full breakfast
Snacks & coffee in room
In room Jacuzzi, fireplace, satellite TV, private portch/entrance, pool

Find contemporary style and Native American flair. . .escape to river views, savor gourmet breakfasts, and relax in "suite comfort" with satellite TV, Jacuzzi, fireplace, and private screened porch. innkeeper@riverhouse.ws http://www.riverhouse.ws/

ROCKFORD (REGION)

Lee Creek
21355 Grade School Rd,
Caledonia 61011
815-292-3519 Fax: 815-292-3520
800-815-8360
Dom & Nelda Ruscitti
All year

130-150-BB
3 rooms, 3 pb
Visa, MC, *Rated*
C-ltd/S-no/P-no/H-no

Full breakfast
Afternoon tea
Sitting room, library, suites, cable TV, accom. bus. travelers, stocked pond

The Inn is located on an 80-acre operating grain farm. Newly constructed, serving peace and tranquility with specialty breakfast. Large front and rear porches and solar room with fireplace. 76627.2102@compuserve.com http://www.bbonline.com/il/leecreek

SPRINGFIELD

Inn at 835
835 South 2nd St 62704
217-523-4466 Fax: 217-523-4468
888-217-4835
Court & Karen Conn
All year

90-190-BB
7 rooms, 7 pb
Visa, MC, AmEx,
Rated, •
C-ltd/S-no/P-no/H-yes

Full breakfast
Snacks, complimentary wine
Sitting room, bicycles, fireplace & Jacuzzi rooms available

National register. Luxurious rooms with fireplaces, Jacuzzis and gorgeous antiques. Walking distance to historic sites. Gourmet breakfast, wine and cheese.
theinnat835@worldnet.att.net http://www.innat835.com

Inn at 835, Springfield, IL

SPRINGFIELD (REGION)

Country Dreams
3410 Park Lane, *Rochester*
62563
217-498-9210
Fax: 217-498-8178
Ralph & Kay Muhs
All year

75-160-BB
Most CC, *Rated*
C-yes/S-no/P-no/H-yes

Full breakfast on weekends
Continental plus breakfast weekdays
Snacks, sitting room, library, bicycles, fireplaces, cable TV

Newly built country hideaway. Perfect for anniversary weekends, short getaways & honeymooners. Located on 16 acres of grass with flowers, fruit trees, gardens, and a small lake.
host@countrydreams.com http://www.countrydreams.com

STOCKTON

Hammond House
323 North Main Street 61085
815-947-2032
LaVonneda & Spencer Haas
All year

45-150-BB
5 rooms, 5 pb
Visa, MC, Disc, *Rated*
C-ltd/S-no/P-no/H-ltd

Continental plus breakfast
Seasonal cookout availible
Picinic table, grill , and a gift shop on premisses

This 1900 Colonial Revival offering year round hospitality. 5 romantic theme rooms. Suites with double whirlpool bath-shower combinations, air conditioning, cable color TV's. Off street parking. haas@blkhawk.net http://www.hammondhouse.org

SYCAMORE

Stratford Inn
355 W. State St 60178
815-895-6789 Fax: 815-895-6563
800-937-8106
Tom & Debbie Carls
All year

80-139-BB
39 rooms, 39 pb
Most CC, *Rated*, •
C-yes/S-ltd/P-no/H-no
Some Spanish on request

Continental
Restaurant, lunch & dinner avail., bar service
Sitting room, suites, cable TV, bike trails, accom. bus. travelers

Located in downtown Sycamore's historical district, our Inn features beautiful tapestries, artwork, oak wainscoting and antiques of very fine quality.
tom@stratfordinnhotel.com

URBANA

Lindley House
312 W Green St 61801
217-384-4800
Carolyn Baxley
All year

85-150-BB
5 rooms, 3 pb
Visa, MC
C-ltd/S-no/P-no

Breakfast in main house only

Lindley House is one of Urbana's finest examples of the Queen Anne style of Victorian architecture. carolyn@basleymedia.com http://www.lindley.cc

WHEATON

The Wheaton Inn
301 W Roosevelt Rd 60187
630-690-2600 Fax: 630-690-2623
800-447-4667
Mary Koerner
All year

145-225-BB
16 rooms, 16 pb
Most CC, *Rated*, •
C-ltd/S-no/P-no/H-ltd

Full breakfast
Afternoon wine & cheese, bedtime cookies and milk
11 rooms with Jacuzzi, fireplace, or both

A charming, European-style B&B reminiscent of Colonial Williamsburg offering a quiet retreat in the heart of bustling DuPage County (suburban Chicago).
sales@wheatoninn.com http://www.wheatoninn.com

Indiana

BLOOMINGTON

Grant Street Inn
310 N Grant St 47408
812-334-2353
Fax: 812-331-8673
800-328-4350
Bob Bohler
All year

100-175-BB
24 rooms, 24 pb
Most CC, *Rated*
S-ltd/P-no/H-yes

Full breakfast buffet
Snacks
Sitting room, TVs & phones in rooms

Suites have fireplaces and whirlpool Jacuzzis. Walk to downtown or Indiana University.
http://www.grantstinn.com/

BOONVILLE

Godbey Guest House
401 S Fourth St 47601
812-897-3902
Fax: 812-897-1423
Cora & Don Seaman
All year

60-80-BB
3 rooms
Visa, MC, Disc, *Rated*
C-yes/S-ltd/P-ltd/H-no
Spanish

Gourmet breakfast
Snacks, afternoon tea, lunch & dinner available
Sitting room, library, suite, cable TV, acc. bus. trav.

Beautifully-restored Victorian home built by one of Boonville's founding fathers in 1865.
godbeyguesthouse@toast.net http://www.godbeyguesthouse@yahoo.com

CAMPBELLSBURG

James Wilkins House
PO Box 40
225 W Oak St 47108
812-755-4274 Fax: 812-755-5239
866-248-9198
Diane Callahan
All year

55-65-BB
3 rooms
Visa, MC, *Rated*, •
C-yes/S-no/P-no/H-no

Full breakfast
Afternoon tea, snacks, comp. wine
Sitting room, library, cable TV, games, puzzles, gazebo

Experience country hospitality in an elegant Victorian setting; gourmet breakfast served by candlelight or in the gazebo.
jwhbnb@blueriver.net http://www.jameswilkinshousebnb.com

CHESTERTON

Gray Goose Inn
350 Indian Boundary Rd 46304
219-926-5781
Fax: 219-926-4845
800-521-5127
Tim Wilk, Charles Ramsey
All year

90-185-BB
8 rooms, 8 pb
Most CC, *Rated*, •
C-ltd/S-ltd/P-no/H-no

Full gourmet breakfast
Complimentary beverages, snacks
Sitting & meeting rooms, telephones in rooms, bicycles, boats

In Dunes Country. English country house on private wooded lake. Charming guestrooms, private baths, fireplaces, Jacuzzis, sun porch. Jogging/hiking trails.
graygoose@niia.net http://www.graygooseinn.com

COLUMBUS

Ruddick-Nugent House
1210 16th St 47201
812-379-1354 Fax: 812-379-1357
800-814-7478
Dennis & Joyce Orwin
All year

69-99-BB
4 rooms, 4 pb
Most CC, •
C-yes/S-no/P-no/H-no

Full breakfast
Snacks
Sitting room, library, Jacuzzis, suites, fireplaces, cable TV

1884 Victorian/Neo-classical on 3 acres, gardens, full candlelight breakfast, antiques, and gift shop. dorwin@transedge.com http://www.ruddick-nugent-house.com

EVANSVILLE

Cool Breeze
1240 SE Second St 47713
812-422-9635
Katelin & David Hills
All year

85-BB
4 rooms, 4 pb
Most CC, *Rated*
C-yes/S-no/H-no

Full breakfast
Sitting room, library, family friendly facility, meetings for small groups

A quiet, peaceful retreat ideal for a memorable romantic interlude and personal renewal. All rooms have queen beds, private baths, phones & cable TV.
coolbreeze27@juno.com http://www.coolbreezebb.com

Oliver House
420 SE Riverside Dr 47713
812-434-0029 866-876-8920
Kathy & Orson Oliver
All year

125-175-BB
4 rooms, 4 pb
Visa, MC
C-ltd/S-no/P-ltd/H-no

Full breakfast
Snacks
Sitting room, Jacuzzis, suites, fireplaces, cable, accom. bus. trvlrs.

The Oliver House is an Italianate villa style home located in he heart of the riverside historic district of Evansville, overlooking a beautiful bend of the Ohio River.
kap47713@yahoo.com http://www.oliverhousebnb.com

FORT WAYNE

Carole Lombard House
704 Rockhill St 46802
260-426-9896 888-426-9896
Bev & Dave Fiandt
All year

70-90-BB
4 rooms, 4 pb
Visa, MC, *Rated*, •
C-ltd/S-no/P-no/H-ltd

Full breakfast
Sitting room, cable TV, Carole Lombard movies & books

Decor reminiscent of the 1930's to commemorate Carole Lombard's fame. Enjoy a self-guided tour of historic West Central neighborhood. Located right on River Greenway.

GOSHEN

Prairie Manor
66398 US 33 S 46526
219-642-4761 Fax: 219-642-4762
800-791-3952
Jean & Hesston Lauver
All year

72-95-BB
4 rooms, 4 pb
Visa, MC, Disc, *Rated*
C-yes/S-no/P-no/H-no

Full breakfast
Snacks
Library, swimming pool, cable TV, accommodate business travelers

Come visit Indiana Amish country. Relax in our spacious historic English country manor home, enjoy our bountiful breakfast, find your treasure in Grandma's Attic.
jeston@npcc.net http://www.prairiemanor.com

Prairie Manor, Goshen, IN

GOSHEN (REGION)

Rust Hollar
55238 CR 31, *Bristol* 46507
219-825-1111 Fax: 219-825-4614
800-313-7800
Tim & Janine Rust
All year

79-89-BB
4 rooms, 4 pb
Most CC, *Rated*
C-yes/S-ltd/P-no/H-ltd

Full breakfast
Sitting room, cable TV, conferences.

Rustic log home situated in a secluded "hollar."
tim@rusthollar.com http://www.rusthollar.com/RHBB/index.html

INDIANAPOLIS

Speedway
1829 Cunningham Rd 46224
317-487-6531 Fax: 317-481-1825
800-975-3412
Robert & Pauline Grothe
All year

65-135-BB
5 rooms, 5 pb
Most CC, *Rated*
C-ltd/S-ltd/P-no/H-no

Full breakfast
Bicycles, suites, fireplaces, cable TV, accommodate business travelers

Located in the little town of Speedway. Surrounded by the city of Indianapolis, you'll find a feeling of home.
speedwaybnb@msn.com http://www.speedwaybb.com

Tranquil Cherub
2164 N Capitol Ave 46202
317-923-9036 Fax: 317-923-8676
Barb & Thom Feit
All year

85-125-BB
4 rooms, 4 pb
Visa, MC, AmEx, *Rated*, •
C-ltd/S-ltd/P-no/H-no

Full gourmet breakfast
Snacks
Airport pickup, library, sitting room, transportation downtown

This lovingly restored, antique filled, 100 year old B&B is located minutes from downtown in a safe, culturally diverse urban neighborhood.
tranquilcherub@aol.com http://www.tranquilcherub.com

JASPER

Powers Inn
325 W 6th St 47546
812-482-3018
Larry & Alice Garland
All year

60-BB
3 rooms, 3 pb
Visa, MC, *Rated*
C-ltd/S-no/P-no/H-no

Full breakfast
Sitting room, cable TV, accommodate business travelers

Renovated Second Empire home from 1880's. Original wood floors, pleasant mix of antiques. Three cozy guestrooms with private baths. Enjoy a full breakfast in spacious dining room.

JEFFERSONVILLE

The Beck Haus 911 East Court Ave 47130 812-284-5330 Fax: 812-284-9730 866-201-3244 Judy Beck All year	75-110-BB 3 rooms, 3 pb Visa, MC, AmEx, *Rated*, • C-ltd/S-ltd/P-no/H-yes	Full breakfast Snacks, dinner Sitting room, library, bikes, cable TV, extended stay, biz travelers

A beautifully restored 1924 house filled with antiques. Just 9 miles from Louisville (KY) Int'l airport. Located in downtown Jeffersonville within walking distance of Ohio River.
thebeckhaus@aol.com http://www.thebeckhaus.com

LAPORTE

Arbor Hill Inn 263 W Johnson Rd 46350 219-362-9200 Fax: 219-326-1778 L. Kobat/M. Wedow/K. Demoret All year	71-229-BB 7 rooms, 7 pb Most CC, *Rated* C-yes/S-ltd/P-no/H-yes	Full breakfast Lunch/dinner available (fee) Sitting room, Jacuzzis, suites, fireplaces, cable TV, VCR

Historic 1910 Greek Revival Structure. Elegant, peaceful surroundings create a haven for business and leisure travelers. arborh@netnitco.net http://www.arborhillinn.com

LEAVENWORTH

The Leavenworth Inn PO Box 9 930 West State Road 62 47137 812-739-2120 Fax: 812-739-2012 888-739-2120 Bert Collins All year	69-119-BB 11 rooms, 11 pb Most CC, *Rated* C-yes/S-no/P-no/H-yes	Full breakfast Afternoon snacks Sitting room, library, bicycles, tennis court, suites, fireplaces, cable TV.

Country hideaway overlooking the Ohio River, beautifully landscaped grounds with gazebo, tennis court, and walking and biking paths. Jacuzzi and Fireplace Suites available.
leavenworthinn@aol.com http://www.leavenworthinn.com

LOGANSPORT

Inntiquity, A Country Inn 1075 St Rd 25 N 46947 219-722-2398 Fax: 219-739-2217 877-230-7870 George & Lee Nafzger Season Inquire	80-125-BB 11 rooms, 11 pb Most CC, *Rated*, • C-ltd/S-ltd/P-ltd/H-ltd	Gourmet breakfast Dinner by Reservation Cable TV, air-conditioning, Jacuzzis, telephones, business facilities

Catering to customers as to those "to the manor born" is INNTIQUITY INN'S primary goal. We aim to indulge the tastes of those who enjoy a by-gone atmosphere.
inntiqui@ffni.com http://www.inntiquity.com

MADISON

Schussler House 514 Jefferson St 47250 812-273-2068 800-392-1931 Ann & Larry Johnson All year	130-155-BB 3 rooms, 3 pb Most CC, *Rated*, • C-ltd/S-no/P-no/H-no	Full breakfast Snacks Private parking, A/C, gift certificates available

Gracious accommodations in the heart of the Historic District; a sumptuous breakfast served in the formal dining room.
schussler@voyager.net http://www.schusslerhouse.com

MICHIGAN CITY

The Hutchinson Mansion Inn 220 W 10th St 46360 219-879-1700 Mary DuVal All year	95-150-BB 10 rooms, 10 pb Visa, MC, AmEx, *Rated*, • C-ltd/S-ltd/P-no/H-ltd	Full breakfast Snacks Sitting room, piano, whirlpools, fax, tennis & golf nearby

Elegant Victorian mansion filled with antiques, stained glass, friezes. Near Nat'l Lakeshore, dunes, beaches, antique stores, and shopping.

Spring Mill Inn, Mitchell, IN

MIDDLEBURY

Bee Hive PO Box 1191 51129 CR 35, Bristol 46540 574-825-5023 Herb & Treva Swarm All year	60-80-BB 3 rooms, 1 pb Visa, MC, *Rated* C-yes/S-no/P-no	Full breakfast Complimentary refreshments Sitting room, restaurant nearby, guest cottage available

Welcome to our cozy country B&B, built with rough-hewn timber and open beams. Snuggle under hand-made quilts. Amish Heartland tours available.

MISHAWAKA

Beiger Mansion Inn 317 Lincoln Way E 46544 219-255-6300 Ron Montandon, Dennis Slade All year	115-195-BB 10 rooms, 4 pb	

The Beiger Mansion Inn is one of the most unique Bed and Breakfast establishments you will ever visit. The four-level Neo-Classical limestone structure was built in 1903–1909.
beiger@michiana.org http://business.michiana.org/beiger/

MITCHELL

Spring Mill Inn PO Box 68 Hwy 60 East 47446 812-849-4081 Fax: 812-849-4647 877-9SPRING Brian J. Ferguson All year	49-89-EP 74 rooms, 74 pb Most CC, • C-yes/S-ltd/P-no/H-yes	American cuisine & bountiful buffet Full service restaurant Sitting room, indoor/outdoor swimming pool, fireplaces, accom. bus. traveler

Snuggled into a backdrop of stately oaks and scenic hills in Southern Indiana. Built in 1939 of picturesque rough hewn limestone, the Inn offers 74 cozy country guestrooms.
bferguson@dnr.state.in.us http://www.springmillinn.com

NASHVILLE

Allison House Inn
PO Box 1625
90 S Jefferson 47448
812-988-0814
Tammy Galm
All year

95-95-BB
5 rooms, 5 pb
Rated
C-ltd/S-no/P-no/H-no

Full breakfast
Library, sitting room, art gallery, gift shop

In the heart of Brown County, the center for the arts and craft colony. Coziness, comfort and charm. tammy@kiva.net http://browncountry.org/allisonhouse.html

---

Always Inn
8072 E State Rd 46 47448
812-988-2233 Fax: 812-988-9688
888-457-2233
Freda Counceller
All year

100-200-BB
6 rooms, 6 pb
Most CC, *Rated*, •
C-yes/S-no/P-ltd/H-yes

Full breakfast
Lunch, dinner, tea, snack, wine
Sitting room, library, Jacuzzis, fireplaces, cable TV, accom. bus. travelers

Relax, refresh, renew, restore, recharge and connect at the Always Inn. An intimate country Inn tucked away in the beautiful hills of Brown County, Indiana.
innkeeper@alwaysinn.com http://www.alwaysinn.com

Story Inn at Story Village
PO Box 847
6404 S State Road 135 47448
812-988-2273 Fax: 812-988-6516
800-881-1183
Frank Mueller & Richard Hoffstetter All year

90-160-BB
13 rooms, 13 pb
Visa, MC, *Rated*, •
C-ltd/S-no/P-ltd/H-no
German

Full country breakfast
Lunch, dinner, aftn. tea
Restaurant, bar, sitting room, larger units available, for 2-6 persons

Story Village is an 1850's rural town nestled in the hills of Brown County, IN, a place known for covered bridges, clapboard churches, weather-beaten barns, and splendid fall foliage. reservations@storyinn.com http://www.storyinn.com

SOUTH BEND

English Rose Inn
116 S Taylor St 46601
574-289-2114 Fax: 574-287-1311
Susan & Barry Kessler
All year

75-125-BB
Visa, MC, AmEx, *Rated*
C-ltd/S-no/P-no/H-no
Sign Language

Full breakfast
Snacks, complimentary wine
Sitting room, library, Jacuzzis, fireplaces, cable TV, accom. bus. travelers

English gardens surround this charming 1892 inn furnished with antiques and lace, stripes and florals, quilts and comforters. The inn offers a full private breakfast and warm hospitality. info@englishroseinn.com http://www.englishroseinn.com

SOUTH BEND (REGION)

Hidden Pond
5342 N US Hwy 35, *LaPorte* 46350
219-879-8200 Fax: 219-879-1770
Sue & Ed Berent
All year

99-159-BB
4 rooms, 3 pb
Visa, MC, *Rated*
C-yes/S-ltd/P-ltd/H-no

Full breakfast
Afternoon tea, snacks
Sitting room, library, Jacuzzis, pool, fireplaces, cable TV, acc. bus. travl

Comfortable country home close to everything, although you feel far away. You can do as much or as little as you want-experience the magic that is in Hidden Pond. Only minutes from Michigan City. edberent@adsnet.com http://www.bbonline.com/in/hiddenpond

SYRACUSE

Anchor Inn
11007 N State Rd 13 46567
574-457-4714 888-347-7481
Robert & Jean Kennedy
All year

90-100-BB
4 rooms, 4 pb

A haven for the tired traveler seeking a quiet evening, or the guest from nearby cities looking for a few days of R and R!
Anchorinn@kconline.com http://www.bbonline.com/in/anchorinn/index.html

TERRE HAUTE

Farrington
931 South 7th St 47807
812-238-0524 Fax: 812-242-8335
Mike & Connie Mutterspaugh
All year

85-BB
5 rooms, 3 pb
Visa, MC, *Rated*, •
C-yes/S-yes/P-no/H-no

Full breakfast
Snacks
Sitting room, fireplaces, covered porches in rooms, family friendly facility

A Colonial Revival home adapted to Queen Anne style. Built in 1898. Located in the heart of Terre Haute's Historical District.

abednbkfst@aol.com http://members.aol.com/abednbkfst

VALPARAISO

Inn at Aberdeen, Ltd.
3158 S State Rd 2 46385
219-465-3753 Fax: 219-465-9227
Bill Simon
All year

99-190-BB
11 rooms, 11 pb
Most CC, *Rated*
C-yes/S-no/P-no/H-yes

Full gourmet breakfast
Evening dessert, snacks
Sitting room, library, bikes, hot tubs, pool, conference center, tennis

Travel back to the 1800s while enjoying your own Jacuzzi, balcony, cozy fire & truly regal service/amenities. 18-hole championship golf course.

inn@innataberdeen.com http://www.innataberdeen.com

Songbird Prairie
174 N 600 W 46385
219-759-4274
Fax: 219-759-4233 877-SONGBRD
Barbara & Efrain Rivera
All year

125-155-BB
2 rooms, 2 pb
Visa, MC, *Rated*
C-ltd/S-ltd/P-no/H-yes

Full 3 course breakfast
Hot tea, coffee, cold beverages, evening snacks
Common room, satellite TV, VCR, fireplaces, Jacuzzis for two, data ports

We offer personal attention or perfect freedom.

efnbarb@aol.com http://www.songbirdprairie.com

WINCHESTER

Winchester Guest House Inn
1529 S Old US 27 47394
765-584-3015
Fax: 765-584-4135
Ted & Debra Davenport
All year

79-119-BB
6 rooms, 5 pb
Most CC, •
C-ltd/S-no/P-no/H-ltd

Full breakfast
Coffee, tea, wine & cheese, evening snacks
Indoor pool, theatre, fireplaces, golf, volleyball, workout facilities

7200 sq. ft. executive quality country inn featuring six acres of park-like grounds, indoor pool, theatre w/free DVD movies, billiard room, and six guestrooms-five with private baths. Fireplace rooms.

reservations@winchesterguesthouseinn.com http://www.winchesterguesthouseinn.com

ZIONSVILLE

Country Gables
9302 E Indiana 334 46077
317-873-5382
Fax: 317-873-5382
Jean & Garland Elmore
All year

88-135-BB
3 rooms, 3 pb
Visa, MC, Disc
C-yes/S-no/P-no/H-ltd

Continental breakfast
Dessert, welcome basket-fruit, snacks, candy
private living rooms, porches, deck, gardens

Newly renovated Victorian farmhouse with 3 spacious suites, located in historic Zionsville 25 minutes from Indianapolis. Relax, enjoy the antiques and hand-crafted furniture.

countrygables@indy.rr.com http://countrygables.com

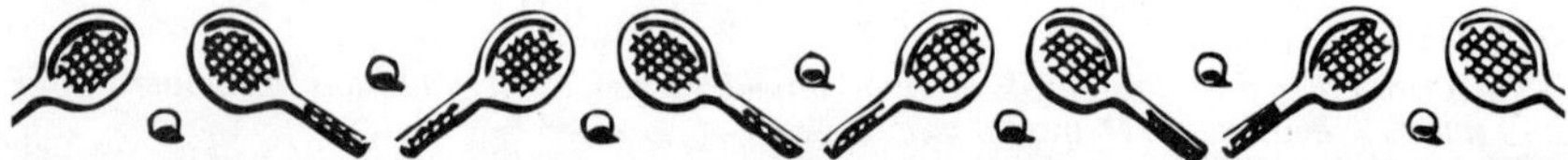

Iowa

ALGONA

Heartland 400 E Nebraska St 50511 515-295-9445 Vickie Woods & Randy Roeber All year	85-130-BB 4 rooms, 4 pb *Rated* C-ltd/S-no/P-no/H-no	Full breakfast Sitting room, bicycles, Jacuzzis, fireplaces, cable TV, massage next door

Constructed 1913 restored 1990's, heirlooms, oak floors, trim, window seats, marble fireplace, suites, private baths, whirlpools, central air, breakfast in dining room or wrap around porches.

rlroeber@ncn.net http://www.heartlandbnb.com

ATLANTIC

Chestnut Charm 1409 Chestnut St 50022 712-243-5652 Barbara Stensvad All year	70-225-BB 9 rooms, 9 pb Visa, MC, *Rated*, • S-no/P-no/H-ltd	Full breakfast Sitt. room, piano, sauna, sun rooms, A/C, antiques, fountain patio, gazebo

Enchanting 1898 Victorian mansion on large estate. Just a short drive to the famous bridges of Madison County. Gourmet dining. One suite is fully handicapped accessible.

chestnut@metc.net http://www.chestnutcharm.org/

BATTLE CREEK

The Inn at Battle Creek PO Box 58 201 Maple St 51006 712-365-4949 Fax: available 877-365-4949 Jeff & Nancy Decker All year	49-79-BB 5 rooms, 4 pb Visa, MC, *Rated* C-ltd/S-no/P-no/H-ltd	Full breakfast Dinner, snacks, restaurant, beer & wine list Cable TV, accomm. bus. travelers, free movies, FAX svc

Historic Queen Anne Victorian. Near Sioux City, Loess Hills in Western Iowa. All guestrooms have private baths; furnished with period antiques.

theinn@pionet.net http://elwood.pionet.net/~theinn

BELLEVUE

Mont Rest 300 Spring St 52031 563-872-4220 Fax: 563-872-5094 877-872-4220 Christine Zraick All year	115-195-BB 12 rooms, 12 pb Visa, MC, *Rated*, • C-ltd/S-no/P-no/H-ltd	Full breakfast A gourmet desert is included with your stay! All our luxury rooms feature heated towel bars, Egyptian cotton towels, Turt

From the moment you walk through the door, Mont Rest transports you back to a lost era of grace and beauty.

innkeeper@montrest.com http://www.montrest.com

BURLINGTON

Mississippi Manor 809 N 4th 52601 309-753-2218 Francesca Harris All year	55-75-BB 4 rooms, 4 pb Visa, MC, *Rated*, • C-ltd/S-no/P-no/H-no	Continental breakfast Full breakfast available Lunch, dinner (fee), sitting room, porch, bicycles

Enjoy peace & quiet, elegance & hospitality at this handsome Victorian Italianate home (circa 1877), located in a charming river town.

fhdjd@aol.com http://www.mississippimanor.com

BURLINGTON

The Schramm House
616 Columbia St 52601
319-754-0373 Fax: 319-754-0373
800-683-7117
Sandy & Bruce Morrison
All year

85-150-BB
5 rooms, 5 pb
Most CC, *Rated*, •
S-no/P-no/H-no

Full breakfast
Complimentary wine, snacks
Sitting room, library bicycles

Charming Victorian in historic district. Furnished with antiques throughout.
visit@schramm.com http://www.visit.schramm.com

CEDAR RAPIDS

Belmont Hill Victorian
1525 Cherokee Dr NW 52405
319-366-1343 Fax: 319-366-1351
Ken & Shelley Sullens
All year

99-152-BB
3 rooms, 3 pb
Visa, MC
C-ltd/S-no/P-no/H-yes

Full breakfast
Afternoon tea
Suites, fireplace, accommodate business travelers, wooded grounds, gardens

Experience a unique level of pampering and privacy. Restored 1882 National Register home and carriage house. Immaculate accommodations, private baths. Lovely secluded grounds, terrace and gardens. belmonthil@aol.com http://www.belmonthill.com

CEDAR RAPIDS (REGION)

The Lion & The Lamb
913 2nd Ave, *Vinton* 52349
319-472-5086 Fax: 319-472-5086
888-390-5262
Richard & Rachel Waterbury
All year

85-109-BB
6 rooms, 6 pb
Most CC, *Rated*, •
C-yes/S-no/P-no/H-no

Full breakfast
Five course Murder Mystery dinner
Sitting room, many attractions nearby, historic town

1892 Victorian mansion with seven fireplaces. Each guestroom has a private bath, queen size bed, air conditioning, ceiling fan and TV. Murder Mystery Dinners are our specialty.
lionlamb@lionlamb.com http://www.lionlamb.com

DELMAR

Lee Ar's Victorian Retreat
PO Box 238
401 Market 52037
319-674-4157 800-550-1449
Leroy & Arlene Regenwether
All year

100-BB
2 rooms, 2 pb
Rated
C-yes/S-ltd/P-no/H-no

Full breakfast
Snacks, complimentary wine coolers or soft drinks
Sitting room, tennis court, Jacuzzis, pool, suites, fireplaces, cable TV

Enjoy the enchanting Victorian era in rooms decorated with candles, roses & lace. Queen beds, cable TV, A/C, private baths w/double whirlpools.
leears@netins.net http://www.inntravels.com

DES MOINES

Butler House on Grand
4507 Grand Ave 50312
515-255-4096 866-455-4096
Clark Smith & Lauren Kernan Smith
All year

90-160-BB
7 rooms, 7 pb
Most CC, *Rated*
C-ltd/S-no/P-no/H-no

Full breakfast
Jacuzzis, fire places, book and video library

Butler House on Grand is one of the top places to stay while visiting Des Moines. Come enjoy nostalgic elegance at its finest!
info@butlerhouseongrand.com http://www.butlerhouseongrand.com

---

The Cottage
1094 28th Street 50311
515-277-7559 Fax: 515-663-0514
Dan Weese
All year

89-BB
4 rooms, 4 pb
Most CC
C-ltd/S-ltd/P-no/H-ltd

Full gourmet breakfast
Fresh daily dessert, comp. beer, wine, soda
Cable TV, hot tub, A/C, meeting & wedding space

Savor the warmth and charm of our Georgian Brick, built in 1929, in the historic Drake Neighborhood. Experience the tranquility of the enchanting cottage gardens and fountain. DanRWeese@hotmail.com http://www.thecottagedsm.com

The Hancock House, Dubuque, IA

DUBUQUE

The Hancock House 1105 Grove Terrace 52001 563-557-8989 Fax: 563-583-0813 Susan & Chuck Huntley All year	80-175-BB 9 rooms, 9 pb Most CC, *Rated* C-ltd/S-no/P-no/H-no	Full breakfast Snacks, complimentary wine Sitting room, Jacuzzis, suites, fireplaces, cable, accom. bus. trvl.

Situated on the bluffs overlooking the city to the Mississippi River Valley. Furnished in Victorian period antiques, full breakfast.

chuckdbq@aol.com http://www.thehancockhouse.com

Lighthouse Valleyview 15937 Lore Mound Rd 52002 563 583 7327 800 407 7023 Jo Ann & Bill Klauer All year	85-150-BB 5 rooms, 2 pb Most CC, • C-ltd/S-ltd/P-no/H-ltd	Full breakfast Coffee, stash tea, cappuccino, wine, soda, snacks Great Room, library, sundeck, spa, fitness, lighthouse

A unique country inn located NW of historic Dubuque, Iowa. A year-round Inn, 3 charming Queen rooms and a King Safari Suite with Jacuzzi and fireplace, a full country breakfast and close to skiing & golf.

lhthse@mcleodusa.net http://www.lighthousevalleyview.com

The Mandolin Inn 199 Loras Blvd 52001 563-556-0069 Fax: 563-556-0587 800-524-7996 Amy Boynton All year	85-175-BB 8 rooms, 6 pb Most CC, *Rated* C-ltd/S-no/P-no/H-yes Spanish, French	Full breakfast Sitting room, parlor, music room, suites, cable TV, resident cat

Beautifully restored 1908 Edwardian mansion dedicated to sharing elegance & comfort. Perfect for kindling romance, or unwinding after business, as well as exploring the upper Mississippi River.

innkeeper@mandolininn.com http://www.mandolininn.com

DUBUQUE

The Redstone Inn & Suites
504 Bluff St
5th & Bluff St 52001
563-582-1894 Fax: 563-582-1893
Jerry & Kelly Lazore
All year

75-195-BB
14 rooms, 14 pb
Most CC, •
C-yes/S-no/P-ltd/H-no

Full breakfast
Tea/coffee in the Parlor
Cable TV, phones w/data ports, ironing boards/irons, off-street parking

A beautifully restored Queen Ann Victorian in the heart of the historic Cable Car Square shopping district. info@theredstoneinn.com http://www.theredstoneinn.com

---

The Richards House
1492 Locust St 52001
563-557-1492
Michelle Stuart
All year

45-105-BB
5 rooms, 4 pb
Most CC, *Rated*, •
C-yes/S-ltd/P-ltd/H-no

Full breakfast
Snacks
Sitting room, antiques, concealed TVs, phones, fireplaces

1883 Stick-style Victorian mansion with over 80 stained-glass windows. Seven varieties of woodwork and period furnishings.
info@therichardshouse.com http://www.therichardshouse.com

FORT MADISON

Kingsley Inn
707 Ave H 52627
319-372-7074 Fax: 319-372-7096
800-441-2327
Alida Willis
All year

85-185-BB
18 rooms, 18 pb
Most CC, *Rated*, •
C-ltd/S-no/P-no/H-no

Full breakfast
Cookies & beverages at check-in
Parlor with piano, VCR/movies, restaurant with room service and gift shop.

Historic inn on Mississippi River. Antique furnishings, whirlpool tubs, fireplaces, elevator. Near museums, shops, casino riverboat, 15 miles to Nauvoo, IL.
kingsley@interl.net http://www.kingsleyinn.com

GRINNELL

Carriage House
1133 Broad St 50112
641-236-7520 Fax: 641-236-5085
Ray & Dorothy Spriggs
All year

55-75-BB
5 rooms, 5 pb
Visa, MC, *Rated*, •
C-ltd/S-no/P-no/H-no

Full breakfast
Afternoon tea, snacks
Sitting room, library, Jacuzzis, fireplaces, accommodate business travelers

Victorian home restored with your comfort in mind; gourmet breakfast, afternoon tea available. Enjoy the wicker on the porch or read by the fire.
irishbnb@iowatelecom.net http://www.bedandbreakfast.com/bbc/p216752.asp

IOWA CITY

The Brown Street Inn
430 Brown St 52245
319-338-0435 Fax: 319-351-8271
Janet & Steve Panther
All year

59-99-BB
5 rooms, 5 pb
Visa, MC, AmEx
C-yes/S-ltd/P-no/H-no

Full or continental breakfast
Continental breakfast served at reduced price
Pillared porch, fireplace centered livingroom, guest home office/internet

This 1913 Gambrel Cottage Style Mansion in the quiet Brown Street Historical District is within casual walking distance of downtown Iowa City, Hancher Auditorium, and the University of Iowa campus. info@brownstreetinn.com http://www.brownstreetinn.com

---

Haverkamp Linn Street Homestay
619 N Linn St 52245
319-337-4363 Fax: 319-354-7057
Clarence & Dorothy Haverkamp
All year

45-50-BB
3 rooms
Rated, •
C-yes/S-no/P-no/H-no

Full breakfast
Sitting room, library, cable TV

Short walk to University of Iowa campus and downtown. Relax in our front porch swing.
havb-b@soli.inav.net http://www.bbhost.com/haverkampslinnstbb

LANSING

Suzanne's Inn
120 N 3rd 52151
319-538-3040 Fax: 319-538-3040
Suzanne Cansler
Closed January

65-85-BB
4 rooms, 2 pb
Rated
C-ltd/S-ltd/P-no/H-no

Full breakfast
Afternoon tea
Sitting room, suites, fireplaces, sauna in the root cellar

Antique-filled gothic revival perched on the bluffs of the Mississippi River.
suzanneinn@aol.com http://www.suzanneinn.com

MAQUOKETA

Squiers Manor
122 McKinsey Dr
418 W Pleasant St 52060
563-652-6961 Fax: 563-652-5995
Virl & Kathy Banowetz

80-195-BB
8 rooms, 8 pb
Visa, MC, AmEx, *Rated*
C-yes/S-no/P-no/H-no
All year

Full gourmet breakfast
Sitting room, library, bridal suite available, fireplaces, whirlpool

Experience Victorian elegance, ambiance & hospitality at its finest. Private whirlpool baths, fireplaces, antiques.
innkeeper@squiersmanor.com http://www.squiersmanor.com

MARENGO

Loy's Farm
2077 KK Ave 52301
319-642-7787
Loy & Robert Walker
All year

80-BB
3 rooms, 1 pb
Rated, •
C-yes/S-ltd/P-ltd/H-ltd

Full gourmet breakfast
Dinner available, snacks
Sitting room, library, fireplaces, TV, accom. bus. travel

Contemporary 1976 farm home on a working 1500 acre farm. Hostess serves a gourmet farm breakfast, lively conversation, farm tour, pheasant hunting.
LBW20771@zeus.ia.net

MCGREGOR

McGregor Manor
320 4th St 52157
563-873-2600 Fax: 563-873-2218
Carolyn & David Scott
All year

70-80-BB
4 rooms, 4 pb
Visa, MC, *Rated*, •
C-ltd/S-no/P-no/H-no

Full breakfast
Snacks, dinner (fee)
Sitting room, bicycles, fireplaces, whirlpool

Come share the warmth and hospitality of our home, one that will transport you back to an era of Victorian elegance and charm.
mmanor@mhtc.net http://www.mcgregorinn.com

MONTEZUMA

English Valley
4459 135th St 50171
641-623-3663 888-462-1060
Sue & Jim Eichhorn
April–December

70-200-BB
5 rooms, 3 pb
Visa, MC, Disc, *Rated*, •
C-yes/S-no/P-ltd/H-ltd

Full breakfast
Lunch & dinner avail., snacks
Sitting room, library, Jacuzzis, suites, fireplaces, cable TV

Nestled in the English River Valley of central Iowa, the English Valley B&B is just south of I-80. It's a real farm, with chickens, turkeys, sheep, calves, horses, hogs, dogs, kittens & quail. jeichorn@netins.net http://www.ia-bednbreakfast-inns.com/englishvalley.htm

NEWTON

La Corsette Maison Inn
629 First Ave E 50208
641-792-6833
Kay Owen
All year

85-200-BB
7 rooms, 7 pb
Visa, MC, AmEx, *Rated*, •
C-ltd/S-no/P-ltd/H-no

Full breakfast
Gourmet dinner, restaurant
Whirlpools, fireplaces, sitting room, near I-35, near Des Moines on I-80

Turn-of-the-century mission-style mansion. Charming French bedchambers, beckoning hearths. Gourmet Dining 4 1/2 star rating. http://www.lacorsette.com

La Corsette Maison Inn, Newton, IA

ST. ANSGAR

Blue Belle Inn
PO Box 205
513 West 4th St 50472
641-713-3113 877-713-3113
Sherrie Hansen
All year

70-160-AP
6 rooms, 5 pb
Most CC, *Rated*
C-yes/S-no/P-no/H-no
German

Full breakfast
Dinner, popcorn, hot chocolate, coffee, soda
TV/VCRs, movies, kitchenette, library, piano, conference rooms

Creatively restored Victorian with gourmet dining by candlelight, stained glass windows, maple woodwork, lofty tin ceilings, queen/king beds, A/C, fireplaces & private Jacuzzis for two. innkeeper@bluebelleinn.com http://www.BlueBelleInn.com

Kansas

ATCHISON

Saint Martin's
324 Santa Fe St 66002
913-367-4964
Fax: 913-367-7014
877-367-4964
John & Janet Settich
All year

75-95-BB
5 rooms, 5 pb
Visa, MC, Disc, *Rated*, •
C-ltd/S-no/P-no/H-no

Full breakfast
Snacks
Sitting room, Jacuzzis, fireplaces, cable TV, accom. bus. travelers

Hospitality is an art form in this comfortably historic, elegant home. Details will delight you. Made for scratch baked goods, secluded outdoor whirlpool and engaging, savvy hosts. stmartinsbandb@aol.com http://www.stmartinsbandb.com

COUNCIL GROVE

The Cottage House
25 N Neosho 66846
620-767-6828 Fax: 620-767-6414
800-727-7903
Connie Essington
All year

75-165-BB
26 rooms, 26 pb
Most CC, *Rated*, •
C-yes/S-yes/P-ltd/H-yes

Continental plus breakfast
Restaurant nearby
Sitting room, sauna room, 6 rooms w/whirlpool tubs, next to Neosho Riverwalk

Beautifully renovated Victorian hotel with modern comforts & lovely antique furnishings-in historic "Birthplace of the Santa Fe Trail."
cotthouse@cgtelco.net http://www.cottagehousehotel.com

The Castle Inn Riverside, Wichita, KS

HOLTON

The Parsonage Guesthouse	79-129-BB	Full breakfast
425 W Fourth St 66436	5 rooms, 5 pb	Homemade cookies, tea,
785-364-2240	Visa, MC, Disc, *Rated*,	lemonade, wine
Joni A. White	•	Library with fireplace, parlor
All year	C-yes/S-no/P-no/H-no	with piano, wraparound
		front porch, gazebo

1870's restored parsonage; antique-furnished. Visit on-site gift shop, sit on the wraparound front porch or stroll the garden; near historic town square; central to 3 area casinos.

jwhite@holtonks.net http://www.holtonks.net/parsonage

LAKIN

Windy Heights	50-60-BB	Full breakfast
PO Box 347	3 rooms, 3 pb	
697 Country Heights 67860	Visa, MC	
316-355-7699	C-yes/S-no/P-yes/H-no	
Chuck & DiAnne Jaeger		
All year		

Relaxing, quiet, country atmosphere; enjoy a challenging 9-hole golf course located across the backyard; the best pheasant and deer hunting in the state.

djaeger@pld.com http://innsite.com/inns/A003120.html

WICHITA

The Castle Inn Riverside	125-275-BB	Full breakfast
1155 N River Blvd 67203	14 rooms, 14 pb	Light hors d'oeuvres, wine,
316-263-9300	Most CC, *Rated*, •	home made desserts
Fax: 316-263-4998	C-ltd/S-no/P-no/H-yes	6 guestrooms with in-room
800-580-1131		Jacuzzi tubs
Paula & Terry Lowry		
All year		

114 years-old, this luxurious home has 14 guestrooms, each individually appointed. Guests enjoy a selection of wine, cheese, gourmet coffees, teas, liqueurs, homemade desserts & full breakfast.

info@castleinnriverside.com http://www.castleinnriverside.com

WICHITA

The Inn at Willowbend
3939 Comatara 67226
316-636-4032 Fax: 316-634-2190
800-553-5775
George M. Sloyer II,CHA
All year

69-159-BB
44 rooms, 44 pb
Most CC, *Rated*, •
C-yes/S-yes/P-yes/H-yes
Spanish

Full breakfast
Willowbends Championship Driving Range and putting greens HSI & Business Ctr

Near the intersection of 37th & Rock Road, The Inn at Willowbend is a quiet business hotel overlooking a championship golf course. Competitive Rates with exclusive environment and service. icthotelier@yahoo.com http://www.theinnatwillowbend.net/

Little River House
6141 Fairfield Rd 67204
316-838-3127 Fax: 316-838-3127
Michael & Karen Coup
All year

109-149-BB
1 rooms, 1 pb
Visa, MC
C-yes/S-no/P-ltd/H-ltd

Full breakfast
Dinner, snacks, complimentary wine
Sitting room, library, bicycles, suites, cable TV

Charming guest cottage on quiet wooded acre, on Little Arkansas River.
coupmk@aol.com

Kentucky

BARDSTOWN

Arbor Rose
209 E Stephen Foster Ave
40004
502-349-0014 Fax: 502-349-7322
888-828-3330
Judy & Derrick Melzer
All year

99-139-BB
5 rooms, 5 pb
Most CC, *Rated*, •
C-yes/S-no/P-ltd/H-ltd

Full breakfast
Snacks
Gardens, Porch Swing, fireplaces, TV/VCR movies, garden terrace, Spa/hot tub

1820 home on National Historic Register. Thoroughly updated and renovated with central heat/air. 5 rooms, private baths, centrally located 1½ blocks from downtown dining and shopping. arborrose@bardstown.com http://www.arborrosebardstown.com

---

Beautiful Dreamer
440 E Stephen Foster Ave
40004
502-348-4004 800-811-8312
Lynell & Dan Ginter
All year

109-149-BB
4 rooms, 4 pb
Most CC, *Rated*
C-no/S-no/P-no/H-no

Full 5 course breakfast
Snacks
Sitting room, Jacuzzis, fireplaces, cable TV, conference facilities

Federal design home in historic district complemented with antiques and cherry furniture. Striking view of My Old Kentucky Home from double front porches.
bdreamerbb@yahoo.com http://www.geocities.com/bdreamerbb/

Jailer's Inn
111 W Stephen Foster Ave
40004
502-348-5551 Fax: 502-349-1837
800-948-5551
C. Paul McCoy
March–Dec.

70-125-BB
6 rooms, 6 pb
Visa, MC, *Rated*, •
C-yes/S-ltd/H-yes

Full breakfast
Complimentary wine & cheese
Sitting room, gazebo, landscaped courtyard, roses, 2 rooms w/Jacuzzis

Jailer's Inn is a place of wonderful, thought-provoking contrasts. Each of our guestrooms is beautifully decorated w/antiques & heirlooms, all located in the renovated front jail.
cpaul@jailersinn.com http://www.jailersinn.com

BARDSTOWN

The Mansion
1003 N Third St 40004
502-348-2586 Fax: 502-349-6098
877-909-2586
Charmaine & Dennis Downs
All year

100-130-BB
8 rooms, 8 pb
Most CC, *Rated*, •
S-ltd/P-no/H-no

Full breakfast
Sitting room, piano, mimosa trees, roses, 2 rm. w/Jacuzzi

Bardstown's most elegant B&B. Greek revival mansion with beautiful period antiques.
ddowns@bardstown.com http://www.bardstownmansion.com

BARDSTOWN (REGION)

1851 Historic Maple Hill Manor
2941 Perryville Rd, *Springfield* 40069
859-336-3075 Fax: 859-336-3075
800-886-7546
J. Todd Allen & R. Tyler Horton All year

85-125-BB
7 rooms, 7 pb
Visa, MC, Disc, *Rated*, •
C-yes/S-ltd/P-yes/H-yes

Full breakfast
Lunch, dinner, afternoon tea, snacks, comp. wine
Sitt. rm, library, Jacuzzi, suites, frplace, gardens, gift gallery & studio

Rediscover romance at this beautiful, historic 1851 Greek Revival Plantation Home. Stately. Built on tranquil farmland in the heart of Kentucky's Bluegrass Region.
stay@maplehillmanor.com http://www.maplehillmanor.com

BOWLING GREEN

Alpine Lodge
5310 Morgantown Rd 42101
270-843-4846 Fax: 270-843-4833
888-444-3791
Dr. & Mrs. David Livingston
All year

45-90-BB
5 rooms, 3 pb
Rated, •
C-yes/S-ltd/P-ltd/H-ltd

Full breakfast
Sitting room, bicycles, Jacuzzis, swimming pool, suites, fireplace, cable TV

Alpine Lodge is a large Swiss-Chalet style home, 6,000 sq. ft. on 12 acres of lawn & gardens of flowers. alplodge@aol.com http://www.travelguides.com/home/Alpine_Lodge/

BOWLING GREEN (REGION)

Victorian House
PO Box 104
110 N Main Street, *Smiths Grove* 42171
270-563-9403 800-843-5210
Dave & Sharon Dahle

95-110-BB
4 rooms, 4 pb
Visa, MC, AmEx, *Rated*
C-ltd/S-ltd/P-no/H-ltd
All year

Full breakfast
Lunch, dinner, afternoon tea
Day spa, sitting room, library, cable TV, accommodate bus. travelers

Historic 1875 brick mansion offers wrap-around porch, large guestrooms furnished with antiques; two acres with garden and fountain; ten antique shops within walking distance.
dandsdahle@msn.com http://www.bbonline.com/ky/victorian

BURLINGTON

Burlington's Willis Graves B&B
5825 Jefferson St 41005
859-689-5096 888-226-5096
Nancy and Bob Swartzel
All year

75-135-BB
3 rooms, 3 pb
Most CC, *Rated*, •
C-ltd/S-no/P-no/H-no

Full breakfast
Sitting room, suites, fireplaces, cable TV, accom. bus. travelers

Relax, and enjoy country charm, privacy, attention to detail, excellent food and friendly innkeepers in our 1830s preservation awarded B&B.
inn@burligrave.com http://www.burligrave.com

GEORGETOWN

Jordan Farm
4091 Newtown Pike 40324
502-863-1944 Fax: 502-868-9002
Harold & Rebecca Jordan
All year

85-100-BB
4 rooms, 4 pb
Rated
C-yes/S-no/P-no/H-yes

Continental Plus breakfast
Afternoon tea, snacks
Family friendly facility near shops, restaurants

Jordan Farm offers a unique opportunity to stay on a beautiful 100-acre working Bluegrass thoroughbred farm. hjordan@mis.net http://www.jordanfarmbandb.com

Shaker Village Pleasant Hill, Harrodsburg, KY

GEORGETOWN

Pineapple Inn
645 S Broadway 40324
502-868-5453 Fax: 502-868-5453
Muriel & Les
All year

75-100-BB
4 rooms, 4 pb
Visa, MC, *Rated*, •
C-ltd/S-ltd/P-no/H-no

Full breakfast
Snacks, complimentary wine
Sitting room, bar service, Heart of Bluegrass, horse country, spa available

Built in 1876—on historical register—gourmet breakfast in country French dining room.

HARRODSBURG

Shaker Village Pleasant Hill
3501 Lexington Rd 40330
859-734-5411 Fax: 859-734-7278
800-734-5611
James C. Thomas, CEO

74-89-EP
81 rooms, 81 pb
Visa, MC, *Rated*, •
C-yes/S-yes/P-no/H-ltd
All year

Full breakfast (fee)
Lunch, dinner
Afternoon tea in winter, meeting facilities, sitting room, hiking trails, ho

America's largest restored Shaker Village. National Historic Landmark. 33 restored buildings amid 2,800 acres of bluegrass farmland. Offering tours, riverboat excursions and special events. diana@shakervillageky.org http://www.shakervillageky.org/

LEXINGTON (REGION)

1823 Historic Rose Hill Inn
233 Rose Hill, *Versailles* 40383
859-873-5957 Fax: 859-873-1813
800-307-0460
Sharon Amberg All year

109-169-BB
6 rooms, 6 pb
Most CC, *Rated*, •
C-ltd/S-ltd/P-ltd/H-ltd

Full breakfast
Snacks
Sitting room, library, bikes, suites, fireplaces

Victorian home with estate-like yard in historic district. Easy walk for antiquing and dining. Lovingly restored with original stained glass windows, hardwood floors.
Innkeepers@rosehillinn.com http://www.rosehillinn.com

LOUISVILLE

1888 Historic Rocking Horse Manor
1022 S Third St 40203
502-583-0408 Fax: 502-283-6077
888-HORSEBB
Diana Jachimiak & Brad Vossberg All year

79-169-BB
5 rooms, 5 pb
Most CC, *Rated*, •
C-yes/S-ltd/P-yes/H-no
German

Full two course breakfast
Snacks and beverages
Whirlpools, suites, fax on site, exercise facility, guest refrigerators

Renovated mansion in historical "Old Louisville." Complete with all amenities for today's traveler. Close to many attractions, downtown and the airport.
rockinghorsebb@webtv.net http://www.rockinghorse-bb.com

1888 Historic Rocking Horse Manor, Louisville, KY

LOUISVILLE

Dupont Mansion 1317 S Fourth St 40208 502-638-0045 Sharon Portman All year	119-199-BB 5 rooms, 5 pb Visa, MC, AmEx C-ltd/S-ltd	Full gourmet breakfast Afternoon tea Library, gardens; fireplaces, Jacuzzi, TV, dataports in each room

Beautifully restored mansion in historic Old Louisville offers 15 ft ceilings, ornate working fireplaces, a banquet style dining room, antique furnishings, crystal chandeliers & formal gardens. info@dupontmansion.com http://www.dupontmansion.com

Fleur de Lis 1452 S Fourth St 40208 502-635-5764 Fax: 502-485-0451 Sharon Portman All year	119-159-BB 5 rooms, 5 pb Visa, MC, AmEx, *Rated*, • C-ltd/S-no/P-no/H-no	Full gourmet breakfast Tea, snacks, wine Sitting room, Jacuzzis, suites, fireplace, cable TV

Beautiful Victorian Mansion restored to period. Comfortable and modern conveniences.
Fleurdelis@kentucky-lodging.com http://www.kentucky-lodging.com

Inn at the Park 1332 S Fourth St 40208 502-637-6930 Fax: 502-637-2796 800-700-PARK John and Sandy Mullins All year	89-169-BB 7 rooms, 7 pb Visa, MC, AmEx, *Rated*, • S-ltd/P-no/H-no German	Full breakfast Afternoon tea, snacks Complimentary wine, sitting room, library, tennis court

Southern charm & hospitality await you at Inn at the Park.
innatpark@aol.com http://innatpark.com

LOUISVILLE

Inn at Woodhaven
401 S Hubbards Ln 40207
502-895-1011 Fax: 502-896-0449
888-895-1011
Marsha Burton
All year

85-225-BB
7 rooms, 7 pb
Visa, MC, AmEx,
Rated, •
C-ltd/S-no/P-ltd/H-ltd

Full breakfast
Snacks
Sitting room, library, Jacuzzis, suites, fireplaces, cable TV

Elegant and comfortable inn in beautiful suburb 8 minutes from downtown and close to attractions, fine dining, and shopping. Furnished in antiques.
info@innatwoodhaven.com http://www.innatwoodhaven.com

Pinecrest Cottage & Gardens
2806 Newburg Rd 40205
502-454-3800 Fax: 502-452-9791
Nancy & Alaln Morris
All year

95-165-BB
1 rooms, 1 pb
Visa, MC, AmEx, *Rated*
C-yes/S-ltd/P-no/H-yes

Continental plus breakfast
Snacks
Sitting room, fireplace, tennis court, cable TV, swimming pool

Traditionally decorated, well-appointed guest house affording complete privacy.
pinecrestbb@prodigy.net http://www.pinecrestcottageandgardens.com

---

Samuel Clubertson Mansion
1432 S 3rd St 40208
502-634-3100 Fax: 502-636-3096
Rudy Van Meter
All year

99-179-BB
Most CC, •
C-ltd/S-ltd/P-no/H-no
German

Full breakfast
Snacks
Sitting room, library, suites, fireplaces, cable TV, accom. bus. trav.

Louisville's most historic B&B, opulently furnished, southern gourmet breakfasts, close to downtown and Churchill Downs.
bandb@culbertsonmansion.com http://www.culbertsonmansion.com

LOUISVILLE (REGION)

1877 House
2408 Utica-Sellersburg Rd, *Jeffersonville, IN* 47130
812-285-1877 Fax: 812-280-1877
888-284-1877
Steve & Carol Stenbro
All year

89-149-BB
3 rooms, 3 pb
Most CC, *Rated*
C-yes/S-no/P-no/H-ltd

Full breakfast
Snacks
Sitting room, library, Jacuzzis, fireplaces, cable TV, hot tub

This historic farm house on 2 1/2 acres has a fantastic view of the Louisville skyline. Guests will enjoy a 40-ft front porch with ceiling fans and an outdoor hot tub/spa.
house1877@peoplepc.com http://www.bbonline.com/in/1877house

The Old Bridge Inn
131 W Chestnut St, *Jeffersonville, IN* 47130
812-284-3580 Fax: 812-284-3561
Linda Williams
All year

65-115-BB
3 rooms, 3 pb
Most CC, *Rated*, •
C-yes/S-no/P-ltd/H-no

Full breakfast
Afternoon tea, snacks, dinner (fee)
Sitting room, Jacuzzis, fireplace, accom. bus. travelers

This historic home is located in Jeffersonville's historic district, seconds to I-65 and Louisville, KY. innbridge@aol.com http://www.oldbridgeinn.com

---

Sulphur Trace Farm
PO Box 127
8793 Sulphur Rd, *Sulphur* 40070
502-743-5956 Fax: 502-743-5464
K. Penny Sanders & Francis C. Thiemann
March 1-October 31

70-BB
2 rooms, 2 pb
Rated
C-yes/S-ltd/P-ltd/H-yes

Full breakfast
Afternoon tea, snacks
Sitting room, patio

A lovely, spacious, contemporary B&B nestled in the trees, w/a feeling of the great outdoors. Breakfast is served in the great room with sheep and goats not far from the door.
sulphtrace@aol.com

MURRAY

Diuguid House
603 Main St 42071
270-753-5470 888-261-3028
Karen & George Chapman
All year

45-BB
3 rooms
Visa, MC, Disc, *Rated*, •
C-yes/S-no/P-no/H-no

Full breakfast
Afternoon tea, snacks
Formal parlor, porch, piano, TV, laundry, children welcome

Historic Queen Anne centrally located in beautiful university town; close to Kentucky Lake and many antique shops. Nice retirement area.
gachap@hotmail.com http://www.diuguid.homestead.com

NEWPORT (REGION)

Cincinnati's Weller Haus
319 Poplar St, *Bellevue* 41073
859-431-6829 Fax: 859-431-4332
800-431-4287
Valerie & David Brown

89-175-BB
5 rooms, 5 pb
Most CC, *Rated*, •
C-ltd/S-no/P-no/H-ltd
All year

Full breakfast
Snacks and beverages
Gathering kitchen, patio and gardens, Jacuzzi suites

Choose from five spacious, uniquely decorated guestrooms to ensure your comfort; all with private bath, TV and telephone. Need a romantic getaway? Our Jacuzzi suites are just what you're looking for. innkeepers@wellerhaus.com http://www.wellerhaus.com

PADUCAH

Trinity Hills Farm Inn
10455 Old Lovelaceville Rd
42001
270-488-3999 800-488-3998
Ann Driver
All year

90-175-BB
6 rooms, 6 pb
Visa, MC, Disc, •
C-ltd/S-no/P-ltd/H-yes

Full breakfast
Complimentary beverages & refreshments
Private bath, romantic whirlpool, fireplace, queen bed, TV/VCR/CD/radio, etc

Visit a peaceful haven designed for your perfect retreat to the country. Enjoy the best of everything: nature, atmosphere, amenities & hospitality.
info@trinityhills.com http://www.trinityhills.com

RENFRO VALLEY

Brush Arbor
PO Box 57
Hummel Rd 40473
606-256-2450
All year

90-125-BB
3 rooms, 1 pb
Visa, MC, AmEx
C-no/S-no/P-no/H-no

Full breakfast

Brush Arbor Bed & Breakfast is a Swiss Chalet private home, which sits at the top of a hill overlooking peaceful Renfro Valley. The house is surrounded by beautiful trees and breathtaking views. janine@brusharborbb.com http://www.brusharborbb.com

RUSSELLVILLE

Washington House
283 W 9th St 42276
270-726-1240 Fax: 270-726-1240
866-850-9282
Regina C. Phillips
All year

75-125-BB
2 rooms, 2 pb
C-ltd/S-ltd/P-no/H-no

Weekdays=continental; Weekends=full
Well-stocked guest kitchen, snacks & sodas
Sitting room, screened porch w/ swing, parlor, fireplace, formal dining room

Washington House B&B, c. 1824, is in a large historic district, has queen size beds and big comfortable chairs in each bedroom. It is furnished with period antiques, many of which are for sale. chucklp@bellsouth.net
http://www.visitlogancounty.com/where_can_we_stay/washington_house_bed_and_breakfa.htm

SOUTH UNION

Shaker Tavern
PO Box 30
Highway 73 42283
270-542-6801 Fax: 270-542-7558
800-929-8701
Jo Ann Moody All year

65-120-BB
6 rooms, 4 pb
Visa, MC, *Rated*

Full breakfast

Beautiful historic bed & breakfast located just west of Bowling Green, Kentucky, fifteen miles from I-65. shakmus@logantele.com http://www.shakermuseum.com

Louisiana

BATON ROUGE

A Sunrise on the River
1825 False River Dr 70760
225-638-3642 Fax: 225-638-3642
800-644-3642
Darlene Fuehring and Dr. Charlotte Stinson
All year

125-240-BB
3 rooms, 3 pb
Visa, MC, AmEx, *Rated*, •
C-ltd/S-no/P-no/H-yes

Full breakfast
Snacks
Suites, cable TV, accommodate business travelers

Come enjoy a warm, elegant home on the bank of the beautiful False River. Relax on the shady porches, listen to the flicker of bird wings, the flutter of butterflies, a beautiful sunrise. . . .

info@newroadslakeside.com http://www.newroadslakeside.com

BATON ROUGE (REGION)

Tree House in the Park
16520 Airport Dr, *New Roads* 70769
225-622-3885 Fax: 225-622-2850
800-532-2246
Vic & Vikki Hotopp
All year

110-175-BB
4 rooms, 3 pb
Visa, MC, *Rated*, •
S-no/P-no/H-no

Full breakfast
Dinner included 1st night
Gazebo, pool table, ping, pong, kayak & pirogues, heated swimming pool

Cajun cabin in the swamp. Rooms have private entrance, queen waterbed, TV/VCR, hot tub on deck under stars. Comp. first supper. Cypress trees, moss, ponds. Satellite TV

lecabin@netzero.net http://www.treehouseinthepark.com

BOURG

Julia's Cajun Country
4021 Benton Dr. 70343
985-851-3540 Fax: 985-851-2508
Julia & Enis J. White
All year

60-BB
4 rooms, 2 pb
C-yes/S-ltd/P-no/H-yes
French

Full breakfast
Aft. tea, comp. wine. Dinner $10.00 per person fee
Sitting room

Cajun hospitality & Cajun Cuisine at its finest. Located near swamp tours, plantations, museums, fishing, horseback riding.

Juliawcajunctry@aol.com

CARENCRO

Bechet House
313 N Church St 70520
337-896-3213 Fax: 337-886-1155
866-896-3211
Jan Barber & Harris Rowzie
All year

85-125-BB
6 rooms, 6 pb
Most CC, •
C-yes/S-ltd/P-ltd/H-ltd

Full breakfast
Lunch, dinner, snacks, and comp. wine upon request
Sitting room, 2 bed/2 bath cottage for families, acc. business travelers

Innkeepers Jan Barber & Harris Rowzie are pleased to share w/you a soft touch in an otherwise hi-tech world. More than just a place to sleep, our charming home offers nourishment the body and soul.

bechethouse@eatel.net http://www.bechethouse.com

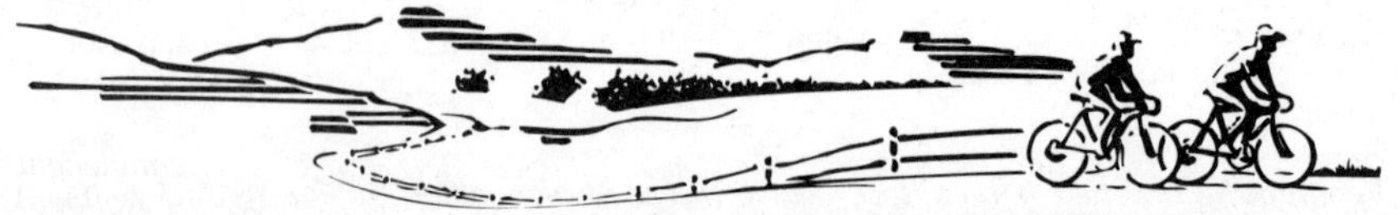

FRANKLIN

Hanson House
114 E Main St 70538
337-828-3271 Fax: 337-828-0497
877-928-3271
Bette & Caunse Kemper
All year

125-BB
4 rooms, 3 pb
Most CC, *Rated*, •
C-ltd/S-ltd/P-ltd/H-no
Limited French &
German

Full breakfast
Snacks, wine
Sitting room, library, the house has been in, the family since 1860

In the heart of Franklin's historic district, this 10,000 sq. foot antebellum cottage sits on 4 1/2 acres on the banks of Bayou Teche some 50 miles from the Evangeline Oak.
caunse@aol.com http://www.hansonhouse.bigdogz.com

HAMMOND

Michabelle Inn & Rest.
1106 S Holly St 70403
985-419-0550 Fax: 985-542-1746
Chef Michel & Isabel Marcais
All year

85-125-BB
6 rooms, 6 pb
Most CC, *Rated*
C-ltd/S-ltd/P-no/H-ltd
French, Portuguese

Full breakfast
Full service bar & restaurant
Library, reception hall

A Greek Revival Estate decorated in authentic French antiques, located in serene surroundings, draped by oaks, azaleas and camellias. Full service restaurant & bar, banquet facilities available. michabelle@i-55.com http://www.michabelle.com

HOUMA

Grand Bayou Noir
PO Box 308
1143 Bayou Black Dr 70361
985-873-5849
Tim & Debbie Ellender

90-130-BB
3 rooms, 3 pb
Most CC, •
C-yes/P-no/H-yes
All year

Full breakfast
Dinner available
Balconies, patio,bbq pits,screen porch,bikes,cajun cooking instructions

Grand old home on serene Big Black Bayou, surrounded by four acres of beautiful old oak trees. The perfect place for a romantic escape or peaceful getaway.
tce@cajun.net http://www.grandbayounoir.com

LAKE CHARLES

Walter's Attic & C.A.'s House
618 Ford St
618 & 624 Ford St 70601
337-439-6672 866-439-6672
Tanis Robinson

115-140-BB
5 rooms, 3 pb
Most CC, *Rated*
C-ltd/S-ltd/P-ltd/H-no
All year

Full breakfast
Snacks, coffee, refreshments
Bikes, hot tub, kayaks

Walter's Attic & C.A.'s House offers superb luxury accommodations. There are a range of rooms, from single rooms to luxury suites. Located in the heart of Lake Charles' Charpentier Historic District. waltersatt@aol.com http://www.waltersattic.com

MONROE (REGION)

Rose Lee
318 Trenton St, *West Monroe* 71291
318-366-2412 Fax: 318-323-9958
Ken & Kathryn Huff

75-95-BB
5 rooms, 5 pb
Visa, MC, AmEx, •
C-ltd/S-no/P-no/H-no
All year

Southern breakfast
Sitting room, cable TV, kitchen & laundry facility, accomm. business travel

You might enjoy breakfast in bed or on the quaint balcony overlooking Antique Alley, a shoppers paradise. A wonderful place to unwind and enjoy peaceful surroundings.
roseleebnb@aol.com

NAPOLEONVILLE

Madewood Plantation House
4250 Hwy 308 70390
985-369-7151 Fax: 985-369-9848
800-375-7151
Keith & Millie Marshall
All year

209-259-MAP
8 rooms, 8 pb
Most CC, *Rated*, •
C-yes/S-ltd/P-ltd/H-no
French

Full breakfast
Wine & cheese reception, honor bar
Candlelit dinners, canopied beds, private baths, parlor, library, porches

Greek Revival mansion featuring canopied beds, antiques, wine and cheese, candlelight dinner, full breakfast. A house party in the cane field. Rated in top 54 inns by National Geographic Traveler. madewoodpl@aol.com http://www.madewood.com

NATCHITOCHES

Casa Rio
1326 Williams Ave 71457
318-356-5698
Patricia & Terence Elliott
All year

85-95-BB
2 rooms, 2 pb
Visa, MC
C-ltd/S-ltd/P-no/H-ltd
Spanish

Full breakfast
Complimentary wine
River deck and pier for fishing

Enjoy the tranquil Cane River from our deck. Casually elegant home on two park-like acres close to historic Front Street. Queen or twin iron canopied beds, private entrances and gourmet breakfast. patti@casariobandb.com http://www.casariobandb.com

---

Chateau D'Terre
109 Jamar Dr 71457
318-354-7929 Fax: 318-356-8745
888-798-6566
Terrie & Lee McCallister
All year

95-135-BB
2 rooms, 2 pb
Visa, MC, AmEx
C-ltd/S-no/P-no/H-no

Full breakfast
Snacks, complimentary wine
Sitting room, Jacuzzi, cable TV

French country style inn on Sibley Lake. 5 minutes from historic Natchitoches. 2 rooms with private bath, 1 with Jacuzzi.
terrieandlee@chateaudterre.com http://www.chateaudterre.com

Judge Porter House
314 Rue Poete
321 Second St. 71457
318-352-9206 1-800-441-8343
John Puckett
All year

95-150-BB
5 rooms, 5 pb
Visa, MC, AmEx
C-ltd/S-no/P-no/H-no
English

Full multi-course breakfast
Wine, coffee, tea, soft drinks, chocolates
Swimming pool, hair dryers, irons, TV/VCR, monogrammed robes, videos

Elegant rooms, exquisite antiques, Queen sized full tester beds, private spacious baths, landscaped gardens, swimming pool, full multi-course breakfast, located in Historic District. judgeporter@judgeporterhouse.com http://www.judgeporterhouse.com

---

Levy-East House
358 Jefferson St 71457
318-352-0662 800-840-0662
Judy & Avery East
All year

105-200-BB
4 rooms, 4 pb
Visa, MC, AmEx,
Rated, •
C-no/S-no/P-no/H-no

Full gourmet breakfast
Champagne, cream sherry, coffee/tea, chocolates
Sitting room, off-street parking, front & back galleries, ceiling fans

In this quaint historic town, The Levy-East House invites you to step back in time. Located in the Natchitoches Historic Landmark District and listed on the National Register of Historic Places. judy@levyeasthouse.com http://www.levyeasthouse.com

---

Maison Louisiane
332 Jefferson St 71457
318-352-1900 800-264-8991
Keri & Ben Fidelak
All year

75-150-BB
5 rooms, 5 pb
Most CC
C-ltd/S-ltd/P-no/H-no

Full Gourmet Breakfast
Bar service
Sitting room, Jacuzzis, suites, cable TV, accommodate business travelers

Recently restored back to its original luster, "Maison Louisiane" has been described as one of the "best examples of the Queen Anne styles in Natchitoches."
kfidelak@aol.com http://www.maisonlouisiane.com

Queen Anne
125 Pine St 71457
888-685-1585 Fax: 318-352-9500
888-685-1585
All year

85-150-BB
5 rooms, 5 pb
Most CC, •
C-ltd/S-ltd/P-no/H-no

Full breakfast
Wine, tea, snacks, bottled water and soft drinks
Whirlpool & clawfoot tubs, refrigerator, in room TV/w VCR and phones.

1905 two-story Victorian with a double wraparound porch. Five spacious bedrooms with queen and king beds, beautifully decorated, w/private bath. A full breakfast is served.
queenanne@cp-tel.net http://www.queenannebandb.com

NEW IBERIA

Cook's Cottage 5505 Rip Van Winkle Rd 70560 318-365-3332 Fax: 318-365-3354 800-375-3332 Carolyn Doerle & Dr. Ron Ray All year	198 3 rooms Visa, MC, AmEx, • C-yes/S-ltd/P-no/H-yes Some French	Continental plus breakfast Afternoon tea, snacks Restaurant, bar service, lunch/dinner available, sitting room, Jacuzzis

Acasian cottage furnished in antiques. Complimentary continental breakfast, gourmet coffees and liqueurs. Handmade 4 poster king size mahogany bed, deluxe linens, CDs, Jacuzzi tub, aromatherapy soaps/lotions.

A New Iberian 416 Iberia St 70560 337-367-5888 Michael David LeBoeuf All year	75-140-BB 5 rooms, 3 pb Most CC, *Rated*, • C-yes/S-ltd/P-ltd/H-ltd	Full breakfast Snacks, lunch Sitting room, suites, fireplaces, cable TV, accomm. bus. travelers

Enchanted Cajun Victorian built in 1898 entirely out of local cypress. Suites and charming 2-bedroom carriage house. Lush gardens with fragrant colorful flora, birds, fish, butterflies and squirrels. anewiberian@aol.com http://www.anewiberian.com

NEW ORLEANS

1822 Bougainvillea House 841 Bourbon St 70116 504-525-3983 Fax: 504-525-5000 Flo Cairo & Pat Kahn All year	125-250-BB 2 rooms, 2 pb AmEx, • C-ltd/P-no/H-no	Continental breakfast All rooms have A/C, TV, and phones, courtyard, patio, off-street parking

In the heart of the French Quarter, antique ambience with all of the modern conveniences. Off-street parking for cars. Private phone, cable TV, central A/C.
patkahn@aol.com http://www.1822bougainvillea.com

1830 Dauphine House 1830 Dauphine St 70116 504-940-0943 Karen Jeffries All year	65-125-BB 3 rooms, 3 pb *Rated*, • S-no	Continental breakfast Host lives on property, daily maid service

Built in 1860 and located one and a half blocks from the enchanting French Quarter near Bourbon and Esplanade, Dauphine House offers cozy rooms with hardwood floors and 12 foot ceilings. info@dauphinehouse.com http://www.dauphinehouse.com

---

1870 Banana Courtyard French Qt. PO Box 70556 French Quarter Station 70130 504-947-4475 Fax: 504-949-5689 800-842-4748 Mary Ramsey High season Sept-May	55-165-BB 8 rooms, 6 pb Most CC, *Rated*, • C-ltd/S-ltd/P-ltd/H-ltd	Generous Cont. breakfast B&B only Soft drinks, wine, beer, coffee, tea, cordials Library/sitting rm, phone, TV, fax, H+A/C, clock, hammock, courtyard veranda

1st French Quarter visit? Safe location, BOURBON ST. 3 blocks, LAID BACK, courtyard, antiques, ROMANTIC Victorian. Off season $55+/n 7 days. Web site info: sightsee, music, food, Voodoo, plantations. bananacour@aol.com http://bananacourtyard.com

---

1890 St Charles Guest House 1748 Prytania St 70130 504-523-6556 Fax: 504-522-6340 Dennis Hilton All year	55-95-BB 26 rooms, 26 pb Visa, MC, AmEx, *Rated* C-ltd/S-ltd/P-no Spanish	Continental breakfast Bakery Swimming pool, library, ample reading material (books/magazines)

Historic Garden District near French quarter, sweet, unpretentious, inexpensive, like Grandma's! Family owned business for 50 years.
dhilton111@aol.com http://www.stcharlesguesthouse.com

1870 Banana Courtyard, French Quarter, New Orleans, LA

NEW ORLEANS

1891 Castle Inn of New Orleans 1539 Fourth St 70130 504-897-0540 Fax: 504-895-2231 888-826-0540 Miss Karen All Year	79-350-EP 9 rooms, 8 pb Most CC, *Rated*, • C-ltd/S-no/P-ltd/H-no French	Sitting room, suites, fireplaces, cable TV

The Castle Inn is a nine suite mansion tucked in right off of St. Charles Avenue, in the quiet and exclusive Garden District.

info@castleinnofneworleans.com http://www.castleinnofneworleans.com

1930 Canal Street Guesthouse 3700 Magellan 1930 Canal Street 70112 504-525-1928 Sam & Kathey Kranzthor All year	27-35-EP 10 rooms, 2 pb Visa, MC C-yes/S-ltd/P-ltd/H-no Spanish	Community Kitchen, personal refrig. Vending machine with snacks Weekly rates, Great location, Clean rooms, Refrigerators, Balconies, Kitchen

Turn-of-the-century rooming house restored to provide simple, clean, inexpensive, comfortable lodgings. One week minimum. Favored by professors, newcomers, researchers, international travelers.

canalstgst@aol.com http://www.BestGuesthouse.com

A Creole House 1013 St Ann 70016 504-524-8076 Fax: 504-581-3277 800-535-7858 Lakenya Johnson All year	49-150-BB 27 rooms, 25 pb Most CC, *Rated*, • C-yes/S-yes/P-no/H-no	Continental breakfast canopied beds

27 rooms in a quiet residential neighborhood of the French Quarter, yet only two blocks from exciting Bourbon Street and four blocks from historic Jackson Square.

info@acreolehouse.com http://www.acreolehouse.com

NEW ORLEANS

A Crescent City Guest House
612 Marigny St 70117
504-944-8722 Fax: 504-945-0904
877-203-2140
Matthew
September–May

70-100-BB
4 rooms, 4 pb
Most CC, •
C-no/S-yes/P-yes/H-no

Continental plus breakfast

Enjoy all of the excitement and charm that New Orleans has to offer. We are in the historic Faubourg Marigny, just three blocks from the French Quarter and the Riverfront Street Car Lines. matlynccgh@msn.com http://www.crescentcitygh.com

---

A Henry Howard Inn
2041 Prytania St 70130
504-586 0858 Fax: 504-566-1518
Peter Schrieber
All year

29-69-BB
24 rooms, 15 pb
Most CC, *Rated*, •
C-yes/S-yes/P-ltd/H-no
German

Full breakfast
Sitting room, suites, balconies

In 2 historic Antebellum mansions in the majestic Garden District, Henry Howard Inn provides guests with Old World charm at unbeatable prices. Five minutes from the Quarter on the street car line.
PeterSchreiber@compuserve.com http://www.henryhowardinn.com

A Olivier Estate B&B
1425 N Prieur Street 70116
504-949-9600 Fax: 504-948-2219
800-429-3240
Lance Gaulon
All year

100-450-BB
7 rooms, 7 pb
Most CC, *Rated*, •
C-yes/S-ltd/P-ltd/H-yes

Full breakfast
Tea, snacks, bar
Sitting room, jacuzzi, swimming pool, suites, fireplace, cable TV

New Orleans finest service will pamper your every need. The "Olivier Estate Mansion" host everything you will need, plus a whole lot more.
oebb@bellsouth.net http://www.olivierestate.com

A Quarter Esplanade
719 Esplanade Ave 70116
504-948-9328
Fax: 504-940-6190
800-546-0076
Steve & Andrea Kudelich
All year

75-200-BB
5 rooms, 5 pb
Most CC, *Rated*, •
C-yes/S-ltd/P-ltd/H-ltd
German

Continental breakfast
Bicycles, Jacuzzi, suites, fireplace, cable TV, conferences, heated pool

We offer spacious, well appointed accommodations in a charming old mansion with an excellent French Quarter location.
info@quarteresplanade.com http://www.quarteresplanade.com

Aaron's Ingram Haus
1012 Elysian Fields 70117
504-949-3110
Scott Graves
All year

EP
C-ltd/S-yes/P-no/H-no

Coffee
Courtyards

Located six blocks from world-famous Bourbon Street and within easy walking distance to most New Orleans attractions. ingramhaus@yahoo.com http://www.ingramhaus.com

---

An Elephant Walk
230 Bermuda St 70114
504-368-5559 Fax: 503-907-9444
888-895-6361
Sharon Giles
All year

125-150-BB
2 rooms, 2 pb
Visa, MC, AmEx, •
C-ltd/S-ltd/P-ltd/H-no

Continental breakfast
Coffee, snacks, juices
Private entrance, cable TV, private telephone, separate kitchen/dining area

Luxury multi-room suites with kitchens, in historic and serene Algiers Point, a free five-minute ferry ride to the foot of Canal Street, then a few minutes walk to the heart of the French Quarter. sgiles@cox.net http://www.elephantwalknola.com

NEW ORLEANS

Annabelle's House
1716 Milan St 70115
504-899-0701
Fax: 504-899-0095
Grey Rayburn
All year

90-185-BB
5 rooms, 5 pb
Visa, MC, •
C-yes/S-no/P-yes/H-no

Continental plus breakfast
Complimentary wine
Sitting room, family friendly facility, canopied beds

Experience peaceful antique atmosphere with the luxury of every modern amenity. Elegant 1840s Greek Revival mansion in uptown. One block to street car. Open since 1984.

Avenue Inn
4125 St. Charles Avenue 70115
504-269-2640 Fax: 504-269-2641
800-490-8542
Joe & Bebe Rabhan
All year

99-299-BB
17 rooms, 17 pb
Most CC, *Rated*, •
C-ltd/S-no/P-no/H-ltd
Spanish

Continental plus breakfast
Afternoon tea, wine & cheese upon request
Grand parlor & master dining, private baths, voice mail, data port

1891 Mansion on famed St. Charles, minutes to the French Quarter via the streetcar. Enjoy the "Avenue" on our veranda, rest in our restored guestrooms and drift back to the splendor of the past.
info@avenueinnbb.com http://www.avenueinnbb.com

Beau Sejour
1930 Napoleon Ave 70115
504-897-3746 Fax: 504-891-3340
888-897-9398
Kim & Gilles Gagnon
All year

110-175
6 rooms, 6 pb
Rated

Welcome . . .Relax among the live oaks and Spanish moss on Beau Sjour's cool, columned front porch and you'll understand where New Orleans got the name 'the Big Easy.'
bosejour@aol.com http://www.beausejourbandb.com/

Bonne Chance
621 Opelousas Ave 70114
504-367-0798
Fax: 504-368-4643
Dolores Watson
All year

100-150-BB
5 rooms, 5 pb
Visa, MC, *Rated*, •
C-ltd/S-ltd/P-no/H-no
French

Continental plus breakfast
Sitting room, library, Jacuzzis, suites, cable TV, accom. bus. travelers

Twice award winner, beautiful Victorian, four balconies, historic, quiet neighborhood, minutes from French Quarter, gorgeous courtyard, antiques, and luxury.
watsondolores@aol.com http://www.bonne-chance.com

Bracket House
1020 Kerlerec St 70116
504-940-6330
Hugh Wilson
All year

95-150-BB
2 rooms, 2 pb
Visa, MC, AmEx
C-no/S-no/P-no/H-no

Continental plus breakfast

One block to the French Quarter. Secure, off-street parking available. Spacious rooms, high ceilings, distinct character. Typical French Quarter courtyard.
innkeeper@brackethouse.com http://www.brackethouse.com

Bywater
1026 Clouet St 70117
504-944-8438
Fax: 504-947-2795
Betty-Carol & Marti
All year

65-125-BB
4 rooms, 1 pb
Visa, MC
C-ltd/S-no/P-ltd/H-no

Continental plus breakfast
Sitting room, library, cable TV, covered porches, patio

Completely renovated "double shotgun" house in National Historic District, full of contemporary Louisiana folk art, antiques, books, and music. Lovely brick patio with fishpond and porch swing. bywaterbnb@juno.com http://www.bywaterbnb.com

NEW ORLEANS

Chateau Louisiane
1216 Louisiana Ave 70115
504-723-3926
Fax: 504-269-2603
800-734-0137
Penny Toohey
All year

79-159-BB
5 rooms, 5 pb
Most CC, *Rated*, •
C-yes/S-no/P-ltd/H-no

Continental breakfast
Complimentary wine
Bar service, sitting room, bicycles, suites, cable TV

Historic B&B, circa 1885, featuring antique furnishings, high ceilings and hardwood floors. Located in historic Garden District. Via the St. Charles Avenue Streetcar, the city is at your fingertips. chateau@accesscom.net http://www.chateaulouisiane.com

---

Chimes B&B & Reserv. Agency
PO Box 52257
1146 Constantinople St 70152
504-488-4640 Fax: 504-488-4639
800-729-4640
Jill Abbyad & Hazell Boyce
All year

89-150-BB
5 rooms, 5 pb
Most CC, *Rated*, •
C-yes/S-ltd/P-ltd/H-no
French, Arabic

Continental Plus
Suites, cable TV, accommodate business travelers, data ports, private phones

Fodor's Guidebook "Choice" (one of top 5 places in New Orleans). A special place ... cherished by many returning guests for comfort, charm and location.
chimes@historiclodging.com http://www.HistoricLodging.com/chimes.html

---

Cindee's Southern Comfort
1739 Marengo St 70115
504-895-3680
Fax: 504-895-3682
888-769-3868
Cindee Quick
All year

125-200-BB
2 rooms, 2 pb
Most CC, *Rated*, •
C-ltd/S-ltd/P-no/H-no

Continental breakfast
Comp. sodas, bottled water, iced tea
Conference room, private phones w/data ports, cable TV, sitting room.

1890's raised center hall cottage with Greek Revival influence, located 2 blocks from streetcar line. Furnished with period pieces and 21st century amenities.
scomfortbb@aol.com http://www.southerncomfort-bnb.com

The Cornstalk Hotel
915 Royal St 70116
504-523-1515 Fax: 504-522-5558
Debi & David Spencer
All year

145-185-BB
14 rooms, 14 pb
Visa, MC, AmEx, *Rated*
C-yes/S-yes/P-no/H-no
French, German

Continental plus breakfast
Complimentary tea, wine, paper
Stained-glass windows, oriental rugs, fireplaces

Small, elegant hotel in heart of French Quarter. All antique furnishings. Recent renovation. dbspencer@mindspring.com http://www.travelguides.com/bb/cornstalk/

La Dauphine
2316 Dauphine St 70117
504-948-2217 Fax: 504-948-3420
Ray Ruiz & Kim Pedersen
All year

85-250-BB
4 rooms, 4 pb
Visa, MC, Disc, *Rated*
S-no/P-no/H-no
French

Continental breakfast
Sitting room, library, bathrobes

Located in the bohemian, artsy, and gay Faubourg Marigny. A non-smoking, European style guest house for the budget-minded. ladauphine@aol.com http://www.ladauphine.com

---

The Dusty Mansion
2231 Gen Pershing 70115
504-895-4576
Fax: 504-891-0049
Cynthia Riggs
All year

60-120-BB
4 rooms, 2 pb
Most CC, *Rated*, •
C-yes/S-ltd/P-no/H-no
Spanish, French

Continental plus breakfast
Sunday champagne brunch
Complimentary wine, beverages, sitting room, hot tub, pool table, sun deck

Charming turn-of-the-century home, spacious, comfortable. Near St. Charles Street Car; easy access to French Quarter. Dusty_mansion@hotmail.com

The Cornstalk Hotel, New Orleans, LA

NEW ORLEANS

Elysian Fields Inn
930 Elysian Fields Ave 70117
504-948-9420 Fax: 504-948-0053
866-948-9420
Gregg Smith & Sal Sapienza
All year

95-225-BB
8 rooms, 8 pb
Most CC
C-yes/S-ltd/P-yes/H-yes

Continental plus breakfast
Snacks, complimentary wine
Sitting room, library, Jacuzzis, suites, cable TV, accom. bus. trav.

Historic 1850's Urban Inn. 8 tastefully decorated guestrooms each with cable flat-screen TV, DVD/VCR player, private bath, most with Jacuzzi tub.
innkeeper@elysianfieldsinn.com http://www.elysianfieldsinn.com

---

Fairchild House
1518 Prytania St 70130
504-524-0154 Fax: 504-568-0063
800-256-8096
Beatriz Aprigliano-Ziegler
All year

75-165-BB
18 rooms, 18 pb
Visa, MC, AmEx, *Rated*, •
C-yes/S-no/P-no/H-no
Spanish, Portuguese

Continental plus breakfast
Afternoon tea, wine
Sitting room, suites, accommodate business travelers

Classic, comfortable B&B in antique setting, located in the lower Garden District, one block from streetcar line, 15 blocks to French Quarter.
info@fairchildhouse.com http://www.fairchildhouse.com

French Quarter
1132 Ursulines St 70116
504-525-3390 Fax: 504-593-9859
800-823-6785 (PIN: GO)
Elmo F. Orgeron Jr.
All year

100-EP
2 rooms, 2 pb
Visa, MC, AmEx, •
C-yes/S-yes/P-ltd/H-no

Continental breakfast
Coffee & tea
Swimming pool, cable TV/VCR, accommodate business travelers

Built in 1822, this Creole cottage is located just one block from the French Quarter. This spacious inn has 2 bedrooms, sitting areas, private bath, full kitchen, and pool.
elmofq@bellsouth.net

NEW ORLEANS

Frenchmen Hotel 417 Frenchmen 70016 504-948-2166 Fax: 504-948-2258 800-831-1781 Thelma Dordain All year	49-205-BB 27 rooms, 27 pb Most CC, *Rated*, • C-yes/S-yes/P-no/H-yes	Continental breakfast Sitting room, hot tub & swimming pool, sun deck

Each of the rooms is decorated with period furniture, ceiling fan & high ceiling. Located just steps away from the French Quarter.
info@frenchmenhotel.com http://www.frenchmenhotel.com

The Girod House 835 Esplanade Ave 70116 504-944-2255 866-877-1024 Steve Kudelich Season Inquire	89-225-BB 6 rooms, 6 pb Visa, MC, AmEx, • C-ltd/S-no/P-no/H-no	Continental Suites, cable TV, accommodate business travelers, balcony-2 suites

Girod House is a charming bed and breakfast with lofty rooms, balconies, antique furnishings and a tropical patio filled with exotic flowers.
info@girodhouse.com http://www.girodhouse.com

House of the Rising Sun 335 Pelican Ave 70114 504-367-8461 Fax: 504-367-6544 888-842-2747 Kevin & Wendy Herridge All year	75-150-BB 2 rooms, 2 pb • C-ltd/S-no/P-no/H-no	Continental plus breakfast Afternoon tea Sitting room, library, cable TV, garden, pond, deck

Historic District home built in 1896. Walking distance to French Quarter, Central Business District, Convention Center. Situated in charming neighborhood of Algiers Point, established in 1719. cockney@bellsouth.net http://www.HouseOfTheRisingSunBnB.com

---

House on Bayou Road 2275 Bayou Rd 70119 504-945-0992 Fax: 504-945-0993 800-882-2968 Cynthia Reeves All year	135-320-BB 8 rooms, 8 pb Visa, MC, AmEx, *Rated*, • C-ltd/S-ltd/P-no/H-no Spanish	Full breakfast Dinner, snacks, restaurant Sitting room, Jacuzzi, pool, suites, fireplaces, cable TV, acc. bus. trav.

Situated on 2 acres of manicured land, The House on Bayou Road offers our guests a historic plantation experience, fine food, welcoming service, and amenities found in fine hotels. hobr@hobr.nocoxmail.com http://www.houseonbayouroad.com

---

Inn the Quarter Dunaine St 70116 888-523-5235 Robin Kaplan All year	59-250-EP 4 rooms, 4 pb Visa, MC, AmEx, • C-ltd/S-ltd/P-no/H-ltd	In-room coffee Cable TV, French Quarter, courtyard and balcony, free local calls

The perfect French Quarter location in historic 1840's townhouse. A rooftop view or real street site balcony and a cool plant-filled courtyard. Ideal for both business and leisure travelers.
ourvacationrentals@hotmail.com http://www.10kvacationrentals.com/innthequarter/

Jana's B&B 628 Baronne St 70113 504-524-6473 Fax: 504-524-6473 888-751-3273 Jana Napoli & Kevin McCaffrey All year	125-375-BB 4 rooms, 3 pb Visa, MC, AmEx, • C-yes/S-ltd/P-ltd/H-no Spanish, Italian, French	Continental breakfast Snacks Sitting room, library, Jacuzzis, suites, fireplace, cable TV, restaurant

Urban getaway in historic 1840's townhouse, which also houses two art galleries. Furnished with antiques and unique art. Numerous services available upon request.
busykev@yahoo.com http://www.628baronne.com

NEW ORLEANS

Lafitte Guest House
1003 Bourbon St 70116
504-581-2678 Fax: 504-581-2677
800-331-7971
Andrew Crocchiolo
& Edward Dore
All year

129-219-BB
14 rooms, 14 pb
Visa, MC, AmEx,
Rated, •
C-ltd/S-ltd/P-no/H-ltd

Continental plus breakfast
Wine & hors d'oeuvres
Sitt. rm., clock radios,
balconies, courtyard, queen
& king-size beds

This fine French manor building greets you with elegance & tradition. Fine antique pieces and reproductions.
lafitteguesthouse@travelbase.com http://www.lafitteguesthouse.com/v3.0/noframes.htm

---

Lamothe House
621 Esplanade Ave 70016
504-947-1161 Fax: 504-943-6536
800-367-5858
Cheryl Hedrick
All year

49-200-BB
29 rooms, 29 pb
Most CC, *Rated*, •
C-yes/S-yes/P-no/H-no

Continental breakfast
Afternoon sherry
Sitting room, courtyard,
Jacuzzi and pool, parking

An elegantly restored historic old mansion located on the eastern boundary of the French Quarter. info@lamothehouse.com http://www.lamothehouse.com

---

Macarty Park Guest House
3820 Burgundy St 70117
504-943-4994 Fax: 504-943-4999
800-521-2790
John Maher
All year

59-190-BB
8 rooms, 8 pb
Most CC, •
C-ltd/S-yes/P-no/H-no

Continental plus breakfast
Pool, suites, accommodate
business travelers

Go for a splash in our in-ground heated pool. Cottages and rooms beautifully furnished primarily in antiques. All have private baths, color cable TV and phone. Free parking.
macpar@aol.com http://www.macartypark.com

Maison DuBois
3115 Napoleon Avenue
1421 Dauphine St 70016
504-896-9977 800-886-3709
Eric Freeman & Maggie
Shimon
All year

89-179-BB
5 rooms, 5 pb
MC, •
C-no/S-ltd/P-no/H-no

Continental plus breakfast
Swimming Pool, Hot Tub,
Color TV, VCR, Private
Phone

Located in the oldest and most famous neighborhood in North America. Yesterday's charms blend with today's comforts. The sights, sounds and adventures are limitless in the French Quarter. nolabandb@earthlink.net http://www.Nolabandb.com

---

Maison Esplanade Guest House
1244 Esplanade Ave 70116
504-523-8080 Fax: 504-527-0040
866-418-8080
Lisa Ross
All year

59-189-BB
10 rooms, 10 pb
Most CC, *Rated*, •
C-yes/S-no/P-ltd/H-no

Continental breakfast
Sitting room, suites, cable TV,
accomm. bus. travelers

Just two blocks from the world famous French Quarter, this 1846 Crede Mansion offers visitors the ambiance and charm of this historic period.
maison@accesscom.net http://www.maisonesplanade.com

Maison Perrier
4117 Perrier 70115
504-897-1807 Fax: 504-897-1399
888-293-2088
Tracewell Bailey/Paige Bailey
All year

79-260-BB
8 rooms, 8 pb
Most CC, *Rated*, •
C-yes/S-ltd/P-no/H-ltd
Spanish

Snacks all day; wine, draft
and cheese evenings
Library, Den, Parlor, Guest
Bar, professional and
personal concierge service

Beautiful American Victorian built in 1892 located in the Uptown/Garden district. Victorian charm, modern conveniences. Hot breakfast every morning. Minutes to the Quarter, all attractions. madame@maisonperrier.com http://www.maisonperrier.com

NEW ORLEANS

Mandevilla B&B
7716 St Charles Ave 70118
504-862-6396 Fax: 504-866-4104
800-288-0484
Marnie & Allen Borne
All year

129-159-BB
5 rooms, 5 pb
Visa, MC, Disc, *Rated*, •
C-yes/S-ltd/P-no/H-ltd

Continental plus breakfast
Afternoon tea, complimentary wine
Sitting room, library, bicycles, Jacuzzi, suites, fireplaces, cable TV

On streetcar line near universities. Beautifully restored 19th century mansion, fine antiques, safe area. mandevla@bellsouth.net http://www.mandevilla.com

---

McMurphy's
3115 Napoleon Ave 70125
504-896-9977 Fax: 504-896-2482
800-886-3709
Maggie Shimon
All year

125-BB
2 rooms, 2 pb
Most CC, •
C-ltd/S-no/P-no/H-no

Full gourmet breakfast
Afternoon tea, snacks, complimentary wine
Sitting room, bicycles, cable TV, accommodate business travelers

McMurphy's is a tropical paradise with large, airy rooms that are beautifully decorated. Welcoming at first glance with an ambiance totally New Orleans.
nolabandb@earthlink.net http://www.nolabandb.com/mcmurphys.html

---

New Orleans 1st, B&B/Essems House
PO Box 8163
3660 Gentilly Blvd 70182
504-947-3401 Fax: 504-838-0140
888-240-0070
Sarah Margaret Brown
All year

95-350-BB
4 rooms, 3 pb
Most CC, *Rated*
C-ltd/S-no/P-ltd

Continental breakfast
Sitting room, library, New Orleans first B&B, Near zoo, aquarium, park

There is safety, comfort and convenience. Off street parking.
nobba@bellsouth.net http://www.neworleansbandb.com

Nine-O-Five Royal Hotel
905 Royal St 70116
504-523-0219
Fax: 504-525-3905
J.M.
All year

95-250-EP
14 rooms, 14 pb
Visa, MC, *Rated*
C-yes/S-yes/P-no/H-no

Kitchens in all rooms
Daily maid service, three suites, near zoo, aquarium, park, Jackson Square

Quaint European-style hotel located in the heart of the French Quarter. Features 10 rooms and 3 suites beautifully decorated with period furnishings—balconies overlooking Royal Street. info@905royalhotel.com http://www.905royalhotel.com

---

Old World Inn
1330 Prytania St 70130
504-566-1330
Jean & Charlie Matkin
All year

45-75-BB
20 rooms, 10 pb
Visa, MC, •
C-ltd/S-yes/P-no/H-no
French, Spanish, Arabic

Continental plus breakfast
Comp. wine, juice
Sitting room, library, common rm w/piano, chess, fireplaces, A/C

French cafe style with unique ambiance, excellent concierge. Hosts are professional broadcasters/musicians. oldworldinn@usa.net http://www.angelfire.com/biz/oldworldinn

---

Olde Victorian Inn
914 N Rampart St 70116
504-522-2446 Fax: 504-522-8646
800-725-2446
Keith & Andre West-Harrison
All year

135-250-BB
6 rooms, 6 pb
Most CC, *Rated*, •
C-ltd/S-no/P-no/H-no
German

Full gourmet JAZZ breakfast
Afternoon tea with Check-in
Sitting room, fireplaces, cable TV, accom. bus. travel

Old French Quarter home with period antiques, private baths, fireplaces, balconies and tropical courtyard. oldeinn@aol.com http://www.oldevictorianinn.com

NEW ORLEANS

Park View Guest House
7004 St Charles Ave 70118
504-861-7564 Fax: 504-861-1225
888-533-0746
Jo-Ann Bird
All year

119-395-BB
22 rooms, 14 pb
Visa, MC, AmEx, •
C-yes/S-no/P-no/H-no
Spanish

Continental breakfast
Complimentary wine
Sitting room, cable TV, accommodate business travelers

A European style grand Victorian guest house, the Park View is affordable, comfortable and conveniently located. Some of our guestrooms are furnished with simple to grand elegant antiques. info@parkviewguesthouse.com http://www.parkviewguesthouse.com

---

Parkview Marigny
726 Frenchmen St 70116
504-945-7876 Fax: 504-945-7886
877-645-8617
Chris Liddy & Larry Molaison
All year

75-185-BB
5 rooms, 5 pb
Rated, •
S-ltd/P-no/H-no

Continental plus breakfast
Sitting room, next to French Quarter, summer rates available

130-year-old Creole townhouse on Washington Square Park. Two blocks from the French Quarter. pmarigny@aol.com http://www.neworleansbb.com

---

Pecan Tree Inn
2525 N Rampart St 70117
504-943-6195 Fax: 504-943-6388
800-460-3667
Tim L. Fields
All year

99-495-BB
5 rooms, 5 pb
•
C-yes/S-ltd/P-ltd/H-no
Spanish

Continental plus breakfast
Snacks, wine
Sitting room, suites, fireplaces, cable TV, 2 & 3 bedroom houses

A row of 3 19th century Creole houses built in the late 1800s. In the heart of the Old Bernard de Marigny Plantation. Furnished with fine antiques & reproductions
PecanTreeInn@aol.com http://www.pecantreeinn.com

Rose Manor B&B
7214 Pontchartrain Blvd 70124
504-282-8200 Fax: 504-282-7283
877-886-7673
Peter & Ruby Verhoeven
All year

75-125-BB
5 rooms, 5 pb
Visa, MC, AmEx, •
C-ltd/S-ltd/P-no/H-ltd
Chinese, German

Continental plus breakfast
Tea, coffee, soft drinks, snacks
Free membership to West End Tennis Club, two blocks away

All the elegance and decor of an English country house, situated only 10 minutes from the French Quarter, area attractions and convention center. Extremely comfortable, friendly atmosphere. info@rosemanor.com http://www.rosemanor.com

---

St. Peter Guest House
1005 St Peter 70016
504-524-9232 Fax: 504-523-5198
800-535-7815
Amy Clark
Season Inquire

49-200-BB
Most CC, *Rated*, •
C-yes/S-yes/P-no/H-no

Continental breakfast
Period antiques and quain courtyards

In the heart of French Quarter, located 2 blocks from fabulous Bouron St. Built as a private residence in the early 1800's, the St. Peter House is distinctly more intimate than conventional hotels. info@stpeterhouse.com http://www.stpeterhouse.com

---

St. Vincent's Guest House
1507 Magazine St 70130
504-523-3144 Fax: 504-566-1518
Peter & Sally Schreiber
All year

59-89-BB
75 rooms, 75 pb
Most CC, *Rated*, •
C-yes/S-ltd/P-ltd/H-yes
German, French, Spanish

Full breakfast
Lunch, aft. . tea, rest.
Sitting room, swimming pool, suites, free on site parking lot

Historical, beautiful and affordable, St. Vincent's is a European style Inn just a 10–15 minute walk from the French Quarter and Convention Center.
peterschreiber@compuserve.com http://www.stvincentsguesthouse.com

NEW ORLEANS

The Sully Mansion
2631 Prytania St 70130
504-891-0457 Fax: 504-269-0793
800-364-2414
Raymond Manci
All year

165-250-BB
7 rooms, 7 pb
Visa, MC, AmEx, •
S-no/P-no/H-ltd

Continental plus breakfast
Sitting room, suites, fireplaces, cable TV, accommodate bus. travelers

Circa 1890. Only inn nestled in the renowned Garden District. Well appointed rooms, antiques, and today's furnishings.
reservations@sullymansion.com http://www.sullymansion.com/

Sun & Moon
1037 N Rampart St 70116
504-529-4652 Fax: 504-529-4652
800-638-9169
Glinda Mantle
All year

61-121-BB
4 rooms, 4 pb
Visa, MC, AmEx
C-ltd/S-ltd/P-no/H-no

Continental Breakfast

French Quarter historic Creole cottage with suites overlooking a luscious courtyard with fountain. sunmoon4@bellsouth.net http://www.sunandmoon.qpg.com

NEW ORLEANS (REGION)

Poche Plantation
6554 LA Hwy 44, *Convent* 70723
225-562-7728 Fax: 225-562-0550
Tammy Kinler
All year

119-139-BB
5 rooms, 5 pb
Visa, MC, AmEx, *Rated*, •
C-yes/S-no/P-yes/H-yes

Full breakfast
Swimming pool, Jacuzzi, fireplaces, cable TV

Historic Mississippi River plantation home furnished in period antiques. Full plantation breakfast served in the main house.
innkeeper@pocheplantation.com http://www.pocheplantation.com

The Dansereau House
506 St. Philip St, *Thibodaux* 70301
985-447-1002 Fax: 985-447-1003
888-746-0122
Jim & Joan Rogers
All year

99-135-BB
4 rooms, 4 pb
Most CC, *Rated*
C-ltd/S-no/P-no/H-no
French

Continental plus breakfast
Snacks, complimentary wine, bar service
Sitting room, suites, cable TV, 2nd story gallery, accom. bus. travelers

An open door to Southern hospitality. Most unusual architecture in Louisiana. 14,000 sq. ft. home of Italianate and Second Empire design.
danhouse@bellsouth.net http://www.danhouse.com

Bay Tree Plantation
3785 Hwy 18, *Vacherie* 70090
225-265-2109 Fax: 225-265-7076
800-895-2109
Dinah & Rich Laurich
All year

89-199-BB
7 rooms, 7 pb
Most CC, *Rated*, •
C-yes/S-no/P-no

Full Southern breakfast

C 1850 French Creole Cottage on National Historic Register, Bay Tree offers a truly Southern Bed & Breakfast experience in an authentic antebellum ambience in the heart of Plantation Country. info@baytree.net http://www.baytree.net

OPELOUSAS

The Estorge House
417 N Market St 70570
337-942-8151 Fax: 337-942-8151
888-655-9539
Sherl Picchioni & Judith Estorge
All year

125-BB
2 rooms, 2 pb
Visa, MC, *Rated*
C-ltd/S-ltd/P-no/H-no

Full breakfast
Afternoon tea, snacks, complimentary wine
Sitting room, library, swimming pool, cable TV, tour of home

Return to a time of genteel elegance in the heart of Cajun Country. Your room is appointed with fresh flowers, antiques and a clawfoot tub.
whatbayou@aol.com http://www.whatbayou.com/estorge

SHREVEPORT

2439 Fairfield
2439 Fairfield Ave 71104
318-424-2424 Fax: 318-459-1839
877-251-2439
Brian Resmond
All year

135-225-BB
4 rooms, 4 pb
Most CC, *Rated*, •
S-no/P-no/H-no

Full breakfast
Whirlpools, private garden, gazebo, sitting room, library

1905 Victorian with balconies overlook English gardens featuring gazebo, fountain, Victorian swing.

SLIDELL (REGION)

Woodridge of Louisiana
40149 Crowe's Landing Rd, *Pearl River* 70452
985-863-9981 Fax: 985-863-0820
877-643-7109
Debbi & Tim Fotsch All year

65-140-BB
5 rooms, 5 pb
Most CC, •
C-ltd/S-ltd/P-no/H-no

Full Gourmet breakfast
Veranda, balcony, swing, gardens, sitting room, Pavilion, guest refrigerator

Located in a serene area 30 minutes from New Orleans & MS Gulf Coast. Five suites exquisitely decorated with queen beds, private baths. Gourmet breakfast! A true Southern Hospitality experience. tfotsch@aol.com http://www.woodridgebb.com

ST. FRANCISVILLE

Barrow House Inn
PO Box 1461
9779 Royal St 70775
225-635-4791 Fax: 225-635-1863
Shirley Dittloff All year

95-160-BB
7 rooms, 5 pb
Rated, •
C-ltd/S-yes/P-no/H-no

Continental breakfast
Full breakfast (fee)
Dinner (res), comp. wine, sitting room, bicycles, cassette walking tours

Circa 1809, located in Historic District. Balconies & period antiques. Cassette walking tours. Honeymoon packages. staff@topteninn.com http://www.topteninn.com

---

Butler Greenwood Plantation
8345 US Hwy 61 70775
225-635-6312 Fax: 225-635-6370
Anne Butler
All year

125-BB
7 rooms, 7 pb
Visa, MC, *Rated*, •
C-yes/S-ltd/P-ltd/H-no
French

Continental plus breakfast
Meeting facilities, library, balloon trips, nature walk, pool, bikes

7 private cottages with plenty of historic charm, scattered across peaceful landscaped plantation grounds. All cottages have Jacuzzis, porch or deck. On National Register of Historic Places.
butlergree@aol.com http://www.butlergreenwood.com

The Myrtles Plantation
PO Box 1100
7747 Hwy 61 70775
225-635-6277
Fax: 225-635-5837
John & Teeta Moss
All year

115-230-BB
10 rooms, 10 pb

The Myrtles Plantation, circa 1796, invites you to step into the past to experience antebellum splendor. You will see fine antiques and architectural treasures of the South.
myrtles@bsf.net http://www.myrtlesplantation.com

Shadetree Inn
PO Box 1818
9704 Royal 70775
225-635-6116 Fax: 225-635-0072
K. W. Kennon
All year

95-195-BB
3 rooms, 3 pb
Visa, MC, Disc, *Rated*, •
C-ltd/S-ltd/P-ltd/H-ltd

Continental plus breakfast
Snacks, comp. wine
Cocktails, appetizers, Jacuzzis, bicycles, cable TV

Three very private and romantic suites. Each has king bed, stereo, private phone and cable.
shadetreeinn@webtv.net http://www.shadetreeinn.com

SUNSET

La Caboose	75-95-BB	Full breakfast
PO Box E	4 rooms, 4 pb	Complimentary wine, gift of
145 S Budd St 70584	*Rated*, •	Jam and Jelly
337-662-5401 Fax: 337-662-5401	S-no/P-no/H-yes	
Margaret & Armand Brinkhaus		
All year		

4 distinctive B&Bs–Depot, caboose, ticket office, 1800s mail/passenger car–4 private bathrooms, refrigerators, coffee pots, toaster ovens. All in the heart of the country.

THIBODAUX

Naquin's	60-BB	Full breakfast
1146 W Camellia Dr 70301	4 rooms	Afternoon tea, snacks
985-446-6977	•	Sitting room, cable TV,
Frank & Joyce Naquin	C-yes/S-no/P-ltd/H-ltd	accommodate business
All year	French	travelers

Magic on the Bayou. Enjoy Cajun hospitality with a family of Acadian descent. We welcome you to a Cajun experience. naquinsbb@hotmail.com

WHITE CASTLE

Nottoway Plantation Inn	135-250-BB	Full and/or continental breakfast
PO Box 160	13 rooms, 13 pb	Restaurant serving lunch/dinner
30970 Hwy 405 (Great River Rd) 70788	Most CC, *Rated*, •	Swimming pool, meeting space, sitting room, piano, tennis & golf nearby
225-545-2730 Fax: 225-545-8632	C-yes/S-no/P-no/H-ltd	
Cindy A. Hidalgo	French	
All year exc. Christmas		

Rooms include a guided tour of the mansion, chilled champagne or sherry, a wake-up tray of hot sweet potato muffins, coffee and juice delivered to your room, and a full plantation breakfast. nottoway@att.net http://www.nottoway.com

Maine

ACADIA (REGION)

Surry Inn	62-82-BB	Full breakfast
PO Box 25	8 rooms, 6 pb	Full service dining room;
Route 172, *Surry* 04684	Visa, MC, Disc	wines and cocktails.
207-667-5091 800-742-3414	C-yes/S-no/P-no/H-yes	Sitting rooms, canoe, row
Annelise & Peter Krinsky		boat, large grounds,
All year		swimming in cove

Award-winning cuisine and beautiful water views await you at the Surry Inn. This picturesque 1830s farmhouse is conveniently located on the coast between Acadia National Park and Blue Hill. http://www.surryinn.com

ACADIA SCHOODIC

Acadia's Oceanside Meadows Inn	128-208-BB	Full gourmet breakfast
PO Box 90	14 rooms, 14 pb	Afternoon tea
Prospect Harbor, Rte 195 04669	Most CC	Sitting room, library,
207-963-5557 Fax: 207-963-5928	C-yes/S-no/P-yes/H-yes	fireplace, lawn games,
Sonja Sundaram, Ben Walter		flowers, private beach
All year		

Historic sea captain's home with magnificent ocean views, on 100+ acres with private sand beach, Acadia National Park, great hiking, biking, swimming, sea kayaking, canoeing. oceaninn@oceaninn.com http://www.oceaninn.com

AUBURN

The Munroe Inn
123 Pleasant St 04210
207-782-4984 Fax: 207-784-0938
800-668-0638
Connie & Clint Zimmerman
All year

74-119-BB
4 rooms, 4 pb
Most CC, *Rated*, •
C-ltd/S-no/P-no/H-no

Full breakfast
Restaurant, complimentary wine, snacks
Sitting room, fireplaces, cable TV, accommodate business travelers

The Munroe Inn is a three-story Queen Anne Victorian structure, recognized on the National Register of Historic Places. munroeinn@munroeinn.com http://www.munroeinn.com

AUGUSTA (REGION)

Maple Hill Farm Inn
RR1 Box 1145
Outlet Rd, *Hallowell* 04347
207-622-2708
Fax: 207-622-0655
800-622-2708
Scott Cowger & Vince Hannan
All year

65-190-BB
8 rooms, 8 pb
Most CC, *Rated*, •
C-ltd/S-no/P-no/H-yes

Full breakfast
Afternoon tea, snacks
Lunch (fee), bar service, sitting room/art gallery, swimming hole, trails

"Best of Maine, hands down" (Maine Times). Unique combination of country farm serenity on 130 acres, set back from road, and full-service room accommodations.
stay@maplebb.com http://www.maplebb.com

BAILEY ISLAND

Captain York House
PO Box 298
8 Garrison Cove Rd 04003
207-833-6224
Alan & Jean Thornton
All year

70-130-BB
5 rooms, 3 pb
Visa, MC, *Rated*, •
C-ltd/S-no/P-no/H-no

Full breakfast
Flowers, private beach

A restored Captain's home located on a small, quiet island in mid-coast Maine.
athorn7286@aol.com http://www.iwws.com/captainyork

Log Cabin, An Island Inn
PO Box 410
5 Log Cabin Ln 04003
207-833-5546 Fax: 207-833-7858
Matt & Aimee York
April-October

109-249-BB
8 rooms, 8 pb
Most CC, *Rated*
C-ltd/S-no/P-no/H-yes

Full breakfast
Dinner, restaurant, bar
Hot tubs, flowers, private beach, swimming pool

8 luxurious rooms, all with private baths & private decks. All have spectacular ocean views. Some with Jacuzzi tubs, some gas fireplace, some with kitchens.
info@logcabin-maine.com http://www.logcabin-maine.com

BAR HARBOR

Acadia Hotel
20 Mt Desert St 04609
207-288-5721 888-876-2463
Chris Coston
Season Inquire

60-160-EP
11 rooms, 11 pb
Visa, MC, AmEx
C-yes/S-ltd/P-no/H-no

Jacuzzis, cable TV, porch & balcony, A/C, queen/king beds all rms

Tastefully restored Victorian home on historic corridor in heart of picturesque village of Bar Harbor. acadiahotel@aol.com http://www.acadiahotel.com

---

Anne's White Columns Inn
57 Mt Desert St 04609
207-288-5357 Fax: 207-288-5357
800-321-6379
Anne & Robert Bahr
May-November

90-135-BB
10 rooms, 10 pb
Visa, MC, AmEx, *Rated*
C-ltd/S-no/P-no/H-ltd

Continental plus breakfast
Afternoon tea, complimentary wine
Sitting room, cable TV, in rooms, queen beds, covered porch, gardens

Impressive Georgian structure located in the historical corridor in downtown Bar Harbor. "As contemporary a Victorian B&B as you can find" —Weekending in New England.
anneswci@aol.com http://www.anneswhitecolumns.com

BAR HARBOR

The Atlantean Inn
11 Atlantic Ave 04609
207-288-5703 Fax: 207-288-0452
800-722-6671
Marian Burns
May-Nov

160-275-BB
8 rooms, 8 pb
Most CC, *Rated*, •
C-ltd/S-no/P-no/H-ltd

Full breakfast
Tea & afternoon refreshments
Gourmet breakfast, gardens with pergola, ""live"" chess game, very quiet

A stay in the Atlantean Inn will usher you back to the golden days of Victorian Bar Harbor where opulence was a way of life.
mzeiher@atlanteaninn.com http://www.atlanteaninn.com

Balance Rock Inn
21 Albert Meadow 04609
207-288-9900 Fax: 207-288-5534
800-753-0494
Michael Miles
May-October 27

95-555-BB
14 rooms, 14 pb
Most CC, *Rated*, •
C-ltd/S-ltd/P-no/H-no
French

Full breakfast
Full breakfast (fee)
Aftn. tea, sitting room, hot tubs, fireplaces, oceanside heated pool

Turn-of-the-century oceanfront mansion with lovely rooms & spectacular views. Ideal spot for romantic vacations.
barhbrinns@aol.com http://www.barharborvacations.com/welcomebri.htm

---

Black Friar Inn
10 Summer St 04609
207-288-5091 Fax: 207-288-4197
Perry & Sharon Risley, Falke
All year

70-150-BB
7 rooms, 7 pb
Visa, MC, Disc, *Rated*
C-ltd/S-no/P-no/H-no

Full gourmet breakfast
Afternoon tea & refreshments
Sitting room, fishing guide available, Sea Kayak School-June

Voted 1999 Inn of the Year by our guests. Lovingly restored eclectic Victorian Inn features antiques & architectural finds from the island. One mile to Acadia National Park.
perry@blackfriarinn.com http://www.blackfriarinn.com

Canterbury Cottage
12 Roberts Ave
12 Roberts Avenue 04609
207-288-2112 Fax: 207-288-5681
Armando & Maria Ribeiro
All year

BB
4 rooms, 4 pb
Visa, MC, Disc, *Rated*
C-ltd/S-no/P-no/H-no
Portuguese

Full breakfast
Afternoon tea, snacks
Sitting room, fireplace, cable TV

Cozy and comfortable accommodations just minutes away from Acadia National Park and within walking distance to downtown Bar Harbor.
canterbury@gwi.net http://www.canterburycottage.com

Castlemaine Inn
39 Holland Ave 04609
207-288-4563 Fax: 207-288-4525
800-338-4563
Terence O'Connell
All year

50-225-BB
12 rooms, 12 pb
Visa, MC, *Rated*
C-ltd/S-ltd/P-no

Continental plus breakfast
All A/C, all cable TV, Main street 3 blocks, water 2 blocks, Fax, VCR

The inn is nestled on a quiet side street in Bar Harbor Village, surrounded by the magnificent Acadia National Park. http://www.castlemaineinn.com

---

Chiltern Inn
3 Cromwell Harbor Rd 04609
207-288-0114
Fax: 207-288-0124
800-404-0114
Pat & John Shaw
All year

275-450-BB
4 rooms, 4 pb
Most CC, *Rated*, •
S-no/P-no

Full breakfast
Snacks
Sitting room, library, Jacuzzis, indoor pool, fireplaces, cable TV, sauna

Complete luxury in a 1905 Edwardian Carriage House furnished with period antiques, fine art & luxurious linens. Enjoy your Jacuzzi & fireplace in your own suite.
pat@chilterninn.com http://www.chilterninn.com

BAR HARBOR

Cleftstone Manor
92 Eden St 04609
207-288-8086 Fax: 207-288-2089
888-288-4951
Kelly & Steve Hellmann
Late April through October

70-200-BB
16 rooms, 16 pb
Visa, MC, Disc, *Rated*
C-ltd/S-no/P-no/H-no

Full breakfast with modest menu
Afternoon tea and fresh baked cookies
Sitting rooms, library, many rooms with TV and phone, some with fireplace.

The Cleftstone Manor is an 1881 historic mansion listed on the National Register of Historic Places. innkeeper@cleftstone.com http://www.cleftstone.com

---

Coach Stop Inn
PO Box 266
Bar Harbor Rd (Rt 3) 04609
207-288-9886 Fax: 207-288-4241
Kathy Combs
Mid May–mid October

59-129-BB
5 rooms, 5 pb
Visa, MC, AmEx, *Rated*
C-ltd/S-ltd/H-ltd

Full gourmet breakfast
Snacks, complimentary wine, afternoon refreshments
Suites, fireplaces, cable TV in common room

Built in 1804, this historic Inn was formerly a stage coach stop and tavern.
info@coachstopinn.com http://www.coachstopinn.com

Graycote Inn
40 Holland Ave 04609
207-288-3044
Fax: 207-288-2719
Pat & Roger Samuel All year

75-165-BB
12 rooms, 12 pb
Most CC, *Rated*
C-ltd/S-ltd/P-no/H-no

Full breakfast
Afternoon refreshments
All rooms have king or queen bed, some w/sitting room, fireplace, balcony

Light and airy Victorian: Spacious rooms, all with private baths. Large landscaped yard on quiet village street. Walk to shops, galleries, and restaurants. Early morning coffee and full hot breakfast. Info@graycoteinn.com http://www.graycoteinn.com

---

Hatfield
20 Roberts Ave 04609
207-288-9655
Jeff & Sandy Miller
All year

95-125-BB
6 rooms, 6 pb
Most CC, *Rated*
C-ltd/S-no/P-no/H-no

Full breakfast
Afternoon tea
Living room, dining room, porch, 3rd floor sun deck, outdoor smoking area

Kick off your shoes and enjoy Country Comfort in Bar Harbor. Located on a quiet side street, within walking distance to everything in town and only 5 minutes to beautiful Acadia National Park. lanier@hatfieldinn.com http://www.hatfieldinn.com

---

Hearthside
7 High St 04609
207-288-4533 Fax: 207-288-9818
Susan & Barry Schwartz
All year

100-145-BB
9 rooms, 9 pb
Visa, MC, *Rated*
C-ltd/S-no/P-no/H-no

Full breakfast
Afternoon tea & cookies
All rooms have A/C, 3 rooms w/fireplaces, 3 bath w/whirlpool jets

Small, gracious hostelry in quiet, in-town location; elegant blend of antiques & traditional furniture. lanier@hearthsideinn.com http://www.hearthsideinn.com

---

Holbrook House
74 Mt Desert St 04609
207-288-4970 Fax: 207-288-4994
800-860-7430
Phil & Lesley DiVirgilio
Feb. to Nov.

90-165-BB
12 rooms, 12 pb
Visa, MC, *Rated*
C-ltd/S-no/P-no/H-no

Full breakfast
Afternoon refreshments
Sitting room, library, enclosed bike storage, ample parking & scenic flights

Relax amid the charm & ambience of Bar Harbor's "Golden Years."
info@holbrookhouse.com http://www.holbrookhouse.com

Holland Inn
35 Holland Ave 04609
207-288-4804
Evin & Tom Hulbert
All year

90-145-BB
5 rooms, 5 pb
Visa, MC, *Rated*
C-ltd/S-no/P-no/H-no

Full breakfast
Sitting room, library, suites, fireplace, cable TV

Short stroll to center of town, minutes from the park.
info@hollandinn.com http://www.hollandinn.com

BAR HARBOR

The Inn at Bay Ledge
1385 Sand Point Rd 04609
207-288-4204 Fax: 207-288-5573
Jack & Jeani Ochtera
May-Oct/June 15-Oct. 1

100-375-BB
10 rooms, 10 pb
Rated
S-no/P-no

Full breakfast
Heated pool, fireplaces, sauna, steam rooms, Jacuzzis, meeting room

Amidst towering pines, the inn literally clings to the cliffs of Mt. Desert Island. Many tiered decks overlook spectacular coastline. Priv. beach. All rooms with ocean views.
bayledge@downeast.net http://www.innatbayledge.com

Ivy Manor Inn
194 Main Street 04609
207-288-2138 Fax: 207-288-0038
888-670-1997
Judi & Bob Stanley
Spring, Summer, Fall

150-350-BB
8 rooms, 8 pb
Most CC, *Rated*, •
C-ltd/S-no/P-no/H-yes

Full breakfast
Restaurant, dinner
Sitting room, suites, fireplace, cable TV, conference

Romance, elegance, antiques & the "finest dining on the island" depicts the Ivy Manor Inn & Michelle's Fine Dining Bistro. ivymanor@acadia.net http://www.ivymanor.com

---

The Ledgelawn Inn
66 Mount Desert St 04609
207-288-4596 Fax: 207-288-9968
800-274-5334
Nancy Cloud
April—November

65-275-BB
33 rooms, 33 pb
Visa, MC, AmEx, *Rated*, •
C-yes/S-yes/P-no/H-no

Continental plus breakfast
Bar service, comp. tea
Sitting room, library, piano, pool, sauna, modern exercise room

A graceful turn-of-the-century mansion with antiques, sitting areas, fireplaces, hot tub; in a quiet location. barhbrinns@aol.com http://www.barharborvacations.com/welcomelli.htm

---

Manor House Inn
106 West St 04609
207-288-3759 Fax: 207-288-2974
800-437-0088
Mac Noyes
May-mid-Oct.

65-235-BB
14 rooms, 14 pb
Visa, MC, AmEx, *Rated*, •
C-ltd/S-no/P-no/H-no

Full breakfast
Afternoon tea
Sitting room, fireplaces, swimming pool, piano, gardens, tennis courts

Many special touches. Restored Victorian, National Register, antique furniture. Bedrooms include parlor, bath. Near Acadia National Park.
manor@acadia.net http://www.barharbormanorhouse.com

Mansion at the Oakes
PO Box 3
119 Eden St 04609
207-288-5801 Fax: 207-288-8402
800-33-MAINE
The Cough Family
May to mid-October

73-252-BB
9 rooms, 9 pb
Visa, MC, AmEx, *Rated*, •
C-ltd/S-no/P-no/H-ltd

Continental plus breakfast
Sitting room, tennis court, indoor swimming pool, suites, cable TV

Restored Bar Harbor summer "cottage" built on the ocean in 1913. Gardens and stone walls recall Bar Harbor's "Cottage Era." An additional 144 hotel rooms are available separate from the B&B. oakes@barharbor.com http://www.barharbor.com

---

The Maples Inn
16 Roberts Ave 04609
207-288-3443 Fax: 207-288-0356
Tom & Sue Palumbo
All year

70-160-BB
6 rooms, 6 pb
Visa, MC, Disc, *Rated*
C-ltd/S-no/P-no/H-no
Spanish

Full gourmet breakfast
Afternoon tea
Sitting room, library, suites, fireplaces, A/C

Our 1903 Victorian inn is perfectly located on an attractive side street, a five-minute walk to Bar Harbor's restaurants, shops, activities, waterfront, and a short drive to Acadia National Park. info@maplesinn.com http://www.maplesinn.com

BAR HARBOR

Mira Monte Inn & Suites
69 Mt Desert St 04609
207-288-3115 Fax: 207-288-3115
800-553-5109
Marian Burns
Mid-Apr. to Early Nov.

160-240-BB
16 rooms, 16 pb
Visa, MC, AmEx,
Rated, •
C-ltd/S-ltd/P-no/H-yes

Full breakfast buffet
Complimentary wine & cheese
Juice, snacks, piano, sitting & meeting rooms, all rms: phones, A/C, TV

Renovated 1864 Victorian estate with period furnishings and fireplaces. A quiet, in-town location, walk to waterfront. mburns@miramonte.com http://www.miramonte.com

---

Moseley Cottage Inn
12 Atlantic Avenue 04609
207-288-5548 Fax: 207-288-9406
800-458-8644
Joe Paluga & Christine Sweeting
April-November

105-175-BB
9 rooms, 9 pb
Most CC, *Rated*, •
C-yes/S-no/P-no/H-ltd

Full breakfast
Private off-street parking, sitting room, piano, courtesy phone, fax

Beautiful Victorian inn in a quiet location close to downtown. Enjoy period furniture, working fireplaces, private porches and delicious breakfast served daily.
http://www.townmotelmoseleycottageinn.com

Primrose Inn
73 Mt Desert St 04609
207-288-4031 877-846-3424
Pamela & Bryan
May-Oct.

90-200-BB
15 rooms, 15 pb
Most CC, *Rated*
C-ltd/S-no/P-ltd

Full breakfast
Afternoon tea featuring fresh-baked treats
In town, private parking, spacious living room w/fireplace, piano, library

Beautifully preserved 1878 Stick-Style Victorian on "Historic Corridor," in downtown Bar Harbor near Acadia National Park.
relax@primroseinn.com http://www.primroseinn.com

Sunset on West
115 West Street 04609
207-288-4242 Fax: 207-288-4545
877-406-4242
Nancy & Mel Johnson
May 1-October 31

135-295-BB
4 rooms, 4 pb
Visa, MC, *Rated*
C-ltd/S-no/P-no/H-no
French

Full breakfast
Tea, snacks, wine
Sitting room, library, suites, fireplace, conference, ocean views

Ideally situated in historic district overlooking Frenchman Bay. Magnificent, landmark Bar Harbor Cottage built in 1910. sunsetonwest@gwi.net http://www.sunsetonwest.com

---

The Tides
119 West St 04609
207-288-4968 Fax: 207-288-2997
Ray & Loretta Harris
All year

195-375-BB
3 rooms, 3 pb
Visa, MC, Disc, *Rated*
C-ltd/S-no/P-no/H-no

Full breakfast
Sitting room, 2nd floor guest living room with gas fireplace

Magnificent water views from every bed chamber. Private, but walk to town. Sumptuous full breakfast on the verandah, with sweeping views of Frenchman's Bay. 3 suites.
info@barharbortides.com http://www.barharbortides.com/

BATH

Benjamin F. Packard House
45 Pearl St 04530
207-443-6069 Fax: 207-443-5453
800-516-4578
Debby & Bill Hayden
All year

75-100-BB
3 rooms, 3 pb
Most CC, *Rated*
C-ltd/S-no/P-no/H-no
French

Full breakfast
Sitting room, library

The Benjamin F. Packard House is a treasure in historic Bath, a perfect place in which to return to the mid 19th century.
packardhouse@clinic.net http://www.mainecoast.com/packardhouse

Galen C. Moses House, Bath, ME

BATH

Fairhaven Inn
118 N Bath Rd 04530
207-443-4391 Fax: 207-443-6412
888-443-4391
Susie & Dave Reed All year

80-140-BB
8 rooms, 6 pb
Rated, •
C-ltd/S-no/P-no/H-no

Full breakfast
Tea, soda
Piano, library, bicycles, hiking trail

Quiet country inn on 16 acres of woods, meadows, lawns. Antique & country furnishings. Occasional baking lessons from pastry chef/owner.

fairhvn@gwi.net http://www.mainecoast.com/fairhaveninn

Galen C. Moses House
1009 Washington St 04530
207-442-8771 888-442-8771
Jim Haught & Larry Kieft
All year

99-159-BB
5 rooms, 4 pb
Most CC, *Rated*, •
C-ltd/S-no/P-no/H-no

Full breakfast
Afternoon tea, wine
Turn down service, A/C

Built in 1874, the Galen C. Moses House is reminiscent of the 19th century grand Victorian style. Selected for the National Register of Historic Homes.

stay@galenmoses.com http://www.galenmoses.com

The Inn at Bath
969 Washington St 04530
207-443-4294 Fax: 207-443-4295
800-423-0964
Nick Bayard All year

125-185-BB
9 rooms, 9 pb
Most CC, *Rated*, •
C-ltd/S-no/P-yes/H-yes
French

Full breakfast
Complimentary tea, coffee
2 rooms with Jacuzzis and/or fireplaces, cable TV, VCRs, phones, A/C

The Inn at Bath is an elegant, comfortable B&B on the mid-coast of Maine. Antique-filled 1810 Greek Revival home surrounded by lovely gardens. Located in Bath's Historic District. innkeeper@innatbath.com http://www.innatbath.com

BELFAST

1 Church St./The White House
1 Church Street 04915
207-338-1901 Fax: 207-338-5161
888-290-1901
Bob Hansen & Terry Prescott
All year

95-165-BB
6 rooms, 6 pb
Visa, MC, Disc, *Rated*
C-ltd/S-no/P-no/H-no

Full breakfast
Special dietary needs met*Afternoon refreshments
View our website for guest chamber photos and descriptions

This 1840 Greek Revival mansion was designed to create the showcase of coastal Maine. Explore elegant classical European styled decor.

whitehouse@mainebb.com http://www.mainebb.com

BELFAST

The Alden House
63 Church St 04915
207-338-2151 Fax: 207-338-2151
877-337-8151
Bruce & Susan Madara
All year

90-130-BB
7 rooms, 5 pb
Visa, MC, Disc
C-yes/S-no/P-no

Full breakfast
Afternoon tea
Sitting room, library, fireplaces, in-room VCR/TV

Recently renovated 1840's Greek Revival home, antique appointed, modern amenities; full, hearty, healthy breakfast.
innkeeper@thealdenhouse.com http://www.thealdenhouse.com

Belfast Bay Meadows
192 Northport Ave
Route 1 04915
207-338-5715 800-335-2370
Karin & Richard Jensen
All year

85-155-BB
19 rooms, 19 pb
Most CC, *Rated*, •
C-yes/S-no/P-yes/H-ltd

Full gourmet breakfast
Sitting room, library, park-like setting on the Penobscot Bay

Stroll our 7 acres of flowered meadows and follow the grassy path to the blue waters of the Penobscot Bay. Our Inn is just 350 yards from its own private beachfront.
bbmi@baymeadowsinn.com http://www.baymeadowsinn.com

Belhaven Inn
14 John St 04915
207-338-5435
Anne & Paul Bartels
All year

85-130-BB
5 rooms, 3 pb
Visa, MC, *Rated*
C-yes/S-no/P-yes/H-no

Full breakfast
Evening tea
3 sitting rooms with fireplaces,1 Efficiency Suite with kitchen & cable TV

An 1851 family oriented Victorian B&B. Children all ages welcome. Delightful guestrooms. Efficiency/kitchen. Pet friendly. Gourmet breakfasts. Fireplaces. Walk to waterfront, near Acadia/Bar Harbor. stay@belhaveninn.com http://www.belhaveninn.com

---

The Jeweled Turret Inn
40 Pearl St 04915
207-338-2304 800-696-2304
Carl & Cathy Heffentrager
All year

95-145-BB
7 rooms, 7 pb
Visa, MC, *Rated*, •
C-ltd/S-ltd/P-no/H-no

Full breakfast
Afternoon tea
Sitting rooms, parlors, antiques, tennis & pool nearby

Intimate turrets, verandahs, beautiful woodwork. Walk to town, shops & harbor. On National Register.
info@jeweledturret.com http://www.jeweledturret.com

Londonderry Inn
133 Belmont Ave 04915
207-338-2763 Fax: 207-338-6303
877-529-9566
Marsha & Fletcher Oakes
All year

95-145-BB
5 rooms, 5 pb
Most CC, *Rated*, •
C-ltd/S-no/P-no/H-ltd

Full breakfast
Evening beverage and dessert
Large common rooms, porch, deck, spacious grounds, function facilities

Come to our beautifully restored country farmhouse on 10 acres, with large sunny rooms, many sitting areas, a large fireplaced country kitchen, and a full country breakfast.
info@londonderry-inn.com http://www.londonderry-inn.com

BELGRADE LAKES

Wings Hill
PO Box 386
Route 27 04918
207-495-2400 Fax: 207-495-3400
866-495-2400
Christopher & Tracey Anderson All year

95-140-BB
8 rooms, 8 pb
Visa, MC, Disc, •
C-ltd/P-no/H-ltd
French, Spanish

Full breakfast
Afternoon tea, dinner available
Sitting room, suites, cable TV

A picturesque village setting, unexpected touches and service, superb food. Ideal getaway for relaxing romance. Steps from hiking, boating, and Maine's best golf, skiing, shopping, coastal points. wingshillinn@earthlink.net http://www.wingshillinn.com

BETHEL

Briar Lea Inn & Restaurant
150 Mayville Rd
04217
207-824-4717 Fax: 207-824-7121
Gary & Carol Brearley
All year

69-119-BB
7 rooms, 7 pb
C-yes/S-no/P-yes/H-ltd
German

Full breakfast

Experience the comfort and ambiance of this 150 year old renovated Maine farmhouse. Our 6 cozy rooms all have private baths, cable TV, phones, air conditioning and casual eclectic antique decor. briarlea@megalink.net http://www.briarleainnrestaurant.com

Rivendell House
PO Box 74
16 Park St 04217
207-824-0508

Recently renovated 1860 farm house. Two guest rooms, each with private bath, queen bed. Full breakfast, afternoon tea included. Walk to restaurants and shops. 10 minutes to Sunday River Ski Resort. ajcressy@megalink.net http://www.rivendellhouse.com

BLUE HILL

Blue Hill Inn
PO Box 403
Union St Route 177 E 04614
207-374-2844 Fax: 207-374-2844
800-826-7415
Don Hartley May 15-Oct 31

138-265-BB
12 rooms, 12 pb
Visa, MC, AmEx,
Rated, •
C-ltd/S-no/P-no/H-ltd

Full breakfast
Afternoon refreshments, hors d'oeuvres
Day trip consultation, beverage service, cocktail hour, turn-downs

Blue Hill Inn c1830, a romantic bed and breakfast in sea coast village of Blue Hill, ME, 30-45 mins to Acadia, Bar Harbor, Deer Isle. Distinctive lodging, hors d'oeuvres, fireplaces, down comforters. mary@bluehillinn.com http://www.bluehillinn.com

BOOTHBAY (REGION)

Coveside
6 Gotts Cove Lane,
Georgetown 04548
207-371-2807 Fax: 207-371-2952
800-232-5490
Carolyn & Tom Church
May-Oct.

110-175-BB
7 rooms, 7 pb
Visa, MC, Disc, *Rated*, •
C-ltd/S-no/P-no/H-no
French

Full gourmet breakfast
Complementary beer and soft drinks, cookies
Two sitting rooms, private porches, in-room fireplaces, canoe

Stylish retreat on 5 waterfront acres, reminiscent of turn-of-century coastal cottages. All rooms overlook rocky Gotts cove and Sheepscot Bay; several have fireplaces, private balconies, and spa tub. innkeeper@covesidebandb.com http://www.covesidebandb.com

BOOTHBAY HARBOR

1830 Admiral's Quarters Inn
71 Commercial St 04538
207-633-2474 Fax: 207-633-5904
800-644-1878
Les & Deb Hallstrom
Mid Feb-Nov

95-195-BB
6 rooms, 6 pb
Visa, MC, Disc, *Rated*
C-ltd/S-no/P-no/H-ltd

Full breakfast
Afternoon tea, snacks
Sitting room, library, fireplaces, cable TV, accom. bus. travelers

Newly renovated sea captain's home blending antiques with white wicker; hearty full homemade breakfast served overlooking the harbor and meticulously manicured gardens. loon@admiralsquartersinn.com http://www.admiralsquartersinn.com/

Anchor Watch
9 Eames Rd 04538
207-633-7565
Diane Campbell, Kathy Campbell Reed
All year

95-160-BB
5 rooms, 5 pb
Rated, •
C-ltd/S-no/P-no/H-no

Full breakfast
4 rooms with ocean views, whirlpool, fireplace, fishing and boating

Scenic shore; winter ducks feed near the rocks; flashing lighthouses; lobstermen hauling traps, walk to restaurants, shops, boats.
diane@lincoln.midcoast.com http://www.anchorwatch.com

BOOTHBAY HARBOR

Atlantic Ark Inn
64 Atlantic Ave 04538
207-633-5690
Donna
May-Oct.

95-169-BB
7 rooms, 7 pb
Rated
C-ltd/S-ltd/P-no/H-no

Full gourmet breakfast
Complimentary afternoon beverage
Sitt. rm., wrap around, veranda with arbor, fresh flowers, walk to town

Quaint & intimate, this small inn offers lovely harbor views, balconies, Oriental rugs, mahogany furnishings, flowers.
donnz@atlanticarkinn.com http://www.atlanticarkinn.com/

Bayside Inn
55 Union St 04538
207-633-3992
Peter & Kathryn Sullivan
All year

65-100-BB
5 rooms, 5 pb
C-yes/S-no/P-no

Full breakfast
Antiques & family treasures, creating a feeling of warmth & casual elegance

Welcome to Bayside Inn—a bed and breakfast with the flavor of the historic seaside town, overlooking beautiful Boothbay Harbor, Maine.
bayside@wiscasset.net http://www.wiscasset.net/bayside

Five Gables Inn
PO Box 335
107 Murray Hill Rd 04544
207-633-4551 800-451-5048
Mike & De Kennedy
Mid-May to End of Oct

130-195-BB
15 rooms, 15 pb
Visa, MC, *Rated*, •
C-ltd/S-no/P-no/H-no

Full breakfast
Afternoon tea
Fireplaces, games, wraparound verandah, pool & boating nearby

Have you ever heard your parents or grandparents reminisce about vacations at a rambling old hotel somewhere on the coast of New England and wondered what it was like back in those days? info@fivegablesinn.com http://www.fivegablesinn.com

---

The Footbridge Inn
15 Atlantic Ave 04538
207-633-9965 Fax: 207-633-9965
888-633-9965
Barbara Ford-Latty
5/1-10/31

85-165-BB
8 rooms, 8 pb
Visa, MC, Disc, •
C-ltd/S-ltd/P-no/H-no

Full breakfast
Sitting room, suites, fireplaces, cable TV, accom. bus. travelers

An historic sea captain's home located at the water's edge, just across the famous footbridge. Large, open decks for sunset viewing or just relaxing.
thefootbridgeinn@gwi.net http://www.thefootbridgeinn.com

The Harborage Inn
75 Townsend Avenue 04538
207-633-4640 800-565-3742
Troy Chapman
All year

70-160-BB
9 rooms, 9 pb
Visa, MC, *Rated*
C-ltd/S-no/P-no/H-no

Continental breakfast
Waterfront lawn w/seating, Wraparound porches, Laura Ashley rooms

A seaside inn since the 1920's. We offer the quality and tradition of a three generation Boothbay Harbor family.
info@harborageinn.com http://www.harborageinn.com

Harbour Towne Inn on the Waterfront
71 Townsend Ave 04538
207-633-4300 Fax: 207-633-2442
800-722-4240
George Thomas & Family
Most of year

79-299-BB
12 rooms, 12 pb
Most CC, *Rated*, •
C-ltd/S-no/P-no/H-yes

Continental plus buffet breakfast
Deck available to all rooms, 2-5 minute walk to everything, A/C

The Finest B&B on the Waterfront. Famous for our flower displays. New dock & float for harbor & village scenic views or launch a kayak/canoe, etc. Off season packages including dinner from $99 for 2!
gtme@gwi.net http://www.harbourtowneinn.com

BOOTHBAY HARBOR

Kenniston Hill Inn PO Box 125 988 Wiscasset Rd 04537 207-633-2159 Fax: 207-633-2159 800-992-2915 Jim & Gerry Botti All year	85-130-BB 10 rooms, 10 pb Most CC, *Rated*, • C-yes/S-no/P-no/H-ltd	Full breakfast Afternoon refreshments

Come immerse yourself in the warmth of old New England. Beautiful grounds and gardens. Today, we invite you to step back to those days when the country was young and hospitality was still an art. innkeeper@maine.com http://www.maine.com/innkeeper/

Lion d'Or 106 Townsend Ave 04538 207-633-7367 800-887-7367 Greg & Lucy Barter All year	65-135-BB 5 rooms, 5 pb Visa, MC C-ltd/S-no/P-no/H-ltd	Full breakfast PM treats Cable TV, private baths, parking, intown.

At Lion d'Or, a warm welcome awaits you in a comfortable Victorian home built in 1886. Cozy and intimate, Lion d'Or has 5 spacious rooms, all with private bath and queen beds, cable TV and parking. liondor@gwi.net http://www.liondorboothbay.com

BOOTHBAY HARBOR (REGION)

Hodgdon Island Inn PO Box 603 Barters Island Road, *Boothbay* 04537 207-633-7474 Fax: 207-633-0571 Peter Wilson & Peter Moran All year	105-140-BB 8 rooms, 8 pb Visa, MC, Disc C-ltd/S-no/P-no/H-no	Full breakfast Sitting room, library, swimming pool, fireplaces, cable TV

Quiet waterfront getaway, outdoor heated swimming pool, well-groomed gardens. All rooms have water-views, private baths.
mail@hodgdonislandinn.com http://www.hodgdonislandinn.com

Ocean Point Inn PO Box 409 Shore Rd, *East Boothbay* 04544 207-633-4200 800-552-5554 Dave & Beth Dudley	118-190-EP 61 rooms, 61 pb Most CC, *Rated* C-yes/S-ltd/P-no/H-no All year	Restaurant, bar service Dinner available, swimming pool, family friendly facility, game room, hot tub

Traditional seacoast inn on beautiful Ocean Point. A natural, unspoiled oceanfront setting in a relaxed atmosphere with a spectacular open ocean view.
opi@oceanpointinn.com http://www.oceanpointinn.com

Ocean Gate Inn PO Box 240 70 Ocean Gate Rd, *Southport* 04576 207-633-3321 Fax: 207-633-2900 800-221-5924 Dennis W. Clark	75-165-BB 66 rooms, 66 pb Visa, MC, *Rated*, • C-yes/S-no/P-no/H-ltd Memorial Day–Columbus Day	Full breakfast (buffet) 5 PM until closing, light fare at the Snack Shack Free tennis courts, playground, heated pool, fitness center, fishing. . .

Cross the bridge to scenic Southport Island, five minutes from the center of Boothbay Harbor. Removed from the crowds, you can explore 85 secluded wooded acres nestled on the waterfront. ogate@oceangateinn.com http://www.oceangateinn.com

BRIDGTON

Tarry-a-While Resort On Highland Lake RR 3, Box 1067 Highland Ridge Rd. 04009 207-647-2522 Fax: 207-647-5512 800-451-9076 Marc & Nancy Stretch	60-150-BB 28 rooms, 23 pb *Rated*, • All year	Continental plus breakfast

The natural beauty of this vacation paradise is something that makes vacation memories that last a lifetime. tarryayl@megalink.net http://www.tarryawhile.com

BROOKSVILLE

Oakland House Seaside Resort
435 Herrick Rd 04617
207-359-8521 Fax: 207-359-9865
800-359-7352
Jim & Sally Littlefield
All year

155-269-MAP
25 rooms, 23 pb
Visa, MC, *Rated*, •
C-ltd/S-ltd/P-no/H-no
Polish, German, Russian

Full breakfast
Box lunches, catered events, wine & beer
On Premises lake & ocean beaches, gazebo, boating, lobster picnics, weddings

Spectacular location! Shore Oaks Seaside Inn and 15 cottages are sprinkled along 1/2 mile of shorefront. In its 114th season. Simple, elegant, fine dining, lake/ocean beaches, dock, trails, gardens. jim@oaklandhouse.com http://www.oaklandhouse.com

BROWNFIELD

Brownfield
PO Box 160
Rt 160 S Firelane 44 04010
207-935-4014
Cullen Carpenter All year

50-BB
3 rooms, 2 pb
Rated
C-yes/S-no/P-yes/H-no

Full, hearty Maine breakfast
Jacuzzis, large deck, swimming, fishing,

Three sunny rooms on the side of Burnt Meadow Mountain and overlooking Burnt Meadow Pond.

BRUNSWICK

Brunswick
165 Park Row 04011
207-729-4914 800-299-4914
Steve & Mercie Normand
Closed January

95-200-BB
8 rooms, 8 pb
Visa, MC
C-ltd/S-no/P-no/H-no

Full breakfast
Snacks
Sitting room, suites, fireplaces, cable TV, accom. bus. travel

Gracious lodging in Greek Revival home decorated with quilts and antiques. Easy walk to restaurants, shops, museums, Bowdoin College.
mercie@brunswickbnb.com http://www.brunswickbnb.com

CAMDEN

A Little Dream
60 High St 04843
207-236-8742 800-217-0109
Joanna Ball & Bill Fontana
All year

120-250-BB
7 rooms, 7 pb
Visa, MC, AmEx, *Rated*
C-no/S-no/P-no

Full gourmet breakfast
Afternoon refreshements
Private baths, A/C, turndown service

Sweet dreams and little luxuries abound in this lovely white Victorian with wicker and flower filled wrap-around porch. dreamers@mint.net http://www.littledream.com

---

Abigail's Inn
8 High St 04843
207-236-2501 Fax: 207-230-0657
800-292-2501
Ed & Donna Misner
All year

110-175-BB
4 rooms, 4 pb
Visa, MC, *Rated*
C-ltd/S-no/P-no/H-no

Full breakfast
Afternoon tea
Sitting room, library, Jacuzzi, suites, fireplace, cable TV, A/C

Let yourself be pampered; cozy four-poster bed, tempting breakfast, Jacuzzi, fireplaces, afternoon tea, a short walk to Camden harbor & village.
abigails@midcoast.com http://www.abigailsinn.com

Blackberry Inn
82 Elm St 04843
207-236-6060 Fax: 207-236-9032
800-388-6000
Jim & Cyndi Ostrowski
All year

80-210-BB
11 rooms, 11 pb
Visa, MC, Disc, •
C-yes/S-no/P-no/H-no

Full breakfast
Afternoon tea, snacks
Three spacious parlors, gardens, fireplaces, whirlpools, A/C, cable TV

Maine's only "painted lady" Victorian, just a 3 block stroll to windjammer harbor, shops and restaurants. Gracious parlors, original tin ceilings, beautiful parquet floors.
blkberry@midcoast.com http://www.blackberryinn.com

CAMDEN

Camden Windward House
6 High St 04843
207-236-9656 Fax: 207-230-0433
877-492-9656
Del & Charlotte Lawrence
All year

99-259-BB
8 rooms, 8 pb
Visa, MC, AmEx, *Rated*
C-ltd/S-no/P-no/H-no

Full breakfast from menu
Afternoon tea
Sitting room, library, Jacuzzis, suites, fireplaces, cable, accom. bus. trvl

Luxurious in-town inn with large, comfortable rooms, oversized beds, full complement of amenities, full choice of menu breakfast, close to all Camden has to offer.
bnb@windwardhouse.com http://www.windwardhouse.com

The Elms B&B
84 Elm St 04843
207-236-6250 Fax: 207-236-7330
800-755-ELMS
Ted & Jo Panayotoff
All year

75-115-BB
6 rooms, 6 pb
Visa, MC, *Rated*, •
C-ltd/S-no/P-no/H-ltd

Full breakfast
Afternoon tea, restaurants
Cottage gardens, frplcs., period furniture, lib., phone/data ports in rooms

Experience the casual warmth of this restored 1806 Colonial, with a lighthouse theme. Walk to harbor and shops. theelms@midcoast.com http://www.elmsinn.net

---

Hartstone Inn
41 Elm St 04843
207-236-4259 Fax: 207-236-9575
800-788-4823
Mary Jo & Michael Salmon
All year

85-160-BB
10 rooms, 10 pb
Most CC, *Rated*
C-ltd/S-no/P-no/H-no

Full breakfast
Dinner, picnic sails
Comp. tea, cookies, sitting room, fireplaces, library, TV room, phones

Come fall under the spell of one of Camden's grandest historic homes located in the heart of the village. info@hartstoneinn.com http://www.hartstoneinn.com

---

Hawthorn Inn
9 High St 04843
207-236-8842 Fax: 207-236-6181
866-381-3647
Maryanne Shanahan
All year

90-240-BB
10 rooms, 10 pb
Visa, MC, *Rated*, •
C-ltd/S-no/P-no/H-no
Spanish

Full breakfast
Afternoon refreshments
Library w/ wood fire, parlor, Jacuzzi tubs, TV/VCR, fireplaces. decks

Stately Victorian mansion with spacious, light, airy rooms. Beautiful garden. Views of mountains and Camden Harbor.
hawthorn@midcoast.com http://www.camdenhawthorn.com

Inn at Oceans Edge
PO Box 704
Rte 1 04843
207-236-0945 Fax: 207-236-0609
Ray and Marie Donner
All year

159-265-BB
27 rooms, 27 pb
Visa, MC, *Rated*, •
C-ltd/S-no/P-no/H-yes

Full breakfast
Sitting room, Jacuzzis, fireplaces, cable TV

Exquisite oceanfront lodging on seven private acres. Style and charm of a country inn, perfectly blended with the warmth of a B&B and the polished hospitality of a full-service hotel. ray@innatoceansedge.com http://www.innatoceansedge.com

---

Maine Stay Inn
22 High St 04843
207-236-9636 Fax: 207-236-0621
Bob & Juanita Topper
All year

100-190-BB
8 rooms, 8 pb
Visa, MC, AmEx, *Rated*, •
C-ltd/S-no/P-no/H-no

Full breakfast
Afternoon tea
2 parlors with fireplaces, TV room, 4 rooms with fireplace, deck

Built in 1802, the inn is situated in the high street historic district on two acres of lovely grounds only two blocks from the harbor and village center.
innkeeper@camdenmainstay.com http://www.camdenmainstay.com

CAMDEN

Swan House
49 Mountain St, Rt 52 04843
207-236-8275 Fax: 207-236-0906
800-207-8275
Lyn & Ken Kohl All year

95-160-BB
6 rooms, 6 pb
Visa, MC, *Rated*
C-ltd/S-no/P-no/H-ltd

Full country breakfast
Sitting rooms, gazebo, enclosed sunporch, mountain hiking trail

Located in a quiet neighborhood, away from busy Route 1. Short walk to Camden's beautiful harbor. hikeinn@swanhouse.com http://www.swanhouse.com

CAMDEN (REGION)

Lakeshore Inn
184 Lakeview Dr, *Rockland* 04841
207-594-4209 Fax: 207-596-6407
Joseph McCluskey/Paula Nicols All year

135-155-BB
4 rooms, 4 pb
Visa, MC, *Rated*, •
C-ltd/S-no/P-no/H-no
Greek

Full gourmet breakfast
Refreshments 3-5 PM
Sitting room, library, close to boat rentals, fishing, parasailing

Elegant c.1767 New England farmhouse. Special soaps, gels, robes. Ladies spa weekends. Close to Rockland, Schooner-lobster capital, home of Wyeth Art. Shop Camden.
info@lakeshorebb.com http://www.lakeshorebb.com

FeatherBed
705 Commercial St, *Rockport* 04856
207-596-7230 Fax: 207-596-7657
Michelle Painchaud & Ted Skowronski
All year

85-125-BB
2 rooms, 2 pb
Visa, MC, Disc, •
C-ltd/S-ltd/P-no/H-ltd

In-room continental breakfast
Home baked cookies & refreshments
Heated pool, in-room refrg., coffee, TV/VCR, whirlpool, scented toiletries

Indulge your senses! Romantic rooms, stenciled ceilings and feather beds. Private baths featuring whirlpools. Breakfast in bed. Quiet location. Ocean access. Heated pool.
chelted@midcoast.com http://www.featherbedspa.com

CAPE ELIZABETH

Inn by the Sea
40 Bowery Beach Rd 04107
207-799-3134 Fax: 207-799-4779
800-888-4287
Maureen McQuade All year

209-639-EP
43 rooms, 43 pb
Most CC, •
C-yes/S-no/P-yes/H-yes

Restaurant

Inn By The Sea is a charming coastal resort located only minutes from the historic city of Portland, Maine. The setting is spectacular. The accommodations are rated 4-Diamond by AAA. info@innbythesea.com http://www.innbythesea.com/

CASTINE

Castine Harbor Lodge
PO Box 215
147 Perkins St 04421
207-326-4335 Fax: 207-326-0900
Sara Brouillard All year

85-245-BB
16 rooms, 16 pb
Visa, MC, Disc
C-yes/S-ltd/P-yes/H-ltd

Continental plus breakfast
restaurant, bar, dock, waterviews, private baths

We have 16 guest rooms all with water-views and private baths. Our 250 feet of porches are a great place to sip a glass of wine and watch the boats go by. Come relax with us.
chl@acadia.net http://www.castinemaine.com

COREA

Black Duck Inn on Corea Harbor
PO Box 39
Crowley Island Rd 04624
207-963-2689 Fax: 207-963-7495
877-963-2689
Barry Canner & Bob Travers
All year

105-160-BB
5 rooms, 3 pb
Visa, MC, *Rated*, •
C-ltd/S-no/P-no/H-no
Danish, French

Full breakfast
Special diets catered
Sitting room, library, bicycles, hiking trails

Casual elegance, antiques and art. Overlooking working lobster harbor. Village charm with rural atmosphere. Near national park and bird sanctuary.
bduck@acadia.net http://www.blackduck.com

Brewster House, Freeport, ME

DAMARISCOTTA (REGION)

Brannon Bunker Inn
349 State Route 129, *Walpole* 04573
207-563-5941 800-563-9225
Jeanne & Joe Hovance

70-85-BB
9 rooms, 4 pb
Visa, MC, *Rated*, •
C-yes/S-no/P-no/H-ltd
All year

Continental plus breakfast
Kitchen facilities
Sitting room, porch, antique shop, 3 room suite for family

Charming rooms furnished w/antiques; close to all mid-coast recreation facilities including ocean, beach, boating, golf, antiquing. brbnkinn@lincoln.midcoast.com

EASTPORT

The Milliken House
29 Washington St 04631
207-853-2955
Bill& Mary Williams
All year

65-75-BB
5 rooms, 3 pb
Visa, MC, AmEx
C-yes/S-no/P-yes/H-no

Full breakfast
Complimentary wine
Sitting room, library, family friendly facility

Elegant accommodations in large, gracious 1846 home furnished with ornately carved Victorian marble-topped furniture.
millikenhouse@eastport-inn.com http://www.eastport-inn.com

FREEPORT

Brewster House
180 Main St 04032
207-865-4121 Fax: 207-865-4221
800-865-0822
Matt & Amy Cartmell
All year

85-150-BB
7 rooms, 7 pb
Most CC, *Rated*
C-ltd/S-no/P-no/H-ltd

Full breakfast
Snacks
Sitting room, suites, discount coupons to some area restaurants

Newly renovated 1888 Queen Anne. Family suites, full-size private bathrooms, delicious full breakfast with a variety of choices.
info@brewsterhouse.com http://www.brewsterhouse.com

Captain Briggs House
8 Maple Ave 04032
207-865-1868 Fax: 207-865-6083
888-217-2477
Rob & Celia Elberfeld
All year

75-130-BB
6 rooms, 6 pb
Visa, MC, *Rated*
C-ltd/S-no/P-no/H-no

Full breakfast
Sitting room with cable TV, VCR, books, games, or conversation

Quaint village on the sea coast of Maine. Historic 1853 Federal house with six beautiful guestrooms. Colorful garden with blooming shrubs and flowers, watch and listen to our wild birds. briggsbb@suscom-maine.net http://www.bbonline.com/me/johnbriggs

FREEPORT

Harraseeket Inn 162 Main St 04032 207-865-9377 Fax: 207-865-1684 800-342-6423 The Gray Family All year	160-375-BB 93 rooms, 93 pb Most CC, *Rated*, • C-yes/S-no/P-yes/H-yes	Full breakfast buffet 2 restaurants, afternoon tea Indoor pool, 23 fireplaces, ballroom, Tavern w/open kitchen, 7 meeting rooms

Luxury Country Inn. 84 rooms, 9 townhouses, 2 restaurants (fine dining & casual open kitchen tavern), 23 fireplaces, indoor pool. Zagat & Wine Spectator Awards of Excellence. harraseeke@aol.com http://www.stayfreeport.com

Isaac Randall House 10 Independence Dr 04032 207-865-9295 800-865-9295 Jim & Glynrose Friedlander All year	75-175-BB 12 rooms, 12 pb Most CC, *Rated*, • C-yes/S-no/P-yes/H-ltd Spanish, French	Full breakfast Snacks Sitting room, library, fireplaces, cable TV, accommodate business travelers

Quiet Federal-style 1823 farmhouse, furnished in antiques, less than a half mile from Freeports exciting business district. ikesspot@aol.com http://www.isaacrandall.com

Kendall Tavern 213 Main St 04032 207-865-1338 800-341-9572 Carrie McBride All year	85-140 7 rooms, 7 pb Visa, MC, *Rated* C-ltd/S-no/P-no/H-no	Full breakfast Sweets in the evening Two parlors with fireplaces, large front porch, all rooms with A/C

The Kendall Tavern is located on 3 acres at the north end of Freeport Village, just a short stroll to shops and restaurants and a perfect location from which to explore the coast of Maine. info@kendalltavern.com http://www.kendalltavern.com

Maple Hill B&B 18 Maple Ave 04032 207-865-3730 Fax: 207-865-6727 800-867-0478 Susie and Lloyd Lawrence All year	85-175-BB 3 rooms, 3 pb Most CC C-yes/S-no/P-yes/H-no	Full breakfast Snacks, teas Sitt. rm., bikes, tennis, cable, fireplace, hiking, shopping, beach

Historic home built in 1831. Quiet, peaceful, romantic, 2 blocks from LL Bean, scrumptious breakfasts, beautiful gardens, cozy fireplace, your home away from home.
mplhll@aol.com http://www.web-knowledge.com/maplehill

White Cedar Inn 7 Merganser Way 178 Main St 04032 207-865-9099 Fax: 207-865-6636 800-853-1269 Gwen Sartoris All year	80-140-BB 7 rooms, 7 pb Most CC, *Rated* C-ltd/S-no/P-no/H-no	Full breakfast Sitting room, picnic table, patio, all rooms have A/C

Recently restored 100-year-old home with large uncluttered antique-furnished rooms. Located just 2 blocks from L.L. Bean. capandphil@aol.com http://www.whitecedarinn.com

FREEPORT (REGION)

The Bagley House 1290 Royalsborough Rd, *Durham* 04222 207-865-6566 Fax: 207-353-5878 800-765-1772 S. O'Connor & S. Backhouse All year	115-165-BB 8 rooms, 8 pb Most CC, *Rated*, • C-yes/S-no/P-ltd/H-yes	Full breakfast Complimentary beverages, cookies Sitting room, library, cross country skiing, 6-acre yard, BBQ

Peace, tranquility & history abound in this magnificent 1772 country home. A warm welcome awaits you from us & resident dog & cat.
bglyhse@aol.com http://www.bagleyhouse.com

FRYEBURG

Admiral Peary House
9 Elm St 04037
207-935-3365 Fax: 207-935-3365
800-237-8080
Alberta Robinson, Leo Rogers & Carol Arsenault
All year

85-145-BB
7 rooms, 7 pb
Most CC, *Rated*, •
C-ltd/S-no/P-no/H-no

Full breakfast
Complimentary beverage
Sitting room, library, fireplace, tennis court, hot tub, billiards, A/C

Charming historical home in a picturesque White Mountain village. Near antique shopping and restaurants.
admpeary@nxi.com http://www.admiralpearyhouse.com

The Oxford House Inn
105 Main St
Route 302 04037
207-935-3442 Fax: 207-935-7046
800-261-7206
John & Phyllis Morris
All year

95-125-BB
4 rooms, 4 pb
Most CC, *Rated*
C-yes/S-no/P-no/H-no

Full breakfast
Dinner available, snacks
Restaurant, bar, sitting room, cable TV, conference facilities

Charming country inn/bed and breakfast with a gourmet restaurant and spectacular mountain views. Famous for the area's best dining.
innkeeper@oxfordhouseinn.com http://www.oxfordhouseinn.com

GREENVILLE

Blair Hill Inn
PO Box 1288
Lily Bay Road 04441
207-695-0224 Fax: 207-695-4324
Dan & Ruth McLaughlin
All year

200-395-BB
8 rooms, 8 pb
Most CC
C-ltd/S-no/P-no/H-no

Full Gourmet Breakfast
Fresh fruit, spring water, fine wines
Fine dining summer/fall weekends, Jacuzzi under the stars, spa services

Historic hill top estate with soaring lake and mountain views. Elegant yet casual, it is "The Diamond" of Maine's unspoiled northwoods. Outstanding cuisine, gardens, spa services, fresh air, magical! blairhill@moosehead.net http://www.blairhill.com

---

Greenville Inn
PO Box 1194
40 Norris St 04441
207-695-2206 Fax: 207-695-0335
888-695-6000
Elfi & Susie Schnetzer All year

140-255-BB
12 rooms, 12 pb
Most CC, *Rated*, •
C-ltd/S-no/P-no/H-ltd
German

Continental plus breakfast
Dinner, wine & bar
Two sitting rooms with fireplace and lake views, library, porches, gardens

A restored lumber baron's mansion with individually appointed guest rooms, suites and cottages. The inn features fireplaces, flower gardens, porches, lawns, gourmet dining, lake and mountain views. gvlinn@moosehead.net http://www.greenvilleinn.com

---

Lodge at Moosehead Lake
PO Box 1167
Upper Lily Bay Rd 04441
207-695-4400 Fax: 207-695-2281
800-825-6977
Sonda & Bruce Hamilton

225-425-BB
8 rooms, 8 pb
Most CC, *Rated*
C-ltd/S-no/P-no/H-ltd
All year

Full breakfast
Dinner available, snacks, bar
Sitting room, library, bikes, Jacuzzis, suites, fireplace, cable TV

Outdoor persons' paradise in pampered luxury. Spectacular panoramic views of lake and mountains. innkeeper@lodgeatmooseheadlake.com
http://www.lodgeatmooseheadlake.com

GUILFORD

The Trebor Mansion Inn
PO Box 722
11 A Golda Court 04443
207-876-4070 888-280-7575
The Shaffer Family All year

30-110-BB
8 rooms, 3 pb
Visa, MC, Disc, •
C-yes/S-ltd/P-ltd/H-no
German, Spanish

Dinner, afternoon tea
Sitting room, library, fireplace, 3 acre lawn, accommodate bus. travelers

Unique and mysterious hilltop mansion on three acres of gardens with mature oaks and maples overlooking the Pisquataquis River, on the National Register of Historic Places.
info@trebormansioninn.com http://www.trebormansioninn.com

HANCOCK

Le Domaine Inn & Rest.
HC 77 PO Box 496
US Route #1 04640
207-422-3395 Fax: 207-422-3252
800-554-8498

200-285-BB
7 rooms, 7 pb
Rated
Nicole L. Purslow
All year

Continental plus breakfast

A jewel of French Country charm on the coast of Maine: Deluxe Rooms & Suites, Provençal Cuisine and a Superb French Wine Cellar with over 5000 bottles.
nicole@ledomaine.com http://www.ledomaine.com

HARRINGTON

Harrington House Inn
PO Box 126
Main St 04643
207-483-4044 Fax: 207-483-2459
1-866-308-8493
Chuck & Cindy Cason

65-70-BB
5 rooms, 5 pb
Visa, MC
C-ltd/S-no/P-no/H-ltd
French, Spanish
All year

Full breakfast
Gift basket (fruit, cheese, & wine) upon request
Tidal river access, library, living area, outdoor activities

Harrington House has 5 air conditioned guestrooms with private baths. Lighted gables & gingerbread trim are a part of its charm. A full breakfast is served including fresh baked breads & fruit. harringtonbb@hotmail.com http://www.harringtonhouseinn.com

HARRISON

Greenwood Manor Inn
PO Box 551
52 Tolman Road 04040
207-583-4445 Fax: 207-583-2480
866-583-4445
All year

99-199-BB
9 rooms, 9 pb
Visa, MC, •
C-ltd/S-no/P-no/H-no
Patty Douthett & Mike Rosenbauer

Full country breakfast
Afternoon snacks
Sitting rooms, fireplaces, cable TV, canoes, gardens, walking trails, river

Romantic rooms with private baths, A/C, and some with gas fireplaces. Luxury suite with Jacuzzi, wet bar, sitting room, fireplaces. Situated on over 100 acres with extensive lawn and perennial gardens. info@greenwoodmanorinn.com
http://www.greenwoodmanorinn.com

ISLAND FALLS

Sewall House
PO Box 254
1027 Crystal Rd 04747
207-463-3428 Fax: 646-463-3429
888-235-2395
Donna Davidge

100-140-MAP
5 rooms, 1 pb
C-yes/S-no/P-yes/H-no
July 4–Columbus Day

Continental plus breakfast
Dinner, no alcohol
Sitting room, library, bicycles

Experience history of a simpler time, where Theodore Roosevelt learned healing attributes of native nature guide Bill Seavall. Now Seavall's great grand-daughter continues the tradition. info@sewallhouse.com http://www.sewallhouse.com

ISLE AU HAUT

The Keeper's House
PO Box 26
Lighthouse Road 04645
207-335-2551
Jeff & Judi Burke
May–October

294-350-AP
4 rooms
Rated
C-yes/S-no/P-no/H-no
Spanish

Full breakfast
All meals included in rate
Vegetarian dining, snacks, hiking, bicycles, ocean swimming

Operating lighthouse station on island in Acadia National Park. Tiny fishing village, spectacular natural surroundings. http://www.keepershouse.com

KENNEBUNK

The Kennebunk Inn
45 Main St 04043
207-985-3351 Fax: 207-985-8865
John & Kristen Martin
All year

75-165-BB
27 rooms, 27 pb
Most CC, *Rated*, •
C-yes/S-ltd/P-yes/H-yes
French, Italian

Continental breakfast
4* restaurant, garden patio dining, quaint pub
Fireside reception, TV & game rm, A/C, garden patio

Gracious inn located in the heart of charming Kennebunk. Individually -appointed guest rooms, 4 restaurant, quaint pub, garden patio, & warm hospitality await you at The Kennebunk Inn.* info@thekennebunkinn.com http://www.thekennebunkinn.com

KENNEBUNK (REGION)

Arundel Meadows Inn
PO Box 1129, Kennebunk, ME 04043
Rte 1, *Arundel* 04046
207-985-3770 Fax: 207-967-4704
Mark Bachelder, Murray Yaeger
All year

95-150-BB
7 rooms, 7 pb
Visa, MC, *Rated*, •
C-ltd/S-no/P-no/H-ltd

Full breakfast
Library, sitting room, ocean swimming, Barney the cat, hot tub, small pool

Rooms individually decorated with art, antiques. Some with fireplaces; all with private baths. bach12@adelphia.com http://www.arundelmeadowsinn.com

KENNEBUNK BEACH

The Ocean View
171 Beach Ave 04043
207-967-2750 Fax: 207-967-5418
Carole & Bob Arena
April-mid Dec.

150-350-BB
9 rooms, 9 pb
Most CC, *Rated*
C-ltd/S-no/P-no/H-no
French

Full breakfast
Late afternoon refreshments
Living room, library, TV room, exclusive boutique, concierge service

"The closest you'll find to a bed on the beach." An intimate oceanfront Inn. Immaculate and sparkling. A jewel of distinct quality.
arena@theoceanview.com http://www.theoceanview.com

KENNEBUNKPORT

1802 House
PO Box 646-A
15 Locke St 04046
207-967-5632 Fax: 207-967-0780
800-932-5632
Edric & Mary Ellen Mason
All year

169-389-BB
6 rooms, 6 pb
Most CC, *Rated*
C-ltd/S-no/P-no/H-ltd

Full country gourmet breakfast
Homemade cookies, coffee, tea, lemonade

Tucked away, along the fifteenth fairway of the Cape Arundel Golf Club, in the quaint seaside village of Kennebunkport, Maine, the 1802 House B&B is a nineteenth century inn for all seasons. inquiry@1802inn.com http://www.1802inn.com

---

The Beach House Inn
211 Beach Avenue 04046
207-967-3850 Fax: 207-967-4719
Maureen Violette
All year

190-295-BB
34 rooms, 34 pb
Visa, MC, AmEx, *Rated*, •
C-ltd/S-no/P-no/H-yes
French

Continental plus breakfast
Afternoon tea (winter)
Sitting room, whirlpool tubs, beach & ocean views

On Kennebunkport beach. Country Victorian antiques, beautiful ocean views. An elevator for your convenience. innkeeper@beachhseinn.com http://www.beachhseinn.com

---

Bufflehead Cove
PO Box 499
Gornitz Lane 04046
207-967-3879 Fax: 207-967-3879
Harriet a&Jim Gott
May through Oct.

155-350-BB
6 rooms, 6 pb
Visa, MC, Disc, *Rated*
C-ltd/S-no/P-ltd/H-no
Spanish

Full breakfast
Tea, hot chocolate, wine, snacks
Whirlpool tubs, dock and rowboats, water views, fireplaces, gardens,6 acres

Hidden away in the woods on a bank of the Kennebunkport tidal river, Bufflehead Cove offers peace, privacy and pampering in a beautiful setting.
info@buffleheadcove.com http://www.buffleheadcove.com

Captain Fairfield Inn
PO Box 2690
Pleasant & Green St 04046
207-967-4454 Fax: 207-967-8537
800-322-1928
Janet & Rick Wolf
Season Inquire

110-295-BB
9 rooms, 9 pb
Most CC, *Rated*
C-yes/S-no/P-no/H-no

Full four-course gourmet breakfast
Afternoon tea & sweets
Sitting room, music room w/piano, library, gardens, beach, boats

Romantic, historic inn, elegant rooms w/private baths, fireplaces, bounteous gourmet breakfasts. Exceptionally warm hospitality. Near village, shopping, beaches, galleries, restaurants. jrw@captainfairfield.com http://www.captainfairfield.com

KENNEBUNKPORT

Captain Jefferds Inn
PO Box 691
5 Pearl St 04046
207-967-2311 Fax: 207-967-0721
800-839-6844
Pat & Dick Bartholomew
April-Dec.

165-350-BB
16 rooms, 16 pb
Visa, MC, *Rated*, •
C-ltd/S-no/P-yes/H-yes

Full breakfast
Afternoon tea
Library, garden, breakfast on terrace, suites, sitting room, whirlpool tubs

Especially beautiful, quiet, private. In "House Beautiful" and "Country Living" 12/92. Completely redecorated. captjeff@captainjeffersinn.com http://www.captainjefferdsinn.com

---

Captain Lord Mansion
PO Box 800
6 Pleasant St 04046
207-967-3141 Fax: 207-967-3172
Bev Davis & Rick Litchfield
All year

199-449-BB
16 rooms, 16 pb
Most CC, *Rated*, •
C-ltd/S-no/P-no/H-no

Full 3-course breakfast
Afternoon tea, sweets
Accessories in bathrooms, sitting room, piano, A/C, beach towels, umbrellas

An unforgettable, romantic experience is your reward when you reserve one of the 16 large, beautifully-appointed, guestrooms at the Captain Lord Mansion.
innkeeper@captainlord.com http://www.captainlord.com

Crosstrees
PO Box 1333
6 South St 04046
207-967-2780 Fax: 209-967-2610
800-564-1527
Merle & John Hoover
Closed March

120-250-BB
4 rooms, 4 pb
Visa, MC, *Rated*
C-ltd/S-no/P-no/H-no

Full gourmet breakfast
Complimentary wine, beverages
Sitting room, porch, lawn, A/C, 4 rooms with fireplaces, warm, inviting rooms

Crosstrees provides casually elegant lodging—four romantic, charming guestrooms. Beds are either king or queen; rooms are light and airy, awash in sunlight with fireplaces and en suite baths. info@crosstrees.com http://www.crosstrees.com

---

English Meadows Inn
141 Port Rd 04043
207-967-5766 800-272-0698
Pete & Kathy Smith All year

90-170-BB
12 rooms, 10 pb
Visa, MC, AmEx
C-ltd/S-no/P-no/H-ltd

Full breakfast
Afternoon beverage and snack, Evening candies
Library, garden with patio, beach parking pass

Attractive 1860's Victorian Farmhouse on a lovely knoll in Kennebunkport. The English Meadows Inn, adorned with all of its classic Victorian style inside and out, exudes a warm and homely feeling. eminn@adelphia.net http://www.englishmeadowsinn.com

---

Inn at Harbor Head
41 Pier Rd 04046
207-967-5564
Fax: 207-967-1294
Eve & Dick Roesler
February–December

130-330-BB
5 rooms, 5 pb
Visa, MC, *Rated*
C-ltd/S-no/P-no/H-no

Full gourmet breakfast
Afternoon tea, wine
Sitting room, library, Jacuzzis, suites, fireplace

Nestled on a rocky knoll on Cape Porpoise Harbor, this romantic inn is a base for your visit to historic Kennebunkport & surrounding area.
harborhead@cybertours.com http://www.harborhead.com

Inn on South Street
PO Box 529A
5 South St 04046
207-967-5151
Fax: 207-967-4385
800-963-5151
Tom & Patti
All year

105-250-BB
4 rooms, 4 pb
Visa, MC, *Rated*
C-ltd/S-ltd/P-no/H-no

Full breakfast
Afternoon tea and lemonade served with cookies
Air conditioning, cable TV, refrigerators; suite has whirlpool tub

Attractive, spacious rooms with traditional furnishings. This Bed and Breakfast is on a quiet historical street, yet 5 blocks to the village with shopping, whale watching, sailing and dining. innkeeper@innonsouthst.com http://www.innonsouthst.com

Inn on South Street, Kennebunkport, ME

KENNEBUNKPORT

The Kennebunkport Inn
PO Box 111
One Dock Square 04046
207-967-2621
Fax: 207-967-3705
800-248-2621
Debra Lennon & Tom Nill
All year

89-299-EP
34 rooms, 34 pb
Visa, MC, AmEx,
Rated, •
C-yes/P-no/H-yes
French

Continental breakfast (Nov–Apr) fee
Cont. plus breakfast May–Oct-fee
Pub, restaurant, pool, color TV, phones, golf, tennis, whirlpools, fireplace

Country inn, in old sea captain's home. All rooms with private baths. Gourmet patio dining, turn-of-the-century bar, piano bar.

stay@kennebunkportinn.com http://www.kennebunkportinn.com

Kilburn House
PO Box 424
6 Chestnut St 04046
207-967-4262 Fax: 207-967-1065
877-710-4762
Rose Mary & Arthur Wyman
All year

110-325-BB
4 rooms, 4 pb
Visa, MC, *Rated*
C-ltd/S-no/P-no/H-no

Full gourmet breakfast
Tea, snacks, fruit basket
Lovely sitting and reading rooms

Steps away from Kennebunkport's historical Dock Square village, this peaceful turn-of-the-century Victorian offers all the comforts of home without the responsibilities.

info@kilburnhouse.com http://www.kilburnhouse.com

Lake Brook
PO Box 762
57 Western Ave (Lower Village) Rte 9 04046
207-967-4069
Carolyn A. McAdams.

90-130-BB
4 rooms, 4 pb
Visa, MC, *Rated*, •
C-ltd/S-no/P-no/H-no
Spanish
Late April thru Feb

Full breakfast
Golf, tennis nearby, just 1/2 mile from, downtown Kennebunkport

A charming turn-of-the-century home located on the edge of a salt marsh and tidal moor. All rooms have private baths and ceiling fans.

carolyn@lakebrookbb.com http://www.lakebrookbb.com

KENNEBUNKPORT

Maine Stay Inn & Cottages
PO Box 500 A
34 Maine St 04046
207-967-2117 Fax: 207-967-8757
800-950-2117
George & Janice Yankowski
All year

105-275-BB
17 rooms, 17 pb
Visa, MC, AmEx,
Rated, •
C-yes/S-no/P-no/H-no

Full breakfast
Afternoon tea, snacks
Sitting room, swing set, garden, porch, 9 rooms with fireplaces

Elegant bed & breakfast inn located in Kennebunkport's Historic District. Walk to shops, galleries, restaurants and harbor. Noted for exceptional hospitality, great breakfasts and romantic cottages. lindsay@innvisibility.com http://www.mainestayinn.com

---

Old Fort Inn
PO Box M
8 Old Fort Ave 04046
207-967-5353 Fax: 207-967-4547
800-828-3678
David & Sheila Aldrich
Season–Inquire

160-390-BB
16 rooms, 16 pb
Visa, MC, AmEx,
Rated, •
C-ltd/S-no/P-no/H-no

Full breakfast
Cable TV, phone in room, tennis, pool, Jacuzzis, A/C, some fireplaces

A luxurious resort in a secluded, charming setting. The inn has yesterday's charm with today's conveniences. info@oldfortinn.com http://www.oldfortinn.com

---

Shorelands Guest Resort
PO Box 769
247 Western Ave, Rt 9, 04046
207-985-4460 800-99-BEACH
Sonja Haag Ducharme & Family April–Oct.

49-165
30 rooms, 30 pb
Most CC, •
C-yes/S-ltd/P-yes/H-yes
French, German

Continental breakfast
Afternoon tea
Sitting room, library, bikes, Jacuzzis, pool, suites, cable TV, gas grills

A typical Maine country cottage resort, far from noise and congestion. Lawn & flower areas for relaxing, a short walk to secluded, sandy beach.
idlease@cybertours.com http://www.shorelands.com

The Welby Inn
PO Box 774
92 Ocean Ave 04046
207-967-4655 Fax: 207-967-8654
800-773-4085
Christopher Farr All year

99-165-BB
7 rooms, 7 pb
Visa, MC, Disc, *Rated*, •
C-ltd/S-no/P-no/H-no

Full breakfast
Eve. homemade Amaretto, afternoon tea
Guest pantry, large, welcoming living room, 5 queen, 2 full beds

Gracious turn-of-the-century home in historic Kennebunkport. Walk to beach, marina and shops. Deep-sea fishing and harbor cruises available.
innkeeper@welbyinn.com http://www.welbyinn.com

MONHEGAN ISLAND

Island Inn
PO Box 128
1 Ocean Ave 04852
207-596-0371 Fax: 207-594-5517
Krista Lisajus
Memorial Day–Columbus Day

105-295-BB
33 rooms, 23 pb
Visa, MC, *Rated*, •
C-yes/S-no/P-yes/H-no

Full breakfast
Afternoon tea, restaurant
Lunch, dinner (fee), Barnacle coffee house, sitting room, library

A turn-of-the-century summer hotel overlooking Monhegan Harbor and the ocean. Relax on the porch & admire the setting sun as it displays its glorious colors in front of you.
islandin@midcoast.com http://www.islandinnmonhegan.com

NAPLES

Inn at Long Lake
PO Box 806
Lake House Rd 04055
207-693-6226 Fax: 207-693-6226
800-437-0328
Buddy Marcum & Todd Fuja
All year

99-180-BB
16 rooms, 16 pb
Visa, MC, Disc, *Rated*, •
C-ltd/S-no/P-no/H-no

Full country breakfast
Complimentary coffee/tea/hot cocoa
Sitting room, library, great room with fireplace

A charming Victorian inn nestled by Long Lake offering a cozy, relaxed atmosphere and Maine hospitality at its best! info@innatlonglake.com http://www.innatlonglake.com

NEW HARBOR

The Bradley Inn
3063 Bristol Rd 04554
207-677-3367 Fax: 207-677-3367
800-942-5560
Warren & Beth Busteed
All year

145-250-BB
16 rooms, 16 pb
Most CC, *Rated*, •
C-yes/S-no/P-no/H-no

Full breakfast
Dinner, afternoon tea, restaurant, bar service
Sitting room, library, bicycles

A coastal destination, a moment's walk from the Pemaquin Lighthouse. Lovely rooms and award-winning restaurant. bradley@lincoln.midcoast.com http://bradleyinn.com

---

Gosnold Arms
146 State Route 32 04554
207-677-3727 Fax: 207-677-2662
The Phinney Family
Mid-May to Oct.

89-165-BB
26 rooms, 26 pb
Visa, MC, *Rated*
C-yes/S-ltd/P-no/H-ltd

Full breakfast
Sitting room, wharf, cable TV available in some rooms & cottages

Charming country inn & cottages, most with harbor or ocean views. Located on the Pemaquid Peninsula, in a true Maine working harbor. The wharf is an ideal spot to view the activities of the harbor. info@gosnold.com http://www.gosnold.com

NOBLEBORO

Mill Pond Inn
50 Main St 04555
207-563-8014
Bobby & Sherry Whear
All year

125-BB
6 rooms, 6 pb
C-ltd/S-ltd/P-no

Full breakfast

On a pond tucked away in the antique village of Damariscotta Mills is the Mill Pond Inn.
http://www.millpondinn.com

NORRIDGEWOCK

Norridgewock Colonial Inn
PO Box 932
15 Upper Main St 04957
207-634-3470
Nancy & Lincoln Fickett
All year

85-95-BB
3 rooms, 3 pb
C-yes/S-no/P-ltd/H-no

Full breakfast
Afternoon tea
Sitting room, fireplaces, cable TV

Lovely Victorian Inn. Cozy and friendly atmosphere always present. Full breakfast in a beautifully decorated area.

OCEAN PARK

Nautilus By The Sea
PO Box 7276
2 Colby Ave 04063
207-934-2021 Fax: 207-934-2022
800-981-7018
Dick & Patte Kessler
All year

50-160-BB
13 rooms, 9 pb
Most CC
C-yes/S-no/P-no/H-no

Continental plus breakfast
Guest living room with cable TV/VCR

The Nautilus By The Sea has 13 rooms, suites, or apartments, with our continental plus breakfast served on the dune front enclosed porch.
info@nautilusbythesea.com http://nautilusbythesea.com

OGUNQUIT

The Admiral's Inn
PO Box 2241
#79 US Rt I South Main St 03907
207-646-7093 Fax: 207-646-5241
888-263-6318
David Mills
All year

49-130-BB
16 rooms, 10 pb
Most CC, *Rated*
C-no/S-ltd/P-no/H-no

Continental breakfast
Lunch and dinner available, restaurant & bar
Sitting room, Jacuzzi, swimming pool, cable TV

Heritage Inn, premier accommodations, casual fine dining, intimate cocktail lounge.
office@theadmiralsinn.com http://www.theadmiralsinn.com

OGUNQUIT

Distant Sands
PO Box 148
632 Main St 03907
207-646-8686
John Stand & Steve Wilkos
All year

95-195-BB
6 rooms, 5 pb
Visa, MC, Disc, *Rated*
C-ltd/S-no/P-no/H-no

Full breakfast

Romantic six-bedroom B&B decorated with artwork and antiques. Enjoy full gourmet breakfast surrounded by lush flower gardens. Relax in the backyard patio overlooking the Ogunquit River. innkeeper@distantsands.com http://www.distantsands.com

---

Gorges Grant Hotel
PO Box 2240 239 Route 1
03907
207-646-7003 Fax: 207-646-0660
800-646-5001
Karen and Bob Hanson
All year

81-176-BB
81 rooms, 81 pb
Rated
C-yes/S-no/P-no/H-yes

Full breakfast
Restaurant, bar
Hot tub, fitness room, indoor & outdoor pool

Elegant, small, modern hotel operated with an inn flavor.
gorgesgrant@ogunquit.com http://www.ogunquit.com/gorgesgrant/index.html

---

Morning Dove
PO Box 1940
13 Bourne Lane 03907
207-646-3891
Jane and Fred Garland
All year

90-150-BB
7 rooms, 5 pb
Visa, MC
C-ltd/S-no/P-no/H-no

Full breakfast
Victorian front porch, fireplaced gathering room, country gardens with pond

An intimate bed and breakfast offering year round accommodations in the heart of Ogunquit.
info@themorningdove.com http://www.themorningdove.com

The Nellie Littlefield House
PO Box 1599
27 Shore Rd 03907
207-646-1692 Fax: 207-361-1206
Eric & Maria Haselton
May-October

150-210-BB
8 rooms, 8 pb
Visa, MC, Disc, *Rated*
S-no/P-no/H-ltd
German

Full breakfast
Snacks
Sitting room, library, cable TV, exercise room

Spectacular 1889 three-story grand Victorian house on Shore Road was built by J. H. Littlefield for his wife, Nellie.
fhaselt@aol.com http://www.visit-maine.com/nellielittlefieldhouse/

Puffin Inn
PO Box 2232
433 Main St 03907
207-646-5496 Fax: 207-646-1449
Lee & Maurice Williams
April-October 25

75-145-BB
10 rooms, 10 pb
Visa, MC, *Rated*
C-ltd/S-ltd/P-no/H-ltd
French

Generous homemade buffet breakfast

A charming country inn by the sea, offering a peaceful and relaxed atmosphere.
puffin@maine.rr.com http://www.puffininn.com

Rockmere Lodge
PO Box 278
150 Stearns Rd 03907
207-646-2985 Fax: 207-646-6947
Andy Antoniuk & Bob Brown
All year

100-200-BB
8 rooms, 8 pb
Visa, MC, *Rated*
C-ltd/S-no/P-no/H-no

Continental plus breakfast
Afternoon tea, complimentary wine
Sitting room, library, beach chairs, cool drinks for beach

Seaside, shingled cottage in out-of-the-way location. Very quiet. Listen to the ocean and relax. Walking distance to everything.
info@rockmere.com http://www.rockmere.com

OGUNQUIT

The Trellis House
PO Box 2229
10 Beachmere Place 03907
207-646-7909 800-681-7909
Pat & Jerry Houlihan
All year

115-185-BB
8 rooms, 8 pb
Visa, MC
C-ltd/S-no/P-no/H-no

Full breakfast
Afternoon beverages
Sitting room, porches, ocean views, trolley stop

A year-round inn close to all that is special to Ogunquit. Furnished with an eclectic blend of antiques, coupled with some ocean views and quiet surroundings.
trellishouse@cybertours.com http://www.trellishouse.com

The West Highland Inn
PO Box 1667
14 Shore Rd 03907
207-646-2181
Linda & Steve William/Westies
All year

75-150-BB
11 rooms, 9 pb
Visa, MC
C-ltd/S-no/P-ltd

Full breakfast
Complimentary wine and cheese Saturday afternoons

The West Highland Inn is an Island of Serenity in a New England village setting, in the heart of Ogunquit, close to everything it has to offer.
westhigh@cybertours.com http://www.westhighlandinn.com

OLD ORCHARD BEACH

Atlantic Birches Inn
20 Portland Ave 04064
207-934-5295 Fax: 207-934-3781
888-934-5295
Ray and Kim DeLeo
All year

69-135-BB
10 rooms, 10 pb
Most CC, *Rated*
C-yes/S-no/P-no/H-ltd

Continental Plus
Teas, coffee, cider, hot chocolate
Sitting rooms, heated outdoor pool, TV's, A/C , wraparound porch

The Atlantic Birches is an elegant yet casual Inn in Old Orchard Beach. It is comprised of two buildings, the Victorian Main House built in 1903, and the 1920's bungalow called The Cottage. info@atlanticbirches.com http://www.atlanticbirches.com

POLAND

Wolf Cove Inn
5 Jordan Shore Dr 04274
207-998-4976 Fax: 207-998-7049
Rose Aikman
All year

73-250-BB
10 rooms, 8 pb
Visa, MC, AmEx, •
C-ltd/S-no/P-no/H-ltd

Full breakfast
Afternoon tea
Sitting room, Jacuzzis, suites, fireplaces, cable TV, accom. bus. travelers

Romantic, elegant country inn with spectacular lake view and setting; full breakfast is served in the Grand Room or Glassed-in Porch.
wolfcove@exploremaine.com http://www.wolfcoveinn.com

POLAND SPRINGS

Country Abundance
509 White Oak Hill Rd 04274
207-998-2132
Mary & Francis Bauer
All year

80-90-BB
3 rooms, 3 pb
Visa, MC, *Rated*, •
C-yes/S-ltd/P-ltd/H-ltd

Full breakfast
Afternoon tea, snacks
Sitting rm, library, cable TV, bikes; lake on property, canoes, inner tubes

Quaint 1870's country home centrally located in the western mountain, close to skiing. Enjoy a short walk through giant Maine pines to Tripp Lake.
info@countryabundance.com http://www.countryabundance.com

PORTLAND

Andrews on Auburn
417 Auburn St 04103
207-797-9157 Fax: 207-797-9040
Elizabeth
All year

99-185-BB
5 rooms, 5 pb
Most CC, *Rated*
C-ltd/S-no/P-yes/H-no

Full breakfast
Snacks, guest kitchen
Sitting room, library, whirlpool in suite, deck, solarium

Formerly Andrews Lodging, Andrews on Auburn offers New England charm for all seasons. Five guestrooms, each/private bath come complete w/antiques, quilts & cozy comforter for our chilly Maine nights. dandrew2@maine.rr.com http://www.andrewsonauburn.com

PORTLAND

Inn at St. John
939 Congress St 04102
207-773-6481 Fax: 207-756-7629
800-636-9127
Paul Hood
All year

45-190-BB
36 rooms, 20 pb
Visa, MC, Disc, *Rated*,
•
C-yes/S-yes/P-yes/H-yes

Continental breakfast
Family friendly

A most unique 100 year-old Inn noted for its European charm and quiet gentility. Tastefully decorated with traditional and antique furnishings.
theinn@maine.rr.com http://www.innatstjohn.com

Percy Inn
15 Pine St 04102
207-871-POET Fax: 207 775-2599
888-41-PERCY
Dale Northrup, CTC
All year

89-269-BB
10 rooms, 10 pb
Visa, MC, *Rated*, •
C-ltd/S-no/P-no/H-no

Continental plus breakfast
24 hour pantry with comp snacks, soft drinks
Parlor with 400 movies and CDs, pantry, bricked garden courtyard, sundeck.

Hotel critic Dale Northrup delivers sumptuous romance in this 1830 Federal brick row-house at Longfellow Sq., in the Historic District. Amenity-rich rooms complement the artistic landmark neighborhood. innkeeper@percyinn.com http://www.percyinn.com

---

Victorian Terrace
84 Eastern Promenade 04101
207-774-9083 Fax: 207-775-0530
888-393-9083
Eva Horton
All year

150-250-EP
17 rooms, 17 pb
Visa, MC, AmEx, *Rated*
C-yes/S-no/P-ltd/H-no
Norwegian

Sitting room, suites, fireplace, cable TV

Our three turn-of-the-century Victorian buildings house our fully furnished luxury apartments and rooms. evahorton@earthlink.net http://www.victorianterrace.com

---

West End Inn
146 Pine St 04102
207-772-1377 Fax: 207-828-0984
800-338-1377
Rosa & Nicholas Higgins
All year

99-225-BB
6 rooms, 6 pb
Most CC, *Rated*
C-yes/S-no/P-no/H-no

Full breakfast
Afternoon tea, snacks
Cable TV, remodeled & redecorated, old port, dining, museum

Very comfortable, relaxing home atmosphere in the heart of the city in historical district. Art Museum, theaters and Old Port within walking distance.
westendbb@aol.com http://www.Westendbb.com

Enchanted Nights
29 Wentworth St
Scenic Coastal Rte 103, *Kittery* 03904
207-439-1489
Peter Lamardia
All year

50-275-BB
8 rooms, 7 pb
Most CC, *Rated*, •
C-yes/S-ltd/P-yes/H-yes

Full or continental breakfast
Sitting room, family friendly facility, bikes, tennis, sauna

Victorian/Country French. Whimsical, colorful, fanciful. Whirlpool for 2 in 3 rooms, elegant breakfasts. info@enchanted-nights-bandb.com http://www.enchanted-nights-bandb.com

---

Inn at Portsmouth Harbor
6 Water St, *Kittery* 03904
207-439-4040 Fax: 207-438-9286
Tim & Paula Miller
All year

85-195-BB
6 rooms, 6 pb
Visa, MC, *Rated*, •
S-no/P-no/H-ltd
French

Full breakfast
Sitting room, games, porch, patio, garden

Comfortable brick Victorian with beautifully appointed rooms, water views, stroll to historic Portsmouth. Recommended by NY Times.
info@innatportsmouth.com http://www.innatportsmouth.com

1794 Watchtide by the Sea, Searsport, ME

ROCKLAND

Old Granite Inn
546 Main St 04841
207-594-9036 800-386-9036
Ragan & John Cary
All year

130-160-BB
11 rooms, 9 pb
Visa, MC, Disc, *Rated*, •
C-ltd/S-no/P-no/H-yes

Bountiful full breakfast
Sitting room, library, garden, piano

Comfortable historic inn overlooking a busy harbor filled with boats.
ogi@midcoast.com http://www.oldgraniteinn.com

S. WATERFORD

Bear Mountain Inn
R.R. 35 37 04081
207-583-4404 Fax: 207-583-4404
Lorraine Blais All year

90-275-BB
10 rooms, 6 pb
•

Full breakfast

Bear Mountain Inn is nestled on 52 acres of country charm. Location is in Western ME between the lakes & mountains. Bear Mountain Inn's property includes 3 acres of private beachfront on Bear Lake. bearmtin@megalink.net http://www.bearmtninn.com

SACO

Crown 'N' Anchor Inn
PO Box 228
121 North St 04072
207-282-3829 Fax: 207-282-7495
800-561-8865
John Barclay, Martha Forester

65-120-BB
6 rooms, 6 pb
Most CC, *Rated*, •
C-ltd/S-no/P-ltd/H-ltd
French
All year

Full breakfast
Afternoon tea
Sitting room, library, fireplaces, cable TV, conference facilities

The Inn is a National Historic Register House situated on 3 acres in the heart of Saco Historic District. Rooms are antique furnished and the Inn is close to many beaches.
cna@gwi.net

SEARSPORT

1794 Watchtide by the Sea
190 W Main St 04974
207-548-6575 Fax: 207-548-0938
800-698-6575
Nancy-Linn Nellis &
Jack Elliott

105-185-BB
6 rooms, 5 pb
Visa, MC, Disc, •
C-ltd/S-no/P-no/H-no
French
All year

Full gourmet breakfast, afternoon refreshments
60' sunporch; guest lounge w/lg. screen TV, game table, library, sitting rm.

18th century Historic Register inn features 60' all season sunporch where scrumptious breakfasts are served overlooking Penobscot Bay. Upscale, National Register, seaside inn.
stay@watchtide.com http://www.watchtide.com

Homeport Inn
PO Box 647
121 E Main St, Rte 1 04974
207-548-2259 Fax: 207-548-2259
800-742-5814
George & Edith Johnson
All year

75-125-BB
7 rooms, 7 pb
Most CC, *Rated*, •
C-ltd/S-ltd/P-no/H-yes

Full breakfast
Soda fountain, garden, antique shop, ocean view, bicycles, golf, tennis

On Historic Register. Ideal mid-coast location for an extended stay on coast of Maine. Victorian cottage available by the week.
hportinn@acadia.net http://www.bnbcity.com/inns/20015

SEARSPORT

Inn Britannia
132 W Main St 04974
207-548-2007 Fax: 207-548-2006
866-Inn-Brit
Caren & Susan
All year

70-200-BB
8 rooms, 8 pb
Visa, MC, Disc
C-yes/S-no/P-ltd/H-no
Slight French

Multi-course gourmet breakfast
Homemade cookies in a "bottomless" fox cookie jar
TV/VCR, beach towels, hair dryer, toiletries, refrigerator, binoculars

Nestled on 5 acres with beautiful gardens and a peek at the ocean, Inn Britannia offers comfortable elegance and memorable breakfasts in the English tradition of fine lodging!
info@innbritannia.com http://www.innbritannia.com

SEBASCO ESTATES

Rock Gardens Inn
PO Box 178
Route 217 04565
207-389-1339 Fax: 207-389-9112
Ona Barnet June-Sept

200-300-MAP
13 rooms, 13 pb
Rated
C-yes/S-ltd/P-no/H-ltd

Full breakfast
Picnic lunch, dinner
Sitting room, library, tennis court and bicycles nearby, swimming pool

Maine style cottages on private peninsula facing Casco Bay. New England breakfast and dinner daily, lobster cookouts weekly. http://www.rockgardensinn.com

SORRENTO

Bass Cove Farm
312 Eastside Rd 04677
207-422-3564 Fax: 207-422-3564
Mary Solet & Michael Tansey
All year

50-85-BB
3 rooms, 1 pb
Visa, MC
C-ltd/S-no/P-ltd

Full breakfast
Library, porch, gardens, sitting room

Coastal Maine farmhouse in active summer colony. Convenient to Acadia National Park. Comfortable beds, delicious breakfast. Explore, shop, relax.
basscove@downeast.net http://www.basscovefarm.com

SOUTHPORT (REGION)

Lawnmeer Inn & Restaurant
PO Box 505
65 Hendricks Hill Road, *West Boothbay Harbor* 04576
207-633-2544 800-633-7645
Lee & Jim Metzger

100-200-EP
32 rooms, 32 pb
Visa, MC, *Rated*, •
C-ltd/S-no/P-ltd/H-ltd
May–Oct.

Full breakfast
Breakfast and dinner available
Restaurant, bar, sitting room, complimentary coffee

Handsome 1898 Maine Country Inn & modern annex located on 3 attractive acres of lawn descending to oceanfront. cooncat@lawnmeerinn.com http://www.lawnmeerinn.com

SOUTHWEST HARBOR

The Inn at Southwest
PO Box 593
371 Main St 04679
207-244-3835 Fax: 207-244-9879
Sandy Johnson & Andrea Potapovs May–November

75-185-BB
7 rooms, 7 pb
Visa, MC, *Rated*
C-ltd/S-ltd/P-no/H-no

Full breakfast
Afternoon tea & cookies

Overlooking the serene waters of Southwest Harbor, the Inn at Southwest combines Victorian charm and gracious hospitality. The inn is within walking distance of restaurants, shopping, and the marina. innatsw@acadia.net http://www.innatsouthwest.com

---

Island Watch
73 Freeman Ridge 04679
207-244-7229
Maxine Clark
All year

85-BB
6 rooms, 4 pb
Rated

Full breakfast

Island Watch offers a panoramic view of Maine mountains, islands, and the sea at Southwest Harbor, a year-round fishing village.
mmclark@prexar.com

SOUTHWEST HARBOR

The Kingsleigh Inn 1904 PO Box 1426 373 Main St 04679 207-244-5302 Fax: 207-244-7691 Ken & Cyd Collins All year	75-220-BB 8 rooms, 8 pb Visa, MC, *Rated* C-ltd/S-no/P-no/H-ltd	Full candlelight breakfast Afternoon Homebaked 'Treats,' refreshments Living room with working fireplace, wicker filled wrap-around porch, library

Overlooking picturesque Southwest Harbor. Full gourmet breakfast, rooms with harbor views, private balconies, private baths, secluded 3-room turret suite w/fireplace.
relax@kingsleighinn.com http://www.kingsleighinn.com

Lindenwood Inn PO Box 1328 118 Clark Point Rd. 04679 207-244-5335 800-307-5335 James King All year	95-295-BB 9 rooms, 9 pb S-ltd/P-no	

Built in 1904 as a sea captain's home, the Inn derives its name from the graceful linden trees that line the front lawn. lindenwood@acadia.net http://www.lindenwoodinn.com

Penury Hall 374 Main St 04679 207-244-7102 Fax: 207-244-5651 Toby & Gretchen Strong All year	80-105-BB 3 rooms, 3 pb *Rated* C-ltd/S-no/P-no/H-no	Full breakfast Complimentary wine, coffee, tea Sitting room, sauna, picnic day sails, canoeing

Comfortable rambling Maine home for us and our guests. Decor reflects hosts' interests in art, antiques, books, gardening, sailing.
tstrong@penuryhall.com http://www.penuryhall.com

SPRUCE HEAD

Craignair Inn 5 Third St 533 Clark Island Rd 04859 207-594-7644 Fax: 207-596-7124 800-320-9997 Neva & Steve Joseph All year	54-130-BB 21 rooms, 12 pb Visa, MC, AmEx, *Rated*, • C-yes/S-no/P-yes/H-no	Full breakfast Restaurant, coffee, tea Full liquor service, library, flower garden, coastal activities

Area alive with history of quarrying days. Extensive hiking. Delightful swimming in abandoned granite quarry. innkeeper@craignair.com http://www.craignair.com

VINALHAVEN

Payne Homestead @ Moses Webster House PO Box 216 Atlantic Avenue 04863 207-863-9963 Fax: 207-863-2295 888-863-9963 Lee & Donna Payne All year	90-145-BB 4 rooms C-yes/S-ltd/P-no/H-yes	Full breakfast Sitting room, cable TV, game room with video collection for children

Step back in time and experience life as it ought to be . . . non-commercial and uncluttered. A wonderful combination of Victorianna and family comfort.
payne@foxislands.net http://www.paynehomestead.com

WALDOBORO

Broad Bay Inn & Gallery PO Box 607 1014 Main Street 04572 207-832-6668 800-736-6769 Libby Hopkins All year	75-85-BB 5 rooms, 3 pb Visa, MC, • C-ltd/S-no/P-no/H-no French	Full gourmet breakfast Wine Library, cable TV, conference facilities

Center of small quiet village mid-coast gives easy access to most of the interesting areas of Maine. brdbayin@midcoast.com http://www.broadbayinn.com

The Roaring Lion, Waldoboro, ME

WALDOBORO

The Roaring Lion	80-90-BB	Full breakfast
995 Main St 04572	4 rooms, 1 pb	Afternoon tea
207-832-4038 Fax: 207-832-7892	•	Sitting room, library,
Bill & Robin Branigan	C-yes/S-no/P-no/H-no	fireplaces, cable TV, accom.
All year		bus. travelers

1905 Victorian with screened-in porch on two acres of lawn and gardens in small, quiet village in mid-coast Maine. Book store on premises.
innkeeper@roaringlion.com http://www.roaringlion.com

WATERFORD

Kedarburn Inn	75-130-BB
Route 35, Box 61	7 rooms, 3 pb
Valley Rd. 04088	
207-583-6182 Fax: 207-583-6424	
Margaret & Derek Gibson	
All year	

Beautiful white frame house, built in 1858, set beside Kedar Brook in historic Waterford Village. kedarburn@cybertours.com http://www.members.aol.com/kedar01

Lake House	115-170-BB	Full breakfast
PO Box 82	7 rooms, 7 pb	Dinner, snacks, restaurant
686 Waterford Rd 04088	Most CC, •	Sitting room, suites
207-583-4182 Fax: 207-583-2831	C-ltd/S-no/P-no/H-ltd	
800-223-4182	Spanish	
Michale & Doreen Myers		
All year		

Built in the 1790's, on the National Register of Historic Places; located on the Village Green. 7 wonderfully restored guestrooms.
info@lakehousemaine.com http://www.lakehousemaine.com

WISCASSET

Squire Tarbox Inn	
1181 Main Rd	11 rooms, 11 pb
Westsport Island 04578	Most CC, *Rated*, •
207-882-7693	C-ltd/S-ltd/P-no/H-no
Mid May to Late October	

.". pastoral setting . . . while the guests find comfort at the Inn, the goats luxuriate in their own three-star accommodations." Bostonia Magazine.
squiretarbox@ime.net http://www.squiretarboxinn.com/

YORK (REGION)

The Cape Neddick House
PO Box 70
1300 Rt 1, *Cape Neddick* 03902
207-363-2500 Fax: 207-363-4499
Diane Goodwin
All year

95-165-BB
5 rooms, 5 pb
Rated
C-ltd/S-ltd/P-no/H-no

Full breakfast
Complimentary wine, tea, coffee
Parlor & living room, bicycles, trails, horseshoes, picnic area

Coastal, country, 4th-gen. Victorian home. Close to beach, antiques, Kittery outlets, boutiques. dianne@capeneddickhouse.com http://www.capeneddickhouse.com

YORK HARBOR

Inn at Tanglewood Hall
PO Box 490
611 York St 03911
207-351-1075 Fax: 207-351-1296
Bonnie & Bill Alstrom
May-November

115-195-BB
6 rooms, 6 pb
Visa, MC
C-no/S-no/P-no/H-no

Creative continental
Port & chocolates in the afternoon

Built in 1889, Tanglewood Hall is set among tall oak trees and gardens. Rocky ocean views and beaches are just around the corner.
tanglewoodhall@aol.com http://tanglewoodhall.com

York Harbor Inn
PO Box 573
Coastal Route 1A 03911
207-363-5119 Fax: 207-363-7151
800-343-3869
Garry Dominguez
All year

99-349-BB
47 rooms, 47 pb
Most CC, *Rated*, •
C-yes/S-ltd/P-no/H-ltd

Continental breakfast
Lunch, dinner, Sunday brunch, pub menu
Hot tub, restaurant, pub, A/C, CCTV, phone w/data port, many rms w/FP, spas

Historic Oceanview Inn featured on "Great Country Inns." Dining recognized by Food & Wine Magazine. English Style Pub, Hot Tub. Open Year Round.
info@yorkharborinn.com http://www.yorkharborinn.com

YORK HARBOR (REGION)

Dockside Guest Quarters
PO Box 205
Harris Island Rd, *York* 03909
207-363-2868 Fax: 207-363-1977
800-270-1977
The Lusty Family
All year

85-230-EP
25 rooms, 25 pb
Visa, MC, Disc, *Rated*, •
C-yes/S-no/P-no/H-yes

Continental plus (fee)
Lunch, dinner in adjacent restaurant
Restaurant, sitting room, porches, lawn games, marina, boat rentals, phones

The essence of Maine is captured on this private peninsula, providing panoramic views of the harbor and ocean. Distinctive accommodations and dinning at the water's edge.
info@docksidegq.com http://www.docksidegq.com

Maryland

ANNAPOLIS

1908-William Page Inn
8 Martin St 21401
410-626-1506 Fax: 410-263-4841
800-364-4160
Robert L. Zuchelli
All year

125-250-BB
5 rooms, 3 pb
Visa, MC, •
C-ltd/S-no/P-no/H-no

Full breakfast
Afternoon tea
Sitting room, suites, Jacuzzis, cable TV

1908, Historic District, 5 guestroom Inn. Furnished in antiques and family collectibles.
info@williampageinn.com http://www.williampageinn.com

Barn on Howard's Cove, Annapolis, MD

ANNAPOLIS

201 B&B
201 Prince George St 21401
410-268-8053 Fax: 410-263-3007
Graham W. Gardner & Robert A. Bryant
All year

150-225-BB
4 rooms, 4 pb
Most CC
C-ltd/S-no/P-no/H-no

Full breakfast
Library, Jacuzzis, fireplaces, cable TV, accommodate business travelers

Georgian mansion in premium location with parking and grounds. Spacious rooms with fine antiques. All bedrooms have attached baths, TV/VCR, A/C and refrigerator.
bbat201@aol.com http://www.201bb.com

---

55 East
55 East St 21401
410-295-0202 Fax: 410-295-0203
Tricia Herban
All year

140-175-BB
3 rooms, 3 pb
Visa, MC, AmEx
C-ltd/S-no/P-no/H-no
French

Full breakfast
Sweet treat in the evening
Two living rooms, one with cable TV; library; courtyard with fountain

55 East offers you a special interlude. Just steps from historic sites and the harbor, it is tastefully decorated with antiques and original art, a fountained courtyard, Japanese Room and Library. triciah@erols.com http://annearundelcounty.com/hotel/55east.htm

---

Annapolis Inn
144 Prince George Sr 21401
410-295-5200 Fax: 410-295-5201
Joseph Lespier
All year

250-375-BB
3 rooms, 3 pb
Visa, MC, AmEx,
Rated, •
C-no/S-no/P-no/H-no
Spanish, Italian

Full breakfast
Afternoon tea, chocolates in rooms, soft drinks
A/C, heated Jacuzzi, towel warmers, heated marble floors, business telecom

Breathtaking antiques, spacious suites & excellent service are the hallmarks of this recently restored Georgian townhouse that once belonged to Thomas Jefferson's physician.
annapolisinn@att.net http://www.annapolisinn.com

Barn on Howard's Cove
500 Wilson Rd 21401
410-266-6840 Fax: 410-266-7293
Graham & Libbie Gutsche
All year

125-BB
2 rooms, 2 pb
Rated, •
C-yes/S-no/P-no/H-no

Full breakfast
Snacks
Sitting rm, near pool, tennis, dock, deep water docking avail, canoes/kayak

Charming restored 1850s horse barn just outside Annapolis, overlooking a cove off the Severn River. gdgutsche5@aol.com http://www.bnbweb.com/howards-cove.html

Chez Amis
85 East St 21401
410-263-6631 Fax: 410-295-7889
888-224-6455
Don & Mickie Deline
All year

135-165-BB
4 rooms, 4 pb
Visa, MC, AmEx, •
C-ltd/S-no/P-no/H-no

Full breakfast
Soft drinks, beer, wine, peanuts, M&Ms, cookies
Sitting room, "European Country" decor, theme rooms, robes, TV, A/C, antiques

Former circa 1900 grocery store, transformed into a B&B in 1989. Perfect location for enjoying historic area, harbor & Academy.
stay@chezamis.com http://www.chezamis.com

Dolls' House
161 Green St 21401
410-626-2028 Fax: 410-626-9884
Barbara & John Dugan
All year

120-150-BB
3 rooms, 3 pb
Rated
C-ltd/S-no/P-no/H-no

Full breakfast
Parlor, flower garden, all bedrooms have private baths and sitting rooms

Late Victorian home decorated with period antiques and dolls. Located in the heart of the Historic District. Old fashioned front porch and English garden.
dugan@dollshousebandb.com http://www.annapolis.net/dollshouse

---

Georgian House
170 Duke of Gloucester 21401
410-263-5618 Fax: 410-263-5618
800-557-2068
Sandy & Hank Mayer
All year

140-185-BB
4 rooms, 4 pb
Most CC
C-no/S-no/P-no/H-no
Spanish

Full breakfast
Guest lounge has beverages and snacks
Outside patio

Sandy and Hank invite you to come and enjoy their elegant Bed & Breakfast in Annapolis' Historic District. The four guestrooms in this pre-Revolutionary home have queen size beds and private baths. georgian@erols.com http://www.georgianhouse.com

---

Gibson's Lodgings of Annapolis
110 Prince George St 21401
410-268-5555 Fax: 410-268-2775
877-330-0057
Beverly Snyder
All year

99-239-BB
20 rooms, 17 pb
Visa, MC, AmEx
C-ltd/S-no/P-no/H-yes

Full continental breakfast
Complimentary Sherry

In the heart of historic Annapolis is this distinctive and internationally known Bed & Breakfast Inn with courtyard parking and unique conference facilities.
gibsonslodgings@starpower.net http://www.gibsonslodgings.com

Mary Rob
243 Prince George St 21401
410-268-5438 Fax: 410-268-9623
Mary-Stuart Taylor & Robert Carlson
All year

150-BB
1 rooms, 1 pb
Visa, MC, AmEx
C-ltd/S-no/P-no/H-no

Full breakfast to order
Special diet requests, snacks
A/C, off-street parking, fax, copier, modem hookup, piano, bicycles, TV

Circa 1864 Victorian Italianate villa with tower. Furnished in antiques and in the heart of the Historic District. Walk to many fine restaurants, antique and decorator shops.

Scotlaur Inn
165 Main St 21401
410-268-5665 Fax: 410-269-6738
Ted & Beth Levitt
All year

85-130-BB
10 rooms, 10 pb
Visa, MC, *Rated*, •
C-yes/S-no/P-ltd/H-no

Full breakfast
Snacks, restaurant, lunch/dinner
Suites, accommodate business travelers.

Our 10 beautifully decorated guestrooms are set in the heart of historic Annapolis with the look and feel of the early 1900s.
scotlaurinn@aol.com http://www.scotlaurinn.com

ANNAPOLIS

State House Inn
25 State Circle 21401
410-990-0024 Fax: 410-990-9508
Patrick Donegan
All year

120-165-BB
7 rooms, 7 pb
Visa, MC, AmEx, •
C-ltd/S-no/P-no/H-ltd

Continental breakfast
Snacks
Sitting room, Jacuzzis, cable TV, suites, accom. bus. travelers

All the amenities of a hotel, combined with the charm of a B&B in the heart of historic Annapolis. shinn25@aol.com http://www.statehouseinn.com

ANNAPOLIS (REGION)

Chester Peake Waterfront
101 Swan Cove Ln, *Chester* 21619
410-604-0588 Fax: 410-604-0588
Bill & Janice Costello
All year

75-145-BB
4 rooms, 4 pb
Visa, MC, *Rated*, •
C-ltd/S-no/P-no/H-ltd

Continental breakfast
Snacks
300-foot pier, TV, game room, pool table, fishing, canoe, bikes

Beautiful white sandy beach on the Chesapeake Bay; hiker/biker trail runs in front; public fishing pier, boat rentals restaurants. 14 miles from historic Annapolis and Naval Academy.

BALTIMORE

1870 Guest House
21 S Stricker St 21223
410-947-4622
Frank & Dana Trovato
All year

115-125-BB
1 room, 1 pb
Visa, MC
C-yes/S-no/P-no/H-no

Full breakfast
Complimentary sherry, soda, tea, cheese plate
Sitting area, desk, phone with answering, internet hook-up

Large suite located in a restored row home. Includes full kitchen and bath with all amenities. Close to Inner Harbor and Convention Center.
dhtrovato@aol.com http://www.innsite.com/a005349

Abacrombie Badger
58 W Biddle St 21201
410-244-7227 Fax: 410-244-8415
888-9-BADGER
Mr. & Mrs. Edward M. Sweetman
All year

88-155-BB
12 rooms, 12 pb
Most CC, *Rated*, •
C-ltd/S-no/P-no/H-no
German, Dutch, French

Continental plus breakfast
Restaurant
Bar, sitting room, A/C, private phones, parlor, cable TV

1880 house in the heart of Baltimore's Cultural Center. Walk to symphony, opera, museums, Antique Row. Near Inner Harbor.
info@badger-inn.com http://www.badger-inn.com

Celie's Waterfront
1714 Thames St 21231
410-522-2323 Fax: 410-522-2324
800-432-0184
Sara J. Backstrom
All year

129-239-BB
7 rooms, 7 pb
Most CC, *Rated*, •
C-ltd/S-no/P-no/H-yes

Continental plus breakfast
Refrigerators
Private phones/answering machines, cable TV, A/C, whirlpools, fireplaces

Urban inn in Fell's Point historic maritime community. Near Harbor Place, business district & Orioles Park by water taxi.
innkeeper@celieswaterfront.com http://celieswaterfront.com

Gramercy Mansion
1400 Greenspring Valley 21153
410-486-2405 Fax: 410-486-1765
800-553-3404
Anne Pomykala & Cristin Kline
All year

90-275-BB
13 rooms, 8 pb
Most CC, *Rated*, •
C-yes/S-ltd/P-no/H-ltd
Spanish

Full breakfast
Snacks
Sitting room, library, tennis, Jacuzzis, swimming pool, suites, fireplace

English Tudor Mansion on 45 acres. Guests will enjoy flower and herb gardens and organic farm. Just fifteen minutes from downtown Baltimore.
gramercy@erols.com http://www.gramercymansion.com

BALTIMORE

Inn at 2920
2920 Elliott St 21224
410-342-4450 Fax: 410-342-6436
877-774-2920
David & Debbie Schwartz
All year

140-225-BB
4 rooms, 4 pb
Most CC, •
C-ltd/S-no/P-no/H-no

Full Gourmet Breakfast
Jacuzzi tubs, Satellite TV/VCR, High-speed Internet Access

Inn at 2920 is an upscale, contemporary bed and breakfast located in one of downtown Baltimore's most desirable waterfront neighborhoods.
reservations@theinnat2920.com http://www.theinnat2920.com

Mr. Mole
1601 Bolton St 21217
410-728-1179 Fax: 410-728-3379
Collin Clarke & Paul Bragaw
All year

119-150-BB
5 rooms, 5 pb
Most CC, *Rated*, •
C-ltd/S-no/P-no/H-no

Dutch Style continental breakfast
Sitting room, A/C, garage parking, parlor, phones, modem connection

Elegant and spacious 1870 Baltimore row house on historic Bolton Hill.
info@MrMoleBB.com http://www.MrMoleBB.com

Scarborough Fair
1 East Montgomery St 21230
410-837-0010 Fax: 410-837-0010
Ashley & Ellen Scarborough
All year

149-189-BB
6 rooms, 6 pb
Most CC
C-ltd/S-no/P-no/H-no

Full gourmet breakfast
Afternoon tea & sweets or wine & cheese
Gathering room with library, private phones, fireplaces, Jacuzzis, tour info

1801 Georgian residence two blocks from the Inner Harbor in charming historic Federal Hill. Walk to business district, ballparks, convention center, and Harbor Place.
scarborough-fair@starpower.net http://www.scarborough-fair.com

BERLIN

Merry Sherwood Plantation
108 Williams St
8909 Worcester Hwy 21811
410-641-2112 Fax: 410-641-9528
800-660-0358
W. Kirk Burbage
All year

150-175-BB
8 rooms, 5 pb
Visa, *Rated*, •
S-no/P-no/H-no

Full breakfast
Afternoon tea
Sitting room, library, bikes, Jacuzzi, suite, fireplace, cable TV

Elegant c.1859 Victorian home restored to its former grandeur with Gothic Italianate architectural additives. info@merrysherwood.com http://www.merrysherwood.com

BETTERTON

Lantern Inn
PO Box 29
115 Ericsson Ave 21610
410-348-5809 Fax: 410-348-2323
800-499-7265
Ray & Sandi Sparks
All year

75-90-BB
13 rooms, 4 pb
Visa, MC
C-ltd/S-no/P-no/H-no

Continental plus breakfast
Complimentary wine
Beach & tennis, 2 blocks, sitting room, library

Small quiet town on Chesapeake Bay. One and one half hours from Philadelphia, Baltimore, D.C. Sandy beaches, great cycling, seafood, wildlife preserves, antiquing, tennis.
lanterninn@dmv.com

CHESAPEAKE CITY

Blue Max Inn
PO Box 30
300 Bohemia Avenue 21915
410-885-2781 Fax: 410-885-2809
877-725-8362
Wayne & Wendy Mercer
All year

110-225-BB
8 rooms, 8 pb
Most CC, *Rated*, •
C-ltd/S-ltd/P-no/H-yes

Full breakfast
Tea, snacks
Sitting room, library, Jacuzzis, fireplace, cable TV, conference

Located in the heart of town, this elegant historic Inn offers charm and Southern hospitality. Eight luxurious rooms, private baths.
innkeeper@bluemaxinn.com http://www.bluemaxinn.com

CHESAPEAKE CITY

Inn at the Canal PO Box 187 104 Bohemia Ave 21915 410-885-5995 Fax: 410-885-3585 Mary & Al Ioppolo All year	85-175-BB 6 rooms, 6 pb Most CC, *Rated*, • C-ltd/S-no/P-no/H-no	Full breakfast Complimentary iced tea, cider Sitting room, porch, guests receive 10% dsc'nt at our antique shop

Elegant waterside Victorian in quaint historic district on banks of Chesapeake and Delaware Canal. innkeeper@innatthecanal.com http://www.innatthecanal.com

CHESTERTOWN

Brampton Inn 25227 Chestertown Rd 21620 410-778-1860 Fax: 410-778-1805 Michael & Danielle Hanscom All year	145-250-BB 10 rooms, 10 pb Visa, MC, *Rated* C-ltd/S-no/P-no/H-ltd French, German	Full breakfast Complimentary wine, afternoon tea Sitting room, library, bicycles, one suite, one room sleeps 4

1860 National Register manor house. 35-acre estate one mile south of historic Chestertown. Luxurious rooms, furnished in antiques and with Wood-burning fireplaces.
innkeeper@bramptoninn.com http://www.bramptoninn.com

Imperial Hotel 208 High St 21620 410-778-5000 Fax: 410-778-9622 800-295-0014 Jan Macdonald & Richard O'Neill All year	95-225-BB 13 rooms, 13 pb Visa, MC, AmEx C-ltd/S-no/P-no/H-yes	Continental breakfast

The Imperial is a unique building with a distinctive double veranda over the front entrance. The guestrooms are individually decorated with period furnishings.
imperial@friend.ly.net http://www.imperialchestertown.com

Inn at Mitchell House 8796 Maryland Pkwy 21620 410-778-6500 Jim & Tracy Stone All year	95-120-BB 5 rooms, 5 pb Visa, MC, *Rated* C-yes/S-ltd/P-no/H-no	Full breakfast Complimentary wine Sitting room, tennis court, fireplace, private beach, acc. bus. travelers

Take a step back in time. 18th century manor house in a quiet rural setting. Enjoy gardens, pond, and the Chesapeake Bay a mere 1/2 mile away. Nature lovers paradise.
innatmitch@friend.ly.net http://www.chestertown.com/mitchell

Lauretum Inn 954 High St 21620 410-778-3236 Fax: 410-778-1922 800-742-3236 Peg & Bill Sites All year	75-150-BB 5 rooms, 3 pb Most CC C-yes/S-no/P-no	Continental breakfast

Lauretum (1881) sits splendidly atop a tree graced knoll on six acres in Chestertown, MD. A long winding lane invites you to Lauretum.
lauretum@aol.com http://www.chestertown.com/lauretum

COLUMBIA

Peralynna Manor Guesthouse 10605 Route 108 21044 410-715-4600 Fax: 410-715-0046 877-737-2596 David Lynn All year	99-175-BB 5 rooms, 5 pb C-yes/S-no/P-no	Complimentary breakfast foods

Peralynna Manor is a majestic 14,000 square foot European-styled Country Manor located in Columbia, Maryland.
peralynna@aol.com http://www.howardcounty.com/hotel/peralynna.htm

CUMBERLAND

The Inn at Walnut Bottom	89-147-BB	Full breakfast
120 Greene St 21502	12 rooms, 10 pb	Afternoon refreshments
301-777-0003 Fax: 301-777-8288	Most CC, *Rated*, •	Sitting room, in-room TV,
800-286-9718	C-yes/S-no/P-no/H-ltd	telephones, bicycles,
Kirsten Hansen & Grant Irvin		massage therapy
All year		

Beautiful rooms, delightful breakfasts, and excellent service in the heart of historic Cumberland. Easy stroll to scenic train, restaurants, and canal towpath.
iwb@iwbinfo.com http://www.iwbinfo.com

DEALE

Creekside	75-BB	Full breakfast
6036 Parkers Creek Drive	2 rooms, 2 pb	Use of living room, library,
20751	C-ltd/S-no/P-ltd/H-ltd	canoes, decks, garden
301-261-9438 Fax: 410-867-1253	Spanish	
Betty-Carol Sellen & Marti Burt		
All year		

Creek-side B&B is located in a small community on the western shore of the Chesapeake Bay, 20 miles south of Annapolis. It is tastefully furnished in a blend of old oak & contemporary furniture. bcsellen@juno.com

DERWOOD

Reynolds of Derwood	85-95-BB	Continental breakfast
16620 Bethayres Rd 20855	2 rooms, 2 pb	Sitting room, outside hot tub,
301-963-2216	Visa, MC, AmEx, •	inside sauna, exercise room,
Joan Reynolds	C-yes/S-ltd/P-no/H-yes	waterfall
All year		

Walking distance to metro subway station to DC metropolitan area. 30 min ride to Washington, DC mall, to visit the museums and see the monuments.
HomerTheGolfer@yahoo.com http://www.reynolds-bed-breakfast.com

EASTON

The Bishop's House	110-120-BB	Full breakfast
PO Box 2217	5 rooms, 5 pb	Complimentary wine &
214 Goldsborough St 21601	*Rated*, •	beverages
410-820-7290 Fax: 410-820-7290	C-ltd/S-no/P-no/H-no	Sitting rooms, bikes, A/C,
800-223-7290		whirlpool tubs, fireplaces,
D. & J. Ippolito		parking
All year		

Romantically furnished in-town circa 1880 Victorian centrally located for visiting all points of interest in Talbot County.
bishopshouse@skipjack.bluecrab.org http://www.bishopshouse.com

---

Chaffinch House	100-130-BB	Full breakfast
132 S Harrison St 21601	5 rooms, 5 pb	Sitting room, fireplaces, A/C,
410-822-5074 800-861-5074	Visa, MC, •	overhead sprinkler system
Laura C. Brandt	C-yes/S-no/P-no/H-no	
All year		

Elegant Queen Anne Victorian, circa 1893, Historic District. Individually decorated rooms with period furnishings. Two-course gourmet breakfast served in dining room.
innkeeper@chaffinchhouse.com http://www.chaffinchhouse.com

ELLICOTT CITY

The Wayside Inn	95-200-BB	Full breakfast
4344 Columbia Rd 21042	4 rooms, 2 pb	Afternoon refreshments
410-461-4636 Fax: 410-750-2070	Visa, MC, AmEx, •	Cable TV/VCR/movies,
Susan & David Balderson	C-yes/S-no/P-no/H-no	phones w/dataport,
All year		concierge service, library

History awaits you at the Wayside Inn. Located in historic Ellicott City, Maryland, near Baltimore or Washington, D.C., the Wayside Inn is the perfect place to escape to the past.
bnbboy@aol.com http://www.waysideinnmd.com

FREDERICK

McCleery's Flat
121 E Patrick St 21701
301-620-2433 800-774-7926
Jutta & George Terrell
All year

100-135-BB
5 rooms, 5 pb
Visa, MC, AmEx
C-ltd/S-ltd/P-no/H-no
German

Full breakfast
Sitting room, library, Jacuzzis, suites, cable TV, garden, courtyard

An 1876 French Empire home in the center of Frederick's downtown historic district. Comfortable lodging and luxurious breakfasts within the stately setting of the home's historic past. http://www.fwp.net/mccleerysflat

---

Middle Plantation Inn
9549 Liberty Rd 21701
301-898-7128
Shirley & Dwight Mullican
All year

90-110-BB
4 rooms, 4 pb
Visa, MC, *Rated*, •
C-ltd/S-no/P-no/H-no

Continental plus breakfast
Afternoon tea (Tues–Thur), fee
Sitting room, garden, hen house, brook, four golf courses nearby

A charming stone and log B&B, furnished with antiques, television and A/C. In-room phones available. bandb@mpinn.com http://www.MPInn.com

---

Spring Bank Inn
7945 Worman's Mill Rd 21701
301-694-0440 800-400-INNS
Beverly & Ray Compton
All year

105-120-BB
5 rooms, 1 pb
Most CC, *Rated*, •
C-ltd/S-no/P-no/H-no

Continental plus breakfast
Double parlors, library, view from observatory, 10 acres for roaming

On National Register of Historic Places. Antiques. Near Baltimore, Washington, D.C., and Civil War battlefields. Exceptional dining in Frederick Historic District 2 mi. away.
rcomp1880@aol.com http://www.bbonline.com/md/springbank

GRANTSVILLE

Walnut Ridge
PO Box 368
92 Main 21536
301-895-4248 Fax: 301-895-4054
888-419-2568
Tim Fetterly & Candace Fetterly
All year

85-135-BB
4 rooms, 4 pb
Visa, MC, *Rated*, •
C-ltd/S-no/P-yes/H-ltd

Full breakfast
Snacks
Hot tub, Sitting room, Videos, Fireplaces, Cable TV, Suites

Find refuge and romance in western Maryland. Quiet charm and grace will greet you! Wrap up in comfort. walnutridge@usa.net http://www.walnutridge.net

HAVRE DE GRACE

Spencer Silver Mansion
200 S Union Ave 21078
410-939-1097 800-780-1485
Carol Nemeth
All year

65-125-EP
4 rooms, 2 pb
Rated, •

Full breakfast

Built in 1896, the Spencer-Silver Mansion offers the perfect lodging while visiting historic Havre de Grace and the upper Chesapeake Bay region.
spencersilver@erols.com http://www.spencersilvermansion.com

NORTH EAST

Chesapeake Lodge at Sandy Cove
60 Sandy Cove Rd 21901
410-287-5433 Fax: 410-287-3196
800-234-COVE
Kevin Bitler
All year

75-140-BB
153 rooms, 153 pb
Visa, MC, Disc, •
C-yes/S-no/P-no/H-yes

Full breakfast
Lunch and dinner may be purchased
Sitting areas, TV room/DIRECTV, Fitness Center, vending machines, laundry

Located at the headwaters of the Chesapeake Bay, Chesapeake Lodge at Sandy Cove Christian Conference Center is situated on 206 acres of Maryland woodland. We are conveniently close to I-95. info@sandycove.org http://www.sandycove.org

OCEAN CITY

Atlantic House B&B
501 N Baltimore Ave 21842
410-289-2333 Fax: 410-289-2430
Paul Cook & Debi Thompson
Presidents'–Columbus day

75-225-BB
12 rooms, 8 pb
Most CC, *Rated*, •
C-ltd/S-ltd/P-no/H-no

Full breakfast
Snacks, afternoon tea
Sitting room, bicycles, swimming pool, suites, cable TV

Comfort convenience, and service provided by knowledgeable life-long resident with a breakfast to excite and ocean sunsets to remember.
ocbnb@Atlantichouse.com http://www.atlantichouse.com

Lighthouse Club Hotel/The Eagle
201 60th St
56th Street on the Bay 21842
410-524-5400 Fax: 410-524-3928
888-371-5400 All year

79-375-BB
35 rooms, 35 pb
Most CC, *Rated*, •
C-no/S-ltd/P-no/H-no

Continental breakfast
Restaurant on site

Set amidst the gentle rushes of the natural wetlands, with the Isle of Wight Bay lapping at your doorstep, we have created 23 very special one-bedroom suites.
lthouse@dmv.com http://www.fagers.com

OXFORD

Robert Morris Inn
PO Box 70
314 N Morris St 21654
410-226-5111 Fax: 410-226-5744
888-823-4012
Jay Gibson
Apr-Nov, Winter varies

130-280-EP
35 rooms, 35 pb
Visa, MC, AmEx, *Rated*, •
C-ltd/S-no/P-no/H-ltd

All meals available
Restaurant, bar service, non-smoking inn, private beach

Historic Chesapeake Bay romantic inn. Featuring the best crab cakes on the eastern shore. robertmorrisinn@webtv.net http://www.robertmorrisinn.com

QUEENSTOWN

Queenstown Inn
PO Box 2012
7109 Main Street 21658
410-827-3396 888-744-3407
Shyam & Denise All year

70-145-BB
5 rooms, 5 pb
Visa, MC, AmEx
C-ltd/S-ltd/P-no/H-yes

Full breakfast
Snacks
Sitting room, library, bikes, cable TV, accom. bus. travelers

1830's historic home with many wonderful additions, including large screened porch. Five rooms decorated with a theme include private baths and air conditioning.
qtbb@dmv.com http://www.queenstowninn.com

RIDGE

Bard's Field in Trinity Manor
15671 Pratt Rd 20680
301-872-5989
James & Audrey Pratt
All year

75-BB
2 rooms
C-no/S-no/P-no/H-no

Full breakfast
Sitting room, library

The modest 18th century manor house, Bard's Field, built about 1798 is typical of Tidewater Architecture. Located on the beautiful Rawley Bay overlooking the Potomac River.
ajpratt@erols.com

Longpoint Cottage
PO Box 505
Wynne Road 20680
301-872-0057
Cameron Kashani
All year

75-150-EP
6 rooms
C-yes/S-no/P-no/H-no

Library, satellite TV, VCR, CD/tape/radio, laundry, porch, deck, games

Longpoint Cottage: A charming waterfront getaway on 13 acres, with park like settings, 1800 feet of shoreline, private beach and dock, and expansive water views.
longpoint@birdwave.com http://www.birdwave.com

ROCK HALL

Huntingfield Manor	95-145	Semi-public pool
4928 Eastern Neck Rd 21661	6 rooms, 6 pb	
410-639-7779 Fax: 410-639-2924		
George & Bernie Starken		
All year		

The Manor House stands in the center of 70 acres of rich farm land that borders the Eastern Shore of the Chesapeake Bay. manorlord@juno.com http://www.huntingfield.com

Swan Haven	98-138-BB	Continental plus breakfast
20950 Rock Hall Ave 21661	7 rooms, 7 pb	Waterfront, screened
410-639-2527	Visa, MC, AmEx	porches, bicycles, boat
Diane & Harry	C-no/S-ltd/P-no/H-no	rentals
All year		

Waterfront accommodations in the finest boating area of the Chesapeake Bay. Small boat rentals & bicycles are available on site. 7 tastefully decorated guestrooms w/private baths, central air, cable. swanhaven@friend.ly.net http://www.swanhaven.com

SALISBURY (REGION)

Waterloo Country Inn	125-255-BB	Full gourmet breakfast
28822 Mt Vernon Blvd,	6 rooms, 6 pb	Snacks, candlelight dining by
Princess Anne 21853	Most CC, *Rated*, •	the fireplace
410-651-0883 Fax: 410-651-5592	C-yes/S-no/P-ltd/H-yes	A/C, bikes, golf nearby,
Erwin & Theresa Kraemer	German, French, Italian,	outdoor pool, lounge, canoes
March–Dec.	Swiss German	on property

Beautiful, historic, breathtaking, relaxing & fulfilling Eastern Shore 1750's waterfront estate, with elegant & comfortable rooms, all w/private bath. Gourmet breakfast, canoes, bikes, outdoor pool.
innkeeper@waterloocountryinn.com http://www.waterloocountryinn.com

SHARPSBURG

The Inn at Antietam	110-175-BB	Full Breakfast
PO Box 119	5 rooms, 5 pb	Sitting room, piano, bicycles,
220 E Main St 21782	Visa, MC, AmEx,	library
301-432-6601 Fax: 301-432-5981	*Rated*, •	
877-835-6011	C-ltd/S-ltd/P-no/H-no	
Charles Van Metre & Robert LeBlanc	Closed January	

Lovely 1908 Victorian fully restored and furnished in antiques, on Antietam Battlefield in Civil War historic area. Featuring five suites.
innatantietam@juno.com http://www.innatantietam.com

Jacob Rohrbach Inn	94-119-BB	Full multi-course breakfast
PO Box 706	4 rooms, 3 pb	Complimentary Home Baked
138 W. Main St 21782	Visa, MC, AmEx,	Cookies and Soft Drinks
301-432-5079 Fax: 413-473-1797	*Rated*, •	Jacuzzi Spa "Under the
877-839-4242	C-ltd/S-ltd/P-no/H-no	Stars"
Joanne & Paul Breitenbach		
All year		

A local landmark since around 1800. This Federal Period Inn in the heart of quaint Sharpsburg, is surrounded by the Antietam Battlefield.
info@jacob-rohrbach-inn.com http://www.jacob-rohrbach-inn.com

SNOW HILL

The Mansion House	110-160-BB	Full breakfast
4436 Bayside Rd 21863	4 rooms, 4 pb	Refreshments
410-632-3189	Visa, MC, AmEx, *Rated*	10 fireplaces, 3 porches,
Fax: 410-632-1980	C-ltd/S-no/P-ltd/H-no	private pier, bikes, upstairs
C. Pauley and		coffee service
G. Hogeboom		
All year		

Escape from life's hectic pace and surround yourself in the warmth and comfort of The Mansion House. mansionhouse@earthlink.net http://www.mansionhousebnb.com

Waterloo Country Inn, Princess Anne, MD

SNOW HILL

River House Inn 201 E Market St 21863 410-632-2722 Fax: 410-632-2866 Larry & Susanne Knudsen All year	150-250-BB 6 rooms, 6 pb Most CC, *Rated*, • C-yes/S-no/P-ltd/H-yes	Full breakfast Lunch & dinner available, comp. snacks, wine, tea Porches, A/C, fishing, boating, country club golf, bikes

Come relax at our elegant 1860s riverfront country home in historic Snow Hill. Canoe or bike inn-to-inn. Enjoy Maryland's eastern shore, beaches, bayou, AARP. 6 rooms and suites. innkeeper@riverhouseinn.com http://www.riverhouseinn.com

SOLOMONS

Solomons Victorian Inn PO Box 759 125 Charles St 20688 410-326-4811 Fax: 410-326-0133 Helen Bauer All year	95-195-BB 8 rooms, 8 pb Visa, MC, AmEx C-ltd/S-no/P-no/H-no	Full breakfast Boating, shops, hiking, 3 rooms w/whirlpool tubs, restaurants nearby

Let the Chesapeake romance you from the porch of this charming Queen Anne Victorian. Convenient to Washington, Baltimore, and Richmond.
info@solomonsvictorianinn.com http://www.solomonsvictorianinn.com

ST. GEORGE ISLAND

Camp Merryelande Vacation PO Box 222 Camp Merryelande Rd 20674 301-994-1722 Fax: 301-994-3482 800-382-1073 Mike Evans & Debbie Sapp All year	55-375-EP 22 rooms, 14 pb Visa, MC, • C-yes/S-yes/P-no/H-ltd	We will help you purchase local seafood Cable TV, AC, gas fireplaces, fishing pier, beach, private decks, kitchens

Modern clean, fully furnished 1 to 6 bdrm Olde Time cottages. Cable TV & AC, Lighted fishing pier, 1200 ft. sandy beach, river view decks, picnic table, BBQ grill. See the waves from the living room. escape@campmd.com http://www.campmd.com

ST. MARY'S CITY

Brome-Howard Inn
PO Box 476
11821 Rosecroft Rd 20686
301-866-0656 Fax: 301-866-9660
Michael & Lisa Kelley
All year

125-185-BB
4 rooms, 4 pb
Visa, MC, AmEx, •
C-yes/S-ltd/P-no/H-no

Full breakfast
Dinner, snacks, bar service
Sitting room, library, bicycles, suites, fireplaces, cable TV, bus. trav., beach

30 acres of farmland, raised flower beds and working gardens surround the 19th century Brome-Howard Inn Bed and Breakfast and its original carriage house and smokehouse, dairy house and former slave quarters.
kelleyms@tqci.net http://www.bromehowardinn.com

ST. MICHAELS

Barrett's B&B & Tea Room
PO Box 279
204 N Talbot Street 21663
410-745-3322 Fax: 410-745-3888
Jim Barrett
All year

120-280-BB
7 rooms, 7 pb
Most CC, *Rated*, •
S-no/P-no/H-ltd

Full gourmet breakfast
Snacks
Tea Room, Jacuzzis, fireplaces, cable TV, gift shop, espresso bar

Double Jacuzzi tub in front of fireplace, priv. bathroom, candles, fresh flowers, handmade quilts, cable TV, central air, queen beds, shopping, boating, golf, biking.
JWBarrett@yahoo.com http://www.barrettbb.com

Five Gables Inn & Spa
209 North Talbot Street 21663
410-745-0100 Fax: 410-745-2903
877-466-0100
Lynsey Rochon
All year

140-325-BB
15 rooms, 15 pb
Visa, MC, AmEx
C-ltd/S-no/P-yes/H-ltd

Continental breakfast
Romantic, whirlpools, non-smoking, fireplaces, Spa, Indoor Pool

Rooms feature gas fireplaces, porches and whirlpools with fluffy robes and Aveda amenities. Enjoy the Heated Indoor Pool, steam room and sauna with massage therapy and facials by appointment. fivegables@crosslink.net http://www.fivegables.com

---

Kemp House Inn
PO Box 638
412 S Talbot St 21663
410-745-2243 Fax: 410-745-4315
Steve & Diane Cooper
All year

95-130-BB
7 rooms, 7 pb
Visa, MC, •
C-yes/S-no/P-ltd/H-no

Continental plus breakfast
Bicycles, queen-sized beds, private cottage available

1805 Georgian house with four-poster beds and working fireplaces in historic eastern shore village. info@kemphouseinn.com http://www.kemphouseinn.com

---

The Old Brick Inn
PO Box 987
401 S Talbot St 21663
410-745-3323 Fax: 410-745-3320
Martha Strickland
Feb 13- Jan 1

95-250-BB
12 rooms, 12 pb
Visa, MC, AmEx
C-ltd/S-no/P-no/H-yes

Continental breakfast
Sitting room, library, tennis court, pool, fireplaces, cable TV

Centrally located, The Old Brick Inn is an elegant, historic (circa 1816) inn with European charm. mstrickland@expresshost.com http://www.oldbrickinn.com

---

Victoriana Inn
PO Box 449
205 Cherry St 21663
410-745-3368 888-316-1282
Maria and Charles McDonald
All year

129-315-BB
7 rooms, 7 pb
Visa, MC
C-ltd/S-no/P-no/H-no
Spanish, French

Full breakfast
Tea, wine, beer, cokes, etc.
Each room includes a private bath, 3 have fireplaces

The Victoriana Inn is located on the harbor in St. Michaels. Situated next to the Chesapeake Bay Maritime Museum, the inn is just 2 blocks from the main street yet removed from the bustle of town.
info@victorianainn.com http://www.victorianainn.com

ST. MICHAELS

Wades Point Inn on the Bay
PO Box 7, 21663
410-745-2500 Fax: 410-745-3443
888-923-3466
The Feiler Family

115-230-BB
24 rooms, 16 pb
Rated
All year

Continental plus breakfast

Grand Georgian style home on the edge of Chesapeake Bay. Two thousand feet of gently curving shoreline wrap the Inn's private grounds, giving spectacular views to its 24 rooms. wadesinn@wadespoint.com http://www.wadespoint.com

ST. MICHAELS (REGION)

Lowes Wharf Marina Inn
PO Box 12
21651 Lowes Wharf Rd,
Sherwood 21665
410-745-6684 Fax: 410-745-5085
888-484-9267
Paul & Tracy Zelinske

89-159-BB
10 rooms, 10 pb
Visa, MC, Disc
C-yes/S-yes/P-ltd/H-yes
All year

Continental breakfast
Dinner available, snacks, restaurant
Bar service, suites, cable TV

Country waterfront Inn located on the Chesapeake Bay proper. Featuring 10 guestrooms, all of which enjoy water views, private bath, A/C-heat, coffee service, and satellite TV.
info@loweswharf.com http://www.loweswharf.com

Chesapeake Wood Duck Inn
PO Box 202
21490 Dogwood Harbor Rd,
Tilghman 21671
410-886-2070 Fax: 413-667-7256
800-956-2070
Kimberly & Jeffrey Bushey

139-219-BB
7 rooms, 7 pb
Visa, MC, *Rated*, •
S-no/P-no/H-no
All year

Full gourmet breakfast
Afternoon tea, snacks
Sitting rooms, fireplaces, sunroom, 3 porches, kayaking, nearby restaurants

Tucked in a quaint waterman's village, there's a place where time stands still. The Wood Duck Inn offers guests a choice of 6 bedrooms & 1 cottage, boasting casual elegance on the Eastern shore. woodduck@bluecrab.org http://www.woodduckinn.com

SYKESVILLE

Inn at Norwood
7514 Norwood Ave 21784
410-549-7868
Kelly & Stevon Crum
All year

90-150-BB
4 rooms, 4 pb
Visa, MC
C-ltd/S-ltd/P-no/H-no

Full breakfast
Tea, snacks, soft drinks, water
Sitting room, library, bicycles, movies, Jacuzzi tubs, fireplaces

The Inn at Norwood is a Romantic Bed & Breakfast. We have four spectacular guest rooms, all newly renovated and decorated to reflect Marylands colorful seasons. It is the perfect escape. kelly@innatnorwood.com http://www.innatnorwood.com

TAKOMA PARK

Davis Warner Inn
8114 Carroll Ave 20912
301-408-3989 Fax: 301-408-4840
888-683-3989
Robert Patenaude All year

85-145-BB
4 rooms, 1 pb
Most CC, *Rated*
C-ltd/S-ltd/P-no/H-no

Full breakfast
Afternoon tea
Sitting room, library, Jacuzzi in master suite, fireplace

An elegant and fully restored Victorian mansion, the Davis Warner Inn is ideally suited to business and vacation travelers to the Nation's Capital region.
reservations@daviswarnerinn.com http://www.daviswarnerinn.com

TANEYTOWN

Antrim 1844
30 Trevanion Rd 21787
410-756-6812 Fax: 410-756-2744
800-858-1844
Dorothy & Richard Mollett
Closed Dec. 24-25

160-375-BB
22 rooms, 22 pb
Visa, MC, AmEx, *Rated*, •
C-ltd/S-ltd/P-no/H-ltd

Full breakfast
Dinner, afternoon tea, restaurant, bar service
Sitting rm., tennis, Jacuzzi, pool, suites, frplce, cable, accom. bus. trav.

Antrim 1844 antebellum elegance and nationally acclaimed restaurant has earned the Inn a place in connoisseur's hearts. antrim1844@erols.com http://www.antrim1844.com

Woods Gain, Linwood, MD

TANEYTOWN

Glenburn
3515 Runnymede Rd 21787
410-751-1187
Robert Neal
All year

85-125-BB
3 rooms, 2 pb
•
C-yes/S-ltd/P-no/H-no

Full breakfast
Refrigerator, kitchen
2 bedroom cottage with kitchen, swimming pool, porches, golf, A/C

Georgian house with Victorian addition, antique furnishings, featured in Maryland House & Garden Pilgrimage. Historic rural area close to Gettysburg.

TILGHMAN ISLAND

Black Walnut Point Inn
PO Box 308
Black Walnut Rd 21671
410-886-2452 Fax: 410-886-2053
Brenda & Tom Ward

120-225-BB
7 rooms, 7 pb
Rated
S-ltd/P-no/H-yes
All year

Continental plus breakfast
Screened porches with rock rocking chairs, 57-acre wildlife reserve

The inn at the end of the road. Key West sunsets. Hammocks by the bay. Quiet and peaceful. Fishing. mward@shore.intercom.net
http://www.tilghmanisland.com/blackwalnut

Sinclair House
PO Box 145
5718 Black Walnut Point Rd
21671
410-886-2147 Fax: 410-886-2171
888-859-2147
William Jacobsen/Monica Stecher de Jacobsen

109-119-BB
4 rooms, 4 pb
Most CC
C-ltd/S-no/P-no/H-no
Spanish, German, French, Portuguese
All year

Full breakfast
Sitting room, library, bicycles, dish TV & VCR

Historic residence decorated and furnished by multilingual world traveler innkeepers. Africa Room, Indonesia Room, Peru Room, Morocco Room—each with private bath.
sinclairhousebandb@yahoo.com http://www.tilghmanisland.com/sinclair

VIENNA

The Tavern House
PO Box 98, 111 Water St 21869
410-376-3347
Harvey & Elise Altergott
All year

70-80-BB
3 rooms
Visa, MC, *Rated*, •
C-ltd/S-yes
Spanish, German

Full breakfast
Afternoon tea, complimentary wine
Sitting room, tennis courts nearby, 1830s grand piano

Restored Colonial tavern on Nanticoke River. Simple elegance; stark whites, detailed woodwork. Looks out over river and marshes. oldgod@shore.intercom.net

WESTMINSTER (REGION)

Woods Gain
421 McKinstry's Mill Rd, *Linwood* 21791
410-775-0308
Bev & Steve Kerkam

85-140-BB
4 rooms, 4 pb
•
C-ltd/S-ltd/P-no/H-yes
Weekends Sept–June

Full breakfast
Snacks
Sitting room, fireplaces, separate cottage

Enjoy the serenity of country surroundings, antiques, hearty breakfast and friendly hospitality as you step back in time at Wood's Gain, a homestay B&B, in the historic village of Linwood. steve@woodsgainbnb.com http://www.woodsgainbnb.com

WHITEHAVEN

Whitehaven
23844 River St 21856
410-873-3294 Fax: 410-873-2162
888-205-5921
Maryen, Carlton, Mark Herrett
All year

75-100-BB
5 rooms, 3 pb
Most CC, *Rated*, •
C-ltd/S-ltd/P-no/H-ltd

Full breakfast
Complimentary wine, snacks
Sitting rooms, library, cable TV, 1830s grand piano

19th century charm in tiny, historic village, scenic, all rooms water view, lovely country Victorian furnishings. whavnbb@dmv.com http://www.whitehaven.com/

Massachusetts

AMHERST

Allen House Victorian Inn
599 Main St 01002
413-253-5000 Fax: 413-253-7625
Alan & Ann Zieminski
All year

75-175-BB
7 rooms, 7 pb
Visa, MC, Disc, *Rated*
C-ltd/S-no/P-no/H-no

Full breakfast
Afternoon tea
Evening refreshments, sitting room, library, veranda, gardens, A/C

Authentic 1886 stick-style Victorian on 3 acres. Spacious bed chambers, private baths, personal phones with modems, ceiling fans and central air conditioning. allenhouse@webtv.net http://www.allenhouse.com

AMHERST (REGION)

An Old Indian Trail
664 Amherst Rd, *Granby* 01033
413-467-3528 Fax: 413-467-3528
Peter & Dolores Reis
All year

85-135-BB
5 rooms, 5 pb
Most CC, •
C-yes/S-no/P-no/H-ltd

Full breakfast
Complimentary beverages
TV/VCR, selection of movies, many books

An Old Indian Trail is conveniently located between Amherst & South Hadley in rural Granby, Massachusetts. reispd@att.bi.com http://www.bbonline.com/ma/oit

BARRE

Jenkins Inn & Restaurant
PO Box 779
7 West St 01005
978-355-6444 Fax: 978-355-6444
800-378-7373
Joe Perrin and David Ward
All year

155-185-BB
Rated
S-no/P-ltd

Full breakfast

Our c.1834 Gothic Revival Inn is located on a lovely New England Town Common and is dedicated to offering romantic lodging and dining to those looking for quality and comfort! jenkinsinn@juno.com http://www.bbhost.com/jenkinsinn

BERKSHIRES (REGION)

Thornewood Inn
453 Stockbridge Rd, *Great Barrington* 01230
413-528-3828 Fax: 413-528-3307
800-854-1008
Terry & David Thorne
All year

145-275-BB
15 rooms, 15 pb
Most CC, *Rated*, •
C-ltd/S-no/P-no/H-no

Continental plus breakfast
Dinner, afternoon tea, restaurant, bar service
Sitting room, library, Jacuzzis, pool, suites, frplc., Cable TV, bus. trav.

Exceptional turn of the century Dutch Colonial Inn located in the heart of the Berkshire Hills. Beautiful antique-appointed rooms, fabulous restaurant, periodic live entertainment. inn@thornewood.com http://www.thornewood.com

BERKSHIRES (REGION)

Windflower Inn
684 S Egremont Rd, Rte 23, *Great Barrington* 01230
413-528-2720 Fax: 413-528-5147
800-992-1993
Claudia & John Ryan, Barbara & Gerald Liebet
All year

100-200-BB
13 rooms, 13 pb
AmEx, *Rated*
C-yes/S-no/P-no/H-ltd

Full breakfast
Afternoon tea, snacks
Sitting room, library, swimming pool

Elegant small country Inn. Beautiful rooms, some with fireplaces. Produce from our organic garden. wndflowr@windflowerinn.com http://www.windflowerinn.com

---

Brook Farm Inn
15 Hawthorne Street, *Lenox* 01240
413-637-3013 Fax: 413-637-4751
800-285-7638
Linda and Phil Halpern
All year

105-250-BB
12 rooms, 12 pb
Most CC, *Rated*
C-ltd/S-no/P-no/H-no
Spanish, Hebrew

Full breakfast
Tea and scones daily at 4:00
Sitting room, library, heated pool, fireplaces, gardens, guest pantry

Gracious Victorian with modern comforts. Gardens, pool, and fireplaces provide serene oasis in the heart of the Berkshires. English tea served every afternoon in the library.
innkeeper@brookfarm.com http://www.brookfarm.com

Cornell Inn
203 Main St, *Lenox* 01240
413-637-0562 Fax: 413-637-0927
800-637-0562
Billie & Doug McLaughlin
All year

100-350-BB
30 rooms, 30 pb
Most CC, *Rated*
C-ltd/S-no/P-no/H-yes

Continental plus breakfast
Full service pub
Japanese style garden

Choose a cozy bedroom., a fully equipped suite with fireplace and kitchen or a four poster fireplace & Jacuzzi in our newly renovated 200 year old MacDonald House.
info@cornellinn.com http://www.cornellinn.com

The Gables Inn
81 Walker St, *Lenox* 01240
413-637-3416 Fax: 413-637-3416
800-382-9401
Frank Newton
All year

90-250-BB
17 rooms, 17 pb
Most CC, *Rated*
C-ltd/S-yes/P-no/H-no
Spanish

Full breakfast
Complimentary wine, dinner packages
Sitting room, library, tennis courts, swimming pool

Built in 1885, this gracious "cottage" was home of Edith Wharton at the turn-of-the-century. Lovingly furnished in period style. gable@berkshire.net http://www.gableslenox.com

---

Kemble Inn
2 Kemble St, *Lenox* 01240
413-637-4113 Fax: 416-637-8259
800-353-4113
All year

105-305-BB
15 rooms, 15 pb
Visa, MC, AmEx, *Rated*
S-no/P-no/H-yes

Continental breakfast
A/C, fireplaces, tennis

Elegant 1881 Georgian mansion, magnificent mountain views, spacious rooms with private baths, fireplaces, A/C, TV. kemble@bcn.net http://www.kembleinn.com

---

Seven Hills Country Inn
40 Plunkett St, *Lenox* 01240
413-637-0060 Fax: 413-637-3651
800-869-6518
Patricia & Jim Eder All year

85-350-BB
52 rooms, 52 pb
Rated

Continental plus breakfast

The Seven Hills Inn invites you to enjoy the romantic luxuries of a time long since past. Stay at the inn and enter a world that others have been discovering since the turn of the last century. 7hills@berkshire.net http://www.sevenhillsinn.com

BERKSHIRES (REGION)

The Village Inn
PO Box 1810
16 Church St, *Lenox* 01240
413-637-0020 Fax: 413-637-9756
800-253-0917
Clifford Rudisill & Ray Wilson
All year

60-270-BB
32 rooms, 32 pb
Most CC, *Rated*, •
C-ltd/S-ltd/P-no/H-yes
Spanish, French, German

Full or Continental plus breakfast
Dinner available
Sitting room, library, TV/VCRs in rooms, movies, voice mail, hair dryers

Built in 1771, this authentic New England inn has been lovingly restored and renovated to include modern amenities such as bathrooms with hairdryers, magnifying mirrors, and most with whirlpool tubs. villinn@vgernet.net http://www.villageinn-lenox.com

---

Walker House
64 Walker St, *Lenox* 01240
413-637-1271 Fax: 413-637-2387
800-235-3098
Peggy & Richard Houdek
All year

80-220-BB
8 rooms, 8 pb
Rated
C-ltd/S-no/P-ltd/H-ltd
Spanish, French

Continental plus breakfast
Complimentary wine, afternoon tea
Sitting room, piano, library video theatre, opera/film weekends

Our guests feel like special pampered friends. Lovely country atmosphere on 3 acres.
phoudek@vgernet.net http://walkerhouse.com

Whistler's Inn
5 Greenwood St, *Lenox* 01240
413-637-0975 Fax: 413-637-2190
866-637-0975
Lisa Mears All year

90-225-BB
14 rooms, 14 pb
Rated, •

Full breakfast

Celebrating our 30th year, Whistler's Inn is an 1820 English Tudor country manor house in the heart of New England's beautiful Berkshires.
mail@whistlersinnlenox.com http://www.whistlersinnlenox.com

A B&B in the Berkshires
1666 Dublin Rd, *Richmond* 01254
413-698-2817 Fax: 413-698-3158
800-795-7122
Doane Perry
All year

95-300-BB
3 rooms, 3 pb
Visa, MC, AmEx, *Rated*, •
C-yes/S-no/P-ltd/H-ltd
Frrench, German, Greek, Swahili

Continental plus breakfast
Afternoon tea, snacks
Sitting room, library, bicycles, comp. wine, cable TV

Gracious hosts offer great beds and breakfasts, private baths, hammock in the orchard, rolling lawns and meadows.
doaneperry@compuserve.com http://www.berkshirelodgings.com/abed.html

---

The Inn at Richmond
802 State Rd (Rt 41), *Richmond* 01254
413-698-2566 Fax: (413) 698-2100
(888) 968-4748
Jerri Buehler All year

125-325-BB
9 rooms, 9 pb
Visa, MC, *Rated*
C-ltd/S-no/P-no/H-ltd

Full gourmet breakfast
Comp. Port-Sherry-soft-drinks-chocolate truffles
Library, books/videos, greenhouse/gardens, equestrian ctr, snowshoes

The Inn at Richmond, a Berkshires Bed and Breakfast, is a historic country inn situated on twenty-seven magnificent acres in western Massachusetts. The inn is romantic, tranquil and casually elegant. innkeepers@innatrichmond.com http://www.innatrichmond.com

---

Federal House
PO Box 248
1560 Pleasant St, Rt 102, *South Lee* 01260
413-243-1824 Fax: 800-243-1828
800-243-1824
Dick & Sue Cody All year

100-245-BB
9 rooms, 9 pb
Most CC
C-ltd/S-no/P-no/H-ltd

Full candlelight breakfast
Complimentary sherry, wine list, liquor cabinet

Historic 1824 Greek Revival home, gracious common areas, bright sunny guestrooms, some with fireplaces, queen beds, pvt baths, full candlelight breakfast. A mile from Stockbridge, mins to Tanglewood.
innkeeper@federalhouseinn.com http://www.federalhouseinn.com

BERKSHIRES (REGION)

Arbor Rose
8 Yale Hill Rd, *Stockbridge* 01262
413-298-4744 Fax: 413-298-4235
877-298-4744
Christina Alsop
All year

110-175-BB
6 rooms, 6 pb
Visa, MC, *Rated*, •
C-yes/S-no/P-ltd/H-no
French

Full or continental plus
Full breakfast on weekends
Sitting room, family friendly facility, fireplaced dining rooms

Charming 1810 mill and farmhouse with flowing pond & gardens, country antiques, new 4-poster beds, lovely fabrics and rural paintings. The mill has post & beam rafters and sounds of the flowing stream. innkeeper@arborrose.com http://www.arborrose.com

---

Inn at Stockbridge
PO Box 618
Rt 7 N, *Stockbridge* 01262
413-298-3337 Fax: 413-298-3406
888-466-7865
Alice & Len Schiller
All year

130-325-BB
16 rooms, 16 pb
Most CC, *Rated*, •
C-ltd/S-no/P-no/H-no

Full breakfast
Complimentary wine
Sitting room, library, antiques, phones, A/C, pool, fireplace

Experience peaceful charm and elegance in a 1906 Georgian style mansion secluded on 12 acres. Sixteen well appointed guest rooms, many with a fireplace, double whirlpool, and wonderful amenities. innkeeper@stockbridgeinn.com http://www.stockbridgeinn.com

---

The Red Lion Inn
PO Box 954
30 Main St, *Stockbridge* 01262
413-298-5545 Fax: 413-298-5130
Brooks Bradbury
All year

125-220-EP
109 rooms, 95 pb
Visa, MC, AmEx, *Rated*, •
C-yes/S-no/P-no/H-yes
Spanish, French

Restaurant, full service dining and room service

The Berkshires' ultra-savvy new inn. Spacious rooms and suites with a contemporary-retro decor. Attitude-free service. Fully wired rooms with high-speed Internet.
reservations@redlioninn.com http://www.redlioninn.com

House On Main Street
1120 Main St, *Williamstown* 01267
413-458-3031 Fax: 413-458-2254
Timothy Hamilton & Donna Riley
All year

85-175-BB
6 rooms, 3 pb
Visa, MC, AmEx, *Rated*, •
C-yes/S-no/P-no/H-ltd

Full breakfast
Sitting room, fireplace in living room, cable TV in 1 bedroom & living room

The charm of the Victorian era with the luxury of the 21st century nestled in a tree-lined setting, with the convenience of walking to the Clark Art Museum, Williams College, WTF, shopping and dining. Relax@HouseOnMainStreet.com http://www.houseonmainst.com

---

Steep Acres Farm
520 White Oaks Rd, *Williamstown* 01267
413-458-3774
Mary & Marvin Gangemi
All year

90-150-BB
4 rooms, 3 pb
Rated
C-ltd/S-no/P-no/H-no

Full gourmet breakfast
Complimentary wine
Sitting room, swimming, 1 1/2 acre pond, fishing, hiking trails, boating

Country home on a high knoll—spectacular views of Berkshire Hills & Vermont's Green Mts. Furnished in country antiques. jmgangemi@adelphia.net

BOSTON

198 Clarendon Square Inn
198 West Brookline St 02118
617-536-2229
Stephen Gross & Michael Selbst
All year

119-259-BB
3 rooms, 3 pb
Most CC, •
C-ltd/S-no/P-no/H-no
French

Continental plus breakfast
Broadband & Dial-up Access, fax machine, formal parlors, rooftop hot-tub

Boston's finest small inn experience! Tranquil and spacious guestrooms, marble baths, CD stereo, high-speed Internet, fireplaces. Featured in Travel & Leisure, Yankee, Interiors Mag. and CBS News. stephen@clarendonsquare.com http://www.clarendonsquare.com

BOSTON

Appleton Studios
PO Box 57166
32 Appleton St 02457
781-647-4949 Fax: 781-647-7437
888-486-6019
Marie Kemmler
All year

100-155-EP
2 rooms, 2 pb
Visa, MC, AmEx, •
C-yes/S-no/P-no/H-no

2 furnished studio apartments on the 2nd floor. Occupancy up to 4/apt.

In a 19th Century South End townhouse, three blocks from Copley Square, and on one of Boston's prettiest residential streets, are two furnished studio apartments.
marie@bnbboston.com http://www.bnbboston.com

Beacon Hill
27 Brimmer St 02108
617-523-7376
Susan Butterworth
All year

200-275-BB
3 rooms, 3 pb
Rated, •
C-yes/S-no/P-no/H-no
French

Full breakfast
Restaurants, convenience stores one block away
Sitting room, garage nearby, elevator for luggage, a/c

Superb location in most exclusive historically preserved downtown neighborhood. Private home in elegant 1869 Victorian townhouse overlooking river, spacious rooms, private baths, home-cooked breakfast bhillbb@aol.com

---

Bunker Hill
80 Elm St 02129
617-241-8067 Fax: 617-886-9367
Christiane Wolff
All year

125-150-BB
2 rooms, 2 pb
Visa, MC
C-yes/S-yes/P-yes/H-no
German, French

Full breakfast
Afternoon tea, snacks
Library, central air, Jacuzzis, cable TV, video library, deck, yard, pond

Home away from home. I supply amenities: slippers, bathrobes, toiletries, VCRs, video & book library, curling irons, hairdryers, snacks, umbrellas and more . . . just bring yourself!
crawolff@cs.com http://www.bunkerhillbedandbreakfast.com

Carruth House
30 Beaumont St 02124
617-436-8260 Fax: 617-436-5320
888-838-8900
Heidi Kieffer-Higgins
All year

85-125-BB
3 rooms, 1 pb
C-ltd/S-ltd/P-no/H-no

Continental plus breakfast

An affordable Private Home Bed & Breakfast in a gracious neighborhood setting—convenient to downtown Boston by subway and offering a comfortable place to relax after a busy day in Boston.
carruthhouse@yahoo.com http://www.geocities.com./carruthhouse

---

The Charles Street Inn
94 Charles St 02114
617-314-8900 Fax: 617-371-0009
877-772-8900
Sally Deane & Louise Venden
All year

220-395-BB
9 rooms, 9 pb
Most CC, •
C-yes/S-no/P-no/H-yes

Continental plus breakfast
Snacks
Library, Jacuzzis, fireplaces, cable TV, accom. bus. travel

Historic luxury urban Inn furnished in Victorian antiques with all modern amenities.
info@charlesstreetinn.com http://www.charlesstreetinn.com

The Gryphon House
9 Bay State Rd 02215
617-375-9003 Fax: 617-425-0716
877-375-9003
Teresa Blagg
All year

150-260-BB
8 rooms, 8 pb
Most CC, •
C-ltd/S-no/P-no/H-no

Continental breakfast
Fruit is always available in the lobby
Video & CD library, high speed internet, internet station in lobby, Cable TV

The Gryphon House is set in the heart of Boston, MA. We offer charm and hospitality in a fully renovated four-story brownstone in Boston's Back Bay area overlooking the Charles River. innkeeper@gryphonhouseboston.com http://www.gryphonhouseboston.com

BOSTON

Oasis Guest House
22 Edgerly Rd 02115
617-267-2262 Fax: 617-267-1920
Joe Haley
All year

90-139-BB
16 rooms, 10 pb
Visa, MC, AmEx,
Rated, •
C-ltd/S-ltd/P-no/H-no

Continental breakfast
Snacks
Sitting room, cable TV, fax capabilities

Two townhouses in the heart of Boston. Telephone, televisions, central air, outdoor decks, parking on a quiet residential street. info@oasisgh.com http://www.oasisgh.com

---

Taylor House
50 Burroughs St 02130
617-983-9334 Fax: 617-522-3852
888-228-2956
Dave Elliott & Daryl Bichel
All year

100-190-BB
6 rooms, 6 pb
Most CC
C-ltd/S-no/P-ltd/H-no

Continental plus breakfast
Snacks
TV/VCR in room, tape library, common room, modem access, phones

Italianate Victorian home with spacious rooms, high ceilings, private baths, near public transportation, restaurants & shopping.
Dave@taylorhouse.com http://www.taylorhouse.com

BOSTON (REGION)

Vine & Ivy
212 Hart St, *Beverly Farms* 01915
978-927-2917 Fax: 978-927-4610
800-975-5516
Jim Glesener
All year

150-250-BB
5 rooms, 5 pb
Most CC, •
C-yes/S-no/P-no/H-yes
Spanish

Full breakfast
Sitting room, pool, suites, cable TV, accom. bus. travelers

Charming New England renovated carriage and barn buildings filled with antiques, opening to beautiful gardens and pool, courtyard. Gourmet breakfast menu.
vineandivy@aol.com http://www.vineandivy.com

Anthony's Town House
1085 Beacon St, *Brookline* 02446
617-566-3972 Fax: 617-232-1085
Barbara A. Anthony
All year

75-95-EP
14 rooms
Rated, •
C-yes/S-no/P-no/H-no

Restaurant, stores nearby
Near major league sports, A/C, sitting room, historical sites, cable TV

Turn-of-the-century Brownstone townhouse; spacious rooms in Victorian atmosphere; family-operated for over 50 years; 10 min. to Boston. Non-smoking Inn.
info@anthonystownhouse.com http://www.anthonystownhouse.com

The Bertram Inn
92 Sewall Avenue, *Brookline* 02446
617-566-2234 Fax: 617-277-1877
800-295-3822
Bryan Austin
All year

109-239-BB
14 rooms, 14 pb
Most CC, *Rated*, •
C-ltd/S-no/P-yes/H-no
Spanish, Italian

Continental plus breakfast
Afternoon tea, snacks
Iron & board, hairdryers in all rooms, A/C, fax on premises

Come home to Victorian elegance. Ten minutes to Boston by trolley. Furnished with period antiques. innkeeper@bertraminn.com http://www.bertraminn.com

---

The Samuel Sewall Inn
143 St. Paul St, *Brookline* 02446
617-713-0123 888-713-2566
Naida, Tara and Jen
All year

89-209-BB
14 rooms, 14 pb
Most CC, •
C-ltd/S-ltd/P-no/H-yes
English, French, Spanish, Portuguese

Deluxe Breakfast
Tea, snacks, cakes & cookies, early breakfast
Living room, patio, porch

We would love to welcome you to The Samuel Sewall Inn, where enchanting Victorian elegance, contemporary comforts and exceptional service are united at their finest.
innkeeper@samuelsewallinn.com http://www.samuelsewallinn.com

BOSTON (REGION)

Harding House 288 Harvard St, *Cambridge* 02139 617-876-2888 Fax: 617-497-0953 877-489-2888 David Fishman All year	109-300-BB 14 rooms, 14 pb Visa, MC, AmEx, *Rated*, • C-yes/S-no/P-no/H-yes	Continental plus breakfast Afternoon tea Sitting room, voice mail, fax

Located within an easy walk of Harvard Square, Harding House offers quiet, friendly charm in its 14 rooms on a tree-lined residential street. harding@irvinghouse.com

---

Irving House at Harvard 24 Irving St, *Cambridge* 02138 617-547-4600 Fax: 617-576-2814 877-547-4600 Rachael Solem All year	99-199-BB 44 rooms, 29 pb Visa, MC, AmEx, *Rated*, • C-yes/S-no/P-ltd/H-yes Swahili, Hindi	Continental plus breakfast Sitting room, library, cribs, central A/C, fax, laundry, conference room

Friendly accommodations in the heart of Cambridge since 1945. Off-street parking. 10 min. walk to Harvard Square. reserve@irvinghouse.com http://www.irvinghouse.com

---

Prospect Place 112 Prospect St, *Cambridge* 02139 617-864-7500 Fax: 617-576-1159 800-769-5303 Eric Huenneke All year	90-170-BB 4 rooms, 2 pb Visa, MC C-ltd/S-no/P-no/H-no	Full breakfast Afternoon tea Sitting room, accommodate business travelers

The most historic B&B in Cambridge—19th century charm at its best with terrific and discreet modern updates. Gourmet quality full breakfast served on fine china and linens. info@prospectpl.com http://www.prospectpl.com

---

Park Lane 11 Park Lane, *Newton Centre* 02459 617-964-1666 Fax: 617-964-8588 800-772-6759 Pat Pransky All year	85-115-BB 3 rooms, 1 pb Visa, MC, AmEx, *Rated*, • C-yes/S-ltd/P-no/H-no	Continental breakfast Fresh bread Sitting room, bikes, Jacuzzi, cable TV, room seats 20 people

A 10 minute walk to Newton Center T Station (high speed light rail) in a quiet tree-lined neighborhood. info@bostonbandb.com http://bostonbandb.com

---

1810 House 147 Old Oaken Bucket Rd, *Norwell* 02061 781-659-1810 Fax: 781-659-1810 888-833-1810 Susanne & Harold Tuttle All year	95-105-BB 3 rooms, 2 pb • C-ltd/S-no/P-no/H-no	Full breakfast Sitting room, family suite, antique 1915 Model T

Enjoy a memorable stay in an antique home, with great beds, good food and friendly hosts. Wonderful location near Boston and Plymouth.
tuttle1810@earthlink.net http://www.1810house.com

Joan's RR 210 Lynn St, *Peabody* 01960 978-532-0191 Fax: 978-536-2726 Joan Hetherington All year	55-85-BB 3 rooms, 1 pb C-ltd/S-no/P-no/H-no	Continental plus breakfast Afternoon tea, snacks Sitting room, patio, swimming pool, laundry, use of whole house

Located 10 min. from historic Salem, 25 min. from Boston, and 25 min. from picturesque Gloucester and Rockport. All rooms have A/C. joanbandb@rcn.com

BOSTON (REGION)

Morrison House
221 Morrison Ave, *Somerville* 02144
617-627-9670 877-627-9670
Ron & Linde Dynneson
All year

60-100-BB
2 rooms
Visa, MC
C-ltd/S-no/P-no/H-no
Some German

Continental plus breakfast
Tea, snacks available
Sitting room, patio, computer with high-speed Internet access

This charming, 11-room, Italianate, turn-of-the-century house is your tranquil home-away-from-home right in the heart of one of North America's most vibrant neighborhoods. innkeeper@morrisonhousebnb.com http://www.morrisonhousebnb.com

BREWSTER

The Blue Cedar
699 Main St 02631
508-896-4353
Diane & Clyde Mosher
May 1–October 31

95-135-BB
3 rooms, 3 pb
Visa, MC
C-ltd/S-no/P-no

Full breakfast
Cable TV, Air conditioning, guest fridge

Our home was originally an 1840's farmhouse in the Greek Revival Style. It is located on historic Old King's Highway on the west side of Brewster.
cmosher@cape.com http://www.thebluecedar.com

The Bramble Inn & Rest.
PO Box 807
2019 Main St 02631
508-896-7644
Ruth & Cliff Manchester
All year

135-175-BB
8 rooms, 8 pb
Rated
C-ltd/S-no/P-no

Full breakfast
Restaurant

The Main Inn, built in 1861, houses a restaurant on the first floor, with lodging rooms on the second floor. Short stroll to Cape Cod Bay. chefola@aol.com
http://www.brambleinn.com

BROOKLINE

The Beech Tree Inn
83 Longwood Ave 02446
617-277-1620 Fax: 617-277-0657
800-544-9660
Katherine Anderson
All year

120-150-BB
11 rooms, 7 pb
Visa, MC, AmEx, •
C-yes/S-no/P-yes/H-no
German

Continental breakfast
Coffee, Tea, and Cookies in the Afternoon
Sitting room, cable TV, tennis courts nearby, historical sites

Victorian style B&B boasts individually decorated guestrooms, all with TV's, Cable, phones and A/C. Enjoy downtown Boston in 15 minutes via nearby trolley. beechtre@gis.net

CAMBRIDGE

Antrim House
16 Antrim St 02139
617-491-5477
Jean LoPresti
All year

125-BB
S-no/P-no

Den w/ TV/VCR and a radio/CD

Whether visiting Cambridge for pleasure, business, or academia, Antrim House is the perfect location. Subways and buses easily accessible.
antrimhouse@aol.com http://www.antrimhouse.com

A B&B in Cambridge
1657 Cambridge St 02138
617-868-7082 Fax: 617-876-8991
800-795-7122
Doane Perry
All year

125-180-BB
3 rooms
Visa, MC, AmEx,
Rated, •
C-ltd/S-no/P-no/H-no
Fr.,Ger., Greek, Swahili

Full breakfast
Afternoon tea, snacks, wine
Sitting room, library, swimming pool, cable TV

1897 Colonial Revival home, close to Harvard Square, affordable elegance near museums, theaters, restaurants. Fresh flowers, antiques, great beds.
doaneperry@compuserve.com http://www.cambridgebnb.com

CAMBRIDGE

Blue's
82 Avon Hill St 02140
617-354-6106
Mary Magruder
All year

110-150-BB
2 rooms
C-ltd/S-no/P-no/H-no
French

Continental plus breakfast

A comfortable, antiques-filled B&B on a quiet, tree-lined street just north of the Harvard campus offers spacious sunlit rooms, 4 blocks walk to Porter Square subway, shops and restaurants. bluesbnb@attbi.com

---

The Mary Prentiss Inn
6 Prentiss St 00140
617-661-2929 Fax: 617-661-5989
Jennifer Fandetti
Season Inquire

99-259-BB
20 rooms, 20 pb
Visa, MC, AmEx,
Rated, •
C-yes/S-no/P-no/H-yes

Full breakfast
Afternoon tea, snacks
Sitting room, large, outdoor deck, laundry, conference room

Historic house in neoclassical Greek Revival style. Rooms furnished with genuine antiques. Near Harvard Square. njfandetti@aol.com http://www.maryprentissinn.com

CAMBRIDGE (REGION)

A Cambridge House
2218 Massachusetts Ave, *Somerville* 02143
617-491-6300 Fax: 617-868-2848
800-232-9989
Ellen Riley
All year

109-275-BB
16 rooms, 14 pb

Full breakfast buffet
Hors d'oeuvres, pasta w/lots of toppings, cookies

A Cambridge House Bed and Breakfast is a unique turn-of-the-century inn offering warm hospitality in an elegant setting convenient to Cambridge and the Boston area.
innach@aol.com http://www.acambridgehouse.com

CAPE COD (REGION)

Ashley Manor
PO Box 856
3660 Main St, *Barnstable* 02630
508-362-8044 Fax: 508-362-9927
888-535-2246
Kathy Callahan
All year

140-225-BB
6 rooms, 6 pb
Most CC, *Rated*, •
C-ltd/S-no/P-no/H-no

Full gourmet breakfast
Complimentary wine, sherry, port
Sitting rm, A/C, bikes, tennis, garden, imported bedside chocolates

1699 mansion in the historic district. Rooms & suites have antiques, fireplaces and some with Jacuzzis & private baths. Walk to beach, village & harbor.
stay@ashleymanor.net http://www.ashleymanor.net

Cobb's Cove Inn
PO Box 208
31 Powder Hill Rd, *Barnstable* 02630
508-362-9356 Fax: 508-362-9356
877-378-5172
Evelyn Chester All year

149-189-BB
6 rooms, 6 pb
Rated, •
S-ltd/P-no/H-no
French

Full breakfast
Dinner, complimentary wine, tea
Whirlpool tubs, robes, toiletries, piano, sitting room, library

Secluded getaway inn for couples. Two fabulous honeymoon suites with water views.
cobbscove@webtv.net http://www.cobbscove.com

Honeysuckle Hill
591 Main St
591 Old King's Hwy, *West Barnstable* 02668
508-362-8418 Fax: 508-362-8386
866-444-5522
Bill & Mary Kilburn
All year

100-210-BB
5 rooms, 4 pb
Most CC, *Rated*
C-ltd/S-ltd/P-no/H-no

Full breakfast
Chocolates & sherry
A/C, screened porch, near beaches, fresh, flowers, am coffee

On National Register, c.1810, this enchanting cottage offers comfortably elegant rooms & graciously served breakfasts.
stay@honeysucklehill.com http://www.honeysucklehill.com

CAPE COD (REGION)

Lamb and Lion Inn PO Box 511 2504 Main Street (Route 6A), *Barnstable* 02630 508-362-6823 Fax: 508-362-0227 800-909-6923 Alice Pitcher, Tom Dott All year	125-250-BB 10 rooms, 10 pb Visa, MC, *Rated*, • C-ltd/S-no/P-ltd/H-no	Heated pool, outdoor Jacuzzi, 11 fireplaces, sitting room, conference room

A classic 1740's Inn on 4 acres boasting 10 suites, 12 fireplaces and rambling "open-air" hallways, creating a central courtyard with full-sized heated pool and year-round outdoor hot tub spa. info@lambandlion.com http://www.lambandlion.com

Beechwood Inn 2839 Main St (Rt 6A), *Barnstable Village* 02630 508-362-6618 Fax: 508-362-0298 800-609-6618 Ken & Debbie Traugot	150-185-BB 6 rooms, 6 pb Most CC, *Rated*, • C-ltd/S-no/P-no/H-no All year	Full gourmet breakfast Afternoon snacks & bev. Parlor, veranda, croquet, bikes, garden, all rooms have A/C

Award winning romantic Victorian inn along the historic "Old King's Way." Spacious antique-filled guestrooms offer fireplaces & views of Cape Cod Bay.
info@beechwoodinn.com http://www.beechwoodinn.com

Captain Isaiah's House 33 Pleasant St, *Bass River* 02664 508-394-1739 Marge & Alden Late June–early Sept.	55-80-BB 6 rooms, 2 pb *Rated* C-ltd/S-no/P-no/H-no	Continental breakfast Home-baked goodies Sitting room, fireplaces, 2 studio apartments, whale watching nearby

Charming, restored old sea captain's house in historic Bass River area. Most rooms have fireplaces. info@captainisaiahs.com http://www.captainisaiahs.com

Candleberry Inn 1882 Main St, *Brewster* 02631 508-896-3300 Fax: 508-896-4016 800-573-4769 Gini & David Donnelly All year	105-225-BB 9 rooms, 9 pb Most CC, *Rated* C-ltd/S-no/P-no/H-no	Full breakfast Afternoon tea, snacks, wine Sitting room, library, Jacuzzis, fireplaces, suites, cable TV

Elegant, 250 yr. old inn. 2 acres priv. gardens. Rooms furnished with antiques; some with fireplaces or Jacuzzi. House for weekly rental also available.
candle@cape.com http://www.candleberryinn.com

Captain Freeman Inn 15 Breakwater Rd, *Brewster* 02631 508-896-7481 Fax: 508-896-5618 800-843-4664 Carol & Tom Edmondson All year	150-250-BB 12 rooms, 12 pb Visa, MC, AmEx, *Rated*, • C-ltd/S-no/P-no/H-no	Full breakfast Afternoon tea, al fresco dining Sitting room, Jacuzzi, bicycles, badminton, A/C, swimming pool, croquet

Lovingly restored Victorian mansion. Queen canopy beds, romantic wrap- around porch, fireplaces and whirlpool spas. Full breakfast, afternoon tea. In-ground pool, walk to Beautiful Breakwater Beach.
stay@captainfreemaninn.com http://www.captainfreemaninn.com

The Old Manse Inn & Rest. PO Box 745 1861 Main St, *Brewster* 02631 508-896-3149 Fax: 508-896-1546 David & Suzanne Plum March-Dec.	120-148-BB 9 rooms, 9 pb Visa, MC, AmEx, *Rated* C-ltd/S-yes/P-no/H-yes	Full breakfast Gourmet dinner, bar, afternoon tea Coffee, library, patio, garden, A/C, 6 rooms have cable TV

Enjoy salt air from room in antique sea captain's home. Walk to Cape Cod's attractions. Gourmet dining by reservation. oldmanse@c4.net http://www.oldmanseinn.com

CAPE COD (REGION)

Old Sea Pines Inn PO Box 1026 2553 Main St, *Brewster* 02631 508-896-6114 Fax: 508-896-7387 Stephen & Michele Rowan April-Dec. 22	75-150-BB 24 rooms, 15 pb Most CC, *Rated*, • C-ltd/S-no/P-no/H-ltd Italian, German	Full breakfast Beverage on arrival, restaurant Parlor with, fireplace, deck, Sunday, dinner theatre summers only

Turn-of-the-century mansion furnished with antiques. Near beaches, bicycle trails, quality restaurants & shops. innkeeper@oldseapinesinn.com http://www.oldseapinesinn.com

---

The Ruddy Turnstone 463 Main St, *Brewster* 02631 508-385-9871 Fax: 508-385-5696 800-654-1995 Sally & Swanee All year	125-175-BB 5 rooms, 5 pb *Rated*, •	Full breakfast

The Ruddy Turnstone B&B captures the flavor of old Cape Cod. The restored early 19th century house & carriage house are situated on three acres of land with a magnificent view of Cape Cod Bay! rturnstone@msn.com http://www.theruddyturnstone.com

---

Adam's Terrace Gardens Inn 539 Main St, *Centerville* 02632 508-775-4707 Fax: 508-775-4707 Louise Pritchard All year	100-125-BB 8 rooms, 5 pb Visa, MC, *Rated*, • C-yes/S-ltd/P-no/H-no French	Full breakfast Afternoon tea Sitting room, bikes, beach chairs, parasols, fireplaces, cable TV, fridge

Historic Captain home located on Captain's Row in beautiful Centerville, 10 minute walk to churches and beach. louise@adamsterrace.com http://www.adamsterrace.com

---

Cyrus Kent House Inn 63 Cross St, *Chatham* 02633 508-945-9104 Fax: 508-945-9106 800-338-5368 Steve & Sandra Goldman All year	100-300-BB 10 rooms, 10 pb Most CC C-ltd/S-no/P-no/H-ltd German	Continental plus breakfast Afternoon tea upon request Porch, deck, gardens, ample parking, phones, art & antique gallery

Gardens surround the award winning Cyrus Kent House, providing beautiful views from all 10 rooms. Just off Main St. in the Village Center the only thing you'll hear is the chiming of the church bell. cyrus@cape.com http://www.cyruskent.com

---

Moses Nickerson House Inn 364 Old Harbor Rd, *Chatham* 02633 508-945-5859 Fax: 508-945-7087 800-628-6972 Linda & George Watts	149-209-BB 7 rooms, 7 pb Most CC, *Rated*, • C-ltd/S-no/P-no/H-no All year	Full breakfast Tea or lemonade with cookies In-room phones, antiques, TV, A/C

Elegant sea captain's home built 1839. Canopy beds, fireplaces, romantic, quiet. Walk to village & beaches. tmnhi@attbi.com http://www.mosesnickersonhouse.com

---

Acworth Inn PO Box 256 4352 Main St, Rt 6A, *Cummaquid* 02637 508-362-3330 Fax: 508-375-0304 800-362-6363 Lisa Callahan All year	120-185-BB 5 rooms, 5 pb Visa, MC, AmEx, *Rated*, • C-ltd/S-no/P-no/H-no German	Full breakfast Afternoon tea, snacks Sitting room, bicycles, flower and herb gardens

Cape Cod charm in the center of the historic district; especially noted for the hand painted furnishings; easy access to islands.
host@acworthinn.com http://www.acworthinn.com

CAPE COD (REGION)

Isaiah Hall
PO Box 1007
152 Whig St, *Dennis* 02638
508-385-9928 Fax: 508-385-5879
800-736-0160
Marie Brophy

105-185-BB
10 rooms, 10 pb
Most CC, *Rated*, •
C-ltd/S-no/P-no/H-ltd
May 4–October 20

Continental plus breakfast
Complimentary tea, coffee, chocolate chip cookies
AC, TV/VCR's, Phones, robes, Internet access, guest fridge, garden, library

This lovely AAA 3 Diamond Inn surrounded by gardens is in the heart of Cape Cod. Walk to beach & village. Guestrooms are comfortably appointed with antiques, Orientals & modern amenities. info@isaiahhallinn.com http://www.isaiahhallinn.com

---

Scargo Manor
909 Main St, *Dennis* 02638
508-385-5534 Fax: 508-385-9791
800-595-0034
Richard & Lin Foa All year

95-195-BB
6 rooms, 6 pb
Most CC
C-yes/S-no/P-no/H-no
Italian, French

Full breakfast
Snacks, restaurant next door
Sitting room, library, bikes, suites, fireplaces, cable TV, lakefront, boats

Elegant, comfortable lodging on Scargo Lake in historic sea captain's home. Gardens, docks, small boats, bikes, art & antique collections. Families welcome.
scargomanor@attbi.net http://www.scargomanor.com

By-the-Sea Guests B&B & Suites
PO Box 507
57 Chase Avenue & Inman Road Extension, *Dennisport* 02639
508-398-8685 Fax: 508-398-0334
800-447-9202

78-175-BB
17 rooms, 17 pb
Visa, MC, AmEx, *Rated*, •
C-yes/S-no/P-no/H-no
Greek, German, Portuguese, French
May 1–December 1

Continental plus breakfast
Afternoon tea, snacks
Sitting room, HBO/cable TV, private beach

Owned & operated by By The Sea Guests LLC

Oceanfront B breakfast served overlooking private beach; quaint villages; lighthouses; antique shops; bicycle paths and golf courses.
bythesea@capecod.net http://www.bytheseaguests.com

Nauset House Inn
PO Box 774
143 Beach Rd, *East Orleans* 02643
508-255-2195 Fax: 508-240-6276
Diane Johnson, Cindy and John Vessella

75-160-BB
14 rooms, 8 pb
Visa, MC, Disc, *Rated*
C-ltd/S-no/P-no/H-no
Apri–October

Full breakfast
Wine & hors d'oeuvres
Commons room, conservatory, dining room

Intimate 1810 inn, unique turn-of-the-century conservatory, warm ambiance, only 1/2 mile to the beautiful Nauset Beach.
info@nausethouseinn.com http://www.nausethouseinn.com

Ship's Knees Inn
PO Box 756
186 Beach Road, *East Orleans* 02643
508-255-1312 Fax: 508-240-1351
Lesley & George Sloane

55-150-BB
25 rooms, 11 pb
Visa, MC, *Rated*, •
C-ltd/S-no/P-no/H-no
All year

Continental breakfast
Sitting room, pool, tennis

The Ship's Knees Inn is a 180-year-old restored sea captain's home–three minute walk to beautiful sand duned Nauset Beach. Pool and Tennis on the Premises. Continental Breakfast–Open year round. skinauset@aol.com http://capecodtravel.com/shipskneesinn

---

Overlook Inn
PO Box 771
3085 County Rd, Route 6, *Eastham* 02642
508-255-1886 Fax: 508-240-0345
Pam & Don Andersen

145-200-BB
14 rooms, 14 pb
Most CC, •
C-ltd/S-ltd/P-ltd/H-ltd
All year

Full breakfast
Dinner occ., Afternoon tea
Sitting room, billiard room, 3 family suites in our Carriage House

Victorian mansion across from the Cape Cod National Seashore offering Danish hospitality. Antique-filled guestrooms with private baths, some fireplaces, includes a full breakfast. stay@overlookinn.com http://www.overlookinn.com

CAPE COD (REGION)

Penny House Inn 4885 Route 6, *Eastham* 02642 508-255-6632 Fax: 508-255-4893 800-554-1751 Margaret & Rebecca Keith All year	150-315-BB 12 rooms, 12 pb Most CC, *Rated*, • C-ltd/S-no/P-no/H-no	Full breakfast Afternoon refreshments Sunroom, outside patio, great room w/fireplace

Built in 1690, this luxury B&B inn has 12 elegantly decorated guestrooms and suites. pennyhouse@aol.com http://www.pennyhouseinn.com

---

Whalewalk Inn 220 Bridge Rd, *Eastham* 02642 508-255-0617 Fax: 508-240-0017 800-440-1281 Elaine and Kevin Conlin All year	190-325-BB 16 rooms, 16 pb Most CC, *Rated*, • C-ltd/S-no/P-no/H-ltd	Full gourmet breakfast Comp. hors d'ouevres Bar, sitting room, patio, all rooms are A/C, all suites with fireplaces

Restored 1830s whaling master's home. Elegance, hospitality. Uniquely decorated. On quiet road by bay, ocean. information@whalewalkinn.com http://www.whalewalkinn.com

---

Captain Tom Lawrence House 75 Locust St, *Falmouth* 02540 508-548-9178 Fax: 508-457-1790 800-266-8139 Anne Grebert & Jim Cotter All year	90-220-BB 6 rooms, 6 pb Visa, MC, AmEx, *Rated* C-ltd/S-no/P-no/H-ltd	Full gourmet breakfast Complimentary afternoon home-baked snacks Sitting room, A/C, porch, cable TV and refrigerator in each room

Elegant, historic whaling captain's home. Close to sea beaches, numerous golf courses, restaurants, ferries to Martha's Vineyard & Nantucket.
CaptTomHouse@aol.com http://www.CaptainTomLawrence.com

Grafton Inn 261 Grand Ave South, *Falmouth* 02540 508-540-8688 Fax: 508-540-1861 800-642-4069 Rudy J. Cvitan Mid-April-Nov.	110-260-BB 10 rooms, 10 pb Visa, MC, *Rated*, • C-ltd/S-no/P-no/H-no Croatian	Full Breakfast Complimentary wine/cheese Sitting room, porch, phones available, A/C, cable TV

Oceanfront B&B—Queen Anne Style Victorian. Completely restored. Breathtaking views of Nantucket Sound and Martha's Vineyard. Ten rooms with private shower baths, period antiques throughout. graftoninn12@aol.com http://www.graftoninn.com

---

Hewins House 20 Hewins St, *Falmouth* 02540 508-457-4363 Fax: 508-540-5891 877-4-HEWINS Virginia Price All year	115-125-BB 3 rooms, 3 pb Disc, • C-yes/S-no/P-no/H-no	Full breakfast Kitchen facility Sitting room, porch, walk to free shuttle for Martha's Vineyard ferry

Your home on Olde Cape Cod-National Register Historic District. Gardens, porch, breakfast in dining room. Convenient location for all Cape attractions.
hewhousebb@aol.com http://www.hewinshousebb.com

Inn on the Sound 313 Grand Ave S, *Falmouth* 02540 508-457-9666 Fax: 508-457-9631 800-564-9668 Renee Ross & David Ross All year	150-295-BB 10 rooms, 10 pb Most CC, *Rated*, • C-no/S-no/P-no/H-no	Breakfast; 8:30 to 11:00 AM Comp. hot/cold beverages; sweet treat each evening Fabulous ocean views, footsteps to the beach; short stroll to Vineyard Ferry

This special oceanfront Bed & Breakfast boasts breathtaking views of Vineyard Sound & Martha's Vineyard. Professionally decorated, meticulously maintained and highly acclaimed in all publications. info@innonthesound.com http://www.innonthesound.com

CAPE COD (REGION)

Inn at One Main
1 Main St, *Falmouth* 02540
508-540-7469 888-281-6246
Christi & Ray Stoltz
All year

110-185-BB
6 rooms, 6 pb
Most CC, *Rated*, •
C-yes/S-no/P-no/H-no

Full breakfast
Coffee, teas and homemade cookies
Sitting room, A/C, cable TV, Martha's Vineyard ferry

This light and airy 1892 Victorian welcomes guests year-round. Walk to shops, beaches, Shining Sea Bike path, ferry shuttle to Martha's Vineyard
innat1main@aol.com http://www.innatonemain.com

La Maison Cappellari @ Mostly Hall
27 Main St, *Falmouth* 02540
508-548-3786 Fax: 508-548-5778
800-682-0565
Christina & Bogdan Simcic
Apr. .-Dec.

185-225-BB
6 rooms, 6 pb
Most CC, *Rated*
S-no/P-no/H-no
German, French, Italian

Full gourmet breakfast
To be decided upon the customer's needs
Sitting room, gazebo, veranda, porch, bicycles, gardens

Hidden splendor, this Italianate Villa brings sophisticated style in a relaxed atmosphere. Unique mural paintings and full gourmet European breakfast will make your stay unforgettable. mostlyhall@aol.com http://www.mostlyhall.com

---

Village Green Inn
40 Main St, *Falmouth* 02540
508-548-5621 Fax: 508-457-5051
800-237-1119
Don & Diane Crosby
April-January

90-225-BB
5 rooms, 5 pb
Visa, MC, AmEx, *Rated*, •
C-ltd/S-no/P-no/H-no

Full gourmet breakfast
Seasonal beverages, afternoon cookies
Parlor, piano, A/C, fireplaces, open porches, bikes, color cable TV

Old Victorian inn ideally located on Falmouth's historic village green. Nineteenth century charm & warm hospitality in lovely spacious rooms.
vgi40@aol.com http://www.villagegreeninn.com

Wildflower Inn
167 Palmer Ave, *Falmouth* 02540
508-548-9524 Fax: 508-548-9524
800-294-5459
Phil & Donna Stone
All year

95-250-BB
6 rooms, 6 pb
Visa, MC, AmEx, *Rated*, •
C-ltd/S-no/P-no/H-no

Full gourmet breakfast
Tea, coffee, snacks, wine
Sitt. rm., library, A/C, bikes, whirlpool tubs, fish, golf, tennis nearby

VOTED # 1 B&B–Award winning Victorian in historic district close to shops, restaurants & Island Ferry. Enjoy an edible flower breakfast in the gathering room, or a picnic delivered to your room. wldflr167@aol.com http://www.wildflower-inn.com

---

Woods Hole Passage
186 Woods Hole Rd, *Falmouth* 02540
508-548-9575 Fax: 508-540-4771
800-790-8976
Deb Pruitt
All year

100-165-BB
5 rooms, 5 pb
Most CC, *Rated*, •
C-ltd/S-no/P-no/H-no

Full breakfast
Tea and sweets in afternoon
Bicycles, library, spacious grounds, flower & herb gardens, outdoor shower

Graceful 100 year-old carriage house and renovated barn, providing a magical retreat year round. inn@woodsholepassage.com http://www.woodsholepassage.com

---

Augustus Snow House
528 Main St, *Harwich Port* 02646
508-430-0528 Fax: 508-432-6638
800-320-0528
Joyce & Steve Roth
All year

105-395-BB
5 rooms, 5 pb
Most CC, *Rated*, •
C-ltd/S-no/P-no/H-no

Full breakfast
Afternoon tea
Gazebo and verandah, close to quaint shops of Chatham

Romantic Victorian mansion. Exquisite bedrooms, PB (some with Jacuzzis), fireplaces all rooms, TVs. info@augustussnow.com http://www.augustussnow.com

CAPE COD (REGION)

Dunscroft By The Sea
24 Pilgrim Rd, *Harwich Port* 02646
508-432-0810 Fax: 508-432-5134
800-432-4345
Alyce Mundy All year

125-350-BB
9 rooms, 9 pb
Rated, •
C-ltd/S-no/P-no/H-yes

Full breakfast
Juices
Piano, terrace, canopied 4-posters, Jacuzzis, A/C, king suite with fireplace

Breathtaking, private mile-long beach! Quiet & romantic. In-town to restaurants, shops. King/queen canopies & 4 posters.
info@dunscroftbythesea.com http://www.dunscroftbythesea.com

Harbor Breeze of Cape Cod
326 Lower County Rd, *Harwich Port* 02646
508-432-0337 Fax: 508-432-1276
800-455-0247
Jim & Marie David
All year

110-210-BB
10 rooms, 10 pb
Most CC, •
C-yes/S-ltd/P-no/H-no

Continental breakfast
Pool, sitting area, garden courtyard

Harbor Breeze offers an informal setting especially suited to couples and families who prefer casual surroundings.
harborbreeze@yahoo.com http://www.harborbreezeinn.com

Harbor Walk
6 Freeman St, *Harwich Port* 02646
508-432-1675
Marilyn & Preston Barry
May–Oct.

60-80-BB
6 rooms, 4 pb
Rated
C-yes/S-no/P-ltd/H-no
French

Full breakfast
Canopy beds, library, sitting room, tennis & ocean nearby

Victorian charmer featuring antiques, homemade quilts and queen canopy beds. Walk to beach and most photographed harbor on Cape Cod. Summer sports paradise.

Inn on Sea Street
358 Sea St, *Hyannis* 02601
508-775-8030 Fax: 508-771-0878
888-775-8030
Sylvia & Fred LaSelva
May-Nov.

85-150-BB
9 rooms, 7 pb
Visa, MC, AmEx, *Rated*, •
C-ltd/S-no/P-no/H-no

Full gourmet breakfast
Fruit & cheese
Library, sitting room, small weddings, 4-room cottage for two

Elegant Victorian inn, steps from beach & Kennedy Compound. Antiques, canopy beds, goose down pillows, radios, fireplace, home-baked delights.
info@innonseastreet.com http://www.innonseastreet.com

Simmons Homestead Inn
288 Scudder Ave, *Hyannis Port* 02647
508-778-4999 Fax: 508-790-1342
800-637-1649
Bill Putman
All year

200-350-BB
14 rooms, 14 pb
Visa, MC, AmEx, *Rated*, •
C-yes/S-ltd/P-yes/H-no

Full breakfast
Complimentary evening wine
Sitting room, library, wrap-around porch, bikes, huge yard, beaches

Beautifully restored 1820 sea captain's home. Lovely grounds. Everything dedicated to just relaxing and fun. Collection of 35 red classic sports cars is reason enough to visit this unique inn. SimmonsHomestead@aol.com http://www.SimmonsHomesteadinn.com

---

Academy Place
PO Box 1407
8 Academy Place, *Orleans* 02653
508-255-3181 Fax: 508-247-9812
Sandy & Charles Terrell
Mid-May to Mid-Oct.

79-119-BB
5 rooms, 3 pb
Visa, MC, *Rated*
C-ltd/S-no/P-no/H-ltd

Continental plus breakfast
Afternoon tea
Sitting room, phone, Internet, 2-person hammock, swimming & fishing close by

Antique Sea Captain's home on Village Green. Walk to restaurants & shops. Cape Cod Seashore National Park, 10 minute—and beaches 5-minute—drives. Bike path 3 blocks.
academyplace@mindspring.com http://www.academyplace.com

CAPE COD (REGION)

Bay Cottage 44 Captain Linnell, *Orleans* 02653 508-240-5640 Fax: 508-255-6284 Jarvis & Judy Hunt May–December	115-130-BB 3 rooms, 3 pb • C-ltd/S-no/P-no/H-ltd French	Full Gourmet breakfast Afternoon tea, snacks Sitting room, library, The Nest Suite, cable TV, computer hook-up

Located on the edge of marsh overlooking the Bay. Romantically decorated with antiques, gourmet breakfasts, a short walk to the beach and bike trail.
jhunt@C4.net http://www.baycottagecapecod.com

Governor Prence Inn 66 Rt 6A, *Orleans* 02653 508-255-1216 Fax: 508-240-1107 800-342-4300 Linda LeGeyt April 15–October 15	99-159-BB 56 rooms, 56 pb Most CC, • C-yes/S-ltd/P-no/H-no	Continental breakfast Sitting room, library, swimming pool, cable TV, bike path

Great central location—on five acres of rose gardens. Fine, spacious rooms, Olympic size pool, AC/heat, direct dial phones, cable TV, barbecue picnic area.
lindal@c4.net http://www.governorprenceinn.com

Morgan's Way Nine Morgan's Way, *Orleans* 02653 508-255-0831 Fax: 508-255-0831 Page McMahan All year	95-140-BB 3 rooms, 3 pb *Rated*, • C-ltd/S-no/P-no/H-no	Full gourmet breakfast Guest refrigerators Sitting room, library, fresh flowers, chocolate, firm beds, heated pool

Romantic and elegant contemporary hideaway. Five acres of gardens and woodlands, heated pool; a birdwatcher's paradise.
morgnway@capecod.net http://www.capecodaccess.com/morgansway/

A Beachside B&B, Ellisville Harbor 159 Ellisville Rd, *Plymouth* 02360 508-888-3692 Fax: 508-888-5978 888-738-BEDS Jon & Amy Townsend All year	110-150-BB 3 rooms, 3 pb Most CC, *Rated*, • C-ltd/S-ltd/P-ltd/H-no	Full breakfast Cable TV, private baths , and private decks

Beach on Cape Cod Bay, Harbor and Swan pond all viewed from this custom Colonial home. Full country breakfast served. Hidden amongst acres of trees to insure total privacy. amy@ellisville.com http://www.ellisville.com

---

Widow's Walk PO Box 605 152 Clark Rd, *Sagamore Beach* 02562 508-888-0762 Meredith & Bill Chase	90-95-BB 2 rooms C-yes/S-no All year	Continental breakfast Soft drinks Bicycles, beach & sporting equipment, refrig.

Quiet, country style home where you can relax and enjoy the best of old Cape Cod.
http://www.widowswalk@capecod.net

Bay Beach PO Box 151 3 Bay Beach Ln, *Sandwich* 02563 508-888-8813 Fax: 508-888-5416 800-475-6398 Emily Lemieux May 1–November 15	245-345-BB 6 rooms, 6 pb Visa, MC, *Rated* C-ltd/S-no/P-no/H-ltd French	Full breakfast Afternoon tea, complimentary wine Sitting room, CD player, bicycles, phones, A/C, exercise room, fireplaces

Located on secluded & private Bay Beach, offering relaxation & privacy. Compl. fruit/wine/cheese/crackers welcomes your arrival. Jacuzzis in rooms. Boardwalk to private beach. info@baybeach.com http://www.baybeach.com/

CAPE COD (REGION)

Burbank's Windfall House 108 Old Main St, *Sandwich* 02563 508-888-3650 Fax: 508-833-9819 877-594-6325 Ted Diggle All year	65-125-BB 6 rooms, 4 pb Most CC C-ltd/S-ltd/P-no/H-ltd	Full menu breakfast Afternoon tea Sitting room, library, suites, fireplaces, cable TV, accom. bus. travelers

A charming 1818 Colonial set in historic Sandwich Village. This gracious antique has retained many original features, such as wideboard floors and 3 fireplaces, one with beehive oven. windfallhs@aol.com http://www.windfallhouse.com

The Dan'l Webster Inn 149 Main St, *Sandwich* 02563 508-888-3623 Fax: 508-888-5156 800-444-3566 The Catania Family All year	109-359-EP 47 rooms, 47 pb Most CC C-yes/P-no	Cont. brkfst only in off season Restaurant Concierge, room service, bar, conference facil., pool, cable TV, lounge

The Dan'l Webster Inn, the centerpiece of Historic Sandwich Village, is located on the site of a tavern built before the American Revolution. Breakfast included in rate during off-season. dwi@capecod.net http://www.danlwebsterinn.com

Belvedere Inn 167 Old Main St, *South Yarmouth* 02664 508-398-6674 Fax: 508-398-6674 800-288-4080 Marcia & Jack Weiss All year	100-175-BB 5 rooms, 3 pb Most CC, • C-yes/S-no/P-ltd/H-no	Full breakfast Tea, wine, soft drinks Sitting room, library, screened sun porch, sundeck, gazebo

Relaxing old Sea Captain's home on the National Register of Historic Homes. Near beaches and all activity but on quiet street. Cordial in home hosts.
mweiss@belvederebb.com http://www.belvederebb.com

Blue Heron Cove 260 Blue Heron Rd, *Wellfleet* 02667 508-349-0021 Nancy & Ken Reisinger All year	130-215-BB 3 rooms, 2 pb C-no/S-no/P-no/H-no German	Continental plus breakfast Fruit Room service

"Winner in Cape Cod Life's 2001 Best of the Cape & Islands Readers' Poll!" Deluxe B&B on Cape Cod Bay, waterviews from every room across a beautiful tidal marsh, to MA Audubon, & out to Cape Cod Bay! blueheron@gis.net http://www.blueheroncove.net

Inn at Duck Creeke PO Box 364 70 Main St, *Wellfleet* 02667 508-349-9333 Fax: 508-349-0234 Bob Morrill & Judith Pihl May through Oct.	70-110-BB 25 rooms, 17 pb Visa, MC, AmEx C-yes/S-ltd/P-no/H-ltd	Continental plus breakfast Fine Dining and Full Tavern Menu on premises

Located on five acres in Wellfleet, Massachusetts near the tip of Cape Cod. Premiere Bed and Breakfast Country Inn and home to two of the most often visited and well-reviewed restaurants on the Cape. duckinn@capecod.net http://www.innatduckcreeke.com/

CAPE COD (REGION)

Chapoquoite Inn
PO Box 367
495 W. Falmouth Hwy 28A,
West Falmouth 02574
508-540-7232 Fax: 508-540-4402
800-842-8994
Kim & Tim McIntyre

95-200-BB
8 rooms, 8 pb
Visa, MC, *Rated*
C-ltd/S-ltd/P-no/H-ltd
Conversational
Japanese, Spanish
All year

Full breakfast
Tea, coffee and fresh fruit
Bicycles, beach towels and beach chairs

Make our home your home at Chapoquoit Inn, an elegant and romantic B&B located on over 3 acres, in the heart of Historic West Falmouth Village. Experience the best of old Cape Cod at your doorstep! info@chapoquoit.com http://www.chapoquoit.com

---

Cape Cod Claddagh Inn/Fiddlers Green
PO Box 667
77-79 W Main St (Rte 28), *West Harwich* 02671
508-432-9628 Fax: 508-432-6039
800-356-9628

75-150-BB
8 rooms, 8 pb
Visa, MC, *Rated*, •
C-ltd/S-ltd/P-ltd/H-ltd
Eileen, Jack Connell, Cathy Niemisto
All year

Full breakfast
Lunch & dinner available, restaurant
Afternoon tea, bar service, sitting room, library, pool, fireplace, cable TV

As well as the 1880 Victorian Inn, we now have Fiddlers Green, a romantically themed colonial inn set apart from the Irish Pub and restaurant. Four poster queen beds, garden tubs for 2. claddagh@capecod.net http://www.capecodcladdaghinn.com

---

Tern Inn
91 Chase St, *West Harwich* 02671
508-432-3714 Fax: 508-432-5810
800-432-3718
David & Joan Bruce

109-149-BB
8 rooms, 8 pb
Visa, MC
C-yes/S-no/P-no/H-no
All year

Continental plus breakfast
Snacks
Sitting room, swimming pool, Cable TV, business travelers

We are Cape Cod as it should be! Seasonal family cottages for great family get-togethers, and 8 year-round inn rooms offering a bit of luxury at a reasonable price.
stay@theterninn.com http://www.theterninn.com

Inn at Lewis Bay
57 Maine Ave, *West Yarmouth* 02664
508-771-3433 Fax: 508-790-7089
800-962-6679
Janet & Dave Vaughn

68-128-BB
6 rooms, 6 pb
Visa, MC, AmEx, *Rated*, •
C-ltd/S-no/P-no/H-no
All year

Full breakfast
Afternoon refreshments at 4:00
Sitting room, views of the Bay, beach chairs & towels

Lovely B&B just a block from the beach in a quiet seaside neighborhood. Enjoy full breakfast, afternoon refreshments and use of our beach chairs and towels. All rooms have private baths and A/C. stay@innatlewisbay.com http://www.innatlewisbay.com

---

Colonial House Inn
277 Main St, Rt 6A, *Yarmouth Port* 02675
508-362-4348 Fax: 508-362-8034
800-999-3416
Malcolm J. Perna

80-120-BB
21 rooms, 21 pb
Most CC, *Rated*, •
C-yes/S-yes/P-yes/H-yes
All year

Continental plus breakfast
Dinner available (fee)
Game room, bar, pool, cribs/high chair, TV/VCR, Jacuzzi, fitness center

Decorated guestrooms furnished with antiques, canopy beds. Charming grounds by historic homes. Indoor heated pool, conference center. Victorian sitting room, lovely outdoor deck. info@colonialhousecapecod.com http://www.colonialhousecapecod.com

---

Liberty Hill Inn
77 Main St, Rte 6A, *Yarmouth Port* 02675
508-362-3976 Fax: 508-362-6485
800-821-3977
Ann and John Cartwright

95-200-BB
9 rooms, 9 pb
Visa, MC, AmEx, *Rated*, •
C-yes/S-no/P-no/H-yes
All year

Full gourmet breakfast
Afternoon tea
A.C., cable TV, whirlpools, fireplaces, down comforters/pillows and more!

Gracious and elegant Greek Revival inn, c.1825. Romantic getaway, fireplaces, canopy beds, whirlpools, shoppers paradise, antiques. Yankee Magazine's "Editors' Pick" 2002 Travel Guide libertyh@capecod.net http://www.libertyhillinn.com

CAPE COD (REGION)

Olde Captain's Inn on the Cape 101 Main St, Rt 6A, *Yarmouth Port* 02675 508-362-4496 Fax: 508-362-4496 888-407-7161 Sven Tilly & Betsy O'Connor All year	60-120-BB 5 rooms, 3 pb C-ltd/S-no/P-no/H-no	Continental plus breakfast Maid & concierge service

A charming Greek Revival c.1812 former sea Captain's house located in the Historic District. Walk to fine restaurants, craft shops and antique shops.

general@oldecaptainsinn.com http://www.oldecaptainsinn.com

One Centre Street Inn 1 Centre St, *Yarmouth Port* 02675 508-362-9951 Fax: 508-362-9952 866-362-9951 Carla & Robert Masse	80-199-BB 5 rooms, 3 pb Most CC, *Rated*, • C-yes/S-no/P-no/H-no All year	Full gourmet breakfast Tea, snacks, banana bread, evening wine Cable TV/VCR , high speed Internet (parlor), hot tub, refrigerator, garden

English garden courtyard with bubbling water fountains and classical music dress this elegant 1824 c. parsonage with all the amenities of present, but charm of the past.

sales@onecentrestreetinn.com http://www.onecentrestreetinn.com

Wedgewood Inn 83 Main St, *Yarmouth Port* 02675 508-362-5157 Fax: 508-362-5851 Milt & Gerrie Graham All year	115-215-BB 9 rooms, 9 pb Visa, MC, AmEx, *Rated*, • C-ltd/S-ltd/P-no/H-ltd	Full breakfast Afternoon tea, fruit Common room, fireplaces, private porches, gardens/gazebo, A/C

Romantic inn in historic area of Cape Cod. Near beaches & restaurants. Antiques, Wood-burning fireplaces, plank floors, canopy beds.

info@wedgewood-inn.com http://www.wedgewood-inn.com

CHATHAM

Carriage House Inn 407 Old Harbor Rd 02633 508-945-4688 Fax: 508-945-8909 800-355-8868 Patty & Dennis O'Neill All year	115-210-BB 3 rooms, 3 pb Most CC, *Rated*, • C-ltd/S-no/P-no	Full breakfast A/C, private entrances, fireplaces, private garden sitting areas

Welcome to the Carriage House Inn...located one quarter mile from the ocean in the picturesque seaside village of Chatham, on Cape Cod.

carriageh@capecod.net http://www.capecodtravel.com/carriagehouse

The Cranberry Inn of Chatham 359 Main St 02633 508-945-9232 Fax: 508-945-3769 800-332-4667 Kay & Bill DeFord All year	165-280-BB 18 rooms, 18 pb *Rated*, • C-ltd/S-no	Full country breakfast Afternoon tea Telephones, TVs, A/C

Distinctive lodging in the heart of Chatham–since 1830. Located on the quiet outskirts of the Chatham village, The Cranberry Inn offers a memorable getaway in every season.

info@cranberryinn.com http://www.cranberryinn.com

The Old Harbor Inn 22 Old Harbor Rd 02633 508-945-4434 Fax: 508-945-7665 800-942-4434 Judy & Ray Braz All year	169-259-BB 8 rooms, 8 pb Visa, MC, *Rated*, • C-ltd/S-no/P-no/H-no	Continental plus breakfast Restaurants nearby, afternoon tea, soft drinks Sitting room with fireplace, sun room, deck, A/C, Jacuzzi, bathrobes

English country decor. King/Queen/Twin beds. Delectable buffet breakfast. Walk to quaint seaside village attractions. brazohi@capecod.net http://www.chathamoldharborinn.com

CONCORD

Hawthorne Inn 462 Lexington Rd 01742 978-369-5610 Fax: 978-287-4949 Marilyn Mudry All year	175-305-BB 7 rooms, 7 pb Most CC, *Rated*, • C-yes/S-no/P-no/H-no	Continental plus breakfast Tea & coffee at check-in Sitting room, garden, yard, small pond, swings, bicycles, tree house

On the "Battle Road" of 1775, furnished with antiques, quilts and artwork with the accent on New England comfort and charm. Extensive gardens, canopy queen bed.
inn@concordmass.com http://www.concordmass.com

North Bridge Inn 21 Monument St 01742 978-371-0014 Fax: 978-371-6460 888-530-0007 Heidi Senkler Godbout All year	190-250-BB 6 rooms, 6 pb Visa, MC, AmEx C-yes/S-no/P-ltd/H-no	Full breakfast Suites, kitchens, cable TV, accommodate business travelers

European style B&B located in the heart of historic Concord, MA. Each of the Inn's 6 suites is newly renovated and redecorated in its own distinct style.
info@northbridgeinn.com http://www.northbridgeinn.com

CONCORD (REGION)

Amerscot House PO Box 351 61 West Acton Rd., *Stow* 01775 978-897-0666 Fax: 978-897-6914 Doreen S. Gibson All year	130-150-BB 3 rooms, 3 pb Visa, MC, AmEx, *Rated* C-yes/P-no	Full breakfast

Amerscot House is an elegant early American farmhouse where Scottish hospitality is the art of everyday life. doreen@amerscot.com http://www.amerscot.com

DENNIS (REGION)

The Rose Petal PO Box 974 152 Sea St, *Dennis Port* 02639 508-398-8470 Gayle Kelly All year	79-115-BB 3 rooms, 3 pb Visa, MC, AmEx, *Rated*, • C-yes/S-no/P-no/H-no French	Full breakfast Complimentary beverages Sitting rm., TV, gardens, brass beds, piano, A/C, handstitched quilts

Excellence & sophistication in a AAA Three Diamond Awarded property. 1872 Seafarer's home in a delightful seaside resort neighborhood, a short walk to the Sea.
info@rosepetalofdennis.com http://rosepetalofdennis.com/

Pine Cove Inn 5 Old Main St, *West Dennis* 02670 508-760-6690 Fax: 508-760-9453 Chuck Stanko & George Carroll All year	99-179-BB 9 rooms, 7 pb Most CC, *Rated* C-ltd/S-no/P-no/H-no	Homemade Continental breakfast Sitting room, suites, cable TV, accom. bus. trav., Saltwar Beach

Our circa 1850 Inn is filled with antiques and a warm welcome. Beautifully appointed rooms and efficiencies overlook your private salt water cove beach.
reservations@pinecoveinn.com http://www.pinecoveinn.com

DUXBURY

Winsor House Inn 390 Washington St 02332 781-934-0991 Fax: 781-934-5955 David & Patricia O'Connell All year	130-210-BB 4 rooms, 4 pb Most CC, *Rated* C-yes/S-no/P-no/H-no	Full breakfast Dinner daily at 4:30 PM (fee) Sitting room, Plymouth- 10 minutes, handstitched quilts

Charming 19th-Century sea captain's home located in quaint seaside village of Duxbury, 35 miles south of Boston, 10 miles from Plymouth.

FAIRHAVEN

Edgewater 2 Oxford St 02719 508-997-5512 Fax: 508-997-5784 Kathy Reed All year	90-150-BB 6 rooms, 6 pb Most CC, *Rated*, • C-ltd/S-no/P-no/H-no	Continental plus breakfast Complimentary tea, coffee Sitting room, library, spacious lawns, cable TV in all rooms

Gracious waterfront mansion overlooking New Bedford Harbor. Six accommodations; 2 suites with fireplaces. kprof@aol.com http://www.rixsan.com/edgewater/

Fairhaven Harborside Inn & Spa 1 Main St 02719 508-990-7760 Fax: 508-990-7722 888-575-STAY Sandra & Stephen Leddgar All year	85-145-BB 6 rooms, 6 pb Most CC C-ltd/S-no/P-no/H-no	Full breakfast Sitting room, suite, accommodate business travelers

6 rooms located directly on picturesque Fairhaven Harbor, a short walk to Fairhaven center, bike path, and beaches. The inn is on the waterfront site where artist William Bradfords studio was located. fhis@attbi.com http://www.fairhavenharborsideinn.com

GREAT BARRINGTON

Baldwin Hill Farm 121 Baldwin Hill Rd 01230 413-528-4092 Fax: 413-528-6365 888-528-4092 Richard & Priscilla Burdsall All year	89-130-BB 6 rooms, 5 pb Visa, MC, AmEx, *Rated*, • C-ltd/S-no/P-no/H-no	Full country breakfast Afternoon tea, snacks 2 sitting rooms, library, screened porch, pool, fireplace, cross country ski

Spacious Victorian farmhouse. Mountain views, nature hikes. Restaurants nearby. Hiking, tennis, golf, boating, fishing. rpburds@aol.com http://www.baldwinhillfarm.com

GREENFIELD

The Brandt House 29 Highland Ave 01301 413-774-3329 Fax: 413-772-2908 800-235-3329 Full time staff All year	100-225-BB 8 rooms, 6 pb Most CC, *Rated*, • C-ltd/S-ltd/P-ltd/H-no	Full & Continental plus breakfast Afternoon tea, comp. wine, full breakfast wkends. Snacks, sitting room, library, tennis, Jacuzzis, cable, frplcs., fax, phones

An elegant turn-of-the-century Colonial Revival mansion. Has original beautiful woodwork & personally selected furnishings & decor.
info@brandthouse.com http://www.brandthouse.com

HAMILTON

Miles River Country Inn PO Box 149 823 Bay Rd 01936 978-468-7206 Fax: 978-468-3999 Gretel & Peter Clark All year	95-175-BB 8 rooms, 5 pb *Rated* C-yes/S-no/P-no/H-no Spanish, French, German	Full breakfast Afternoon tea Library, gardens, paths in woods, field, wildlife, beaches

200-year-old country Colonial on large estate. Summer breakfast on shaded garden terraces. Winter evenings by your bedroom's fireplace. Outdoor weddings. Apartment available with 2 queen beds and a pull out couch.
gretel@milesriver.com http://www.milesriver.com

IPSWICH

Town Hill 16 N Main Street 01938 978-356-8000 Fax: 978-356-8000 800-457-7799 Robert & Chere Statho Closed part of Feb.	95-170-BB 11 rooms, 9 pb Visa, MC, AmEx, *Rated*, • C-ltd/S-ltd/P-no/H-no	Full breakfast Sitting room, suites, fireplaces, cable TV, huge yard, beaches

1850 Greek Revival property located in historic district, with 11 individually decorated rooms. reserve@townhill.com http://www.townhill.com

LEE

Applegate Inn
279 West Park Street 01238
413-243-4451 Fax: 413-243-9832
800-691-9012
Gloria & Len Friedman
All year

95-330-BB
7 rooms, 7 pb
Visa, MC, AmEx, *Rated*
C-ltd/S-no/P-no/H-no

Full breakfast
Snacks, complimentary wine
Sitting room, library, bicycles, Jacuzzis, swimming pool, suites, fireplace

From the screened porch of this magnificent, white pillared Georgia colonial, view the pool and our 6 landscaped acres. Beyond is tranquillity itself, in the heart of the Berkshires.
LenandGloria@applegateinn.com http://www.applegateinn.com

Parsonage on the Green
20 Park Place 01238
413-243-4364 Fax: 413-243-2372
Donald & Barbara Mahony
All year

80-175-BB
4 rooms, 4 pb
Rated
C-ltd/S-no/P-no/H-no

Full breakfast
Coffee/tea served at 7:00a.m. in upstairs hall
Bathrobes, locally made hand-dipped chocolates at bedtime

1851 Colonial gem furnished with family treasures spanning generations. Hosts create an atmosphere of serenity, enabling guests to feel like family. Candlelight breakfast, afternoon tea. parsonage@berkshire.net http://www.bbhost.com/parsonageonthegreen

LENOX (REGION)

Old Inn on the Green/Gedney Farm
SR 70 Village Green
Route 57, *New Marlborough* 01230
413-229-3131 Fax: 413-229-8236
800-286-3139
Brad Wagstaff & Leslie Miller
All year

175-350-BB
21 rooms, 17 pb
Visa, MC, *Rated*, •
C-yes/S-yes/P-no/H-yes
French, German, Spanish

Continental breakfast
Restaurant, bar
Dinner (Fri-Sun), five public rooms, whirlpools, pool

1830 Georgian colonial inn with 5 deluxe guestrooms with whirlpools and fireplaces.
brad@oldinn.com http://www.oldinn.com

LEXINGTON (REGION)

Col. Roger Brown House
1694 Main St, *Concord* 01742
978-369-9119 Fax: 978-369-8924
800-292-1369
Mrs. Lauri Berlied
All year

95-250-BB
5 rooms, 5 pb
Most CC, •
C-ltd/S-no/P-no/H-no

Continental plus breakfast
Snacks
Sitting room, library, sauna & swimming pool, next door to health club

National historic register 1775 Colonial; private suites, with kitchenettes; DSL and cable TV; near historic areas. innkeeper@colrogerbrown.com http://www.colrogerbrown.com

MARBLEHEAD

A Nesting Place
16 Village St 01945
781-631-6655 877-855-5656
Louise Hirshberg
All year

65-85-BB
2 rooms
Visa, MC, •
C-yes/S-no/P-no/H-no

Full Homemade breakfast
Afternoon tea and cookies
Sitting room, tennis court, Jacuzzis

Bright, cheerful century-old home. Hand-painted whimsical furnishings. Easy walking to harbor, beach, shops, eateries. 1/2 hour from Boston Airport. Delicious homemade breakfasts. louisehir@aol.com http://www.anestingplace.com

---

Harbor Light Inn
58 Washington St 01945
781-631-2186 Fax: 781-631-2216
Peter C. Conway
All year

125-275-BB
20 rooms, 20 pb
Visa, MC, AmEx, *Rated*, •
C-ltd/S-yes/P-no/H-no

Continental plus breakfast
Aftn. tea, coffee/cookies
Sitting rm., conf. room, hot tubs, courtyard, heated swimming pool

The north shore's premier inn. Elegant 18th-century Federalist mansion. Jacuzzis, sundecks, in heart of historic Harbor District.
info@harborlightinn.com http://www.harborlightinn.com

MARBLEHEAD

Harborside House
23 Gregory St 01945
781-631-1032
Susan Livingston
All year

75-95-BB
2 rooms
Rated, •
C-ltd/S-no/P-no/H-no

Continental plus breakfast
Harbor Sweets candy, afternoon tea on request
Living room with fireplace, deck, period dining room, bicycles available

C. 1850 colonial home overlooks picturesque harbor in historic district of Marblehead on Boston's North Shore. Antiques and modern amenities. Homemade baked goods. Period dining room, flower gardens.

stay@harborsidehouse.com http://www.harborsidehouse.com

Pheasant Hill Inn
71 Bubier Rd 01945
781-639-4799 Fax: 781-639-4799
Bill & Nancy Coolidge
All year

95-175-BB
3 rooms, 3 pb
Visa, MC, AmEx,
Rated, •
C-ltd/S-ltd/P-no/H-no

Continental plus breakfast
Snacks
Sitting room, library, phones, TV, A/C, suite with fireplace

Charming 1920 summer estate. Private all-suites getaway. Country-like setting and views to water. Memorable! info@pheasanthill.com http://www.pheasanthill.com

---

The Seagull Inn
106 Harbor Ave 01945
781-631-1893 Fax: 781-631-3535
Skip & Ruth Sigler
All year

125-250-BB
3 rooms, 3 pb
Visa, MC, *Rated*
C-yes/S-no/P-ltd/H-ltd

Continental plus breakfast
Sitting room, library, bikes, suites, cable TV, kayaks, hammock,refrigerator

Shaker-style furniture and artwork by owner. Ocean and harbor views from most rooms. Located on scenic Marblehead Neck. Beautiful gardens.

host@seagullinn.com http://www.seagullinn.com

MARION

Hideaway Haven
86 County Rd 02738
508-748-3336
Bud & Evie Holland All year

75-120-BB
3 rooms, 1 pb
C-ltd/S-no/P-ltd/H-no

Snacks
Sitting room, cable TV/VCR, fishing poles, computer, accom. bus. travel.

Hideaway Haven is a peaceful retreat near a quaint seaside village and Tabor Academy. The open floor plan leads to trompe l'oeil Victorian surprises.

hidehaven@aol.com

MARTHA'S VINEYARD (REGION)

Colonial Inn of Martha's Vineyard
PO Box 68
38 N Water St, *Edgartown*
02539
508-627-4711 Fax: 508-627-5904
800-627-4701
CJ Rivard

75-375-BB
43 rooms, 43 pb
Visa, MC, AmEx,
Rated, •
C-yes/S-yes/P-no/H-yes
Portuguese
April 1–December 1

Continental breakfast
Restaurant, bar
Sitting room, library, nearby tennis, riding, golf, sailing, fishing, beach

Charming, lovingly refurbished inn with brass beds, offers affordable luxury. 2 suites with kitchens. Near museums, galleries, shops. Inn has day spa and fitness room.

info@colonialinnmvy.com http://www.colonialinnmvy.com

Daggett House
PO Box 1333
59 N. Water St, *Edgartown*
02539
508-627-4600 Fax: 508-627-4611
800-946-3400
Judy Rogers All year

85-600-BB
31 rooms, 31 pb
Most CC, *Rated*, •
C-yes/S-no/P-no
H-ltd

Afternoon tea, lemonade, cookies
Continental breakfast served Nov. to April only

A charming historic inn on Edgartown Harbor and within walking distance to many shops, restaurants, Lighthouse Beach. Shuttle bus to other beaches and sites on the island.

innkeeper@thedaggetthouse.com http://www.thedaggetthouse.com

MARTHA'S VINEYARD (REGION)

Dockside Inn
PO Box 1206
9 Circuit Ave Extension, *Oak Bluffs* 02557
508-693-2966 Fax: 508-696-7293
800-245-5979
Mark Luce

80-350-BB
22 rooms, 22 pb
Most CC, *Rated*
C-ltd/S-ltd/P-no/H-yes
Early Apr through Oct

Continental plus breakfast
Bicycles, A/C, sitting room, TV, kitchen suites, garden area w/BBQ grill

The Dockside Inn is located on the enchanted island of Martha's Vineyard in the seaside village of Oak Bluffs. Overlooking Oak Bluffs Harbor, the Inn is within walking distance to all attractions. Inns@vineyard.net http://www.vineyardinns.com/dockside.html

---

Martha's Vineyard Resort
111 New York Ave, *Oak Bluffs* 02557
617-693-5411 Fax: 617-524-3211
800-874-4403
Claudette & Jack E. Robinson

75-300-BB
10 rooms, 10 pb
Most CC, *Rated*, •
C-yes/S-ltd/P-no/H-ltd
All year

Continental breakfast
Complimentary wine, afternoon tea
Sitting room, library, tennis, suites, cable TV

This modern B&B provides modern conveniences, while preserving the quiet idyllic aura of a bygone era. jackerobin@aol.com http://www.marthasvineyardresort.com

---

The Nashua House Hotel
PO Box 2221
30 Kennebec Ave, *Oak Bluffs* 02557
508-693-0043
Caleb Caldwell All year

49-109-EP
15 rooms
Visa, MC, AmEx, •
C-yes/S-ltd/P-no/H-no
Portuguese

Restaurant

Superbly located in the heart of town, The Nashua House Hotel is a beloved Martha's Vineyard Victorian Landmark featuring charming, breezy, sunlight filled rooms with stunning Atlantic Ocean views.
calebcaldwellmv@hotmail.com http://www.nashuahouse.com

Oak House
PO Box 299
75 Seaview Ave, *Oak Bluffs* 02557
508-693-4187 Fax: 508-696-7385
800-245-5979
Betsi Convery-Luce

130-280-BB
10 rooms, 10 pb
Most CC, *Rated*
C-ltd/S-no/P-no/H-no
Early May through Oct.

Continental-plus breakfast
Afternoon tea
Sitting room, piano, sun porch, bicycles, near town, ferry, beach

Romantic Victorian Inn on the beach, richly restored 1872 Governor's home. Oak paneling, wide porches, balconies, leaded windows, water views. Very cozy and attractive rooms and suites. Inns@vineyard.net http://www.vineyardinns.com/oakhouse.html

---

The 1720 House
PO Box 1193
130 Main St, *Vineyard Haven* 02568
508-693-6407 Fax: 508-696-0034
Jennifer & Peter Weno
All year

150-225-BB
6 rooms, 4 pb
Visa, MC, AmEx, *Rated*, •
C-ltd/S-ltd/P-no/H-no
German, French, Spanish

Continental plus breakfast
Snacks
Sitting room, bikes, cable TV, accommodate business travelers

Historic in-town hideaway furnished in antiques. Breakfast served on the sunporch, use bikes to tour the island. info@1720house.com http://www.1720house.com

---

Crocker House Inn
PO Box 1658
4 Crocker Ave, *Vineyard Haven* 02568
508-693-1151 Fax: 508-693-1123
800-772-0206
Jynell and Jeff Kristal

105-385-BB
8 rooms, 8 pb
Visa, MC
C-ltd/S-ltd/P-no/H-no
All year

Continental plus breakfast
Telephones, cable TV hookups, fireplaces, Jacuzzi, outside private porches

The Crocker House Inn is elegance in a comfortable casual atmosphere.
crockerinn@aol.com http://www.crockerhouseinn.com

MARTHA'S VINEYARD (REGION)

Doctor's House	180-225-BB	Full breakfast
PO Box 1653	7 rooms, 7 pb	Sitting room, library, suites,
60 Mt Aldworth Rd, *Vineyard Haven* 02568	Most CC, •	fireplaces, cable TV, accom.
508-696-0859 Fax: 508-696-0489	C-no/S-no/P-no/H-no	bus. travelers
866-507-6670	April–November	
Kathy & John Bondur		

Rambling 2-story, adult-oriented getaway tucked away on two quiet acres, amidst large colorful gardens. Short stroll to village and beach. All rooms with private baths and air conditioning. info@doctorshouse.com http://www.doctorshouse.com

Martha's Place	200-425-BB	Continental plus breakfast
PO Box 1182	6 rooms, 6 pb	Sitting room, bikes, tennis
114 Main St, *Vineyard Haven* 02568	Visa, MC, *Rated*, •	court, Jacuzzis, fireplaces,
508-693-0253	C-ltd/S-ltd/P-no/H-ltd	cable TV
Martin Hicks & Richard Alcott	All year	

The most elegant waterview Inn on Martha's Vineyard. Overlooking Vineyard Haven Harbor, most rooms have water views, fireplaces, Jacuzzi tubs.
info@marthasplace.com http://www.marthasplace.com

Thorncroft Inn	180-500-BB	Full or continental breakfast
PO Box 1022	14 rooms, 14 pb	Continental breakfast
460 Main St, *Vineyard Haven* 02568	*Rated*, •	delivered to room
508-693-3333 Fax: 508-693-5419	C-ltd/S-ltd/P-no/H-no	Afternoon tea, TV, evening
800-332-1236		turndown service, 3.5 acres,
Karl & Lynn Buder		morning paper
All year		

Romantic country inn. AAA 4 diamond; Mobil 3 stars. Fireplaces; central A/C; luxury suites with Jacuzzi or private hot tub. innkeeper@thorncroft.com http://www.thorncroft.com

MIDDLEBORO

On Cranberry Pond	110-180-BB	Continental plus breakfast
43 Fuller St 02346	6 rooms, 4 pb	Snacks
508-946-0768 Fax: 508-947-8221	Visa, MC, AmEx, •	Sitting room, library, suites,
Jeannine LaBossiere & Son Tim	C-ltd/S-ltd/P-ltd/H-no	fireplaces, cable TV,
All year		accomodate business travelers

Nestled between Cranberry Pond and picturesque New England, Cranberry bogs in the peace and quiet of the country and wake to a gourmet breakfast and freshly brewed coffee. oncranberrypond@aol.com http://www.oncranberrypond.com

NANTUCKET

The Carriage House	70-200-BB	Continental plus breakfast
5 Rays Court 02554	7 rooms, 7 pb	Guest refrigerator
508-228-0326	*Rated*, •	Sitting room, library, patio,
Jeanne McHugh & son, Haziel	C-yes/S-no/P-no/H-no	beach towels, discount rates,
All year	Fr., Ger., Sp., Japanese	ask

Converted carriage house on the prettiest country lane; "beautifully quiet, yet right in town." B&B and more, since 1974.
carrhousenant@hotmail.com http://www.carriagehousenantucket.com

The Century House	95-295-BB	Gerry's buffet breakfast
10 Cliff Rd 02554	9 rooms, 9 pb	Happy hour setups
508-228-0530	*Rated*, •	Afternoon tea, munchies,
Gerry Connick & Jeane Heron	C-ltd/S-ltd/P-no/H-no	sitting room, veranda, H.
All year	Fr., Rus., Ger., Jap.	Miller player piano

Historic sea captain's B&B inn in operation since the mid-1800s. Minutes to beaches, restaurants, galleries, shops. centurybnb@aol.com http://www.centuryhouse.com

NANTUCKET

Corner House, Circa 1790
PO Box 1828
49 Centre St 02554
508-228-1530 Fax: 508-228-2000
866-228-1409
John & Sandy Knox-Johnston
All year

75-235-BB
14 rooms, 14 pb
C-ltd/S-ltd/P-no

Continental plus breakfast
Afternoon tea and refreshments

Brought very gently into the 20th century, Corner House provides a special experience of Nantucket for those who appreciate the difference.
cornerhs@nantucket.net http://www.cornerhousenantucket.com

House of the Seven Gables
32 Cliff Road 02554
508-228-4706 Fax: 508-228-2898
Sue Walton
April–December

100-300-BB
10 rooms, 8 pb
Visa, MC, AmEx
C-ltd/S-no/P-no/H-no

Continental breakfast
Sitting room porches

A quiet Victorian in the Old Historic District. Walk to Main Street, beaches, museums and restaurants. A continental breakfast is served to your room each morning.
http://www.houseofthesevengables.com

Jared Coffin House
PO Box 1580
29 Broad St 02554
508-228-2400 Fax: 508-228-8549
800-248-2405
Jonathan & Patty Stone

125-375

The inn is a historic collection of six buildings, either connected to or within steps of the main house. Sixty guest rooms with private baths, phone, TV. Signature restaurant and tap room. jchouse@nantucket.net http://www.jaredcoffinhouse.com

---

Nantucket Whaler Guest House
PO Box 1337
8 N Water Street 02554
508-228-6597 Fax: 508-228-6291
800-462-6882
Calliope Ligelis & Randi Ott

295-575-EP
12 rooms, 12 pb
Visa, MC, AmEx,
Rated, •
C-ltd/S-no/P-no/H-no
April–December

Complimentary coffee & bottled water
Suites, remote control cable TV, cooking facilities in each room, stereo/CD

Luxury guest house with private entrance to each studio, 1 bedroom and 2 bedroom suites, most with deck. Romantic get-away treasure. Deluxe wetbar area in suites. In Historic District. Luxury linens. nanwhaler@aol.com http://www.nantucketwhaler.com

---

Sherburne Inn
10 Gay St 02554
508-228-4425 Fax: 508-228-8114
888-577-4425
Dale & Susan Hamilton
All year

85-295-BB
8 rooms, 8 pb
Most CC, *Rated*
C-ltd/S-no/P-no/H-no
German

Continental plus breakfast
Fruit basket, coffee, tea & hot chocolate all day
Queen or king beds, cable TV/VCR, A/C, telephone

Sherburne Inn is a luxury inn located in the core district of Nantucket. The New York Times Sophisticated Traveler writes "The Sherburne Inn is the place I shall stay when I next visit Nantucket." sherinn@nantucket.net http://www.sherburneinn.com

---

Stumble Inne
109 Orange St 02554
508-228-4482 Fax: 508-228-4752
800-649-4482
Jeanne & George Todor

95-225-BB
8 rooms
Visa, MC, AmEx
C-ltd/S-no/P-no/H-no
All year

Hearty Continental breakfast
Afternoon tea
Sitting room, parking, spacious grounds

Stumble Inne is a lovely, award winning bed & breakfast inn. Greek Revival architecture, spacious grounds outside, lovingly redecorated on the inside.
romance@nantucket.net http://www.stumbleinne.com

NANTUCKET

Tuckernuck Inn
PO Box 629
60 Union St 02554
508-228-4886 Fax: 508-228-4890
800-228-4886
Laddy & Jack McElderry

80-325-BB
19 rooms, 18 pb
Visa, MC, AmEx,
Rated, •
C-ltd/S-no/P-no/H-ltd
All year

Cont'l breakfast (Apr.–Oct.)
Tuckernuck Inn Cafe serves dinner from April-Oct.
Private baths, large yard, private baths, TV/VCR, fridges, parking

Wonderful in-town location; short walk to cobbled Main Street, Harbor Beach, shops and restaurants; spacious lawn with recreational facilities; Colonial ambiance; Cafe on premises. tuckinn@nantucket.net http://www.TuckernuckInn.com

---

The Woodbox Inn
29 Fair St 02554
508-228-0587 Fax: 508-228-7527
Dexter Tutein
May–December

185-315-EP
9 rooms, 9 pb
Rated
C-ltd/S-no/P-no/H-no
French, German, Spanish

Continental breakfast
Gourmet dinner available
Restaurant, suites w/fireplaces, canopy, high-poster beds

Nantucket's oldest inn (c.1709). 9 units, queen beds, 1 and 2 bedroom suites with working fireplaces. Just 1½ blocks from historic Main Street. Award-winning dining room.
woodbox@nantucket.net http://www.woodboxinn.com

NEW BEDFORD

The Orchard Street Manor
139 Orchard St 02740
508-984-3475
Al & Suzanne Saulniers
All year

115-155-BB
3 rooms, 3 pb
Visa, MC, AmEx
C-ltd/S-no/P-no/H-no
French, Spanish

Continental breakfast
Complimentary soft drinks/wine
Formal Parlor, Billiard Room/Library, Gathering Room, fine Dining Room, Deck

Enjoy the luxury of New Bedford's whaling and textile past in our 1845 whaling captain's home renovated and expanded in 1903 by a cotton baron to its current, graceful, Georgian-Revival style.
theorchardstreetmanor@hotmail.com http://www.the-orchard-street-manor.com

NEW SALEM

Bullard Farm
89 Elm St 01355
978-544-6959
Janet Kraft All year

95-BB
4 rooms
Visa, MC
C-ltd/S-no/P-ltd/H-no

Continental plus breakfast
Sitting room, cable TV, accommodate business travelers

1794 historic Colonial farmhouse on 400 acres with groomed hiking trails, one mile from Quabbin Reservoir, 20-30 minutes from Amherst and Northfield.
http://www.bbonline.com/ma/bullardfarm/

NEWBURYPORT

Newburyport
296 High St 01950
978-463-4637 Fax: 978-463-4637
Donna Wilson Irwin & Ken Irwin
All year

125-140-BB
2 rooms, 2 pb
Visa, MC, AmEx, •
C-ltd/S-no/P-ltd/H-no

Continental plus breakfast
Snacks, complimentary wine
Sitting room, bikes, library tennis, pool, suites, Cable TV, bus. travelers

Experience the gracious formal elegance captured in this magnificent turn-of-the-century Georgian Colonial built in 1901.
donnaw@rounder.com http://www.newburyportbedandbreakfast.com

The Windsor House
38 Federal St 01950
978-462-3778 Fax: 978-465-3443
888-TRELAWNY
Judith & John Harris
All year

155-BB
4 rooms, 4 pb
Most CC, *Rated*, •
C-ltd/S-no/P-ltd/H-no

Full English breakfast
Afternoon tea
Common room, meeting room seats 20 people, shops, museums

Celebrating 25 years, with original innkeepers. Federalist mansion/ship's chandlery in restored historic seaport furnished in period antiques.
windsorinn@earthlink.net http://www.bbhost.com/windsorhouse

NORTH ADAMS

The Porches Inn
231 River St 01247
413-664-0400 Fax: 413-664-0401
Olivier Glattfelder & Brooks Bradbury, Mgr.
All year

130-435-BB
52 rooms, 52 pb
Visa, MC, AmEx, *Rated*, •
C-yes/S-no/P-no/H-yes
German, French

Continental plus breakfast
Bar service
Sitting room, swimming pool, suites, cable TV, accom. bus. travelers

The Berkshires' ultra-savvy new inn. Spacious rooms and suites with a contemporary-retro decor. Attitude-free service. Fully wired rooms with Internet. Complimentary in-room continental breakfast. reservations@porches.com http://www.porches.com

NORTHAMPTON (REGION)

The Knoll
230 N Main St, *Florence* 01062
413-584-8164 Fax: 603-308-0357
Leona (Lee) Lesko
All year

70-BB
3 rooms
Rated
C-ltd/S-no/P-no/H-no

Full breakfast

Large Tudor house in quiet rural setting on 16 acres.
theknoll@crocker.com http://www.crocker.com/~theknoll

Lupine House
PO Box 60483
185 North Main, *Florence* 01062
413-586-9766 800-890-9766
Evelyn & Gil Billings
All year

75-100-BB
3 rooms, 3 pb
Visa, MC, Disc
C-ltd/S-no/P-no/H-no

Continental plus breakfast
Sitting room, library, fireplace

Tastefully and comfortably furnished, including many family antiques. The warm hospitality of "Lupine House" offers a home away from home.
Lupinehouse@attbi.com http://www.westmass.com/lupinehouse

PETERSHAM

The Inn at Clamber Hill
111 N Main St 01366
978-724-8800 Fax: 978-724-8829
888-374-0007
Mark & Deni Ellis
All year

135-185-BB
5 rooms, 5 pb
Visa, MC, AmEx, •
C-ltd/S-ltd/P-ltd/H-ltd
German, French

Full breakfast
Tea, wine, beer, cocktails, afternoon tea
Formal library, parlor, wintergarden, terraces, gardens

Peaceful Seclusion in a Grand Style in the heart of our 33-acre estate. Original artwork, antiques, Oriental rugs. Rooms and suites individually decorated. Relax and leave your cares behind. clamber@tiac.net http://www.clamberhill.com

---

Winterwood at Petersham
PO Box 176
19 North Main St 01366
978-724-8885 Fax: 978-724-8884
Jean & Robert Day
All year

119-BB
6 rooms, 6 pb
Visa, MC, AmEx, •
C-yes/S-ltd/P-no/H-no

Continental plus breakfast
Bar service, sitting room, library, working fireplaces

Elegant sixteen-room Greek revival mansion listed on the National Register located in the center of town. Six beautifully appointed guestrooms, all with private baths and most with fireplaces. winterwoodatpetersham@juno.com http://www.winterwoodinn.com

PLYMOUTH

16 Turnberry
16 Turnberry Dr 02360
508-224-2224 Fax: 508-224-7292
888-BNB-1620
Addy & Jeffrey Soilson
All year

125-195-BB
4 rooms, 4 pb
Visa, MC, •
C-yes/S-no/P-no/H-no
Spanish, Russian, Hebrew

Full breakfast
Coffee, tea, hot chocolate, cookies, wine, cheese
Baby grand player piano, TV/DVD, movie library, fireplaces, Jacuzzi

Unique and stately Colonial Revival home on 2 acres that combines the preserved architectural detail of a past age and the comfort of the present day.
info@16turnberry.com http://www.16turnberry.com

PLYMOUTH

A Beach House Oceanfront
429 Center Hill Rd
45 Black Pond Lane 02360
508-224-3517 Fax: 508-224-3517
888-262-2543
Denise & Jack Kedian
All year

130-150-BB
3 rooms, 3 pb
Visa, MC, *Rated*
C-yes/S-ltd/P-ltd/H-no

Full breakfast
Refreshments
Sitting room, bicycles, suites, fireplace, cable TV, conferences, beach

Only direct oceanfront B&B in Plymouth. Others claim it, but we're 20' from the water while they're a 5 minute walk away. Welcoming, casual elegance, light, airy, water's edge on Cape Cod Bay. seacliff@tiac.net http://www.beachhouseplymouth.com

---

Another Place Inn
240 Sandwich St 02360
508-746-0126 Fax: 508-746-0126
800-583-0126
Carol Barnes
March-November

95-125-BB
3 rooms, 3 pb
Rated
C-ltd/S-no/P-no/H-no

Full breakfast
Afternoon tea
Sitting room, suites, fireplaces, cable TV, accom. bus. travel

Only at "Another Place" can you experience the reality of another time in Plymouth.
anotherplace@adelphia.net http://www.anotherplaceinn.com

Foxglove Cottage
101 Sandwich Road 02360
508-747-6576 Fax: 508-747-7622
800-479-4746
Mr. & Mrs. Charles K. Cowan
All year

90-115-BB
3 rooms, 3 pb
Rated

Full breakfast
Afternoon tea
Sitting room, video library, bicycles, breakfast on deck

Charming, romantic restored 1800 Cape in pastoral setting. Furnished with Victorian antiques. Full breakfast on deck.
tranquility@foxglove-cottage.com http://www.foxglove-cottage.com

PLYMOUTH (REGION)

1831 Zachariah Eddy
51 S Main St
51 S Main Street, *Middleborough* 02346
508-946-0016 Fax: 508-947-2603
Cheryl Leonard
All year

79-129-BB
3 rooms, 1 pb
Most CC, •
C-ltd/S-no/P-no/H-no

Full breakfast
Dinner available, snacks, wine
Sitting room, library, bicycles, fireplace, cable TV, conference

This 1831 historic home offers quiet, comfortable elegance and sumptuous breakfasts. Conveniently located within 35 miles of Boston, Providence, Plymouth, Newport and Cape Cod. ZachEddy@aol.com http://www.1831eddyhousebb.com

PROVIDENCE (REGION)

Five Bridge Inn
PO Box 462
154 Pine St, *Rehoboth* 02769
508-252-3190 Fax: 508-252-3190
Ann & Harold Messenger
All year

98-145-BB
6 rooms, 3 pb
Visa, MC, Disc, *Rated*
C-yes/S-ltd/P-yes/H-ltd

Full gourmet breakfast
Complimentary soft drinks, wine and cheese
Gazebo, tennis court, pool, modern parking area

Five Bridge sits on 90 acres in the middle of a nine hundred acre preserve with miles of trails through pastures, woodlands and bogs.
info@fivebridgeinn.com http://www.fivebridgeinn.com

Nichols Guest Rooms
50 Pine St, *Seekonk* 02771
508-761-7146
Dorothy Tameo, Walter Nobriga
All year

60-100-BB
4 rooms, 3 pb
•
C-yes/S-ltd/P-ltd/H-ltd

Full breakfast
Coffee, tea, soda, cookies, candy
Bikes, playground, lawn chairs, hiking trails, golf, health club nearby

Early 1800 New England Colonial. Wide pine floors, fireplaces, air dried sheets, screened porches, hearty farm fresh breakfasts, near many places of interest.
nicholsbnb@aol.com http://bedandbreakfast.com/bbc/p613410.asp

PROVINCETOWN

Revere Guest House
14 Court St 02657
508-487-2292 800-487-2292
Gary A. Palochko
May–October

75-165-BB
8 rooms, 2 pb
Most CC, •
S-ltd/P-no/H-no

Continental breakfast
Sitting room, fireplaces, cable TV

Revere House is listed as an historic home built in 1830. In 1998, the historical commission awarded the Revere House for being maintained in an authentic manner.

info@reverehouse.com http://www.reverehouse.com

QUINCY

Quincy Adams
24 Whitney Rd 02169
617-479-6215 Fax: 617 479-1065
Mary Lee Caldwell
All year

100-BB
3 rooms, 3 pb
Most CC, •
C-yes/S-no/P-no/H-no

Full breakfast
Sitting room with leather furniture, TV and VCR

An elegant Victorian home offering old fashioned New England hospitality at remarkably reasonable rates. All rooms have private baths. Deluxe breakfast included. Near to all Boston's tourist sites.

marylee@quincyadamsbandb.com http://www.quincyadamsbandb.com

REHOBOTH

Gilbert's Tree Farm
30 Spring St 02769
508-252-6416
Jeanne D. Gilbert
All year

65-85-BB
4 rooms, 1 pb
Rated, •
C-yes/S-no/P-no/H-no

Full breakfast
Afternoon tea
Sitting room, swimming pool, fireplaces, accom. bus. travel

New England Cape was built in 1830s. Features original floors, windows & hardware. Has a fireplace, in-ground pool & hiking trails.

glbrtsbb@aol.com http://members.aol.com/glbrtsbb/

ROCKPORT

Addison Choate Inn
49 Broadway 01966
978-546-7543 Fax: 978-546-7638
800-245-7543
Cynthia Francis and Ed Cambron
All year

110-175-BB
8 rooms, 8 pb
Visa, MC, *Rated*
C-ltd/S-no/P-no/H-no

Continental plus breakfast
Tea, lemonade, wine, cookies, crackers, cheese
Verandah, sitting room, TV room, A/C, whale watch discounts, fireplaces

Located in the village of Rockport, a short walk to the beaches, galleries and shops, this 1851 Greek Revival home offers a romantic verandah overlooking perennial gardens.

info@addisonchoateinn.com http://www.addisonchoateinn.com

Emerson Inn by the Sea
1 Cathedral Ave 01966
978-546-6321 Fax: 978-546-7043
800-954-5550
Bruce & Michelle Coates
April–December

95-325-BB
36 rooms, 36 pb
Most CC, *Rated*, •
C-yes/S-no/P-no/H-ltd

Full or continental plus breakfast
Restaurant
Sitting room, hot tubs, sauna, swimming pool, family friendly facility

The Emerson Inn By the Sea is a newly renovated, handsome white clapboard inn, which once welcomed Ralph Waldo Emerson into its peace and comfort.

info@emersoninnbythesea.com http://www.emersoninnbythesea.com

---

Inn on Cove Hill/Caleb Norwood Jr. House
37 Mt Pleasant St 01966
978-546-2701 Fax: 978-546-1095
888-546-2701
Betsy Eck
Mid Apr.–Mid Oct.

75-150-BB
11 rooms, 9 pb
Visa, MC, *Rated*
C-ltd/S-no/P-no/H-no

Continental plus breakfast
Afternoon tea
Canopy beds, garden, panoramic view, porch, all rooms A/C, sitting room

Inn built in 1771 by Caleb Norwood, Jr. Open almost all year round, 8 rooms, 6 private baths, no afternoon tea, but only on request. Park or walk to everything, harbor views, in town location. beck@ziplink.net http://www.innoncovehill.com

ROCKPORT

Linden Tree Inn
26 King St 01966
978-546-2494 Fax: 978-546-3297
800-865-2122
Tobey & John Shepherd
Open mid-April–end of Oct.

100-135-BB
18 rooms, 18 pb
Visa, MC, AmEx,
Rated, •
C-yes/S-yes/P-no/H-no

Continental plus breakfast
Afternoon tea, cookies
Lemonade, sitting room,
guest living room

Easy access by train, romantic inn. Short walk to beach, shops, restaurants, galleries. Widow's walk views of ocean & mill pond.
ltree@shore.net http://www.lindentreeinn.com

Rocky Shores Inn & Cottages
65 Eden Rd 01966
978-546-2823
800-348-4003
Renate & Gunter Kostka
May–Oct.

104-152-BB
20 rooms, 20 pb
Rated, •
C-yes/S-ltd/P-no/H-no
German

Continental plus breakfast
Sitting room, rooms with
ocean views, walk to
beaches

Inn & cottages with unforgettable view of Thatcher Island lights & open sea. Inn has 7 fireplaces & beautiful woodwork. http://www.rockportusa.com/rockyshores

---

Sally Webster Inn
34 Mt Pleasant St 01966
978-546-9251 877-546-9251
John & Kathy Fitzgerald
All year

85-120-BB
7 rooms, 7 pb
Visa, MC, *Rated*
C-ltd/S-no/P-no/H-no

Continental breakfast
Complimentary wine for
special occasion
Sitting room, TV/VCR

Historic, Colonial home built in 1832. Antique decor. Walk to village and sea.
sallywebsterinn@hotmail.com http://www.sallywebster.com

The Tuck Inn
17 High St 01966
978-546-7660
800-789-7260
Liz & Scott Wood
All year

69-109-BB
11 rooms, 11 pb
Visa, MC, *Rated*
C-yes/S-no/P-no/H-no

Continental plus breakfast
Snacks
Sitting room, A/C, swimming
pool, bicycles, scenic walks,
beach

Cozy 1790 Colonial home. Featuring hospitable, comfortable & affordable year 'round lodging. Renowned home-baked breakfast. Antiques, quilts, gardens, pool, non-smoking.
info@thetuckinn.com http://www.thetuckinn.com

Yankee Clipper Inn
127 Granite St 01966
978-546-3407
Fax: 978-546-9730
800-545-3699
Randy & Cathy Marks
All year

141-349-BB
16 rooms, 16 pb
Most CC, *Rated*, •
C-yes/S-no/P-no/H-no

Full breakfast—High Season
Continental Plus breakfast—
off season
Salt water pool, oceanfront
dining room and meeting
room

The Yankee Clipper Inn is an oceanfront, Art Deco mansion located on a bluff, overlooking the open ocean and downtown Rockport, MA.
info@yankeeclipperinn.com http://www.yankeeclipperinn.com

SALEM

Amelia Payson House
16 Winter St 01970
978-744-8304
Ada May & Donald Roberts
April thru November

95-150-BB
4 rooms, 4 pb
Most CC, *Rated*
C-ltd/S-no/P-no/H-no

Continental plus breakfast
Restaurant nearby

Celebrating 17 years of innkeeping in 2001. Elegantly restored 1845 Greek Revival-style home. Five minute stroll finds restaurants, museums, shopping & train station.
bbamelia@aol.com http://www.ameliapaysonhouse.com

SALEM

Coach House Inn
284 Lafayette St 01970
978-744-4092 Fax: 978-745-8031
800-688-8689
Patricia Kessler
All year

95-165-BB
11 rooms, 10 pb
Visa, MC, AmEx, *Rated*
C-yes/S-no/P-no/H-no

Continental breakfast
Non-smoking Inn, completely restored and redecorated rooms

This Victorian mansion, built by a sea captain in 1879, retains the charm and elegance of an earlier era. We are located in one of Salem's Historic Districts, 2 blocks from the Harbor. coachhse@star.net http://www.coachhousesalem.com

---

Inn at Seven Winter Street
7 Winter St 01970
978-745-9520 Fax: 978-745-5052
800-932-5547
Jill Cote, Sally Flint
All year

105-275-BB
10 rooms, 10 pb
Visa, MC, AmEx, •
C-ltd/S-no/P-no/H-no

Continental plus breakfast
Cider, cookies, sherry, chocolates
Dining room, Library, Sitting Room

Romantic, luxurious French Victorian. Masterfully restored, beautifully decorated. Dedicated to your comfort and enjoyment. Each room furnished with antiques and period detail. info@inn7winter.com http://www.inn7winter.com

---

The Salem Inn
7 Summer St 01970
978-741-0680 Fax: 978-744-8924
800-446-2995
Richard & Diane Pabich
All year

139-229-BB
41 rooms, 41 pb
Most CC, *Rated*, •
C-yes/H-no

Continental breakfast
Complimentary sherry
Private garden, sitting room, A/C, canopy beds, fireplaces, Jacuzzi baths

Spacious, luxuriously appointed rooms in three elegantly restored historic homes. Located within easy walk of city's restaurants, attractions, museums and the waterfront. salem.inn@verizon.net http://www.saleminnma.com

---

Stephen Daniels House
One Daniels St 01970
978-744-5709
Mrs. Kay Gill
All year

95-120-BB
5 rooms, 3 pb
Rated, •
C-yes/S-yes/P-yes/H-no

Continental breakfast
Complimentary tea
Sitting rooms, walk-in fireplaces, private garden, bicycles

300-year-old house furnished with canopy beds, antiques throughout, fireplaces in every room.

SCITUATE

The Allen House
18 Allen Place 02066
781-545-8221
Fax: 781-544-3192
Meredith Emmons
All year

115-250-BB
6 rooms, 6 pb
Most CC, *Rated*, •
C-ltd/S-no/P-no/H-yes

Full gourmet breakfast
Massage available, golf course nearby

Gourmet cook serves breakfast on Victorian porch overlooking harbor in unpretentious fishing town 25 miles south of Boston. AAA 3 Diamond rating. sales@allenhousebnb.com http://www.allenhousebnb.com

SHELBURNE FALLS

Bear Haven
22 Mechanic St 01370
413-625-9281
Deane Merrill & Chris Morben
All year

69-99-BB
3 rooms, 1 pb
Most CC, *Rated*, •
C-ltd/S-ltd/P-no/H-no
French, German, Russian

Continental breakfast
Sitting room, cable TV, feather beds, family cats, ceiling fans, A/C

"A Rest Home for Teddy Bears." Moses W. Merrill Homestead, 1852. Cozy Victorian ambiance. info@bearhaven.com http://www.bearhaven.com

SOUTH DEERFIELD

Deerfields Yellow Gabled House
111 N Main St 01373
413-665-4922
Edna J. Stahelek
All year

80-145-BB
3 rooms, 1 pb
Rated, •
C-ltd/S-no/P-no/H-no
Lithuanian

Full breakfast
Antiques, gardens, tennis nearby, library, carriage rides arranged

Old country house in the heart of historical and cultural area.

SOUTH EGREMONT

The Egremont Inn
PO Box 418
10 Old Sheffield Rd 01258
413-528-2111 Fax: 413-528-3284
800-859-1780
Steve & Karen Waller
All year

90-185-BB
19 rooms, 19 pb
Most CC, *Rated*, •
C-yes/S-ltd/P-no/H-no

Continental Plus
Continental breakfast, weekdays
Restaurant/Tavern, Common rooms, fireplaces, tennis courts, pool, porch

Wonderful Colonial inn offering charm & comfort. Tavern, restaurant. Close to antiquing, cycling, hiking, skiing & Tanglewood–Come join us.
egremontinn@taconic.net http://www.egremontinn.com

Weathervane Inn
PO Box 388
17 Main St, Route 23 01258
413-528-9580 Fax: 413-528-1713
800-528-9580
Maxine & Jeffrey Lome
All year

135-250-BB
10 rooms, 10 pb
Visa, MC, AmEx, *Rated*
C-yes/S-no/P-no/H-ltd

Full breakfast
Afternoon tea, bar service
Sitting room, library, pool, 2 suites, fireplaces, cable TV

The Inn began in 1785 as a farmhouse and today sits on 10 beautifully landscaped acres of gardens and trees. innkeeper@weathervaneinn.com http://www.weathervaneinn.com

SOUTH ORLEANS

A little Inn on Pleasant Bay
Box 190
654 S Orleans Rd 02662
508-255-0780 Fax: 508-240-1850
Sandra, Pamela & Bernd
All year

130-175-BB
10 rooms, 10 pb
C-ltd/P-no

European continental breakfast
5:00pm Sherry hour

Main house dates back to 1798 and was part of the "Underground Railroad."
berndzeller@earthlink.net http://www.alittleinnonpleasantbay.com

SPENCER

Zukas Homestead Barn Inc
89 Smithville Rd 01562
508-885-5320 Fax: 508-885-5546
Lynn & Pete Zukas
All year

129-BB
1 rooms, 1 pb
Visa, MC, Disc
C-yes/S-no/P-no/H-no

Continental plus breakfast
Sitting room, suites, fireplaces

Secluded hilltop farm, banquet facility in renovated barn for weddings, reunions or private parties. Outdoor wedding ceremony and tent facilities are our specialty.
zukasfarm@aol.com http://www.zukas.com

STOCKBRIDGE (REGION)

Historic Merrell Inn
1565 Pleasant St, *South Lee* 01260
413-243-1794 Fax: 413-243-2669
800-243-1794
George Crockett
All year

95-185-BB
10 rooms, 10 pb
Visa, MC, *Rated*
C-ltd/S-no/P-no/H-no

Full breakfast
Afternoon refreshments
Fireplace rooms, antiques, telephones, A/C

One of New England's most historic stage coach inns, a few miles from Norman Rockwell Museum, Stockbridge. info@merrell-inn.com http://www.merrell-inn.com

STURBRIDGE

Sturbridge Country Inn
PO Box 60
530 Main St 01566
508-347-5503 Fax: 508-347-5319
Ms. Affenito
All year

59-169-BB
9 rooms, 9 pb
Visa, MC, AmEx,
Rated, •
C-ltd/S-yes/P-no/H-yes

Continental breakfast
Restaurant, bar
Lunch & dinner in tavern, complimentary champagne, hot tubs

Close to Old Sturbridge Village lies our grand Greek Revival structure. Each room has period reproductions, fireplaces, and whirlpool tubs.
info@sturbridgecountryinn.com http://www.sturbridgecountryinn.com

STURBRIDGE (REGION)

Wildwood Inn
121 Church St, *Ware* 01082
413-967-7798 800-860-8098
F. Fenster & R. Watson
All year

65-110-BB
9 rooms, 7 pb
Visa, MC, AmEx,
Rated, •
C-ltd/S-no/P-no/H-yes

Full breakfast
Lemonade, cider
Sitting room, tennis courts, swimming, canoeing, hiking, games

Relax! Enjoy American antiques & heirloom quilts. Near Sturbridge, Deerfield, Amherst. Canoe, swim, bike, hike. We'll spoil you.
freelance@mail.ccsinet.net http://www.wildwoodinn.net

WAREHAM

Mulberry
257 High St 02571
508-295-0684 Fax: 508-291-2909
866-295-0684
Frances A. Murphy
All year

60-80-BB
3 rooms
Visa, MC, *Rated*, •
C-yes/S-no/P-no/H-no

Full breakfast
Afternoon tea, snacks
Sitting room, library, bicycle routes with maps, restaurant discounts

Charming 1840s Cape Cod style home built by blacksmith. Used as a general store by B&B owner's grandfather.
mulberry257@aol.com http://www.virtualcities.com/ons/ma/z/maza801.htm

WEST STOCKBRIDGE

Card Lake Inn
PO Box 38
29 Main St 01266
413-232-0272
Ed & Lisa Robbins All year

85-145-BB
11 rooms, 11 pb
Most CC, •
C-yes/S-no/P-no/H-no

Continental plus breakfast
Lunch and dinner
Restaurant on site, bar service, sitting rooms, library, cable TV

A two hundred year old colonial country inn with a tavern restaurant on premises and an outdoor deck cafe, minutes to Butternut and Jimini Peak ski areas.
cardlake@bcn.net http://www.cardlakeinn.com

The Williamsville Inn
PO Box 138
286 Great Barrington Rd, Rt 41
01266
413-274-6118 Fax: 413-274-3539
800-457-3971
Gail & Kathleen Ryan
All year

130-195-BB
16 rooms, 16 pb
Visa, MC, AmEx,
Rated, •
C-yes/S-ltd/P-yes/H-no
Spanish

Full breakfast
Bar service, picnic baskets
Sitting room, library, tennis court, pool

1797 farmhouse on ten beautiful acres, on a quiet country road in the heart of the Berkshires. williamsville@taconic.net http://www.williamsvilleinn.com

WILLIAMSTOWN

1896 House Country Inn
Route 7 Cold Spring Rd 01267
413-458-1896 888-666-1896
Denise Richer & Suzanne Morelle
All year

65-249-BB
36 rooms, 36 pb
Most CC, *Rated*, •
C-ltd/S-no/P-no/H-yes

Restaurant and Tavern, heated outdoor pool, shuffleboard

Historic 1896 landmark barn, housing six "Barnside" luxury suites and renowned Colonel Bullock's Tavern, is flanked by two charming motels, "Brookside" and "Pondside," on 17 rural acres. celebrate@1896house.com http://www.1896house.com

WINCHENDON

Bona Vista Farm
10 Cummings Rd 01475
978-297-0460
Jean Fincke and Dick Hoyt
All year

80-BB
2 rooms
C-yes/S-no/P-no/H-no
French, Russain, Spanish

Full breakfast
Snacks
Jacuzzis, accom. bus. travelers, pond, hiking, cc trails

A Colonial-era, 80-acre, diversified, organic farm and bed and breakfast. Full farm breakfast of ham, bacon and sausage from our pigs. Fresh eggs and homemade granola and bread. bonavistafarm@aol.com http://bonavistafarm.freeyellow.com/index.html

WORCESTER (REGION)

The Rose Cottage
24 Worcester St
Rts 12 & 140, *West Boylston* 01583
508-835-4034 Fax: 508-835-4043
Michael & Loretta Kittredge
All year

80-BB
5 rooms, 2 pb
Rated
C-yes/S-no/P-no/H-ltd
Little Italian

Full breakfast
Welcoming beverage
Sitting room, suites, fireplaces, cable TV, accommodate business travelers

Gracious 1850 Gothic Revival cottage situated on 4 acres of lawn, overlooking Wachusett Reservoir. Only 20 minutes to Worcester.

Michigan

ANN ARBOR

The Urban Retreat
2759 Canterbury Rd 48104
734-971-8110
Andre Rosalik & Gloria Krys
All year

60-75-BB
2 rooms, 1 pb
Visa, MC, *Rated*
C-ltd/S-ltd/P-no/H-no

Full breakfast
Sitting room, gardens, patio, air conditioning

Comfortable 1950s ranch home on quiet tree-lined street; furnished with antiques.
http://www.theurbanretreat.com

AUBURN HILLS

Cobblestone Manor
3151 University Dr 48326
248-370-8000 Fax: 248-370-1035
800-370-7270
Heather and Paul Crandall
All year

139-219-BB
8 rooms, 8 pb
Most CC, •
C-ltd/S-no/P-no/H-yes

Full breakfast
Complementary soft drinks, popcorn, fresh cookies

Built in 1840 and recently renovated with all the modern amenities required by professional travelers, Cobblestone Manor offers eight beautifully appointed guestrooms.
stay@cobblestonemanor.com http://www.cobblestonemanor.com

AUTRAIN

AuTrain Lake
PO Box 120
N6915 Forest Lake Road 49806
906-892-8892
Susan Larsen
May–October

75-120-BB
3 rooms, 3 pb
Visa, MC, •
C-yes/S-ltd/P-ltd/H-ltd

Full gourmet breakfast
Afternoon refreshments
Comfortable common area with great views and good books.

Traditional B&B in sunny meadow between sparkling AuTrain and Paulson Lakes. Gardens, antiques, French roast. Woodsy retreat offers three guestrooms, view-filled common area, close to nature decks. autrain@juno.com http://www.autrainlake.com

AUTRAIN

Pinewood Lodge
PO Box 176, M-28-W
10 miles west of Munising
49806
906-892-8300 Fax: 906-892-8510
Jerry & Jenny Krieg
All year

105-135-BB
6 rooms, 6 pb
Visa, MC, Disc, *Rated*, •
C-ltd/S-no/P-no/H-ltd

Full breakfast
Snacks
Library, sitting room, sauna, beach on Lake Superior

Enjoy our log home. Breakfast overlooking our sand beach, Lake Superior & AuTrain Island. pinewood@tds.net http://www.pinewoodlodgebnb.com

BATTLE CREEK

Greencrest Manor
6174 Halbert Rd 49017
616-962-8633 Fax: 616-962-7254
Tom & Kathy
All year

95-235-BB
8 rooms, 6 pb
Visa, MC, AmEx, *Rated*
C-yes/S-no/P-no/H-no

Continental plus breakfast
Snacks
Sitting room, library, suites, fireplaces, cable TV, accom.bus.travel

Words truely cannot describe this treasure of a typically "French" rural Manor. Its breathtaking views around every corner, inside or out or in the gardens, will persuade you to stay here and relax. greencrestmanor@aol.com http://www.greencrestmanor.com

BAY CITY

Clements Inn
1712 Center Ave 48708
517-894-4600 Fax: 517-892-9442
800-442-4605
Shirley & David Roberts

75-190-BB
6 rooms, 6 pb
Most CC, *Rated*
C-ltd/S-no/P-no/H-ltd
All year

Continental breakfast
Grandma's famous cookies await guests
TV's, VCR's, phones with modems and coffee makers

Comfortable Victorian Elegance in the heart of the renowned Center Avenue Historic District of Bay City, Michigan–a quaint mid-Michigan waterfront community.
clementsinn@chartermi.net http://www.clementsinn.com

BAY VIEW (REGION)

Terrace Inn
PO Box 266
1549 Glendale, *Petoskey* 49770
231-347-2410 Fax: 231-347-2407
800-530-9898
Tom & Denise Erhart
All year

49-159-BB
43 rooms, 43 pb
Visa, MC, AmEx, *Rated*, •
C-yes/S-no/P-no/H-yes

Continental plus breakfast
Restaurant serves dinner (fee)
Sitting room, bicycles, tennis, private beach, conference/banquet rooms

1910 furnishings are at home in this Victorian inn among 400 Victorian cottages, each room having its own decor and bathroom.
info@theterraceinn.com http://www.theterraceinn.com

BEULAH

Brookside Inn
115 US 31 49617
231-882-9688
Pamela & Kirk Lorenz
All year

215-270-MAP
40 rooms, 40 pb
Most CC, *Rated*, •
C-ltd/S-yes/P-no/H-yes
German, French

Full breakfast
Breakfast, lunch, dinner served daily, compl. wine
Restaurant, bar service, sitting room, bikes, hot tubs, sauna, steambaths

Created for romantics, couples only rooms, hot tubs, waterbeds, some rooms with steam bath & sauna. All rooms have King canopy beds, log stoves and Polynesian Spa.
rsvp@brooksideinn.com http://www.brooksideinn.com

BROOKLYN

Dewey Lake Manor
11811 Laird Rd 49230
517-467-7122 Fax: 517-467-2356
Joe & Barb Phillips
All year

72-130-BB
5 rooms, 5 pb
Visa, MC, *Rated*, •
C-ltd/S-ltd/P-ltd/H-no

Full breakfast
Picnic lunch avail., snacks, tea, always cookies
Sitting room w/piano, croquet, bonfires, ice skating, fireplace, grills

Century-old, Italianate-style home furnished with antiques, original kerosene lamps.
deweylk@frontiernet.net http://www.getaway2smi.com/dewey

Benedict Doll, Coldwater, MI

CHARLEVOIX (REGION)

Easterly Inn PO Box 366 209 Easterly St, *East Jordan* 49727 231-536-3434 Joan Martin May—October	70-85-BB 4 rooms, 4 pb Visa, MC C-yes/S-no/P-no/H-no	Full breakfast Sitting room, library, fireplace, cable TV

A large wrap-around porch embellishes this three story Victorian home with original oak, cherry and birds-eye maple woodwork, period wall coverings and antiques.
http://innsite.com/inns/A001279.html

CLARKSTON

Millpond Inn 155 North Main St 48346 248-620-6520 Fax: 248-625-6108 800-867-4142 Joan Kopietz All year	80-90-BB 5 rooms, 5 pb Most CC, *Rated* C-yes/S-no/P-ltd/H-ltd	Full breakfast Snacks Sitting room, cable TV, accommodate business travelers

A historic home in the village of Clarkston, where comfort, cleanliness and good food are paramount. Fresh flowers from the many gardens surrounding the Inn add a special touch to each room. millpondbb@email.com http://www.millpondinnbb.com

COLDWATER

Benedict Doll 665 W Chicago Rd 49036 517-279-2821 866-279-2821 Christina Towell & Richard Christensen All year	75-95-BB 4 rooms, 1 pb Visa, MC, Disc C-ltd/S-no/P-no/H-yes	Full breakfast Afternoon tea, snacks, complimentary wine Sitting room, fireplace, cable TV

Faithfully restored, historic register Queen Ann on nine secluded acres between two lake chains. Country Victorian charm featuring full breakfast, distinctive room decor and unparalleled hospitality. benedictdoll@cbpu.com http://www.benedictdoll.com

COLDWATER

Chicago Pike Inn 215 E Chicago St 49036 517-279-8744 Fax: 517-278-8597 800-471-0501 Rebecca Schultz All year	100-195-BB 8 rooms, 8 pb Visa, MC, AmEx, *Rated* S-no/P-no	Full breakfast Afternoon refreshments

Come and enjoy a night or weekend in this turn-of-the-century Colonial mansion located in a quiet, historical residential neighborhood. http://www.chicagopikeinn.com

The HideOut 260 Stevens Shore Dr 49036 517-278-4210 866-872-9559 Lee Pierucki All year	70-120-BB Visa, MC	

Located on Beautiful Craig Lake near Coldwater Michigan, which is near Michigan's southern border, about half way between Detroit and Chicago.
hideoutbb@yahoo.com http://www.hideoutbnblakefront.com

DEARBORN

Dearborn 22331 Morley 48124 313-563-2200 Fax: 313-277-2962 888-959-0900 Nancy Siwik & Rick Harder All year	95-165-BB 4 rooms, 4 pb Most CC, • C-ltd/S-no/P-no/H-no	Continental plus breakfast Snacks, complimentary wine Swimming pool, cable TV, accommodate business travelers

Unique, antique filled home, located in quiet, charming neighborhood. Just a short walk to shopping, museums, and fine dining. Perfect place for romantic getaways or business travelers. nancyswork@aol.com http://www.dearbornbb.com

EAST TAWAS

East Tawas Junction 514 West Bay St 48730 989-362-8006 Don & Leigh Mott All year	89-149-BB 5 rooms, 5 pb Visa, MC, Disc S-ltd/P-no	Full breakfast Tea service available Wrap-around porch, parlour w/piano/digital TV/fireplace, library, decks

Lovely country Victorian, in park-like setting overlooking beautiful Tawas Bay. Five rooms, private baths, sumptuous full breakfast, public rooms. Chickadee Guesthouse available for extended stays. info@east-tawas.com http://www.east-tawas.com

FLINT

Avon House 518 Avon St 48503 810-232-6861 Fax: 810-233-7437 888-832-0627 Arletta E. Minore All year	55-BB 3 rooms Most CC, *Rated* C-yes/S-no/P-no/H-no	Full breakfast Formal dining room Sitting room, A/C, play yard, grand piano, extended stay rates

Enchanting Victorian home close to college and cultural center with art and entertainment. Driving distance to Manufacturer's Marketplace.
avonhsebed@aol.com http://www.accessflint.com/~avonhouse

FRANKENMUTH

Frankenmuth Bender Haus 337 Trinklein St 48734 989-652-8897 Bev & Elden Bender May-October	65-75-BB 4 rooms, 2 pb *Rated*, • C-ltd/S-no/P-no/H-no German	Full or continental plus breakfast Sitting room, bicycles, cable TV

Our traditional home in the center of #1 tourist town. Our home is quiet and peaceful.
benderjb@juno.com http://innsite.com/inns/A001221.html

GLEN ARBOR

Glen Arbor B&B & Cottages	BB	Full breakfast
PO Box 580	8 rooms, 6 pb	Air-conditioned, fireplace in
6548 Western Ave 49636	Visa, MC	B&B & cottages, in-room
231-334-6789 Fax: 231-334-6198	C-ltd/S-no/P-no/H-ltd	TV/VCR/cable, parking.
877-253-4200	All year	
Angela & Bryan Ray		

Enjoy warm hospitality, special amenities & all new French Country decor in the heart of great sand beaches, boutique shopping, dining, wineries, golf, fishing, miles of trails and many more adventures. innkeeper@glenarborbnb.com http://www.glenarborbnb.com

Sylvan Inn	65-140-BB	Continental plus breakfast
PO Box 39	14 rooms, 7 pb	Sitting room, whirlpool &
6680 Western Ave (M-109)	Visa, MC, *Rated*, •	sauna room, extended stay
49636	C-ltd/S-no/P-no/H-yes	rates
231-334-4333	May–October	
Ralph & Rose Gladfelter		

Luxuriously renovated 1885 historic inn situated in the heart of Sleeping Bear National Lakeshore. Walking distance to fine dining, shopping, swimming, biking, skiing.
sylvaninn@earthlink.net http://www.sylvaninn.com

GULLIVER

Thistledowne at Seul Choix	180-180-BB	Full breakfast
PO Box 88 49840	3 rooms, 3 pb	Complementary hors
906-283-3559 Fax: 906-283-3564	Visa, MC, AmEx	d'oeuvres, wine, and
800-522-4649	C-no/S-no/P-no/H-ltd	cocktails
Robert "Bob" Hughes		Inroom fireplaces, whirlpool
May 1–October 31		tubs, direct access to beach

Thistledowne at Seul Choix is a newly constructed Bed & Breakfast. The Inn rests on 60 heavily wooded acres on beautiful Seul Choix Bay, on a quarter mile of Lake Michigan sand beach. thistle@up.net http://www.thistledowne.com

HARBOR BEACH

The State Street Inn	65-79-BB	Full breakfast
646 State Street 48441	3 rooms, 3 pb	Evening dessert with coffee,
989-479-3388 Fax: 989-479-3766	Most CC, •	tea, soft drinks
866-424-7961	C-ltd/S-no/P-no/H-no	Parlor, library, veranda, 2-
Janice & Bill Duerr	German	tiered deck overlooking
All year		gardens

Century old Country Victorian B&B on Lake Huron in Michigan's thumb. Old fashioned hospitality, quaint surroundings, unique guestrooms. Quiet, cozy, romantic atmosphere reminiscent of an earlier era.
janice@thestatestreetinn.com http://www.thestatestreetinn.com

HOLLAND

Centennial Inn	100-150-BB	Full breakfast
8 E 12th St 49423	8 rooms, 8 pb	Sitting room, library, Jacuzzi,
616-355-0998 Fax: 616-355-0882	Visa, MC, *Rated*	fireplaces, cable TV,
Rein & Kay Wolfert	C-ltd/S-no/P-no/H-no	beaches, bicycle path
All year	French, German,	
	Spanish, Dutch	

Located across from Centennial Park and next to the Hope College Campus, Centennial Inn B&B is within the heart of the Historic District and walking distance of downtown Holland. centBNB@iserv.net http://www.yesmichigan.com/centennial

Dutch Colonial Inn	100-160-BB	Full breakfast
560 Central Ave 49423	4 rooms, 4 pb	Afternoon tea, snacks
616-396-3664 Fax: 616-396-0461	Most CC, *Rated*	In-room phone with data-
Bob & Pat Elenbaas	S-no/P-no/H-no	port, in-room TV, double
All year		whirlpool tubs

Lovely 1928 Dutch Colonial home. Touches of elegance and antiques. Whirlpool tubs for 2 in private baths; fireplaces; honeymoon suites.
dutchcolonialinn@juno.com http://www.dutchcolonialinn.com

Horse & Carriage, Jonesville, MI

HOLLAND

The Thistle Inn
300 N 152nd Ave 49424
616-399-0409
Gary & Pat Teski
All year

90-110-BB
3 rooms, 3 pb
Visa, MC, *Rated*, •
C-ltd/S-ltd/P-no

Large, memorable breakfasts
Evening dessert, cordials, hors d'oeuvres
Private patio hot tub, in-room coffee, TV, hairdryers; bicycles available

Quiet wooded setting near Lake Michigan beaches and over 200 miles of paved bike paths. Very nicely furnished rooms, twin, queen or king and all open to patio with hot tub.

patteske@triton.net http://web.triton.net/p/patteske/

JONESVILLE

Horse & Carriage
7020 Brown Rd 49250
517-849-2732 Fax: 517-849-2732
Keith L. Brown & Family
All year

50-100-BB
3 rooms, 2 pb
Rated, •
C-yes/S-no/P-no/H-no
Portuguese, Spanish

Full breakfast
Picnic lunch, snacks, bed-time chocolates
Sitting room, library, family-friendly facility, carriage ride by request

Romantic horse-drawn carriage ride awaits you on our peaceful centennial farm. Shetland sheep and baby chicks. Sleigh rides and fireplace in winter. 1898 Schoolhouse. Children welcome. Antiquing.

ccbrown@modempool.com http://www.hcbnb.com

Munro House
202 Maumee St 49250
517-849-9292 Fax: 517-849-7685
800-320-3792
Mike & Lori Venturini
All year

99-199-BB
7 rooms, 7 pb
Most CC, *Rated*, •
C-yes/S-no/P-no/H-ltd

Full breakfast
Complimentary coffee, cookies, soft drinks
Sitting room, library, 2 rooms with Jacuzzis, 5 rooms with fireplaces

"The most comfortable lodging in Michigan" is located midway between Jackson & Coldwater at Hwys 12 & 99. This historic, pre-Civil War mansion (c. 1834) was once a station on the Underground Railroad.

stay@munrohouse.com http://www.munrohouse.com

Munroe House, Jonesville, MI

KALAMAZOO

Hall House
106 Thompson St 49006
269-343-2500 Fax: 269-343-1374
888-761-2525
Scott & Terri Fox
All year

79-155-BB
6 rooms, 6 pb
Visa, MC, AmEx,
Rated, •
C-ltd/S-no/P-no/H-no

Full breakfast on weekends
Continental plus on weekdays
Goodies always available, sitting room, cable TV/VCRs in rooms

Stately 1920s Georgian Colonial home, minutes from downtown, Western Michigan University, and on the edge of the Kalamazoo College campus.

thefoxes@hallhouse.com http://www.hallhouse.com

KALAMAZOO (REGION)

Sanctuary at Wildwood
58138 M-40 N, *Jones* 49061
616-244-5910 Fax: 616-244-9022
800-249-5910
Dick & Dolly Buerkle

159-219-BB
6 rooms, 6 pb
Most CC, *Rated*
S-no/P-no
All year

Full breakfast
Jacuzzis, fireplaces

Three new separate cottages each with two fireplace/Jacuzzi suites.

info@sanctuaryatwildwood.com http://www.sanctuaryatwildwood.com

LAURIUM

Laurium Manor Inn
320 Tamarack St 49913
906-337-2549
Fax: 815-328-3692
Julie & Dave Sprenger
All year

45-139-BB
17 rooms, 15 pb
Visa, MC, Disc, *Rated*,
•
C-yes/S-no/P-no

Full breakfast buffet
Cable TV, phones in guestrooms available, queen/king beds

Largest mansion in western U.P. 13,000 sq. ft 42 rm. Neo-Classic home has 1300 sq. ft ballroom, library, den, parlor, 2 dining rooms, carriage house.

innkeeper@lauriummanorinn.com http://www.lauriummanorinn.com

LELAND

Falling Waters Lodge
PO Box 345
200 W Cedar 49654
231-256-9832
Fax: 231-256-7611
April–November

75-145-BB
21 rooms, 21 pb
Most CC, *Rated*
C-yes/S-yes/P-ltd/H-no

Continental breakfast
Suites, cable TV, Lake Michigan Beach, ferry, fishing, marina

Shops, marina, beach, on the river at the Dam in historical Fishtown. Direct access to beautiful Lake Michigan beach, charter fishing and ferry to Manitou Islands.

gwn@bigfoot.com http://www.angelfire.com/mi/fwl/

LELAND

The Riverside Inn
PO Box 1135
302 River Street 49654
231-256-9971 Fax: 231-256-2217
888-257-0102
Kate, Robin, and Barb Vilter
May through January

60-85-BB
7 rooms, 4 pb
Most CC, *Rated*
C-ltd/S-no/P-no/H-ltd

Continental breakfast
Dinner and Sunday Brunch

Located on the river, we are a historic B&B and gourmet restaurant offering charming guestrooms, innovative menus, and an expertly created wine list to create a memorable stay in Leelanau County. Vilter77@aol.com http://www.theriverside-inn.com

---

Whaleback Inn
PO Box 1125
1757 N Manitou Trail 49654
231-256-9090 Fax: 231-256-2255
800-942-5322
Ron Koehler
All year

59-169-BB
17 rooms, 17 pb
Visa, MC, *Rated*
C-yes/S-ltd/P-no/H-yes

Continental breakfast
Sitting room, hot tubs, sauna, hiking, lake, swimming, basketball

Relaxing getaway. Beautiful scenic area. All accommodations new or recently remodeled with private baths and ground floor entry. wbi@wfn.net

LOWELL

McGee Homestead
2534 Alden Nash NE 49331
616-897-8142
Bill & Ardie Barber
March 1-December 31

55-75-BB
4 rooms, 4 pb
Most CC, *Rated*
C-yes/S-ltd/P-ltd/H-no

Full breakfast
Afternoon tea, snacks
Sitting room, library, guest kitchen with microwave & fridge

Wake up to the rooster crowing. Our 1880's farmhouse is filled with antiques and is very comfy. mcgeebb@iserv.net http://www.iserv.net/~mcgeebb

LUDINGTON

The Inn at Ludington
701 E Ludington Ave 49431
231-845-7055 Fax: 231-845-0794
800-845-9170
Diane Nemitz
All year

90-110-BB
6 rooms, 6 pb
Most CC, *Rated*, •
C-ltd/S-no/P-no/H-no

Full breakfast
Picnic lunches (fee)
Sitting room, library, murder mystery weekends, family country suite

This 1890 Queen Anne painted lady combines the charm of the past with the comforts of today. Fireplace rooms. diane@inn-ludington.com http://www.inn-ludington.com

---

The Ludington House
501 E Ludington Ave 49431
231-845-7769 800-827-7869
Virginia Boegner
All year

70-135-BB
8 rooms, 8 pb
Visa, MC, *Rated*, •
C-yes/S-no/P-ltd/H-no

Full breakfast
Sitting room, library, Jacuzzis, fireplaces, cable TV, parlor games, fridge

1878 Lumber Baron home. Romantic interlude, vacation, or family reunions. House capacity 20. Queen beds. Hearty gourmet breakfast; special diets available. Murder Mysteries. http://www.ludingtonhouse.com

---

Snyder's Shoreline Inn
PO Box 667
903 W Ludington Ave 49431
231-845-1261 Fax: 231-843-4441
Sue Brillhart
Open May–October

69-299-BB
44 rooms, 44 pb
Most CC, *Rated*
S-no/P-no/H-yes

Continental breakfast
Box lunches available
Library, hot tub, swimming pool, in room spas

Country inn with private balconies facing Lake Michigan. In-room spas. sharon@snydersshoreinn.com http://www.snydersshoreinn.com

MACKINAC ISLAND

Cloghaun
PO Box 203
49757
906-847-3885
Dorothy & James Bond

Cloghaun is a large Victorian home located on Market Street, one block from the harbor and close to many fine restaurants, shops and riding stables. All boat docks are within easy walking distance. Cloghaun@aol.com

MANISTIQUE

Royal Rose
230 Arbutus Ave 49854
906-341-4886 Fax: 906-341-4886
877-443-0016
Gilbert & Rosemary Sablack
May 1–December 31

75-110-BB
4 rooms, 4 pb
Visa, MC, Disc, *Rated*
S-no/P-no/H-no

Full breakfast
Snacks
Sitting room, fireplaces, cable TV, Business travelers

Enjoy luxurious accommodations in this 1903 Dutch Colonial home. Sunroom with fireplace and four elegant guestrooms with private baths. One guestroom with a Jacuzzi.
rrbnb@chartermi.net http://www.royalrose-bnb.com

NEW BUFFALO

Sans Souci Euro Inn
19265 S Lakeside Rd 49117
616-756-3141 Fax: 616-756-5511
Wally or Jennifer Siewert
All year

160-240-BB
9 rooms, 9 pb
Most CC, *Rated*, •
C-ltd/S-ltd/P-ltd/H-yes
German, Spanish

In-suite full gourmet breakfast
Full kitchens/houses
Whirlpool, fireplace, TV/VCR/stereo, phones, priv. lake/beach, birdwatching

Euro-homes, honeymoon suites, family cottages offer luxury amenities. King-size bed and private bath in all. Enjoy an unmatched level of privacy. Ideal for reunions, meetings, outdoor weddings. sans-souci@worldnet.att.net http://www.sans-souci.com

NEW BUFFALO (REGION)

Rivers Edge
9902 Community Hall Rd,
Union Pier 49129
616-469-6860 Fax: 616-469-6890
800-742-0592
Gretchen & Mark Robbins

89-155-BB
8 rooms, 8 pb
Visa, MC, AmEx, *Rated*, •
C-ltd/S-no/P-no/H-yes
All year

Full breakfast
Snacks, wine
Sitting room, library, bikes, Jacuzzis, suites, fireplaces, canoes

A pine lodge located on 30 acres of land with close to a mile of frontage on the Galein River. All rooms have fireplaces, double Jacuzzis, TVs.
zigzag@enteract.com http://www.riversedgebandb.com

NORTHVILLE

The Fraser Inn
501 W. Dunlap St 48167
248-449-6699 Fax: 248-449-7499
Dave & Sherry Farhat
All year

80-150-BB
6 rooms, 6 pb
Visa, MC, AmEx
C-yes/S-no/P-no/H-no

Full breakfast
Snacks
Sitting room, library, Jacuzzis, suites, fireplaces, cable TV

1882 Victorian home located in the historical district of Northville, Michigan. Walking distance to restaurants, shops and theatres. A comfortable place to stay.
fraserinn@earthlink.net http://www.thefraserinn.com

ODEN

The Inn at Crooked Lake
PO Box 139
4407 US31 North 49764
231-439-9984 Fax: 231-347-3683
877-644-3339
Diane & Mark Hansell

80-195-BB
5 rooms, 3 pb
Most CC
C-no/S-no/P-no/H-no

Full breakfast
Dessert each evening; wine & cheese p.m.
Beach, front porch overlooking the lake

The Inn At Crooked Lake is a romantic getaway near Petoskey Michigan overlooking beautiful Crooked Lake. Excellent breakfasts, cozy rooms and close to all this area offers.
innatcrookedlake@aol.com http://www.innatcrookedlake.com

PAW PAW

Carrington Country House
43799 60th Ave 49079
616-657-5321
Reva M. Carrington
Easter–Thanksgiving

55-75-BB
3 rooms
C-yes/S-no/P-ltd/H-ltd

Continental plus breakfast
Snacks, complimentary wine
Sitting room, cable TV

Country farmhouse furnished in family antiques, continental to full breakfast served in large glassed-in front porch.

PENTWATER

Historic Nickerson Inn
PO Box 986
262 West Lowell St 49449
231-869-6731 Fax: 231-869-6151
800-742-1288
Harry & Gretchen Shiparski
4/1–12/15; 1/1; 2/14

85-250-BB
13 rooms, 13 pb
Visa, MC, Disc, *Rated*, •
C-ltd/S-no/P-no/H-no
German, Swiss German, Ital, French, Sp

Full breakfast
Tea, snacks, dinner, bar service, restaurant
Sitting room, library, Jacuzzis, fireplaces

Since 1914, the Inn has been known for its charm, gracious hospitality & casual fine dining. nickerson@voyager.net http://www.nickersoninn.com

PETOSKEY

Serenity
504 Rush St 49770
231-347-6171 Fax: 231-439-0337
877-347-6171
David & Peggy Vermeesch
All year

105-145-BB
3 rooms, 3 pb
Visa, MC, *Rated*
C-ltd/S-no/P-no/H-no

Full four course sitdown breakfast
Afternoon snacks and refreshments
Quiet, relaxing porches, romantic atmosphere

1890's Victorian B&B in downtown Petoskey. Antiques, soft music and lace. Exceptional hospitality. Three rooms, queen beds, PB, A/C. Recently featured in TIME and BEST CHOICES magazines. $105-145. stay@serenitybb.com http://www.serenitybb.com

PITTSFORD

The Rocking Horse Inn
8652 North St 49271
517-523-3826
Mary Ann & Phil Meredith
All year

50-90-BB
4 rooms, 4 pb
Visa, MC
C-ltd/S-ltd/P-no/H-no

Full breakfast
Snacks, afternoon tea, lunch & dinner available
Sitting room, cable TV, accommodate business travelers

We are ready to pamper & serve you in our 1852 brick Italianate-style home, especially with our pamper packages. Other packages are also available.
rockingh@frontiernet.net http://www.bbonline.com/mi/rockinghorse

PLYMOUTH

932 Penniman B&B
932 Penniman Ave 48170
734-414-7444 Fax: 734-414-7445
888-548-4887
Carey & Jon Gary
All year

99-175-BB
4 rooms, 4 pb
Most CC, *Rated*, •
C-ltd/S-no/P-no/H-no

Full breakfast
Snacks, wine
Sitting room, library, Jacuzzis, fireplaces, cable TV, accom. bus. travel

Enjoy the informal elegance of this lovingly restored 1903 Victorian home.
http://www.bbonline.com/mi/penniman

PORT AUSTIN

The Garfield Inn
PO Box 366
8544 Lake St 48467
989-738-5254 Fax: 989-738-6384
800-373-5254
Jim & Dianne Pasant
All year

110-125-BB
6 rooms, 3 pb
Most CC, *Rated*
C-yes/S-no/P-no/H-ltd

Full breakfast
Cable TV, in-room coffee

The Inn is a National Historic Site styled in French Second Empire, dating back to the 1830's. garfield_inn@hotmail.com http://www.garfieldinn.com

PORT HURON

The Victorian Inn 1229 7th St 48060 810-984-1437 Fax: 810-984-5777 Marv & Sue Burke All year	100-150-BB 4 rooms, 2 pb Most CC, *Rated*, • C-ltd/S-yes/P-no/H-no	Full breakfast Restaurant, pub Lunch, dinner, near museum, downtown, civic center, marina

The Victorian Inn features fine dining w/ creative cuisine & guestrooms presenting timeless ambiance in authentically restored Victorian. elegance. http://www.victorianinn-mi.com

PORT SANILAC

Raymond House Inn PO Box 439 111 S Ridge St 48469 810-622-8800 Fax: 810-622-8485 800-622-7229 Gary & Cristy Bobofchak All year	75-120-BB 7 rooms, 5 pb Visa, MC, Disc, *Rated* C-ltd/S-no/P-no/H-no	Full breakfast Comp. sherry, snacks A/C, TV, phones, sitting room, deck, VCR & tapes to view.

127 year-old Victorian home on Michigan's Historic Register, furnished in antiques. On Lake Huron—marina, boating, shipwreck, scuba diving, fishing, swimming.
rayhouse@greatlakes.net http://www.bbonline.com/mi/raymond

SAGINAW

Montague Inn 1581 S Washington 48601 517-752-3939 Fax: 517-752-3159 Janet Hoffmann All year	72-176-BB 18 rooms, 16 pb Visa, MC, AmEx, *Rated* C-yes/S-ltd/P-no/H-yes	Continental breakfast Restaurant, bar service Lunch, dinner (fee), library, Jacuzzi suite

Georgian mansion restored to its original splendor. Surrounded by spacious lawns with flower & herb gardens. montaguein@aol.com http://www.montagueinn.com

SAINT CLAIR

William Hopkins Manor 613 N Riverside Ave 48079 810-329-0188 Fax: 810-329-6239 Sharon Llewellyn & Terry Mazzarese All year	80-100-BB 5 rooms, 1 pb Visa, MC, AmEx, *Rated*, • C-ltd/S-no/P-no/H-ltd	Full breakfast Sitting room, fireplaces, accommodate business travelers

This elegant 1876 Victorian home is perched on a hill overlooking the St. Clair River.
whmanor@aol.com http://members.aol.com/whmanor

SAUGATUCK

Bayside Inn PO Box 186 618 Water St 49453 269-857-4321 Fax: 269-857-3912 Kathy & Frank Wilson All year	85-250-BB 10 rooms, 10 pb Most CC, *Rated* C-yes/S-no/P-no/H-ltd	Full breakfast Snacks Converted boathouse, private bath & deck in rooms, cable TV, phones

Bayside is an old boathouse converted to a B&B on the water, near downtown Saugatuck. info@baysideinn.net http://www.baysideinn.net

---

Beachway Resort PO Box 186 106 Perryman Street 49453 269-857-3331 Fax: 269-857-3912 Frank & Kathy Wilson May-end of Oct.	75-250-EP 28 rooms, 28 pb Visa, MC, AmEx, *Rated* C-yes/S-no/P-no/H-yes	Snacks Swimming pool, cable TV, video library

Overlooking the harbor on the banks of the Kalamazoo River, just a 100-foot ferry ride to downtown. info@beachwayresort.com http://www.beachwayresort.com

SAUGATUCK

Hidden Garden Cottages
PO Box 27
247 Butler St 49453
616-857-8109 Fax: 616-857-6098
888-857-8109
Daniel Indurante & Gary Kott
All year

165-185-BB
3 rooms, 3 pb
Most CC, •
C-ltd/S-no/P-no/H-yes

Continental plus breakfast
Snacks
Jacuzzis, suites, fireplaces, cable TV

Luxurious hideaways designed for two, perfect for guests seeking a more private bed & breakfast. Elegantly furnished, steps away from shopping, dining & attractions.
indakott@aol.com http://www.hiddengardencottages.com

The Park House
888 Holland St 49453
616-857-4535 Fax: 616-857-1065
800-321-4535
John & Sallie Cwik
All year

105-235-BB
8 rooms, 8 pb
Most CC, *Rated*, •
C-ltd/S-ltd/P-no/H-yes

Full breakfast
Soft drinks, juice
Jacuzzi suite with fireplaces, cottages, rooms with fireplaces, porches

Stay with us and relive a bit of Saugatuck history. Built in 1857 by H.D. Moore, The Park House is Saugatuck's oldest residence. Special packages include dinners, romance getaways & much more. . . . info@parkhouseinn.com http://www.parkhouseinn.com

---

Sherwood Forest
PO Box 315
938 Center St 49453
616-857-1246 Fax: 616-857-1996
800-838-1246
Susan & Keith Charak
All year

100-200-BB
5 rooms, 5 pb
Visa, MC, Disc, *Rated*, •
C-ltd/S-no/P-no/H-no
Atlantian

Full breakfast
Afternoon tea, snacks
Sitting room, bicycles, heated pool, skiing, Jacuzzi, cottage

Surrounded by woods, this beautiful Victorian-style home offers fireplace-Jacuzzi suites, heated pool, bicycles, wraparound porch. 1/2 block to Lake Michigan & spectacular sunsets. sf@sherwoodforestbandb.com http://www.sherwoodforestbandb.com

---

Twin Gables Inn
PO Box 1150
900 Lake St 49453
616-857-4346 Fax: 616-857-3482
800-231-2185
B. Lawrence & S. Schwaderer
All year

85-185-BB
14 rooms, 14 pb
Most CC, *Rated*
C-ltd/S-no/P-no/H-yes
French

Full gourmet breakfast
Refreshments, fresh-baked treats
Whirlpool, hot tub, pool, A/C, bicycles, pond, garden park

Enjoy personalized service at this relaxing gourmet breakfasts, lake view, spectacular sunsets, fireplaces, spa, pool. relax@twingablesinn.com http://www.twingablesinn.com

---

Twin Oaks Inn
PO Box 818
227 Griffith St 49453
616-857-1600 Fax: 616-857-7446
800-788-6188
Willa Lemken All year

95-135-BB
6 rooms, 6 pb
Most CC, •
C-yes/S-no/P-no/H-no

Full breakfast
Afternoon tea, snacks
Hot tubs, bicycles, TVs, VCRs with movie library

Relax in the warmth and charm of antiques and modern amenities. Six guest rooms with queen/king size beds, Jacuzzi suite.
twinoaks@sirus.com http://www.bbonline.com/mi/twinoaks/

The Wickwood Country Inn
PO Box 1019
510 Butler St 49453
616-857-1465 800-385-1174
Julee & Bill Rosso-Miller
All year

145-325-BB
11 rooms, 11 pb
Visa, MC, *Rated*
S-no/P-no/H-yes

Snacks, bedtime sweets
Library, garden room, fireplaces, game room, fresh flowers

Best selling cookbook author, Julee Rosso of The Silver Palate Cookbook and her husband Bill Miller, have created an exquisite Inn on the shores of Lake Michigan
innkeeper@wickwoodinn.com http://www.wickwoodinn.com

SAUGATUCK (REGION)

Will O'Glenn Irish
PO Box 288, *Glenn* 49416
616-227-3045
Fax: 616-227-3045
888-237-3009
Shelley & Ward Gahan
All year

99-145-BB
4 rooms, 4 pb
Visa, MC, *Rated*, •
C-ltd/S-no/P-no/H-ltd
Some French

Full breakfast
Tea, snacks, wine
Sitting room, library, Jacuzzis, fireplace, conference facilities

Tranquility & serenity are the order of the day in these peaceful surroundings.
shamrock@irish-inn.com http://www.irish-inn.com

SEBEWAING

Antique Inn
4 N Center St 48759
517-883-9424
Dana & Dean Roof

65-85-BB
4 rooms, 4 pb
Visa, MC
C-yes/S-no/P-ltd/H-no

Continental plus breakfast
Snacks
Sitting room, bikes, TV/VCR, books & videos, A/C

Behind the businesslike red brick exterior, there's a secret Victorian hideaway. With four guest rooms, we're small enough to give you personal attention and big enough for a family get together. antique@avci.net http://www.antiqueinn.com

SOUTH HAVEN

Carriage House at Harbor
118 Woodman St 49090
616-639-2161
Fax: 616-639-2308
Jay & Joyce Yelton
All year

95-210-BB
11 rooms, 11 pb
Visa, MC, AmEx, *Rated*
S-no/P-no/H-yes

Lavish 2-course full breakfast
Evening hors d'oeuvres
Sitting room, library, adult get-away, 2 people per room only, screend porch

An exclusive harborside B&B that has been completely restored, featuring individually decorated rooms with cozy fireplaces and private baths. A beautiful getaway, or a haven for the business traveler.
carriagehousebb@email.msn.com http://www.carriagehouseharbor.com

---

Old Harbor Inn
515 Williams St 49090
616-637-8480 Fax: 616-637-9496
800-433-9210
Gwen DeBruyn
All year

75-300-BB
44 rooms, 44 pb
Most CC, *Rated*, •
C-yes/S-yes/P-no/H-yes

Continental breakfast
Comp. paper, Jacuzzis, near fishing/boats/golf, tennis/beaches/sailing

Nestled on banks of the Black River, Old Harbor Inn offers guests the charm & grace of a quaint coastal village. info@oldharborinn.com http://www.oldharborinn.com

---

Sand Castle Inn
203 Dyckman Ave 49090
616-639-1110
Fax: 616-637-1050
Mary Jane & Charles Kindred
All year

95-225-BB
9 rooms, 9 pb
Most CC, *Rated*
S-no/P-no/H-yes

Full breakfast
Afternoon tea, snacks
Sitting room, library, bikes, suites, fireplaces, private balconies.

Beautiful, restored, historic Lake Michigan Resort Hotel. One block to beach, close to downtown, shops, restaurants. Designer decorated. Elegant, private, & exclusive.
innkeeper@thesandcastleinn.com http://www.thesandcastleinn.com

---

The Seymour House
1248 Blue Star Hwy 49090
616-227-3918 Fax: 616-227-3090
Friedl Scimo
All year

85-145-BB
5 rooms, 5 pb
Visa, MC, *Rated*
C-ltd/S-no/P-no/H-no
German

Full breakfast
Afternoon tea
Snacks, Jacuzzis, sitting room, library, pond to swim in

Historic 1862 mansion in picturesque wooded setting near Lake Michigan's sandy beaches.
seymour@cybersol.com http://www.seymourhouse.com

SOUTH HAVEN

Yelton Manor 140 North Shore Dr 49090 616-637-5220 Fax: 616-637-4957 Elaine Herbert & Robert Kripaitis All year	95-270-BB 17 rooms, 17 pb Visa, MC, AmEx, *Rated* C-ltd/S-no/P-no/H-no	Full or Continental breakfast Evening hors d'oeuvres Library, porch, Jacuzzis in 11 rooms, fireplaces in 8 rooms

Fabulous lakeside Victorian mansion. Elegant fireplace and Jacuzzi rooms, lake views. Porches, parlors, antiques. elaine@yeltonmanor.com http://www.yeltonmanor.com

ST. JOSEPH

South Cliff Inn 1900 Lakeshore Dr 49085 616-983-4881 Fax: 616-983-7391 Bill Swisher All year	85-195-BB 7 rooms, 7 pb Most CC, *Rated*, • C-ltd/S-no/P-no/H-no	Continental plus or full breakfast Sunday brunch, snacks Sitting room, library, formal gardens, fireplaces

South Cliff Inn is an English Country Style B&B. The exterior is English Cottage style w/decks overlooking Lake Michigan, lovely formal gardens & sunsets beyond compare. http://www.southcliffinn.com

TRAVERSE CITY

Linden Lea On Long Lake 279 S Long Lake Rd N 49684 231-943-9182 Jim & Vicky McDonnell All year	100-120-BB 2 rooms, 2 pb *Rated*, • C-ltd/S-no Spanish	Full breakfast Complimentary wine, snacks Sitting room, whirlpool, tub, lake frontage, sandy beach, boating

Wooded lakeside retreat with private sandy beach, fishing, swimming, rowboat & raft. Comfortable country furnishings. lindenlea@aol.com http://www.lindenleabb.com

UNION PIER

The Inn at Union Pier PO Box 222 9708 Berrien St 49129 616-469-4700 Fax: 616-469-4720 Mark Pitts & Joyce Erickson Pitts All year	145-215-BB 16 rooms, 16 pb Most CC, *Rated* C-ltd/S-no/P-no/H-yes	Full breakfast Snacks & beverages Great room, library, bikes, outdoor hot tub, Lake Michigan beach

Elegantly refurbished inn blending barefoot informality with gracious hospitality. In "Harbor Country", known for Lake Michigan beaches, antiques, galleries, and wineries. Host corporate retreats. info@innatunionpier.com http://www.innatunionpier.com

Sandpiper Inn PO Box 607 16136 Lakeview Avenue 49129 269-469-1146 Fax: 269-469-8091 800-351-2080 Veronica Lynch All year	80-265-BB 8 rooms, 8 pb Visa, MC, AmEx C-no/S-no/P-no/H-no	Full breakfast Snacks Sitting room, library, bicycles, Jacuzzis, fireplaces

Elegant new Georgian style home, nestled on Southwestern Michigan's shoreline, offering lake views from private screened verandas. Luxurious fireplace and whirlpool rooms. info@sandpiperinn.net http://www.sandpiperinn.net

WATERFORD

Carriage House 5967 Andersonville Rd 48346 248-623-0025 Fax: 248-623-3002 Doug & Mary Ann Johnson All year	85-125-BB 3 rooms, 3 pb Most CC, *Rated*, • C-ltd/S-no/P-ltd/H-ltd	Full and Continental Victorian Teas, Catering Historic Home. Nostalgic antiques. Fireplace. Dual whirlpool. Get-a-ways.

Award winning historic 1865 home in Waterford–Clarkston. Warm and inviting inside. Three unique guest rooms with private baths. Popular for get-a-ways and visiting guests. Private event hosting.
innkeeper@waterfordcarriagehouse.com http://www.waterfordcarriagehouse.com

Minnesota

AFTON

Afton House Inn PO Box 326 3291 S St Croix Trail 55001 651-436-8883 Fax: 651-436-6859 877-436-8883 Gordy & Kathy Jarvis All year	65-250-BB 25 rooms, 25 pb Most CC, *Rated*, • C-yes/S-ltd/P-no/H-yes	Continental plus breakfast Lunch/dinner available, restaurant Bar service, Jacuzzis, fireplaces, cable TV, accommodate business travelers

Historic country inn on St. Croix River. Furnished with antique decor, private baths. Many rooms have gas fireplace & Jacuzzi. Some rooms overlook Marina and St. Croix River. Fine Dining Restaurant. info@aftonhouseinn.com http://www.aftonhouseinn.com

ALEXANDRIA

Cedar Rose Inn 422 7th Ave West 56308 320-762-8430 Fax: 320-762-8044 888-203-5333 Aggie & Florian Ledermann All year	85-145-BB 5 rooms, 4 pb Visa, MC, *Rated*, • C-ltd/S-no/P-no/H-no	Full breakfast Snacks, complimentary wine Sitting room, library, bicycles, hot tubs, swimming, fishing

Cozy 1903 Tudor-Revival style home, walking distance to downtown, many beautiful roses, located in heart of Minnesota lake country.
florian@cedarroseinn.com http://www.echopress.com/cedarose

BATTLE LAKE

Xanadu Island 35484 235th St 56515 218-864-8096 800-396-9043 Janet & Bryan All year	95-155-BB 5 rooms, 5 pb Most CC, *Rated*, • C-no/S-no/P-no/H-no	Grandmotherly full breakfasts Tea, iced tea, snacks Great room, sun room, spa, fireplaces, hammocks, boats, canoe, swimming

Five acre private island retreat on Bass Lake accessed by a small causeway. Peaceful, quiet tastefully decorated rooms complimented by a Grandmotherly type full breakfast. Fireplaces and hot tubs. xanadu@prtel.com http://www.xanadu.cc

BEMIDJI

Beltrami Shores 5554 Island View Dr, NE 56601 218-586-2518 800-746-7373 Dr. Jerry & Barbara Vanek All year	75-115-BB 3 rooms, 3 pb Visa, MC C-ltd/S-no/P-no/H-no	Full & continental plus breakfast Complimentary wine Sitting room, library, fireplaces, cable TV, beach swim, boats, snowshoes

"A quiet place by the lake." Swim, fish, canoe, hike, ski, snowshoe. Northwoods decor, cedar-log queens, private baths, decks, greatroom with fireplace, sitting room/library, glassed-in porch. vacation@beltramishores.com http://www.beltramishores.com

BRAINERD (REGION)

Manhattan Beach Lodge PO Box 719 39051 County Road 66, *Manhattan Beach* 56442 218-692-3381 Fax: 218-692-2774 800-399-4360 John & Mary Zesbaugh All year	69-189-BB 18 rooms, 18 pb Most CC, *Rated*, • C-ltd/S-no/P-no/H-yes	Continental breakfast Lunch, dinner, snacks, restaurant, bar service Sitting room, Jacuzzis, suites, fireplaces, cable TV, conference room

Manhattan Beach Lodge is Minnesota's historic lakeside inn. Enjoy the amenities of a full service hotel and the warm feel of a country inn at the gateway to pristine lakes and woods. info@MBLodge.com http://www.MBLODGE.com

CANNON FALLS

Quill & Quilt
615 W Hoffman St 55009
507-263-5507 800-488-3849
Thomas & Jean Schulte

84-169-BB
5 rooms, 5 pb
Rated
All year

Full breakfast

In 1897, Dr. A.T. Conley, a physician in Cannon Falls for over 40 years, built this grand, three-story home. info@quillandquilt.com http://www.quillandquilt.com

COOK

Ludlow's Island Resort
PO Box 1146
8166 Ludlow Dr 55723
218-666-5407 Fax: 218-666-2488
877-583-5697
Mark & Sally Ludlow
May-October

200-550-EP
56 rooms, 56 pb
Most CC, *Rated*, •
C-yes/S-yes/P-no/H-no

Breakfast by request
Dinner by request
Sitting room, library, tennis court, sauna, family friendly facility

Our private land, with cottages, is situated under a canopy of pine and birch on the water's edge. info@ludlowsresort.com http://www.ludlowsresort.com

DULUTH

A Charles Weiss Inn
1615 E Superior St 55812
218-724-7016 800-525-5243
Dave & Peg Lee All year

95-145-BB
5 rooms, 5 pb
Visa, MC, Disc, *Rated*
C-ltd/S-no/P-ltd/H-no

Full breakfast
Complimentary wine
Sitting room, library, Jacuzzis, suites, fireplaces, cable TV

Historic 1895 Victorian Colonial with 5 fireplaces and whirlpool room. Located 3 blocks from Lake Superior, Lakewalk, quick access to Canal Park, skiing and 3 golf courses.
dglee@uslink.net http://www.visitduluth.com/acweissinn

Firelight Inn on Oregon Creek
2211 E Third St 55812
218-724-0272 Fax: 218-724-0304
888-724-0273
Jim & Joy Fischer
All year

160-240-BB
6 rooms, 6 pb
Most CC, *Rated*
C-ltd/S-no/P-no/H-no

Full breakfast
Snacks
Sitting room, Jacuzzis, suites, fireplaces, cable TV, bathrobes, hair dryers

The Inn is located next to a wooded ravine, adjacent to the babbling creek as it flows to Lake Superior. info@firelightinn.com http://www.firelightinn.com

---

A. G. Thomson House
2617 E Third St 55812
218-724-3464 Fax: 218-724-5177
877-807-8077
Becky & Bill Brakken
All year

119-219-BB
6 rooms, 6 pb
Most CC, *Rated*, •
C-no/S-no/P-no/H-no
French

Full gourmet breakfast
Complimentary wine
Sitting room, library, Jacuzzis, suites, fireplaces, AC, lake views

Historic Elegance Nestled in Nature. Featuring spacious rooms with private baths, whirlpools, fireplaces, Lake Superior views, A/C, and sumptuous breakfasts served in a sun-drenched dining room. info@thomsonhouse.biz http://www.thomsonhouse.biz

---

The Olcott House Inn
2316 E 1st St 55812
218-728-1339 800-715-1339
Don and Barb Trueman
All year

125-185-BB
6 rooms, 6 pb
Visa, MC, Disc, *Rated*, •
C-ltd/S-no/P-no/H-ltd

Full breakfast
Afternoon tea, snacks, complimentary wine.
Sitting room, library, suites, fireplaces, cable TV, accom. bus. travelers

A "Gone With the Wind" beautiful, Southern-style 1904 Georgian Colonial mansion set in the historic east end of Duluth, MN, port city.
info@olcotthouse.com http://www.olcotthouse.com

FERGUS FALLS

Bakketopp Hus
20571 Hillcrest Rd 56537
218-739-2915 800-739-2915
Dennis & Judy Nims
All year

70-105-BB
3 rooms, 3 pb
Visa, MC, Disc, *Rated*
C-ltd/S-no/P-no/H-no

Full special breakfast
Afternoon tea, snacks
Sitting room, antiques, fishing, golf, hot tubs, decks on the lakeside

Wooded hillside lake view. A scenic lake setting. Listen to loons at dusk, enjoy flowers in tiered gardens or relax in spa. Golf, antiques & restaurants nearby.

ddn@prtel.com http://www.bbonline.com/mn/bakketopp

GRAND MARAIS

Gunflint Lodge
143 S Gunflint Lake 55604
218-388-2294 Fax: 218-388-9429
800-328-3325
Bruce & Susan Kerfoot
All year

99-320-BB
25 rooms, 25 pb
Visa, MC, AmEx, *Rated*, •
C-yes/S-yes/P-yes/H-yes

Full breakfast
Lunch, dinner, restaurant, bar
Sauna, outdoor hot tubs, sitting room, sauna, fireplace, suites

Upscale family, fishing and riding resort in northern Minnesota, gourmet chef, guides, family activities, honeymoon packages, women's retreats.

jennifer@gunflint.com http://www.gunflint.com

Old Shore Beach
1434 Old Shore Rd
1434 Old Shore Road 55604
218-387-9707 Fax: 218-387-9811
888-387-9707
Paulette Anholm
All year

125-185-BB
4 rooms, 4 pb
Visa, MC, *Rated*
C-ltd/S-no/P-no/H-no

Full breakfast
Snacks
Sauna, Private beach on Lake Superior, Guest living room with fireplace

Situated on a private beach on Lake Superior, this new B&B offers guests relaxing opportunities: a sauna, beach stroll, lounge by the fireside while wrapped in our deluxe robes.

visit@oldshorebeach.com http://www.oldshorebeach.com

Snuggle Inn
PO Box 915
8 7th Avenue W 55604
218-387-2847 Fax: 218-387-2847
800-823-3174
Tim Nauta & Greg Spanton

85-100-BB
4 rooms, 4 pb
Most CC, *Rated*, •
C-ltd/S-ltd/P-no/H-no
All year

Full breakfast
Snacks
Sitting room, cable TV, harbor/lake view, deck

Warm and inviting lodging in a private comfortable setting. Located near the Gunflint Trail, with a Lake Superior harbor view.

info@snuggleinnbb.com http://www.snuggleinnbb.com

HASTINGS

Thorwood Historic Inns
315 Pine St 55033
651-437-3297 Fax: 651-437-4129
888-THORWOOD
Pam Thorsen All year

97-277-BB
14 rooms, 14 pb
Most CC, *Rated*, •
C-ltd/S-no/P-ltd/H-ltd

Pantry w/cookies, ice cream, juice, hot bev.
library, parlors, full dinner option

Two 1880 mansions in peaceful river town. Most rooms have double whirlpools and fireplaces. Large breakfast to guest's schedule. In room massage and gourmet intimate dinners and packages available. mrthorwood@aol.com http://www.thorwoodinn.com

LITTLE MARAIS

Stone Hearth Inn on Lake Superior
6598 Lakeside Estates Rd 55614
218-226-3020 Fax: 218-226-3966
888-206-3020
Charlie & Susan Michels

94-155-BB
8 rooms, 8 pb
Visa, MC, Disc, *Rated*
C-ltd/S-no/P-no/H-no
All year

Full or continental breakfast
Jacuzzis, suites, fireplaces

Enjoy refined comforts of a classic B&B on the shore of Lake Superior. Private baths, whirlpool tubs and fireplaces, continental and full gourmet breakfast.

michels@lakenet.com http://www.stonehearthinn.com

Lindgren's on Lake Superior, Lutsen, MN

LUTSEN

Cascade Lodge 3719 W Hwy 61 55612 218-387-1112 Fax: 218-387-1113 800-322-9543 Gene & Lawrence Glader All year	69-205-EP 27 rooms, 27 pb Visa, MC, AmEx, *Rated*, • C-yes/S-ltd/P-ltd/H-no	Restaurant Sitting room, bikes, Jacuzzis, suites, fireplaces, accom. bus. travelers

Located in the midst of Cascade River State Park overlooking Lake Superior. Hiking, fishing and sightseeing in summer. Cross-country and downhill skiing in winter.
cascade@cascadelodgemn.com http://www.cascadelodgemn.com

Lindgren's on Lake Superior PO Box 56 5552 County Road 35 55612 218-663-7450 Fax: 218-663-7450 Shirley Lindgren All year	105-150-BB 4 rooms, 4 pb Visa, MC, *Rated*, • C-ltd/S-no/P-no/H-no	Continental plus breakfast Tea, snacks, soda, cocoa Whirlpool/sauna, horseshoes, hike, kayak, fall colors, golf, bike, ski

1920s Northwoods rustic lodge log home in Superior National Forest on Lake Superior's walkable shoreline. info@lindgrensbb.com http://www.lindgrensbb.com

MANKATO

The Butler House 704 S Broad St 56001 507-387-5055 Sharry & Ron Tschida All year	89-139-BB 5 rooms, 5 pb Visa, MC, AmEx, *Rated* C-ltd/S-no/P-no/H-no	Full or continental plus breakfast We offer coffee, tea, iced water Sitting room, bikes, suites, fireplaces, cable TV, two Jacuzzi's for two

Beautiful Fresco paintings in dining room, entrance, and stairway to second floor. Cozy windowseats; two lovely rooms have Jacuzzi's for two.
butler1@hickorytech.net http://www.butlerhouse.com

The Butler House, Mankato, MN

MINNEAPOLIS

Elmwood House
1 East Elmwood Pl 55419
612-822-4558
Fax: 612-823-9107
888-822-4558
Robert & Barbara   All year

75-105-BB
3 rooms, 1 pb
Visa, MC, *Rated*, •
C-yes/S-no/P-no/H-no

Continental plus breakfast
Sitting room, 3rd-floor 2-bedroom suite with private bath

1887 Norman chateau. Historical home on National Register. 3 miles from downtown. 10 miles from Mall of America and airport.
innkeeper@elmwood-hous.com http://www.elmwood-house.com

Evelo's
2301 Bryant Ave S 55405
612-374-9656
Fax: 612-377-2801
David & Sheryl Evelo
All year

70-BB
3 rooms
Most CC, *Rated*
C-ltd/S-no/P-no/H-no

Continental plus breakfast
TV, refrigerator, coffee maker, air conditioning

1897 Victorian, period furnishings. Located on bus line, walk to Guthrie Theater, Minneapolis Art Institute, children's theater. evelosbandb@qwest.net

---

Nan's
2304 Fremont Ave S 55405
612-377-5118
800-214-5118
Nan & Jim Zosel
All year

60-70-BB
3 rooms
Visa, MC, AmEx, *Rated*
C-yes/S-no/P-no/H-no

Full breakfast
Beautiful porch, antique furnishings, near many restaurants

Comfortable urban 1890s Victorian family home near best theaters, galleries, restaurants, Minneapolis. zosel@mcad.edu http://www.virtualcities.com/mn/nan.htm

MINNEAPOLIS (REGION)

Inn on the Farm
6155 Earle Brown Dr, *Brooklyn Center* 55430-2138
763-569-6330 Fax: 763-569-6321
800-428-8382
All year

110-150-BB
10 rooms, 10 pb
Visa, MC, AmEx, *Rated*
C-ltd/S-no/P-no/H-yes

Full wknds, continental plus wkdys
Snacks
Sitting room, accomodate business travelers

Beautifully restored Victorian gentlemen's country estate. Extensive lawns, beds of flowers, informal sitting areas and fountain pools.
inn@earlebrown.com http://www.innonthefarm.com

MINNEAPOLIS (REGION)

PJ's B&B
5757 Berquist Rd, *Duluth* 55804
218-525-2508 Fax: 218-525-0249
Phil & Jan Hanson
All year

85-155-BB
5 rooms, 5 pb
•
C-ltd/S-no/P-no/H-ltd

Full & continental breakfast
Sitting room, Jacuzzi, pool, fireplace, TV/VCR in rooms, acc. bus. travelers

PJ's Bed and Breakfast, the "Inn with the Superior View" offers a breathtaking view of Lake Superior as it is perched hight on a ridge. pjsbb@duluth.com http://www.pjsbb.com

---

The Rand House
1 Old Territorial Rd, *Monticello* 55362
612-295-6037 Fax: 612-295-6037
Duffy & Merrill Busch
All year

105-155-BB
4 rooms, 4 pb
Visa, MC, Disc, *Rated*,
•
C-ltd/S-no/P-no/H-ltd

Full breakfast
Afternoon tea, snacks
Complimentary wine, sitting room, library, bicycles, tennis court, fireplace

One of the last remaining great Victorian country estates established by one of Minneapolis' most prominent families. info@randhouse.com http://www.randhouse.com

NEW PRAGUE

Schumachers' Hotel & Rest.
212 W Main St 56071
612-758-2133 Fax: 612-758-2400
800-283-2049
John & Kathleen Schumacher
All year

140-275-EP
16 rooms, 16 pb
Most CC, *Rated*, •
S-yes/P-no/H-ltd

Breakfast (fee)
Lunch, dinner, bar
Comp. wine, piano, all rooms with TV's, whirlpools, fireplaces

National and regional award-winning country inn and restaurant. Central European theme. snph@schumachershotel.com http://www.schumachershotel.com

NORTHFIELD

The Magic Door
818 Division St South 55057
507-664-9096 Fax: 507-664-9047
Pamela Simonson
All year

100-195-BB
3 rooms, 3 pb
Most CC
C-ltd/S-no/P-no/H-ltd

Four course candlelight breakfast
Afternoon snack tray, complimentary wine & beer
Whirlpools, fireplaces, in room TV/VCR, video library, mini-fridges, cookies

The Magic Door is a lovely 1899 Victorian, located in the charming town of Northfield MN. Just 35 miles south of Minneapolis, Northfield is the home of two top-rated colleges; Carleton & St Olaf. magicdoorbb@hotmail.com http://www.magicdoorbb.com

OWATONNA (REGION)

Historic Tea House
425 Main St S, *Medford* 55049
507-446-0002
Jessica & Andrew Miller
All year

70-125-BB
5 rooms, 2 pb
Visa, MC, *Rated*, •
C-ltd/S-no/P-no/H-no

Full & continental plus breakfast
Afternoon tea, snacks, complimentary wine
Sitting room, Jacuzzis, suites, fireplaces, cable TV

Come experience the atmosphere of a more elegant time in a beautiful Victorian estate that once served as the headmaster's house for the only Minnesota orphanage.
info@historicteahouse.com

RED WING

Candlelight Inn
818 W 3rd St 55066
651-388-8034 800-254-9194
Lynette and Zig Gudrais
All year

109-199-BB
5 rooms, 5 pb
Visa, MC, AmEx, *Rated*
C-ltd/S-no/P-no/H-no

Full breakfast
Snacks
Sitting room, Library, Jacuzzis, Fireplaces

Beautifully appointed Victorian home with fireplaces in every room. Three blocks to historic and beautiful downtown Red Wing.
info@candlelightinn-redwing.com http://www.candlelightinn-redwing.com

RED WING

Golden Lantern Inn
721 East Ave 55066
651-388-3315 Fax: 651-385-8509
888-288-3315
Rhonda & Tim McKim
All year

99-215-BB
5 rooms, 5 pb
Most CC, *Rated*, •
C-ltd/S-no/P-no/H-no

Full breakfast
Lunch, dinner, snacks
Sitting room, library, bicycles, Jacuzzi, suites, fireplace, cable TV

Wonderful Tudor Revival formerly home to Red Wing Shoe presidents.
info@goldenlantern.com http://www.goldenlantern.com

Lawther Octagon House
927 W 3rd St 55066
651-388-1778 800-388-0434
Penny Stapleton
All year

125-225-BB
5 rooms, 5 pb
Visa, MC, Disc
C-no/S-no/P-no/H-ltd

Full breakfast
Complimentary wine
Sitting room, library, Jacuzzis, suites, fireplaces, accom. bus. travelers

Rare, eight-sided carefully restored Victorian home built in 1857.
info@octagon-house.com http://www.octagon-house.com

Moondance Inn
1105 West Fourth St 55066
651-388-8145 Fax: 651-388-9655
866-388-8145
Chris Brown Mahoney & Mikel Waulk
All year

110-189-BB
5 rooms, 5 pb
Most CC
C-no/S-no/P-no/H-no

Full breakfast
Snacks, complimentary wine
All king or queen size beds, whirlpools, gourmet breakfast, fireplaces

Elegant limestone home built in 1874; beautiful wood, grand staircase, Tiffany chandeliers. All rooms have private baths and double whirlpools.
moondanceinn@charter.net http://www.moondanceinn.com

St. James Hotel
406 Main St 55066
651-388-2846 Fax: 651-388-5226
Gene Foster
All year

89-200-BB

Valet service and twice daily maid service, cable TV

Established in 1875, the St. James Hotel offers guests a choice of 61 authentically appointed rooms, some with whirlpool. Two distinguished restaurants and a lounge with entertainment. info@St-James-Hotel.com http://www.st-james-hotel.com

RED WING (REGION)

Hearthwood
17650 200th St East, *Hastings* 55033
651-437-1133
Ann & Gary Berg
All year

135-150-BB
5 rooms, 5 pb
Most CC, *Rated*, •
C-ltd/S-no/P-no/H-no

Full breakfast
Snacks
Jacuzzis, fireplace

Tucked into the bluffs of the Mississippi Valley, this home blends a timber facade with Cape Cod architecture. Five suites have double whirlpools, fireplaces, queen size beds and private baths. berg123@aol.com http://www.hearthwood.com

ST. CLOUD (REGION)

Thayer's Historic B&B
PO Box 246
60 W Elm St–Hwy 55, *Annandale* 55302
320-274-8222 Fax: 320-274-5051
800-944-6595
Sharon Gammell

99-225-BB
13 rooms, 13 pb
Rated
All year

Full breakfast

Thayer's is rumored to be haunted–interesting! Thayer's offers interactive mystery dinners "To Die For!" thayers@hotmail.com http://www.thayers.net

ST. PAUL

Chatsworth
984 Ashland Ave 55104
651-227-4288 Fax: 651-665-0388
Neelie Forrester
All year

75-155-BB
5 rooms, 3 pb
Most CC, *Rated*
C-ltd/S-no

Continental plus breakfast
Tea, coffee, cocoa
Sitting room, library, 2 rooms with whirlpools

Peaceful retreat in city near Governor's Mansion. Down comforters, lace curtains. Excellent restaurants & unique shops within walking distance
chats@isd.net http://www.chatsworth-bb.com

STILLWATER

Aurora Staples Inn
303 N Fourth St 55082
651-351-1187 Fax: 651-430-1974
Cathy & Jerry Helmberger
All year

119-199-BB
5 rooms, 5 pb
Visa, MC, *Rated*
C-ltd/S-no/P-no/H-no

Full breakfast
Sitting room, library, Jacuzzis, suites, fireplaces

Queen Anne Victorian close to downtown shopping and restaurants. Wraparound porch, formal gardens with a fountain. River view.
info@aurorastaplesinn.com http://www.aurorastaplesinn.com

Cover Park Manor
15330 58th St North 55082
651-430-9292 Fax: 651-430-0034
877-430-9292
Chuck & Judy Dougherty
All year

99-199-BB
4 rooms, 4 pb
Most CC, *Rated*, •
C-ltd/S-no/P-no/H-yes
Spanish, German

Full breakfast
P.M. tea, snacks, compl. wine
Sitting room, Jacuzzis, suites, fireplaces, cable TV, business travelers

This romantic 1890's home is situated on six city lots and borders Cover Park.
coverpark@coverpark.com http://www.coverpark.com

James Mulvey Inn
622 W. Churchill St 55082
651-430-8008 Fax: 651-430-2801
800-820-8008
Truett and Jill Lawson
All year

99-219-BB
7 rooms, 7 pb
Most CC, *Rated*, •
C-ltd/S-no/P-no/H-no

Full breakfast
Tea, outside eating
Sitting room, bicycles, Jacuzzis, swimming pool, suites, conference
Welcome refreshments

This is an enchanting place. Built by lumberman James Mulvey in 1878, the Italianate residence and stone carriage house grace the most visited historic river town in the upper Midwest. Truettldem@aol.com http://www.jamesmulveyinn.com

---

The Rivertown Inn
306 W Olive St 55082
651-430-2955 Fax: 651-430-0034
800-562-3632
Judy & Chuck Dougherty
All year

89-169-BB
9 rooms, 8 pb
Visa, MC, *Rated*, •
C-yes/S-ltd/P-no/H-no

Full breakfast
Complimentary wine on weekends
Sitting areas, A/C, screen porch, gazebo, whirlpool bath, bicycles

The Rivertown Inn's nine rooms are each named and decorated in the spirit of a 19th century poet. rivertown@rivertowninn.com http://www.rivertowninn.com

VERGAS

The Log House & Homestead
PO Box 130
44854 E Spirit Lake 56587
218-342-2318 Fax: 218-342-3294
800-342-2318
Suzanne Tweten
All year

110-195-BB
5 rooms, 5 pb
Visa, MC, *Rated*
S-ltd/P-no/H-no
French

Full breakfast
Private candlelit dinners available
Sitting room, hike, bike, whirlpool, skiing, boats, large suite w/balconies

Romantic, elegant retreat in restored 1889 loghouse and turn-of-the-century homestead with in-room fireplaces. loghouse@tekstar.com http://www.loghousebb.com

WINONA

Windom Park
369 W Broadway 55987
507-457-9515 Fax: 507-452-1680
866-737-1719
Craig & Karen Groth
All year

99-175-BB
6 rooms, 6 pb
Most CC, *Rated*
C-ltd/S-ltd/P-no/H-no
Polish

Full breakfast
Evening wine and cheese
Fireplaces, Jacuzzis, suites, cable TV, business facilities

Enjoy the quiet charm of our 1900 Colonial Revival home.
ckgroth@hbci.com http://www.windompark.com

Mississippi

BAY ST. LOUIS

Blue Meadow Inn
828 Blue Meadow Rd 39520
228-467-2900 Fax: 228-466-6662
877-952-2900
Mike & Joy Zuppardo

79-105-BB
6 rooms, 6 pb
Most CC, •
C-ltd/S-ltd/P-no/H-ltd
All year

Full breakfast

A Victorian cottage built circa 1887 with high ceilings, brass chandeliers, many antiques, and hardwood floors throughout. Front and side porches with wicker chairs and tables to relax. Bluemeadowinn@aol.com http://www.bluemeadowinn.com

BILOXI

Green Oaks
580 Beach Blvd 39530
228-436-6257 Fax: 228-436-6225
888-436-6257
Jennifer Diaz
All year

125-170-BB
8 rooms, 8 pb
Most CC, *Rated*, •
C-yes/S-ltd/P-no/H-yes

Full breakfast
Afternoon tea with Mint Juleps
Sitting room, library, bicycles, located on the, Gulf of Mexico on beach

Mississippi's oldest beachfront mansion. Circa 1826 National Historic Register, 3 acres with 28 live oaks overlooking white sand beaches and Gulf of Mexico.
greenoaks4@aol.com http://www.gcww.com/greenoaks

The Old Santini House Inn
964 Beach Blvd 39530
228-436-4078 Fax: 228-432-9193
800-686-1146
James & Patricia Dunay
All year

75-150-BB
5 rooms, 5 pb
Visa, MC, AmEx, *Rated*, •
C-ltd/S-ltd/P-no/H-no

Full gourmet breakfast
Tea, wine
Sitting room, library, bikes, Jacuzzis, suites, fireplace, cable TV

Relive the quaint charm of the early 1800s in our 160 year-old "American Cottage." Antiques & fine furnishings, located downtown across from beach.
jad39530@cs.com http://www.santinibnb.com

BILOXI (REGION)

Red Creek Inn
7416 Red Creek Rd, *Long Beach* 39560
228-452-3080
Fax: 228-452-4450
800-729-9670
Karl & Toni Mertz
All year

65-138-BB
7 rooms, 5 pb
Rated, •
C-yes/S-ltd/P-ltd
Spanish

Continental breakfast
Full breakfast upon request
Coffee, afternoon tea, hot tub, racing stable

Three-story "raised French cottage" with 6 fireplaces, 64-foot porch, and antiques. Amid 11 acres of live oaks & magnolias, near beaches.
karlmertz@aol.com http://www.redcreekinn.com

Red Creek Inn, Long Beach, MS

CORINTH

The Generals' Quarters Inn	80-120-BB	Full breakfast
924 Fillmore St 38834	10 rooms, 9 pb	Beverages and snacks
662-286-3325	Visa, MC, Disc, *Rated*	Library, Gift Shop, Veranda,
Fax: 662-287-8188	C-ltd/S-ltd/P-no/H-ltd	Hot Tub, Gardens
800-664-1866		
Luke and Charlotte Doehner		
All year		

Two beautifully restored Victorian homes circa 1872 and 1909, connected by lovely gardens. Located in the Historic District of an old Civil War town. All rooms with private baths and many amenities.

genqtrs@tsixroads.com http://www.thegeneralsquarters.com

JACKSON

Fairview Inn	115-290-BB	Full breakfast
734 Fairview St 39202	18 rooms, 18 pb	Snacks, complimentary
601-948-3429	Most CC, *Rated*, •	wine, dinner available
Fax: 601-948-1203	C-ltd/S-no/P-no/H-yes	Dataports, sitting room,
888-948-1908	French	library, special occasion
Carol & Bill Simmons		facilities
All year		

Colonial Revival mansion on National Register of Historic Places. Luxury accommodations. Fine dining for groups. AAA Four Diamond Award.

fairview@fairviewinn.com http://www.fairviewinn.com

Millsaps Buie House	105-185-BB	Full breakfast
628 N. State St 39202	11 rooms, 11 pb	Wine, beer, cocktails
601-352-0221	Most CC, *Rated*, •	available for purchase.
Fax: 601-709-3315	C-ltd/S-no/P-no/H-yes	
800-784-0221		
Judy Loper		
All year		

An elegant inn, in the heart of Jackson, Mississippi. National Register of Historic Places, c. 1888.

info@millsapsbuiehouse.com http://www.millsapsbuiehouse.com

NATCHEZ

1888 Wensel House
206 Washington St 39120
601-445-8577 Fax: 801-849-2726
888-775-8577
Ron & Mimi Miller
All year

85-120-BB
4 rooms, 4 pb
Most CC, •
C-ltd/S-no/P-no/H-no
Spanish

Full hot Southern breakfast
Help yourself to free beverages & fruit any time
Cable color TV with remote, telephone, hair dryer, iron & board.

Great value: perfect location in heart of historic district, restrained antique furnishings, generous hot breakfasts, moderate rates, complimentary drinks and fruit, and knowledgeable hosts. info@1888WenselHouse.com http://www.1888WenselHouse.com

---

The Briars Inn
PO Box 1245
31 Irving Ln 39120
601-446-9654 Fax: 601-445-6037
800-634-1818
Newt Wilds & R.E. Canon
All year

150-295-BB
14 rooms, 14 pb
Visa, MC, AmEx, *Rated*, •
C-ltd/S-ltd/P-no/H-yes

Full breakfast
Bar service, snacks
Sitting room, library, swimming pool, porch, gardens

Circa 1812, retreat into unique 19th century splendor with modern amenities. National Register. thebriarsinn@bkbank.com http://www.thebriarsinn.com

---

Burn Antebellum Inn
712 N Union St 39120
601-442-1344 Fax: 601-445-0606
800-654-8859
Ty & Sonja Taylor
All year

125-200-BB
7 rooms, 7 pb
Most CC, *Rated*, •
C-yes/S-ltd/P-yes/H-yes

Plantation style southern breakfast
Wine, Coffee, Tea, Nuts,
Dinners by arrangement
Swimming pool, brick patios, gardens, library sitting room, verandas

A spectacular Greek Revival (c.1834) home set on two exquisitely landscaped acres covered with camellias. Entry noted for graceful semi-spiral staircase.
theburn1@bellsouth.net

Glenfield Plantation
6 Providence Rd 39120
601-442-1002
Marjorie & Lester Meng
All year

80-135-BB
4 rooms, 4 pb
Rated, •
C-yes/S-ltd/P-no/H-yes

Full breakfast
Complimentary wine
Sitting room, all rooms with private bath, banquet facilities

Family owned-5th generation c.1778 Spanish and 1840 English Gothic architecture. On the National Register of Historic Places. http://www.travelguides.com/home/glenfieldplantation/

Linden
1 Linden Place 39120
601-445-5472
Fax: 601-442-7548
800-2-LINDEN
Jeanette Feltus
All year

105-135-BB
7 rooms, 7 pb
Rated, •
C-ltd/S-yes/P-no/H-yes

Full breakfast
Early morning coffee
Sitting room, piano, banquet facilities

Antebellum home furnished with family heirlooms. Park-like setting of mossy live oaks. Occupied by same family since 1849. http://www.natchezms.com/linden

---

Magnolia Hill Plantation
16 Wild Turkey Rd 39120-9772
601-445-2392 Fax: 601-442-5782
877-642-2392
Pam White
All year

125-250-BB
4 rooms, 4 pb
Visa, MC, AmEx, *Rated*, •
C-yes/S-yes/P-yes/H-yes
French

Full breakfast
Afternoon tea, snacks, lunch and dinner available
Sitting room, library, bikes, swimming pool, suites, accom. bus. travelers

Built in 1834, Magnolia Hill offers the guest a secluded retreat.
mwheelis@aol.com http://magnoliahillplantation.com

NATCHEZ

Monmouth Plantation
36 Melrose Avenue 39120
601-442-5852 Fax: 601-446-7762
800-828-4531
Ron & Lani Riches
All year

150-270-BB
30 rooms, 30 pb
Most CC, *Rated*, •
C-ltd/S-no/P-no/H-no
French on request

Full breakfast
Dinner, bar
Sitting room, Jacuzzis, suites, fireplaces, cable TV, conf. facility

26 wooded acres of landscaped grounds, with stocked fishing ponds, period buildings, and superbly renovated mansion house.
luxury@monmouthplantation.com http://www.monmouthplantation.com

OCEAN SPRINGS

Ruskin Carriage Inn
410 Ruskin Ave 39564
228-872-8161 Fax: 228-872-8161
Ernest and Aimee Cantrell
All year

69-75-BB
1 rooms, 1 pb
•
C-ltd/S-ltd/P-no/H-ltd

Continental breakfast
Coffee, tea, juice, milk, soft drinks
Health club passes available, private patio, private entrance

Near the historic Ruskin Oak, the Ruskin Carriage Inn offers private accommodations within walking distance of Historic Ocean Springs and its quiet beachfront.
RuskinCarriageInn@hotmail.com

OXFORD

The Oliver-Britt House
512 Van Buren Ave 38655
662-234-8043 Fax: 662-281-8065
Mary Ann Britt, Glynn Oliver
All year

60-95-BB
5 rooms, 5 pb
Rated, •

Full breakfast weekends only

Greek Revival Inn, circa 1905 between historic town square and the University of Mississippi. This is our 20th. year we have been in business. oliv6448@bellsouth.net

PASS CHRISTIAN

Harbour Oaks Inn
126 W Scenic Dr 39571
228-452-9399 Fax: 228-452-9321
800-452-9399
Tony & Diane Brugger
All year

83-128-BB
5 rooms, 5 pb
Most CC, *Rated*, •
C-ltd/S-ltd/P-no/H-no

Full breakfast
Snacks, complimentary wine
Sitting room, Jacuzzis, cable TV, accommodate business travelers, billiards

Overlooking historic Pass Christian Yacht Harbor and beaches, Harbour Oaks is the only remaining 19th century hotel on the Mississippi coast.
harbour@dellepro.com http://www.harbouroaks.com

Woodland Oaks Inn
23095 Woodland Way 39571
228-452-3266 800-452-0070
Janie Koch
All year

79-119-BB
3 rooms, 1 pb
C-yes/S-ltd/P-ltd/H-no

Full breakfast
Complimentary cold drinks, fruit, coffee, tea
Living Room (with CATV), pool, kitchen w/microwave, stove, fridge

Come stay in a quiet, peaceful setting. We're on three acres, with antique furnishings, hardwood floors, majestic oaks & magnolias, swimming pool. We are 1 hour to New Orleans and close to casinos.
janie@woodlandoaksinn.com http://www.woodlandoaksinn.com

PORT GIBSON

Bernheimer House
212 Walnut St 39150
601-437-2843 800-735-3407
Loren & Nancy Ouart
All year

105-135-BB
4 rooms, 4 pb
Most CC, •
C-yes/S-no/P-no/H-no

Dinner at additional cost

Outstanding example of Queen Anne architecture, the Bernheimer House is on the National Register and is located in the historic downtown district. Featuring four spacious rooms with private baths. lorenou@bernheimerhouse.com http://www.bernheimerhouse.com

PORT GIBSON

Oak Square
1207 Church St 39150
601-437-5300 Fax: 601-437-5768
800-729-0240
Mrs. William D. Lum
All year

105-135-BB
11 rooms, 11 pb
Most CC, *Rated*, •
C-ltd/S-ltd/P-no/H-ltd

Full southern breakfast
Complimentary wine & tea
Victorian parlor, piano, TV, courtyard, fountain, gazebo

Step back to an era of gracious living and Antebellum splendor in this luxurious 1850, Greek Revival mansion of the Old South. Overnight guests will be surrounded by a "Gone With the Wind" setting. oaksquarebandb@cs.com

TUPELO

The Mockingbird Inn
305 N Gloster 38804
662-841-0286 Fax: 662-840-4158
Sharon Robertson
All year

69-129-BB
7 rooms, 7 pb
Most CC, *Rated*
C-no/S-no/P-no/H-yes

Full breakfast
Light afternoon/evening snack or sweet treat
Queen beds, cable TV, private phones

Each of the seven unique and lovely guestrooms reflects the decorating style, character and charm from different corners of the world.
sandbird@netdoor.com http://www.bbonline.com/ms/mockingbird

TYLERTOWN

Merry Wood
26 Dillons Bridge Rd 39667
601-222-1415 Fax: 601-222-1449
866-222-1415
Merry Caplan
All year

130-180-BB
5 rooms, 4 pb
Visa, MC, •
C-no/S-no/P-no/H-no

Continental plus breakfast
Country afternoon tea, snacks
Full kitchen & living area, library, exercise room, conference facility

Luxury accommodations in a 300 acre wilderness preserve. Library, exercise room, conference facility. Quality linens and tableware, country antiques, full kitchens.
merrywoodcottage@aol.com http://www.merrywoodcottages.com

VICKSBURG

Annabelle
501 Speed St 39180
601-638-2000 Fax: 601-636-5054
800-791-2000
George & Carolyn Mayer
All year

98-135-BB
7 rooms, 7 pb
Most CC, *Rated*, •
C-ltd/S-no/P-ltd/H-no
Ger., Sp., Portuguese

Full breakfast
Afternoon tea
Jacuzzis, swimming pool, turn-down service, fireplaces, cable TV

At Annabelle, built in 1868, you'll experience the grand feeling of a bygone era. An era of the genteel life. In this romantic refuge you'll find true grace, charm and luxurious comfort. annabelle@vicksburg.com http://www.annabellebnb.com

Cedar Grove Mansion Inn
PO Box B
2200 Oak St 39180
601-636-1000 Fax: 601-634-6126
800-862-1300
Ted Mackey
All year

100-190-BB
34 rooms, 34 pb
Most CC, *Rated*, •
C-yes/S-ltd/P-ltd/H-yes

Full breakfast
Dinner (fee), afternoon tea, turndown, soda (fee)
Restaurant, bar service, bikes, tennis court, Jacuzzis, pool, suites

Experience Vicksburg in style. Cedar Grove Mansion offers a warm, Southern welcome to all travelers to Vicksburg. info@cedargroveinn.com http://www.cedargroveinn.com

Missouri

ANNAPOLIS

Rachel's
202 W Second St 63620
573-598-4656
Fax: 573-598-3439
888-245-7771
Sharon & Joe Cluck
All year

65-130-MAP
6 rooms, 6 pb
Most CC, *Rated*, •
C-ltd/S-ltd/P-no/H-yes

Full breakfast
Dinner, snacks
Sitting room, library, Jacuzzis, suites, hot tub, satellite & cable TV

Elegant country inn, designed for comfort surrounded by rivers, lakes, mountains & streams!

info@rachelsbb.com http://www.rachelsbb.com

BLUFFTON (REGION)

Rendleman Home
173 Hwy 94, *Rhineland* 65069
573-236-4575
Doug
April-October

60-90-BB
4 rooms
C-ltd/S-no/P-no/H-no

Full breakfast
Dinner available
Bicycles, swimming pool, bonfires

Secluded stop on 225 mile bike trail run by a cyclist for trail users, but all are welcome.

BONNE TERRE

Victorian Veranda
207 E School St 63628
573-358-1134
800-343-1134
Galen & Karen Forney
All year

70-125-BB
4 rooms, 4 pb
Most CC, *Rated*, •
C-ltd/S-ltd/P-no/H-no

Full breakfast
Snacks, afternoon tea
Sitting room, Jacuzzis, suites, fireplaces, cable TV, accomm. bus. travelers

Our historic home was built circa 1880 as a boarding house for St. Joe Lead Co.

victoriaveranda@ldd.net http://www.victorianveranda.com

BOONVILLE (REGION)

Rivercene
127 County Rd 463, *New Franklin* 65233
660-848-2497
Fax: 660-848-2142
800-531-0862
Ron Lenz
All year

90-150-BB
8 rooms, 8 pb
Most CC, *Rated*, •
C-ltd/S-no/P-no/H-no

Full breakfast
Sitting room, Jacuzzi, suites, fireplaces, accom. bus. travelers

Take a walk back in time: Stay at the 1869 home of Riverboat Captain Kinney. Retire to a spacious room with queen-size beds, private bath, and marble fireplace for your complete renewal.

jalenz@mid-mo.net http://www.rivercene.com

BRANSON

Branson Hotel B&B Inn
PO Box 158
214 W Main 65616
417-335-6104
Fax: 417-339-3224
800-933-0651
Randy & Cynthia Parker
All year

75-105-BB
7 rooms, 7 pb
Visa, MC, AmEx, *Rated*, •
C-yes/S-ltd/P-no/H-no

Full gourmet breakfast
Afternoon tea, coffee, snacks
Sitting room, 2 large verandas, guest refrigerator, cable TV, private baths

Branson's elegant little hotel built in 1903 is also a B&B inn. Beautifully restored in 1992. Perfectly located in historic downtown Branson.

info@bransonhotelbb.com http://www.bransonhotelbb.com

BRANSON

Emory Creek B&B & Gift Shop
143 Arizona Dr 65616
417-334-3805 Fax: 417-337-7045
800-362-7404
Sammy & Beverly Gray Pagna
All year

95-140-BB
6 rooms
Visa, MC, *Rated*, •
C-ltd/S-no/P-no/H-no

Full breakfast
Afternoon tea, snacks
Sitting room, library, Jacuzzis, suites, fireplaces

A magnificent Victorian Inn with refinement and grandeur, yet a welcome home feeling of the country. 18th century antiques, elegant bathrooms, oversized Jacuzzis & fireplaces.
emorycreekbnb@pcis.net http://www.emorycreekbnb.com

Fall Creek
4988 Fall Creek Rd 65616
417-334-3939 Fax: 417-332-2439
800-482-1090
Bob Doyle
All year

65-90-BB
19 rooms, 15 pb
Visa, MC, AmEx, *Rated*, •
C-yes/S-ltd/P-ltd/H-yes

Full breakfast buffet
Free morning coffee
Sitting room, library, whirlpool Jacuzzis, pool, cable TV

Pamper yourselves at the Victorian B&B Inn. Full country buffet breakfast. Double queen beds, walkout wooden decks! http://www.fallcreekbedbreakfast.bizonthe.net

BRANSON (REGION)

Cameron's Crag
PO Box 526
738 Acacia Club Rd, *Point Lookout* 65726
417-335-8134 Fax: 417-335-8134
800-933-8529
Kay & Glen Cameron
All year

85-135-BB
3 rooms, 3 pb
Visa, *Rated*, •
C-ltd/S-no/P-no/H-no

Full hearty breakfast
Video library, area sites, private entrance & tubs, hot tubs, cable TV/VCR

Contemporary hideaway on bluff overlooking Lake Taneycomo. Fantastic views! Three separate guest areas, delightful accommodations.
mgcameron@aol.com http://www.camerons-crag.com

CAPE GIRARDEAU

Bellevue
312 Bellevue 63701
573-335-3302 Fax: 573-332-7752
800-768-6822
Marsha Toll
All year

75-115-BB
4 rooms, 4 pb
Most CC, *Rated*, •
C-yes/S-ltd/P-no/H-no

Full breakfast
Complimentary beverages, snacks
Sitt. rm. w/large-screen TV, business facility, massage by app't., mtg. rms.

1891 Queen Anne Victorian faithfully restored, furnished with period antiques and modern amenities. BellevueBb@compuserve.com http://www.bbim.org/bellevue

COLUMBIA

The Gathering Place
606 S College Ave 65201
573-815-0606 Fax: 573-817-1653
877-731-6888
Ross & Shirley Duff
All year

85-145-BB
5 rooms, 5 pb
Most CC, *Rated*
C-ltd/S-no/P-no/H-yes

Full breakfast
Snacks
Sitting room, library, tennis court, exercise fac. nearby

College town B&B. University of Missouri is our front yard. Bountiful Missouri breakfasts. Jacuzzis. King & queen suites. rossduff@aol.com http://www.gatheringplacebb.com

---

University Ave
1315 University Ave 65201
573-499-1920 Fax: 573-256-8335
800-499-1920
Willa Adelstein
All year

80-90-BB
4 rooms, 4 pb
Most CC, *Rated*
C-ltd/P-no/H-ltd

Full breakfast
Snacks
Sitting room, Jacuzzis, fireplaces, accom. bus. travelers

In Columbia's historic and eclectic East Campus neighborhood. Situated along the eastern edge of the University of Missouri campus.
universityavenue@aol.com http://www.universityavenuebnb.com

COLUMBIA (REGION)

Clifton Lodge
700 W Reed St, *Moberly* 65270
660-269-8548
Elizabeth Clifton
All year

60-95-BB
3 rooms, 2 pb
AmEx, •
C-yes/S-yes/P-ltd/H-no
German

Full breakfast
Snacks, complimentary wine
Sitting room, suites

Comfortable, 1906 home; beautiful woodwork; parlor has fireplace, sofas, games, puzzles; breakfast to your specifications.

elizabethclifton@cliftonlodge.com http://www.cliftonlodge.com

DIXON

Rock Eddy Bluff Farm
10245 Maries Rd 511 65459
573-759-6081 800-335-5921
Kathy & Tom Corey
All year

70-110-BB
4 rooms, 4 pb
Visa, MC, Disc, *Rated*
C-yes/S-ltd/P-ltd/H-no

Full breakfast
Snacks
Sitting room, library, hot tub, fireplaces, fishing, bird watching

Escape to river & Ozark Hills! Scenic cottages, secluded cabin in the trees, and an inviting 3-room suite. Peace & quiet in country atmosphere.

innkeeper@rockeddy.com http://www.rockeddy.com

FULTON

Romancing the Past Victorian
830 Court St 65251
573-592-1996
Jim & ReNee Yeager
All year

100-175-BB
3 rooms, 3 pb
Visa, MC, AmEx, *Rated*
C-ltd/S-ltd/P-ltd/H-ltd

Full breakfast
Afternoon tea, snacks, comp. wine
Sitting room, bicycles, Jacuzzis, suites, fireplaces, cable TV

Enchanting Victorian in beautiful historic neighborhood surrounded by trees and gardens. Grand hall with magnificent arch and staircase.

innkeeper@sockets.net http://www.romancingthepast.com

HANNIBAL

Garth Woodside Mansion
11069 New London Rd 63401
573-221-2789 Fax: 573-221-9941
888-427-8409
Col (Ret) John & Julie Rolsen
All year

109-295-BB
8 rooms, 8 pb
Visa, MC, *Rated*, •
C-ltd/S-ltd

Full breakfast
Cookies, cider, teas, coffee
Library, tour planning

Mark Twain was a frequent guest at this 33-acre estate. Most furnishings are original to the Victorian home. Elegance/privacy/hospitality galore.

innkeepers@garthmansion.com http://www.garthmansion.com

HERMANN

Nestle Inn
215 W 2nd St 65041
573-486-1111 Fax: 573-486-5981
866-637-8534
Donna Nestle
All year

135-155-BB
2 rooms, 4 pb
Visa, MC, AmEx, *Rated*, •
C-yes/S-ltd/P-no/H-no

Full breakfast
Snacks
Sitting room, Jacuzzis, suites, fireplaces, cable TV, accom. bus. travelers

Nestled cozily atop a bluff overlooking the scenic Missouri River, the Nestle Inn is the perfect getaway for romance and relaxation.

nestle@ktis.net http://www.nestleinn.com

Patty Kerr Gasthaus & Massage
PO Box 434
109 E Third 65041
573-486-2510
Todd & Nancy Satre
All year

98-110-BB
2 rooms, 2 pb
Visa, MC
C-no/S-no/P-no/H-no
English

Full breakfast
Tea and coffee in the room
Outdoor hot tub in private garden, massage available, VCRs with movies

A great romantic getaway, located in historic Hermann. Enjoy the privacy of a small guesthouse! Your continental breakfast is served in your room.

nljohnston@ktis.net http://www.pattykerrgasthaus.com

INDEPENDENCE

Ophelia's Restaurant & Inn
201 N Main 64050
816-461-4525 Fax: 816-836-4248
Cindy McClain
All year

75-125-BB
8 rooms, 8 pb
Visa, MC, AmEx
C-yes/S-no/P-no/H-yes

Continental breakfast
Restaurant, snacks
Jacuzzis, suites, cable TV, accom. bus. travel

This is a historic building totally remodeled in 1998. Each room has its own look with down comforters and pillows. http://ophelias.net

JACKSON

Trisha's B&B, Tea Room & Gifts
203 Bellevue 63755
573-243-7427 800-651-0408
Gus & Trisha Wischmann
All year

55-85-BB
4 rooms, 3 pb
Most CC
C-ltd/S-ltd/P-no

Full breakfast

Experience our type of hospitality–warm, relaxed and at home. Even though our 1905 Victorian house features turn-of-the-century quality, we think you will find our modern amenities comfortable. http://www.rosecity.net/trishabb

JOPLIN

The John Wise Home
504 S Byers Ave 64801
417-627-9657 Fax: 417-627-9676
Tom & Alice Ward
All year

90-125-BB
3 rooms, 3 pb
Most CC
C-yes/S-no/P-no/H-ltd

Full breakfast
A Gathering Place restaurant in The John Wise Home

Walking through the front door is like stepping back in time. You are greeted by hospitality, antiques, stained glass, & wood features reminiscent of years gone by.
johnwisehome@prodigy.net http://www.angelfire.com/folk/thejohnwisehome

KANSAS CITY

Brookside House
6315 Walnut 64113
913-491-8950 Fax: 913-381-6256
Vern & Brenda Otte
All year

110-BB
3 rooms, 2 pb
Rated
C-yes/S-no/P-no/H-no

Continental plus breakfast
Complimentary wine
2nd & 3rd bedrooms are, $35 each., yard, airport shuttle

Guests have entire house: 3 bedroom, 2 bath, kitchen, living room, fireplace, dining room, piano, cable TV, stereo. murphyotte@aol.com

KANSAS CITY (REGION)

The Inn on Crescent Lake
1261 St. Louis Ave, *Excelsior Springs* 64024
816-630-6745
Anne & Bruce Libowitz
All year

135-250-BB
8 rooms, 8 pb
Visa, MC, *Rated*, •
C-ltd/S-ltd/P-no/H-ltd

Full breakfast
Dinner, bar service available
Color TV, inner tubes

1915 mansion on 22 acres surrounded by two ponds. Boats, swimming pool and walking path. Extensively renovated in 1997.
info@crescentlake.com http://www.crescentlake.com

The Porch Swing Inn
702 East St, *Parkville* 64152
816-587-6282
Ellen Underkoffler & Rhonda Weimer
All year

80-100-BB
4 rooms, 4 pb
Visa, MC, Disc
C-ltd/S-ltd/P-ltd/H-no

Full breakfast
Afternoon tea, snacks, complimentary wine
Sitting room, Jacuzzis, suites, frplces, cable TV, accom. bus. trav., phones

Enjoy a wonderful breakfast, relax on the front porch or back deck, soak in the hot tub. Venture out for shopping, walking in the park, and dinner–all witting walking distance.
theporchswinginn@kc.rr.com http://www.theporchswinginn.com

KANSAS CITY (REGION)

Cedarcroft Farm & Cottage
431 SE County Rd Y,
Warrensburg 64093
660-747-5728 800-368-4944
Sandra & Bill Wayne
All year

125-220-BB
2 rooms, 2 pb
Most CC, *Rated*
C-no/S-ltd/P-no/H-no

Full breakfast
Complimentary evening snack
Cottage, Jacuzzis, suites, fireplace, dish TV

The Cottage on the Knoll at Cedarcroft Farm has all romantic amenities in a secluded meadow. Explore 80 acres of woods, meadows & streams at our National Register farm.
info@cedarcroft.com http://www.cedarcroft.com

MARTHASVILLE

Concord Hill
473 Concord Hill Rd 63357
636-932-4228
Jim & Vicki Cunningham
All year

90-BB
4 rooms, 3 pb
Rated
C-yes/S-no/P-no/H-no

Full breakfast
Snacks
Sitting room, fireplaces, hot tub

19th century farm house, combination of simple elegance and rural ambiance.
chickenman@socket.net http://www.aoh.org/concordhill

OSAGE BEACH

Inn at Harbour Ridge
PO Box 496
65065
573-302-0411 877-744-6020
Sue & Ron Westenhaver
All year

95-175-BB
5 rooms, 5 pb
C-ltd/S-no/P-ltd/H-yes

Jacuzzi, hot tub, in room fireplace

Enjoy private baths (twosome tubbies), fireplaces, hot tub, sinfully good breakast, private decks, & boat dock at "The Lake's Most Inviting B&B," circa 2000. Happy Hearts!
info@harbourridgeinn.com http://www.harbourridgeinn.com

PLATT CITY

A Planter's Wheel
PO Box 78
1112 4th Street 64079
816-858-2079 Fax: 816-858-2079
866-437-2079
Wilbur & Karon Roberts
All year

70-120-BB
4 rooms, 3 pb
Most CC, *Rated*, •
C-ltd/S-no/P-no/H-ltd

Full breakfast
Afternoon tea, snacks
Sitting room, library, bicycles, suites, cable TV, accom. bus. travelers

"Small town getaway," with great access to entertainment, biking, sports & family fun park. Just minutes from Kansas City International Airport.
karon@aplanterswheelbb.com http://aplanterswheelbb.com

ROCHEPORT

School House
504 Third St 65279
573-698-2022 Fax: 573-698-2022
John & Vicki Ott, Penny Province
All year

95-225-BB
10 rooms, 10 pb
Rated, •

Full, Cont. or Cont Plus breakfast

In 1987 John and Vicki Ott purchased the old Rocheport School circa 1914. After 15 months of extensive renovation, they opened the School House B&B in spring of 1988.
innkeeper@schoolhousebandb.com http://www.schoolhousebandb.com

---

Yates House
PO Box 10
305 Second St 65279
573-698-2129
Conrad & Dixie Yates
All year

115-225-BB
6 rooms, 6 pb
Visa, MC
S-ltd/P-no

Full Gourmet Breakfast

The Yates House Bed and Breakfast graciously accommodates Honeymooners, Anniversaries, Adult Family and Friend Retreats, as well as that very special Romantic Interlude.
yateshouse@webchoice.net http://www.yateshouse.com

Virginia Rose, Springfield, MO

SPRINGFIELD

Virginia Rose
317 E Glenwood St 65807
417-883-0693
Fax: 417-883-0693
800-345-1412
Jackie & Virginia Buck
All year

60-120-BB
3 rooms, 3 pb
Most CC, *Rated*, •
C-ltd/S-no/P-no/H-ltd

Full breakfast
Afternoon tea, snacks
Sitting room, accom. bus. travel., large parking area

Lovely country-Victorian hideaway on tree-covered acre right in town. Private yet close to walking trail, antique & mall shopping and restaurants.
vrosebb@sisna.com http://bbonline.com/mo/virginiarose

Walnut Street Inn
900 E Walnut St 65806
417-864-6346 Fax: 417-864-6184
800-593-6346
Gary & Paula Blankenship
All year

69-169-BB
12 rooms, 12 pb
Most CC, *Rated*, •
C-yes/S-no/P-no/H-yes

Full breakfast
Cookies, snacks, tea/coffee, beer, wine available
Sitting room, hot tubs, tennis nearby
4 rooms with Jacuzzi, tennis nearby

1894 Victorian showcase inn in Historic District. Gourmet breakfast; walking distance to shops, theater, live music. Great place for business/pleasure!
stay@walnutstreetinn.com http://www.walnutstreetinn.com

SPRINGFIELD (REGION)

The Dickey House B&B
331 South Clay St, *Marshfield* 65706
417-468-3000
Fax: 417-859-2775
800-450-7444
Michaelene & Larry Stevens
All year

65-145-BB
7 rooms, 7 pb
Most CC, *Rated*, •
C-ltd/S-no/P-ltd/H-ltd

Full breakfast
Dinner, snacks
Sitting room, library, Jacuzzis, suites, fireplace, cable TV, conference.

1913 Greek Revival Mansion nestled among ancient oak trees on 2 acres of manicured gardens. AAA Four Diamond Rated. Featured in Time Magazine as "A Refug in the Hills.". .One of the Best in the USA!
info@dickeyhouse.com http://www.dickeyhouse.com

ST. CHARLES

Boone's Lick Trail Inn
1000 So Main St 63301
636-947-7000 888-940-0002
V'anne & Paul Mydler
All year

105-175-BB
6 rooms, 6 pb
Most CC, *Rated*, •
C-yes/S-no/P-no/H-ltd

Full breakfast
In room beverage service
Hiking/biking, sitting room, conference, folk art, rollaways available

Escape to restored 1840 Inn. Flower gardens, regional antiques, duck decoys in historic river settlement. Duck hunting. info@booneslick.com http://www.booneslick.com

ST. LOUIS

Napoleon's Retreat
1815 Lafayette Ave 63104
314-772-6979 Fax: 314-772-7675
800-700-9980
J. Archuleta & M Lance
All year

95-135-BB
5 rooms, 5 pb
Most CC, *Rated*, •
C-ltd/S-no/P-no/H-no

Full breakfast
Snacks, afternoon tea
Sitting room, Jacuzzis, suites, fireplaces, cable TV

Elegant Victorian townhouse with 5 beautiful guestrooms, all featuring private bath, queen-sized bed, cable TV, & numerous amenities. The perfect retreat for business or pleasure.
info@napoleonsretreat.com http://www.napoleonsretreat.com

The Winter House
3522 Arsenal St 63118
314-664-4399
Kendall Winter
All year, not Chritsmas

100-120-BB
3 rooms, 3 pb
Most CC, *Rated*, •
C-yes/S-ltd/P-no/H-no

Full breakfast
Complimentary refreshments
Sitt. room w/gas logs and, piano, 24 hr Kinko nrby, near shops & restaurants

1897 Victorian 9-room house with turret. Hand-squeezed O.J. and live piano at breakfast by reservation. kmwinter1@juno.com http://www.thewinterhouse.com

ST. LOUIS (REGION)

Bilbrey Farms, Exotic Animal Farm
8724 Pin Oak Rd, *Edwardsville, IL* 62025
618-692-1950 Fax: 618-659-9764
Linda & Mike Bilbrey
All year

95-185-BB
5 rooms, 2 pb
Visa, MC, *Rated*
C-yes/S-no/P-ltd/H-yes

Full Breakfast
Sitting room, Jacuzzis, suites, fireplaces, cable TV, sauna, whirlpool

Our home is your castle. 11,000 sq. ft country estate offers the finest amenities, modern facilities and old country charm. Come—be treated like royalty.
bilbreyfarms@email.com http://www.bilbreyfarms.com

Geery's
720 N 5th St, *Saint Charles* 63301
636-916-5344 Fax: 636-916-4702
Peter & Marilyn Geery
All year

80-125-BB
3 rooms, 3 pb
Most CC, *Rated*, •
C-yes/S-ltd/P-no

Full breakfast
Afternoon tea, snacks, complimentary wine
Library, fireplaces, Jacuzzi, Cable TV, off-street parking

Return to Victorian era. 3 guestrooms with private bathroom. Hospitality at its finest! Relax and pamper yourselves in a beautifully decorated home.
pgeeryktj1@aol.com http://www.geerys.com

STE. GENEVIEVE

Hotel Sainte Genevieve
9 N Main St 63670
573-883-3562 877-272-2588
Jami & Jacque Inman
All year

40-EP
14 rooms, 14 pb
Visa, MC, AmEx, *Rated*
C-yes/S-yes/P-ltd/H-ltd

Restaurant, breakfast, lunch & dinner avail.
Bar service, cable TV

Founded in 1735, historic Ste. Genevieve allows you to experience life as it was centuries ago. The Hotel Ste. Genevieve has one of today's finest restaurants.

STE. GENEVIEVE

The Inn St. Gemme Beauvais
78 N Main St 63670
573-883-5744 Fax: 573-883-3899
800-818-5744
Janet Joggerst All year

89-189-BB
9 rooms, 9 pb
Most CC, *Rated*, •
C-yes/S-ltd/P-no/H-ltd

Full breakfast
Tea with dessert, hors d'oeuvres with drinks
Special packages available, Jacuzzi tubs, fireplaces, gardens, 2-room suites

AAA rated 3 diamonds with warm, but non-intrusive hospitality. Many 2 room suites with private baths. Individual breakfast tables, waitress service, 8 entree choices!
Buffin@msn.com http://www.bbhost.com/innstgemme

Southern Hotel
146 S Third St 63670
573-883-3493 Fax: 573-883-9612
800-275-1412
Mike & Barbara Hankins

93-138-BB
8 rooms, 8 pb
Visa, MC, *Rated*
C-ltd/S-no/P-no/H-no
All year

Full breakfast
Complimentary wine
Sitting room, pool room, parlors, free bicycles, Jacuzzis, gift shop

Step gently into the time when Riverboats plied the mighty Mississippi and weary travelers looked forward to the hospitality of this famous 1800s hotel.
mike@southernhotelbb.com http://www.southernhotelbb.com

STEELVILLE

Parkview Farm
117 E Hwy 8 65565
573-775-4196 877-221-2314
Tom & Jan Weisel
All year

55-95-BB
4 rooms
Most CC
C-ltd/S-ltd/P-no/H-ltd

Full breakfast
Sitting room, bikes, Jacuzzis, "Greenway" walking path

Conveniently located in a beautiful valley with a wonderful view of Steelville's park and recreation area.
tweisel@misn.com http://msnhomepages.talkcity.com/CommercialSt/tweisel/parkview.html

TRENTON

Hyde Mansion
418 E 7th St 64683
660-359-5631 Fax: 660-359-5632
Robert & Carolyn Brown
All year

65-110-BB
5 rooms, 5 pb
Visa, MC, AmEx, *Rated*
C-ltd/S-ltd/P-no/H-no

Full breakfast
Complimentary beverages, snacks
Sitting room, library, Baby grand piano, patio, scr. porch

Inviting hideaway in rural America, 1949 mansion refurbished for your convenience.
brown@lyn.net

WASHINGTON

Schwegmann House
438 W Front St 63090
636-239-5025 Fax: 636-239-3920
800-949-2262
Cathy & Bill Nagel
All year

120-160-BB
9 rooms, 9 pb
Visa, MC, AmEx, *Rated*
C-ltd/S-no/P-no/H-yes

Full breakfast
Breakfast served in parlor or on patio
Private baths and direct dial phones, patios, parlors, porch

Missouri Wine Country with 11 wineries & historic communities. Rekindles local flour miller's hospitality of more than 100 years ago. Business meetings.
cathy@schwegmannhouse.com http://www.schwegmannhouse.com

Washington House
100 W Front St 63090
636-390-0200 Fax: 636-451-0737
888-229-8341
Terry & Susan Black All year

85-BB
2 rooms, 2 pb
Most CC
C-yes/H-yes

Full or continental breakfast
Tea, coffees
Private, romantic getaway

Our historic 1837 inn on the Missouri River features antique furnishings and decor, queen-size canopy beds and river views.

WEBSTER GROVES

Old Orchard
915 Newport Ave 63119
314-961-6026
Marian D. Briedenbach

80-85-BB
3 rooms, 2 pb
C-ltd/S-ltd/P-no/H-no
All year

Full breakfast
Fireplaces, cable TV

We are located in a suburb of St. Louis. There is a small town feeling here because of the old trees, two small business shopping districts and friendly people.
http://www.oldorchardbedandbreakfast.com

WESTPHALIA

Werner House
PO Box 257
202 West Main St 65085
573-455-2885
Linda & Sergio Fernandez
All year

60-BB
3 rooms
C-yes/S-ltd/P-no/H-no
Spanish

Full breakfast
Sitting room, cable TV, extensive movie library

Restored 1885 vernacular Missouri German home in historic small town. Excellent example of urban farmstead. Guaranteed homey, friendly atmosphere. Free roses in season.

Montana

BIG SKY

Lone Mountain Ranch
PO Box 160069
Lone Mountain Access Rd
59716
406-995-4644 Fax: 406-995-4670
800-514-4644
Bob & Vivian Schaap

BB
23 rooms, 23 pb
Rated, •
All year

Full breakfast

Comfortable log cabins and the luxurious RidgeTop Lodge offers a wide range of accommodations. lmr@lmranch.com http://www.lmranch.com

Mountain Meadows Guest Ranch
PO Box 160072
7055 Beaver Creek Rd 59716
406-995-4997 Fax: 406-995-2097
888-644-6647
Elizabeth Severn-Erikson
Nov 15-April 15,June-Oct

400-600-AP
7 rooms, 7 pb
Most CC, •
C-yes/S-no/P-no/H-yes
Swedish, Spanish

Full breakfast
Breakfast, lunch, dinner, snacks
Two cabins and log lodge, sauna, Jacuzzi, dining room, Thirty Moose Bar

Big Sky's newest guest ranch! Family-owned & operated, MMGR specializes in the complete Montana experience. Great views, gourmet food, outdoor activities, wildlife, and great accommodations. mmgr@mcn.net http://www.mountainmeadowsranch.com

BIGFORK

Burggraf's Countrylane
1 Rainbow Dr on Swan Lake
677 Cedar Bay Dr 59911
406-837-4608 Fax: 406-837-2468
800-525-3344
Natalie & R.J. Burggraf
May-Sept.

100-145-BB
5 rooms, 5 pb
Visa, MC, *Rated*, •
C-ltd/S-ltd/P-no/H-yes

Full or Continental Plus breakfast
Complimentary wine, cheese, fruit
Picnic baskets, fishing, lake, snowmobiles, boating, canoes, Jacuzzi

True log home nestled in heart of Rocky Mountains; 7 acres on the shores of Swan Lake; panoramic view; country breakfast. nburggraf@yahoo.com

BIGFORK

Candlewycke Inn
311 Aero Ln 59911
406-837-6406 Fax: 406-837-9921
888-617-8805
Megan Vandegrift All year

100-125-BB
6 rooms, 4 pb
Visa, MC, AmEx, *Rated*, •
C-yes/S-ltd/P-ltd/H-no

Full country breakfast
Afternoon tea, truffles on your pillow
Hot tub with bathrobes, campfire & BBQ picnic area

Country theme rooms offer an inviting and warm atmosphere in this authentic lodge style B minutes away from Flathead Lake and the village of Bigfork.
candle@digisys.net http://www.candlewyckeinn.com

O'Duachain Country Inn
675 Ferndale Dr
675 Ferndale Drive 59911
406-837-6851 Fax: 406-837-0778
800-837-7460
William & Mary Corcoran
Knoll All year

110-180-BB
5 rooms, 4 pb
Most CC, *Rated*, •
C-yes/S-ltd/P-ltd/H-ltd

Full gourmet breakfast
Sitting room, hot tubs, water sports, will help w/tours, dinner plans

Elegant, rustic log home nestled in the woods and mountain meadows.
knollmc@aol.com http://www.MontanaInn.com

BILLINGS

The Josephine
514 North 29th St 59101
406-248-5898 800-552-5898
Douglas & Becky Taylor
All year

75-150-BB
6 rooms, 4 pb
Most CC, *Rated*, •
C-ltd/S-no/P-no/H-no

Full breakfast
Afternoon tea, comp. liqueur
Snacks, sitting room, library, tennis/pool/, hot tubs/sauna nearby

Lovely historic home within walking distance to downtown. Comfortably elegant, delicious gourmet breakfasts–a refreshing alternative.
josephine@imt.net http://www.thejosephine.com

BOZEMAN

Cottonwood Inn
13515 Cottonwood Canyon
59718
406-763-5452 Fax: 406-763-5639
888-879-4667
Joe and Debbie Velli
All year

85-129-BB
5 rooms, 5 pb
Visa, MC, AmEx, *Rated*, •
C-ltd/S-ltd/P-no/H-no
Italian

Full breakfast
Snacks, complimentary beverages
Hot tubs, sitting room, library, nightly turndown service

Mountain hideaway, 10 minutes from Bozeman, built in 1996.
info@cottonwood-inn.com http://www.cottonwood-inn.com

Fox Hollow
545 Mary Rd 59718
406-582-8440 Fax: 406-582-9752
800-431-5010
Nancy & Michael Dawson
All year

75-135-BB
5 rooms, 5 pb
Most CC, *Rated*, •
C-ltd/S-no/P-no/H-no

Full gourmet breakfast
Sitting room, hot tub, art gallery, washer game

Luxury accommodations, panoramic mountain views, hospitality–uniquely Montana. Five guestrooms with private baths. Guesthouse with kitchen. Romantic honeymoon suite.
foxhollow@bozeman-MT.com http://www.bozeman-mt.com

Gallatin Gateway Inn
PO Box 376
76405 Gallatin Rd 59719
406-763-4672 Fax: 406-763-4672
800-676-3522
Catherine Wrather
All year

85-160-BB
34 rooms, 34 pb
Visa, *Rated*, •
C-yes/S-ltd/P-no/H-yes

Continental plus breakfast
Restaurant, dinner available, bar service
Sitting room, bicycles, pool, suites, cable TV, accom. bus. travelers

Stunningly restored 1927 grand railroad hotel, located 12 miles southwest of Bozeman, MT amid spectacular scenery. Fine dining and casual pub, well appointed, comfortable rooms. gatewayinn@gallatingatewayinn.com http://www.gallatingatewayinn.com

BOZEMAN

Gallatin River Lodge
9105 Thorpe Rd 59718
406-388-0148 Fax: 406-388-6766
888-387-0148
Steve & Christy Gamble
All year

100-500-BB
6 rooms, 6 pb
Visa, MC, *Rated*, •
C-yes/S-ltd/P-ltd/H-yes

Full Breakfast
Snacks, lunch & dinner available, Restaurant
Bar service, sitting room, library, Jacuzzis, suites, fireplaces, cable TV

New elegant inn offering fine dining, fly fishing, horseback tours on acreage near the Gallatin River, hardwood floors, mission furnishings and spectacular mountain views from suites. info@grlodge.com http://www.grlodge.com

---

Lehrkind Mansion
719 N Wallace Ave 59715
406-585-6932 800-992-6932
Jon Gerster/Christopher Nixon
All year

79-159-BB
5 rooms, 3 pb
Visa, MC, AmEx, *Rated*
C-ltd/S-no/P-no/H-no
German

Full breakfast
Afternoon tea
Sitting rm, library, bikes, hot tubs, large yard, mountain views, fax, piano

Queen Anne Victorian mansion furnished in 1890s antiques. Tea served in our music parlor to Montana's largest music box, 7 feet tall!
lehrkindmansion@imt.net http://www.bozemanbedandbreakfast.com

---

Lindley House
202 Lindley Pl 59715
406-587-8403 Fax: 406-582-8112
Stephanie Volz
All year

90-350
6 rooms, 6 pb
Visa, MC, Disc, *Rated*, •
C-yes/S-no/P-no/H-no

Full breakfast
Cookies, candy, sherry
hot tub, fireplaces

Victorian Bed & Breakfast elegantly restored with French wall coverings, antiques, comfortable beds and an excellent downtown location. Attention to detail.
lindley@lindley-house.com http://www.lindley-house.com

Voss Inn
319 S Willson Ave 59715
406-587-0982 Fax: 406-585-2964
Bruce & Frankee Muller
All year

105-125-BB
6 rooms, 6 pb
Most CC, *Rated*, •
C-ltd/S-ltd/P-no/H-no
Spanish, Africaans

Full breakfast in parlor or room
Afternoon tea; Friday night dinners by reservation
Sitting room, parlour, piano, telephones, fax, rose & perennial garden

The Voss Inn is a warm, elegant circa 1883 Victorian Italianate mansion beautifully restored and decorated with period wallpaper & furniture, surrounded by a lush English cottage garden. vossinn@bigsky.net http://www.bozeman-vossinn.com

EMIGRANT

Johnstad's Guesthouse
PO Box 981
03 Paradise Ln 59027
406-333-9003 Fax: 406-333-9003
800-340-4993
Ron & Mary Ellen Johnstad
All year

85-150-BB
6 rooms, 4 pb
Most CC, •
C-ltd/S-no/P-ltd/H-yes
Spanish, Norwegian, German

Full breakfast
Afternoon tea, snacks
Sitting room, library, fireplace, conference, facilities

Classic Montana hospitality in the heart of Paradise Valley, just north of Yellowstone Park. Stay in our B&B with spacious rooms and majestic views or in our log guest house.
rjohnstad@aol.com http://www.johnstadsbb.com

GARDINER

Headwaters of the Yellowstone
PO Box 25
9 Olson Ln 59030
406-848-7073 Fax: 406-848-7420
Joyce & Merv Olson All year

85-125-BB
6 rooms, 6 pb
Visa, MC, AmEx
C-yes/S-no/P-no/H-ltd

Full breakfast
Sitting room, library, satellite TV

Our home on the Yellowstone River, 5 minutes from Yellowstone Park, is a quiet place to enjoy spectacular views and native wildlife, fish, or relax after touring the Park.
mervo@headwatersbandb.com http://www.headwatersbandb.com

The Hostetler House, Glendive, MT

GARDINER

Yellowstone Suites
PO Box 277
506 4th St 59030
406-848-7937 800-948-7937
Vicki LaPlante, John & Anita Vorley All year

47-98-BB
4 rooms, 2 pb
Most CC
C-yes/S-ltd/P-ltd/H-no

Full breakfast
Tea, & coffee
Sitting room, TV/VCR, hot tub, Yellowstone reference library, garden

Yellowstone Suites, a historic home, is 3 blocks from the Entrance to Yellowstone Park. Amenities include: antiques, historical photos, verandahs, a hot tub, peaceful gardens, & a resource library. bandb@montanads1.com http://www.wolftracker.com/ys

GLENDIVE

Charley Montana
PO Box 1192
103 N Douglas 59330
406-365-3207 Fax: 406-365-3207
888-395-3207
Katherine & Jim Lee All year

65-90-BB
7 rooms, 5 pb
Visa, MC, AmEx, *Rated*, •
C-ltd/S-no/P-ltd/H-ltd

Full breakfast
Sitting room, library, bikes, suites, accommodate business travelers

Explore eastern Montana's Badlands vistas and rich heritage. Casual, comfortable 1907 Krug Mansion; on National Register. Guests say it's "the real thing" – by a noted rancher.
charley@midrivers.com http://www.charley-montana.com

The Hostetler House
113 N Douglas St 59330
406-377-4505 Fax: 406-377-8456
800-965-8456
Craig & Dea Hostetler
All year

50-BB
2 rooms
Rated, •
C-ltd/S-no/P-no/H-no
Basic German

Full gourmet breakfast
Sitting room/library, hot tub/gazebo, tandem mountain bike

Charming 1912 historic home with two comfortable guestrooms in casual country.
hostetler@midrivers.com http://wtp.net/go/montana/sites/hostetler.html

GREAT FALLS

Collins Mansion
1003 2nd Ave NW 59404
406-452-6798 Fax: 406-452-6787
877-452-6798
Connie Romain & Diana Unghire All year

78-99-BB
5 rooms, 5 pb
Visa, MC, AmEx, *Rated*, •
C-ltd/S-no/P-no/H-no

Full breakfast
Snacks
library, fireplaces, cable TV, telephones in rooms, internet capable

Our 1891 historic Victorian B&B has 5 beautiful guestrooms, all with private baths, comfortable beds and plenty of quiet. Close to area attractions, wonderful breakfasts.
cmansionbb@aol.com http://www.collinsmansion.com

HAMILTON

Deer Crossing
396 Hayes Creek Rd 59840
406-363-2232 Fax: 406-375-0771
800-763-2232
Mary Lynch
All year

89-149-BB
6 rooms, 5 pb
Visa, MC, AmEx,
Rated, •
C-yes/S-ltd/P-ltd/H-no

Full country breakfast
Complimentary beverages, fruit & homemade cookies
Fishing guide, shuttle, horseback riding, Bunk house with full bath

Experience Old West charm & hospitality. 25 acres of tall pines and lush pastures. Incredible views. Hearty ranch breakfast.
deercrossing@montana.com http://www.deercrossingmontana.com

Red Willow Inn
147 West Bridge Rd 59840
406-375-1101
Susan Gudmundsson
All year

75-85-BB
4 rooms, 4 pb
Visa, MC, *Rated*
C-ltd/S-no/P-ltd/H-no

Full breakfast
Snacks
Sitting room, beautiful views

This 1904 Victorian, located at the base of the Bitterroot Mountains, 1/2 mile from the River. 1 mile to downtown. 4 bedrooms, 4 baths, decks, healthy breakfast.
info@redwillowinn.com http://www.redwillowinn.com

Roaring Lion Inn
830 Timberbrook Ln 59840
406-363-6555 Fax: 406-363-9056
877-LION-INN
Suzanne & Gregg Couch
All year

95-135-BB
3 rooms, 3 pb
Visa, MC, *Rated*
C-yes/S-ltd/P-ltd/H-yes

Full breakfast
Snacks, complimentary wine
Sitting room, fireplaces

Nestled in the woods a few short miles from wilderness area; summer and winter activities. rli@cybernet1.com http://www.roaringlioninn.com

HELENA

Birdseye
1001 Knight St
6890 Raven Rd 59601
406-449-4380 Fax: 406-449-4380
888-449-4380
BJ Block All year

55-95-BB
5 rooms, 1 pb
Visa, MC, *Rated*
C-yes/S-ltd/P-yes/H-no

Full or Continental breakfast
Snacks, dinner available
Sitting room, library

Press an authentic slice of Montana in your memory book. Wind your way up a mountain road and discover a quiet lifestyle. Hard to describe.
birdseyebb@aol.com http://www.birdseyebb.com

The Sanders-Helena B&B
328 N. Ewing 59601
406-442-3309 Fax: 406-443-2361
Bobbi Uecker & Rock Ringling
All year

90-115-BB
7 rooms, 7 pb
Most CC, *Rated*
C-yes/S-no/P-no/H-ltd

Full breakfast
Afternoon cookies, tea, coffee, iced tea, lemonade
Front porch, parlor, sitting room, library of books about Helena

The Sanders offers elegant 1875 accommodations in a mansion that is centrally located in the heart of historic Helena. thefolks@sandersbb.com http://www.sandersbb.com

KALISPELL

Cottonwood Hill Farm Inn
2928 Whitefish Stage Rd 59901
406-756-6404 Fax: 406-756-8507
800-458-0893
Jennifer & Charlie Horvath
All year

105-135-BB
3 rooms, 3 pb
Visa, MC, AmEx,
Rated, •
C-ltd/S-ltd/P-no/H-no

Full breakfast
Full meal plan option
TV/VCR, library, chess, croquet, bocce, fax, phone, exercise equipment

A beautiful renovated farmhouse on 14 acres. 3 elegant guestrooms each with private bath. Spectacular views of the valley and mountains.
cei1@digisys.net http://www.cottonwoodhillfarm.com

KALISPELL

The Keith House
538 Fifth Ave E 59901
406-752-7913 Fax: 406 752-7933
800 972-7913
Don and Rebecca Bauder
All year

115-220-BB
6 rooms, 6 pb
Visa, MC, AmEx,
Rated, •
C-ltd/S-no/P-no/H-ltd

Full breakfast
cookies, lemonade, wine and cheese reception
robes, designer linens, luxury soaps, turndown service, in-room telephones

Montana's most elegant lodging and gateway to Glacier National Park. This meticulously restored historic mansion is walking distance to downtown's galleries and restaurants.
keithbb@digisys.net http://www.keithhousebb.com

MISSOULA

Gibson Mansion
823 39th Street 59803
406-251-1345 Fax: 406-251-9872
866-251-1345
Tom & Nancy Malikie
All year

99-149-BB
4 rooms, 4 pb
Visa, MC, AmEx
C-yes/S-ltd/P-no/H-ltd

Full breakfast
Afternoon snacks
Parlor, library, porch, hammock, flower gardens and grounds

Historic Mansion fully restored with stained glass and hard wood floors. iron beds with down comforters. Beautiful grounds with flower gardens, ideal for weddings and receptions. info@gibsonmansion.com http://www.gibsonmansion.com

MISSOULA (REGION)

Montana Hotel
PO Box 423
702 Railroad Ave, *Alberton*
59820
406-722-4990 888-271-9317
Rebecca Hazlitt & Steve Young
All year

59-95-BB
10 rooms, 8 pb
Visa, MC, •
C-yes/S-no/P-ltd/H-ltd

Continental plus breakfast
Home-made brownies, cakes, other snacks; lemonade
Shady courtyard

Historic railroad inn is a charming reminder of simpler times. Ten pretty rooms, private baths. Great for small group gatherings and reunions. An easy day's drive from Seattle, just off I-90. montanahotel@blackfoot.net http://www.montanahotel.net

---

Blue Damsel
1081 Rock Creek Rd, *Clinton*
59825
406-825-3077 Fax: 406-825-3077
Niki
April 1–Jan 2

110-195-BB
7 rooms, 4 pb
Visa, Disc, *Rated*, •
C-ltd/S-no/P-no/H-ltd
Italian, Croatian

Full breakfast
Lunch & dinner available, snacks
Sitting room, library, Jacuzzis, suites, fireplaces, cable TV

Fantasy log B blue ribbon trout stream designated as wild and scenic river. Antiques and art make your stay comfortable; fireplaces and Jacuzzis.
niki@thebluedamsel.com http://www.thebluedamsel.com

NOXON

Big Horn Lodge
2 Bighorn Lane 59853
406-847-4676 Fax: 406-847-0069
888-347-8477
Dave & Cindy Nye
All year

75-150-BB
5 rooms, 5 pb
Visa, MC, *Rated*
C-yes/S-no/P-no/H-ltd

Full breakfast
Wine and cheese upon arrival
Fireplaces, bicycles, cable TV, accommodate business travelers

For a little luxury with your wilderness.... Enjoy hiking, mountain biking, canoeing, rafting, horseback riding, skiing & spectacular fishing, or just relax and enjoy breath-taking views. bhl@blackfoot.net http://www.bighornlodgemontana.com

POLSON

Hawthorne House
304 Third Ave E 59860
406-883-2723 800-290-1345
Karen & Gerry Lenz
All year

40-EP
4 rooms
C-ltd/S-no/P-no/H-no

Full breakfast (fee)
Sitting room, cable TV

Hawthorne House is a two story English Tudor house with seven gables. It expresses a diversity of cultures. http://www.visitmt.com

RED LODGE

Willows Inn
PO Box 886
224 S Platt Ave 59068
406-446-3913
Kerry, Carolyn, Elven Boggio
All year

65-120-BB
6 rooms, 4 pb
Visa, MC, *Rated*, •
C-yes/S-no/P-no/H-no
Finnish, Spanish

Full breakfast
Gourmet picnics available
TV/VCR parlor with movies, games/books, local menus, ski racks, sun decks

Charming Victorian. Delicious home-baked pastries. Spectacular mountain scenery.
willowinn@earthlink.net http://www.bbhost.com/willowsinn

RONAN

The Timbers
1184 Timberlane Rd 59864
406-676-4373 Fax: 406-676-4370
800-775-4373
Doris & Leonard McCravey

95-160-BB
2 rooms, 1 pb
Visa, MC, *Rated*, •
C-yes/S-ltd/P-ltd/H-no
All year

Full or continental breakfast
Refreshments
Robes, sherry, bicycles, horse boarding

Located in Montana's spectacular Mission Valley enroute to Glacier Park, near Flathead Lake and Bison Range. Stables and corrals for guest horses, pond, barbecue and picnic area. timbers@ronan.net http://www.timbers.net

SEELEY LAKE

The Emily A. B&B
PO Box 350
MM20; Hwy 83 N 59868
406-677-3474 Fax: 406-677-3474
800-977-4639
Marilyn & Keith Peterson

95-150-BB
5 rooms, 2 pb
Visa, MC, *Rated*, •
C-yes/P-ltd
Spanish
All year

Full breakfast
Snacks, complimentary wine
Bar service, sitting room, library, bicycles, fireplaces, conference

The lodge, named for Marilyn's grandmother, is the perfect place for adventure and relaxation. slk3340@blackfoot.net http://www.theemilya.com

ST. IGNATIUS

Stoneheart Inn B&B
PO Box 236
26 North Main 59865
406-745-4999 Fax: 406-745-3060
800-866-9197
Mike Tholt & Judith Ellis-Tholt

30-50-BB
4 rooms, 4 pb
Visa, MC, Disc, *Rated*
C-yes/S-ltd/P-yes/H-no
All year

Full breakfast
Afternoon tea, snacks, complimentary wine
Sitting room, fireplaces, cable TV, accom. business travelers

Historic hotel nestled in Mission Mountains reflects uniqueness of Montana. Air-conditioned, optional feather beds, home-baked treats on arrival, brandy at your bedside.
http://www.stoneheart.com

VIRGINIA CITY

Just an Experience
PO Box 98
1570 Mt Hwy 287 59755
406-843-5402 Fax: 406-843-5235
866-664-0424
John & Carma Sinerius

60-95-BB
5 rooms, 3 pb
Most CC, •
C-yes/S-ltd/P-no/H-ltd
All year

Full breakfast
Dinner
Sitting room, tennis court, Jacuzzis, historic sites

The perfect get-away! Fully furnished cabins & guest rooms with excellent Montana hospitality. Delicious meals, mountain scenery and historic attractions. Open year round!
john@justanexperience.com http://www.justanexperience.com

WEST GLACIER (REGION)

Paola Creek
PO Box 97
Mile Marker 172.8 Hwy 2 East, *Essex* 59936
406-888-5061 Fax: 406-888-5063
888-311-5061
Kelly & Les Hostetler All year

90-170-BB
5 rooms, 5 pb
Visa, MC, *Rated*
C-no/S-no/P-ltd/H-yes

Full breakfast

Paola Creek B&B is the perfect base for exploring Montana's Glacier National Park. Our view of Mount Saint Nicholas is unequalled.
paola@in-tch.com http://wtp.net/go/paola

WHITEFISH

Good Medicine Lodge
537 Wisconsin Ave 59937
406-862-5488 Fax: 406-862-5489
800-860-5488
Betsy & Woody Cox All year

85-215-BB
9 rooms, 9 pb
Most CC, *Rated*, •
C-yes/S-no/P-no/H-yes
German, French

Full breakfast
Guest bar
Ski boot & glove dryers, hot tubs, library, sitting room, guest laundry

A classic Montana getaway. Built of solid cedar; has balconies with stunning views, crackling fireplaces, outdoor spa, and loads of western hospitality.
info@goodmedicinelodge.com http://www.goodmedicinelodge.com

Gasthaus Wendlingen
700 Monegan Rd 59937
406-862-4886 Fax: 406-862-4886
800-811-8002
Barbara & Bill Klein
All year

60-125-BB
4 rooms, 3 pb
Visa, MC, *Rated*, •
C-ltd/S-no/P-no/H-ltd
German

Full breakfast
Afternoon tea, snacks, comp. wine or beer
Sitting room, library, fireplaces, cable TV, accommodate business travelers

German-Western hospitality. Private 8 acre setting. A real Montana feeling. Home baked specialties. Relax on patio, front porch or around our fieldstone fireplace.
gasthaus@aboutmontana.net http://www.whiefishmt.com/gasthaus

Nebraska

AINSWORTH

The Upper Room
409 N Wilson 69210
402-387-0107
Greg & Joan Felton
All year

60-BB
4 rooms, 3 pb
Rated
C-yes/S-no/P-ltd/H-no

Full breakfast
Afternoon Tea
Sitting room, library, bikes, fireplace, turn-down serv., accom. bus. travel

Return to the charm and romance of the Victorian era. Historic 1910 landmark. Vacation in the Nebraska outback where the sandhills meet the scenic Niobrara River; top 10 in the nation for tubing & canoeing.
upperroom@bloomnet.com http://www.bbhost.com/upperroom

CAMBRIDGE

Cambridge
606 Parker St 69022
308-697-3220 Fax: 308-697-3267
Gloria Hilton
All year

75-90-BB
4 rooms, 4 pb
Visa, MC
S-no/P-no/H-no

Full breakfast
Beverages, snacks, prearranged lunch or dinner
Private telephones, modem hook-ups, TV/VCR, porches, parlors

1907 landmark mansion of Neoclassic architecture on the National Register brings modern luxury to a small rural town. Preserved original details, stained glass, fine art, and antiques. hilton@swnebr.net http://bedandbreakfast.com/bbc/p211133.asp

COLUMBUS

Traditions Inn
2905 14th St 68601
402-563-3333 Fax: 402-246-2084
877-563-3311
Patricia & Scott Mueller
All year

59-89-BB
4 rooms, 3 pb
Visa, MC, Disc, *Rated*, •
C-ltd/S-no/P-no/H-ltd

Full breakfast
Snacks, comp. wine, lunch & dinner available
Restaurant, bar service, sitting room, library, bikes, Jacuzzis, suites

Two historic homes linked by a sunlit conservatory overlooking the gazebo/garden. Antiques, gift shoppe, restaurant serving certified Angus beef, and pub.
samuell@megavision.com http://www.megavision.com/traditions

IMPERIAL

The Balcony House B&B
1006 Court St 69033
308-882-5597
866-882-5597
Jim & Linda Pirog

65-110-BB
5 rooms, 5 pb
Most CC
C-yes/S-no/P-ltd/H-no

Full breakfast
Coffee, tea, soda. Homemade cookies & baked goods.
Sitting room w/ TV/VCR, enclosed sun porch, guest kitchen.

Relax in the warmth of old fashioned hospitality away from the hustle of city life. After a restful night's sleep, enjoy a delicious hearty homemade breakfast. Experience comfort, privacy & pampering. balconyhouse@chase3000.com http://www.balconyhouse.com

LINCOLN

The Atwood House
740 S 17th St 68508
402-438-4567 Fax: 402-477-8314
800-884-6554
Ruth & Larry Stoll
All year

85-179-BB
4 rooms, 4 pb
Most CC, *Rated*
C-ltd/S-no/P-no/H-no

Full breakfast
Snacks, complimentary soft drinks
Sitting room, library, Jacuzzis, suites, fireplace, cable TV

"Experience the Elegance" of a suite in this 7,500-plus square foot 1894 Neoclassical Georgian Revival mansion. Larry@atwoodhouse.com http://www.atwoodhouse.com

OMAHA

The Cornerstone
140 N 39th St 68131
402-558-7600 Fax: 402-551-6598
Mark O'Leary
All year

75-110-BB
7 rooms, 7 pb
Most CC, *Rated*
C-yes/S-no/H-no

Full or continental breakfast
Sitting room, library, suites, fireplaces, cable TV, accom. bus. travelers

Built in 1894, the 10,000 sq. ft mansion is located in Omaha's Historic Gold Coast area. Guests have a choice of 6 rooms, or the Carriage House, each with private bath.
cornerstonebnb@aol.com http://www.thecornerstonebandb.com

VALPRAISO

Pine Crest Farms
PO Box 206
2550 County Rd A 68065
402-784-6461 Fax: 402-784-6462
Harriet & Jack Gould
All year

65-100-BB
6 rooms, 6 pb
C-ltd/S-no/P-no/H-no

Full breakfast
Snacks
Pool, library, sitting rooms, TV/VCR, beautiful grounds

Escape to the country just 16 miles north of Lincoln! Decorated in Colonial style, the inn's premier rooms are romantic. The property includes 1800 acres of farm/ranch land and a 25x50 swimming pool.
harrietgould@earthlink.net

VERDIGRE

The Commercial Hotel
PO Box 269
217 Main St 68783
402-668-2386
Fax: 402-668-2328
Mike & Jenete Maslonka
All year

46-46-BB
7 rooms, 7 pb
Most CC
C-yes/S-ltd/P-no/H-yes
Spanish

Continental breakfast
Parlor,lg 2 story deck,pvt landscaped yard w/BBQ.
Bicycles avail.for rent.

An historic hotel, built in 1900, fully renovated in 1995. Large dining room, 2 story deck, private yard. On the National Register of Historic Places.
jenete@aol.com

Nevada

BOULDER CITY

Boulder Dam Hotel 1305 Arizona St 89005 702-293-3510 Fax: 702-293-3093 Non-profit Boulder Dam Hotel Assn. All year	99-149-BB 22 rooms, 22 pb *Rated*, • C-yes/S-no/P-no/H-yes	Full breakfast Lunch, dinner, comp. wine reception, restaurant, b Suites, free use of gymn, free museum passes, accommodate bus. travelers

With a legacy of hosting celebrities and ghosts alike, this charming Dutch Colonial-style hotel is distinguished as Nevada's only entry in the prestigious Historic Hotels of America guide. info@boulderdamhotel.com http://www.boulderdamhotel.com

CARSON CITY

Bliss Mansion 710 W Robinson St 89703 775-887-8988 Fax: 775-887-0340 800-887-3501 Joyce Harrington & Ron Smith All year	145-195-BB 5 rooms, 5 pb Most CC, *Rated*, • C-yes/S-no/P-no/H-no	Full breakfast Snacks, complimentary wine Sitting room, library, fireplaces, cable TV, DSL/datalines, acc. bus. trav.

Nevada's historical Bed & Breakfast, Bliss Mansion. Built by lumber tycoon Duane L. Bliss in 1879. Across from the Governor's Mansion at the foot of the Sierra Mountains. innkeeper@blissmansion.com http://www.blissmansion.com

CARSON CITY (REGION)

Deer Run Ranch 5440 Eastlake Blvd, *Washoe Valley* 89704 775-882-3643 David & Muffy Vhay All year	95-125-BB 2 rooms, 2 pb Most CC, *Rated* C-ltd/S-no/P-no/H-ltd	Full breakfast Complimentary wine, beverages Snacks, refrigerator, sitting room, library, TV, VCR, private entry

Western ambiance in a unique architect-designed & built ranch house between Reno & Carson City overlooking Washoe Lake. http://bbonline.com/nv/deerrun/

LAKE TAHOE (REGION)

Haus Bavaria B&B PO Box 9079, Incline Village, NV, 89452 593 N Dyer Circle, *Incline Village* 89452 775-831-6122 Fax: 775-831-1238 800-731-6222 Bick Hewitt All year	99-245-BB 5 rooms, 5 pb Most CC, *Rated*, • C-ltd/S-no/P-no/H-no	Full breakfast Large family room, TV, frplc., ski packages, horse accommodations

There's much to do and see in this area, from gambling casinos to all water sports and golf, hiking, tennis and skiing at 12 nearby sites.
info@hausbavaria.com http://www.hausbavaria.com

UNIONVILLE

Old Pioneer Garden 2805 Unionville Rd 89418 775-538-7585 Mitzi & Lew Jones All year	75-85-BB 11 rooms, 3 pb *Rated*, •	Full breakfast

The Old Pioneer Garden Country Inn, in an oasis of Northern Nevada's high desert, dates to 1861. The inn was built the same year that silver prospectors toured the area & established Unionville. http://www.virtualcities.com/nv/oldpioneer.htm

New Hampshire

ALBANY

The Darby Field Inn
185 Chase Hill Rd 03818
603-447-2181 Fax: 603-447-5726
800-426-4147
Marc & Maria Donaldson
All year

90-270-BB
13 rooms, 13 pb
Visa, MC, *Rated*, •
C-ltd/S-ltd/P-no/H-no
Spanish

Full breakfast
Dinner, bar, MAP avail.
Spa services, video library, sitting room, piano, pool, hiking, birding

Cozy country inn overlooking Mt. Washington Valley & Presidential Mountains, and scenic rivers.

marc@darbyfield.com http://www.darbyfield.com

ASHLAND

Glynn House Inn
PO Box 719
59 Highland St 03217
603-968-3775 Fax: 603-968-9415
800-637-9599
Jim and Gay Dunlop
All year

99-239-BB
14 rooms, 14 pb
Most CC, *Rated*, •
C-ltd/S-no/P-no/H-no
French

Full gourmet breakfast
Afternoon refreshments daily from 4:30 to 6:30 PM
Sitting room, cable TV/VCR, A/C, lake, golf, canopy beds, CD players, robes

Located in the heart of New Hampshire's majestic White Mountains and pristine Squam Lake. Less than 2 hours from Boston, 1 hour Manchester.

theglynnhouseinn@aol.com http://www.glynnhouse.com

BARTLETT

The Bartlett Inn
Route 302, PO Box 327
Route 302 03812
603-374-2353 Fax: 603-374-2547
800-292-2353
Mark Dindorf
All year

79-175-BB
17 rooms, 17 pb
Visa, MC, AmEx, *Rated*, •
C-yes/S-ltd/P-ltd

Full breakfast
Comp. tea/coffee, snacks
Sitting room, outdoor hot tub, cross-country ski trails

A B&B inn for hikers, skiers & outdoors enthusiasts in the White Mountains. New addition of 2-room cottage with fireplace. Expert hiking & trail advice.

stay@bartlettinn.com http://www.bartlettinn.com

BEDFORD

Bedford Village Inn
2 Village Inn Ln 03110
603-472-2001 Fax: 603-472-2379
800-852-1166
Jack & Andrea Carnevale
All year

195-350-EP
14 rooms, 14 pb
Rated
S-no/P-no/H-yes

Lunch, dinner, afternoon tea, snacks, restaurant
Sitting room, library, Jacuzzis, suites, fireplaces, cable TV

A multi-million dollar farm estate restoration. The Bedford Village Inn is elegant country dining and lodging in the middle of historical New England.

guestservices@bedfordvillageinn.com http://www.bedfordvillageinn.com

BETHLEHEM

Adair Country Inn
80 Guider Ln 03574
603-444-2600 Fax: 603-444-4823
888-444-2600
Judy & Bill Whitman
All year

175-345-BB
10 rooms, 9 pb
Most CC, *Rated*, •
C-ltd/S-no/P-no/H-no

Full breakfast
Afternoon tea, comp. cheese & crackers
Living room, activity room with pool table, large screen TV, video library

Casually elegant country home in a breathtaking setting w/views of the White Mountains. Romantic retreat on 200 acres surrounded by sweeping lawns, gardens, stone walls, woods, and numerous wildlife.

innkeeper@adairinn.com http://www.adairinn.com

BETHLEHEM

Angel of the Mountains
PO Box 487
2007 Main St 03574
603-869-6473 Fax: 603-869-5490
888-704-4004
Sally & Ben Gumm
All year

95-225-BB
5 rooms, 4 pb
Visa, MC, AmEx, •
C-ltd/S-no/P-no/H-ltd

Full breakfast
Evening wine & cheese
Tennis Courts, Lantern Tour, Concierge Service, Fireplaces

Step into a world of Victorian elegance, gracious hospitality and enchanting scenery. Step into Angel of the Mountains. All guestrooms feature queen beds, private baths and views of Mt. Washington. info@angelofthemountains.com http://www.angelofthemountains.com

---

Mulburn Inn at Bethlehem
2370 Main St 03574
603-869-3389 800-457-9440
Christina & Alecia
All year

85-175-BB
7 rooms, 7 pb
Most CC, *Rated*, •
C-yes/S-no/P-no/H-no

Full breakfast
Afternoon tea, snacks
Library, ski & golf packages, wraparound porches, hot tub, exercise equip.

Sprawling 1913 summer cottage and family retreat known as the Ivy House on the Woolworth Estate. Warm, fireside dining, hot country breakfast.
info@mulburninn.com http://www.mulburninn.com

The Wayside Inn
PO Box 480
3738 Main St, Rte 302 03574
603-869-3364 Fax: 603-869-5765
800-448-9557
Victor & Kathe Hofmann
May-Oct. & Dec.-March

88-148-BB
26 rooms, 26 pb
Most CC, *Rated*
C-yes/S-ltd/P-no/H-yes
French, German

Full breakfast
Dinner available
Restaurant, bar, sitting rooms, cable TV, frplc, bocce court

New England Country Inn with a European flavour, where the whole family is welcome. Located by the Ammonoosuc River, our inn has invited travelers since it was built as a homestead in 1825. info@thewaysideinn.com http://www.thewaysideinn.com

BRADFORD

Candlelite Inn
5 Greenhouse Lane 03221
603-938-5571 Fax: 603-938-2564
888-812-5571
Marilyn & Les Gordon
All year

90-125-BB
6 rooms, 6 pb
Most CC, *Rated*
C-ltd/S-no/P-no/H-no

Full gourmet breakfast
Snacks
Fireplace in parlor, gazebo porch, woodstove, sun rooms, games

Lovely country Victorian Inn w/ handmade cross stitch, tole painting, quilts. Breakfast served in sun room overlooking pond & countryside.
candlelite@conknet.com http://www.candleliteinn.com

Mountain Lake Inn
PO Box 443
2871 Rt 114 03221
603-938-2136 Fax: 603-938-5622
800-662-6005
Bob & Tracy Foor
All year

80-85-BB
9 rooms, 9 pb
Most CC
C-yes/S-no/P-ltd/H-no
Spanish

Full country breakfast
Afternoon tea
Sitting room, library, full porch, beach, piano

An 18th century inn overlooking lovely Lake Massasecum and the splendid mountain peaks. innkeeper@mountainlakeinn.com http://www.mountainlakeinn.com

---

Rosewood Country Inn
67 Pleasant View Rd 03221
603-938-5253 800-938-5273
Dick & Lesley Marquis
All year

119-269-BB
11 rooms, 11 pb
Most CC, *Rated*, •
C-ltd/S-ltd/P-no/H-ltd
French

3 course candlelight & crystal
In-room sherry
Sitting room, Jacuzzis, suites, fireplace, cable TV, conference

Selected as NH's and Pamela Lanier's "Inn of the Year!" Romantic country hideaway furnished in antiques, with award-winning gardens, pond and Victorian gazebo.
rosewood@conknet.com http://www.rosewoodcountryinn.com

Candlelite Inn, Bradford, NH

BRADFORD

Thistle & Shamrock Inn & Rest.
11 W Main St 03221
603-938-5553 Fax: 603-938-5554
888-938-5553
Jim & Lynn Horigan
All year

85-140-BB
10 rooms, 10 pb
Most CC, •
C-yes/S-no/P-no/H-yes

Full breakfast
Restaurant, bar service
Dinner (fee), Sitting room, library, family friendly facility

Discover the quiet corner of New Hampshire in our historic 1898 Inn. B&B accommodations, great breakfasts, and casual gourmet dining.
stay@thistleandshamrock.com http://www.thistleandshamrock.com

CAMPTON

Mountain Fare Inn
PO Box 553
Mad River Road 03223
603-726-4283 Fax: 603-726-4285
Susan & Nick Preston
All year

75-145-BB
10 rooms, 10 pb
Visa, MC, Disc, *Rated*, •
C-yes/S-no/P-ltd/H-ltd
French

Full breakfast
Tea, snacks, wine
Sitting room, suites, fireplace, cable TV, conference, sauna, soccer field

Lovely 1830's village farmhouse. Summer gardens, foliage in fall, a skiers lodge in winter.
mtnfareinn@cyberportal.net http://www.mountainfareinn.com

CHARLESTOWN

Maple Hedge Inn
PO Box 638
355 Main St 03603
603-826-5237 Fax: 603-826-3237
800-9-MAPLE9
Joan & Dick DeBrine

90-145-BB
5 rooms, 5 pb
Visa, MC, *Rated*, •
C-ltd/S-ltd/P-no/H-no
Closed January–March

Full 3-course breakfast
Wine & cheese hour 5-6pm
Sitting room, library, fireplace, biking, golf, horseshoes, antiquing

Luxurious accommodations in elegant home set among lovely gardens & 200 year-old maples. Part of longest National District in New Hampshire.
debrine@fmis.net http://www.maplehedge.com

CLAREMONT

Goddard Mansion
25 Hillstead Rd 03743
603-543-0603 Fax: 603-543-0001
800-736-0603
Debbie Albee All year

75-125-BB
10 rooms, 3 pb
Visa, MC, AmEx, *Rated*
C-yes/S-no/P-no/H-ltd
French

Full breakfast
Snacks
Sitting room, library, bicycles, 1 king-size room, golf & tennis nearby

Delightful, c.1902, 18 room English Manor style mansion, acres of lawns, gardens, easy elegance yet comfortable/homey atmosphere.
deb@goddardmansion.com http://www.goddardmansion.com

Mountain Lake Inn, Bradford, NH

DIXVILLE NOTCH

The Balsams Grand Resort Hotel
Route 26 03576
603-255-3400 800-255-0600
Steve Barba
May-Oct; Dec-Mar

AP
203 rooms
Rated, •
C-yes/S-ltd/P-no/H-yes
French

Full breakfast
3 meals except winter (2 mls); snacks, rest./bar
Sitting rm, library, bikes, tennis, Jacuzzis, pool, suites

15,000-acre private estate high in New Hampshire mountains. American plan hospitality—one rate includes accommodations, meals, facilities use, entertainment and much more.
thebalsams@aol.com http://www.thebalsams.com

DURHAM (REGION)

Under the Elm
308 Ridge Rd, *Northwood* 03261
603-942-8318 Fax: 603-942-5244
Rosemary James All year

75-110-BB
4 rooms, 2 pb
C-ltd/S-no/P-no/H-no

Full breakfast
Social Room, Reading Alcove, Three season porch, beaver pond, 40 acres

Restored 1782 Cape historic landmark, shaded by one of the few surviving Elm Trees in NH. On 40 acres and at the area's highest elevation. Centrally located for relaxing & enjoying all that NH offers. info@undertheelm.com http://www.undertheelm.com

EAST ANDOVER

Highland Lake Inn
PO Box 164
32 Maple Street 03231
603-735-6426 Fax: 603-735-5355
Steve & Judee Hodges
All year

85-125-BB
10 rooms, 10 pb
Most CC, *Rated*
C-ltd/S-no/P-no/H-no

Full country breakfast
Complimentary soda, snacks and tea
Common Area with cable TV, VCR, stone fireplace, library; private beach

Graciously restored 1767 farmhouse on seven acres, with scenic lake and mountain views. Year round recreation. Ten spacious guestrooms, all with private baths, some fireplaces. AAA three diamonds. highlandlakeinn@msn.com http://www.highlandlakeinn.com

ENFIELD

Mary Keane House
93 Chosen Vale Ln 03748
603-632-4241 888-239-2153
Sharon & David Carr
All year

85-155-BB
4 rooms, 4 pb
Most CC, •
C-yes/S-no/P-yes/H-no

Full breakfast
Snacks
Sitting room, bicycles, suites, cable TV, private beach, canoes

Gracious lakeside Victorian style B&B, with spacious rooms, balconies and porches, furnished with antiques, vintage linens and touches of whimsy.
mary.keane.house@valley.net http://www.marykeanehouse.com

ENFIELD

Shaker Hill
259 Shaker Hill Rd
RR 4 Box 100 03748
603-632-4519 Fax: 603-632-4082
877-516-1370
Nancy & Allen Smith
All year

75-95-BB
4 rooms, 4 pb
Visa, MC
C-ltd/S-no/P-no/H-no

Full breakfast
Afternoon tea, snacks
Sitting room, accommodate business travelers

Newly renovated 1790's Colonial farmhouse. Gardens and wrap-around porch, newly decorated rooms with down comforters and pillows. All private baths.
info@shakerhill.com http://www.shakerhill.com

EXETER (REGION)

The Curtis Field House
735 Exeter Rd, *Hampton* 03842
603-929-0082
Mary Houston
May-October

85-90-BB
3 rooms, 2 pb
Visa, MC, *Rated*
C-ltd/S-ltd/P-no

Full breakfast
Dinner upon request
Afternoon tea, sundeck, sitting room, library, tennis courts, pool, A/C

Royal Bairy Wills Cape-country setting. Near Phillips Exeter, antiques, historical area, ocean. Breakfast served on terrace. gadabout@ttlc.net

FRANCONIA

Franconia Inn
1300 Easton Rd 03580
603-823-5542 Fax: 603-823-8078
800-473-5299
The Morris Family
Mem. Day–Oct; 12/15-4/1

150-210-BB
35 rooms, 34 pb
Most CC, *Rated*, •
C-yes/S-yes/P-no/H-no

Full breakfast
Restaurant, full bar
Lounge with movies, library, bicycles, heated pool

Since1863, The Franconia Inn has welcomed guests with the tranquil appeal of country life, in an elegant setting that is both unpretentious and inviting.
info@franconiainn.com http://www.franconiainn.com

Historic Lovetts Inn
1474 Profile Rd
Rt 18 03580
603-823-7761 Fax: 603-823-8802
800-356-3802
Janet & Jim Freitas
All year

125-235-BB
21 rooms, 21 pb
Visa, MC, Disc
S-no

Full country breakfast
Afternoon tea

Built in 1904 and listed on the National Register of Historic Places, the Lovetts Inn offers a variety of accommodations in either the historic inn or intimate cottages, most with fireplaces. lovetts@earthlink.net http://www.lovettsinn.com

---

Horse and Hound Inn
205 Wells Rd 03580
603-823-5501 Fax: 603-823-5501
800-450-5501
Bill Steele & Jim Cantlon
All year

90-135-BB
10 rooms, 8 pb
Most CC, *Rated*, •
C-yes/S-yes/P-yes/H-no

Full breakfast

1830 Farmhouse renovated in 1946 to an old fashioned New England B&B.
hound@together.net

Sugar Hill Inn
Route 117
Sugar Hill 03580
603-823-5621 Fax: 603-823-5639
800-548-4748
Judy& Orlo Coots
All year

125-375-BB
16 rooms, 16 pb
Visa, MC, AmEx, *Rated*, •
C-yes/S-no/P-no/H-no

Full 3-course breakfast
Dining Thursday-Sunday, Pub
Guitar, Jacuzzi, gardens, picnic lunches, massages, facials

Incredible lodging, food and hospitality. Considered to have some of the finest mountain views in New Hampshire. info@sugarhillinn.com http://www.sugarhillinn.com

FRANCONIA (REGION)

Sunset Hill House–A Grand Inn 231 Sunset Hill Rd, *Sugar Hill* 03585 603-823-5522 Fax: 603-823-5738 800-SUN-HILL Lon, Nancy, Mary Pearl & Adeline Henderson	100-495-BB 28 rooms, 28 pb Most CC, *Rated*, • C-ltd/S-no/P-no/H-yes German, French All year	Full breakfast Tea, coffee all day, afternoon home-baked cookies Htd pool, onsite golf, 3 parlors, fine dining, casual tavern, conf rm, gdns

New England's most spectacular mountain views ("Best views with a Room," Yankee '99). "NH's most spectacular Meal," NH Magazine '01.

innkeeper@sunsethillhouse.com http://www.sunsethillhouse.com

FRANKLIN

Atwood Inn 71 Hill Rd, Rt#3A 03235 603-934-3666 Sandy Hoffmeister All year	80-90-BB 7 rooms, 7 pb Most CC S-no/P-no	Full breakfast Compl. snacks, beverages, fruit & cookies

Surrounded by lush green trees & shrubbery, lies the Maria Atwood Inn. You will be taken back into a different time by the allure and mystique of this house.

atwoodinn@cyberportal.net http://www.atwoodinn.com

GLEN

Bernerhof Inn PO Box 240 Rte 302 03838 603-383-9132 Fax: 603-383-0809 800-548-8007 Carla Schneider All year	79-175-BB 9 rooms, 9 pb Most CC, *Rated* C-ltd/S-no/P-no/H-no	Full breakfast Lunch (limited), dinner Restaurant, pub, sitting room, cooking school, outdoor pool, cable TV, phone

Elegant Victorian Inn. Individually appointed rooms w/ Jacuzzi, fireplace & suites. Romantic escape packages. Host of A Taste of the Mountains Cooking School. Pamper yourself. you deserve it! stay@bernerhofinn.com http://www.bernerhofinn.com

GREENFIELD

Greenfield Inn PO Box 400 749 Forest Rd 03047 603-547-6327 Fax: 603-547-2418 800-678-4144	49-149-BB 13 rooms, 10 pb Visa, MC, *Rated*, • C-yes/S-ltd/P-no/H-no Vic All year	Full breakfast Lunch (for groups to 12) Comp. wine, tea, coffee, Jacuzzis, hayloft suite, conf., cottage, phones

Play hooky. Make it together. 90 minutes from Boston.

greenfieldinn@earthlink.net http://www.greenfieldinn.com

HAMPSTEAD

Stillmeadow at Hampstead PO Box 565 545 Main St 03841 603-329-8381 Fax: 603-329-0137 Lori Offord All year	65-100-BB 4 rooms, 4 pb Most CC, *Rated* C-ltd/S-no/P-no/H-no Some French, Ger., Sp.	Continental plus breakfast Comp. wine and cookies Croquet, gardens, bikes, near lake & cross-country skiing, conf., phones

Discover Southern New Hampshire's best kept secret. Memorable, charming getaway. Inviting Greek Revival Colonial with 5 chimneys and 3 staircases.

stillmeadowb@yahoo.com

HAMPTON (REGION)

D.W.'s Oceanside Inn 365 Ocean Blvd, *Hampton Beach* 03842 603-926-3542 Fax: 603-926-3549 866-OCEANSIDE Duane & Debbie Windemiller	125-215-BB 10 rooms, 10 pb Most CC, *Rated*, • C-no/S-no/P-no/H-no Mid-May to Mid-Oct.	Choice of breakfast items off menu Self-service bar on back deck, sitting room/library, beach chairs & towels

Elegantly appointed inn, unique to NH seacoast. Directly across from sandy beach. During mid-summer, area has an active, resort-type atmosphere. Inn itself is very quiet. Many recent renovations. info@oceansideinn.com http://www.oceansideinn.com

HANOVER

The Trumbull House
49 Etna Rd 03755
603-643-2370 Fax: 603-643-2430
800-651-5141
Hilary Pridgen
All year

100-280-BB
5 rooms, 5 pb

Conference center

Hanover's first and finest Bed & Breakfast offers luxury country lodgings just four miles east of Dartmouth College and three miles from the Dartmouth-Hitchcock Medical Center. bnb@valley.net http://www.trumbullhouse.com

HAVERHILL

Gibson House
341 DCH
Rt 10 & Court St 03765
603-989-3125 Fax: 603-989-5749
Keita Colton

140-190-BB
7 rooms, 4 pb
Rated, •
P-ltd/H-no
All year

Full breakfast
Complimentary wine, snacks, afternoon tea
Sitting room, library, tennis court, fireplaces

1850s Stagecoach Inn beautifully redone by artist/owner. Gallery, antiques throughout, murals. 50 ft porches with sunset views of Connecticut River Valley, overlooks gardens, lilypond, wildflower meadow.
gibsonhs@ix.netcom.com http://www.gibsonhousebb.com

HENNIKER

Colby Hill Inn
PO Box 779
3 The Oaks 03242
603-428-3281 Fax: 603-428-9218
800-531-0330
Cynthia & Mason Cobb

110-200-BB
16 rooms, 16 pb
Most CC, *Rated*, •
C-ltd/S-no/P-no/H-ltd
All year

Full breakfast
Dinner, complimentary beverages, full bar
Bar, cookies, sitting room, library, A/C, croquet, badminton, pool

Classic New England country inn. 16 romantic and antique-filled guestrooms, all with private baths and some with fireplaces. Candlelit fine dining overlooking perennial gardens and antique barns. innkeeper@colbyhillinn.com http://www.colbyhillinn.com

HOLDERNESS

The Inn on Golden Pond
PO Box 680
Route 3 03245
603-968-7269 Fax: 603-968-9226
Bill & Bonnie Webb All year

120-175-BB
8 rooms, 8 pb
Visa, MC, *Rated*, •
C-ltd/S-no/P-no/H-no

Full breakfast
Piano, air conditioned rooms, full service restaurant

Located on 55 wooded acres across the street from Squam Lake, setting for "On Golden Pond." innongp@lr.net http://www.innongoldenpond.com

---

The Manor on Golden Pond
PO Box T
Rt 3 & Shepard Hill Rd 03245
603-968-3348 Fax: 603-968-2116
800-545-2141
Brian & Mary Ellen Shields

175-375-BB
27 rooms, 27 pb
Most CC, *Rated*, •
C-ltd/S-no/P-no/H-no
All year

Full breakfast
Afternoon Tea
Clay Tennis Court, Pool, Private Beach, Lawn Games

Elegant, AAA 4 diamond country inn on 15 hillside acres overlooking Squam Lake. Many rooms have working fireplaces and beautiful views; several have Jacuzzis for two.
info@manorongoldenpond.com http://www.manorongoldenpond.com

JACKSON

Carter Notch Inn
PO Box 269
Carter Notch Rd 03846
603-383-9630 Fax: 603-383-9642
800-794-9434
Jim & Lynda Dunwell & Tucker (chocolate lab)

79-189-BB
8 rooms, 8 pb
Most CC, *Rated*, •
C-ltd/S-no/P-no/H-no
Dec–March, May–Oct

Full breakfast
Afternoon tea, complimentary wine
Sitting room, tennis court, Jacuzzis, swimming pool, cable TV, suites

Perched on a hillside overlooking the river & golf course with panoramic mountain views. Wraparound front porch, impeccably clean rooms. Honeymoon suites with Jacuzzis & private balconies. jimdunwell@earthlink.net http://www.carternotchinn.com

JACKSON

Crowes' Nest
Thorn Mountain Rd 03846
603-383-8913 Fax: 603-383-8241
800-511-8383
Christine & Myles Crowe
All year

99-215-BB
7 rooms, 7 pb
Most CC, *Rated*, •
C-ltd/S-no/P-no/H-ltd
French

Gourmet breakfast
Afternoon tea
Three beautifully appointed common areas, patio, access to pool, tennis,golf

We offer exquisite views, impeccably appointed rooms minutes to the splendor of Mt Washington. tcnest@crowesnest.net http://www.crowesnest.net/

Dana Place Inn
PO Box 48
Route 16, Pinkham Notch 03846
603-383-6822 Fax: 603-383-6022
800-537-9276
The Levine Family
All year

155-250-BB
35 rooms, 31 pb
Most CC, *Rated*, •
C-yes/S-yes/P-yes/H-no
French

Full breakfast in season
Dinner, pub, wine list, dinner, box lunch
Piano, river swimming, indoor pool, tennis courts, Jacuzzi

Historic country inn, fine dining, three 2-room family suites, pub, views of Mount Washington. contact@danaplace.com http://www.danaplace.com

---

Ellis River House
PO Box 656
Route 16 03846
603-383-9339 Fax: 603-383-4142
800-233-8309
Monica & Jim Lee
All year

95-255-BB
20 rooms, 20 pb
Most CC, *Rated*, •
C-ltd/S-no/P-no/H-yes
Italian

Full country breakfast
Tea, coffee, cookies
Tavern with billiards, darts, cable, fishing, atrium with Jacuzzi, sauna

An enchanting country inn offering romance and rejuvenation nestled in the heart of the White Mts. Let the serenity of the Ellis River House rekindle relationships and create unforgettable memories. innkeeper@erhinn.com http://www.ellisriverhouse.com

---

Inn at Jackson
PO Box 807
Main St & Thorn Hill Rd 03846
603-383-4321 Fax: 603-383-4085
800-289-8600
Lori Tradewell All year

99-199-BB
14 rooms, 14 pb
Most CC, *Rated*, •
C-ltd/S-ltd/P-no/H-no

Full breakfast
Library, sitting room, fireplaces, A/C, TVs, outdoor hot tub Jacuzzi

Stanford White mansion in the heart of the White Mountains. Adjacent to Jackson ski touring trails. info@innatjackson.com http://www.innatjackson.com

---

Nestlenook Farm on the River
PO Box Q
Dinsmore Road 03846
603-383-9443 Fax: 603-383-4515
800-659-9443
Robert C. Cyr All year

125-320-BB
7 rooms, 7 pb
Visa, MC, Disc, *Rated*, •
C-ltd/S-no/P-no/H-no

Full breakfast
Social hour wine/snacks
Sitting room, bikes, pool, skating, snowshoeing, Austrian sleigh rides

Experience the romance of Victorian elegance on our 65-acre estate. 7 guestrooms, w/private 2-person Jacuzzi bathroom & period antiques.
inn@lmgnh.com.com http://www.nestlenook.com

Paisley and Parsley
PO Box 298
Black Mountain Rd 03846
603-383-0859 Fax: 603-383-3629
Bob & Suzanne Scolamiero
All year

100-135-BB
2 rooms, 2 pb
Visa, MC, AmEx, •
C-ltd/S-no/P-no

Full breakfast

Beautifully situated on a birch-covered hill, surrounded by lush perennial and herb gardens, grape and rose arbors, and woodland paths. Spectacular mountain views including Mt. Washington. welcome@paisleyandparsley.com http://www.paisleyandparsley.com

JAFFREY (REGION)

Woodbound Inn
62 Woodbound Rd, *Rindge* 03461
603-532-8341 Fax: 603-532-8341
800-688-7770
Kohlmorgen Family
All year

79-149-BB
40 rooms, 36 pb
Most CC, *Rated*, •
C-yes/S-ltd/P-no/H-yes

Full breakfast
Restaurant, aftn. tea
Sitting room, library, tennis court, lake, 9-hole golf, cross-country skiing

1890 inn, quintessentially New England; classic American cuisine.
woodbound@aol.com http://www.woodbound.com

JEFFERSON

The Jefferson Inn
6 Renaissance Lane
Route #2 03583
603-586-7998 Fax: 603-586-7808
800-729-7908
Mark & Cindy Robert, Bette Bovio
All year

75-175-BB
11 rooms, 11 pb
Most CC, *Rated*, •
C-yes/S-no/P-no/H-yes

Full breakfast
Tea, cocoa, homemade baked goods
Two common rooms, board games, spring-fed swimming pond

A charming 1896 Victorian nestled in the Northern White Mountains, near Mount Washington. Spectacular views and outdoor adventures year-round. Perfect for a romantic getaway or a family vacation. jeffinn@ncia.net http://www.jeffersoninn.com

KEENE

The Wright Mansion Inn
695 Court St. 03431
603-355-2288 Fax: 603-355-8829
800-352-5890
William Hermann
All year

80-175-BB
6 rooms, 4 pb
Visa, MC, AmEx, Most CC, *Rated*, •
C-ltd/S-no/P-no/H-ltd

Continental breakfast
Afternoon snacks, tea, dinner, restaurant, bar
Library, bicycles, tennis court, fireplaces, cable TV

The Inn is a restored Georgian manor house with antique and reproduction furnishings and lovely landscaped grounds. innkpr@cheshire.net http://www.flythere.com/wright/

KEENE (REGION)

Inn of the Tartan Fox
350 Old Homestead Hwy, *Swanzey* 03446
603-357-9308 877 836 4319
Wayne or Meg
All year

80-150-BB
4 rooms, 4 pb
Visa, MC, AmEx
C-ltd/S-no/P-no/H-yes

Four Course Gourmet Breakfast
Library, gardens

1832 Manorhouse with Celtic styled rooms. Antiques, private baths, heated marble floors, fireplaces, gift shop. One fully accessible room. Scrumptious gourmet breakfast. 3 miles to Main St. Keene. travelguides@tartanfox.com http://www.tartanfox.com

LACONIA (REGION)

The Inn at Smith Cove
19 Roberts Rd, *Gilford* 03249
603-293-1111 Fax: 603-293-7660
Bob & Maria Ruggiero
All year

90-170-BB
11 rooms, 11 pb
Most CC, *Rated*
C-ltd/S-no/P-no/H-no

Continental breakfast
Sitting room, Jacuzzis, private beach, gazebo, boat slips, antiques

Circa 1898 Victorian on Lake Winnepesaukee. Close to Gunstock ski area, outlet shopping, golf courses, health club, fishing, hiking. http://www.innatsmithcove.com

LEBANON

B&B of Bank Street
93 Bank St 03766
603-448-2041
Charles & Alean Hunnewell
All year

70-100-BB
5 rooms, 3 pb
Visa, MC, AmEx
S-no/P-ltd/H-ltd

Full breakfast

Lovely 1875 Gingerbread Victorian home with lovely rooms and a nutritious, full breakfast. Walking distance to downtown restaurants, recreation center, biking/hiking trails.
bbbankst@aol.com

LINCOLN

The Red Sleigh Inn PO Box 562 Pollard Rd 03251 603-745-8517 Fax: 603-745-8517 Bill & Loretta Deppe All year	85-110-BB 7 rooms, 3 pb Visa, MC, *Rated* C-ltd/S-no/P-no/H-no	Full vegetarian breakfast Complimentary tea Sitting room, library

Mountains surrounding us abound in ski touring trails. Bedrooms are tastefully decorated with many antiques. redsleigh@adelphia.net http://www.redsleighinn.com

LISBON

Ammonoosuc Inn 641 Bishop Rd 03585 603-838-6118 Fax: 603-838-5591 888-838-6118 Jeni & Jim Lewis All year	75-130-BB 9 rooms, 9 pb Visa, MC, *Rated*, • C-yes/S-ltd/P-ltd/H-ltd	Full Breakfast Tea & hot chocolate anytime Large wrap-around porch, wicker furniture, common rooms & pub

Tucked away on a wooded hillside overlooking the Ammonoosuc River, sits our peaceful, quiet, and restful inn, surrounded by a golf course and the foothills of the White Mountains. info@amminn.com http://www.amminn.com

LITTLETON

The Beal House Inn 2 W Main St 03561 603-444-2661 Fax: 603-444-6224 888-616-BEAL Catherine & Jose Luis Pawelek All year	115-235-BB 8 rooms, 8 pb Visa, MC, AmEx, *Rated*, • C-no/S-no/P-no/H-no French, German, Dutch, Spanish, Italian	Full gourmet breakfast Dinner, snacks, tea, bar Restaurant, parlor, phone, suites, fireplace, satellite TV, spa

Historic 1833 Inn on Main Street in the quaint town of Littleton, ranked 9th best small town in the U.S. The Inn is furnished with antiques and has 3 guestrooms & 5 suites, all with private bathroom. info@bealhouseinn.com http://www.bealhouseinn.com

Edencroft Inn 120 North Littleton Road 03561 603-444-1158 Fax: 603-444-5671 877-460-7101 Dan & Kathy Hinds All year	110-210-BB 7 rooms, 7 pb Most CC, *Rated* C-ltd/S-no/P-no/H-ltd	Full breakfast Fireplaces, whirlpool tubs, spacious guest com. areas, gift shop, antiques

"Fall in Love with the North Country" at EDENCROFT INN, where guests are given a warm welcome and a stay filled with pampering and special touches ... the perfect romantic getaway. stay@edencroftinn.com http://www.edencroftinn.com

LYME

Loch Lyme Lodge 70 Orford Rd, Route 10 03768 603-795-2141 Paul & Judy Barker All year	BB	

Loch Lyme Lodge has been offering affordable family vacations for over 80 years. lochlymelodge@valley.net http://www.lochlymelodge.com

MADISON

Maple Grove House PO Box 340 21 Maple Grove Rd 03849 603-367-8208 877-367-8208 Don and Celia Pray All year	85-105-BB 6 rooms, 6 pb C-ltd/P-no	Full breakfast

Set on a knoll and over looking the White Mountains of New Hampshire, this turn-of-the-century guest house has been completely renovated.
info@maplegrovehouse.com http://www.maplegrovehouse.com

MANCHESTER (REGION)

Breezy Hill
119 Adams Rd, *Londonderry* 03053
603-432-0122 Fax: 603-432-0511
Emily & Ron Foley
All year

75-95-BB
4 rooms, 2 pb
Visa, MC
C-yes/S-ltd/P-no/H-no

Full breakfast
Sitting room, cable TV, swimming pool, fishing, canoeing, books

An 1850s New England farmhouse, wonderful farm fresh breakfasts. Guests enjoy beautiful views of acres of orchardland; seasonal pool.
breezyhill@worldnet.att.net http://www.breezyhill.com

Stepping Stones
6 Bennington Battle Trail, *Wilton Center* 03086
603-654-9048 888-654-9048
Ann Carlsmith All year

65-75-BB
3 rooms, 3 pb
Rated, •
C-yes/S-ltd/P-ltd/H-no

Full breakfast
Complimentary tea, wine
Stereo, color TV, looms, library, sitting room, breakfast room, gardens

Quiet country setting in Monadnock hills, near picture-book village. Summer theater & music. acarlsmith@steppingstonesbb.com http://www.steppingstonesbb.com

MARLBOROUGH

Peep-Willow Farm
51 Bixby St 03455
603-876-3807
Noel Aderer All year

75-BB
3 rooms, 1 pb
•
C-yes/S-no/P-yes/H-no

Full breakfast
Complimentary wine
Snacks, sitting room, trails, cross country skiing

18-acre working thoroughbred horse farm Bed and Breakfast. Relax on the farm, visit with the livestock, sit on the terrace and enjoy breathtaking views. No riding available.
naderer@cheshire.net http://www.peepwillowfarm.com

MEREDITH

Inns at Mill Falls
312 Daniel Webster Hwy
Route 3 & 25 03253
603-279-7006 Fax: 603-279-6797
800-622-6455
Gail Batstone All year

99-289-EP
101 rooms, 101 pb
Most CC, *Rated*, •
C-yes/S-ltd/P-no/H-yes

Lunch, dinner, restaurant, snacks
Jacuzzis, swimming pool, suites, fireplaces, cable TV, fitness room

The Inns offer the ultimate in comfort & relaxation. Three lovely distinctive Inns surround our 40' waterfall & 19th century restored linen mill.
info@millfalls.com http://www.millfalls.com

MOULTONBORO

Olde Orchard Inn
RR 1 Box 256
108 Lee Rd 03254
603-476-5004 Fax: 603-476-5419
800-598-5845
Jim & Mary Senner All year

75-175-BB
9 rooms, 6 pb
Visa, *Rated*, •
C-yes/S-no/P-ltd/H-ltd
French, Finnish

Full breakfast
Sitting room, fishing, library, bicycles, spa, sauna, conferences

C.1790 Federal nestled in twelve acre apple orchard. Furnished with antiques collected by former diplomat owners. Near large lake.
innkeep@oldeorchardinn.com http://www.oldeorchardinn.com

NEW LONDON

The Inn at Pleasant Lake
PO Box 1030
125 Pleasant Street 03257
603-526-6271 Fax: 603-526-4111
800-626-4907
Linda & Brian MacKenzie
All year

110-175-BB
10 rooms, 10 pb
Visa, MC, Disc, *Rated*
C-yes/S-no/P-no/H-ltd

Full breakfast
Continental breakfast, aft. . tea
Dinner, aftn. tea, rest., Bar service, sitting rm., Lake, conference

Ten well-appointed guestrooms. Full breakfast and aft. tea included. Panoramic views of Mt. Kearsarge and Pleasant Lake. Reservations required for five course pre-fixe dinner avail. Wed.-Sun. bmackenz@tds.net http://www.innatpleasantlake.com

NEW LONDON (REGION)

Follansbee Inn on Kezar Lake
PO Box 92
2 Keyser St, *North Sutton* 03260
603-927-4221 Fax: 603-927-6307
800-626-4221
Cathy & Dave Beard

90-165-BB
20 rooms, 16 pb
Visa, MC, *Rated*, •
C-ltd/S-no/P-no/H-no
All year except Mar–Apr, & Nov.

Full breakfast
Snacks, bar
Sitting room, bicycles, lake

You will find our Inn nestled in a quiet rural village with porch views of the town green and peaceful Kezar Lake. follansbeeinn@mcttelecom.com http://www.follansbeeinn.com

NORTH CONWAY

The 1785 Inn & Rest.
PO Box 1785
3582 White Mountain Hwy
03860
603-356-9025 Fax: 603-356-6081
800-421-1785
Becky & Charlie Mallar

69-199-BB
13 rooms, 8 pb
Visa, MC, AmEx, *Rated*, •
C-yes/S-ltd/P-ltd/H-ltd
French
All year

Full country breakfast
Restaurant, lounge
2 sitting rooms, piano, classical guitar Sat-Sun, ski/honeymoon pkgs, pool

Newly redecorated historic inn at the Scenic Vista, overlooking the Saco River Valley.
the1785inn@aol.com http://www.the1785inn.com

The Buttonwood Inn
PO Box 1817
Mt. Surprise Rd 03860
603-356-2625 Fax: 603-356-3140
800-258-2625
Peter & Claudia Needham

105-225-BB
10 rooms, 10 pb
Most CC, *Rated*, •
C-ltd/S-ltd/P-no/H-no
All year

Full breakfast
Large common rooms w/wood burning fireplaces, pool, TV/VCR & movies

1820's farmhouse on 17 secluded acres of fields and forests. Ten newly renovated guestrooms all with private baths.
innkeeper@buttonwoodinn.com http://www.buttonwoodinn.com

Cabernet Inn
PO Box 489
3552 White Mountain Hwy
03860
603-356-4704 Fax: 603-356-5399
800-866-4704
Debbie & Rich Howard

85-225-BB
11 rooms, 11 pb
Most CC, *Rated*, •
C-ltd/S-ltd/P-no/H-ltd
All year

Full breakfast
Aft. . tea, comp. wine on Spec. occasion, sitt. rm, 2 common rms. w/frplcs., upper deck for breakfast

Enjoy warmth and elegance of this romantic 1842 inn set among towering pines, just a stroll away from breathtaking view of Mt. Washington.
info@cabernetinn.com http://www.cabernetinn.com

Cranmore Inn
PO Box 1349
80 Kearsarge 03860
603-356-5502 800-526-5502
Chris & Virginia Kanzler
Closed December 24-25

64-115-BB
18 rooms, 14 pb
Visa, MC, AmEx, *Rated*, •
C-ltd/S-no/P-no/H-no
Spanish

Full breakfast
Afternoon tea
Sitting room, library, swimming pool, suites, cable TV

The Cranmore Inn is an authentic country inn, continuously operated since 1863. Antique furnishings and country prints lend charm to comfortably modern queen beds & facilities.
stay@cranmoreinn.com http://www.cranmoreinn.com

Eastman Inn
PO Box 882
Route 16/302 03860
603-356-6707 Fax: 603-356-7708
800-626-5855
Lea Greenwood & Tom Carter
All year

90-240-BB
14 rooms, 14 pb
Most CC
C-no/S-no/P-no/H-no

Full breakfast

Experience gracious Southern hospitality with New England flair in this award-winning bed and breakfast with a wraparound porch and spectacular views. Gourmet breakfasts and afternoon refreshments. innkeeper@eastmaninn.com http://www.eastmaninn.com

NORTH CONWAY

Locust Hill
PO Box 427
267 Kearsarge Rd 03860
603-356-6135
Cynthia & Conrad Briggs
All year

65-80-BB
1 rooms, 1 pb
Visa, MC, *Rated*, •
C-yes/S-no/P-no/H-no

Full breakfast
Sitting room, library, swimming pool, suites, cable TV

A Bed and Breakfast in the English tradition; vacation accommodations in a private home. innkeeper@locusthillnh.com http://www.locusthillnh.com

---

Merrill Farm Resort
428 White Mountain Hwy
Rte 16 03860
603-447-3866 Fax: 603-447-3867
800-445-1017
Michael R. Wilson All year

49-149-BB
60 rooms, 60 pb
Most CC, •
C-yes/S-yes/P-no/H-yes

Continental breakfast
Complimentary cookies, cider, beverages
A/C, color cable TV, private baths, telephones

Once a working farm over 100 years ago, Merrill Farm Resort offers rustic country charm with modern amenities in the heart of New Hampshire's White Mountains.
merrill2@ncia.net http://www.merrillfarm.com

Nereledge Inn
PO Box 547
94 River Rd 03860
603-356-2831 Fax: 603-356-7085
888-356-2831
Dave Halpin & Betsy Brisbois

64-159-BB
11 rooms, 5 pb
Most CC
C-yes/S-no/P-no/H-no
All year

Full breakfast
Afternoon refreshments
Large common areas w/fireplace, guest pantry with fridge & electric kettle

Old-fashioned 1787 inn, off Main Street in the village. Hearty country breakfasts, close to skiing, climbing, hiking, & biking. Walk to river for fly-fishing, swimming, and canoeing.
info@nereledgeinn.com http://www.nereledgeinn.com

Old Red Inn, LLC
PO Box 467
2406 White Mountain Hwy
03860
603-356-2642 Fax: 603-356-6626
800-338-1356
Terry & Dick Potochniak

78-158-BB
17 rooms, 15 pb
Most CC, *Rated*, •
C-yes/S-ltd/P-no/H-no
French
All year

Full breakfast
Kitchenettes
Living room w/woodstove, piano, herb garden, gardens, park, cable TV, pool

Enjoy warm hospitality in our four-season circa 1810 country inn and individually decorated cottages, featuring gas log fireplaces.
oldredinn@adelphia.com http://www.oldredinn.com

A Romantic Escape/Wyatt House
PO Box 777
Main St 03860
603-356-7977 Fax: 603-356-2183
800-527-7978
Bill & Arlene Strickland
All year

99-229-BB
7 rooms, 7 pb
Most CC, *Rated*, •
C-ltd/S-ltd/P-no/H-no

Multi-course gourmet by candlelight
Afternoon Tea w/homebaked goodies; Box Lunches
Romance and Elegance awaits you in a Two Person Jacuzzi with Fireplace!

Romance, Views, Pampering; Jacuzzi/Fpl; Bkfst in Bed or Gourmet Multicourse Bkfst by candlelight; walk Vlg/restaurants/shopping; swim/ski; Afternoon Tea Opulent and Intentionally Memorable. innkeeper@wyatthouseinn.com http://www.wyatthouseinn.com

---

Stonehurst Manor
PO Box 1937
Route 16 03860
603-356-3113 Fax: 603-356-3217
800-525-9100
Peter Rattay All year

116-176-MAP
25 rooms, 23 pb
Visa, MC, AmEx, *Rated*
C-yes/S-yes/P-no/H-yes
German

Full breakfast
Dinner included, tea/coffee
Library, piano, bar, swimming pool, hot tub, tennis, fireplaces

Turn-of-the-century mansion with old oak and stained glass. Relax by our fireplace in the library. Guided walking and hiking tours.
smanor@aol.com http://www.stonehurstmanor.com

NORTH CONWAY

The Victorian Harvest Inn	75-200-BB	Full breakfast
PO Box 1763	8 rooms, 8 pb	Sitting room, library,
28 Locust Ln 03860	Visa, MC, AmEx, *Rated*	swimming pool, suites,
603-356-3548 Fax: 603-356-8430	C-ltd/S-no/P-no/H-no	fireplaces, cable TV, Jacuzzi
800-642-0749		
David & Judy Wooster	All year	

1850s restored Victorian on quiet side street close to village, outlet shopping, restaurants, hiking trails. All private baths, pool, antiques and gardens.
info@victorianharvestinn.com http://www.victorianharvestinn.com

NORTH CONWAY (REGION)

The Notchland Inn	185-295-BB	Full country breakfast
Route 302, *Hart's Location*	14 rooms, 14 pb	Dinner, restaurant, bar
03812	Most CC, *Rated*, •	beverages, wines & beer
603-374-6131 Fax: 603-374-6168	C-ltd/S-no/P-ltd/H-ltd	Sitting room, library,
800-866-6131		Jacuzzis, suites, fireplaces,
Ed Butler & Les Schoof	All year	conference, hot tub

Comfortably elegant 1860s mansion on 100 forested acres. 7 spacious rooms & 6 suites, each appointed with Wood-burning fireplaces. Recently added, a separate cottage where children & pets are welcome. innkeepers@notchland.com http://www.notchland.com

---

Snowvillage Inn	129-249-BB	Full breakfast
Stuart Rd, Box 68, *Snowville*	18 rooms, 18 pb	
03832	*Rated*, •	
603-447-2818 Fax: 603-447-5268	C-ltd/S-no/P-no	
800-447-4345		
Kevin, Caitlin, Maggie Flynn	All year	

As visitors ascend the hill, they see why Yankee Magazine said the Snowvillage Inn is as perfect as an Inn gets. kevin@snowvillageinn.com http://www.snowvillageinn.com

NORTH WOODSTOCK

Wilderness Inn	65-155-BB	Full gourmet breakfast
RFD 1, Box 69	8 rooms, 8 pb	(menu)
Route 3 & 112 03262	Visa, MC, AmEx,	Aft. . tea, hot cider, cocoa,
603-745-3890 800-200-9453	*Rated*, •	lemonade
Michael & Rosanna Yarnell	C-yes/S-no/P-no/H-no	3 porches, fireplace living rm
All year	French, Italian, Hindi,	& cottage, cable TV all rms, 3
	Amharic	rms w/Jacuzzis

"The quintessential country inn." Circa 1912, located in quaint New England town. Inn & rooms furnished with antiques & Oriental carpets.
info@thewildernessinn.com http://www.thewildernessinn.com

Woodstock Inn	63-215	
80 Main Street 03262	19 rooms, 11 pb	
603-745-3951 800-321-3985		
Scott & Eileen Rice		

One of the most visited country inns in the White Mountains. 24 rooms with cable TV, A/C, and in-room phone; some with Jacuzzis and gas fireplaces. Hearty breakfast at Clement Room Grille included.

NORTHWOOD

Meadow Farm	70-85-BB	Full breakfast
454 Jenness Pond Rd 03261	3 rooms	Private beach, canoeing,
603-942-8619 Fax: 603-942-5731	C-ltd/S-ltd/P-ltd/H-no	sitting room, antiquing,
Janet & Doug Briggs	All year	cottage on lake for rent

Restored charming 1770 Colonial home—50 acres of fields, woods. Private beach on lake. Ideal setting for country weddings.
amcalan@worldpath.net http://www.bbonline.com/nh/meadowfarm/

PETERBOROUGH

Peterborough Manor
50 Summer St 03458
603-924-9832
Peter & Ann Harrison
All year

65-75-BB
7 rooms, 6 pb
Most CC
C-yes/S-no/P-ltd/H-ltd
Australian

Continental breakfast

The Peterborough manor offers simple affordable accommodations, All rooms are spacious clean and comfortable Queen beds, Private baths TV, and phones.

himanor@weaver.mv.com http://www.peterboroughmanor.com

PLYMOUTH

Colonel Spencer Inn
PO Box 206
Route 3, Campton 03264
603-536-3438
Carolyn & Alan Hill
All year

55-75-BB
7 rooms, 7 pb
Rated
C-yes/S-no/P-no/H-no

Full breakfast
Snacks
Sitting room, tennis court, cable TV

PORTSMOUTH

The Governor's House
32 Miller Ave 03801
603-427-5140 Fax: 603-427-5145
866-427-5140
Bob Chaffee
All year

175-275-BB
4 rooms, 4 pb
Most CC, •
C-ltd/S-no/P-no/H-no

Continental plus breakfast
Wine, tea, chocolate, bottled water, soda, juice
Tennis court, hot tub, library, bikes

Built in 1917, this stately Georgian colonial was the home of NH Governor Charles Dale from 1930 to 1964. The Governor's House offers an atmosphere of casual elegance to discriminating travelers.

info@governors-house.com http://www.governors-house.com

Inn at Strawbery Banke
314 Court St 03801
603-436-7242 800-428-3933
Sarah Glover O'Donnell
All year

100-150-BB
7 rooms, 7 pb
Visa, MC, AmEx, *Rated*
C-ltd/S-no/P-no/H-ltd

Full breakfast
Sitting room, outdoor garden, bikes, all guest rooms have A/C

This colonial inn charms travelers with its beautiful rooms and outdoor garden. Located in heart of Portsmouth with its quaint shops, working port, parks and historical homes.

http://innatstrawberybanke.com

Martin Hill Inn
404 Islington St 03801
603-436-2287
Jane & Paul Harnden
All year

120-150-BB
7 rooms, 7 pb
Visa, MC, *Rated*
C-ltd/S-no/P-no/H-no

Full breakfast
All rooms have writing, tables and sofas or, separate sitting areas

1810 Colonial has beautifully appointed rooms with period antiques. Elegant yet comfortable.

http://www.portsmouthnh.com/martinhillinn

PORTSMOUTH (REGION)

Three Chimneys Inn
17 Newmarket Rd, *Durham* 03824
603-868-7800
Fax: 603-868-2964
888-399-9777
Ron Peterson
All year

119-199-BB
24 rooms, 24 pb
Most CC, *Rated*, •
C-ltd/S-no/P-no/H-yes

Full breakfast
Lunch, dinner, aft. . tea
Snacks, rest., bar serv., sitt. rm., lib., cable, Jacuzzis, fireplaces

A newly restored 1649 Homestead offers 24 guestrooms, Georgian furnishings.

chimney3@threechimneysinn.com http://www.threechimneysinn.com

PORTSMOUTH (REGION)

High Meadows
2 Brixham Rd, Rt 101, *Eliot, ME* 03903
207-439-0590 Fax: 207-439-6343
Elaine & Ray Michaud
April-November

80-110-BB
4 rooms, 4 pb
Rated

Full breakfast
Afternoon wine, tea
Sitting room, Barn available for parties and weddings

1736 colonial house in the country. Walking & cross-country ski trails.
info@highmeadowsbnb.com http://www.highmeadowsbnb.com

ROCHESTER

Agnes Pease House
1 May St 03867
603-332-5509 Fax: 603-332-7276
M. Susan Clemons
All year

75-160-BB
5 rooms, 5 pb
Visa, MC, AmEx
C-yes/S-ltd/P-ltd/H-no

Full breakfast
Complimentary brandy
Sitting room, library, suites, cable TV, TV/VCR, phones, internet

Wonderfully restored Victorian and Gardens. The flavor of a small European hotel but with all the amenities of large, four star establishments.
msclemons@ttlc.net http://www.agnespeasehouse.com

SANBORNTON

Shaker Woods Farm
30 Lower Smith Rd 03269
603-528-1990 Fax: 530-481-5153
Eva Dunn & Jack Potter
All year

50-85-BB
6 rooms, 2 pb
Visa, MC, Disc
C-ltd/S-no/P-no/H-no

Full breakfast
Sitting room, cable TV, accom. bus. travelers

Your hosts, Eva & Jack, have built their dream farm with a B&B furnished from their worldwide Air Force assignments. They are nestled against the woods on a quiet road.
info@shakerwoodsfarm.com http://www.shakerwoodsfarm.com

SHELBURNE

Mt. Washington
421 SR 2 03581
603-466-2669 877-466-2399
Mary Ann Mayer
All year

50-160-BB
7 rooms, 7 pb
Visa, MC
C-yes/S-no/P-no/H-no

Full breakfast
Afternoon snack, soda/tea available all day.
Sitting rooms, fluffy robes, scented glycerin soaps, bath scents...

Come be pampered at this late 1800's Federal Farmhouse nestled in the White Mountains! Watch breathtaking sunsets over Mts. Washington, Madison, and Adams from the swing on our porch. mtwashbb@yahoo.com

SILVER LAKE

Lake View Cottage
PO Box 1
99 Route 113 03875
603-367-9182 Fax: 603-367-9289
800-982-0418
Becky Knowles All year

95-200-BB
4 rooms, 4 pb
Visa, MC, AmEx
C-yes/S-no/P-no/H-no

Full candlelight breakfast
Afternoon refreshments
Library, sitting area, boats, dock, fishing, romance packages

This restored lakeside Victorian Inn offers spectacular views, romantic getaways, swimming, boating, snowmobiling from our door and many lake and mountain region activities. info@lakeviewcottage.com http://www.lakeviewcottage.com

SOUTH EFFINGHAM

Chebacco Dude Ranch
HC 66 Box 11
Rt 153 03882
603-522-3211 Fax: 603-522-8970
Merlyn & Jim Rutherford

69-EP
5 rooms, 5 pb
Visa, MC, Disc, •
C-yes/S-ltd/P-no/H-no
All year

Lunch, trail lunch and dinner
Hot Tub, LGB electric train layout, entertainment center, canoe, paddle boat

Relax in a quiet country setting, set out on an adventure on horseback, play a round of golf or day trip to activities nearby. Stay in a 17th Century farmhouse or renovated barn with a Western flavor. chebaccodr@aol.com http://chebaccoduderanch.com/

SUNAPEE

Dexter's Inn & Tennis Club
PO Box 703
258 Stagecoach Rd 03782
603-763-5571 800-232-5571
John & Emily Augustine
All year

115-195-BB
21 rooms, 21 pb
Most CC, *Rated*, •
C-yes/S-no/P-ltd/H-ltd
German, French

Full breakfast
Afternoon refreshments
Tennis, swimming, volleyball, basketball, game room, kids playroom, library.

Warm, welcoming, family-friendly country inn with magnificent views and spacious, idyllic grounds. Tennis, swimming, game room, library on-site. Minutes to golf, skiing, shopping, mountain and lake. dexters@tds.net http://www.dextersnh.com

---

The Inn at Sunapee
PO Box 336
125 Burkehaven Hill Rd 03782
603-763-4444 Fax: 603-763-9456
800-327-2466
Ted and Susan Harriman

100-BB
16 rooms, 16 pb
Most CC
C-yes/S-no/P-no/H-ltd
All year

Full breakfast
Diner with reservations
Lounge

On a hilltop above pristine Lake Sunapee, The Inn at Sunapee presents its guests with a unique combination of hospitality, history and activities that will draw you back time and again. stay@innatsunapee.com http://www.innatsunapee.com

TAMWORTH

The Tamworth Inn
15 Cleveland Hill Rd 03886
603-323-7721 Fax: 603-323-2026
800-642-7352
Bob Schrader
Closed in April

115-300-BB
16 rooms, 16 pb
Visa, MC, AmEx, *Rated*
C-yes/S-no/P-ltd

Full country breakfast
Afternoon tea, beverages, dinner & pub style food
Sitting room, library, fireplaces, bicycles, Jacuzzis, pool, suites, cableTV

Escape to the Tamworth Inn where Simple Elegance in lodging, food and service transport you back to a simpler time. Every room is uniquely decorated w/period antiques & original artwork. inn@tamworth.com http://www.tamworth.com

WARNER

Turtle Pond Farm, Cottages
4 Bean Rd 03278
603-456-2738 Fax: 603-456-2187
877-861-8623
Deb & Walt
All year

85-105-BB
4 rooms, 4 pb
Visa, MC, AmEx
C-yes/S-no/P-no/H-no

Full breakfast
Tea available upon request
pool, spa, TV/VCR, clay tennis court, fridge, gas fireplace

B&B cottages nestled in the Mink Hills & Mt. Kearsarge on 16+ acres. Turtle Pond Farm affords intimacy with the amenities of a B&B.
bury@turtlepondfarm.com http://www.turtlepondfarm.com

WHITEFIELD

Spalding Inn
199 Mountain View Rd 03598
603-837-2572 Fax: 603-837-3062
800-368-8439
Diane & Michael Flinder

99-160-BB
42 rooms, 42 pb
All year

Full breakfast

Perfect family getaway on over 200 acres with mountain views, swimming pool, and tennis courts. dianeec@ncia.net http://www.spaldinginn.com

WILTON

The Fountain House
PO Box 1199
55 Burns Hill Rd
603-654-5000 Fax: 603-804-0400
888-222-7330
Tony Mason
All year

85-195-BB
4 rooms, 2 pb
AmEx, Most CC, •
C-ltd/S-no/P-no/H-no
Pig Latin

M–F—Continental, Weekend—Full
Coffee and Tea are available 24 hours a day.
Sitting/Game Room, Parlor/TV Room. Licensed Massage Therapy

A restored 19th century Italianate Victorian. Originally built as a summer home, it has a lively history. Once again we make it available as an inn. Enjoy our luxurious yet casual surroundings! info@fountain-house.com http://www.fountain-house.com

New Jersey

ATLANTIC CITY (REGION)

Dr. Jonathan Pitney House
57 North Shore Road, *Absecon* 08201
609-569-1799 Fax: 609-569-9224
888-7-PITNEY
Don Kelly & Vonnie Clark
All year

99-209-BB
11 rooms, 11 pb
Visa, MC, *Rated*, •
S-no/P-no/H-yes

Full breakfast
Afternoon tea
Sitting room, library, Jacuzzi, fireplaces, cable, suites, sm. conf.

The home of the "Father of Atlantic City." Built in 1799 and restored and renovated in 1997. Furnished with antiques from both Colonial and Victorian eras.
drpitney@pitneyhouse.com http://www.pitneyhouse.com

White Manor Inn
739 S Second Ave, *Absecon Highlands* 08205
609-748-3996 Fax: 609-652-0073
Howard R. Bensel Jr/Anna Mae Bensel
All year

65-105-BB
7 rooms, 5 pb
•
C-ltd/S-no/P-no/H-no

Continental Plus breakfast
Snacks
Sitting room, suites, accom. bus. travelers, gazebo, onsite parking

Homespun hospitality abounds at this quiet country inn. Renovated extensively, the inn offers today's conveniences while retaining its original country charm.
info@whitemanorinn.com http://www.whitemanorinn.com

Carisbrooke Inn
105 S Little Rock Ave, *Ventnor* 08406
609-822-6392
Fax: 609-822-9710
Lori McIntyre
February–November

89-240-BB
8 rooms, 8 pb
Visa, MC, Disc, *Rated*, •
C-yes/S-no/P-no/H-ltd

Full breakfast
Afternoon tea
Beach tags, Cable TV, ceiling fans, clock radio

Located just 1 mile from the excitement of Atlantic City, and a few steps from the beach & world famous boardwalk, Carisbrooke Inn is the perfect place to enjoy the pleasures of the Jersey Shore!
info@carisbrookeinn.com http://www.carisbrookeinn.com

AVON BY THE SEA

Atlantic View Inn
20 Woodland Ave 07717
732-774-8505 Fax: 732-869-0187
Nita & Pete Rose
All year

160-295-BB
Visa, MC, AmEx, *Rated*, •
C-ltd/S-no/P-no/H-no

Full breakfast
Afternoon refreshments and cookies
Sitting room, fireplaces, suites with TV/VCR, beach badges and chairs.

The charm of an English seashore home, overlooking the ocean. Full gourmet breakfast served on an open porch.
nita@monmouth.com http://www.atlanticviewinn.com

Cashelmara Inn
22 Lakeside Ave 07717
732-776-8727 Fax: 732-988-5819
800-821-2976
Mary Wiernasz
All year

83-310-BB
14 rooms, 14 pb
Visa, MC
C-ltd/S-no/P-no/H-no

Full breakfast
Tea & goodie table, ice machine
Beach chairs, umbrellas, wind breaks, resident retrievers: Cody & Lucy

European antiques, water views complemented by designer fabrics & window treatments. In-season complimentary beach badges.
cashelmara@monmouth.com http://www.cashelmara.com

AVON BY THE SEA

Inn-to-the-Sea
101 Sylvania Ave 07717
732-775-3992 Fax: 732-775-2538
John and Roberta Gunn
All year

100-255-BB
8 rooms, 8 pb
Most CC, *Rated*, •
C-no/S-ltd/P-no/H-ltd

Full home cooked breakfast
ocean views, air conditioning, small refrigerators, TVs with VCRs, phones

1890's Queen Anne Victorian bed and breakfast located one block from the beach and boardwalk in the quiet shore community of Avon-by-the-Sea.
john@inntothesea.com http://www.inntothesea.com

BAY HEAD

Bay Head Gables
200 Main Ave 08742
732-892-9844 Fax: 732-295-2196
800-984-9536
Don Haurie & Ed Laubusch
Wkends only in winter

110-225-BB
11 rooms, 11 pb
Most CC, *Rated*, •
C-ltd/S-no/P-no/H-no

Full breakfast
Snacks, complimentary wine
Sitting room, 75 yards to ocean, in-room phones & A/C

A 3-story Georgian Colonial overlooking ocean. Elegant Victorian to ultra contemporary—to please the most discriminating guest.
bhgables@monmouth.com http://www.bayheadgables.com

BEACH HAVEN

Victoria Guest House
126 Amber St 08008
609-492-4154 Fax: 609-492-1420
Marilyn & Leonard Miller
May thru September

75-300-BB
17 rooms, 15 pb
C-ltd/S-ltd/P-no/H-ltd

Continental plus breakfast
Bicycles, beachchairs, heated pool

Situated four houses from the Ocean. We offer spacious guestrooms, attractively decorated with cheerful exposure. Linger on our wrap around porches or take a cooling dip in our heated pool. lbivictorian@yahoo.com http://www.nealcomm.com/victoria

BELMAR

Down the Shore
201 7th Ave 07719
732-681-9023
Annette Bergins
All year

80-120-BB
3 rooms, 3 pb
Visa, MC, *Rated*, •
C-ltd/S-no/P-no/H-no

Full breakfast
Snacks
Sitting room, library, cable TV, accommodate business travelers

Cozy, comfortable but only six years old. One block to boardwalk and beach, attentive, not intrusive service provided by friendly well-informed hosts.
lodgings@monmouth.com http://www.downtheshorenj.com

The Inn at the Shore
301 Fourth Ave 07719
732-681-3762 Fax: 732-280-1914
Tom & Rosemary Volker
All year

110-200-BB
10 rooms, 4 pb
Visa, MC, AmEx, *Rated*, •
C-yes/S-ltd/P-no/H-no

Full breakfast
Tea, snacks, beverages
Jacuzzi, fireplaces, aquarium, phones, TV/VCR, patio & gas grill, A/C

Let us pamper you at our seashore, family friendly, Victorian country inn, while you rock away & enjoy sea & lake breezes on a wraparound porch.
tomvolker@aol.com http://www.theinnattheshore.com

Morning Dove Inn
204 5th Ave 07719
732-556-0777
Carol Lee Tieman
All year

100-220-BB
8 rooms, 8 pb
Visa, MC, AmEx, *Rated*
C-ltd/S-ltd/P-no/H-no

Full specialty breakfast
Afternoon refreshments
Porch, solarium, fireplace, beach admission & chairs, Jacuzzis, suites

Overlooking Silver Lake and one block from the Atlantic Ocean, the Inn provides a year-round peaceful setting. Large sunny rooms, private baths, Jacuzzi.
info@morningdoveinn.com http://www.morningdoveinn.com

CAPE MAY

The Abbey 34 Gurney St 08204 609-884-4506 Fax: 609-884-2379 Jay & Marianne Schatz Easter–Dec.	100-295-BB 14 rooms, 14 pb Visa, MC, *Rated* C-ltd/S-ltd/P-no/H-no	Full breakfast buffet on veranda Complimentary wine, snacks 2 parlors, piano, harp, off-street parking, fax

Elegantly restored villa, with period antiques. Genuine merriment in a warm atmosphere. A/C available. One block from Atlantic Ocean.
theabbey@bellatlantic.net http://www.abbeybedandbreakfast.com

---

The Albert G. Stevens Inn 127 Myrtle Ave 08204 609-884-4717 Fax: 609-884-8320 800-890-2287 Jim & Lenanne Labrusciano All year	100-230-BB 10 rooms, 10 pb Visa, MC, • C-ltd/S-ltd/P-no/H-no	Full breakfast Afternoon tea with refreshments Evening tea, sherry, Stress-Reduction Center, large, lighted Jacuzzi

Built in 1898 as a wedding gift from his new in-laws, this Queen Anne Victorian was owned by Cape May's prominent and life-long resident Dr. Albert G. Stevens and his wife Bessie.
albertstevensinn@hotmail.com http://www.beachcomber.com/Capemay/Bbs/stevens.html

---

Angel of the Sea 5 Trenton Ave 08204 609-884-3369 Fax: 609-884-3331 800-848-3369 Greg Whissill All year	95-285-BB 27 rooms, 27 pb Visa, MC, AmEx, *Rated*, • C-ltd/S-no/P-no/H-no	Full breakfast Wine, tea, sitting room, oceanfront porch, fireplaces, bicycles

Cape May's most luxurious B fabulous ocean views. Rooms have private baths, ceiling fans, ocean views, clawfoot tubs.

The Ashley 120 Decatur St 08204 609-898-1099 Fax: 215-230-8986 Patricia & Ashley Tedesco Closed Dec. 15–Jan. 5	EP 2 rooms, 2 pb C-yes/S-no/P-no/H-no	Cable TV, VCR, beach chair, reading library, A/C

The Ashley has two oversized apartments that cater to families.
theashleycm@aol.com

Barnard Good House 238 Perry St 08204 609-884-5381 Fax: 609-884-2871 Nan & Tom Hawkins April 1–Nov 1	100-175-BB 5 rooms, 5 pb Visa, MC, *Rated* C-ltd/S-ltd/P-no/H-no	Full 4-course breakfast Wine, snacks (sometimes) Sitting room, antique, organ, private baths, A/C in rooms

Victorian splendor in landmark-dotted town. Breakfast is a taste thrill ... sumptuous & lovingly created for you.
bargood@snip.net http://www.beachcomber.com/Capemay/Bbs/barnard.html

---

Bedford Inn 805 Stockton Ave 08204 609-884-4158 Fax: 609-884-6320 Cindy & James Schmucker March–December	150-225-BB 10 rooms, 10 pb Most CC, *Rated*, • C-ltd/S-ltd/P-no/H-no	Full memorable breakfast Afternoon refreshments Dining room, parlor, sun & outdoor, limited on-site parking

Elegant 1880 Italianate seaside inn with unusual double staircase; lovely, antique-filled rooms, suites. Full gourmet breakfast and afternoon tea.
info@bedfordinn.com http://www.bedfordinn.com

CAPE MAY

Captain Mey's Inn
202 Ocean St 08204
609-884-7793 Fax: 609-884-7793
800-981-3702
George & Kathleen Blinn
All year

85-225-BB
7 rooms, 7 pb
Visa, MC, *Rated*, •
C-ltd/S-no/P-no/H-no

Full country breakfast
Complimentary wine, refreshments
A/C, on-site parking, 1 block to beach, shops, restaurants, veranda

Victorian 1890 inn with wraparound verandah. Period antiques, fireplace in dining room, Victorian parlor, 2 bedroom suite. innkeeper@ship.net http://www.captainmeys.com

---

Carroll Villa
19 Jackson St 08204
609-884-9619 Fax: 609-884-0264
Mark Kulkowitz & Pam Huber
Jan 14–Dec 31,

80-185-BB
22 rooms, 22 pb
Most CC, *Rated*, •
C-yes/S-no/P-no/H-no

Full breakfast
Great lunch & dinner in season
Fireplace, garden terrace, A/C, front porch

National landmark hotel with critically acclaimed restaurant located in historic Cape May. We are a small family run business with 22 rooms all with private shower.
cvres@eticomm.net http://www.carrollvilla.com

The Chalfonte Hotel
PO Box 475
301 Howard St 08204
609-884-8409 Fax: 609-884-4588
888-411-1998
Anne LeDuc & Judy Bartella
Memorial Day–Colum. Day

135-285-MAP
70 rooms, 10 pb
Most CC, *Rated*, •
C-yes/S-no/P-no/H-no
French, Russian, Polish

Full breakfast
Dinner, restaurant, snacks, bar service
Sitting room, library, accomm. business travelers, children

Victorian Cape May's oldest continually operating B&B Hotel, serving guests since 1876. Simply appointed rooms and Southern hospitality provide a perfect vacation spot for family gatherings. chalfontnj@aol.com http://www.chalfonte.com

---

Cliveden Inn & Cottage
709 Columbia Ave 08204
609-884-4516 800-884-2420
Susan & Al DeRosa
All year

110-165-BB
10 rooms, 10 pb
Visa, MC, AmEx, *Rated*
C-ltd/S-ltd/P-no/H-no

Full breakfast buffet
Afternoon tea, snacks
Library, veranda, rocking chairs, Victorian cottage available

Fine accommodations, delicious breakfast and gracious hospitality have made the Cliveden one of the popular inns of Cape May.
http://www.clivedeninn.com

The Dormer House
800 Columbia Ave 08204
609-884-7446 Fax: 609-884-7446
800-884-5052
Lucille & Dennis Doherty
All year

79-240-BB
10 rooms, 10 pb
Visa, MC, AmEx, *Rated*
C-ltd/S-no/P-no/H-no

Full breakfast
Afternoon tea
Sitting room, glass enclosed breakfast porch, bikes, Jacuzzi room

One of the great summer houses of the 1890s. Long porches, enjoy full breakfast/tea. An inn for all seasons.
http://www.dormerhouse.com

Duke of Windsor Inn
817 Washington St 08204
609-884-1355 Fax: 609-884-1887
800-826-8973
Patricia Joyce
All year

95-225-BB
10 rooms, 10 pb
Visa, MC, *Rated*
C-ltd/S-no/P-no/H-no

Full breakfast
Afternoon tea
Sitting rooms, cable TV, on-site parking, suites, veranda

Grand & elegant home built in 1896. Dramatic 45 ft tower provides for 2 unique guestrooms. Original oak woodwork & wainscoting, 9 ft sliding doors, Tiffany stained glass window.
innkeeper@dukeofwindsorinn.com http://www.dukeofwindsorinn.com

CAPE MAY

Fairthorne
PO Box 2381
111 Ocean St 08204
609-884-8791 Fax: 609-898-6129
800-438-8742
Ed & Diane Hutchinson
All year

145-245-BB
9 rooms, 9 pb
Most CC, *Rated*, •
C-ltd/S-no/P-no/H-no

Full breakfast
Afternoon tea
Public library across street, bicycles, sitting room, near ocean

Voted B&B with best front porch by Inn goers in Arrington's B&B Journal. "The Discerning Traveler" chose us as one of the East's most delightful and delicious destinations–Romantic Hideaways 2002. fairthornebnb@aol.com http://www.fairthorne.com

---

Gingerbread House
28 Gurney St 08204
609-884-0211
Fred & Joan Echevarria
All year

98-260-BB
6 rooms, 3 pb
Rated
C-ltd/S-ltd/P-no/H-no

Full breakfast
Afternoon tea with baked goods
Wicker-filled porch, parlor with fireplace, Victorian antiques, A/C

The G.B.H. offers period furnished rooms–comfortable accommodations within walking distance to major sights. Half block from the beach.
info@gingerbreadinn.com http://www.gingerbreadinn.com

The Humphrey Hughes House
29 Ocean St 08204
609-884-4428 800-582-3634
Lorraine & Terry Schmidt
Mid-April–Oct.

140-290-BB
10 rooms, 10 pb
Visa, MC, AmEx, *Rated*
S-ltd/P-no/H-no

Full breakfast
Afternoon tea & treats
Library, veranda, beach, tags, rocking chairs, Victorian cottage

Enjoy full breakfast & afternoon tea & treats on our large, wraparound verandah. Cozy Victorian cottage. Center of Historic District. http://www.humphreyhugheshouse.com

---

Inn at 22 Jackson
22 Jackson St 08204
609-884-2226 Fax: 609-884-0055
800-452-8177
Chip & Barbara Masemore
All year

95-375-BB
7 rooms, 7 pb
Visa, MC, AmEx, *Rated*
C-ltd/S-no/P-no/H-no

Full breakfast
Afternoon tea, snacks, wine
Sitting room, bicycles near beach, fireplaces

Whimsical, yet romantic Victorian; center of historic district; collections of majolica, toys and bawdy women. innat22@nwip.net http://www.innat22jackson.com

---

The Inn on Ocean
PO Box 551
25 Ocean St 08204
609-884-7070 Fax: 609-884-1384
800-304-4477
Victoria Clayton & Richard White
All seasons

129-299-BB
5 rooms, 5 pb
Most CC, *Rated*
C-ltd/S-no/P-no/H-no

Full breakfast
Golf, tennis, antiques, birdwatching, fishing, near beach/ocean's edge

Intimate, elegant restored Victorian. Steps to beach. Romantic ocean view porches. Victorian Billiard Room. Luxurious Honeymoon Suite.
innocean@bellatlantic.net http://www.theinnonocean.com

John F. Craig House
609 Columbia Ave 08204
609-884-0100 Fax: 609-898-1307
877-544-0314
Chip & Barbara Masemore
March–December

125-205-BB
8 rooms, 8 pb
Most CC, *Rated*, •
C-ltd/S-ltd/P-no/H-no
French

Full gourmet breakfast
Afternoon tea, snacks
Parlor with fireplace, library, A/C in all rooms, 2 cats in residence

Victorian inn, period furnishings & decor. Wrap-around veranda with swing, enclosed sun porches. English cottage perennial garden. All private baths and A/C.
fe6119@bellatlantic.net http://www.johnfcraig.com

CAPE MAY

John Wesley Inn 30 Gurney St 08204 609-884-1012 Rita Tice & Capt John All year	125-200-BB 6 rooms, 4 pb • C-ltd/S-no/P-no/H-no	Continental plus breakfast Sitting room, library, beach tags, beach chairs, parking

Elegant Victorian interior designed for relaxation & romance. Centrally located in Historic District, 1/2 block from beach. http://www.johnwesleyinn.com

Leith Hall Historic Seashore Inn 22 Ocean St 08204 609-884-1934 Susan & Elan Zingman-Leith All year	105-240-BB 7 rooms, 7 pb *Rated* C-ltd/S-no/P-no/H-no French, Yiddish	Full breakfast Afternoon English tea Whirlpool tubs, fireplaces, cable TV, A/C in all rooms & suites, ocean views

Elegantly restored 1880s home in the heart of the Victorian district. Only half block from the beach, with ocean views. stay@leithhall.com http://www.leithhall.com/

The Mainstay Inn 635 Columbia Ave 08204 609-884-8690 Tom & Sue Carroll All year	110-350-BB 16 rooms, 16 pb *Rated* C-ltd/S-no/P-no/H-ltd	Full breakfast (spring/fall) Continental breakfast (summer) Afternoon tea, 16 A/C rooms, piano, 3 sitting rooms

An elegant Victorian Inn within a lovely garden setting. The Inn and adjacent Cottage feature wide rocker-lined verandas, and large rooms, which are lavishly and comfortably furnished. http://www.mainstayinn.com

The Mason Cottage 625 Columbia Ave 08204 609-884-3358 800-716-2766 Joan E. Mason Open Feb.–Dec.	85-250-BB 9 rooms, 9 pb Visa, MC, AmEx, *Rated*, • C-ltd/S-no/P-no/H-no	Full gourmet breakfast Afternoon tea Sitting room, veranda, parlor, fireplaces, A/C, whirlpool, beach towels

An elegant seaside inn located on a quiet, tree-lined street in the center of historic district, 1 block to beach & close to other attractions. http://www.themasoncottage.com

The Mission Inn 1117 New Jersey Ave 08204 609-884-8380 Fax: 609-884-4191 800-800-8380 Susan Babineau-Roberts	100-225-BB 8 rooms, 8 pb Visa, MC, AmEx C-ltd/S-no/P-no/H-no	Juice, fresh fruit, meat entree Afternoon refreshment, complimentary wine/appetizer Fireplace, great room, solarium, veranda, bikes, TV, business travelers

The Mission Inn is the only California Spanish mission style B&B in historic, Victorian Cape May. This Spanish revival Inn stands alone in its comfort, charm and attention to guests' desires. info@missioninn.com http://www.missioninn.net

The Mooring 801 Stockton Ave 08204 609-884-5425 Fax: 609-884-1357 Leslie Valenza April 3–Dec. 30	75-180-BB 12 rooms, 12 pb Visa, MC, *Rated*, • C-ltd/S-no/P-no/H-no	Full breakfast Afternoon tea Sitting room

Victorian mansard structure furnished in original period antiques. One block to ocean and easy walking distance to five different restaurants.
info@themooring.com http://www.themooring.com

Perry Street Inn 29 Perry St 08204 609-884-4590 Fax: 609-884-8444 800-29-PERRY John & Cynthia Curtis April–November	60-170-BB 20 rooms, 13 pb Visa, MC, *Rated*, • C-ltd/S-yes/H-yes	Full breakfast Afternoon tea, snacks Sitting room, bicycles, in-room phones, Mystery!, oceanfront porch, phones

National historic landmark city. Victorian guest house close to unique shopping, fine restaurants. info@perrystreetinn.com http://www.perrystreetinn.com

The Queen Victoria, Cape May, NJ

CAPE MAY

Poor Richard's Inn 17 Jackson St 08204 609-884-3536 Fax: 609-884-2329 Harriett Sosson Valentines–New Year's	65-165-BB 9 rooms, 4 pb *Rated*, • C-ltd/S-yes/P-no/H-no	Continental breakfast Sitting room, oriental rock garden, near beach

Classic gingerbread guesthouse offers accommodations with eclectic Victorian & country decor. http://www.poorrichardsinn.com

---

The Queen Victoria 102 Ocean St 08204 609-884-8702 Dane & Joan Wells All year	95-300-BB 21 rooms, 21 pb Visa, MC, *Rated* C-ltd/S-ltd/P-no/H-ltd French	Full buffet breakfast Afternoon tea, comp. beverages Bikes, evening turn-down, refrigerators in all rooms, luxury suites

Welcoming guests since 1980, The Queen Victoria is one of America's most famous Victorian B&B Inns. Centrally located one block to the Atlantic Ocean and shops.
qvinn@bellatlantic.net http://www.queenvictoria.com

Queen's Hotel 102 Ocean St Columbia Ave at Ocean St 08204 609-884-1613 Joan & Dane Wells All year	90-270-EP 11 rooms, 11 pb Visa, MC, *Rated* C-ltd/S-no/P-no/H-no	Continental breakfast Bikes, whirlpools, suites, fireplace, TV, A/C, telephones, some parking

Historic hotel centrally located one block to Atlantic Ocean & shops. Elegant luxury rooms and suites with modern amenities. Open all year.
qvinn@bellatlantic.net http://www.queenshotel.com

Rhythm of the Sea 1123 Beach Dr 08204 609-884-7788 Fax: 609-884-7799 800-498-6888 Robyn & Wolfgang Wendt All year	165-365-BB 9 rooms, 9 pb Most CC, *Rated* C-ltd/S-no/P-no/H-no German	Full breakfast Beverage service daily, dinner w/advance arrngmnt Gathering rooms, parking, bikes, beach towels, beach chairs, concierge

With the ocean as our front yard, we provide fragrant breezes & a wealth of seaside activities. We invite you to come savor our sumptuous meals, peaceful privacy and 'gemuetlichkeit'. rhythm@algorithms.com http://www.rhythmofthesea.com

CAPE MAY

Saltwood House 28 Jackson St 08204 609-884-6754 Fax: 609-884-1749 800-830-8232 Don Schweikert April–December	100-200-BB 4 rooms, 4 pb Visa, MC, AmEx, *Rated* C-ltd/P-no/H-no	Full breakfast Afternoon tea, complimentary wine Sitting room, suites, cable TV, VCRs & video library

Ideally located mid-block on Cape May's oldest street, this meticulously restored and authentically furnished 1906 Inn captures the essence of a historic private residence.
innkeeper@saltwoodhouse.com http://www.saltwoodhouse.com

Victorian Lace Inn 901 Stockton Ave 08204 609-884-1772 Fax: 609-884-0983 Carri & Andy O'Sullivan Mid-February–New Years	85-220-BB 5 rooms, 5 pb *Rated* C-yes/S-no/P-no/H-no	Full breakfast Sitting room, library, Jacuzzis, suites, cable TV

Beautiful all-suite Colonial Revival inn, with ocean views and fireplaces. Cottage with fireplace and Jacuzzi. viclace@bellatlantic.net http://www.victorianlaceinn.com

Woodleigh House 808 Washington St 08204 609-884-7123 Fax: 609-884-8065 800-399-7123 Joe & Jo Anne Tornambe All year	110-275-BB 5 rooms, 5 pb Visa, MC, *Rated* C-ltd/S-no/P-no/H-no	Full breakfast Afternoon refreshments Sitting room w/firepl, queen beds, gardens, guest phone, A/C, romantic suite

Nestled in Cape May's historic district, surrounded by porches and courtyards. This attractive example of "Country Victorian" is charmingly hosted.
http://www.woodleighhouse.com

CHESTER (REGION)

The Neighbour House 143 W Mill Rd, *Long Valley* 07853 908-876-3519 Fax: 908-876-5813 Rafi & Iris Kadosh All year	85-120-BB 4 rooms, 2 pb Visa, MC, AmEx, • C-ltd/S-no/P-no/H-no Hebrew	Full breakfast Afternoon tea Sitting room, bicycles, fireplaces, cable TV, hiking, antique shops,fishing

Our guests enjoy elegantly furnished rooms in an enchanting, pastoral setting (we're surrounded by 800 beautiful green acres).
rkadosh@worldnet.att.net http://www.bbonline.com/nj/neighbour

FLEMINGTON

Jerica Hill, A B&B Inn 96 Broad St 08822 908-782-8234 Fax: 908-237-0587 V. Eugene Refalvy All year	85-125-BB 5 rooms, 5 pb Visa, MC, AmEx, *Rated*, • C-ltd/S-no/P-no/H-no	Full breakfast Sherry, refreshments Picnic & wine tours, guest pantry, refrig., fax on premises

Gracious Victorian in heart of historic Flemington. Spacious, sunny guestrooms with A/C. Phones/TV by request.

Main Street Manor 194 Main St 08822 908-782-4928 Fax: 908-782-7229 Margaret & Henry Ferreira All year	100-145-BB 5 rooms, 5 pb Most CC, *Rated*, • C-ltd/S-no/P-no/H-no Portuguese	Full breakfast on weekends Continental breakfast (weekdays) Snacks, complimentary wine, sitting room, cable TV

Historic home restored to elegance. Period antiques, two parlors, satellite TV, paneled dining room. innkeeper@mainstreetmanor.com http://www.mainstreetmanor.com

FRENCHTOWN

Widow McCrea House	95-225-BB	Candelite Gourmet breakfast
53 Kingwood Ave 08825	5 rooms, 5 pb	Afternoon tea,
908-996-4999 Fax: 908-806-4496	Visa, MC, AmEx, *Rated*	complimentary wine
Burt Patalano, Lynn Marad	C-ltd/S-no/P-no/H-yes	Sitting room, bicycles,
All year		fireplaces, cable TV, accommodate business travelers

Charming 1878 Victorian with private cottage & spacious suite with working fireplace & Jacuzzis. Three elegant guestrooms. Fine antiques, Queen-size feather beds, private baths, Candlelit breakfast. bpatalano@sprintmail.com http://www.widowmccrea.com

GLENWOOD

Apple Valley Inn	110-150-BB	Full breakfast
PO Box 302	9 rooms, 3 pb	Dinner available, tea/coffee,
967 Rte 517 07418	Most CC, *Rated*, •	homemade bread
973-764-3735 Fax: 973-764-1050	C-ltd/S-no/P-no/H-yes	Complimentary wine, sitting
Elizabeth and Brendan Leen		room, library, pool, porches
All year		

Historic 1831 mansion located in Skylands Region, adjacent to Appalachian Trail. Located at the intersection of Rt. 517 and Rt. 565 in Glenwood, New Jersey.
appleinn@warwick.net http://www.applevalleyinn.com

HACKETTSTOWN

Everitt House	115-150-BB	Full breakfast
200 High Street 07840	4 rooms, 4 pb	Hot and cold beverages and
908-684-1307 Fax: 908-684-8049	Most CC, •	snacks available.
Lotis & Russ Markowitz	C-ltd/S-no/P-no/H-no	All rooms have a small sitting
All year		area.

Spacious Victorian bedrooms with private baths; elegant sitting rooms.
everitthouse@email.com http://www.everitthouse.com

HADDONFIELD

Haddonfield Inn	120-215-BB	Full breakfast
44 West End Ave 08033	9 rooms, 9 pb	Snacks, tea, coffee, beer,
856-428-2195 Fax: 856-354-1273	Most CC, *Rated*, •	wine, soda
800-269-0014	C-ltd/S-ltd/P-ltd/H-yes	Fireplaces, elevator, free
Nancy & Fred Chorpita	Spanish	local calls, concierge service,
All year		parking

Elegant hotel for business traveler or tourist in historic village near Philadelphia. Fireplaces, phones w/voicemail, Internet, cable, private baths (whirlpools). Concierge. Elevator. Full breakfast. Innkeeper@haddonfieldinn.com http://www.haddonfieldinn.com

HIGHLANDS

SeaScape Manor	110-165-BB	Full breakfast
3 Grand Tour 07732	4 rooms, 4 pb	Complimentary wine
732-291-8467 Fax: 732-872-7932	Visa, MC, AmEx, *Rated*	Sitting room, library, bikes,
Sherry Ruby, Gloria Miller,	C-ltd/S-no/P-no/H-no	ocean swimming, fireplace,
Bob Adamec All year		fish

Secluded manor nestled in the tree covered hills overlooking the blue Atlantic and Sandy Hook National Recreation area. Escape to elegance. 45 minutes from NYC.
seascape25@comcast.net http://www.bbianj.com/seascape

LAMBERTVILLE

Chimney Hill Farm Estate	125-350-BB	Full breakfast
207 Goat Hill Rd 08530	12 rooms, 12 pb	Afternoon tea, snacks,
609-397-1516 Fax: 609-397-9353	Visa, MC, AmEx,	sherry
800-211-4667	*Rated*, •	Sitting room, library, nature
Terry Ann & Richard	C-ltd/S-no/P-no/H-ltd	trails, Jacuzzis, suites, cable
Anderson All year		TV

Romantic, elegant 1820 Fieldstone House on acres of gardens, fields & woods. Less than a mile from the arts & dining of the antique Mecca of Lambertville, NJ and New Hope, PA.
chbb@comcast.com http://www.chimneyhillinn.com

LAMBERTVILLE

Lambertville House
32 Bridge St 08530
609-397-0200 Fax: 609-397-0511
888-867-8859
Brad Michael
All year

168-328-BB
26 rooms, 26 pb
Most CC, *Rated*, •
C-ltd/S-no/P-no/H-yes

Continental plus breakfast
Bar service, cable TV, suites, Jacuzzis, fireplaces, bike path

26-room National Historic Inn, jetted tubs, balconies, fireplaces, conference facilities, AAA Four Diamond Award, Left Bank Libations Lounge.
innkeeper@lambertvillehouse.com http://www.lambertvillehouse.com

---

York Street House
42 York St 08530
609-397-3007 Fax: 609-397-3299
888-398-3199
Laurie & Mark Weinstein
All year

100-195-BB
6 rooms, 6 pb
Most CC, *Rated*, •
C-ltd/S-no/P-no/H-no

Full breakfast
Compl. beverages, homemade cookies
Sitting room, fireplaces, gardens, cable TV, Jacuzzi tub

Quiet elegant Georgian Colonial Revival inn. Fireplaces. Canopies. Jacuzzi. Waterford chandelier. Complimentary beverages.
innkeeper@yorkstreethouse.com http://www.yorkstreethouse.com

LONG BEACH ISLAND (REGION)

Amber Street Inn
118 Amber St, *Beach Haven* 08008
609-492-1611 Fax: 609-492-9165
Joan & Michael Fitzsimmons
Mid February-Nov.

130-245-BB
6 rooms, 6 pb
Visa, MC, *Rated*
C-ltd/S-no/P-no/H-ltd
Spanish

Full breakfast
Afternoon tea & lemonade
Fireplace in parlor & dining room, beach passes/chairs, bicycles, phones

A romantic, Victorian, seaside B&B, 1/2 block to the beach and ocean. Antiques, great breakfasts, some fireplaces. inn118@aol.com http://www.amberstreetinn.com

LONG BRANCH

Cedars & Beeches
247 Cedar Ave 07740
732-571-6777 Fax: 732-728-9428
800-323-5655
Esther Cohen
All year

100-300-BB
12 rooms, 12 pb
Visa, MC, AmEx
C-ltd/S-no/P-no/H-no
Spanish

Full breakfast
Full Breakfast-weekends, continental plus-weekdays
On site parking

Located 3 blocks from the beach, Monmouth University & Medical Center, this deluxe 12 room inn features private baths, A/C, color cable TV, telephone with dataport/voice mail and delicious breakfasts.
ecohen@smartsinc.com http://www.cedarsandbeeches.com

MANASQUAN

Nathaniel Morris Inn
117 Marcellus Ave 08736
732-223-7826 Fax: 732-223-7827
Joe and Barbara Jackson
All year

110-215-BB
6 rooms, 6 pb
Rated, •
C-ltd/S-ltd/P-no/H-no
Spanish, French

Full breakfast
Snacks, wine
Sitting room, library, bicycles, suites, cable TV, beach chairs

1882 Victorian Inn with six romantic, antique filled rooms, all with private baths, three with private porches. joej@monmouth.com http://www.nathanielmorris.com

NEWARK (REGION)

The Pillars of Plainfield
922 Central Ave, *Plainfield* 07060
908-753-0922 888-PILLARS
Chuck & Tom Hale
All year

124-250-BB
6 rooms, 6 pb
Visa, MC, AmEx, *Rated*, •
C-ltd/S-no/P-ltd/H-no
Swedish

Full breakfast
Evening sherry, cookies, chocolates
Swedish home baking, sitting room, library, woodburning fireplaces, turndown

Close to NYC and Newark Liberty International Airport. An 1870 Victorian mansion in the Van Wyck Brooks Historic District, where homes on acre lots offer "Sylvan Seclusion with Urban Access." info@pillars2.com http://www.pillars2.com

The Pillars of Plainfield, Plainfield, NJ

NORTH WILDWOOD

Candlelight Inn
2310 Central Ave 08260
609-522-6200
Fax: 609-522-6125
800-992-2632
Bill & Nancy Moncrief
All year

95-240-BB
10 rooms, 10 pb
Most CC, *Rated*, •
S-no/P-no/H-no

Full breakfast
Refreshments
Sitting room, piano, hot tub, sun deck, TV, 3 suites, Jacuzzi, A/C

Seashore B&B with genuine antiques, fireplace, wide verandah. Getaway specials and murder mystery parties available. Close to beach & boardwalk.
info@candlelight-inn.com http://www.candlelight-inn.com

OCEAN CITY

Barnagate
637 Wesley Ave 08226
609-391-9366
Frank & Lois Barna
All year

85-190-BB
5 rooms, 1 pb
Visa, MC, AmEx, *Rated*, •
C-ltd/S-ltd/P-no/H-no

Full breakfast (winter)
Continental breakfast (summer)
Afternoon tea, sitting room, library, tennis court, cable TV, suites

A Seashore Country Victorian that returns guests to an era when hospitality was a matter of pride.
barnagate@aol.com http://www.barnagate.com

Castle By The Sea
701 Ocean Avenue 08226
609-398-3555
Fax: 609-398-8742
800-622-4894
Renee & Jack Krutsick
All year

105-235-BB
9 rooms, 9 pb
Most CC, *Rated*, •
C-ltd/S-ltd/P-no/H-no

3 course gourmet breakfast
Afternoon Tea & Sweets, Evening Soda & Juice
Private Bath, A/C, TV-VCR, Movie Library, Hairdryers, Clock Radios, Irons

ONCE UPON A TIME, There Was A Very Romantic B&B. . .With Lavish Accommodations, Spectacular Cuisine, Bedside Chocolates.
castle701@aol.com http://www.castlebythesea.com

OCEAN CITY

The Ebbie
820 E 6th St 08226
609-399-4744
Dave, Liz & Jake Warrington
Mem.Wknd–Columbus wknd

65-100-BB
7 rooms, 5 pb
Visa, MC
C-yes/S-no/P-no/H-no

Continental breakfast
Coffee and donuts
Tennis court across the street, cable TV

Established by the Warrington family in 1945. All rooms, efficiency, studio and 2-bedroom apartments, have been refurbished with AC, color TV, fridge and daily maid service.
http://www.ebbie.com

Northwood Inn
401 Wesley Ave 08226
609-399-6071
Marj & John Loeper
All year

85-230-BB
7 rooms, 7 pb
Visa, MC, AmEx, *Rated*
C-ltd/S-no/P-no/H-no

Full breakfast
Continental plus breakfast on weekdays
Snacks, roof-top deck w/year round whirlpool, bikes, game room, pool table

Award winning 1894 Victorian with 21st century comforts including Jacuzzis. Located between Atlantic City & Cape May. Enjoy our romantic rooftop whirlpool spa with magnificent sunsets all seasons. info@northwoodinn.com http://www.northwoodinn.com

---

Rose Garden Inn
1214 Ocean Ave 08226
609-398-4889
Susan & Jack Masters
Memorial Day–Oct 15

115-135-BB
6 rooms, 6 pb
Visa, MC, AmEx
C-yes/S-no/P-no/H-no

Full breakfast
Sitting room, fireplaces, cable TV, suites

This spacious Arts & Crafts period home, across from the beach and boardwalk, offers guests a comfortable and memorable visit to Ocean City, New Jersey.
msamtab3@aol.com http://www.bbonline.com/nj/rosegarden

Scarborough Inn
720 Ocean Ave 08226
609-399-1558 Fax: 609-399-4472
800-258-1558
Gus & Carol Bruno
May 1–October 20

80-220-BB
24 rooms, 24 pb
Most CC, *Rated*, •
C-ltd/S-ltd/P-no/H-no
Italian

Full Gourmet Breakfast
Afternoon refreshments
Wraparound porch, library, patio garden w/fountain

The Scarborough Inn is reminiscent of a European-style inn, small enough to be intimate, yet large enough for privacy. This AAA Three Diamond bed & breakfast is known for its gracious hospitality. info@scarboroughinn.com http://www.scarboroughinn.com

---

The Sea Bean
1330 Wesley Ave 08226
609-399-1956
Dave & Andrea Porter
All year

80-110-BB
3 rooms, 3 pb
C-ltd/S-no/P-no/H-ltd

Continental plus breakfast
Afternoon tea, snacks
Fireplaces

1920's restored seashore cottage, one block from beach and boardwalk. Relax by the fireplace or on the garden-lined back deck.
cbeanocnj@aol.com http://www.bbonline.com/nj/seabean

Sea Cottage Inn
1136 Ocean Ave 08226
609-399-3356 Fax: 609-399-3004
888-208-1927
Pamela Gibbs
All year

75-150-BB
8 rooms, 8 pb
Visa, MC, Disc, *Rated*
C-ltd/S-no/P-ltd/H-ltd

Full breakfast
Afternoon and evening beverages & treats
Dinner by arrangement, sitting room, tropical garden w/outdoor fireplace

Nestled on one of Ocean City's historic beach block streets, with homes dating from the early teens & twenties. All rooms have private baths, A/C, TV/VCR, limited onsite parking and free beach passes. seacottinn@aol.com http://www.seacottageinn.info

OCEAN CITY

Serendipity
712 Ninth St 08226
609-399-1554 Fax: 609-399-1554
800-842-8544
Clara & Bill Plowfield
All year

79-159-BB
6 rooms, 4 pb
Most CC, *Rated*, •
C-ltd/S-no/P-no/H-no

Full breakfast
Snacks, beverages all day
Free parking, garden verandah, fireplace, video library, beach Passes/Chairs

Fabulous location, 1/2 block to Ocean City beach & boardwalk. California-style full breakfast with vegetarian & healthful choices. Fireplace & vine-shaded garden verandah and bountiful amenities. info@serendipitynj.com http://www.serendipitynj.com

OCEAN GROVE

The Cordova
26 Webb Ave 07756
732-774-3084 Fax: 732-897-1666
Peter & Sue Gioulis
All year

55-189-BB
20 rooms, 7 pb
Most CC, *Rated*, •
C-yes/S-ltd/P-no/H-no
Greek

Continental plus breakfast
Guest kitchen
Sitting room, bikes, BBQ, garden, picnic tables

Newly renovated Century-old Victorian Inn with antiques, lovely historic beach community. Feel like one of the family—experience Old World charm!

House by the Sea
14 Ocean Avenue 07756
732-774-4771 Fax: 732-502-0403
Sally & Alyn Heim
May 25 to September 09

65-110-BB
18 rooms, 10 pb
C-ltd/S-no/P-no/H-no

Continental breakfast
Sitting rooms, porch, TV

The House by the Sea offers a lifestyle rather than a typical hotel experience.
housebysea@monmouth.com http://www.travelguides.com/home/house_by_the_sea/

The Love Letter Inn
19 Broadway 07756
732-897-0700
Lynne & Philip Bruno
All year

125-225-BB
8 rooms, 8 pb
C-ltd/S-no/P-no/H-no

Full breakfast
Afternoon tea, snacks, complimentary wine
Bikes, Jacuzzis, suites, fireplaces, cable TV,accommodate business travelers

Romantic French Victorian providing 8 intimate guestrooms all with private baths and most with panoramic ocean and lake views. Each room has been uniquely decorated to charm and romance you. loveletterinnog@aol.com http://www.loveletterinn.com

---

Manchester Inn
25 Ocean Pathway 07756
732-775-0616
Clark & Margaret Cate
All year

100-140-BB
35 rooms, 25 pb
Most CC, *Rated*
C-yes/S-no/P-no/H-ltd

Full breakfast
Open for dinner in season, coffee/tea all day
Porches, family rooms, guest kitchen, rocking chairs on front porch

Circa 1870, The Manchester Inn boasts Victorian decor and 35 uniquely decorated rooms; one block from the ocean. The on-premise Restaurant can be reserved for private events. Exit 100B off the GSP. thenjinn@aol.com http://www.themanchesterinn.com

PITTSTOWN

Seven Springs Farm
14 Perryville Rd 08867
908-735-7675
Jim & Dina Bowers
All year

85-175-BB
4 rooms, 4 pb
Rated, •
C-yes/S-ltd/P-no/H-no

Full breakfast
Snacks
Sitting room, library, Jacuzzis, suite, fireplaces, cable TV, gardens, farm

The farmhouse serving as Seven Springs Farm Bed and Breakfast has undergone an extensive restoration to make the transition from the 18th century to the new millennium.
http://www.sevenspringsfarmbandbnj.com

PRINCETON

Peacock Inn
20 Bayard Ln 08540
609-924-1707 Fax: 609-924-2229
Canice J. Lindsay
All year

145-175-BB
17 rooms, 17 pb
Visa, MC, AmEx, •
C-ltd/S-no/P-yes/H-ltd
French, Russian, Polish

Continental Plus breakfast
Lunch & dinner avail, snacks, afternoon tea
Restaurant, bar service, cable TV

The Peacock Inn is one of Princeton's most historic buildings.
info@peacockinn.com http://www.peacockinn.com

SPRING LAKE

La Maison Inn
404 Jersey Ave 07762
732-449-0969 Fax: 732-449-4860
800-276-2088
Julie Corrigan
All year

155-350-BB
8 rooms, 8 pb
Most CC, *Rated*, •
C-ltd/S-ltd/P-no/H-no

Full breakfast
Special cheeses w/fruit, complimentary beverages
Sitting rm, bikes, Jacuzzis, suites, CATV, free access premiere health club

La Maison is a getaway for the soul–it is like a private European residence, filled with antiques & private art collected by the owner. Experience a place like no other.
lamaisonnj@aol.com http://www.lamaisoninn.com

The Normandy Inn
21 Tuttle Ave 07762
732-449-7172 Fax: 732-449-1070
800-449-1888
The Valori Family
All year

132-396-BB
17 rooms, 17 pb
Rated, •
C-yes/S-ltd/P-no/H-no

Full breakfast
Complimentary wine
Sitting/meeting room, bicycles, front porch, newly built suite

A country inn at the shore, decorated with lovely Victorian antiques, painted with 5 different Victorian colors. normandy@bellatlantic.net http://www.normandyinn.com

---

Sea Crest by The Sea
19 Tuttle Ave 07762
732-449-9031 Fax: 732-974-0403
800-803-9031
Barbara & Fred Vogel
All year

190-495-BB
11 rooms, 11 pb
Visa, MC, AmEx, *Rated*, •
S-no/P-no/H-no

Full breakfast
Afternoon tea
Bicycles, beach chairs, beach towels, beach umbrellas, croquet

A Spring Lake B&B just for the two of you. A lovingly restored 1885 Queen Anne Victorian with beautiful antiques, ocean views, fireplaces, our famous Sea Crest buttermilk scones.
capt@seacrestbythesea.com http://www.seacrestbythesea.com

Spring Lake Inn
104 Salem Ave 07762
732-449-2010 Fax: 732-449-4020
Barbara & Andy
All year

99-350-BB
16 rooms, 16 pb
Most CC, *Rated*, •
C-ltd/S-no/P-no/H-no
Spanish

Great breakfast
Jersey Fresh fruit, candy, cookies, daily snacks
cable, beach badges, chairs, towels, onsite parking

The heart of an intimate hotel. The soul of a B&B. One short block to the ocean & boardwalk. Circa 1888, 80-foot Victorian porch. Quiet, private. Great breakfast! Parlor with cable, games, library. sprnglkinn@aol.com http://www.springlakeinn.com

---

Victoria House
214 Monmouth Ave 07762
732-974-1882 Fax: 732-974-2132
888-249-6252
Lynne & Alan Kaplan
All year

189-345-BB
8 rooms, 8 pb
Most CC, *Rated*
S-no/P-no/H-no

Full breakfast served
TV, VCR, bicycles, tennis pass, fireplaces, Jacuzzis

The perfect retreat in Victorian splendor. "One of Top Ten Inns in New Jersey" 2002.
info@victoriahouse.net http://www.victoriahouse.net

Alpine Haus Inn, Vernon, NJ

STANHOPE

Whistling Swan Inn 110 Main St 07874 973-347-6369 Fax: 973-347-3391 Liz & Ron Armstrong All year	99-179-BB 10 rooms, 10 pb Most CC, *Rated*, • C-ltd/S-no/P-no/H-no	Full breakfast buffet Complimentary sherry, snacks, juices, sodas Sitting rooms, fireplace, TV/VCRs, phones in room, dataports, irons/boards

We cordially welcome you to the Whistling Swan Inn, an elegantly restored 1905 Victorian home. Take a step back in time, and experience true Victorian ambience.
info@whistlingswaninn.com http://www.whistlingswaninn.com

TUCKERTON

J.D. Thompson Inn 149 E Main St 08087 609-294-1331 Fax: 609-294-2091 888-393-5723 Joe & Gloria Gartner All year	95-155-BB 7 rooms, 7 pb Visa, MC, AmEx, *Rated*, • C-ltd/S-no/P-no/H-ltd	Full breakfast Afternoon tea, snacks, complimentary wine Sitting room, bikes, suites, cable TV, outdoor spa and gazebo

Romantic, c.1823, fully restored Gothic Revival located in historic seaport town. Beautifully furnished in period antiques.
jdthompsoninn@worldnet.att.net http://www.jdthompsoninn.com

VERNON

Alpine Haus Inn 217 Route 94 07462 973-209-7080 Fax: 973-209-7090 Jack and Allison Smith All year	110-225-BB 10 rooms, 10 pb Most CC, *Rated* C-yes/S-no/P-no/H-yes	Full breakfast Sitting room, Jacuzzis, suites, fireplaces, cable TV, accom.bus.travel, deck

1887 Colonial Inn & Carriage House with fireplaces, Jacuzzis, suites, antiques.
alpinehs@warwick.net http://www.alpinehausbb.com

WHITEHOUSE STATION

Holly Thorn House 143 Readington Rd 08889 908-534-1616 Fax: 908-534-9017 Anne & Joseph Fosbre All year	125-145-BB 5 rooms, 5 pb *Rated*, •	Full breakfast Sitting room—leather sofas, wet bar, TV, library; pool, billiards

Sophisticated library with books, games, videos and snacks. 3 Diamond rating.
http://www.hollythornhouse.com

New Mexico

ABIQUIU

Casa Del Rio
PO Box 702
19946 Hwy 84 87510
505-753-2035 Fax: 505-753-2035
800-920-1495
Eileen Sopanen & Mel Vigil
All year

100-125-BB
2 rooms, 2 pb
Most CC, *Rated*, •
C-ltd/S-no/P-ltd/H-no
Spanish

Full breakfast
Wakeup tray to room, refrigerators in rooms, handmade crafts & rugs

A Gold Medallion certified B&B that offers intimate luxury in a country setting. Situated halfway between Taos and Santa Fe. Voted "Best Weekend Getaway" by B&B Journal.
casadelrio@newmexico.com http://www.bbonline.com/nm/casadelrio/

ALBUQUERQUE

Brittania & W.E. Mauger Estate
701 Roma Ave NW 87102
505-242-8755 Fax: 505-842-8835
800-719-9189
Mark Brown & Keith Lewis
All year

79-199-BB
10 rooms, 9 pb
Most CC, *Rated*, •
C-yes/S-no/P-yes/H-no

Full breakfast
Snacks, complimentary wine
Sitting room, family friendly facility, handmade crafts & rugs

Wonderful Queen Anne Victorian on the National Register. Within walking distance of old town, downtown, convention center and many restaurants.
maugerbb@aol.com http://www.maugerbb.com

Casa Del Granjero
414 C de Baca Lane NW 87114
505-897-4144 Fax: 505-897-9788
800-701-4144
Victoria & Butch Farmer
All year

79-189-BB
6 rooms, 6 pb
Visa, MC, Disc, *Rated*, •
C-yes/S-ltd/P-ltd/H-ltd
English, Spanish

Full breakfast
Dinner, snacks
Sitting room, library, suites, fireplaces, cable TV

Historic hacienda and guest house on 3 secluded acres. Quiet, spacious suites, antiques, fireplaces, gardens, hearty breakfasts.
granjero@prodigy.net http://www.innewmexico.com

Cinnamon Morning
2700 Rio Grande Blvd NW 87104
505-345-3541 Fax: 505-342-2283
800-214-9481
Sue & Dick Percilick
All year

79-195-BB
7 rooms, 6 pb
Most CC, •
C-yes/S-ltd/P-yes/H-ltd
Spanish

Full breakfast
Iced Tea, Lemonade, Sodas
Fireplaces, Garden & Pond in Courtyard, Cable TV/VCR, Outdoor Kitchen

Experience the true atmosphere of Old and New Mexico just minutes from Old Town. Enjoy our gracious hospitality and delicious food. Pets always welcome!
dpercilick@aol.com http://www.cinnamonmorning.com

Hacienda Antigua
6708 Tierra Dr NW 87107
505-345-5399
Fax: 505-345-3855
800-201-2986
Mark Brown & Keith Lewis
All year

99-229-BB
5 rooms, 5 pb
Most CC, *Rated*, •
C-ltd/S-ltd

Full breakfast
Sitting room, library, hot tubs, swimming pool, great for small reunions

Peaceful gardens, kiva fireplaces, antique furnishings, and warm hospitality fill this 200 year-old hacienda.
info@haciendantigua.com http://www.haciendantigua.com

ALBUQUERQUE

Hacienda de Colores/Old Town 1113 Montoya NW 87104 505-247-0013 Fax: 505-242-7063 877-265-6737 Rey & Kim Vejih All year	115-185-BB 3 rooms, 3 pb Visa, MC, AmEx, *Rated*, • C-ltd/S-ltd/P-ltd/H-ltd Spanish	Full breakfast Afternoon tea, snacks, comp. wine Sitting room, library, bicycles, Jacuzzis, fireplaces, cable TV, pool

Spanish hacienda a heartbeat away from Old Town Plaza and downtown Albuquerque with an inviting covered portal for refreshments nestled among ageless native trees shading a six-acre pastoral setting. hdecolores@aol.com http://www.haciendadecolores.com

---

The Inn at Paradise 10035 Country Club Ln NW 87114 505-898-6161 Fax: 505-890-1090 800-938-6161 Antoni Neimczak All year	55-80-BB 16 rooms, 16 pb Visa, MC, AmEx, • C-yes/S-no/P-yes/H-yes Polish, Russian	Continental plus breakfast Afternoon tea, lunch, restaurant Sitting room, Jacuzzis, suites, fireplaces, Cable TV

We would like to invite you to experience living, New Mexico style... a blend of people, food, art, history, wildlife and culture; all spaced between the sunrise and sunset of the great Southwest. theinn@flash.net http://www.innatparadise.com

---

Nuevo Dia Guest Accom. 11110 San Rafael Ave NE 87122 505-856-7910 Fax: 505-797-9806 Gretchen & Norman Helm All year	60-100-BB 3 rooms, 3 pb Visa, MC, Disc, *Rated* C-yes/S-ltd/P-yes/H-ltd	Full breakfast Homemade pastries Suites, cable TV, conference

Fantastic view of mountains and city at night from a sunroom or deck. Our guesthouse is self-contained and offers complete privacy. A sunroom with wood stove is attached.
nuevodiaNM@aol.com

Old Town B&B 707 17th St NW 87104 505-764-9144 888-900-9144 Nancy Hoffman All year	80-115-BB 2 rooms, 2 pb *Rated*, • C-ltd/S-no/P-no/H-no	Full breakfast Refreshment in room

Old Town B&B provides the comforts of home in a quiet, secluded garden setting with a wealth of interesting activities just minutes away from its doorstep.
nancyhoffman@earthlink.net http://www.inn-new-mexico.com

ALBUQUERQUE (REGION)

La Hacienda Grande 21 Baros Ln, *Bernalillo* 87004 505-867-1887 Fax: 505-771-1436 800-353-1887 Troy & Melody Scott All year	109-139-BB 6 rooms, 6 pb Most CC, *Rated*, • C-ltd/S-ltd/P-no/H-no	Full breakfast Snacks Weddings, retreats, Jacuzzi for 2, business meetings

250-year-old authentic hacienda with two-foot thick walls; wood ceilings, fireplaces, private baths, air cooled. lhg@swcp.com http://www.lahaciendagrande.com

---

Angels' Ascent B&B PO Box 4, *Cedar Crest* 87008 505-286-1588 Fax: 505-286-1588 Betty Hawk All year	85-160-BB 3 rooms, 2 pb *Rated*, • C-yes/S-ltd/P-yes/H-ltd	Full breakfast Snacks Sitting room, library, Jacuzzis, suites, cable, video lib., spec. pkgs.

A little bit of heaven in the heart of the Sandias with magnificent views on the historic Turquoise Trail. The decor is English country with antiques, outdoor Jacuzzi, waterfall & fishpond. angelsasc1@aol.com http://www.angelsascent.com

ALBUQUERQUE (REGION)

Chocolate Turtle
1098 W Meadowlark, *Corrales* 87048
505-898-1800 Fax: 505-898-5328
800-898-1842
Carole Morgan
All year

85-125-BB
4 rooms, 4 pb
Most CC, *Rated*, •
C-ltd/S-no/P-no

Full & Cont. plus bkfsts
Handmade chocolates
TV/videos, dining room, spa,
Romantic packages

Relax in historic Corrales. Located on the northern boundary of Albuquerque, yet in a country-like setting with incredible mountain views, horses, and great golfing.
turtlebb@aol.com http://www.collectorsguide.com/chocturtle

Nora Dixon Place
312 Dixon Rd, *Corrales* 87048
505-898-3662 Fax: 505-898-6430
888-667-2349
Norris & Cynthia C. Tidwell
All year

80-155-BB
3 rooms, 3 pb
Most CC, *Rated*, •
C-yes/S-no/P-ltd/H-ltd

Continental breakfast weekdays
Full breakfast on weekends
Sitting room, suites, fireplaces, conference facilities, TV, phones

Quiet New Mexico Territorial Style B&B, facing Sandia Mountain in Corrales. Located Northside Albuquerque where historic sites are easily visited on day excursions.
noradixon@aol.com http://www.noradixon.com

CHAMA

The Parlor Car
PO Box 967
311 Terrace Ave 87520
505-756-1946 Fax: 505-756-1057
888-849-7800
Wendy & Bonsall Johnson
All year

79-99-BB
3 rooms, 3 pb
Most CC, *Rated*, •
C-ltd/S-no/P-no/H-ltd

Full breakfast
Box lunches on request, snacks, welcome basket
Sitting room, library, Jacuzzi in 1 room, cable TV

Luxuriate in cool, clean mountain air in historic Victorian banker's home. Guests are treated to the luxury enjoyed by the socially elite of the early 20th century at economy pricing. http://www.parlorcar.com

---

Posada Encanto
PO Box 536
277 Maple Ave 87520
505-756-1048 Fax: 505-756-1843
800-756-1925
Teresa & Steve Smith All year

79-115-BB
5 rooms, 5 pb
Most CC, *Rated*, •
C-ltd/S-no/P-no/H-no
Spanish

Full breakfast
Afternoon tea, snacks
Library

Posada Encanto B&B, once an old church, is now a charming Old New Mexico style Inn, with rustic Southwestern appeal.
teresa@posadaencanto.com http://www.posadaencanto.com

CORRALES

Casa de Koshare
122 Ashley Ln NW 87048
505-898-4500 Fax: 505-898-8900
877-729-8100
Dar Robertson All year

82-155-BB
4 rooms, 2 pb
Most CC, •
C-ltd/S-no/P-ltd/H-ltd

Full breakfast
Snacks and beverages available in the afternoon
Courtyard, sitting room

Casa de KOSHARE is a "territorial" style Bed & Breakfast located in historic Corrales, New Mexico. darvinr@worldnet.att.net http://www.casadekoshare.com

---

Hacienda Manzanal B&B
PO Box 2667
300 West Meadowlark Ln
87048
505-922-1909 Fax: 505-922-1909
877-922-1662
Sue & Norm Gregory

85-135-BB
4 rooms, 4 pb
Most CC
All year

Full country breakfast
Afternoon tea, coffee, sodas, snacks
Gas fireplace, TV in great room, covered patio, spa, phone jack in room

Located in historic Corrales, New Mexico the newly built Hacienda Manzanal (House in the Apple Orchard) B&B offers luxurious accommodations in a warm and relaxed atmosphere. info@haciendamanzanal.com http://www.haciendamanzanal.com

FARMINGTON

Casa Blanca Inn
999 S 1200 E, Salt Lake City, UT, 84105
505 E La Plata St 87401
505-327-6503 Fax: 505-326-5680
800-550-6503
Rosalita Velasques & daughter Charlotte Latham
All year

78-135-BB
8 rooms, 7 pb
Most CC, *Rated*
C-yes/S-ltd/P-no/H-ltd
Spanish

Full gourmet breakfast
Lunch & dinner available, afternoon tea, snacks
Sitting rm, library, Jacuzzis, suites, fireplaces, cable TV, acc. bus. trav.

Beautiful Mediterranean style home built and handcrafted by the owner's father in the 1950s; has made a perfect transition to a bed and breakfast inn.

casablancanm@hotmail.com http://www.4cornersbandb.com

Silver River Adobe Inn
PO Box 3411
3151 West Main St 87499
505-325-8219 Fax: 505-325-5074
800-382-9251
Diana Ohlson & David Beers
All year

105-175-BB
3 rooms, 3 pb
Visa, MC, *Rated*, •
C-ltd/S-no/P-no/H-yes

Continental plus breakfast
Dinner upon request
River walk, wildlife, 5 star golfing, weddings, workshops

New Mexico adobe with large timbers. Day trips to Chaco Canyon, Mesa Verde, Aztec ruins, Salmon ruins, Canyon de Chelly.

sribb@cyberport.com http://www.cyberport.com/silveradobe

JEMEZ SPRINGS

Desert Willow
PO Box 255
15975 Hwy 4 87025
505-829-3410 Fax: 505-829-3410
Leone Wilson
All year

99-109-BB
2 rooms, 2 pb
Most CC, *Rated*, •
C-ltd/S-no/P-no/H-ltd

Full breakfast
Snacks
Sitting room, library, cable TV, 2 bedroom cottage with fireplace

Charming northern New Mexico style home on the Jemez River, nestled between red rock cliffs. wilsons@desertwillowbandb.com http://www.desertwillowbandb.com

---

Riverdancer Retreat
16445 Scenic Hwy 4 87025
505-829-3262 Fax: 505-829-3262
800-809-3262
All year

109-159-BB
7 rooms, 7 pb
Visa, MC, Disc, *Rated*, •
C-ltd/S-no/P-no/H-ltd

Full gourmet, mostly vegetarian
Retreat and groups

Comfortable adobe inn nestled by a river, beneath canyons & cottonwoods. Individual & intimate group retreats, massage/energy treatments, spirituality, creativity, nature hikes, yoga. info@riverdancer.com http://www.riverdancer.com

LAS CRUCES

Happy Trails Ranch in Old Mesilla
1857 Paisano Rd 88005
505-527-8471 Fax: 505-532-1937
Barry & Sylvia Byrnes
All year

85-100-BB
3 rooms, 1 pb
Visa, MC, AmEx, •
C-yes/S-ltd/P-yes
Spanish

Full breakfast
Snacks
Sitting room, library, bikes, Jacuzzis, cable TV

Hideaway, magnificent views of 4 mountain ranges, swimming pool, Jacuzzi in season. Children and pets welcome.

htrails@zianet.com http://www.las-cruces-new-mexico.com

T.R.H. Smith Mansion
909 N Alameda Blvd 88005
505-525-2525 Fax: 505-524-8227
800-526-1914
Marlene K. & Jay Tebo
All year

70-110
4 rooms, 4 pb
Rated

Prairie-style architecture featuring high-beamed ceilings, hardwood floors, stained glass windows and a brick & stucco exterior. smithmansion@zianet.com

LAS VEGAS

Plaza Hotel
230 Plaza 87701
505-425-3591 Fax: 505-425-9659
800-328-1882
Wid & Kak Slick
All year

59-129-BB
36 rooms, 36 pb
Most CC, *Rated*, •
C-yes/S-ltd/P-ltd/H-yes
Spanish, German

Full breakfast
Full breakfast, lunch & dinner avail 7 days a week
Business center, high-speed Internet

Historic hotel built in 1882, when Las Vegas was New Mexico's mercantile center. Now offering a restaurant, saloon, meeting space, high-speed Internet, and spacious rooms with private baths and HBO. lodging@plazahotel-nm.com http://www.plazahotel-nm.com

LOS ALAMOS

Casa del Rey B&B
305 Rover Blvd 87544
505-672-9401
Virginia King
All year

50-BB
2 rooms, 1 pb
Rated
C-ltd/S-no/P-no/H-no

Continental plus breakfast
Homemade breads, granola
Sitting room, patio, sun porch, garden, tennis courts nearby

Quiet residential area, friendly atmosphere, beautiful Mt. views from patios. Excellent library, restaurants and recreational facilities. nearby. vlking@aol.com

MESILLA

Meson de Mesilla Boutique
PO Box 1212
1803 Avenida de Mesilla 88046
505-525-9212
Chuck Walker
All year

75-105-BB
15 rooms, 13 pb
Most CC, *Rated*
C-no

Full breakfast
Restaurant/Cafe

Delightful boutique hotel with individually decorated rooms. Full service cocktail lounge. 3 star restaurant. http://www.mesondemesilla.com

OJO CALIENTE

Black Mesa
34328 US Highway 285 87549
505-583-2545 Fax: 505-583-2545
Lara Fitzgerald
All year

125-150-BB
2 rooms, 2 pb
AmEx, •
C-ltd/S-ltd/P-yes/H-no

Full breakfast
Decanter of sherry in room
Natural springs hot pool, library/sitting room

An oasis in the high desert. Friendly personalized service. Leisurely gourmet breakfast. Natural springs hot pool, porch surrounding the B&B with hammock and chairs, outdoor dining available. lara@blackmesabnb.com http://www.blackmesabnb.com

ROSWELL

The Pecos Diamond
200 S Kentucky Ave 88203
505-623-4534 Fax: 505-627-7694
877-321-7903
Sara & Randy Grill
All year

65-75-BB
3 rooms, 3 pb
•
C-ltd/S-yes/P-yes/H-no

Full gourmet breakfast
Afternoon tea, snacks
Sitting room, library, bikes, Jacuzzis, suites, fireplaces, cable TV, fax

In National Historic District; close to museums (5); dog run; antiques. Victorian suite; Southwest Pioneer suite; TV/VCR's; micro & fridge. padreone@trailnet.com

SANTA FE

Adobe Abode
202 Chapelle St 87501
505-983-3133 Fax: 505-983-3132
Andy Duettra
All year

135-175-BB
6 rooms, 6 pb
Visa, MC, Disc, *Rated*, •
C-yes/S-no/P-no/H-ltd
Spanish

Full gourmet breakfast
Complimentary cookies & sherry
Just 4 blocks from Santa Fe Plaza; designer linens, fireplaces, decor

Named Santa Fe's "Best Southwestern B&B" by Frommer's, this restored, historic adobe just 4 blocks from the Plaza offers a sophisticated mix of Southwest decor and European touches. Perfection! adobebnb@sprynet.com http://www.adobeabode.com

Adobe Abode, Santa Fe, NM

SANTA FE

Alexander's Inn
529 E Palace Ave 87501
505-986-1431
Fax: 505-982-8572
888-321-5123
Keith Spencer-Gore
All year

85-180-BB
7 rooms, 7 pb
Visa, MC, *Rated*, •
C-ltd/S-no/P-yes/H-no
French

Full breakfast
Afternoon tea, beverages
Sitting room w/fireplace, hot tub in back garden, dbl. Jacuzzi in cottage

Our traditional Southwestern casitas and historic inn are near both The Plaza and Canyon Road. We offer the warmth of staying with good friends and the comforts of a fine hotel.

alexandinn@aol.com http://www.alexanders-inn.com

Arius Compound
PO Box 1111
1018 Canyon Rd 87504
505-982-2621 Fax: 505-989-8280
800-735-8453
Len & Robbie Goodman
All year

100-120-EP
3 rooms, 3 pb
Most CC
C-yes/S-no/P-yes/H-no
Spanish

Full Kitchens in all Casitas
Fireplaces in all Casitas, outdoor red cedar Hot Tub, fruit trees, gardens

One-bedroom and two-bedroom Adobe Casitas on Canyon Road ("the Heart and Soul of Santa Fe"), next to restaurants and galleries. All with fireplaces and kitchens. Old world charm at affordable rates.

len@ariuscompound.com http://www.ariuscompound.com

Camas de Santa Fe
323 E Palace Ave 87501
505-984-1337 Fax: 505-984-8449
800-632-2627
John Gundzik, Vivian Margolis
All year

79-175-BB
15 rooms, 14 pb
Most CC, *Rated*, •
S-no/H-yes

Continental breakfast
Air-conditioning, telephones and cable television

Organically prepared, all natural continental breakfast.

camasdesantafe@aol.com http://www.camasdesantafe.com

SANTA FE

Casa De La Cuma
105 Paseo de la Cuma 87501
505-983-1717 Fax: 505-983-2241
888-366-1717
Alex & Nancy Leeson
All year

75-145-BB
4 rooms, 2 pb
Most CC, *Rated*, •
C-ltd/S-ltd/P-no/H-no

Continental plus breakfast
Complimentary beverages, snacks
Cable TV, solarium, garden, patio, outdoor hot tub, on-site parking

Southwestern adobe home with original artwork and furniture in 4 unique rooms. Mountain views! Walking distance to Plaza, shopping, restaurants, galleries, library, museums, banks and Ft. Marcy park. casacuma@casacuma.com http://www.casacuma.com

---

Casitas de las Palomas
511 Douglas St 87501
505-984-2270 Fax: 505-474-5675
866-832-0589
Wendy Kapp
All year

85-200-EP
4 rooms, 4 pb
Rated
C-yes/S-ltd/P-ltd/H-ltd

Fireplaces, cable TV

Old Authentic Adobe casitas located on one of Santa Fe's most charming streets. 1 block from Canyon Rd gallery district on historic eastside.
twocasitas@aol.com http://www.twocasitas.com

Crystal Mesa Farm
3547 State Rd 14 87505
505-474-5224 Fax: 505-474-5224
Marie Willey, Marie Bartels
All year

85-110-BB
C-yes/H-no
German

Continental plus breakfast
Snacks
Sitting room, library, suites, fireplaces, cable TV, hot tub, TIDI

Unique adobe hacienda hideaway, elegantly and eclectically furnished. Miniature animal farm with country solitude, but close to everything, and we have many off-beat recommendations. crysmefa@aol.com http://www.crystalmesafarm.com

---

Dos Casas Viejas
610 Agua Fria 87501
505-983-1636 Fax: 505-983-1749
Susan & Michael Strijek
All year

195-295-BB
8 rooms, 8 pb
Visa, MC, •
C-yes/S-ltd/P-no/H-yes

Continental plus breakfast
Snacks, complimentary wine
Lib., pool, stes., fireplaces, cable TV, accommodate business travelers.

A unique, intimate & sophisticated collection of charming adobe buildings housed w/in a walled & gated half acre adobe compound in heart of Santa Fe. Aspens, native grasses & flowering plants abound. doscasas@rt66.com http://www.doscasasviejas.com

---

Dunshee's
986 Acequia Madre 87501
505-982-0988
Susan Dunshee
All year

125-140-BB
2 rooms, 2 pb
Visa, MC, *Rated*
C-yes/S-no/P-no/H-no

Full or continental plus breakfast
Continental plus in casita, full brkfst in suite
Sitting room, refrigerator, homemade cookies, TV, private patio & gardens

Romantic hideaway in adobe compound in historic zone. Choice of 2-room suite or 2-bedroom guesthouse furnished with antiques.
sdunshee@aol.com http://www.dunshees.com

El Farolito
514 Webber St
514 Galisteo St 87501
505-988-1631 Fax: 505-988-4589
888-634-8782
Walt Wyss, Wayne Mainus
All year

140-230-BB
8 rooms, 8 pb
Most CC, *Rated*, •
C-yes/S-no/P-no/H-no

Continental plus breakfast
Sitting room, A/C, family friendly facility, private entrances, fireplaces

In the city's historic district, just a short walk to the plaza, El Farolito offers 8 romantic casitas. All accoms. feature patios, authentic Southwestern decor and art.
innkeeper@farolito.com http://www.farolito.com

Dunshee's, Santa Fe, NM

SANTA FE

Four Kachinas Inn
512 Webber St 87505
505-982-2550 Fax: 505-989-1323
888-634-8782
Walt Wyss, Wayne Mainus
All year

100-195-BB
5 rooms, 5 pb
Most CC, *Rated*, •
C-yes/S-no/P-no/H-yes
Spanish

Continental plus breakfast
Afternoon tea
Sitting room

Only 4 blocks from historic Plaza; furnished with handcrafted furniture, Navajo rugs breakfast, award-winning baked goods.
info@fourkachinas.com http://www.fourkachinas.com

Grant Corner Inn
122 Grant Ave 87501
505-983-6678 Fax: 505-983-1526
800-964-9003
Louise Stewart
All year

130-240-BB
10 rooms, 10 pb
Visa, MC, AmEx,
Rated, •
C-ltd/S-yes/P-no/H-yes
Spanish

Full breakfast
Wine & beer list (fee)
Gourmet picnic lunches, private club access, pool, sauna, tennis

Elegant colonial home located in the heart of downtown Santa Fe, nine charming rooms furnished with antiques; friendly, warm atmosphere.
gcinn@qwest.net http://www.grantcornerinn.com

Hacienda Nicholas
320 E Marcy St 87501
505-992-8385 Fax: 505-982-8572
888-284-3170
Glennon Grush
All year

100-175-BB
Rated, •

Full breakfast

Located on a quiet street on Santa Fe's east side, Hacienda Nicholas is just blocks away from the historic plaza and galleries of Canyon Road.
Haciendanicholas@aol.com http://www.haciendanicholas.com

Inn of the Turquoise Bear
342 E Buena Vista St 87505
505-983-0798 Fax: 505-988-4225
800-396-4104
Ralph Bolton & Robert Frost
All year

95-220-BB
10 rooms, 8 pb
Most CC, *Rated*, •
C-ltd/S-ltd/P-ltd/H-ltd
Spanish, French, German, Norwegian

Continental plus breakfast
Complimentary afternoon refreshments
Sitting room, library, cable TV/VCRs, book/film library, concierge services

Authentic adobe villa in a garden setting close to the Plaza. Winner of Heritage Preservation Awards (City of Santa Fe, 1999; State of NM, 2000). Out & About Editor's Choice: 1999, 2000, 2001. bluebear@newmexico.com http://www.turquoisebear.com

SANTA FE

The Madeleine
106 Faithway St 87501
505-982-3465 Fax: 505-982-8572
888-877-7622
George Padilla
All year

85-180-BB
8 rooms, 6 pb
Visa, MC, *Rated*, •
C-ltd/S-ltd/P-no/H-no

Full breakfast
Afternoon tea & dessert
Sitting room, lawn, quiet location, 3 blocks from Plaza

Historic 100-year-old Queen Anne house on Nat'l Register with fireplaces and antiques. Sensational English garden with hot tub for relaxing under the stars.
madeleineinn@aol.com http://www.madeleineinn.com

El Paradero
220 W Manhattan 87501
505-988-1177 Fax: 505-988-3577
Matt & Jennifer Laessig
All year

75-160-BB
14 rooms, 12 pb
Visa, MC, *Rated*, •
C-ltd/S-no/P-ltd/H-ltd
Spanish

Full gourmet breakfast
Open courtyard w/ garden, common rooms, piano, central cooling in rooms

180-year-old adobe in quiet downtown location near plaza. Gourmet breakfasts, warm atmosphere, detailed visitor information.
info@elparadero.com http://www.elparadero.com

Pueblo Bonito, Inc.
138 W Manhattan Ave 87501
505-984-8001 Fax: 505-984-3155
800-461-4599
Herb & Amy Behm
All year

75-160-BB
14 rooms, 14 pb
Most CC, *Rated*, •
C-yes/S-ltd/P-no/H-ltd

Continental plus breakfast to room
Afternoon tea, snacks
Laundry, cable TV, A/C, tours, sightseeing arr., airport pickup, hot tub

Secluded historic adobe; 5-minute walk from Santa Fe Plaza. Traditional New Mexico living and decor. 15 guestrooms w/private bath & fireplace.
pueblo@cybermesa.com http://www.pueblobonitoinn.com

Spencer House
222 McKenzie St 87501
505-988-3024 Fax: 505-984-9862
800-647-0530
Jan McConnell & John Pitlak
All year

115-165-BB
6 rooms, 6 pb
Visa, MC, AmEx, *Rated*, •
C-ltd/S-no/P-no/H-no

Full gourmet breakfast
Afternoon tea, homemade cookies
Sitting room, English patio garden, airport pickup

Cozy cottage-like charm around corner from the new Georgia O'Keefe Museum.
jan@spencerhse-santafe.com http://www.spencerhse-santafe.com

La Tienda Inn & Duran House
445 W San Francisco 87501
505-989-8259 800-889-7611
Leighton & Barbara Watson, James Meyer
All year

100-195-BB
11 rooms, 11 pb
Visa, MC, *Rated*, •
C-ltd/S-ltd/P-no/H-yes

Continental plus breakfast
Afternoon tea
Sitting room, library, bottled water and fresh flowers in room

A romantic adobe compound just 4 blocks from the Plaza. Private entrances; private baths; fireplaces. info@latiendabb.com http://www.latiendabb.com

---

Water Street Inn
427 W Water St 87501
505-984-1193 Fax: 505-984-6235
800-646-6752
Mindy Mills
All year

100-250-BB
12 rooms, 12 pb
Most CC, *Rated*
C-yes/S-no/P-yes/H-ltd
Spanish

Continental plus breakfast
Snacks, complimentary wine
Sitting room, Jacuzzis, suites, fireplaces, cable TV, CD players

Award-winning adobe restoration two blocks from the Plaza.
info@waterstreetinn.com http://www.waterstreetinn.com

SANTA FE (REGION)

Hacienda Vargas B&B Inn
PO Box 307
1431 El Camino Real,
Algodones 87001
505-867-9115 Fax: 505-867-1902
800-261-0006
Cynthia & Richard
Spence All year

79-149-BB
7 rooms, 7 pb
Visa, MC, *Rated*, •
C-ltd/S-no/P-no/H-ltd
Spanish, German

Full country breakfast
Complimentary wine
Hot tubs, sitting room, library, golf courses, nearby, private Jacuzzis

Conveniently located between Albuquerque and Santa Fe. Suites with double Jacuzzi's, fireplaces and private entrances.
stay@haciendavargas.com http://www.haciendavargas.com

Casa Escondida
PO Box 142
CR 0100 #62-64, *Chimayo* 87522
505-351-4805 Fax: 505-351-2575
800-643-7201
Belinda Bowling All year

80-140-BB
8 rooms, 8 pb
Visa, MC, *Rated*, •
C-yes/S-no/P-ltd/H-ltd

Full breakfast
Snacks, teas, coffees, lemonade
Hot tub, fireplaces, private decks, oversized tubs, CD player, copier

We are a secluded B&B in the mountains, on 6-acres. Located in the historic village of Chimayo (just 35 minutes north of Santa Fe). The perfect location for touring & skiing northern New Mexico. casaes@newmexico.com http://www.casaescondida.com

---

Rancho De San Juan
PO Box 4140
34020 Highway 285, *Espanola* 87533
505-753-6818 Fax: 505-757-8976
800-726-7121
David Heath & John H. Johnson III

200-400-BB
17 rooms, 17 pb
Visa, MC, AmEx, *Rated*, •
C-ltd/S-no/P-no/H-yes
Closed in January

Continental breakfast
Dinner available, Restaurant
Bar service, sitting room, suites, fireplaces

Intimate luxury on 225 scenic acres; award winnning gourmet restaurant and wine list. In-suite "spa services. Relais & Chateaux.
ranchosj@cybermesa.com http://www.ranchodesanjuan.com

The Galisteo Inn
HC 75-Box 4
9 La Vega, *Galisteo* 87540
505-466-8200 Fax: 505-466-4008
Chris Griscom
Feb.-Dec.

115-190-BB
12 rooms, 9 pb
Visa, MC, Disc, *Rated*, •
C-ltd/S-ltd/P-no/H-yes
Spanish

Full breakfast
Lunch, dinner, tea
Rest., bar, lib., bikes, hot tubs, sauna, massage, spa, horseback riding

Magical 250 year old Spanish hacienda on eight country acres, half hour from Santa Fe. Romantic dinners & buffet breakfasts, serene and retreat like.
galisteoin@aol.com http://www.galisteoinn.com

SILVER CITY

The Carter House
101 N. Cooper St 88061
505-388-5485 Fax: 505-534-0123
Lucy Dilworth
All year

70-80-BB
5 rooms, 5 pb
Visa, MC, AmEx, *Rated*
C-yes/S-no/P-no/H-ltd

Full breakfast included
Tea and home baked cookies

Silver City at its best! The stately Carter House was built in 1906 and offers five rooms each with private bath, personal service and a full, home cooked breakfast. THIS INN FOR SALE BY OWNER. carterhouse@zianet.com http://www.gilanet.com/carterhouse/

The Cottages
PO Box 2562
2037 Cottage San Rd 88062
505-388-3000 800-938-3001
Colleen & Mike All year

89-199-AP
5 rooms, 5 pb
Most CC, *Rated*, •
S-no/P-no/H-no

Full breakfast
Breakfast, lunch, dinner
Sitting room, library, suites, fireplaces, hot mineral baths

Secluded Country French cottages nestled in hundreds of acres of virgin forest, canyons, mountains and meadows with abundant wildlife! http://www.zianet.com/cottages

TAOS

Adobe & Pines Inn
PO Box 837
4107 Highway 68 87557
505-751-0947 Fax: 505-758-8423
800-723-8267
David/KayAnn Tyssee & C. Connelly All year

95-185-BB
9 rooms, 9 pb
Visa, MC, •
C-yes/S-no/P-yes/H-ltd

Full breakfast
Snacks
Fireplaces, Jacuzzis, CD players, music/book library, kitchens, lounge areas

Historic adobe hacienda transformed into charming/luxurious hideaway in Southwest says Frommer's/Fodor's. Jacuzzis, fireplaces, CD players, full breakfasts, snacks, gardens, views, romantic portals. adobepines@taosnet.com http://www.adobepines.com

---

Adobe and Stars
PO Box 2285
584 State Hwy 150 87571
505-776-2776 Fax: 505-776-2872
800-211-7076
Judy Salathiel All year

75-185-BB
8 rooms, 8 pb
Most CC, *Rated*, •
C-yes/S-no/P-ltd/H-yes
Spanish

Full breakfast
Get acquainted hour w/beverage, snacks. . .etc
Beautiful commmon area, hot tub under the stars, Jacuzzi/robes/hairdryers

Southwestern pueblo adobe style Inn with kiva fireplaces, beamed ceilings, hot tub under the stars, Jacuzzi tubs, 360 degree mountain views, full breakfasts, skiing/mountain biking/hiking access. stars@taosadobe.com http://www.taosadobe.com

---

Alma del Monte/Spirit of the Mountain
PO Box 1434
372 Hondo Seco Rd 87571
505-776-2720 Fax: 505-776-8888
800-273-7203

150-245-BB
5 rooms, 5 pb
Visa, MC, AmEx, *Rated*, •
C-ltd/S-ltd/P-no/H-ltd
Suzanne Head All year

Full breakfast
Afternoon tea, snacks, wine
Sitting room, library, Jacuzzis, fireplaces, suites, conference facilities

"Best Romantic Getaway" -Frommer's. Built for romance and luxury, this exquisite hacienda exudes casual elegance with magnificent vistas.
info@almaspirit.com http://www.AlmaSpirit.com

American Artists Gallery
PO Box 584
132 Frontier Ln 87571
505-758-0497 Fax: 505-758-0497
800-532-2041
LeAn & Charles Clamurro
All year

80-195-BB
10 rooms, 10 pb
Visa, MC, AmEx, *Rated*, •
C-ltd/S-no/P-ltd/H-ltd
Spanish

Full breakfast
Afternoon snacks & goodies
Hot tub, sitting room, skiing, hiking, art gallery, kiva fireplace

One of Taos' most romantic bed and breakfast inns. Inroom Jacuzzi 'tubs for two', fireplaces, outdoor hot tub and gourmet breakfasts. Discover the magic of Taos at this charming Southwest hacienda. aagh@newmex.com http://www.taosbedandbreakfast.com

---

Brooks Street Inn
PO Box 4954
119 Brooks St 87571
505-758-1489 Fax: 505-758-7525
800-758-1489
All year

79-145-BB
6 rooms, 6 pb
Most CC, *Rated*, •
C-ltd/S-no/P-ltd/H-ltd
Spanish
Cheryl Reed, Connie Sadler, Deb Bolk

Full breakfast
Complimentary espresso bar, afternoon snacks
Sitting area, library, lovely secluded garden, hammock

Near Taos Plaza. Our adobe home is a place of Southwest style and warmth. Full breakfasts, fine amenities, gracious hospitality. Offering the personal attention that only a small inn can provide. brooks@newmex.com http://www.brooksstreetinn.com

---

Casa Encantada
6460 NDCBU
416 Liebert Street 87571
505-758-7477 Fax: 505-737-5085
800-223-TAOS
Sharon Nicholson All year

105-195-BB
9 rooms, 9 pb
Visa, MC, AmEx, *Rated*, •
C-yes/S-no/P-yes/H-no

Full breakfast
Snacks
Sitting room, suites, fireplace, cable TV, conference facilities, hammocks

Welcome home to our peaceful, "enchanted" hacienda with its soft adobe walls, gardens and kivas. encantada@newmex.com http://www.casaencantada.com

TAOS

Casa Europa Inn & Gallery
HC 68, Box 3F
840 Upper Ranchitos Rd 87571
505-758-9798 888-758-9798
Rudi & Marcia Zwicker
All year

95-165-BB
6 rooms, 6 pb
Visa, MC, *Rated*, •
C-yes/S-no/P-no/H-no
German

Full breakfast
Wine, snacks, afternoon tea
Hot tub in one room, art gallery, shaded patio, hammock

Luxury country inn-historical Southwest estate; horses, views, ambiance. Romantic rooms and suites; marble baths (hot tubs), fireplaces.
casa-europa@travelbase.com http://www.travelbase.com/destinations/taos/casa-europa/

Cottonwood Inn B&B
HCR 74 Box 24609
#2 State Rt. 230 87529
505-776-5826 Fax: 505-776-1141
800-324-7120
Bill & Kit Owen
All year

95-175-BB
7 rooms, 7 pb
Most CC, *Rated*, •
C-yes/S-ltd/P-no/H-yes
Spanish, German

Full breakfast
Afternoon tea, snacks
Concierge service, sitting room, library, hot tubs, sauna

Exceptional views. Extensive gardens. Distinctive rooms with fireplaces, whirlpools, Southwestern art display & gallery. Outdoor hot tub.
cottonbb@newmex.com http://www.taos-cottonwood.com

Dreamcatcher
PO Box 2069
87571
505-758-0613 Fax: 505-751-0115
888-758-0613
Bob & Jill Purtee
All year

89-134-BB
7 rooms, 7 pb
Most CC, *Rated*, •
C-ltd/S-ltd/P-no/H-yes
Spanish

Full breakfast
Afternoon tea, snacks
Sitting room, fireplaces, hot tub, hammocks

A unique NM adobe inn situated in a secluded wooded setting a short 10 minute walk to Historic Taos Plaza. dream@taosnm.com http://dreambb.com

---

Hacienda Del Sol
PO Box 177
109 Mabel Dodge Ln 87571
505-758-0287 Fax: 505-758-5895
866-333-4459
Dennis Sheehan
All year

95-425-BB
11 rooms, 11 pb
Visa, MC, *Rated*, •
C-yes/S-no/P-no/H-ltd

Full breakfast
Complimentary snacks
Library, fireplaces, gallery, outdoor hot tub, robes, golf nearby, gardens

180-yr-old large adobe hideaway purchased by Mabel Dodge for Indian husband, Tony. Adjoins vast Indian lands yet close to Plaza. Tranquility, mountain views.
sunhouse@newmex.com http://www.taoshaciendadelsol.com

Historic Taos Inn
125 Paseo del Pueblo Norte
87571
505-758-2233 Fax: 505-758-5776
800-TAOS-INN
Carolyn Haddock & Doug Smith
All year

60-225-EP
36 rooms, 36 pb
Most CC
C-yes/S-ltd/P-no/H-yes

The Inn was founded on a rich legacy of excellence. Our guests are eager to sample the atmosphere of old Taos yet expect modern amenities. So our goal is to deliver just that.
taosinn@newmex.com http://www.taosinn.com

Inger Jirby's Casitas
207 Ledoux St 87571
505-758-7333 Fax: 505-758-7333
Inger Jirby
All year

150-250-BB
2 rooms, 2 pb
Most CC, *Rated*, •
C-yes/S-no/P-no/H-ltd

Self-prepared breakfast
Kiva fireplaces, phones in room, kitchen, entertainment ctr, washer/dryer

Inger's Guest Houses are located on Historic Ledoux Street, one block from Taos Plaza, in a 200 year old adobe compound located right across from the Blumenshein Museum.
jirby@newmex.com http://www.jirby.com

An Inn on La Loma Plaza
PO Box 4159
315 Ranchitos Rd 87571
505-758-1717 Fax: 505-751-0155
800-530-3040
Jerry & Peggy Davis
All year

85-250-BB
7 rooms, 7 pb
Most CC, *Rated*, •
C-yes/S-ltd/P-ltd/H-ltd
French & Spanish

Full breakfast
Afternoon tea, snacks
Sitting room, library, Jacuzzis, swimming pool, suites, fireplaces, cable TV

An elegant historic Inn, featuring exceptional hospitality, Southwestern ambiance, romantic rooms with fireplaces, mountain views, patios, and outdoor hot tub.

laloma@vacationtaos.com http://www.vacationtaos.com

Laughing Horse Inn
PO Box 4889
729 Paseo del Pueblo No 87571
505-758-8350 Fax: 505-751-1123
800-776-0161
Bob Bodenhamer All year

63-135-BB
13 rooms, 3 pb
Most CC, •
C-yes/S-no/P-yes/H-no
Spanish

Full breakfast
Guest kitchen
Fireplaces, 500 videos, free mountain bikes, hot tub, pets welcome

An eclectic 1887 adobe that was once home to the publisher of The Laughing Horse magazine and his guests, D.H. Lawrence and Georgia O'Keeffe.

laughinghorse@laughinghorseinn.com http://www.laughinghorseinn.com

---

The Little Tree
PO Drawer ii
226 County Road B-143 87571
505-776-8467 Fax: 505-776-3870
800-334-8467
Maggie and Gordon Johnston
All year

95-155-BB
4 rooms, 4 pb
Visa, MC, *Rated*, •
C-ltd/S-no/P-ltd/H-ltd

Full breakfast
Afternoon refreshments
Jacuzzi for 2, kiva fireplaces, private garden courtyrds, concierge services

Autumn in Taos! Come away to the serenity of our secluded four room B&B nestled halfway between the Mountains and the Plaza.

little@littletreebandb.com http://www.littletreebandb.com

Orinda
4451 NDCBU
461 Valverde 87571
505-758-8581 Fax: 505-751-4895
800-847-1837
Adrian & Sheila Percival
All year

95-145-BB
5 rooms, 5 pb
Most CC, *Rated*, •
C-ltd/S-no/H-no

Full breakfast
Snacks
Sitting room w/kiva fireplace, library, tennis ct, hottubs, sauna/pool, golf, mountain views

Quiet, pastoral setting on 2 acres, southwest adobe home close to town, shops, galleries and skiing (16 miles). orinda@newmex.com http://www.orindabb.com

---

La Posada de Taos
PO Box 1118
309 Juanita Ln 87571
505-758-8164 Fax: 505-751-4696
800-645-4803
Sandy & Alan Thiese All year

99-234-BB
6 rooms, 6 pb
Most CC, *Rated*, •
C-ltd/S-ltd/P-no/H-yes

Full breakfast
Large dining room
Sitting room, patios, sun room, portals, fireplaces, courtyards

We have a new large dining room with 13' high beamed ceiling overlooking the garden & Taos Mountain. Also added private patios for 2 rooms. Garden off sunroom with natural stone waterfall. laposada@laposadadetaos.com http://www.laposadadetaos.com

---

Touchstone Inn, Spa & Gallery
PO Box 1885
110 Mabel Dodge Ln 87571
505-758-0192 Fax: 505-758-3498
800-758-0192
Bren Price All year

135-300-BB
8 rooms, 8 pb
Visa, MC, AmEx, *Rated*, •
C-ltd/S-no/P-no

Full or continental breakfast
Jacuzzi tubs, fireplaces

Destination Spa and Gallery, a seven room inn with historic significance to Taos. The original portion of the traditional adobe is 200 years-old.

touchstone@taosnet.com http://www.touchstoneinn.com

TAOS (REGION)

Salsa del Salto
PO Box 1468
543 Highway 150, *El Prado*
87529
505-776-2422 Fax: 505-776-5734
800-530-3097
Theresa O'Connor
All year

85-160-BB
10 rooms, 10 pb
Visa, MC, AmEx,
Rated, •
C-ltd/S-no/P-no/H-no
English, French,
German, Spanish

full gourmet breakfast
afternoon snacks
hot tub, swimming
pool(summer only), tennis
courts

Beautiful southwestern Inn offering 10 years of fine food and hospitality. Ten guest rooms, private baths, hot tub, swimming pool, tennis court and stunning mountain views.
salsa@taosnm.com http://BandBTaos.com

Columbine Inn & Conf. Ctr.
PO Box 19
1288 Hwy 150, *Taos Ski Valley*
87525
505-776-5723 Fax: 505-776-1326
888-884-5723
Susie & Paul Geilenfeldt

55-150-BB
20 rooms, 20 pb
Visa, MC, AmEx, •
C-yes/S-no/P-ltd/H-no
May–Oct, Nov–April

Continental plus breakfast
Sitting room, Jacuzzis, board
games, accom. bus. travelers

Authentic, alpine Inn located in the heart of the Taos Mountains. Come to the mountains and let us be your home away from home. Friendly, fun and convenient.
psgeilen@taosnet.com http://www.columbineinntaos.com

TAOS SKI VALLEY

Austing Haus
PO Box 8
1282 State Hwy 150 87525
505-776-2649 Fax: 505-776-8751
800-748-2932
Brian Iffert

49-175-BB
23 rooms, 23 pb
Most CC, *Rated*, •
C-yes/S-ltd/P-yes/H-ltd
Closed April 10–May 10

Continental plus breakfast
Sitting room, Jacuzzis,
fireplaces, cable TV,
accommodate business
travelers

A mountain inn nestled in the southern Rockies of northern New Mexico, specializing in romantic getaways. austing@newmex.com http://www.taoswebb.com/hotel/austinghaus

ZUNI MOUNTAINS (REGION)

Cimarron Rose
689 Oso Ridge, *Grants* 87020
505-783-4770 800-856-5776
Sheri McWethy
All year

50-105-BB
3 rooms, 2 pb
Rated
C-ltd/S-no/P-no/H-ltd

Full breakfast
Evening dessert
Sitting room, library, suites,
woodstove, gallery, full
kitchen

Relax, nurture your soul in the rustic comfort of our Mountain Southwest Inn. Enjoy ecclectic decor, plants, viga ceilings, pine and Mexican tile floors.
http://www.cimarronrose.com

New York

ADIRONDACK MOUNTAINS (REGION)

Glenmoore Lakeside Cottages
330 Glen Lake Rd, *Lake George*
12845
518-792-5261
Dave & Denise Paddock
May–October

68-120-BB
11 rooms, 11 pb
Visa, MC
C-yes/S-ltd/P-ltd/H-no

Continental plus breakfast
Sitting room, rowboats,
canoes, accommodate
business travelers

Lakeside cottages and lodge accommodations on beautiful Glen Lake in the southern Adirondack Mountains. World famous Lake George & Saratoga Springs nearby.
http://www.glenmoorelodge.com

ADIRONDACK MOUNTAINS (REGION)

Glenmoore Lakeside Cottages
330 Glen Lake Rd, *Lake George* 12845
518-792-5261
Dave & Denise Paddock

68-120-BB
11 rooms, 11 pb
Visa, MC
C-yes/S-ltd/P-ltd/H-no
May–October

Continental plus breakfast
Sitting room, rowboats, canoes, accommodate business travelers

Lakeside cottages and lodge accommodations on beautiful Glen Lake in the southern Adirondack Mountains. World famous Lake George & Saratoga Springs nearby.
http://www.glenmoorelodge.com

ALBANY

Pine Haven
531 Western Ave 12203
518-482-1574
All year

74-89-BB
5 rooms, 5 pb
Most CC, *Rated*, •
C-ltd/S-no/P-no/H-no

Continental plus breakfast
Living room, TV, books, board games, antiques, original oak woodwork

Victorian ambience in the heart of the city. Century-old Victorian in a beautiful residential area of the state's capital. Features iron & brass beds, feather mattresses
http://www.pinehavenbedandbreakfast.com

ALBANY (REGION)

River Hill
PO Box 253
Route 144, *New Baltimore* 12124
518-756-3313
Julia Coryell All year

90-BB
2 rooms, 2 pb
Visa, MC, AmEx
C-yes/P-ltd/H-no
Spanish

Full breakfast
Afternoon tea, complimentary wine
Sitting room, library, family friendly facility, rooms with A/C

Charming Victorian overlooking the Hudson River, boasting antiques, four poster beds, bountiful breakfast served on the terrace or by fire, with nearby marina.
riverhillbb@aol.com

AMENIA

Troutbeck
Leedsville Rd 12501
914-373-9681 Fax: 914-373-7080
800-978-7688
Garret Corcoran
All year

350-600-AP
42 rooms, 37 pb
AmEx, *Rated*, •
C-ltd/S-yes/P-no/H-no
Spanish, Port., It., Fr.

Full breakfast excluding Sunday
All meals & open bar included
Pub. rooms, piano, library, tennis courts, ballroom, 2 pools, exercise room

Historic English country estate on 422 acres, with indoor & outdoor pools, fine chefs, 12,000 books, lovely grounds, gazebo brookside for weddings.
innkeeper@troutbeck.com http://www.troutbeck.com

AUBURN

A Wicher Garden
5831 Dunning Ave Rd 13021
315-252-1187 Fax: 315-282-0028
800-356-8556
Gail & Gary Wichers
All year

85-160-BB
4 rooms, 4 pb
Most CC, *Rated*, •
C-ltd/S-no/P-ltd/H-no

Full breakfast
Snacks & Beverages
Sitting room, Jacuzzis, fireplaces, cable TV, accommodate business travlers

Relaxing porches, nature walks and starry nights; our unique and inviting custom themed rooms and country treed lawns welcome you. Minutes from fine dining, wine trail, lakes and museums. wgarden@localnet.com http://www.wichergardeninn.com

AVON

Serenity, A B&B
2284 Dutch Hollow Rd 14414
716-226-9252 Fax: 716-226-6274
Steve & Kimberle Miller
All year

70-225-BB
5 rooms, 3 pb
Most CC, *Rated*, •
S-no/P-no/H-no

Full breakfast
Afternoon tea, snacks
Sitting room, Jacuzzis, suites, fireplaces, outdoor spa

"Comfortably Posh", this newly renovated 1823 7000 sq ft manor is splended for a romantic getaway or relaxing retreat. serenity1@prodigy.net http://www.Serenitybandb.com

AVON

White Oak
277 Genessee St 14414
585-226-6735
Barbara B. Herman
All year

95-105-BB
3 rooms, 3 pb
Visa, MC
C-ltd/S-no/P-no/H-no

Full breakfast
Cable TV, sitting room, library, accommodate business travelers

An 1860 Second Empire Victorian home set in a country village, but affording convenient access to Western New York attractions and activities.
avon-bnb@frontiernet.net http://www.whiteoakbandb.com

BELLEAYRE MOUNTAIN (REGION)

Alpine Osteria
PO Box 443
Belleayre Mtn Rd, *Highmount* 12441
845-254-9851
Scott F.
All year

BB
5 rooms, 5 pb
Visa, MC, AmEx
C-yes/S-no/P-no/H-ltd
Italian

Breakfast served in dining room
Delicious breakfast, homemade wine, coffee, tea
Professional chef, game room, Jacuzzi, family room, in room VCR's with tapes

All new beautiful Bed and Breakfast Inn located on Belleayre Mountain access road in the heart of the Catskills. Sparkling clean King and Queen size bedrooms. Perfect for families and couples! info@alpineosteria.com http://www.alpineosteria.com

BERKSHIRES (REGION)

Sedgwick Inn
PO Box 250
17971 State Route 22, *Berlin* 12022
518-658-2334 Fax: 518-658-3998
Diane and Chet Niedzwiecki
All year

75-195-BB
11 rooms, 11 pb
Most CC, *Rated*, •
C-ltd/S-ltd/P-ltd/H-yes
Polish, Russian

Full breakfast
Lunch/dinner, restaurant
Bar service, sitting room, library, tennis nearby, swimming lakes, spa, pool

Circa 1791 "quintessential country inn"–A place of old-world charm, casual elegance, of good food, and gracious hospitality. The two-hundred eleven-year-old Colonial Inn is a true New England gem. sedgwickin@aol.com http://www.sedgwickinn.com

BLOOMFIELD

Melody Farm & Teddy Inn
6700 State Route 5 14469
585-657-4863 Fax: 585-657-4863
Patti and Mark Watkins
All year

85-150-BB
3 rooms, 3 pb
Visa, MC
C-ltd/S-ltd/P-no/H-no

Full breakfast
Various holiday snacks
Jacuzzis, fireplaces, TVs, radios, tape players and A/C

Fully restored 1820's farmhouse offering three rooms with private baths and a full breakfast buffet. Relax after breakfast on the enclosed porch or just wile away some time on the gazebo swing. mldytdybnb@aol.com http://www.melodyteddybnb.com

BLUE MOUNTAIN LAKE

The Hedges
PO Box 209
Hedges Road 12812
518-352-7325 Fax: 518-352-7672
Rip & Pat Benton

160-295-MAP
29 rooms, 29 pb
Rated
C-yes/S-no/P-no/H-yes
May through Oct.

Full breakfast
Tea, coffee, evening snack
Boat & Swimming docks, beach, tennis courts, library, porches, game room

On the shores of Blue Mountain Lake in the heart of America's largest State Park, The Hedges offers the relaxation & recreation of a unique Adirondack resort.
hedges@capital.net http://www.thehedges.com

BOUCKVILLE

Ye Olde Landmark Tavern
PO Box 5
US Route 20 & Canal Rd 13310
315-893-1810 Fax: 315-893-1810
Stephen Hengst
April-December

80-110-BB
4 rooms, 4 pb
Most CC
C-yes/S-no/P-no/H-no

Continental plus breakfast
Dinner, restaurant, bar service
Suites, cable TV

Historic cobblestone building on National Register, in antique center of New York State. Near Colgate University, Hamilton College. http://www.hamsltonny.com/landmark/

BOVINA

Swallows Nest
159 Miller Ave 13740
602-832-4547 Fax: 602-832-4547
Walter & Gunhilde Kuhnle
All year

50-75-BB
4 rooms, 2 pb
Visa, MC
C-ltd/S-ltd/P-ltd/H-no
German

Full 3-course breakfast
Afternoon tea, snacks
Sitting room, fireplaces, cable TV, accommodate business travelers

Tranquil country setting. Quiet pond and babbling brook. 1840 farm house full of warmth and ambiance. http://www.delinns.com/snbb.htm

BROCKPORT

The Victorian
320 Main St 14420
716-637-7519 Fax: 716-637-7519
800-836-1929
Sharon M. Kehoe
All year

66-99-BB
7 rooms, 7 pb
Rated, •
C-yes/S-no/P-no/H-no

Full breakfast
Afternoon tea
Sitting room, library, bikes, Jacuzzis, fireplaces, fax, cable TV

Late 19th-century Queen Anne home with pleasing blend of antiques and modern furnishings. Short walk from historic Erie Canal.
sk320@aol.com http://www.victorianbandb.com

BRONXVILLE

The Villa
90 Rockledge Rd 10708
914-337-5595 Fax: 914-337-5661
800-457-5595
Pam Humbert
All year

150-BB
4 rooms, 4 pb
Most CC
C-ltd/S-yes/P-ltd

Continental plus breakfast
Snacks and beverages
hot tub, home office w/ personal computer, typewriter, copier, fax

Four bedroom suites, each with a queen bed, private bath, fireplace, air-conditioning and cable TV. pam@thevillainbronxville.com http://www.bbhost.com/villa

BUFFALO

Beau Fleuve Inn
242 Linwood Ave 14209
716-882-6116 800-278-0245
Ramona & Rik Whitaker
All year

100-140-BB
Most CC, *Rated*
S-no

Full breakfast
Down comforters, ceiling fans, coffeemakers, central A/C

Come, enjoy the gracious hospitality and elegance of the finest Bed & Breakfast Buffalo has to offer, where the beds are oh-so-comfortable and the candlelight breakfasts superb.
innkeeper@beaufleuve.com http://www.beaufleuve.com/

BUFFALO (REGION)

Asa Ransom House
10529 Main St, Rt 5, *Clarence* 14031
716-759-2315 Fax: 716-759-2791
800-841-2340
Robert Lenz, Abigail Lenz
All year exc. Jan.

95-155-BB
9 rooms, 9 pb
Visa, MC, Disc, *Rated*, •
C-ltd/S-no/P-no/H-yes

Full breakfast
Dinner (except Mon), bar, snacks
Sitting room, library, most rooms with fireplaces, herb garden, bicycles

Village inn furnished with antiques, period reproductions; gift shop, herb garden, regional dishes, homemade breads & desserts.
innfo@asaransom.com http://www.asaransom.com

BURDETT

The Red House Country Inn
4586 Picnic Area Rd
Finger Lakes Nat'l Forest 14818
607-546-8566 Fax: 607-546-4105
Sandy Schmanke & Joan Martin
All year

79-99-BB
5 rooms
Most CC, *Rated*, •
C-ltd/S-no/P-no

Full breakfast
Complimentary tea, coffee
Large in-ground pool, sitting room, nature trails

Within national forest; 28 miles of trails. Beautiful rooms in gorgeous setting. Near famous Watkins Glen, Eastside Seneca Lake.
redhsinn@aol.com http://www.fingerlakes.net/redhouse

CAMPBELL

Halcyon Place B&B
11 Maple St
14825
607-529-3544
Yvonne & Douglas Sloan
All year

55-85
3 rooms, 1 pb
Rated

Peacefulness, tranquility, and gracious hospitality are the hallmarks of this elegant and historic bed and breakfast. herbtique@aol.com http://www.bbonline.com/ny/halcyon

CANANDAIGUA

Acorn Inn
4508 Bristol Valley Rd
4508 Bristol Valley Rd (Rte 64 S) 14424
585-229-2834 Fax: 585-229-5046
888-245-4134
Louis & Joan Clark
All year

130-225-BB
4 rooms, 4 pb
Most CC, *Rated*, •
C-ltd/S-no/P-no/H-no

Full gourmet breakfast
Snacks, complimentary beverages
Sitting room, library, hot tubs, wineries, golf/skiing/tennis nearby

Charming 1795 inn furnished with period antiques, canopy beds, luxury baths, colonial fireplace in book-lined gathering room. Beautiful gardens with spa.
acorninn@rochester.rr.com http://acorninnbb.com

Chambery Cottage
6104 Monks Rd 14424
585-393-1405 Fax: 585-393-1405
Terry & Zora Molkenthin
All year

95-145-BB
4 rooms, 4 pb
Visa, MC
C-no/S-no/P-no/H-no
Czech, Polish, Russian

Full breakfast
Tea, coffee, cookies, snacks, water, soda
Sitting room, library, 30 acres of privacy

Chambery Cottage is a fully renovated 100 year-old farmhouse. The decor is Old World or French Country. All four guestrooms feature private bath, TV/VCRs, CD players, alarm clocks, some fireplaces. euroctge@frontiernet.net http://www.chamberycottage.com

---

Morgan Samuels Inn
2920 Smith Rd 14424
585-394-9232 Fax: 585-394-8044
John & Julie Sullivan
All year

119-325-BB
6 rooms, 6 pb
Most CC, *Rated*, •
C-ltd/S-no/P-no/H-no

Full breakfast
Dinner, afternoon tea
Library, bicycles, tennis court, Jacuzzis, suites, fireplaces, bus. trav.

Travel the 2,000 foot tree-lined drive to the secluded 1810 English style mansion and sense the difference between ordinary and legendary. Afternoon tea and appetizers are welcome treats. morsambb@aol.com http://www.morgansamuelsinn.com

---

Oliver Phelps Country Inn
252 N Main St 14424
716-396-1650 800-724-7397
John & Joanne Sciarratta
All year

90-155-BB
4 rooms, 4 pb
Visa, MC, AmEx, *Rated*, •
C-ltd/P-no/H-no

Full breakfast
Afternoon tea, snacks
Fireplaces, cable TV, accommodate business travelers

A historic Inn built in the 1800's chockfull of antiques and country charm. A delicious breakfast featuring homemade bread and pastries.
js1145@aol.com http://www.oliverphelps.com

CANANDAIGUA (REGION)

Greenwoods Inn
8136 Quayle Rd, *Honeoye* 14471
585-229-2111 Fax: 585-229-0034
800-914-3559
Lisa & Mike Ligon
All year

99-165-BB
5 rooms, 5 pb
Most CC, *Rated*, •
C-ltd/S-ltd/P-no/H-no

Full breakfast
Sitting room, library, Jacuzzis, suites, fireplaces, cable TV

Country log inn displaying influences from the Adirondack "Great Camps" of yesterday. Hilltop setting provides panoramic lake/valley views.
innkeeper@greenwoodsinn.com http://www.greenwoodsinn.com

CANTON

Misty Meadows
1609 State Highway 68 13617
315-379-1563
Fax: 315-379-1563
Peter & Marcia Syrett
All year

55-65-BB
3 rooms, 3 pb
Visa, MC, AmEx, *Rated*
C-yes/S-no/P-ltd/H-no

Full Country Breakfast
Complementary beverages, fruit & Full Cookie Jar!
Cozy garden seating area, game room, Internet access, video & book library.

Modern center hall colonial located on rolling meadows. We provide that special place to stay when you visit the Canton-Potsdam area. A short drive to any of our four area colleges. info@mistymeadowsny.com http://www.mistymeadowsny.com

---

Ostrander's
1675 State Hwy 68 13617
315-386-2126 Fax: 315-386-3843
877-707-2126
Rita & Al Ostrander
All year

65-75-BB
4 rooms, 4 pb
Visa, MC, AmEx, *Rated*, •
C-ltd/S-no/P-no/H-no

Full breakfast
Snacks, evening dessert
Sitting rm, cable TV, phones, A/C, cottages w/full kitchen, acc. bus. trvl.

Whether you arrive for business or for pleasure, we offer the perfect combination of convenience & quiet comfort. Visit the sheep barn, play with border collie dogs or shop in our gift shop. ostbbinn@northnet.org http://www.ostranders.com

CATSKILLS (REGION)

River Run
PO Box 9
882 Main St, *Fleischmanns* 12430
845-254-4884
Melissa & Ben Fenton All year

75-165-BB
9 rooms, 5 pb
Visa, MC, AmEx, *Rated*, •
C-yes/S-ltd/P-yes/H-no

Continental plus breakfast
Fireplace, stained glass, beautiful grounds, piano, front porch/trout stream

Exquisite country village Victorian, at the edge of the Catskill Forest. Enjoy hiking trails, superb skiing, antiquing, auction, fishing, golf & tennis.
riverrun@catskill.net http://www.catskill.net/riverrun

CAZENOVIA

Brae Loch Inn
5 Albany St 13035
315-655-3431 Fax: 315-655-4844
James & Valerie Barr
All year

80-155-BB
12 rooms, 12 pb
Visa, MC, AmEx, *Rated*
C-yes/S-yes/P-no/H-no
Spanish

Continental breakfast
Dinner available; brunch on Sunday
Fireplaces, gift shop, cigar lounge w/ pool table

Family owned & operated since 1946. As close to a Scottish Inn as you will find this far west of Edinburgh! braeloch1@aol.com http://www.braelochinn.com

---

Brewster Inn
PO Box 507
6 Ledyard Ave 13035
315-655-9232 Fax: 315-655-2130
Richard Hubbard All year

70-235-EP
17 rooms, 17 pb
Visa, MC, *Rated*

Continental breakfast

Elegant Country Inn overlooking Cazenovia Lake serving dinner nightly and Sunday Brunch. Award winning wine list. http://www.cazenovia.com/brewster

CHAPPAQUA

Crabtree's Kittle House
11 Kittle Rd 10514
914-666-8044 Fax: 914-666-2684
800-235-6186
Judith Kissel,
Proprietor: John Crabtree
All year

147-BB
12 rooms, 12 pb
Most CC
C-yes/S-ltd/P-ltd/H-ltd
Spanish

Continental breakfast
Lunch, dinner
Restaurant, bar, cable TV, accommodates business travelers

Built in 1790, country charm, historic character with world-class Progressive American cuisine. New York Times rated excellent. Grand Award wine cellar.
kittlemimi@aol.com http://www.kittlehouse.com

CHATHAM (REGION)

Inn at Silver Maple Farm
PO Box 358
1871 Route 295, *Canaan* 12029
518-781-3600 Fax: 518-781-3883
Bill Hutton and Joell Weisman
All year

80-290-BB
11 rooms, 11 pb
Most CC, *Rated*
C-ltd/S-no/P-no/H-ltd

Full breakfast
Afternoon tea
Sitting room, Jacuzzi, suites, fireplaces, cable TV, accom.bus.travelers

Lovely accommodations in a beautifully converted post and beam barn, furnished with Shaker-inspired furnishings; gourmet breakfast in our Great Room.
billjoel@silvermaplefarm.com http://www.silvermaplefarm.com

CHAUTAUQUA

Plumbush
PO Box 864
4541 Chautauqua-Stedman R 14722
716-789-5309 Fax: 716-357-9727
Gary & Mary Doebler
All year

85-130-BB
5 rooms, 5 pb
Visa, MC, AmEx, *Rated*
S-no/P-no/H-no

Continental breakfast plus
Sitting room, library, cable TV, conference facilities, hiking/skiing trails

Plumbush is a gracious circa 1865 Italianate villa restored to its original grandeur.
plumbush@yahoo.com http://chautauquainfo.com

CHESTERTOWN

Landon Hill
10 Landon Hill Rd 12817
518-494-2599 Fax: 518-494-7324
888-244-2599
Carl & Judy Johnson
All year

80-144-BB
5 rooms, 4 pb
Visa, MC, *Rated*, •
C-yes/S-ltd/P-ltd/H-yes

Full breakfast
Sitting room, fireplaces, cable TV, canoe, snowshoe rental

Landon Hill is an historic house built in the 1860s. There are 5 large, distinctive guestrooms with queen or king beds. landon@bedbreakfast.net http://bedbreakfast.net

CLINTON

The Artful Lodger
7 East Park Row 13323
315-853-3672 Fax: 315-853-1489
888-563-4377
Tim & Susan Ostinett Sweetland
All year

99-130-BB
5 rooms, 5 pb
Most CC, *Rated*
C-yes/S-no/P-no/H-ltd
French

Full breakfast on weekends
Continental breakfast on weekdays
Sitting room, library, art gallery, piano, family friendly facility

Located on a historic Village Green, this 1835 federal-style inn showcases the work of regional artists. artful@dreamscape.com

COLDEN

Back of the Beyond
7233 Lower E Hill Rd 14033
716-652-0427
Shash Georgi
All year

65-BB
3 rooms
Rated
C-yes/S-no/P-no/H-no

Full country breakfast
Complimentary beverages & snacks
Kitchen, fireplace, pool table, gift shop, swimming pond

Charming mini-estate 50 minutes from Niagara Falls. Organic herb, flower and vegetable gardens. Hiking. shashibotb@aol.com

CONESUS

Eastlake
5305 East Lake Rd 14435
716-346-3350 Fax: 716-346-5255
866-222-1544
Charlotte & Dennis Witte
All year

95-175-BB
4 rooms, 4 pb
Most CC, *Rated*, •
C-ltd/S-ltd/P-no/H-ltd

Full breakfast
Evening dessert
Sitting room, Jacuzzis, suites, fireplaces, cable TV, docking privileges

Elegant Arts many amenities for your pleasure. Use our boats, bring your own or rent nearby. Great restaurants. eastlake@rochester.rr.com

COOPERSTOWN

Angelholm
14 Elm St 13326
607-547-2483 Fax: 607-547-2309
Jan & Fred Reynolds
All year

105-125-BB
5 rooms, 5 pb
Visa, MC, *Rated*, •
C-ltd/S-no/P-no/H-no

Full breakfast
Deluxe & afternoon tea
Sitting room, library, porch, piano, TV room, specialty diets, A/C

Historic 1805 Federal Colonial with off-street parking. Walking distance to shops, restaurants and Hall of Fame Museum. anglholm@telenet.com http://www.angelholmbb.com

---

Chestnut Street Guest House
79 Chestnut St 13326
607-547-5624
John & Pam Miller
May 1–October 31

125-190-BB
4 rooms, 4 pb
C-ltd/S-no/P-no/H-no

Continental plus breakfast
Restaurants nearby
Sitting room, walk to 3 museums, tennis nearby

Park your car and enjoy the beauty of our delightful village. Warm hospitality and a lovely home await you. stay@chestnut79.com http://www.chestnut79.com

---

The Cooper Inn
PO Box 311
15 Chestnut St 13326
607-547-2567 Fax: 607-547-1271
800-348-6222
Steven C. Walker
All year

115-290-BB
15 rooms, 15 pb
Rated, •
C-yes/S-no/P-no/H-no

Continental breakfast
Facilities of Otesaga Resort Hotel available to inn guests during season

Classic Federal brick landmark Inn built in 1812 & located on its stately grounds in the heart of Cooperstown. reservations@cooperinn.com http://cooperinn.com

---

Country Lion
4 Glen Ave 13326
607-547-8264 Fax: 607-544-1431
Maureen & Richard Haralabatos
All year

99-159-BB
5 rooms, 4 pb
Rated, •
C-yes/S-no/P-no/H-no

Full breakfast
Afternoon tea
Sitting room, library, Jacuzzis, suites, fireplaces, cable TV

Beautiful 1883 restored Queen Anne home, centrally located in the village of Cooperstown. countrylion@countrylion.com http://www.countrylion.com

---

Green Apple Inn
81 Lake St 13326
607-547-1080 Fax: 607-544-1441
866-547-1080
Melanie Jane Crawford
All year

135-210-BB
4 rooms, 3 pb
Visa, MC, *Rated*, •
C-ltd/S-no/P-no/H-no

Full breakfast
Afternoon tea, snacks, complimentary wine
Sitting room, library, bicycles, tennis court, swimming pool, suites

Enchanted Bed & Breakfast, built on Lake Otsego in 1840. Beautiful suites and gardens with beautiful gourmet breakfasts.
grnapple@dmcom.net http://www.greenappleinn.com

The Inn at Cooperstown
16 Chestnut St 13326
607-547-5756 Fax: 607-547-8779
Michael Jerome
All year

110-315-BB
17 rooms, 17 pb
Most CC, *Rated*, •
C-ltd/S-yes/P-no/H-yes

Continental breakfast
1986 NY State Historic Preservation award winner, conf. facilities

Restored Victorian inn providing genuine hospitality; clean, comfortable guestrooms.
theinn@telenet.net http://www.innatcooperstown.com

The Landmark Inn
64 Chestnut Street 13326
607-547-7225 Fax: 607-547-7240
Linda & Bob Schuermann
All year

95-135-BB
9 rooms, 9 pb
Most CC
C-yes/S-no/P-no/H-yes

Full Gourmet Breakfast
Sitting room, A/C, cable TV, suites, large yard, acc. bus. travelers

1856 Victorian; nine rooms/suites, private baths, TV, A/C, full gourmet breakfast; walk to Baseball Hall of Fame, shops, restaurants; near lake, golf, breweries, Farmer's and Art Museums, opera. landmarkinn@yahoo.com http://www.landmarkinnbnb.com

Green Apple Inn, Cooperstown, NY

COOPERSTOWN

Litco Farms PO Box 1048 6231 St Hwy 28, Fly Creek 13326 607-547-2501 Fax: 607-547-7079 Jim & Margaret Wolff All year	89-129-BB 4 rooms, 2 pb Most CC, *Rated*, • C-yes/S-no/P-no/H-no	Full breakfast Sitting room, swimming, library, pool, hikes, cross-country ski trails,ponds

Families marvelous breakfasts litcofarms@stny.rr.com

Thistlebrook 316 County Hwy 28 13326 607-547-6093 800-596-9305 Paula & Jim Bugonian Open May-Nov.	135-155-BB 5 rooms, 5 pb *Rated*, • C-ltd/S-no/P-no/H-yes	Full breakfast Complimentary port & sherry Sitting room, library, oversized guestrooms, pool, 4 private acres

Voted as a "Top Twelve Inn" in 1992 by Country Inns magazine. Circa 1866 barn with European, American, antique furnishings. Beautiful valley views.
bugonian@aol.com http://www.thistlebrook.com

COOPERSTOWN (REGION)

Sunrise Farm 331 County Hwy 17, *New Berlin* 13411 607-847-9380 Janet Schmelzer All year	50-60-BB 1 rooms, 1 pb C-yes/S-no/P-no/H-no	Full breakfast Complimentary wine

Quiet, hill farm on paved road. Scottish Highland cattle. Lake swimming, hiking at nearby State Parks. Private bathroom. Full breakfast. Small enough for hosts to be flexible. Cooperstown 20 miles. jluddite@mycidco.com

Edgefield PO Box 152 153 Washington St, *Sharon Springs* 13459 518-284-3339 Daniel M. Wood All year	110-175-BB 5 rooms, 5 pb • C-yes/S-no/P-no/H-no	Full breakfast Afternoon tea, complimentary wine and refreshments Living room, veranda, fireplace, friendly host & cat

A well-appointed Edwardian home in historic village near Cooperstown & Glimmerglass Opera. Comfortable, elegant English country-house decor, antiques. Five guestrooms (queen or twin), private baths.
dmwood71@hotmail.com http://www.sharonsprings.com/edgefield.htm

COOPERSTOWN (REGION)

Westwood Guest Cottage
215 W 90th St #4E
286 Fred Braun Rd, *Unadilla* 13849
607-369-7306 Fax: 607-369-7306
Lisa Moskowitz & Doren Slade
April–November

150-EP
2 rooms, 2 pb
Rated, •
C-yes/S-ltd/P-yes/H-no
Spanish

Full kitchen and outside grill
Sitting room

Magical 2-bedroom hideaway w/fully equipped kitchen, nestled on 11 acres of woods. Furnished w/comfortable antiques; complete patio w/ outdoor grill. Located in the heart of historic New York. ldjinc@concentric.net http://www.westwoodguestcottage.com/

CORNING (REGION)

Rufus Tanner House
60 Sagetown Rd, *Pine City* 14871
607-732-0213 Fax: 607-735-0620
Donna & Rick Powell
All year

77-110-BB
4 rooms, 4 pb
Visa, MC, *Rated*, •
C-ltd/S-ltd/P-ltd/H-ltd

Full breakfast
Snacks, soda, tea, candy
Sunroom, Jacuzzi, fireplaces, A/C, TV/CD player, ceiling fans, aromatherapy

An 1864 farmhouse tastefully updated that offers classy comfort in relaxing surroundings at a reasonable price. Convenient to Corning, Elmira, Watkins Glen and winery trails.
rthouse@stny.rr.com http://www.rufustanner.com

CROWN POINT

Crown Point
PO Box 490
2695 Main St, Rte 9 N 12928
518-597-3651 Fax: 518-597-4451
Hugh & Sandy Johnson
All year

70-140-BB
6 rooms, 5 pb
Visa, MC, *Rated*, •
C-ltd/S-no/P-no/H-yes
Spanish

Full breakfast
Afternoon tea, wine, snacks
Sitting room, gift shop, bicycles, Jacuzzi, robes/slippers, croquet

Victorian manor house rich in raised paneled woodwork, decorated with antiques & customized linens. Home baking done daily.
crwnptbb@cptelco.net http://www.crownpointbandb.com

CUTCHOGUE

Freddy's House
1535 New Suffolk Rd 11935
631-734-4180
Prudence and Dan Heston
All year

100-210-BB
2 rooms, 2 pb
C-ltd/S-no/P-no/H-no

Full breakfast
Afternoon tea
Sitting room, farm and private beach

Built in 1798, Freddy's House has been meticulously restored. Guests enjoy our 300 acre fruit farm and 1/2 mile of private sandy beach.
freddyshouse@aol.com http://www.wickhamsfruitfarm.com

DEPOSIT

Alexander's Inn
770 Oquaga Lake Rd 13754
607-467-6023 Fax: 607-467-5355
Alexander Meyer
All year

79-119-BB
5 rooms, 5 pb
Most CC, *Rated*, •
C-yes/S-ltd/P-yes/H-ltd
German, French

Full breakfast
Dinner by appointment
Boats, bicycles, hiking, sauna, hot tub, pool

Beautiful lake, elegant & relaxing meeting place for world travelers.
alexinn@aol.com http://www.tempotek.com/alexinn

EAST HAMPTON

The 1848 Guest House
100 Pantigo Rd 11937
631-329-9330
Tom Christman
Spring, Summer, Fall

130-150-BB
5 rooms, 2 pb
Rated
C-no/S-no/P-no/H-no

Continental breakfast
Beach passes

A historic house in the village of East Hampton, NY, on an acre and a half of grounds.
the1848guesthouse@aol.com http://www.1848guesthouse.com

EAST HAMPTON

Getaway House
PO Box 2609
4 Neighborhood House Dr
11937
631-324-4622
Johnny Kelman All year

185-270-BB
4 rooms, 2 pb
Visa, MC, •
C-no/S-no/P-no/H-no

Continental breakfast
Large pool, central air conditioning, bicycles, beach passes, fireplace

A charming bed and breakfast nestled in a wooded setting, yet close to the village and ocean beaches. Central air conditioning and 20 x 40' swimming pool. Continental breakfast served on the patio. windsigh@earthlink.net http://www.getawayhouse.com

---

Maidstone Arms
207 Main St 11937
631-324-5006 Fax: 631-324-5037
Coke Anne M. Wilcox
All year

215-555-BB
19 rooms, 19 pb

Full or Continental breakfast

This beautifully restored 1740 inn nestled in the charming village of East Hampton offers visitors historic charm with modern comfort.
maidstay@aol.com http://www.maidstonearms.com

Mill House Inn
31 N Main St 11937
631-324-9766 Fax: 631-324-9793
877-324-9753
Sylvia & Gary Muller
All year

200-600-BB
10 rooms, 10 pb
Most CC, *Rated*, •
C-yes/S-no/P-yes/H-yes

The best breakfast on the East End!
Cookies around the clock & afternoon beverages
A/C, in-room fireplaces, whirlpool tubs

The Mill House Inn is a luxurious, 1790 Colonial B&B Inn featuring the warmth and charm of the past, with today's comforts and conveniences. 8 rooms and 2 new luxury suites.
innkeeper@millhouseinn.com http://www.millhouseinn.com

The Pink House
26 James Ln 11937
631-324-3400 Fax: 631-324-5254
Mercedes Dekkens
All year

165-425-BB
5 rooms, 5 pb
Most CC, *Rated*
C-ltd/S-no/P-no/H-no
Spanish

Full breakfast
Sitting room, porch, swimming pool

A distinctive B&B located in the historic district of East Hampton. Newly renovated with marble bathrooms, lush bathrobes & special emphasis on personal service.
roso@hamptons.com http://thepinkhouse.net

EAST MARION

Quintessentials B&B & Spa
PO Box 574
8985 Main Rd, Rt 25A 11939
631-477-9400 877-259-0939
Sylvia Daley
All year

150-260-BB
6 rooms, 6 pb
Most CC, *Rated*
C-yes/S-ltd/P-no/H-ltd
German, Portuguese, Spanish

Full breakfast
Afternoon High Tea
Full-service spa, steam room, whirlpool tub, lounge, library, fireplace, cab

Deluxe lodging and full-service day spa in a romantic, 16-room Victorian Sea Captain's House in Long Island's North Folk wine country in the village of East Marion between Greenport and Orient.
innkeeper@quintessentialsinc.com http://www.QuintessentialsInc.com

ELLICOTTVILLE

Jefferson Inn of Ellicottville
PO Box 1566
3 Jefferson St 14731
716-699-5869 Fax: 716-699-5758
800-577-8451
Donna Gushue & Jim Buchanan
All year

79-199-BB
7 rooms, 7 pb
Most CC, *Rated*, •
C-ltd/S-no/P-yes/H-yes

Full breakfast
Sitting room, library, suites, fireplace, cable TV, catering, in-room phones

Stroll to restaurants & boutiques, when escaping Cleveland, Toronto, Rochester & Pittsburgh. Base to visit Niagara Falls, Chautauqua Inst. Air-conditioning and hot tub.
info@thejeffersoninn.com http://www.thejeffersoninn.com

ELMIRA

The Painted Lady
520 W Water St 14905
607-732-7515 Fax: 800-398-1377
Kim & Marty Molisani
All year

99-149-BB
5 rooms, 5 pb
Visa, MC, AmEx
C-ltd/S-no/P-no/H-ltd

Full upscale breakfast
Wine, beer, coffee, tea and snacks
Herbal tea baths, spa robes, hair dryers, TV/VCR, billiard room, CD players

Elegant Victorian accommodations in National Register property. Located between NYC & Niagara Falls. Convenient to Finger Lakes wineries, Corning Museum of Glass, NASCAR, antique trails, & shopping. info@thepaintedlady.net http://www.thepaintedlady.net

ESSEX

Cupola House
PO Box 57
S Main St 12936
518-963-7222 Fax: 518-963-7209
Donna Lou Sonnett–licensed NYS Outdoor Guide

150-185-EP
3 rooms, 3 pb
Visa, MC
C-yes/S-no/P-ltd/H-no
French
All year

Continental breakfast by request-1st morning only
Library, bikes, suites, cable TV, full service marina, kayaks & canoes

Lakeside getaway in beautifully restored 1840's house and 1930's carriage house; accommodations have lake and garden views, lots of amenities.
essexmarina@hotmail.com http://www.virtualcities.com/ny/cupolahouse.htm

FAIR HAVEN

Black Creek Farm
PO Box 390
13615 Mixer Rd 13143
315-947-5282 Fax: 315-947-5282
Bob & Kathy Sarber
All year

75-125-BB
3 rooms, 3 pb
Visa, MC, *Rated*, •
C-ltd/S-ltd/P-no/H-no

Full breakfast
Snacks
Sitting room, cable TV, pond for fishing, peddle boat

Our main house, a restored Victorian B&B, was built in 1888 and is full of antiques. Our secluded, private guest house was built in 1996 and has everything you need except food and PJ's! ksarber@redcreek.net http://www.lakeontario.net/bcf/

FAIRPORT

Clematis Inn
2513 Penfield Rd 14450
585-388-9442
Theda Ann Burnham
All year

75-90-BB
3 rooms, 1 pb
C-yes/S-no/P-ltd/H-no

Vegetarian fare, no refined sugar
Attention given to special diets, afternoon tea
Sitting room, Library, and Sunroom, terry cloth robes, hair dryers

A 1900 Historic National Folk House is the perfect lodging for your comfort when you visit Upstate New York. The warm hospitality of The Clematis Inn will make your stay most Innjoyable. theclematisinn@aol.com

FINGER LAKES (REGION)

Villa Serendip
10849 River Rd, State Rte 371
Cohocton 14826
716-384-5299 Fax: 716-384-9228
888-266-8597+4663
Fran Ambroselli

85-165-BB
5 rooms, 5 pb
Most CC, *Rated*, •
C-yes/S-ltd/P-ltd/H-yes
All year

Full breakfast
Afternoon tea, snacks, dinner avail.
Sitting room, Jacuzzis, suites, fireplaces, cable TV, accom. bus. travel

An elegant, upscale Victorian villa, located in New York's Finger Lakes Region, just off I-390 and only a few minutes from Naples.
innhost@yahoo.com http://www.villaserendip.com

Buttermilk Falls
110 E Buttermilk Falls Rd,
Ithaca 14850
607-272-6767
Margie Rumsey & Kristen
All year

95-295-BB
5 rooms, 5 pb
C-ltd/S-no/P-no

Double Jacuzzi, TV, fireplace

At the foot of the falls is swimming, gorge hiking, and forest trails.

FINGER LAKES (REGION)

Fox Inn
158 Main St, *Penn Yan* 14527
315-536-3101 800-901-7997
Cliff & Michele Orr
All year

105-169-BB
6 rooms, 6 pb
Visa, MC, AmEx,
Rated, •
C-yes/S-ltd/P-no/H-no

Full breakfast
Bar service, sitting room, library, Jacuzzis, suites, fireplaces, cable TV

1820 Greek Rovival Inn, furnished with Empire furnishings, marble fireplaces, sun porch, parlor with billiards table and formal rose gardens.
mawhite@eznet.net http://www.foxinnbandb.com

FORT PLAIN

A White Rose
105 Reid St 13339
518-993-3339
Richard & Melissa Brown
All year

90-100-BB
4 rooms, 2 pb
C-yes/S-no/P-no/H-ltd

Full breakfast
Tea, lemonade, soda, juices. Homemade cookies.
Sitting room has TV, VCR A/C; hammock; bicycle built for two

One of the village's first farmhouses, built in the mid-1800's, now a comfortable four bedroom B&B where one can unwind from a day's activities and then get a fresh beginning to the new day. awhiterose@adelphia.net http://www.awhiterosebnb.com

FREDONIA

Brookside Manor
3728 Route 83 14063
716-672-7721 800-929-7599
Andrea Andrews & Dale Mirth
All year

75-85-BB
4 rooms, 4 pb
Visa, MC, Disc, *Rated*
C-yes/S-no/P-yes/H-no

Full breakfast
Sitting room, cable TV, accommodate business travelers, garden, patio, brook

Enchanting Victorian manor near Historic Fredonia, Lake Erie, Lily Dale; spacious, comfortable, tastefully appointed, non-smoking guestrooms.
brookbnb@yahoo.com http://www.bbonline.com/ny/brookside/

FULTON

Battle Island Inn
2167 State Rt 48N 13069
315-593-3699 Fax: 315-593-3699
Richard & Joyce Rice
All year

65-125-BB
6 rooms, 6 pb
Rated

Full breakfast

The ordinary doesn't exist at Battle Island Inn, an 1840's Italianate perched on a hill in the heart of Central New York.
battleislandinn@usadatanet.net http://www.battle-island-inn.com

GARRISON

Bird & Bottle Inn
1123 Old Albany Post Rd
Route 9 & Albany Post Rd
10524
845-424-3000 Fax: 845-424-3283
800-783-6837
Ira Boyar
All year

220-260-MAP
4 rooms, 4 pb
Visa, MC, AmEx,
Rated, •
C-ltd/S-ltd/P-no/H-no

Full breakfast
Dinner included, bar
Gazebo near brook, cedar shake roof, special diets available

Established in 1761, the inn's history predates Revolutionary War. Each room has period furniture, working fireplace, four-poster or canopy bed.
info@birdbottle.com http://www.birdbottle.com

GLENS FALLS

The Glens Falls Inn
25 Sherman Ave 12801
518-743-9365 Fax: 518-743-0696
Eric & Denise Olson
All year

90-155-BB
5 rooms, 5 pb
Visa, MC, AmEx, *Rated*
C-ltd/S-ltd/P-no/H-yes

Full breakfast
Snacks
Sitting room, bicycles, cable TV, accommodate business travelers, phones

Restored Victorian Inn furnished with a blend of antiques and traditional. Located in the city within walking distance to restaurants, museums and park.
info@glensfallsinn.com http://www.glensfallsinn.com

GLENS FALLS (REGION)

Crislip's 693 Ridge Road, *Queensbury* 12804 518-793-6869 Ned & Joyce Crislip All year	65-85-BB 3 rooms, 3 pb	Full breakfast

This Federal-style house (c.1802) was built by Quakers and was once owned by the area's first doctor, who used it as a training center for young interns. nedbc@capital.net

GREENE

The Inn at Serenity Farms 386 Pollard Rd 13778 607-656-4659 Fax: 253-423-3525 Gregg Nasarenko All year	60-89-BB 8 rooms, 2 pb Visa, MC, AmEx, *Rated*, • C-yes/S-ltd/P-yes/H-no	Coffee, tea, snacks, Rec room with fireplace and pool table, main dining area seats 40

The Inn at Serenity Farms is located in historic Greene, New York. Tucked away 100 acres of property, the refurbished barn was converted to an Inn in 1999.
NYSerenity@aol.com http://www.geocities.com/serenityofny/SERENITY

GROTON

Gleasons 307 Old Stage Rd 13073 607-898-4676 Fax: 607-898-4676 Irene & Roger Gleason All year	44-BB 2 rooms C-yes/S-no/P-ltd/H-no	Continental plus breakfast

We are a true B&B. Share our house, enjoy the country backyard away from the noise of a large city, but within a few minutes drive.

GUILFORD

Tea & Sympathy PO Box 133 1302 City Route #35 13780 607-895-6874 Fax: 607-895-6874 800-524-3394 Angela Jochim All year	75-125-BB 7 rooms AmEx, Disc, *Rated*, • C-ltd/S-ltd/P-no/H-ltd	Full breakfast Afternoon tea, lunch & dinner avail. (by arrang.) Sitting room, library, bikes, Jacuzzis, suites, cable TV, accom. bus. trav.

Country hideaway furnished in antiques; gourmet breakfast served in our French country dining room. ajochim@ascent.net

HADLEY

Saratoga Rose Inn & Rest. PO Box 238 4274 Rockwell St 12835 518-696-2861 Fax: 518-696-5319 800-942-5025 Nancy & Chef Anthony Merlino All year	155-185-BB 4 rooms, 4 pb Visa, MC, AmEx, *Rated*, • C-ltd/S-ltd/P-no/H-no	Full gourmet breakfast Restaurant, bar, dinner Library, some in-room, fireplace &/or Jacuzzi, gift shop, garden/gazebo

Romantic Queen Ann Victorian inn and restaurant. Six comfortable suites all with private bath, A/C, and fireplace. Four suites with private hot tub either on deck or in your room.
saratogarose@adelphia.net http://www.saratogarose.com

HAMMONDSPORT

Amity Rose Inn 8264 Main St 14840 607-569-3402 Fax: 607-569-3402 800-982-8818 Ellen & Frank Laufersweiler May 1-Dec 31	95-135-BB 4 rooms, 4 pb *Rated* C-ltd/S-ltd/P-no/H-ltd	Full breakfast Afternoon tea Sitting room, Jacuzzis, tennis court, suites, fireplaces, conference

A 1900 country house. 2 rooms have 6 foot whirlpool soaking tubs, one a 2 room suite. Nice large living room with fireplace. Dinner boat nearby.
bbam@infoblvd.net http://www.amityroseinn.com

HARLEM (REGION)

The Urban Jem Guest House
2005 Fifth Ave, *New York City* 10035
212-831-6029 Fax: 212-831-6940
Jane Mendelson
All year

90-220-BB
4 rooms, 2 pb
Most CC, •
C-yes/S-ltd/P-no/H-no
Some French, Spanish

Continental
Sitting room, suites, Cable TV/VCR/CD, conference, A/C, in room phones

Renovated 1878 brownstone, just steps from the Marcus Garvey Memorial Park in the historic community of Mount Morris Park, Harlem, New York.
JMendel760@aol.com http://www.urbanjem.com

HARTSDALE

Krogh's Nest
4 Hillcrest Rd 10530
914-946-3479
Claudia & Paul Krogh
All year

75-BB
2 rooms, 2 pb
AmEx
C-yes/S-ltd/P-no/H-ltd

Full breakfast
Sitting room, hammock, lawn swing, picnic table

100 year old home on hillside acre with country atmosphere. Walk to 10 restaurants and train.

HERKIMER

Portobello Inn
PO Box 169
5989 State Route 5 13350
315-823-8612
Roland S. Randall
all year

75-95-BB
5 rooms, 5 pb
Most CC
C-ltd/S-no/P-no/H-no

Continental Plus & Full on Weekends
Coffee, Tea, Juices, Softdrinks & Snacks
Fireplaces, Internet, Antique Shop, Library, Country Club use.

Classic Italianate home, overlooking the Mohawk River Valley and the Erie Canal since the 1840's. From our wraparound porch and Victorian veranda, enjoy views reminiscent of the Tuscan hills of Italy. stay@portobelloinn.com http://www.portobelloinn.com

HILLSDALE

The Bell House
9315 State Rte 22 12529
518-325-3841 Fax: 518-325-3832
Marilyn Simon
All year

100-150-BB
5 rooms, 3 pb
Visa, MC, AmEx
C-ltd/S-no/P-no/H-no
Spanish

Full breakfast
Sitting room, library, swimming pool, bikes, fireplaces, cable TV

Gracious country lodging in an 1830's home filled with American antiques. In-ground swimming pool in a garden setting; gourmet breakfast in dining room or on wraparound porch. info@bellhousebb.com http://www.bellhousebb.com

---

The Honored Guest
20 Hunt Rd 12529
518-325-9100
Deborah Kinney
All year

125-175-BB
4 rooms, 4 pb
Visa, MC, AmEx, •
C-yes/S-no/P-no/H-no
German

Full breakfast
Afternoon tea, snacks
Sitting room, fireplace, cable TV, turn-down service every night

Beautiful 1910 Arts and Crafts house furnished with authentic Mission style furniture.
stay@honoredguest.com http://www.honoredguest.com

Swiss Hutte Inn & Rest.
PO Box 357
Rte 23 12529
518-325-3333 Fax: 413-528-6201
Gert & Cindy Alper
April 15-March

85-180-EP
16 rooms, 16 pb
Visa, MC, *Rated*
C-yes/S-yes/P-yes/H-yes
German

Restaurant, bar service
Vegetarian dishes, in-room phones, parlor room, tennis, pool, skiing

Swiss chef & owner. Nestled in hidden wooded valley. French continental decor. Indoor/outdoor garden dining, banquets, conference facilities.
8057@msn.com http://www.swisshutte.com

HOPEWELL JUNCTION

Aaron Stockholm House
101 Beekman Rd 12533
845-226-7790 Fax: 845-227-8649
John & Kathleen McHugh and Kelly Joseph
All year

100-170-BB
5 rooms, 2 pb
Visa, MC, AmEx
C-ltd/S-no/P-no/H-no

Continental plus breakfast
4:00 tea wine
Sitting room w/fireplace, coin-op laundry facilities on site

1817 restored Colonial ideal for weddings and business functions. Selected as the exclusive overnight accommodation for the Branton Woods Championship Golf Club located in Stormville, NY. AStockholmHouse@aol.com

HUDSON VALLEY (REGION)

Greenville Arms 1889 Inn
PO Box 659
Rt 32 South St, *Greenville* 12083
518-966-5219 Fax: 518-966-8754
888-665-0044
Eliot & Letitia Dalton
May-October

115-195-BB
15 rooms, 15 pb
Visa, MC, *Rated*, •
C-ltd/S-no/P-no/H-no

Full breakfast from menu
Elegant country dining
Library, secluded 50' pool, living/sitting rms, art workshops, croquet, A/C

A Historic Victorian Inn, welcoming guests for 50 years. Gardens, outdoor pool and an atmosphere of warmth & charm invite guests to relax. A delicious breakfast completes a memorable stay. stay@greenvillearms.com http://www.greenvillearms.com

---

Mead-Tooker House
136 Clinton St, *Montgomery* 12549
845-457-5770 Fax: 845-457-4585
Nancy Michaels
All year

105-225-BB
8 rooms, 4 pb
Most CC, •
C-ltd/S-no/P-no/H-no

Full breakfast
Sitting rooms, suites, fireplaces, cable TV, competitive corporate rate

1790 Colonial On National Register, fireplaces, feather beds and antique furnishings add to the comfort and charm of this wonderful house. Dedicated to making your stay with me an unforgettable one. meadtook@frontiernet.net http://www.meadtooker.com

---

Sparrow Hawk
4496 Route 209, *Stone Ridge* 12484
845-687-4492
Betsy & Howard Mont
All year

115-160-BB
5 rooms, 4 pb
•
C-ltd/S-ltd/P-no/H-ltd
Italian, Spanish, French

Full gourmet breakfast
Afternoon tea
Suites, fireplaces, Cable TV, bus. travelers, music/library

A registered 1770 brick colonial, located in the picturesque Hudson Valley, 15 min. from Kingston, New Paltz.
info@sparrowhawkbandb.com http://www.sparrowhawkbandb.com

HUNTER

Washington Irvin Lodge
PO Box 675
Route #23 A 12442
518-589-5560 Fax: 518-589-5775
Stefania Jozic
All year

85-145-BB
20 rooms, 7 pb
Visa, MC, AmEx, *Rated*, •
C-yes/S-yes/P-no/H-no
Serbo-Croatian

Full breakfast
Restaurant on premises
Sitting room, TV, tennis courts, pool, near slopes, cross country skiing

A classic Catskills country inn built in 1890. Accommodations are homey and comfortable. http://www.washingtonirving.com

HUNTER (REGION)

Greene Mountain View Inn
S Main Street, *Tannersville* 12485
518-589-9886 Fax: 518-589-5886
Glenn & Donna Weyant
All year

75-150-BB
12 rooms, 12 pb
Most CC
C-yes/S-yes/P-no/H-no

Continental plus breakfast
Restaurant, bar
Sitting room, fireplace, cable TV, game room, Newly renovated 3rd flr.

Quaint B mountain views and immaculate accommodations. Relaxing atmosphere.
info@GreenMountainViewInn.com http://www.greenemountainviewinn.com

HYDE PARK

Costello's Guest House
21 Main St 12538
845-229-2559
Patsy Newman Costello
All year

45-75-EP
2 rooms
Rated
C-yes/S-no/P-no/H-no

Small refrigerator in den for guests
Close to F.D. Roosevelt home & library, Culinary Institute of America

Federal style home built in the mid-1850's. Located in the Historic District of the Village of Hyde Park. Comfortable, A/C guestrooms. patsyc97@aol.com

---

Journey Inn
1 Sherwood Place 12538
845-229-8972
Diane & Michele DiNapoli
All year

95-155-BB
6 rooms, 6 pb
C-ltd/S-ltd/P-no/H-no

Full gourmet breakfast
A butler's pantry
2 large, comfortable living rooms to relax, read and enjoy in

We are situated directly across from the Vanderbilt Mansion's entrance & 3 miles north of The Culinary Institute of America. stay@journeyinn.com http://www.journeyinn.com

---

The Willows
53 Travis Rd 12538
845-471-6115
Lisa & Lee Fraitag
All year

110-BB
2 rooms, 2 pb
C-ltd/S-ltd/P-no/H-no

Full breakfast
Snacks
Sitting room, library, fireplace, cable TV

Country farmhouse from 1765 where you will be indulged by a Culinary Institute of America graduate. stay@willowsbnb.com http://www.willowsbnb.com

ITHACA

Besemer Station Inn
2024 Slaterville Rd 14850
607-539-6319
Becky & Don Bilderback
All year

80-110-BB
2 rooms, 2 pb
Visa, MC, •
C-ltd/S-no/P-no/H-no
German

Full breakfast
Snacks
Sitting room

This country farmhouse from the early 1800s is located 5 miles from Ithaca, Cornell University and wineries. dhb2@cornell.edu http://www.lightlink.com/donald/inn.html

---

Brookton Hollow Farm
18 Banks Rd 14817
607-273-5725
Deborah Halpern
All year

85-110-BB
3 rooms, 1 pb
C-ltd/S-no/P-no/H-no

Full breakfast
Vegetarian breakfasts with organic ingredients

Located on a 135-acre horse-powered organic farm just 10 minutes from Cornell University, Brookton Hollow Farm offers bird-watching, walking paths, Six Mile Creek, an outdoor deck, and picnic areas.
relax@brooktonhollowfarm.com http://www.brooktonhollowfarm.com

---

The Hound & Hare
1031 Hanshaw Rd 14850
607-257-2821 Fax: 607-257-3121
800-652-2821
Zetta Sprole
All year

85-125-BB
5 rooms, 4 pb
Most CC, *Rated*
C-yes/S-no/P-no/H-no

Full gourmet breakfast
Afternoon tea, snacks
Sitting room, library, bicycles, Jacuzzi, cable, suites, fireplaces

White brick Colonial built on land given to my forbears by General George Washington for service in Revolutionary War.
info@houndandhare.com http://www.houndandhare.com

Log Country Inn B&B
PO Box 581 14851
607-589-4771 Fax: 607-589-6151
800-274-4771
Slawomir & Wanda Grunberg
All year

55-200-BB
5 rooms, 4 pb
Most CC, *Rated*, •
C-yes/S-no/P-yes/H-no
Polish, Russian

Full breakfast
Afternoon tea in winter
Sitting room, library, sauna, fireplace, Jacuzzi in some rooms.

Enjoy Wanda's blintzes & Russian pancakes. Rest in cozy rooms furnished with custom made furniture. Family friendly facility. wanda@logtv.com

ITHACA

Rose Inn
PO Box 6576
813 Auburn Rd, Rt 34 N 14851
607-533-7905 Fax: 607-533-7908
Charles Rosemann
All year

125-330-BB
20 rooms, 20 pb
AmEx, *Rated*, •
C-ltd/S-no/P-no/H-no
German, Spanish

Full breakfast
Gourmet dinner by reservation
Antique shop, parlor, piano, bikes, Jacuzzis, garden w/wedding chapel

The inn has a non-smoking Jazz Club with a-la-carte dinner on Tues. & Sat. night April-Dec. Prix Fixe dinner Jan.-Mar. Conference facility in restored 1850s Carriage House for 60 people. info@roseinn.com http://www.roseinn.com/

La Tourelle Country Inn
1150 Danby Rd 14850
607-273-2734 Fax: 607-273-4821
800-765-1492
Leslie Marie Leonard
All year

99-299-EP
35 rooms, 35 pb
Visa, MC, AmEx, *Rated*, •
C-yes/S-ltd/P-ltd/H-ltd

Continental Breakfast
Library, tennis court, cable TV, high speed internet, hairdryers, irons

Perfect blend of Old World charm and contemporary comfort. Beautifully appointed guest rooms. Reminiscent of the delightful country hotels of Europe.
latourel@lightlink.com http://www.latourelleinn.com

William Henry Miller Inn
303 North Aurora St 14850
607-256-4553 Fax: 607-256-0092
877-256-4553
Lynnette Scofield
All year

95-155-BB
9 rooms, 9 pb
Most CC, *Rated*, •
C-ltd/S-no/P-no/H-yes

Full breakfast
Evening dessert
Sitting room, library, Jacuzzis, fireplace, cable TV, conference

Stately Ithaca landmark quietly convenient to the heart of Ithaca, Cornell University and Ithaca College. MillerInn@aol.com http://www.MillerInn.com

ITHACA (REGION)

The Edge of Thyme
PO Box 48
6 Main St, *Candor* 13743
607-659-5155 Fax: 607-659-5155
800-722-7365
Frank & Eva Mae Musgrave
All year

75-135-BB
7 rooms, 3 pb
Most CC, *Rated*, •
C-yes/S-no/P-no/H-no

Full breakfast
High tea by appointment
Sitting rms w/fireplaces, piano, indoor games, lawn games, gift shoppe

Featured in Historic Inns of the Northeast. Visit a turn-of-the-century Georgian home. Enjoy leaded glass windowed porch, marble fireplaces, period sitting rooms, gardens and pergola. innthyme@twcny.rr.com http://www.edgeofthyme.com/

JAMESPORT

Red Barn
PO Box 1002
733 Herricks Lane 11947
631-722-3695 Fax: 631-722-3695
Linda Slezak All year

150-250-BB
3 rooms, 3 pb
Visa, MC, *Rated*
C-ltd/S-ltd/P-ltd/H-no

Delicious 3 course breakfast/afternoon tea & cake
TV/VCR, bicycles, porch, hammock, bathrobes, sherry

Surrounded by vineyards, orchards and farms with the original barn and out-buildings on the property, Red Barn B&B has one of the most picturesque settings on the North Fork.
lindaslezak@hotmail.com http://www.northfork.com/redbarn

KINDERHOOK

Kinderhook
16 Chatham St 12106
518-758-1850
Bill & Jayne All year

BB

Center Hall Colonial in a village setting. Tastefully decorated, friendly, and comfortable. We are in the Hudson Valley, 1/2 hour to Albany, the Capital District.
kinderhoob-b@berk.com

KINGSTON

Rondout
88 W Chester St 12401
845-331-8144 Fax: 845-331-9049
Adele & Ralph Calcavecchio
All year

85-115-BB
4 rooms, 2 pb
Visa, MC, AmEx, •
C-yes/S-ltd
Italian, French

Full breakfast
Snacks
Sitting room, piano, library, in-room A/C, glassed-in porch, garden

Art, antiques, and light-filled 1906 spacious house near the Hudson River with gardens and woods. Near buses, trains, airports. Glassed-in porch with rattan.
calcave@attglobal.net http://www.rondoutbandb.com

LAKE GEORGE (REGION)

Boathouse
PO Box 1576
44 Sagamore Rd, *Bolton Landing* 12814
518-644-2554 Fax: 518-644-3065
Joseph Silipigno & Patti Gramberg All year

125-325-BB
5 rooms
Visa, MC, AmEx, *Rated*
C-yes/S-ltd/P-no/H-no

Full breakfast

Historic bed & breakfast located directly on Lake George, open year round. This famous and unique B&B has been featured in Motor Boat & Sailing, The Great and the Gracious, and Unique Homes. Stay@boathousebb.com http://www.boathousebb.com

---

Friends Lake Inn
963 Friends Lake Rd, *Chestertown* 12817
518-494-4751 Fax: 518-494-4616
Sharon Taylor
All year

195-425-BB
17 rooms, 17 pb
Visa, MC, AmEx, *Rated*, •
C-ltd/S-ltd/P-no/H-no

Full country breakfast
Full dinner service available, full bar service
Library, swimming, Adirondack suites w/view, outdoor sauna, lake view rooms

Fully restored 19th century inn with lake view. Award-winning restaurant & wine list, 3 rooms with working fireplaces, x-country skiing, snow-shoeing, private beach canoes and kayaks on Friends Lake. friends@friendslake.com http://www.friendslake.com

---

Lamplight Inn
PO Box 130
231 Lake Ave, *Lake Luzerne* 12846
518-696-5294 Fax: 518-696-4914
800-262-4668
Gene & Linda Merlino

85-239-BB
16 rooms, 16 pb
Visa, MC, AmEx, *Rated*, •
C-ltd/S-no/P-no/H-yes
All year

Full breakfast
Complimentary tea & coffee
Sitting rm w/fireplaces, porch with swing, gardens, lake swimming, Jacuzzi

Lake George and Saratoga Springs area. 1890 Victorian plus Carriage House, 8 fireplace bedrooms, 6 suites with Jacuzzi and fireplace. Full breakfast. Romantic getaway. Our 16th year. stay@lamplightinn.com http://www.lamplightinn.com

---

Country Road Lodge
115 Hickory Hill Rd, *Warrensburg* 12885
518-623-2207 Fax: 518-623-4363
Steve & Sandi Parisi All year

58-72-BB
4 rooms, 2 pb
Rated, •
C-ltd/S-no/P-no/H-no

Full breakfast of choice
Cold drinks, coffee and tea always available
Sitting room, library, bird watching, hiking

Quiet, idyllic setting along Hudson River at the end of a country road. Discreetly sociable host. No traffic or TV. Southern Adirondack Mountains, near Lake George.
mail@countryroadlodge.com http://www.countryroadlodge.com

LAKE PLACID

Interlaken Inn
15 Interlaken Ave 12946
518-523-3180 Fax: 518-523-0117
800-428-4369
Roy & Carol Johnson
Exc. April & November

90-180-MAP
11 rooms, 11 pb
Visa, MC, *Rated*, •
C-ltd/S-yes/P-no/H-no

Full breakfast
Dinner incl, rest., bar
Comp. wine, high tea, sitting room, croquet, lake swimming, Jacuzzi

Adirondack inn; heart of Olympic country; quiet setting-half block from Main St. between Mirror Lake & Lake Placid. Balconies.
interlkn@northnet.org http://www.innbook.com

LAKE PLACID

South Meadow Farm Lodge
HCR 1 Box 44
Rte 73 (Cascade Rd) 12946
518-523-9369 Fax: 515-523-8749
800-523-9369
Tony & Nancy Corwin
All year

85-125-BB
6 rooms
Most CC, •
C-yes/S-no/P-no/H-yes

Full breakfast
Family style dinner and trail lunch are optional.
Free x-country skiing & mountain biking. Beautiful peaceful view.

Enjoy the 50 klms of Olympic cross-country ski trails that cross our small farm, the view, our fireplace, and homemade meals.
reservations@southmeadow.com http://www.southmeadow.com

Spruce Lodge
31 Sentinel Rd 12946
518-523-9350 Fax: 518-523-7898
800-258-9350
Carol Hoffman
All year

58-114-BB
7 rooms, 2 pb
Visa, MC, *Rated*
C-yes/S-no/P-no/H-no

Continental breakfast
Sitting room

Located within Lake Placid. Close to all area activities. This has been a family run lodge since 1949. sprucelodge@juno.com http://www.sprucelodgebnb.com

LAKE PLACID (REGION)

Book & Blanket
PO Box 164
Route #9N, *Jay* 12941
518-946-8323
Kathy, Fred, Sam & Zoe the Basset Hound All year

70-90-BB
3 rooms, 1 pb
Rated
C-yes/S-no/P-no/H-no

Full breakfast
Afternoon tea–request
Sitting room, library, fireplace, porch swing, piano, village green

1850s Greek Revival near Lake Placid. Picturesque Adirondack hamlet with village green & swimming hole. Bedrooms honor famous authors.
bookinnjay@aol.com http://www.bookandblanket.com

LITTLE FALLS

Gansevoort House Inn
42 W Gansevoort St 13365
315-823-1833
Linda Stivala
All year

85-115-BB
5 rooms, 3 pb
Most CC
C-yes/S-no/P-no/H-ltd
Spanish, Italian, French, German

Full breakfast
Afternoon Tea
Sitting and reading room, guest pass to fitness facility

Between Albany and Syracuse on I-90 at exit 29A, this inn offers three guestrooms, 2 with private baths, and a guest suite in the carriage house.
lstivala@twcny.rr.com http://www.thebookfinderbandb.com

LIVINGSTON MANOR

Lanza's
839 Shandelee Road 12758
845-439-5070 Fax: 845-439-5003
Richard & Mary Lanza
All year

89-129-BB
7 rooms, 7 pb
Visa, MC, AmEx, *Rated*
C-ltd/S-no/P-no/H-no

Full breakfast
Dinner, p.m. tea, snacks, comp wine, restaurant
Bar service, sitting room

The personal attention and service you receive at Lanza's sets it apart. This is coupled with clean comfortable rooms and great food.
dickl400@aol.com http://www.lanzascountryinn.com

LOCKPORT

Hambleton House
130 Pine St 14221
716-439-9507 Fax: 716-634-3650
Hambleton Family
All year

55-95-BB
3 rooms, 3 pb
Visa, MC, •
C-ltd/S-ltd/P-no/H-no

Continental plus breakfast
Snacks
Sitting room, private baths all rooms, air conditioning

Gracious, historic city home where Lockport carriage maker resided in the 1850s. This old house has a wraparound porch and additional back porch to be enjoyed by guests.
hambletbb@aol.com http://www.niagarabedandbreakfastinn.com

Lanza's, Livingston Manor, NY

LONG EDDY

Rolling Marble Guest House
PO Box 33
Delaware Road 12760
845-887-6016
Karen Gibbons & Peter Reich
Memorial Day–Labor Day

75-85-BB
5 rooms
Visa, MC
C-yes/S-ltd/P-no/H-no

Full breakfast
Snacks
Sitting room, bicycles, use of canoes

Enjoy a magical atmosphere where each room is special, breakfasts bountiful, and beauty abounds. Our sundappled paths lead to a stone beach and the pristine waters of the Delaware River.

scuro@aol.com http://www.doorwaytothedelaware.com

LONG ISLAND (REGION)

Centerport Harbor
129 Centershore Rd, *Centerport* 11721
631-754-1730
Fax: 631-754-6241
Jean & Jim Vavrina
All year

179-199-BB
1 rooms, 1 pb
Visa, MC, *Rated*, •
C-yes/S-no/P-no/H-no

Full breakfast
In-room tea kettle, beverages
Cable TV, waterfront, private beach, private balcony

Romantic accommodations overlooking scenic harbor, private beach and dock. Gourmet breakfast served in-room, or on private balcony.

centerport.hrbr.bnb@eudoramail.com http://www.bbonline.com/ny/centerport

---

Harbor Knoll
424 Fourth St, *Greenport* 11944
631-477-2352
Fax: 631-477-2352
Leueen Miller
All year

175-250-BB
4 rooms, 4 pb
Visa, MC, AmEx
C-ltd/S-no/P-no/H-no
French, Spanish, Italian

Full breakfast
Afternoon tea, complimentary wine
Sitting room, library, fireplaces, cable TV

1880 Dutch Colonial on a spectacular waterfront location with fantastic views. Decorated like an English country home. Walk to historic whaling village.

lmiller7@optonline.com http://www.harborknoll.com

Old Seamens Guest Church
248 Fifth Avenue, *Greenport* 11944
631-477-8691 Fax: 631-477-1559
WM Kranker
All year

EP
1 rooms, 1 pb
Visa, MC, AmEx, *Rated*
C-ltd/S-yes/P-ltd/H-no

Full kitchen for guest use
Sitting room, fireplaces, cable TV, accomodate business travelers

Historic Seamen's Church, 120 yr. old, in excellent condition, 14 stained glass windows, cathedral ceiling. $750.00 weekly, $1250.00 bi-weekly, $2500.00/month.

Hambleton House, Lockport, NY

LONG ISLAND (REGION)

Coeur des Vignes L'Hotel & Rest. Francais
57225 Main Road, *Southold* 11971
631-765-2656 Fax: 631-765-2656
Donna Marie & George Pavlou
All year

155-225-BB
4 rooms, 4 pb
Most CC, *Rated*, •
C-ltd/S-ltd/P-ltd/H-no
French, Greek

Continental breakfast
Sunday Champagne Brunch, lunch, dinner, tea, snack
Cable TV, Accommodates. bus. travelers

Dine, wine & spend the night. All in one lovely jewel box.
hotel@coeurdesvignes.com http://www.coeurdesvignes.com

MILLBROOK

The Porter House
PO Box 1282
17 Washington Ave 12545
845-677-3057
Timothy Tice
All year

115-175-BB
5 rooms, 5 pb
Most CC
C-ltd/S-no/P-no/H-no

Continental plus breakfast

A charming turn-of-the-century renovated stone house in the Village of Millbrook. Conveniently located 4 miles off the Taconic Parkway.
porterhousebandb@aol.com http://www.porterhousebandb.com

MONTAUK

Shepherds Neck Inn
PO Box 639
Second House Rd. 11954
631-668-2105 Fax: 631-668-0171
George & Marie Hammer
All year

59-220-BB
70 rooms, 70 pb
Rated, •

Full or Continental Breakfast
Putting green, driving net

You will enjoy the friendly ambience at Shepherds Neck Inn, where you'll feel relaxed and at home.

NEW BERLIN

The Preferred Manor
45 S Main St, Rt 8 13411
607-847-6238 Fax: 607-847-9414
Julia A. King
All year

54-65-EP
5 rooms, 1 pb
Visa, MC, *Rated*
C-yes/S-no/P-no/H-no

Continental plus breakfast
Sitting room, fireplaces, cable TV, accommodate business travelers

Built in 1831, this spacious stone house was entered in 1974 on the National Register of Historic Places. preferred.manor@pminsco.com http://www.preferredmanor.com

NEW PALTZ

Mountain Meadows
542 Albany Post Rd 12561
845-255-6144 Fax: 845-255-6144
Corinne D'Andrea & Art Rifenbary
All year

115-125-BB
4 rooms, 4 pb
Visa
C-yes/S-no/P-no/H-ltd

Full breakfast
Afternoon refreshments
Recreation room, pool, hot tub, lawn games, A/C

Beautiful grounds and panoramic views of the Shawangunk Mountains provide the backdrop for our contemporary B&B, an ideal place for nature lovers who enjoy casual and comfortable living. mtnmead542@aol.com http://www.mountainmeadowsbnb.com

NEW PALTZ (REGION)

Captain Schoonmaker's
913 St Rt 213, *High Falls* 12440
845-687-7946
Judy & Bill Klock
All year

110-140-BB
4 rooms, 4 pb
Rated, •
C-ltd/S-no/P-no/H-no

Elegant 5 Course Breakfast
Evening snacks

Fish our trout stream, relax in romantic antique rooms in 1810 Carriage House, on private balcony overlooking waterfalls; enjoy an elegant 5 course bkfst by the fireplace in the 1760 Stone House. info@captainschoonmakers.com http://www.captainschoonmakers.com

---

Whispering Pines
60 Cedar Hill Rd, *High Falls* 12440
914-687-2419
Celia & HD Seupel
May-November

99-139-BB
3 rooms, 3 pb
Visa, MC, Disc, *Rated*
C-ltd/S-no/P-no/H-no
German, French

Full buffet breakfast
Afternoon tea
Sitting room, library, babysitting available, VCR, 2 rooms with Jacuzzis

Light filled B historic sightseeing, crafts, woodland-walking, fine dining, antiquing, biking, enjoy the quiet.
CSeupel@cs.com http://www.whisperingpinesbb.com

Fox Hill
55 So Chodikee Lake Road, *Highland* 12528
845-691-8151 Fax: 845-691-4051
Jeri & Jerry Luke
All year

100-115-BB
3 rooms, 3 pb
AmEx
C-ltd/S-no/P-no

Full breakfast weekends & holidays
Continental breakfast served on weekdays
Complimentary train pickup at Poughkeepsie station.
Restaurant reservations

Quiet, country comfort all suite B&B. 5 miles to New Paltz, landscaped hillside setting, gourmet breakfast, perennial gardens, heated pool.
http://www.foxhillbnb.com

NEW YORK CITY

102 Brownstone
102 W 118th St Ste 1 10026
212-662-4223
Lizette Agosto
All year

70-140-EP
6 rooms, 4 pb
Visa, MC, AmEx
C-ltd/S-no/P-no/H-no
Spanish, French

Coffee, tea, champagne, candy, crackers, popcorn
Full kitchens, Jacuzzi tubs, local phones/ans. machine, cable TV, DVD

Stay with us! Experience New York like a true native! Make 102 Brownstone your home away from home!
stay@102brownstone.com

1871 House
Upper East Side 10021
212-756-8823 Fax: 212-588-0995
Lia & Warren Raum
All year

139-249-EP
10 rooms, 10 pb
Most CC, •
C-yes/S-no/P-no/H-no

Suites, cable TV, fireplace

Located on the fashionable Upper East Side of Manhattan on a tree-lined block in the East 60s, 1871 House is within walking distance of Central Park, boutiques, museums and art galleries. infotravelguides@1871house.com http://www.1871house.com

NEW YORK CITY

Chelsea Pines Inn
317 W 14th St 10014
212-929-1023 Fax: 212-620-5645
888-546-2700
Jay Lesiger & Al Ridolfo
All year

89-139-BB
25 rooms, 15 pb
Most CC, *Rated*, •
S-yes/P-no/H-no
Spanish

Continental plus breakfast
Coffee & cookies all day
Outdoor patio, greenhse., all rms. have A/C, color, cable TV, phone, refrig.

One of the most popular gay & lesbian inns in the city. Chelsea Pines is charmingly decorated with original vintage film posters from the Golden Age of Hollywood.
cpiny@aol.com http://www.chelseapinesinn.com

Country Inn the City
270 W 77th St., Apt 7
270 W 77th St 10024
212-580-4183
Fergus O'Brien
All year

150-210
4 rooms, 4 pb
Rated, •
C-ltd/S-no/P-no/H-no

Self-serve continental breakfast
Tea, fresh gourmet coffee

"Country Inn the City is a dreamlike place. Staying here gives the sense of being a real New Yorker, living in a real neighborhood in a really nice apartment." "NY's 60 Best Wonderful Little Hotels." ctryinn@aol.com http://www.countryinnthecity.com

---

The Gorham Hotel
136 W 55th St 10019
212-245-1800 Fax: 212-582-8332
800-735-0710
Mr. David Sabo
All year

235-440-EP
115 rooms, 115 pb
Visa, MC, AmEx, *Rated*, •
C-yes/S-yes/P-no/H-yes
Spanish, Italian, Hebrew, Bosnian, Thai, Tagolog, French

Weekday a.m. coffee/pastries; in-room coffee/tea
Fitness room, bkfst. Room, comp. Internet access, cable TV, HBO

Charming European boutique hotel near Rockefeller Center, 5th Ave., theatres/concert sites. New York's Premier Boutique Hotel.
reservations@gorhamhotel.com http://www.gorhamhotel.com

The Inn on 23rd
131 W 23rd St 10011
212-463-0330 Fax: 212-463-0302
877-387-2323
The Fisherman Family
All year

175-350-BB
12 rooms, 12 pb
Visa, MC, AmEx, *Rated*
C-yes/S-no/P-no/H-ltd

Continental plus breakfast
Sitting room, library, cable, suites, fax, coier, hair dryers, iron, A/C

The Inn on 23rd is a classic 5 story, 19th century townhouse, which has been renovated into a B&B and the home of your host Annette Fisherman. InnOn23rd@aol.com

---

Ivy Terrace
230 E 58th St #1A 10022
516-662-6862 Fax: 212-353-9193
Vinessa & Sue
All year

169-200-BB
3 rooms, 3 pb
Visa, MC, AmEx, •
C-yes/S-ltd/P-ltd/H-no

Continental breakfast
Restaurant downstairs, afternoon tea
Cable TV, accom. bus. travelers, extra jack for laptop hookup

Private, elegantly furnished apartments in the heart of New York's Eastside. Enjoy your own terrace as well as a full kitchen, and fresh flowers waiting for you!
smar3650@aol.com http://www.ivyterrace.com

Wyman House
36 Riverside Dr 10023
212-799-8281 Fax: 212 362-1747
Pamela & Ron Wyman
All year

175-EP
6 rooms, 6 pb
Rated, •
C-ltd/S-no/P-no/H-no

Complimentary ""get started"" breakfast basket upon arrival

Located on sunny Riverside Park, Wyman House has been lauded by hundreds of happy travelers for its gracious hospitality. You will find the finest accommodations with the utmost attention to detail. pam@wymanhouse.com http://www.wymanhouse.com

NEW YORK CITY (REGION)

Angelique B&B
405 Union St, *Brooklyn* 11231
718-852-8406 Fax: 718-923-0060
Johanna Spoerri & Family
All year

125-BB
4 rooms
Most CC
C-ltd/S-ltd/P-ltd/H-no

Continental breakfast
Sitting room, cable TV, accom. bus. travelers, gardens

Experience historic Brownstone Brooklyn in our Victorian Lady. Enjoy the antique furnishings and oil paintings; appreciate the original layout and appointments of our antique home. sspoerri@ezaccess.net http://www.sspoerri.com/abb

---

Eve's
1375 Coney Island Ave
751 Westminster Rd, *Brooklyn* 11230
212-560-5373 Fax: 718-338-2350
All year

125-BB
1 rooms, 1 pb
Visa, MC, AmEx, •
C-ltd/S-ltd/P-yes/H-ltd
Spanish

Full breakfast
Afternoon tea, snacks, complimentary wine
Library, fireplaces, accommodate business travelers

Luxurious private 2 bedroom apartment for your exclusive use. Safe, beautiful residential area close to Manhattan and major attractions.
evesplace_2001@yahoo.com http://www.virtualcities.com/ons/ny/n/nyn1902.htm

---

De Bruce Country Inn on the Willowemoc
85 Mercer St
982 De Bruce Rd, *De Bruce* 10012
845-439-3900
All year

200-250-MAP
15 rooms, 15 pb
Rated, •
C-yes/S-yes/P-yes/H-no
French

Full breakfast
Dinner included, bar
Library, sauna, pool, private forest preserve, trout pond, art gallery

W/in the Catskill Forest Preserve, w/ its trails, wildlife, famous trout stream; our turn-of-the-century inn offers superb dining overlooking the valley.
http://www.debrucecountryinn.com

Rose Hill Guest House
44 Rose Hill Ave, *New Rochelle* 10804
914-632-6464
Marilou Mayetta
All year

80-125-BB
3 rooms
Rated, •
C-yes/S-ltd/P-ltd/H-no

Continental plus breakfast
Complimentary wine, tea
Sitting room, library, VCR, cable TV

Beautiful French Normandy home 20 minutes from Manhattan or Greenwich. Enjoy "Big Apple" & country living in one. rosehillguests@webtv.net

NEWPORT

What Cheer Hall
PO Box 417
7482 Main Street 13416
315-845-8312
Jim & Phyllis Fisher
All year

55-65-BB
2 rooms, 2 pb
C-yes/S-ltd/P-no/H-no

Full breakfast
Sitting room, fireplaces, cable TV

Georgian Federal Limestone home built in 1812, situated in a 19th century village, furnished with Federal antiques. jimmer@borg.com http://www.borg.com/~jimmer

NIAGARA FALLS

Cameo Inn & Cameo Manor
3881 Lower River Rd
Route 18F 14174
716-745-3034 Fax: 716-745-7444
Greg & Carolyn Fisher
All year

75-140-BB
8 rooms, 4 pb
Visa, MC, Disc, *Rated*, •
C-ltd/S-no/P-no/H-no

Full breakfast
Antiquing, fishing, bicycling, cross-country ski, relax by river, library

Choose Victorian elegance in a romantic river setting, or a secluded English manor, both just minutes from Niagara Falls. info@cameoinn.com http://www.cameoinn.com

NIAGARA FALLS

The Red Coach Inn
2 Buffalo Ave 14303
716-282-1459 Fax: 716-282-2650
800-282-1459
Tom Reese
All year

89-179-BB
14 rooms, 16 pb
Most CC, *Rated*, •
C-ltd/S-no/P-no/H-ltd

Continental plus breakfast
Lunch, dinner (fee), snacks
Restaurant, bar service, sitting room, library, Jacuzzis, suites

Overlooking the breathtaking Upper Rapids and just steps away from the American Falls, the Inn is Niagara's most distinctive historic structure with its English Tudor exterior.
innkeeper@redcoach.com http://www.redcoach.com

NIAGARA FALLS (REGION)

Maplehurst
4427 Ridge Rd, *Lockport* 14094
716-434-3502
Mark & Peggy Herbst
All year

60-75-BB
4 rooms, 3 pb
Rated, •
C-ltd/S-ltd/P-no/H-no
Some German

Full breakfast
Afternoon tea, snacks
Sitting room, cable TV, accommodate business travelers

Historic, spacious, antique filled country bed & breakfast located minutes from world famous scenic and historic sites. Large, comfortable guestrooms tastefully decorated.

NORFOLK

Paradico Farms & Resort
PO Box 585
3456 State Hwy 310 13667
315-384-8915 Fax: 315-384-4872
877-75-BISON
June Hitsman
All year

85-150-BB
4 rooms
Visa, MC, AmEx
C-yes/S-no/P-ltd/H-ltd

Full breakfast
Drinks and snacks

Paradico Farms is an 800 acre working buffalo farm in the heart of St. Lawrence County.

OGDENSBURG

Professor's Place
4777 St Hwy 68 13669
315-344-1237
Betty Marino
All year

60-60-BB
2 rooms, 2 pb
C-ltd/S-no/P-ltd/H-no
English

Full breakfast
Tea, snacks, fruit
Wicker sitting room, library, pool, gardens

Relaxing tranquil location in St. Lawrence County, cross Ogdensburg Prescott Bridge to Canada. Fish Black Lake and St Lawrence River areas. Visit Universities and Colleges, ten to twenty minutes away.
bma7082376@aol.com http://hometownaol.com/bma7082376/index.html

OLIVEREA

Slide Mt. Forest House
805 Oliverea Rd 12410
845-254-5365 Fax: 845-254-6107
Ralph & Linda Combe
All year

50-120-BB
21 rooms, 17 pb
Visa, MC, Disc, *Rated*
C-yes/S-yes/P-no/H-no
German

Full breakfast
Lunch & dinner available (fee)
Restaurant, bar, pool, sitting room, hiking, tennis courts, fishing

Fresh air, nature & a touch of Old World charm await you at our German/American Catskill Mountains Inn. slide_mtn@yahoo.com http://www.slidemountain-inn.com

ONEONTA (REGION)

Charlotte Valley Inn
480 County Hwy 40, *Worcester* 12197
607-397-8164
Lawrence & Joanne Kosciusko
All year

90-125-BB
5 rooms, 3 pb
Rated
C-yes/S-ltd/P-no/H-ltd

Full breakfast
Afternoon tea, snacks
Sitting room, tennis court, suite, fireplaces, cable TV

Elegance in the country. Historic Stagecoach Stop built in 1832. Fine period antiques—historic experience in idyllic Charlotte Valley, where the sidewalk ends.
charlottevalley@yahoo.com http://www.cooperstownchamber.org/cvinn

PENN YAN

Finton's Landing On Keuka Lake
661 E Lake Rd 14527
315-536-3146
Doug & Arianne Tepper
Spring, Summer, Fall

99-129-BB
4 rooms, 4 pb
Visa, MC, *Rated*
C-ltd/S-no/P-no/H-no
Dutch

Full breakfast
Sitting room, library, wraparound porch, lakefront, hammock, gazebo

Waterfront Victorian, all private baths and A/C, 165-ft. secluded beach on Keuka Lake, romantic porch, rocking chairs, whimsical period pieces, parlor fireplace.
tepperd@eznet.net http://home.eznet.net/~tepperd

Trimmer House
145 East Main St 14527
315-536-0522 Fax: 315-536-8304
800-968-8735
Gary Smith
All year

99-199-BB
5 rooms, 5 pb
Visa, MC, AmEx, *Rated*
C-ltd/S-ltd/P-no/H-ltd

Full breakfast
Snacks
Sitting room, library, Jacuzzis, suites, fireplaces, cable TV

1891 Queen Anne Victorian. Romantic atmosphere in the heart of New York wine country. Let us pamper you in our luxurious surroundings. Close to wineries, shops and restaurants. innkeeper@trimmerhouse.com http://www.trimmerhouse.com

PINE HILL

Birchcreek Inn
Route 28, Box 323 12465
914-254-5222 Fax: 914-254-5812
Julie Odato
All year

95-145-BB
7 rooms, 7 pb
Most CC, *Rated*, •
C-yes/S-ltd/P-no/H-no
Spanish

Full breakfast
Snacks, complimentary drinks, in room coffee, tea
Great hall, library, billiard rm, bikes, wraparound porch, frplcs., Cable TV

Award-winning country inn on 23 wooded acres with streams, mountains, beautiful views. Full breakfast. Secluded, yet close to all activities, "...a gem of an Inn." Recommended by NY Daily News. birchcreek@hvc.rr.com http://www.abirchcreekinn.com

POUGHKEEPSIE

Inn at the Falls
50 Red Oaks Mill Rd 12603
845-462-5770 Fax: 845-462-5943
800-344-1466
Dr. Ashok Dhabuwala
All year

170-205-BB
36 rooms, 36 pb
Rated, •
C-yes/S-yes/P-no/H-yes

Continental plus breakfast
Complimentary evening snacks & port
Hiking, whirlpool tubs in all suites, landscaped grounds, swimming pool

Quiet country inn, well off the main highway. Glass-enclosed common area with fireplace. innatfalls@aol.com http://www.innatthefalls.com

PRATTSBURGH

Feather Tick 'N Thyme
7661 Tuttle Rd 14873
607-522-4113
Ruth & Deb Cody
All year

80-100-BB
4 rooms, 2 pb
Most CC, *Rated*
C-ltd/S-ltd/P-no/H-no

Full breakfast
Afternoon tea, complimentary wine
Sitting room, iron and board, robes for shared bath, maps for guest use

An "unforgetable stop in Thyme." Country Victorian offers romantic getaway, luxurious furnishings, antiques, quiescent sleep, gracious hospitality, hiking, campfires and lawn games. info@bbnyfingerlakes.com http://www.bbnyfingerlakes.com

PULTNEYVILLE

Captain Throop House
PO Box 145
4184 Washington St 14538
315-589-8595
Dory Driss and John Wilson
All year

60-95-BB
3 rooms, 1 pb
•
C-ltd/S-ltd/P-no/H-no
Spanish, Italian

Continental plus breakfast
Afternoon tea
Sitting room, fireplaces, cable TV

Landmark 1832 cobblestone in lakeside historic district. Located on Seaway Trail. Antiques, fireplaces, perennial gardens, casual, homey atmosphere. Continental plus breakfast. ddriss@rochester.rr.com

PURLING

Bavarian Manor Country Inn
866 Mt Ave 12470
518-622-3261 Fax: 518-622-2338
All year

59-213-BB
19 rooms, 19 pb
Visa, MC, *Rated*
C-yes/S-yes/P-yes/H-yes
German, Polish

Full breakfast
Restaurant, dinner avail.
Bar service, Jacuzzis, swimming pool, fireplaces, cable TV, massage sessions

Nestled on 100 acres in the Catskill Mountains, this 4-story Victorian Inn overlooking a private lake has been welcoming guests since 1865 with its friendly, relaxed casual atmosphere. bavarian@mhonline.net http://www.bavarianmanor.com

RENSSELAER

Tibbitt's House Inn
100 Columbia Turnpike
Routes 9 & 20 12144
518-472-1348
Claire & Herb Rufleth
All year

75-85-EP
5 rooms, 1 pb
Rated
C-yes/S-yes/P-no/H-ltd

Full or Continental, for a fee
Enclosed porch, garden, patio, maid service, one apartment available

Comfortable, 135-year-old, antique-furnished farmhouse.

RHINEBECK

Beckrick House
27 Beckrick Dr 12572
845-876-6416
866-384-3450
David & Michelle Andrick
All year

80-175-BB
4 rooms, 2 pb
C-ltd/S-no/P-no/H-no

Full & continental breakfast
Snacks
Sitting room, fireplaces, dish TV, accommodate business travelers

Private retreat on 3.3 acres of shaded glens and gardens. Paddle boat on the large pond. Savor gourmet breakfast on the screened porch.
stay@beckrickhouse.com http://www.beckrickhouse.com

Beekman Arms/Delamater Inn
Rt 9, Center of Village 12572
845-876-7080 Fax: 845-876-7062
800-361-6517
Andrea Johnson
All year

95-170-BB
59 rooms, 59 pb
Most CC, *Rated*

Continental breakfast
Conference room (seats 40)

Romantic Country Inn in the Historic Village of Rhinebeck, located in New York's Hudson Valley. delamaterinn@aol.com http://www.delamaterinn.com

---

Stone Church Road
339 Stone Church Rd 12572
845-758-2427
Fax: 845-758-2427
Richard and Marsha DeBlasi
All year

95-115-BB
4 rooms, 2 pb
Visa, MC, AmEx
C-ltd/S-ltd/P-no/H-no

Full breakfast
Snacks
Sitting room, library, Cable TV, nature trail, badminton, croquet, patios

Peaceful country setting 10 minutes from the village of Rhinebeck and convenient to area attractions. Four comfortable rooms with scenic views.
stay@stonechurchroadbedandbreakfast.com
http://www.stonechurchroadbedandbreakfast.com

Veranda House
6487 Montgomery St 12572
845-876-4133 Fax: 845-876-4133
877-985-6800
Linda & Ward Stanley
All year

110-150-BB
5 rooms, 5 pb
Visa, MC, AmEx
C-yes/S-no/P-no/H-no

Full gourmet breakfast
Breakfast on terrace
Sitting room, library, A/C, concierge service, veranda with wicker

Charming 1845 Federal house located in historic Hudson Valley. Restaurants, fairs, antiques. Gourmet breakfasts.
visit@verandahouse.com http://www.verandahouse.com

RHINEBECK (REGION)

The Lombards Antiques & Lodgings
15 Spring Lake Rd, *Red Hook* 12571
845-758-3805 Fax: 845-758-6351
Peggy Anne & Peter Lombard
All year

95-125-BB
1 rooms, 1 pb
S-no/P-no/H-no

Full breakfast
Sitting room, library, bikes, cable TV, grounds, smoking porch

1760 Dutch Colonial with large sunny rooms furnished in antiques. Hearty breakfasts, cozy beds and free bikes to explore historic area and u-pick farms.
thelombards@webjogger.net

Red Hook Inn
7460 S Broadway, *Red Hook* 12571
845-758-8445 Fax: 845-758-3143
Beth Pagano & John Fraioli
All year

125-195-BB
6 rooms, 6 pb
Most CC
C-yes/S-no/P-no/H-no

Continental plus breakfast
Lunch & dinner, restaurant, bar service
Sitting room, Jacuzzis, suites, fireplaces, cable TV

Your casual place for elegant dining, lodging, and catering.
innkeeper@citlink.net http://www.theredhook.com

Lakehouse Inn
419 Shelley Hill Rd, *Stanfordville* 12581
845-266-8093 Fax: 845-266-4051
Judy Kohler
All year

125-750-BB
8 rooms, 8 pb
Visa, MC, AmEx, *Rated*, •
C-ltd/S-no/P-no/H-no

Full gourmet breakfast
Afternoon appetizers
7-acre private lake, swimming, boating, bass fishing

Circa 1898 country farmhouse on 6 separate and rolling acres, with 2 fireplaces, Jacuzzi, kitchen and in-ground pool for seasonal rental or weekend rental.
judy@lakehouseinn.com http://www.lakehouseinn.com

ROCHESTER

428 Mount Vernon
428 Mt Vernon Ave 14620
585-271-0792 Fax: 585-271-0946
800-836-3159
Philip & Claire Lanzatella
All year

125-BB
7 rooms, 7 pb
Most CC, *Rated*, •
C-ltd/S-ltd/P-no

Full breakfast from menu
Afternoon tea
Sitting room, library TV, games, refrigerator

Elegant estate home on two wooded acres at the entrance to historic Highland Park.
planzat1@rochesterrr.com http://www.428mtvernon.com

A B&B at Dartmouth House
215 Dartmouth St 14607
585-271-7872 Fax: 585-473-0778
800-724-6298
Ellie & Bill Klein
All year

120-150-BB
4 rooms, 4 pb
Most CC, *Rated*, •
C-ltd/S-no/P-no/H-no

Full candlelight breakfast
Bottomless cookie jar
Library, porches, organ, grand piano, A/C, movies, TV/VCRs & phones in rooms

Quiet, spacious Tudor in city's cultural district. Architecturally fascinating, residential neighborhood. Hosts are well-traveled & love people.
stay@dartmouthhouse.com http://www.dartmouthhouse.com

ROCHESTER (REGION)

The Country Corner
317 Redman Rd, *Hamlin* 14464
716-964-9935
John & Linda DeRue
All year

65-75-BB
3 rooms, 1 pb
Visa, MC
C-ltd/S-no/P-no/H-ltd

Full breakfast
Snacks
Sitting room, antique shop onsite in season.

Located in a serene country setting near Lake Ontario beaches and Rochester, we offer the perfect environment for relaxing and reading.
linda@thecountrycorner.com http://www.TheCountryCorner.com

ROCHESTER (REGION)

Rosewood
68 Geddes St, *Holley* 14470
585-638-6186 Fax: 585-638-7568
Karen Cook & Roy Nichols
All year

69-89-BB
5 rooms, 2 pb
Most CC, *Rated*
C-no/S-no/P-no/H-no

Full gourmet breakfast
Snacks
Sitt. rm., lib., bikes, fireplaces, cable TV, antique & gift shop

Rosewood offers Victorian elegance for business or pleasure. rosewdbnb@aol.com

---

Genesee Country Inn, C1833
PO Box 340
948 George St, *Mumford* 14511
585-538-2500 Fax: 585-538-4565
800-697-8297
Glenda Barcklow & Kim Rasmussen
All year

95-165-BB
12 rooms, 12 pb
Most CC, *Rated*, •
C-ltd/S-no/P-no/H-ltd

Full breakfast
Afternoon tea, snacks
Common rooms, fireplaces, canopy beds, gift shop, A/C, fly fishing, TVs

Historic Stone Mill. Relax on our 8 unique acres on Spring Creek, surrounded by woods & waterfalls. roomzescapeinn@aol.com http://geneseecountryinn.com

ROME

Maplecrest
6480 Williams Rd 13440
315-337-0070
Diane Saladino
All year

75-BB
3 rooms, 1 pb
Rated, •
C-ltd/S-no/P-no/H-no
Italian

Full gourmet breakfast
Beverage on arrival
Refrig. use, central A/C, sitting room, grill, picnic facilities

Modern split-level home. Close to historic locations. Adirondack foliage, lakes, & skiing. Near Griffins Business Park.

SAMSONVILLE

Dream House
128 Haver Rd 12461
914-657-2004
Ellen Iwanowski
All year

85-140-BB

Dream House offers country charm, solitude, breathtaking views, private decks for sunning and porches for shading dream@ulster.net http://www.dreamhousebandb.com

SARANAC LAKE

Sunday Pond
5544 State Route 30 12983
518-891-1531
Fax: 518-891-1531
Lesley & Dick Lyon
All year

75-BB
4 rooms, 4 pb
C-yes/S-no/P-no/H-no

Full breakfast
Lunch, dinner, snacks
Sitting room, accommodate business travelers

Adirondack style lodging in a peaceful forest setting. Catering to outdoor enthusiasts for over 15 years. Hearty breakfasts.
info@sundaypond.com http://www.sundaypond.com

SARANAC LAKE (REGION)

The Wawbeek Resort
Panther Mountain Rd, Rt 30, *Tupper Lake* 12986
518-359-2656 800-953-2656
All year

90-290-BB
20 rooms, 20 pb
Visa, MC, AmEx, •
C-yes/S-ltd/P-ltd/H-yes

Dine with spectacular views of Upper Saranac Lake
Canoes and kayaks, sand beach, sailboats, mountain bikes, hiking trails

Six bedroom Great Camp lodge circa 1902 and new 8-bedroom Lake House. Both with spectacular lake views. Cabins with kitchens. Boats, canoes, sand beach, tennis, daily housekeeping all complimentary.
wawbeek@capital.net http://www.wawbeek.com

SARATOGA (REGION)

Cambridge Hotel
4 West Main St, *Cambridge* 12816
518-677-5626 Fax: 518-677-0837
John La Posta
All year

135-155-BB
17 rooms, 17 pb
Visa, MC, AmEx
C-ltd/S-no/P-no/H-yes

Full breakfast
Lunch, dinner, afternoon tea, snacks, restaurant
Bar service, sitting room, library, cable TV, accom. bus. travelers

1885 Victorian Train hotel fully restored in 1999. Five star restaurant.
fhotelcl@nycap.rr.com http://www.cambridgehotel.com

Agape Farm LLC
4839 Rt 9 N, *Corinth* 12822
518-654-7777 Fax: 518-654-7777
Fred & Sigrid Koch
All year

89-175-BB
6 rooms, 6 pb
Visa, MC, Disc, *Rated*
C-yes/S-no/P-no/H-yes

Full breakfast
Snacks
Gardens, trout stream, farm animals, dogs, cats, family friendly facility

Enjoy an old farm atmosphere in our large country home. Six guestrooms, one handicapped equipped. agapefarmbnb@adelphia.net http://www.geocities.com/agapefarm/

SARATOGA SPRINGS

Adelphi Hotel
365 Broadway 12866
518-587-4688 Fax: 518-587-0851
Sheila Parkert
May-November

120-400-BB
20 rooms, 20 pb
Visa, MC, AmEx, *Rated*, •
C-yes/S-yes/P-no/H-no

Continental breakfast
Bar
Sitting room, swimming pool, large lobby, courtyard, front porch

Charming accommodations. Opulently restored high Victorian hotel located in the historic district of the renowned resort and spa of Saratoga Springs. http://www.adelphihotel.com

---

Chestnut Tree Inn
9 Whitney Place 12866
518-587-8681 888-243-7688
Cathleen & Bruce DeLuke
Mid-April-Nov.

95-165-BB
7 rooms, 7 pb
Visa, MC, •
C-ltd/S-no/P-no/H-no

Continental plus breakfast
Afternoon tea, lemonade
Comp. wine, snacks, sitting room, antiques, porch, spas, A/C

Restored turn-of-the-century guest house. Walk to racetrack large wicker porch. All rooms have private bath and air-conditioning. http://www.chestnuttreeinn.net

---

Saratoga Arms
495-497 Broadway 12866
518-584-1775 Fax: 518-581-4065
Noel & Kathleen Smith
all year

150-450-BB
16 rooms, 16 pb
Most CC, *Rated*, •
C-ltd/S-no/P-no/H-yes

Continental plus breakfast
Private bath, TV, telephone, voice mail, data ports, air conditioning

In the heart of historic downtown district, near shopping, restaurants, museums. Award-winning, recently refurbished, 16 room, concierge hotel. Ideal for meetings, business and leisure travelers. hotel@saratoga-lodging.com http://www.saratogaarms.com

---

Six Sisters
149 Union Ave 12866
518-583-1173 Fax: 518-587-2470
Kate Benton & Steve Ramirez
All year

85-320-BB
4 rooms, 4 pb
Visa, MC, AmEx, *Rated*, •
C-ltd/S-no/P-no

Full gourmet breakfast
Complimentary beverages
Sitting room, porch, A/C, rooms have TV & refrig., mineral bath/massage

Beautifully appointed 1880 Victorian, recommended by Gourmet, NY Times, & McCall's.
stay@sixsistersbandb.com http://www.sixsistersbandb.com

Westchester House
102 Lincoln Ave 12866
518-587-7613 Fax: 518-583-9562
800-581-7613
Bob & Stephanie Melvin
All year

95-325-BB
7 rooms, 7 pb
Most CC, *Rated*, •
C-ltd/S-ltd/P-no/H-no
French, German

Continental Plus breakfast
Complimentary beverages
Fireplace, guest fridge, in-room phones w/voice mail, data ports

Gracious Queen Anne Victorian Inn surrounded by old fashioned gardens. Elegant bedrooms combine Old World ambiance with up to date comforts.
innkeeper@westchesterhousebandb.com http://www.westchesterhousebandb.com

SARATOGA SPRINGS (REGION)

Apple Tree 49 West High St, *Ballston Spa* 12020 518-885-1113 Fax: 518-885-9758 Dolores & Jim Taisey All year	95-200-BB 5 rooms, 5 pb Visa, MC, AmEx, *Rated*, • C-ltd/S-no/P-no/H-no	Full breakfast Sitting room, TV/VCR, tennis court, whirlpool tub

Second Empire Victorian with romantic ambiance. Close to SPAC, Spa Park and Saratoga attractions. mail@appletreebb.com http://www.appletreebb.com

Wayside Inn 104 Wilton Rd, *Greenfield Center* 12833 518-893-7249 Fax: 518-893-2884 800-893-2884 Karen & Dale Shook All year	85-205-BB 4 rooms, 4 pb Visa, MC, • C-yes/S-no/P-no/H-no	Full breakfast Snacks, tea, coffee, etc. Pond, pool, herb gardens, walking / hiking areas, cable TV, patios, etc.

Friendly original 1786 stagecoach inn with easy access to downtown Saratoga Springs, thoroughbred track, performing arts center and Adirondack Mountains.
waysidein@aol.com http://www.Waysidein.com

Country Life 67 Tabor Rd, *Greenwich* 12834 518-692-7203 Fax: 518-692-9203 888-692-7203 Richard & Wendy Duvall All year	85-175-BB 3 rooms, 3 pb *Rated*, • C-yes/S-no/P-no/H-no Spanish, German, French	Full breakfast Afternoon tea or cocoa, cookies, sherry in room Patio, library, swimming hole, sunsets, sitting room, hammock, porch swing

Beautifully restored 1829 farmhouse near Saratoga horse racing, bridges, fishing, hiking, museums, shopping. 118 quiet acres with waterfalls, meadows, sunsets. Full breakfast. Non-smokers only please. stay@countrylifebb.com http://www.countrylifebb.com

The Mansion PO Box 77 801 Route 29, *Rock City Falls* 12863 508-885-1607 Fax: 518-373-8799 888-996-9977 Jeff Wodicka & Neil Castro All year	90-280-BB 10 rooms, 10 pb Visa, MC, AmEx, • C-ltd/S-no/P-ltd/H-yes	Full breakfast Wine-cheese & snacks afternoon, coffee-tea 24 hrs Phone, cable TV, comp. hookup, ponds/waterfalls/fountains, Bentley Transport

Step back in time & experience the romance of the 19th Cent. Built in 1866, the historic Mansion is a luxurious villa located 7mi from the action of Saratoga Spgs & 25 min from Spectacular Lake George.
infodesk@themansionsaratoga.com http://themansionsaratoga.com

SCHROON LAKE

Schroon Lake B&B PO Box 638 Route 9 12870 518-532-7042 800-523-6755 Rita & Bob Skojec All year	90-115-BB 5 rooms, 4 pb Visa, MC, AmEx, *Rated* C-ltd/S-ltd/P-no/H-ltd	Full breakfast Sitting room, library, cable TV, accom. bus. travelers, secure bike storage

Romantic country Victorian Inn located in the Adirondack Mountains in upstate New York. schroonbb@aol.com http://www.schroonbb.com

SILVER CREEK

Pinewoods Cottage 11634 York Rd 14136 716-934-4173 Fax: 716-934-2415 Estelle M. Crino All year	65-85-BB 3 rooms, 3 pb Visa, MC C-ltd/S-ltd/P-no/H-no	Full breakfast Snacks Sitting room, fireplaces, direct TV

Surrounded by woodlands and walking trails. Three beautifully appointed bedrooms with private baths, queen beds, A/C. An eclectic atmosphere of antiques and family history. Gourmet breakfast daily.
estelle@crinopinewoodscottage.com http://www.crinopinewoodscottage.com

SODUS

Tanniquetil
6237 Snyder Rd 14551
315-483-4046
Judith Moss
All year

40-45-BB
2 rooms, 1 pb
C-yes/S-no/P-yes/H-no
some French

Full country breakfast
Afternoon tea
Sitting room, library, fireplaces, walking trails, screened porch

Secluded wooded country setting with paths for walking or cross-country skiing. Organic mini-farm with goats and chickens. Full country breakfast with homemade breads.

SODUS BAY (REGION)

Bonnie Castle Farm
PO Box 188
6603 Bonnie Castle Rd, *Wolcott* 14590
315-587-2273 Fax: 315-587-4003
800-587-4006
Eric & Georgia Pendleton
All year

89-165-BB
8 rooms, 8 pb
Most CC, *Rated*, •
C-yes/S-no/P-no/H-no

Full breakfast
Hot tubs, sitting room, library, A/C, swimming, fishing, boating

"Turn of the Century" waterfront home on Sodus Bay, Northern Finger Lakes, between Rochester & Syracuse. http://www.virtualcities.com/ons/ny/r/nyr9701.htm

SOUTH NYACK (REGION)

RiverView
PO Box 22, *Piermont* 10968
845-353-0778 Fax: 845-353-0778
800-643-7225
Carolla Dost
All year

110-150-BB
3 rooms, 2 pb
C-ltd/S-no

Full breakfast
Prepared to your specifications
Central parlor, laundry facilities, fax and computer (fee)

Charming, historic, Colonial (cir. 1835) home situated on 2 secluded acres overlooking the Hudson River. info@riverviewbnb.com http://www.riverviewbnb.com

SOUTHAMPTON

Mainstay
579 Hill St 11968
631-283-4375 Fax: 631-287-6240
Elizabeth Main
All year

100-450-BB
8 rooms, 5 pb
Most CC, *Rated*, •
C-ltd/S-no/P-no/H-no

Continental breakfast
Restaurant nearby
Sitting room, bikes, tennis court, swimming pool

1870s Colonial guest house, all antique iron beds & country pine furniture.
elizmain@hamptons.com http://www.TheMainstay.com

ST. JOHNSVILLE

Inn by the Mill
1679 Mill Rd 13452
518-568-2388 Fax: 518-568-6060
866-568-2388
Ron and Judith Hezel
5/1-11/1;winter holidays

110-350-BB
5 rooms, 5 pb
Most CC, *Rated*
C-ltd/S-no/P-no/H-no

Continental plus breakfast
Afternoon tea, snacks
Sitting room, library, fireplaces, bicycles, waterfall, gardens, hot tub

Historical 1835 stone grist mill and miller's home, flower & watergardens. Elegant rooms, private baths. romance@innbythemill.com http://www.innbythemill.com

STONE RIDGE

Bakers
24 Old Kings Hwy 12484
845-687-9795 Fax: 845-687-4153
888-623-5513
Doug & Linda Baker
All year

98-138-BB
6 rooms, 4 pb
C-ltd/S-no/P-no

Full breakfast

A restored 1780 farm house located in the Rondout Valley with its memorable views of streams, fields, woods and mountains.
dbakersbandb@aol.com http://www.bakersbandb.com

STONE RIDGE

The Inn at Stone Ridge
PO Box 76
3805 Main St 12484
914-687-0736 Fax: 914-687-0112
Suzanne & Dan Hausping
All year

195-425-BB
11 rooms, 2 pb
Rated

Full breakfast
Restaurant & Bar

18th century Dutch colonial mansion. Set on 150 acres in rural Ulster County, New York. The Inn includes a full service Restaurant & Bar.
innfuse@aol.com http://www.innatstoneridge.com

SYRACUSE

B&B Wellington
707 Danforth St 13208
315-474-3641 Fax: 315-474-2557
800-724-5006
Wendy Wilber & Ray Borg
All year

95-135-BB
5 rooms, 5 pb
Most CC, *Rated*, •
C-yes/S-no/P-no/H-no

Full breakfast weekends
Continental plus weekdays
Aftn. tea, sitting room, suites, frplcs., cable, fax, copier, porches

The finest Arts & Crafts home in Central New York. Built in 1914 as a brick and stucco Tudor style home. Currently registered on the National and New York State Register of Historic properties. innkeepers@bbwellington.com http://www.bbwellington.com

Dickenson House on James
1504 James St 13203
315-423-4777 Fax: 315-425-1965
888-423-4777
Pam & Ed Kopiel
All year

105-350-BB
5 rooms, 5 pb
Most CC, *Rated*, •
C-ltd/S-no/P-no/H-ltd

Full gourmet breakfast
Afternoon tea, snacks, comp. wine, home bake goods
Sitting room, library, bicycles, tennis court, Jacuzzi, fireplaces, cable TV

Retreat to a haven of Old World elegance & hospitality with all the modern conveniences. Breakfast will delight your senses.
innkeeper@dickensonhouse.com http://www.dickensonhouse.com

SYRACUSE (REGION)

High Meadows
3740 Eager Rd, *Jamesville* 13078
315-492-3517 Fax: 315-492-0343
800-854-0918
Nancy Mentz

55-140-BB
4 rooms, 2 pb
Most CC, *Rated*, •
C-yes/S-no/P-no/H-no
March–December

Full breakfast
Jacuzzis, suites, fireplaces, cable TV

We are an owner designed & built California contemporary with a lot of light. Furnished with traditional comfortable pieces, you will experience quiet and serenity in one of the custom designed areas. nancy@himeadows.com http://www.himeadows.com

Ancestor's Inn, The Bassett House
215 Sycamore St, *Liverpool* 13088
315-461-1226 888-866-8591
Mary & Dan Weidman
All year

75-95-BB
4 rooms, 4 pb
Most CC, *Rated*
C-yes/S-ltd/P-no/H-no

Full breakfast
Afternoon tea, soft drinks & juices
In-Room TV/VCR, movies, books, central AC, porch

Ancestors is located in the village of Liverpool NY, in the historic Bassett House. The house is decorated in the high Victorian style & has all of today's comforts.
innkeeper@ancestorsinn.com http://www.ancestorsinn.com

River Edge Mansion
1 County Rt 10, *Pennellville* 13132
315-695-3021 Fax: 315-695-3021
Kelly & Dean Wright
All year

129-179-BB
3 rooms, 3 pb
Visa, MC, AmEx, *Rated*, •
C-yes/S-ltd/P-no/H-no

Full, three course breakfast
Beverage & snack in the evening
Large movie library, bicycles, canoe, gazebo and deck on the river.

Historic 1818 Greek Revival Mansion features whirlpool suites, fireplaces, private balcony, and docking on the Erie Canal, minutes from Syracuse.
innkeeper@riveredgemansion.com http://www.riveredgemansion.com/

TANNERSVILLE

The Eggery Inn
SR 1 Box 4, County Rd 16
12485
518-589-5363 Fax: 518-589-5774
800-785-5364
Julie & Abe Abramczyk

99-130-BB
15 rooms, 15 pb
Visa, MC, AmEx, *Rated*
C-yes/S-ltd/P-no/H-ltd
All year

Full breakfast from menu
Group dinners, wine list, in-room cable TV, cozy fireside parlor lounge, bar

Majestic setting, panoramic views, dining in a garden setting, cozy fireside lounge, bar, wraparound porch, atmosphere & individualized attention. Facing Hunter Mountain ski slopes. eggeryinn@aol.com http://www.eggeryinn.com

TARRYTOWN (REGION)

Alexander Hamilton House
49 Van Wyck St, *Croton-on-Hudson* 10520
914-271-6737 Fax: 914-271-3927
888-414-ALEX
Barbara Notarius, Jonathan Wright All year

100-250-BB
7 rooms, 7 pb
Most CC, *Rated*, •
C-yes/S-no/P-no/H-no
French, German

Full gourmet breakfast
Chocolate chip cookies
Sitting room, bicycles, Jacuzzis, swimming pool, suites, fireplace, cable TV

We are a romantic, Victorian Inn close to all the attractions of the lower Hudson Valley, 48 minutes from the heart of NYC, river view, village setting, with pool.
info@alexanderhamiltonhouse.com http://www.alexanderhamiltonhouse.com

UTICA

Adam Bowman Manor
197 Riverside Dr 13502
315-738-0276 Fax: 315-738-0276
877-724-7268
Marion & Barry Goodwin
All year

70-95-BB
4 rooms, 2 pb
Visa, MC, *Rated*
C-yes/S-no/P-no/H-yes
Italian, German

Full breakfast
Snacks, afternoon tea on weekends
Sitting room, library, A/C, fountain, antique gazebo, lush landscaping

Nestled in the foothills of the Adirondacks beside the Erie Canal, this historic 1823 brick Federal Manor offers the elegance once enjoyed by the Duke & Duchess of Windsor.
bargood@adelphia.net

The Pratt Smith House
10497 Cosby Manor Rd 13502
315-732-8483
Anne & Alan Frederick
All year

60-65-BB
2 rooms, 2 pb
Rated
C-yes/S-no/P-no/H-no

Full breakfast
Cable TV, sitting room

1815 brick Colonial, wide plank floors, antiques; set on 22 acres in woodsy residential area convenient to city, area attractions, NY's thruway.
alannem@borg.com http://www.cnybb.com/pratt.htm

VERNON

Lavender Inn
5950 State Rt 5 13476
315-829-2440
Rose Degni & Lyn Doring

90-BB
3 rooms, 3 pb
C-yes/P-no
All year

TV and phone available in common area, A/C

Located along Historic Seneca Turnpike between Utica and Vernon, New York, is a quiet country getaway.
rdegni@hotmail.com http://lavenderinn.homestead.com/homepage.html

WARRENSBURG

Cornerstone Victorian
3921 Main St 12885
518-623-3308 Fax: 518-623-3979
Doug & Louise Goettsche
All year

68-165-BB
5 rooms, 5 pb
Visa, MC, •
C-ltd/S-no/P-no/H-no

Five course gourmet breakfast
Complimentary homemade desserts & beverages
Sitting room, TV lounge, bicycles, wrap-around porch overlooking mountain

Grand Victorian home replete with gleaming woodwork, exquisite stained glass, and terra-cotta fireplaces. Five delightful bedchambers, with private bath and A/C.
stay@cornerstonevictorian.com http://www.cornerstonevictorian.com

WARRENSBURG

The Merrill Magee House
PO Box 391
3 Hudson St 12885
518-623-2449 Fax: 518-623-3990
888-MMH-INN1
James Carrington &
Pamela Converse

115-145-BB
13 rooms, 10 pb
Rated, •
All year

Full breakfast

Centrally located in the Adirondack 5 miles north of Lake George Village.
mmhinn1@capital.net http://www.merrillmageehouse.com

White House Lodge
3760 Main St 12885
518-623-3640
Ruth & Jim Gibson
All year

85-BB
3 rooms, 2 pb
Visa, MC
C-ltd/S-ltd/P-no/H-no

Continental breakfast
Complimentary wine, cookies
Homemade cakes, pies, sitting room, television, front porch

An 1847 Victorian in the heart of the Adirondacks. The home is furnished with many antiques.

WARWICK

Warwick Valley
24 Maple Ave 10990
845-987-7255 Fax: 845-988-5318
888-280-1671
Loretta Breedveld
All year

100-145-BB
5 rooms, 5 pb
Most CC, *Rated*, •
C-ltd/S-ltd/P-no/H-no

Full breakfast
Sitting room, bicycles, fireplaces, cable TV, covered porch, back lawn

Located in the Historic District of the village of Warwick.
loretta@warwick.net http://www.wvbedandbreakfast.com

WARWICK (REGION)

The Glenwood House
49 Glenwood Road, *Pine Island* 10969
845-258-5066 Fax: 845-258-4226
Andrea & Kevin Colman
All year

110-295-BB
7 rooms, 5 pb
Most CC, *Rated*
C-yes/S-ltd/P-no/H-no
Italian, German

Full breakfast
Library, fireplaces, whirlpool tubs for two, bkfst. in bed, modem hookup

Restored Victorian Farmhouse. Cottage suites and private rooms featuring Jacuzzis for two. Fireplaces, antiques, candles and full candlelight breakfast.
info@glenwoodhouse.com http://www.glenwoodhouse.com

WATER MILL

Seven Ponds
PO Box 98
261 Seven Ponds Towd Rd. 11976
631-726-7618
Carol Conover
All year, closed July

115-175-BB
3 rooms, 3 pb
C-ltd/S-ltd/P-no/H-no
Spanish, limited French

Continental plus breakfast
Glass of wine

Our traditional saltbox home has three bedrooms, 2 queen & 1 twin, each with private bath. Lots of privacy in a quiet wooded setting and a large deck with 20' x 40' pool.
zindalo@aol.com

WEST POINT (REGION)

Cromwell Manor Inn
174 Angola Rd, *Cornwall* 12518
845-534-7136
Jack Trowell & Cynthia Krom
All year

150-345-BB
13 rooms, 13 pb
Visa, MC, AmEx, *Rated*, •
C-ltd/S-no/P-no/H-yes

Full breakfast
Afternoon tea, fresh cookies, picnics arranged
Fireplaces, spa and fitness options, 7-acre garden, Internet, art gallery

This stunning 1820 Greek Revival Mansion is set on 7 lush acres with scenic Hudson Valley views. Top 10 Inns, Best Romantic Inns, National Register of Historic Places. Weddings and corporate retreats. cmi@hvc.rr.com http://www.cromwellmanor.com

WEST POINT (REGION)

Caldwelll House
PO Box 425
25 Orrs Mills Road, *Salisbury Mills* 12577
845-496-2954 Fax: 845-496-5924
Carmela Turco & Eugene Sheridan
All year

135-245-BB
4 rooms, 4 pb
Visa, MC, AmEx, •
C-ltd/S-ltd/P-no/H-no
Spanish, Italian

Full breakfast
Snacks
Sitting room, fireplaces, TV/VCR, telephone in each room

Elegant and romantic 1803 Hudson Valley Colonial on three landscaped acres, furnished with antiques, fine linens and fresh flowers.
caldwel@frontiernet.net http://www.caldwellhouse.com

WESTFIELD

Westfield House
PO Box 505
7573 E Main Rd 14787
716-326-6262 Fax: 716-326-2543
877-299-7496
Kathy Grant & Marianne Heck
All year

75-125-BB
7 rooms, 7 pb
Visa, MC, *Rated*, •
C-yes/S-no/P-no/H-ltd

Full breakfast
Snacks, coffee & tea
Large common areas, billiard room

Brick Gothic Revival architecture. Seven guestrooms, all with private bath.
whouse@adelphia.net http://www.westfieldhousebnb.com

WESTHAMPTON

Westhampton Country Manor
28 Jagger Lane 11977
631-288-9000 Fax: 516-288-3292
888-288-5540
Susan & Bill Dalton All year

138-250-BB
5 rooms, 5 pb
Visa, MC, AmEx
C-ltd/S-no/P-no/H-no

Full breakfast
Sitting room, library, tennis court, pool, fireplace, guesthouse

Simple elegance. Quiet, romantic getaway in historic (c.1865) home decorated with many antiques. Frplc., piano & a gourmet breakfast. Har-tru tennis court & heated pool in season. innkeeper@hamptonsbb.com http://www.hamptonsbb.com

WESTHAMPTON BEACH

1880 House
PO Box 648
2 Seafield Ln 11978
631-288-1559 Fax: 631-288-7696
800-346-3290
Elsie Collins All year

150-250-BB
3 rooms, 3 pb
Rated, •
C-yes/S-no/P-no/H-no

Full breakfast
Complimentary sherry & muffins
Sitting room, piano, tennis court, library, pool

Country hideaway with 3 suites furnished in antiques.
elsie.collins@verizon.net http://www.1880-house.com

1900 South Winds
91 Potunk Lane 11978
631-288-5505 Fax: 631-288-5506
866-332-3344
Rosemary & Randy Dean
All year

150-235-BB
4 rooms, 4 pb
Visa, MC, AmEx, *Rated*, •
C-ltd/S-no/P-no/H-no

Full breakfast
Afternoon beverage, cookies, fruit
Pool

The former estate of Governor A. Smith family has been newly renovated and features up-to-date amenities and plenty of space to relax in our spacious rooms, country parlor, or large front porch. info@southwindsbnb.com http://www.southwindsbnb.com

---

Woodland B&B
12 Woodland Ave 11978
631-288-1681 Fax: 631-288-8453
Amanda Downing
All year

85-150-BB
3 rooms, 1 pb
AmEx, •
C-ltd/S-ltd/P-ltd/H-ltd

Continental breakfast
Sitting room, outdoor pool, fireplace, cable TV

This private residence bed and breakfast is one of the best kept secrets of the Hamptons.
WoodlandBandB@aol.com
http://hometown.aol.com/woodlandbandb/myhomepage/profile.html

WESTPORT

All Tucked Inn
PO Box 324
53 S Main St 12993
518-962-4400 Fax: 518-962-4400
888-ALL-TUCK
Claudia Ryan & Tom Haley
All year

65-125-BB
9 rooms, 9 pb
Rated, •
C-ltd/S-no/P-no/H-no

Full breakfast
Dinner, snacks, wine
Championship golf, beach, marina close by, sitting room

Four season inn overlooking Lake Champlain. Cozy rooms, fireplaces. Enjoy championship golf and the year round activities of the Adirondacks.
haleyt@westelcom.com http://www.alltuckedinn.com

The Inn on the Library Lawn
PO Box 390
One Washington St 12993
518-962-8666 Fax: 518-962-2007
888-577-7748
Don & Susann Thompson
All year

75-125-BB
10 rooms, 10 pb
Most CC, *Rated*
C-ltd/S-no/P-no/H-no

Full breakfast
Beer, wine & dinner available
Lunch served on weekends, May-Oct. library, sitting room, snacks

Elegant Victorian inn w/period decor & furnishings. Lake Champlain views. Walk to restaurants, marina, beach, golf, theater & shopping.
innthompson@msn.com http://www.theinnonthelibrarylawn.com

WHITEFACE MOUNTAIN (REGION)

Willkommen Hof
PO Box 240
Rt 86, *Wilmington* 12997
518-946-7669 Fax: 518-946-7626
800-541-9119
Heike & Burt Yost
Closed Nov.

64-165-BB
8 rooms, 3 pb
Visa, MC, *Rated*, •
C-yes/S-no/P-yes/H-no
German

Full breakfast
Afternoon tea, bar service
Dinner available (fee), hot tubs, sauna, near golf, cross-country skiing

European tradition in the heart of the Adirondack Mountains with indoor sauna & outdoor hot tub. WillkommenHof@Whiteface.net http://www.lakeplacid.net/willkommenhof

WILLSBORO

Champlain Vistas
183 Lake Shore Rd 12996
518-963-8029 Fax: 518-963-7040
Barbara and Bob Hatch
All year

85-110-BB
5 rooms, 3 pb
Visa, MC
C-ltd/S-no/P-no/H-yes

Full breakfast
Snacks, afternoon tea
Sitting room, trails for hiking & biking nearby, near golf, swimming

Lake wrap-around porch special wedding site; artists' paradise.
rdehatch@aol.com http://www.virtualcities.com/ny/champlainvistas.htm

WINDHAM

Albergo Allegria
PO Box 267
#43 Rt 296 12496
518-734-5560 Fax: 518-734-5570
Leslie & Marianna Leman
All year

73-299-BB
21 rooms, 21 pb
Visa, MC, *Rated*, •
C-ltd/S-no/P-no/H-yes
Croatian, Italian

Full gourmet breakfast
Sitting room, fireplaces, cable TV/VCR, videos, bikes & tennis (fee)

Highly awarded 1892 Victorian mansion nestled in the northern Catskill Mountains. Set on 2 acres of manicured lawns & country gardens. Voted 2000 Inn of the Year!
mail@albergousa.com http://www.AlbergoUSA.com

WOODSTOCK

Enchanted Manor
23 Rowe Rd 12401
845-679-9012
Claudia & Rolan
All year

165-325-BB
4 rooms, 3 pb
Visa, MC, AmEx, •
C-ltd/S-no/P-ltd/H-no

Tea, wine, fruit
Heated pool, outdoor hot tub, massage therapy, gym

Elegant yet comfortable home with beautiful furnishings on eight storybook acres. Extraordinary 6-level deck overlooking pond; cascading waterfall; serenity and peace.
enchantedmanor@aol.com http://www.enchantedmanorinn.com

WOODSTOCK

Twin Gables of Woodstock
73 Tinker St 12498
845-679-9479 Fax: 845-679-5638
Frederic Vercauteren
All year

64-110-EP
9 rooms, 3 pb
Most CC, *Rated*
C-ltd/S-no/P-no/H-no
French, Flemish

Continental breakfast
Parlor, front patio to enjoy a sunny day, meditation room, in-house reiki

1930's ambience revives the easy living of the time. Woodstock "Colony of the Arts," world-wide reputation for art, literature and music.
info@twingableswoodstockny.com http://www.twingableswoodstockny.com

---

The Wild Rose Inn
66 Rock City Rd 12498
845-679-8783
Fax: 845-679-8783
Ms. Marti Ladd
All year

100-200-BB
5 rooms, 5 pb
Visa, MC
C-yes/S-no/P-no/H-no

Continental Plus Breakfast
Snacks, complimentary wine
Jacuzzis, suites, cable TV, accom. bus. travel

Victorian Revival furnished with magnificent antiques, sumptuously draped beds, all private baths with whirlpool tubs. An elegant experience in the heart of downtown.
wildrosebb@aol.com http://www.woodstock-online.com/wildrose

The Woodstock Inn on the Millstream
2399 Glasco Turnpike
48 Tannery Brook Rd 12498
845-679-8211 800-697-8211
Karen Pignataro
All year

99-149-BB
18 rooms, 18 pb
Visa, MC, AmEx, *Rated*
C-yes/S-yes/P-no/H-no
French

Continental plus breakfast
Cable TV

Your retreat in the heart of Woodstock. Beautiful grounds & gardens along the cascading Millstream. Easy walk to shopping & dining.
http://www.woodstock-inn-ny.com

North Carolina

ANDREWS

Hawkesdene House
PO Box 670
381 Phillips Creek Rd 28901
828-321-6027 Fax: 828-321-5007
800-447-9549
Roy & Daphne Sargent
All year

85-212-BB
5 rooms, 5 pb
Most CC, *Rated*, •
C-ltd/S-no/P-ltd/H-yes

Full breakfast
No breakfast in cottages
Sitting room, library, suites, fireplaces, cable TV

Romantic English country inn & family cottages nestled in the Great Smoky Mountains. Hiking or llama treks from the inn. hawke@dnet.net http://www.hawkesdene.com

ASHEBORO

Victorian Country
711 Sunset Avenue 27203
336-626-4706
Joyce Tucker
All year

75-140-BB
4 rooms, 4 pb
Visa, MC
C-ltd/S-ltd/P-ltd/H-ltd

Full breakfast
Snacks are provided in the evening
Sitting room, library, full country porch, music room with baby grand

Victorian Country B&B is a restored 1905 Queen-Anne treasure. Nestled in the heart of NC and convenient to the mountains or the coast. vcbb@asheboro.com

ASHEVILLE

1899 Black Walnut
288 Montford Ave 28801
828-254-3878 Fax: 828-236-9393
800-381-3878
Sandra & Randy Glasgow
All year

95-200-BB
7 rooms, 7 pb
Most CC, *Rated*, •
C-yes/S-ltd/P-no/H-no
Italian, French

Full gourmet breakfast
Vegetarian dining available
Sitting room, fireplace, tennis & golf nearby, cottage, carriage house

Turn-of-the-Century shingle-style home in heart of historic district. Minutes from downtown & Biltmore Estate. info@blackwalnut.com http://www.blackwalnut.com

---

A Hill House B&B Inn
120 Hillside St 28801
828-232-0345 Fax: 828-255-9855
800-379-0002
Carol Winter & Al Ganzenhuber
All year

95-300-BB
9 rooms, 9 pb
Visa, MC, AmEx, *Rated*, •
C-ltd/S-no/P-ltd/H-no
German

Full breakfast
Afternoon tea, snacks
Sitting room, Jacuzzi, suites, fireplace, cable TV

Commanding view of downtown and Western Mountains. Guest pampering with whirlpool tubs, fireplaces, bedside breakfast. withzak@home.com http://www.hillhousebb.com

---

Abbington Green
46 Cumberland Cir 28801
828-251-2454 Fax: 828-251-2872
800-251-2454
V., J. & G. Larrea
All year

135-295-BB
7 rooms, 6 pb
Visa, MC, AmEx, *Rated*, •
C-ltd/S-no/P-no

Full breakfast
Afternoon tea
Sitting room & library with piano, chess, etc., bicycles, A/C

Elegant, light-filled, historic home–English garden theme with antiques throughout and 6 working fireplaces. Sumptuous, full breakfast.
info@abbingtongreen.com http://www.abbingtongreen.com

Aberdeen Inn
64 Linden Ave 28801
828-254-9336 Fax: 828-281-4005
888-254-9336
Bonnie Chase
All year

95-130-BB
6 rooms, 6 pb
Most CC
C-ltd/S-ltd/P-no

Full breakfast

The majestic oak and maple trees surrounding the Aberdeen Inn will welcome you home, where for a while, you can step away from your busy world and rediscover simple, peaceful pleasures. aberdeeninn@aol.com http://www.lookingup.com/aberdeen

---

Albemarle Inn
86 Edgemont Rd 28801
828-255-0027 Fax: 828-236-3397
800-621-7435
Cathy and Larry Sklar
All year

145-295-BB
11 rooms, 11 pb
Visa, MC, Disc, *Rated*, •
C-ltd/S-no/P-no/H-no

Full breakfast
Afternoon tea, snacks
Sitting room, suites, fireplaces, gardens, private balcony, private sunporch

Elegant 1907 Greek Revival mansion on 3/4 acre of landscaped grounds in the residential Grove Park section of Asheville. Features exquisite carved oak staircase and exceptionally spacious guestrooms. info@albemarleinn.com http://www.albemarleinn.com

---

AppleWood Manor Inn
62 Cumberland Circle 28801
828-254-2244 Fax: 828-254-0899
800-442-2197
Johan & Coby Verhey
All year

110-125-BB
4 rooms, 4 pb
Visa, MC, *Rated*, •
C-ltd/S-no/P-no/H-no

Full gourmet breakfast
Complimentary beverages
Sitting room, library, bikes, badminton, croquet

Balconies, fireplaces, private baths, delicious breakfasts & aftn. tea-just to mention a few pleasures. Come romance yourselves with a stay.
innkeeper@applewoodmanor.com http://www.applewoodmanor.com

ASHEVILLE

At Cumberland Falls
254 Cumberland Ave 28801
828-253-4085 Fax: 828-253-5566
888-743-2557
Patti & Gary Wiles
All year

180-250-BB
5 rooms, 5 pb
Visa, MC, Disc, *Rated*,
•
C-ltd/S-no/P-no/H-no

Full breakfast
Afternoon tea, snacks, comp. wine & cheese on Fri.
Jacuzzis, fireplaces, cable TV, accommodate business travelers

We are a turn-of-the-century home located in historic Asheville. Our home features waterfalls and gardens, Jacuzzis and fireplaces.
fallsinn@aol.com http://www.cumberlandfalls.com/

Beaufort House Victorian
61 N Liberty St 28801
828-254-8334 Fax: 828-251-2082
800-261-2221
Jacqueline & Robert Glasgow
All year

95-235-BB
10 rooms, 10 pb
Visa, MC, *Rated*, •
C-yes/S-no/P-no/H-no

Full breakfast
Afternoon tea
Sitting room, bicycles, hot tubs

National Historic property. Lovely tea garden & manicured lawns. All homemade baked goods. info@beauforthouse.com http://www.beauforthouse.com

---

Biltmore Village Inn
119 Dodge St 28803
828-274-8707 Fax: 828-274-8779
866-274-8779
Ripley Hotch & Owen Sullivan
April-December

175-285-BB
5 rooms, 5 pb
Visa, MC, AmEx, •
C-ltd/S-no/P-no/H-no
French

Full breakfast
Tea with refreshments
Two sitting rooms, wraparound porches

Welcome to the Biltmore Village Inn Bed and Breakfast, just a stone's throw from the gates of the Biltmore Estate, and the shopping, restaurants, and attractions of Biltmore Village of Asheville. info@biltmorevillageinn.com http://www.biltmorevillageinn.com

---

Bridle Path Inn
30 Lookout Rd 28804
828-252-0035 Fax: 828-252-0221
Carol & Fred Halton
All year

90-125-BB
8 rooms, 8 pb
Visa, MC, AmEx,
Rated, •
C-yes/S-ltd/P-no/H-yes

Full breakfast
Dinner by great cooks
Sitting room, verandah, picnic baskets, hiking trails

Comfortable and secluded on mountain overlooking downtown Asheville. Full breakfast served on verandah.
fjhalton3@aol.com http://www.BridlePathInn.com

Carolina
177 Cumberland Ave 28801
828-254-3608 Fax: 828-252-0640
888-254-3608
David Feinstein and Susan Birkholz
All year

110-175-BB
7 rooms, 7 pb
Rated

Full breakfast

Located in the Montford Historic District, we are close to downtown Asheville and the Biltmore Estate. All rooms have private bath, A/C, TV.
info@carolinabb.com http://www.carolinabb.com

Cedar Crest Victorian Inn
674 Biltmore Ave 28803
828-252-1389
Fax: 828-253-7667
800-252-0310
Bruce and Rita Wightman
All year

150-285-BB
11 rooms, 11 pb
Most CC, *Rated*, •
C-ltd/S-no/P-no/H-no

Full breakfast
Beverages, cookies, evening desserts
A/C, cable TV, phones, piano, parlor & study, staff massage therapist

Three blocks to the Biltmore Estate. The essence of Victoriana- magnificent woodwork, stained glass, guestroom fireplaces, period antiques throughout. Full gourmet breakfast. Evening dessert. Gardens.
stay@cedarcrestinn.com http://www.cedarcrestinn.com

ASHEVILLE

Corner Oak Manor 53 Saint Dunstans Rd 28803 828-253-3525 888-633-3525 Karen & Andy Spradley All year	115-175-BB 4 rooms, 4 pb Most CC, *Rated*, • C-ltd/S-no/P-no/H-no	Full breakfast Snacks Sitting room, A/C, fireplace, hot tub, cottage has TV & fireplace

Elegant full gourmet breakfast; queen-size beds; outdoor deck with Jacuzzi; flowers/chocolates. info@corneroakmanor.com http://www.corneroakmanor.com

---

Dogwood Cottage Inn 40 Canterbury Rd N 28801 828-258-9725 Joan & Don Tracy All year	110-125-BB 4 rooms, 4 pb Visa, MC, AmEx, *Rated*, • C-yes/S-ltd/P-yes/H-yes	Full breakfast Afternoon tea, snacks, wine Sitting room, library, swimming pool, veranda, Blue Ridge views

Historical, rustic brown shingled lodge, wood floors, French doors, wood-burning fireplaces, beamed ceilings, 40 foot porch, stunning views. http://www.dogwoodcottageinn.com

---

Katherine's 43 Watauga St 28801 828-236-9494 Fax: 828-236-2218 888-325-3190 Ineke Strongman All year	95-145-BB 5 rooms, 5 pb Visa, MC, Disc, • C-ltd/S-no/P-no/H-no Dutch	Full gourmet breakfast Afternoon tea, snacks, complimentary wine Sitting room, library, tennis court, accom. bus. travelers

Situated on a quiet tree-lined street in the Montford Historic District. The decor can be described in superlatives such as elegant and rich, yet comfortable.
http://www.katherinesbandb.com

The Lion and The Rose 276 Montford Ave 28801 828-255-7673 Fax: 828-285-9810 800-546-6988 Chris & Janis Ortwein All year	155-255-BB 5 rooms, 5 pb Most CC, *Rated*, • C-ltd/S-no/P-no/H-no	Full breakfast Afternoon tea, snacks Sitting room, Jacuzzis, suites, fireplace, cable TV, water fountain garden

Biltmore Estate (8 minutes away), Chimney Rock Park, Blue Ridge Parkway, Great Smoky National Park, canoeing, white water rafting, hiking, antiquing, shopping, golf.
info@lion-rose.com http://www.lion-rose.com

North Lodge on Oakland 84 Oakland Rd 28801 828-252-6433 Fax: 828-252-3034 800-282-3602 Herb & Lois Marsh All year	95-130-BB 4 rooms, 4 pb Most CC, • C-ltd/S-no/P-no/H-no	Full breakfast Afternoon tea, snacks Sitting room, library, enclosed porch, front parlor, TV, phones

Warm, friendly environment. English antiques and contemporary decor. Deluxe breakfasts! stay@northlodge.com http://www.northlodge.com

---

Old Reynolds Mansion 100 Reynolds Heights 28804 828-254-0496 800-709-0496 Fred & Helen Faber All year	95-150-BB 10 rooms, 10 pb Most CC, *Rated* C-ltd/S-ltd/P-no/H-no	Full breakfast Snacks, beverage, complimentary wine Sitting room, verandahs, pool, A/C, televisions, refrigerator, telephone

A restored 1850 Antebellum mansion in a country setting. Wide verandahs, mountain views, wood-burning fireplaces, huge old swimming pool.
innkeeper@oldreynoldsmansion.com http://www.oldreynoldsmansion.com/

ASHEVILLE

Pinecrest
249 Cumberland Ave 28801
828-281-4275 Fax: 828-281-2215
888-811-3053
Barbara & Richard Newell
All year

145-175-BB
4 rooms, 4 pb
Visa, MC, *Rated*, •
C-ltd/S-no/P-no/H-no

Full gourmet breakfast
Afternoon tea, snacks, complimentary wine
Sitting room, library, fireplaces, cable TV, accom. bus. travelers, sunroom

Turn-of-the-century residence with European elegance. Two parlors, with fireplaces, sunroom, and beautifully appointed guestrooms. Stone patio and landscaped gardens for outdoor enjoyment! innkeeper@pinecrestbb.com http://www.pinecrestbb.com

---

Richmond Hill Inn
87 Richmond Hill Dr 28806
828-252-7313 Fax: 828-252-8726
800-545-9238
Susan Michel
All year

175-485-BB
36 rooms, 36 pb
Visa, MC, AmEx, *Rated*, •
C-yes/S-no/P-no/H-ltd

Full gourmet breakfast
2 gourmet restaurants
Library, garden rooms, turndown, phone, TV, conference facilities

Historic 1889 Victorian inn, magnificently renovated, with gracious service and fine dining. Elegant setting for meetings & small weddings.
info@RichmondHillInn.com http://www.richmondhillinn.com

WhiteGate Inn & Cottage
173 E Chestnut St 28801
828-253-2553 Fax: 828-281-1883
800-485-3045
Ralph Coffey & Frank Salvo
All year

155-265-BB
5 rooms, 5 pb
Rated, •
S-ltd

Full 3-course gourmet breakfast

Circa 1889 shingle-style house, surrounded by beautifully landscaped grounds with a greenhouse/conservatory filled with orchids and tropical plants.
innkeeper@whitegate.net http://www.whitegate.net

Wright Inn & Carriage House
235 Pearson Dr 28801
828-251-0789 Fax: 828-251-0929
800-552-5724
Vicki & Mark Maurer All year

140-325-BB
11 rooms, 11 pb
Visa, MC, AmEx, *Rated*
C-ltd/S-no/P-no/H-no

Full breakfast in inn
Snacks, comp. beverages, afternoon social hour
Sitting Rm, centrl A/C, whirlpools, fireplaces, TVs & phones

The Wright Inn & Carriage House represents one of the finest examples of Queen Anne architecture found in the Historic Montford District.
info@wrightinn.com http://www.wrightinn.com

ASHEVILLE (REGION)

Bent Creek Lodge
10 Parkway Crescent, *Arden* 28704
828-654-9040 Fax: 828-654-7597
877-231-6574
Doug & Jodee Sellers and Kathy Courtney All year

110-160-BB
6 rooms, 6 pb
Visa, MC, Disc, •
C-ltd/S-ltd/P-no/H-yes

Full breakfast
Snacks, wine list, dinner by reservation
Walking trails, pool table, gardens

Surrounded by 160 wooded acres, this mountain retreat was designed to sit serenely amid the scenery yet be close to all you want to see and do. We believe that nature can "soothe the soul." bentcreek@ioa.com http://www.bentcreeknc.com

---

Red Rocker Inn
136 N Dougherty St, *Black Mountain* 28711
828-669-5991 888-669-5991
The Lindberg Family
All year

95-155-BB
17 rooms, 17 pb
Visa, MC
C-ltd/S-no/P-no/H-ltd

Full breakfast
Afternoon & evening tea, coffee, baked goods
Sitting room, library, gardens, large porch

Named the Best B&B in Asheville and all of Western North Carolina for 2000, 2001 and 2002. One of the Atlanta Journal's "Top 12 Favorites in the Southeast."
info@redrockerinn.com http://www.redrockerinn.com

ASHEVILLE (REGION)

NuWray Inn
PO Box 156
Town Square, *Burnsville* 28714
828-682-2329 Fax: 828-682-1113
800-368-9729
Rosemary & Chuck Chandler
All year

55-100-BB
26 rooms, 26 pb
Most CC, •
C-yes/S-ltd/P-ltd/H-yes

Continental, Full English/Southern
High Tea w/reservation, Full Dinner menu
TV, fireplace, gardens, private baths

Historic 1833 inn. Romantic retreat. Full service dining. For vacation and business travelers. King, queen, single rooms/suites. Support for all wedding activities and business conferences. nuwrayinn@aol.com http://www.nuwrayinn.com

---

Owl's Nest Inn at Engadine
2630 Smokey Park Hwy, *Candler* 28715
828-665-8325 Fax: 828-667-2539
800-665-8868
Marg Dente & Gail Kinney

130-195-BB
5 rooms, 5 pb
Most CC, *Rated*, •
S-no/P-no/H-no
All year

Full breakfast
Afternoon tea, snacks, comp. wine
Sitting room, Jacuzzis, suites, fireplaces, cable TV, accom. bus. travelers

Historic Victorian Inn built in 1885; mountain views; fireplaces; Jacuzzi suite; situated on 12 acres of beautiful rolling hills, yet just 15 minutes from downtown Asheville and Biltmore Estate. info@engadineinn.com http://www.engadineinn.com

---

The Inn at Old Fort
PO Box 1116
106 W Main St, *Old Fort* 28762
828-668-9384 800-471-0637
Debbie & Chuck Aldridge
All year

60-80-BB
4 rooms, 4 pb
Rated, •
C-yes/S-ltd/P-no/H-no

Continental plus breakfast
Snacks
Parlor and library, cable TV, large porch, pin for #800 is 1709

1880s Victorian cottage, furnished with antiques, set on 3½ acres overlooking Blue Ridge town near Asheville, Lake Lure.

Inn On Mill Creek
PO Box 185
3895 Mill Creek Rd, *Ridgecrest* 28770
828-668-1115 Fax: 828-668-8506
877-735-2964
Aline & Jim Carillon All year

100-175-BB
7 rooms, 7 pb
Visa, MC, AmEx, *Rated*
C-yes/S-no/P-ltd/H-yes

Full breakfast
Tea, snacks
Sitting room, library, bicycles, Jacuzzis, suites, fireplace, cable TV, A/C

Seek the nourishment of your soul that only a wilderness venue provides. Seven acres in the midst of the Pisgah National Forest, with lake, orchard, berries, trails, and more.
jim@inn-on-mill-creek.com http://www.inn-on-mill-creek.com

Dry Ridge Inn
26 Brown St, *Weaverville* 28787
828-658-3899 Fax: 828-658-9533
800-839-3899
Howard & Kristen Dusenbery
All year

95-155-BB
8 rooms, 8 pb
Most CC, *Rated*
C-yes/S-no/P-no/H-no

Full breakfast
Sodas, juice, beer, wine
Sitting room, A/C, outdoor spa, gift shop, antiques

Our charming three story home has eight rooms with private baths, some with fireplaces, and some can be combined to make suites for large families.
innkeeper@dryridgeinn.com http://www.dryridgeinn.com

BALD HEAD ISLAND

Theodosia's
PO Box 3130
Harbour Village 28461
910-457-6563 Fax: 910-457-6055
800-656-1812
Donna and Gary Albertson

175-275-BB
14 rooms, 14 pb
Most CC, *Rated*, •
C-ltd/S-no/P-no
All year

Full breakfast
Afternoon hors d'oeuvres + comp. coffee & snacks
Sitting room, bikes, elec carts & scooters, golf, tennis, pool, fireplace

Stay in the most beautiful inn on an incredible island. Modern Victorian structure with every comfort. Wonderful food. Great setting for a getaway "just for the two of you," or corporate retreat. stay@theodosias.com http://www.theodosias.com

BALSAM

Balsam Mountain Inn
PO Box 40
68 Seven Springs Dr 28707
828-456-9498 Fax: 828-456-9298
800-224-9498
Merrily Teasley, Forest Ray
All year

115-170-BB
50 rooms, 50 pb
Visa, MC, Disc, *Rated*, •
C-ltd/S-ltd/P-no/H-yes
French

Full breakfast
Restaurant
Game room, porches, 26 acres, springs, rhododendron forest

Rest, read, ramble, romp and revel in the easy going hospitality of our Southern mountains. balsaminn@earthlink.net http://www.balsaminn.com

BANNER ELK

1902 Turnpike House
317 Old Turnpike Rd 28604
828-898-5611 Fax: 828-898-5612
888-802-4487
Cindy & Paul Goedhart
All year

75-120-BB
5 rooms, 5 pb
Most CC, •
C-ltd/S-ltd/P-no/H-no
Spanish

Full breakfast
Snacks, bar service
Sitting room, library, Jacuzzi, fireplace, cable TV, accom. bus. travelers

"I feel like I'm coming home" is most often expressed to describe the 1902 Turnpike House. The comforts of today are experienced in the beauty and richness of a bygone era.
info@1902turnpikehouse.com http://www.1902turnpikehouse.com

BEAUFORT

The Cedars Inn
305 Front St 28516
252-728-7036 Fax: 252-728-1685
Linda & Sam Dark
All year

125-165-BB
12 rooms, 12 pb
Most CC, *Rated*, •
C-ltd/S-ltd/P-no/H-no

Full breakfast
Wine bar
Private cottage, Jacuzzi, cooking classes, TV, A/C, sitting room, bikes

Selected as one of North Carolina's 10 best inns. Perfect for romantic and intimate getaways. Waterfront setting, shopping, restaurants, tours, and golfing.
http://www.cedarsinn.com

Langdon House
135 Craven St 28516
252-728-5499 Fax: 252-728-1717
Jimm & Lizzet Prest
All year

141-BB
4 rooms, 4 pb
Rated
C-ltd/S-ltd/P-no/H-no

Full breakfast
Dinner reservations
Refreshments, sitting room, bicycles, fishing & beach supplies

Friends who help you make the most of your visit. Restored 18th-century home in historic seaside hamlet on the outer banks.
innkeeper@coastalnet.com http://www.langdonhouse.com

Pecan Tree Inn
116 Queen St 28516
252-728-6733 Fax: 252-728-3909
David & Allison DuBuisson
All year

80-150-BB
7 rooms, 7 pb
Visa, MC, Disc, *Rated*
C-ltd/S-no/P-no/H-no

Continental plus breakfast
Soda & juices
Jacuzzis, bikes, beach supplies

Romantic, antique-filled 1866 Victorian home in the heart of Beaufort's Historic District.
pecantree@ec.rr.com http://www.pecantree.com

BEAUFORT (REGION)

Harborlight Guest House
332 Live Oak Dr, *Cape Carteret* 28584
252-393-6868 Fax: 252-393-6868
800-624-VIEW
Anita & Bobby Gill
All year

140-250-BB
7 rooms, 7 pb
Visa, MC, AmEx, Most CC, *Rated*
C-no/S-no/P-no/H-yes

Full breakfast
Snacks
Fireplaces,Jacuzzis,In-suite bkfst.,TV/VCR,Refrigerator,Coffee Service

Romantic coastal inn located on the central NC coast. Luxury suites feature two-person whirlpools, fireplaces, water-views, & in-suite breakfast. Recently named a top undiscovered inn in America! inn@clis.com http://www.harborlightguesthousenc.com

BLACK MOUNTAIN

Black Mountain Inn
718 W Old Hwy 70 28711
828-669-6528 Fax: 828-669-4809
800-735-6128
June Bergeron
All year

98-158-BB
7 rooms, 7 pb
Visa, MC, AmEx, •
C-yes/S-ltd/P-yes/H-no

Spa services, garden

Discover a peaceful retreat, steeped in the spirit of the North Carolina Mountains.
ijbergeron@mindspring.com http://blackmountaininn.com

Guesthouse Over Yonder
433 N Fork Rd 28711
828-669-6762
Wilhelmina K. Headley
May–November

70-BB
5 rooms, 5 pb
Rated, •
C-ltd/S-no/P-no/H-no

Full breakfast
Comp. wine (occ.),snacks
Sitting room, library, wildflower gardens, near tennis, pool, golf

Secluded & comfortable on wooded hillside. Breakfast of mountain trout served on rock terraces surrounded by flowers, views of highest peaks in eastern U.S.

Monte Vista Hotel
308 W State St 28711
828-669-2119
Rosalie Phillips
All year

65-75-EP
40 rooms, 40 pb
Most CC, •
C-yes/S-yes/P-yes/H-ltd
Spanish

Lunch, dinner, snacks, restaurant, bar service
Sitting room, swimming pool, live entertainment Saturday nights

Family owned and operated "boarding house" inn—still going strong for over 80 years.
mvdeskclerk@aol.com http://www.montevistahotel.com

BLOWING ROCK

Maple Lodge
PO Box 1236
152 Sunset Dr 28605
828-295-3331 Fax: 828-295-9986
866-866-7013
Marilyn & David Bateman
All year

100-200-BB
11 rooms, 11 pb
Most CC, *Rated*, •
C-ltd/S-no/P-no/H-no

Full breakfast
Parlors, fireplace, canopy beds, quilts, splendor packages

Perennial gardens. Gracious charm in the heart of village, offering privacy, personal attention & understated elegance.
innkeeper@maplelodge.net http://www.maplelodge.net

BOONE (REGION)

Green Park Inn
PO Box 7
9239 Valley Blvd, *Blowing Rock* 28605
828-295-3141 Fax: 828-295-3141
800-852-2462
Stephen P. Love
All year

79-159-EP
87 rooms, 87 pb
Most CC, •
C-yes/S-no/P-no/H-ltd

Dinner, restaurant, bar service
Swimming pool, suites, cable TV, accomm. business travelers, library

120-year-old historic Victorian Inn located in the mountains of NC. Restaurant, bar, pool in season, moderate climate. greenparkinn@boone.net http://www.greenparkinn.com

BOONE (REGION)

Prospect Hill
801 W Main St/Hwy 67, *Mountain City, TN* 37683
423-727-0139 Fax: 423-727-6979
800-339-5084
Robert & Judy Hotchkiss
All year

70-235-BB
5 rooms, 5 pb
Most CC, •
C-yes/S-no/P-no/H-ltd

Full breakfast—fruit, of course
Snacks, complimentary wine
Porch/balcony, fireplace, whirlpool tubs, cable TV, garden, views, fireflies

Enjoy Tennessee's First Sunrise ... in America's First Frontier. Relax in this gracious 1889 mountain mansion. A romantic getaway with whirlpools, fireplaces, tranquility, views.
Lanier@prospect-hill.com http://www.prospect-hill.com

Buffalo Tavern
958 W Buffalo Rd, *West Jefferson* 28694
336-877-2873 Fax: 336-877-2874
877-615-9678
Karon Torrence
All year

110-135-BB
3 rooms, 3 pb
Visa, MC, AmEx
S-ltd/P-ltd/H-no

Full breakfast
Complimentary wine
Fireplaces

Elegant Southern Colonial circa 1872. A popular tavern during prohibition with patrons such as former NC Governors. katorr@skybest.com http://www.buffalotavern.com

BREVARD

The Inn at Brevard
410 E Main St 28712
828-884-2105 Fax: 828-885-7996
Faye & Howard Yager
All year

99-225-BB
15 rooms, 15 pb
Most CC, *Rated*, •
C-yes/S-ltd/P-yes/H-ltd

Full breakfast
Dinner on Thursday, Friday, Saturday, and Sunday

The Inn at Brevard, beautifully located in the Heart of Brevard. Antiques, shopping, dining, and more are just minutes away! Come join us and experience the magic of the mountains!!! brevardinn@citcom.net http://www.innatbrevard.8m.net

---

A Place To Remember
300 West Probart St 28712
828-862-6660 Fax: 828-862-6660
Claudia Beck
All year

95-175-BB
4 rooms, 4 pb
Rated
C-no/S-no/P-no/H-no
German

Full breakfast
Sitting areas/table, library, suites, beautiful Mt. views from porches

Unique "Arts & Crafts" style house designed by supervising architect of the Biltmore Estate! Unusual interior design (Feng-Shui) and lots of art and books. Gorgeous mountain views from two porches.

The Red House
412 Probart St 28712
828-884-9349
All year

69-125-BB
5 rooms, 3 pb
•
C-ltd/S-ltd/P-no/H-no

Full breakfast
Complimentary wine
Sitting room, porches, air conditioned, off-street parking

Lovingly restored antebellum home. Former trading post, courthouse, school and more. Near park, outlets, theater and sights.
redhouseinn@hotmail.com http://www.brevardnc.com/accom

Womble Inn
301 W Main St 28712
828-884-4770 Fax: 828-862-3492
888-884-4770
Beth & Steve Womble
All year

77-125-BB
6 rooms, 6 pb
Rated
C-yes/S-yes/P-no/H-yes

Full breakfast
Lunch available, Mon-Fri
Sitting room, piano, off-street parking

Gracious atmosphere of antiquity, private baths, near town and Brevard Music Center, wonderful Christmas shop. wombleinn@citcom.net http://www.thewombleinn.com

BRYSON CITY

Folkestone Inn
101 Folkestone Rd 28713
828-488-2730 888-812-3385
Kay Creighton & Peggy Myles
All year

98-129-BB
10 rooms, 10 pb
Most CC, *Rated*, •
C-ltd/S-no/P-no/H-no

Full gourmet breakfast
Complimentary snacks, wine
Sitting room, library, porch, rocking chairs, balconies, antiques, AC

An old-fashioned bed & breakfast at the Deep Creek entrance to the Great Smoky Mountains National Park just two miles north of Bryson City, a sleepy mountain town.

innkeeper@folkestone.com http://www.folkestone.com

Fryemont Inn
PO Box 459
1 Fryemont St 28713
828-488-2159 800-845-4879
Monica & George Brown Jr., Sue & George Brown
April–November

95-220-MAP
46 rooms, 46 pb
Visa, MC, Disc, *Rated*
C-yes/S-no/P-no/H-no

Full breakfast menu
Full dinner included
Full service lounge, library, sitting room, swimming pool

Price includes breakfast and dinner! Located on a mountain shelf overlooking the Great Smoky Mountains National Park. A tradition in mountain hospitality since 1923.

fryemont@dnet.net http://www.fryemontinn.com

Nantahala Village Mt. Resort
9400 Hwy 19 W 28713
828-488-2826 Fax: 828-488-9634
800-438-1507
John Burton & Jan Letendre
Mid March–Dec

55-125-EP
54 rooms, 54 pb
Most CC, *Rated*
C-yes/S-ltd/P-no/H-ltd

Restaurant, meals available
Pool, Rec Hall, rafting, tennis court, volleyball, horseback riding

Family mountain resort with 11 rooms and 45 guest cabins, cottages, condos and private homes; 200 acres in the Great Smoky Mountains, Western NC.

nvinfo@nvnc.com http://www.nvnc.com

Randolph House Country Inn
PO Box 816
223 Fryemont St 28713
828-488-3472 800-480-3472
Bill & Ruth Randolph Adams

95-160-MAP
6 rooms, 3 pb
Most CC, *Rated*, •
C-ltd/S-yes/P-no/H-yes
April–November

Full country breakfast
Dinner, tea on request
Wine, set-ups, sitting room, library, piano

Country Inn circa 1885–listed in Nat'l Register of Historical Places. Contains orig. furnishings. The Inn is a mountain estate tucked among hemlock trees & dogwoods.

http://www.randolphhouse.com

CASHIERS

Knoll Top Lodge
PO Box 818
71 Brocade Dr 28717
818-743-3033 Fax: 818-743-0199
877-595-3600
Judy & Gordon Gray All year

95-BB
4 rooms, 4 pb
Visa, MC, *Rated*
C-ltd/S-ltd/P-no/H-no

Full breakfast
Afternoon tea, snacks
Sitting room, library,cable TV, fireplaces, accom. bus. travelers

10 acre mountain haven for all seasons; comfortable lodge setting surrounded by natural and man-made attractions of the Southern Appalachians.

cottage@dnet.net http://www.cottageinncashiers.com

CHAPEL HILL

Inn at Bingham School
PO Box 267, 27514
NC 54 @ Mebane Oaks Rd
919-563-5583 Fax: 919-563-9826
800-566-5583
Francois,Christina, Zinho & Loften Deprez All year

80-140-BB
5 rooms, 5 pb
Visa, MC, AmEx, *Rated*, •
C-yes/S-no/P-no/H-no
French, Spanish

Full breakfast
Snacks, complimentary wine
Sitting room, library, small meetings, wedding facilities

Step back to a slower time, a slower pace. Rock by the fire with your wine, or stroll the surrounding woodlands; four rooms have fireplaces.

fdeprez@aol.com http://www.chapel-hill-inn.com

CHAPEL HILL

Windy Oaks Inn
1164 Old Lystra Rd 27517
919-942-1001 Fax: 919-942-8919
Kim Oglesby
All year

135-195-BB
5 rooms, 3 pb
Visa, MC, *Rated*
C-ltd/S-ltd/P-yes/H-no

Full breakfast
Snacks, complimentary wine
Sitting room, library, suites, fireplaces, cable TV, accom. bus. trav.

Chapel Hill's most convenient B&B and event site. Located five miles from campus. Charming farmhouse with antiques and folkart.
windyoaksinn@aol.com http://www.windyoaksinn.com

CHAPEL HILL (REGION)

The Fearrington House
2000 Fearrington Village Center, *Pittsboro* 27312
919-542-2121 Fax: 919-542-4202
Richard M. Delany
All year

220-450-BB
33 rooms, 33 pb
Most CC, *Rated*, •
C-no/S-ltd/P-no/H-yes

Full breakfast
Lunch/dinner available (fee)
Afternoon tea, weddings, sitting room, pool/bikes, meeting facilities

Classic countryside elegance in suites furnished with English antiques. Charming courtyard and gardens. Delicately prepared regional cuisine.
fhouse@fearrington.com http://www.fearringtonhouse.com

CHARLOTTE

The Duke Mansion
400 Hermitage Road 28210
704-714-4400 888-202-1009
Patricia Martin
All year

BB

Gourmet made-to-order breakfast
Dinner, beverages, snacks
Sitting room, library, cable TV/VCR, voice mail

The Duke Mansion is your weekend haven. In larger accommodations, you may feel like a number, but at our twenty room bed and breakfast you are recognized by name and treated like family. marketingmatters@carolina.rr.com http://www.dukemansion.org

---

The Morehead Inn
1122 E. Morehead St 28204
704-376-3357 Fax: 704-335-1110
Billy Maddalon & Helen Price
All year

120-190-BB
11 rooms, 11 pb
Most CC, *Rated*, •
C-yes/S-ltd/P-no/H-ltd
Sp., Fr., It., Port.

Continental plus breakfast
Complimentary wine, tea
Meeting/social functions, piano, whirlpool, bikes, YMCA fitness privileges

Restored estate in historic district; furnished with American quiet elegance. Churchill Galleries on-site: exclusive antiques.
morehead@charlotte.infi.net http://www.moreheadinn.com

Still Waters
6221 Amos Smith Rd 28214
704-399-6299
Janet & Rob Dyer
All year

65-105-BB
4 rooms, 4 pb
Visa, MC, *Rated*, •
C-ltd/S-no/P-no/H-no

Full breakfast
Sport court, tennis, basketball, volleyball, boat ramp, dock, gazebo

Log resort home on two wooded acres overlooking Lake Wylie. Near Charlotte downtown & airport. rdyer399@aol.com http://members.aol.com/bbdyer399/homepage/index.html

CHIMNEY ROCK

The Wicklow Inn
PO Box 246
307 Main St, Hwy 64/74A 28720
828-625-4038 Fax: 828-625-0435
877-625-4038
Sharon & Jack Ryan
All year

110-135-BB
6 rooms, 5 pb
Visa, MC, *Rated*
C-ltd/S-no/P-no/H-no

Full breakfast
Sitting room, cable TV, fax and photocopy service available

Small, quaint inn on banks of Rocky Broad River in Blue Ridge Mountains. Rustic furniture, antiques, contemporary mountain crafts. 2 blocks from Chimney Rock Park. 45 mins. from Biltmore Estate. wicklowinn@blueridge.net http://www.thewicklowinn.com

CLINTON

The Ashford Inn 615 College Ave 28328 910-596-0961 Fax: 910-596-0961 888-ATTHEINN C.H. Parrish & A.M. Carberry All year	75-130-BB 4 rooms, 4 pb Most CC, *Rated* C-ltd/S-no/P-yes/H-no	Full breakfast Gourmet menu with full ABC permits.

Historic inn for the selective traveler with facilities for business and social gatherings.
annec97757@aol.com http://www.travelguides.com/home/ashford/

DANBURY (REGION)

Southwyck Farm 1070 Southwyck Farm Rd, *Lawsonville* 27022 336-593-8006 Fax: 336-593-9180 866-593-8006 Diana Carl & David Hoskins	90-125-BB 6 rooms, 4 pb Visa, MC, Disc, *Rated*, • C-yes/S-no/P-no/H-no All year	Full breakfast Lunch, dinner, afternoon tea Snacks, comp. wine, library, sitting room, fishing pond, walking trails

Blue Ridge Foothills, fully stocked bass pond, "Murder Mystery" weekends, canoeing on Dan River, gourmet meals at Southwyck, & antiques.
bnb@southwyckfarm.com http://www.southwyckfarm.com

DAVIDSON

Davidson Village Inn PO Box 1463 117 Depot St 28036 704-892-8044 Fax: 704-896-2184 800-892-0796 Gordon & Rebecca Clark All year	94-175-BB 18 rooms, 18 pb Most CC, *Rated*, • C-yes/S-ltd/P-no/H-yes	Continental plus breakfast Afternoon tea, snacks Library, sitting room, lakefront recreation, 4 new ""executive rooms""

Warm relaxed inn, located in quaint college town serving a unique blend of historic & contemporary Southern pleasures.
info@davidsoninn.com http://www.davidsoninn.com

DILLSBORO

The Chalet Inn 285 Lone Oak Dr 28725 828-586-0251 800-789-8024 George & Hanneke Ware 3rd Fri in Mar-New Years	87-120-BB 6 rooms, 6 pb Most CC, *Rated*, • C-ltd/S-no/P-no/H-ltd German, Dutch, French	Full breakfast Snacks, comp. imported beer or wine Great room w/fireplace, private balconies, A/C, CD Players, robes & slippers

Views of the Smoky Mountains, private flower-bedecked balconies, a babbling brook and bountiful breakfast beckon you to this Romantic Inn, in Western NC between Dillsboro, Bryson City and Cherokee. paradisefound@chaletinn.com http://www.chaletinn.com

The Dillsboro Inn PO Box 270 146 North River Rd 28725 828-586-3898 T. J. Walker All year	85-200-BB 8 rooms, 8 pb Visa, MC C-ltd/S-no/P-no/H-ltd	Full breakfast Waterfall, camp fire, suites, fireplaces, river views

Come visit our front yard, a river falls through it. Next to waterfall and riverfront park. Riverside suites with balconies, river views, kitchens and fireplaces. Nightly campfires and trout fishing. info@dillsboroinn.com http://www.dillsboroinn.com

The Jarrett House PO Box 219 100 Haywood St 28725 828-586-0265 Jim & Jean Hartbarger All year	80-90 22 rooms, 18 pb C-ltd/S-ltd/P-no	Restaurant

The Jarrett House is one of the oldest inns in Western North Carolina, a throwback to the days of the horse and buggy and the wood-burning passenger train.
http://www.jarretthouse.com

DILLSBORO

Olde Towne Inn
PO Box 485
300 Haywood Road 28725
828-586-3461 888-528-8840
Lera Chitwood
All year, except January

65-105-BB
5 rooms, 4 pb
Most CC, *Rated*
C-yes/S-ltd/P-no

Full breakfast
Drinks offered at night. Small gift for special occasions.

Cozy comfort in quilt covered beds, country cooking, and views of mountains. The sounds of trains can be heard in the historic Olde Towne Inn in the tiny town of Dillsboro.
oldetown@gte.net http://www.dillsboro-oldetowne.com

Squire Watkins Inn
PO Box 430
657 Haywood Rd 28725
828-586-5244 800-586-2429
Tom & Emma Wertenberger
All year

85-95-BB
5 rooms, 5 pb
Rated

Full breakfast

This year marks our 20th anniversary at Squire Watkins. We still enjoy innkeeping and are now hosting the children of our first year guests.

DILLSBORO (REGION)

The Freeze House
71 Sylvan Heights, *Sylva* 28779
828-586-8161 Fax: 828-631-0714
P. & M. E. Montague
All year

85-100-BB
4 rooms, 4 pb
Rated, •
C-ltd/S-no/P-no/H-no
French, German

Full breakfast
Sitting room, library, tennis court, swimming pool, cable TV, health club

On a tree-shaded knoll overlooking the village, we offer excellent accommodations in the middle of a varied vacationland. Two cottages also available.
freezeh@dnet.net http://www.freezehousebnb.com

Mountain Brook Cottages
208 Mountain Brook Rd #18, *Sylva* 28779
828-586-4329
Gus, Michele, Maqelle McMahon
All year

90-140-EP
12 rooms, 12 pb
Rated, •
C-yes/S-yes/P-no/H-ltd
French

Jacuzzis, fireplaces, all cottages equipped for homemaking

Quaint c.1930s cottages with fireplaces & porch swings. Nestled on a brook filled wooded mountainside in Smokies. Near historic Dillsboro.
michele@mountainbrook.com http://www.mountainbrook.com

Mountain Creek Cottages
2672 Dicks Creek, *Whittier* 28789
828-586-6042
MaryBeth Druzbick & Patrick Hinkle
All year

60-150-EP
12 rooms, 12 pb
Rated
C-yes/S-ltd/P-ltd/H-ltd

Fireplaces, cable TV, accomodate business travelers

Twelve completely furnished cabins in the Smoky Mountains of western North Carolina.
mtncrk@aol.com http://www.mountaincreekcottages.com

DURHAM

The Blooming Garden Inn
513 Holloway St 27701
919-687-0801 Fax: 919-688-1401
888-687-0801
Frank & Dolly Pokrass
All year

110-220-BB
5 rooms, 5 pb
Most CC, *Rated*, •
C-yes/S-no/P-no/H-no

Full gourmet breakfast
Comp. wine, tea, snacks
Sitting rooms, library, 145 foot porch, antiques, 2 rm. suite w/footed tub

Vibrant colors and floral gardens transform this restored, gated Victorian into a cozy, memorable retreat in downtown historic Durham. http://BloomingGardenInn.tripod.com

DURHAM

Mineral Springs Inn
718 S Mineral Springs Rd 27703
919-596-2162 Fax: 919-596-2162
Michael Sullivan
All year

69-BB
4 rooms, 4 pb
Most CC
S-ltd/P-ltd/H-no

Full breakfast
Snacks, complimentary wine
Sitting room, library, Jacuzzis, pool, fireplaces, cable TV

Restored 1895 farmhouse with modern amenities. Ideal for the business traveler to RTP or those passing through on I-85. IGLTA member.
mineralspringsinn@yahoo.com

EDENTON

Albemarle House
204 West Queen St 27932
252-482-8204
Reuel & Marijane Schappel
All year

85-85-BB
3 rooms, 3 pb
Visa, MC, AmEx, *Rated*, •
C-ltd/S-no/P-no/H-no

Full breakfast
Welcoming Refreshments, Morning Coffee, Evening Sn

Enjoy Historic Edenton in our charming 1900 circa Victorian home. Our spacious guest rooms all contain queen size beds, cable TV, and private baths. Each morning, a full gourmet breakfast awaits you.
albemarlehouse@inteliport.com http://www.bbonline.com/nc/albemarle/

The Lords Proprietors' Inn
300 N Broad St 27932
252-482-3641 Fax: 252-482-2432
800-348-8933
Arch & Jane Edwards
All year

155-260-BB
18 rooms, 18 pb
Most CC, *Rated*, •
C-yes/S-ltd/P-no/H-ltd

Full breakfast
Four-course dinner by Reservation
Tea, homemade cookies, sitting room, bicycles, private pool privileges

Edenton's oldest and most elegant inn offering the finest dining in eastern North Carolina.
stay@edentoninn.com http://www.edentoninn.com

Trestle House Inn
632 Soundside Rd 27932
252-482-2282 Fax: 252-482-7003
800-645-8466
Peter L. Bogus
All year

90-125-BB
5 rooms, 5 pb
Most CC, *Rated*, •
C-ltd/S-ltd/P-no/H-no

Full breakfast
BYOB
Waterfront birding, fishing, canoeing, swimming, golfing, relaxing

On a wildlife refuge surrounded on three sides by water in historic Edenton, North Carolina. Birding, fishing, swimming, golfing, boating, sightseeing and relaxing are our guests' favorite activities. thinn@coastalnet.com http://www.edenton.com/trestlehouse

EMERALD ISLE

Emerald Isle Inn by the Sea
502 Ocean Dr 28594
252-354-3222 Fax: 252-354-3222
Elaine & Jim Normile
All year

85-160-BB
4 rooms, 4 pb
Most CC, *Rated*, •
C-yes/S-ltd/P-no/H-ltd

Continental plus breakfast
Sitting room, library, direct ocean access, beach chairs, umbrellas

Enjoy a warm, relaxing getaway at the best beach on the coast! The Crystal Coast! All suites have private baths and entrances, with ocean or sound views.
jimnormile@coastalnet.com http://www.emeraldisleinn.com

FLAT ROCK

Woodfield Inn
PO Box 98
2905 Greenville Hwy 28731
828-693-6016 Fax: 828-693-0437
800-533-6016
Rhonda & Mike Horton
All year

129-189-BB
19 rooms, 19 pb
Rated, •

Full breakfast
Full service restaurant
Evening social & turndown service

150 year old house on 28 acres circa 1852. NC original country inn, 5 dining rooms, special events & wedding facilities. http://www.woodfieldinn.com

FRANKLIN

Buttonwood Inn	65-95-BB	Full breakfast
50 Admiral Dr 28734	4 rooms, 4 pb	Sitting room, TV, golf nearby,
828-369-8985 888-368-8985	*Rated*, •	entertainment
Liz Oehser	C-ltd/S-ltd/P-no/H-no	
All year		

Completely surrounded by tall pines, small and cozy Buttonwood will appeal to the person who prefers simplicity and natural rustic beauty.
innkeeperbwbb@myexcel.com http://www.bbonline.com

Franklin Terrace	52-69-BB	Full breakfast
159 Harrison Ave 28734	9 rooms, 9 pb	Complimentary
828-524-7907 800-633-2431	Most CC, *Rated*, •	refreshments
Ed & Helen Henson	C-ltd/S-ltd/P-no/H-no	2 beautiful sitting rooms,
April-mid november		color/cable TV, A/C, 2
		porches with rockers

All rooms furnished with antiques. Gift shop and antiques for sale.
stay@franklinterrace.com http://www.franklinterrace.com

Hummingbird Lodge	85-95-BB	Full breakfast
1101 Hickory Knoll Rd	3 rooms, 3 pb	Aft. tea, evening dessert
28734	Visa, MC, *Rated*	Sitting room, Jacuzzis,
828-369-0430 Fax: 828-349-3350	C-ltd/S-ltd/P-no/H-ltd	fireplaces, satellite TV,
Rota & Harvey Krape	Latvian	assistance w/travel plans
All year		

Country log home set in the mountains provides peace and quiet whether sitting on the large porch or in front of the fireplace. Adventurous guests have hiking, biking, rafting, shopping and crafting. rotakrape@myexcel.com
http://www.bbonline.com/nc/hummingbird

FUQUAY VARINA

Fuquay Mineral Spring Inn	80-150-BB	Full breakfast
333 S Main St 27526	4 rooms, 4 pb	Tea, wine, beer, coffee, soda,
919-552-3782 Fax: 919-552-5229	Most CC, *Rated*	& juice
866-552-3782	C-ltd/S-ltd/P-no/H-ltd	Sitting Room, library, and
John & Patty Byrne	Spanish, French	garden
All year		

The Fuquay Mineral Spring Inn and Garden is a Historic Landmark Inn and Garden located in the Heart of the Fuquay Springs Historic District across from the Fuquay Mineral Spring Park. jbyrne@fuquayinn.com http://www.fuquayinn.com

GREENVILLE (REGION)

Big Mill	55-75-BB	Continental breakfast
1607 Big Mill Rd, *Williamston*	Most CC, *Rated*	Bikes, suites, fireplace,
27892	C-ltd/S-ltd/P-no/H-ltd	fishing, accommodate
252-792-8787		business travelers
Chloe G. Tuttle		
All year		

Shaded by old pecan trees amid landscaped grounds, this is the perfect country hide-away. bigmill@coastalnet.com http://www.bigmill.com

HATTERAS

Seaside Inn	75-140-BB	Full breakfast
PO Box 688	10 rooms, 10 pb	Sitting room, library,
57303 Monitor Trail 27943	Visa, MC, *Rated*	spacious porches, small,
252-986-2700 Fax: 252-986-2923	C-yes/S-no/P-ltd/H-no	gatherings, Jacuzzis
866-986-2700		
Cindy Foster All year		

Established in 1928, the inn has been refurbished as one of the most unique, comfortable, convenient places to stay on Hatteras Island.
SeasideBB@aol.com http://www.seasidebb.com

HENDERSONVILLE (REGION)

Highland Lake Inn PO Box 1026 Highland Lake Rd, *Flat Rock* 28731 828-693-6812 Fax: 828-696-8951 800-635-5101 The Grup Family All year	89-399-BB 52 rooms, 52 pb Most CC, *Rated*, • C-yes/S-no/P-no/H-ltd Spanish, French	Full breakfast Restaurant, lunch, dinner Fireplaces, whirlpool tubs, lake, pool, organic gardens, massage, yoga

Country farm setting. Families welcome! Canoes, trails, paddleboats, pool & more. Historic lodge, elegant Inn, family style cottages, cozy cabins. Award-winning restaurant. Organic garden & yoga. frontdesk@hlinn.com http://www.hlinn.com

HIGHLANDS

4-1/2 Street Inn 55 4-1/2 Street 28741 828-526-4464 Fax: 828-526-5102 888-799-4464 Helene & Rick Siegel	110-140-BB 10 rooms, 10 pb Visa, MC C-ltd/S-no/P-no/H-yes March–December	Homemade cookies, wine hour, juice, fruit Hot tub, bicycles, library, outside sitting & common areas, bird watching

Tucked away on a quiet street in the heart of Highlands, the 4 1/2 Street Inn offers the ultimate in comfort, charm, and convenience.
relax@4andahalfstinn.com http://www.4andahalfstinn.com

Colonial Pines Inn 541 Hickory St 28741 828-526-2060 Chris & Donna Alley All year	85-150-BB 8 rooms, 8 pb Visa, MC, *Rated* C-ltd/S-no/P-no/H-no	Full breakfast Cider, hot chocolate, tea, sherry, cookies, snacks Suites, kitchens, fireplaces, grand piano, cable TV, videos, library

On two acres in town with a mountain view from moderately priced rooms, spacious suites, private cottages. Sumptuous breakfasts, afternoon refreshments, and berry gardens. sleeptight@colonialpinesinn.com http://www.colonialpinesinn.com

---

Highlands Suite Hotel PO Box 459 200 Main St 28741 828-526-4502 Fax: 828-526-4840 800-221-5078 Cathy Dixon All year	70-215-BB 28 rooms, 28 pb Visa, MC, AmEx, *Rated* C-yes/S-yes/P-no/H-yes	Continental breakfast Snacks, complimentary wine Sitting room, Jacuzzis, suites, fireplaces, cable TV

Highlands "the South's most exclusive mountain top" features fine dining, golf, shopping & fishing. mtnhi@gte.net http://www.highlandssuitehotel.com

---

Kelsey & Hutchinson Lodge PO Box 2129 450 Spring St 28741 828-526-4746 Fax: 828-526-4921 888-245-9058 Nancy Plate All year	95-250-BB 33 rooms, 33 pb Visa, MC, AmEx C-yes/S-no/P-ltd/H-yes	Continental plus breakfast Snacks, complimentary wine Sitting room, library, bicycles, Jacuzzis, fireplace, cable TV

Quiet deluxe mountain rustic lodge overlooking downtown Highlands. Known for friendly, personalized service. 2 blocks from the boutiques and fine dining restaurants of Main Street. innkeeper@k-hlodge.com http://k-hlodge.com

---

Main Street Inn 270 Main St 28741 828-526-2590 Fax: 828-787-1142 800-213-9142 Farrel and Jan ZehrApril-Dec.	95-185-BB 19 rooms, 19 pb Visa, MC, AmEx, • C-ltd/S-no/P-no/H-no	Full breakfast Afternoon tea Sitting room, fireplaces, cable TV

1885 Federal Farmhouse style renovated in 1998. In the center of a quaint mountain town of Highlands. info@mainstreet-inn.com http://www.mainstreet-inn.com

HIGHLANDS

Mitchell's Lodge & Cottages
PO Box 1717
264 Dillard 28741
828-526-2267 Fax: 818-526-1643
800-522-9874
Al & Renee Bolt
All year

49-214-BB
27 rooms, 27 pb
Most CC, •
C-yes/S-no/P-no/H-yes

Continental plus breakfast
Sitt. rm, Jacuzzi, suites, frplces, cable TV, outdoor pavilion by small pond

From our 4118 ft elevation, Mitchell's Lodge & Cottages has been a part of Highlands, NC history for over 63 years. relax@mitchellslodge.com http://www.mitchellslodge.com

HILLSBOROUGH

Hillsborough House Inn
PO Box 880
209 East Tryon St 27278
919-644-1600 Fax: 919-644-1308
800-616-1660
Lauri & Kirk Michel
Closed Xmas–New Years

105-200-BB
6 rooms, 6 pb
Most CC, *Rated*, •
C-ltd/S-no/P-no/H-no

Full breakfast buffet
Complimentary soft drinks & snacks
Library with TV/VCR, swimming pool, robes

Italianate-style mansion on 7 acres in the Hillsborough Historic District. Convenient to Durham, Chapel Hill, Research Triangle Park and Raleigh-Durham International Airport. info@hillsborough-inn.com http://www.hillsborough-inn.com

KENANSVILLE

The Murray House Inn
PO Box 534
201 NC Highway 24-50 28349
910-296-1000 Fax: 910-296-1000
800-276-5322
Lynn & Joe Davis All year

75-110-BB
7 rooms, 7 pb

Full breakfast
Jacuzzis, weddings & retreats, par terre made of our 400 boxwoods

murrayhi@gsiwave.com http://www.murrayhouseinn.com

LAKE TOXAWAY

Earthshine Mountain Lodge
Route 1, Box 216-C
Golden Rd. 28747
828-862-4207
Kim Heinitsh
All year

255-300-AP
13 rooms, 13 pb
Visa, MC, Disc, *Rated*, •
C-yes/S-ltd/P-no/H-yes

Full country breakfast
Lunch, Hors., Fruit, Beverages, Set Ups & Dinner
Horseback, High Ropes, "Flight thru the Treetops" Zip, Children's Programs

Earthshine—the storybook grandmother's farm family vacation you've always dreamed about. Surrounded by 70 gorgeous acres, our 1½ story log lodge overlooks the beautiful Blue Ridge Mountains. earthshine@citcom.net http://www.earthshinemtnlodge.com

LITTLE SWITZERLAND

Big Lynn Lodge
PO Box 459
10860 Hwy 226-A 28749
828-765-4257 Fax: 828-765-0301
800-654-5232
Gale & Carol Armstrong
April 15–Oct.

87-133-MAP
40 rooms, 40 pb
Visa, MC, Disc, *Rated*, •
C-ltd/S-yes/P-no/H-ltd
German

Full breakfast and dinner
Fruit
Sitting room, library, player piano lounge, TV, billiards, shuffleboard

Old-fashioned country inn. Cool mountain air; elevation 3200 ft. Breathtaking view. Rocking chairs on porches. info@biglynnlodge.com http://www.biglynnlodge.com

MOUNT AIRY

The William E. Merritt House
618 N. Main St 27030
800-290-6090 877-786-2174
Pat Mangels
All year

80-125
4 rooms, 4 pb
Visa, MC, AmEx, *Rated*
C-ltd/S-ltd/P-no/H-no

Full breakfast
snacks and soft drinks

The Merritt House is a beautiful Victorian home nestled in the foothills of the Blue Ridge Mountains. DMAC2895@advi.net http://bbonline.com/nc/merritthouse/

MURPHY

Huntington Hall
272 Valley River Ave 28906
828-837-9567 Fax: 828-837-2527
800-824-6189
Curt & Nancy Harris
All year

75-135-BB
5 rooms, 5 pb
Visa, MC, AmEx, *Rated*, •
C-yes/S-no/P-no/H-ltd

Full breakfast
Complimentary beverages
Sitting room, library, public pool & tennis, white water rafting package

A Bed & Breakfast well done! Circa 1881, former mayor's home, delightful country Victorian. Sumptuous breakfast, cool mountain breezes await you! huntington@grove.net http://www.bed-breakfast-inn.com

NEW BERN

Harmony House Inn
215 Pollock St 28560
252-636-3810 Fax: 252-636-3810
800-636-3113
Ed & Sooki Kirkpatrick
All year

99-160-BB
10 rooms, 10 pb
Visa, MC, AmEx, *Rated*, •
C-yes/S-no/P-no/H-no

Full breakfast
Complimentary drinks, wine, sherry
Victorian pump organ, 1 suite, parlor, porch with swings, rocking chairs

Unusually spacious c.1850 home, rocking chairs on porch, lovely yard. In historic district, near Tryon Palace; shops, fine restaurants.
harmony@cconnect.net http://www.harmonyhouseinn.com/

OCRACOKE

Island Inn & Dining Room
PO Box 9
25 Lighthouse Rd 27960
252-928-4351 Fax: 252-928-4352
877-456-3466
Bob & Cee Touhey All year

49-89-EP
39 rooms, 34 pb
Most CC, *Rated*
C-ltd/S-ltd/P-ltd/H-ltd

Full breakfast
Restaurant, dinner avail.
Sitting room, Jacuzzis, swimming pool, suites, cable TV

Ocracoke's oldest and most historic Inn offers old time charm and modern conveniences. Beautiful harbor views, delicious food, island hospitality, all moderately priced.
bctouhey@hotmail.com http://www.ocracokeislandinn.com

OUTER BANKS (REGION)

Inn at Corolla Lighthouse
1066 Ocean Trail, *Corolla* 27927
252-453-0335 Fax: 252-453-6947
800-215-0772
Bob and Sally White All year

95-350-BB
42 rooms, 42 pb
Visa, MC, AmEx
C-yes/P-no

Deluxe continental breakfast

Nestled among stately water oaks and tall pines along the historic Currituck Sound, The Inn at Corolla Light offers guests luxurious accommodations and a variety of activities.
the-inn@outer-banks.com http://www.corolla-inn.com

Advice 5 Cents
PO Box 8278
111 Scarborough, *Duck* 27949
252-255-1050 800-238-4235
Donna Black & Nancy Caviness
Feb.–Nov.

135-205-BB
5 rooms, 5 pb
Visa, MC, *Rated*
C-ltd/S-no/P-no/H-no

Continental plus breakfast
Afternoon tea
Sitting rm., library, tennis, cable TV, beach chairs/towels, outdoor showers

Celebrating our 9th year! Tucked away in Sea Pines, sits Advice 5 Cents, situated between the waters of the Atlantic Ocean and Currituck Sound. advice5@pinn.net
http://www.advice5.com

Cypress House
500 N Virginia Dare Trail, *Kill Devil Hills* 27948
252-441-6127 Fax: 252-441-2009
800-554-2764
Karen & Leon Faso All year

75-150-BB
6 rooms, 6 pb
Most CC, *Rated*, •
C-ltd/S-no/P-no/H-no

Full breakfast
Afternoon tea
Wrap around porches, overhead fans, bikes, Senior Citizen discount

Romantic seaside inn ideally located on the outer banks of North Carolina. Only 150 yards from the Atlantic Ocean. cypresshse@aol.com http://www.cypresshouseinn.com

OUTER BANKS (REGION)

Cameron House Inn
PO Box 308
300 Budleigh St, *Manteo* 27954
252-473-6596 Fax: 252-473-9874
800-279-8178
Beth & Michael McOwen

109-209-BB
7 rooms, 7 pb
Visa, MC, •
C-yes/S-no/P-no/H-no
French
All year

Full breakfast
Snacks, stocked fridge with soft drinks and water
Bicycles, outdoor fireplace, huge front porch swing, sitting room

Cameron House welcomes you with island ease. Our restored 1919 inn features wonderfully decorated rooms and tiled baths, a huge outdoor fireplace, and an Outer Banks style that makes you feel relaxed. bpstorie@yahoo.com http://www.cameronhouseinn.com

The First Colony Inn
6720 S Virginia Dare Tr, *Nags Head* 27959
252-441-2343 Fax: 252-441-9234
800-368-9390
The Lawrences All year

170-295-BB
26 rooms, 26 pb
Most CC, *Rated*, •
C-yes/S-ltd/P-no/H-yes

Full breakfast
Afternoon tea, complimentary wine on weekends
Library, verandas, pool, croquet, ocean, fishing, weddings

Elegant 26-room inn with Southern hospitality, verandahs along all four sides; English antiques, wonderful big beds. Walkway to our private gazebo on the dune; oceanview and soundviews on third floor.
innkeeper@firstcolonyinn.com http://www.firstcolonyinn.com

Thurston House Inn
PO Box 294
685 Highway 12, *Ocracoke Island* 27960
252-928-6037 Fax: 252-928-6051
Marlene & Randal Mathews
All year

79-139-BB
9 rooms, 9 pb
Visa, MC, Disc, •
C-ltd/S-ltd/P-no/H-ltd

Continental plus breakfast
Sitting room, cable TV

Covered porches with swing and rockers, private grounds with lush native plants and graying cedar shake buildings set the scene for a perfect island retreat.
thurstonhouseinn@ocracokenc.net http://www.thurstonhouseinn.com

PILOT MOUNTAIN (REGION)

Scenic Overlook
144 Scenic Overlook Ln, *Pinnacle* 27043
336-368-9591
Gayle & Alan Steinbecker
All year

125-165-BB
5 rooms, 5 pb
Most CC, *Rated*, •
S-no/P-no/H-no

Full breakfast
Sitting room, Jacuzzis, suites, fireplaces, cable TV, accom. bus. trav.

A unique romantic getaway on 50 acres, large luxurious suites and rooms with spectacular views of lake and mountains. Whirlpools for 2, fireplaces, in-ground pool.
info@scenicoverlook.com http://www.scenicoverlook.com

PINEHURST (REGION)

Knollwood House
1495 W Connecticut Ave, *Southern Pines* 28387
910-692-9390 Fax: 910-692-0609
Dick & Mimi Beatty
All year

115-175-BB
6 rooms, 6 pb
Visa, MC, *Rated*, •
C-ltd/S-ltd/P-no/H-no

Full breakfast buffet
Golf packages includes, breakfast, lodgings, dinner and greens fee

A luxurious English manor house with 18th century antiques & contemporary comforts in the heart of golf country. knollwood@pinehurst.net http://www.knollwoodhouse.com

PISGAH FOREST

The Pines Country Inn
719 Hart Rd 28768
828-877-3131
Tom & Mary McEntire
Memorial Day-end of Oct.

65-BB
22 rooms, 19 pb
Rated
C-yes/S-yes/P-no/H-ltd

Full breakfast
Sitting room, piano, children play yard, great biking & hiking

Quiet, homey country inn. Fantastic view. Accommodations in the Inn or the 4 cabins and cottages. http://www.pinescountryinn.bizonthe.net

RALEIGH

The Oakwood Inn
411 N Bloodworth St 27604
919-832-9712 Fax: 919-836-9263
800-267-9712
Doris & Gary Jurkiewicz
All year

95-165-BB
6 rooms, 6 pb
Disc, Most CC, *Rated*, •
C-ltd/S-no/P-no/H-no

Full breakfast
Complimentary wine, snacks, soda, afternoon tea
Sitting room, piano, parlor, porch, massage therapist

Victorian retreat nestled in the heart of Raleigh's Historic Oakwood District. Six guestrooms, each with Private Bath, remote control fireplaces, cable TV.
innkeepers@oakwoodinnbb.com http://www.oakwoodinnbb.com

William Thomas House
530 North Blount St 27604
919-755-9400 Fax: 919-755-3966
800-653-3466
Jim & Sarah Lofton
All year

113-165-BB
4 rooms, 4 pb
Most CC
P-no

For comfort and charm, personal attention with respect for privacy, Southern hospitality at its very best, come be our guests at The William Thomas House Bed and Breakfast.
lofton@williamthomashouse.com http://www.williamthomashouse.com

ROBBINSVILLE

Blue Boar Inn
200 Santeetlah Rd 28771
828-479-8126 Fax: 828-479-2415
Pamela Glenn
April–mid November

85-135-BB
8 rooms, 8 pb
Most CC, *Rated*, •
C-yes/S-no/P-no/H-yes

Full breakfast
Lunch, picnic lunch, dinner
TV, Telephone, AC/Heat, private porches, lake access, trout pond

An upscale country house hotel nestled in the heart of the misty Smoky Mountains and the unspoiled shores of Lake Santeetlah.
innkeeper@blueboarinn.com http://www.blueboarinn.com

Snowbird Mountain Lodge
275 Santeetlah Rd 28771
828-479-3433 Fax: 828-479-3473
800-941-9290
Karen & Robert Rankin
April 15–Nov. 6

185-350-AP
21 rooms, 21 pb
Most CC, *Rated*
C-ltd/S-ltd/P-no/H-ltd

Full breakfast
Lunch & dinner included
Sitting room, piano, vegetarian meals, wildflower hikes

Located in the heart of the National Forest. Fishing, hiking, mountain stream swimming, canoeing, whitewater rafting, shuffleboard, and horseback riding.
innkeeper@snowbirdlodge.com http://www.snowbirdlodge.com

RUTHERFORDTON

Pinebrae Manor
1286 NC 108 Hwy 28139
828-286-1543 Fax: 828-288-1161
Allen & Charlotte Perry
March 15-November 30

59-69-BB
4 rooms, 4 pb
Visa, MC, AmEx, *Rated*, •
C-yes/S-ltd/P-no/H-yes

Full breakfast
Snacks
Sitting room, library, firepalces, accommodate business travelers, VCR

A large Georgian style home located in an area steeped in Revolutionary and Civil war history. pinebrae@blueridge.net http://www.pinebrae.blueridge.net

SALUDA

The Oaks
339 Greenville St 28773
828-749-9613 800-893-6091
Crowley & Terry Murphy
All year

115-175-BB
6 rooms, 6 pb
Most CC, *Rated*, •
C-ltd/S-ltd/P-no/H-no

Full breakfast
Sitting room, library, decks, porches, AC in all rooms

Charming Victorian with wrap-around porch furnished with American and Oriental antiques. In small town in western North Carolina mountains.
oaks@tds.net http://www.theoaksbedandbreakfast.com

SILER CITY

Inn at Celebrity Dairy
2106 Mount Vernon Hickory Road 27344
919-742-5176 Fax: 919-742-1432
877-742-5176
Brit & Fleming Pfann
All year

80-130-BB
6 rooms, 6 pb
Visa, MC, Disc, *Rated*
C-yes/S-no/P-no/H-yes

Full breakfast
vegetarian, wheat-free
featherbeds

The Inn at Celebrity Dairy welcomes you to the peace and comfort of an old home-place, and the purposeful life of a 200 acre working dairy.
theinn@celebritydairy.com http://www.celebritydairy.com

STATESVILLE

Tower House B&B
530 W Front St 28677
704-883-0328 Fax: 435-330-7982
800-844-1883
Cindy & Jim Castle
All year

70-80-BB
3 rooms, 3 pb
Most CC, •
C-ltd/S-ltd/P-no/H-no

Full breakfast
TV, clock/radio, laundry facilities, iron and ironing board, smoke detectors

We invite you to take a step in time and capture the charm and mood of the Victorian era at Tower House. Located at I-40 & I-77.
towerhouse@abts.net http://www.tower-house.com

TARBORO

Little Warren BB&
304 E Park Ave 27886
252-823-1314 Fax: 252-823-1314
800-309-1314
Patsy & Tom Miller
All year

75-BB
3 rooms, 3 pb
Most CC, *Rated*, •
C-ltd/S-yes/P-no/H-no
Spanish

Full English and American Southern
Complimentary beverage
Sitting room, tennis courts, sitting room, library, fireplace

Gracious, Edwardian home full of antiques & collectibles. In quiet neighborhood, historic district. lwarrenbb@tarboronc.com

TRYON

Pine Crest Inn
85 Pine Crest Ln 28782
828-859-9135 Fax: 828-859-9135
800-633-3001
Debby & Barney DuBois
All year

110-550-BB
35 rooms, 35 pb
Most CC, *Rated*, •
C-yes/S-ltd/P-no/H-ltd
French

Full breakfast
Restaurant & bar (fee)
Sitting room, library, 27 fireplaces, gazebo, volleyball, Country Club

Elegant mountain inn with views of the Blue Ridge Mountains. Near the Blue Ridge Parkway and Biltmore House. Gourmet restaurant, library, bar and wide verandas add to the casual elegance. info@pinecrestinn.com http://www.pinecrestinn.com

Stone Hedge Inn
PO Box 366
300 Howard Gap Rd 28782
828-859-9114 Fax: 828-859-5928
800-859-1974
Tom and Shaula Dinsmore
All year

100-125-BB
6 rooms, 6 pb
Visa, MC, *Rated*
C-ltd/S-no/P-no/H-ltd

Full breakfast
Restaurant, dinner available
Swimming pool, hiking in wooded meadows, receptions & reunions, weddings

Restaurant and lodge on peaceful 28-acre estate. Small meetings, conferences, weddings.
stonehedgeinn@alltel.net http://www.stone-hedge-inn.comj

VALLE CRUCIS

The Baird House
1451 Watauga River Rd 28679
828-297-4055 Fax: 828-297-3506
800-297-1342
Tom & Deede Hinson
All year

85-129-BB
5 rooms, 5 pb
Visa, MC, AmEx, •
C-ltd/S-no/P-no/H-no

Full breakfast
Snacks
Sitting room, bikes, Jacuzzis, fireplaces, cable TV, accom. bus. travelers

The Baird House was built in 1790 and is a restored Colonial farmhouse on 16 private acres on the Watauga River. bairdhouse@boone.net http://www.bairdhouse.com

VALLE CRUCIS

The Mast Farm Inn
PO Box 704
2543 Broadstone Road 28691
828-963-5857 Fax: 828-963-6404
888-963-5857
Wanda Hinshaw & Kay Philipp
All year

125-250-BB
15 rooms, 15 pb
Most CC, *Rated*, •
C-yes/S-no/P-no/H-yes

Full country breakfast
Cookie jar, restaurant & bar on site
A large wraparound porch, spacious grounds, organic gardens, pond and creek

The Mast Farm Inn has been welcoming guests since the 1800's ... and while we have added modern amenities, the hospitality remains the same ... attentive and sincere. Come make yourself at home. stay@mastfarminn.com http://www.mastfarminn.com

WASHINGTON

Carolina House
227 E 2nd St 27889
252-975-1382
Toni & Peter Oser
All year

60-90-BB
4 rooms, 4 pb
Most CC, *Rated*, •
C-ltd/S-ltd/P-no/H-no
German

Full breakfast
Tea, coffee, milk, sodas
Bicycles, parlor, enclosed smoking area

Welcome to the Carolina House Bed and Breakfast. Enjoy a quiet get-away for the weekend, or come and relax for the night as you head on your way to the Outer Banks of North Carolina. carolinahsebnb@coastalnet.com http://www.carolinahousebnb.com

---

Moss House
129 Van Norden St 27889
252-975-3967 Fax: 252-975-1148
888-975-3393
Mary Havens Cooper
January 4-Dec. 15

85-175-BB
4 rooms, 4 pb
Most CC, *Rated*, •
C-ltd/S-no/P-no/H-no

Full breakfast
Sitting room, library, fax, copier, modem access, private baths

Located in the historic district of Washington, one block from the Pamlico River. Walking distance from local gourmet restaurants, shops, and sailboat rentals and cruises. info@themosshouse.com http://www.themosshouse.com

WAYNESVILLE

Andon House
92 Daisey Ave 28786
828-452-3089 Fax: 828-452-7003
800-293-6190
Ann & Don Rothermel
All year

75-130-BB
4 rooms, 4 pb
Most CC, *Rated*
C-no/S-ltd/P-no/H-no

Our special four-course breakfast
Refreshments all day
Garden sitting room, library books

The beauty of the mountains, the quaint town of Waynesville, the comfort and relaxation of the Andon House is yours but a phone call away. info@andonhouse.com http://www.andonhouse.com

---

Haywood House
675 S Haywood St 28786
828-456-9831 Fax: 828-456-4400
Lynn & Chris Sylvester
All year

85-105-BB
4 rooms, 2 pb
Visa, MC, AmEx, •
C-ltd/S-no/P-no/H-no

Full breakfast
Comp. beverage, snacks
Sitting room, library, laundry fac., Fax, veranda & picnic areas

Rock, relax, view the mountains and enjoy small town charm. Comfortable, beautifully furnished historic home. info@haywoodhouse.com http://haywoodhouse.com

---

Herren House
94 E Street 28786
828-452-7837 Fax: 828-452-7706
800-284-1932
Jackie & Frank Blevins
All year

85-140-BB
6 rooms, 6 pb
Most CC, *Rated*, •
C-ltd/S-no/P-no/H-yes

Full breakfast
Afternoon tea, snacks, wine
Lunch available (fee), sitting room, library, cable TV

A special place filled with Victorian charm and casual elegance. Unique 19th century boardinghouse, completely and exquisitely restored. Gourmet breakfast by candlelight. herren@brinet.com http://www.herrenhouse.com

Andon House, Waynesville, NC

WAYNESVILLE

Mountain Creek
146 Chestnut Walk Dr 28786
828-456-5509 800-557-9766
Hylah & Guy Smalley
All year

95-125-BB
6 rooms, 6 pb
Visa, MC, *Rated*, •
C-ltd/S-no/P-yes/H-no

Full breakfast
Sitting room, 1600 sq foot deck, cable TV

Nestled on 6 acres with 2 creeks, a pond & mill wheel, this ex-corporate retreat has a rustic, but contemporary lodge feeling. guylah@aol.com

---

Mountain Inn at Windsong
459 Rockcliffe Lane 28721
828-627-6111 Fax: 828-627-8080
Russ & Barbara Mancini
All year

120-180-BB
7 rooms, 7 pb
Most CC, *Rated*, •
C-ltd/S-no/P-no/H-ltd
German

Full gourmet breakfast
Ploughman's Lunch or Supper, Llama Dinner Treks
Hot tub, hiking, pool table, swimming pool, Jacuzzi, tennis, llamas

Romantic Inn awesome views, tennis, hiking, swimming. Renowned breakfasts. From $120. Near Asheville, Smoky Mt Pk.
russ@windsongbb.com http://www.windsongbb.com

October Hill, A 1920's
421 Grimball Dr 28786
828-452-7967 Fax: 828-452-2780
877-628-4455
Judy & Roger Winge
All year

95-155
6 rooms, 6 pb
Visa, MC, Disc
C-ltd/S-no/P-no/H-no

Full breakfast
sun room

October Hill is a stately mansion in the beautiful mountains of North Carolina. Built in the 1920's, on 3 beautiful, park-like acres, it is within walking distance of charming downtown Waynesville. octhill5@aol.com http://www.octoberhillbedandbreakfast.com

---

Old Stone Inn
109 Dolan Rd 28786
828-456-3333 800-432-8499
Robert & Cindy Zinser
April to mid-December

120-180-BB
22 rooms, 22 pb
Most CC, *Rated*
S-no/P-no/H-no

Full breakfast
Wine & beer service, award winning dining.
Sitting room, library, outdoor deck, gift shop, color TV in rooms

Secluded mountain inn with classic lodging and superb candlelight fireside dining. Conveniently located on 6.5 acres, yet has the feeling of being deep in the woods.
http://www.oldstoneinn.com

Old Stone Inn, Waynesville, NC

WAYNESVILLE

The Swag Country Inn
2300 Swag Rd 28785
828-926-0430 Fax: 828-926-2036
800-789-7672
Deener Matthews
April 29—November 18

265-580-AP
15 rooms, 15 pb
Most CC, *Rated*, •
C-ltd/S-ltd/P-no/H-yes

Full breakfast
All meals included in rate
Library, piano, sauna, racquetball, hiking, croquet, badminton, pond

Tucked, snuggled, positioned, located and sitting spectacularly atop a 5000' mountain ridge, this log & rock lodge offers the ultimate high country wilderness experience.
swaginnkeeper@aol.com http://www.theswag.com/

The Yellow House on Plott Creek Rd
89 Oakview Dr 28786
828-452-0991 Fax: 828-452-1140
800-563-1236
Ron & Sharon Smith

125-250-BB
6 rooms, 6 pb
Visa, MC, *Rated*, •
C-ltd/S-no/P-no/H-no
All year

Full breakfast
Hors d'oeuvres hour
Sitting room, library, bikes, tennis court, hot tubs, swimming pool

Western North Carolina's most romantic inn. Gourmet breakfast may be served in your room. 3½ acres of lawn, lily pond & gardens.
yelhouse@asap-com.com http://www.theyellowhouse.com/

WAYNESVILLE (REGION)

WindDancers Lodging & Llama Treks
1966 Martins Creek Rd, *Clyde* 28721
828-627-6986 Fax: 828-627-0754
877-627-3300
Donna & Gale Livengood, family

130-195-BB
9 rooms, 9 pb
Visa, MC, *Rated*, •
C-yes/S-no/P-no/H-no
All year

Continental plus or full breakfast
Snacks
Sitting room, library, suites, fireplace, llama dinner, lunch hikes

Our contemporary log lodging is nestled in a peaceful mountain cove of woodlands, stream & llama-scaped pastures. info@winddancersnc.com http://www.winddancersnc.com

WEAVERVILLE (REGION)

Inn on Main Street
PO Box 6071
88 S Main St, *Asheville* 28787
828-645-4935 877-873-6074
Dan & Nancy Ward
All year

85-145-BB
7 rooms, 7 pb
Visa, MC, Disc, *Rated*, •
C-ltd/S-no/P-no/H-no
Spanish, German, French

Full breakfast
Complimentary evening refreshments
Sitting room, picnic lunches by request for extra $$

Romantic Victorian getaway near Asheville, Biltmore Estate, antiques, crafts, golf, rafting, hiking, skiing and the Blue Ridge Parkway.
relax@innonmain.com http://www.innonmain.com

WELDON

Weldon Place Inn
500 Washington Ave 27890
252-536-4582 800-831-4470
Bill & Cathy Eleczko
All year

65-75-BB
4 rooms, 3 pb
Most CC
S-ltd/P-no/H-no

Full breakfast
Sitting room, cable TV, music room, accommodate business travelers

Relaxed lodgings in 1914 Colonial Revival home. Large restful front porch. Many instruments for our musical guests.
weldonplaceinn@email.com http://www.allaboutbootleg.com/WPI

WILMINGTON

4 Porches B&B
312 S 3rd St 28401
910-763-6603 Fax: 910-763-5116
800-763-6603
Vickie & Greg Stringer
All year

79-119-BB
3 rooms, 3 pb
Visa, MC, AmEx,
Rated, •
C-ltd/S-no/P-no/H-no

Full breakfast
Afternoon tea, snacks
Sitting room, library, cable TV, accommodate business travelers

Three large guest rooms, two with king beds, 1 with queen bed. Central air, cable/VCR, guest robes, telephone, ceiling fans in each room. http://www.bbonline.com/nc/curran

---

Anderson Guest House
520 Orange St 28401
910-343-8128 888-265-1216
Connie Anderson
All year

80-95-BB
2 rooms, 2 pb
Rated
C-ltd/S-yes/P-yes/H-no

Full breakfast
Complimentary wine, mixed drinks
Afternoon tea, fireplace, restaurant nearby, baby-sitting service

1851 Italianate townhouse; separate guest quarters overlooking private garden. Furnished with antiques; ceiling fans, fireplaces. anderlancon@aol.com

---

C.W. Worth House
412 S Third St 28401
910-762-8562 800-340-8559
All year

115-150-BB
7 rooms, 7 pb
Most CC, *Rated*, •
C-ltd/S-no/P-no/H-no

Full breakfast
Complimentary beverages and snacks
3 sitting rooms, porches, gardens, decorative fireplaces, 1 room w/whirlpool

The Worth House Bed & Breakfast is known for its striking Queen Anne architecture, romantic atmosphere and gardens. Your hosts greet you warmly and make you feel at home. relax@worthhouse.com http://www.worthhouse.com

---

Camellia Cottage
118 S 4th St 28401
910-763-9171 Fax: 910-362-8791 1-800-763-9171
P. Tirrito & S. Skavroneck
All year

129-179-BB
4 rooms, 4 pb
Visa, MC, Disc
C-yes/S-ltd/P-yes/H-no

Full breakfast
Snacks and refreshments offered all day.

Located in the heart of the Historic District, The Camellia Cottage has four intriguing guest rooms, a lush perennial garden and features a 3-course breakfast each morning.
camelliacottage@earthlink.net http://www.camelliacottage.net

Catherine's Inn
410 S Front St 28401
910-251-0863 Fax: 910-772-9550
800-476-0723
Catherine & Walter AcKiss
All year

85-125-BB
3 rooms, 3 pb
Visa, MC, AmEx,
Rated, •
C-yes/S-yes/P-no/H-no

Full breakfast
Complimentary wine, snacks, tea
Bar service, sitting room, library, baby-sitting service

In heart of the historical district. Experience warm gracious hospitality, tasty breakfasts.
catherin@wilmington.net http://www.catherinesinn.com

WILMINGTON

Front Street Inn
215 S Front St 28401
910-762-6442 Fax: 910-762-8991
800-336-8184
Jay & Stefany Rhodes
All year

110-188-BB
9 rooms, 9 pb
Most CC, *Rated*
C-ltd/S-ltd/P-no/H-ltd
Spanish, French

Continental plus breakfast
Snacks, Sol y Sombra Bar
Phones, TVs, modems, massage, room service, parking, exercise room

Intimate European style inn. Privacy and charm. One block from river in historic downtown. Abundant healthful breakfast served all morning.
jay@frontstreetinn.com http://www.frontstreetinn.com

Graystone Inn
100 S Third St 28401
910-763-2000 Fax: 910-763-5555
888-763-4773
Paul & Yolanda Bolda
All year

159-299-BB
7 rooms, 7 pb
Most CC, *Rated*, •
C-ltd/S-ltd/P-no/H-no

Full Gourmet breakfast
Complimentary wine & fruit
Sitt. rm., piano, robes, library, fitness center, phones with voice mail

Recently named "One of America's Top 10 Most Romantic Inns" by American Historic Inns. Wilmington's only AAA Four Diamond property.
reservations@graystoneinn.com http://www.graystoneinn.com

Rosehill Inn
114 S Third St 28401
910-815-0250 Fax: 910-815-0350
800-815-0250
Laurel Jones & Dennis Fietsch
All year

99-229-BB
6 rooms, 6 pb
Most CC, *Rated*, •
C-ltd/S-no/P-no/H-no

Full breakfast
Sitting room, library, premium cable TV in rooms, some VCRs

Rosehill is a beautifully restored Victorian/neo-classical home in the heart of Wilmington's historic district. rosehill@rosehill.com http://www.rosehill.com

---

The Verandas
202 Nun Street 28401
910-251-2212 Fax: 910-251-8932
Dennis Madsen
All year

145-200-BB
8 rooms, 8 pb
Most CC, *Rated*, •
C-ltd/S-no/P-no/H-no
American Sign Language

Full breakfast
Complimentary wine
Sitting room, cable TV, piano

Grand, yet affordable luxury on a quiet street two blocks from river-walk, restaurants, shopping. Large rooms with marble baths, phone & modem jacks.
verandas4@aol.com http://www.verandas.com/

The Wilmingtonian
101 S Second St 28401
910-348-1800 Fax: 910-251-1149
800-525-0909
Mike Compton & Tom Scott
All year

129-299-BB
40 rooms, 40 pb
Visa, MC, AmEx, *Rated*, •
C-ltd/S-no/H-yes

Continental plus breakfast
In suites–kitchen included
Concierge, conservatory, billiard room, courtyard, in-house pub, conference

Elegant accommodations for discriminating travelers, located in romantic Historic District. Walk along Cape Fear River paths to fine restaurants, museums and specialty shops.
director@thewilmingtonian.com http://www.thewilmingtonian.com

WILMINGTON (REGION)

Beacon House Inn & Cottages
715 Carolina Beach Ave, *Carolina Beach* 28428
910-458-6244
Mary & Larry Huhn All year

55-110-BB
Most CC, *Rated*
S-ltd

Full country breakfast

The atmosphere at The Beacon House is relaxed, warm and friendly. Enjoy our ocean view from the veranda of our restored 1950's beach house while sipping your morning coffee.
innkeeper@beaconhouseinnb-b.com http://www.beaconhouseinnb-b.com

WILMINGTON (REGION)

Darlings by the Sea
PO Box 373
329 Atlantic Ave, *Kure Beach* 28449
910-458-8887 Fax: 910-458-6468
800-383-8111
Kip & Maureen Darling

139-249-BB
5 rooms, 5 pb
Most CC, *Rated*, •
S-yes/P-no/H-no
Spanish
All year

Continental plus breakfast
Bicycles, Jacuzzis, suites, cable TV, fitness center, beach

Fabulously appointed, oceanfront, whirlpool suites. King beds, down comforters. Satellite TV, music, VCR, dbl. whirlpools. Oceanfront fitness center.
reservations@darlingsbythesea.com http://www.darlingsbythesea.com

---

Docksider Oceanfront Inn
PO Box 373
202 N Ft Fisher Blvd, *Kure Beach* 28449
910-458-4200 Fax: 910-458-6468
800-815-8636
Kip & Maureen Darling

75-175-EP
34 rooms, 34 pb
Most CC, *Rated*, •
C-yes/S-yes/P-no/H-yes
All year

Swimming pool, family friendly facility, fitness center, beach

The nicest selection of ocean front hotel rooms on the coast. "Oceanfront Queens"–Queen bed on a pedestal overlooking the sea. Private porch. Seaworthy nautical decor.
reservations@docksiderinn.com http://www.docksiderinn.com

WILSON

Miss Betty's
600 W Nash St 27893
252-243-4447 Fax: 252-243-4447
800-258-2058
Betty & Fred Spitz All year

60-80-BB
14 rooms, 14 pb
Most CC, *Rated*
S-yes/P-no/H-yes

Full breakfast
3 parlors, antique shop, A/C, golf, swimming pool, games, executive suites

Selected as one of "best places to stay in the South." A touch of Victorian elegance & beauty. info@missbettysbnb.com http://www.missbettysbnb.com

WINSTON-SALEM

Augustus T. Zevely Inn
803 S Main St 27101
336-748-9299 Fax: 336-721-2211
800-928-9294
Regina Johnson All year

80-205-BB
12 rooms, 12 pb
Visa, MC, AmEx, *Rated*, •
C-yes/S-ltd/P-yes/H-yes

Continental plus-wkdy, full-wknds
Wine & cheese, freshly baked cookies, soda
Fireplaces, steam baths, whirlpool tubs, parking, heated porch

Circa 1844 Moravian-style inn restored to museum quality. Only lodging in historic Old Salem. Rooms individually furnished, heated covered porch. Featured in County living. AAA & Mobile rated. ctheall@dddcompany.com http://www.winston-salem-inn.com

---

Colonel Ludlow Inn
434 Summit at W 5th 27101
336-777-1887 Fax: 336-777-0518
800-301-1887
Ken Land
All year

89-189-BB
9 rooms, 9 pb
Most CC, *Rated*, •
C-ltd/S-ltd/P-no/H-no

Full breakfast in your room.
Tea, popcorn, sodas, snack, buy alcohol, desserts
Nautilus exercise room, billiard room, 400-plus movie/300-plus CD library

IN YOUR ROOM: Victorian antiques, 2-person Jacuzzi, King bed, stereo, TV/VCR/DVD, phones, bathrobes, coffee/tea maker, microwave, mini-refrig. Two adjacent 1887 & 1895 Nat. Historic Register homes. innkeeper@bbinn.com http://www.bbinn.com

---

Lady Anne's Victorian
612 Summit St 27101
336-724-1074
Shelley Kirley
All year

60-185-BB
4 rooms, 3 pb
Rated

Full or continental plus breakfast

Lady Anne's Victorian B&B, listed on the National Register circa 1890, graciously accommodates romantic getaways, special occasions and business stays.
http://www.bbonline.com/nc/ladyannes/

North Dakota

COOPERSTOWN (REGION)

Volden Farm
11943 County Rd 26, *Luverne*
58056
701-769-2275 Fax: 701-769-2610
Jim & JoAnne Wold
All year

60-95-BB
4 rooms, 1 pb
Rated, •
C-yes/S-ltd/P-ltd/H-no
Russian, Norwegian

Full breakfast
Lunch, dinner, snacks, wine
Canoeing, sitt. rm., hammock swing, bikes, billiard, library, fireplaces

An unexpected old world atmosphere on the wide prairie of eastern North Dakota. We have collected things Russian and Norwegian, which reflect our years in Moscow and family heritage. voldenfarm_bb@broadvu.com http://www.broadvu.com/voldenfarm

FARGO

Chez Susanne
1100 3rd Ave S 58103
701-293-9023 866-787-2663
Amie Dexter
All year

85-BB
4 rooms, 4 pb
C-ltd/S-no/P-no/H-no
Spanish

Continental plus breakfast
Afternoon tea, snacks
Sitting rm, library, tennis, suites, fireplaces, cable TV, acc. bus. trav.

Victorian Bed and Breakfast offering spacious and elegant suites with up-to-date amenities catering to business travel and weekend getaways.
chezsusanne@aol.com http://www.chezsusanne.com

MEDORA

Rough Riders Hotel
PO Box 198
58645
701-623-4444
Paul Herringer
All year
medora@medora.com

REGENT

Prairie Vista
Box 211
101 Rural Ave, SW 58650
701-563-4542 Fax: 701-563-4519
Marlys A. Prince
All year

65-BB
10 rooms, 2 pb
C-ltd/S-ltd/P-ltd/H-ltd

Full breakfast
Indoor swimming pool, sauna, rec room with wet bar,pool table

Located at the end of "The Enchanted Highway" is a brick ranch style home. Seven bedrooms, three baths, recreation room with wet bar, fireplace, sauna, indoor swimming pool. prince@prairievista.com http://www.prairievista.com

Ohio

ALEXANDRIA

WillowBrooke
4459 Morse Rd 43001
740-924-6161 Fax: 740-924-0224
800-772-6372
Sandra Gilson All year

100-150-BB
5 rooms, 5 pb
Most CC
C-ltd/S-ltd/P-no/H-ltd

Full breakfast
Jacuzzi suites w/microwave, fridge, frplces, TV/VCRs, sofas, outdoor hot tub

Elegant English Tudor Manor House with separate Guest House secluded in 34 acres of woods. Huge suites with candlelight, fireplaces, featherbeds & Jacuzzi tubs add to the romantic atmosphere. wilbrk@aol.com http://www.willowbrooke.com

AMANDA

Dum-Ford House
PO Box 496
123 W Main St 43102
740-969-3010 877-271-9598
Anna Ford
All year

70-85-BB
2 rooms, 2 pb
Visa, MC, *Rated*
C-ltd/S-ltd/P-no/H-no

Full breakfast
Homebaked cookies, hot & cold beverages
Sitting room, garden and courtyard, chimney, fireplace, paperback exchange

Are you tired of the hustle and bustle of life? The Dum-Ford House offers a quiet, romantic place to relax while surrounded by fresh flowers, soothing music, and homecooked food.
dum-fordbb@buckeyenet.net http://www.dum-fordbb.com

ARCHBOLD

Sauder Heritage Inn
PO Box 235
22611 St. Route 2 43502
419-445-6408 Fax: 419-445-2609
800-590-9755
Andy Brodbeck All year

98-129-BB
35 rooms, 35 pb
Rated
S-no

Continental plus breakfast

At the Sauder Heritage Inn, we've combined the amenities of a city hotel with the ambiance of a country inn to create the ideal place to stay in northwestern Ohio.
sauderheritageinn@bright.net http://www.saudervillage.com

ASHLAND

Winfield
1568 St Rt 60 44805
419-281-5587 800-269-7166
Bill & Sally Davidson
All year

75-125-BB
3 rooms, 3 pb
Most CC, *Rated*
C-ltd/S-ltd/P-no/H-no

Full breakfast
Snacks, complimentary wine
Suite, fireplaces, cable TV, accommodate business travelers

Grand 1876 Italianate home, beautiful architecture, luxurious French-English decor, lush gardens, sweeping lawns. http://www.bbonline.com/oh/winfield

ATWOOD LAKE (REGION)

Whispering Pines
PO Box 340
1268 Magnolia Rd SW, *Dellroy* 44620
330-735-2824 Fax: 330-735-7006
866-4lakevu

140-220-BB
9 rooms, 9 pb
Most CC, *Rated*, •
C-ltd/S-no/P-no/H-yes
Bill & Linda Horn
All year

Full breakfast
Afternoon tea and coffee
Spa tubs, fireplace, balcony, lakeviews, great food, romance & privacy

The ultimate romantic getaway nestled on 7 rolling acres with a million-dollar view of beautiful Atwood Lake. Relax in a spa-tub, sip wine on your balcony & wake up to a delicious breakfast. linda@atwoodlake.com http://www.atwoodlake.com

BARNESVILLE

Georgian Pillars
128 E Walnut St 43713
740-425-3741 888-425-3741
Janet Thompson All year

60-80-BB
4 rooms
Visa, MC
C-yes/S-ltd

Full breakfast
Fireplace, Victorian Parlor, gift shoppe

The Georgian Pillars is a 1900 Georgian Revival Home, with lavish oak woodwork and stained glass windows, that has been lovingly decorated in the teal and mauve hues of the Victorian era. janet.thompson@attbi.com http://www.georgianpillars.8m.com

BERLIN

Donna's Premier Lodging
PO Box 307
East St 44610
330-893-3068 Fax: 330-893-0037
800-320-3338
Johannes and Donna Marie Schlabach All year

55-369-BB
19 rooms, 19 pb
Visa, MC, Disc, *Rated*
C-ltd/S-ltd/P-no/H-ltd

Please inquire about breakfast
Fresh fruit and pastry platter, sparkling cider
Jacuzzi, fireplace, TV/VCR, CD stereo, mood lighting, kitchenette

Welcome to Donna's! Experience a romantic, luxurious stay in one of our beautifully appointed Honeymoon/Anniversary Cottages, Cedar Log Cabins, Chalets, Bridal Suites or Villas. info@donnasb-b.com http://www.donnasofberlin.com

BERLIN (REGION)

Gilead's Balm Manor
8690 CR 201, *Fredricksburg* 44627
330-695-3881 Fax: 330-6695-3881
888-612-3436
Ilene & John Hess All year

110-175-BB
6 rooms, 6 pb
Most CC, *Rated*, •
C-yes/S-ltd/P-no/H-ltd

Full breakfast
Snacks, complimentary sparkling juice
Jacuzzis, fireplaces, satellite TV, free videos, small lake, paddleboat

European elegance in Amish Country. 6 luxurious rooms, 12 ft ceiling, waterfalls Jacuzzi, fireplaces, kitchenette, private bath, A/C, satellite TV, VCR, CD player.
gileadbalmmanor@valkyrie.net http://www.gileadsbalmmanor.com

The Barn Inn
6838 CR 203, *Millersburg* 44654
330-674-7600 Fax: 330-674-0761
877-674-7600
Paul & Loretta Coblentz
All year

69-159-BB
7 rooms, 7 pb
Most CC, *Rated*
C-ltd/S-ltd/P-no/H-yes

Full breakfast
Snacks
Fireplaces, satellite TV

A beautifully restored barn featuring original beams and Victorian elegance in a country setting. http://www.bbonline.com/oh/thebarn/

BUCYRUS

HideAway Inn
1601 State Route 4 44820
419-562-3013 Fax: 419-562-3003
800-570-8233
Debbie A. Miller
All year

87-287-BB
12 rooms, 12 pb
Visa, MC, Disc, *Rated*, •
C-yes/S-ltd/P-no/H-yes

5 course breakfast
Candlelight dinner available
Sitting room, library, 3 rooms with Jacuzzi, frplcs., priv. garden

First in Ohio to be featured in the New York Times. Enjoy private Jacuzzis for two, fireplaces, & a 5-course breakfast served in your room. 1 hour north of Columbus, 1.5 hours from Cleveland & Toledo.
innkeeper@hideawayinn.com http://www.hideawayinn.com

CAMBRIDGE

The Colonel Taylor Inn
633 Upland Rd 43725
740-432-7802 Fax: 740-435-3152
Patricia Irvin
All year

105-175-BB
4 rooms, 4 pb
Visa, MC, Disc, *Rated*, •
C-ltd/S-no/P-no/H-no

Full gourmet breakfast
Snacks, coffee, tea
Central A/C, 3 porches, dining, library, 2 parlors, big screen TV, frplaces

The Colonel Taylor Inn is a beautiful, three story, 9000 sq. ft. Victorian mansion located in the scenic part of southeastern Ohio.
coltaylor@peoplepc.com http://www.coltaylorinnbb.com

Misty Meadow Farm
64878 Slaughter Hill Rd 43725
740-439-5135 Fax: 740-439-5408
Jim & Vicki Goudy
All year

BB
4 rooms, 4 pb
Visa, MC, Disc, *Rated*
C-ltd/S-ltd/P-no/H-ltd
Spanish

Full breakfast
Snacks, dinner available
Sitting room, Jacuzzis, swimming pool, fireplaces, accom. bus. travelers

A sumptuous, sunset picnic dinner complete with hayride to your private hilltop. A uniquely romantic escape. misty@cambridgeoh.com http://www.mistymeadow.com

CANTON (REGION)

Elson Inn
225 N Main St, *Magnolia* 44643
330-866-9242 Fax: 330-866-3398
Jo Lane & Gus Elson
All year

100-120-BB
5 rooms, 5 pb
Visa, MC, Disc, *Rated*
C-ltd/S-ltd/P-no/H-no

Full breakfast
Snacks
Sitting room, library, tennis court, accommodate business travelers

Victorian brick furnished in original antiques of building in 1879. Full breakfast served with linens, crystal, silver, etc. Hike the low path of the Sandy & Beaver Canal.
jelson@neo.rr.com http://www.elsoninn.com

The Colonel Taylor Inn, Cambridge, OH

CANTON (REGION)

The Lodge at Fair Oaks 1717 Seven Mile Dr, *New Philadelphia* 44663 330-343-3460 Fax: 330-343-3460 877-546-1884 Ron & Mary Fotheringham	75-95-BB 3 rooms, 3 pb • C-ltd/S-no/P-ltd/H-yes All year	Continental Plus breakfast Sitting room, library, bicycles, Jacuzzis, pool, suites, fireplaces

Wooded hideaway furnished in antiques; Starbucks coffee and homemade baked goods served on our patio or by the fireplace; use our bikes to tour our quaint small town and antique browse. http://www.lodgeatfairoaks.com

CHESTERLAND

Marigold PO Box 1 12647 Caves Rd 44026 440-729-4000 Fax: 440-729-6666 John Oberle All year	75-175-BB 6 rooms, 6 pb *Rated*, • C-yes/S-no/P-no/H-yes	Full breakfast Afternoon tea, complimentary wine Library, fireplace, Jacuzzi, suites, cable TV, accommodates bus. travelers

100+ acres of serenity, yet within 30 minutes of downtown, airport, Six Flags. University Circle and all major attractions.

CINCINNATI

Hyde Park House 3572 Lilac Ave 45208 513-314-3149 Fax: 513-321-6944 Ron Romero All year	40-60-BB 3 rooms C-ltd/S-no/P-ltd Japanese	Coffee and Quiche

Overnight stay: $35–$60 per night – Convenient to X.U., U.C., Downtown, & I-71 – Hyde Park house is designed to accommodate students and orofessionals while traveling or in between housing. ronromero@aol.com http://www.hydeparkhouse.com

CINCINNATI (REGION)

Victorian Manor 219 Oxford Rd, *Franklin* 45005 513-746-0050 Fax: 937-746-3023 866-833-9805 Stella Turner All year	95-125-BB 5 rooms, 5 pb Visa, MC, *Rated*, • C-ltd/S-no/P-no/H-no	Full breakfast Sitting room, fireplaces, cable TV

Whether your stay is for a night or a weekend, for business or pleasure, add the extra dimension that only we can bring: an atmosphere from the unhurried days of the past.
victorianmanor@hotmail.com http://www.bbonline.com/oh/victorian/index.html

CINCINNATI (REGION)

Ohio River House
PO Box 188
101 Brown St, *Higginsport* 45131
937-375-4395 Fax: 937-375-4394
Andrew & Judy Lloyd
All year

85-165-BB
8 rooms, 8 pb
Visa, MC, *Rated*
C-yes/S-no/P-yes/H-no

Full breakfast
Snacks, complimentary wine
Sitting room, bikes, pool, family friendly

Beautiful river valley setting. 1830 built Federal Colonial furnished with comfortable antiques. fdsinc@bright.net http://www.OhioRiverHouse.com

---

First Farm Inn Kentucky
2510 Stevens Rd, *Petersburg, KY* 41080
859-586-0199 800-277-9527
Jen Warner & Dana Kisor
All year

90-126-BB
2 rooms, 2 pb
Visa, MC, Disc, •
C-ltd/S-no/P-ltd/H-ltd

Full breakfast
Ask about special treats, birthday cakes, etc.
Horseback riding, in-room massages, sitting room, library, spa, fireplace

First Farm Inn Kentucky is an elegant, updated 1870s farmhouse on 20 acres of rolling hills. Horseback riding, spacious rooms, sumptuous breakfasts, outdoor hot tub, in-room massages, and more.
firstfarm@goodnews.net http://bbonline.com/ky/firstfarm

CLEVELAND

Brownstone Inn Downtown
3649 Prospect Ave 44115
216-426-1753 Fax: 216-431-0648
Mr. Robin Yates
All year

85-115-BB
5 rooms, 1 pb
•
C-ltd/S-ltd/P-ltd/H-no

Full breakfast
Snacks
Sitting room, fireplaces, cable TV, accommodate business travelers

Beautiful townhouse located minutes from all cultural, educational and musical activities. ryates@iopener.net http://www.brownstoneinndowntown.com

---

Glidden House
1901 Ford Dr 44106
216-231-8900 Fax: 216-231-2130
Thomas Farinacci
All year

149-229-BB
60 rooms, 60 pb
Most CC, •
C-yes/S-ltd/P-no/H-yes

Continental plus breakfast
Atrium, sitting area with fireplace, pub

This French Gothic mansion, built in 1910, is located in the heart of Cleveland's cultural district, University Circle. tfarinacci@gliddenhouse.com http://www.gliddenhouse.com

CLEVELAND (REGION)

Red Maple Inn
14707 S Cheshire St, *Burton* 44021
440-834-8334 Fax: 440-834-8356
888-646-2753
Gina N. Holk
All year

99-175-BB
18 rooms, 18 pb
Most CC, *Rated*, •
C-yes/S-yes/P-no/H-yes

Deluxe Continental Breakfast
Wine and Cheese and light appetizers
Music in room and special chocolates, sitting room, library, Jacuzzis, bikes

Overlooking peaceful Amish country. Antique and Amish craft shops, 7 golf courses, and more. Relax, refresh, and recharge in our rooms. Jacuzzis, balconies, fireplaces, library all with great staff.
info@redmapleinn.com http://www.redmapleinn.com

C.M. Spitzer House
504 West Liberty St, *Medina* 44256
330-725-7289 Fax: 330-725-7289
888-777-1379
Dale & Janet Rogers
All year

65-125-BB
4 rooms, 4 pb
Visa, MC, Disc, *Rated*, •
C-ltd/S-no/P-no/H-no

Full breakfast
Snacks
Sitting room, Jacuzzis, fireplace, cable TV, rose garden

Beautifully restored 1890 Queen Anne filled with warm antiques, lacey linens and Victorian charm. spitzer@apk.net http://www.victorianinns.com/spitzerhouse

CLEVELAND (REGION)

Fitzgerald's Irish
47 Mentor Avenue, *Painesville* 44077
440-639-0845
Debra & Tom Fitzgerald
All year

72-90-BB
3 rooms, 3 pb
Most CC, *Rated*
C-ltd/S-no/P-no/H-no

Full-weekends; continental+-weekday
Beverages
Sitting room, TV room with satellite TV

Irish hospitality awaits you in our 16-room French Tudor, which will charm you with its unique castle-like architecture. 3 miles from Lake Erie beaches and 30 minutes from Cleveland. info@fitzgeraldsbnb.com http://www.fitzgeraldsbnb.com

---

Inn at Brandywine Falls
8230 Brandywine Rd, *Sagamore Hills* 44067
330-467-1812 Fax: 330-467-2162
888-306-3381
George & Katie Hoy
All year

108-250-BB
6 rooms, 6 pb
Most CC, *Rated*, •
C-ltd/S-no/H-yes

Full breakfast
Library, sitting room

The Inn, built in 1848, is an impeccable Country Place and a part of the tapestry of 33,000 acres of parkland (Cuyahoga Valley National Recreation Area) and adjacent to Brandywine waterfall. brandywinefallsinn@prodigy.net http://www.innatbrandywinefalls.com

COLUMBUS

House of the Seven Goebels
4975 Hayden Run Rd 43221
614-761-9595 Fax: 614-761-9595
Pat & Frank Goebel
All year

75-90-BB
2 rooms, 2 pb

Full and Continental breakfast

From the pineapple hospitality sign above the front walk, to the warmth of the music room and parlor, The House of the Seven Goebels beckons to those that enjoy and appreciate the past. fgoebel@columbus.rr.com http://www.bbhost.com/7goebels

COLUMBUS (REGION)

Penguin Crossing
3291 State Rt 56 W, *Circleville* 43113
740-477-6222 Fax: 740-420-6060
800-PENGUIN
Ross & Tracey Irvin
All year

100-225-BB
5 rooms, 5 pb
Most CC, *Rated*, •
C-yes/S-no/P-no/H-yes

Full breakfast on weekends
Continental plus breakfast midweek
Sitting room, hot tubs, star gazing, hiking, kennel nearby, snacks

Penguin Crossing Bed and Breakfast is an 1820 brick farmhouse situated on about 300 acres, just NW of Circleville, Ohio. Only 25 miles south of downtown Columbus in the midst of farmland. innkeepers@penguin.cc http://www.penguin.cc

---

Alexandra's
117 N Main St, *London* 43140
740-852-5993 Fax: 740-852-6484
Ron and Susan Brown
All year

70-130-BB
6 rooms, 5 pb
Visa, MC, AmEx
C-ltd/S-no/P-no/H-ltd

Full breakfast

Walking into Alexandra's Bed and Breakfast may give the feeling of stepping back in time, but amongst the beautiful antiques you will find all the necessities of modern life.
ronbrown@netwalk.com http://www.alexandrasbb.com

The College Inn
63 W College Ave, *Westerville* 43081
614-794-3090 Fax: 614-895-9337
888-794-3090
Becky Rohrer
All year

95-115-BB
3 rooms, 3 pb
Most CC, •
C-yes/S-no/P-ltd/H-no

Full breakfast
Afternoon tea, snacks
Sitting rm, library, bikes, cable TV, outdoor patio/gardens, acc. bus. trav.

Elegant 1870's 2-story home on tree lined street fully restored in 1996. Eclectic furnishings, beautiful gardens, spacious guestrooms. Gourmet breakfast, caters to business travelers.
cibnb@aol.com http://www.bbonline.com/oh/collegeinn

DANVILLE

Red Fox Country Inn PO Box 717 26367 Danville Amity Rd 43014 740-599-7369 Fax: 740-599-7369 877-600-7310 Denny & Sue Simpkins All year	75-95-BB 5 rooms, 5 pb Visa, MC, Disc, *Rated*, • C-ltd/S-ltd/P-no/H-no	Full breakfast Afternoon tea, snacks Sitting room, library, cable TV, accommodates business travelers

1830s Inn in the country. Less than 30 minutes from Amish country or Mohican County.
sudsimp@aol.com http://www.redfoxcountryinn.com

The White Oak Inn 29683 Walhonding Rd 43014 740-599-6107 877-908-5923 Ian & Yvonne Martin All year	90-195-BB 12 rooms, 12 pb Most CC, *Rated*, • C-ltd/S-no/P-no/H-yes Some French	Full breakfast Dinner with notice, afternoon snacks Common room with books, boardgames and fireplace, porch, screen house, lawn games

Large country home nestled in wooded area. Outdoor enthusiasts' paradise. Comfortable antique decor. Four rooms with fireplaces and two luxury cottages.
info@whiteoakinn.com http://www.whiteoakinn.com

FINDLAY

Lambs Ear 17429 Co Rd 7 St Rt 568 45840 419-424-5810 Lorena Oman All year	69-99-BB 4 rooms, 3 pb Visa, MC, *Rated* C-ltd/S-no/P-yes/H-no	Full breakfast Lunch, dinner upon request Sitting room, whirlpool tubs, firelaces, accommodate business travelers

1915 homestead with original 1850's barn. Antique & country decor, 2 fireplaces, walking trails, pond with canoe, whirlpool tubs. Close to shopping, 5 golf coursers, many parks, and antique shops. lambsear@turbosurf.net http://www.lambsear.com

FRANKLIN FURNACE

Riverview Inn 91 Riverview Dr 45629 740-355-4004 Fax: 740-354-9813 888-388-8439 George & Bobbie Sich All year	92-109-BB 4 rooms, 4 pb Most CC, *Rated* C-yes/S-no/P-no/H-yes	Full breakfast Snacks; soft drinks; fruit drinks; fruit juices Exercise Room; whirlpool tub; satellite TVs; direct phone lines; Internet

RiverView Bed Franklin Furnace, OH; Ohio River vacation 4 Rooms, Private Baths; Boat Docks; Meeting Facility. innkeepers@riverhost.com http://www.riverhost.com

GRAND RAPIDS

The Sisters of Thurston House 24401 2nd St 43522 419-832-0915 Carol McNair All year	75-BB 2 rooms C-ltd/S-no/P-ltd/H-no	Full breakfast Afternoon tea, snacks, complimentary wine Sitting room, cable TV

Go back in time to this historic 1860 home: veranda, charming parlour, lots of antiques, lots of antiques. victoria@danberry.com

HOCKING HILLS (REGION)

Shaw's Restaurant & Inn 123 N Broad St, *Lancaster* 43130 740-654-1842 Fax: 740-654-7032 800-654-2477 Bruce & Nancy Cork All year	70-198-BB 24 rooms, 24 pb Visa, MC, *Rated* S-ltd/P-no/H-ltd	Full breakfast Lunch & dinner available, restaurant Bar service, library, Jacuzzis, suites, cable TV, accom. bus. travel

Shaw's, located on historic downtown square, features 24 individually decorated rooms, nine with whirlpools for two.
borncork@computechnow.com http://www.hockinghills.com/shaws

HURON

Captain Montague's
229 Center St 44839
419-433-4756 800-276-4756
Judy and Mike Tann
April-October

95-175-BB
6 rooms, 6 pb
S-no/P-no/H-no
English

Continental plus breakfast
Lunch (picnic basket)
Afternoon tea, snacks, swimming pool, parlor, garden and gazebo

Captain Montague's Guest House is near a summer theater, waterfront parks, a boat harbor and Cedar Point. judytann@aol.com http://www.captainmontagues.com

KELLEYS ISLAND

A Water's Edge Retreat
PO Box 839
827 E Lakeshore Dr 43438
419-746-2455 Fax: 419-746-2242
800-884-5143
Tim & Beth
All year

179-350-BB
6 rooms, 6 pb
•
C-ltd/S-no/P-no/H-no
Some French, ASL

Full breakfast
Snacks, comp. wine
Sitting room, library, bridal suite, fireplaces, Jacuzzis, beach, bikes

Waterfront, elegant Queen Anne Victorian style. Travel & Leisure rated "... best of the Great Lakes." watersedge@mindspring.com http://WatersEdgeRetreat.com

---

Cricket Lodge
PO Box 323
111 E Lakeshore Dr 43438
419-746-2263
Frank & Chris Yako
All year

110-130-BB
3 rooms, 1 pb
C-ltd/S-no/P-no/H-no

Full breakfast
Snacks
Lakefront, screened porch, sitting room

Cricket Lodge, built in 1905, is a lovely lakefront home where guests can enjoy a leisurely breakfast on our screened-in front porch overlooking Lake Erie.
cricketlodge@aol.com http://www.kelleysisland.com/cricketlodge

LOGAN

Inn at Cedar Falls
21190 State Rt 374 43138
740-385-7489 Fax: 740-385-0820
800-65-FALLS
Ellen Grinsfelder
Rooms closed on X-mas

85-245-BB
19 rooms, 19 pb
Visa, MC, *Rated*, •
C-ltd/S-no/P-no/H-yes

Full breakfast
Lunch & dinner available (fee)
Restaurant, bar service, sitting room, library, Call for winter rates

1840s log cabin houses-open kitchen. Gourmet meals prepared from inn's organic garden. Antique furnished rooms (9), log cabins (6), cottages with whirlpool tubs (4). Three cabins with whirlpool tubs. innatcedarfalls@hockinghills.com http://www.innatcedarfalls.com

MARIETTA

The Buckley House B&B
332 Front St 45750
740-373-3080 Fax: 740-373-8000
888-282-5540
Alf & Dell Nicholas
All year

80-90-BB
3 rooms, 3 pb
Visa, MC, *Rated*
C-ltd/S-no/P-no/H-no

Full breakfast
Sitting room, library, Jacuzzi, suites, fireplace, cable TV, accom. bus. tr.

Unwind in the spa, lounge on the deck overlooking the southern style garden, fish pond and gazebo. dnicholas@wscc.edu

MARYSVILLE

Brodrick House B&B
275 W Fifth St 43040
937-644-9797 Fax: 937-644-3242
877-644-9797
Harold and Bonnie Green
All year

89-99-BB
4 rooms, 4 pb
Visa, MC, AmEx, *Rated*, •
C-ltd/S-ltd/P-no/H-no

Continental breakfast
Tea, freshly baked snacks
Freshly baked continental-style goods, fireplace, cable TV, media room

The Victorian, turn-of-the-century home in downtown Marysville, offers all of the privacy and hospitality of a small town, with all of the luxuries of a big city.
brodrick@midohio.net http://www.brodrickhouse.com

MILLERSBURG

Fields of Home Guest House
7278 CR 201 44654
330-674-7152
Mervin & Ruth Yoder
All year

65-155-BB
5 rooms, 5 pb
Visa, MC, Disc, *Rated*
C-yes/S-no/P-no/H-ltd
German

Continental breakfast
Snacks, complimentary sodas
Suites, fireplaces, accommodate business travelers

Our log cabin B&B invites you to relax and enjoy the peace and quiet of rural Amish Country. Enjoy perennial gardens, fish pond and paddle boat.
http://www.bbonline.com/oh/fieldsofhome

MOUNT VERNON

Chaney Manor Inn
7864 Newark Rd 43050
740-392-2304
Freda & Norman Chaney
all year

100-BB
2 rooms
Visa, MC, Disc, •
C-ltd/S-no/P-no/H-no
French, German

Full breakfast
Gourmet Dinners, afternoon tea on request, snacks
Music Room, library, Jacuzzi, Game Room, Gift Shop

One of the most unusual, romantic, historic Inns in Ohio. Huge suites, gourmet meals, Roman Jacuzzi room, gift shop, located on six acres with gardens, pond, covered dock and bridge. chaney@ecr.net http://www.placestostay.com

NAPOLEON

The Augusta Rose
345 W Main St 43545
419-592-5852 Fax: 419-592-7279
877-590-1960
Ed & Mary Hoeffel
All year

65-85-BB
4 rooms, 4 pb
Visa, MC, AmEx
C-yes/S-no/P-no/H-no

Full breakfast
2 sitting rooms–1 with TV, recreational assistance

Stately Victorian, with wrap-around porch located one block from scenic Maumee River. Tranquil small town. Wonderful antique shops.
augrose@bright.net http://www.augustarose.com

NEW CONCORD

Friendship House
62 West Main St 43762
740-826-7397 877-968-5501
Dan & Diane Troendly
All year

75-85-BB
5 rooms, 5 pb
Visa, MC, *Rated*
C-ltd/S-no/P-no/H-no

Continental plus breakfast
Snacks
Sitting room, cable TV, accommodate business travelers

Relax in the comfort of our 1830's landmark home, lovingly furnished with antiques. We can recommend a favorite museum or restaurant.
dtroendly@msn.com http://www.bedandbreakfastohio.com

NEW PLYMOUTH

Ravenwood Castle
65666 Bethel Rd 45654
740-596-2606 Fax: 740-596-5818
800-477-1541
Sue & Jim Maxwell
All year

95-185-BB
16 rooms, 16 pb
Visa, MC, Disc, *Rated*, •
C-yes/S-no/P-no/H-yes

Full breakfast
Lunch & dinner available
Afternoon tea, snacks, suites, fireplaces, Jacuzzis, library

Re-creation of a 12th century Medieval Castle with two "villages" of cottages, shops, tearoom, etc. Many special "Medieval" or "British" events.
ravenwood@ohiohills.com http://www.Ravenwoodcastle.com

OBERLIN

Ivy Tree Inn & Garden
195 S Professor St 44074
440-774-4510
Ron Kelly & Steve Coughlin
All year

79-109-BB
3 rooms, 3 pb
Visa, MC
C-ltd/S-no/P-no/H-no

Full breakfast
Afternoon tea
Sitting room, cable TV, garden tours, small meetings

1860's Colonial Revival; professionally landscaped gardens; Lorain County "Beautiful Award"; scenic town/campus views, walk to Oberlin College.
komonr@hotmail.com http://innsite.com/inns/A031258.html

PAINESVILLE

Riders 1812 Inn 792 Mentor Ave 44077 440-942-2742 Fax: 440-350-9385 Elaine, Courtney & Gary All year	75-101-BB 12 rooms, 7 pb Most CC, *Rated*, • C-yes/P-ltd	Full breakfast

We've redecorated our rooms and change our restaurant menu seasonally.
ridersinn@ncweb.com http://www.ridersinn.com

PORT CLINTON

Scenic Rock Ledge Inn & Cabins 2772 E Sand Rd 43452 419-734-3265 877-994-ROCK Jim Jachimiak All year	69-169-BB 7 rooms, 5 pb Visa, MC, AmEx C-ltd/S-no/P-no/H-no	Deluxe continental breakfast buffet Evening coffee/tea service (Nov–Feb) Lake view pool, hammocks & swings, great lake swimming, sunset view

Welcome to the Scenic Rock Ledge Inn and Cabins. Enjoy the history of a 120 year old Inn, combined with the comforts of a 1995 renovation, and a 2000 ownership change.
scenicinns@hotmail.com http://www.TheScenicRockLedgeInn.com

RIPLEY

The Signal House 234 N Front St 45167 937-392-1640 Fax: 937-392-1640 Vic & Betsy Billingsley May-October	85-BB 2 rooms • C-ltd/S-ltd/P-no/H-no	Full breakfast Snacks, complimentary wine Sitting room, library, fireplaces, cable TV

Share historic 1830's home on the banks of the scenic Ohio River.
signalhouse@webtv.net http://www.thesignalhouse.com

ROCKBRIDGE

Glenlaurel Inn 14940 Mount Olive Rd 43149 740-385-4070 Fax: 740-385-9669 800-809-7378 Michael Daniels All year	115-245-BB 11 rooms, 11 pb S-no/P-no	Full breakfast

Glenlaurel, a Scottish Country Inn with Wooded Cottages and Crofts, has been labeled the "premier romantic getaway in the Midwest." Located one hour southeast of Columbus, Ohio in the Hocking Hills. michael@glenlaurelinn.com http://www.glenlaurelinn.com

SANDUSKY

Wagner's 1844 Inn 230 E Washington St 44870 419-626-1726 Fax: 419-626-0002 Barbara Wagner All year	70-100-BB 3 rooms, 3 pb Visa, MC, *Rated* S-no/P-yes/H-ltd	Continental plus breakfast Complimentary wine, chocolates Billiard room with TV, air-conditioning, weddings, receptions

Elegantly restored Victorian home. Listed on National Register of Historic Places. Near Lake Erie attractions. wagnersinn@sanduskyohio.com http://www.lrbcg.com/wagnersinn

SHEFFIELD LAKE

Lake Breeze Inn 4233 Lake Rd 44054 440-949-2545 Mary Fran & Roger Urban All year	BB C-yes/S-ltd	Full breakfast

Lake Breeze Inn is a charming, new, stone front, contemporary Bed & Breakfast nestled in a manicured, park-like setting with endless views of Lake Erie. lakebreeze@core.com

TIFFIN

Zelkova Country Manor
2348 S County Rd #19 44883
419-447-4043 Fax: 419-447-6473
Michael Pinkston
All year

75-150-BB
8 rooms, 8 pb
Most CC
C-yes/P-no/H-yes

Full English breakfast
Gourmet dinner, afternoon tea, Manor Reception
Rooms have TVs, phones, CD players

Our Zelkova tree-lined drive welcomes you to a world of country elegance and manor life. The manor rests on 27 acres of sprawling green lawns, country gardens, lush woodland and wetlands. Zelkova@BPSom.com http://www.zelkovacountrymanor.com

WAKEMAN

Melrose Farm
727 Vesta Rd 44889
419-929-1867 877-929-1867
Eleanor & Abe Klassen
All year

85-100-BB
3 rooms, 3 pb
Visa, MC, AmEx
C-yes/S-no/P-no/H-no
German

Full breakfast
Afternoon tea, snacks
Sitting room, library, tennis court, suites, fireplaces

Peaceful country retreat. Tennis court, stocked pond, perennial gardens at an 1867 Ohio farmhouse inn. Full gourmet breakfast.
melrose@accnorwalk.com http://www.melrosefarmbb.com

WEST UNION

Murphin Ridge Inn
750 Murphin Ridge Rd 45693
937-544-2263 877-687-7446
Sherry & Darryl McKenney
All year

100-195-BB
10 rooms, 10 pb
C-yes/S-no/P-no

Country breakfast
Homebrewed tea, homemade muffins & cookies

Murphin Ridge Inn, a perfect spot for pleasure and relaxation, is nestled in Southwestern Ohio's Amish country. murphinn@bright.net http://www.murphinridgeinn.com

WILMINGTON

The Lark's Nest at Caesar's Creek
619 Ward Rd 45177
937-382-4788
Carla & Colin Stimpert
All year

75-105-BB
3 rooms, 3 pb
C-yes/S-no/P-no

Full breakfast
Living room, conference room, TV/VCR, training & workout facilities

Travel down a country lane, kick off your shoes, hang up your hat & sit back & enjoy. Great for bird watching, nature lovers & book readers. The "Best" Place to stay for the Ohio Renaissance Fest. http://www.ohiobba.com/larksnest.htm

YOUNGSTOWN (REGION)

Inn At The Green
500 S Main St, *Poland* 44514
330-757-4688
Ginny & Steve Meloy
All year

70-BB
5 rooms, 4 pb
Visa, MC, *Rated*, •
C-ltd/S-no/P-no/H-no

Continental plus breakfast
Complimentary wine
Oriental rugs, deck, patio, antiques, garden, sitting room, fireplaces

Authentically restored Victorian townhouse in preserved Western Reserve Village near Youngstown. Convenient to Turnpike and I-80. http://www.acountryvillage.com/innatgreen

ZOAR

Cowger House
PO Box 527
197 4th St 44697
330-874-3542 Fax: 330-874-4172
800-874-3542
Ed & Mary Cowger
All year

70-150-BB
9 rooms, 9 pb
Rated
C-ltd/S-yes/P-no/H-no

Full country breakfast
Lunch & dinner by RSVP
Entertainment, honeymoon suite with fireplace & Jacuzzi

A little bit of Williamsburg. 1817 log cabin with 2-acre flower garden maintained by the Ohio Historic Society. cowgerhous@aol.com http://www.zoarvillage.com

Oklahoma

ARDMORE

St. Agnes Inn
118 E Street SW 73401
580-223-5679
Fax: 580-223-4668
Maxine Huggins
All year

75-110-BB
5 rooms, 5 pb
Most CC, *Rated*
C-ltd/S-no/P-no/H-no

Full breakfast
Snacks
Sitting room, library, suites, fireplaces, cable TV, accom. bus. travelers

Historic home beautifully decorated offering comfort and attentive innkeepers! Wake to delicious breakfast served in elegant style. Enjoy the beautiful garden from the deck!
stagnes@ardmore.com http://www.bbonline.com/ok/stagnes

BETHANY

Rosewood
7000 NW 39th St 73008
405-787-3057
Fax: 405-787-3057
888-786-3057
Val & Dana Owens
All year

89-149-BB
4 rooms, 4 pb
Most CC
C-yes/S-no/P-no/H-no

Rosewood Inn is a fine Bed and Breakfast in Bethany, Oklahoma located just one block south of old Route 66. We welcome you to central Oklahoma and will strive to make your stay memorable. innkeeper@rosewoodinnbb.com http://www.rosewoodinnbb.com

NORMAN

Montford Inn
322 W Tonhawa 73069
405-321-2200
Fax: 405-321-8347
800-321-8969
Phyllis, Ron & William Murray
All year

90-200-BB
16 rooms, 16 pb
Most CC, *Rated*, •
C-yes/S-no/P-no/H-yes

Full breakfast
Afternoon tea, wine
Sitting room, library, fireplaces in rooms, 2 outdoor/private hot tubs

Urban 16-room inn with 6 cottage suites. Restaurants, shops, parks, University of Oklahoma nearby. Off-street parking.
innkeeper@montfordinn.com http://www.montfordinn.com/

SULPHUR

Sulphur Springs Inn
1102 W Lindsay 73086
580-622-5930
877-622-5930
All year

Rated

Our historic Inn, sits at the edge of the old Platt National Park: allowing our guests easy access to a beautiful sanctuary of healing waters & wildlife.
innkeeper@sulphurspringsinn.com http://www.sulphurspringsinn.com

TULSA

McBirney Mansion B&B
1414 S Galveston 74127
918-585-3234
Fax: 918-585-9377
Kathy Collins & Renita Shofner
All year

119-225-BB
8 rooms, 8 pb
Most CC, *Rated*, •
C-ltd/S-no/P-no

Full breakfast
Afternoon tea, snacks, complimentary wine
Sitting room, library, fireplaces, cable TV

One of Tulsa's most treasured historic dwellings, each luxury bedroom boasts spectacular views and its own unique decor. http://www.mcbirneymansion.com

WILBURTON

Windsong Inn 100 W Cedar 74578 918-465-5174 Gayle & Monte Carnahan All year	69-99-BB 6 rooms, 6 pb • C-ltd/S-no/P-no/H-no	Full breakfast Snacks, complimentary wine Sitting room, fireplaces, cable TV, accom. bus. travelers

A 1911 Arts and Crafts private house situated on a hill top. Filled with antiques. New section includes a huge deck and 3 new rooms on a higher level with another deck.
windsonginn@aol.com http://www.bedandbreakfast.com

Oregon

ASHLAND

Anne Hathaway's Cottage 586 E Main St 97520 541-488-1050 Fax: 541-482-1969 800-643-4434 David & Deedie Runkel All year	105-180-BB 6 rooms, 6 pb Visa, MC C-ltd/S-no/P-ltd/H-no	Full breakfast Afternoon tea, snacks Sitting room, library, suites, front porch, accommodate business travelers

Art and antique-filled 1908 boarding house conveniently located just four blocks to Shakespeare festival theatres in the Ashland business district.
innkeeper@ashlandbandb.com http://www.ashlandbandb.com

Ashland Creek Inn 70 Water St 97520 541-482-3315 Fax: 541-482-1092 Graham, George & Carolyn Sheldon All year	175-250-BB 7 rooms, 7 pb Visa C-ltd/P-no/H-no	Multi-course gourmet breakfasts Luxury suites in a shaded, creekside park, private entrance, kitchen, deck

Seven Luxury Suites in a cool, shaded private park on Ashland Creek, 3 blocks from Shakespearean theaters. Gourmet breakfast is served in our garden.
reservations@ashlandcreekinn.com http://www.ashlandcreekinn.com

Cadbury's Cottage PO Box 3373 353 Hargadine St 97520 541-488-5970 Jennifer Nidalmia All year	180-240-EP 3 rooms, 2 pb C-yes/S-no/P-no/H-no	Sitting room, library, deck & grill, washer, dryer, kitchen

Newly updated Victorian 3 bedroom, 2 bath home on quiet street overlooking downtown Ashland. Only 1 block from theatre, shops & restaurants.
http://www.ashland-oregon.com

Country Willows B&B Inn 1313 Clay St 97520 541-488-1590 Fax: 541-488-1611 800-WILLOWS Dan Durant All year	110-225-BB 9 rooms, 9 pb Most CC, *Rated*, • C-ltd/S-ltd/P-no/H-yes	Full breakfast Sitting room, hot tubs, library, outdoor Jacuzzi, heated swimming pool

Romantic, peaceful, rural setting. 1896 farmhouse, 5 acres. Rooms in house, cottage & barn with mountain views. willows@willowsinn.com http://www.willowsinn.com

ASHLAND

Grapevine Inn
486 Siskiyou Blvd 97520
541-482-7944 Fax: 541-482-0389
800-500-8463
Susan Yarne
All year

85-150-BB
3 rooms, 3 pb
Visa, MC, *Rated*, •
C-ltd/S-no/P-no/H-no

Full breakfast
Afternoon refreshments
firelace in two rooms, personal refrigerators

Discover Ashland hospitality and charm at the GrapeVine Inn, a romantic Bed & Breakfast built in 1909. An intimate inn with lovely gardens, walking distance to theaters, restaurants and shopping. vinemail@mind.net http://www.mind.net/grapevineinn

---

Lithia Springs Inn
2165 W Jackson Rd 97520
541-482-7128 Fax: 541-488-1645
800-482-7128
Duane Smith
all year

135-295-BB
26 rooms, 26 pb
Most CC, *Rated*, •
C-ltd/S-no/P-no/H-yes

Full Gourmet Buffet Breakfast
Wine and cheese from 3pm to 6pm. Sweets at 6pm.
Hot springs fed whirlpools in privacy of the cottages, suites, and rooms. I

Country-setting hideaway, 2 miles from Ashland's theatres and fine dining. Enjoy a hot springs-fed whirlpool in the peace and privacy of your own cottage, suite, or room.
lithia@ashlandinn.com http://www.ashlandinn.com

Neil Creek House
341 Mowetza Dr 97520
541-482-6443 Fax: 541-482-1074
800-460-7860
Paul & Gayle Negro
All year

90-120-BB
2 rooms, 2 pb
Rated
C-ltd/S-no/P-no/H-no

Full breakfast
Library, swimming pool, suites, fireplace

Enjoy the ambiance of this country hideaway with all the luxury of a fine hotel. Breakfast is served al fresco at this intimate, pristine setting.
bnb@neilcreek.com http://www.neilcreekhousebnb.com

ASTORIA

Benjamin Young Inn
3652 Duane St 97103
503-325-6172 800-201-1286
Carolyn & Ken Hammer
All year

85-140-BB
5 rooms, 5 pb
Most CC, •
C-ltd/S-no/P-no/H-ltd

Afternoon tea, snacks
Sitting room, accom. bus. travelers

Elegant but relaxed ambiance in this 1888 Victorian listed in the National Register. Columbia River views from all rooms.
benjamin@benjaminyounginn.com http://www.benjaminyounginn.com

---

Franklin St. Station
1140 Franklin 97103
503-325-4314 Fax: 801-681-5641
800-448-1098
Becky & Sharon
All year

75-135-BB
6 rooms, 5 pb
Most CC, *Rated*
C-yes/S-no/P-no/H-no

Full breakfast
Fresh fruit for your enjoyment
A warm welcome awaits you, breakfast at 3 settings.

Come enjoy this ornate, lovely home on the Oregon Coast in Astoria.
franklinststationbb@yahoo.com http://www.franklin-st-station-bb.com

---

Grandview
1574 Grand Ave 97103
503-325-5555 Fax: 707-982-8790
800-488-3250
Charleen Maxwell
All year

75-101-BB
9 rooms, 7 pb
Most CC, *Rated*, •
C-ltd

Full breakfast
Snacks
Sitting room, canopy beds, books, games, binoculars, liquor not permitted

Light, airy, cheerful Victorian close to superb Maritime Museum, Lightship, churches, golf, clam-digging, fishing, beaches and rivers.
grandviewbedandbreakfast@usa.net http://www.pacifier.com/~grndview

ASTORIA

Rose River Inn
1510 Franklin Ave 97103
503-325-7175 Fax: 503-325-7188
888-876-0028
Kati Tuominen
All year

85-130-BB
4 rooms, 4 pb
Visa, MC, Disc
C-ltd/S-no/P-ltd/H-no
Finnish, Swedish, German

Full breakfast
Afternoon coffee, tea & snack
Sitting room, suites, fireplaces, cable TV, sauna, massage

Rose River Inn is a beautiful 1912 home in historic Astoria, Oregon, the oldest American city west of the Mississippi. Specialties of the inn are sauna, relaxing massage, and Finnish pastries. jaska@pacifier.com http://www.roseriverinn.com

BANDON

Beach Street
PO Box 217
200 Beach Street 97411
541-347-5124 888-335-1076
Sharon & Karlena
All year

125-180-BB
6 rooms, 6 pb
Visa, MC, Disc, *Rated*
C-ltd/S-no/P-no/H-ltd

Sumptuous breakfast
We address all dietary issues of our guests.
Rooms with private decks,two person spa tubs,pillow top beds.Some fireplace.

Tranquil retreat welcomes. Oceanview rooms with private decks allow observation of the moods of the Pacific Whale watch. Walk unspoiled beaches; golf Bandon or Pacific Dunes. Relax, romance, recharge. Sfishaut@adelphia.net http://www.beach-street.com

---

Lighthouse
PO Box 24
650 Jetty Rd SW 97411
541-347-9316
Shirley Ann Chalupa
All year

115-200-BB
5 rooms, 5 pb
Visa, MC, *Rated*
C-ltd/S-no/P-no/H-no

Full breakfast
Complimentary teas, hot cocoa
Sitting room, bicycles, hot tub in one room, on the beach

Located on the beach across from historic lighthouse. Panoramic views, quiet location. Walk to fine restaurants. 2 rooms with whirlpool and fireplace.
lthousbb@harborside.com http://www.lighthouselodging.com

Sea Star Guesthouse
375 2nd St
370 1st St 97411
541-347-9632 Fax: 541-347-8329
Misty Berry
All year

45-110-EP
4 rooms, 4 pb
Most CC
C-yes/S-no/P-no/H-no

Comp. tea/coffee in room
Restaurant, deck, mini-kitchen, fireplace, cable TV, harbor and river view

Coastal getaway on harbor in "Oldtown" with restaurant. Romantic retreat with European flair. seastarban@earthlink.net http://www.seastarbandon.com

BEND

Lara House
640 NW Congress 97701
541-388-4064 Fax: 541-388-4064
800-766-4064
Doug & Bobbye Boger
All year

95-150-BB
5 rooms, 5 pb
Visa, MC, *Rated*, •
C-yes/S-ltd/P-no/H-no

Full breakfast
Snacks
Sitting room w/fireplace, sun room, flower gardens, bicycles, hot tub

A magnificent 1910 historical home overlooking Drake Park and Sechutes River.
larahousebnb@aol.com http://www.larahouse.com

The Sather House
7 NW Tumalo Ave 97701
541-388-1065 Fax: 541-330-0591
888-388-1065
Robbie Giamboi
All year

88-126-BB
4 rooms, 4 pb
Most CC, *Rated*, •
C-no/S-ltd/P-no

Full breakfast
Cable TV

This carefully restored stately craftsman style Bed and Breakfast home is located in a neighborhood of older historical homes. It is featured on the cover of The Heritage Walk Tour Guide. satherhouse@aol.com http://www.satherhouse.com

BROOKINGS

Chetco River Inn
21202 High Prairie Rd 97415
541-670-1645 800-327-2688
Sandra Brugger
Exc. Thanksgiving & Xmas

115-135-BB
6 rooms, 6 pb
Visa, MC, *Rated*, •
C-ltd/S-ltd/P-no/H-no

Full breakfast
Lunch, dinner with res.
Beverages & cookies, sitting room, library, games, hiking, river

Relax in the peaceful seclusion of our private 35-acre forest, bordered on 3 sides by the Chetco River. chetcoriverinn@chetcoriverinn.com http://www.chetcoriverinn.com

---

Pacific View
18814 Montbretia Ln 97415
541-469-6837 800-461-4830
Mac & Ursula Mackey
All year

85-90-BB
1 rooms, 1 pb
Visa, MC
S-no/P-no/H-no
German

Full breakfast
Snacks, complimentary wine
Sitting room, suite, fireplace

One suite with beautiful ocean view, gourmet breakfast served at your convenience in suite. cmackey@wave.net http://www.pacificviewbb.com

BURNS (REGION)

Blue Bucket at 3E Ranch
PO Box 225
82543 Ahmann Ranch Rd, *Drewsey* 97904
541-493-2375 Fax: 541-493-2528
Judy & John Ahmann
All year

65-85-BB
4 rooms, 2 pb
•
C-ltd/S-no/P-ltd/H-yes
Spanish

Full breakfast
Lunch, dinner, afternoon tea, snacks
Sitting room, library, wood stoves

Historic working cattle ranch in Oregon's Outback; enjoy hiking, wildlife, star-gazing; surrounded by lush meadows, sagebrush, mesas and pine-covered mountains.
http://www.moriah.com/bluebucket

COOS BAY

Old Tower House
476 Newmark Ave 97420
541-888-6058 Fax: 541-888-6058
Thomas & Stephanie Kramer
All year

75-145-BB
5 rooms, 5 pb
Visa, MC, •
C-ltd/S-no/P-no/H-no

Full breakfast
Sitting room, cable TV in the 2 outer cottages

Historic home in Coos Bay filled with history, antiques, and ambiance. Gourmet breakfasts served in the main house. oldtowerhouse@yahoo.com http://www.oldtowerhouse.com

CORVALLIS

Harrison House
2310 NW Harrison Blvd 97330
541-752-6248 Fax: 541-754-1353
800-233-6248
Charlie & Maria Tomlinson
All year

100-110-BB
4 rooms, 4 pb
Most CC, *Rated*, •
C-ltd/S-no/P-no/H-no
French, German

Full breakfast
Afternoon tea, snacks, wine, beer/cold soda
Sitting room, cable TV, telephones, welcome gifts

Harrison House is a lovely restored Dutch Colonial style historic home. Elegant furnishings & delicious full breakfast.
stay@corvallis-lodging.com http://www.corvallis-lodging.com

DAYTON

Wine Country Farm
6855 Breyman Orchards Rd 97114
503-864-3446 Fax: 503-864-3109
800-261-3446
Joan Davenport
All year

95-135-BB
7 rooms, 7 pb
Visa, MC, •
C-ltd/S-no/P-no/H-yes
Spanish

Full breakfast
Snacks, complimentary wine
Sitting room, library, bikes, Jacuzzi, suites, fireplaces, movie library

Spectacular views from a historic French style, eclectic farmhouse surrounded by its own vineyards. Wonderful country farm breakfast. Complimentary wine from our own tasting room. innkeeper@winecountryfarm.com http://www.winecountryfarm.com

EUGENE

Campbell House Inn 252 Pearl St 97401 541-343-1119 Fax: 541-343-2258 800-264-2519 Myra Plant All year	82-345-BB 18 rooms, 18 pb Most CC, *Rated*, • C-yes/S-no/P-no/H-yes	Full breakfast Lunch & dinner arranged Jetted tubs, beer & wine for sale, sitting room, library

Built in 1892 and restored in the tradition of a small European hotel. "Classic elegance, exquisite decor and impeccable service."

campbellhouse@campbellhouse.com http://www.campbellhouse.com/

Enchanted Country Inn 29195 Gimpl Hill Rd 97402 541-465-1869 Fax: 877-465-1507 Leslie Conway All year	75-125-BB 4 rooms, 3 pb Visa, MC, AmEx, *Rated*, • C-ltd/S-ltd/P-ltd/H-no	Full gourmet breakfast Afternoon tea, snacks, compl. wine, dinner avail. Sitting room, fireplaces, cable TV, acccom. bus. travelers

Nestled in a quiet forest just minutes from downtown. Three suites and a cozy cottage. Library with fireplace. Serenity surrounds you. Decks, gardens and gazebo.

http://www.enchantedcountryinn.com

The Oval Door 988 Lawrence St 97401 541-683-3160 Fax: 541-485-0260 800-882-3160 Nicole Wergeland & Melissa Coray All year	75-195-BB 5 rooms, 5 pb Visa, MC, AmEx, *Rated*, • C-ltd/S-no/P-no/H-no	Full breakfast Tea, soft drinks, cookies Sitting room, library, Jacuzzi, sitting room, wrap-around porch

Offering warm hospitality in the heart of Eugene. Private baths, bountiful breakfast, home-baked treats, walk to shops and restaurants. Private phone lines and TV/VCR in every room. ovaldoor@ovaldoor.com http://www.ovaldoor.com

Pookie's on College Hill 2013 Charnelton St 97405 541-343-0383 Fax: 541-431-0967 800-558-0383 Pookie & Doug Walling All year	75-115-BB 3 rooms, 2 pb Visa, MC, *Rated* C-ltd/S-ltd/P-no/H-no	Full breakfast Snacks Sitting room, library, shade trees, antiques, gas BBQ in back

Built in 1918, located in quiet, older neighborhood. Antique decor. Great breakfasts. Close to downtown and University of Oregon campus.

pookiesbandb@aol.com http://www.pookiesbandblodging.com

The Secret Garden Inn 1910 University St 97403 541-484-6755 Fax: 541-431-1699 888-484-6755 Becky Drobac All year	105-235-BB 10 rooms, 10 pb Most CC, *Rated*, • C-yes/S-no/P-no/H-yes Spanish	Full breakfast Other meals by reservation Sitting room, library, suites, fireplaces, cable TV, accom.bus.travel

Near University, this old world inn has large, elegant public rooms, ten strikingly unique and luxurious guest rooms furnished with art, antiques, and unusually comfortable beds.

gardenbb@att.net http://www.secretgardenbbinn.com

EUGENE (REGION)

McKenzie View—A Riverside B&B 34922 McKenzie View Dr., *Springfield* 97478 541-726-3887 Fax: 541-726-6968 888-625-8439 Roberta & Scott Bolling	75-250-BB 4 rooms, 4 pb Most CC, *Rated*, • C-ltd/S-no/P-no/H-no All year	Full breakfast Snacks Sitting room, tennis court, suites, fireplaces, cable TV, accom. bus. trav.

Large riverside home and gardens on 6 acres. Deluxe comfort inside and out. Memorable breakfasts. Country seclusion 15 minutes from town.

mckenzieview@worldnet.att.net http://www.mckenzie-view.com

FLORENCE

Blue Heron Inn
PO Box 1122
6536 Highway 126 97439
541-997-4091 800-997-7780
Maurice Souza
All year

55-125-BB
5 rooms, 5 pb
Rated

Full breakfast

Enjoy the ambiance of this charming bed & breakfast on the Siuslaw River just 5 minutes from the center of historic Florence. http://www.blue-heroninn.com

GARIBALDI

Pelican's Perch B&B
PO Box 543
114 E Cypress Ave 97118
503-322-3633
Thomas and Marielle Ham
All year

108-128
4 rooms, 4 pb
C-ltd/S-no

We love our location because Garibaldi, Oregon has remained true to its fishing village roots. The pace of life recalls a more relaxed time.
thomas@pelicansperchlodge.com http://www.pelicansperchlodge.com

GOLD BEACH

Endicott Gardens
95768 Jerry's Flat Rd 97444
541-247-6513
Fax: 541-247-6513
Patrick & Beverly Endicott
All year

60-70-BB
4 rooms, 4 pb

Full or continental breakfast

Spectacular grounds with several fruit trees, flowers, shrubs and exotic plants. The home features four guestrooms in a separate wing, each with private bath.
http://www.endicottgardens.com

GRANTS PASS

Flery Manor
2000 Jumpoff Joe Cr Rd 97526
541-476-3591 Fax: 541-471-2303
Marla & John Vidrinskas
All year

85-150-BB
5 rooms, 4 pb
Visa, MC, *Rated*, •
C-ltd/S-no/P-no/H-no
Lithuanian, Russian

Full 3 course gourmet breakfast
Afternoon tea, snacks, wine
Sitting room, library, frplc., piano, gazebo with waterfall, stream, pond

"Elegant, Romantic, Secluded." Suites with fireplace, Jacuzzi, and private balcony. Library, parlor with piano, huge balcony and extraordinary views. Ponds, waterfall, streams, and gazebo. flery@flerymanor.com http://www.flerymanor.com

---

The Ivy House
139 SW I St 97526
541-474-7363
All year

60-75-BB
5 rooms, 1 pb
Visa, MC, Disc
C-yes/S-no/P-ltd/H-no

Full English Breakfast
Tea & biscuits are offered in bed prior to breakfast upon request

Step down from the busy street into the quiet green lawn and rose edged path of The Ivy House and you immediately feel that you've entered a quieter, more genteel era.

Lawnridge House
1304 NW Lawnridge 97526
541-476-8518
B. H. Head
All year

85-130-BB
4 rooms, 2 pb
Rated, •
C-yes/S-no
Spanish, French

Full breakfast
Room refrig w/beverages
Alfresco dining, secluded deck & porch, filled bookshelves, VCR

1909 Craftsman (restored) in quiet, wooded, in-town location convenient to shopping, river and freeway/highway. lawnhouse@yahoo.com

GRANTS PASS

Weasku Inn
5560 Rogue River Hwy 97527
541-471-8000 Fax: 541-471-7038
800-4-WEASKU
Dave Hagert
All year

110-295-BB
17 rooms, 17 pb
Visa, MC, AmEx,
Rated, •
C-yes/S-no/P-no/H-yes

Continental plus breakfast
Evening wine & cheese reception, seasonal BBQ
Sitting room, fireplaces, cable TV, conference facility & outdoor deck

A cozy, riverfront inn, built around a colorful historical fishing lodge. Decorated with locally hand-crafted furniture, one of a kind lamps, hand-quilted bed covers, chairs and fishing memorabilia. info@weasku.com http://www.weasku.com

HOOD RIVER

Columbia Gorge Hotel
4000 Westcliff Dr 97031
541-386-5566 Fax: 541-387-5414
800-345-1921
Karl Wells
All year

169-299-BB
40 rooms, 40 pb
Most CC, •
C-ltd/S-no/P-ltd/H-ltd
Spanish, French, German

World Famous Farm Breakfast
Lunch, dinner, full service lounge, room service
Champagne massage therapists on site

On acres of gardens at the top of a 208' waterfall, "Oregon's finest Country Inn" offers a rare blend of comfort, service, and award-winning cuisine. Voted "Best Romantic Hotel in the Nation." cghotel@gorge.net http://www.ColumbiaGorgeHotel.com

KLAMATH FALLS

Crystalwood Lodge
PO Box 1117
38625 Westside Rd 97601
541-381-2322 Fax: 541-381-2328
866-381-2322
Elizabeth Parrish &
Peggy O'Neal All year

105-275-MAP
7 rooms, 7 pb
Visa, MC, AmEx, •
C-yes/S-no/P-yes/H-no

Continental plus breakfast
Excellent wines & micro-brews with hors d'ouvres
Great room, deck, vista porch, snowshoes, boats/canoes, meadows/woods/ponds

Pet-friendly Crystalwood Lodge features informal excellence, world-class dining, and superb wines and micro-brews ... the place to base your all-seasons adventures in the Southern Oregon Cascades. k9crusr@earthlink.net http://www.crystalwoodlodge.com

LA GRANDE

Stang Manor Inn
1612 Walnut Ave 97850
541-963-2400 1-888-286-9463
Ron & Carolyn Jensen
All year

98-115-BB
4 rooms, 4 pb
Visa, MC, Disc, *Rated*
C-ltd/S-no/P-no/H-no

Full breakfast
Gardens, fireplaces, oodles of books, flowers in rooms

Capturing the romance and elegance of a former era, Stang Manor is a lovingly preserved Georgian Colonial mansion, which beckons even the casual traveler to bask in its comfort and hospitality. innkeeper@stangmanor.com http://www.stangmanor.com

LINCOLN CITY

Brey House Oceanview Inn
3725 NW Keel Ave 97367
541-994-7123 Fax: 541-994-5941
Milt & Shirley Brey
All year

80-145-BB
4 rooms, 4 pb
Visa, MC, Disc, *Rated*, •
C-yes/S-ltd/P-no/H-no

Full breakfast
Sitting room, hot tub, ocean view deck, landscaped yard

The ocean awaits you just across the street. We are located within the city limits of Lincoln City. breysinn@webtv.net http://www.breyhouse.com

---

O'Dysius Hotel
120 NW Inlet Ct 97367
541-994-4121 Fax: 541-994-8160
800-869-8069
Todd Taylor
All year

149-299-BB
30 rooms, 30 pb
Visa, MC, AmEx,
Rated, •
C-ltd/S-no/P-ltd/H-yes

European Continental Breakfast
Coffee, fruit in lobby, evening wine get-together
Library, fireplace lounge, covered parking, elevators, interior corridors

A place where you can expect the amenities and services that only a 4-diamond hotel can provide. Romantically nostalgic overlooking the Pacific ocean. It's all here for you. Come stay, enjoy, relax. toddandcharli@hotmail.com http://www.odysius.com

LINCOLN CITY

Pacific Rest
1611 Northeast 11th St 97367
541-994-2337 888-405-7378
R. & J. Waetjen, B. Beard
All year

100-110-BB
2 rooms, 2 pb
C-yes/S-no/P-no/H-yes

Full gourmet breakfast
Snacks, coffee, tea
Family friendly facility, suites for families, books. . .old and new

Newer home especially designed with the "B&B" guest in mind. Relaxed, restful atmosphere, just 4 blocks to beach. . .a special place to find respite for the body, soul and spirit.
jwaetjen@wcn.net http://pacificrestbb.hypermart.net/

MCMINNVILLE

Mattey House
10221 NE Mattey Ln 97128
503-434-5058 Fax: 503-434-6667
Jack & Denise Seed
All year

90-110-BB
4 rooms, 4 pb
Rated

Full breakfast

In the heart of wine country, this 1892 Queen Anne Victorian, nestled behind its vineyard, is a perfect country retreat. mattey@matteyhouse.com http://www.matteyhouse.com

---

Steiger Haus
360 SE Wilson St 97128
503-472-0821 Fax: 503-472-0100
888-220-1142
Dale & Susan DeRette
All year

70-130-BB
5 rooms, 5 pb
Rated

Full breakfast

In the heart of Oregon Wine Country. Unique architecture in a park-like town setting. Close to gourmet restaurants. Charm and hospitality plus!
steigerhaus@onlinemac.com http://www.steigerhaus.com

MEDFORD

Waverly Cottages
305 N. Grape Street 97501
541-779-4716 Fax: 541-732-1718
David Fisse All year

60-80-EP
2 rooms, 2 pb
Most CC, *Rated*, •
C-yes/S-no/P-ltd/H-ltd

Sitting room, suites, Jacuzzi, cable TV, accomodate business travelers

Located in historic district just North of downtown.
dfisse@aaaabb.com http://www.aaaabb.com/waverly/

MONMOUTH

Howell House
17950 Hwy 22
212 N Knox Street 97361
503-838-2085 866-403-6951
Clint & Sandra Boylan

70-110-BB
5 rooms, 3 pb
Visa, MC, Disc
C-yes/S-no/P-ltd/H-no
All year

Full breakfast
Gazebo, Hot Tub

This charming 3 story Queen Anne, built by an Oregon Trail pioneer family, features historic gold-leaf wallpapers and original woodwork throughout.
howellbnb@yahoo.com http://www.howellhousebb.com/

MT. HOOD

Mt. Hood Hamlet
6741 Hwy 35 97041
541-352-3574 Fax: 541-352-7685
800-407-0570
Paul & Diane Romans

105-145-BB
3 rooms, 3 pb
Most CC, •
C-ltd/S-no/P-no/H-ltd
All year

Full breakfast
Complimentary juices/soft drinks
3 guestrooms with private baths, outdoor spa

"Reach out and touch Mt. Hood" from our 18th century New England Colonial style home with modern convenience and amenities. 13 miles rooftop to mountain top, and a world apart from your daily cares.
innkeeper@mthoodhamlet.com http://www.mthoodhamlet.com

MT. HOOD (REGION)

Brightwood Guesthouse
PO Box 189
64725 E Barlow Trail Rd, *Brightwood* 97011
503-622-5783 Fax: 503-622-5783
888-503-5783
Jan Estep All year

113-127-BB
1 rooms, 1 pb
Rated, •
C-ltd/S-ltd/P-no/H-ltd
German

Full gourmet breakfast
Snacks, beverages, occasional comp. wine
Living room, library, bikes, washer & dryer, TV/VCR, games, flowers

Peaceful, private, romantic , forested–mountain house of your own; Japanese water garden; Oriental antiquities; fantastic breakfasts. Everything provided including all the tea in China. brightwoodbnb@hotmail.com http://www.Mounthoodbnb.com

---

Falcon's Crest Inn
PO Box 185
87287 Gov't Camp Loop Hwy, *Government Camp* 97028
503-272-3403 Fax: 503-272-3454
800-624-7384

125-179-BB
5 rooms, 5 pb
Most CC, *Rated*, •
C-ltd/S-no/P-no/H-no
B.J. & Melody Johnson
All year

Full breakfast
Gourmet restaurant
Dinner, VCR, fishing, alcoholic beverages, hot tubs, golf, hiking

Elegance in heart of Mt. Hood National Forest. Conference facilities. Inn special events, movie collection, outdoor recreation, ski packages, Christmas Holiday Specialists.
info@falconscrest.com http://www.falconscrest.com

Old Welches Inn & Cottage
26401 E Welches Rd, *Welches* 97067
503-622-3754 Fax: 503-622-5370
Judi & Ted Mondun

107-175-BB
4 rooms, 2 pb
Most CC, *Rated*, •
C-ltd/S-ltd/P-ltd/H-no
All year

Full breakfast
Afternoon tea
Sitting room with fireplace, custom robes, all rooms w/ beautiful views

Memories are made in this 19th century riverside retreat on 2 acres of lush mountain greenery. This quiet oasis will restore your mind and spirits. Private cottage available with kitchen. Innmthood@cs.com http://www.mounthoodlodging.com

NEWPORT

Oar House
520 SW 2nd St 97365
541-265-9571 800-252-2358
Jan LeBrun
All year

90-150-BB
5 rooms, 5 pb
Visa, MC, *Rated*
C-ltd/S-no/P-no/H-no
Spanish

Full breakfast
Tea, soft drinks, bottled water, nuts, candies
Living room; sitting room—fireplace libraries art music lighthouse tower

Lincoln Country historic landmark built 1900. Renovated, expanded 1993, remodeled yearly. Lighthouse tower with widow's walk panoramic views. Centrally located in historic Nye Beach area of Newport.
oarhouse@newportnet.com http://www.oarhouse-bed-breakfast.com

---

Ocean House, An Oceanfront Inn
4920 NW Woody Way 97365
541-265-6158 800-562-2632
Marie & Bob Garrard
All year

100-225-BB
8 rooms, 8 pb
Most CC, *Rated*
C-ltd/S-no/P-no/H-yes

Full breakfast
Snacks, coffee, tea
All rooms with ocean views & fireplaces, 4 rooms with whirlpool, oceanfront gardens

Near center of coastal activities & fun. Large comfortable home with beautiful surroundings, expanded garden with ocean decks.
garrard@oceanhouse.com http://www.oceanhouse.com

Tyee Lodge Oceanfront
4925 NW Woody Way 97365
541-265-8953 888-553-8933
Mark & Cindy McConnell
All year

105-145-BB
5 rooms, 5 pb
Most CC, *Rated*
C-ltd/S-ltd/P-no/H-no
Spanish, French, German

Full breakfast
Convenience bar
Private trail to beach, sitting room, fireplaces, accom. special diets

Our park-like setting is unequaled on the Oregon Coast. Sit by your window, or by the fire, and watch the waves. All rooms have gas fireplaces.
mcconn@teleport.com http://www.tyeelodge.com

Hostess House, Portland, OR

PENDELTON

Dorie's Inn 203 NW Despain Ave 97801 541-276-1519 Fax: 541-276-7974 877-276-7974 Doris Chryst All year	75-95-BB 4 rooms, 2 pb Visa, MC S-ltd/P-no/H-no German	Full breakfast Afternoon tea, complimentary wine Library, cable TV, pool nearby, accom. bus. travel

Dorie's Inn was built in 1912. The style is an excellent example of the Craftsman Bungalow. On the Historical Register. dorieinn@uci.net
stay@homebythesea.com

PORTLAND

Georgian House 1828 NE Siskiyou 97212 503-281-2250 Fax: 503-281-3301 888-282-2250 Willie Jean & Dick Canning Season Inquire	65-95-BB 4 rooms, 2 pb Visa, MC, *Rated* C-ltd/S-ltd/P-no/H-no	Full breakfast Afternoon tea, restaurant Sitting room, library, tennis court, TV, VCR, phones in rooms

Take a romantic step back to "Olde England." Enjoy gazebo, gardens, tree-lined, historic streets. webmaster@thegeorgianhouse.com http://www.thegeorgianhouse.com

Hostess House 5758 NE Emerson St 97218 503-282-7892 Fax: 503-282-7892 877-860-4600,2 Milli Laughlin All year	67-BB 2 rooms Most CC, *Rated* C-yes/S-ltd/P-no/H-ltd	Full gourmet breakfast Afternoon tea Outstanding hospitality since 1988, sitting rm, fireplace, parklike backyard

An affordable tranquil getaway (since 1988) accented with blond antique Heywood Wakefield furniture, located in modest neighborhood. City close and country quiet. Gourmet breakfasts. hostess@hostesshouse.com http://www.hostesshouse.com

MacMaster House 1041 SW Vista Ave 97205 503-223-7362 Fax: 503-224-8808 800-774-9523 Cyndie Nelson & Krista Hagenbuch All year	85-140-BB 7 rooms, 2 pb Most CC C-ltd/S-no/P-no/H-no	Full breakfast Complimentary popcorn and beverages Spacious living room with fireplace, video and book library

Colonial mansion near Washington Park. Convenient to Rose & Japanese Gardens, cafes, galleries, boutiques, theater and commercial districts.
innkeeper@macmaster.com http://www.macmaster.com

PORTLAND

Portland Guest House
1720 NE 15th Ave 97212
503-282-1402
Susan Gisvold
All year

75-105-BB
7 rooms, 5 pb
Visa, MC, AmEx, *Rated*
C-yes/S-no/P-no

Full breakfast
Complimentary beverages
Room phones, antiques, jogging routes, crtyard, bus & light rail tickets

1890 Victorian in historic Irvington neighborhood. All rooms have phones, antiques, heirloom linens, great beds. Luscious breakfasts. Family suite with 3 beds.
pgh@teleport.com http://www.teleport.com/~pgh

Terwilliger Vista
515 SW Westwood Dr 97201
503-244-0608
Fax: 503-293-8042
888-244-0602
Dick & Jan Vatert
All year

85-145-BB
5 rooms, 5 pb
Visa, MC, *Rated*, •
C-ltd/S-no/P-no/H-ltd

Full or continental breakfast
Complimentary wine
Sitting room, library, suites, fireplaces, cable TV

The B&B is situated on over a ½ acre of gardens, featuring mature trees, manicured lawns, camellias, rhododendron and fruit trees. http://www.terwilligervista.com

ROCKAWAY BEACH

Ocean Locomotion Motel
19130 Alder Ave 97136
503-355-2093
David & Ginger Dixon
All year

48-115-EP
10 rooms, 10 pb
Most CC, •
C-yes/S-ltd/P-ltd/H-no

In-room coffee
Suites, fireplaces, cable TV, crab-cooker, BBQ, picnic/play area, firepit

Just steps from the oceanfront, each unit is unique. Cottage with kitchen and fireplace, or guestroom, all are non-smoking, clean and comfortable, and most have kitchens and ocean views. Canines OK.
alandsyl@pacifier.com http://www.bedandbreakfast.com/bbc/p218412.asp

ROSEBURG (REGION)

Idleyld Park Lodge
PO Box 98
23834 N Umpqua Hwy, *Idleyld Park* 97447
541-496-0088 Fax: 541-496-0088
Jim & Barbara Pruner
All year

62-82-BB
4 rooms, 4 pb
Visa, MC, Disc
C-yes/S-ltd/P-ltd/H-ltd

Full breakfast
Lunch, restaurant
Gift & antique shop plus wedding & formalwear shop, fireplaces, sitting room

Old mountain retreat furnished with heirloom antiques & over 4000 formal and wedding gowns to browse through. Eatery open to public during summer months.
pruner@internetcds.com

SALEM

A Creekside Inn, The Marquee House
333 Wyatt Ct NE 97301
503-391-0837 Fax: 503-391-1713
800-949-0837
Rickie Hart
All year

65-95-BB
5 rooms, 3 pb
Visa, MC, Disc, *Rated*, •
C-ltd/S-no/P-no/H-no

Full breakfast
Snacks
Sitting room, movies, comports for business, traveler, hammock chairs

Mt. Vernon Colonial; has antiques, fireplace. Nightly film showing with "bottomless" popcorn bowl. Walk to the capitol. rickiemh@open.org http://www.marqueehouse.com

SEASIDE

Gilbert Inn
341 Beach Dr 97138
503-738-9770 Fax: 503-717-1070
800-410-9770
Carole & Dick Rees
All year

105-125-BB
10 rooms, 10 pb
Most CC, *Rated*
P-no/H-no

Full breakfast

Upon entering this special Queen Anne Victorian you are transported back into yesterday. gilbertinn@seasurf.net http://www.gilbertinn.com

SHERIDAN

Bethell Lodging in Wine Country
17950 Hwy 22 97378
503-623-1300 866-842-2686
All year
BB

Come stay with us at our comfortable family estate and view our private collection of memorabilia from Oregon Logging History!
innkeeper@bethell-lodging.com http://www.bethell-lodging.com

Middle Creek Run
25400 Harmony Rd 97378
503-843-7606
John Tallerino
All year
115-125-BB
3 rooms, 2 pb
Rated
C-ltd/S-ltd/P-no/H-no
Full breakfast
Afternoon tea, snacks
Sitting room, library,
Jacuzzis, suites, fireplaces

Historic Victorian offers quietude & old world comfort. The proprietors designed their home around their collection of art, antiques, Asian and ethnic treasures. Three course breakfast, flowers and truffles await you. http://www.middlecreekrun.com

SILVERTON

The Magnolia Cottage
PO Box 596
504 W Main 97381
503-873-6712
Elsie Tittle
All year
60-100-BB
2 rooms, 2 pb
Visa, MC
C-ltd/S-no/P-no/H-ltd
Full breakfast
Sitting room, in-room
Jacuzzi, suites, cable TV

Quaint 1938 gabled English cottage near the Oregon Gardens. Walk easily to town to antique shops. Warm, cozy and private. elise7777@juno.com

SISTERS

Conklin's Guest House
69013 Camp Polk Rd 97759
541-549-0123 Fax: 541-549-4481
800-549-4262
Frank & Marie Conklin
All year
90-150-BB
5 rooms, 5 pb
Rated, •
C-ltd/S-ltd/P-ltd/H-yes
Spanish
Full breakfast
Snacks, complimentary wine
Sitting room, heated
swimming pool, trout ponds

A spectacular country paradise, with spacious grounds, ponds, & mountain vistas.
conklins@outlawnet.com http://www.conklinsguesthouse.com

STEAMBOAT

Steamboat Inn
42705 N. Umpqua Hwy 97447
541-498-2230
Fax: 541-498-2411
800-840-8825
S. & J. Van Loan & P. Lee
135-250
12 rooms, 12 pb
Rated
All year

Cozy country inn nestled along the North Umpqua River.
stmbtinn@rosenet.net http://www.thesteamboatinn.com

SWEET HOME

Santiam River Resort
PO Box 473
27945 Santiam Hwy 97386
541-367-4837 Fax: 541-367-7007
Chuck & Pennie Farrington
All year
90-180-BB
3 rooms, 3 pb
Most CC
Full breakfast
Candy, snacks, sodas,
coffee/teas, dessert
Pinball, jukebox, heated pool
& spa
Quiet reading areas with
river views

Our amazing river views will soothe and relax you. At SRR, our desire is for you to have a very enjoyable, romantic getaway when you vacation with us. We cater to individual tastes and desires. moviebuf@direcpc.com http://www.relax-here.com

WALDPORT

Cliff House
PO Box 2076
1450 SW Adahi Rd 97394
541-563-2506
Fax: 541-563-3903
Sharon & Keith Robinson
All year

110-225-BB
4 rooms, 4 pb
Visa, MC, *Rated*
C-no/S-no/P-no/H-no
Dutch

Full breakfast
Afternoon tea, coffee, fresh lemonade, cookies
Sitting room, hot tubs, sauna, decks, ocean gazing

Pampered elegance by the sea. Perched high on a cliff, we offer gourmet breakfasts, spa, sauna, plush robes, gazebo for massage (by appointment), and luxury rooms.
innkeeper@cliffhouseoregon.com http://www.cliffhouseoregon.com

YACHATS

Overleaf Lodge
PO Box 291
97498
541-547-4880 Fax: 541-547-4888
800-338-0507
David Locke All year

90-225-BB
39 rooms, 39 pb
Visa, MC, Disc, *Rated*, •
C-yes/S-no/P-no/H-yes

Continental breakfast
Microwave, refrigerator, coffee maker
Sitting room, Jacuzzi, suites, cable TV, balconies

Located in the tiny village of Yachats. Oceanfront property with luxurious rooms, each with a spectacular view. reservations@overleaflodge.com http://www.overleaflodge.com

YAMHILL

Willakenzie House
19700 Adcock Rd 97148
503-662-4297
Debbie Gorham
All year

BB

bluesky@aracnet.com

Pennsylvania

ADAMSTOWN (REGION)

Living Spring Farm
2614 Rt 568, *Mohnton* 19540
610-775-8525 Fax: 610-775-1399
Debra Cazille
All year

85-150-BB
4 rooms, 4 pb
C-ltd/S-no/P-no/H-no

Full breakfast
Snacks, wine
Sitting room, fireplace, cable TV

A 200 year old, 32 acre gentleman's farm decorated with antiques. Enjoy breakfast or a snack outside on the veranda overlooking beautiful farmland or do some bird watching.
DebCaz@worldnet.att.net http://www.livingspringfarm.com

The Barnyard Inn & Carriage House
2145 Old Lancaster Pike, *Reinholds* 17569
717-484-1111
Fax: 717-484-0722
888-738-6624
Pam & Jerry Pozniak
All year

80-155-BB
5 rooms, 5 pb
Most CC, *Rated*, •
C-yes/S-no/P-no/H-no

Full 5 entree gourmet breakfast
Complimentary beverages & snacks
Sitting room, bikes, pool & golf nearby, petting zoo onsite

A 150-year-old restored German schoolhouse on 2 1/2 wooded acres overlooking countryside. Located in the Antique Capital of USA & minutes from outlet shopping and Pennsylvania Dutch attractions.
pam@barnyardinn.com http://www.barnyardinn.com

AKRON

Boxwood Inn
PO Box 203
12 Tobacco Rd 17501
717-859-3466
Fax: 717-859-4507
800-238-3466
Robyn & Robert Carter
All year

110-210-BB
5 rooms, 5 pb
Visa, MC, AmEx,
Rated, •
C-ltd/S-no/P-no/H-no

Full breakfast
Amish dinners arranged
Sitting room, library,
Jacuzzis, suites, fireplaces,
cable TV

Located in the heart of Pennsylvania Dutch country. Five rooms with private baths; full breakfast. Beautifully restored 1768 stone home on 3½ acres. Quiet country setting.
http://www.800padutch.com/boxwood.html

ALBURTIS

Prospect Hill Farm
298 Conrad Rd 18011
610-845-2880
Jane & Aurel Arndt
All year

125-275-BB
3 rooms, 3 pb
Visa, MC
C-ltd/S-no/P-no/H-no

Full breakfast
Complimentary wine
Sitting room, Jacuzzi,
fireplaces, cable TV

Historic 1860 Pennsylvania Stone Farmhouse and Cottage on a 60 acre estate; private candlelight breakfast in the dining room, gardens or veranda.
arndt7950@aol.com http://www.prospecthillfarm.com

ALLENTOWN

Coachaus Inn
107 North 8th St 18101
610-821-4854 Fax: 610-821-6862
800-762-8680
Rebecca Day
All year

68-128-BB
22 rooms, 22 pb
Visa, MC, AmEx, *Rated*
C-ltd/S-ltd/P-ltd/H-no

Full breakfast
Sitting room, suites, cable TV

Center city inn located in the historic District, furnished with antiques and reproductions.

BEAVER FALLS

McKinley Place
132 McKinley Road 15010
724-891-0300
Holly Flechner
All year

75-105-BB
4 rooms, 4 pb
Visa, MC, AmEx,
Rated, •
C-yes/S-no/P-no/H-ltd

Full breakfast
AC, Cable TV/VCRs, Private
Baths, Phones in Rooms

McKinley Place is a classic, Colonial home appointed with the crisp, springtime fresh decor of the English countryside. mckinleypl@aol.com http://www.mckinleyplace.com

BEDFORD

Bedford House
203 W Pitt St 15522
814-623-7171
Lyn & Linda Lyon
All year

90-145-BB
10 rooms, 10 pb
Most CC, •
C-ltd/S-no/P-no/H-yes

Full breakfast
Afternoon tea
Sitting rm, library nook,
Frplc. in 5 guestrooms,
tennis, golf nearby

The in-town B&B, c.1800 brick Federal, is near shops, restaurants and churches. A path through the flower garden leads to the guesthouse.
bedhouse@bedford.net http://www.bedfordcounty.net/bedfordhouse

---

Jean Bonnet Tavern
6048 Lincoln Hwy 15522
814-623-2250
Melissa R. Jacobs
All year

BB
Most CC
C-yes/P-no

Hearty country breakfast

On the National Register of Historic Places, this sturdy inn was licensed to Jean Bonnet as a Public House in 1780, although it has been serving the public since it was built in the 1760's. jbonnet@pennswoods.net http://www.bedfordcounty.net/bandb/jbt/index.htm

BIRD IN HAND

Mill Creek Homestead
2578 Old Philadelphia 17505
717-291-6419 Fax: 717-291-2171
800-771-2578
Vicki & Frank Alfone
All year

99-129-BB
4 rooms, 4 pb
Most CC, *Rated*, •
C-ltd/S-no/P-no/H-no

Full breakfast
Snack, beverages
Sitting room, library, swimming pool, fireplaces

Country hideaway in restored stone farmhouse amidst Amish farmland. Decorated with family heirlooms & quilts. valfone@yahoo.com http://www.millcreekhomestead.com

---

Village Inn of Bird-in-Hand
PO Box 253
2695 Old Philadelphia Pike 17505
717-293-8369 Fax: 717-768-1117
800-914-2473
Nancy Papac
All year

79-155-BB
11 rooms, 11 pb
Most CC, *Rated*
C-yes/S-ltd/P-no/H-no

Continental plus breakfast
Evening snacks
Sitting room, Dutch Country bus tour, hot tubs in 2 suites

Beautifully restored historic inn located in Pennsylvania Dutch Country. Country setting. Victorian-style architecture and furnishings.
lodging@bird-in-hand.com http://www.bird-in-hand.com/villageinn

BLOOMSBURG

Inn at Turkey Hill
991 Central Rd 17815
570-387-1500 Fax: 570-784-3718
Andrew B. Pruden
All year

105-195-BB
23 rooms, 23 pb
Most CC, *Rated*, •
C-yes/S-yes/P-yes/H-yes

Continental breakfast
Dinner every evening
Cozy tavern, whirlpools & fireplaces, duck pond & gazebo

Nestled amid PA's rolling hills & farmlands. Inn extends warmth, comfort, charm & hospitality. info@innatturkeyhill.com http://www.innatturkeyhill.com

BOYERTOWN

The Enchanted Cottage
22 Deer Run Rd 19512
610-845-8845
Peg & Richard Groff
All year

100-110-BB
1 rooms, 1 pb
Rated, •
C-ltd/S-ltd/P-no

Full gourmet breakfast

Hidden in the forest is a storybook house, the Enchanted Cottage, almost out of Grimm's Fairy Tales. admin@choice-guide.com http://www.choice-guide.com/pa/enchanted

BRANDYWINE VALLEY (REGION)

Hedgerow B&B Suites
268 Kennett Pike
Rt 52, *Chadds Ford* 19317
610-388-6080 Fax: 610-388-0194
Barbara & John Haedrich
All year

135-175-BB
3 rooms, 3 pb
Most CC, *Rated*, •
C-ltd/S-no/P-no/H-no

Full breakfast
Afternoon tea, snacks
Sitting room, library, Jacuzzi, fireplaces, gardens, privacy, cable TV

Between Longwood/Winterthur. Beautifully restored Carriage House. Three luxurious, private suites with amenities plus A/C. Personal service.
hedgerowbb@aol.com http://www.brandywine-valley.com

Kennett House
503 W State St, *Kennett Square* 19348
610-444-9592 Fax: 610-444-7633
800-820-9592
Carol & Jeff Yetter
All year

119-149-BB
4 rooms, 4 pb
Most CC, *Rated*, •
C-ltd/S-no/P-no/H-no

Full breakfast
Afternoon homemade cookies & brownies and snacks
Library, sitting room, A/C, fireplaces, porch, gardens

Granite Arts & Craft mansion minutes from Longwood Gardens/Winterthur/ Brandywine Valley attractions. Old-fashioned hospitality in a comfortable & relaxing atmosphere. Magnificent chestnut woodwork. innkeeper@kennetthouse.com
http://www.kennetthouse.com

CANADENSIS

The Brookview Manor Inn
RR 2 Box 2960
RR 447 18325
570-595-2451 Fax: 570-595-7154
800-585-7974
Gaile & Marty Horowitz

130-200-BB
10 rooms, 10 pb
Most CC, *Rated*, •
C-ltd/S-no/P-no/H-no
All year

Full gourmet breakfast
Afternoon tea, snacks, dinner available
Sitting room, library, lawn games, waterfall, hiking

We invite you to recapture the art of relaxation in an enchanting country Inn. We are nestled in the heart of the Poconos on 4 hilly acres across from the Brodhead Creek. Hike, golf, ski, antiquing.
innkeepers@TheBrookviewManor.com http://www.thebrookviewmanor.com

---

Pine Knob Inn
PO Box 295
Rt 447 18325
570-595-2532 Fax: 570-595-6429
800-426-1460
Cheryl & John Garman

80-250
28 rooms, 19 pb
All year

We want to welcome you to a very special place in the country. Far from the hustle and bustle of modern life. innkeepers@pineknobinn.com http://www.pineknobinn.com/

CARLISLE

Jacob's Resting Place
1007 Harrisburg Pike 17013
717-243-1766 Fax: 717-241-5010
888-731-1790
Terry & Marie Hegglin
March 1-Jan 1

75-95-BB
5 rooms, 2 pb
Most CC, •
C-ltd/S-ltd/P-no/H-no

Full breakfast
Snacks and beverages
Hot tub, swimming pool, hiking, trout fishing, colonial gardens, fireplaces

Historical Inn from 1790. Antique decor, working fireplaces, trout stream, colonial & cottage gardens, pool, exercise equipment, hot tub, air conditioning & gourmet breakfasts for your enjoyment. jacobsrest@pa.net http://www.jacobsrestingplace.com

---

Pheasant Field
150 Hickorytown Rd 17013
717-258-0717 Fax: 717-258-1352
877-258-0717
Dee Fegan & Chuck DeMarco
All year

90-150-BB
4 rooms, 4 pb
Visa, MC, AmEx, *Rated*, •
C-ltd/S-ltd/P-ltd/H-no

Full breakfast
Snacks
Sitting room, tennis courts, horse boarding available

Lovely 200-year-old brick farmhouse. History, antiques, fly fishing, car shows. Appalachian trail nearby. stay@pheasantfield.com http://www.pheasantfield.com

CHADDS FORD

Brandywine River Hotel
PO Box 1058
Rte 1 & Rte 100 19317
610-388-1200 Fax: 610-388-1200
Jeffrey T. Yamas
All year

125-169-BB
40 rooms, 40 pb
Most CC, *Rated*
C-yes/S-yes/P-yes/H-yes

Continental plus breakfast
Restaurant, afternoon tea, snacks, wine (fee)
Sitting room, Jacuzzis, suites, fireplaces, cable TV, accom. bus. travelers

40 elegant guestrooms. Rates include a European Plus Breakfast in Ashley Dining Room & Afternoon Tea in lobby w/ delicious homemade specialties.
brhdos@aol.com http://www.virtualcities.com/ons/pa/a/paa7601.htm

---

Fairville Inn
506 Kennett Pike, Rt 52 19317
610-388-5900 Fax: 610-388-5902
877-285-7772
Thomas & Eleanor Everitt
All year

150-250-BB
15 rooms, 15 pb
Visa, MC, AmEx, *Rated*, •
C-ltd/S-no/P-no/H-ltd

Full breakfast
Afternoon refreshments
Suites, fireplaces, cable TV, accommodate business travelers

The Fairville Inn is ideally located for all major attractions in the Brandywine Valley. All rooms are individually decorated. info@fairvilleinn.com http://www.fairvilleinn.com

CHADDS FORD

The Pennsbury Inn 883 Baltimore Pike 19317 610-388-1435 Fax: 610-388-1436 Cheryl & Chip Grono All year	72-225-BB 7 rooms, 6 pb Most CC, • C-yes/S-no/P-ltd/H-no French, German	Full or continental plus breakfast Afternoon tea Sitting room, library, fireplaces, cable TV, accom. bus. travel

The c.1714 Inn is a large, yet cozy retreat with uneven floors, slanted doorways, winder staircases and huge, open fireplaces. Eight acres of gardens, ponds and wooded trails provide tranquil beauty. info@pennsburyinn.com http://www.pennsburyinn.com

CLEARFIELD

Christopher Kratzer House 101 E Cherry St 16830 814-765-5024 888-252-2632 Bruce & Ginny Baggett All year	75-90-BB 3 rooms, 1 pb Visa, MC, Disc, *Rated*, • C-yes/S-ltd/P-ltd/H-no	Full breakfast Afternoon tea, complimentary wine Snacks, sitting room, library, attic flea market for browsing, A/C

1840 historic house overlooking river shared bath. Honeymoon suite with breakfast in room; complimentary champagne.
bbaggett@pennswoods.net http://www.travelguides.com/home/kratzerhouse/

COOKSBURG

Gateway Lodge & Restaurant Route 36 Box 125 16217 814-744-8017 Fax: 814-744-8017 800-843-6862 The Burney Family All year	90-340-BB 39 rooms, 34 pb *Rated* C-ltd/S-no/P-no/H-ltd	Full breakfast Snacks, lunch/dinner available Piano, buggy rides, sitting room, hot tubs, heated pool, sauna

A Full Service Country Inn. info@gatewaylodge.com http://www.gatewaylodge.com

CRESSON

The Station Inn 827 Front St 16630 814-886-4757 Fax: 814-866-5350 800-555-4757 Tom Davis All year	73-80-BB 7 rooms, 7 pb C-ltd/S-ltd/P-no/H-no	Continental plus breakfast Restaurant, bar service, sitting room, library

The Station Inn is a restored 1866 railroad hotel. Our specialty is catering to serious rail buffs. Our staff provides guests with area maps, information, and guidance that insures a good visit. http://www.stationinnpa.com

DANVILLE

Pine Barn Inn 1 Pine Barn Pl 17821 570-275-2071 Fax: 570-275-3248 800-627-2276 Martin Walzer All year	70-125-EP 102 rooms, 102 pb Most CC, *Rated*, • C-yes/S-yes/P-yes/H-ltd Spanish	Full breakfast (fee) Lunch, dinner, bar Dining patio, hiking, fitness room, all rooms have A/C

Main inn is a 19th-century barn; guestrooms located in new lodge building. Located in residential part of community. Especially popular locally for fine food.
mwalzer@pinebarninn.com http://www.pinebarninn.com

DELAWARE WATER GAP

The Shepard House PO Box 486 108 Shepard Ave 18327 570-424-9779 Ruth and Wayne MacWilliams All year	99-120-BB 4 rooms, 4 pb Visa, MC C-ltd/S-ltd/P-ltd/H-no	Full breakfast Afternoon tea, snacks Sitting room, cable TV

Country Victorian decorated with beautiful antiques and lace curtains along with many special touches. Relax on our wrap around veranda and enjoy a special full course gourmet breakfast. shepardhouse@enter.net http://www.shepardhouse.com

EAGLES MERE

A Eagles Mere Inn
PO Box 356
Mary & Sullivan Ave 17731
570-525-3273 Fax: 570-525-3273
800-426-3273
Susan & Peter Glaubitz
All year

155-245-MAP
19 rooms, 19 pb
Visa, MC, *Rated*, •
C-yes/S-ltd/P-no/H-ltd

Full Country breakfast
5-course dinner included.
Excellent wine list
Pub, sitting room, tennis, swimming, golf, skiing, fishing, bicycles, canoe

Ultimate stress relief! Guests enjoy warm hospitality, gourmet meals included in rates, outstanding wines and peaceful relaxation.
relax@eaglesmereinn.com http://www.eaglesmereinn.com

EASTON

The Lafayette Inn
525 W Monroe St 18042
610-253-4500 Fax: 610-253-4635
Scott & Marilyn Bushnell
All year

110-175-BB
16 rooms, 16 pb
Most CC, *Rated*
C-yes/S-no/P-no/H-ltd

Full breakfast
Snacks
Sitting room, Jacuzzis, suites, fireplaces, cable TV, VCRs, fax, dataports

Our 16 antique filled rooms and landscaped grounds offer distinctive accommodations in Pennsylvania's historic Lehigh Valley. lafayinn@fast.net http://www.lafayetteinn.com

---

Seipsville Inn
2912 Old Nazareth Rd 18045
610-252-3620 Fax: 610-253-4733
Dero Pettinelli
All year

79-150-BB
7 rooms, 7 pb
Visa, MC, AmEx, *Rated*, •
C-yes/S-no/P-no/H-yes
Italian, German

Full breakfast
Dinner & comp. wine upon request, bar service
Sitting room, library, fireplaces, cable TV, dining area, accom. bus. travel

Built in 1760 and recently restored to its original 18th century design. B&B travelers will enjoy the beauty and charm of this unique country inn.
dino@nac.net http://www.seipsvilleinn.com

ELIZABETHTOWN

Conewago Manor Inn
2048 Zeager Rd 17022
717-361-0826 Fax: 717-361-0111
Keith & Laura Murphy
All year

150-200-BB
9 rooms, 9 pb
Visa, MC, *Rated*
C-ltd/S-no/P-no/H-no

Full breakfast
Sitting room, library, Jacuzzi, fireplaces, TV with VCR

1739 Stone Manor on the Conewago Creek. Unique Victorian rooms w/whirlpool baths, fireplaces, most with balconies.
kmurphyco@dejazzd.com http://www.conewagomanorinn.com

ELIZABETHVILLE

Inn at Elizabethville
PO Box 236
30 W Main St 17023
717-362-3476 Fax: 717-362-1444
Heidi Milbrand
All year

54-70-BB
7 rooms, 7 pb
Visa, MC
C-ltd/S-no/P-no/H-no

Full breakfast
Afternoon tea, snacks
Sitting room, bikes, tennis court, pool, fireplaces, cable, accom. bus. trav

Country Inn furnished comfortably. We want to make you feel like you are at home. Full country breakfast served. theinnwench@adelphia.net

EPHRATA

Historic Smithton Inn
900 W Main St 17522
717-733-6094 877-755-4590
Dorothy Graybill
All year

85-175-BB
8 rooms, 8 pb
Visa, MC, *Rated*, •
C-ltd/S-no/P-ltd/H-ltd

Full breakfast
Complimentary tea, snacks
Sitting room, fireplaces, whirlpool baths, gardens, library, canopy beds

A 1763 historic village inn in picturesque Lancaster County, home of the PA Dutch people. Amish, Mennonite, Bretherin, etc. http://www.historicsmithtoninn.com

EPHRATA

Inns at Doneckers
318-324 N State St 17522
717-738-9502 Fax: 717-738-9554
800-377-2009
Cyndi Boozer
All year

69-210-BB
40 rooms, 39 pb
Visa, MC, AmEx
C-yes/S-no/P-no/H-ltd

Continental plus breakfast
Snacks, restaurant
Sitting room, Jacuzzis, suites, fireplace, cable TV

40 rooms with private baths, continental breakfast, cozy chambers and luxurious suites restored to the spirit of early America. Jacuzzi, fireplaces, restaurant.
theinns@doneckers.com http://www.doneckers.com

Jacob Keller House
990 Rettew Mill Rd 17522
717-733-4954
B. Long
All year

80-95-BB
4 rooms, 2 pb
Visa, MC, •
C-ltd/S-no/P-no/H-no

Full breakfast
Sitting room, library, prefer adults

1814 stone house in Ephrata. Near antique alley. On the Nat'l Historic Register. Minutes from the Ephrata Cloister. 17 miles from Hershey. Near Landis Museum. In the heart of the Amish country. jacobkellerhouse@yahoo.com

---

Meadow Valley Farm Guest Home
221 Meadow Valley Rd 17522
717-733-8390 Fax: 717-733-9068
877-562-4530
Marlene Hurst
All year

35-45-BB
3 rooms, 1 pb
C-yes/S-no/P-ltd/H-no

Fully stocked kitchen

We have a wonderful experience awaiting you. We think you will enjoy relaxing by our pond and watching the swans! walterhurst@juno.com

EQUINUNK

Sault Falls Inn
PO Box 267
Braman Rd 18417
570-224-6897 1-877-487-0435
Peter, Richard & Tasha Grunn
All year

85-100-BB
7 rooms, 1 pb
Visa, MC
C-ltd/S-no/P-no/H-ltd
French, Portuguese

Full breakfast
Afternoon Tea
Sitting room, library, verandahs, gardens, Swimming Pool

For the "overworked and underplayed." Near the Upper Delaware River, offers 46 acres, gardens, swimming pool, eclectic comfort in a rambling old farm house and the restful sounds of the Sault Falls. braman@ptd.net http://www.saultfallsinn.com

ERIE

The Boothby Inn LLC
311 West 6th St 16507
814-456-1888 Fax: 814-456-1887
866-BOOTHBY
Wally & Gloria Knox
All year

90-145-BB
4 rooms, 4 pb
Most CC
C-no/S-no/P-no/H-no

Guest kitchen with snacks
TV, phone, dataport, conference

Experience the finest accommodations downtown Erie has to offer. Catering to the business traveler and vacationer, the Inn boasts warm and sophisticated hospitality. Opened June 1, 2001. info@theboothbyinn.com http://www.theboothbyinn.com

ERWINNA

Evermay on-the-Delaware
PO Box 60
889 River Rd 18920
610-294-9100 Fax: 610-294-8249
877-864-2365
William & Danielle Moffly
All year exc. Christmas

145-350-BB
16 rooms, 16 pb
Visa, MC, *Rated*, •
C-ltd/S-ltd/P-no/H-yes

Continental plus breakfast
Complimentary sherry in parlor
Cordial in rm., bar, tea, restaurant (weekends), sitting room, piano

Romantic Victorian inn on 25 acres of gardens, woodlawn paths and pastures. Elegant dinner served Friday-Sunday & holidays.
moffly@evermay.com http://www.evermay.com

FAWN GROVE

Horse Lover's 405 Throne Rd 17321 866-382-4171 866-382-4171 Barb & Dale Trobert All year	90-180-BB 5 rooms, 5 pb C-ltd/S-no/P-no/H-no	Full breakfast Tea, coffee, snacks, wine, etc. Jacuzzis, balcony, water garden with Koi

Voted one of the top 15 B&Bs for the horse lover by inn goers from across the country for year 2002. Country setting with a stable of 20 fine horses on the property.
barb@ixiusa.com http://www.horseloversb-b.com

FOGELSVILLE

Glasbern Inn 2141 Pack House Rd 18051 610-285-4723 Fax: 610-285-2862 Susan Drexinger All year	145-360-BB 37 rooms, 37 pb Visa, MC, AmEx, *Rated* C-ltd/S-ltd/P-no/H-ltd	Full breakfast Dinner served nightly Fitness Room, pool, bikes, whirlpools, fireplaces, DVD player, Movie Library

Guests enjoy pastoral landscapes, ponds, and paths throughout this restored mid-19th century farm. 37 unique guest rooms and suites are embellished with country charm and modern amenities. innkeeper@glasbern.com http://www.glasbern.com

FRANKLIN

The Lamberton House 1331 Otter St 16323 814-432-7908 800-481-0776 Jack & Sally Clawson All year	60-80-BB 6 rooms, 4 pb Visa, MC S-ltd/P-no	Full breakfast

Restored 1874 Queen Anne Victorian Mansion. Located mid-way between Pittsburgh, PA & Erie PA.

GETTYSBURG

Baladerry Inn at Gettysburg 40 Hospital Rd 17325 717-337-1342 Suzanne Lonky All year	125-200-BB 8 rooms, 8 pb Most CC, *Rated*, • C-ltd/S-no/P-no/H-no	Full breakfast Snacks, coffee and tea Sitting room, library, tennis, fireplace, conferences, in-room phones

Private, quiet, historic and spacious, country location at the edge of the Gettysburg National Historic Park. baladerry@blazenet.net http://www.baladerryinn.com

The Brafferton Inn 44 York St 17325 717-337-3423 Bill and Maggie Ward All year	95-175-BB 12 rooms, 12 pb Most CC, *Rated*, • C-ltd/S-no/P-no/H-yes	Full country breakfast Complementary coffee, tea, and snacks Library, atrium, piano, hat collection, old mags, primitive mural

Stone and clapboard inn circa 1786 near the center square of Gettysburg. The rooms have stenciled designs, antiques. innkeepers@brafferton.com http://www.brafferton.com

Brickhouse Inn 452 Baltimore St 17325 717-338-9337 Fax: 717-338-9265 800-864-3464 Craig & Marion Schmitz All year	95-145-BB 10 rooms, 10 pb Most CC, *Rated*, • C-yes/S-no/P-no/H-no	Full breakfast Snacks Sitting room, walk to restaurants, shops and battlefield

1898 brick Victorian nestled in the historic district. Walk to battlefields, great restaurants, antique and gift shops.
stay@brickhouseinn.com http://www.brickhouseinn.com

Brickhouse Inn, Gettysburg, PA

GETTYSBURG

The Doubleday Inn
104 Doubleday Ave 17325
717-334-9119 Fax: 717-334-7907
Charles & Ruth Anne Wilcox
All year

100-140-BB
9 rooms, 5 pb
Visa, MC, Disc, *Rated*, •
C-ltd/S-no/P-no/H-no

Full breakfast
Afternoon tea, snacks
Sitting room, battlefield guide, presentations

The only inn directly on Gettysburg Battlefield. Cozy antiques, Civil War accents and splendid views. doubledayinn@blazenet.net http://www.doubledayinn.com

---

Farnsworth House
401 Baltimore St 17325
717-334-8838 Fax: 717-334-5862
Loring Shultz
All year

95-180-BB
9 rooms, 9 pb
Most CC, *Rated*
C-yes/S-ltd/P-no/H-ltd

Full breakfast
Restaurant, bar, tea
Treats, sitt. rm., lib., garden, gallery, cable, fireplaces, whirlpools

Surround yourself with the enchanting blend of intimate atmosphere and Victorian elegance. farnhaus@mail.cvn.net http://www.farnsworthhousedining.com

---

The Gaslight Inn
33 East Middle Street 17325
717-337-9100 Fax: 717-337-1100
Denis and Roberta Sullivan
All year

100-195-BB
9 rooms, 9 pb
Most CC, *Rated*, •
C-ltd/S-ltd/P-no/H-yes

Full breakfast
Snacks
Sitting room, library, Jacuzzi, fireplaces, cable, conference room

Luxurious touches, wonderful outdoor living spaces and gardens, and the best food in town are complimented by hosts' pampering & concierge service.
info@thegaslightinn.com http://www.thegaslightinn.com

James Gettys Hotel
27 Chambersburg St 17325
717-337-1334 Fax: 717-334-2103
888-900-5275
Stephanie McSherry
All year

125-145-BB
11 rooms, 11 pb
Most CC, *Rated*
C-yes/S-no/P-no/H-yes
French, German

Continental breakfast
Sitting room, suites, cable TV

Restored in 1996, this 198 year old hotel, located in downtown Gettysburg, offers 11 tastefully appointed suites, gracious amenities and exceptional service.
info@jamesgettyshotel.com http://www.jamesgettyshotel.com

GETTYSBURG

Keystone Inn
231 Hanover St 17325
717-337-3888
Doris & Wilmer Martin
All year

79-119-BB
5 rooms, 5 pb
Visa, MC, *Rated*
C-yes/S-ltd/P-no

Full breakfast from menu
Lemonade, coffee, tea
Sitting room, library, suite with TV, microwave & fridge, tennis nearby

A wonderful three-story late Victorian. Great house with a lot of natural chestnut & oak. Lovely flower gardens. Comfort our priority. Country breakfasts.
http://www.virtualcities.com/pa/keystone.htm

GETTYSBURG (REGION)

Cashtown Inn
PO Box 103
1325 Old Route 30, *Cashtown* 17310
717-334-9722 Fax: 717-334-1442
800-367-1797

100-150-BB
7 rooms, 7 pb
Most CC, *Rated*
C-ltd/S-ltd/P-no/H-ltd
Eileen & Dennis Hoover
All year

Full breakfast
Restaurant–lunch and dinner, bar service
Comp. wine, sitting room, library, suites, cable TV, biz travelers

Civil War landmark; antiques, artwork, country decor. Relax on the porches or fireside in the Tavern. Delectable food, gracious hosts and history that comes alive!
cashtowninn@mail.cvn.net http://www.cashtowninn.com

Bechtel Victorian Mansion
PO Box 688
400 West King St, *East Berlin* 17316
717-259-7760 800-331-1108
Carol & Richard Carlson

85-150-BB
9 rooms, 9 pb
Visa, MC, AmEx, *Rated*, •
C-yes/S-ltd/P-no/H-no
All year

Full breakfast
Complimentary tea
Sitting room, library, A/C, meeting room, garden

1897 Victorian Mansion w/9 guestrooms. All rooms have private bath & A/C. Beautifully decorated in country Victorian style, furnished w/period antiques, accented w/porcelain dolls, teddy bears & toys.
bechtelvictbnb@aol.com http://www.bbonline.com/pa/bechtel/

The Old Barn B&B & Country Inn
PO Box 556
1 Main Trail, *Fairfield* 17320
717-642-5711 800-640-BARN
All year

85-130-BB
12 rooms, 12 pb
Most CC, *Rated*, •
C-yes/S-no/P-no/H-ltd
Jim Cook & Jim Richardson

Full breakfast
Lunch & dinner available
Afternoon tea, swimming pool, sitting room, library, suites, cable TV

Historic 1853 Stone Barn used as field hospital by Confederates during battle of Gettysburg. Restored into unique B&B with 12 guestrooms & suites, including a private three bedroom, two bath suite. oldbarn@adelphia.net http://www.theoldbarnbandb.com

---

Angelic Inn at Ragged Edge
PO Box 244
1090 Ragged Edge Inn, *Fayetteville* 17222
717-261-1195 Fax: 717-263-2118
888-900-5880

89-189-BB
10 rooms, 10 pb
Most CC, *Rated*
C-ltd/S-no
Darlene Elders
All year

Continental breakfast
Refreshments
A/C

Travel the same route that General Robert E. Lee rode into Gettysburg. Stay in this beautiful Victorian Mansion in the country close to the battlefields.
raggededge@gettysburginns.com http://www.gettysburginns.com

Sheppard Mansion
PO Box 475
117 Frederick St, *Hanover* 17331
717-633-8075 Fax: 717-633-8074
877-762-6746

140-220-BB
9 rooms, 5 pb
Most CC, *Rated*
C-ltd/S-no/P-no/H-no
Kathryn Sheppard & Timothy Bobb All year

Full breakfast
Snacks
Cable TV, accommodate business travelers

Restored to its original elegance and splendor, our 1913 neo-classical mansion is perfect for a romantic getaway or the weary business traveler.
reservations@sheppardmansion.com http://www.sheppardmansion.com

GETTYSBURG (REGION)

Country Escape
PO Box 195
275 Old Rt 30, *McKnightstown* 17343
717-338-0611 Fax: 717-334-5227
800-484-3244 c
Merry V. Bush All year

65-125-BB
3 rooms, 1 pb
Most CC, *Rated*, •
C-yes/S-no/P-ltd/H-no

Full breakfast
Homemade cookies, tea, soda, coffee
Family friendly facility, crib available, code for 800# is 4371

Laid back country decor, peaceful and quiet, near Gettysburg. Extensive garden, hot tub under the stars, children's play area.

merry@innernet.net http://gettysburgcountrybnb.com

Hickory Bridge Farm
96 Hickory Bridge Rd, *Orrtanna* 17353
717-642-5261 Fax: 717-642-6419
Robert & Mary Lynn Martin
All year

85-145-BB
9 rooms, 8 pb
Visa, MC, *Rated*
C-ltd/S-yes/P-no/H-no

Full breakfast
Dinner available Friday-Sunday
Sitting room, fireplaces, bicycles, fishing, 8 miles from Gettysburg

Relax in the country by enjoying a cozy cottage by the stream, a hearty breakfast at the farmhouse, and dining in restored PA barn on weekends.

hickory@innbook.com http://www.hickorybridgefarm.com

GLEN MILLS

Old Country & Antiques
1260 Middletown Rd 19342
610-358-0504 Fax: 610-358-0504
877-358-1260
Claire & Roger Poulet All year

100-120-BB
4 rooms, 4 pb
C-ltd/S-no/P-no/H-no
French, Spanish

Continental plus breakfast
Sitting room, Jacuzzi

We are located in Gradyville, Edgemont Township, the heart of Delaware County, outside of Philadelphia in southeastern Pennsylvania.

oldcbnb@voicenet.com http://www.oldcountrybnb.com

Sweetwater Farm
50 Sweetwater Rd 19342
610-459-4711 Fax: 610-358-4945
Deirdre Conwell & Victor Cancelmo All year

125-275-BB
12 rooms, 12 pb
Most CC
C-yes/P-yes

Full breakfast
Billiards room, library, swimming pool

1734 C Estate on 50 manicured acres. Seven elegantly decorated rooms in Main House with fireplace, and 5 private cottages.

deirdre @sweetwaterfarmbb.com http://www.sweetwaterfarmbb.com

GROVE CITY (REGION)

As Thyme Goes By
PO Box 493
214 North Main Street, *Harrisville* 16038
724-735-4003 877-278-4963
Susan M. Haas All year

60-85-BB
3 rooms, 3 pb
Rated
C-ltd/S-ltd/P-no/H-no

Full breakfast
Afternoon tea, snacks
Sitting room, Library, fireplaces, cable TV, classical music, picnics

We do for our guests what they don't take time to do for themselves, come prepared to be pampered during your stay at As Thyme Goes By. Candlelit breakfasts, homemade baked goods/jams asthymegoesby@pathway.net http://www.asthymegoesby.com/

HANOVER

Beechmont Inn
315 Broadway 17331
717-632-3013 Fax: 717-632-2769
800-553-7009
Kathryn & Thomas White
All year

90-155-BB
7 rooms, 7 pb
Visa, MC, AmEx, *Rated*, •
C-ltd/S-no/P-no/H-no

Full breakfast
Help yourself cookie jar with homemade cookies
Library, in-room telephones with data port, fax, copier, guest refrigerator

Centuries of charm greet you. Sumptuous breakfasts and warm hospitality are our hallmarks. Whether on holiday or business, enjoy gardens, patios and porches, creating treasured memories of your stay.

innkeeper@thebeechmont.com http://www.thebeechmont.com

HARRISBURG (REGION)

Farm Fortune
204 Limekiln Rd, *New Cumberland* 17070
717-774-2683 Fax: 717-774-5089
Phyllis Combs
All year

95-185-BB
4 rooms, 4 pb
Most CC, •
C-ltd

Full breakfast
Lunch & dinner nearby
Sitting room, library

1790's limestone home overlooking the Yellow Breeches Creek, known for its trout fishing. Home furnished in period antiques with many amenities. Thought to be part of Underground Railroad. FrmFortune@aol.com http://members.aol.com/FrmFortune/

Kanaga House
6940 Carlisle Pike, *New Kingstown* 17072
717-766-8654 Fax: 717-697-3908
877-952-6242
Dave & Mary Jane Kretzing
All year

85-125-BB
6 rooms, 5 pb
Visa, MC, AmEx, *Rated*, •
C-ltd/S-no/P-no/H-ltd

Full breakfast
Snacks
Spacious common areas, fireplaces, phones/cable TV, great breakfasts

Elegant 1775 limestone mansion. On U.S. 11, only 2.2 miles from I-81 and 3.5 miles from PA Turnpike (I-76). Gettysbury, Hershey are an easy drive. Antiques, history, and hospitality await. stay@kanagahouse.com http://www.kanagahouse.com

HATFIELD

John Kindig House
244 W Orvilla Rd 19440
215-361-3200
Edward & Barbara Frazer
All year

95-105-BB
4 rooms, 4 pb
Most CC, *Rated*
C-ltd/S-ltd/P-no/H-ltd

Full breakfast
Sitting room, private deck, gazebo, pond, pool, cable TV, off street parking

1864 farmhouse furnished with antiques and artwork, located on 2 acres in central Montgomery County. Convenient to Philadelphia, Valley Forge, New Hope and Doylestown. Relaxed and comfortable.
info@johnkindighouse.com http://www.johnkindighouse.com

HAWLEY

The Falls Port Inn & Rest.
330 Main Ave 18428
570-226-2600 Fax: 570-226-6409
Dorothy S. Fenn
All year

75-120-BB
9 rooms, 5 pb
Visa, MC, AmEx, *Rated*
C-yes/S-ltd/P-ltd/H-ltd

Continental breakfast
Lunch, dinner, restaurant
Bar service, sitting room, cable TV, brunch on Sunday

Restored Victorian Inn. Guest rooms & dining rooms filled with antiques & elegant decor. Restaurant creates an oasis of both elegant & casual affordable dining with superior cuisine.

Morning Glories
204 Bellemonte Ave
Rt 6/Rt 590 18428
570-226-0644
Roberta & Natalie Holcomb
All year

55-75-BB
3 rooms, 1 pb
Visa, MC, Disc
C-ltd/S-ltd/P-ltd/H-no

Full breakfast
Sitting room, cable TV, conservatory (plants), exersize room

Nestled on a hillside overlooking the charming village of Hawley, enjoy Morning Glories newly added conservatory filled with plants, a Koi pond and wonderful views of a Japanese style garden.

The Settlers Inn at Bingham Park
4 Main Ave 18428
570-226-2993 Fax: 570-226-1874
800-833-8527
Grant & Jeanne Genzlinger
All year

110-200-BB
20 rooms, 18 pb
Most CC, *Rated*
C-yes/S-yes/P-ltd/H-no

Full breakfast
Lunch, dinner, bar
Sitting room, library, phones in rooms, bikes, tennis, piano, gift shop

Delightful country inn of Tudor architecture, with gift shops and art gallery.
settler@thesettlersinn.com http://www.thesettlersinn.com

HAWLEY (REGION)

Beech Tree Gardens
RR#10 Box 3100
State Route 590, *Lake Ariel*
18436
570-226-8677 Fax: 570-226-7461
Lynn & Kevin Schultz
All year

85-115-BB
3 rooms, 3 pb
Visa, MC, •
C-no/S-ltd/P-no/H-no

Full breakfast
Sitting Room, Pond House, trails

Beech Tree Gardens B&B is a Victorian home situated on 81 private forested acres in the Lake Region of the Pocono Mountains. beech@ptd.net

HERSHEY

Hershey Highland
PO Box 222
1601 Sandbeach Rd 17033
717-533-6166
Robert C. Richardson All year

80-100-BB
Most CC
S-no

Rest and relax as you visit or vacation in Hershey, PA. Make Hershey Highland your base as you tour Lancaster County and the Pennsylvania Dutch Country or Gettysburg, each within a one hour drive. hersheyhighland@aol.com http://hersheyhighland.com

HUNTINGTON MILLS

Hart's Content
PO Box 97
18622
717-864-2499
Gerry & Ken Hart All year

55-65-BB
3 rooms, 3 pb
C-yes/S-no/P-no/H-no

Full breakfast
Pool, pond

Harts' Content is nestled on 27 wooded acres. The area abounds in wildlife. Spring, summer, winter or fall brings beauty, each in its own way
kahart@epix.net http://innsite.com/inns/A005457.html

INTERCOURSE

Intercourse Village Suites
PO Box 340
Rt 340 Main St 17534
717-768-2626 800-664-0949
Ruthann Thomas
All year

119-199-BB
9 rooms, 9 pb
Most CC, *Rated*
C-no/S-no/P-no/H-no

Gourmet Candlelit breakfast
Sodas, Pretzels, Fruit
Sitting room, Jacuzzis, Suites, Fireplaces, Cable TV, steam showers

AAA 4 Diamond Award. A Romantic B&B for Couples in an Amish Country Village. K/Q Beds, Private in Room Baths, Fireplaces, Honeymoon Suites w/Jacuzzis. Walk to Craft Shoppes. ivbbs@aol.com http://amishcountryinns.com/bed-breakfast-inn.htm

INTERCOURSE (REGION)

Circa 1766 Osceola Mill
313 Osceola Mill Rd,
Gordonville 17529
717-768-3758 Fax: 717-768-7539
800-878-7719
Elaine & John Lahr All year

85-135-BB
5 rooms, 5 pb
Visa, MC, *Rated*
C-ltd/S-no/P-no/H-no

Gourmet Breakfast
Afternoon tea, snacks, Can arrange Amish Dinners
Sitting room, fireplace, cable TV, air conditioning

Beautiful stone Georgian Colonial c.1766 set amongst Old Order Amish farms. Fireplaces, antiques, canopy beds, quilts adds to the charm of the tranquil setting.
elalahr@epix.net http://www.lancaster-inn.com

JIM THORPE

The Inn at Jim Thorpe
24 Broadway 18229
570-325-2599 Fax: 570-325-9145
800-329-2599
David Drury All year

89-279-BB
45 rooms, 45 pb
Most CC, *Rated*, •
C-yes/S-ltd/P-no/H-yes

Continental plus breakfast
Snacks, lunch & dinner available
Restaurant, bar, sitting room, game room, suites

Historic New Orleans style inn combines Victorian splendor with 21st century comforts.
innjt@ptd.net http://www.innjt.com

JOHNSTOWN (REGION)

Dillweed B&B & Trailside Shop
PO Box 1
Main St, *Dilltown* 15929
814-446-6465
Corey & Cindy Gilmore

65-70-BB
4 rooms
Visa, MC, Disc
C-yes/S-no/P-no/H-no
All year

Full breakfast
Snacks, ice cream/snack bar
Sitting room, bicycles, fireplace, accom. bus. travelers

Country getaway adjacent to historic Ghost Town Trail, a scenic Rail-Trail suitable for biking, hiking and cross-country skiing.
dillweed@floodcity.net http://www.dillweedinc.com

KENNETT SQUARE (REGION)

B&B at Walnut Hill
541 Chandler Mill Rd
Kennett Square, *Avondale* 19311
610-444-3703 Fax: 610-444-6889
Sandy & Tom Mills
All year

75-100-BB
2 rooms, 2 pb
C-yes/S-ltd/P-no/H-no
Spanish, French

Full breakfast
Afternoon tea, snacks
Keeping room, hot tub, fireplaces, cable TV, canoeing and tennis nearby

Warm, cozy, antique filled B&B, bucolic setting, minutes to major attractions. Creative, all-natural, full country breakfast.
millsjt@magpage.com http://www.bbonline.com/pa/walnuthill

KINTNERSVILLE

The Bucksville House
4501 Durham Rd 18930
610-847-8948 Fax: 610-847-8948
888-617-6300
Joe & Barb Szollosi
All year

125-150-BB
5 rooms, 5 pb
Most CC, *Rated*
C-ltd/S-no/P-no/H-yes

Full breakfast
Afternoon tea, complimentary wine
Sitting room, library, suite, fireplaces, cable TV, accom. bus. travel

Almost 2 decades of experience. Featured in 4 national magazines for decor & furnishings. Cover of Country Inn Magazine. http://www.bucksvillehouse.com

KINZER

Country View PA
5463 Old Philadelphia Pike
17535
717-768-0936
Ely & Barbara Smucker

59-79
5 rooms, 5 pb
Visa, MC
All year

Relax and enjoy the incredible views of the Amish farm country at this friendly inn. Near to Sight and Sound Millennium Theater, quilt and craft shops, and much more!
http://www.countryviewpa.com

LANCASTER

1725 Historic Witmer's Tavern Inn
2014 Old Philadelphia Pike
17602
717-299-5305
Brant Hartung All year

70-110-BB
7 rooms, 2 pb
Rated, •
C-ltd/S-ltd/P-no/H-no

Continental plus breakfast
Popcorn popper when using fireplace
Antique shop, sitting room, on-site massage therapist/reflexologist

Lancaster's only pre-Revolutionary Inn & Museum still lodging travelers. Fireplaces, antiques, quilts & fresh flowers in romantic rooms. Mapping of local interests by Innkeeper.
witmerstavern@cs.com http://www.witmerstavern.com

Artist's Inn & Gallery
PO Box 26
117 East Main 17581
717-445-0219 Fax: 717-445-0219
888-999-4479
Jan & Bruce Garrabrandt

95-179-BB
3 rooms, 3 pb
Most CC, •
C-ltd/S-ltd/P-no/H-ltd
All year

Four-course gourmet breakfast
Snacks, aft.. tea, wine
Art gallery, sitting room, tennis, suites, puzzle room, fireplaces, Jacuzzi

Spend the night in an art gallery! Antique-filled B&B in small town surrounded by Amish farms; gourmet candlelight breakfasts, innkeepers artwork. Let passing buggies take you back in time. stay@artistinn.com http://www.artistinn.com

LANCASTER

Flowers & Thyme B&B
238 Strasburg Pike 17602
717-393-1460 Fax: 717-399-1986
Don & Ruth Harnish
All year

85-115-BB
3 rooms, 3 pb
Visa, MC, *Rated*
C-ltd/S-no/P-no/H-no

Full breakfast
Snacks, cold drinks
Sitting rooms, library, patio & porch, A/C, winter & group discounts

Spacious house in the heart of PA Dutch country. Your choice of a room with canopy bed, fireplace, or Jacuzzi. Beautiful gardens.
padutchbnb@aol.com http://members.aol.com/padutchbnb

Gardens of Eden
1894 Eden Rd 17601
717-393-5179 Fax: 717-393-7722
Marilyn & Bill Ebel
All year

100-150-BB
4 rooms, 4 pb
Visa, MC, *Rated*, •
C-ltd/S-no/P-no/H-no

Full breakfast
Amish dinners arranged
Canoe, tours, tea/cookies on arrival, private baths, bike, maps, storage

Eden exists along the Conestoga River, where wild flowers, herbs, and perennials bloom among the trees and lawns of this circa 1867 Iron Masters mansion.
info@gardens-of-eden.com http://www.gardens-of-eden.com

Hollinger House
2336 Hollinger Rd 17602
717-464-3050 Fax: 717-464-3053
866-873-7370
Gina & Jeff Trost
All year

100-120-BB
5 rooms, 5 pb
C-yes/S-no/P-ltd/H-no

Full, country breakfast included
Evening dessert offered, picnic lunches
Den with TV/reading material, outdoor balconies and porch

1870 Adams Period mansion with wraparound veranda and balconies on 5½ acres with woodland stream. Fully restored original hardwood floors, columns, high ceilings and fireplaces. mywillow99@aol.com

---

King's Cottage
1049 E King St 17602
717-397-1017 Fax: 717-397-3447
800-747-8717
Janis Kutterer & Ann Willets
All year

145-240-BB
8 rooms, 8 pb
Visa, MC, Disc, *Rated*, •
C-ltd/S-no/P-no/H-ltd

Full Gourmet Breakfast
Afternoon tea, evening cordials
Sitting room, Spa, water garden, dinner with Amish family available

A Top 10 Most Romantic Inn. Enjoy National Register award-winning architecture & elegance. Kg/Qn bed, private baths, gourmet breakfasts. Near Amish farms, antiques, outlets, quilts, historic sites. info@kingscottagebb.com http://www.kingscottagebb.com

---

Lovelace Manor
2236 Marietta Ave 17603
717-399-3275 866-713-6384
Lark & Michael McCarley
All year

95-110-BB
4 rooms, 4 pb
Most CC
C-ltd/S-ltd/P-no/H-no

Full breakfast
Refreshments available in the Butler's Pantry
Game room with billiard table, in-room TV/VCRs, some modem hookups

A gracious Second Empire Victorian home offering guests an opportunity to step back in time. Located in historic Lancaster County, Lovelace Manor is conveniently located to all area attractions. hostess@lovelacemanor.com http://www.lovelacemanor.com

---

O'Flaherty's Dingeldein House
1105 E King St 17602
717-293-1723 Fax: 717-293-1947
800-779-7765
Nancy & Danny Whittle
All year

95-150-BB
5 rooms, 4 pb
Most CC, *Rated*, •
C-yes/S-no/P-no/H-no

Full gourmet breakfast
Amish meal if reserved
Sitting room, library, Amish farmlands nearby, farmers mkt, mall outlet

For the business traveler, why spend another night in impersonal hotel room, greeted by a lonely cup of coffee. Instead, join us for all the comforts of home in our home.
rooms@dingeldeinhouse.com http://www.dingeldeinhouse.com

LANCASTER (REGION)

Adamstown Inn PO Box 938 62 W Main St, *Adamstown* 19501 717-484-0800 Fax: 717-484-1384 800-594-4808 Tom & Wanda Berman All year	75-175-BB 8 rooms, 8 pb Visa, MC, AmEx, *Rated*, • C-ltd/S-no/P-no/H-no	Continental plus breakfast Afternoon tea Private baths, Jacuzzis, fireplaces, private balconies

Victorian B&B featuring rooms w/ Jacuzzis, fireplaces, balconies & sauna. Inn is located in the Antique District & is minutes from outlets, Lancaster's Amish attractions & golf. HIGHLY RECOMMENDED! stay@adamstown.com http://www.adamstown.com

---

Bella Vista B&B 1216 Main St, *Akron* 17501 717-859-4227 Fax: 717-859-4071 888-948-9726 Sarah & Jeff Shirk All year	80-95-BB 6 rooms, 5 pb Visa, MC, *Rated* C-ltd/S-no/P-no/H-no	Full breakfast Afternoon tea, snacks Sitting room, bikes, tennis, cable TV, conference facilities

Quite, country setting et within 15 minutes of all Lancaster County attractions (antiquing, outlets, Amish). jshirk@epix.net http://www.bellavistabandb.com

---

Churchtown Inn 2100 Main St, *Churchtown* 17555 717-445-7794 Fax: 717-445-0962 800-637-4446 Diane and Michael Franco All year	85-145-BB 8 rooms, 8 pb Visa, MC, • C-ltd/S-ltd/P-no	Full multi-course breakfast Dinner with Amish or Mennonite family/Evening tea Glass garden room, piano, den, carriage house, theme weekends, fireplaces

1735 stone mansion in Pennsylvania Dutch country. Queen beds, lovely antiques and handmade Amish quilts. Multi-course breakfast served in glass garden room. Amish/Mennonite dinners arranged. innkeepers@churchtowninn.com http://www.churchtowninn.com

---

Inn at Twin Linden 2092 Main St, *Churchtown* 17555 717-445-7619 Fax: 717-445-4656 Bob & Donna Leahy All year	125-265-BB 8 rooms, 8 pb Most CC, *Rated*, • C-ltd/S-no/P-no/H-ltd	Full breakfast Afternoon tea, snacks, sherry, brandy, Sat. dinner Jacuzzi, suites, fireplaces, cable TV, accommodate business travelers

Elegant accommodations in historic estate for discriminating inn-goers. Private baths, Jacuzzis, fireplaces, renowned gourmet cuisine.
info@twinlinden.com http://www.innattwinlinden.com

The Columbian 360 Chestnut St, *Columbia* 17512 717-684-5869 800-422-5869 Chris & Becky Will All year	70-125-BB 8 rooms, 8 pb Most CC C-yes/S-no/P-no/H-no	Full breakfast Complimentary beverages Sitting room, A/C, TVs, fireplaces, porches, patio, garden railroad

Circa 1897 restored turn-of-the-century mansion. Includes wraparound sun porches, stained-glass window, & tiered staircase. Decorated with antiques in Victorian or Country style. inn@columbianinn.com http://www.columbianinn.com

---

West Ridge Guest House 1285 West Ridge Rd, *Elizabethtown* 17022 717-367-7783 Fax: 717-367-8468 877-367-7783 Sue Miller All year	80-140-BB 8 rooms, 8 pb Most CC, *Rated* C-ltd/S-ltd/P-no/H-yes	Full breakfast Whirlpools, TV/VCR, A/C, fireplaces, phones, tennis court.

Country setting, each room decorated in a different decor. Some rooms with decks, fireplaces, and whirlpool tubs. wridgeroad@aol.com http://www.westridgebandb.com

LANCASTER (REGION)

Lincoln Haus Inn
51 King Rd
1687 Lincoln Hwy E, *Honey Brook* 19344
717-392-9412
Verna Fisher
All year

65-90-BB
8 rooms, 8 pb
Rated, •
C-ltd/S-no/P-no/H-ltd
German

Full breakfast
No alcohol on premises, honeymoon suite available, Amish crafts nearby

Unique suburban home, built in late 1800s, with rooms & apts. Natural oaks woodwork, antiques. Owner is a member of the old order Amish church.
http://www.800padutch.com/linchaus.html

Carriage Corner
PO Box 371
3705 E Newport Rd, *Intercourse* 17534
717-768-3059 Fax: 717-768-0691
800-209-3059
Gordon & Gwen Schuit
All year

68-90-BB
5 rooms, 5 pb
Visa, MC, *Rated*, •
C-ltd/S-no/P-no/H-no

Full breakfast
Afternoon tea, use of refrigerator
Common room, central AC, library, cable TV, bike rentals, gazebo

Located in the hub of the Amish farmland and tourist area; relaxing country atmosphere. Dinner with an Amish family can be arranged. The B&B is a unique blend of hospitality, laughter and kindness. gschuit@dejazzd.com http://www.carriagecornerbandb.com

---

Australian Walkabout Inn
PO Box 294
837 Village Rd, *Lampeter* 17537
717-464-0707 Fax: 717-464-2501
Richard & Margaret Mason
All year

99-289-BB
3 rooms, 3 pb
Visa, MC, AmEx, *Rated*, •
C-ltd/S-no/P-no/H-no

Full Aussie breakfast
Goldfish pond & fountain, in-room whirlpools/hot tubs, cable TV, fireplaces

Victorian restored 1925 Mennonite house, landscaped, in a quaint village setting. Dinner and tour with Amish family can be arranged. Extensive gardens.
http://www.800PAdutch.com/walkinn.html

The Alden House
62 E Main St, *Lititz* 17543
717-627-3363 800-584-0753
Tom & Lillian Vasquez
All year

85-120-BB
5 rooms, 5 pb
Visa, MC, *Rated*
C-ltd/S-no/P-no/H-no

Full breakfast
Dinner with Amish arranged
Sitting room, suites with fireplaces, route maps, bike storage

1850 brick Victorian home in the heart of Pennsylvania Dutch Country. Walk to all local attractions and fine dining. inn@aldenhouse.com http://www.aldenhouse.com/

Casual Corners
301 N Broad St, *Lititz* 17543
717-626-5299 800-464-6764
Ruth & Glen Lehman
All year

70-90-BB
4 rooms, 2 pb
Visa, MC, *Rated*, •
C-ltd/S-no/P-no/H-no

Full breakfast
Sitting room, guest private entrance, off-street parking

Charming turn-of-the-century home, with wrap-around porch and wicker furniture. Close to Lancaster County Amish. ccbb@desupernet.net http://www.casualcornersbnblititz.com

---

Penns Valley Farm & Guest House
6182 Metzler Rd, *Manheim* 17545
717-898-7386 Fax: 717-898-8489
Mel & Gladys Metzler
All year

65-75-BB
2 rooms, 1 pb
Visa, MC, AmEx, *Rated*
C-yes/S-no/P-no/H-no

Full breakfast
Farmhouse, open hearth, TV, A/C

A cozy, getaway guest house that sleeps up to seven people in beautiful Lancaster County farmland, but close to attractions.

LANCASTER (REGION)

Rose Manor
124 S Linden St, *Manheim* 17545
717-664-4932 Fax: 717-664-1611
800-666-4932
Susan
All year

70-130-BB
5 rooms, 4 pb
Visa, MC, AmEx, *Rated*, •
C-ltd/S-no/P-no/H-no

Full breakfast
Afternoon tea (fee), complimentary sherry
Picnic baskets, sitting room, gift shop, conservatory, gardens

Lancaster County 1905 manor house. Comfortable, elegant Victorian decor & cooking reflect "herbal" theme. Surrounded by rose & herb gardens. Full breakfast.
inn@rosemanor.net http://www.rosemanor.net

B.F. Hiestand House
722 E Market St, *Marietta* 17547
717-426-8415 Fax: 717-426-8417
877-560-8415
Pam & Dallas Fritz
All year

95-139-BB
4 rooms, 3 pb
Most CC
C-ltd/S-no/P-ltd/H-no

Full breakfast
Snacks
Sitting room, suites, cable TV

Historic 1887 High Queen Anne Victorian. Experience the elegance of a bygone era. Enjoy breakfast in our charming dining room. Exquisite parlors with 12-foot ceilings, pocket doors and fireplaces. info@bfhiestandhouse.com http://www.bfhiestandhouse.com

---

Railroad House Restaurant
280 W Front St, *Marietta* 17547
717-426-4141
Rick & Donna Chambers
All year

89-129-BB
8 rooms, 8 pb
Visa, MC
C-yes/S-no/P-no/H-ltd
Spanish, French

Full breakfast
Lunch/dinner avail, aft. . tea
Restaurant, bar service, suites, sitting room.

Restored historic 1820s Victorian country inn. Complex includes historic hotel, train station, carriage house, summer kitchen and gardens with patio. Eight unique rooms!
http://www.lancnews.com/railroadhouse/

Vogt Farm
1225 Colebrook Rd, *Marietta* 17547
717-653-4810 Fax: 717-653-5288
800-854-0399
Keith & Kathy Vogt All year

90-125-BB
3 rooms, 3 pb
Visa, MC, AmEx, *Rated*, •
C-yes/S-no/H-no

Full breakfast
Snacks
Sitting room, suites, fireplaces, cable TV, accom. bus. travelers

Small farm with cows, in Lancaster County. Breakfast is all you can eat.
lanier@vogtfarmbnb.com http://www.vogtfarmbnb.com

Maytown Manor
PO Box 275
25 W High St, *Maytown* 17550
717-426-2116 Fax: 717-426-2116
866-426-2116
Jeff & Julie Clouser All year

80-90-BB
3 rooms, 3 pb
Visa, MC, *Rated*
C-ltd/S-no/P-no/H-no

Full breakfast
Afternoon tea and complimentary snacks offered.
guest pantry, FP, A/C, PB, CBTV, VCR, radios, fans, hairdryers, Q/F beds.

Maytown Manor B&B provides an inviting and relaxing retreat near Lancaster, PA. Leave the hectic world behind, 'come home' to a peaceful sanctuary, and capture that 'renewed' feeling! innkeepers@maytownmanorbandb.com http://www.maytownmanorbandb.com

---

Hillside Farm
607 Eby Chiques Rd, *Mount Joy* 17552
717-653-6697 Fax: 717-653-9775
888-249-3406
Deb & Gary Lintner All year

90-215-BB
3 rooms, 3 pb
Most CC, *Rated*, •
C-ltd/S-no/P-no/H-no

Full breakfast
Afternoon & evening snacks
Sitting room, library, baby grand piano, A/C, barn cats, 6-person spa

Quiet, secluded, 1863, 2-acre farm homestead located in the heart of Amish Country, overlooking Chickies Creek with dam and waterfall, entirely surrounded by working farms. hillside3@att.net http://www.hillsidefarmbandb.com

LANCASTER (REGION)

The Olde Square Inn
127 E Main St, *Mount Joy* 17552
717-653-4525 Fax: 717-653-0976
800-742-3533
Fran & Dave Hand
All year

99-225-BB
5 rooms, 5 pb
Visa, MC, AmEx, Most CC, •
C-ltd/S-no/P-no/H-ltd

Full breakfast
All rooms equipped with cable color TV/VCR and phone jacks, coffee maker, hot tubs

Romantic Bed & Breakfast located on the historic square in Mount Joy, PA, which is surrounded by the peaceful Lancaster County farmlands. Enjoy gracious accommodations with in-town convenience. oldesquare@dejazzd.com http://www.oldesquareinn.com

---

Creekside Inn
PO Box 435
44 Leacock Rd, *Paradise* 17562
717-687-0333 Fax: 717-687-8200
866-604-2574
Cathy & Dennis Zimmermann

85-110-BB
5 rooms, 5 pb
Most CC, *Rated*
C-no/S-no/P-no/H-no
All year

Full breakfast
Afternoon tea, snacks
Sitting room, air conditioning, 2 guestrooms with fireplaces

Beautifully restored 1781 stone house on 2 acres along the Pequea Creek in the heart of Amish country. Private baths, antique furnishings, fireplace rooms, full breakfast.
cathy@thecreeksideinn.com http://www.thecreeksideinn.com

Candlelight Inn
2574 Lincoln Hwy E, *Ronks* 17572
717-299-6005
Fax: 717-299-6397
800-77-CANDLE
Tim & Heidi Soberick

79-159-BB
7 rooms, 7 pb
Most CC, *Rated*, •
C-ltd/S-no/P-no/H-no
French, Italian
All year

Full breakfast
Afternoon tea & snacks
Sitting room, antiques & oriental rugs, Victorian style

Large country home, elegantly decorated with Victorian antiques & Oriental rugs. Surrounded by Amish farms in the heart of PA Dutch country.
candleinn@aol.com http://www.candleinn.com

Homestead Lodging
PO Box 26
184 E Brook Rd (Rt 896), *Smoketown* 17576
717-393-6927
Fax: 717-393-1424

44-69-BB
5 rooms, 5 pb
Visa, MC, Disc, *Rated*, •
C-yes/S-no/P-no/H-no
Bob & Lori Kepiro
All year

Continental breakfast
Microwave
A/C, heat, cable TV, refrigerator in room, relax on porch or enjoy walking

Christian family owned B&B where you can rest, relax & recharge. Bob & Lori provide personal attention, warm hospitality and knowledge of area. Centrally located in heart of Amish farms & country. lkepiro@juno.com http://www.bbonline.com/pa/homestead/

Smoketown Village Guest House
PO Box 21
2495 Old Philadelphia Pike, *Smoketown* 17576
717-393-5975

36-42-BB
4 rooms, 2 pb
C-yes/S-ltd/P-no/H-no
Paul & Margaret Reitz
All year except Christmas

Continental breakfast
Sitting room, cable TV, comfortable porch, picnic table

Sleep under colorful quilts; relax in our spacious antique filled sitting room; watch the Amish buggies trot by from the porch; your hosts have helpful sightseeing ideas from our central location.

The Apple Bin Inn
2835 Willow Sreet Pike, *Willow Street* 17584
717-464-5881 Fax: 717-464-1818
800-338-4296
Mike & Dottie Mcloughlin

95-155-BB
5 rooms, 5 pb
Visa, MC, *Rated*
C-ltd/S-no/P-no/H-no
All year

Full breakfast
Afternoon tea, snacks
Sitting room, patios, 2 story Carriage House, w/frplc., living room

Warm Colonial charm with country flavor and antiques. Near Amish community, antique & craft shops, excellent restaurants & historical sites.
bininn@aol.com http://www.applebininn.com/

LANCASTER COUNTY (REGION)

Cocalico Creek	92-110-BB	Full breakfast
224 S 4th St, *Denver* 17517	4 rooms, 4 pb	Afternoon tea, snacks
717-336-0271 888-208-7334	Most CC, *Rated*	Sitting room, cable TV,
Charlene Sweeney	C-ltd/S-no/P-no/H-no	board/card games, puzzles,
All year		therapeutic massages

Casual elegance in a country setting overlooking pastures and gardens; a tranquil retreat blended with sounds of ducks splashing in ponds and Cocalico Creek, or the occasional Amish buggy passing by. cocalicocrk@dejazzd.com http://www.cocalicocrk.com

LANDENBERG

Cornerstone Inn	75-275-BB	Full breakfast
300 Buttonwood Rd 19350	8 rooms, 8 pb	Snacks, hot and cold
610-274-2143 Fax: 610-274-0734	Most CC, *Rated*	beverages
Kelle Anne Lafferty	C-yes/S-no/P-no/H-no	Sitting room, swimming pool,
All year	Spanish	therapeutic massage

A fine 18th century country house in the heart of the Brandywine Valley. Just minutes from Longwood gardens, Winterthur, and Amish country.
corner3000@aol.com http://www.cornerstoneinn.net

LEHIGH VALLEY (REGION)

Inn At Heyers' Mill	55-85-BB	Full breakfast
568 Heyer Mill Rd, *Nazareth*	4 rooms, 4 pb	Tennis court, cable TV,
18064	Most CC	fishing, accommodate bus.
610-759-6226 Fax: 610-759-6226	S-ltd/P-no/H-no	travelers
800-755-7829	Spanish	
Carl L. Mancino All year		

Located on 40 acres at the foothills of the Poconos. 2 acre pond bass fishing, Bushkill Creek, trout, and boating. http://www.innatheyersmill.com

LEWISBURG

Pineapple Inn	72-92-BB	Full country breakfast
439 Market St 17837	6 rooms, 6 pb	Comp. tea, snacks
570-524-6200	Most CC, *Rated*	A/C, pool nrby, piano, tea
Charles & Deborah North	C-ltd/S-ltd/P-no/H-no	room, sitt. room, tennis,
All year	German	wonderful restaurants

1857 Federal Victorian home decorated completely with 19th century antiques. Just blocks from Bucknell University. Beautiful architecture, great antiquing.
pineappl@jdweb.com http://www.jdweb.com/pineappleinn/

LEWISBURG (REGION)

The Inn at New Berlin	99-169-BB	Full breakfast
PO Box 390	9 rooms, 9 pb	Lunch & dinner available
321 Market St, *New Berlin*	Most CC, *Rated*, •	Evening dining available
17855	C-ltd/S-no/P-no/H-no	Wednesday to Sunday,
570-966-0321 Fax: 570-966-9557		closed Mondays & Tuesdays
800-797-2350		
John & Nancy Showers		
Closed 3 weeks in Jan.		

Uptown experience in a rural setting-the wooded hills & rolling farmlands of Central Pennsylvania. Wine Spectator acclaimed fine dining. A luxurious base for indulging in a clutch of quiet pleasures. lodging@newberlin-inn.com http://www.innatnewberlin.com

MCCLURE

Mountain Dale Farm	90-BB	Some meals available
RR 02, Box 985 17841	10 rooms, 10 pb	(arrange prior to arrival)
570-658-3536	C-yes/S-ltd/P-ltd/H-no	
Ken and Sally Hassinger		
All year		

Working farm in scenic rolling country, animals, fishing, hiking, antiques, cottages with bathrooms and kitchens. mtndale@sunlink.net http://www.pafarmstay.com

Ashcombe Mansion, Mechanicsburg, PA

MECHANICSBURG

Ashcombe Mansion	120-180-BB	Full breakfast, three courses
1100 Grantham Rd 17055	8 rooms, 6 pb	Afternoon tea, soft drinks
717-766-6820	Most CC, *Rated*, •	Sitting room, library,
Fax: 717-790-0723	C-ltd/S-ltd/P-no/H-no	fireplaces, cable TV/VCR,
Mira Stankovic	German, Yugoslavian	telephone,
All year		

"Ashcombe Mansion is one of the grandest bed & breakfasts in all of Pennsylvania," PA Visitor's Guide. Ashcombe offers the romance and style of a bygone era.
ashcombe@pa.net http://www.Ashcombemansion.com

MERCERSBURG

Mercersburg Inn	135-275-BB	Full breakfast
405 S Main St 17236	15 rooms, 15 pb	Aft. tea/scones-weekends,
717-328-5231	Most CC, *Rated*, •	evening refreshments
Fax: 717-328-3403	C-ltd/S-ltd/P-no/H-ltd	
Walt & Sandy Filkowski		
All year		

A stately 20,000 sq. ft Georgian Mansion on 5 acres of terraced lawns. Once the private residence of Ione and Harry Byron, the home is now a 15 guestroom country Inn.
sandy@mercersburginn.com http://www.mercersburginn.com

The Steiger House	85-125-BB	Full breakfast
33 N Main St 17236	4 rooms, 4 pb	Complimentary wine or
717-328-5757 Fax: 717-328-5627	Most CC	other beverage
Ron L. Snyder	C-ltd/S-ltd/P-no/H-no	Sitting room, TV room with
All year		VCR/DVD, courtyard

Circa 1820, the Steiger House is a federal style home located in the Historic District of Mercersburg, PA. Near Whitetail Ski Resort, Whitetail Golf Course and the Mercersburg Academy. steiger@steigerhouse.com http://www.steigerhouse.com

MERTZTOWN

Longswamp	93-125-BB	Full breakfast
1605 State St 19539	10 rooms, 10 pb	Early coffee and tea
610-682-6197 Fax: 610-682-4854	Visa, MC, AmEx, *Rated*	Bocce court, horseshoes,
JoAnn and John Swenson	C-ltd/S-ltd/P-no/H-ltd	fireplaces, suites; rooms w/
All year		fridge, MW's and TV's

Historic country mansion and cottage in Lehigh Valley. Full breakfast included. Beautiful gardens and fruit orchards on premises.
innkeeper@longswamp.com http://www.longswamp.com

MILFORD

Black Walnut Country Inn 179 Firetower Rd 18337 570-296-6322 Fax: 570-296-7696 Stewart Schneider, Awilda Torres All year	60-175-BB 14 rooms, 8 pb Visa, MC, AmEx, *Rated*, • C-yes/S-ltd/P-no/H-no	Full breakfast Restaurant, complimentary sherry, BBQ on weekends Pool table, lawn games, piano, pond, hot tub, riding lessons, trails

Large secluded estate for an exclusive clientele. Tudor-style stone house w/ marble fireplace, charming bedrooms. with antiques/brass beds.
awilda@theblackwalnutinn.com http://www.theblackwalnutinn.com

Laurel Villa Country Inn 2nd & E Ann St 18337 570-296-9940 Janice Halsted & Carl Muhlhauser Mid-March–Dec. 31	75-145-BB 10 rooms, 10 pb Most CC C-yes/S-yes/P-ltd/H-no	Continental breakfast Restaurant, dinner, bar service Sitting room, suites, fireplaces, cable TV, A/C

Country inn on quiet side street. Candlelight dining; cozy sitting room with fireplace. Extensive gardens in a park-like setting with koi pond and benches for relaxing.
info@laurelvilla.com http://www.laurelvilla.com

MILFORD (REGION)

Roebling Inn on the Delaware PO Box 31 155 Scenic Drive, *Lackawaxen* 18435 570-685-7900 Fax: 570-685-1718 Don & JoAnn Jahn All year	75-150-BB 6 rooms, 6 pb Most CC, *Rated* C-ltd/S-ltd/P-no/H-no	Full breakfast Afternoon tea & cookies Sitting room with fireplace & books, porch with riverview

A profound escape from urban stress amid scenery to soothe the senses. Enjoy a backroad ride through our beautiful region. Canoe the river. See an eagle. View waterfalls. Have a great meal. Star gaze. roebling@ltis.net http://www.roeblinginn.com

MILTON

Pau-lyn's Country RR 3, Box 676 17847 570-742-4110 Paul & Evelyn Landis All year	65-75-BB 7 rooms, 4 pb *Rated* C-yes/S-no/P-no/H-ltd	Full breakfast Sitting room, fireplaces, cable TV, accom. bus. travelers

1857 Built Victorian Brick House furnished in antiques and working musical instruments. Large patio and yard, many trees and birds.
paulyns@uplink.net http://www.welcome.to/paulyns

MONTROSE

Ridge House 6 Ridge St 18801 570-278-4933 888-600-4933 Thomas & Veea Calcaine All year	55-BB 4 rooms, 2 pb *Rated*, • C-yes/S-ltd/P-yes/H-no	Continental plus breakfast

Warm hospitality; comfortable rooms; antique furnishings; ideal for peaceful getaway, relaxing business travel. We make every effort to make guests feel this is their extended home.

MOUNT JOY

Cedar Hill Farm 305 Longenecker Rd 17552 717-653-4655 Fax: 717-653-9242 Gladys Swarr All year	85-105-BB 5 rooms, 5 pb Most CC, *Rated*, • C-ltd/S-ltd/P-no/H-no	Continental plus breakfast Central A/C, porch, 1 room with private balcony, 1 room with whirlpool tub

Host born in this 1817 Fieldstone farmhouse. Quiet area overlooks stream. Near Lancaster's Amish country & Hershey. cedarhill@supernet.com http://www.cedarhillfarm.com

NEW HOPE

1830 Porches on the Towpath
20 Fishers Alley 18938
215-862-3277 Fax: 215-862-1833
John, Billy & Chrissie
All year

95-195-BB
6 rooms, 6 pb
Visa, MC, AmEx
C-ltd/S-ltd/P-ltd/H-ltd

Full country breakfast
Refreshments
Library, bicycles, gardens

A gracious Country Inn located in the heart of historic New Hope, Bucks County, with six beautifully furnished guest rooms. Two story wrap around porch overlooking the Delaware Canal. info@porchesnewhope.com http://www.porchesnewhope.com

---

1870 Wedgwood Inn – New Hope
111 W Bridge St
Route 179 18938
215-862-3936 Fax: 215-862-3937
Carl & Nadine Glassman
All year

95-260-BB
14 rooms, 14 pb
Visa, MC, AmEx, *Rated*, •
C-ltd/S-no/P-ltd/H-yes
French, Hebrew, Dutch, Italian

Continental plus breakfast in Bed
Aft.. tea on Sat & refreshments on arrival daily
Victorian gazebo, dbl Jacuzzis, in-room massage, frplcs, parlors

Bucks County Victorian mansion. Two-person Jacuzzi tubs/frplces, Wedgwood china, fresh flowers, gingerbread porches. OUR 1989 INN OF THE YEAR! On 2 private, park-like acres in New Hope. Open year round.
carl.glassman@erols.com http://www.1870WedgwoodInn.com

Aaron Burr House Inn
80 W Bridge St
Corner of Chestnut St 18938
215-862-2570 Fax: 215-862-3937
Nadine & Carl Glassman
All year

90-199-BB
8 rooms, 8 pb
Visa, MC, AmEx, *Rated*, •
C-ltd/S-no/P-ltd/H-yes
French, Spanish, Italian, Hebrew

Continental plus breakfast
Comp. liqueur, snacks. Welc ref and Sat Tea.
Afternoon tea, library, 2 new fireplace suites, white wicker porch, pool

Lace Canopy beds and fireplaces! Discover "safe haven" in vintage village Victorian inn—Aaron Burr did after his famous pistol duel with Alexander Hamilton in 1804! A "Wedgwood Inn." stay@new-hope-inn.com http://www.aaronburrhouse.com

---

Fox and Hound – New Hope
246 W Bridge St 18938
215-862-5082 Fax: 215-862-5082
800-862-5082
Art and Colleen Menz
All year

85-170-BB
8 rooms, 8 pb
Visa, MC, AmEx, *Rated*, •
C-no/S-no/P-no/H-no

Full breakfast daily
Afternoon refreshments

Elegant 1850 stone manor on 2 acres. 8 queen or king rooms w/private bath, air cond, color TV; some with fireplaces. Full breakfast served daily.
info@foxhoundinn.com http://foxhoundinn.com

Pineapple Hill
1324 River Rd 18938
215-862-1790 Fax: 215-862-5273
888-866-8404
Kathryn & Charles "Cookie" Triolo
All year

94-279-BB
9 rooms, 9 pb
Most CC, *Rated*, •
C-ltd/S-no/P-no/H-no

Full breakfast
Afternoon tea, snacks, evening sherry
Sitting room, library, bicycles, pool, cable TV, fireplaces, telephones

Romantic rooms and suites, all with private baths. Full gourmet breakfast daily, served at individual candlelit tables. innkeeper@pineapplehill.com http://www.pineapplehill.com

---

The Whitehall Inn
1370 Pineville Rd 18938
215-598-7945 Fax: 215-598-0378
888-37-WHITE
Mike & Suella Wass
All year

160-230-BB
6 rooms, 4 pb
Most CC, *Rated*, •
C-ltd/S-no/P-no/H-no

Full candlelight breakfast
High tea, complimentary sherry
Pool & rose garden, library, sun room, piano & pump organ

Experience our four-course candlelit breakfast using European china and crystal and heirloom sterling silver. whitehall@hotmail.com http://www.selectregistry.com

NEW HOPE (REGION)

Golden Pheasant Inn on the Delaware
763 River Rd, *Erwinna* 18920
610-294-9595 Fax: 610-294-9882
800-830-4474
Barbara & Michael Faure

95-225-BB
6 rooms, 6 pb
Visa, MC, *Rated*, •
C-ltd/S-ltd/P-ltd
French, Spanish, Italian
All year

Continental plus breakfast
Dinner (Tues.–Sun.)
Restaurant, bar, canoes, Delaware Canal & River, wine in rm., hiking/bike

1857 fieldstone inn situated between river and canal. Six rooms furnished with incredible blend of antiques. barbara@goldenpheasant.com http://www.goldenpheasant.com

---

Barley Sheaf Farm
PO Box 10
5281 York Rd, Route 202, *Holicong* 18928
215-794-5104 Fax: 215-794-5332
Veronika & Peter Suess

110-300-BB
12 rooms, 12 pb
Rated, •
C-ltd/S-no/P-no/H-yes
French, German
All year

Full farm breakfast
Afternoon tea
Swimming pool, sitt. rm., one room with Jacuzzi, conference center

30-acre working farm–raise sheep. Rooms all furnished in antiques. Good antiquing and historic sights in area. info@barleysheaf.com http://www.barleysheaf.com

---

Hollyleaf Inn
677 Durham Rd, *Newtown* 18940
215-598-3100 Fax: 215-598-3423
Janice Sullivan
All year

125-175-BB
5 rooms, 5 pb
Visa, MC, AmEx, *Rated*, •
C-ltd/S-ltd/P-ltd/H-ltd

Full breakfast
Afternoon coffee, tea & desserts
Accommodate special diet, volleyball, croquet, badminton, horseshoes

A peaceful 18th Century farm house situated on 5 1/2 acres of rolling Buck County countryside. info@hollyleaf.com http://www.hollyleaf.com

---

Tattersall Inn
PO Box 569
Cafferty & River Rds, *Pt. Pleasant* 18950
215-297-8233 Fax: 800-297-5093
800-297-4988
Donna & Bob Trevorrow
All year

120-155-BB
6 rooms, 6 pb
Visa, MC, *Rated*, •
C-ltd/S-ltd/P-no/H-no

Full breakfast
Apple cider, snacks
Library, sitting room, piano, veranda, conference, walk-in fireplace

Circa 1750. This Bucks County plastered fieldstone house with its 18" thick walls, broad porches and wainscoted entry hall offers a peaceful place to relax, rebuild and enjoy the bucolic surroundings. tattersallinn@aol.com http://www.tattersallinn.com

---

Woolverton Inn
6 Woolverton Rd, *Stockton, NJ* 08559
609-397-0802 Fax: 609-397-0987
888-264-6648
C. McGavin, M. Lovette, M. Smith
All year

100-295-BB
9 rooms, 9 pb
Visa, MC, AmEx, *Rated*, •
C-ltd/S-no/P-no/H-ltd
Some Spanish and German

Full country breakfast
Snacks
Sitting room, suites, fireplaces, Jacuzzis, gardens, meeting facilities

A 1792 stone manor house on 10 acres of lawns and gardens, surrounded by 400 acres of rolling farmland. So close to everything, but a world away. Elegant hearty breakfasts. Sheep@WoolvertonInn.com http://www.woolvertoninn.com

---

The Bridgeton House on the Delaware
1525 River Rd, *Upper Black Eddy* 18972
610-982-5856 888-982-2007
Charles & Bea Briggs
All year

99-279-BB
11 rooms, 11 pb
Visa, MC, *Rated*, •
C-ltd/S-ltd/P-no/H-ltd

Full gourmet breakfast
Afternoon tea & cakes
Rocking chairs & river views, swim, fish & tube, phones/data ports, TV/VCR

Bucks county's only Riverfront B&B Inn! 1836 inn on Delaware River. French Doors, Private Riverfront Balconies, Canopy Beds, Fireplaces & Featherbeds. Swim, Fish & Birdwatch from our Riverbank & Dock. innkeeper@bridgetonhouse.com http://www.bridgetonhouse.com

NEW HOPE (REGION)

Inn to the Woods
150 Glenwood Dr, *Washington Crossing* 18977
215-493-1974 Fax: 215-493-7592
800-982-7619
Carol & Chris Bolton All year

99-225-BB
7 rooms, 7 pb
Most CC, *Rated*, •
C-ltd/S-no/P-no/H-no

Full breakfast on weekends
Afternoon refreshments and evening sweets.
Indoor atrium, king or queen beds, tubs for two, fireplaces

Nestled on 7.5 wooded acres in Washington Crossing/Bucks County. "Every Room Tells A Story." Seven unique guestrooms some with double tubs and fireplaces. Outdoor gardens & pond. inn2woods@inn-bucks.com http://www.inn-bucks.com/

NEW MILFORD

Lynn-Lee House
143 Main St 18834
570-465-3505
Chuck and Eleanor Lempke
All year

95-105-BB
4 rooms, 2 pb
Rated, •
C-ltd/S-no/P-no/H-no

Full breakfast
Afternoon tea
Sitting room, fireplaces, cable TV, accom. bus. travelers

A lovingly restored 1868 Victorian, furnished with antiques and period furnishings. Cozy quilts, fresh flowers, fireplaces in parlor, early morning coffee and tea.
http://www.lynn-lee.com

NORTH WALES

Joseph Ambler Inn
1005 Horsham Rd 18901
215-362-7500 Fax: 215-361-5924
Richard Allman
All year

100-250-BB
36 rooms, 36 pb
Most CC, *Rated*, •
C-yes/S-yes/P-no/H-ltd
French, German

Full breakfast
Restaurant
3 sitting rooms, banquet/meeting room, special diet cooking

1735 estate house set on 13 acres and furnished with antiques, four-poster beds, walk-in fireplace. 6 rooms have spa tubs.
jai@josephamblerinn.com http://www.josephamblerinn.com

OXFORD

Troll Hollow
371 Street Rd 19363
610-998-1007
Don Nilsen
All year

75-150-BB
7 rooms, 5 pb
Visa, MC
C-ltd/S-no/P-no/H-no

Full breakfast
Afternoon tea, snacks
Sitting room, library, accommodate business travelers

Huge country manor house, beautifully furnished with antiques. Desks and comfortable chairs with reading lamps in each room.
troll35@epix.net http://www.bbonline.com/pa/trollhollow

PARADISE

After Eight B&B
PO Box 24
2942 Lincoln Hwy E 17562
717-687-3664 Fax: 717-687-7620
888-314-3664
Toni & Lorin Wortel
All year

99-159-BB
8 rooms, 8 pb
Visa, MC, Disc, *Rated*, •
C-ltd/S-ltd/P-no/H-ltd
Dutch

Gourmet Full Served Breakfast
Coffee, tea, fruit, fruit drinks
Sitting room, antique decor, landscaped grounds with gazebo & fountains

Renovated colonial brick home from 1818 in the center of the Pennsylvania Dutch, Amish heartland. Elegantly decorated and antique filled guestrooms with modern amenities and private baths. aftereight_bb@yahoo.com http://www.theplacetostay.com

PHILADELPHIA

Alexander Inn
301 South 12th St
Spruce at 12th St 19107
215-923-3535 Fax: 215-923-1004
877-ALEX-INN
George Blum All year

129-BB
48 rooms, 48 pb
Most CC, *Rated*, •
C-ltd/S-ltd/P-no/H-ltd
Spanish, French

Continental plus breakfast
Snacks
Cable TV, accommodate business travelers, fitness center-24 hour

A beautiful, small hotel with B&B hospitality. Designer rooms, big fluffy towels, complimentary breakfast with fresh baked goods, great artwork, 4 complimentary movie channels, 24-hour fitness center. info@alexanderinn.com http://www.alexanderinn.com

PHILADELPHIA

Anam Cara
52 Wooddale Ave 19118
215-242-4327
Fax: 215-242-4327
Teresa Vesey & Jack Gann
All year

95-125-BB
3 rooms, 3 pb
Visa, MC, Disc, *Rated*, •
C-ltd/S-no/P-no/H-no

Continental plus breakfast
Complimentary wine
Sitting room, fireplaces, cable TV, accommodate business travlers

At Anam Cara Bed & Breakfast a special ambiance is created by owner and hostess Teresa Vesey. acarabandb@aol.com http://www.anamcarabandb.com/

Antique Row
341 S 12th St 19107
215-592-7802 Fax: 215-592-9692
Barbara Pope
All year

70-110-BB
C-ltd/S-ltd/P-no/H-no

Full breakfast

A small, European-style guesthouse, recommended by Lonely Planet, Let's Go USA, Globe-trotter, etc., for centrally-located, comfortable and civilized lodging at a reasonable cost. bp341@aol.com http://www.antiquerowbnb.com

---

The Gables
4520 Chester Ave 19143
215-662-1918 Fax: 215-662-1918
Warren Cederholm & Don Caskey
All year

85-125-BB
10 rooms, 8 pb
Most CC
C-ltd/S-no/P-no/H-no

Full breakfast
Snacks
Sitting room, fireplaces, cable TV, accom. bus. travelers, private phones

Restored Victorian mansion. Winner of Historic Preservation Award. Near University of Pennsylvania, Drexel and hospitals; 12 minutes to center city by easy public transportation. gablesbb@aol.com http://www.gablesbb.com

---

Gaskill House
312 Gaskill St 19147
215-413-0669
Guy M. Davis
All year

145-200-BB
3 rooms, 3 pb
•
C-ltd/S-no/P-ltd/H-no

Full breakfast
Living Room, Parlor, Music and Video Library

Gaskill House is a small, European type luxury B&B in Philadelphia's historic Society Hill district. Built in 1828, Gaskill House has been totally renovated and beautifully furnished. gaskillbnb@aol.com http://www.gaskillhouse.com

---

Grier House
322 S 12th St 19107
215-732-4415
Fax: 215-732-4415
Cathy Grier
All year

85-135-BB
5 rooms, 5 pb
Visa, MC
C-ltd/S-ltd/P-ltd/H-ltd

Continental plus breakfast
Suites, cable TV, accommodate business travelers

Urban inn—perfect for business or leisure travel. Walking distance to Convention Center, Liberty Bell, shopping, dining, entertainment, museums. grierc@bellatlantic.net http://www.grierhouse.com

---

Mellow Manor B&B in Overbrook Farms
6359 Woodbine Ave 19151
215-477-3311 Fax: 215-878-0475
800-820-9876
Ted Gentner
All year

90-125-BB
8 rooms, 1 pb
Visa, MC, *Rated*
C-ltd/S-no/P-no/H-ltd

Full breakfast
Lunch, dinner, tea, snacks, wine
Sitting room, library, fireplace, cable TV, conferences

Unique home designed in 1896 in a planned community. In 1915 changed from twin into single. The porches & plazas offer a homey invitation for browsing the gardens. fwg@aol.com http://www.travelguides.com/home/mellow_manor/

PHILADELPHIA

Penn's View Inn Hotel
14 N Front St
Front & Market Streets 19106
215-922-7600 Fax: 215-922-7642
800-331-7634
The Sena Family
All year

108-195-BB
38 rooms, 38 pb
Most CC, *Rated*, •
C-yes/S-yes/P-no/H-no
Italian, Spanish

Continental plus breakfast
Lunch & dinner available
Restaurant, bar service, Jacuzzis, fireplaces, individual wine tasting

Charming European-style hotel. Short walk to historic attractions. 2 meeting rooms.
http://pennsviewhotel.com

Society Hill Hotel
301 Chestnut St @ 3rd 19106
215-925-1919
Judith Kleinman
All year

85-175-BB
12 rooms, 12 pb
Most CC, *Rated*, •
C-yes/S-yes/P-ltd

Continental breakfast
Restaurant
Piano bar, telephones, individual wine tasting

An "urban inn" located in the midst of Philadelphia's Historic Park. Fresh flowers, chocolates and brass double beds grace each room.

Thomas Bond House
129 S Second St 19106
215-923-8523 Fax: 215-923-8504
800-845-BOND
Rita McGuire
All year

95-175-BB
12 rooms, 12 pb
Visa, MC, AmEx, *Rated*, •
C-yes/S-ltd/P-no/H-no

Continental plus and Full breakfast
Full breakfast on weekends, wine & cheese, cookies
Hair dryers, TV, phone, fireplaces, whirlpool tubs, local calls, soda

Circa 1769, listed in Nat'l Register. Individually decorated rooms. Only lodging in Independence Nat'l Historical Park. One of top 25 historic inns, AAA & Mobile rated.
ctheall@dddcompany.com http://www.winston-salem-inn.com/philadelphia

PHILADELPHIA (REGION)

General Lafayette Inn & Brewery
646 Germantown Pike, *Lafayette Hill* 19444
610-941-0600 Fax: 610-941-0766
800-251-0181
Michael & Ellen McGlynn
All year

99-159-BB
5 rooms, 4 pb
Visa, MC, AmEx, *Rated*, •
C-ltd/S-ltd/P-no/H-ltd

Continental breakfast
Lunch & dinner avail, aft. tea, snacks
Restaurant, bar service, sitting rm, library, suites, fireplace in living rm

Quiet and secluded with Victorian charm. Set amongst tall oaks and connected to the restaurant and brewery by a brick pathway.
ellen.mcglynn@generallafayetteinn.com http://www.generallafayetteinn.com

PITTSBURGH

The Priory—A City Inn
614 Pressley St 15212
412-231-3338 Fax: 412-231-4838
Mary Ann Graf
All year

121-160-BB
24 rooms, 24 pb
Most CC, *Rated*, •

Continental Plus breakfast
Complimentary wine, snacks
Honor Bar, cable TV, accom. bus. travelers

The Priory—A City Inn, is a European style hotel, with the appointments of a large establishment, and the personality and personal service that only a small inn can offer.
edgpgh@stargate.net http://www.thepriory.com

The Waterford
3337 Brownsville Rd 15227
412-881-1111 Fax: 412-881-7777
Jason Coll & Lisa Klein
All year

125-195-BB
6 rooms, 3 pb
Most CC, *Rated*
C-ltd/S-ltd/P-no/H-no

Continental breakfast
Complimentary wine
Sitting room, cable TV, accom. bus. travel

The Waterford B&B provides its guests with stunning landscaping and plenty of free parking. waterfordbb@msn.com http://www.waterfordbb.com

La Anna Guesthouse, Cresco, PA

PITTSBURGH (REGION)

Kane Manor Country Inn 230 Clay St, *Kane* 16735 814-837-6522 Fax: 814-837-6522 Joyce Benek All year	89-149-BB 10 rooms, 6 pb Visa, MC, AmEx, *Rated* C-yes/P-no/H-ltd	Continental breakfast Restaurant, bar, afternoon tea Sitting room, piano, banquet room

Kane Manor is one of the best kept secrets of the Alleghanies. The historical landmark boast 250 acres of property.

PLEASANT MOUNT

Pleasant View RR 1 Box 186 18453 570-448-9627 Fax: 570-448-3146 800-450-2544 Eileen Fella & Laura Mirarchi All year	60-90-BB 5 rooms, 3 pb Most CC, • C-ltd/S-ltd/P-no/H-no	Full breakfast Snacks Sitting room, cable TV, woodstove in gathering room, front porch

Cozy, warm 100 year old Victorian nestled in the woodlands. Activities for every season nearby. Full country breakfast served daily. Homemade "goodies" available all day.
plsntvw@nep.net http://www.bedandbreakfast.com/bbc/p603727.asp

POCONO MOUNTAINS (REGION)

La Anna Guesthouse RR 2, Box 2801, *Cresco* 18326 570-676-4225 Fax: 570-676-4225 Kay Swingle & Jill Porter All year	50-BB 4 rooms, 2 pb *Rated* C-ltd/S-yes/P-ltd/H-no	Continental plus breakfast Sitting room, piano, cross-country skiing, fishing, swimming, golf

Private Victorian home nestled in Pocono Mountain village welcomes guests. Furnished with antiques.

RIDGWAY

Towers Victorian Inn 330 South St 15853 814-772-7657 Dale & Dan Lauricella All year	70-125-BB 5 rooms, 5 pb Visa, MC, AmEx C-ltd/S-no/P-no/H-ltd	Continental plus breakfast Snacks, complimentary wine Sitting room, bikes, suites, cable TV, accom. bus. travelers

Elegant and historic B&B in Elk County, five minutes from Allegheny National Forest.
lauricde@ncentral.com http://www.ncentral.com/~towers

RIVERTON (REGION)

Belle Reve
7757 Martin's Creek/ Belvidere Rd, *Bangor* 18013
610-498-2026 Fax: 610-498-2163
888-549-8608
Shirley Creo
All year

80-125-BB
5 rooms, 3 pb
Visa
C-ltd/S-no/P-no/H-no

Full & Continental Plus breakfast
Afternoon tea, snacks
Sitting room, cable TV, accommodate business travelers, riverside gazebo

Belle Reve, our "beautiful dream," is located on the Delaware River, the boundary between Pennsylvania and New Jersey, making attractions in both states easily accessible.
bellereve@enter.net http://www.bellereveriverside.com

SCRANTON (REGION)

Red Barn Village
1826 Red Barn Village, *Clarks Summit* 18411
570-587-2567 800-531-2567
Bert & Nancy Ayers
All year

109-199-BB
3 rooms, 3 pb
Most CC, •
C-ltd/S-no/P-no/H-no

Full breakfast

Red Barn Village B&B is a comfortable, relaxing, truly unique accommodation set in the countryside 20 min. from Scranton, & 45 min. from Wilkes Barre, PA.
bertayrs@uplink.net http://www.redbarnvillage.com/b&b/

SEWICKLEY (REGION)

The Whistlestop
195 Broad St, *Leetsdale* 15056
724-251-0852
Joyce & Stephen Smith
All year

70-80-BB
3 rooms, 3 pb
Visa, MC, AmEx, •
C-yes/S-no/P-ltd/H-ltd

Full breakfast
Cable TV, nearby trains

Built in 1888 by the Harmonists, our brick Victorian is located 20 minutes from Pittsburgh and the airport. http://www.pittsburghbnb.com/whistle.html

SHIPPENSBURG

Field & Pine
2155 Ritner Hwy 17257
717-776-7179 Fax: 717-776-0076
Mary Ellen & Allan Williams
All year

70-85-BB
3 rooms, 1 pb
Visa, MC, *Rated*, •
C-ltd/S-no/P-no/H-no

Full breakfast
Afternoon tea, snacks, wine
Sitting room, library, fireplaces, antiques, fly fishing streams

Historic limestone house c.1790, on 80 acre farm. Antiques, fireplaces, gourmet country breakfast. Come stay with us–homemade cookies await you.
fieldpine@aol.com http://www.cubedandbreakfasts.com

SOMERSET

Bayberry Inn
611 N Center Ave 15501
814-445-8471
Marilyn & Bob Lohr
All year

55-65-BB
11 rooms, 11 pb
Most CC, *Rated*, •
C-ltd/S-no/P-no/H-no

Continental plus breakfast
Snacks
Sitting room, library, TV room with VCR/stereo, swimming pool

One and one-half blocks from turnpike exit, near Georgian Place Outlet Mall.
robertlohr498@msn.com http://www.bayberry-inn.com

Glades Pike Inn
2684 Glades Pike 15501
814-443-4978 Fax: 814-443-2562
800-762-5942
Janet L. Jones
All year

70-90-BB
5 rooms, 5 pb
Most CC, *Rated*, •
C-ltd/S-no/P-no/H-no

Full breakfast
Complimentary wine on weekends
Swimming pool

Built in 1842 as a stagecoach stop; located on a 200-acre dairy farm in the center of Laurel Highlands. Close to skiing, golf, state parks, falling water.
fwmjj@sprynet.com http://www.gladespike.com/

ST. MARYS

Towne House Inn 138 Center St 15801 814-781-1556 Fax: 814-834-4449 800-851-9180 Aimee Renner All year	52-125-BB 14 rooms, 14 pb Most CC	Continental breakfast Full country breakfast/luncheon menu & dinner menu

We now have 8 homes with 58 guestrooms all in one location.
townhous@penn.com http://www.townehouseinn.com

STARLIGHT

The Inn at Starlight Lake PO Box 27 Route 4020, Lake Road 18431 570-798-2519 Fax: 570-798-2672 800-248-2519 Jack & Judy McMahon Exc. late Mar-Apr 16	165-255-MAP 26 rooms, 21 pb Visa, MC, *Rated*, • C-yes/S-ltd/P-no/H-no	Full breakfast Lunch, dinner, full bar Sitting room, piano, tennis court, boating, bicycles, hiking trails

A congenial recreation for every season. Breakfast and dinner included in rate.
theinn@unforgettable.com http://www.innatstarlightlake.com

STATE COLLEGE (REGION)

Harmon House PO Box 61 3947 Main St, *Belleville* 17004 717-935-2291 Fax: 717-935-2291 800-299-8849 Phyllis Harmon All year	40-90-BB 3 rooms, 1 pb *Rated*, • C-ltd/S-no/P-no/H-no Interpreter available for 8 languages	Full breakfast Snacks, complimentary wine, lunch/dinner available Sitting room, library, pool, cable TV, accom. bus. travelers

Relax in our quiet, casual Greek colonial that once housed the village bank. Shop for handmade Amish quilts and crafts. pharmon@acsworld.net

STRASBURG

The Decoy B&B 958 Eisenberger Road 17579 717-687-8585 Fax: 717-687-9713 800-726-2287 Robert & Carol Kroth All year	70-80-BB 5 rooms, 5 pb C-yes/S-no/P-no/H-yes	Full breakfast

Quietly and peacefully set in the Amish farmland just south of Strasburg, PA, close to the special attractions of the area, our blue Amish farmhouse gives you the feeling of home in Lancaster County. decoybnb@aol.com http://www.kroth.com/decoybnb

The Limestone Inn 33 E Main St 17579 717-687-8392 Fax: 717-687-8366 800-278-8392 Denise & Richard Waller & Daughters All year	89-115-BB 5 rooms, 5 pb Most CC, *Rated* C-ltd/S-no/P-no/H-no	Full gourmet breakfast Tea, coffee, snacks, cold drinks Sitting rooms, library, bicycle storage, patio

The Limestone Inn B situated in the heart of Lancaster's Amish country.
limestoneinn@yahoo.com http://www.thelimestoneinn.com

SUMMIT

The Inn at Nichols Village 1101 Northern Blvd 18411 570-587-1135 Fax: 570-586-7140 800-642-2215 George A. Nichols All year	69-219-BB 134 rooms, 134 pb Most CC, *Rated*, • C-yes/S-yes/P-no/H-yes	Continental bkfst. midweek Special pkgs. avail.; lunch; dinner; 2 restaurants Jacuzzis, swimming pool, suites, cable TV, accom. bus. trav.

Our 12-acre inn is a blend of luxury and familiarity.
roomsnv@epix.net http://www.nicholsvillage.com

THORNTON

Pace One Restaurant & Country Inn
PO Box 108
Glen Mills & Thornton Rd.
19373
610-459-3702 Fax: 610-558-0825
Ted Pace All year

95-BB
6 rooms, 6 pb
S-no/P-no

Continental breakfast
In-room television, phone

Pace One Country Inn is located in the heart of Brandywine Valley, an area rich in history and natural beauty. augustpace@msn.net http://www.paceone.net

UNIONTOWN

Inne at Watson's Choice
234 Balsinger Rd 15401
724-437-4999 888-820-5380
William & Nancy Ross
All year

94-275-BB
7 rooms, 7 pb
Most CC, *Rated*, •
C-ltd/S-no/P-no/H-yes
French

Full breakfast weekend
Continental breakfast midweek, snacks
Sitting room, library, accommodate business travelers

Restored circa 1820 Western PA farmhouse offering charm and ambiance of yesteryear and just a short distance drive to Frank Lloyd Wright's "Fallingwater and Kentuck Knob."
innkeeper@watsonschoice.com http://www.watsonschoice.com

VALLEY FORGE

Great Valley House of Valley Forge
1475 Swedesford Rd 19355
610-644-6759 Fax: 610-644-7019
Pattye Benson All year

95-115-BB
3 rooms, 3 pb
Most CC
C-yes/S-no/P-ltd/H-no

Full breakfast
Swimming pool, cable TV, guest refrigerator and microwave

Built before the Revolutionary War, the Great Valley House retains original fireplaces and random-width wood floors. As you enjoy breakfast, there may be a fire in the old kitchen walk-in fireplace. pattye@greatvalleyhouse.com http://www.greatvalleyhouse.com

VALLEY FORGE (REGION)

Shearer Elegance
1154 Main St, *Linfield* 19468
610-495-7429 Fax: 610-495-7814
800-861-0308
Shirley and Malcolm Shearer
All year

90-140-BB
7 rooms, 7 pb
Most CC, *Rated*, •
C-ltd/S-no/P-no/H-ltd

Full breakfast
Sitting room, private baths, Jacuzzi tubs

22 room Victorian with 3 acres of gardens in summer and 35 decorated Christmas trees in winter. shearerc@aol.com http://www.shearerelegance.com

---

Coddington House
441 S Whitehorse Rd
441 S Whitehorse Road, *Phoenixville* 19460
610-935-2454 Fax: 610-935-8422
Cara Walker All year

100-150-BB
2 rooms, 2 pb
Visa, MC, AmEx
C-ltd/S-ltd/P-no/H-no

Full breakfast
Snacks, complimentary bar
Sitting room, Jacuzzis, pool, fireplace, cable TV, conference facilities

1730 farmhouse, adjacent to 300 acre farm, with antique furniture, fireplaces, pool, hot tub, golf, complimentary bar, toiletries, bathrobes.
bigcoddi@cs.com http://www.bbhost.com/coddingtonhouse

WARFORDSBURG

Buck Valley Ranch LLC
Rt 2 Box 1170
1344 Negro Mountain Road
17267
717-294-3759 Fax: 717-294-6413
800-294-3759
Leon Fox All year

65-125-MAP
4 rooms
AmEx, Disc, •
C-yes/S-ltd/P-no/H-no

Full breakfast
Lunch
horseback riding, outdoor pool, hot tub, air conditioned

Buck Valley Ranch LLC, a year round resort located in the Appalachian Mountains of south central Pennsylvania, offers trail riding and other outdoor activities in a secluded setting.
bvranch@nb.net http://www.buckvalleyranch.com

WARREN

Horton House
504 Market St 16365
814-723-7472 Fax: 814-726-3633
888-723-7472
Scalise Family All year

89-98-BB
5 rooms, 5 pb
Most CC, *Rated*, •
C-yes/S-ltd/P-ltd/H-no

Full breakfast
Beverages & snacks
Hot Tub, woodburning fireplaces,private line phones,private baths,

Stately, historical, 22-room Victorian mansion at gateway to Allegheny National Forest. Inn offers 5 bedrooms with private baths, Wood-burning fireplaces, music room, sun deck and year-round hot tub. hh504bb@aol.com http://www.hortonhousebb.com

WATTSBURG

TimberMist
11050 Backus Rd 16442
814-739-9004 888-739-9004
Karen & Steve Rzepecki
All year

120-135-BB
2 rooms, 2 pb
Visa, MC, Disc.
C-no/S-no/P-no/H-ltd

Full breakfast
Beverages and snacks
Therapeutic massage, hot tub spa, game room with billiards

TimberMist is the perfect romantic getaway! Explore nature on the 100-acre estate. Gaze at the stars from the outdoor hot tub spa. Exquisite rooms, private baths, robes, on-site massage. info@timbermist.com http://www.timbermist.com

WELLSBORO

Kaltenbach's
RD #6 Box 106A
Stonyfork Rd & Kelsey St
16901
570-724-4954 800-722-4954
Lee Kaltenbach All year

80-150-BB
10 rooms, 10 pb
Visa, MC, *Rated*, •
C-yes/S-no/P-no/H-yes
Spanish

Full breakfast
Afternoon tea, snacks, wine
Lunch/dinner by res., sitting room, library, tennis court, Jacuzzis

Featuring antique quilts made by the owner's grandmother 80 years ago. Nearby rails to trails, hiking and biking through the canyon. http://www.kaltenbachsinn.com

WEST CHESTER

1732 Folke Stone
777 Copeland School Rd 19380
610-429-0310 Fax: 610-918-9228
800-884-4666
Marcy & Walter Schmoll
All year

75-99-BB
3 rooms, 3 pb
Visa, MC, *Rated*
C-ltd/S-no/P-no/H-no

Full gourmet breakfast
Snacks
Sitting room, fireplaces, cable TV, accommodate business travelers

Enjoy the ambience of yesteryear in this charming beautifully furnished 1732 William Penn land grant manor house. folkbandb@aol.com http://www.bbonline.com/pa/folkestone

WEST CHESTER (REGION)

Inn at Whitewing Farm
PO Box 98
370 Valley Rd, *Kennett Square*
19348
610-388-2664 Fax: 610-388-3650
Wanda & Ed DeSeta
All year

135-259-BB
10 rooms, 10 pb
Rated
C-ltd/S-no/P-no/H-ltd
Spanish

Full breakfast
Tea, snacks & sodas
Outdoor pool & Jacuzzi, tennis court, 10 hole chip and putt golf, fishing

Situated on 43 acres, this late 1700's era estate offers spacious luxury throughout. Enjoy a full country breakfast in the converted Hay Barn before touring the beautiful Brandywine Valley. info@whitewingfarm.com http://www.whitewingfarm.com

WHEELING (REGION)

Dodson's Valentine House
99 Old National Pike, *West Alexander* 15376
724-484-7843 Fax: 724-484-7304
Bryce & Pam Dodson
All year

60-BB
2 rooms, 2 pb
C-ltd/S-no/P-no/H-no

Full breakfast
Afternoon tea, snacks
Sitting room, fireplaces, accommodate business travelers

Historic 1810 Inn on Old National Pike, one mile from I-70 Exit, minutes from Wheeling. Quiet 10-acre location.
bpdodson@pulsenet.com http://www.geocities.com/valentinehsbb

YORK (REGION)

Red Lion
PO Box 587
101 S Franklin St, *Red Lion* 17356
717-244-4739 Fax: 717-246-3219
George & Danielle Sanders
All year

65-85-BB
4 rooms, 1 pb
Visa, MC, *Rated*
C-ltd/S-no/P-no/H-no

Full breakfast
Complimentary snacks & drinks available
Common area with fireplace, sunroom

Quietly tucked away in the small town of Red Lion, the Red Lion B&B is a cozy, inviting retreat. Shaded by swaying blue spruce, this early 1930's Federal brick home welcomes all who pass by. staywithus@redlionbandb.com http://www.redlionbandb.com

---

Warrington Farm
7680 Carlisle Rd, *Wellsville* 17365
717-432-9053 Fax: 717-432-4537
Brad & Megan Hakes All year

64-90-BB
5 rooms, 5 pb
Visa, MC, Disc, *Rated*
C-ltd/S-no/P-no/H-ltd

Full breakfast
Snacks
Sitting room, fireplace.

1860's Gentleman's Farm with Shaker decor. Full country breakfast served on enormous back porch, dining area or by fireplace when available.
wfarm@conewago.com http://www.conewago.com/wfarm/

Rhode Island

BLOCK ISLAND

Atlantic Inn
PO Box 1788
High Street 02807
401-466-5883 Fax: 401-466-5678
800-224-7422
Anne & Brad Marthens
Mid Apr.–Mid-late Oct.

130-250-BB
22 rooms, 22 pb
Visa, MC, Disc, *Rated*
C-yes/S-no/P-no/H-ltd
English, German

Fresh Baked Breakfast Buffet
Candlelit–four course dinner, tea
Bar, sitting rm, tennis, beaches, nature walks, antiques, horseback riding.

An 1879 Victorian inn set high on a hill overlooking the ocean & harbor. The Atlantic Inn is surrounded by 6 landscaped acres, sloping lawns, numerous gardens & two of six tennis courts on the island. AtlanticInn@BIRI.com http://www.atlanticinn.com

---

The Blue Dory Inn & The Adrianna Inn
PO Box 488
Old Town Rd 02807
401-466-5891 Fax: 401-466-9910
800-992-7290
Ann Law May–October

95-525-BB
10 rooms, 10 pb
Most CC, •
C-yes/S-no/P-yes/H-no

Continental plus breakfast
Afternoon tea, complimentary wine
Sitting room, cable TV

100 year-old Victorian. rundezvous@aol.com http://www.blockislandinns.com

---

Gables Inn
1319 Dodge St 02807
401-466-2213 Fax: 401-466-5739
Barbara & Stanley Nyzio
Mid May to November

60-190-BB
21 rooms, 8 pb
Visa, MC
C-yes/S-no/P-no/H-ltd

Continental breakfast
Coffee, tea, and cocoa available anytime
complimentary beach supplies, access to refrigerator, grills & picnic tables

1880 Victorian inn at the edge of the village, close to beaches & restaurants. Relax in the ambience of ornate tin ceilings & antique furniture in comfortable sitting rooms or on our shaded verandas. gablesinn@aol.com http://www.gablesinnblockisland.com

BLOCK ISLAND

The Rose Farm Inn PO Box E 1005 Roslyn Rd 02807 401-466-2034 Fax: 401-466-2053 Judith B. Rose April–October	129-250-BB 19 rooms, 17 pb Most CC, *Rated* C-ltd/S-no/P-no/H-yes	Continental plus breakfast Afternoon tea Parlor, bicycle rental

The Rose Farm Inn is known for its natural setting, romantic rooms and informal hospitality. rosefarm@riconnect.com http://www.rosefarminn.com

BRISTOL

Point Pleasant Inn 333 Poppasquash Rd 02809 401-253-0627 Fax: 401-253-0371 Trish & Gunter Hafer April-November	250-575-BB 5 rooms, 5 pb Visa, MC, • C-ltd/S-no/P-no/H-ltd English, German, Spanish, Latvian, Portuguese	Full breakfast Tea, open bar, snacks, complimentary wine Sitting room, library, bikes, tennis, Jacuzzis, swimming, suites, fireplaces

Waterfront estate, restored English manor. Step back in time and enjoy life as it was. Terrace dining, biking, full resort. On a hillside overlooking Narragansett Bay and Bristol, RI. info@pointpleasantinn.com http://www.pointpleasantinn.com

---

William's Grant Inn 154 High St 02809 401-253-4222 Fax: 401-254-0987 800-596-4222 Diane & Warren Poehler All year	95-180-BB 5 rooms, 3 pb Most CC, *Rated*, • C-ltd/S-ltd/P-no/H-ltd	Full breakfast Afternoon tea, complimentary sherry Complimentary coffee/cookies, bikes, sitting room, library, picnic lunches

On a quiet tree-lined street. Filled with family antiques and artist's fine work. Ceiling fans and A/C in all rooms. wmgrantinn@earthlink.net http://www.wmgrantinn.com

LITTLE COMPTON

Stone House Club 122 Sakonnet Point Rd 02809 401-635-2222 Margaret & Peter Tirpaeck All year	58-125-BB 13 rooms, 9 pb Visa, MC, *Rated* C-yes/S-ltd/P-no/H-ltd	Continental plus breakfast Restaurant, bar service Beach, nature trails, yacht club closeby, sitting room, library

Private ocean view Victorian Inn, Early American tavern and restaurant, banquet facility and executive retreat. info@stonehouseclub.com http://www.stonehouseclub.com

NARRAGANSETT

1900 House 59 Kingstown Rd 02882 401-789-7971 Sandra & Bill Panzeri All year	65-115-BB 3 rooms, 1 pb *Rated* C-ltd/S-no/H-no	Full breakfast Winter cider, summer tea Book Swap, antique postcards, porch, homemade quilts

Walk to the beach, browse the shops, or tour the Mansions, then return to reflections of the past in our Victorian home. Enjoy sea breezes on the porch or inside.
http://www.1900house.com

The Richards 144 Gibson Ave 02882 401-789-7746 Fax: 401-789-7168 Steven & Nancy Richards All year	100-175-BB 4 rooms, 4 pb *Rated*, • C-ltd/S-no/P-no/H-no	Full gourmet breakfast Complimentary sherry in room Library with fireplace, tennis courts nearby, fireplaces in bedrooms

Gracious accommodations in an English country setting. Awaken to the smell of gourmet coffee and freshly baked goods.

1900 House, Narragansett, RI

NARRAGANSETT

Sea Gull Guest House
50 Narragansett Ave 02882
401-783-4636
Kimber Wheelock
Memorial Day-Labor Day

50-110-EP
7 rooms, 4 pb
Visa, MC, *Rated*
C-ltd/S-no/P-no/H-no

Tennis courts nearby, near gambling casino, ocean beach 1 block

Large rooms cooled by ocean breezes. Close to everything. Swim, sun, sail and fish. 2 efficiency apts., 1 cottage available.
contact@seagullguesthouse.com http://www.seagullguesthouse.com

NEWPORT

1760 Francis Malbone House
392 Thames St 02840
401-846-0392 Fax: 401-848-5956
800-846-0392
Will Dewey, Mark & Jasminka Eads All year

155-450-BB
20 rooms, 20 pb
Visa, MC, AmEx, *Rated*, •
C-ltd/S-ltd/P-no/H-yes
Italian, French, Bosnian

Full Gourmet Breakfast
Afternoon tea from 3:00pm–6:00pm
Manicured secret garden, six guest parlors, library, honor bar, newspapers.

Historic Inn, c. 1760, recently awarded a rating of "Extraordinary" from ZagatSurvey 2002, offers a warm and luxurious, yet relaxed atmosphere in the heart of Newport on the harborfront. innkeeper@malbone.com http://www.malbone.com

1855 Marshall Slocum Guest House
29 Kay St 02840
401-841-5120 Fax: 401-846-3787
800-372-5120
Joan & Julie Wilson
All year

99-199-BB
5 rooms, 5 pb
Visa, MC, AmEx, *Rated*, •
S-no/P-no/H-no

Full breakfast
Afternoon tea, comp. wine, sitting room, library, front porch w/rockers

Charming Victorian private home with rooms for guests. Serving an extra-ordinary breakfast each morning. info@marshallslocuminn.com http://www.marshallslocuminn.com

1886 Sherman House
24 Mann Ave 02840
401-848-0436 800-828-0000
Carla O'Rourke All year

155-195-BB
2 rooms, 2 pb
Most CC
C-ltd/S-ltd/P-no/H-no

Full gourmet breakfast
Breakfast served in room

Queen Anne Victorian "painted lady", minutes by foot from Newport's attractions. The decor reflect the gilded age but come complete with all the amenities of the 21st century.
innkeeper@1886shermanhouse.com http://www.1886shermanhouse.com

NEWPORT

Adele Turner Inn 93 Pelham St 02840 401-847-1811 Fax: 401-848-5850 800-845-1811 Stephan Nicolas All year	175-475-BB 13 rooms, 13 pb Most CC C-ltd/S-no/P-no	Full breakfast Afternoon tea service Fireplaces, library, rooftop deck, cable TV/VCR

Nestled among century-old homes on the first gas-lit street in America, The Adele Turner Inn awaits your arrival and discovery.
innkeeper@legendaryinnsofnewport.com http://www.adeleturnerinn.com

---

Aurelea 130 Eustis Ave 12840 401-848-9687 Maria Aureli All year	140-150-BB 1 rooms, 1 pb S-no/P-no Italian	Continental breakfast 2 bicycles

Aurelea is a lovely, one room bed & breakfast overlooking Easton's Pond, just three blocks from the Cliff Walk and Newport Beach and a short walk to Bellevue Avenue.
cfma@cox.net http://www.aurelea.com

Black Duck Inn 29 Pelham St 02840 401-841-5548 Fax: 401-846-4873 800-206-5212 Mary A. Rolando All year	99-199-BB 8 rooms, 6 pb Visa, MC, AmEx, *Rated*, • C-yes/S-no/P-no/H-no	Continental plus breakfast Sitting room, cable, Jacuzzis, fireplaces, A/C

A charming inn located in the waterfront area. Shops, restaurants, historic mansions and sailing in walking distance. MaryA401@aol.com http://www.blackduckinn.com

---

The Brinley Victorian Inn 23 Brinley St 02840 401-849-7645 Fax: 401-845-9634 800-999-8523 John & Jennifer Sweetman All year	119-229-BB 17 rooms, 12 pb *Rated*, • C-ltd/S-no/P-no/H-no	Continental plus breakfast Wine & lobster dinner Sitting room, Jacuzzi tubs, landscaped courtyard, A/C, gardens

Romantic Victorian uniquely decorated with antiques, period wallpapers. Brick courtyard planted with flowers. john@brinleyvictorian.com http://www.brinleyvictorian.com

---

The Captain James Preston House 378 Spring St 02840 401-847-7077 866-238-3952 Chad & JoAnn Smith All year	95-225-BB 4 rooms, 4 pb Visa, MC, *Rated* C-no/S-no/P-no/H-no	Full breakfast Afternoon snacks Period sitting room w/fireplace, A/C, cable TV, sun room, large front porch

This charming B&B is a large 1861 Victorian house authentically restored. Situated in the heart of downtown Newport, it's within walking distance to the harbor, beach, mansions, cliffwalk & more. prestonhouse@aol.com http://www.captainpreston.com

---

Castle Hill Inn & Resort 590 Ocean Ave 02840 401-849-3800 Fax: 401-849-3838 888-466-1355 Chuck Flanders All year	145-750-BB 35 rooms, 35 pb Most CC, *Rated* C-ltd/S-no/P-no/H-no	Full gourmet breakfast Restaurant, bar service Sitting room, whirlpool baths, private beach, trails, fireplaces, ocean view

Experience Victorian splendor-private waterfront retreat on Newport's picturesque Ocean Drive. info@castlehillinn.com http://www.castlehillinn.com

NEWPORT

Chambord
25 Ayrault Street 02840
401-849-9223 800-379-3244
Robert & Regina Morrissey
All year
BB
C-ltd/S-no/P-no
Full breakfast
Living room, outdoor spa, fireplaces, bicycles

The Chambord Bed & Breakfast is a circa 1863, 137-year-old restored Victorian in the heart of Newport. hosts@ChambordNewport.com http://ChambordNewport.com

---

Chestnut Inn
99 3rd St 02840
401-847-6949
Bill, Eileen & Cheryl Nimmo
All year
75-150-BB
2 rooms
•
C-yes/S-yes/P-yes/H-no
Full breakfast
Snacks
Sitting room, library, tennis, Jacuzzis, suites, cable TV, accom. bus. trav.

We are one block from Narragansett Bay in the historic "Point" section. It is a perfect getaway for couples and families.
chstnut99@aol.com http://members.aol.com/chstnut99/

Claddaugh House Inn
3 Prairie Ave 02840
401-846-0886
All year
Most CC
C-yes/S-ltd
Full Continental Breakfast

The Claddaugh House is an 1880s Victorian home recently restored by native Newporters Michael and Beth Grimes. CladdaughHouse@aol.com http://www.claddaughhouse.com

---

Claire's B&B
26 Greenough Place 02840
401-846-4773 Fax: 401-849-0690
Claire Ball
All year
75-165-BB
2 rooms, 2 pb
Visa, MC
C-yes/S-no/P-no/H-no
Full breakfast

Property is located in the most architecturally diverse neighborhood in Newport called the "Top of the Hill." claire@clairesbnb.com http://www.clairesbnb.com

---

Cliff View
4 Cliff Terrace 02840
401-846-0885
Pauline Shea
May 1–Nov. 1
85-95-BB
4 rooms, 2 pb
Visa, MC, *Rated*
C-ltd/S-ltd/P-no/H-no
Continental breakfast
Sitting room, piano, 2 rooms with A/C

Two-story Victorian c.1870. East side has view of Atlantic Ocean. Two porches, open sun deck. Walk to beach or Cliff Walk.

Cliffside Inn
2 Seaview Ave 02840
401-847-1811 Fax: 401-848-5850
800-845-1811
Stephan Nicolas
All year
235-495-BB
16 rooms, 16 pb
Most CC, *Rated*, •
C-ltd/S-no/P-no/H-no
French
Full breakfast
Afternoon tea
Sitting room, Jacuzzis, suites, fireplaces, cable TV

Newport's most celebrated inn. Formerly the summer home of legendary Newport artist Beatrice Turner, the inn is a magical, one-of-a-kind place to stay.
innkeeper@legendaryinnsofnewport.com http://www.cliffsideinn.com

---

Hydrangea House Inn
16 Bellevue Ave 02840
401-846-4435 Fax: 401-846-6602
800-945-4667
Dennis Blair, Grant Edmondson
All year
145-310-BB
8 rooms, 8 pb
Visa, MC, *Rated*, •
S-no/P-no/H-no
Full breakfast buffet
Sitting room, parlor with fireplace, A/C, private parking

Within Newport's "Walking District." A gratifying hot breakfast buffet served in our contemporary art gallery. Fireplace suite with 2 person whirlpool & king bed.
hydrangeahouse@cox.net http://www.hydrangeahouse.com

NEWPORT

InnTowne Inn
6 Mary St 02840
401-846-9200 Fax: 401-846-1534
800-457-7803
Carmella L. Gardner
All year

100-224-BB
26 rooms, 26 pb
Visa, MC, AmEx
C-ltd/S-yes/P-no/H-no

Continental plus breakfast
Afternoon tea
Sitting room, library, swimming pool, health club facilities, sundeck

Elegant traditional Inn situated in the heart of Newport. Sun deck, four poster beds, use of health club/pool nearby. Close to Mansions, shopping, beaches & fine restaurants.
innkeeper@inntowneinn.com http://www.Inntowneinn.com

Melville House
39 Clarke St 02840
401-847-0640 Fax: 401-847-0956
Vincent DeRico, David Horan
All year

125-175-BB
7 rooms, 5 pb
Rated

Full gourmet breakfast
Afternoon tea, refreshments, soup on cold days

Staying at The Melville House is like a step back into the past. Built c. 1750 and on the National Register of Historic Places, The Melville House is located in Newport's Historic Hill District. innkeeper@ids.net http://www.melvillehouse.com/

Old Beach Inn
19 Old Beach Rd 02840
401-849-3479 Fax: 401-847-1236
888-303-5033
Cyndi & Luke Murray
All year

85-300-BB
7 rooms, 7 pb
Most CC, *Rated*
C-ltd/S-no/P-no/H-no

Continental plus breakfast
Full breakfast Sundays
Gazebo, fish pond, patio, Sitting room, fireplaces, garden, some A/C & TVs

Elegant Victorian B&B filled with romance, history and charm. Ideal location, lovely gardens, comfortable guestrooms.
info@oldbeachinn.com http://www.oldbeachinn.com

Pilgrim House Inn
123 Spring St 02840
401-846-0040 Fax: 401-848-0357
800-525-8373
Barry & Debbie Fonseca
All year

95-225-BB
10 rooms, 8 pb
Visa, MC, *Rated*, •
C-ltd/S-no/P-no/H-no

Continental plus breakfast
Complimentary sherry, shortbread
Deck with view of harbor, living room with fireplace, close to attractions

Elegant Victorian inn, two blocks from the harbor in Newport's historic district. Rooftop deck with view of Newport Harbor. Walking distance to shops, dining & sights, cliff walk.
innkeeper@pilgrimhouseinn.com http://www.pilgrimhouseinn.com

Samuel Durfee House
352 Spring St 02840
401-847-1652 877-696-2374
Heather & Michael de Pinho
All year

85-185-BB
5 rooms, 5 pb
Visa, MC, *Rated*, •
C-ltd/S-no/P-no/H-no

Full breakfast
Afternoon tea and snacks
Cable TV in sitting room only

An elegant 1803 Federal period inn located downtown just a block from the harbor and two blocks from Bellevue Avenue.
samueldurfeeinn@mindsping.com http://www.samueldurfeehouse.com

---

Savanas' Inn
41 Pelham St 02840
401-847-3801 Fax: 401-841-0994
888-880-FROG
"Ande" & Philip Savana
All year

110-290-BB
4 rooms, 4 pb
Most CC, *Rated*, •
S-ltd/P-no/H-no

Full breakfast
Cheese/cracker/fruit on arrival
Sitting room, library, suites, fireplaces, cable TV, hot tub, VCRs, A/C

1865 second empire restored to its original splendor, nestled in the heart of Historic Hill. Robes, turn down, Victorian porch.
savanasinn@efortress.com http://www.savanasinn.com

NEWPORT

Spring Street Inn 353 Spring St 02840 401-847-4767 Patricia Golder & Jack Lang Closed January	119-279-BB 7 rooms, 5 pb Visa, MC, *Rated*, • C-yes/S-no/P-no/H-no	Full gourmet breakfast Afternoon tea Sitting room, parking, bus loop, two blocks from harbor

Charming restored Empire Victorian house, c.1858. Harbour-view suite with private deck & living room. sprngstinn@aol.com http://www.springstreetinn.com

Stella Maris Inn 91 Washington St 02840 401-849-2862 Dorothy & Ed Madden All year	95-225-BB 8 rooms, 8 pb *Rated*, • C-ltd/S-no/P-no/H-no Minimal French	Continental plus breakfast Afternoon tea, complimentary wine Sitting room, library, small meetings possible

1861 Victorian mansion. Newly renovated, water view rooms, fireplaces, spacious porch & gardens, antique decor, homemade muffins, walk to town. Elevator on premises. ukrunner@earthlink.net http://www.stellamarisinn.com

Wayside Guest House 406 Bellevue Ave 02840 401-847-0302 Fax: 401-848-9374 800-653-7678 Don Post All year	150-195-BB 8 rooms, 8 pb C-yes/S-yes/P-no/H-no	Continental plus breakfast BBQ facilities Sitting room, flower beds, outdoor swimming pool

Large, attractive, comfortable Georgian-style island home. Ideally located within short walk of mansions, cliff walk, & harborfront activities. wayside406@earthlink.net

NEWPORT (REGION)

The Inn at Shadow Lawn 120 Miantonomi Ave, *Middletown* 02840 401-847-0902 Fax: 401-848-6529 800-352-3750 Selma & Randy Fabricant All year	99-225-BB 8 rooms, 8 pb Most CC, *Rated*, • C-yes/S-no/P-no/H-no	Full or continental plus breakfast Complimentary wine Sitting room, library, Tiffany lighting, cable TV, wicker

Step back in time & take a leisurely stroll around the beautiful rolling lawns at our 1853 Victorian mansion. randy@shadowlawn.com http://www.shadowlawn.com

PROVIDENCE

AAA Jacob Hill Inn PO Box 41326 02940 508-336-9165 Fax: 508-336-0951 888-336-9165 Bill & Eleonora Rezek All year	179-299-BB 10 rooms, 10 pb Most CC, *Rated*, • C-ltd/S-ltd/P-no/H-ltd Polish	Full gourmet breakfast Snacks, complimentary wine, tea Sitting room, fireplaces, A/C, tennis, pool, gazebo, Jacuzzis, canopy beds

Located on a peaceful country estate, 10-minute drive from downtown, the Convention Center, Rhode Island School of Design & Brown University. Recipient of the prestigious AAA 4-diamond award. host@jacobhill.com http://www.Inn-Providence.com

C.C. Ledbetter 326 Benefit St 02903 401-351-4699 Fax: 401-351-4699 CC Ledbetter All year	85-130-BB 5 rooms, 2 pb Most CC C-ltd/S-ltd/P-ltd/H-no French, Italian	Continental plus breakfast Afternoon tea, snacks Sitting room, 3 ultra wedding rooms

On historic Benefit Street, close to Brown University, Rhode Island School of Design, Johnson & Wales, and Providence College.

PROVIDENCE

The Cady House 127 Power St 02906 401-273-5398 Fax: 401-273-5398 Anna & Bill Colaiace All year	90-100-BB 3 rooms, 3 pb Most CC, • C-yes/S-no/P-ltd/H-no Hebrew, French, German, Spanish	Continental plus breakfast Library, fireplaces, suites, cable TV

A 1839 Victorian, centered in the historic district, near all major universities and best restaurants. Rooms are decorated with antiques and misc. artifacts.
wcolaiace@aol.com http://www.cadyhouse.com

Edgewood Manor & The Newhall House 232 Norwood Ave 02905 401-781-0099 800-882-3285 Joy Generali All year	99-279-BB 15 rooms, 15 pb Most CC, *Rated* C-ltd/S-no/H-no French	Full gourmet breakfast Sitting room, Jacuzzis, suites, A/C, fireplace, cable TV, bicycles

Greek Revival mansion & architectural jewel, adorned with leaded & stained glass, fine art & period antiques. Guestrooms & suites luxuriously decorated in Victorian & Empire style.
edgemanor@aol.com http://www.providence-lodging.com

The Old Court 144 Benefit St 02903 401-751-2002 Fax: 401-272-4830 David "Dolby" Dolbashian All year	95-165-BB 10 rooms, 10 pb Most CC, *Rated*, • C-ltd/S-yes/P-no/H-no French	Full breakfast Complimentary tea, assorted bread Antiques, common TV room, wet bars in some rooms

Built in 1863, Italianate in design and in ornate details; combines tradition with contemporary standards of luxury. reserve@oldcourt.com http://www.oldcourt.com

SOUTH KINGSTOWN

Admiral Dewey Inn 668 Matunuck Beach Rd 02879 401-783-2090 800-457-2090 Joan LeBel All year	100-140-BB 10 rooms, 8 pb Visa, MC, *Rated*, • C-ltd/S-ltd/P-no/H-no Polish	Continental plus breakfast Snacks Sitting room, bicycles, cable TV

The past comes alive in this 1898 Victorian, which has been lovingly restored and furnished with antiques in the Victorian style. Listed on the National Historic Register.
http://www.admiraldeweyinn.com

The Kings' Rose 1747 Mooresfield Rd 02879 401-783-5222 Fax: 401-783-9984 888-230-ROSE B. Larsen-Viles & Perry Viles All year	130-180-BB 5 rooms, 4 pb *Rated* C-ltd/S-no/P-yes/H-no French	Full breakfast Dinner, afternoon tea, snacks Complimentary wine, bar service, sitting room, library, tennis court, suites

Country mini-estate, gardens; private entrance to gracious public rooms; bountiful breakfast al fresco or by firelight; nearby pristine beaches, wildlife refuges, bike paths.
kingsrose@earthlink.net

WAKEFIELD

Brookside Manor 380-B Post Road 02879 401-788-3527 Fax: 401-788-3530 Allyson Huskisson & Robert Vitale All year	150-225-BB 5 rooms, 5 pb Visa, MC, AmEx, *Rated* C-ltd/S-no/P-no/H-no Italian	Full breakfast Afternoon tea, wine, snacks Sitting room, library, fireplace, cable TV, phone in room, A/C

Built in 1890, this meticulously restored New England mansion is beautifully decorated with antiques & Oriental rugs. Eight acres of gardens, together with brook & pond, complete the perfect setting. allyson@brooksidemanor.net http://www.brooksidemanor.net

Brookside Manor, Wakefield, RI

WAKEFIELD

Larchwood Inn
521 Main St 02879
401-783-5454 Fax: 401-783-1800
800-275-5450
Francis & Diann Browning
All year

35-150-EP
19 rooms
Most CC, *Rated*, •
C-yes/S-yes/P-yes/H-no
Spanish, French

Restaurant, cocktail lounge
Sitting room, conference facilities

Intimate country inn in New England townhouse style circa 1831. Conveniently located near Newport, Mystic Seaport, Block Island and University of Rhode Island.
larchwoodinn@xpos.com http://www.larchwoodinn.com

WESTERLY

Kismet on the Park
71 High St 02891
401-596-3237
Cindy Slay
All year

85-150-BB
4 rooms, 4 pb
Rated
C-yes/S-ltd/P-ltd

Light breakfast
Kitchen is always open

The last and only privately owned grand old home situated directly at the entrance to Wilcox Park in downtown Westerly.
kismetbandb@webtv.net http://www.kismetbandb.com

The Villa
190 Shore Rd 02891
401-596-1054
Fax: 401-596-6268
800-722-9240
Angela Craig & Peter Gagnon
All year

95-255-BB
6 rooms, 6 pb
Most CC, *Rated*, •
C-no/S-no/P-no/H-ltd

Continental plus breakfast
Full breakfast on weekends
Hot tub, swim pool, 2 fireplces/4 Jacuzzi suites, 1.5 acres of lawn/garden

Escape to our Mediterranean style villa. We set the stage for your romantic get-away. You'll fall in love and want to return. Outdoor pool and hot tub. Adjacent to golf course. Private & romantic. villa@riconnect.com http://www.thevillaatwesterly.com

---

Woody Hill
149 S Woody Hill Rd 02891
401-322-0452
Ellen L. Madison
All year

95-150-BB
4 rooms, 4 pb
Rated, •
C-yes/S-no/P-no/H-ltd

Full country breakfast
Porch with swing, pool, winter hearth cooking

Relaxed 18th century ambiance on 20 country acres, with a 40' in-ground pool, antiques, two miles from ocean beaches. woodyhill@riconnect.com http://www.woodyhill.com

South Carolina

ABBEVILLE (REGION)

Latimer Inn
PO Box 295
1387 Highway 81 N, *Calhoun Falls* 29628
864-391-2747 Fax: 864-391-2747
877-481-5095
Harrison & Anne Sawyer
All year

49-129-BB
17 rooms, 14 pb
Visa, MC, AmEx, *Rated*, •
C-yes/S-yes/P-yes/H-no

Full or continental breakfast
Dinner available
Fishing & water sports, hiking, horseshoes, swimming pool

A fisherman's paradise located near historic Abbeville, with its rich Civil War heritage. Three luxury rooms with Jacuzzis and fireplaces, and 14 room Motel.
latimerinn@wctel.net http://www.latimerinn.com

BEAUFORT

Cuthbert House Inn
1203 Bay St 29902
843-521-1315 Fax: 843-521-1314
800-327-9275
Gary & Sharon Groves
All year

155-265-BB
7 rooms, 7 pb
Most CC, *Rated*
C-ltd/S-no/P-no/H-ltd

Full breakfast
Sunset refreshments
Bay view verandahs, formal parlor, bikes, library, quiet courtyard garden

Highly recommended, the Inn is the only Antebellum Inn on Beaufort's picturesque waterfront c.1790. cuthbert@hargray.com http://www.cuthberthouseinn.com

Old Point Inn
212 New St 29902
843-524-3177 Fax: 843-524-3177
Julie and Paul Michau
All year

85-145-BB
5 rooms, 5 pb
Most CC, •
C-ltd/S-ltd/P-no/H-no
French, Afrikaans

Full breakfast
Complimentary wine
Access to private club dining, golf, tennis and beach. Boating.

1898 Queen Anne, the only inn in Beaufort's Historic Old Point District. Near shops, restaurants, park. oldpointinn@islc.net http://www.oldpointinn.com

The Rhett House Inn
1009 Craven St 29902
843-524-9030 888-480-9530
Marianne & Stephen Harrison
All year

160-350-BB
10 rooms, 10 pb
Visa, MC, AmEx
C-ltd/S-ltd/P-no

Full gourmet breakfast
Afternoon refreshments

The Rhett House Inn dates back to 1820, when Beaufort was a prominent coastal town noted for its rich culture and politics.
rhetthse@hargray.com http://www.rhetthouseinn.com

TwoSuns Inn
1705 Bay St 29902
843-522-1122 Fax: 843-522-1122
800-532-4244
Henri & Patricia Safran
All year

130-168-BB
6 rooms, 6 pb
Most CC, *Rated*, •
C-ltd/S-no/P-no/H-yes
French

Full breakfast
Afternoon tea, complimentary wine and champagne.
Sitting room, bicycles, public tennis courts, computer, fax, cable TV

1917 Certified Historic Building with finest bayview. Gourmet Breakfast fare, modern amenities and the personal attention of caring hosts.
twosuns@islc.net http://www.twosunsinn.com

CAMDEN

A Camden SC B&B
127 Union St 29020
803-432-2366 Fax: 803-432-9767
Janie Erickson
All year

85-190-BB
3 rooms, 3 pb
Most CC, •
C-yes/S-yes/P-yes/H-ltd

Full breakfast
Cottages and Suites

Away from rumbling trucks and traffic! Wonderful bed and breakfast with lovely cottages and suites in a charming and beautiful Southern town.
jerixon@tech-tech.com http://www.camdenscbandb.com

TwoSuns Inn, Beaufort, SC

CAMDEN

Candlelight Inn 1904 Broad St 29020 803-424-1057 Jo Ann Celani All year	80-125-BB 3 rooms, 3 pb Most CC, *Rated*, • C-ltd/S-no/P-no/H-no	Full breakfast Snacks, complimentary wine Sitting room, library, suites, fireplaces, cable TV

Candlelight, comfort, camellias, charm, cookies, conversations & cooking all add up to Candlelight Inn. candlelightinncamden@yahoo.com http://www.candlelightinn.org

Greenleaf Inn of Camden 1308 Broad St 29020 803-425-1806 Fax: 803-425-5853 800-437-5874 Catania Family All year	79-119-BB 12 rooms, 12 pb Most CC, *Rated*, • C-ltd/S-ltd/P-no/H-yes	Full breakfast Restaurant on premise with dinner served Private sitting areas and verandahs available to lodging guests only

A step back in time when life was tranquil and travelers were pampered. Beautifully decorated with antiques and reproductions in keeping with the period.
greenleafinn@aol.com http://www.greenleafinncamden.com

CHARLESTON

1843 Battery Carriage House Inn 20 S Battery 29401 843-727-3100 Fax: 843-727-3130 800-775-5575 Howard M. Vroon All year	150-299-BB 11 rooms, 11 pb Most CC, *Rated* C-ltd/S-ltd/P-no/H-no	Continental breakfast Complimentary wine 3 whirlpool baths, 4 steam showers, bicycles

Very romantic, elegant. Located in garden of historic mansion on the Battery; silver tray breakfast. bch@mymailstation.com http://www.batterycarriagehouse.com

27 State Street 27 State St 29401 843-722-4243 Fax: 843-722-6030 Paul & Joye Craven All year	175-BB 5 rooms, 5 pb *Rated* C-yes/S-no/P-no/H-no	Continental plus breakfast In-room snacks Sitting room, cable TV, newspapers, fresh flowers, bicycles, library

Enjoy Southern hospitality in the midst of "ages past." Walk in any direction for wonderful adventures in shopping, touring, dining, entertainment. http://www.charleston-bb.com

CHARLESTON

36 Meeting Street 36 Meeting St 29401 843-722-1034 Fax: 843-723-0068 Vic & Anne Brandt All year	95-160-BB 3 rooms, 3 pb Visa, MC, Disc, *Rated* C-yes/S-ltd/P-no	Sitting room, suites, fireplace, cable TV, conferences

abrandt@awod.com http://www.36meetingstreet.com

Ann Harper's 56 Smith St 29401 843-723-3947 Ann D. Harper All year	100-135-BB 2 rooms, 1 pb *Rated* C-ltd/S-ltd/P-no/H-no	Full breakfast Small garden, cable TV, off-street parking, golf/swimming nearby

Charming circa 1870 home located in Charleston's historic district. Walled garden, newspaper daily.
http://www.virtualcities.com/s.c./annharpers.htm

Ansonborough Inn 21 Hasell St 29401 843-723-1655 Fax: 843-577-6888 800-522-2073 Allison Fennell All year	139-350-BB 37 rooms, 37 pb Most CC, *Rated*, • C-ltd/S-no/P-no/H-yes	Continental breakfast Wine & Cheese, coffee, tea, lemonade, cookies. Guest business center (Internet, fax, printer), rooftop terrace, Anson's pub

This all suite inn is located in the historic district. Decorated and furnished in period antiques and reproductions, the inn boasts heart-pine beams, exposed brick walls, and a three-story atrium.
slove@fennellholdings.com http://www.ansonboroughinn.com

Ashley Inn 201 Ashley Ave 29403 843-723-1848 Fax: 843-579-9080 800-581-6658 Barry Carroll All year	79-265-BB 7 rooms, 7 pb Visa, MC, • C-ltd/S-ltd/P-no/H-no	Full breakfast Afternoon tea, sandwiches & cookies, comp. wine Sitting room, fireplace, complimentary bikes, free off-street parking.

Sleep until the fragrance of southern cooking lures you to garden breakfast. Featured in Gail Greco's Nationally Televised "Country Inn Cooking."
ashleyinnbb@aol.com http://www.charleston-sc-inns.com/ashley/index.htm

---

Belvedere 40 Rutledge Ave 29401 843-722-0973 800-816-1664 David Spell & Joanne Kuhn All year	135-195-BB 3 rooms, 3 pb *Rated*, • C-ltd/S-no/P-no/H-no	Continental plus breakfast Afternoon sherry & refreshments Sitting room w/ cable TV/VCR, newspaper, TV, A/C, porch with view of lake

Hospitable accommodations in large gracious downtown mansion in Historic District overlooking Colonial Lake. Exquisite decor & collections. http://www.belvedereinn.com

---

Cannonboro Inn 184 Ashley Ave 29403 843-723-8572 Fax: 843-723-8007 800-235-8039 Barry Carroll All year	79-210-BB 6 rooms, 6 pb Visa, MC, • C-ltd/S-no/P-no/H-no	Full breakfast Afternoon tea, sandwiches, goodies Sitting room, garden, complimentary bikes, free off-street parking

Antebellum home c.1850 in Charleston's historic district. Breakfast served on a piazza overlooking a country garden. Fireplaces in rooms.
cannonboroinn@aol.com http://www.charleston-sc-inns.com/cannonboro/index.htm

CHARLESTON

Charleston Governor's House
117 Broad St 29401
843-720-2070 Fax: 843-805-6549
800-720-9812
Karen Spell Shaw
Closed Christmas Day

179-355-BB
11 rooms, 11 pb
Rated
C-ltd/S-ltd/P-no/H-ltd

Continental plus breakfast
Low country tea of local recipes; Evening sherry
3 living rooms, whirlpools, wet bars, concierge, verandah, free parking.

The majestic former Governor's mansion, a National Landmark, reflects Charleston's romantic history and grandeur, with elegant living areas, 9 fireplaces, 12' ceilings, crystal chandeliers, antiques. innkeeper@govhouse.com http://www.governorshouse.com

---

Charlotte Street Cottage
32 Charlotte St 29403
843-577-3944 Fax: 843-577-6768
Lisa Flaggman
All year

225-375-BB
2 rooms, 2 pb
Rated, •
C-ltd/S-no/P-no/H-no
French (un petit peu)

self serve in your kitchen
light refreshments, welcome basket
parking, private garden, phone, cable/VCR, A/C, fireplace, washer/dryer

Elegant superbly refurbished 1820's guest home in an exclusive neighbor hood of historic downtown Charleston available by day, week or month.
info@charlestoncottage.com http://www.charlestoncottage.com

Country Victorian
105 Tradd St 29401
843-577-0682
Diane Deardurff Weed
All year

110-200-BB
2 rooms, 2 pb
Rated
C-ltd/S-no/P-no/H-no

Continental plus breakfast
Afternoon tea, snacks
Parking, bicycles, TV, restaurants nearby, piazzas, tour info

Private entrances, antique iron and brass beds, old quilts, antique oak and wicker furniture. Situated in the historic district.

Fulton Lane Inn
212 1/2 King St
202 King St 29401
843-720-2600 Fax: 843-720-2940
800-720-2688
Michelle Woodhull
All year

140-285-BB
27 rooms, 27 pb
Most CC, *Rated*, •
C-yes/S-no/P-no/H-yes

Continental plus breakfast
Bar service, complimentary wine
Sitting room, suites available, babysitters, hot tubs, conf. facility

Victorian inn built in 1870 by Confederate blockade runner John Rugheimer, on quiet pedestrian lane. Furnished with antiques and historically accurate reproductions.
melissa@charminginns.com http://www.

John Rutledge House
116 Broad St 29401
843-723-7999 Fax: 843-720-2615
800-476-9741
Linda Bishop
All year

165-375-BB
19 rooms, 19 pb
Most CC, *Rated*, •
C-yes/S-ltd/P-no/H-yes

Continental breakfast
Afternoon iced tea, evening sherry and brandy
Parlor room, concierge, turndown service, babysitters, whirlpools

John Rutledge, a signer of the US Constitution, built this elegant home in 1763. Visit and re-live history. Downtown location near shopping & historic sites.
jrutledgehouse@aol.com http://www.charminginns.com/rutledgehouse.cfm

---

King George IV Inn
32 George St 29401
843-723-9339 Fax: 843-723-7749
888-723-1667
Terry & Debra Flowers
All year

99-185-BB
10 rooms, 8 pb
Visa, MC, AmEx, *Rated*, •
C-yes/S-no/P-no/H-ltd

Continental plus breakfast
Complimentary coffees & teas
Three levels of porches, parking, refrigerators, sitting room

Originally the 1790's home of a Charleston writer. A 4 story Federal style home furnished in antiques. All rooms have fireplaces, hardwood floors, high ceilings with moldings.
info@kinggeorgeiv.com http://www.kinggeorgeiv.com

CHARLESTON

Kings Courtyard Inn
212 1/2 King St
198 King St 29401
843-723-7000 Fax: 843-720-2608
800-845-6119
Michelle Woodhull
All year

99-270-BB
41 rooms, 41 pb
Most CC, *Rated*, •
C-yes/S-ltd/P-no/H-yes

Continental breakfast
Afternoon wine and sherry, turndown, wine tasting
Sitting room, parking available, hot tub, conference room

Located in the heart of the Historic District and surrounded by countless interesting boutiques and antique shops, it is a mere stroll from the famous harbor, historic homes and attractions. charminginns3@aol.com http://www.charminginns.com/kingscourtyard.cfm

---

The Kitchen House
126 Tradd St 29401
843-577-6362 Fax: 843-965-5615
Lois Evans
All year

175-400-BB
2 rooms, 2 pb
Visa, MC, *Rated*, •
C-ltd/S-ltd/P-no/H-no

Full breakfast
Sherry, tea
Sitting room, library,Cable T.V., VCR,parking, concierge service

Located in the heart of Charleston's Historic District, The Kitchen House is a heart warming return to the charm of a simpler time. Private patio, colonial herb garden, fish pond & fountain. loisevans@worldnet.att.net http://www.cityofcharleston.com/kitchen.htm

---

The Lodge Alley Inn
195 E. Bay St 29401
843-722-1611 Fax: 843-577-7497
800-845-1004
David Price
All year

159-375-BB
93 rooms, 93 pb
Rated, •

Continental plus breakfast

Located downtown in the historic district within strolling distance to area attractions.
alleyinn@bellsouth.net http://www.lodgealleyinn.com

The Palmer Home
5 E Battery 29401
843-853-1574 Fax: 843-723-7983
888-723-1574
Francess, David, & Joe Sam Hogan
All year

165-300-BB
3 rooms, 3 pb
Visa, MC, AmEx, *Rated*
C-ltd/S-no/P-ltd/H-no

Continental breakfast
Sitting room, piazzas, historic district, swimming pool, parking

Enjoy a room with a view. One of the fifty famous homes in the city; furnished in period antiques; piazzas overlook harbor and Fort Sumter where Civil War began.
palmerbnb@aol.com http://www.palmerhomebb.com

Philip Porcher House
19 Archdale St 29401
843-722-1801
Dr. Price & Louisa Cameron
All year

250-350-BB
2 rooms, 1 pb
C-ltd/S-no/P-no/H-no

Continental breakfast
Sitting room, fireplaces, cable TV

Luxury ground floor apartment of Georgian house (c.1765) located in heart of Historic District. Within walking distance of antique stores, house museums and restaurants.
porcherh@comcast.net http://www.bbonline.com/sc/porcher

Phoebe Pember House
26 Society St 29401
843-722-4186 Fax: 843-722-0557
Carolyn Rivers
All year

125-215-BB
6 rooms, 6 pb
Visa, MC, AmEx, *Rated*
C-ltd/S-ltd/P-no/H-no

Continental breakfast
Afternoon tea, wine & cheese, chocolates nightly
Accommodate business traveler, concierge, turndown service, Yoga Studio

200 year-old Charleston Single house, Carriage house and Kitchen house, with beautiful piazzas overlooking private walled gardens.
info@phoebepemberhouse.com http://www.phoebepemberhouse.com

CHARLESTON

Planters Inn
112 N Market St 29401
843-722-2345 Fax: 843-577-2125
800-845-7082
Larry Spelts
All year

195-295-EP
Most CC, *Rated*, •
C-yes/S-yes/P-no/H-yes

Breakfast available (fee)
Complimentary hors d'oeuvres
Wine by Chef Nuetzi, valet parking, full turndown service

Beautifully restored and furnished 1840's building at the center of Charleston's historic district. High ceiling rooms all individually decorated.
reservations@plantersinn.com http://www.plantersinn.com

The Thomas Lamboll House
19 King St 29401
843-723-3212 888-874-0793
Marie & Emerson Read
All year

125-185-BB
2 rooms, 2 pb
Visa, MC, Disc
C-yes/S-no/P-no/H-no

Continental plus breakfast
Tennis and golf nearby, off street parking

Built in 1735 in the historic district. Bedrooms have queen size beds, private baths and French doors leading to piazza.
lamboll@aol.com http://www.Lambollhouse.com/home.htm

Vendue Inn
27 Vendue Range
19 Vendue Range 29401
843-577-7970 Fax: 843-577-2913
800-845-7900
Coyne & Linda Edmison
All year

135-285-BB
65 rooms, 65 pb
Most CC, *Rated*, •
C-yes/S-no/P-no/H-ltd

Full breakfast
Afternoon wine and cheese, nightly milk & cookies
Wine and cheese, milk and cookies, turndown service, evening cordials

Four star property located in the heart of Charleston's Historic District. Steps from Waterfront Park and Charleston Harbor.
vendueinnresv@aol.com http://www.vendueinn.com

Victoria House Inn
208 King St 29401
843-720-2944 Fax: 843-720-2930
800-933-5464
All year

150-255-BB
18 rooms, 18 pb
Visa, MC, Disc, *Rated*, •
C-yes/S-ltd/P-no/H-ltd

Continental plus breakfast
Bar service
Conference facilities, some hot tubs, babysitter available

Victorian inn built in 1889. Document wallpapers and paint colors. Furnished with antiques and historically accurate reproductions. melissa@charminginns.com

---

Villa de La Fontaine
138 Wentworth St 29401
843-577-7709
Aubrey Hancock, William Fontaine
All year

125-165-BB
6 rooms, 6 pb
Visa, MC, *Rated*
C-ltd

Full breakfast
Garden, terraces, tennis, Canopy beds, off-street parking

Southern Colonial mansion, circa 1838, in historic district; half-acre garden; fountain and terraces. http://charleston.cityinformation.com/villa/

Wentworth Mansion
149 Wentworth St 29401
843-853-1886 Fax: 843-720-5290
888-INN-1886
Bob Seidler
All year

195-695-BB
21 rooms, 21 pb
Most CC, *Rated*, •
C-yes/S-ltd/P-no/H-yes

European buffet breakfast
Afternoon welcome with wine and sherry
Bar service, sitting room, library, suites, cable, fireplaces, conference

This world-class AAA 4-diamond hotel is furnished with antiques and has original fireplaces and crystal chandeliers. Beautifully renovated, it is located in the heart of downtown Historic District. wentworthmansion@aol.com http://www.wentworthmansion.com

CHARLESTON (REGION)

Woodlands Resort & Inn
125 Parsons Rd, *Summerville* 29483
843-875-2600 Fax: 843-875-2603
800-744-9999
Marty Wall Spring & Fall

295-395-EP
19 rooms, 19 pb
Most CC, *Rated*, •
C-ltd/S-no/P-yes/H-yes
German, French, Spanish

Lunch, Dinner available, p.m. tea
Five Diamond Dining Room, spa, bikes, clay tennis courts, pool, croguet

South Carolina's only AAA, Five Diamond exclusive resort and dining room. Meticulously restored 1906 Classic Revival mansion rests on 42 acres.
reservations@woodlandsinn.com http://www.woodlandsinn.com

FAYETTE

Columbus Street Inn
108 May Apple Way
1043 Columbus St W 35555
205-932-0826 Fax: 205-932-2907
Vicki Fowler
All year

55-65-BB
5 rooms, 5 pb
Visa, MC, AmEx
C-yes/S-no/P-ltd/H-ltd
French

Continental plus breakfast
Snacks
Sitting room, fireplaces, cable TV, exercise room

Carefully renovated historic home filled with antiques. Relax and enjoy the beauty of the grounds from our shady porch rockers. SF4013@bellsouth.net

FLORENCE (REGION)

Breeden Inn-Carriage House
404 East Main St, *Bennettsville* 29512
843-479-3665 Fax: 843-479-1040
888-335-2996
Wesley & Bonnie Park
All year

105-150-BB
10 rooms, 10 pb
Most CC, •
C-ltd/S-no/P-no/H-no

Full breakfast
Tea/soda offered upon arrival. Bedtime chocolates
Pool,private phones,TV's VCR's,Southern porches,whirlpool,bikes

Memorable halfway NY&FL stay. Ten lovely rooms in three 19th-century houses, in a village-like setting. Gardens include pool, 6 original outbldgs. & 3 Koi ponds. Comfortably historic. breedeninn@att.net http://www.breedeninn.com

---

Abingdon Manor
307 Church St, *Latta* 29565
843-752-5090 Fax: 843-752-6034
888-752-5080
Michael & Patty Griffey
All year

120-175-BB
5 rooms, 5 pb
Most CC, *Rated*, •
C-ltd/S-ltd/P-no/H-no

Full breakfast
Fine dining, full service liquor, beer & wine
Sitting room, library, bikes, suites, hot tub, turndown service, cable TV

Only luxury inn (AAA-4 diamond) with such close proximity to I-95 in Georgia or the Carolinas (5 miles east). Historic, elegant, comfortable.
am@abingdonmanor.com http://www.abingdonmanor.com

GEORGETOWN

1790 House
630 Highmarket St 29440
843-546-4821 Fax: 843-520-0609
800-890-7432
Denise Heurich & Captain Bill Gower
All year

99-195-BB
6 rooms, 6 pb
Most CC, *Rated*, •
C-ltd/S-ltd/P-ltd/H-ltd

Full breakfast
Afternoon tea, snacks, evening nightcap, cruise lu
Bath robes, hair dryers, fresh flowers, cable TV, VCR, telephones, bicycles

Let us pamper you within the 212-year-old walls of the 1790 House.
info@1790house.com http://www.1790house.com

Alexandra's Inn
620 Prince St 29440
843-527-0233 Fax: 843-520-0718
888-557-0233
Vit & Diane Visbaras
All year

95-135-BB
5 rooms, 5 pb
Most CC, *Rated*
C-ltd/S-no/P-ltd/H-ltd

Full breakfast
Snacks
Sitting room, Jacuzzis, pool, fireplaces, cable TV

Our Inn provides a romantic and comfortable atmosphere for our guests. All of our rooms are named after the characters in "GONE WITH THE WIND" and decorated with them in mind. alexinn@sccoast.net http://www.alexandrasinn.com

GEORGETOWN

DuPre House
921 Prince St 29440
843-546-0298 Fax: 843-520-0771
877-519-9499
Richard & Judy Barnett
All year

99-135-BB
5 rooms, 5 pb
Visa, MC, AmEx,
Rated, •
C-ltd/S-no/P-no/H-no

Full breakfast
Afternoon tea, snacks, complimentary wine
Sitting room, library, spa, pool, TV, fireplaces, accom. bus. travel.

No agenda is necessary while experiencing this c. 1740 pre-Revolutionary home in National Register Historic District. Walking distance to the waterfront boardwalk, shopping, dining and marina. richardbarnett@sc.rr.com http://www.duprehouse.com

---

Harbor House
15 Cannon St 29440
843-546-6532
877-511-0101
Meg Tarbox
All year

135-155-BB
4 rooms, 4 pb
Visa, MC, *Rated*, •
C-ltd/P-no/H-no

Full breakfast
Snacks, complimentary wine
Bicycles, fireplaces, cable TV, waterfront, accom. bus. travelers

Harbor House is the only waterfront bed and breakfast in Georgetown, SC. Enjoy the breezes from the harbor on our porch. Stroll through the historic district and dine on the waterfront. info@harborhousebb.com http://www.harborhousebb.com

---

Live Oak Inn
515 Prince St 29440
843-545-8658 Fax: 843-545-8948
888-730-6004
Fred & Jackie Hoelscher
All year

85-150-BB
5 rooms, 5 pb
Most CC, *Rated*, •
C-ltd/S-ltd/P-no/H-no

Full breakfast
Snacks
Sitting room, library, bicycles, Jacuzzis, fireplace, cable TV, conference.

1905 Victorian home nestled between two 500 year-old live Oak trees, in-room fireplaces, whirlpool tubs, full breakfast. info@liveoakinn.com http://www.liveoakinn.com

---

The Shaw House
613 Cypress Ct 29440
843-546-9663
Mary & Joe Shaw
All year

60-75-BB
3 rooms, 3 pb
Rated, •
C-yes/S-yes/P-no/H-ltd

Full breakfast
Complimentary wine, tea, coffee
Sitting room, piano, bicycles, bird watching

Spacious two-story home in serene natural setting, with beautiful view overlooking miles of marshland formed by 4 rivers which converge and flow into the Intracoastal Waterway.

GREENVILLE (REGION)

Walnut Lane Inn
110 Ridge Rd, *Lyman* 29365
864-949-7230 Fax: 864-949-1633
David Ades & Hoyt Dottry
All year

95-130-BB
6 rooms, 6 pb
Most CC, *Rated*, •
C-ltd/S-ltd/P-no/H-ltd

Full breakfast
Snacks, complimentary evening tea, coffee, wine
Sitting room, 2 bedroom suite, cable TV, conferences, weddings

Nestled deep in the South between Greenville and Spartanburg SC, Walnut Lane Inn offers you a tradition in Southern hospitality.
walnutlaneinn@charter.net http://www.walnutlaneinn.com

LANDRUM

The Red Horse Inn
310 N Campbell Rd 29356
864-895-4968 Fax: 864-895-4968
Mary & Roger Wolters
All year

95-210-BB
9 rooms, 9 pb
Rated, •
C-yes/S-ltd/P-yes/H-yes

Continental breakfast
Each cottage has kitchen
Dining area, living room, fireplace, bedroom, bath, sitting area, TV, A/C

Situated on 190 rolling acres in the midst of horse country with extraordinary mountain views. 5 cottages and 4 Inn rooms.
theredhorseinn@aol.com http://www.theredhorseinn.com

MARION

Montgomery's Grove	80-110-BB	Full breakfast
408 Harlee St 29571	5 rooms, 4 pb	Afternoon tea, snacks
843-423-5220 877-646-7721	*Rated*, •	Lunch, dinner (fee), sitting
Coreen & Rick Roberts	C-ltd/S-ltd/P-no	room, library, bikes, hot tub
All year		

1893 Victorian manor in historic village between I-95 and Myrtle Beach. Dramatic architecture, stunning rooms. http://www.bbonline.com/sc/montgomery/

MYRTLE BEACH

Brustman House	65-145-BB	Full breakfast
400 25th Ave S 29577	5 rooms, 5 pb	Afternoon tea,
843-448-7699 Fax: 843-626-2478	Visa, MC, AmEx,	complimentary wine
800-448-7699	*Rated*, •	Bikes, phones, TVs, A/C,
Dr. Wendell Brustman	C-ltd/S-ltd/P-no/H-no	whirlpool tubs for two, golf,
All year		tennis nearby

Estate property only 300 yards to beach. Rose and herb gardens, honeymoon suites with private whirlpool tubs. Rose Garden Cottage with kitchenette and whirlpool tub.
wcbrustman@worldnet.att.net http://www.brustmanhouse.com

PAWLEYS ISLAND

Litchfield Plantation	200-620-BB	Full breakfast
PO Box 290	38 rooms, 38 pb	Dinner (fee), restaurant
Kings River Rd 29585	Most CC, *Rated*, •	Tennis courts, pool, golf,
843-237-9121 Fax: 843-237-1041	C-ltd/S-ltd/P-no/H-ltd	concierge service,
800-869-1410	German	oceanfront beachhouse
Karl Friedrich		
All year		

Escape down our avenue of live oaks to the Plantation House c.1750 or other well appointed rooms. Premier amenities, fine dining. Romance packages.
vacation@litchfieldplantation.com http://www.litchfieldplantation.com

PICKENS

The Schell Haus	BB	Full breakfast
117 Hiawatha Trail 29671	6 rooms, 6 pb	Picnic & backpack lunches
864-878-0078	Most CC	w/ advance request
Sharon & Jim Mahanes	C-ltd/S-ltd/P-no	Coffee makers, hidden TV's
All year		& VCR's

We welcome you to the Schell Haus, A Victorian style home tucked away in the foothills of the Blue Ridge mountains. schellhs@bellsouth.net http://www.schellhaus.com

ROCK HILL

Park Avenue Inn	70-85-BB	Continental plus breakfast
347 Park Ave 29730	3 rooms, 3 pb	Afternoon tea
803-325-1764 Fax: 803-325-1998	C-ltd/S-ltd/P-ltd/H-no	Library, bicycles
877-422-0127		
Sharon & Donny Neely		
All year		

Like your grandmothers house, all antiques. Large front porch swings and rocking chairs.

SALEM

Sunrise Farm	85-120-BB	Full gourmet or country
325 Sunrise Dr 29676	6 rooms, 6 pb	breakfast
864-944-0121 Fax: 864-944-6195	Visa, MC, *Rated*	Snacks & refreshments
888-991-0121	C-yes/S-no/P-ltd	
Barbara & Ron Laughter		
All year		

Sunrise Farm Bed & Breakfast is located on a 10-acre farm, in The Blue Ridge Mountain foothills of northwest South Carolina. The farm is the last part of an early 1900s cotton plantation. sfbb@bellsouth.net http://www.bbonline.com/sc/sunrisefarm

SUMMERVILLE

Price House Cottage
224 Sumter Ave 29483
843-871-1877 Fax: 843-873-7991
Jennifer & David Price
All year

145-BB
1 rooms, 1 pb
Visa, MC, AmEx
C-ltd/S-ltd/P-ltd/H-ltd

Full gourmet breakfast on weekends
Kitchen stocked with soft drinks, juice, teas, hot
Tennis court, Jacuzzi, fireplace, cable TV, accommodate business travelers

Restored 1812 servants' quarters; gourmet continental breakfast in cottage weekdays; full gourmet breakfast in Main House weekends; luxurious appointments Summerville's historic district. phcbb@aol.com http://www.bbonline.com/sc/pricehouse

UNION

The Inn at Merridun
100 Merridun Place 29379
864-427-7052
Fax: 864-429-0373
888-892-6020
Jim & Peggy Waller & JD (cat)
All year

99-125-BB
5 rooms, 5 pb
Rated, •
C-ltd/S-ltd/P-no/H-yes

Full breakfast
Meals by prior arrangement
Evening dessert, sitting room, library, 1 room with whirlpool bath

City close, country quiet. 1855 Antebellum mansion with many interesting architectural details. info@merridun.com http://www.merridun.com

South Dakota

CANOVA

Skoglund Farm
24375 438th Ave 57321
605-247-3445
Alden & Delores Skoglund
All year

30-60-MAP
6 rooms
Rated, •
C-yes/S-ltd/P-yes/H-no
Swedish

Full breakfast
Dinner included
Sitting room, piano, bicycles, newspaper, fax, A/C

Enjoy overnight on the South Dakota prairie. Return to your childhood–animals, country walking, home-cooked meals.

CUSTER

Custer Mansion
35 Centennial Dr 57730
605-673-3333
Fax: 605-673-6696
877-519-4948
Bob & Pat Meakim
All year

74-125-BB
6 rooms, 5 pb
Visa, MC, *Rated*, •
C-yes/S-no/P-no/H-no

Full breakfast
Afternoon tea
Sitt. rm., bikes, tennis, hiking & golf nearby, honeymoon & family stes.

Historic 1891 Victorian on 1 acre in heart of beautiful Black Hills. Western hospitality & delicious, home-baked food.
cusmanbb@gwtc.net http://www.gwtc.net/~cusmanbb/custer.html

Raspberry and Lace
12175 White Horse Rd 57730
605-574-4920
Fax: 605-574-4920
Loretta & Roland Daigle
All year

75-140-BB
4 rooms, 4 pb
Visa, MC, AmEx
C-yes/S-ltd/P-no/H-ltd

Full breakfast
Jacuzzis

Remodeled homestead in a beautiful mountain meadow along a trout stream and the Mickelson Trail. Quiet, comfortable rooms with king or queen beds.
RaspLaceBB@aol.com http://www.raspberryandlace.com

CUSTER

Strutton Inn B&B	70-135-BB	Full breakfast
RR 1, Box 555 57730	9 rooms, 9 pb	Afternoon tea, snacks
605-673-4808 Fax: 605-673-5297	Visa, MC, *Rated*, •	evening desserts
800-226-2611	C-no/S-ltd/P-no/H-no	Sitting room, Jacuzzis,
Cary & Denice Strutton		fireplace, satellite dish, hot
All year		tub under the stars

Elegant, romantic hideaway, Country Victorian home on four acres with veranda, gazebo, antiques out door hot tubs. Nine rooms, each with private baths, whirlpool tubs, king beds. strutton@gwtc.net http://www.gwtc.net/users/strutton

DEADWOOD

Black Hills Hideaway	105-179-BB	Full breakfast
11744 Hideaway Rd 57732	9 rooms, 9 pb	Lun./din.(fee), snacks
605-578-3054 Fax: 605-578-2028	Visa, MC, *Rated*, •	Comp. wine, sitt. rooms,
Kathy & Ned Bode	C-ltd/S-ltd/P-no/H-ltd	bikes, Jacuzzis, frplcs.,
All year		decks, hot tubs, conf.

Mountain. inn with cathedral ceiling & wood interior, tucked in National Forest. You'll be pampered on 67 wooded acres with fresh mountain. air, the aroma & whispering of pines, peace & solitude hideaway@enetis.net http://www.enetis.net/~hideaway

HILL CITY

Coyote Blues Village	50-139-BB	Full specialty breakfast
PO Box 966	4 rooms, 4 pb	Dinner optional
23165 Horsemans Ranch Road	Visa, MC, Disc, *Rated*,	Sitting rm w/ fireplace, large
57745	•	deck, 1 suite, satellite TV,
605-574-4477 Fax: 605-574-2101	C-yes/S-ltd/P-ltd/H-yes	Ping Pong table
888-253-4477	German, French	
Christina/Hans-Peter Streich	All year	

Experience inter-cultural ambiance. Secluded yet centrally located in pine trees near lake. Weight lifting equipment.
coyotebb@dtgnet.com http://www.coyotebluesvillage.com

Pine Rest Cabins	59-249-EP	Bring your own breakfast
PO Box 377	12 rooms, 12 pb	Equipped kitchens
24063 Hwy 385 57745	Visa, MC, Disc	Restaurant, tennis, bike
605-574-2416 800-333-5306	C-yes/S-ltd/P-ltd/H-ltd	rentals, nearby, hot tub,
Jan & Steve Johnson	All year	hiking, cable TV

Perfect location for day trips anywhere in the Black Hills! Mount Rushmore, Crazy Horse, Custer State Park, less than 20 minutes. Mickelson trail access less than 1 mile.
pinerestcabins@aol.com http://www.pinerestcabins.com

RAPID CITY

Carriage House	115-149-BB	Full breakfast
721 West Blvd 57701	5 rooms, 5 pb	Dinner (fee), snacks, tea
605-343-6415 Fax: 603-925-0061	Visa, MC, Disc, *Rated*,	Library, sitting room, piano,
888-343-6415 All year	•	whirlpools for two, music
Janice & Jay Hrachovec	C-no/S-ltd/P-no/H-no	libraries

Step back in time when you enter the 1900 Carriage House. We welcome you with amenities, such as feather down beds and pillows, whirlpools for two, and breakfasts fit for a king and queen.
info@carriagehouse-bb.com http://www.carriagehouse-bb.com

Willow Springs Cabins	110-175-BB	Full gourmet breakfast
11515 Sheridan Lake Rd 57702	2 rooms, 2 pb	Coffee, tea, hot chocolate,
605-342-3665	*Rated*	popcorn, cookies
Joyce & Russell Payton	C-ltd/S-no/P-no/H-no	TV/VCR, stereo, outdoor hot
All year		tubs, hiking trails, mountain
		stream

Privacy at its best! Secluded, antique filled, log cabins in the beautiful Black Hills National Forest. Great views, gourmet breakfasts in your cabin, private hot tubs. A relaxing romantic retreat!
wilosprs@rapidnet.com http://www.willowspringscabins.com

RAPID CITY (REGION)

A Rosemary For Remembrance
HC 89 Box 204, *Hermosa* 57744
605-394-5431
1-800-577-3952
Gary Benson & Cheri Santana

125-139-BB
3 rooms, 3 pb
Visa, MC, Disc
C-yes/S-ltd/P-ltd/H-yes
All year

Coffee & tea, early evening dessert, or cookies
Videos, books & games, BBQ, hot tub

Bed & Breakfast Escape on nearly 10 acres. . .Panoramic views. Deer, red fox. Views of several thousand acres off porch, near Mt. Rushmore and Custer State Park.
rosemarygrows@earthlink.net http://www.rosemarygrows.com

WEBSTER

Lakeside Farm
13476 437th Ave 57274
605-486-4430
Glenn & Joy Hagen
All year

50-BB
3 rooms
Rated
C-yes/S-no/P-no/H-no

Full breakfast
Other meals possible
Comp. coffee, tea, snack, sitting room, bicycles, museum, factory outlet

Sample country life with us. A family-owned farm. Northeastern SD lakes area. Fresh air, open spaces. Fresh milk, homemade cinnamon rolls.
gjhagen@sbtc.net http://www.webstersd/lakesidefarm.com

Tennessee

ATHENS

Black Bear Trace
310 County Rd 121 37303
423-745-0439 Fax: 423-745-0566
Kathy King
All year

95-125-BB
2 rooms, 2 pb
Visa, MC
C-no/S-ltd/P-no/H-yes

Full breakfast
Coffee, tea, soda pop, snacks, baked goodies
Gathering room with fireplace, porch—rockers/swing, telescope, library

Cozy Log Home retreat on 45 acres of forest in the Smoky Mountains. Sit on the porch and enjoy the beautiful view with a fresh baked treat. Conveniently located to I75 and area attractions. blackbeartrace@earthlink.net http://www.blackbeartrace.com

BUTLER

Iron Mountain Inn
PO Box 30
138 Moreland Dr 37640
423-768-2446 Fax: 423-768-2451
888-781-2399
Vikki Woods All year

155-250-BB
7 rooms, 5 pb
Most CC, *Rated*, •
C-ltd/S-no/P-ltd/H-ltd
French

Full breakfast
Lunch/dinner available (fee) tea, bottomless jar
Library, whirlpool baths, balconies, steam showers, hot tub, hiking trails

Romance abounds in the chalet w/ starlit hot tub by Crossover Creek. Pampering Perfected service at the B&B. Spectacular mountain views, birdsong instead of alarm clocks, "Paradise Found," guests say. ironmtn@preferred.com http://www.ironmountaininn.com

CHATTANOOGA

The Pettit House
109 Ochs Hwy 37409
423-821-4740
Marcie Pettit
All year

125-195-BB
2 rooms, 2 pb
Visa, MC, AmEx, •
C-yes/S-ltd/P-no/H-no
Geramn, Dutch, French, Spanish, Japanese

Full breakfast
Snacks, complimentary wine
Sitting room, bicycles, suites, cable TV, accommodate business travelers

Elegant, spacious bed and breakfast suites are beautifully furnished with antiques. Located downtown at the foot of Lookout Mountain with a spectacular view!
rroypettit@juno.com http://www.pettithouse.com

CLEVELAND

Candlewycke Manor	85-125-BB	Bountiful Southern breakfast
500 Davis Lane NW 37312	4 rooms, 2 pb	Homemade evening desserts
423-584-2337	Visa, MC, AmEx	Reading nook, deck, swing,
Wacoe Lineberry, Herschel &	C-yes/S-no/P-no	croquet, horseshoes
Regenia Collier All year		

Located in Cleveland, TN, Candlewycke's guests enjoy the quiet of the country, and still have the luxury of being a few minutes from town. Quaint & comfortable–it feels like home, without the work! info@candlewyckemanor.com
http://www.candlewyckemanor.com

COLLEGE GROVE

Peacock Hill Country Inn	135-245-BB	Full breakfast
6994 Giles Hill Rd 37046	10 rooms, 10 pb	Snacks, lunch & dinner
615-368-7727 Fax: 615-368-7933	Most CC, *Rated*, •	available with reservations
800-327-6663	C-ltd/S-no/P-no/H-ltd	Sitting room, Jacuzzis,
Anita & Walter Ogilvie		fireplaces, accommodate
All year		business travelers

Romantic retreat located on a 1000-acre working cattle farm, with trails for hiking luxurious rooms & suites, all with king beds & large baths. AAA four diamond rating.
suzannes@peacockhillgh.com http://www.peacockhillinn.com

DANDRIDGE (REGION)

The Barrington Inn	65-125-BB	Full breakfast
1174 McGuire Rd, *New Market*	7 rooms, 7 pb	Restaurant, dinner available
37820	Most CC, •	Sitting room, library,
865-397-3368 Fax: 865-397-6370	C-ltd/S-ltd/P-ltd/H-ltd	fireplaces, satellite TV,
888-205-8482	Afrikans	fridges, iron & board
Vince & Sharlene Barrington	All year	

European elegance with American country charm. The only fine dining restaurant in the county and quite a large surrounding area. A far away feel and yet so close!
bvinshar2@aol.com http://www.bbonline.com/tn/barrington

DICKSON

East Hills Inn	75-135-BB	Full breakfast
100 E Hill Terrace 37055	7 rooms, 7 pb	Afternoon tea, snacks
615-441-9428 Fax: 615-446-2181	Most CC, *Rated*, •	Sitting room, library,
John & Anita Luther	C-ltd/S-ltd/P-no/H-yes	bicycles, fireplaces, cable
All year		TV, 3 rooms with kitchen

The historic Inn, built in the late forties on 4.5 acres, has a country setting in the city with today's amenities. jaluther@comcast.net http://www.easthillsbb.com

DUCKTOWN

The Company House Inn	79-89-BB
PO Box 154	7 rooms, 7 pb
125 Main Street 37326	
423-496-5634 Fax: 423-496-4324	
800-343-2909	
Margaret Tonkin & Mike	
Fabian All year	

The Company House was built in 1850 by Dr. Lewis Kinsey. Dr. Kinsey served the miners who worked in the area copper mines.
companyhousemt@tds.net http://www.bbonline.com/tn/companyhouse

The White House	70-79-BB	Full breakfast
PO Box 668	3 rooms, 3 pb	Afternoon tea, snacks
104 Main St 37326	Visa, MC, *Rated*, •	Evening dessert buffet, wrap-
423-496-4166 Fax: 423-496-9778	C-ltd/S-ltd/P-no/H-no	around porches, rocking
800-775-4166	All year	chairs, TV
Mardee & Dan Kauffman		

Beautiful mountain area, close to whitewater rafting, 4 TVA lakes 1 hour away, trout fishing, golf. Lovely porch with rocking chairs.
mardan@tds.net http://www.ocoee-whitehousebb.com

FAYETTEVILLE

Fayetteville
1111 W Washington St 37334
931-433-9636
Eugenia Lancaster
All year

75-85-BB
2 rooms, 2 pb
C-ltd/S-no/P-no/H-yes

Full breakfast
Afternoon tea
Sitting room, library, fireplaces.

1914 charming vintage home with quiet, spacious bedrooms, private baths, library, and gardens. Candlelight gourmet breakfast customized to your needs. Near Towne Square, antiques and shops. fayettevillebb@webTV.net

---

Old Cowan Plantation
126 Old Boonshill Rd 37334
931-433-0225
Paul & Betty Johnson
All year

60-BB
2 rooms, 2 pb
C-yes/S-no/P-no/H-no

Continental breakfast
Sitting room, fireplaces, cable TV

The 1886 Colonial home offers a peaceful atmosphere with two well-appointed guest rooms. Sleep on crisp, freshly ironed sheets in the peaceful Tennessee countryside.

FRANKLIN

Namaste Acres Country Ranch Inn
5436 Leipers Creek Rd 37064
615-791-0333 Fax: 615-591-0665
Lisa and Bill Winters
All year

75-85-BB
3 rooms, 3 pb
Most CC, *Rated*, •
S-ltd/P-no/H-no

Full country breakfast
In-room coffee, fridge
Hot tub, phone, pool, TV/VCR, hiking, horseback riding trails

Quiet valley setting, poolside deck and hot tub plus hiking. Horseback trails with guided rides on the original Natchez Trace. Inn offers 4 theme suites, each with fireplace.
namastebb@aol.com http://www.namasteacres.com

GATLINBURG

Buckhorn Inn
2140 Tudor Mtn Rd 37738
865-436-4668 Fax: 865-436-5009
Lee & John Mellor
All year

115-150-BB
20 rooms, 20 pb
Most CC, *Rated*
C-ltd/S-ltd/P-no/H-yes
Spanish, French, Latin

Full breakfast
Dinner, sack lunches, afternoon refreshments
Fireplaces, Jacuzzis, coffeemakers, nature trail, library, bathrobes

Set on a ridge facing spectacular views of the mountains, Buckhorn Inn is the area's most historic inn and the only inn in the area that serves dinner every evening.
buckhorninn@msn.com http://www.buckhorninn.com

Eight Gables Inn
219 N Mtn Trail 37738
865-430-3344 Fax: 865-430-3344
800-279-5716
Don & Kim Cason
All year

99-199-BB
12 rooms, 12 pb
Visa, MC, AmEx, *Rated*, •
C-ltd/S-ltd/P-no/H-no

Full breakfast
Sitting room, TV lounge, 2 rooms with whirlpools, hot tubs

Eight Gables Inn is a luxurious four diamond rated bed and breakfast nested at the foot of the Great Smoky Mountains. 8gables@eightgables.com http://www.eightgables.com

---

Tennessee Ridge Inn
507 Campbell Lead 37738
865-436-4068 800-737-7369
Dar Hullander
All year

85-159-BB
7 rooms, 7 pb
Most CC, *Rated*, •
S-ltd/P-no/H-yes

Full gourmet breakfast
Afternoon tea, snacks
Sitting room, library, fireplaces, balconies, Jacuzzi, honeymoon stes.

View the Smokies by day & the city lights of Gatlinburg by night. Jacuzzis, fireplaces, private balconies, king beds, swimming pool.
innkeeper@tn-ridge.com http://www.tn-ridge.com

GATLINBURG (REGION)

Christopher Place, An Intimate Resort
1500 Pinnacles Way, *Newport* 37821
423-623-6555 Fax: 423-613-4771
800-595-9441
Drew Ogle
All year

175-325-BB
8 rooms, 8 pb
Most CC, *Rated*, •
C-ltd/S-ltd/H-yes

Full breakfast
Snacks, restaurant
Sitting room, library, tennis court, pool, hot tubs, sauna

Rated as one of the "10 Most Romantic Inns in America" by Vacations Magazine. We are an intimate resort located in East Tennessee!

thebestinn@aol.com http://www.christopherplace.com

GREAT SMOKY MOUNTAINS (REGION)

Bonny Brook
2301 Wears Valley Rd, *Sevierville* 37862
865-908-4745 Fax: 865-908-4745
Coleen Thomason All year

125-140-BB
2 rooms, 2 pb
Visa, MC, *Rated*
C-ltd/S-no/P-no/H-no

Full breakfast
Afternoon tea
Sitting room, suites, cable TV, stone fireplace, Celtic music, tartan robes

Log structure w/Scottish decorative influence. Deck near large stream, large shady porches surrounded by woods. Scots-Irish items for sale.

bonnybrookbb@msn.com http://www.bonnybrook.net

GREENEVILLE

Kennel Lane House
485 Kitchen Branch Rd
89 Kennel Ln 37743
423-917-0817

BB
Katherine Rollins
All year

Central Heat and Air, Large Covered Porch with Gas Grill, Wrought Iron Chairs, Porch Swing, and Table

rental_info@greatandsmall.net http://www.greatandsmall.net/rental/rental.html

---

Nolichuckey Bluffs
295 Kinser Park Ln 37743
423-787-7947 Fax: 423-787-9247
800-842-4690
Brooke & Patricia Sadler
All year

85-125-BB
7 rooms, 7 pb
Visa, MC, Disc, *Rated*, •
C-yes/S-no/P-ltd/H-ltd

Full breakfast
Afternoon tea, snacks
Sitting room, library, bicycles, Jacuzzis, fireplaces

Quiet luxury in country setting. Gazebos, trails, rose gardens and spectacular views.

cabins@usit.net http://www.tennessee-cabins.com

HILLSBORO

Lord's Landing
375 Lord's Landing Ln 37342
931-467-3830 Fax: 931-467-3032
Denny & Pam Neilson
All year

95-150-BB
7 rooms, 7 pb
Most CC, *Rated*, •
C-ltd/S-ltd/P-no/H-no

Full Brkfst Su-Fr, Deluxe Cont Sat
Popcorn, Sodas, Chocolates, Private Label Wine
Whirlpool tubs, fireplaces, swimming, billiards, campfire, farm animals

Central Tennessee's 50 acre paradise awaits. Located at the base of the Cumberland Plateau. Farmland and mountains as far as the eye can see. Peaceful setting. Whirlpool tubs and fireplaces. lordslanding@blomand.net http://www.lordslanding.com

JACKSON

Highland Place
519 N Highland Ave 38301
731-427-1472 Fax: 731-427-2430
877-614-6305
Cindy & Bill Pflaum
All year

95-155-BB
4 rooms, 4 pb
Visa, MC, AmEx, •
C-ltd/S-no/P-ltd/H-no

Full breakfast
Gourmet romantic or business dinners

A 1911 Colonial Revival mansion, Highland Place guestrooms all have private bath, cable TV, VCR and stereo. Beautifully refurbished. Gourmet breakfasts served every morning.

relax@highlandplace.com http://www.highlandplace.com

JOHNSON CITY

Hart House
207 East Holston Ave 37604
423-926-3147
Vanessa Johnson
All year

70-BB
3 rooms, 3 pb
Visa, MC, *Rated*
C-yes/S-no/P-no/H-no

Full breakfast
Afternoon tea, snacks
Sitting room, library, basketball court, weight rm, tapes/toys for children

1910 Dutch Colonial home lovingly restored to its original grandeur. Relax on the front porch, or spend an evening by the fireplace. harthouseinn@worldnet.att.net

JONESBOROUGH

Blair-Moore House
201 W Main St 37659
423-753-0044 Fax: 423-753-0044
888-453-0044
Jack and Tami Moore
All year

95-150-BB
3 rooms, 3 pb
Most CC, *Rated*
C-no/S-no/P-no/H-ltd

Exceptional multi-course breakfast
Complimentary refreshments
Sitting room, large veranda, lovely gardens

Recognized by Arrington's B&B Journal as one of the "Top 15 B&B/Inns in US & Canada" and we ranked #3 in the "Best Breakfast" category. This survey was conducted among inn-goers nationwide. blairmoorehouse@aol.com http://www.blairmoorehouse.com

---

Eureka Hotel
127 W Main St 37659
423-913-6100 Fax: 423-913-0429
877-734-6100
Baxter Bledsoe
All year

89-199-BB
16 rooms, 16 pb
Most CC, *Rated*
C-yes/S-no/P-no/H-yes

Continental Plus breakfast
Afternoon tea
Sitting room, suites, fireplace, cable TV, accom. business travelers

Built as a residence in 1797, the structure was enlarged into the Eureka Hotel in 1900. After a multi-million dollar restoration the hotel has re-opened.
eureka@naxs.net http://www.eurekajonesborough.com

KINGSTON

Whitestone Country Inn
1200 Paint Rock Road 37763
865-376-0113 Fax: 865-376-4554
888-247-2464
Paul and Jean Cowell
All year

120-200-EP
16 rooms, 16 pb
Rated

Full breakfast
Dinner (fee)

Whitestone Country Inn's 360 secluded acres on the shores of Watts Bar Lake provide lodging with a peaceful country pace.
moreinfo@whitestones.com http://www.whitestones.com

Woodland Cove
PO Box 791
144 Helton Vojt Kofsky Ln
37763
865-717-3719 877-700-2683
Bruce & Della Marshall
All year

95-125-BB
3 rooms, 3 pb
Visa, MC, Disc, *Rated*, •
C-yes/S-no/P-no/H-no

Full breakfast
Afternoon tea, snacks
Sitting room, Jacuzzis, cable TV, accom. bus. travel, located on lake

Delight in the tranquil beauty of romantic, secluded Woodland Cove B&B on Watts Bar Lake. Enjoy canoeing, paddle-boating, fishing, swimming, or just relaxing!
woodlandcove@earthlink.net http://www.woodlandcovebb.com

KNOXVILLE

Maplehurst Inn
800 W Hill Ave 37705
423-523-7773 800-451-1562
Sonny & Becky Harben
All year

79-149-BB
11 rooms, 11 pb
Visa, MC, AmEx, *Rated*, •
C-yes/S-ltd/P-ltd/H-no

Full breakfast
Snacks
Sitting room, library, suites, conference, facilities, Penthouse

European style B&B in downtown Knoxville. Walk to University of Tennessee, Neyland Stadium and World's Fair Park.
sonny@maplehurstinn.com http://www.maplehurstinn.com

KNOXVILLE (REGION)

Bushrod Hall
422 Cumberland St NE,
Harriman 37748
423-882-8406 Fax: 423-882-6056
888-880-8406
All year

75-110-BB
3 rooms, 3 pb
Visa, MC, AmEx,
Rated, •
C-ltd/S-no/P-no/H-ltd
Spanish

Full breakfast
Snacks
Sitting room, library, fireplaces, cable TV, conference, kitchen

Historic home, furnished in period antiques, with exquisite woodwork. Represents long forgotten days of a bygone era and small town life. Victorian gardens.
bushrodbb@aol.com http://www.bbonline.com/tn/bushrod

LENOIR CITY

The Captain's Retreat
3534 Lakeside Dr 37772
865-986-4229 877-531-7421
Kelley Honea
All year

105-BB
4 rooms, 4 pb
Visa, MC, Disc, *Rated*,
•
C-ltd/S-ltd/P-no/H-yes

Continental plus breakfast
Snacks
Sitting room, Jacuzzis, fireplaces, cable TV, accommodate bus. trav.

Quiet lakehouse on Fort Loudon Lake, close to Knoxville, Smokey Mountains, and water activities. Fourteen minutes from I40 and I75.
kelley@captainsretreat.com http://www.captainsretreat.com

LOUDON

The Mason Place
600 Commerce St 37774
865-458-3921
Bob & Donna Siewart
All year

88-120-BB
5 rooms, 5 pb
Rated

Full breakfast

Listed on the National Registry of Historic Places, the Mason Place proudly oversees 3 acres of lawn, gardens and large shade trees where Civil War artifacts are still being found.
thempbb@aol.com http://www.themasonplace.com

LYNCHBURG

Lynchburg B&B
PO Box 34
107 Mechanic Street 37352
931-759-7158
Virginia & Mike Tipps
All year

65-78-BB
3 rooms, 3 pb
Visa, MC, *Rated*
C-yes/S-no/P-no/H-yes

Continental breakfast
Afternoon tea
Tennis court, pool

Stay in one of the oldest homes in historic Lynchburg, home of Jack Daniel Distillery. Antique furnished. Private baths.
lynchburgbb@cafes.net http://www.bbonline.com/tn/lynchburg/

MCDONALD

BrockHaus
500 Brock Rd 37353
423-559-0457 800-745-4119
Sandra & Ralph Brock
All year

85-BB
3 rooms, 3 pb
Visa, MC
C-ltd/S-ltd/P-no/H-no

Snacks, drinks
Evening desserts
Sitting room with TV/VCR/CD, videos, board games, portable TV/VCR

Welcome to Our Home! The house is modeled after the famous Black Forest homes in southern Germany and features a kachelofen (ceramic tile stove), balconies, and German furniture.
brockllc@aol.com http://hometown.aol.com/brockllc/myhomepage/business.html

MONTEAGLE

Adams Edgeworth Inn
Monteagle Assembly 37356
931-924-4000 Fax: 931-924-3236
1-87-RELAXINN
Wendy & David Adams
All year

125-250-BB
12 rooms, 12 pb
Visa, MC, AmEx,
Rated, •
C-ltd/S-ltd/P-no/H-ltd
French

Full gourmet breakfast
Candle-lit dinner available
Gift shop, library, Verandas, swim, hike, summer program

Historic Country Inn in a Victorian village on mountain top. Canopy beds, fireplaces, antiques, A/C, gourmet dinners available. We feature 8 rooms, 3 suites, and a dinner with new 'a la carte' menu. innjoy@blomand.net http://www.assemblyinn.com

MOUNTAIN CITY

Butler House
309 N Church St 37683
423-727-4119 Fax: 423-727-4119
Bill & Joan Trathen
All year

65-80-BB
4 rooms, 4 pb
Most CC, *Rated*
C-ltd/S-no/P-no/H-no

Full breakfast
Tea, snacks, complimentary wine
Sitting room, library, cable TV, accommodate business travelers

Elegant but comfortable historic home on fifteen acres in the charming town of Mountain City, the heart of Tennessee's Mountain paradise.
info@thebutlerhouse.com http://www.thebutlerhouse.com

MURFREESBORO

Byrn-Roberts Inn
346 E Main St 37130
615-867-0308 Fax: 615-867-0280
888-877-4919
David & Julie Becker
All year

125-205-BB
4 rooms, 4 pb
Most CC, *Rated*, •
S-no/P-no/H-no

Full breakfast
Snacks, complimentary wine
Sitting room, library, bicycles, Jacuzzis, suites, fireplaces, cable TV

Exquisite woodwork, 11 fireplaces adorn this restored and renovated 1903 Victorian mansion. byrnrobert@aol.com http://www.byrn-roberts-inn.com/

Carriage Lane Inn
411 N Maney Avenue 37130
615-890-3630 Fax: 615-893-5707
800-357-2827
Sharon Petty
All year

105-135-BB
5 rooms, 5 pb
Most CC, •
C-ltd/S-no/P-no/H-ltd

Full breakfast
Wedding ceremony, and reception site

History abounds in Middle Tennessee and you are in the middle of it all at Carriage Lane Inn. Newly restored, elegantly decorated 100-year-old home in historic district.
info@carriagelaneinn.com http://www.carriagelaneinn.com

Simply Southern
211 N Tennessee Blvd 37130
615-896-4988 Fax: 615-867-2899
888-723-1199
Carl & Georgia Buckner
All year

89-149-BB
5 rooms, 5 pb
Visa, MC, Disc, *Rated*, •
S-no/P-no/H-no

Full breakfast
Snacks
Sitting room, library, suites, fireplaces, cable TV

Four story, fine old 1907 home with wraparound veranda, antiques, eclectically elegant, professionally decorated, private baths, gourmet breakfast, romantic.
InnSouth@aol.com http://www.simplysouthern.net

NASHVILLE

End O'The Bend Lodge
2523 Miami Ave 37214
615-883-0997
Betty Blackwell
All year

165-220-EP
5 rooms, 2 pb
Rated
C-ltd/S-ltd/P-no/H-ltd

Coffee and Coffee Pot in Kitchen
Daily housekeeping services

Spend your visit to Nashville in a luxurious log cabin, on the banks of the Cumberland River, a mile from the Opryland Hotel~ Opry Mills. Named in "BEST PLACES TO STAY IN THE SOUTH." river200mi@aol.com http://www.bbonline.com/tn/bend/

Four Walls
1804 Blair Blvd 37212
615-292-7162 Fax: 615-292-1538
Marilyn Warren
All year

145-BB

Full breakfast
Covered off-street parking available

Four Walls is like a small European hotel dropped into the historic Belmont-Hillsboro area, within walking distance of Vanderbilt & Belmont Universities, great shops and restaurants, and Music Row. mk4walls@aol.com http://www.fourwallsbedandbreakfast.com

NASHVILLE (REGION)

Morning Star 460 Jones Ln, *Hendersonville* 37075 615-264-2614 Fax: 615-264-2640 Bob & Faith Murray All year	100-175-BB 4 rooms, 2 pb *Rated* P-yes	Full breakfast

This Custom Country Victorian, which was featured in the January 1995 special edition of ELITE UNIQUE HOMES magazine.

PIGEON FORGE

Hilton's Bluff 2654 Valley Heights Dr 37863 865-428-9765 Fax: 865-428-8997 800-441-4188 Bob & JoAnn Quandt All year	69-129-BB 10 rooms, 10 pb Most CC, *Rated*, • C-ltd/S-ltd/P-no/H-ltd	Full breakfast Afternoon tea, snacks Sitting room, library, Jacuzzis, fireplace, cable TV, accom. bus. travelers

Romantic hilltop hideaway, very quiet and peaceful setting, yet within a mile of most major attractions. info@hiltonsbluff.com http://www.hiltonsbluff.com

PIKEVILLE

Fall Creek Falls B&B & Meadowbrook Cabin Rt 3, Box 298B 37367 423-881-5494 Fax: 423-881-5040 Rita & Doug Pruett Closed 12/22-2/1	79-140-BB 8 rooms, 8 pb Most CC, *Rated*, • C-ltd/S-no/P-no/H-no	Full breakfast Sitt. rm., AC, phones, room with whirlpool, cabin rental for 2 available

Romantic mountain getaway, one mile from nationally acclaimed Fall Creek Falls State Resort Park, featuring golfing, fishing, hiking, swimming, boating, suite with fireplace. FCFBandB@bledsoe.net http://www.fallcreekfalls.com

---

MountainTop Retreat Rt 1 Box 129E 37367 423-533-2995 Nita Formby All year	BB C-ltd/S-ltd/P-ltd/H-ltd	Full breakfast Other meals upon special request Patio, picnic baskets, VCR, TV in parlor, A/C

This is a modern residence nestled in 19 acres of wooded privacy overlooking the Sequatchie River Valley. Great views from all locations. mtntopretreat@hotmail.com

SAVANNAH

White Elephant 200 Church St 38372 731-925-6410 Sharon & Ken Hansgen All year	100-120-BB 3 rooms, 3 pb *Rated*, • C-ltd/S-no/P-no/H-no	Full breakfast Afternoon refreshments Sitting room, library, guided tours of Shiloh National Military Park

Elegant Victorian inn, closest B&B to Shiloh National Military Park, in Historic District, features Civil War guide service, antique furnishings, full breakfasts, library. stay@whiteelephantbb.com http://www.WhiteElephantBB.com

SEVIERVILLE

Blue Mountain Mist Country Inn & Cottages 1811 Pullen Rd 37862 423-428-2335 800-497-2335 Norman & Sarah Ball All year	115-169-BB 17 rooms, 17 pb Most CC C-yes/S-ltd/P-no/H-ltd	Full country breakfast and evening desserts Wraparound porch and sitting room

The Blue Mountain Mist is a distinguished Smoky Mountain inn where luxury, history and nature abound. 12 guestrooms and 5 romantic cottages are decorated with antiques and heirlooms. blumtnmist@aol.com http://www.bluemountainmist.com

SEVIERVILLE

Calico Inn
757 Ranch Way 37862
865-428-3833 800-235-1054
Lill & Jim Katzbeck
All year

99-115-BB
3 rooms, 3 pb
Visa, MC, *Rated*, •
C-yes/S-ltd/P-no/H-no

Full delicious breakfast
Afternoon tea, snacks
Nature lovers delight, near malls/outdoor sport, shopping/entertainment

Log inn w/magnificent Mt. views, antiques and country decor. Near all attractions. Minutes from outlet stores, Dollywood, live entertainment, theaters and Smoky Mt. Nat'l Park.

calicoinn@aol.com http://www.calico-inn.com

Chilhowee Bluff, A Great Smokey Mountains Inn
1887 Bluff Mountain Rd 37876
865-908-0321 Fax: 865-774-3308
888-559-0321
Judy & Joe Hudak
Feb. 1-Jan. 1

105-165-BB
4 rooms, 4 pb
Most CC, *Rated*
C-no/S-ltd/P-no/H-no

Three course gourmet breakfast
Snacks/beverages; casual fine dining restaurant
Pvt. entrance, fireplace, Jacuzzi, TV/VCR, phone, hot tub, robes, hair dryer

Created to pamper the weary and inspire the romantic. Great location, great food, great accommodations. A great Smoky Mountains Bed & Breakfast Inn!

reservations@chilhoweebluff.com http://www.chilhoweebluff.com

---

Little Greenbrier Lodge
3685 Lyon Springs Rd 37862
865-429-2500 Fax: 865-429-4093
800-277-8100
Charles & Susan LeBon
All year

115-125-BB
9 rooms, 9 pb
Visa, MC, Disc, *Rated*, •
C-ltd/S-no/P-no/H-no

Full breakfast
Lunch & dinner available (fee)
Snacks, sitting room, shopping/entertainment

We are the oldest Lodge bordering the Great Smoky Mountain National Park. Genuine antiques furnish the old place.

littlegreenbrier@worldnet.att.net http://www.littlegreenbrierlodge.com

---

River Piece Inn
PO Box 6872
1970 Pittman Center Rd 37864
865-428-6547 Fax: 865-453-7099
888-265-3097
Bob & Janene Allen
All year

81-125-BB
5 rooms, 5 pb
Most CC, *Rated*
C-ltd/S-no/P-no/H-yes

Full country breakfast
Snacks, evening dessert
Jacuzzis, fireplaces, shopping/entertainment

Farmhouse inn offering 5 guestrooms, private baths with whirlpools, queen beds, antiques, 7 fireplaces, gazebo, river benches, river tubing, & fishing.

rpiallen@earthlink.net http://www.riverpieceinn.com

Von Bryan Mountaintop Inn
2402 Hatcher Mtn Rd 37862
865-453-9832 Fax: 865-428-8634
800-633-1459
Vaughn Family
All year

125-170-BB
9 rooms, 9 pb
Rated, •
C-yes/S-ltd/P-no/H-no

Full breakfast
evening refreshments and desserts
mountain views, swimming pool, hot tub, hiking trails, library

A curving, climbing road leads to a log mountaintop hide-a-way with views of sensational smoky mountain ranges and peaceful valley farmland.

von-bryan-inn@juno.com http://www.vonbryan.com

TOWNSEND

Gracehill
1169 Little Round Top 37882
865-448-3070
Katherine Janke
All year

200-300-BB
3 rooms, 3 pb
Visa, MC, AmEx
S-ltd/P-no

Full breakfast
Complimentary stocked snack area
Internet, fax and copy Machine, satellite TV/VCR, fitness center

Gracehill Bed & Breakfast, award winning and unforgettable, one guest says, "... this is beyond elegant ... it's exquisite."

gracehil@bellsouth.net http://www.gracehillbandb.com

Texas

ABILENE

BJ's Prairie House
508 Mulberry St 79601
915-675-5855 Fax: 915-677-4694
800-673-5855
B.J. & Bob Fender
All year

75-85-BB
4 rooms, 2 pb
Most CC, *Rated*
C-ltd/S-no/P-no/H-no

Full breakfast
Snacks, wine, bar
Sitting room, cable TV
complimentary movies,
conferences

Built in 1902, nestled in the heart of old Abilene, remodeled in 1920 to favor a Frank Lloyd Wright "prairie style" design.
bfender@earthlink.net http://abilenebedandbreakfast.com

ALPINE

Historic Holland Hotel
PO Box 444
209 W Holland Ave 79830
915-837-3844
Fax: 915-837-7346
800-535-8040
Carla McFarland
All year

45-80-BB
14 rooms, 14 pb
Visa, MC, AmEx
C-yes/S-yes/P-yes/H-yes
Spanish

Continental breakfast
Lobby restaurant,
microwave, refrigerator
Sitting room, catering &
banquet rooms

1928 Historic Landmark across from the Amtrack station; Lobby Restaurant.
info@hollandhotel.net http://www.hollandhotel.net

AMARILLO

Parkview House
1311 S Jefferson St 79101
806-373-9464
Fax: 806-373-3166
Carol & Nabil Dia
All year

75-135-BB
6 rooms, 4 pb
Visa, MC, AmEx, •
C-ltd/S-no/P-no/H-ltd
Arabic

Continental plus breakfast
Beverages, wine
Bicycles, tennis, Jacuzzi,
fireplaces, cable TV, suite,
garden cottage

Amarillo's first historic Victorian B&B, Parkview House, is known for its friendly Texas hospitality. Charming romantic rooms furnished with distinct antiques are both cozy and homey. parkviewbb@aol.com http://Parkviewbb.20M.com

AUSTIN

1110 Carriage House Inn
1110 W 22 1/2 St 78705
512-472-2333 Fax: 512-476-0218 1-866-472-2333
Tressie Damron
All year

100-150-BB
5 rooms, 5 pb
Most CC, •
C-ltd/S-no/P-no/H-no

Full breakfast
Coffee, tea. Delicious treat
upon arrival.
Private bathrooms, Jacuzzi,
private entrances, deck,
gazebo, lily pond, coff

Carriage House Inn was voted one of the Top Ten Country Breakfasts in the US. This Austin, Texas bed and breakfast will spoil you with romantic rooms, relaxing grounds, and a delicious breakfast. dcarriagehouse@aol.com http://www.carriagehouseinn.org

---

1888 Miller-Crockett House
112 Academy Dr 78704
512-441-1600 Fax: 512-447-6532
888-441-1641
Kathleen Mooney
All year

89-149-BB
6 rooms, 6 pb
Visa, MC, AmEx
C-yes/S-ltd/P-yes/H-yes
Spanish

Full gourmet breakfast
Complimentary wine
Bikes, Jacuzzis, suites, cable
TV, accom. bus. travelers

Elegant, historic New Orleans style Queen Anne Victorian Estate overlooking spectacular view of downtown skyline. Walk to downtown and river.
kat@millercrockett.com http://www.millercrockett.citysearch.com

Adams House, Austin, TX

AUSTIN

Adams House
4300 Avenue G 78751
512-453-7696
John & Sidnney Lock
All year

80-125-BB

Adams House is located in historic and central Hyde Park. It was recently renovated and the original pine floors, sash windows, slate flooring and 12-foot ceilings have all been restored.

reservations@theadamshouse.com http://www.theadamshouse.com

Austin Brook House
609 W 33rd St 78705
512-459-0534
Fax: 512-476-4769
800-871-8908
Lisa Wiedemann
All year

79-129-BB
6 rooms, 6 pb
Most CC, *Rated*
C-yes/S-no/P-ltd/H-ltd
Spanish

Full breakfast
Tea, lemonade, ice cream & cookies
Gazebo, sitting room

Built in 1922 & lovingly restored to its present country charm, the high ceilings, original windows & antique-filled rooms provide a relaxed atmosphere and a comfortable retreat from your busy world.

brookhouse@earthlink.net http://www.austinbedandbreakfast.com

---

Austin Folk House
506 West 22nd St 78705
512-472-6700 866-472-6700
Sylvia Mackey
All year

89-139-BB
9 rooms, 9 pb
Most CC
C-yes/S-ltd/P-yes/H-yes
Spanish

Full breakfast
Afternoon sweets and evening wine
Cable TV and VCR, private phone lines and voice mail, robes, fine toiletries

Beautifully restored in 2001, this B&B offers historic charm without sacrificing modern comfort and convenience. Decorated with antiques and a large collection of folk art. Centrally located.

sylvia@austinfolkhouse.com http://www.austinfolkhouse.com

AUSTIN

Austin's Governors' Inn
611 W 22nd St 78705
512-477-0711 Fax: 512-476-4769
888-397-8677
Lisa Wiedemann
All year

59-129-BB
10 rooms, 10 pb
Most CC, *Rated*
C-yes/S-ltd/P-ltd/H-ltd
Spanish, French

Full breakfast
Afternoon tea, snacks
Vegetarian dining available, sitting room, library

Grand neo-classical Victorian mansion built in 1897. Historical designation, lovely rooms with private baths, cable TV, phones, and beautiful antiques.
governorsinn@earthlink.net http://www.governorsinnaustin.com

Austin's Wildflower Inn
1200 W 22½ St 78705
512-477-9639 Fax: 512-474-4188
Kay Jackson
All year

94-139-BB
3 rooms, 3 pb
Most CC, *Rated*
C-ltd/S-no/P-no/H-no

Full breakfast
Afternoon tea, snacks
Sitt. rm., deck, gardens, nearby public tennis, hiking & biking trails

Lovely old home w/spacious porch that graces the front of the house; furnished with antiques; located on tree-shaded street; near Univ. of Texas & State Capitol.
kjackson@io.com http://www.austinswildflowerinn.com

Brava House
1108 Blanco St 78703
512-478-5034 Fax: 800-545-8200
888-545-8200
Shelley Seale
All year

99-125-BB
4 rooms, 4 pb
Most CC, •
C-yes/S-ltd/P-yes/H-yes

Continental plus and Full breakfast
Tea and snacks available each afternoon
Wireless Internet, TV with cable, private phone, hair dryers, ironing board

Brava House offers private suites located in central Austin. Minutes to State Capital, 6th Street, Convention Center and The University of Texas. Antiques & fireplace suites create character & charm. travelguides@bravahouse.com http://www.bravahouse.com

---

Lazy Oak
211 West Live Oak 78704
512-447-8873 Fax: 512-912-1484
877-947-8873
Renee & Kevin Buck
All year

89-125-BB
5 rooms, 5 pb
Most CC, •
C-ltd/S-ltd/P-no/H-no

Full breakfast
Homemade goodies, snacks, wine and beer
Hot tub on back deck in winter; front porch; fish pond

Near downtown, UT and the State Capitol, the Lazy Oak B&B is perfect for the business traveler and vacationer. The 1911 farmhouse is furnished with all the amenities of a small hotel. lazyoakinn@aol.com http://www.lazyoakbandb.com

AUSTIN (REGION)

Trails End
12223 Trails End Rd #7, *Leander* 78641
512-267-2901 800-850-2901
JoAnn Patty All year

85-125-BB
Most CC, •
C-yes/S-no/P-no/H-no

Full breakfast
Dinner by reservation
Sitting room, library, gazebo, bikes, swimming pool, hiking

Austin-Lake Travis area. Truly unique, elegant, comfortable country B&B. Porches, decks with panoramic view of hill country. Fireplaces, hospitality.
jpjobnb@aol.com http://www.trailsendbb.com

BASTROP

Pecan Street Inn
1010 Pecan St 78602
512-321-3315 Fax: 512-321-3880
Shawn & Bill Pletsch
All year

75-100-BB
5 rooms, 4 pb
Rated, •
C-yes/S-ltd/P-ltd/H-ltd
Spanish

Special full gourmet breakfast
Complimentary hors d'oeuvres & wine
Parlor, TV/VCR, games, library, fireplaces, bikes, featherbeds, flowers

Unparalleled hospitality & heritage in Texas' heart: Nat'l Register "inn" the Victorian manner. Luxury accommodations & amenities, gracious grounds. Rent 1 room or the whole Inn. Famous breakfasts!
innkeeper@pecanstreetinn.com http://www.pecanstreetinn.com

BOERNE

Ye Kendall Inn
128 W Blanco 78006
830-249-2138 Fax: 830-816-6441
800-364-2138
Elisa McClure
All year

109-170-BB
17 rooms, 17 pb
Most CC, *Rated*, •
C-yes/S-no/P-no/H-yes

Full breakfast
On-site shopping; spa services; restaurant

The Ye Kendall Inn, established in 1859 as the stagecoach stop in the quaint hill country town of Boerne, is a pristine registered state and national historic landmark.
info@yekendallinn.com http://www.yekendallinn.com

BRENHAM

Mariposa Ranch
8904 Mariposa Ln 77833
979-836-4737 Fax: 979-836-4712
877-647-4774
Johnna & Charles Chamberlain All year

85-175-BB
11 rooms, 11 pb
Visa, MC, AmEx, •
C-yes/S-ltd/P-no/H-no
Spanish

Full breakfast
Snack baskets, picnic baskets, dinners available. Parlor, library, and video library available

Private cabins, cottages and suites including an 1860 Texas Plantation home, an early Texas antique log cabin, and more. All with private baths, some with Jacuzzis-for-two or antique clawfoot tubs. info@mariposaranch.com http://www.mariposaranch.com

BROWNWOOD

Star of Texas
650 Morelock Lane 76801
915-646-4128 800-850-2003
Don & Debbie Morelock
All year

95-115-BB
3 rooms, 3 pb
Visa, MC
C-ltd/S-ltd/P-ltd/H-no

Full breakfast
Homemade chocolates await you.
Hot tub; hiking or biking trail, covered garden deck

At our secluded peaceful nature retreat, you will find yourself hidden among a tranquil Central Texas hillside. Here you will experience the natural beauty and quiet serenity we all value highly. relaxing@star-of-texas.com http://www.star-of-texas.com

BRYAN

Reveille Inn
4400 Old College Rd 77801
979-846-0858 Fax: 979-846-0859
Janet Friddle
All year

120-BB
4 rooms, 4 pb
Most CC, *Rated*
C-ltd/S-no/P-no/H-yes

Full breakfast
Tea, coffee, juice and snacks
Sitting Room Patios, and Picnic area

This Southern Colonial style B&B, standing stately on one acre of land, is shaded by old sentinel oaks. Each room is furnished & decorated in the rich traditions of Texas A&M University. howdy@reveilleinn.com http://www.reveilleinn.com

CLIFTON

The River's Bend
PO Box 228
76634
254-675-4936
Helen M. Hubler
All year

95-240-BB
3 rooms, 2 pb
•
C-yes/S-ltd/P-yes/H-yes

Full breakfast
Sitting room, fireplaces, accommodate business travelers

Unoccupied home rented to one party at a time. Nature lovers paradise. Long covered porch with swing, glider, tables and chairs, looking up the Bosque River.

COLUMBUS

Magnolia Oaks
634 Spring St 78934
978-732-2726 Fax: 978-733-0872
888-677-0593
Bob & Nancy Stiles

125-195-BB
8 rooms, 7 pb
Visa, MC, *Rated*, •
C-ltd/S-no/P-no/H-no

Full breakfast
Afternoon tea, snacks
Sitting room, library, bicycles, suites, fireplaces, cable TV, antiques

The day starts with a refreshing "Toast to the Morning" greeting song by Bob with guitar. Then comes a full 'knock your socks off' breakfast to ensure guests return.
rmstiles@aol.com http://www.magnoliaoaks.com

COMFORT

La Luna Linda
Rte 1, Box 127
127 Allerkamp Rd 78013
830-995-5062
Melinda Luna
All year

80-EP
4 rooms, 4 pb
Most CC, •
C-yes/S-ltd/P-no/H-ltd
French, German, Spanish

Optional: Fixings in Fridge. Coffee, tea, cream & sugar at no extra charge.
Optional: Add $5/person for breakfast fixings you can prepare.

Relax on the farm! Three separate, private guesthouses with kitchens on 70 acres with a creek in the beautiful Texas Hill Country.
luna@lalunalinda.com http://www.lalunalinda.com

CORPUS CHRISTI

Fortuna Bay
15405 Fortuna Bay Dr #12
78418
361-949-7554
John & Jackie Fisher
All year

125-135-BB
6 rooms, 6 pb
Rated, •
C-ltd/S-ltd/P-no/H-yes
Spanish

Continental plus breakfast
Snacks, restaurant
Fishing off deck, pool, conference center, golf, tennis, boat dock

Hideaway on Texas North Padre Island with white sand beaches. Country Club privileges, fishing off our deck. fortunabay@msn.com http://www.ccinternet.net/fortunabay/

CRYSTAL BEACH

Out By The Sea
PO Box 2046
2134 Vista Dr 77650
409-684-1555 888-522-5926
Carole P. Hamadey
All year

100-175-BB
5 rooms, 5 pb
Visa, MC, *Rated*, •
C-ltd/S-no/P-no/H-no

Full hot breakfast
Snacks and wine
Sitting room, 2 Jazzes, suite, fireplace, satellite TV

Located one block from the beach on the Gulf of Mexico on the Boliver Peninsula (15 miles from Galveston Island). mistyg@wans.net http://www.outbythesea.com

DALLAS

Hotel St. Germain
2516 Maple Ave 75201
214-871-2516 Fax: 214-871-0740
800-683-2516
Claire Heymann
All year

290-650-BB
7 rooms, 7 pb
Rated, •

Continental plus breakfast

Champagne Bar in downstairs parlors, offering 130 different champagnes, pate and caviar–all by advanced reservation. http://www.hotelstgermain.com

DALLAS (REGION)

The Heritage Inns
815 N Locust, *Denton* 76201
940-565-6414 Fax: 940-565-6515
888-565-6414
John & Donna Morris
All year

65-135-BB
11 rooms, 11 pb
Most CC, *Rated*, •
C-yes/S-ltd/P-ltd/H-yes
Spanish

Full breakfast
Snacks, restaurant
Sitting room, library, Jacuzzis, suites, fireplaces, cable TV

We are a B&B Cluster Group, which includes 3 restored historic houses and a gourmet Italian restaurant. We are located within walking distance to Historic Courthouse Square.
redbudbb@gte.net http://www.theheritageinns.com

Tartan Thistle
513 W Louisiana St, *McKinney*
75069
214-680-2744 Fax: 972-548-1048
Tom Watson
All year

85-135-BB
6 rooms, 6 pb
Most CC
C-ltd/S-ltd/P-ltd/H-yes

Full breakfast
Snacks and beverages included in rate
TV/VCR with HBO/CNN, “”sound machine”” clock radios, hair dryers, telephones

Historic Victorian B&B listed in the National Register. Located three blocks from the historic McKinney shopping/restaurant district. Single rates available Sunday through Thursday nights. tom@tartanthistle.net http://www.tartanthistle.net

DALLAS (REGION)

Oaklea Mansion
407 S Main, *Winnsboro* 75494
903-342-6051 Fax: 903-342-5013
Norma Wilkinson
All year

89-250-BB
12 rooms, 12 pb
Most CC, *Rated*, •
C-ltd/S-no/P-no/H-yes
Spanish

Full breakfast
Afternoon tea
Sitting room, suites, fireplaces, spa house with hot tub/Jacuzzi

Accommodations in this 1903 historically marked mansion include luxurious suites and guestrooms filled with antique treasures.
oaklea@bluebonnet.net http://www.bluebonnet.net/oaklea

DENTON

Wildwood Inn
2602 Lillian Miller Pkwy 76210
940-243-4919 Fax: 940-387-9029
Carolyn Moore
All year

125-225-BB
11 rooms, 11 pb

Full breakfast
Dinner by reservation: Th–Sa
Old World elegance in a modern setting on four acres of woodlands.

On four wooded acres in the Dallas-Fort Worth area. Eleven guest rooms with whirlpools and fireplaces; swimming pool and spa. Private room for weddings, receptions, and business meetings. info@denton-wildwoodinn.com http://www.denton-wildwoodinn.com

FORT WORTH

Azalea Plantation
1400 Robinwood Dr 76111
817-838-5882 800-687-3529
Martha & Richard Linnartz
All year

125-159-BB
4 rooms, 4 pb
Most CC, •
C-ltd/S-no/P-no/H-no

Full buffet breakfast
Complimentary sherry, special group meals avail.
Sitting room, library, whirlpool, suites, fireplaces, accom. bus. travelers

A wooded estate furnished in antiques. Full buffet breakfast served in elegant dining room. Located 8 minutes from Sundance Square & downtown Fort Worth. 10 minutes to Stockyards Historic District. rmlinnartz@aol.com http://www.azaleaplantation.com

FREDERICKSBURG

Alte Welt Gasthof
PO Box 628
142 E Main St 78624
830-997-0443 Fax: 830-997-0040
888-991-6749
Ron & Donna Maddux

150-165-BB
2 rooms, 2 pb
Most CC, *Rated*, •
C-ltd/S-no/P-no/H-no
German
All year

Continental breakfast
Afternoon tea, snacks, comp. wine
Jacuzzis, suites, cable TV, accommodate business travelers

Beautiful European antique decor. Vintage fabrics, Ralph Lauren and Frette linens add to the Old World ambiance.
stay@texas-bed-n-breakfast.com http://www.texas-bed-n-breakfast.com

---

Das College Haus
106 W College St 78624
830-997-9047 Fax: 830-990-5047
800-654-2802
Bitsy & Bob Neuser
All year

110-135-BB
4 rooms, 4 pb
Visa, MC, *Rated*, •
C-ltd/S-no/P-no/H-ltd

Full breakfast
Snacks, comp. wine
Library porches, rocking chairs, sitting room, suites, fireplace, cable TV

Built in 1916, this beautiful example of a turn-of-the-century Victorian home will receive you with all the warmth of its time.
ibneuser@hctc.net http://www.dascollegehaus.com

The Full Moon Inn
3234 Luckenback Rd 78624
830-997-2205 Fax: 830-997-1115
800-997-1124
Capt. Matthew Carinhas
All year

125-200-BB
6 rooms, 6 pb
Visa, MC, Disc, *Rated*
C-yes/S-no/P-yes/H-yes
Spanish

Full breakfast
Dinner, restaurant
Bar service, Jacuzzi, suites, fireplace, accommodates business travlers

A romantic country getaway rich with charm and class. The inn is minutes away from three great wineries and Fredericksburg, Texas.
info@fullmooninn.com http://www.fullmooninn.com

The Full Moon Inn, Fredericksburg, TX

FREDERICKSBURG

Magnolia House
101 East Hackberry 78624
830-997-0306 Fax: 830-997-0766
800-880-4374
Dee & David Lawford

95-140-BB
5 rooms, 5 pb
Visa, MC, *Rated*, •
C-ltd/S-no/P-no/H-ltd
All year

Full breakfast
Snacks, complimentary wine
Sitting room, patio, waterfall, koi pond

1923 Texas historical home. Elegant southern hospitality. Your home-away-from-home.
magnolia@hctc.net http://www.magnolia-house.com

Schandua Suite
PO Box 1532
205 E Main St 78624
830-990-1415 Fax: 830-990-8626
888-990-1415
Sharla & Jonathan Godfrey
All year

150-BB
1 rooms, 1 pb
Visa, MC, Disc, *Rated*
S-ltd/P-no/H-no

Continental plus breakfast
Snacks, complimentary wine
Sitting room, library, suites, cable TV, robes, chocolates, phone

Luxury suite located in the heart of the historic district; Pullman kitchen; quaint shops all within walking distance; private balcony overlooking secluded courtyard.
sharla44@hctc.net http://www.schandua.com

A Way of the Wolf Country Inn
458 Wolf Way 78624
830-997-0711 888-WAY-WOLF
Ron & Karen Poidevin
All year

85-150-BB
7 rooms, 5 pb
C-ltd/S-ltd/P-no/H-no

Full breakfast
Coffee, tea, soft drinks
Living room, kitchen, pool, screened porches, gas grills

60+acres Texas Hill Country. Tastefully furnished with antiques. Setting is ideal for a romantic getaway or retreat. Screened porches/swimming pool. Guided individual & group retreats are available. wawolf@ktc.com http://www.wayofthewolf.com

FREDERICKSBURG (REGION)

Rose Hill Manor
2614 Upper Albert Rd, *Stonewall* 78671
830-644-2247 Fax: 830-644-2248
877-767-3445
Bob Vander Lyn
All year

115-150-BB
6 rooms, 6 pb
Most CC, •
C-ltd/S-no/P-no/H-ltd
German

Continental Plus on weekdays only
Tea, bar service, restaurant & dinner on weekends
Sitting room, library, bicycles, suites, accom. business travelers

Luxurious country inn with fabulous suites and porches with spectacular views. On-site bookstore and lending library, bar, and gourmet dinner served on weekends.
bobv@fbg.net http://www.rose-hill.com

GAINESVILLE

Alexander Acres, Inc
3692 County Road 201 76240
903-564-7440 Fax: 903-564-7440
800-887-8794
Jimmy & Pamela Alexander
All year

60-125-BB
8 rooms, 5 pb
Most CC, *Rated*, •
C-ltd/S-ltd/P-no/H-ltd

Full breakfast in main house
Lunch & dinner avail. by reservation, snacks
Sitting room, bicycles, hot tub, swimming pool, suites, fireplace

Three story Queen Anne country Inn and two story Guesthouse on 65 acres of woods, meadows and walking trails. Enjoy star gazing or help us feed the livestock.
abba@texoma.net http://www.alexanderbnb.com

GALVESTON

1887 Coppersmith Inn
1914 Avenue M 77550
409-763-7004 800-515-7444
Patrick and Karen Geary
All year

94-170-BB
5 rooms, 5 pb
Visa, MC, Disc, •
C-ltd/S-no/P-no/H-no

Full and Hardy Country Breakfast
Soda, bottled water
Hot tub, bicycles

Charming 1887 Victorian, for that special time and special experience. Five bedrooms with baths on Galveston Island. Exquisite heirloom antiques. A full, hearty country breakfast served family style. coppersmithinn@att.net http://www.coppersmithinn.com

---

Inn at 1816 Postoffice
1816 Postoffice St 77550
409-765-9444 888-558-9444
Bettye Hall & Judy Wilkie
All year

90-220-BB
6 rooms, 6 pb
Most CC
C-ltd/S-no/P-no/H-ltd

Full breakfast
Snacks
Sitting room, bikes, Jacuzzis, cable TV in game room w/pool table

Inn at 1816 Post Office, circa 1886, is a beautiful Victorian home lovingly restored with antiques and fine furnishing. inn1816@aol.com http://www.bbonline.com/tx/1816/

The Queen Anne
1915 Sealy Ave 77550
409-763-7088 Fax: 409-765-6525
800-472-0930
Ron & Jackie Metzger
All year

90-180-BB
6 rooms, 6 pb
Most CC, •
C-ltd/S-no/P-no/H-no

Full breakfast
Afternoon snacks, beverages
Shaded deck, ground floor Jacuzzi suite, bicycles available

Regal accommodations define this favorite Galveston bed and breakfast. Recommended by Southern Living. Jacuzzi "hideaway" suite.
queenanne@ev1.net http://www.galvestonqueenanne.com

GLADEWATER

Honeycomb Suites
111 N Main St 75647
903-845-4430 Fax: 903-844-1859
800-594-2253
Susan and Bill Morgan
All year

95-150-BB
7 rooms, 7 pb
Most CC, •
C-ltd/S-no/P-no/H-no

Full gourmet breakfast
Lunch, restaurant, Candlelight dinners Sat. night
Sitting room, Jacuzzi, suites, cable TV, accommodate business travelers

A unique country inn catering to the romantically inclined. 7 spacious accommodations, all with private baths, some with whirlpool tubs for 2.
gloryb@cox-internet.net http://honeycombsuites.com

GLEN ROSE

Best Western Dinosaur Valley Inn
PO Box 1460
1311 NE Big Bend Trail 76043
800-280-2055
All year

73-375-BB
53 rooms, 53 pb
Most CC, *Rated*
P-ltd

Microwave, frig, VCR, coffee maker, business center, pool, laundry, porches

We invite you to enjoy your home away from home at Dinosaur Valley Inn and Suites. Come and enjoy our Texas-size hospitality.
webmaster@dinosaurvalleyinn.com http://www.dinosaurvalleyinn.com

GLEN ROSE

Bussey's Something Special PO Box 1425 202 Hereford St 76043 254-897-4843 Fax: 254-897-9881 877-426-2233 Morris & Susan Bussey All year	80-125-BB 3 rooms, 2 pb Most CC, • C-yes/S-no/P-no/H-no	Continental plus breakfast Snacks Suites, books, games, full kitchen, un-hosted, porch & yard, jet tub

Private guest cottages, family friendly, relax with a good book, large breakfast provided, 2 blocks from downtown square, 2 blocks from the river. Ask about our special tours. Very relaxing. Unhosted. msbussey@busseys.net http://www.busseys.net

Hill Street Inn PO Box 750 302 Hill Street 76043 Fax: 817-389-4448 888-256-7535 Ben & Becky Newsom All year	100-115-BB 4 rooms, 4 pb Visa, MC, Disc C-yes/S-no/P-no/H-no	Full breakfast Common gathering area

The Hill Street Inn is a stylish getaway in Glen Rose, Texas. Offering 4 rooms with private baths upstairs. Downstairs is large and great for gathering. Perfect for groups. Full breakfast served. bandbhillstreet@aol.com http://www.hillstreetinn.com

GRANBURY

Alfonso's Loft 202 S Crocket 137 E Pearl 76048 817-573-3308 Kay Collerain All year	90-BB 1 rooms, 1 pb Visa, MC C-ltd/S-no/P-ltd/H-no	Full breakfast Coffee, cookies, Perrier in p.m. Sitting room, cable TV, accommodate business travelers

Alfonso's Loft is an unhosted bed and breakfast in the historic district of Granbury. alfonsosloft@granbury-tx.com http://www.granbury-tx.com/alfonsosloft/

Arbor House 530 E Pearl St 76048 817-573-0073 Fax: 817-579-6119 800-641-0073 Eric & Peggy Matsko All year	100-165-BB 11 rooms, 11 pb Most CC, *Rated*, • C-no/S-no/P-no/H-yes	Full breakfast Afternoon desert, soft drinks, coffee and tea. Parlor, Jacuzzi's, suites, cable TV, business travelers, women's groups.

A new Queen Anne Victorian home with the atmosphere of yesterday, the comforts of today and quality service that is timeless. Located across the street from Lake Granbury. Many rooms have lakeview.
stay@granbury-bed-and-breakfast.com http://www.granbury-bed-and-breakfast.com

The Iron Horse Inn 616 Thorp Spring Rd 76048 817-579-5535 Bob & Judy Atkinson All year	95-165-BB 6 rooms, 6 pb	Full gourmet breakfast

This large Craftsman style home featuring ornate mill work and intricate leaded glass has been pristinely restored. http://www.theironhorseinn.com

Nutt House Hotel & Dining 121 E. Bridge St 76048 830-997-0443 Fax: 830 997-0040 888 678 0813 Ron Maddux All year	125-175-EP 7 rooms, 7 pb Most CC, • C-ltd/S-no/P-no/H-ltd	Continental breakfast Private Jacuzzi baths, king beds, Frette Linens, spa, antiques

Beautiful Historic Hotel located on the Square in Granbury, Texas. This landmark hotel is the most well known building in the Lake Granbury area.
stay@nutt-house-hotel.com http://www.nutt-hotel.com

GRUENE (REGION)

Hunter Road Stagecoach Stop
5441 FM 1102, *New Braunfels* 78132
830-620-9453 800-201-2912
Jeff and Bettina
All year

105-145-BB
4 rooms, 4 pb
Visa, MC, AmEx, *Rated*, •
C-ltd/S-no/P-no/H-no

Full breakfast
Sitting room, dog trot, porches, TV, walking and bike trails

Texas landmark constructed 150 years ago by Amish settlers. Authentically restored Fachwerk house & log cabin. All are surrounded by gardens of antique roses and herbs.
stagecoach@satx.rr.com http://www.stagecoachbedandbreakfast.com

HILL COUNTRY (REGION)

Rockin River Inn
PO Box 7
106 Skyline Rd, *Center Point* 78010
830-634-7043 866-424-0576
Ken & Betty Wardlaw
All year

105-115-BB
4 rooms, 4 pb
C-yes/S-ltd/P-ltd/H-ltd

Gourmet breakfast
Texas wine & beer
Homemade desserts
Swimming pool, access to river for fishing, floating, kayaking

Historical Texas Bed and Breakfast on the Guadalupe River located central to the Hill Country near Kerrville, Comfort, Bandera, Boerne, Fredericksburg, and San Antonio.
relax@rockriverinn.com http://www.rockinriverinn.com

HILLSBORO

Windmill
Rt 2, Box 448
441 Hill County Road 2421E 76645
254-582-7373 800-951-0033
Ruben & Gerry Marentes

90-110-BB
3 rooms, 3 pb
Most CC, •
C-ltd/S-no/P-no/H-no
Spanish
All year

Full breakfast
Afternoon tea, snacks, wine
Sitting room, bicycles, Jacuzzis, suites, cable TV.

Charming Victorian, nestled among pecan & oak trees on 21 acres.
windmillbb@aol.com http://www.windmillbb.com

HOUSTON

Angel Arbor
848 Heights Blvd 77007
713-868-4654 Fax: 713-861-3189
888-810-0092
Marguerite Swanson
All year

95-125-BB
6 rooms, 6 pb
Visa, MC, AmEx, *Rated*, •
C-ltd/S-no/P-no/H-no
German, Spanish

Full breakfast
Afternoon tea, snack basket, soft drinks
Whirlpool tubs, sitting rms, solariums, gardens, ceiling fans, bassett hound

Impeccably appointed accommodations with luxurious bedrooms, relaxing atmosphere, inviting common rooms & gardens, and mouthwatering breakfasts combine to make any stay a truly memorable one. b-bhoutx@wt.net http://www.angelarbor.com

---

The Lovett Inn
501 Lovett Blvd 77006
713-522-5224 Fax: 713-528-6708
800-779-5224
Tom Fricke
All year

75-175-BB
8 rooms, 8 pb
Visa, MC, AmEx, *Rated*, •
C-ltd/S-ltd/P-yes/H-no
Spanish

Continental breakfast
Library, swimming pool, hot tubs

Charming 1920s former mayor's mansion near downtown, museums, convention and medical centers and Galleria. lovettinn@aol.com http://www.lovettinn.com

---

The Patrician Inn
1200 Southmore Blvd 77004
713-523-1114 Fax: 713-523-0790
800-553-5797
Patricia Thomas
All year

100-165-BB
7 rooms, 7 pb
Most CC, *Rated*, •
C-ltd/S-no/P-no/H-no

Full breakfast
Bottled water, soft drinks
Sitting room, near golf, perfect for weddings, parties or receptions

1919 mansion minutes to downtown Houston, Texas Medical Center, Museum of Fine Arts and Rice University. Some 2 person whirlpool tubs and walk in showers. Telephone data ports & cable TV in all rooms. southmore@ev1.net http://www.texasbnb.com

HOUSTON (REGION)

Roses & the River
2434 Country Road 506, *Brazoria* 77422
979-798-1070 Fax: 979-798-1070
800-610-1070
Dick & Mary Jo Hosack
All year

125-150-BB
3 rooms, 3 pb
Most CC, *Rated*, •
C-ltd/S-ltd/P-no/H-no

Full breakfast
Snacks
Jacuzzis, fireplaces, cable TV, VCRs in each room with video library

Beautifully decorated Texas farmhouse on banks of San Bernard River, landscaped with 250 rose bushes. "You deserve a little R&R" is our motto.
hosack@roses-and-the-river.com http://www.roses-and-the-river.com

---

Heather's Glen
200 E Phillips, *Conroe* 77301
936-441-6611 Fax: 936-441-6603
800-66-JAMIE
Jamie & Ed George
All year

79-195-BB
8 rooms, 8 pb
Most CC, *Rated*, •
C-ltd/S-ltd/P-ltd/H-ltd
Spanish

Full breakfast
Snacks, soft drinks
Color T/V in rooms, phones, goosedown comforters

Heather's Glen B&B & Carriage House—restored to authentic period look w/out sacrificing modern conveniences. Furnishings reflect grace & elegance of past w/lace curtains & antique glassed windows. heathersbb@aol.com http://www.heathersglen.com

---

Beacon Hill Guest House
3705 NASA Rd One
3701 NASA Rd One, *Seabrook* 77586
281-326-7643 Fax: 281-326-2883
Delaina Hanssen
All year

95-500-BB
6 rooms, 6 pb
Most CC, •
C-yes/S-ltd/P-no/H-yes

Full breakfast
Snacks
Private sun decks, pier, boat dock, ofc serv., shaded grounds.

Unique, private, choice waterfront lodging for a romantic getaway or event. Central base to points of interest. Spiritual healing and self-improvement programs available.
hanssen@aol.com http://www.visitbeaconhill.com

The Pelican House
1302 First St, *Seabrook* 77586
281-474-5295 Fax: 281-474-7840
Suzanne Silver
All year

100-125-BB
4 rooms, 4 pb
Most CC, *Rated*, •
C-ltd/S-ltd/P-no/H-no

Full breakfast
Complimentary wine
Sitting room, library, cable TV, hot tub, champagne & chocolate 2 nite

Whimsical country house overlooking the Back Bay. Gourmet breakfast served on our back deck where water-bird viewing is at its best.
pelicanhouse@usa.net http://www.pelicanhouse.com

JACKSONVILLE

English Manor
540 El Paso St 75766
903-541-4694 800-866-0946
Lynette Sarnoski
All year

85-110-BB
6 rooms, 6 pb
Rated
C-ltd/S-ltd/P-yes/H-ltd
Spanish

Full breakfast
Afternoon tea, snacks, complimentary wine
Sitting room, library, suites, cable TV, accommodate business travelers

Privately gated, 6000 sq. ft. Tudor style 1932 home with lovely gardens and aviary. Restored antique furnishings from nearby malls.
lsarnoski@hotmail.com http://www.englishmanorbedandbreakfast.com

JEFFERSON

Kennedy Manor
217 W Lafayette St 75657
903-665-2528
Chris & Laura Graham
All year

79-139-BB
6 rooms, 6 pb
Most CC
C-ltd/S-no/P-no/H-yes

Full breakfast
Complimentary snacks, cokes, tea, hot chocolate.
library, music room with piano and organ.

Built in 1860 and 1 block from historic downtown Jefferson, Texas. 6 guest rooms full of antiques with private baths, climate control, TV, phones. Full breakfast and narrated home tour included. kennedymanor@jeffersontx.com http://www.kennedy-manor.com

JEFFERSON

Maison Bayou Waterfront
300 Bayou St 75657
903-665-7600 Fax: 240-218-8135
Jan & Pete Hochendel
All year

79-145-BB
12 rooms, 12 pb
Visa, MC, Disc, *Rated*, •
C-yes/S-ltd/P-no/H-ltd

Full breakfast
Wine, Champagne, Beer & Ale on premise
Experience privacy in individual cabins, railcars, bunkhouses

Private Cabins & Cabanas... private ponds, riverfront, wildlife. Full breakfast served on glassed-in gallery overlooking cypress pond. Historic downtown Jefferson, just a short walk across the bridge. cabins@maisonbayou.com http://www.maisonbayou.com

---

Wise Manor
312 Houston St 75657
903-665-2386 Fax: 318-226-4780
318-218-0398
Susan Wise
All year

95-125-BB
3 rooms, 3 pb
Visa, MC, *Rated*, •
C-ltd/S-no/P-no/H-no

Full breakfast
Margaritas, wine, beer, soft drinks available
Sitting room with fireplace, antiques, suites, cable TV, in-room coffee

Built in 1851 on the ferry road into pre-Civil War Jefferson, this charming two-story cottage has been in the same family since 1927.
wises@aol.com http://hometown.aol.com/wises

KERRVILLE

River Run
120 Francisco Lemos St 78028
830-896-8353 Fax: 830-896-5402
800-460-7170
Jean & Ron Williamson
All year

105-139-BB
6 rooms, 6 pb
Most CC, *Rated*, •
C-ltd/S-no/P-no/H-yes
Spanish

Full breakfast
Sitting room, library, Jacuzzis, suites, cable TV, accom. bus. travelers

In the heart of the beautiful Texas Hill Country. 6 spacious rooms, queen beds and whirlpool tubs. Relaxed elegance and real comfort.
riverrun@ktc.com http://www.riverrunbb.com

KINGSLAND

The Antlers Hotel
1001 King 78639
915-388-4411 Fax: 915-388-6488
800-383-0007
Jay Littlepage All year

110-150-EP
16 rooms, 16 pb
Most CC, *Rated*
C-ltd/S-no/P-no/H-ltd

Restaurant
Cabins and train cars, suites, cable TV

Turn of the century railroad resort in the Texas hill country on Lake LBJ. Six luxury suites in the historic hotel, six cabins and four train car accommodations.
Innkeeper@TheAntlers.com http://www.theantlers.com

LAKE TEXOMA (REGION)

Terralak B&B on Lake Texoma
2661 Tanglewood Blvd, *Irving* 75063
214-532-8062 Fax: 972-401-2715
877-Terralak
Kathy Bachand All year

85-200-BB
5 rooms, 4 pb
Most CC, *Rated*, •
C-yes/S-no/P-no/H-no

Full breakfast-weekends
Continental plus breakfast-weekdays
Afternoon tea, snacks, family friendly facility, fishing charters available

Your lake home away from home, located on 13 beautiful wooded acres on the #1 lake in Texas, Lake Texoma. Sailing, skiing, hiking and lots more to see and do.
terralak@aol.com

LAMPASAS

Historic Moses Hughes
7075 W FM 580 76550
512-556-5923
Al & Beverly Solomon
All year

80-100-BB
3 rooms, 3 pb
Visa, MC, *Rated*, •
S-no/P-no/H-no
French, Spanish

Full breakfast
Afternoon tea, snacks
Sitting room, library, 45 acres of creek, springs, wildlife

Sparkling springs, turquoise skies, and star-filled nights set the mood for rest, recreation, and romance. mhrbb@n-link.com http://www.moseshughesranch.com

MADISONVILLE

The Woodbine Hotel & Rest.
209 N Madison St 77864
936-348-3333 Fax: 936-348-6268
888-woodbine
Chef Reinhard & Susan Warmuth
All year

75-165-BB
8 rooms, 8 pb
Visa, MC, AmEx, *Rated*, •
C-ltd/S-no/P-no/H-no
French, German

Full breakfast
Lunch & dinner avail, restaurant, bar service
Sitting room, library, whirlpools in rooms, cable TV, bus. travelers welcome

Built as a hotel in 1904, the Woodbine is a Victorian and Eastlake National and Texas Historic Landmark. World-class restaurant, romantic rooms and beautiful grounds create a perfect romantic getaway.

woodbinehotel@aol.com http://www.woodbinehoteltexas.com

MINEOLA

Munzesheimer Manor
202 N Newsom 75773
903-569-6634 Fax: 903-569-9940
888-569-6634
Bob & Sherry Murray

90-110-BB
7 rooms, 7 pb
Most CC, *Rated*, •
C-ltd/S-ltd/P-no/H-ltd
All year

Full gourmet breakfast
Sitting room, fireplaces, cable TV, accom. bus. travelers

1898 Victorian with wraparound porches; Victorian nightgowns, gourmet breakfasts, and special pampering. Featured in national magazines and named as one of "Best Twelve B&Bs in Texas." innkeeper@munzesheimer.com http://www.munzesheimer.com

NACOGDOCHES

Hardeman Guest House
316 N Church St 75961
409-569-1947
Buzz & Laura Dutton
All year

75-95-BB
5 rooms, 5 pb
Most CC
C-no/S-ltd/P-no/H-ltd

Full breakfast
Tea, coffee, bottled water, wine.
Pvt. baths, King Beds, Cable, Sitting Room, VCR, Fax/copy, DSL comp. avail.

Listed on the National Register of Historic Places. All rooms feature private baths, cable TV, full carpeting. Most rooms feature King Beds.

hardemanhouse@cox-internet.com http://www.hardemanhouse.com

NEW BRAUNFELS

The Faust Hotel
240 S. Seguin 78130
830-625-7791 Fax: 830-620-1530
Bob Abbey All year

59-175-EP
62 rooms, 62 pb
Rated, •

Originally opened in 1929 as the Travelers Hotel, the building & rooms have been completely renovated in the original decor providing today's traveler w/comfort & antiquity.

innkeeper@fausthotel.com http://www.fausthotel.com

Karbach Haus
487 West San Antonio St 78130
830-625-2131 Fax: 830-629-1126
800-972-5941
Kathy & Ben Jack Kinney
All year

120-250-BB
6 rooms, 6 pb
Visa, MC, Disc, *Rated*, •
C-ltd/S-no/P-no/H-no
German

Full gourmet breakfast
Snacks, comp. beverages
Great room w/grand piano, fireplace, sun parlor, swimming pool, TVs, Jacuzzi

Historically significant mansion, downtown, romantic, luxurious, genuine antiques. Acre estate, pool, spa, all amenities of a small resort. Owner/hosts on premises.

KHausBnB@aol.com http://www.bbhost.com/karbach

Kuebler-Waldrip Haus/Danville Schoolhouse
1620 Hueco Springs Loop 78132
830-625-8300 800-299-8372
Margaret K. Waldrip & son, Darrell Waldrip All year

115-175-BB
10 rooms, 10 pb
Most CC, *Rated*, •
C-yes/S-no/P-ltd/H-yes
Spanish

Full candlelight breakfast
Snacks, comp. drinks
Sitting room, library, gift shop, TV/VCR, walking trails, pet deer

Relax! 43 beautiful hill country acres near rivers, Gruene, New Braunfels, San Antonio, Austin. Delicious candlelight breakfast brunch.

kwbandb@compuvision.net http://www.kueblerwaldrip.com

NEW BRAUNFELS

Lamb's Rest Inn
1385 Edwards Blvd 78132
830-609-3932 Fax: 830-620-0864
888-609-3932
Judy Rothell All year

95-225-BB
5 rooms, 5 pb
Visa, MC, Disc, *Rated*, •
C-ltd/S-ltd/P-no/H-no

Full breakfast
Afternoon tea
Sitting room, library, bikes, Jacuzzis, pool, suites, fireplaces, cable TV

Enjoy true Texas hospitality on the Guadalupe River near the historic village of Gruene. A peaceful, romantic atmosphere awaits you in tranquil gardens.

lambsbb@aol.com http://www.bbhost.com/lambsrestbb

PALACIOS

Moonlight Bay
506 South Bay Blvd 77465
361-972-2232 Fax: 361-972-0463
877-461-7070
Earl & Gaye Hudson
All year

95-200-BB
7 rooms, 7 pb
Most CC, *Rated*, •
C-no/S-no/P-no/H-ltd
Thai

Full breakfast
Dinner avail., afternoon tea, snacks, comp. wine
Sitting room, library, Jacuzzis, suites, fireplaces, cable TV, live piano

Spectacular waterfront view from recorded Texas historical landmark. 1910 Craftsman bungalow home featuring themes of 1940's music and literature.

grogers@wcnet.net http://www.bbhost.com/moonlightbaybb/

PITTSBURG

Carson House Inn
302 Mt Pleasant St 75686
903-856-2468 Fax: 903-856-0709
888-302-1878
Eileen & Clark Jesmore
All year

85-145-BB
8 rooms, 8 pb
Most CC, *Rated*
C-ltd/S-ltd/P-ltd/H-no

Full breakfast
Lunch & dinner available, restaurant and bar
Sitting room, Jacuzzi, suites, cable TV, accom. bus. travelers

Historic Victorian Inn built in 1878, featuring rare curly pine wainscoting.

mailus@carsonhouse.com http://www.carsonhouse.com

ROCKPORT

Anthony's By the Sea
732 S Pearl St 78382
361-729-6100 Fax: 361-729-2450
800-460-2557
Anthony & Denis All year

85-100-BB
7 rooms, 4 pb
Visa, MC, *Rated*, •
C-yes/S-yes/P-yes/H-no

Full gourmet breakfast
Sitting room, hot tubs, swimming pool, family friendly facility

Anthony's is causal, friendly & affordable. Pool, hot tub & covered lanai with fountains & chandeliers add to its ambiance. http://www.rockport-fulton.org/ads/anthonys/anthonys.htm

ROUND TOP

Briarfield at Round Top
219 FM 954 78954
979-249-3973 Fax: 979-249-3961
800-472-1134
Mary Stanhope & Roland Nester
All year

95-115-BB
7 rooms, 7 pb
Visa, MC, Disc, •
C-ltd/S-no/P-no/H-ltd

Full breakfast
Snacks
Sitting room, library, VCR/movies

Refined country setting. Walk in the gardens or rock on the porch. Minutes away from historical sites, cultural events, shopping and dining.

stanhope@cvtv.net http://www.briarfieldatroundtop.com

The Settlement at Round Top
PO Box 176
2218 Hartfield Rd 78954
979-249-5015 Fax: 979-249-5587
888-ROUNDTOP
Karen & Larry Beevers

110-225-BB
10 rooms, 10 pb
Most CC, *Rated*, •
S-ltd/P-no/H-no
All year

Full breakfast
Afternoon tea, snacks
Sitting room, library, Jacuzzis, suites, fireplaces

An historic retreat for adults within a wonderfully restored pioneer-era complex of log cabins, German cottages, and period houses.

stay@thesettlement.com http://www.thesettlement.com

SALADO

The Inn at Salado
PO Box 320
307 N Main Street 76571
254-947-0027 Fax: 254-947-3144
800-724-0027
Rob & Suzanne Petro

70-160-BB
9 rooms, 9 pb
Most CC, *Rated*
C-ltd/S-no/P-no/H-ltd
All year

Full breakfast
Sitting room, fireplaces, cable TV, conference, weddings & receptions

The Inn displays both a Texas Historical Marker & a Nat'l Register listing. Walking distance to shopping & dining. The Inn is a great place for couples to get away and for business retreats. rooms@inn-at-salado.com http://www.inn-at-salado.com

SAN ANTONIO

A Beckmann Inn & Carriage House
222 E Guenther St 78204
210-229-1449 Fax: 210-229-1061
800-945-1449
Betty Jo & Don Schwartz

110-150-BB
5 rooms, 5 pb
Rated
C-ltd/S-ltd/P-no/H-ltd
All year

Full breakfast
Welcome tea
Sitting room, concierge, scenic river walk, trolley, TVs, phones

Beautiful historic district, scenic river-walk, Alamo, trolley, gourmet breakfast with dessert, ornate antique beds, warm/gracious hospitality.
beckinn@swbell.net http://www.beckmanninn.com

A Victorian Lady Inn
421 Howard St 78212
210-224-2524 800-879-7116
Joe Bowski
All year

89-135-BB
10 rooms, 10 pb
Most CC, *Rated*
C-ltd/S-no/P-no/H-ltd

Full breakfast
Sitting room, swimming pool, Jacuzzis, fireplaces, wet bars, coffee makers

Experience grand guestrooms, fabulous breakfasts in majestic dining room, outdoor pool in a tropical setting, & unsurpassed hospitality.
info@viclady.com http://www.viclady.com

A Yellow Rose
229 Madison St 78204
210-229-9903 Fax: 210-229-1691
800-950-9903
Deborah & Justin Walker
All year

100-200-BB
5 rooms, 5 pb
Visa, MC, AmEx, *Rated*, •
C-ltd/S-ltd/P-no/H-no
Spanish

Full breakfast
Full, Continental or no breakfast
Private entrances, porches, whirlpool tubs, refrigerators, coffee makers

We love to travel and our goal is to provide our guests with the same quality and comforts that we appreciate. Ask about a packages that include massages, flowers, etc.
yellowrose@ddc.net http://www.ayellowrose.com

Academy House of Monte Vista
9158 Windgarden
2317 North Main Ave 78212
210-731-8393 Fax: 210-733-1661
888-731-8393
Kenneth & Johnnie Staggs

95-155-BB
4 rooms, 4 pb
Rated
All year

Full breakfast

An elegant 1897 Victorian bed & breakfast, be your doorway to the romance of a fondly remembered past. johnniewalkerstaggs@yahoo.com http://www.ahbnb.com

---

Adams House Inn
231 Adams St 78210
210-224-4791 Fax: 210-223-5125
800-666-4810
Nora Peterson & Richard Green
All year

99-169-BB
4 rooms, 4 pb
Most CC, *Rated*, •
C-ltd/S-ltd/P-no/H-no

Full gourmet breakfast
Sitting room, library, copier, fax, computer, net access, carriage house

Three story brick; King William Historic District, near River-walk/downtown; furnished in period antiques; spacious verandahs.
adams@adams-house.com http://www.adams-house.com

SAN ANTONIO

An Oge' Inn Riverwalk
209 Washington St 78204
210-223-2353 Fax: 210-226-5812
800-242-2770
Patrick & Sharrie Magatagan
All year

155-325-BB
10 rooms, 10 pb
Most CC, *Rated*
C-ltd/S-ltd/P-no/H-no

Full gourmet breakfast
Sitting room, library, A/C, cable TV, phone, set on 1/5 acres

Elegant, romantic, Antebellum mansion on 1½ acres on the River-walk. European antiques, quiet comfort & luxury. Shopping, dining & Alamo 5 blocks.
ogeinn@swbell.net http://www.ogeinn.com

Bonner Garden
145 E Argarita 78212
210-733-4222 Fax: 210-733-6129
800-396-4222
Noel & Jan Stenoien
All year

85-125-BB
5 rooms, 5 pb
Most CC, *Rated*, •
C-ltd/S-no/P-no/H-no

Full breakfast
Snacks
Sitting room, library, rooftop patio, pool, TV, VCR, phone

Award-winning (National Historic Association) Italian villa built in 1910 for Mary Bonner, the internationally known artist. noels@onr.com http://www.bonnergarden.com

---

Brackenridge House
230 Madison 78204
210-271-3442 Fax: 210-226-3139
800-221-1412
Bennie & Sue Blansett
All year

110-300-BB
5 rooms, 5 pb
Visa, MC, AmEx, *Rated*, •
C-yes/S-no/P-yes/H-no

Full breakfast
Snacks, complimentary wine
Bikes, Jacuzzis, suites, cable TV, VCR, phone

Native Texan owners & innkeepers will guide you through your visit from their beautiful Greek Revival home in historic King William.
benniesueb@aol.com http://www.brackenridgehouse.com/

Christmas House
2307 McCullough 78212
210-737-2786 Fax: 210-734-5712
800-268-4187
Penny & Grant Estes
All year

85-125-BB
5 rooms, 5 pb
Visa, MC, *Rated*, •
C-ltd/S-ltd/H-yes

Full breakfast
Sitting room, library, private/semi private veranda, catering

1½ miles from River-walk and Alamo. This historic 1910 home is in the Monte Vista National Registered Historic District.
christmashsb@earthlink.net http://www.christmashousebnb.com

Columns on Alamo
1037 South Alamo St 78210
210-271-3245 Fax: 210-271-3245
800-233-3364
Ellenor & Art Link
All year

92-230-BB
13 rooms, 13 pb
Most CC, *Rated*
C-ltd/S-no/P-no
German

Full breakfast
Queen & king beds, in-room TV & phones, off-street parking

1892 mansion & guesthouse—historic district, antiques, Oriental rugs, spacious common areas, verandahs. 7 Jacuzzis for two and 7 fireplaces.
artlink@columnssanantonio.com http://www.columnssanantonio.com

---

Gardenia Inn
307 Beauregard St 78204
210-223-5875 800-356-1605
Nicki and Peter Luescher
All year

100-140-BB
5 rooms, 5 pb
Most CC, *Rated*, •
C-ltd/S-no/P-ltd/H-no
German

Full breakfast
Free sparkling water
Walk to Riverwalk, sitting room, verandas, gazebo, and cable TV.

The Historic Inn, built 1905, is located in the middle of the famous King William District, decorated with elegant antiques. Kingsize bedrooms, verandas, fireplaces and soaking tubs are all yours. relax@gardenia-inn.com http://www.gardenia-inn.com

SAN ANTONIO

The Inn at Craig Place
117 W Craig Place 78212
210-736-1017 877-427-2447
Tamra Black
All year

100-125-BB
4 rooms, 4 pb

At the Inn at Craig Place, we offer you a warm welcome to an atmosphere of casually elegant comfort. stay@craigplace.com http://www.craigplace.com

---

Inn on the River
129 Woodward Place 78204
210-225-6333 Fax: 210-271-3992
800-730-0019
Dr. A.D.Zucht III
All year

69-175-BB
12 rooms, 12 pb
Most CC, *Rated*, •
C-yes/S-no/P-no/H-ltd

Full breakfast
Bicycles, Jacuzzis, fireplaces, cable TV, accommodate business travelers

Restored turn-of-the-century Victorian home situated on the quiet banks of the San Antonio River. The interior has period furnishings and hardwood floors.
innkeeper@innonriver.com http://www.innonriver.com

Little Flower Inn
225 Madison St 78204
210-354-3116 Fax: 210-354-3116
Phil & Christine Touw
All year

80-95-BB
2 rooms, 2 pb
•
C-yes/S-ltd/P-no/H-no
German

Full breakfast
Afternoon tea, snacks
Sitting room, library, swimming pool, cable TV

Our pledge to you: a B&B that is elegant & intimate yet perfect for families, at a reasonable cost. Come experience "Pampered Privacy" at the Little Flower!
littleflower@satexas.com http://www.littleflowerinn.com

Noble Inns
102 Turner St
107 Madison St 78204
210-225-4045 Fax: 210-227-0877
800-221-4045
Don & Liesl Noble
All year

120-250-BB
9 rooms, 9 pb
Most CC, *Rated*, •
C-ltd/S-no/P-no/H-yes
Spanish

Full and cont. plus breakfast
Afternoon tea, snacks
Sitting room, library, hot tub, heated pools, kitchens, phones, TV

Luxurious, meticulously restored Victorian homes. King William District. Beautiful antiques, fireplaces, marble baths, Jacuzzis.
stay@nobleinns.com http://www.nobleinns.com

O'Casey's B&B
225 West Craig Place 78212
210-738-1378 Fax: 210-733-9408
800-738-1378
John & Linda Fay Casey
All year

79-114-BB
7 rooms, 7 pb
Most CC, •
C-yes/S-no/P-yes/H-no

Full breakfast
Sitting room, cable tv, conference

Friendly, home-style B quiet, residential historic district close in; 5 guestrooms + 2 carriage house apartments; private baths; hearty, full breakfast; reasonable rates; families welcome. info@ocaseybnb.com http://www.ocaseybnb.com

---

Tara Inn
307 Beauregard 78204
210-824-8036 Fax: 210-479-1172
800-356-1605
Donna & Douglas West
All year

100-175-BB
6 rooms, 6 pb
Most CC, *Rated*, •
S-ltd/H-no

Continental plus breakfast
Snacks
Sitting room, Jacuzzis, suites, fireplaces, cable TV, accom. bus. travelers

Gone With the Wind flair. Beautiful antiques, very spacious suites and a feeling of going back in time. http://www.xyber.com/tarainn

SAN MARCOS

Crystal River Inn
326 W Hopkins 78666
512-396-3739 Fax: 512-353-3248
888-396-3739
Mike, Cathy & Sarah Dillon
All year

90-160-BB
12 rooms, 12 pb
Visa, MC, AmEx,
Rated, •
C-ltd/S-ltd/P-no/H-yes

Full breakfast
Complimentary brandy, chocolates
Fireplaces, courtyard, piano, fountain, bikes, 2-room suites, picnics

Romantic, luxurious Victorian captures matchless spirit of Texas Hill Country. Fresh flowers, homemade treats. 4-room garden cottage available–fireplace.
dillons@crystalriverinn.com http://www.crystalriverinn.com

SEABROOK

Back Bay B&B
PO Box 353
77586
281-474-3869
Marian Kidd
All year

85-90-BB
3 rooms, 3 pb
Most CC, *Rated*
C-ltd/S-ltd/P-no/H-no

Continental breakfast

Located in an historic building with an intriguing history and charm all its own.
backbay@ev1.net http://www.backbaybnb.com

SMITHVILLE

9E Ranch
1803 Bay Hill Dr
2158 Highway 304 78746
512-497-9502 Fax: 512-327-0248
Joan & Kent Bohls
All year

95-135-BB
3 rooms, 3 pb
Visa, MC, •
C-yes/S-no/P-yes/H-no

Full breakfast basket delivered.
Coffee and tea in cabins
18 hole frisbee golf course

Experience the beauty and tranquility of Texas by staying in the Texas Lone Star log cabin, Eagles' Nest log cabin, or De Colores Artist Barn on the 9E Ranch located in Lost Pine Forest, Bastrop. logcabins@9eranch.com http://www.9eranch.com

---

Katy House
PO Box 803
201 Ramona 78957
512-237-4262 Fax: 512-237-2239
800-843-5289
Sallie Blalock
All year

95-145-BB
5 rooms, 5 pb
Most CC, *Rated*, •
C-ltd/S-no/P-ltd/H-no

Full country breakfast
One suite w/kitchen
Sitting room, queen-size beds, TV, VCR, Ceiling fans,fireplace, balcony

Historic pecan-shaded home in beautiful central Texas. Railroad memorabilia & antique furnishings. innkeeper@katyhouse.com http://www.katyhouse.com

SOUTH PADRE ISLAND

Casa de Siesta
PO Box 3050
4610 Padre Blvd 78597
956-761-5656 Fax: 956-761-1313
Ron & Lynn Speier
All year

99-150-BB
12 rooms, 12 pb
Visa, MC, AmEx,
Rated, •
C-ltd/S-no/P-yes/H-yes
Spanish

Continental breakfast
Pool, bicycles, beach 1/2 block away, sitting room, cable TV, in-room phone

"An Oasis within an oasis," Casa de Siesta is for the discriminating traveler, who likes the best. Rooms are beautifully decorated in southwestern decor, & each has courtyard views of fountain & pool. reservations@casadesiesta.com http://www.casadesiesta.com

---

Moonraker
PO Box 1-9
107 East Marisol 78597
956-761-2206
Robert & Marcy Burns
All year

80-140-BB
4 rooms, 4 pb
Visa, MC
C-ltd/S-no/P-no/H-no
Spanish

Champagne breakfast
Afternoon Snacks
Beach Access, Whirlpool Hot Tub, Entertainment Center, Family Home

This Bed-n-Breakfast is a home. It is a true Bed-n-Breakfast, less than 5 rooms and is not a motel. See the photo gallery for a map of our location.
islatex@flash.net http://www.moonrakerbb.com

SUNRISE BEACH

Sandyland Resort 212 Skyline Dr 78643 915-388-4521 Fax: 915-388-3794 Brad & Krista Foster All year	80-160-BB 14 rooms, 14 pb Most CC, • C-yes/S-ltd/P-yes/H-ltd German, Spanish	Continental plus breakfast Meals for groups by reservation, snacks, wine Lakefront Club Room, Sailing, pool, suites, kitchenette studios

Beautiful lakefront lodge with lush landscaping and flowers; all rooms & suites have lakeview. Pool, Pavilion, Clubroom, lakefront decks, boardwalk, extended pier. Sailing lessons, Watercraft rental. sandy@tstar.net http://www.sandylandresort.com

TRINITY

Parker House PO Box 2373 300 North Maple 75862 936-594-3260 Fax: 936-594-0329 800-593-2373 Mary Anne & Steve Tyler All year	75-100-BB 4 rooms, 3 pb Visa, MC C-yes/S-ltd/P-no/H-no Spanish	Full breakfast Snacks, soft drinks, gourmet coffee, juice

Relive the past in a true Texas Landmark, with fine antiques, warm hospitality, lavish breakfasts and forest trail rides.
styler@lcc.net http://www.bbonline.com/tx/parkerhouse

TYLER

Rosevine Inn 415 S Vine 75702 903-592-2221 Fax: 903-592-5522 Bert & Rebecca Powell All year	95-150-BB 6 rooms, 6 pb *Rated*, • C-ltd/S-no/P-no/H-no French	Full breakfast Sitting room, library, spa, outdoor hot tub, courtyard, gameroom

Original bed and breakfast in the rose capital of the world. Pleasant accommodations with delicious breakfast. rosevine@iamerica.net http://www.rosevine.com

WACO

Judge Baylor House 908 Speight Ave 76706 254-756-0273 Fax: 254-756-0711 888-522-9567 Bruce & Dorothy Dyer All year	72-105-BB 4 rooms, 4 pb Visa, MC, *Rated*, • C-ltd/S-no/P-no/H-ltd	Full breakfast Aft. . tea, snacks Sitting room, library historical landmark

Decorated with antiques & Texas Hill Country art. Quiet & comfortable bedrooms. Near Baylor University and IH-35. jbaylor@iamerica.net http://www.judgebaylorhouse.com

WIMBERLEY

Southwind B&B and Cabins 2701 FM 3237 78676 512-847-5277 Fax: 512-847-5277 800-508-5277 All year	75-90-BB 3 rooms, 3 pb C-yes/S-no/P-yes/H-ltd	Full gourmet breakfast

Located 3 miles northeast of the quaint village of Wimberley, this early Texas style Inn and three rustic secluded cedar cabins are located on 25 hillside wooded acres.
southwind701@att.net http://www.southwindbedandbreak.com

Baker House, Cedar City, UT

Utah

CEDAR CITY

Baker House 1800 Royal Hunte Dr 84720 435-867-5695 Fax: 435-867-5694 888-611-8181 Lori & Tony Baker All year	109-159-BB 5 rooms, 5 pb Most CC, *Rated* C-ltd/S-ltd/P-no/H-no	Full breakfast Cookies, soft drinks, snacks King beds, fireplaces, Jacuzzi tubs, TV/VCRs

The most luxurious bed & breakfast in Cedar City. Experience yesterday's charm with today's comforts. Five beautifully decorated rooms featuring king beds, fireplaces, Jacuzzi tubs, TVs and VCRs. thebakers@netutah.com http://www.bakerhouse.net

GLENDALE

Smith Hotel PO Box 106 295 N Main St 84729 435-648-2156 Fax: 435-648-2156 800-528-3558 Rochelle & Bunny All year	44-80-BB 7 rooms, 7 pb Visa, MC, *Rated*, • C-ltd/S-no/P-no/H-ltd	Full breakfast Sitting room, screened porch, 2 acres to roam, swing, BBQ & picnic table

Historic 1927 hotel; lovely view of nearby bluffs from guest porch. Located in beautiful Long Valley between Zion & Bryce Canyon Nat'l Parks. Two acres to roam.
smith_hotel@email.com

Windwhisper Cabin PO Box 127 Hwy 89 Mile Marker 92 84729 702-648-2162 800-654-3003 Terry & Audrey Behling Closed winter	65-95-BB 3 rooms, 2 pb Most CC C-yes/S-ltd/P-no/H-ltd	Full breakfast

People are attracted to our inn, located between Zion National Park and Bryce Canyon, because of our location but, are pleasantly surprised to find a peaceful home-away-from-home! windwhisper@color-country.net http://www.windwhisperbb.com

MIDWAY

Johnson Mill
100 Johnson Mill Rd 84049
435-654-4333 Fax: 435-657-1454
888-272-0030
Robert Johnson
All year

115-250-BB
6 rooms, 6 pb
Most CC, *Rated*, •
C-ltd/S-no/P-no/H-no

Full breakfast
Tea, evening treats
Lake, streams, paths, 25 acres, fireplaces, jetted tubs, waterfalls, TV/VCR

25 acres situated on Provo River. Trout-stocked ponds, spring creek fishing. Beautiful grounds, walking paths, peaceful, quiet retreat. Outdoor hot tub overlooks 30-ft. waterfall.
bob@johnsonmill.com http://www.johnsonmill.com

MOAB

Cali Cochitta Inn
110 South 200 East 84532
435-259-4961 Fax: 435-259-4964
888-429-8112
David & Kim Boger
All year

69-150-BB
5 rooms, 5 pb
Rated, •
C-yes/S-no/P-no/H-yes

Full breakfast
Lunch, dinner, afternoon tea, snacks
Sitting room, library, Jacuzzis, suites, cable TV, acc. bus. travelers

Located in the heart of spectacular "Red Rock Country . . . a wonderland of breathtaking panoramas, Cali Cochitta, the "House of Dreams" is secluded, yet close to local shops and activities. calicochitta@lasal.net http://www.moabdreaminn.com

---

Sunflower Hill
185 N 300 E 84532
435-259-2974 Fax: 435-259-3065
800-MOAB-SUN
Stucki family
All year

90-210-BB
11 rooms, 11 pb
Visa, MC, *Rated*, •
C-ltd/S-no/P-no

Full breakfast
Sitting room, library, laundry room, hot tub, gardens, patio, BBQ

Inviting country retreat adorned w/antiques, hand painting, stenciling. Serene setting w/lush flower gardens. Healthy, homemade breakfast.
innkeeper@sunflowerhill.com http://www.sunflowerhill.com

PARK CITY

1904 Imperial Hotel
PO Box 1628
221 Main St 84060
435-649-1904 Fax: 435-645-7421
800-669-8824
Marie or Gretchen
All year

80-250-BB
10 rooms, 10 pb
Most CC, *Rated*, •
C-ltd/S-no/P-no/H-no

Full breakfast
Evening refreshments, snacks
Pub & art gallery nearby, ski storage, TV, phones

Superbly restored 1904 hotel in heart of Park City. Private baths with large Roman tubs, phone, cable TV. stay@1904imperial.com http://www.1904imperial.com

---

Angel House Inn
PO Box 159
713 Norfolk Avenue 84060
435-647-0338 Fax: 435-655-8524
800-264-3501
Joe & Jan Fisher-Rush
All year

85-285-BB
9 rooms, 9 pb
Most CC, *Rated*, •
C-ltd/S-no/P-no/H-no
Spanish, English

Full breakfast
Afternoon tea, wine
Sitting room, library, jacuzzi, fireplace, cable TV, soaking tub, ski locker

Found in the rugged Wasatch Mountains, the inn offers gourmet breakfast.
jrush@ditell.com http://www.angelhouseinn.com

The Old Miners' Lodge
PO Box 2639
615 Woodside Ave 84060
435-645-8068 Fax: 435-645-7420
800-648-8068
Susan Wynne & Liza Simpson
All year

75-270-BB
12 rooms, 12 pb
Most CC, *Rated*, •
C-yes/S-no/P-no/H-no

Full country breakfast
Evening refreshments
Sitting room, library, fireplace, hot tub, games

An original miner's lodge—antique-filled rooms, down comforters, full breakfast, complimentary refreshments and fine hospitality.
stay@oldminerslodge.com http://www.oldminerslodge.com

PARK CITY

Old Town Guest House PO Box 162 1011 Empire Ave 84060 435-649-2642 Fax: 435-649-3320 800-290-6423 ext. 3710 Deb Lovci All year	55-195-BB 4 rooms, 4 pb Visa, MC, AmEx, *Rated*, • C-ltd/S-no/P-ltd/H-no	Healthy ""Park City"" breakfast Afternoon snacks Hot tub, common room, boot dryers, ski storage, robes and inspiration!!!

Nestled in the heart of Park City, Old Town Guest House is the perfect place for active skiers, hikers and bikers wishing to enjoy the mountains of Utah. This Inn is Park City's best kept secret!!! info@oldtownguesthouse.com http://www.oldtownguesthouse.com

Washington School Inn PO Box 536 543 Park Ave 84060 435-649-3800 Fax: 435-649-3802 800-824-1672 Delphine Covington All year	95-425-BB 15 rooms, 15 pb Most CC C-yes/S-no/P-no/H-yes	Full breakfast Afternoon wine and appetizers Spa, sauna, ski lockers. Mezzanine area; dining room

Guests delight in unexpected luxuries and a wide range of services at this limestone inn nestled among the majestic mountains of Park City.
washinn@xmission.com http://washingtonschoolinn.com

Woodside Inn PO Box 682680 1469 Woodside Ave 84060 435-649-3494 Fax: 435-649-2392 888-241-5890 Bob McCallister All year	89-289-BB 6 rooms, 6 pb Visa, MC, AmEx, *Rated*, • C-ltd/S-no/P-no/H-yes	Full breakfast Snacks, complimentary wine Sitting rm, Jacuzzis, suites, cable TV, accom bus trav, elevator, cvrd prkg

The only newly-constructed B&B in Park City! Fully air-conditioned with elevator.
info@woodsideinn.com http://www.woodsideinn.com

PARK CITY (REGION)

The Blue Boar Inn & Rest. 1235 Warm Springs Rd, *Midway* 84049 435-654-1400 Fax: 435-654-6459 888-650-1400 Jay & Sandy Niederhauser All year	150-295-BB 14 rooms, 14 pb Most CC, *Rated*, • C-ltd/S-no/P-no/H-yes	Full breakfast Lunch, dinner, restaurant, bar service Sitting room, library, bikes, Jacuzzis, swimming pool, fireplaces, cable TV

The Inn is reminiscent of a romantic European hunting lodge. Fourteen elegant rooms are named after literary figures and accented with fireplaces, fresh flowers and jetted tubs.
Innkeeper @theblueboarinn.com http://www.theblueboarinn.com

SAINT GEORGE

Green Gate Village Inn 76 W Tabernacle 84770 435-628-6999 Fax: 435-628-6989 800-350-6999 Ed Sandstrom All year	65-395-BB 15 rooms, 15 pb Most CC, *Rated*, • C-ltd/S-no/P-no/H-ltd Spanish	Full breakfast Pool, Business & Reception Ctrs, Mtg Rooms, Restaurant, Snack Bar, Gift Shop

Eight fully restored upscale pioneer homes (1800s) gently nestled on the "Historic Walk" of old town St. George, Utah. greengate@usa.com http://www.greengatevillage.com

SALT LAKE CITY

Anton Boxrud Inn 57 South 600 E 84102 801-363-8035 Fax: 801-596-1316 800-524-5511 Jane E. Johnson All year	98-150-BB 6 rooms, 3 pb Visa, MC, *Rated* C-ltd/S-no/P-no/H-no	Full breakfast Hot tubs (winter), sitting room, robes, down comforters

The interior of this "Grand Old Home" is replete with beveled and stain-glass windows, burled woodwork, hardwood floors and pocked doors.
antonboxrud@attbi.com http://www.antonboxrud.com

SALT LAKE CITY

Ellerbeck Mansion
140 North B Street 84103
801-355-2500 Fax: 801-530-0938
800-966-8364
Debbie Spencer
All year

115-150-BB
6 rooms, 6 pb
Most CC, *Rated*, •
C-ltd/S-no/P-no/H-ltd

Continental plus breakfast
Telephone and TV in room.
Soft drinks, turn-down service, treats available

The Ellerbeck is a restored, historic Victorian home with hardwood floors, original moldings and stained glass, and period theme decor, located in the charming Avenues District of downtown SLC. ellerbeckmansion@qwest.net http://www.ellerbeckbedandbreakfast.com

---

Haxton Manor
943 E South Temple 84102
801-363-4646 Fax: 801-363-4686
877-930-4646
Buffi & Douglas King
All year

99-169-BB
7 rooms, 7 pb
Visa, MC, AmEx, *Rated*, •
C-ltd/S-no/P-no/H-yes
Spanish

Continental plus breakfast
Tea, snacks
Sitting room, library, Jacuzzi, fireplace, cable TV, conferences

English styled historic country Inn, conveniently located within walking distance of the university and downtown Salt Lake City.
innkeepers@haxtonmanor.com http://www.haxtonmanor.com

Log Cabin on the Hill
2275 East 6200 S 84121
801-272-2969 800-639-2969
Geri & Marlene Yardley
All year

85-105-BB
4 rooms, 4 pb
Most CC
C-yes/S-no/P-no/H-yes

Full breakfast
Cookies and cheese/crackers, soda, coffee, tea
Hot tub, living room, fireplace

Nestled in natural hollow of the canyon foothills, the Log Cabin on the Hill B&B is minutes from every major Salt Lake ski resort and area attraction.
info@logcabinonthehill.com http://www.logcabinonthehill.com

The Royal Scotsman at Pinecrest
6211 Emigration Canyon 84108
801-583-6663
Dave Phillips
All year

75-195-BB
7 rooms, 7 pb
S-no

Full breakfast

Well known for its superior luxury and hospitality, The Pinecrest Bed and Breakfast Inn takes great pride in providing its guests the personal attention enjoyed by travelers of the past info@theroyalscotsman.com http://www.theroyalscotsman.com

---

Saltair
164 South 900 East 84102
801-533-8184 Fax: 801-595-0332
800-533-8184
Jan Bartlett, Nancy Saxton
All year

79-129-BB
17 rooms, 14 pb
Most CC, *Rated*, •
C-ltd/S-no/P-no/H-no

Full or continental breakfast
Snacks, complimentary wine
Sitting room, A/C, hot tubs, fresh flowers, robes, down comforters

Historic Victorian charm compliments queen brass beds & period furnishings. Near Univ. of Utah, historic downtown, skiing & canyons.
saltair@saltlakebandb.com http://www.saltlakebandb.com

Wildflowers
936 E 1700 S 84105
801-466-0600 Fax: 801-466-4728
800-569-0009
Cill Sparks & Jeri Parker
All year

85-145-BB
5 rooms, 5 pb
Most CC, *Rated*, •
S-no/P-no/H-no
French

Full breakfast
Restaurant nearby
Sitting room, library, reading room, deck, stained glass windows

Nat'l Historic 1891 Victorian offering delights of past and comforts of the present. Wildflower gardens, close to park, downtown, ski resorts.
lark2spur@aol.com http://www.wildflowersbb.com

SALT LAKE CITY (REGION)

Jackson Fork Inn
7345 East 900 S, *Huntsville* 84317
801-745-0051 800-255-0672
Vicki Petersen
All year

70-120-BB
8 rooms, 8 pb
Visa, MC, AmEx, *Rated*, •
C-yes/S-no/P-ltd/H-no

Continental breakfast
Restaurant
Hot tubs, skiing, golf, fishing, water sports, Jacuzzis & VCRs in some rooms

Old dairy barn renovated into a restaurant & inn. Quiet getaway without phones. Private whirlpool tubs. http://www.jacksonforkinn.com

---

Castle Creek Inn
11463 Nicklaus Rd
7391 S Creek Rd, *Sandy* 84092
801-567-9437
Fax: 801-553-2669
Sallie Calder
All year

99-225-BB
10 rooms, 10 pb
Rated
C-ltd/S-no/P-no/H-yes

Full breakfast
Afternoon tea, snacks
Jacuzzis, fireplaces, cable TV, accom. bus. travelers, suites

An authentic Scottish castle, nestled among tall oak trees, provides ten elegant suites each uniquely decorated with castle decor. sal@castleutah.com http://www.castleutah.com

SPRING CITY (REGION)

The Garden B&B Inn
PO Box 425
11650 Canal Canyon Rd, *Ephrain* 84662
435-462-9285 877-537-2337
Phyllis & Bud Snedecor
All year

75-125-BB
4 rooms, 2 pb
Most CC, •
C-yes/S-ltd/P-ltd/H-yes

Continental plus breakfast
Snacks
Wood stove, piano, sitting room, firepit, trails, view

Get Away To A Mountain Retreat! We are located in the heart of Utah, near Spring City, a unique Mormon village overshadowed by beautiful mountains.
thegardeninn@hotmail.com http://www.BedsAndRoses.com

ST. GEORGE

Seven Wives Inn
217 N 100 West 84770
435-628-3737 Fax: 435-628-5646
800-600-3737
David & Shellee Taylor
All year

60-125-BB
13 rooms, 13 pb
Most CC, *Rated*, •
C-yes/S-no/P-no/H-ltd

Full breakfast
Lunch & tea room
Pool, conference facility, sitting room, organ, golf & tennis nearby

1870s pioneer home on National Register, furnished in antiques. Heart of St. George, close to national parks. seven@infowest.com http://www.sevenwivesinn.com

TORREY

SkyRidge Inn
PO Box 750220
950 E. Hwy 24 94775
435-425-3222
Jerry & Shauna Agnew

115-172-BB
Rated
C-ltd/S-ltd/P-no
All year

Full breakfast
Beverages; hors d'oeuvres, sangria, tea in PM

Nationally recognized for its magnificent views and artfully decorated rooms, SkyRidge Bed and Breakfast Inn has been featured in NATIONAL GEOGRAPHIC TRAVELER.
skyridge@color-country.net

TORREY (REGION)

Muley Twist Inn
PO Box 117
249 West 125 St, *Teasdale* 84773
435-425-3640
Fax: 435-425-3641 800-530-1038
Eric & Penny Kinsman
April 1–Oct 28

99-109-BB
5 rooms, 5 pb
Visa, MC, AmEx, *Rated*, •
C-yes/S-no/P-no/H-yes

Full breakfast
Afternoon tea, snacks
Sitting room, library, accommodate business travelers, wheelchair accessible

Distinctive lodging at the edge of the world. Newly built 5-room B&B with private baths, delicious breakfasts, gourmet coffee and magnificent views from large porches. Come and enjoy the quiet! muley@rof.net http://www.go-utah.com/muleytwist

Muley Twist Inn, Teasdale, UT

TROPIC

Bryce Point
PO Box 96
61 North 400 West 84776
435-679-8629
Fax: 435-679-8629
888-200-4211
Lamar & Ethel Le Fevre

70-120-BB
5 rooms, 5 pb
Rated, •

All year

Full breakfast

Located in picturesque Tropic on Utah's Scenic Highway 12, only 8 miles east of the entrance to Bryce Canyon National Park.

Vermont

ALBURG

Alburg Dunes
166 Route 129 05440
802-796-3388
Guy Marion
All year

75-85-BB
4 rooms, 1 pb
Visa, MC
C-yes/S-no/P-no/H-no
French

Full breakfast
Decks by the lake, screened porch, fireplace.

Our modern lake-front bed and breakfast is a comfortable place to enjoy the beauty of Lake Champlain.
innkeeper@alburgdunes.com http://www.alburgdunes.com

Thomas Mott Homestead
63 Blue Rock Rd 05440
802-796-4402
800-348-0843
Lee and Linda Mickey
May-Nov

85-150-BB
4 rooms, 4 pb
Visa, MC, Disc, *Rated*, •
S-no/P-no/H-no

Full breakfast
Complimentary Ben & Jerry treat
Fireplace, Cable TV, bicycles, canoe, swim at Lake Champlain, hiking trails

The B&B has been renovated to English cottage style. Cozy comfort in a rustic yet refined setting. Lake views from all rooms, beautiful mountain backdrop.
lmickey164@aol.com http://www.thomas-mott-bb.com

ANDOVER

Inn at Highview 753 E Hill Rd 05143 802-875-2724 Fax: 802-875-4021 Greg Bohan & Sal Massaro All year, exc. 2 wk. May	135-195-BB 8 rooms, 8 pb Visa, MC, *Rated*, • C-yes/S-no/P-ltd/H-no Italian, Spanish	Full breakfast Dinner–Sat. only Sitting room, library, sauna, pool, hiking

Vermont of your dreams. Secluded elegance; breathtaking views. 8 luxurious rooms with private baths, fabulous food. Tennis/golf nearby.
hiview@aol.com http://www.innathighview.com

Rowell's Inn 1834 Simonsville Rd 05143 802-875-3658 Fax: 802-875-3680 800-728-0842 Louise Riehl-Haley	120-175-BB 7 rooms, 7 pb Most CC, *Rated*, • C-ltd/S-no/P-no/H-no Closed part of April	Full breakfast Dinner available Fri. & Sat. Tavern, parlor, sunroom, patio, horseshoes, badminton

An 1820 stagecoach stop listed on the National Register of Historic Places.
innkeep@rowellsinn.com http://www.rowellsinn.com

ARLINGTON

Arlington Inn PO Box 369 3904 Historic Route 7A 05250 802-375-6532 Fax: 802-375-6534 800-443-9442 Eric & Elizabeth Berger All year	125-310-BB 18 rooms, 18 pb Most CC, *Rated*, • C-yes/S-ltd/P-no/H-yes	Full breakfast Afternoon snack & fresh iced tea or lemonade Gourmet dining, full tavern w/porch, Victorian parlor, country gardens

Exquisite romantic 1848 Greek Revival Mansion. Gourmet dining, extensive wine list, 18 luxurious rooms, two person Jacuzzis, fireplaces, gardens, gazebo, "2002" Editor's Pick Yankee Travel Guide. arlinn@sover.net http://www.arlingtoninn.com

Arlington's West Mountain Inn PO Box 40 144 West Mountain Inn Rd 05250 802-375-6516 Fax: 802-375-6553 The Carlson Family All year	169-300-MAP 15 rooms, 15 pb Visa, MC, AmEx, *Rated*, • C-yes/S-ltd/P-no/H-yes French	Full breakfast Dinner included, bar Fruit, chocolate llama, piano, dining room, flowers, conference room

150-acre hillside estate; hike or ski woodland trails. Fish the Battenkill. Hearthside dining, charming rooms. Relax & enjoy the llamas, goats and rabbits.
info@westmountaininn.com http://www.westmountaininn.com

Country Willows c.1850 332 E Arlington Rd 05250 802-375-0019 Fax: 802-375-8054 800-796-2585 Anne & Ron Weber All year	95-160-BB 5 rooms, 5 pb Visa, MC, AmEx C-ltd/S-no/P-no/H-no	Bountiful breakfast Late afternoon light refreshments (optional) Sitting room, suites, fireplace, cable TV, conferences

Gracious Queen Anne Victorian Inn, c.1850. National Register Historic Landmark. Intimate and romantic! cw@sover.net http://www.countrywillows.com

Hill Farm Inn 458 Hill Farm Rd 05250 802-375-2269 Fax: 802-375-9918 800-882-2545 Kathleen & Craig Yanez All year	105-198-BB 15 rooms Most CC, *Rated* C-yes/S-no/P-no/H-no	Full country breakfast Afternoon tea, snacks Sitting room, cable TV, families welcome, accommodate business travelers

One of Vermont's first country inns. Fifty peaceful acres on the Battenkill River. Large farmhouse plus four cottages with beautiful mountain & valley views.
hillfarm@vermontel.com http://www.hillfarminn.com

BENNINGTON

Alexandra Inn
916 Orchard Rd
Rt 7A, Orchard Rd 05201
802-442-5619 Fax: 802-442-5592
888-207-9386
Alex & Andra All year

85-150-BB
12 rooms, 12 pb
Most CC, *Rated*, •
C-ltd/S-no/P-ltd/H-yes
French, German, Dutch

Full breakfast
Sitting room, library, Jacuzzis, suites, firepalces, cable TV, VCR

A tasteful restored cape from 1859 with 6 deluxe rooms in main building and 6 more in recent colonial. Modern deluxe amenities. Gourmet breakfasts.
alexandr@sover.net http://www.alexandrainn.com

Four Chimneys Inn & Rest.
21 West Rd (Rte 9) 05201
802-447-3500 Fax: 802-447-3692
800-649-3503
Chris & Harold Cullison
Peak June thru October

105-215-BB
11 rooms, 11 pb
Most CC, *Rated*, •
C-ltd/S-no/P-no/H-no

Continental plus breakfast
Restaurant, bar
Dinner, sitting room, library, golf close by

One of New England's premier inns. Classic French cuisine. Beautiful 11-acre estate, plush guestrooms with modern amenities and cocktail lounge.
innkeeper@fourchimneys.com http://www.fourchimneys.com/

Molly Stark Inn
1067 E Main St 05201
802-442-9631 Fax: 802-442-5224
800-356-3076
Reed Fendler
All year

70-175-BB
9 rooms, 7 pb
Most CC, *Rated*, •
C-ltd/S-no/P-no/H-no

Full gourmet breakfast
Evening snack
Den with woodstove, TV, hardwood floors, antique, quilts, claw foot tubs

Charming 1860 Victorian, including romantic private cottages with fireplace & Jacuzzi. Decorated with country Americana, antiques, classical music playing. Sunporch, wood stoves, homey & comfortable. mollyinn@vermontel.net http://www.mollystarkinn.com

BONDVILLE

Bromley View Inn
RR1, Box 161, Route 30 05340
802-297-1459 Fax: 802-297-3676
800-297-1459
Richard & Theresa Rogers
All year

120-140-BB
Most CC
C-yes/S-ltd/P-yes/H-no

Full breakfast
Lunch & dinner avail, restaurant, bar service
Sitting room, library, pool, suites, fireplaces, accom. bus. travelers

Nestled in the heart of the Green Mountains, beautiful views, great food.
bvi@sover.net http://www.bromleyviewinn.com

BRANDON

Churchill House Inn
3128 Forest Dale Rd
Route 73 East 05733
802-247-3078 877-248-7444
Linda & Richard Daybell
Closed April

120-220-MAP
9 rooms, 9 pb
Visa, MC, AmEx, *Rated*, •
S-no/P-no/H-no

Full breakfast and dinner
Lower rate for breakfast only, bar
Swimming pool, golf, library, piano, fishing, biking, hiking, skiing

Century-old farmhouse on the edge of Green Mountain National Forest. Welcoming ambiance and gourmet dining.
innkeeper@churchillhouseinn.com http://www.churchillhouseinn.com

---

The Lilac Inn
53 Park St 05733
802-247-5463 Fax: 802-247-5499
800-221-0720
Shelly and Doug Sawyer
All year

145-325-BB
9 rooms, 9 pb
Visa, MC, AmEx, *Rated*, •
C-ltd/S-no/P-ltd/H-ltd

Full breakfast
Fine dining on weekends
Romantic gardens, front veranda, copper topped bar, library & six fireplaces

Leading romantic destination for fine dining, weddings and civil unions, Middlebury College events, Lake Dunmore, summer & winter in the Green Mountains, corporate retreats & special occasions. lilacinn@sover.net http://www.lilacinn.com

BRATTLEBORO

1868 Crosby House 175 Western Avenue 05301 802-257-4914 800-528-1868 Lynn Kuralt All year	115-145-BB 3 rooms, 3 pb Most CC, • C-ltd/S-no/P-no/H-no	Full breakfast Snacks Sitting room, library, Jacuzzi, Suite, cable TV, fireplaces

Historic home decorated with family heirlooms and collected antiques, luxurious accommodations, elegant gourmet breakfasts. Private baths, fireplaces, whirlpool, delightful amenities. lynn@crosbyhouse.com http://www.crosbyhouse.com

BRIDGEWATER CORNERS

October Country Inn PO Box 66 Upper Rd 05035 802-672-3412 Fax: 802-672-1163 800-648-8421 Edie & Chuck Janisse All year	MAP 10 rooms, 8 pb Most CC, • C-yes/S-no/P-no/H-no Spanish	Full country breakfast Coffee, tea, cookies, beer and wine licensed Pool, gardens, library, games, hiking, bicycling

Relaxed and comfortable, 19th Century Inn, offers warmth and intimacy in the finest innkeeping tradition. We are known throughout the region for our wonderful meals and hospitality. oci@vermontel.com http://www.vermontinns.net

BRISTOL

The Cliff Hanger 308 Many Waters Rd 05443 802-453-2013 Ken & Kim All year	65-90-BB 3 rooms, 1 pb C-yes/S-ltd/P-yes/H-no French, Spanish	Continental breakfast Afternoon tea Sitting room, library, bikes, accommodate business travelers

Spectacular cliff views and a great setting to enjoy nature at the foothills to the Green mountains. There are many hiking, biking & cross country trails from our house, which is on 4 acres. hewitts@gmavt.net

BROOKFIELD

Birch Meadow Luxury Log Cabins RR1 Box 294A 597 Birch Meadow Ln 05036 802-276-3156 Fax: 802-276-3423 Mary & Matt Comerford All year	99-120-BB 4 rooms, 4 pb Visa, MC, *Rated* C-yes/S-yes/P-ltd/H-ltd	Full breakfast Cont. breakfast- cabins Fireplaces, horseback riding, pool, antique stove

"A place to get away from it all, yet close to everything." Cozy cabins for that special time together. Great for a honeymoon or family vacation.
birchmedow@aol.com http://www.bbhost.com/birchmeadow

BROWNSVILLE

Autumn Mist Farm 1073 Bible Hill Rd 05037 802-484-9730 Rice Yordy All year	BB

Travel through a covered bridge and along one of Vermont's prettiest country roads to this intimate bed and breakfast. The home was built in 1861 and was one of the original farms on Bible Hill Road. info@autumnmistfarm.com http://autumnmistfarm.com

BURLINGTON (REGION)

Black Bear Inn 4010 Bolton Access Rd, *Bolton* 05477 802-434-2126 Fax: 802-434-5161 800-395-6335 Ken Richardson All year	79-225-MAP 24 rooms, 24 pb Visa, MC, *Rated*, • C-yes/S-no/P-ltd/H-ltd	Full breakfast Dinner, bar service, restaurant Sitting room, bikes, tennis court, Jacuzzis, pool, suites, fireplaces, cable

True Mountain top country inn on 500 private acres to explore. Features 25 tastefully decorated rooms offering private hot tubs, fireplaces, and fantastic views.
blkbear@wcvt.com http://www.blkbearinn.com

BURLINGTON (REGION)

1804 Potter House B&B
2 Plains Rd., *Jericho* 05465
802-899-5072 888-869-5263
Mike & Bear Mumley
All year

60-80-BB
3 rooms
Most CC, *Rated*, •
C-ltd/S-no/P-no/H-no

Full breakfast
Afternoon tea, snacks
Sitting room, fireplaces, cable TV, accommodates business travelers

Historic Colonial used as stagecoach stop & tavern. Wide board floors, antiques, quilts, 4-poster beds. Potrhowz@together.net

---

Richmond Victorian Inn
PO Box 652
191 E Main St, *Richmond* 05477
802-434-4410 Fax: 802-434-4411
888-242-3362
Frank & Joyce Stewart
All year

85-125-BB
6 rooms, 6 pb
Most CC, *Rated*
C-ltd/S-no/P-no/H-no
French

Full breakfast
Please advise on dietary restrictions
Sitting room, TV/VCR, good conversation

1850's Queen Anne Victorian B nestled in a small Vermont town minutes from Burlington and Lake Champlain.
innkeeper@richmondvictorianinn.com http://www.richmondvictorianinn.com

---

Heart of the Village Inn
PO Box 953
5347 Shelburne Road, *Shelburne* 05482
802-985-2800 Fax: 802-985-2870
877-808-1834
Bobbe, Stephanie, LouAnn

95-225-BB
9 rooms, 9 pb
Visa, MC, AmEx, •
C-yes/S-no/P-no/H-yes
All year

Full breakfast
Afternoon tea
Sitting room, Jacuzzi, cable TV, conferences

Casually elegant and restored Queen Anne Victorian in a beautiful, historic Vermont village; just across from the Shelburne Museum.
innkeeper@heartofthevillage.com http://www.heartofthevillage.com

CHAMPLAIN ISLANDS (REGION)

North Hero House Inn & Restaurant
PO Box 207
Route 2, *North Hero Island* 05474
802-372-4732 Fax: 802-372-3218
888-525-3644

69-249-BB
26 rooms, 26 pb
Most CC, *Rated*, •
C-yes/S-yes/P-no/H-yes
Spanish, French
Walter Blasberg
All year

Full or continental breakfast
Restaurant, coffee, tea
Lounge, sitting room, tennis, lake swimming, bicycles, sauna

The Historic North Hero House Inn and Restaurant is a quintessential Vermont Country Inn with all the conveniences required by today's traveler.
nhhlake@aol.com http://www.northherohouse.com

CHELSEA

Shire Inn
PO Box 37
277 VT Rte 110 05038
802-685-3031 Fax: 802-685-3871
800-441-6908
Jay & Karen Keller All year

115-155-BB
6 rooms, 6 pb
Visa, MC, *Rated*, •
C-ltd/S-no/P-no/H-no

Full breakfast
Dinner by reservation
Sitting room & porch, fireplaces in guestrooms, bicycles

1832 brick mansion. Large, wonderful guestrooms. 23 acres & river. Gracious candlelight dining. Pure romance in a vintage Vermont village!
desk@shireinn.com http://www.shireinn.com

CHESTER

Fullerton Inn
PO Box 188
40 The Common 05143
802-875-2444 Fax: 802-875-6414
Jerry & Robin Szawerda

99-149-BB
21 rooms, 21 pb
Most CC
C-ltd/S-no/P-no/H-no
All year

Continental breakfast
Dinner available
Restaurant, bar, sitting room, suites, fireplace, cableTV, conference room

Elegant yet comfortable country inn on the Village Green. Immaculate rooms, professional, courteous staff. Casual dining in Ye Olde Bradford Tavern Restaurant. Walk to antiques & specialty shops. getaway@fullertoninn.com http://www.fullertoninn.com

CHESTER

Henry Farm Inn 2206 Green Mountain Turnpike 05143 802-875-2674 800-723-8213 Patricia & Paul Dexter All year	90-135-BB 9 rooms, 9 pb Most CC, *Rated*, • C-yes/S-ltd/P-no/H-ltd	Full breakfast Fireplaced sitting room, swimming/skating pond, cross-country ski trail

1700's Colonial in country setting, 1 mile from Chester Village. Fifty-six acres including pond, meadow, woods and river. Nine spacious guestrooms all with private baths. Children very welcome. info@henryfarminn.com http://www.henryfarminn.com

---

Hugging Bear Inn & Shoppe 244 Main St 05143 802-875-2412 800-325-0519 Georgette Thomas Closed Xmas/Thanksgiving	95-145-BB 6 rooms, 6 pb Most CC, *Rated* C-yes/S-no/P-no/H-no	Afternoon beverages, snacks 2 living rooms, library, den-games, toys, 10% shoppe discount, AC

Elegant Victorian in National Historic District, on the Village Green, thousands of teddy bears throughout, extensive teddy bear shop.
georgette@huggingbear.com http://www.huggingbear.com

The Inn at Cranberry Farm 61 Williams River Rd 05143 802-463-1339 Fax: 802-463-8169 800-854-2208 Susan Morency & Paul Florindo All year	130-179-BB 11 rooms, 11 pb Visa, MC, Disc, *Rated*, • C-ltd/S-no/P-no/H-yes	Full breakfast Afternoon tea, snacks, hiking, bike routes, sitting room, library

Leave your world behind and enter ours. Discover why our country inn will be your destination for rest, relaxation and rejuvenation. All the comforts of home with none of the demands. paulansue@msn.com http://www.cranberryfarminn.com

---

Inn Victoria PO Box 788 321 Main St 05143 802-875-4288 Fax: 802-875-2504 800-732-4288 Jack & Janet Burns All year	110-195-BB 7 rooms, 7 pb Visa, MC, *Rated*, • C-no/S-no/P-no/H-yes	Full breakfast Afternoon tea Sitting room with color TV, Jacuzzis, fireplaces, A/C, luxurious robes

Romantic, elegant getaway On The Green in Chester. Enjoy gourmet breakfasts and afternoon tea. Fireplaces, private Jacuzzis, color TVs, and queen-sized beds in antique filled bedrooms. innkeeper@innvictoria.com http://www.innvictoria.com

---

Popple Fields PO Box 636 1300 Popple Dungeon Rd 05143 802-875-4219 Fax: 802-875-2011 Marylin & Conrad Delia All year	90-150-BB 4 rooms, 2 pb Visa, MC, Disc, *Rated* C-ltd/S-no/P-no/H-no	Full breakfast Snacks Sitting room, fireplaces, satellite TV

18th century reproduction Ct. saltbox on 18 acres. Stunning mountain views.
popplfld@sover.net http://www.popplefields.com

Stone Cottage Collectables 196 North St 05143 802-875-6211 Chris & Ann Curran All year	80-100-BB 2 rooms, 2 pb Most CC C-yes/S-no/P-no/H-no	Full breakfast Tea, Cold drinks, snack Sitting rooms,Sunroom,Deck,Gardens, Pond,Fireplaces,Antique Shop,Stamps

Our 1840 stone house in Chester's Historic Stone Village is filled with antiques and collectibles but provides all modern conveniences and comforts. Queen/Full beds, Priv. Baths, Fireplaces, A/C. stonebb@vermontel.net http://www.chesterlodging.com/stonecc.htm

CHESTER

The Stone Hearth Inn
698 Vt Rt 11 W 05143
802-875-2525 Fax: 802-875-1588
888-617-3656
Chris Clay & Brent Anderson
All year

69-149-BB
10 rooms, 10 pb
Most CC, *Rated*, •
C-yes/S-ltd/P-ltd/H-no

Full breakfast
Tavern menu (sandwiches, baskets, chili)
Full tavern with lunch or dinner, fireplace, library, piano, hot tub, games

Historic Vermont Inn, built in 1810, features 10 unique accommodations all w/private bath; tavern w/pub menu; sitting area w/fireplace; hot tub; library.
info@thestonehearthinn.com http://www.thestonehearthinn.com

CHITTENDEN

Fox Creek Inn
49 Dam Rd 05737
802-483-6213 Fax: 802-483-2623
800-707-0017
Ann & Alex Volz
Closed Apr, Nov-Thksgvg

190-409-MAP
9 rooms, 9 pb
Visa, MC, AmEx, *Rated*, •
C-ltd/S-no/P-ltd/H-ltd

Full breakfast
Dinner included
Full bar & wine cellar, sitting room, library

Small, antique-filled country inn, hidden away in the Green Mountains. Gracious dining, homemade breads and desserts, wine list. New room decor.
ttinn@sover.net http://www.foxcreekinn.com

CRAFTSBURY COMMON

The Inn on the Common
PO Box 75
North Main St 05827
802-586-9619 Fax: 802-586-2249
800-521-2233
Penny & Michael Schmitt

240-290-MAP
18 rooms, 18 pb
Visa, MC, *Rated*, •
C-ltd/S-yes/P-ltd/H-no
All year

Full breakfast
Dinner (MAP), bar
Sitting rooms, library, pool, sauna, tennis, walking & biking

Superbly decorated, meticulously appointed, wonderful cuisine, complete recreation facilities. info@innonthecommon.com http://www.innonthecommon.com

DANBY

The Quail's Nest
PO Box 221
81 S Main St 05739
802-293-5099 Fax: 802-293-6300
800-599-6444
Greg & Nancy Diaz

70-115-BB
6 rooms, 6 pb
Most CC, *Rated*, •
C-ltd/S-no/P-no/H-no
All year

Full breakfast
Complimentary tea & snacks
Sitting room with fireplace, library, deck & garden, bicycles

Step back in time in a picturesque village inn, six romantic air conditioned guestrooms wrapped in handmade quilts. Four course candlelit breakfasts prepare you for your day's events. quailsnest@quailsnestbandb.com http://www.quailsnestbandb.com

DERBY LINE

Derby Village Inn
PO Box 1085
440 Main St 05830
802-873-3604 Fax: 802-873-3047
C. McCormick & S. Steplar

80-105-BB
5 rooms, 5 pb
Most CC
C-yes/S-no/P-no/H-no
All year

Full breakfast
Snacks, complimentary wine
Sitting room, library, fireplace, cable TV, suites, conf. facilities

5 gracious rooms, private baths, 3 tiled fireplaces, original woodwork, library, sunporch, full breakfast, activities galore.
pampered@derbyvillageinn.com http://www.derbyvillageinn.com

DORSET

Cornucopia of Dorset
PO Box 307
3228 Route 30 05251
802-867-5751 Fax: 802-867-5753
800-566-5751
Donna Butman Closed April

150-270-BB
5 rooms, 5 pb
Visa, MC, AmEx, *Rated*
C-ltd/S-no/P-no/H-no

Full unique breakfast
Cookies & apples in room upon arrival
Sitting room, library, suites, fireplace, cable TV

Five gracious accommodations including a cottage suite. Candlelit breakfasts, simple elegance, unmatched service and amenities.
innkeepers@cornucopiaofdorset.com http://www.cornucopiaofdorset.com

DORSET

Marble West Inn
PO Box 847
Dorset West Rd 05251
802-867-4155 Fax: 802-867-5731
800-453-7629
Bonnie & Paul Quinn

90-175-BB
8 rooms, 8 pb
Visa, MC, AmEx, *Rated*
C-ltd/S-no/P-no/H-no
All year

Full breakfast
Dinner included with MAP
Refreshments, afternoon tea, sitting room, library

Historic 1840 Greek Revival inn– elegant, quiet, peaceful, off busy main road, with mountain views, gardens, and ponds. marwest@sover.net http://www.marblewestinn.com

DOVER (REGION)

Cooper Hill Inn
PO Box 146
117 Cooper Hill Rd, *East Dover* 05341
802-348-6333 Fax: 802-348-7139
800-783-3229
Gordon & Carolyn Lucas

80-160-BB
10 rooms, 10 pb
Visa, MC, •
C-yes/S-no/P-yes/H-no
French, Spanish
All year

Full breakfast
Lunch or dinner (second meal included)
Sitting room, Jacuzzi, fireplace, cable TV

A hill top inn with one of the most spectacular views in New England. The perfect place for weddings, retreats, or family reunions.
cooperhill@juno.com http://www.cooperhillinn.com

ENOSBURG FALLS

Berkson Farms
1205 W Berkshire Rd
Rt. 108 W Berkshire Rd 05450
802-933-2522
Sam & Lisa Hogaboom
All year

55-65-BB
4 rooms, 1 pb
C-yes/S-no/P-yes/H-no

Full breakfast
Special menus by arrangement
Sitting room, bicycles, working dairy farm, farm animals, near golf

Old restored farmhouse, full working dairy farm with large variety of animals.
berkson@together.net http://www.berksonfarms.com

FAIRLEE

Silver Maple Lodge
520 US Route 5 S 05045
802-333-4852 800-666-1946
Scott & Sharon Wright
All year

49-99-BB
15 rooms, 13 pb
Most CC, *Rated*, •
C-yes/S-ltd/P-ltd/H-ltd

Continental breakfast
Sitting room, fireplaces, picnic area, cottages, bicycle & canoe rental

Quaint country inn located in scenic resort area; convenient to antique shops, fishing, golf, swimming, tennis & winter skiing.
scott@silvermaplelodge.com http://www.silvermaplelodge.com

FREDONIA

The White Inn
52 E Main St 14063
716-672-2103 Fax: 716-672-2107
888-FREDONIA
R. Contiguglia & K. Dennison
All year

79-189-BB
23 rooms, 23 pb
Most CC, *Rated*, •
C-ltd/S-no/P-no/H-no

Full breakfast
Please advise on dietary restrictions

A favorite travelers' sojourn for well over half a century, The White Inn welcomes you with all the comfort and charm of a country manor.
inn@whiteinn.com http://www.whiteinn.com

GAYSVILLE

Laolke Lodge
PO Box 107
466 Laury Road 05746
802-234-9205
Ms. Olive Pratt
All year

25-40-BB
5 rooms
Rated, •
C-yes/S-yes/P-ltd/H-no

Full breakfast
Evening meal
Sitting room, piano, pool, color TV, tennis, river swimming, tubing

Family-style vacations in modern, rustic log cabin. Home cooking.
laolke@juno.com

GREENSBORO

Highland Lodge
1608 Craftsbury Rd
Caspian Lake Road 05841
802-533-2647 Fax: 802-533-7494
David & Wilhelmina Smith
5/24–10/14; 12/21–3/17

204-280-MAP
22 rooms, 22 pb
Visa, MC, Disc, •
C-yes/S-ltd/P-no/H-yes
Dutch

Full breakfast
Lunch (fee), dinner included
Sitting rooms, library, tennis, beach, lawn game, golf, lake

A most comfortable, extremely clean, nicely furnished family resort with rooms & cottages. Lakeside beach & 30 miles of packed cross-country ski trails.

highland.lodge@verizon.net http://www.highlandlodge.com/

HARDWICK

Somerset House
PO Box 1098
130 Highland Ave 05843
802-472-5484 800-838-8074
Judith D. Waible All year

79-99-BB
4 rooms, 4 pb
Visa, MC
C-yes/S-no/P-no/H-no

Full breakfast
Beverage and snack upon arrival

An elegant turn-of-the-century house located 1 block from the Lamoille River. Close to hiking trails, lakes, and x-country skiing.

judy@somersethousebb.com http://www.somersethousebb.com

HARTFORD

House of Seven Gables Inn
PO Box 526
1625 Maple St 05047
802-295-1200 Fax: 802-295-1200
800-947-1200
Lani & Kathy Janisse All year

85-150
8 rooms, 2 pb

JAMAICA

Three Mountain Inn
PO Box 180
Main St, Rte 30 05343
802-874-4568 Fax: 802-874-4745
800-532-9399
David & Stacy Hiler
All year

125-325-BB
15 rooms, 15 pb
Visa, MC, AmEx, *Rated*, •
C-ltd/S-no/P-ltd/H-ltd
German

Full breakfast
Dinner, bar
Pub, two large common areas, private night-lit pool

Three Mountain Inn is all about you. Our mission is to exceed your expectations. We hope you will give us the opportunity.

threemtn@sover.net http://www.threemountaininn.com/

JEFFERSONVILLE

Mannsview Inn
916 Rt 108 S Smugglers' Notch 05464
802-644-8321 Fax: 802-644-2006
888-937-6266
Bette & Kelly Mann
All year

75-185-BB
6 rooms, 2 pb
Visa, MC, AmEx, *Rated*, •
C-yes/S-no/P-no/H-no

Full country breakfast
Complimentary wine
Sitting room, library, tournament billiard room, antiques, whirlpool

Nationally recognized c.1855 Colonial on Vermont's most scenic highway, 15 minutes from Stowe. On premises: canoe rentals, shuttle & 10,000 sq.ft. antique center. Closest inn to ski slopes. rsvp@mannsview.com http://www.mannsview.com

KILLINGTON

Birch Ridge Inn
37 Butler Rd 05751
802-422-4293 Fax: 802-422-3406
800-435-8566
Bill Vines & Mary Furlong
All year

80-295-BB
10 rooms, 10 pb
Most CC, *Rated*, •
C-ltd/S-no/P-no/H-yes

Full breakfast
Dinner plans available
Restaurant, fireplace lounge, many rooms have fireplaces and whirlpool tubs

Experience Vermont in style. 10 rooms surrounded by gardens, nestled in the Green Mtns. Start with a country breakfast, finish with fine dining.

innkeepers@birchridge.com http://www.birchridge.com

KILLINGTON

Cortina Inn and Resort 103 US Route 4 05751 802-773-3333 Fax: 802-775-6948 800-451-6108 Robert & Breda Harnish All year	124-199-BB 96 rooms, 96 pb Most CC, *Rated*, • C-yes/S-yes/P-yes/H-yes Spanish, German, French	Hearty Vermont Buffet Breakfast 2 restaurants, lounge, afternoon tea & treats 8 tennis courts, indoor pool, sleigh rides, health spa

Killington's most luxurious inn. Indoor pool, fitness center, game room, ice skating, 2 restaurants, award-winning cuisine. The amenities of a resort hotel, the hospitality of a country inn. cortina1@aol.com http://cortinainn.com

---

Inn at Long Trail PO Box 267 Route 4, Sherburne Pass 05751 802-775-7181 Fax: 802-747-7034 800-325-2540 Murray & Patty McGrath Summer, fall, winter	68-230-BB 19 rooms, 19 pb Visa, MC, AmEx, *Rated*, • C-yes/S-yes/P-ltd/H-ltd	Full breakfast Irish pub (lunch/dinner) Sitting room, hot tub, weekend Irish music

Rustic country inn/ski lodge high in the Vermont mountains. McGrath's Irish Pub serves pub menu daily and has live entertainment on weekends.
ilt@vermontel.net http://www.innatlongtrail.com

Mountain Meadows Lodge 285 Thundering Brook Rd 05751 802-775-1010 Fax: 802-773-4459 800-370-4567 Mark and Michelle Werle	85-140-BB 18 rooms, 18 pb Visa, MC, *Rated*, • C-yes/S-ltd/P-no/H-ltd Ex. 4/15-6/1;10/15-11/21	Full breakfast Dinner (fee), coffee, tea Sitting room, pool, farm animals, mountain getaway packages

A casual, friendly family lodge in a beautiful secluded mountain and lake setting. Complete cross-country ski center.
havefun@mtmeadowslodge.com http://www.mtmeadowslodge.com

The Peak Chalet PO Box 511 184 South View Path 05751 802-422-4278 Diane & Greg Becker All year	64-202-BB 5 rooms, 5 pb Visa, MC, AmEx, *Rated*, • C-ltd/S-no/P-no/H-no German	Continental plus breakfast Private guest living room beautiful with stone fireplace

A peaceful getaway within the heart of the Green Mountains. Each of our guestrooms features a queen-sized four poster, iron, panel or sleigh bed. All have private bath with shower. home@thepeakchalet.com http://www.thepeakchalet.com

---

Snowed Inn 104 Miller Brook Rd 05751 802-422-3407 Fax: 802-422-8126 800-311-5406 Manfred & Jeanne Karlhuber 6/15-4/15	80-200-BB 19 rooms, 19 pb Most CC, *Rated*, • C-yes/S-no/P-no/H-ltd German	Continental plus breakfast Sitting room, Jacuzzis, suites, cable TV, fireplaces

Distinctive country rooms and suites complemented by a fieldstone fireplace lounge, greenhouse breakfast room, outdoor hot tub overlooking brook.
snowedinn@vermontel.net http://www.snowedinn.com/

The Vermont Inn HC 34, Box 37J Rt 4 05751 802-775-0708 Fax: 802-773-9810 800-541-7795 Megan & Greg Smith Memorial Day-April 15	50-205-BB 18 rooms, 18 pb Most CC, *Rated*, • C-ltd/S-no/P-no/H-yes French, Spanish	Full Country breakfast Map available, bar Pool, sauna, whirlpool, tennis, meeting room, A/C & fireplace in some rooms

Award-winning cuisine; fireside dining (winter), spectacular mountain views. Screened porch, weddings. Minutes to Killington and Pico ski area.
relax@vermontinn.com http://www.vermontinn.com

KILLINGTON (REGION)

Mountain Top Inn
195 Mountain Top Rd,
Chittenden 05737
802-483-2311 Fax: 802-483-6373
800-445-2100
Louise Atwood All year

135-375-EP
41 rooms, 41 pb
Visa, MC, AmEx
C-yes/S-no/P-yes/H-yes

MAP available, includes breakfast & dinner
Sauna, game room, endless summer & winter resort activities (see above)

Four-season resort on 345 acres, eleven miles from Killington, Vermont. "Breathtaking views," endless activities. Equestrian and cross-country ski center (85 km of trails). Fine dining. info@mountaintopinn.com http://www.mountaintopinn.com

LINCOLN (REGION)

Firefly Ranch
PO Box 152
Rd.# 1, Bull Run Road, *Bristol*
05443
802-453-2223
Marie-Louise (Issy) Link
All year

75-79-BB
3 rooms, 1 pb
C-ltd/S-no/P-yes/H-no
German, French, Spanish, Dutch

Hearty Country breakfast
Afternoon tea, dinner, wine
Sitting room, jacuzzi, fireplace, swimming pond

A country getaway with emphasis on outdoor activities: hiking, mountain biking, fishing, swimming, Nordic skiing, downhill skiing, snowboarding at Mad River Glen or Sugarbush, within 15 to 30 minutes. link@together.net http://fireflyranch.com

LONDONDERRY (REGION)

Londonderry Inn
8 Melendy Hill Rd
Route 100, *South Londonderry*
05155
802-824-5226 Fax: 802-824-3146
Chrisman & Maya Kearn

136-176-BB
20 rooms, 20 pb
Most CC, *Rated*, •
C-yes/S-no/P-no/H-ltd
All year

Full breakfast
Afternoon cookies/tea; wine/beer, soda, ice cream
Fireplaces, billiards, movie room, pool

Historic Vermont Family Lodge overlooking the West River. Relaxed hospitality, fireplaces, family suites, children welcome, hot buffet breakfast, fresh-baked cookies, spring-fed pool, sledding hill. londinn@sover.net http://www.londonderryinn.com

LUDLOW

Andrie Rose Inn
13 Pleasant St 05149
802-228-4846 Fax: 802-228-7910
800-223-4846
Michael & Irene Maston
All year

80-330-BB
23 rooms, 23 pb
Visa, MC, AmEx, *Rated*, •
C-ltd/S-no/P-no/H-no

Continental plus breakfast
Tea, snacks, bar
Sitting room, library, bicycles, Jacuzzi, suites, fireplace, cable TV

A Triple A 4 Diamond property in elegant c.1829 country village, Okemo Ski Mountain. andrie@mail.tds.net http://www.andrieroseinn.com

---

The Combes Family Inn
953 E Lake Rd 05149
802-228-8799 Fax: 802-228-8704
800-822-8799
Ruth & Bill Combes
Closed 4/15-5/15

65-160-BB
11 rooms, 11 pb
Visa, MC, AmEx, *Rated*, •
C-yes/S-ltd/P-ltd/H-yes
French

Full breakfast
Dinner available
Sitting room, piano, bicycles, with bath & sitting room

The Combes Family Inn is a century-old farmhouse located on a quiet country back road. billcfi@tds.net http://www.combesfamilyinn.com/

The Governor's Inn
86 Main St 05149
802-228-8830 Fax: 802-228-2961
800-468-3766
Jim & Cathy Kubec
All year

105-325-BB
9 rooms, 9 pb
Most CC, *Rated*, •
C-ltd/S-no/P-no/H-no

Full 3 course breakfast
Afternoon tea, Prix Fixe Dinner available weekends
Fully Air conditioned, fireplaces in some rooms

Stylish, romantic, antique furnished, intimate Victorian village Inn c.1890. Extraordinary slate fireplaces, excellent food, cozy rooms, and generous hospitality. info@thegovernorsinn.com http://www.thegovernorsinn.com

LUDLOW

Inn at Water's Edge
45 Kingdom Rd 05149
802-228-8143 Fax: 802-228-8443
888-706-9736
Bruce Verdrager
All year

175-275-MAP
11 rooms, 11 pb
Visa, MC, AmEx, *Rated*
C-ltd/S-no/P-no/H-yes

Full breakfast
Afternoon refreshments
Lakefront English Pub, hot tub, canoeing, bikes, bocce

Rated AAA Four Diamond and recommended by Frommer's, this romantic Victorian inn is located on Echo Lake between Okemo and Killington Resorts.
innatwatersedge@mail.tds.net http://www.innatwatersedge.com

LUDLOW (REGION)

Hawk Inn & Mountain Resort
HCR70 Box 64 Route 100, *Plymouth* 05056
802-672-3811 Fax: 802-672-5585
800-685-HAWK
James N. Nielsen All year

275-600-BB
50 rooms, 50 pb
Most CC, *Rated*, •
C-yes/S-ltd/P-no/H-yes

Full breakfast
Snacks, din., restaurant, lunch in season
Bar service, sitt. rm., library, bikes, tennis, hot tub, sauna, pool

Luxury resort Inn situated in the heart of the Green Mountains. Okomo, Killington & Woodstock nearby. Luxury private villas available.
hawkinn@vermontel.net http://www.hawkresort.com

Golden Stage Inn
PO Box 218
399 Depot Street, *Proctorsville* 05153
802-226-7744 Fax: 802-226-7882
800-253-8226
Sandy & Peter Gregg
All year

75-375-BB
12 rooms, 8 pb
Visa, MC, AmEx, *Rated*, •
C-yes/S-no/P-no/H-yes

Full breakfast
Dinner, afternoon tea, snacks
Sitting room, library, swimming pool, fireplaces, cable TV, wine & beer

State coach stop in the 1790's, later an Underground Railroad link, this historic Colonial inn offers Vermont hospitality. goldenstageinn@tds.net http://www.goldenstageinn.com

---

Whitney Brook
2423 Twenty Mile Stream, *Proctorsville* 05153
802-226-7460
Ellen & Jim Parrish All year

65-102-BB
4 rooms, 2 pb
Most CC
C-ltd/S-no/P-no/H-no

Full breakfast
Afternoon tea
Sitting room, library, Oriental rugs

Restored 1870 country farmhouse, private and quiet, fine dining nearby, centrally located for touring, shopping, hiking, biking, swimming or relaxing near the brook.
whitney_brook@yahoo.com http://www.whitneybrook.com

LYNDONVILLE

The Wildflower Inn
2059 Darling Hill Rd 05851
802-626-8310 Fax: 802-626-3039
800-627-8310
Jim & Mary O'Reilly
All year

95-280-BB
21 rooms, 21 pb
Visa, MC, *Rated*
C-yes/S-no/P-no/H-ltd
Nepali

Full breakfast
Afternoon tea, snacks, dinner available, snack bar
Pool, hot tub, sauna, tennis & basketball courts, nature trails, restaurant

You're sure to enjoy roaming over the Inn's property, discovering the amenities the Wildflower Inn has to offer the single traveler, family, or group.
info@wildflowerinn.com http://www.wildflowerinn.com

MANCHESTER

1811 House
PO Box 39
route 7 A 05254
802-362-1811 Fax: 802-362-2443
800-432-1811
M. Bruce Duff & C. Jorge Veleta All year

140-280-BB
14 rooms, 14 pb
Most CC, *Rated*, •
C-ltd/S-no/P-no/H-no

Full breakfast
Complimentary sherry
Sitting room, library, canopy beds, fireplaces, gardens, pond, Mt. view

Unequaled charm in a Revolutionary War-era building furnished with English & American antiques. house1811@adelphia.net http://www.1811house.com

MANCHESTER

The Inn at Manchester PO Box 41 3967 Main St 05254 802-362-1793 Fax: 802-362-3218 800-273-1793 Ron & Mary Blake All year	129-249-BB 18 rooms, 18 pb Most CC, *Rated*, • C-ltd/S-no/P-no/H-no	Full breakfast Complimentary wine, afternoon tea Sitting room, library, fireplace, piano, swim pool, 3 lounges, porch, A/C

Casual elegance & warm hospitality. Charming guestrooms, comfortable & inviting common areas. Beautiful grounds, gardens, pool, patio.
stay@innatmanchester.com http://www.innatmanchester.com

Manchester Highlands Inn PO Box 1754 216 Highland Ave 05255 802-362-4565 Fax: 802-362-4028 800-743-4565 Patricia & Robert Eichorn	105-175-BB 15 rooms, 15 pb Visa, MC, AmEx, *Rated*, • C-ltd/S-yes/P-no/H-no Exc. midweek Apr & Nov	Full breakfast Dinner by arrangement Sitting rm., bar, snacks, 7 rooms with canopy beds, carriage house remodeled

Romantic Victorian inn, charming rooms. Resident cat. Homemade country breakfast-in-bed. Gas fireplaces in 3 rooms and dining room.
relax@highlandsinn.com http://www.highlandsinn.com

Reluctant Panther Inn & Rest. PO Box 678 39 West Rd 05254 802-362-2568 Fax: 802-362-2586 800-822-2331 Maye & Robert H. Bachofen	139-479-BB 21 rooms, 21 pb Most CC, *Rated*, • C-ltd/S-no/P-no/H-no French, German, Spanish All year	Full breakfast Dinner, restaurant Fireplaces, cable TV, accommodate business travelers

Romantic country Inn for couples only. Well known for spectacular suites with Jacuzzis for two, fireplace in bathroom, and a second fireplace in the bedroom. Exquisite restaurant on premises. stay@reluctantpanther.com http://www.reluctantpanther.com

MANCHESTER (REGION)

Landgrove Inn 132 Landgrove Rd, *Landgrove* 05148 802-824-6673 Fax: 802-824-6790 800-669-8466 Tom & Moreen Checkia	90-285-BB 18 rooms, 16 pb Visa, MC, AmEx, • C-yes/S-no/P-yes/H-ltd 5/20–10/20; 11/20–4/1	Full breakfast Dinner, afternoon tea, restaurant, bar service Sitting room, tennis, swimming pool, suites, fireplcs, accom. bus. travel.

Over the river and through the woods, a true country inn. Family run for over 40 years, groomed cross country with rentals, horse drawn sleigh and carriage.
vtinn@sover.net http://www.landgroveinn.com

Macartney House 24 VT RTE 11, *Landgrove* 05148 802-824-6444 Fax: 802-824-4335 802-824-6444 James & Elaine Nelson-Parker Mid May–Mid April	105-250-BB 7 rooms, 7 pb Visa, MC, AmEx C-no/S-no/P-no/H-no French, German	Full breakfast Afternoon tea; fully licensed Pub Living room; 2 person whirlpool tubs, fireplaces, private decks

Beautiful, newly refurbished country Inn. Peaceful, romantic farmhouse surrounded by National Forest with trails for guests. English antiques and art. Minutes from Manchester, Stratton, Bromley. Stay@MacartneyHouse.com http://www.MacartneyHouse.com

The Inn at Ormsby Hill 1842 Main St Historic Route 7A, *Manchester Center* 05255 802-362-1163 Fax: 802-362-5176 800-670-2841 Ted & Chris Sprague	150-BB 10 rooms, 10 pb Visa, MC, *Rated*, • C-ltd/S-no/P-no/H-yes All year	Full breakfast Afternoon tea Sitting room, library, all rooms have a fireplace and Jacuzzi for two

Renowned for comfort, heartfelt hospitality and profound attention to detail. Canopies, fireplaces, and air-conditioning. stay@ormsbyhill.com http://www.ormsbyhill.com

MANCHESTER (REGION)

Johnny Seesaw's PO Box 68 3574 VT Route 11, *Peru* 05152 802-824-5966 Fax: 802-824-5533 800-424-CSAW Gary & Nancy Okun All year exc. April–May	80-198-BB 30 rooms, 27 pb Visa, MC, Disc, *Rated*, • C-yes/S-yes/P-yes/H-ltd French	Full breakfast Dinner (MAP winter) Afternoon tea, full bar, tennis, swimming pool, library, sitting room

Unique country lodge, rooms with private baths, cottages with king beds & fireplaces, licensed pub, full dining room, quarter mile E. of Bromley Mt.
gary@jseesaw.com http://www.johnnyseesaw.com

Ira Allen House PO Box 251 6311 Rte 7A, *Sunderland* 05250 802-362-2284 Fax: 802-362-2284 888-733-8666 Sandy & Ray Walters All year	90-120-BB 5 rooms, 5 pb C-yes/S-no/P-ltd/H-no	Full breakfast Afternoon tea Sitting room, library, Jacuzzi, suite, fireplace, families welcome, cable TV

Historic inn home of Ethan located on the Battenkill River in a four season resort area; lovely suites, sumptuous breakfasts.
stay@iraallenhouse.com http://www.iraallenhouse.com

Village Country Inn PO Box 408 Historic Route 7A 05254 802-362-1792 Fax: 802-362-7238 800-370-0300 Anne & Jay Degen All year	129-295-BB 32 rooms, 32 pb Most CC, *Rated*, • C-ltd/S-no/P-no/H-ltd	Full breakfast Candlelight dinner available-special guest price Tavern, sitting room, pool, fireplaces in luxury rooms, dining room, A/C

"A Boutique Hotel" with country inn personalized service. Located in the heart of the Green Mountains. mauve@vermontel.net http://www.villagecountryinn.com

The Wilburton Inn PO Box 468 River Road 05254 802-362-2500 Fax: 802-362-1107 800-648-4944 G. Levis All year	125-250-BB 35 rooms, 35 pb Visa, MC, AmEx, *Rated*, • C-yes/S-ltd/P-ltd/H-ltd	Full breakfast Afternoon tea, bar service Swimming pool, library, tennis court, canoeing, bicycle touring, hiking

A twenty acre Victorian estate overlooking spectacular Battenkill Valley. Sculptures, flowers, and artworks adorn the estate. wilbuinn@sover.net http://www.wilburton.com

MENDON

Red Clover Inn 7 Woodward Road 05701 802-775-2290 Fax: 802-773-0594 800-752-0571 M. & D. Strelecki & M. Davis All year	170-495-MAP 14 rooms, 14 pb Most CC, *Rated*, • C-ltd/S-no/P-ltd/H-ltd	4 course candlelit gourmet dinner In ground pool, Keeping Room with library, pub, fireplaces

Nestled on 13 majestic areas in central Vermont is a flower of a country inn. Red clover, the state flower of Vermont and the Inn, the former 1840's summer home of General John Woodward, awaits you. innkeepers@redcloverinn.com http://www.redcloverinn.com

MIDDLEBURY (REGION)

The Inn at Lovers Lane PO Box 66 3740 Rte 125, *Bridport* 05734 802-758-2185 Pam & John Freilich All year	75-145-BB 3 rooms, 3 pb Visa, MC, Disc, *Rated* C-ltd/S-no/P-no/H-no French	Full breakfast Snacks, wine Sitting room, suites, fireplace, A/C, sunroom, breakfast room & deck

Magnificent mountain & meadow views, expansive grounds, elegantly appointed rooms await at our spacious, yet intimate, c.1830 Greek Revival Inn.
innatloverslane@gmavt.net http://www.bbhost.com/loverslane

MILTON

Wright's Bay 1820
81 Eagle Mtn Harbor Rd 05468
802-893-6717 Fax: 802-524-0084
Bette Wood
May -November

85-125-BB
7 rooms, 7 pb
Visa, MC, AmEx
C-yes/S-no/P-no/H-ltd

Continental plus breakfast
Sitting room, tennis court, cottages, private beach

Private guest suite in 1820 farmhouse. Cottages on Lake Champlain. Private beach, tennis, biking, in country setting. bette81@aol.com http://www.vermontbedbreakfast.com

MONTGOMERY

The Black Lantern Inn
PO Box 128
2057 N Main St, Rte 118 05470
802-326-4507 Fax: 802-326-4077
800-255-8661
Deb Winders
All year

104-195-MAP
15 rooms, 15 pb
Most CC, •
C-yes/S-ltd/P-no/H-no

Full breakfast
Dinner, restaurant, bar
Sitting room, bicycles, Jacuzzi, suites, fireplace, cable TV, conferences

Winter: Cross-country skiing from door; 15 minutes from Jay Peak Ski Area. Summer: Swimming in natural waterfalls, near long trail, country auctions.
blantern@together.net http://www.blacklantern.com

MONTGOMERY CENTER

The Inn on Trout River
PO Box 76
241 Main Street 05471
802-326-4391 Fax: 802-326-3194
800-338-7049
Lee & Michael Forman
All year

83-125-BB
10 rooms, 10 pb
Most CC, *Rated*, •
C-yes/S-no/P-no/H-no

Full breakfast
Dinner available, bar service
Sitting room, library, bicycles, tennis court, fireplaces

Vermont Historic District; 7 covered bridges; downhill vast snowmobiles trails. 10 rooms, private baths, queen beds, down comforters.
info@troutinn.com http://www.troutinn.com

Phineas Swann
PO Box 43
Main St 05471
802-326-4306 Fax: 802-326-4306
G. Bartolomeo & M. Bindler
All year

89-175-BB
6 rooms, 6 pb
Most CC, •
C-ltd/S-no/P-no/H-no

Full gourmet breakfast
Afternoon tea, snacks
Sitting room, library, tennis court, Jacuzzis, fireplaces, gardens, sun deck

A light hearted country Victorian, with hard wood floors French doors and a cozy fireplace to set the relaxed atmosphere. Guests have the choice of fine B&B or superlative suites.
phineas@sover.net http://www.phineasswann.com

MONTPELIER

Betsy's
74 East State St 05602
802-229-0466 Fax: 802-229-5412
Jon & Betsy Anderson
All year

75-105-BB
12 rooms, 12 pb
Most CC, *Rated*, •
C-yes/S-no/P-no/H-no
Spanish

Full breakfast
Snacks, fruit
Parlor, living rooms, kitchens, gardens

Set in a quiet historic district two blocks from town, Betsy's is both comfortably homey and romantically Victorian. The beds are so comfortable, breakfast just has to be good.
betsysbnb@adelphia.net http://www.betsysbnb.com

The Inn at Montpelier
147 Main St 05602
802-223-2727 Fax: 802-223-0722
Rick & Rita Rizza
All year

104-177-BB
19 rooms, 19 pb
Most CC, *Rated*
C-yes/S-no/P-no/H-no

Generous continental plus breakfast
Full bar, snacks
Sitting room, fireplaces, cable TV, accommodate businss travelers

An elegant, historic Inn, in the capital city. Each room is furnished with unique antiques, art and fine reproductions. Best porch in Vermont.
mail2inn@aol.com http://www.InnatMontpelier.com

MONTPELIER (REGION)

Northfield Inn
228 Highland Ave, *Northfield* 05663
802-485-8558
Aglaia Stalb All year

85-159-BB
12 rooms, 8 pb
Visa, MC, *Rated*, •
C-ltd/S-no/P-no/H-no
Greek

Full gourmet breakfast
Lunch & dinner for groups by arrangement
Complimentary wine, snacks, new fitness room

Turn-of-the-century mansion, once occupied by a princess, has been restored to its original Victorian elegance. Tastefully decorated with period furnishings.
northfieldinn@aol.com

MORGAN

Seymour Lake Lodge
28 Valley Rd 05853
802-895-2752 Fax: 802-895-2752
Brian & Joan DuMoulin
All year

65-BB
8 rooms, 1 pb
Visa, MC, •
C-yes/S-ltd/P-yes/H-yes
French

Continental plus breakfast
Full breakfast buffet for $6.00 extra per person.
Library, beach, boats, kitchen, camp fires, fireplaces

Vermont lodge B&B, waterfront, lake, beach, boats, fishing, antique shop, hiking, biking, hunting, swimming, snowmobiling, vast trails, skiing, kitchen facilities.
seymourlodge@fcgnetworks.net http://www.seymourlakelodge.com

MOUNT SNOW (REGION)

Deerfield Valley Inn
PO Box 1834
Rt 100, *West Dover* 05356
802-464-6333 Fax: 802-464-6336
800-639-3588
Doreen Cooney All year

89-179-BB
9 rooms, 9 pb
Most CC, *Rated*
C-yes/S-no/P-no/H-no

Full breakfast
Afternoon tea, snacks
Sitting room, fireplace, cable TV, conference facilities

Charming country inn built in 1885. All guestrooms are individually decorated, some Wood-burning fireplaces, all w/ private bathrooms & TVs.
deerinn@vermontel.com http://www.deerfieldvalleyinn.com

Snow Goose Inn at Mt. Snow
PO Box 366
Route 100, *West Dover* 05356
802-464-3984 Fax: 802-464-5322
888-604-7964
Philip Waller All year

95-395-BB
13 rooms, 13 pb
Visa, MC, AmEx, *Rated*, •
C-yes/S-no/P-yes/H-yes

Full country breakfast
Complimentary wine, snacks
Full housekeeping, waitress service, reception message center, mail posting

Ideal for that romantic getaway from the hassle of city life. Comfort and charm amid 3 wooded acres, pond and country gardens, antique filled rooms, in-room fireplaces and Jacuzzis. reservations@snowgooseinn.com http://www.snowgooseinn.com

NEWFANE

The Four Columns Inn
On the Green 05345
802-365-7713 Fax: 802-365-0022
800-787-6633
Pam & Gorty Baldwin
All year

115-340-BB
15 rooms, 15 pb
Most CC, *Rated*, •
C-yes/S-no/P-ltd/H-ltd

Continental plus breakfast
Afternoon tea, dinner available, Restaurant
Bar service, sitting room, Jacuzzis, pool, suites, fireplaces, cable TV

Innkeepers are friendly and hospitable, making the Inn a happy and comfortable place to be. Recently featured in Country Home Magazine, Travel Holiday and Country Inns Magazine. innkeeper@fourcolumnsinn.com http://www.fourcolumnsinn.com

NEWFANE (REGION)

Inn at South Newfane
369 Dover Rd, *South Newfane* 05351
802-348-7191 877-548-7191
Neville & Dawn Cullen
All year

89-130-BB
6 rooms, 6 pb
Most CC, *Rated*, •
C-ltd/S-no/P-no/H-no

Full or Continental Plus breakfast
Lunch/dinner available, restaurant
Bar service, sitting room, library, fireplaces

Quiet country inn, spacious rocking chair porch overlooking spring fed pond, al fresco dining, int'l cuisine nightly, wedding destination.
cullinn@sover.net http://www.innatsouthnewfane.com

NORTH HERO ISLAND

Charlie's Northland Lodge	70-75-BB	Continental or Continental Plus
3829 US Rt 2 05474	3 rooms, 1 pb	Complimentary wine
802-372-8822	Visa, MC, Disc, *Rated*, •	Sitting room, bicycles, lake, sailing, canoeing, fishing, kayaking
Dorice Clark	C-ltd/S-no/P-no/H-no	
All year		

A snug B&B in a quiet village setting on Lake Champlain. A place to go to fish, sail, bike or just plain relax. dorclrk@aol.com

NORTHEAST KINGDOM (REGION)

Guildhall Inn	49-59-BB	Full breakfast
PO Box 129	4 rooms	Dinner, snacks
Route 102, *Guildhall* 05905	C-ltd/S-no/P-no/H-no	Sitting room, cable TV
802-676-3720 800-987-8240		
Steve & Eleanor Degnan		
All year		

Tranquil historic village inn surrounded by mountains. The inn is located along the Connecticut River within short driving distance to many nearby attractions.
elinvt@aol.com http://www.guildhallinn.com

PUTNEY

Beckwood Pond	95-160-BB	Three Course Gourmet Breakfast
1107 Route 5 05346	5 rooms, 5 pb	Complimentary tea, coffee, wine, homebaked treats
802-254-5900 Fax: 802-254-8456	Visa, MC, AmEx, *Rated*, •	Antiques, English Gift Shop, Gardens, Woods, Fireplace in Great Room
866-228-6868	C-ltd/S-no/P-no/H-ltd	
Helene & Alan Saxby	Some Spanish	
All year		

English Innkeepers of an 1803 Colonial on 14 acres with Gardens, woodlands, Antiques, family heirlooms. beckwood@sover.net http://www.beckwoodpond.com

Hickory Ridge House	125-185-BB	Full breakfast
53 Hickory Ridge Rd South 05346	8 rooms, 8 pb	Afternoon tea
802-387-5709 Fax: 802-387-4328	Visa, MC, AmEx, *Rated*	Sitting room, fireplaces, cable TV, accommodate business travelers
800-380-9218	C-ltd/S-no/P-no/H-yes	
Miriam & Cory Greenspan	Spanish	
All year		

Located on a quiet country road in Putney, Vermont, and listed in the National Register of Historic Places, Hickory Ridge House offers modern convenience in a private, rural setting. hickory@sover.net http://www.hickoryridgehouse.com

Ranney-Crawford House	110-135-BB	Full breakfast
1097 Westminster W Rd 05346	4 rooms	Fireplace
802-387-4150 800-731-5502	Visa, MC, AmEx	
Arnie & Diane Glim	C-ltd/S-no/P-no/H-no	
All year		

An elegant, historic, brick Federal bed and breakfast, near Putney, Vermont, located on a scenic country road, surrounded by farms and meadows. Full gourmet breakfast and comfortable accommodations.
arnyglim@zdnetmail.com http://www.ranney-crawford.com

RANDOLPH

Sweetserenity	75-110-BB	Full breakfast
40 Randolph Ave 05060	3 rooms, 1 pb	Tea, coffee, hot chocolate, cookies, pie or cake
802-728-9590 Fax: 775-414-9487	Most CC, •	Library
888-491-9590	C-ltd/S-no/P-no/H-no	
Don & Evelyn Sweetser		
All year		

Our 1870, 11 room house welcomes you with 3 guest bedrooms. Each room with its own character. We are at the edge of the Montague Golf Course and at the edge of town.
comment@sover.net http://www.sweet-serenity.com

RANDOLPH

Three Stallion Inn
Stock Farm Rd 05060
802-728-5575 Fax: 802-728-4036
800-424-5575
Martina Rutkovsky
All year

102-162-BB
15 rooms, 13 pb
Most CC, •
C-yes/S-no/P-yes/H-ltd

Continental plus breakfast
Full service restaurant and pub
Pool, fitness center, whirlpool, sauna, tennis courts, 35 km trails

In the center of Vermont on 1,300 acres, the Three Stallion Inn offers the most modern of amenities; comfortable guest rooms, a restaurant and pub. Come and enjoy the unspoiled beauty of Vermont. info@3stallioninn.com http://www.threestallioninn.com

RIPTON

The Chipman Inn
PO Box 115
Route 125 05766
802-388-2390 Fax: 802-388-2390
800-890-2390
Joyce Henderson & Bill Pierce
Closed Apr. & Nov.

85-135-BB
8 rooms, 8 pb
Most CC, *Rated*
C-ltd/S-ltd/P-no/H-no
French, Arabic, Swahili

Full breakfast
Dinner available
Bar service, sitting room, candlelit dining room

Beautiful 1828 inn in a Green Mountain village. Fine dining for guests. Skiing, country walking & sightseeing. Warm hospitality.
smudge@together.net http://www.chipmaninn.com

ROYALTON (REGION)

Fox Stand Inn
5615 Rt 14, *South Royalton* 05068
802-763-8437
Jean & Gary Curley
All year

75-85-BB
5 rooms
Visa, MC, *Rated*
C-ltd/S-no/P-no/H-no

Full breakfast (Inn guests only)
Restaurant open Tue. thru Sat. nights
Licensed tavern, river fishing, and swimming

Three-story brick building, originally a stage coach stop. Chef owned and operated for the last 18 years. Conveniently located 1 mile off I-89 on RT14 bordering the White River.
foxstand@aol.com http://www.foxstandinn.com

RUTLAND

Harvest Moon
1659 N. Grove St 05701
802 773-0889
Matthew, Susan, & Jesse
All year

75-135-BB
2 rooms, 2 pb
Visa, MC, Disc, •
C-yes/S-no/P-ltd/H-ltd

Full breakfast
Tea, home baked goods
Living room with TV/VCR, parlor with gas stove, piano and antiquatian books,

Set amidst green hills and rolling hayfields in the Rutland Valley, this Classic 1835 Greek Revival farmhouse conjures old New England.
relax@harvestmoonvt.com http://www.harvestmoonvt.com

The Inn at Rutland
70 N Main St 05701
802-773-0575 Fax: 802-775-3506
800-808-0575
Leslie & Steven Brenner

100-205-BB
11 rooms, 11 pb
Most CC, *Rated*, •
C-yes/S-no/P-no/H-no
All year

3 course gourmet breakfast
Afternoon tea
A/C, TV & phone in rooms, library, 3 ski areas nearby

Beautifully restored 1889 Victorian home with 11 guestrooms furnished with antiques, fine linens & comfortable seating areas. Wonderful mountain views.
relax@innatrutland.com http://www.innatrutland.com

SHREWSBURY (REGION)

Maple Crest Farm
2512 Lincoln Hill Rd, *Cuttingsville* 05738
802-492-3367 Fax: 802-492-3367
William & Donna Smith
February-December

55-85-BB
9 rooms, 4 pb
Rated
C-yes/S-no/P-no/H-ltd

Full breakfast
Afternoon tea, snacks
Sitting room, library, suites, fireplaces

1808 Federal style, 27 room home, high in the Green Mountains, lovingly preserved for 7 generations. 320 acres to hike or walk. Furnished with antiques, 10 miles south of Rutland, 12 miles to Ludlow. maplecrestbandb@aol.com

SPRINGFIELD

Hartness House Inn
30 Orchard St 05156
802-885-2115 Fax: 805-885-2207
800-732-4789
Carolyn & Michael Hofford
All year

89-150-BB
Most CC, *Rated*, •
C-yes/S-yes/P-no/H-no
German

Full country breakfast
dinner available, dining room, bar
Sitting room, swimming pool with deck, brookside nature trails

A 1903 historic landmark built by Governor James Hartness. Nightly tours of underground museum & operating Turret Equatorial Tracking Telescope.
innkeeper@hartnesshouse.com http://www.hartnesshouse.com

ST. ALBANS (REGION)

Inn at Buck Hollow Farm
2150 Buck Hollow Rd, *Fairfax* 05454
802-849-2400 Fax: 802-849-9744
800-849-7985
Brad Schwartz
All year

73-93-BB
4 rooms
Visa, MC, *Rated*, •
C-yes/S-no/P-yes/H-no

Full breakfast
Beer & wine
Sun room, Jacuzzi, pool, hot tub/spa, play area, antique shop

Our intimate inn features canopy beds, antique decor, beamed ceilings, heated pool, fireplace, Jacuzzi and 400 spectacular acres.
inn@buckhollow.com http://buckhollow.com

STOWE

1066 Ye Olde England Inne
433 Mountain Rd 05672
802-253-7064 Fax: 802-253-8944
800-477-3771
Christopher & Linda Francis
All year

99-299-BB
23 rooms, 23 pb
Visa, MC, *Rated*, •
C-yes/S-yes/P-ltd/H-no
French, Arabic

Full gourmet breakfast
Dinner available, afternoon tea
Library, piano, pool, pub, banquet center, polo & gliding packages

Award-winning, full service, luxury country hotel for couples. Offering beautiful Laura Ashley rooms and spacious, romantic suites. Fine and casual dining plus an authentic English Country Pub. englandinn@aol.com http://www.englandinn.com

---

Andersen Lodge–Austrian Inn
3430 Mountain Rd 05672
802-253-7336 Fax: 802-253-4715
800-336-7336
Dietmar & Getrude Heiss
Season Inquire

68-145-BB
17 rooms, 16 pb
Most CC, *Rated*, •
C-yes/S-yes/P-ltd/H-no
German, French

Full breakfast
Piano, game room, spa, Jacuzzi, tennis court, heated pool, golf nearby

Set in relaxing surroundings with lovely view of mountains. Trout fishing, horseback riding, mountain hiking.
trude@stoweaccess.com http://www.andersensaustrianinn.com

Auberge de Stowe
692 S Main St 05672
802-253-7787 800-387-8789
Chantal & Shawn Kerivan
All year

59-98-BB
8 rooms, 4 pb
Most CC
C-yes/S-no/P-no/H-no
French, German

Continental plus breakfast
Sitting room, Jacuzzis, swimming pool, fireplaces

Something for everyone in this charming old farmhouse turned B&B.
info@aubergedestowe.com http://aubergedestowe.com

Brass Lantern Inn
717 Maple St 05672
802-253-2229 Fax: 802-253-7425
800-729-2980
Andy Aldrich
All year

90-225-BB
9 rooms, 9 pb
Visa, MC, AmEx, *Rated*, •
C-yes/S-no/P-no/H-no

Full country breakfast
Afternoon tea, snacks, bar
Gourmet dining, shops nearby, sit. room w/piano, library, fireplaces, A/C

1810 farmhouse & carriage barn, features: antiques, quilts, stenciling, whirlpool baths, fireplaces, activity packages. Award winning breakfast & building restoration.
brasslntrn@aol.com http://www.brasslanterninn.com

STOWE

Buccaneer Country Lodge
3214 Mountain Rd 05672
802-253-4772 Fax: 802-253-9486
800-543-1293
Karen & Rod Zbikowski
All year

69-295-BB
12 rooms, 12 pb
Most CC, *Rated*, •
C-yes/S-no/P-ltd/H-no

Full breakfast
Jacuzzis, swimming pool, suites, fireplaces, cable TV

Cozy lodge that blends the atmosphere of country inn with privacy and convenience of contemporary lodging. Charming, mountain view rooms or full kitchen suites with antiques, canopy beds & fireplaces.
buclodge@sover.net http://www.buccaneerlodge.com

Butternut Inn
2309 Mountain Rd 05672
802-253-4277 Fax: 802-253-5263
800-3-BUTTER
Janis & Parker Diamond
6/15-10/20; 12/18-4/20

65-250-BB
18 rooms, 18 pb
Visa, MC, *Rated*, •
C-yes/S-no/P-no/H-no

Full country breakfast
Dinner (winter)
Comp. sherry, aftn. tea, sitting room, piano, sunroom, courtyard, pool

A country estate-like setting on 8 riverfront acres. Enjoy the courtyard filled with perennials, relax by the fountain, enjoy the koi fish pond.
innstowe2@aol.com http://www.travelguides.com/home/butternut/

The Gables Inn
1457 Mountain Rd 05672
802-253-7730 Fax: 802-253-8989
800-GABLES-1
Monachelli & Stern
All year

85-250-BB
18 rooms, 18 pb
Most CC, *Rated*, •
C-yes/S-no/P-ltd/H-ltd

Full breakfast
Summer Lunch, Autumn and Winter Dinner.
Sitting room, fireplace, swimming pool, hot tub, Jacuzzis, A/C

Stowe's Classic Vermont Country inn-antiques, wide plank floors, panoramic view. Rooms range from cozy inn rooms to luxury accommodations with Jacuzzis and fireplaces. Our breakfast is legendary. inngables@aol.com http://www.gablesinn.com

---

Green Mountain Inn
PO Box 60
18 S Main St 05672
802-253-7301 Fax: 802-253-5096
800-253-7302
Patti Clark All year

109-359-EP
100 rooms, 100 pb
Most CC, *Rated*, •
C-yes/S-no/P-ltd/H-ltd

Full & continental available
Complimentary afternoon tea
Unique shops, heated outdoor pool, health club, conference/banquet fac.

Enjoy a beautifully restored 1833 resort in the heart of historic Stowe. The Inn offers the perfect blend of classic country elegance & modern comfort, in antique-furnished rooms & luxurious suites. webmaster@gminn.com http://www.greenmountaininn.com

---

Honeywood Inn
4527 Mountain Rd
4583 Mountain Rd 05672
802-253-4124 Fax: 802-253-7050
1-800-821-7891
Carolyn & Bill Cook
All year

85-199-BB
10 rooms, 10 pb
Most CC, *Rated*, •
C-ltd/S-no/P-no/H-no

Full breakfast
Afternoon tea, during regular and high season
Large livingroom, satellite TV room, heated pool(summer), 2 hot tubs

Warm hospitality awaits you in our cozy 3 diamond awarded B&B, nestled at the base of the highest mountain in Vermont. Babbling brook, waterfall, wooded walking trail on our 9 beautiful acres. honeywd@aol.com http://www.honeywoodinn.com

---

The Siebeness Inn
3681 Mountain Rd 05672
802-253-8942 Fax: 802-253-9232
800-426-9001
William Ruffing
All year

75-225-BB
12 rooms, 12 pb
Most CC, •
S-no/P-no/H-ltd

Full breakfast
Compl. beverages & snacks, aft. tea/hot cider
Lounge, hot tub, biking, pool, AC, fieldstone fireplace, sitting rm.

Let our charming B&B inn be the setting for your next romantic getaway. Guestrooms are tastefully decorated with country antiques, canopy, brass or four-poster beds, fluffy quilts and stenciling. siebeness@aol.com http://www.siebeness.com

STOWE

Ski Inn
Rt 108
Mountain Road 05672
802-253-4050
Mrs. Larry Heyer
All year

45-65-BB
10 rooms, 5 pb
Rated
C-ltd/S-no/P-ltd/H-no
French

Continental breakfast
Full breakfast (winter)
Dinner (optional) golf & tennis nearby

This comfortable inn, noted for good food and good conversation, is a great gathering place for interesting people. http://ski-inn.com/pl

---

Stone Hill Inn
89 Houston Farm Rd 05672
802-253-6282 Fax: 802-253-7415
Amy & Hap Jordan
Closed early April–May

250-375-BB
9 rooms, 9 pb
Most CC
C-no/S-no/P-no/H-yes

Full breakfast
Snacks, soft drinks & mixers provided
Sitting room, Jacuzzi, fireplace, cable TV

Romantic and luxurious. Nine lavishly decorated guestrooms, each with fireside two-person Jacuzzi and king-size bed. stay@stonehillinn.com http://www.stonehillinn.com

---

Stowe Inn at Little River
123 Mountain Rd 05672
802-253-4836 Fax: 802-253-7308
800-227-1108
Miranda & Steve Batiste
All year

65-219-BB
43 rooms, 43 pb
Most CC, •
C-yes/S-ltd/P-ltd/H-yes

Continental breakfast
Lunch, dinner, restaurant
Restaurant, sitting rooms, hot-tub, swimming pool, suite, fireplaces

Beautiful 1825 Village Inn and riverside restaurant, perfectly located. Full service Inn with 43 deluxe or traditional rooms with king or twin double beds, private bath and cable TV.
info@stoweinn.com http://www.stoweinn.com

Three Bears at The Fountain
1049 Pucker St Rte 100 05672
802-253-7671 Fax: 802-253-8804
800-898-9634
Stephen & Suzanne Vazzano
All year

85-300-BB
6 rooms, 6 pb
Visa, MC, AmEx, *Rated*
C-ltd/S-no/P-ltd/H-no

Full breakfast
Afternoon tea and sweets always available
Hot tub, Living room w/fireplace and video library, player piano, game area

"Where everything is just right." Romance and relaxation await you in Stowes oldest guest house. Full breakfast, mountain views and hot tub.
threebears@stowevt.net http://www.threebearsbandb.com

Timberholm Inn
452 Cottage Club Rd 05672
802-253-7603 Fax: 802-253-8559
800-753-7603
Darrick Pitstick
All year

79-159-BB
10 rooms, 10 pb
Rated, •

Full breakfast

Nestled in the woods, perfect for the active outdoorsman or the couple that just wants to sit on the deck and enjoy the mountain view.
info@timberholm.com http://www.timberholm.com

STOWE (REGION)

Fitch Hill Inn
258 Fitch Hill Rd, *Hyde Park* 05655
802-888-3834 Fax: 802-888-7789
800-639-2903
Sharon & Gary Coquillette
All year

85-205-BB
6 rooms, 6 pb
Most CC, *Rated*, •
C-ltd/S-no/P-no/H-no
Spanish

Full breakfast
Tea, cocoa, cider or lemonade, cookies
Hot tub, video tape library, games

Quiet retreat on 3+ acres overlooking Green Mountains. Beautifully renovated 200-year-old farmhouse with 6 guestrooms including 2 deluxe rooms with fireplace/Jacuzzi. Award-winning breakfasts. fitchinn@sover.net http://www.fitchhillinn.com

STOWE (REGION)

Village Victorian
107 Union St, *Morrisville* 05661
802-888-8850 Fax: 802-888-8976
1-866-266-4672
Ellen & Philip Wolff
All year

60-120-BB
4 rooms, 4 pb
Visa, MC, AmEx, •
C-yes/S-no/P-no/H-no

Full breakfast
Queen beds, TV/VCRs, videos, air conditioners, hair dryers, fireplace area

Enjoy the grace and charm of our beautiful 1890's Victorian in the heart of the village of Morrisville, just 7 miles from Stowe, where everything says "welcome"! Let us be your home away from home. lan@villagevictorian.com http://www.villagevictorian.com

---

Thatcher Brook Inn
PO Box 490
1017 Waterbury Stowe Rd, *Waterbury* 05676
802-244-5911 Fax: 802-244-1294
800-292-5911
John & Lisa Fischer
All year

80-195-BB
21 rooms, 21 pb
Most CC, *Rated*, •
C-ltd/S-no/P-no/H-yes
French

Full country breakfast
Dinner packages (fee)
Restaurant, pub, in-room whirlpools, fireplaces, gazebo porches

Charming country inn with exceptional dining by candlelight, or on our long wraparound porch. info@thatcherbrook.com http://www.thatcherbrook.com

---

The Black Locust Inn
5088 Waterbury-Stowe Rd, *Waterbury Center* 05677
802-244-7490 Fax: 802-244-8473
800-366-5592
Len, Nancy & Valerie Vignola

125-225-BB
6 rooms, 6 pb
Visa, MC, Disc, *Rated*
C-ltd/S-no/P-no/H-ltd
All year

Full 3 course candlelite breakfast
Afternoon hors doeuvres, complimentary wines.
Sitting room, day spa, hammock

A tranquil getaway you can call home! Elegantly restored 1832 farmhouse. 6 pristine guestrooms. 3 course candlelit breakfast.
relax@blacklocustinn.com http://www.blacklocustinn.com

VERGENNES

Strong House Inn
94 W Main St 05491
802-877-3337 Fax: 802-877-2599
Mary Bargiel
All year

90-275-BB
14 rooms, 14 pb
Visa, MC, AmEx, *Rated*, •
C-ltd/S-no/P-no/H-yes

Full country breakfast
Lunch/dinner avail., snacks, tea
Sitting room, suites, fireplaces, beverage license for beer/wine, cable TV

Atmosphere abounds at this historic inn. From the restored inn furnished in period furniture and antiques to the six acres of gardens, ponds and walking trails.
innkeeper@stronghouseinn.com http://www.stronghouseinn.com

WAITSFIELD

Featherbed Inn
5864 Main St
Rt 100 05673
802-496-7151 Fax: 802-496-7933
Clive & Tracey Coutts
All year

95-150-BB
10 rooms, 10 pb
Visa, MC, AmEx, •
C-ltd/S-no/P-no/H-no

Full breakfast
Afternoon tea, snacks
Sitting room, library, suites, fireplace, accom. bus. travelers

Country farmhouse (c.1806) and cottage, spacious, tastefully decorated guestrooms with cozy featherbeds and antiques, specialty breakfast elegantly served.
featherbedinn@madriver.com http://www.featherbedinn.com

Inn at Mad River Barn
2549 Mill Brook Rd 05673
802-496-3310 Fax: 802-496-6696
800-631-0466
Betsy Pratt
All year

77-135-BB
15 rooms, 15 pb

Full breakfast
Gameroom, in-ground pool, mountain environment, private baths

For some a visit to Vermont will include a stay in a ski lodge that was established before 1950 on 800 acres of woodlands and gardens.
madriverbarn@madriver.com http://www.madriverbarn.com

WAITSFIELD

Lareau Farm Country Inn
PO Box 563
48 Lareau Rd 05673
802-496-4949 Fax: 802-496-7979
800-833-0766
Susan Easley All year

80-165-BB
14 rooms, 11 pb
Visa, MC, *Rated*, •
C-yes/S-ltd/P-no/H-no

Full breakfast
Apres-ski hors d'oeuvres
Dinner, wine/beer (fee), sitting room, fireplace, porches, picnic lunches

Picturesque Vermont farmhouse nestled in a picturesque meadow, beside the Mad River. 150-year-old farmhouse is minutes from skiing/shopping.
lareau@lareaufarminn.com http://www.lareaufarminn.com

Mad River Inn
PO Box 75
243 Tremblay Rd 05673
802-496-7900 Fax: 802-496-6892
800-832-8278
Luc Maranda All year

89-150-BB
9 rooms, 9 pb
Visa, MC, AmEx, •
C-ltd/S-no/P-no/H-no

Full breakfast
Afternoon tea
Cable TV, accommodate business travelers

1860's country Victorian Inn, featherbeds, gourmet breakfast served on outdoor porch with picturesque mountain views and distant barns.
madriverinn@madriver.com http://www.madriverinn.com

Millbrook Inn
533 Millbrook Rd
Rt 17 05673
802-496-2405 Fax: 802-496-9735
800-477-2809
Joan & Thom Gorman

80-150-BB
7 rooms, 7 pb
Visa, MC, AmEx, *Rated*
C-ltd/S-no/P-ltd/H-ltd
Closed April–May & Nov.

Full breakfast
Full dinner from restaurant
Complimentary refreshments, 3 sitting rooms, vegetarian dining menu

Charming hand-stenciled guestrooms, with handmade quilts, country gourmet dining, vegetarian choices, in our small candlelit restaurant.
millbrkinn@aol.com http://www.millbrookinn.com

The Waitsfield Inn
PO Box 969, Rt 100
5267 Main St 05673
802-496-3979 Fax: 802-496-3970
800-758-3801
Pat & Jim Masson All year

105-150-BB
14 rooms, 14 pb
Most CC, *Rated*
C-ltd/S-no/P-no/H-no

Full breakfast
Apres ski snacks & cider
Sitting room, fireplaces, down comforters, TV and CD player in Great Room

We offer gracious lodging in an elegant 1825 parsonage in Vermont's beautiful Mad River Valley. Welcoming without the intrusion of TV or phones in the rooms.
lodging@waitsfieldinn.com http://www.waitsfieldinn.com

WALLINGFORD

The I.B. Munson House
PO Box 427
37 S Main St 05773
802-446-2860 Fax: 802-446-3336
888-519-3771
Tom & JoAnn Brem All year

105-195-BB
7 rooms, 7 pb
Most CC, *Rated*, •
C-ltd/S-no/P-no/H-no

Full breakfast
Sitting room, library, suites, fireplaces, breakfast by fire in winter

A charming, elegantly restored 1856 Victorian home transformed into a romantic B&B inn. Count Rumford fireplaces, feather bedding, clawfoot tubs.
stay@ibmunsoninn.com http://www.ibmunsoninn.com

WARREN

Deer Meadow Inn
PO Box 242
3215 Airport Rd 05674
802-496-2850 Fax: 802-496-2850
888-459-9183
Randi Majorell All year

135-BB
3 rooms, 3 pb
Visa, MC, AmEx, •
C-yes/S-no/P-no/H-no

Full breakfast
Afternoon tea, snacks, complimentary wine
Sitting room, library, fireplaces, cable TV, accom. bus. travelers

35 picturesque acres of VT paradise with spectacular mountain views. The accommodations are gracious, elegant and comfortable. Large landscaped grounds, two stocked ponds-fly fishing. Ski country. majorell@accessvt.com http://www.deermeadowinn.com

WARREN

Sugar Lodge
PO Box 652
2197 Sugarbush Access Rd
05674
802-583-3300 Fax: 802-583-1148
800-982-3465
Susan & Robert Cummiskey

69-125-BB
23 rooms, 23 pb
Visa, MC, AmEx
C-yes/S-no/P-no/H-yes
All year

Continental breakfast
Afternoon Tea, Lemonade and Homemade Cookies.
Hot Tub, Outdoor Pool, Beer & Wine Bar, Central A/C.

A Classic Mountain Lodge next to the Sugarbush Resort. Nestled in the Green Mountains and within an hour of Burlington, Montpelier and all of Vermont's most popular attractions. mail@sugarlodge.com http://www.sugarlodge.com

---

The Sugartree Inn
2440 Sugarbush Access Rd
05674
802-583-3211 Fax: 802-583-3203
800-666-8907
Frank & Kathy Partsch

99-175-BB
10 rooms, 10 pb
Most CC, *Rated*, •
C-ltd/S-no/P-no/H-yes
All year

Full country breakfast
Afternoon snacks
Living room with fireplace, in-room phones, brass, antique, canopy beds

Beautifully decorated w/unique country flair & antiques. Enchanting gazebo in flower gardens. Breathtaking views of ski slopes/fall foliage.
info@sugartree.com http://www.sugartree.com

West Hill House
1496 West Hill Rd 05674
802-496-7162 Fax: 802-496-6443
800-898-1427
Dotty Kyle & Eric Brattstrom
All year

115-190-BB
8 rooms, 8 pb
Most CC, *Rated*, •
C-ltd/S-no/P-no/H-ltd

Award-winning full breakfast
Complimentary afternoon tea, snacks, cash bar
Dinner by request, wine cellar, library, TV/VCR, videos, fireplaces, Jacuzzi

Comfortable, well appointed 1850 farmhouse on quiet lane near Sugarbush Resort. Gardens, ponds, gazebo. Near fine restaurants, quaint villages. All guestrooms have fireplaces & whirlpool or steambath. dotty@westhillhouse.com http://www.westhillhouse.com

WATERBURY

Inn at Blush Hill
784 Blush Hill Rd 05676
802-244-7529 Fax: 802-244-7314
800-736-7522
Pamela Gosselin
All year

89-160-BB
5 rooms, 5 pb
Most CC, *Rated*, •
C-ltd/S-no/P-no/H-ltd

Full country breakfast
Afternoon tea and evening refreshments
Featherbeds, down comforters, fabulous views, Jacuzzi bathtub, fireplaces

Cozy, 1790s brick farmhouse adjacent to Ben & Jerry's, just off scenic Route 100, 15 min. to Sugarbush and Stowe. inn@blushhill.com http://www.blushhill.com

---

Old Stagecoach Inn
18 N Main St 05676
802-244-5056 Fax: 802-244-6956
800-262-2206
John Barwick
All year

60-180-BB
11 rooms, 8 pb
Most CC, *Rated*
C-yes/S-no/P-ltd/H-no
German

Full breakfast
Bar service
Sitting room, library/bar

Meticulously restored village Inn on the National Register of Historic Places. Located in the heart of the Green Mountains on scenic route 100, right between the resort areas of Stowe and Sugarbush. lodging@oldstagecoach.com http://www.oldstagecoach.com

WEST DOVER

Austin Hill Inn
PO Box 859
Route 100 05356
802-464-5281 Fax: 802-464-1229
800-332-RELAX
Debbie & John Bailey
All year

95-195-BB
11 rooms, 11 pb
Visa, MC, *Rated*, •
C-yes/S-no/P-ltd/H-no

Full gourmet breakfast
Afternoon wine & cheese
Sitting room, game room, pool, fireplaces, dinner for small groups

Casual elegance, attention to detail and service. Nestled among the pines, making for a quiet romantic stay. info@austinhillinn.com http://www.austinhillinn.com

WEST DOVER

The Deerhill Inn & Rest.
PO Box 136
14 Valley View Rd 05356
802-464-3100 Fax: 802-464-5474
800-99-DEER9
Michael & Linda Anelli
All year

100-320-BB
15 rooms, 15 pb
Most CC, *Rated*
C-ltd/S-ltd/P-no/H-ltd

Full breakfast
Dinner available, restaurant
Sitting room, library, suites, fireplaces, cable, conference facilities

Romantic & relaxed hillside getaway with panoramic mountain views, fireplaces, antiques & art. Unparalleled dining & Wine Spectator Award Winning wine list.
deerhill@sover.net http://www.deerhill.com

West Dover Inn
PO Box 1208
108 Rt 100 05356
802-464-5207 Fax: 802-464-2173
Greg Gramas & Monique Phelan
Closed mid-April–mid-May

100-200-BB
12 rooms, 12 pb
Most CC, *Rated*, •
C-ltd/S-no/P-no/H-no

Full country breakfast
Gourmet dinner(fee)
Cozy pub, fine wines, sitting room, library, fireplace, Jacuzzi suites

Charming, unspoiled, unforgettable. Featuring country elegant guestrooms with antiques & hand-sewn quilts. Hearty breakfasts, innovative gourmet dinners. Save on special ski and golf packages. wdvrinn@sover.net http://www.westdoverinn.com

WESTON

The Darling Family Inn
815 Route 100 05161
802-824-3223
Chapin & Joan Darling
All year

85-145-BB
7 rooms, 7 pb
C-ltd/S-yes/P-ltd/H-no

Full breakfast
Comp. wine, refreshments
Sitting room, cottages, swimming pool, fireplaces, soaking tubs

Restored Colonial in farmland and mountain setting with American and English country antiques. Closest inn to the famous Weston Priory. DFI@vermontel.net

WILMINGTON

The Inn at Quail Run
106 Smith Rd 05363
802-464-3362 Fax: 802-464-7784
800-343-7227
Lorin & Robert Streim
All year

90-220-BB
14 rooms, 14 pb
Most CC, *Rated*, •
C-yes/S-no/P-yes/H-no

Full gourmet breakfast
Afternoon refreshments
Sitting room, sauna, outdoor heated pool, hiking trails

Nestled on 15 private wooded acres, with beautiful views of the Mt. Snow Valley and Haystack Mountain. All rooms have private bath & cable TV with HBO.
quailrunvt@aol.com http://www.theinnatquailrun.com

Red Shutter Inn
PO Box 636
41 W Main St 05363
802-464-3768 Fax: 802-464-5123
800-845-7548
Lacylee & Jerry Gingras
Closed mid-Apr–mid-May

110-260-BB
9 rooms, 9 pb
Most CC, •
C-ltd/S-no

Full breakfast
Restaurant, bar service
Snacks, al fresco dining, fireplaces, guest suites, whirlpool bath

Hillside inn & renovated Carriage House at village edge with candlelight dining. Fireplace suites. innkeeper@redshutterinn.com http://www.redshutterinn.com

---

Trail's End—A Country Inn
5 Trail's End Lane 05363
802-464-2727 Fax: 802-464-5532
800-859-2585
Kevin Stephens
All year

110-190-BB
15 rooms, 15 pb
Most CC, *Rated*, •
C-ltd/S-no/P-no/H-no

Full breakfast from menu
Afternoon refreshments
Heated outdoor pool, fireplace/Jacuzzi suites, clay tennis court

"One of the 10 Best Inns in Vermont" Boston Magazine "One of the top 50 Inns in America" The Inn Times trailsnd@together.net http://www.trailsendvt.com

WILMINGTON

The White House of Wilmington
178 Rt 9 E 05363
802-464-2135 Fax: 802-464-5222
800-541-2135
Robert Grinold
All year

118-230-BB
25 rooms, 25 pb
Most CC, *Rated*, •
C-ltd/S-yes/P-no/H-no
French

Full breakfast
Dinner (included), bar
Sitting room, piano, sauna, pools, weddings

"One of the most romantic inns..." N.Y. Times. Turn-of-the-century mansion, elegant accommodations, fireplaces. whitehse@sover.net http://www.whitehouseinn.com

WILMINGTON (REGION)

Candlelight
PO Box 380
3358 Rt 100, *Jacksonville* 05342
802-368-2004 866-429-1702
Peter & Fran Madden
All year

90-100-BB
4 rooms, 4 pb
•
C-yes/S-no/P-no/H-no

Full breakfast
Afternoon tea
Sitting room, library, fireplaces, in room cable TV, accom. bus. travelers

1850's restored farmhouse in the village of Jacksonville. 3 spacious rooms with private baths, and in room fireplaces. Near skiing on the MOOver (free shuttlebus).
pmadden@candlelightbandb.com http://www.candlelightbandb.com

WINDSOR

Juniper Hill Inn
153 Pembroke Rd 05089
802-674-5273 Fax: 802-674-2041
800-359-2541
Robert & Susanne Pearl
Closed 3 weeks in April

105-195-BB
16 rooms, 16 pb
Visa, MC, Disc, *Rated*, •
C-ltd/S-no/P-no/H-ltd

Full breakfast
Dinner by reservation, tea, snacks
Restaurant, bar, sitting room, library, swimming pool, fireplace

Vermont's luxurious Colonial mansion with unsurpassed location featuring richly appointed guestrooms working fireplaces, four poster beds, canopies, and numerous amenities.
Innkeeper@juniperhillinn.com http://www.juniperhillinn.com

WOODSTOCK

Ardmore Inn
PO Box 466
23 Pleasant St 05091
802-457-3887 Fax: 802-457-9006
800-497-9652
Giorgio Ortiz All year

110-175-BB
5 rooms, 5 pb
Most CC, *Rated*, •
C-ltd/S-no/P-no/H-no
Spanish, French

Full gourmet breakfast
Afternoon tea
Sitting room, library, bicycles, tennis court, intimate gatherings

Spacious, architectural detailed rooms, gracious accommodations, gourmet breakfast, silver service, great fun! ardmoreinn@aol.com http://www.ardmoreinn.com

---

Canterbury House
43 Pleasant St 05091
802-457-3077 Fax: 802-457-4630
800-390-3077
Bob and Sue Frost
All year

120-185-BB
7 rooms, 7 pb
Visa, MC, *Rated*
C-no/S-no/P-no/H-no

Gourmet breakfast
Sitting room, fishing, golf, skiing

An 1880 Victorian townhouse, restored to offer modern comfort & historic authenticity. All 7 rooms have private bath, and in the summer, air-conditioning. Within walking distance of the Village Green. bobfrost@sober.net http://www.thecanterburyhouse.com

---

Carriage House of Woodstock
455 Woodstock Road 05091
802-457-4322 Fax: 802-457-4322
800-791-8045
Debbie & Mark Stanglin
All year

95-180-BB
9 rooms, 9 pb
Most CC
C-ltd/S-no/P-no/H-ltd

Full breakfast
Afternoon snack

1830 Victorian Bed & Breakfast located just one mile west of the village of Woodstock. Nine rooms all with private bath–one with fireplace. Several with TV and whirlpool tub.
stanglin@sover.net http://www.carriagehousewoodstock.com

WOODSTOCK

Deer Brook Inn
535 US Rte 4 05091
802-672-3713
Brian & Rosemary McGinty
All year

80-130-BB
5 rooms, 5 pb
Visa, MC, AmEx, *Rated*
C-ltd/S-no/P-no/H-no

Full breakfast
Sitting room, suite, fireplace, cable TV

Beautifully renovated 1820 farmhouse on 5 acres. Original pine floors, stenciling, hand-made quilts. http://www.bbhost.com/deerbrookinn

---

The Jackson House Inn
114 3 Senior Ln 05091
802-457-2065 Fax: 802-457-9290
800-448-1890
Carl & Linda Delnegro
All year

195-380-BB
15 rooms, 15 pb
Visa, MC, AmEx, *Rated*, •
C-ltd/S-no/P-no/H-yes
Spanish, French, Italian

Full breakfast
Wine & hors d'oeuvres
Sitting room, library, restaurant, cable TV, suites, fireplaces, pond

Immaculate 1880 Victorian mansion in charming historic Woodstock. Period antiques, gourmet breakfast, evening Champagne & snacks, 5 groomed acres, swimming pond, spa/steamroom. innkeepers@jacksonhouse.com http://www.jacksonhouse.com

---

The Lincoln Inn at the Covered Bridge
530 Woodstock Rd
Rte 4 West 05091
802-457-3312
Fax: 802-457-5808
Kurt & Lori Hildbrand
All year

125-175-BB
6 rooms, 6 pb
Visa, MC, *Rated*
C-yes/S-no/P-no/H-no
German, French

Full breakfast
Afternoon tea, complimentary wine
Snacks, restaurant, bar service, biking, sitting room, library

Lovingly restored farmhouse nestled on 6 acres of lovely grounds.
lincon2@aol.com http://www.lincolninn.com

Village Inn of Woodstock
41 Pleasant St 05091
802-457-1255
800-722-4571
Evelyn & David Brey
All year

85-240-BB
7 rooms, 7 pb
Visa, MC, *Rated*
C-ltd/S-ltd/P-no/H-no
German

Full breakfast
Restaurant and tavern on premises, sitting room, perennial shade garden

Lovely 7 room Victorian Inn with a restaurant, tavern and beautiful gardens located in the Village. Private baths, A/C and cable TV. Rates include a 3 course breakfast, with Inn made baked goods. stay@villageinnofwoodstock.com http://www.villageinnofwoodstock.com

---

The Woodstocker
61 River St, Route 4 05091
802-457-3896 Fax: 802-457-3897
Tom & Nancy Blackford
All year

85-175-BB
9 rooms, 9 pb
Visa, MC, *Rated*, •
C-yes/S-no/P-no/H-no

Full buffet breakfast
Afternoon tea, snacks
Sitting room, hot tub

Charming 1830s cape in the village. Walking distance to shops, restaurants & galleries.
woodstocker@valley.net http://www.scenesofvermont.com

WOODSTOCK (REGION)

The Maple Leaf Inn
PO Box 273
Route 12, *Barnard* 05031
802-234-5342
800-51-MAPLE
Gary & Janet Robison
All year

120-230-BB
7 rooms, 7 pb
Most CC, *Rated*
C-no/S-no/P-no/H-yes

Full gourmet breakfast
Afternoon tea, snacks, complimentary wine
Sitting room, library, tennis court, Jacuzzis, fireplaces, satellite TV

Victorian style Inn nestled in woods on sixteen acres. Quiet, private, romantic. Gourmet breakouts served at individual candlelit tables for two. Whirlpool tubs, Wood-burning fireplaces, king beds. mapleafinn@aol.com http://www.mapleleafinn.com

WOODSTOCK (REGION)

Parker House Inn
1792 Quechee Main St,
Quechee 05059
802-295-6077 Fax: 802-296-6696
Walt Forrester
All year

120-150-BB
7 rooms, 7 pb
Visa, MC, *Rated*
C-yes/S-no/P-no/H-no

Full breakfast
Restaurant, bar service
Comp. dessert w/dinner, sitting room, library, bicycles

The Parker House Inn is a classic 19th-century Vermont inn, each room charming with Victorian furnishings. parker_house_inn@valley.net http://www.theparkerhouseinn.com

---

Bailey's Mills
1347 Bailey's Mills Road,
Reading 05062
802-484-7809
800-639-3437
Barbara Thaeder
All year

90-150-BB
3 rooms, 3 pb
•
C-ltd/S-no/P-ltd/H-no

Continental plus breakfast
Afternoon tea, snacks
Sitting room, library, fireplaces, pond, stream, walking paths- 50 acres

History-filled country home overlooking "Spite Cemetery." Colorful breakfast in colonial dining room, solarium or front porch.
goodfarm@vermontel.com http://www.bbonline.com/vt/baileysmills/

Kedron Valley Inn
Rt 106
South Woodstock, *South Woodstock* 05071
802-457-1473 Fax: 802-457-4469
800-836-1193
Max & Merrily Comins

131-248-BB
28 rooms, 28 pb
Most CC, *Rated*, •
C-yes/S-yes/P-yes/H-yes
French, Spanish
All year

Full country breakfast
Contemporary American cuisine
Sitting room, swim pond, piano, TVs, quilts, A/C in some rooms

Distinguished country 1822 inn. Wine list won Award of Excellence (Wine Spectator). Canopy beds, fireplaces in 15 rooms.
kedroninn@aol.com http://www.kedronvalleyinn.com

Virginia

ABINGDON

The Love House
224 Oak Hill St
210 E Valley St 24210
276-623-1281 Fax: 276-676-0780
800-475-5494
Hazel Ramos-Cano & Richard Cano
All year

105-135-BB
4 rooms, 4 pb
Most CC
C-ltd/S-no/P-no/H-no
Spanish, Tagalog, Japanese

Full breakfast
Evening desserts, dinners with advance notice
Sitting room, library, Jacuzzis, fireplaces

A beautifully restored 1850 house, with modern amenities such as control air, heating, and private baths. Four guestrooms, close to the world-renowned Barter Theatre.
lovehouse@naxs.com http://www.abingdon-virginia.com

River Garden B&B
19080 N Fork River Rd 24210
540-676-0335 Fax: 540-676-3039
800-952-4296
Bill Crump & Carol Schoenherr
All year

60-70-BB
4 rooms, 4 pb
Rated, •
C-ltd/S-no/P-ltd/H-yes

Full breakfast
Afternoon tea–request
Library, sitting room, rec. room, covered deck, full private baths

Located in country, private entrances for rooms, antique & period furniture, covered deck facing river. wccrump@preferred.com

ABINGDON

Shepherd's Joy	105-125-BB	Full breakfast
254 White's Mill Rd 24210	4 rooms, 4 pb	Afternoon refreshments
276-628-3273	Visa, MC	Wrap-around porch,Living
Jack & Joyce Ferratt	C-ltd/S-no/P-no/H-no	room, Library, formal dining
All year		room

Genuine hospitality in a lovingly-restored family home. Relax on our wraparound porch. Soak up the peacefulness of sheep grazing in the pasture. Enjoy a gourmet breakfast in the formal dining room. stay@shepherdsjoy.com http://www.shepherdsjoy.com

---

Summerfield Inn	119-159-BB	Full Breakfast
101 West Valley St 24210	7 rooms, 7 pb	Aft. . tea, snacks, beverages,
276-628-5905 Fax: 276-628-7515	Visa, MC, AmEx,	wine
800-668-5905	*Rated*, •	Large Parlors, Library,
Janice & Jim Cowan	C-ltd/S-ltd/P-no/H-yes	Whirlpools, Fireplaces, Cable
All year		TV, Porch, Packages

AAA 3-Diamond-1920's Inn, Historic District. Large parlors, antiques, A/C, whirlpools, porch, swing & rockers, fireplaces. Featured in Southern Living Magazine. Specials & Packages. innkeeper@summerfieldinn.com http://www.summerfieldinn.com

---

Victoria & Albert Inn	115-150-BB	Full breakfast
224 Oak Hill St 24210	5 rooms, 5 pb	Evening desserts, dinner
276-676-2797 Fax: 276-676-0780	Most CC, *Rated*	with advance notice
800-475-5494	C-ltd/S-no/P-no/H-no	Fireplaces, porches,
Hazel Ramos-Cano &	Spanish, Japanese,	whirlpools
Richard Cano All year	Tagalog	

Three story Victorian style home, built in 1892, with five delightful guestrooms, three covered porches and nine working gas log fireplaces.
rcano@naxs.com http://www.abingdon-virginia.com

ALEXANDRIA

Morrison House	175-350-EP	Restaurant, bar service,
109 S Alfred St	45 rooms, 45 pb	sitting room, library, near
116 S Alfred St 22314	Most CC, *Rated*, •	tennis/hot tub/pool
703-838-8000 Fax: 703-548-2489	C-yes/S-ltd/P-no/H-ltd	
800-367-0800	French, Italian, German,	
Wanda McKeon	Japanese	
All year		

Newly renovated (1999) small boutique hotel built in the style of an 18th century manor home. mhresrv@morrisonhouse.com http://www.morrisonhouse.com

ALEXANDRIA (REGION)

Captain McGuire's House	70-325-BB	Continental plus breakfast
512 S 25th St, *Arlington* 22202	2 rooms, 2 pb	Restaurant
703-549-3415 Fax: 703-549-3411	Visa, MC, AmEx, •	Sitting room, library,
888-549-3415	C-ltd/S-ltd/P-ltd/H-ltd	Jacuzzis, fireplaces, suites,
Les Garrison		cable TV
All year		

Historic, charming, authentic 1816 townhouse in middle of Old Town Alexandria. Hospitable hostess. Delightful atmosphere. Guests keep returning!
bbinfo@aabbn.com http://www.aabbn.com/CMH.htm

ARRINGTON

Harmony Hill	65-100-BB	Full breakfast
929 Wilson Hill Rd 22922	5 rooms, 5 pb	Snacks
434-263-7750	Visa, MC, Disc, *Rated*,	Sitting room, library,
Fax: 434-263-4457	•	whirlpool tubs, fireplaces,
877-263-7750	C-ltd/S-no/P-no/H-no	accom. bus. travelers
Joanne & Robert Cuoghi		
All year		

Spacious log home surrounded by hills & farms. Enjoy coffee on the porch while aromas of a country breakfast beckon. Handcrafted quilts and furniture. Rustic, relaxing, romantic.
innkeeper@harmony-hill.com http://www.harmony-hill.com

ASHLAND

The Henry Clay Inn
PO Box 135
114 N Railroad Ave 23005
804-798-3100 Fax: 804-752-7555
800-343-4565
Carol, Ann Carol & Judy

90-165-BB
14 rooms, 14 pb
Most CC, *Rated*, •
C-yes/S-no/P-ltd/H-yes
All year

Continental buffet breakfast
Lunch/dinner available, restaurant
Sitting room, fireplaces, small town pleasures

Southern charm—fireplaces, front porch w/rocking chairs, period- furnished rooms, restaurant, art/gift galleries. Adjacent to Amtrak.

information@henryclayinn.com http://www.henryclayinn.com

BASYE

Sky Chalet Mountain Lodges
PO Box 300
280 Sky Chalet Lane, Rte 263 22810
540-856-2147 Fax: 540-856-2436
877-867-8439 All year

34-79-BB
5 rooms, 5 pb
Visa, MC, Disc, *Rated*, •
C-yes/S-yes/P-yes/H-no
Ken & Mona Seay

Continental breakfast
Sitting room, working stone fireplace, kitchen/kitchenette, decks, views

Rustic, comfortable, mountaintop hideaway in the Shenandoah Valley. Property features spectacular mountain & valley views. Private baths, decks, some fireplaces & kitchens. Mountain Lovers' Paradise. skychalet@skychalet.com http://www.skychalet.com

BEDFORD

Otter's Den
8578 Peaks Road 24523
540-586-2204 Fax: 540-587-6887
1-877-9OTTERS
Michie and Pat Schrock

95-120-BB
4 rooms, 4 pb
Most CC
C-ltd/S-ltd/P-no/H-ltd
All year

Full Country Breakfast
Afternoon tea; lunch and dinner upon request
Fireplace, hot spa, antiques, historic site, hiking trails, game room

Restored 200 year-old homestead farm. 2 miles from the Blue Ridge Parkway and the Peaks of Otter. Scenic, romantic, relaxing getaway only minutes from Bedford and the National D-Day Memorial. ottrsden@aol.com http://www.ottersden.net

---

Reba Farm Inn
1099 Reba Farm Ln 24523
540-586-1906 Fax: 540-587-0917
888-235-3574
Kathleen Donovan-Gore & Ron Gore All year

BB
9 rooms, 9 pb
Visa, MC, •
C-yes/S-ltd/P-no/H-yes

Full breakfast
Lunch, dinner available, bar service
Sitting room, Jacuzzis, pool, suites, cottage, accom. bus. travelers

A unique, full service inn located just off the Blue Ridge Parkway, near Peaks of Otter, D-Day Memorial, Roanoke. A rewarding experience for everyone in Virginia's most beautiful countryside. rebafarm@mindspring.com http://www.rebafarminn.com

BELLE HAVEN

Bayview Waterfront
35350 Copes Dr 23306
757-442-6963 800-442-6966
Wayne & Mary Will Browning
All year

95-BB
2 rooms, 2 pb
Rated
C-yes/S-no

Full country breakfast
swimming pool, croquet, basketball, volleyball

Bay View is on a hill overlooking Occohannock Creek with an expansive view to the Chesapeake Bay and a dock to deep water.

browning@shore.intercom.net http://www.bbhost.com/bvwaterfront

BERRYVILLE

Blue Ridge
2458 Castleman Rd 22611
540-955-1246 Fax: 540-955-4240
800-296-1246
R. Amador & R. Duncan
All year

65-150-BB
4 rooms, 2 pb
Visa, MC, AmEx, *Rated*, •
C-yes/S-ltd/P-ltd/H-yes
Spanish, German

Full breakfast
Complimentary wine
Sitting room, Jacuzzi, library, suites, fireplaces, cable TV, microwave

Close to Skyline Drive & Harper's Ferry—lovely country hideaway furnished in antiques—lovely views of mountains & gardens—full country breakfast—great places to hike. blurdgbb@shentel.net http://www.blueridgebb.com

Evergreen–The Bell Capozzi, Christiansburg, VA

BERRYVILLE

Smithfield Farm B&B 568 Smithfield Lane 22611 540-955-4389 Fax: 540-955-4349 877-955-4389 Betsy Pritchard Spring, Summer, Fall	135-160-BB 5 rooms, 5 pb Visa, MC, AmEx C-ltd/S-ltd/P-no/H-no Italian, French	Full breakfast Sitting room, library, fireplace, hiking on property

A true working beef cattle farm, Smithfield Farm is carefully tucked away from the bustle but close enough to the metropolitan Washington-Baltimore area.

sfarm@visuallink.com http://www.smithfieldfarm.com

BLACKSBURG

Clay Corner Inn 401 Clay St SW 24060 540-953-2604 Fax: 540-951-0541 Joanne Anderson All year	85-145-BB 12 rooms, 12 pb Visa, MC, AmEx, *Rated* C-ltd/S-no/P-no/H-no	Full breakfast Heated pool, A/C, meeting room, hot tub

Cable TV & phones in every room. Healthy breakfast served inside or out on covered deck. Inn consists of the main house and three guest houses.

info@claycorner.com http://www.claycorner.com

BLACKSBURG (REGION)

Evergreen—The Bell-Capozzi 201 E Main St, *Christiansburg* 24073 540-382-7372 Fax: 540-382-0034 800-905-7372 Rocco & Barbara Capozzi All year	105-150-BB 6 rooms, 6 pb Most CC, *Rated*, • C-no/S-no/P-no/H-no	Traditional Southern Breakfast Afternoon tea by reservation from 5-6 p.m. Swimming pool, fireplace, central air, library, Godiva chocolates, Gevalia

Circa 1890 Victorian mansion with private baths, cable TV and VCR. Godiva chocolates, Gevalia coffee, central A/C, in-ground pool, library. In the historic district.

evrgrninn@aol.com http://www.evergreen-bnb.com

BOYCE

The River House
3075 John Mosby Highway
US Route 50 & Shanandoah
22620
540-837-1476 Fax: 540-837-2399
800-838-1476
Cornelia S. Niemann
All year

95-155-BB
5 rooms, 5 pb
Visa, MC, *Rated*, •
C-ltd/S-yes/P-yes/H-yes
French

Full brunch
Fruit, beverages/liqueur
Sitting room, library, phone in room, Fax, modem, special comedy weekends

1780 Fieldstone rural getaway, convenient to scenic, historical, recreational areas, superb rests. Shenandoah river fishing on property.

BRODNAX (REGION)

Three Angels Inn at Sherwood
PO Box 883
236 Pleasant Grove Rd,
Lawrenceville 23868
804-848-0830 Fax: 804-848-9696
877-777-4264

95-105-BB
4 rooms, 4 pb
Visa, MC, *Rated*
C-ltd/S-ltd/P-no/H-no
Pat & Tom Krewson
All year

Full breakfast
Lunch & dinner avail, complimentary wine, snacks
Sitting room, library, fireplaces

Step back in time at our 1883 farmhouse. Lovely porches, rolling hills provide a setting where you breathe deeply, sit down, put your feet up, and be pampered.
innkeeper@threeangelsinn.com http://www.threeangelsinn.com

CAPE CHARLES

Cape Charles House
645 Tazwell Ave 23310
757-331-4920
Fax: 757-331-4960
Bruce & Carol Evans

85-150-BB
5 rooms, 5 pb
Most CC, *Rated*, •
C-no/S-ltd/P-no/H-no
All year

Full Gourmet breakfast
Tea, snacks, wine
Sitting room, bicycles, tennis, Jacuzzis, cable TV, conference

Cape Charles House has recently received the 2000 Governor's Award for Virginia Hospitality. We are a romantic getaway, comfortably elegant, restored Colonial Revival.
stay@capecharleshouse.com http://www.capecharleshouse.com

Pickett's Harbor
28288 Nottingham Ridge Ln
23310
757-331-2212 Fax: 757-331-2212
Sara & Cooke Goffigon

110-175-BB
5 rooms, 3 pb
Rated, •
C-yes/S-no/P-yes/H-no
All year

Full breakfast
Afternoon refreshments
Sitting room, library, acres of private beach, bikes

27 acres of secluded, private beach on Chesapeake Bay, wildlife preserve and state park nearby. Bernice Chesler describes it as "A Real Find" in her MID-ALANTIC BED&BREAKFAST. pickharb@aol.com http://www.pickettsharbor.com

CHARLES CITY

North Bend Plantation
12200 Weyanoke Rd 23030
804-829-5176 Fax: 804-829-6828
800-841-1479
George & Ridgely Copland

115-135-BB
4 rooms, 4 pb
All year

A Bed & Breakfast in James River Plantation Country, just 25 minutes away from Colonial Williamsburg, VA. North Bend is a Virginia Historic Landmark Circa 1819, and a National Register property. ridgely37@aol.com http://www.northbendplantation.com

CHARLOTTESVILLE

200 South Street Inn
200 South St W 22902
804-979-0200 Fax: 804-979-4403
800-964-7008
Brendan Clancy
All year

125-235-BB
20 rooms, 20 pb
Visa, MC, AmEx, *Rated*, •
C-yes/S-yes/P-no/H-yes
French

Continental plus breakfast
Lunch M-F, dinner wkends
Restaurant, comp. wine, sitt. rm., frplcs., lib., whirlpool tubs, TVs

Restored residences in downtown historic district near landmarks, shops, restaurants. Room options include whirlpool tubs, fireplaces, canopy beds.
southst@cstone.net http://www.southstreetinn.com

CHARLOTTESVILLE

Foxfield Inn
2280 Garth Rd 22901
434-923-8892
Fax: 434-923-0963
Mary Pat & John Hulburt
All year

150-190-BB
5 rooms, 5 pb
Visa, MC, *Rated*
C-ltd/S-no/P-no/H-yes

Full breakfast
Snacks, wine
Sitting room, Jacuzzis, fireplace, cable TV, bay windows, outside heated spa

An elegant country Inn only minutes from Monticello and UVA.
foxfieldin@aol.com http://www.foxfield-inn.com

Inn at Monticello
1188 Scottsville Rd
Route 20 South 22902
434-979-3593
Fax: 434-296-1344
Norm & Becky Lindway
All year exc. Christmas

125-185-BB
5 rooms, 5 pb
Visa, MC, *Rated*, •
C-ltd/S-no/P-no/H-no
French

Full gourmet breakfast
Complimentary local beer & wine
Sitting room, hammock, covered porch, croquet, tennis court nearby

19th century manor, perfectly located 2 miles from Thomas Jefferson's beloved "Monticello." stay@innatmonticello.com http://www.innatmonticello.com

---

Inn at Sugar Hollow Farm
PO Box 5705
22905
804-823-7086 Fax: 804-823-2002
Dick & Hayden Cabell
All year

Serene, romantic country retreat, mountain streams near Shenandoah Park and wineries. Fireplaces, double whirlpool tubs, hiking, biking, riding, near Monticello and UVa.
theinn@sugarhollow.com http://www.sugarhollow.com

Inn at the Crossroads
PO Box 6519, 22906
434-979-6452 Fax: 434-979-6452
Jim & Janet Stern
All year

89-169-BB
6 rooms, 6 pb
Visa, MC, *Rated*, •
C-ltd/S-no/P-no/H-no

Full breakfast
Afternoon tea, snacks
Sitting room, tennis court nearby, porch swings, rocking chairs, gazebo

National Historic Register Inn with panoramic mountain views. 10 minutes from the University of Virginia, Charlottesville. Less than 20 min. from Monticello, Skyline Drive and the Blue Ridge Parkway. jimandjanetstern@yahoo.com http://www.crossroadsinn.com

---

Prospect Hill Plantation Inn
PO Box 6960
2887 Poindexter Rd 22906
540-967-0844 Fax: 540-967-0102
800-277-0844
The Sheehan Family
All year

195-425-AP
13 rooms, 13 pb
Rated, •

Full breakfast
All meals included

A complete plantation complex as it existed in the eighteenth and nineteenth centuries. This was Prospect Hill two centuries ago . . . This is Prospect Hill today.
innkeeper@prospecthill.com http://www.prospecthill.com

CHARLOTTESVILLE (REGION)

The Mark Addy Inn
56 Rodes Farm Dr, *Nellysford*
22958
804-361-1101 Fax: 982-832-5277
800-278-2154
John Storck Maddox
All year

100-195-BB
9 rooms, 9 pb
Visa, MC, *Rated*, •
C-ltd/S-no/P-no/H-yes
German, French

Full breakfast
Dinner available, snacks
Sitting room, library, tennis court, Jacuzzis, pool, suites, cable TV

The Mark Addy B&B Inn is situated in Virginia's magnificent Blue Ridge Mountains, near the Parkway, Skyline Drive, Thomas Jefferson's Monticello and home of the University of Virginia. info@mark-addy.com http://www.mark-addy.com

CHARLOTTESVILLE (REGION)

Ridge View
PO Box 13
Rt 231 Scenic Byway, *Rochelle* 22738
540-672-7024 Fax: 540-672-7042
Eleanor & Frank Damico

110-125-BB
3 rooms, 3 pb
Visa, MC, *Rated*, •
C-yes/S-no/P-no/H-no
All year

Full breakfast
Lunch, dinner, afternoon snacks w/48 hr notice
Cable TV, can accommodate business travelers

Situated on 17 acres on Byway 231 and Virginia Civil War Trails. Gourmet breakfast served in dining room or patio.

edamico@virginia-ridgeview.com http://www.virginia-ridgeview.com

---

High Meadows Vineyard Inn
55 High Meadows Lane, *Scottsville* 24590
434-286-2218 Fax: 434-286-2124
800-232-1832
Rose Farber & Jon Storey

99-240-BB
12 rooms, 12 pb
Visa, MC, *Rated*, •
C-yes/S-ltd/P-ltd/H-no
French
All year

Full breakfast
Candlelight dining
Nightly winetasting, library, hot tub, pond, gazebo, bikes, vineyard

Enchanting historical landmark south of Charlottesville. Large, tastefully appointed rooms; fireplaces; period antiques. Private 50 acres for walking & picnics.

peterhmi@aol.com http://www.highmeadows.com

Edgewood Farm
1186 Middle River Rd, *Stanardsville* 22973
804-985-3782 Fax: 804-985-6275
800-985-3782
Norman & Eleanor Schwartz
All year

90-120-BB
3 rooms, 3 pb
Visa, MC, AmEx, *Rated*, •
C-ltd/S-ltd/P-no/H-no

Full breakfast
Compl. cider, snacks on arrival
Sitting room, library, fireplaces, cable TV, accommodate business travelers

Beautifully restored 1790 Virginia farmhouse in the foothills of the Blue Ridge. Secluded yet accessible. Sumptuous breakfast.

edgewoodfarm@firstva.com http://www.edgewoodfarmbandb.com

CHINCOTEAGUE

Miss Molly's Inn
4141 Main St 23336
757-336-6686 Fax: 757-336-0600
800-221-5620
David & Barbara Wiedenheft
March-New Years

79-155-BB
7 rooms, 5 pb
Most CC, *Rated*, •
C-ltd/S-no
French, Dutch, German

Full breakfast
English afternoon tea
Vegetarian breakfast available, sitting room, bicycles, beach items,

Charming Victorian "painted lady" overlooking the Bay. Marguerite Henry stayed here while writing her classic "Misty of Chincoteague."

msmolly@shore.intercom.net http://www.missmollys-inn.com

The Watson House
PO Box 905
4240 Main St 23336
757-336-1564 Fax: 757-336-5776
800-336-6787
The Derricksons & Sneads

79-159-BB
8 rooms, 8 pb
Visa, MC, *Rated*, •
C-ltd/S-ltd/P-no/H-no
March–Nov

Full breakfast
Afternoon tea
Bicycles, beach nearby, beach chairs & towels, wildlife, whirlpool tubs

Beautifully restored Victorian. Furnished with antiques. View of Chincoteague Bay and beach nearby. 2 family cottages. AAA–3 diamond. http://www.watsonhouse.com

CHINCOTEAGUE (REGION)

Year of the Horse Inn
3583 Main St, *Chincoteague Island* 23336
757-336-3221 Fax: 208-728-6305
800-680-0090
Richard Hebert All year

69-165-BB
5 rooms, 3 pb
Visa, MC
C-yes/S-no/P-no/H-no
French, Spanish

Continental Plus breakfast
Library, cable TV, aroma candles, fridges, sundecks, dock, patios, hammock

Chincoteague Island's first and finest waterfront B&B. Three private rooms have sun decks with spectacular sunset views. Spacious yard includes cookout facilities, patios, and crabbing dock. richard@yearofthehorseinn.com http://www.yearofthehorseinn.com

CHINCOTEAGUE (REGION)

Garden and Sea Inn
PO Box 275
4188 Nelson Rd, *New Church*
23415
757-824-0672 800-824-0672
Tom & Sara Baker All year

85-205-BB
8 rooms, 8 pb
Most CC, *Rated*, •
C-ltd/S-no/P-yes/H-yes

Full breakfast
Restaurant, dinner, snacks
Sitting room, library, Jacuzzi, suites, fireplace, cable TV, river cruises

Charming Victorian country inn near Chincoteague and Assateague Islands. Eight whirlpools, some with king beds, most with whirlpools or double whirlpools.

innkeeper@gardenandseainn.com http://www.gardenandseainn.com

COVINGTON

Milton Hall Inn
207 Thorny Ln 24426
540-965-0196 Fax: 540-962-8232
877-7MILTON
Suzanne & Eric Stratmann
All year

120-150-BB
6 rooms, 6 pb
Visa, MC, *Rated*, •
C-yes/S-ltd/P-yes/H-no

Full breakfast
Sunday evening meals for guests
Bar service, comp. wine, afternoon tea, sitting, room, library, patio

English country manor c.1874 set on 44 wooded acres with gardens. This Historic Landmark adjoins national forest, mountains, lakes, springs. Near hunting, fishing.

milton_h@cfw.com http://www.milton-hall.com

CULPEPER

Fountain Hall
609 S East St 22701
540-825-8200 Fax: 540-825-7716
800-29-VISIT
Steve & Kathi Walker All year

105-150-BB
6 rooms, 6 pb
Most CC, *Rated*, •
C-yes/S-no/P-no/H-yes

Continental plus breakfast
Complimentary beverages
3 sitting rooms, books, fireplaces, VCR, porches, golf nearby, bicycles

Gracious accommodations for business & leisure. Centrally located in historic Culpeper, between Washington, D.C., Charlottesville & Skyline Drive.

visit@fountainhall.com http://www.fountainhall.com

EASTERN SHORE (REGION)

The Gladstone House
PO Box 296
12108 Lincoln Ave, *Exmore*
23350
757-442-4614 Fax: 757-442-4678
800-BNBGUEST

65-95-BB
3 rooms, 3 pb
Visa, MC, AmEx, *Rated*, •
S-no/P-no/H-ltd
Pat & Al Egan All year

Full breakfast
Afternoon tea, snacks
Sitting room, bicycles, library

Step back in time in an elegant brick Georgian home. Small town atmosphere. Four-course breakfast. Vegetarian breakfast available.

egan@gladstonehouse.com http://www.gladstonehouse.com

FAIRFAX

The Bailiwick Inn
4023 Chain Bridge Rd 22030
703-691-2266 Fax: 703-934-2112
Christopher & Ann Sheldon
All year

165-350-BB
14 rooms, 14 pb
Visa, MC, AmEx, *Rated*, •
C-no/S-no/P-no/H-yes

Full breakfast
Aft. tea included, (fee) lunch, cocktails, dinner
Feather mattresses; fireplaces; whirlpool tubs; minibars; turn down service

Historic, elegant inn with lovely rooms and pampering service. Dine in our intimate AAA Four Diamond Restaurant with renowned wine list. Perfect for a romantic getaway, business retreat or wedding. theinn@bailiwickinn.com http://www.bailiwickinn.com

FARMVILLE

The Longwood Inn
408 High St 23901
804-392-6500 Fax: 703-738-2243
866-660-8149
Roland Labadan All year

85-125-BB
7 rooms, 7 pb
Visa, MC, AmEx, •
C-ltd/S-ltd/P-no/H-no
Turkish, French, Tagalog

Full breakfast
Ice, soft drinks, snacks available from bar 24/7
Toiletries, phones, bathrobes, gas log fireplaces

The Longwood Inn is the only bed and breakfast in the town of Farmville. It offers exquisitely decorated guestrooms as well as overnight and extended stays in apartments.

innkeeper@longwoodinn.com http://www.longwoodinn.com

FINCASTLE

WoodsEdge Guest Cottage
42 Ridge Trail 24090
540-473-2992 Fax: 540-473-2992
Ferrel & Fred Phillips
All year

110-135-BB
1 rooms, 1 pb
Visa, MC, *Rated*
C-ltd/S-no/P-no/H-no

Full breakfast
Spectacular setting with rocking chairs on porch viewing the Alleghany Mtns

A housekeeping cottage with fireplace nestled on 13+ private acres in a secluded country setting. Furnished with antiques. Modern equipped kitchen.
ffphillips@rbnet.com

FLOYD

Harmony Farm
3510 Black Ridge Rd SW 24091
540-593-2185
Susan & Bill Baker
All year

105-BB
3 rooms, 3 pb
Visa, MC, *Rated*
C-ltd/S-ltd/P-no/H-ltd

Full breakfast, elegantly served
Snacks & beverages
Toiletries, information & maps of local sites & happenings, onsite hiking

Within 1.5-.5 miles of two wineries & the Blue Ridge Pkwy. Rural, mountain setting with wildflower gardens, wildlife viewing, & hiking. Spacious guestrooms with en-suite baths.
susan@harmony-farm.com http://www.harmony-farm.com

FLOYD (REGION)

The Mountain Rose
1787 Charity Hwy, *Woolwine* 24185
276-930-1057 Fax: 276-930-2165
Reeves & Melodie Pogue
All year

105-125-BB
5 rooms, 5 pb
Visa, MC, Disc, *Rated*, •
C-ltd/S-ltd/P-no/H-ltd

Full breakfast
Afternoon snacks, sherry
Pool, fireplaces, satellite TV, trout stream, hiking trails, porches

"Best Bed and Breakfast in the Roanoke area"–City Magazine 2001 Readers Poll. Nestled along the banks of the Rock Castle Creek, the Inn offers country elegance in the Blue Ridge Mountains. info@mountainrose-inn.com http://www.mountainrose-inn.com

FREDERICKSBURG

Fredericksburg Colonial Inn
1707 Princess Anne St 22401
540-371-5666 Fax: 540-371-5884
Vivian West
All year

65-90-BB
32 rooms, 32 pb
Visa, MC, AmEx, *Rated*
C-yes/S-no/P-no/H-yes

Continental breakfast
Conference room avail., honeymoon/anniversary, Colonial Suites

A restored country inn located in the Historic District, has 30 antique appointed rooms with private baths, phones, TV, and fridge. echols@erols.com http://www.fci1.com

FRONT ROYAL

Chester House Inn
43 Chester St 22630
540-635-3937 Fax: 540-636-8695
800-621-0441
Allen Hamblin
All year

105-220-BB
6 rooms, 6 pb
Visa, MC, AmEx
C-ltd/S-ltd/P-no/H-no

Full breakfast
Complimentary wine, beer, sherry, and soft drinks
3 parlors with working fireplaces, laptop phone-line in garden room

Beautiful 1905 Italian Renaissance estate on 2 acres. Walk to restaurants, shops, movies. Separate cottage for 2. Spacious rooms, private baths, A/C, working fireplaces, Comp. wine, beer, & sherry mail@chesterhouse.com http://www.chesterhouse.com

---

Killahevlin
1401 North Royal Ave 22630
540-636-7335 Fax: 540-636-8694
800-847-6132
Susan O'Kelly
All year

135-235-BB
6 rooms, 6 pb
Visa, MC, *Rated*, •
C-ltd/S-no/P-no/H-no

Full breakfast
Complimentary snacks/beer/wine
Scenic, sitting room, Whirlpools, gazebos, screened porch, pub

Historic Edwardian mansion. Civil War encampment hill. Mt. views, working fireplaces, whirlpool tubs, antiques. Prepare to be pampered.
kllhvln@shentel.net http://www.vairish.com

Chester House Inn, Front Royal, VA

GORDONSVILLE

Sleepy Hollow Farm
16280 Blue Ridge Turnpike
22942
540-832-5555 Fax: 540-832-2515
800-215-4804
Beverley Allison & Dorsey Allison-Comer
All year

65-150-BB
7 rooms, 6 pb
Visa, MC, *Rated*, •
C-yes/S-yes/P-yes/H-no
Spanish, French

Full breakfast
Complimentary wine, beverages
Sitting room, conference room, croquet, gazebo, pond fishing & swimming

Old farmhouse & cottage with whirlpool furnished in antiques, accessories. One bedroom with fireplace & Jacuzzi.

shfbnb@ns.gemlink.com http://www.sleepyhollowfarmbnb.com

HARBORTON

Harborton House
PO Box 117
28044 Harborton Rd 23389
757-442-6800 800-882-0922
Helen & Andy Glenn
All year

79-115-BB
3 rooms, 3 pb
Visa, MC, •
C-ltd/S-no/P-no/H-no

Full breakfast
Snacks
Sitting room, bikes, suites, fireplaces, cable TV

Graceful Victorian tucked away in a bayside fishing village minutes to the Chesapeake Bay. Casual, but full of luxuries.

info@harbortonhouse.com http://www.HarbortonHouse.com

IRVINGTON

The Hope and Glory Inn
PO Box 425
65 Tavern Rd 22480
804-438-6053 Fax: 804-438-5362
800-497-8228
Peggy Patteson
All year

135-220-BB
11 rooms, 11 pb
Visa, MC, AmEx
C-ltd/S-no/P-ltd/H-ltd

Full breakfast
Catered events
Sitting room, massages, bikes, tennis court, croquet & bocce on premises

Tatler-Cunard Travel Guide rates it as one of the "101 Best Hotels in the World." Travel + Leisure ranks it one of this country's "30 Great Inns."

hopeandgloryinn@rivnet.net http://www.hopeandglory.com

LEESBURG

Leesburg Colonial Inn
19 S King St 22075
703-777-5000 Fax: 703-777-7000
800-392-1332
Fabian A. Saeidi
All year

110-BB

When you stay at the Colonial Inn, you step back into an era of gracious living.
saeidi@aol.com http://www.leesburgcolonialinn.com

The Norris House Inn
108 Loudoun St SW 20175
703-777-1806 Fax: 703-771-8051
800-644-1806
Pam & Don McMurray
All year

110-150-BB
6 rooms, 3 pb
Most CC, *Rated*, •
C-ltd/S-no/P-no/H-no

Full country breakfast
Parlor, dining room, library & fireplace, sunroom, veranda, gardens

1760 B & B inn in Historic District. Antique furnishings throughout. Three guestrooms have wood-burning fireplaces. Enjoy a forty-foot veranda overlooking award-winning gardens. Walk to fine dining. inn@norrishouse.com http://www.norrishouse.com

LEXINGTON

Applewood Inn & Llama Trekking
PO Box 1348
Buffalo Bend Rd 24450
540-463-1962 Fax: 540-463-6996
800-463-1902
Linda & Chris Best
All year

80-139-BB
4 rooms, 4 pb
Visa, MC, AmEx, *Rated*
C-ltd/S-no/P-ltd/H-ltd
German

Full breakfast
Hot cider, beverages
Fridge, pantry, fireplaces, sitting room, porches, hot tub, pool, hiking

Spectacular solar home on 35 acres. Mountain views. Close to historic Lexington. Miles of trails for hiking & llama treks. Heart healthy breakfasts. For nature lovers.
applewd@cfw.com http://www.applewoodbb.com

A B&B at Llewellyn Lodge
603 S Main St 24450
540-463-3235 Fax: 540-464-3122
800-882-1145
John & Ellen Roberts
All year

65-120-BB
6 rooms, 6 pb
Most CC, *Rated*, •
C-ltd/S-ltd/P-no/H-no

Full breakfast
Afternoon tea, snacks
Sitting room, cable TV, tennis/pool/golf nearby, hiking, fly-fishing

Charming Colonial, walkable to museums, colleges, restaurants.
lll@rockbridge.net http://www.llodge.com

Brierley Hill
985 Borden Rd 24450
540-464-8421 Fax: 540-464-8925
800-422-4925
Al & Jeanne Perkins
All year

95-160-BB
5 rooms, 5 pb
Visa, MC, *Rated*, •
C-ltd/S-ltd/P-no

Full breakfast
Afternoon refreshments
Hiking, canoeing, horseback riding, packages available

English country house atmosphere. Magnificent views of Blue Ridge Mountains and Shenandoah Valley. brierley@cfw.com http://www.brierleyhill.com

---

Inn at Union Run
325 Union Run Rd 24450
540-463-9715 Fax: 540-463-9715
800-528-6466
Roger & Jeanette Serens
All year

95-120-BB
8 rooms, 8 pb
Visa, MC, AmEx, *Rated*, •
C-yes/S-ltd/P-ltd/H-yes
German

Full breakfast
Lunch, dinner, aft. tea, snacks, wine, restaurant
Sitting room, Jacuzzis, fireplaces, accom. bus. travelers

Country quiet on creek fronted mountainside, 1883 inn furnished in antiques. Eight gracious guestrooms, some with fireplaces, Jacuzzis, private porches to view the hills.
unionrun@cfw.com http://www.unionrun.com

LEXINGTON

The Magnolia House Inn
501 S Main St 24450
540-463-2567 Fax: 540-463-4358
877-355-4664
Barney Brown and Antonia Albano All year

105-150-BB
5 rooms, 5 pb
Visa, MC, AmEx, *Rated*
C-ltd/S-ltd/P-no/H-no
Spanish

Full breakfast
Coffee, tea, soft drinks, fine port in the evening
Living Room/Parlor, library, porch, garden

This lovely Shenandoah Victorian style home with its huge magnolia tree, several dogwoods and many azaleas is casual and comfortable, yet elegant.
magnolia@rockbridge.net http://www.magnoliahouseinn.com

Stoneridge
PO Box 38
246 Stoneridge Lane 24450
540-463-4090 Fax: 540-463-6078
800-491-2930
Jim & Evelyn Stallard

115-160-BB
5 rooms, 5 pb
Most CC, *Rated*, •
C-ltd/S-no/P-no/H-no
All year

Full breakfast
Afternoon tea
Sitting room, library, Jacuzzis, suites, fireplaces, cable TV

Romantic 1829 Antebellum home on 36 acres. Elegant rooms have queen beds & private baths, most featuring balconies, fireplaces & double Jacuzzis.
rollo_va@cfw.com http://www.webfeat-inc.com/stoneridge

LEXINGTON (REGION)

Steeles Tavern Manor
PO Box 39
30 Butler Circle, *Steeles Tavern* 24476
540-377-6444 Fax: 540-377-5937
800-743-8666
Eileen Hoernlein All year

130-185-BB
5 rooms, 5 pb
Visa, MC, Disc, *Rated*, •
C-no/S-no/P-no/H-no

Full breakfast
24 hour hot & cold beverages, cookies, sherry
Plush robes, extra pillows, blankets & towels, movies

Rooms have TV/VCRs w/movie library, double Jacuzzis w/private bath, A/C, fireplaces & ceiling fans. 55 acres w/new in-ground pool, fishing pond, separate cottages, birding, wineries, horseback riding. hoernlei@cfw.com http://www.steelestavern.com

---

Sugar Tree Inn
Highway 56, *Steeles Tavern* 24476
540-377-2197 Fax: 540-377-6776
800-377-2197
Terri & Henry Walters

100-160-BB
12 rooms, 12 pb
Most CC, *Rated*, •
C-ltd/S-ltd/P-ltd/H-yes
March thru December

Full breakfast
Dinner by res., pub
Sitting room, biking, library, porches, rocker, creek, waterfall, conf.

Mountain inn nestled in a forest off Blue Ridge Parkway. Fireplaces in every room; 3 whirlpools, VCRs. Premium suites have A/C.
innkeeper@sugartreeinn.com http://www.sugartreeinn.com

LURAY

The Goshen House
120 N Hawksbill St 22835
540-843-0700
Justin Hunsaker & Cheryl Benedict All year

120-190-BB
3 rooms, 3 pb
Most CC
C-ltd/S-ltd/P-no/H-no
German

Continental breakfast
Tea/Coff, Prem Beer, VA/CA Wines, Rail/Soft Drinks
Billiards, Hot tub, Lounging Porch, Fishing, Dinner packages available

A bed and breakfast of historical proportions established in 1805 by the Peter Ruffner family. Originally used as a tavern and stage coach stop.
info@goshenhouse.com http://www.goshenhouse.com

Woodruff Inns
138 E Main St 22835
540-743-1494 Fax: 540-743-1722
866-937-3466
Lucas & Deborah Woodruff
All year

119-289-MAP
9 rooms, 9 pb
Visa, MC, Disc, *Rated*, •
C-ltd/S-no/P-ltd/H-no

Full gourmet breakfast
Afternoon tea and full breakfast included
Candlelight dinner included, library, Jacuzzis for two, outdoor hot tubs

Our Chef owned and operated Victorian Inns offer gourmet dinners, afternoon teas, and breakfast. AAA 3 diamond and Mobil 3 Star.
woodruffinns@woodruffinns.com http://www.woodruffinns.com

LYNCHBURG

Federal Crest Inn
1101 Federal St 24504
434-845-6155 Fax: 434-845-1445
800-818-6155
Ann & Phil Ripley
All year

125-155-BB
5 rooms, 4 pb
Most CC, *Rated*, •
C-ltd/S-no/P-no/H-no

Full breakfast
Afternoon beverages
Snacks, sitting room, library, \xd5 50s cafe with 60\xd3 ” TV

Romantic and elegant! Unique 1909 spacious mansion with BR fireplace, A/C, Jacuzzi, antiques. Theater with 60 inch TV on the 3rd floor.
inn@federalcrest.com http://www.federalcrest.com

Ivy Creek Farm
2812 Link Rd
24503
434-384-3802 800-689-7404
Marilyn & Lynn Brooks

We would like to welcome you to Ivy Creek Farm Bed and Breakfast with memorable, gourmet breakfasts and luxurious accommodations.
info@ivycreekfarm.com http://www.ivycreekfarm.com

LYNCHBURG (REGION)

Crump's Mountain Cottage
2150 Indian Creek Rd, *Amherst* 24521
434-277-5563 866-868-4118
Carolyn & Curtis Crump
All year

65-115-BB
2 rooms, 2 pb
Rated, •
C-yes/S-ltd/P-yes/H-no

Continental plus breakfast
Stocked pond for fishing

Solitary Cottage nestled in Blue Ridge Mountains on 106 wooded acres–panoramic views. Refresh your spirit with nature's sights, sounds, and solitude. cec5e@virginia.edu

MANASSAS

Bennett House
9252 Bennett Dr 20110
703-368-6121 Fax: 703-330-1106
800-354-7060
Jean & Curtis Harrover
All year

95-140-BB
2 rooms, 2 pb
Most CC, *Rated*, •
C-ltd/S-ltd/P-no/H-no

Full breakfast
Afternoon tea, snacks, complimentary wine
Sitting room, library, fireplaces, cable TV, hot tub, A/C, accom. bus. trav.

Charming Victorian setting characterized by exceptional gourmet breakfasts, tastefully appointed facilities, and attentiveness to guests' needs.
jharrover@aol.com http://www.virginia-bennetthouse.com

MANASSAS (REGION)

Shiloh
13520 Carriage Ford Rd, *Nokesville* 20181
703-594-2664 888-447-7210
Alan & Carolee Fischer
All year

185-205-BB
2 rooms, 2 pb
Visa, MC, *Rated*
C-ltd/S-ltd/P-no/H-no

Full breakfast
Snacks
Sitting room, Jacuzzi, suites, wood burning stove

Country hideaway estate on 150 acres; luxury suites with private entrances, full gourmet breakfast service in privacy of your own room, fish our 5 acre, bass filled lake. Come relax! shilohbb@aol.com http://www.shilohbb.com

MATHEWS

Ravenswood Inn
PO Box 1430
Poplar Grove Ln 23109
804-725-7272
Mrs. Ricky Durham
Mid-Feb-early Dec

80-130-BB
5 rooms, 5 pb
Visa, MC, *Rated*
C-ltd/S-ltd/P-no/H-no

Full gourmet breakfast
Complimentary wine at sunset
Living room, library

Excellent waterfront location for unwinding, bicycling and enjoying the pleasures of the Chesapeake Bay (tide water area).
ravenswoodinn@yahoo.com http://www.ravenswood-inn.com

MIDDLEBURG

Briar Patch
23130 Briar Patch Ln 20117
703-327-5911 866-327-5911
Ellen Goldberg & Dan Haendel All year

95-195-BB
8 rooms, 2 pb
Most CC
C-yes/S-ltd/P-ltd/H-ltd

Full breakfast
Snacks, complimentary wine
Sitting room, library, pool, suites, frplcs, hot tub, accom. bus. trav.

Historic farm (c. 1805) on 47 rolling acres in the heart of Virginia horse, antiques and wine country. Large pool, hot tub, mountain views, and grazing horses. We host weddings and other gatherings. info@briarpatchbandb.com http://www.briarpatchbandb.com

---

The Goodstone Inn & Estate
36205 Snake Hill Rd 20117
540-687-4645 Fax: 540-687-6115
877-219-4663
Christopher Crane
All year

195-495-BB
13 rooms, 13 pb
Visa, MC, AmEx, •
C-ltd/S-no/P-no/H-ltd
French, Spanish, Bulgarian

Deluxe continental & full breakfast
An elegant English Tea is offered daily in the Gre
Outdoor pool, Jacuzzi, trail bikes, canoeing, golf, massage, trail riding

Set amidst a 265-acre country estate with the Blue Ridge Mts. in the distance, the Goodstone Inn is a luxury country retreat, 3 miles outside of Middleburg in the heart of Virginia's hunt/wine country. information@goodstone.com http://www.goodstone.com

---

The Inn at Stringfellow Farm
19246 Ebenezer Church Rd
20141
540-554-8652 Fax: 540-554-8722
877-409-4449
Jane Nelson & Mick Mallon

150-250-BB
8 rooms, 8 pb
Most CC
C-ltd/S-no/P-ltd
All year

Full breakfast

The Inn at Stringfellow Farm is an historic rural estate (c.1850) located on 20 acres of lush countryside in the heart of Virginia's horse country.
innkeeper@innatstringfellowfarm.com http://www.innatstringfellowfarm.com

MILLBORO

Fort Lewis Lodge
HCR 3, Box 21A
24460
540-925-2314 Fax: 540-925-2352
John and Caryl Cowden
All year

150-210
13 rooms, 13 pb
Visa, MC, *Rated*
C-yes/P-no

Beer, wine, happy hour, dinner, picnic lunches
Outdoor hot tub, mountain bicycles, fishing, basketball

The richness and sheer beauty of the land led Colonel Charles Lewis to settle here more than two centuries ago. ftlewis@va.tds.net http://www.fortlewislodge.com

MONTEREY

Highland Inn
PO Box 40
Main St 24465
540-468-2143 Fax: 540-468-3143
888-466-4682
Gregg and Deborah Morse
All year

59-119-BB
18 rooms, 18 pb
Most CC
C-yes/S-ltd/P-ltd/H-ltd

Continental breakfast
The Monterey Dining Room & The Black Sheep Tavern
Fine Dining, Guest Parlor, two story porch and local tourist info

The Highland Inn, a classic Country Inn nestled in the foothills of the Allegheny Mountains is in the quaint, picturesque village of Monterey.
highinn@cfw.com

MONTROSS

'Tween Rivers
PO Box 1209
16006 Kings Hwy 22520
804-493-0692 Fax: 804-493-0692
800-485-5777
Rayne & Roy Debski All year

95-110-BB
3 rooms, 3 pb
Visa, MC, AmEx, *Rated*, •
C-ltd/S-no/P-no/H-no

Full candlelight breakfast
Snacks, homemade cookies, soft drinks, restaurant
Sitting room, library, canoes, attraction information

Gentrified country colonial home on one acre with sunlit rooms, fine linens, and period antiques near rivers, winery, plantations, golf, biking.
rooms@tweenrivers.com http://www.tweenrivers.com

MONTROSS

Porterville
14201 King's Hwy 22520
804-493-9394
Mary Porter Hall
All year

75-100-BB
2 rooms
C-yes/S-no/P-no/H-no

Full breakfast
Snacks

Enjoy a relaxed country setting in historic Westmoreland County. Cozy guestrooms are ground level. Full country breakfast served with southern hospitality.
http://www.virtualcities.com/ons/va/f/vaf8801.htm

NELLYSFORD

Meander Inn
3100 Berry Hill Rd 22958
434-361-1121 Fax: 434-361-1380
800-868-6116
Alain San Giorgio
All year

105-125-BB
5 rooms, 5 pb
Most CC, *Rated*, •
C-ltd/S-ltd/P-no/H-no
French, Spanish, Italian

Full breakfast
Dinner, afternoon tea, snacks
Sitting room, library, Jacuzzis, fireplace, cable TV, horse boarding

Romantic getaway with a French "flair", nestled in the foothills of Virginia's Blue Ridge Mountains, The Meander Inn an 85 year old Victorian farmhouse on 40 acres of pasture and woods. meanderinn@aol.com http://www.meanderinn.com

NEW MARKET

Cross Roads Inn
9222 John Sevier Rd 22844
540-740-4157 Fax: 540-740-4255
888-740-4157
Mary-Lloyd Freistzer
All year

65-125-BB
6 rooms, 6 pb
Visa, MC, *Rated*
C-yes/S-no/P-no/H-ltd
German

Full breakfast
Afternoon tea, apple strudel
Sitting room, Jacuzzis, fireplaces, cable TV, evening beverages

Gracious country manor in garden setting with mountain views; bountiful breakfast served in sunny breakfast room. freisitz@shentel.net http://www.crossroadsinnva.com

NORFOLK

B&B at the Page House
323 Fairfax Ave 23507
757-625-5033 Fax: 757-623-9451
800-599-7659
Carl A. Albero
All year

130-220-BB
7 rooms, 7 pb
Visa, MC, AmEx, *Rated*, •
C-ltd/S-no/P-yes/H-no

Full breakfast
In-room continental breakfast In-room Champagne
24hr. self-serve snacks, private in-room phones, cable TV, suites w/refrig

Award-winning restoration. Elegantly appointed. "Year's Best Inn Buy," Country Inns Mag. Many ammenities. Perfect location. AAA 4 Diamond Award.
innkeeper@pagehouseinn.com http://www.pagehouseinn.com

ORANGE

Hidden Inn
249 Caroline St 22960
540-672-3625 Fax: 540-672-5029
800-841-1253
Barbara & Ray Lonick
All year

79-169-BB
10 rooms, 10 pb
Visa, MC, *Rated*, •
C-ltd/S-no/P-no/H-no

Full country breakfast
Afternoon tea
Sitting room, Jacuzzi, A/C, fireplaces, cable TV, sitting room

Comfortably furnished country inn tucked away in rural community. Convenient to D.C., Charlottesville, Blue Ridge Mountains. hiddeninn@ns.gemlink.com

---

Holladay House
155 W. Main St 22960
540-672-4893 Fax: 540-672-3028
800-358-4422
Judy Geary
All year

95-205-BB
6 rooms, 6 pb
Most CC, •
C-ltd/S-no/P-no/H-ltd

Full breakfast
Tea, cordials.
Formal parlor w/library, suites, fireplaces, whirlpool, cable TV, porches

1830 Federal style B&B in the quintessential Virginia town of Orange, VA, where guests call the leisurely breakfast elegant and the highlight of their stay.
jgearyhh@aol.com http://www.holladayhousebandb.com

ORANGE (REGION)

Inn at Meander Plantation
HCR 5, Box 460A, *Locust Dale* 22948
540-672-4912 Fax: 540-672-0405
800-385-4936
S. Thomas, S. & B. Blanchard
All year

125-225-BB
8 rooms, 8 pb
Visa, MC, AmEx, *Rated*, •
C-ltd/S-no/P-ltd/H-no

Full gourmet breakfast
Lunch & Dinner–arranged in advance
Stables, fireplaces, sitting room, library, piano, A/C, grand parlor

Historic, elegantly furnished grand 1776 Colonial manor on 80 majestic acres with spectacular views. Romantic, relaxing getaway. inn@meander.net http://www.meander.net

PENN LAIRD (REGION)

Hearth N' Holly Inn
PO Box 2142
46 Songbird Ln, *Harrisonburg* 22801
540-434-6766 800-209-1379
Dennis & Doris Brown
All year

89-BB
3 rooms, 3 pb
Visa, MC, *Rated*, •
S-no/P-no/H-no

Full breakfast
Afternoon tea, snacks
Sitting room, hot tubs pool, bicycles, trails

Enjoy our hiking trails, spa, great gourmet breakfasts. An Inn where the fresh country air & tranquil surroundings are soothing to the senses.
hhinn@rica.net http://www.hearthnholly.com

PORT HAYWOOD

Inn at Tabb's Creek Landing
PO Box 219
Rt 14 23138
804-725-5136 Fax: 804-725-5136
Catherine Venable

95-125-BB
4 rooms, 4 pb
Rated, •
All year

Full breakfast

Ancient magnolias, taller than main house, screened porches overlooking the water, fragrance drifting from rose garden.

PURCELLVILLE

Middle Grove Inn
37175 Jeb Stuart Rd 20132
540-338-0918 Fax: 540-338-3947
Bob & Vicki Moore
All year

85-110-BB
4 rooms, 2 pb
Visa, MC, AmEx
C-ltd/S-no/P-no/H-no

Full breakfast
Dinner; afternoon tea
Sittg rm, library, pool, Jaccuzzi, frplc, cable TV, billiard table, exercise

Want to escape life's hectic pace? Renew your mind, body and spirit? Plan-your-own or participate in an organized retreat.
middlegroveinn@cswebmail.com http://www.middlegroveinn.com

QUICKSBURG

Strathmore House
658 Wissler Rd 22847
540-477-4141 888-921-6139
Kay & Jim Payne
All year

90-125-BB
4 rooms, 4 pb
C-no/S-no/P-no/H-no
Spanish

Full breakfast
Snacks
Sitting room, library, accom. bus. travelers, wraparound porch

Romantic 1892 Victorian Country House, overlooks Meems Bottom covered bridge and Shenandoah River, exquisite bedchambers, canopy beds, private baths, personalized service. strath@shentel.net http://www.StrathmoreHouse.com

RICHMOND (REGION)

The Virginia Cliffe Inn
2900 Mountain Rd, *Glen Allen* 23060
804-266-1661 Fax: 804 266-2946
1 877 254-3346
James & Margaret Clifton
All year

80-135-BB
7 rooms, 5 pb
Most CC
C-ltd/S-no/P-ltd/H-ltd

Full breakfast
special request accepted

Styled in the tradition of grand plantation homes of the eighteenth century! The Virginia Cliffe Inn is nestled among the trees in Glen Allen, 12 miles north of Richmond, Virginia.
vacliffe@aol.com http://www.bbonline.com/va/cliffeinn/

ROANOKE (REGION)

Inn At Burwell Place, Inc
601 W Main St, *Salem* 24153
540-387-0250 Fax: 540-387-3279
800-891-0250
Mary Workman
All year

99-175-BB
4 rooms, 4 pb
Visa, MC, AmEx, *Rated*
C-ltd/S-no/P-no/H-no

Continental breakfast
Snacks, complimentary wine
Sitting room, Jacuzzis, suites, fireplaces, Cable TV, business travelers

AAA 3-diamond. This 7000-sq.-ft. mansion was built in 1907 with magnificent views of the Blue Ridge Mountains.
burwellplace@yahoo.com http://www.bbonline.com/va/burwellplace

---

Serenity's Edge
4404 Murray Hollow Rd, *Thaxton* 24174
540-947-2468 Fax: 540-947-0111
888-920-4224
Paula Tiara
All year

115-185-EP
5 rooms, 4 pb
Visa, MC, •
C-ltd/S-no/P-no/H-yes

Continental Breakfast Plus for B&B
Keepsake Munchies Basket $15.
Solarium, hot tub, fireplace, exercise equipment, Gazebo, trail,library

Serenity's Edge! Romantic Cottages & Bed and Breakfast is an elegant place of quiet relaxation on a mountain top in Thaxton, Virginia's Blue Ridge, between Roanoke and Bedford. info@serenitysedge.com http://www.serenitysedge.com

SHENANDOAH VALLEY (REGION)

Hotel Strasburg
213 S Holliday St, *Strasburg* 22657
540-465-9191 Fax: 540-465-4797
800-348-8327
Gary & Carol Rutherford
All year

79-175-BB
29 rooms, 29 pb
Most CC, *Rated*, •
C-yes/S-yes/P-no/H-no

Continental breakfast
Restaurant, bar service
Snacks, meeting rooms, sitting room, near beach, Jacuzzi in some rooms

Charming Victorian restoration rooms with period antiques, some Jacuzzi suites. Great food & atmosphere. thehotel@shentel.net http://www.hotelstrasburg.com

---

Inn at Narrow Passage
PO Box 608
U.S. 11 and Chapman Landing Rd, *Woodstock* 22664
540-459-8000 800-459-8002
Ellen & Ed Markel
All year

85-145-BB
12 rooms, 12 pb
Visa, MC, *Rated*, •
C-ltd/S-ltd/P-no/H-yes

Full breakfast
Sitting room, conference facility, fireplace, swimming, fishing, rafting

Historic 1740 log inn on the Shenandoah River. Fireplaces, Civil War Sites, vineyards.
innkeeper@innatnarrowpassage.com http://www.innatnarrowpassage.com/

SMITHFIELD

Isle of Wight Inn
1607 S Church St 23430
757-357-3176 800-357-3245
Bob Hart
All year

59-119-BB
12 rooms, 12 pb
Visa, MC, AmEx, *Rated*, •
C-yes/S-ltd/P-no/H-yes

Full breakfast
Snacks, tea, soft drinks
Sitting room, Jacuzzi, walking tour, golf and fishing nearby

Luxurious inn & antique shop. Famous for Smithfield hams & homes dating from 1750. Saint Lukes church, 1632.

Smithfield Station Inn
PO Box 486
415 S Church St 23431
757-357-7700 Fax: 757-357-7638
Ron & Tina Pack
All year

79-225-BB
23 rooms, 23 pb
Visa, MC, AmEx, *Rated*, •
C-ltd/S-yes/P-no/H-no

Continental breakfast
Full service restaurant (fee), Bar
Riverfront Boardwalk, Marina, Bathhouse, Charter Boat, Packages available

Romantic waterfront Inn modeled after Victorian Coast Guard Station. Full service restaurant & marina. Smithfield Historic District. http://www.smithfieldstation.com

SPERRYVILLE

Conyers House Inn & Stable 3131 Slate Mills Rd 22740 540-987-8025 Fax: 540-987-8709 Sandra & Norman All year	150-300-BB 8 rooms, 8 pb *Rated*, • C-ltd/S-ltd/P-ltd/H-no Fr., Ger., It., Arabic	Hearty gourmet breakfast Comp. afternoon refreshments Candlelight dinners, all rooms w/fireplaces, 2 pianos, 9 porches

18th-century former country store graciously furnished with antiques. Hiking, foxhunting & trail rides. 6 course candlelit dinner by reservation. ABC license.
conyers@monumental.com http://www.conyershouse.com

STANARDSVILLE

South River Cottage 3011 South River Rd 22973 434-985-2901 Fax: 434-985-3833 877-874-4473 Judy & Cliff Braun All year	95-185-BB 4 rooms, 4 pb Visa, MC, AmEx, *Rated*, • C-ltd/S-no/P-no/H-no	Full breakfast Snacks Sitting room, bikes, Jacuzzis, suites, accom. bus. travelers

A cozy country inn located on working farm surrounded by Blue Ridge Mountains. Peace and beauty of farm living with modern conveniences.
cbraun@sprintmail.com http://www.southrivercottage.com

STANLEY

White Fence 275 Chapel Rd 22851 540-778-4680 Fax: 540-778-4773 800-211-9885 Gwen & Tom Paton All year	129-160-BB 3 rooms, 3 pb Visa, MC, Disc, *Rated*, • C-yes/S-no/P-no/H-no	Full breakfast Snacks Parlor, Jacuzzi, fireplace, cable TV, breakfast baskets

Lovely 1890 Victorian on 3 beautiful acres. Luxury accommodations include cottage, carriage house and suite in the house. Pampered service in the heart of the Shenandoah Valley. innkeeper@whitefencebb.com http://www.whitefencebb.com

STAUNTON

Ashton Country House 1205 Middlebrook Ave 24401 540-885-6029 Fax: 540-885-6029 800-296-7819 Vince & Dorie DiStefano All year	85-140-BB 6 rooms, 6 pb *Rated*, • C-yes/S-ltd/P-yes/H-yes	Full breakfast Complimentary hot/cold beverages, baked goodies Sitting room, A/C, TV/VCR

1860's Greek Revival on 25 acres. One mile from town. The best of both worlds.
ashtonhouse@aol.com http://www.bbhost.com/ashtonbnb

Frederick House 28 N New St 24401 540-885-4220 Fax: 540-885-5180 800-334-5575 Joe & Evy Harman All year	85-175-BB 23 rooms, 23 pb Most CC, *Rated*, • C-yes/S-no/P-no/H-no	Full breakfast Vegetarian breakfast available Sitting room, library, conference facilities, National Register listing

The oldest city west of the Blue Ridge Mountains of Virginia, historic Staunton is Woodrow Wilson's birthplace. stay@frederickhouse.com http://www.frederickhouse.com

The Sampson Eagon Inn 238 East Beverley St 24401 540-886-8200 800-597-9722 Frank & Laura Mattingly All year	105-135-BB 5 rooms, 5 pb Visa, MC, AmEx, *Rated* S-ltd/P-no/H-ltd	Full breakfast Complimentary snacks/beverages Sitting area with TV/VCR, video library, phones, porch with swing, cable TV

Affordable luxury accommodations in a preservation award winning Antebellum manor, where comfort and hospitality are key. eagoninn@rica.net http://www.eagoninn.com

THE PLAINS

Grey Horse Inn
PO Box 139
4350 Fauquier Ave 20198
540-253-7000 Fax: 540 253-7031
877 253-7020
Scott and Lori Feely
All year

105-200-BB
6 rooms, 6 pb
Most CC, *Rated*, •
C-yes/S-ltd/P-ltd/H-yes
French, Spanish, Arabic

Full breakfast
Hunt Country Upgrade—Cheese Plate and Wine
Jacuzzi, Private Balcony, Queen & King Beds, Antiques, Gardens, TV/Video, AC

Grey Horse Inn is in The Plains, VA near Middleburg and Warrenton close to Washington. Minutes from the Blue Ridge Mtns, Civil War sites, Great Meadow and wineries. Fine dining is nearby. innkeeper@greyhorseinn.com http://www.greyhorseinn.com

WARM SPRINGS

Anderson Cottage
PO Box 176
Old Germantown Road 24484
540-839-2975
Jean Randolph Bruns
Mar–Nov

70-125-BB
5 rooms, 4 pb
Rated, •
C-ltd/S-no/P-ltd/H-no

Full breakfast
Sitting room, library, parlors, porches, yard, croquet, badminton

Rambling old home in village. Walk to Warm Springs pools. Near Garth Newel Chamber Music Center. Restaurants nearby.
jeanbruns@webtv.net http://www.bbonline.com/va/anderson

Inn at Gristmill Square
PO Box 359
Rte 645 24484
540-839-2231 Fax: 540-839-5770
The McWilliams Family
All year

85-150-BB
17 rooms, 17 pb
Visa, MC, Disc, *Rated*, •
C-yes/S-yes/P-no/H-ltd

Continental breakfast
Dinner, bar
Sauna, swimming pool, tennis courts

Casual country hideaway, historic original mill site dating from 1800s. Each room individually decorated. grist@tds.net http://gristmillsquare.com

WARRENTON

The Black Horse Inn
8393 Meetze Rd 20187
540-349-4020 Fax: 540-349-4242
Lynn Pirozzoli
All year

125-295-BB
7 rooms, 7 pb
Visa, MC, AmEx, *Rated*, •
C-ltd/S-ltd/P-no/H-yes

Full breakfast
Afternoon tea, snacks
Comp. wine, bar service, sitt. room, lib., fishing, bikes, rooms w/Jacuzzis

Historic estate in the heart of hunting country, 45 mins from Washington D.C., horseback riding, rafting. relax@blackhorseinn.com http://www.blackhorseinn.com

WASHINGTON

Bleu Rock Inn
12567 Lee Hwy 22747
540-987-3190 Fax: 540-987-3193
800-537-3652
Bernard & Jean Campagne
All year

99-195-BB
5 rooms, 5 pb
Most CC
C-ltd/S-ltd/P-ltd/H-ltd
French

Hearty French breakfast
Restaurant, bar service
Dinner (fee), wine from, vineyards, Sunday brunch, sitting room

World class cuisine, mountain views, lake, fireplaces, rose gardens and terrace, fountains, and swans all contribute to our Inn's charm.
therock@mns.com http://www.bleurockinn.com

Fairlea Farm
PO Box 124
636 Mt Salem Ave 22747
540-675-3679 Fax: 540-675-1064
Walt & Susan Longyear
All year

95-155-BB
4 rooms, 4 pb
Rated, •
C-ltd/S-ltd/P-no/H-no
French

Hearty full country breakfast
Complimentary drinks
Sitting room with fireplace, hiking, horses, shops, near Civil War battlflds

Spectacular mountain views, a five-minute stroll to The Inn at Little Washington.
longyear@shentel.net http://www.fairleafarm.com

The Black Horse Inn, Warrenton, VA

WASHINGTON

Middleton Inn
PO Box 254
176 Main Street 22747
540-675-2020 Fax: 540-675-1050
800-816-8157
Mary Ann Kuhn
All year

195-425-BB
5 rooms, 5 pb
Most CC, *Rated*, •
C-ltd/S-no/P-ltd/H-no

Dinner with advance notice
Wine & cheese, tea
Nightly turndown service, twice daily maid service, porches, TVs, fireplaces

An elegant historic country estate, Middleton Inn has received the prestigious Four Diamond AAA Award for excellence in accommodations and service in an elegant atmosphere. Fireplaces, mountain views.

innkeeper@middleton-inn.com http://www.middleton-inn.com

WILLIAMSBURG

A Primrose Cottage
706 Richmond Rd 23185
757-229-6421 Fax: 757-259-0717
800-522-1901
Inge Curtis
All year

115-145-BB
4 rooms, 4 pb
Visa, MC, *Rated*, •
C-ltd/S-no/P-no/H-no
German

Full breakfast
Sitting room, garden, all rooms w/TV's, private bath, 2 rooms with Jacuzzis

Cozy Cape Cod style home decorated with antiques and family treasures. Short walk to Colonial Williamsburg. ingecurtis@aol.com http://www.primrose-cottage.com

---

Applewood Colonial
605 Richmond Rd 23185
757-229-0205 Fax: 757-229-9405
800-899-2753
Marty Jones
All year

110-175-BB
4 rooms, 4 pb
Visa, MC, *Rated*, •
C-ltd/S-no/P-no/H-no

Full breakfast
Virginia peanuts, apple pie, comp. beverage
Sitting room, suites, fireplaces, in-room cable TV, perfect location

The perfect location to enjoy all the historic sites, or just relax in one of our elegant and thoughtfully appointed bedchambers, with TVs & phones.

info@williamsburgbandb.com http://www.williamsburgbandb.com

Black Badger Inn
720 College Terrace 23185
757-253-0202 Fax: 757-253-9044
877-334-0641
Rosalind & Derek Revilock-Frost
All year

105-BB
4 rooms, 4 pb
Visa, MC
C-ltd/S-no/P-no/H-no

Full breakfast
Sitting room, suites, cable TV, accommodate business travelers

"A wonderful respite! Great hospitality." "The breakfast was a feast each day. The perfect place to stay." innkeeper@blackbadgerinn.com http://www.blackbadgerinn.com

WILLIAMSBURG

The Cedars
616 Jamestown Rd 23185
757-229-3591 Fax: 757-229-0756
800-296-3591
Thomas Mansfield
All year

110-270-BB
9 rooms, 9 pb
Visa, MC, *Rated*, •
C-yes/S-no/P-no/H-no

Full gourmet breakfast
Afternoon tea
Fireplaces in parlor & cottage, off street parking, A/C, cottage w/2 suites

Brick Georgian Colonial house across the street from William 10 min. walk to Colonial Williamsburg. Separate Cottage. Antiques and canopy beds. Hosts family reunions and weddings. cedars@widomaker.com http://www.cedarsofwilliamsburg.com

---

Colonial Capital Inn
501 Richmond Rd 23185
757-776-0570 Fax: 757-253-7667
800-776-0570
Barbara & Phil Craig
All year

135-175-BB
5 rooms, 5 pb
Most CC, *Rated*, •
C-ltd/S-no/P-no/H-no

Full gourmet breakfast
Afternoon tea & wine
Parlor, porch, patio, deck free bikes, free parking, puzzles, games, videos

Walk three blocks to Colonial Williamsburg from this c.1926 Colonial. Canopied beds, private baths, ceiling fans, inroom phone, TV/VCR. Ticket Discounts, Gift Cards, Romance & Convenience packages. ccbb@widomaker.com http://www.ccbb.com

---

Colonial Gardens
1109 Jamestown Rd 23185
757-220-8087 Fax: 757-253-1495
800-886-9715
Scottie & Wil Phillips
All year

135-165-BB
4 rooms, 4 pb
Most CC, *Rated*, •
C-no/S-no/P-no/H-no

Full breakfast
Early riser coffee, afternoon snacks
Sitting room, sunroom, TV/VCR, phones, desks in rooms, attention to detail

Quiet garden setting, in-town location, magnificent antiques, original art, warm hospitality. Spacious suites with fireplaces. Deluxe Packages and Gift Certificates available.
innkeeper@widomaker.com http://www.colonial-gardens.com

Fox & Grape
701 Monumental Ave 23185
757-229-6914 Fax: 757-229-0951
800-292-3699
Pat & Bob Orendorff
All year

95-120-BB
4 rooms, 4 pb
Most CC, *Rated*
S-no/P-no/H-no

Full breakfast
Sitting room, antiques, counted cross stitch quilts, folk art

This lovely 2-story Colonial with spacious wraparound porch is a perfect place to enjoy your morning coffee, plan your day's activities or relax with your favorite book.
info@foxandgrapebb.com http://www.foxandgrapebb.com

Governor's Trace
303 Capitol Landing Rd 23185
757-229-7552 Fax: 757-220-2767
800-303-7552
Dick & Sue Lake
All year

135-150-BB
3 rooms, 3 pb
Visa, MC, Disc, •
C-no/S-no/P-no/H-no

Full breakfast

Closest B&B to historic Colonial Williamsburg "...vies for the most romantic (in Williamsburg)"—WASHINGTON POST. Candlelit breakfast served in your room. One room has wood burning fireplace. govtrace@widomaker.com http://www.governorstrace.com

---

The Inn at 802
802 Jamestown Rd 23185
757-345-3316 Fax: 757-345-3317
800-672-4086
Jillian Gharavinia & Bill Roebuck
All year

135-160-BB
4 rooms, 4 pb
Most CC, *Rated*, •
C-yes/S-no/P-no/H-no
Farsi

Full breakfast
Snacks, complimentary wine
Library, sitting room, fireplaces, cable TV, fitness center

Great location, Colonial Williamsburg 12 minute walk away. Decorated in period style. Common areas include extensive library, large living room, & dining room.
bill@innat802.com http://www.innat802.com

WILLIAMSBURG

Legacy of Williamsburg
930 Jamestown Rd 23185
757-220-0524 Fax: 757-220-2211
800-962-4722
Marshall Wile
All year

135-195-BB
4 rooms, 4 pb
Visa, MC, *Rated*
C-ltd/S-no

Full breakfast
Billiards, phones, TV, 6 fireplaces, library, 18th Century antiques

Voted best 18th Century B&B-style inn in Williamsburg. Romantic, quaint canopy beds. It will be the highlight of your vacation. The legacy.
legacy@tni.net http://legacyofwilliamsburgbb.com

Liberty Rose Inn
1022 Jamestown Rd 23185
757-253-1260 Fax: 757-253-8529
800-545-1825
Brad & Sandra Hirz
All year

175-245-BB
4 rooms, 4 pb
Visa, MC, *Rated*, •
S-no/P-no/H-no

Full breakfast
Complimentary beverages, chocolates
Sitting room, gift shop, suite with many amenities, TV/VCRs, movies in rooms

"Williamsburg's most romantic B&B." Charming home renovated in perfect detail. Courtyards, gardens, an acre of magnificent trees. First choice for honeymooners.
reservations@libertyrose.com http://www.libertyrose.com

Newport House
710 South Henry St 23185
757-229-1775 Fax: 757-229-6408
877-565-1775
John & Cathy Millar
All year

140-150-BB
2 rooms, 2 pb
Rated, •
C-yes/S-no/P-no/H-no
French

Full breakfast
Sitting room, Library, harpsichord, Ballroom for receptions

Designed in 1756. Completely furnished in period. 5-minute walk from historic area. Colonial dancing every Tuesday evening. http://www.newporthousebb.com

---

Williamsburg Sampler B&B Inn
922 Jamestown Rd 23185
757-253-0398 Fax: 757-253-2669
800-722-1169
Ike Sisane
All year

125-170-BB
4 rooms, 4 pb
Rated, •
C-ltd/S-no/P-no/H-no

Full breakfast
Wet bar/refrig in suites
18th Cent carriage house, antiques/pewter/samplers, suites/fireplaces/tavern

Williamsburg's finest plantation style Colonial home. Richly furnished. Guests have included descendants of John Quincy Adams, Capt. John Smith, Charles Dickens.
wbgsampler@aol.com http://www.williamsburgsampler.com

WILLIAMSBURG (REGION)

Edgewood Plantation
4800 John Tyler Hwy, *Charles City* 23030
804-829-2962 Fax: 804-829-2962
800-296-3343
Julian & Dot Boulware
All year

130-200-BB
8 rooms, 8 pb
Visa, MC, *Rated*, •
C-ltd/S-yes

Full breakfast
Complimentary refreshments
Tea room, shops, fireplaces, formal gardens, gazebos, pool, fishing, TV/VCR

1849 historical 7,000 sq. foot 4 story mansion. Double spiral staircase. Incredible furnishings & antiques-well appointed. http://www.Williamsburg-Virginia.com/edgewood

---

The Jasmine Plantation
4500 N Courthouse Rd, *Providence Forge* 23140
804-966-9836 Fax: 804-966-5679
800-639-5368
Rebecca & Scott Wagar
All year

90-150-BB
6 rooms, 5 pb
Visa, MC, AmEx, *Rated*, •
C-ltd/S-ltd/P-no/H-no

Full breakfast
Snacks, soda's, juices, tea, bottled water
Parlor, Den with TV/VCR, ""Country Store"", bird watching, walking trails

Country at its best! Full "skip-lunch" country breakfast. Antique filled 1750s home on 47 acres. Convenient to I-64, Williamsburg, James River Plantations.
innkeeper@jasmineplantation.com http://www.jasmineplantation.com

WILLIAMSBURG (REGION)

Marl Inn B&B
PO Box 572
220 Church St, *Yorktown* 23690
757-898-3859 Fax: 757-898-3587
800-799-6207
Selden Plumley
All year

95-120-BB
4 rooms, 4 pb
Visa, MC, *Rated*, •
C-ltd/S-no/P-ltd/H-no

Continental plus breakfast
Sitting room, library, bikes for guest use to, tour colonial village

Marl Inn is located in the historic district of the restored town. Bicycles with helmets are offered guests to visit battleground, museums, and Revolutionary reception centers.
plumley@aol.com http://www.marlinnbandb.com

York River Inn B&B
209 Ambler St, *Yorktown* 23690
757-887-8800 Fax: 757-887-5393
800-884-7003
William W. Cole
All year

110-130-BB
3 rooms, 3 pb
Visa, MC, *Rated*
C-no/S-no/P-no/H-no

Full breakfast
snacks and soft drinks; tea in afternoon; other
rooms furnished with hair dryers, irons, TV, VCR, and other

York River Inn exceeds all guest expectations with amenities meeting nearly every need in place, with additional needs easily met.
info@yorkriverinn.com http://www.yorkriverinn.com

WINCHESTER

Brownstone Cottage
161 McCarty Ln 22602
540-662-1962 Fax: 540-665-8948
Chuck & Sheila Brown
All year

110-BB
3 rooms, 2 pb
S-ltd/P-no/H-no

Full breakfast
Comp. pass to local spa club, suites, sitting rm, accommodate bus. travelers

Small, private and very quiet bed and breakfast, conducive to peace and rest. Private weddings–without stress, our specialty. Coffee served in-room, big country breakfast.
cs@brownstonecottage.com http://www.brownstonecottage.com

WINCHESTER (REGION)

L'Auberge Provencale
PO Box 190
13630 Lord Fairfax Hwy, *White Post* 22620
540-837-1375 Fax: 540-837-2004
800-638-1702
Alain & Celeste Borel
Exc. Jan–mid-Feb

150-275-BB
14 rooms, 14 pb
Most CC, *Rated*, •
C-ltd/S-yes/P-no/H-no
French

Full gourmet breakfast
Dinner, restaurant, bar service
Refreshments, flowers, library, sitting room, bicycles, gardens

Master chef from France presents nationally acclaimed cuisine. Extensive wine list. Elegant accommodations with fireplaces, private entrances.
cborel@shentel.net http://www.laubergeprovencale.com

WOODSTOCK

Candlewick Inn
127 N Church St 22664
540-459-8008
Sharon and Dennis Pike
All year

85-150-BB
5 rooms, 5 pb
Visa, MC
C-no/S-no/P-no/H-no

Full breakfast
Five o'clock tea, lemonade or hot cider
A/C, Parlor player piano, Jacuzzi in suite, sitting areas in all rooms

The Candlewick Inn is a beautifully restored pre-Civil War home located in picturesque Shenandoah County, Virginia. The Inn is on the National Historic Registry.
candlewickinnllc@hotmail.com http://www.candlewickinnllc.com

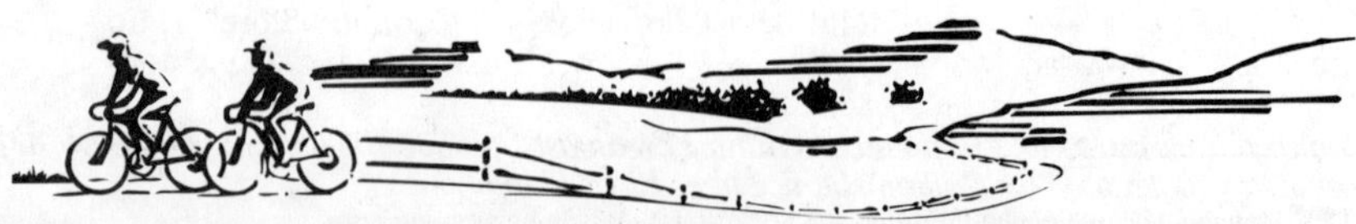

Washington

ABERDEEN

Aberdeen Mansion
807 North M St. 98520
360-533-7079
Allen & Joan Waters
All year

BB

Aberdeen Mansion is a piece of local history as it was built for a lumber baron in 1905. The house is wonderfully decorated with period furnishings and antiques.

reservations@aberdeenmansionbb.com http://www.aberdeenmansionbb.com

ASHFORD

Mountain Meadows Inn
PO Box 291
28912 SR 706 E 98304
360-569-2788
Harry & Michelle Latimer
All year

115-149-BB
6 rooms, 6 pb
Visa, MC, *Rated*
C-ltd/S-ltd/P-no/H-no

Full breakfast most rooms
Picnic lunches available
Luxurious outdoor Jacuzzi spa, maps and guide books to plan your adventures

If seclusion at the base of the most popular tourist attraction is what you are searching for, Mountain Meadows Inn Bed & Breakfast is for you!

mtmeadow@mashell.com http://www.mountainmeadowsinn.com

BAINBRIDGE ISLAND

Agate Pass Waterfront
PO Box 10670
16045 SR 305 NE 98110
206-842-1632
Fax: 800-411-2660
800-869-1632
Penny & Mike McLaughlin
All year

75-125-BB
3 rooms, 3 pb
Most CC, *Rated*, •
C-yes/S-ltd/P-no/H-yes

Breakfast en suite
limitless

7 mi.35 min. and 20 years away from Seattle, our waterfront B&B invites you to smell the salt air, walk the beach, listen to crying gulls, sleep in country quiet far from stress & hurry.

beds@agatepass.com http://www.agatepass.com

The Buchanan Inn
8494 Oddfellows Rd 98110
206-780-9258
Fax: 206-842-9458
800-598-3926
Ron & Judy Gibbs
All year

129-169-BB
4 rooms, 4 pb
Most CC, *Rated*, •
C-ltd/S-ltd/P-no/H-no
Spanish

Full breakfast
Wine
Sitting room, library, Jacuzzi, suites, fireplace, conference facilities

Located just 35 minutes from Seattle by Washington State ferry, features spacious rooms with all the amenities of a four-star hotel. Private hot tub.

jgibbs@buchananinn.com http://www.buchananinn.com

Fuurin-Oka Futon & Breakfast
12580 Vista Dr NE 98110
206-842-4916
All year

149-169-BB
Visa, MC
C-ltd/S-ltd/P-no

Full or continental

Welcome to Fuurin-Oka ("Wind-Bell Hill") Futon and Breakfast, a new, unique bed and breakfast.

molnaire@konzak.com http://www.futonandbreakfast.com

BAINBRIDGE ISLAND

Holly Lane Gardens
9432 Holly Farm Ln 98110
206-842-8959
Patti Dusbabek
All year

BB
C-yes/S-no/P-yes

Enjoyable units include the cottage suite. Each has kitchenette, bathroom, bedroom (queen bed), and relaxing room with couch that opens to a queen-size bed, or a bedroom-bath in the house. dusb2@aol.com

BELFAIR

Selah Inn on Hood Canal
210 NE Cherokee Beach
130 NE Dulalip Landing 98528
360-275-0916 Fax: 360-277-3187
877-232-7941
Bonnie & Pat McCullough
All year

100-205-BB
7 rooms, 7 pb
Visa, MC, *Rated*, •
C-ltd/S-ltd/P-no/H-ltd

Full breakfast
Lunch & Dinner available
Bar service, sitting room, library, Jacuzzis, fireplaces, cable TV

Elegant NW lodge, with majestic view of Hood Canal. Breakfast of Crabcake Eggs Benedict. Dig clams on our beach; we'll steam them for your first of five courses at dinner.
innkeeper@selahinn.com http://www.selahinn.com

BELLEVUE

A Cascade View
13425 NE 27th St 98005
425-883-7078 Fax: 425-702-9326
888-883-7078
Marianne & Bill Bundren
All year

95-120-BB
2 rooms, 2 pb
Visa, MC, AmEx, *Rated*
C-yes/S-ltd/P-no/H-no

Full breakfast
Afternoon tea
Sitting room, library, fireplaces, cable TV, accommodate business travelers

Panoramic views of the Cascade Mountains with extensive colorful and fragrant gardens. 2 beautiful rooms with private baths & extra amenities, fireplace, TV/VCR, sitting room, full breakfasts. innkeepers@acascadeview.com http://www.acascadeview.com

BELLINGHAM

Schnauzer Crossing
4421 Lakeway Dr 98226
360-733-0055 Fax: 360-734-2808
800-562-2808
Monty & Donna McAllister
All year

125-215-BB
3 rooms, 3 pb
Visa, MC, *Rated*
C-yes/S-no/P-ltd
French, Spanish, German

Full breakfast
Sitting room, library, 1/2 acre of gardens, new cottage added 1991

A luxury B&B set amidst tall evergreens overlooking Lake Whatcom. Cottage has fireplace, VCR, private deck, Jacuzzi, skylights.
schnauzerx@aol.com http://www.schnauzercrossing.com

Stratford Manor
4566 Anderson Way 98226
360-715-8441 Fax: 360-671-0840
800-240-6779
Leslie & Jim Lohse All year

125-185-BB
4 rooms, 4 pb
Visa, MC, *Rated*
C-ltd/S-no/P-no/H-no

Full breakfast
Snacks, complimentary wine
Jacuzzis, fireplaces, fresh flowers, robes, outdoor spa, VCRs

Comfortably luxurious English Tudor home on 30 acres. Parklike grounds including perennial gardens and large pond. llohse@aol.com http://www.stratfordmanor.com

BELLINGHAM (REGION)

South Bay B&B
4095 South Bay Dr., *Sedro-Woolley* 98284
360-595-2086 Fax: 360-595-1043
877-595-2086
Dan & Sally Moore
All year

135-150-BB
5 rooms, 5 pb
Visa, MC, *Rated*
C-ltd/S-no/P-no/H-no

Full breakfast
Afternoon tea, snacks, lunch & dinner available
Sitting room, library, bicycles, Jacuzzis, fireplaces

Located in the hillside forest above Lake Whatcom, South Bay with it's lakeview rooms is a quiet retreat that surrounds you with comfortable elegance.
southbay@gte.net http://www.southbaybb.com

CAMANO ISLAND

Camano Blossom
1462 Larkspur Ln 98282
360-629-6784 Fax: 360-629-6794
866-629-6784
Melissa Hsu & Michael Handley
All year

98-128-BB
4 rooms, 4 pb
Most CC, *Rated*
C-ltd/S-no/P-ltd/H-no
Mandarin, Taiwanese

Full breakfast
Dinner, snacks, dinner service available
Sitting room, space for overnight parking of trailerable boats or RV's

Contemporary country home situated on 5 manicured acres looking towards Mt. Baker and Skagit Bay. Unique Asian decor. Beautiful seasonal gardens.
mhandley@worldnet.att.net http://www.camanoblossombandb.com

Camano Island Waterfront Inn
1054 SW Camano Dr 98282
360-387-0783 Fax: 360-387-4173
888-718-0783
Jon & Kari Soth All year

149-195-BB
6 rooms, 6 pb
Most CC, •
C-ltd/S-ltd/P-no/H-yes

Full breakfast
Wine/Beer/Champagne, snack plates, fruit baskets
Tea, snacks, wine, massage, kayaks, Jacuzzis, suites, fireplaces

We are a small, luxurious, waterfront hotel recently ranked the 4th best Bed & Breakfast in the US by Travel and Leisure Magazine!
reservations@camanoislandinn.com http://camanoislandinn.com

Inn at Barnum Point
464 S Barnum Rd 98282
360-387-2256 Fax: 360-387-2256
800-910-2256
Carolin Barnum Dilorenzo
All year

110-199-BB
3 rooms, 3 pb
Most CC, *Rated*, •
C-yes/S-no/P-no/H-no

Full breakfast brunch
Complimentary beverages
Sitting room, library, sidewalks, landscaping, lighting (outside)

All rooms have spectacular water and mountain views. Enjoy our spacious 900 square foot suite. barnum@camano.net http://www.innatbarnumpoint.com

CLE ELUM (REGION)

Iron Horse Inn
PO Box 629
526 Marie Ave, *South Cle Elum* 98943
509-674-5939 Fax: 509-674-1708
800-22-TWAIN
Mary & Doug Pittis All year

55-135-BB
10 rooms, 6 pb
Visa, MC, *Rated*
C-yes/S-no/P-no/H-no

Full breakfast
Afternoon tea
Sitting room, Jacuzzis, cable TV

Filled with historic railroad memorabilia, our former Milwaukee RR train crewman bunk-house has been renovated to provide country comfort and style.
maryp@cleelum.com http://ironhorseinn.uswestdex.com

CLINTON

Home by the Sea Cottages
2388 E Sunlight Beach Rd
Whidbey Island 98236
360-321-2964
S. Fritts Drew, H. Fritts

165-200-BB
7 rooms, 7 pb
S-no/P-yes
All year

Retreat from life's pressures, calm your head and heart, and enjoy the restorative comfort of a country cottage and its gardens on Whidbey Island.
lswalsh@whidbey.com http://www.homebytheseacottages.com

COLVILLE

Lazy Bee Guest House
3651 Deep Lake Boundary Rd 99114
509-732-8917 Fax: 509-732-8917
Bud Budinger & Joann Bender
May-October

60-BB
2 rooms
Visa, MC
C-ltd/S-ltd/P-ltd/H-ltd

Continental breakfast
Lunch, dinner, afternoon tea, snacks
Library, bicycles, fireplaces, accommodate business travelers

Rustic lodge nestled at base of Red Mountain with view of Stone Mountain near Canadian border. budinger.bender@plix.com http://www.travelguides.com/home/Lazy_Bee/

COUPEVILLE

The Captain Whidbey Inn
2072 W Capt. Whidbey 98239
360-678-4097 Fax: 360-678-4110
800-366-4097
Capt. John Colby Stone
All year

85-225-BB
32 rooms, 20 pb
Most CC, *Rated*, •
C-ltd/S-ltd/P-ltd/H-no
French, German, Span.

Full breakfast
All meals available, bar
Sitting room, bicycles, library, sailboats & rowboats

Historic log inn, est. 1907. On the shores of Penn Cove. Antique furnished. Fine restaurant and quaint bar. info@captainwhidbey.com http://www.captainwhidbey.com

DEER HARBOR

Palmer's Chart House
PO Box 51
98243
360-376-4231
Majean Palmer All year

60-100-BB
2 rooms, 2 pb
Rated, •
C-ltd/S-ltd/P-no/H-no
Spanish

Continental breakfast
Library, private deck, flower beds, gardens, fireplaces, cable TV

Quiet, intimate and informal atmosphere. Your hosts know how to pamper you. Fishing, hiking, golf, biking nearby. Day sails on racing-cruising sloop. Sailing on private yacht "Amante."

EASTSOUND

Outlook Inn on Orcas Isle
PO Box 210
Main Street 98245
360-376-2200 Fax: 360-376-2256
888-OUT-LOOK
Starr Farish All year

55-230
29 rooms, 11 pb

Located on the shore of the loveliest of all the American San Juan Islands, the Outlook Inn appears to have been transplanted from the Maine Coast.
info@outlookinn.com http://www.outlookinn.com

EDMONDS

Edmonds Inn
202 Third Avenue South 98020
425-778-1134 888-770-7100
April Waddy
All year

80-120-BB
5 rooms, 5 pb
Most CC
C-ltd/S-ltd/P-no/H-yes

Full breakfast
Complimentary snacks and beverages
Two Patios, a beautiful Yard and a library are available to guests

The Edmonds Inn is located in downtown Edmonds, just three blocks from the waterfront, close to restaurants, beautiful beaches and fine specialty shops. Each morning a home-made breakfast is served. edmonds.inn@verizon.net http://www.edmondsinn.com

ENUMCLAW

White Rose Inn
1610 Griffin Ave 98022
360-825-7194 Fax: 360-802-2472
800-404-7194
Tami & Michael Dunn

85-95-BB
4 rooms, 4 pb
Visa, MC, AmEx, •
C-yes/S-ltd/P-no/H-no
All year

Full breakfast
Sitting room

The gracious hospitality of the past is experienced in this lovely inn today. Escape to the romance of Enumclaw when we turn short stays into lasting memories.
innkeepr@whiteroseinnbb.com http://www.whiteroseinnbb.com

EVERETT

Gaylord House
3301 Grand Ave 98201
425-339-9153 Fax: 425-303-9713
888-507-7177
Gaylord, ShirleyAnne & Theresa
All year

85-150-BB
5 rooms, 5 pb
Most CC, *Rated*, •
C-ltd/S-ltd/P-no/H-no
Italian

Full gourmet breakfast
Lunch, dinner, high tea, snacks
Sitting room, library, Jacuzzi, fireplace, cable TV, business travelers

Our turn-of-the-century home has five theme rooms w/private bath, TV/VCR, data port and private phone line. ShirlyAnne's gourmet breakfasts, afternoon teas and gourmet dinners are wonderful! gaylord_house@gaylordhouse.com http://www.gaylordhouse.com

FRIDAY HARBOR

Beaverton Valley Farm
4144 Beaverton Valley Rd
98250
360-378-3276 877-378-3276
Richard Foote & Angel Michaels
All year

100-165-BB
5 rooms, 5 pb
Most CC, •
C-yes/S-no/P-yes/H-ltd
Scoshi Japanese, French

Full breakfast
Gourmet breakfasts with homemade jams & jellies... Great living room with stone fireplace, night sky full of stars....

Island farmhouse on 3 peaceful acres, 4 mi. from Friday Harbor. Beautiful rooms & carvings. Romantic stone fireplace, gourmet breakfast, private baths. Settler's Cabin is ideal for pets and families. farm@beavertonvalley.com http://www.beavertonvalley.com

---

Friday's Historical Inn
PO Box 2023
35 First St 98250
360-378-5848 Fax: 360-378-2881
800-352-2632
Adam & Laura Saccio
All year

99-219-BB
15 rooms, 11 pb
Visa, MC, *Rated*, •
C-yes/S-no/P-no/H-yes
Span., French, German, Dutch, Japanese

Homemade Continental breakfast
Afternoon snacks and refreshments

Conveniently located just two blocks from the Washington State ferry landing, Friday's Historic Inn is an easy stroll to the Friday Harbor waterfront and the town shops and restaurants. stay@friday-harbor.com http://www.fridayharborinn.com

---

Highland Inn
PO Box 135
439 Hannah Rd 98250
360-378-9450 Fax: 360-378-1693
888-400-9850
Helen Chapman King
All year

175-250-BB
2 rooms, 2 pb
Visa, MC, AmEx, *Rated*, •
S-no/P-no/H-no
Spanish

Full breakfast
Afternoon tea
Sitting room, Jacuzzis, suites, fireplaces, cable, accom. bus. travel.

Nestled in wooded west side with ocean view to Olympics, Victoria B.C., Orca Whales, sunsets, stars from 88 foot veranda.
helen@highlandinn.com http://www.highlandinn.com

Hillside House
365 Carter Ave 98250
360-378-4730 Fax: 360-378-4715
800-232-4730
Cathy & Dick Robinson
All year

120-250-BB
7 rooms, 7 pb
Visa, MC, AmEx, *Rated*, •
C-ltd/S-ltd/P-no/H-no

Full breakfast
Famous banana-chocolate chip cookies

Contemporary B&B in Friday Harbor, 3/4 of a mile from the ferry landing, overlooking harbor and Mt. Baker. info@hillsidehouse.com http://www.hillsidehouse.com

---

Pear Point Inn
2858 Pear Point Rd 98250
360-378-6655
John Darroudi & Lisa Brown
All year

155-225-BB
2 rooms, 2 pb
Visa, MC, *Rated*, •
C-ltd/S-ltd/P-no/H-no

Full breakfast
Snacks, afternoon tea
Sitting room, Jacuzzis, suites, fireplaces, cable TV

Beautiful, modern oceanview Inn on 7+ acres. Spacious rooms with private baths and amenities. pearpointinn@interisland.net http://www.pearpointinn.com

---

Trumpeter Inn
318 Trumpeter Way 98250
360-378-3884 Fax: 360-378-8235
800-826-7926
Aylene Geringer & Mark Zipkin
All year

140-175-BB
6 rooms, 6 pb
Visa, MC, Disc, *Rated*, •
C-ltd/S-no/P-no/H-yes

Full breakfast
Tea, cookies, juices, bottled water in rooms
TV/VCR, living room and den, wheelchair accessible suite, spa, robes.

Our pastoral setting on 5 acres, with views of water, snow-capped mountains, and stunning sunrises and sunsets soothes the soul.
swan@rockisland.com http://www.trumpeterinn.com

GLACIER

the Inn at Mt. Baker
PO Box 5150
8174 Mt Baker Hwy 98244
360-599-1776 Fax: 1-360-599-3000
1-877-567-5526
Carole MacDonald
All year

110-130-BB
5 rooms, 5 pb
Most CC, •
C-no/S-ltd/P-no/H-ltd

Tea, coffee, hot chocolate, popcorn, juices
Hot tub, guest lounge, covered patio

Five guestrooms in this new luxury European style B&B. All have private bath and extraordinary views of Mt Baker, surrounding mountains, the Nooksack River and Valley. Hot tub and guest patio.

tiamb@earthlink.net http://www.theinnatmtbaker.com

GLACIER (REGION)

Mt Baker Lodging, Inc
PO Box 5177
7463 Mt Baker Highway, *Mt. Baker* 98244
360-599-2453 Fax: 360-599-1000
800-709-SNOW
Dan Graham
All year

99-450-EP
50 rooms
Most CC, *Rated*, •
C-yes/S-no/P-ltd/H-ltd

Fully equipped kitchens w/ all cookware, all bed & bath linens provided

An Alternative To The Traditional B&B, Mt. Baker Lodging Is Your #1 Source For Private, Fully Equipped Vacation Rental Home Accommodations. Located At The Magnificent Gateway To Mount Baker, WA!

reservations@mtbakerlodging.com http://www.mtbakerlodging.com

HOQUIAM

Hoquiam Castle
515 Chenault Ave 98550
360-533-2005 Fax: 360-533-2005
877-542-2785
David & Linda Carpenter
All year

75-140-BB
5 rooms, 5 pb
Visa, MC, AmEx, *Rated*, •
C-ltd/S-no/P-no/H-ltd

Full breakfast
Evening dessert, sherry

A Victorian mansion overlooking Gray's Harbor. 5 large bedrooms all with private baths, and featured in National Geographic's America's Great Homes.

carpld@olynet.com http://www.hoquiamcastle.com

KIRKLAND

Shumway Mansion
11410 99th Place NE 98033
425-823-2303 Fax: 425-822-0421
R & S Harris and J. Blakemore
All year

85-120-BB
8 rooms, 8 pb
Visa, MC, *Rated*, •
C-ltd/S-no/P-no/H-ltd

Full breakfast buffet
Evening snack, drinks
Sitting room, piano, weddings, receptions, meetings

Four-story mansion circa 1910. Views of lake and bay. Delicious breakfasts and afternoon goodies. Walk to beach, shops, galleries.

info@shumwaymansion.com http://www.shumwaymansion.com

LA CONNER

Skagit Bay Hideaway
PO Box 497
17430 Goldenview Ave 98257
360-466-2262 Fax: 360-466-7493
888-466-2262
Earlene Beckes & Kevin Haberly
All year

BB
Visa, MC
S-no/P-no

Coffeepot, teapot and refrigerator

For a totally different experience from the lodge or the hotel, check into Skagit Bay Hideaway Bed and Breakfast near La Conner, Washington, with magnificent Puget Sound views. hideaway@skagitbay.com http://www.skagitbay.com

LA CONNER (REGION)

Samish Point by the Bay
4465 Samish Point Rd, *Bow* 98232
360-766-6610 Fax: 360-766-6610
800-916-6161
Theresa L. Goldston All year

175-330-BB
1 rooms, 1 pb
Visa, MC, AmEx, *Rated*, •
C-ltd/S-no/P-no/H-no

Continental Plus breakfast
Afternoon tea, snacks
Sitting room, library, Jacuzzis, fireplaces, cable TV, accom. bus. travelers

Reminiscent of a Cape Cod beach retreat, the cozy, casual cottage accommodates 2-6 in party and is decorated with honey pine and white-washed furnishings with handmade quilts. hgtg@samishpoint.com http://www.samishpoint.com

---

The White Swan Guest House
15872 Moore Rd, *Mount Vernon* 98273
360-445-6805
Peter Goldfarb All year

75-160-BB
3 rooms
Rated, •
C-ltd/S-no/P-no/H-no

Continental plus breakfast
Chocolate chip cookies
Sitting room, library, outdoor patio, garden cottage sleeps 4

A "storybook" Victorian farmhouse 6 miles from La Conner, 1 hour north of Seattle. Honeymoon Cottage. http://www.thewhiteswan.com

LANGLEY

Ashingdon Manor
PO Box 869
5023 Langley Rd 98260
360-221-2334 Fax: 360-221-8503
800-442-4942
Charles & Jennifer Johnson
Mid Feb. to mid Dec.

95-145-BB
6 rooms, 6 pb
Visa, MC, *Rated*, •
C-ltd/S-no/P-no/H-yes

Full breakfast
Complimentary tea & wine, dinner available
Sitting room, library, bikes, suites, fireplaces

Traditional country manor decorated with furnishings and object d'art from around the world. innkeeper@ashingdonmanor.com http://www.ashingdonmanor.com

---

Country Cottage of Langley
215 6th St 98260
360-221-8709 800-713-3860
Jacki Stewart & Tom Felvey
All year

129-179-BB
5 rooms, 5 pb
Visa, MC, AmEx, *Rated*, •
C-yes/S-no/P-ltd/H-ltd

Full gourmet breakfast
Full, hot breakfast served in room or on your deck
Scenic dining room, view deck, gazebo, Croquet lawns and Bocce Ball

1920 farmhouse with 5 separate and distinct cottages on 1½ acres of beautiful gardens. Amazing view of Puget Sound, 2 person Jacuzzis, fireplace, gourmet breakfast, 4 minute walk to Langley Village. stay@acountrycottage.com http://www.acountrycottage.com

---

Eagles Nest Inn
4680 Saratoga Rd 98260
360-221-5331 Fax: 360-221-5331
800-243-5536
Joanne & Jerry Lechner
All year

95-140-BB
5 rooms, 5 pb
Visa, MC, Disc, *Rated*, •
C-ltd/S-no

Full gourmet breakfast
Complimentary bar, tea, coffee
Library, sitting room, TV, fireplace, woodstove, video library, hot tub

Water views, Northwest ambiance with natural art. Hilltop setting on Whidbey Island. One and a half mile from Langley restaurants & shops.
eaglnest@whidbey.com http://www.eaglesnestinn.com

Island Tyme
4940 S Bayview Rd 98236
360-221-5078 800-898-8963
Cliff & Carol Wisman
All year

95-140-BB
5 rooms, 5 pb
Visa, MC, AmEx, *Rated*, •
C-ltd/S-no/P-ltd/H-yes

Full breakfast
Snacks
Jacuzzis, pets in 1 room, fireplaces,

Light a fire, soak in your Jacuzzi, savor your gourmet breakfast at our Victorian B&B, close to Langley, Whidbey Island. islandty@whidbey.com http://www.islandtymebb.com

LANGLEY

Villa Isola Inn
5489 S Coles Rd 98260
360-221-5052 Fax: 360-221-5823
800-246-7323
Bob & Dova Thirsk
All year

95-135-BB
5 rooms, 5 pb
Visa, MC, *Rated*, •
C-no/S-no/P-no/H-no

Full breakfast
Espresso bar/snacks
Charm of Italian villa, professional Bocce court, gardens, Mt. biking

Italian hospitality & Mediterranean charm, contemporary furnishing located on 3 1/2 beautifully landscaped acres. villa@villaisola.com http://www.villaisola.com

LEAVENWORTH

Abendblume Pension
PO Box 981
12570 Ranger Road 98826
509-548-4059 Fax: 509-548-4059
800-669-7634
Randy & Renee Sexauer
All year

77-159-BB
7 rooms, 7 pb

Inspired by fine European country inns, Abendblume is one of Leavenworth's finest award winning bed and breakfasts.
abendblm@rightathome.com http://www.abendblume.com

All Seasons River Inn
PO Box 788
8751 Icicle Rd 98826
509-548-1425 800-254-0555
Jeff & Kathy Falconer
All year

135-180-BB
6 rooms, 6 pb
Visa, MC, *Rated*
S-no/P-no

Full breakfast
Snacks
Sitting room, library, bicycles, Jacuzzis, suites, fireplaces

Cedar home framed by evergreens, just 80 feet from the river. Terraced gardens and pathway to the river. Spacious Jacuzzi suites with decks. Some fireplaces.
info@allseasonsriverinn.com http://www.allseasonsriverinn.com

---

Anna-Hotel Pension
PO Box 127
926 Commercial 98826
509-548-6273 Fax: 509-548-4656
800-509-ANNA
Anne & Robert Smith
All year

89-199-BB
15 rooms, 15 pb
Most CC, *Rated*, •
C-yes/S-no/P-no/H-yes
German, Spanish

Continental plus breakfast
Library, Jacuzzi, suites, fireplace, cable TV

Our 15 rooms are appointed with furniture imported from Germany and Austria with down comforters on each bed. http://www.pensionanna.com

---

Autumn Pond
10388 Titus Rd 98826
509-548-4482 800-222-9661
John & Jennifer Lorenz
All year

89-99-BB
6 rooms, 6 pb
Visa, MC, AmEx, *Rated*, •
C-ltd/S-no/P-no/H-no

Full breakfast
Mountain view lounge, outdoor hot tub

Autumn Pond rests on three quiet country acres, surrounded by panoramic views of the majestic Cascades. info@autumnpond.com http://www.autumnpond.com

---

Mrs. Andersons Lodging House
917 Commercial St 98826
509-548-6173 Fax: 509-548-9113
800-253-8990
Dee & Al Howie
All year

39-70-BB
10 rooms, 8 pb
Visa, MC, Disc, *Rated*
C-yes/S-no/P-no/H-yes

Continental breakfast
Coffee & tea all day
Central heating, A/C, cable TV, massages, views, sundeck, garden, parking

Built in 1895, renovated in 1989. Decorated with turn-of-the-century antiques, quilts and vintage clothing. The decor changes 5 times a year with the seasons.
info@quiltersheaven.com http://www.quiltersheaven.com

LEAVENWORTH

Pine River Ranch
19668 Highway 207 98826
509-763-3959 Fax: 509-763-2073
800-669-3877
Michael & Mary Ann Zenk
All year

135-180-BB
6 rooms, 6 pb
Most CC, *Rated*, •
C-no/S-no/P-no/H-ltd

Full breakfast
Chocolate strawberries, fresh fruit & cheese tray
Snowshoes, mountain bikes, private river front beach, outdoor hot tub

Discover Pine River Ranch all-suite B&B, the perfect romantic mountain retreat. Featuring 6 spacious suites, each with a fireplace, two person whirlpool tub, wet bar, breakfast delivered to your room.

lodger@prranch.com http://www.prranch.com

LONG BEACH

Boreas Inn
PO Box 1344
607 N Ocean Beach Blvd 98631
360-642-8069 Fax: 360-642-5353
888-642-8069
Susie Goldsmith & Bill Verner
All year

130-150-BB
5 rooms, 5 pb
Most CC, *Rated*, •
C-yes/S-no/P-no/H-no

Full gourmet breakfast
Afternoon tea, snacks
Sitting room, library, hot tubs, gazebo, decks, reunions/weddings

Artistically remodeled 1920s beach home. Oceanview bedrooms, spacious living rooms with fireplace. New Dunes Suite added with jetted tub.

boreas@boreasinn.com http://www.boreasinn.com

LONG BEACH (REGION)

The Whalebone House
2101 Bay Ave, *Ocean Park* 98640
360-665-5371 888-298-3330
Deidre & RD Williams
All year

115-BB
4 rooms, 4 pb
Visa, MC, *Rated*, •
C-ltd/S-no/P-no/H-ltd

Full gourmet breakfast
Fresh baked snacks, coffee, tea, fresh fruit
Sitting room, library, country gardens, enclosed sunporch, accom. bus. trav.

This restored 1889 Victorian farmhouse is a blending of the architectural styles of the Pacific Northwest and coastal Maine.

stay@whalebonehouse.com http://www.whalebonehouse.com

Shelburne Inn
PO Box 250
4415 Pacific Way, *Seaview* 98644
360-642-2442 Fax: 360-642-8904
800-INN-1896
Laurie Anderson & David Campiche
All year

119-239-BB
16 rooms, 13 pb
Visa, MC, *Rated*, •
C-ltd/S-yes/P-no/H-yes
French, German, Portuguese

Full country breakfast
Restaurant, pub
Lobby with fireplace, organ, 2 suites

The oldest surviving Victorian hotel in Washington state, with the time-honored tradition of superb service, decor and distinguished cuisine. Can accommodate small meetings of up to 30. innkeeper@theshelburneinn.com http://www.theshelburneinn.com

MT. RAINIER (REGION)

Alexander's Country Inn, Rest.
37515 State Rd 706 E, *Ashford* 98304
360-569-2300 Fax: 360-569-2323
800-654-7615
Melinda J. Simpson
All year

79-140-BB
12 rooms, 12 pb
Visa, MC, *Rated*, •
C-yes/S-no/P-no/H-ltd

Served in Alexander's Retaurant
Complimentary wine served each evening
Hot tub overlooking trout pond, nature trails, full service restaurant

Visit historic Alexander's. Overnight guests enjoy wine and fresh fruit served by the parlor fireplace, a romantic hot tub, full breakfast. Restaurant and 2 Vacation Rentals.

info@alexanderscountryinn.com http://www.alexanderscountryinn.com

MUKILTEO

By the Bay
821 Fourth St 98275
425-347-4997
Mary Epps All year

80-120-BB
2 rooms, 2 pb
C-yes/S-ltd/P-no/H-no

Full breakfast
Sitting room, gardens

Enjoy the comfort and charm of a small village setting while staying in a romantic 1914 bed and breakfast home. Within walking distance of beaches, a state park, famous restaurants and gift shops. bythebay@gte.net http://www.bythebay.net

NORTH BEND

Roaring River
46715 SE 129th St 98045
425-888-4834 877-627-4647
Herschel & Peggy Backues
All year

95-175-BB
4 rooms, 4 pb
Most CC, *Rated*
C-ltd/S-no/P-no/H-no

Full breakfast
Jacuzzis, suites, fireplaces, cable TV, accommodate business travelers

Choose a hot tub, sauna, or Jacuzzi room. Very romantic, very private, wonderful restaurants, and incredible views of mountains, rivers, forests, and occasional wildlife.
info@theroaringriver.com http://www.theroaringriver.com

OLYMPIA

Puget View Guesthouse
7924 61st Ave NE 98516
360-413-9474
Dick & Barbara Yunker
All year

99-129-BB
2 rooms, 1 pb
Visa, MC, *Rated*, •
C-yes/S-yes/P-ltd/H-no

Continental plus breakfast
BBQ
Private dining area/deck, books, games, canoe, 100-acre park next door

Charming waterfront guest cottage suite next to host's log home. Breakfast to your cottage. Peaceful. Picturesque. A "NW Best Places" since 1984.
http://www.bbonline.com/wa/pugetview

Swantown Inn
1431 11th Ave SE 98501
360-753-9123 Fax: 360-943-8047
Lillian & Ed Peeples
Season Inquire

65-120-BB
4 rooms, 4 pb
Visa, MC, *Rated*, •
C-ltd/S-ltd/P-no/H-no
German

Full breakfast
Complimentary afternoon tea

Located in the heart of Olympia, Washington, Swantown Inn can be your headquarters for exploring the Puget Sound Region, or your refuge to escape from it all.
swantown@olywa.net http://www.olywa.net/swantown/

ORCAS (REGION)

Orcas Hotel
PO Box 155
18 Orcas Hill, *Orcas Island* 98280
360-376-4300 Fax: 360-376-4399
888-672-2792
Laura & Doug Tidwell
All year

79-189-BB
12 rooms, 7 pb
Visa, MC, AmEx, *Rated*, •
C-yes/S-no/P-no/H-yes

Cont. Brkfst included peak season
Antiques, books, curios, island art

The Orcas Hotel Bed and Breakfast has been welcoming guests since 1904. The island landmark occupies a place of honor on the National Register of Historic Places.
orcas@orcashotel.com http://www.orcashotel.com

ORCAS ISLAND (REGION)

Kangaroo House B&B
PO Box 334, *Eastsound* 98245
360-376-2175 Fax: 360-376-3604
888-371-2175
Peter & Helen Allen All year

90-150-BB
5 rooms
Most CC, *Rated*, •
C-yes/S-no/P-no/H-no

Full breakfast
Complimentary beverages & snacks
Special diets on request, fireplace, sitting room, hot tub in garden

1907 B&B near Eastsound offers lodging accommodations on Orcas Island in the San Juan Islands of Washington.
innkeeper@KangarooHouse.com http://www.KangarooHouse.com

ORCAS ISLAND (REGION)

Turtleback Farm Inn
1981 Crow Valley Rd,
Eastsound 98245
360-376-4914 Fax: 360-376-4914
800-376-4914
William & Susan C. Fletcher
All year

90-225-BB
11 rooms, 11 pb
Visa, MC, *Rated*, •
C-ltd/S-no/P-no/H-yes

Full breakfast
Complimentary tea & coffee
Bar, complimentary sherry, games, living room, fireplace

Romantic country inn renowned for excellent food, stunning decor, caring hospitality and serene location. New four room Orchard House includes king beds, claw-footed tubs.
info@turtlebackinn.com http://www.turtlebackinn.com

PORT ANGELES

A Hidden Haven & Water Garden Cottages
1428 Dan Kelly Rd 98363
360-452-2719 Fax: 360-417-7585
877-418-0938
Chris & Jodi Jones
All year

95-250-BB
5 rooms, 4 pb
Visa, MC, *Rated*
C-yes/S-ltd/P-no/H-no
Tagalog

Full country breakfast
Tea, snacks, full, continental/plus breakfasts
Sitting room, Jacuzzis

Secluded haven nestled on 20 lush acres at the foot of the Olympics. New elegant luxury cottages! stay@ahiddenhaven.com http://www.ahiddenhaven.com

---

BJ's Garden Gate
397 Monterra Dr 98362
360-452-2322 800-880-1332
BJ & Frank Paton
All year

130-200-BB
5 rooms, 5 pb
Visa, MC, AmEx, *Rated*, •
C-no/S-no/P-no/H-ltd

Full breakfast
Evening sweet
Waterfront, Jacuzzi for 2, fireplace, private bathroom

Pamper yourself in a Victorian waterfront estate with a private fireplace and Jacuzzi for 2. bjgarden@olypen.com http://www.bjgarden.com

---

Colette's
339 Finn Hall Rd 98362
360-457-9197 Fax: 360-452-0711
877-457-9777
Peter & Lynda Clark
All year

175-235-BB
5 rooms, 5 pb
Visa, MC, *Rated*
C-ltd/S-no/P-no

Full breakfast
Afternoon tea, fresh baked cookies, wine & cheese
Special occasions celebration packages, private group retreats, weddings

10-acre waterfront estate nestled between the majestic Olympic Range & the Strait of Juan de Fuca. Suites are luxury king accommodations with private baths, 2-person Jacuzzi, patio, & waterfront views. colettes@olypen.com http://www.colettes.com

---

Domaine Madeleine
146 Wildflower Ln 98362
360-457-4174 Fax: 360-457-3037
888-811-8376
Jeri Weinhold All year

140-225-BB
5 rooms, 5 pb
Most CC, *Rated*
C-ltd/S-ltd/P-no/H-no

Full breakfast
24 hr coffee, tea, hot chocolate, cookies
Sitting room, library, Jacuzzi, lawn games, fireplaces, cable TV

Serene, romantic, contemporary estate w/panoramic Mt European/Asian antiques; fireplace, Jacuzzi, private entrance, renowned 5-course breakfast.
romance@domainemadeleine.com http://www.domainemadeleine.com

Five SeaSuns
1006 S Lincoln St 98362
360-452-8248 Fax: 360-417-0465
800-708-0777
Bob & Jan Harbick
All year

79-135-BB
5 rooms, 5 pb
Visa, MC, *Rated*, •
C-ltd/S-no/P-no/H-no

Full breakfast
Lunch (fee), snacks
Sitting room, Carriage house suite can accommodate four

Peaceful gardens with towering evergreens surrounding an elegant 1926 Dutch Colonial home. Antique furnishings, water and mountain views.
info@seasuns.com http://www.seasuns.com

Five SeaSuns, Port Angeles, WA

PORT TOWNSEND

Ann Starrett Mansion
744 Clay St 98368
360-385-3205 Fax: 360-385-2976
800-321-0644
Edel Sokol
All year

105-205-BB
11 rooms, 11 pb
Visa, MC, *Rated*, •
C-ltd/S-no/P-no/H-ltd

Full breakfast
Complimentary sherry, tea
Sitting room, weddings, honeymoon cottage, Jacuzzi/hot tub, massage

"A destination with a sense of history is a vacation with romance." A tribute to love.
info@starrettmansion.com http://www.starrettmansion.com

Bishop Victorian Guest Suites
714 Washington St 98368
360-385-6122 Fax: 360-379-1840
800-824-4738
Joe & Cindy Finnie
All year

89-199-BB
16 rooms, 16 pb
Most CC, *Rated*, •
C-yes/S-no/P-ltd/H-no

Continental breakfast
Coffee, tea
Internet access, catering, parking lot, conference facilities, kitchenettes

Downtown Victorian-era hotel; beautifully restored. Gracious suites. Mountain and water views. Walk to Port Townsend.
info@rainshadowproperties.com http://www.bishopvictorian.com

The English Inn
718 F St 98368
360-385-5302 800-254-5302
Martin & Jennifer MacGillonie
All year

110-120-BB
4 rooms, 4 pb
Visa, MC, *Rated*
C-ltd/S-ltd/P-no/H-no

Full gourmet breakfast
Afternoon tea, snacks, early morning coffee
Sitting room w/fireplace, gazebo, on-line availability on web site

Where a welcoming English atmosphere awaits you. Stunning Italianate-style Victorian home built c.1885. MacGillonie@english-inn.com http://www.english-inn.com

---

The James House
1238 Washington St 98368
360-385-1238 Fax: 360-379-5551
800-385-1238
Carol McGough
All year

135-225-BB
13 rooms, 11 pb
Visa, MC, *Rated*, •
C-ltd/S-no/P-no/H-ltd

Full breakfast
Complimentary sherry & cookies
Sitting parlors, player piano, fireplaces, porch with swing, garden

1889 Queen Anne Victorian mansion featuring unsurpassed water and mountain views, period antiques. First B&B in the Northwest, still the finest.
info@jameshouse.com http://www.jameshouse.com

PORT TOWNSEND

Lizzie's Victorian
834 Walker St 98368
360-385-4168 Fax: 360-685-9467
800-700-4168
Patti Wickline
All year

70-135-BB
7 rooms, 7 pb
Rated

A wonderful contemporary Bed and Breakfast with a great view.
wickline@olympus.net http://www.lizziesvictorian.com

Old Consulate Inn
313 Walker at Washington
98368
360-385-6753 Fax: 360-385-2097
800-300-6753
Michael & Sue DeLong
All year

110-210-BB
8 rooms, 8 pb
Visa, MC, *Rated*
C-ltd/S-no/P-no/H-no

Full breakfast—banquet
Coffee, tea and cookies; evening desserts
Comp. wine, sitting room, library, tennis, hot tub, billiard and game room

Award-winning Founding Family Mansion-on-the-Bluff. Romantic retreat offering warm hospitality, king beds, comfortable elegance, evening cordials!
mike@oldconsulateinn.com http://www.oldconsulateinn.com

The Swan Hotel
216 Monroe 98368
360-385-1718 800-776-1718
Joe and Cindy Finnie
All year

115-475-EP
9 rooms, 9 pb
Most CC, *Rated*, •
C-yes/S-no/P-yes/H-yes

Small meeting facilities, high speed internet access, and catering

A waterfront hotel overlooking Point Hudson Marina with one-bedroom suites, 2 story penthouse with 4 bedrooms, and garden cottages.
info@rainshadowproperties.com http://www.theswanhotel.com

PORT TOWNSEND (REGION)

Beach Cottages on Marrowstone
10 Beach Dr, *Nordland* 98358
360-385-3077 Fax: 360-385-1181
800-871-3077
Allison & Stephen Willing
All year

60-200-EP
8 rooms, 8 pb
Visa, MC, *Rated*
C-yes/S-no/P-no/H-ltd
German

Full kitchen in each cabin
3 miles undeveloped beach, mountains, wildlife, no one around.

1930s Puget Sound beach hideaway, upgraded to modern basics. Island living, island pace of life (bridge to island). http://www.beachcottagegetaway.com

POULSBO

The Murphy House
PO Box 1960
425 NE Hostmark St 98370
360-799-1600 Fax: 360-697-3832
800-779-1606
Judy & Gordon Buhler
All year

79-119-BB
5 rooms, 5 pb
Visa, MC, AmEx, •
C-ltd/S-no/P-no/H-ltd

Full breakfast
Snacks available
Sitting room, library, fireplaces, Broadband Internet access, cable TV

Get away to comfortable elegance in downtown Poulsbo. Outstanding views of Liberty Bay & Olympic Mountains. Full-service gourmet breakfasts. Five rooms with private baths.
info@murphyhousebnb.com http://www.murphyhousebnb.com

SEATTLE

Amaranth Inn
1451 S Main St 98144
206-720-7161 Fax: 206-323-0772
800-720-7161
Herman and Alea Foster
All year

75-165-BB
8 rooms, 6 pb
Most CC, *Rated*
C-no/S-no/P-no/H-no

Two-course gourmet breakfast
Beautiful sunporch, living room with fireplace, off-street parking available

Grand 1906 Craftsman, just a 20 minute walk (3/4 mile) from downtown Seattle. Lovely restored interior with fireplaces in all rooms but one. Full 2-course breakfast. TVs, phones, parking. visitus@amaranthinn.com http://www.amaranthinn.com

SEATTLE

Bacon Mansion
959 Broadway E 98102
206-329-1864 Fax: 206-860-9025
800-240-1864
Daryl J. King
All year

89-179-BB
11 rooms, 9 pb
Most CC, *Rated*
C-ltd/S-no/P-no/H-no

Continental plus breakfast
Sitt. rm., lib., conference rm., TV, hair dryer, private voicemail/dataport

One of Capitol Hill's gracious mansions c. 1909. Luxury antique-filled rooms, hand-carved woodwork.
info@baconmansion.com http://www.baconmansion.com

Capitol Hill Inn
1713 Belmont Ave 98122
206-323-1955 Fax: 206-322-3809
Joanne and Katie Godmintz
All year

95-170-BB
6 rooms, 6 pb
Visa, MC, AmEx
C-ltd/S-ltd/P-no

Full gourmet breakfast

Located just 6 blocks from downtown Seattle, Capitol Hill Inn is the closest Bed and Breakfast to downtown Seattle, Washington and we're more comfortable than a Hotel.
caphillinn@aol.com http://www.capitolhillinn.com

Chambered Nautilus
5005 22nd Ave NE 98105
206-522-2536 Fax: 206-528-0898
800-545-8459
Steve Poole & Joyce Schulte
All year

89-139-BB
10 rooms, 10 pb
Visa, MC, AmEx, *Rated*
C-ltd/S-no/P-no/H-no
French

Full breakfast
Fireplaces, pvt baths, pvt. phones, robes, tea and cookies,TV, hairdryer

An elegant Colonial home near the University of Washington campus. Minutes from downtown. Rooms are large and quiet.
stay@chamberednautilus.com http://www.chamberednautilus.com

Chelsea Station on the Park
4915 Linden Ave N 98103
206-547-6077 Fax: 206-632-5107
800-400-6077
Carolanne Watner
All year

100-185-BB
9 rooms, 9 pb
Most CC, *Rated*
C-ltd/S-no/P-no/H-no

Full hearty breakfast
Bottomless cookie jar
Walk to restaurants, next to zoo & rose gardens, spacious view rooms

One of Seattle's finest neighborhood inns, circa 1929. Comfortable ambiance, antiques throughout. Minutes north of downtown. Come, refresh your spirit.
info@bandbseattle.com http://www.bandbseattle.com

Gaslight Inn
1727 15th Ave 98122
206-325-3654 Fax: 206-328-4803
Stephen Bennett
All year

88-198-BB
14 rooms, 11 pb
Rated

Continental breakfast

In restoring Gaslight Inn, we have brought out the home's original turn-of-the-century ambiance and warmth.
innkeepr@gaslight-inn.com http://www.gaslight-inn.com

Green Gables Guesthouse
1503 Second Ave West 98119
206-282-6863 Fax: 206-286-8525
800-400-1503
Reonn Rabon
89-159

79-159-BB
Rated

Full breakfast
Off-street parking available, large deck for entertaining and receptions

Warm, in-city retreat close to everything. Located on exclusive Queen Anne Hill, near the Space Needle and the city's performing arts.
greengab@wolfenet.com http://www.greengablesseattle.com

SEATTLE

Mildred's
1202 15th Ave E 98112
206-325-6072 Fax: 206-860-5907
800-327-9692
Mildred & Melodee Sarver
All year

135-175-BB
3 rooms, 3 pb
Rated
C-yes/S-ltd/P-no/H-no

Full breakfast
Afternoon tea or coffee, homemade cookies
Sitting room, fireplace, library, veranda, grand piano, queen beds

1890 Victorian. Wraparound verandah, lace curtains, red carpets. City location near bus, electric trolley, park, art museum, flower conservatory.
mildredsbb@wwdb.org http://www.mildredsbnb.com

Pioneer Square Hotel
77 Yesler Way 98104
206-340-1234 Fax: 206-467-0707
800-800-5514
Jo Thompson
All year

109-299-BB
75 rooms, 75 pb
Most CC, *Rated*, •
C-yes/S-ltd/P-no/H-yes
Spanish, French

Continental deluxe breakfast
Lunch/dinner available
Evening turndown service, full continental brkfst, sitting room, fireplace

Elegant boutique accommodations conveniently located in the downtown Seattle's waterfront district known as the "Pioneer Square Historic District." Close to all major attractions. sales@pioneersquare.com http://www.pioneersquare.com

---

Salisbury House
750 16th Ave E 98112
206-328-8682 Fax: 206-720-1019
Cathryn & Mary Wiese
All year

95-159-BB
5 rooms, 5 pb
Most CC, *Rated*
C-ltd/S-no/P-no/H-no

Full vegy breakfast
Complimentary tea/coffee 24 hours
Sitting room, porch, down comforters, phones with voice mail in each room

Elegant Capitol Hill Inn. Ideal location for business or pleasure. Take advantage of Seattle's excellent transit system. sleep@salisburyhouse.com http://www.salisburyhouse.com

---

Shaefer Baillie Mansion
907 14th Ave E 98112
206-322-4654 Fax: 206-329-4654
800-922-4654
James Carlin, Greg Kerton, Jacob Chase
All year

95-195-BB
13 rooms, 10 pb
Visa, MC
C-ltd/S-ltd/P-no/H-no

Sitting room, fireplaces

Victorian Bed and Breakfast with lavish antiques, red velvet drapes, atrium, formal dining room, all in an amazing historic neighborhood.
smansion@sprynet.com http://www.shaferbaillie.com

Tugboat Challenger
1001 Fairview Av N 1600 98109
206-340-1201 Fax: 206-332-0303
800-288-7521
Jerry Brown/Chariti McIndoe
All year

55-185-BB
10 rooms, 7 pb
Most CC, *Rated*, •
C-ltd/S-no/P-no/H-no

Full breakfast
Soft drinks
Sitting room w/fireplace, TV, VCR, video library, boat rentals nearby

On board a fully functional, exceptionally clean, restored 96' tugboat. Located in the heart of the Seattle area. Breakfast room w/view of city. Cruising packages available.
ctugboat@uswest.net http://gtesupersite.com/tugboatchallenger

---

Villa Heidelberg
4845 45th Ave SW 98116
206-938-3658 Fax: 206-935-7077
800-671-2942
Judy Burbrink
All year

90-150-BB
6 rooms, 2 pb
Visa, MC, AmEx, *Rated*
C-ltd/S-ltd/P-no/H-no

Full breakfast
Sitting room, new king suite w/views, and private bath

1909 Craftsman country home, just minutes from the airport and downtown Seattle. Two blocks to shops, bus and restaurants.
info@villaheidelberg.com http://www.villaheidelberg.com

SEATTLE (REGION)

Palisades B&B at Dash Pt
5162 SW 311th Place, *Federal Way* 98023
253-838-4376 Fax: 253-838-1480
888-838-4376
Dennis & Peggy LaPorte

180-225-BB
1 rooms, 1 pb
Most CC, *Rated*, •
S-no/P-no/H-no
All year

Full breakfast
Afternoon appetizers, snacks, wine
Sitting room, bicycles, Jacuzzis, suites, fireplaces, cable TV

Secluded, private, extremely elegant, waterfront suite; overlooks Puget Sound and breathtaking sunsets beyond Olympic Mt. Range.
laporte2@ix.netcom.com http://www.palisadesbb.com

Peacock Hill Guest House
9520 Peacock Hill Ave, *Gig Harbor* 98332
800-863-2318
Steven & Suzanne Savnov
All year

89-135-BB
2 rooms, 2 pb
Rated, •
C-ltd/S-no/P-no/H-no
Spanish

Full breakfast
Snacks
Sitting room, suites, Jacuzzis, fireplaces, cable TV

Nestled among evergreens. Sitting on a hilltop overlooking the harbor and beyond. Sit back and enjoy all the comforts of home in the Salish Suite or Sedona Room. Stroll down to the harbor and shop. suzannes@peacockhillgh.com http://www.PeacockHillgh.com

---

A Cottage Creek Inn
12525 Avondale Rd NE, *Redmond* 98052
425-881-5606 Fax: 425-881-5606
Steve & Jeanette Wynecoop
All year

89-127-BB
4 rooms, 4 pb
Most CC, *Rated*
C-ltd/P-no/H-no
German

Full breakfast
Afternoon tea
Sitting room, Jacuzzis, suites, hot tub, pond, creek, conference facilities

Romantic English Tudor in beautiful, tranquil garden setting. Enjoy refreshing massage in hydrotherapy hot tub, relaxing afternoon in gazebo by wildlife pond, or walk the nature trail. innkeepers@cottagecreekinn.com http://www.cottagecreekinn.com

---

Branch Colonial House
2420 N 21st St, *Tacoma* 98406
253-752-3565 Fax: 253-752-3956
877-752-3565
Robin Soto
All year

100-195-BB
6 rooms, 6 pb
Visa, MC, AmEx, *Rated*, •
C-yes/S-no/P-no/H-no

Full or continental breakfast
Snacks
Sitting room, jetted tubs, fireplace, cable TV, Bose Waveradio/CD

Nestled above Tacoma's Old Town district and overlooking Puget Sound, Branch Colonial House offers romantic views from its luxury suites.
stay@branchcolonialhouse.com http://www.branchcolonialhouse.com

---

Chinaberry Hill
302 Tacoma Ave N, *Tacoma* 98403
253-272-1282 Fax: 253-272-1335
Cecil & Yarrow Wayman
All year

110-195-BB
5 rooms, 5 pb
Visa, MC, AmEx, *Rated*, •
C-ltd/S-ltd/P-no/H-no
French

Hearty breakfasts & serious coffee
Guest kitchen w/ comp. refreshments
Bright, spacious suites, estate gardens, guest cottage, wraparound porch

1889 Grand Victorian Inn w/bay views, fireplaces, private Jacuzzis. Downtown shops & theatres, Antique Row and waterfront dining are all within a few blocks of this remarkable garden retreat. chinaberry@wa.net http://www.chinaberryhill.com

---

Rose Cottage Guest House
1929 Austin Rd NE, *Tacoma* 98422
253-927-9437 866-767-3268
Myrna & Bill Casey
All year

150-175-BB
1 rooms, 1 pb
Visa, MC, *Rated*
C-no/S-no/P-no/H-no

Full 4 course breakfast
Tea, coffee, soft drinks, cookies, ice cream .
Romance, privacy, luxury bath, web site, data port in library

Winner of the "2003 ARRINGTON'S BED & BREAKFAST JOURNAL'S" Book of Lists, as "BEST INTERIOR DESIGN & DECOR." Located in Dash Point, WA, Rose Cottage offers romance, enchantment & privacy for two.
info@rosecottageguesthouse.com http://www.rosecottageguesthouse.com

SEATTLE (REGION)

Angels of the Sea
26431 99th Ave SW, *Vashon* 98070
206-463-6980 Fax: 206-463-2205
800-798-9249
Marnie Jones All year

75-125-BB
3 rooms, 1 pb
Visa, MC, *Rated*, •
C-yes/S-no/P-yes/H-no

Full breakfast
Afternoon tea
Sitting room, bikes, pool, tennis, summer sailing, country club pool/golf

1917 converted country church in lush woods and meadow on island near Seattle/Tacoma. Live harp with breakfast in sanctuary. $10/room fee for one night stays.
angels@angelsofthesea.com http://www.angelsofthesea.com

Swallow's Nest Guest Cottages
6030 SW 248th St, *Vashon Island* 98070
206-463-2646 Fax: 206-463-2646
800-269-6378
Bob Keller All year

65-180-EP
6 rooms, 6 pb
Most CC, *Rated*, •
C-yes/S-no/P-ltd/H-ltd

Cottages with kitchens
Coffee, tea, cocoa, some hot tubs/fireplaces, golf, boating nearby

Comfortable country cottage on bluffs overlooking Puget Sound & Mt. Rainier, 3 locations, fishing & kayaking available.
anynest@vashonislandcottages.com http://www.vashonislandcottages.com

SEQUIM

Greywolf Inn
395 Keeler Rd 98382
360-683-5889 Fax: 360-683-1487
800-914-WOLF
Peggy & Bill Melang
All year

80-140-BB
5 rooms, 5 pb
Most CC, *Rated*, •
C-ltd/S-ltd/P-no/H-no

Full breakfast
Tea, picnic lunches on request
Fireplace, patio, decks, Japanese hot tub, gazebo, gardens & woods walk

Enjoy fine food & good cheer in this splendid little inn: the perfect starting point for spectacular sightseeing and light adventure on the North Olympic Peninsula or sailing to Victoria, BC. info@greywolfinn.com http://www.greywolfinn.com

---

Juan de Fuca Cottages
182 Marine Dr 98382
360-683-4433 Fax: 360-681-4999
866-683-4433
Sheila & Kathy All year

130-230-EP
6 rooms, 6 pb
Visa, MC, Disc, *Rated*
C-yes/S-no/H-ltd

Coffee & popcorn
Whirlpool tubs, fireplace, CATV, robes, slippers, 200+ classic movies w/VCR

Charming, completely equipped cottages perched on a 50' bluff overlooking Dungeness Spit. We have our own private beach on Dungeness Bay. Sorry no breakfast is served.
juandefucacottages@olypen.com http://www.juandefucacottages.com

SNOHOMISH

Countryman
119 Cedar Ave 98290
360-568-9622 Fax: 360-568-3422
800-700-9622
Larry & Sandy Countryman
All year

85-115-BB
3 rooms, 3 pb
Most CC
S-no/P-yes

Full or continental breakfast

1896 Queen Anne Victorian–private baths, queen beds, choice of breakfast.
sandy@countrymanbandb.com http://www.countrymanbandb.com

SPOKANE

The Fotheringham House
2128 W Second Ave 99204
509-838-1891 Fax: 509-838-1807
Irene & Paul Jensen
All year

95-115-BB
4 rooms, 1 pb
Rated

Full breakfast
Gardens

1891 Queen Anne Victorian with 4 guestrooms on second floor, one with private bath, 3 share two full baths. innkeeper@fotheringham.net http://www.fotheringham.net

SUNNYSIDE

Sunnyside Inn 804 E Edison Ave 98944 509-839-5557 Fax: 509-839-3520 800-221-4195 Karen & Don Vlieger All year	89-119-BB 13 rooms, 13 pb Visa, MC, AmEx, *Rated*, • C-yes/S-no/P-no/H-no	Full breakfast Snacks, hot tubs Sitting room, Jacuzzi, near tennis, golf, and over 20 wineries

Thirteen luxurious rooms, eight with in-room double spa. In the heart of Washington wine country. sunnyside@sunnysideinn.com http://www.sunnysideinn.com

TACOMA

Aussie's Plum Duff House 619 North K St 98403 253-627-6916 Fax: 253-272-9116 888-627-1920 Tulsi & Jennifer Dass All year	85-175-BB 4 rooms, 4 pb C-ltd/S-no/P-no	Full multi-course breakfast Tea/coffee, cookies,cold drinks, choclates, fruits. Sitting room, 15-jets-jaccuzi ,fireplaces fountains,cable TV/Video,phones.

Built in 1901 and listed on the Tacoma Historic Register, this unique charming home has high ceilings, arches, lovely gardens and fountains.
plumduff@harbornet.com http://www.plumduff.com

Austrian B&B and Suites 723 N Cushman 98403 800-495-7097 800-495-4293 Eveline Smith All year	65-115-BB Visa, MC, *Rated*	Full breakfast

The charming European hospitality of the Austrian Bed and Breakfast Suites will delight you. This 1891 classic Residence Inn is filled with authentic Austrian country antiques and decorations. austrianbb@narrows.com http://www.narrows.com/austrianbb

---

DeVoe Mansion 208 E 133rd St 98445 253-539-3991 Fax: 253-539-8539 888-539-3991 Dave & Cheryl Teifke All year	99-130-BB 4 rooms, 4 pb Visa, MC, *Rated*, • C-ltd/S-no/P-no/H-no	Full breakfast 24-hr hot drinks bar w/cookies and fresh fruit

Come, Relax & Revive! This Nat'l Historic Reg Inn is set among the towering pine and fir trees on 1½ acres. The inn offers four luxurious guestrooms with soaking tubs & full multi-course breakfast. innkeeper@devoemansion.com http://www.devoemansion.com

---

The Villa 705 N 5th St 98403 253-572-1157 Fax: 253-572-1805 800-572-1157 Greg & Becky Anglemyer All year	135-245-BB 6 rooms, 6 pb Visa, MC, AmEx, *Rated*, • C-ltd/S-no/P-no/H-yes	Full breakfast Snacks, complimentary wine Sitting room, library, Jacuzzis, suites, fireplaces, cable TV, exercise room

Only B&B in the Seattle/Tacoma area to be accepted into "Unique New Inns", based on the beauty, cleanliness, and amenities offered. villabb@aol.com http://www.villabb.com

TACOMA (REGION)

Inn at Burg's Landing 8808 Villa Beach Rd, *Anderson Island* 98303 253-884-9185 800-431-5622 Ken & Annie Burg All year	80-125-BB 4 rooms, 2 pb Most CC, *Rated*, • C-yes/S-no/P-no/H-no	Full breakfast Lunch and or dinner with notice Outdoor gazebo, golf nearby, deck & hot tub

Magnificent log home loaded with country charm, on the beach with a spectacular view of Mt. Rainier and Puget Sound.
innatburgslanding@mailexcite.com http://bnbinns/burgslanding.inn

WALLA WALLA

Inn at Blackberry Creek
1126 Pleasant St 99362
509-522-5233 877-522-5233
Barbara Knudson
All year

89-132-BB
3 rooms, 3 pb
Most CC, *Rated*
C-ltd/S-no/P-no/H-ltd

Full breakfast
Refrigerators in rooms
Sitting room, library, bikes, fireplaces, cable TV, DSL lines

Quiet country retreat in the middle of town. Victorian charm abounds in this 1906 home. The antique furnishings provide the charm of 1906, but have all the modern conveniences. bknud@nscis.net http://www.innatblackberrycreek.com

WENATCHEE

Apple Country
524 Okanogan Ave 98801
509-664-0400 Fax: 509-664-6448
Jerry & Sandi Anderson
All year

65-95-BB
5 rooms, 4 pb
Most CC
C-ltd/S-no/P-ltd/H-no

Full breakfast
Dinner available
Sitting room, bicycles, cable TV, accom. bus. travelers

Charming 1920 Craftsman home. Gourmet breakfast served daily. Close to downtown, Convention Center, River front & skiing. 18 miles from Leavenworth, Washington. innkeepers@applecountryinn.com http://www.applecountryinn.com

WHIDBEY ISLAND (REGION)

Cliff House & Cottage
727 Windmill Dr, *Freeland* 98249
360-331-1566 800-450-7142
Peggy Moore & Walter O'Toole
All year

195-450-BB
3 rooms, 3 pb
Rated
C-ltd/S-no/P-no/H-no

Continental plus breakfast
Hot tub, fireplaces, kitchens, feather beds, CD & VCR library

The stunning CLIFF HOUSE or gnome-like COTTAGE, each is yours alone. Welcome to a luxurious, secluded world of natural beauty, miles of beach and glorious views in this stunning waterfront hideaway. wink@whidbey.com http://www.cliffhouse.net

---

Island Getaways
397 Cardinal Way
365 Cardinal Way, *Freeland* 98249
360-331-7707
Fran & Thom Moyer
All year

155-200-EP
3 rooms
Visa, MC, •
C-yes/S-ltd/P-no/H-no

Continental plus breakfast
Private hot tubs, gas fireplaces, cable TV, CD/Stereo

Enjoy fabulous view of the shipping lanes, the majestic Olympic Mtns, and the magnificent sunsets on South Whidbey Island from your private view cottage or penthouse suite, each with private hot tub! penthous@whidbey.com http://www.whidbeynet.net/getaways

---

Guest House Log Cottages
24371 S.R. 525, *Greenbank* 98253
360-678-3115 Fax: 360-678-3115
Peggy Walker
All year

125-325-BB
6 rooms, 6 pb
Most CC, *Rated*
S-no/P-no/H-ltd

Full self-serve breakfast
Exercise room, pool, spa, retreat & honeymoon spot

Luxury log mansion for two. Private cottages w/personal Jacuzzis, fireplace, kitchens, TV/VCR. guesthse@whidbey.net http://www.guesthouselogcottages.com

---

Inglewood Haven
5010 S Inglewood Dr, *Langley* 98260
360-221-8641
John & Miriam Raabe
All year

68-90-BB
1 rooms, 1 pb
Most CC
C-ltd/S-ltd/P-no/H-no
Hebrew

Continental breakfast
Tea, coffee in your private mini-kitchen
Private outdoor deck, Japanese style soak tub

A quiet and woodsy B&B up in the trees. A light filled private suite, just a one-mile walk from the small seaside island town of Langley, WA. jraabe@whidbey.com http://www.jshow.com/ihaven

WHITE SALMON

Inn of the White Salmon
PO Box 1549
172 W Jewett Blvd 98672
509-493-2335 800-972-5226
Janet & Roger Holen
All year

112-143-BB
16 rooms, 16 pb
Most CC, *Rated*, •
C-yes/S-ltd/P-yes/H-no

Full breakfast
Beer & wine available
Sitting room, suites, outdoor hot tub

Furnished with antiques, this Inn has the ambiance of a B&B and the privacy of a hotel. The breakfast is |xd3 to die for."
innkeeper@gorge.net http://www.innofthewhitesalmon.com

WINTHROP

Chewuch Inn
223 White Ave 98862
509-996-3107 Fax: 509-996-3107
800-747-3107
Dan & Sally Kuperberb
All year

70-200-BB
14 rooms, 14 pb
Most CC, *Rated*, •
C-yes/S-no/P-no/H-ltd

Continental plus breakfast
Afternoon tea, snacks
Sitting room, library, bicycles, Jacuzzi, fireplaces, cable TV

A Craftsman style country inn with cabins, located within walking distance of an authentic Western theme town. In the foothills of the North Cascade mountains, wildlife and recreation abound. innkeeper@chewuchinn.com http://www.chewuchinn.com

Sun Mountain Lodge
PO Box 1000
Patterson Lake Rd 98862
509-996-2211 Fax: 509-996-3133
800-572-0493
Brian Charlton
All year

120-320-EP
112 rooms, 112 pb
Visa, MC, AmEx, *Rated*, •
C-yes/S-ltd/P-no/H-yes
German

Full breakfast (fee)
Restaurant, bar service, snacks
Sitt. room, library, bikes, tennis court, jacuzzi, pool, suites, fireplaces

Spectacular mountain top location, luxury log and stone lodge, gourmet dining and wine, 3,000 acres of outdoor fun. sunmtn@methow.com http://www.sunmountainlodge.com

YAKIMA

A Touch of Europe
220 N 16th Ave 98902
509-454-9775 Fax: 509-452-1303
888-438-7073
Chef Erika and James A. Cenci
All year

79-110-BB
3 rooms, 3 pb
Visa, MC, AmEx, *Rated*, •
C-ltd/S-no/P-no/H-no
German

Full breakfast
PM high tea, fine dining onsite w/prior arrangmnt
Sitting room, library, fireplaces, nearby bikes, tennis court & pool

Your destination getaway to our historic Queen Anne Victorian home to enjoy luxurious surroundings and private, seasonal multi-course menus creatively prepared.
atoeurope@msn.com http://www.winesnw.com/toucheuropeb&b.htm

West Virginia

AUGUSTA

Almost Heaven Alpaceas & Guest House
HC 52 Box 1121 26704
304-496-1073 Fax: 304-496-9587
Bob & Lee Ciszewski
All year

100-BB
2 rooms, 1 pb
Visa, MC, AmEx, *Rated*
C-yes/S-no/P-no/H-no

Full breakfast
Dinner
Fireplaces, full kitchen, laundry services, accom. bus. travelers

Beautiful, private house on a family-friendly working alpaca farm. Completely outfitted for up to 6 guests. Great views, tranquil atmosphere, full breakfast served.
almsthvn@raven-villages.net http://www.almostheavenguesthouse.com

AURORA

Brookside Inn
Rt 1 Box 217B 26705
304-735-6344 Fax: 304-735-3563
800-588-6344
Bill Reeves & Michele Moure
All year

85-145-MAP
4 rooms, 2 pb
Rated, •
C-yes/S-no/P-no/H-no

Full breakfast
Candlelight dinner; afternoon refreshments; wine
Large front porch; cozy nooks and crannies; relaxing atmosphere

1899 Allegheny Mountain lodge overlooking Cathedral St Pk, a virgin forest of hemlock, rhododendron on National Register.

BUCKHANNON

Post Mansion Inn
8 Island Ave 26201
304-472-8959 800-301-9309
Lawrence & Suzanne Reger
All year

80-BB
3 rooms, 1 pb
Rated
C-ltd/S-ltd/P-no/H-no

Full breakfast
Snacks
Sitting room, accommodate business travelers

Stately three story hand-cut stone mansion. On 6 1/2 acres, originally built in 1860. Spacious air-conditioned rooms beautifully furnished in period antiques.

lham1945@aol.com

CHARLES TOWN

Hillbrook Inn
Route 2, Box 152
Summit Point Rd 25414
304-725-4223 Fax: 304-725-4455
800-304-4223
Gretchen Carroll

200-325-MAP
11 rooms, 11 pb
Visa, MC, *Rated*, •
C-ltd/S-ltd/P-no/H-no
French
Th–Sun only Nov–Apr

Full breakfast
7-course dinner/wine, aft.. tea
Restaurant, sitting room, library, antiques, art collection

Award-winning country inn in the European style. Intimate dining room serves 7-course dinner. Dining terrace with fountain.

info@hillbrookinn.com http://www.hillbrookinn.com

Washington House Inn
216 S George St 25414
304-725-7923 Fax: 304-728-5150
800-297-6957
Nina & Mel Vogel
All year

99-150-BB
6 rooms, 6 pb
Most CC, *Rated*, •
C-ltd/S-ltd/P-no/H-no

Full breakfast
Afternoon tea, snacks, wine
Bar, sitting room, library, bikes, suites, health club access

Relax in the ambience & serenity of this 1899 Victorian built by descendants of Pres. Washington. Period antiques.

emailus@washingtonhouseinnwv.com http://www.washingtonhouseinnwv.com

CHARLES TOWN (REGION)

Gilbert House of Middleway NHD
PO Box 1104
Middleway Nat'l Historic District, *Jefferson County* 25414
304-725-0637
Bernie Heiler All year

80-140-BB
3 rooms, 3 pb
Most CC, *Rated*, •
C-ltd/S-ltd/P-no/H-ltd
German, Spanish

Full gourmet breakfast
Complimentary tea, wine, snacks
Sitting room, library, piano, fireplaces, A/C, bridal suite

Near Harper's Ferry. HABS listed, 18th-century stone house on original settlers' trail into Shenandoah Valley. gilberthousebb@yahoo.com http://www.gilberthouse.com

ELKINS

Graceland Inn & Conf. Center
100 Campus Dr 26241
304-637-1600 Fax: 304-637-1809
800-624-3157
Dick Flack All year

BB
37 rooms, 37 pb
Most CC
C-yes/S-ltd/P-no/H-yes

Continental breakfast

Graceland Inn is a beautifully restored Victorian mansion and is currently a premier lodging, retreat, and meeting facility.

dflack@gracelandinn.com http://www.gracelandinn.com

ELKINS

The Post House
306 Robert E. Lee Ave 26241
304-636-1792
Jo Ann Post Barlow
All year

60-65-BB
5 rooms, 3 pb
Visa, *Rated*
C-yes/S-no/P-no/H-no

Continental plus breakfast
Afternoon tea
AMTA-certified massage, near 5 ski resorts, bikes

Surrounded by mountain and park recreation, yet in town. Park-like backyard with children's playhouse. Handmade quilts for sale, and certified massage on premises.
joanbarlow@aol.com http://www.virtualcities.com

Tunnel Mountain
Route 1, Box 59-1
Old Rt 33 26241
304-636-1684 888-211-9123
Anne & Paul Beardslee
All year

75-85-BB
3 rooms, 3 pb
Rated
C-ltd/S-ltd/P-no/H-no

Full breakfast
Restaurant nearby
Sitting room w/fireplace, patio, wooded paths, A/C, scenic views, cable TV

Romantic country fieldstone B&B nestled in the scenic West Virginia. Mountains next to National Forest and recreational areas. http://www.bbonline.com/wv/tunnel/

The Warfield House B&B
318 Buffalo St 26241
304-636-4555 888-636-4555
Connie & Paul Garnett
All year

75-90-BB
5 rooms, 5 pb
Rated

Full breakfast
Afternoon snacks
Library w/fireplace, parlor w/piano, wraparound porch, herb gardens

Located on the "best corner in town" within a 5-minute walk of restaurants, specialty shops and theater. 1901 property listed on National Register of Historic Places.
warfieldhouse@meer.net http://www.bbonline.com/wv/warfield

FAIRMONT

Acacia House
158 Locust Ave 26554
304-367-1000 Fax: 304-367-1000
888-269-9541
George & Kathy Sprowls
All year

60-70-BB
4 rooms, 2 pb
Most CC, *Rated*, •
C-ltd/S-no/P-no/H-no

Full breakfast
Sitting room, bicycles, cable TV, accommodate business travelers

Four-story brown brick home features beautiful oak throughout and a half-dozen decorative fireplaces. Very nice getaway destination located near hiking/biking trails. Bike rentals available. acacia@acaciahousewv.com http://www.acaciahousewv.com

HARPERS FERRY

Harpers Ferry Guest House
PO Box 1079
800 Washington St 25425
304-535-6955 Fax: 304-535-6955
Al & Alison Alsdorf
All year

75-95-BB
3 rooms, 3 pb
Rated
C-ltd/S-no/P-no/H-ltd

Full breakfast
Snacks, wine
Sitting room, cable TV, conference, off street parking

A wonderfully friendly B&B located right in Historic Harpers Ferry, WV. Walk to shops, restaurants, and Harpers Ferry National Park.
alsdorf@harpersferry-wv.com http://www.harpersferry-wv.com

HARPERS FERRY (REGION)

The Cottonwood Inn
Rt. 5, Box 61-S
Mill Lane off Kabletown Rd., *Charles Town* 25414
304-725-3371 Fax: 304-728-4763
800-868-1188
Joe & Barbara Sobol
All year

75-120-BB
7 rooms, 7 pb
Visa, MC, AmEx, *Rated*
C-ltd/S-no/P-no/H-no
Some French

Full breakfast
Sitting room, library, fireplace, cable TV, conference, grand piano

Escape...to the quiet! Gracious B&B on 6 acres of sylvan land near many historic and recreational attractions. travels@mydestination.com http://www.cottonwoodbb.com

Linger In, Huttonsville, WV

HEDGESVILLE

Farmhouse on Tomahawk Run 1828 Tomahawk Run Rd 25427 304-754-7350 Fax: 304-754-7350 888-266-9516 Judy & Hugh Erskine All year	85-140-BB 5 rooms, 5 pb Most CC, *Rated*, • C-ltd/S-no/P-no/H-no	Full breakfast Afternoon tea Sitting room, Jacuzzis, suites, fireplaces, cable TV, private balconies

Charming Civil War-era farmhouse by historic spring on 280 acres of hills & meadows. Large, comfortable guestrooms w/private baths, private balconies & king or queen beds.

tomahawk@intrepid.net http://www.tomahawkrun.com

HELVETIA

Swiss Village Rt 46 26224 304-924-6435 Eleanor F. Mailloux All year	85-150-BB 3 rooms, 3 pb *Rated* C-ltd/S-ltd/P-ltd/H-yes	Full breakfast The Hutte Restaurant is open noon to 7 PM A common room, airy deck, kitchen and above all seclusion and quiet

The Beekeeper Inn, nestled in the mountains, is a magical place hidden by tall firs and lulled by the nearby mountain stream. It is the perfect place for seclusion and quiet.

dbuls@bellatlantic.net http://www.msys.net/rogersm/index.htm

HUTTONSVILLE

Linger In PO Box 14 US Route 219/250 26273 304-335-4434 Betty & Russell Linger All year	EP 6 rooms *Rated* C-yes/S-ltd/P-no/H-no Spanish, Russian	Sitting room, library, swimming pool, fireplaces, cable TV

Whole house rental with six bedrooms, non-hosted facility. Wooded area with hiking trails.

http://www.bbonline.com/wv/lingerin

MILTON

The Cedar House
92 Trenol Heights 25541
304-743-5516 888-743-5516
Carole Vickers
All year

80-90-BB
3 rooms, 3 pb
Most CC, *Rated*
S-no/P-no/H-ltd

Full breakfast
Snacks
Sitting room, library, fireplaces, cable TV, conference rooms

Hilltop, tri-level ranch style house on 5 1/2 acres, with panoramic view of surrounding hills; quiet and private. vickersc@marshall.edu http://bbonline.com/wv/cedarhouse/

MORGANTOWN

Fieldcrest Manor
1440 Stewartstown Rd 26505
304-599-2686 Fax: 304-599-2853
866-599-2686
Sarah Lough, Cliff & Susan Linkous All year

90-115-BB
5 rooms, 5 pb
Visa, MC, AmEx, *Rated*
C-ltd/S-no/P-no/H-no

Full breakfast
Dinner, bar service
Sitting room, fireplaces, cable TV, special events room for meetings/parties

With its beautifully manicured lawns and romantic natural landscapes, Fieldcrest is the perfect backdrop for relaxation, romance or to reconnect with friends and family.
innkeeper@fieldcrestmanor.com http://www.fieldcrestmanor.com

ROMNEY

Hampshire House 1884
165 N Grafton St 26757
304-822-7171 Fax: 304-822-7582
888-806-1131
Jane & Scott Simmons
All year

75-95-BB
7 rooms, 6 pb
Most CC, *Rated*, •
C-ltd/S-no/P-no/H-yes

Full breakfast
Lunch, dinner
Comp. wine, snacks, sitting room, library, bikes, near tennis, pool

Enjoy the charm of the 1880's in this completely restored period Inn. Central A/C, private baths, TVs, along w/sound proofing, are part of the Inn's modern comforts.
hhouse@raven-villages.net http://www.romneyweb.com/hampshirehouse

SENECA ROCK (REGION)

North Fork Mountain Inn
PO Box 114
Smoke Hole Road, *Cabins* 26855
304-257-1108 Fax: 304-257-2008
Art & Joan Ricker All year

95-135-BB
8 rooms, 8 pb
Visa, MC, *Rated*
C-ltd/S-no/P-no/H-no

Full breakfast
Dinner(fee), snacks
Sitting room, library, Jacuzzis, fireplaces, cable TV, outdoor hot tub

An Outpost of Luxury in the Wilderness, secluded non-resort getaway, located at 2600' on the North Fork Mt. within National Forest.
nfi@access.mountain.net http://www.northforkmtninn.com

WHEELING (REGION)

Bonnie Dwaine
505 Wheeling Ave, *Glen Dale* 26038
304-845-7250 Fax: 304-845-7256
888-507-4569
Bonnie & Sidney Grisell
All year

79-125-BB
5 rooms, 5 pb
Most CC, *Rated*, •
C-ltd/S-ltd/P-no/H-no

Full or continental plus breakfast
Snacks, complimentary wine, sitting room, library, bicycles, fireplaces, A/C

Victorian warmth, style and elegance w/the convenience of modern amenities. This beautiful home displays many antiques.
Bonnie@Bonnie-Dwaine.com http://www.Bonnie-Dwaine.com

WHITE SULPHUR SPRINGS

James Wylie House
208 E. Main St 24986
304-536-9444 Fax: 304-536-2345
800-870-1613
Monica Foos All year

80-150
6 rooms, 6 pb
Visa, MC, AmEx
C-yes/S-no/P-no

Full breakfast

Listed in the National Historic Register in 1990. The Wylie House, completely renovated in 1989-90, offers three non-smoking rooms with private bath or a separate log cabin guest house. mlfoos@access.mountain.net http://www.travelguides.com/home/james_wylie/

Wisconsin

APPLETON

Franklin Street Inn
318 E Franklin St 54911
920-993-1711 Fax: 920-739-6635
888-993-1711
Shelly and Douglas Gabel
All year

85-155-BB
4 rooms, 4 pb
Most CC, *Rated*
C-ltd/S-ltd/P-no/H-no

Full breakfast
Snacks
Sitting room, cable TV, gourmet breakfast, complimentary snacks & soda

Appleton's premier B&B is ideal for vacation, business, wedding/anniversary or weekend get away! 1890s Victorian is walking distance from museums, restaurants, and a short drive to many attractions. info@franklinstreetinn.com http://www.appleton-wisconsin.com

BARABOO

Pinehaven
E 13083 Hwy 33 53913
608-356-3489 Fax: 608-356-0818
Lyle & Marge Getschman
All year

89-BB
4 rooms, 4 pb
Visa, MC, *Rated*
C-ltd/S-ltd/P-no/H-no

Full breakfast
Fishing, rowing, cottage with whirlpool, gazebo, sitting room

Beautiful view of bluffs, small private lake. Tranquil setting. Take a stroll, fish, admire the Belgian draft horses. Relax. Acres to roam. No smoking indoors.
http://www.pinehavenbnb.com

BURLINGTON

Hillcrest Inn & Carriage House
540 Storle Ave 53105
262-763-4706
Fax: 262-763-7871
800-313-9030
Mike & Gayle Hohner
All year

100-190-BB
6 rooms, 6 pb
Visa, MC
C-ltd/S-no/P-no

Full breakfast

Romantic, luxurious and private. Wooded four acre estate with magnificent view. English flower gardens and walking paths. Stately 1908 Edwardian home with elegant Carriage House. hillcrest@thehillcrestinn.com http://www.thehillcrestinn.com

CAMBRIDGE

Cambridge House
PO Box 365
123 Main St 53523
608-423-7008 Fax: 608-423-7008
888-859-8075
Dotti & Bill Krieger
All year

100-150-BB
4 rooms, 4 pb
Visa, MC, Disc, *Rated*, •
C-ltd/S-no/P-no/H-no

Full breakfast
Afternoon tea, snacks, complimentary wine
Sitting room, Jacuzzis, fireplaces, cable TV, accom. bus. travelers

Luxury and privacy in beautifully restored, professionally decorated rooms. Queen or King beds and private Jacuzzi bathrooms. Relaxing living room and secluded courtyard gardens. cambridgehouse@chartermi.net http://www.Cambridgehouse-inn.com

---

Country Comforts
2722 Highland Drive 53523
608-423-3097 Fax: 608-423-7743
877-771-1277
Marian Korth & Mim Jacobson
All year

99-169-BB
4 rooms, 4 pb
Visa, MC, Disc
C-ltd/S-no/P-no/H-yes

Full breakfast
Snacks
Sitting room, library, fireplaces, cable TV, wheelchair accessible

100-year-old family farmhouse with four large guest rooms, all with private baths. Full country breakfast. Wheelchair accessible. Four acres of lawn and gardens. Located 15 miles east of Madison, WI. info@country-comforts.com http://country-comforts.com

CAMP DOUGLAS

Sunnyfield Farm
N6692 Batko Rd 54618
608-427-3686 888-839-0232
John & Susanne Soltvedt
All year

60-98-BB
4 rooms, 1 pb
Rated
C-yes/S-no/P-no/H-no

Full breakfast
Tea, coffee, snacks
Sitting room

Nature lovers paradise. Choose from three bedrooms on second floor. Third floor studio. Aroma of coffee and fresh baked rolls start the day. 160 acres to hike or snooze on the porch. soltvedt@mwt.net http://www.sunnyfield.net

CEDARBURG

The Washington House Inn
W62 N573 Washington Ave
53012
262-375-3550 Fax: 262-375-9422
800-554-4717
Wendy Porterfield All year

89-219-BB
34 rooms, 34 pb
Rated, •
C-yes/S-yes/P-no/H-yes

Continental plus breakfast
Afternoon social
Sitting room, fireplaces, whirlpool baths, sauna, wet bars, bicycles

Country inn in center of historical district. Breakfast in charming gathering room. Shopping, golf, winter sports. Gift certificates & golf packages available.
whinn@execpc.com http://www.washingtonhouseinn.com

EAU CLAIRE

Otter Creek Inn
PO Box 3183
2536 Hwy 12 54702
715-832-2945 Fax: 715-832-4607
866-832-2945
Shelley & Randy Hansen

90-180-BB
6 rooms, 6 pb
Most CC, *Rated*
C-no/S-no/P-no/H-no
All year

Full breakfast
Beverages during check-in times
Rooms have TVs/VCRs, video library for your use

Each guestroom has a whirlpool for two! Many w/fireplaces. Choice of breakfast entree, serving time, breakfast in bed. Spacious 3-story English Tudor, antiques, inground pool. Many restaurants nearby. info@ottercreekinn.net http://www.ottercreekinn.net

EGG HARBOR

Bay Point Inn
7933 Hwy 42 54209
920-868-3297 Fax: 920-868-2876
800-707-6660
Myles Dannhausen All year

189-235-BB
10 rooms, 10 pb
Most CC, *Rated*, •
C-yes/S-ltd/P-no/H-yes

Continental plus breakfast
Dinner, coffee
Jacuzzis, swimming pool, suites, fireplaces, waterview

Bay Point sits high on the edge of the Niagra Escarpment in Door County. Each Villa offers panoramic views of the shoreline, unobstructed by any commercial or residential development. stay@baypointinn.com http://www.baypointinn.com

EPHRAIM

Eagle Harbor Inn
PO Box 588
9914 Water St 54211
920-854-2121 Fax: 920-854-2121
800-324-5427
Nedd & Natalie Neddersen

74-229-BB
21 rooms, 21 pb
Visa, MC, *Rated*
C-ltd/P-no/H-yes
All year

Full gourmet breakfast
Continental plus breakfast Nov-Apr
Pool with current, bakery, cottages have TV & grill, 200 yds to sandy beach

An intimate New England-style country inn. Antique-filled, period wallpapers. Close to boating, beaches, golf course, parks.
nedd@eagleharbor.com http://www.eagleharbor.com

FISH CREEK

Thorp House Inn & Cottages
PO Box 490
4135 Bluff Lane 54212
920-868-2444
C. & S. Falck-Pedersen
All year

75-195-BB
10 rooms, 10 pb
Rated
C-ltd/S-no
Norwegian

Continental plus breakfast
Restaurants nearby
Sitting room w/fireplace, bikes, fireplaces, library, X-C skiing, whirlpools

Antique-filled historic home backed by wooded bluff, overlooking bay. Kids OK in cottages, 5 with fireplace, 4 with whirlpool. On National Register.
innkeeper@thorphouseinn.com http://www.thorphouseinn.com

GILLS ROCK

Harbor House Inn
12666 Hwy 42 54210
920-854-5196
David & Else Weborg
May 1-Oct 31

75-189-BB
15 rooms, 15 pb
Visa, MC, AmEx, *Rated*
C-yes/S-no/P-ltd/H-yes
Danish

Continental plus breakfast
Sitting room, bikes, Jacuzzis, suites, fireplaces, sauna, beach

1904 Victorian with a new Scandinavian country wing, new lighthouse suite & 2 cottages situated across from quaint fishing harbor w/view of sunsets over bay.
http://www.door-county-inn.com

GREEN BAY

The Astor House
637 S Monroe Ave 54301
920-432-3585 Fax: 920-436-3145
888-303-6370
Greg & Barbara Robinson
All year

120-160-BB
5 rooms, 5 pb
Most CC, *Rated*, •
C-ltd/S-no/P-no/H-no

Continental plus breakfast
Complimentary wine
Double whirlpools, sitting rm, gas fireplaces, phone, cable TV, stereo, VCR

Welcome to Green Bay's historic Astor Neighborhood. Five decorative motifs & in-room amenities indulge our guests, including double whirlpools and fireplaces.
astor@execpc.com http://www.astorhouse.com

GREEN BAY (REGION)

James Street Inn
201 James St, *De Pere* 54115
920-337-0111 Fax: 920-337-6135
800-897-8483
Kevin C. Flatley
All year

79-199-BB
36 rooms, 36 pb
Most CC, *Rated*, •
C-yes/S-ltd/P-no/H-yes

Continental plus breakfast
Afternoon tea, snacks
Comp. wine, bar service, sitting room, fireplaces, private decks, whirlpool

A country inn hidden just outside of Green Bay. Built on the foundation of a c.1858 mill, the river literally flows beneath it. jamesst@netnet.net http://www.jamesstreetinn.com

HARTLAND

Monches Mill House
W301 N9430 Hwy E 53029
262-966-7546
Elaine Taylor
All year

50-85-BB
4 rooms, 2 pb
C-yes/S-yes/P-yes/H-yes
French

Continental plus breakfast
Lunch in summer by res., fixed menu w/set price
Sitting room, hot tub, bikes, tennis, canoeing, hiking

House built in 1842, located on the bank of the mill pond, furnished in antiques, choice of patio, porch or gallery for breakfast enjoyment.

HAYWARD

Ross' Teal Lake Lodge
12425 N Ross Rd 54843
715-462-3631
Tim & Prudence Ross
May—October

120-270-EP
25 rooms, 25 pb
Visa, MC, *Rated*, •
C-yes/S-yes/P-yes/H-ltd

Full & continental breakfast (fee)
Restaurant, bar, lunch & dinner available
Sitting room, library, Jacuzzi, swimming pool, suites, fireplaces

A traditional lakeside cottage resort with many log buildings, natural woods and natural lakeshore. vacation@teallake.com http://www.teallake.com

HAZEL GREEN

Wisconsin House Stage Coach Inn
PO Box 71
2105 E. Main St 53811
608-854-2233
Ken & Pat Disch
All year

65-125-BB
8 rooms, 6 pb
Most CC, *Rated*, •
C-yes/S-no/P-no/H-no

Full breakfast
Free soft drinks, cookies.
Library, Garden Gazebo, Porches.

A country furnished bed and breakfast, we're located just 10 miles north of Galena, Illinois, 13 miles west of Dubuque, Iowa, and 15 miles south of Platteville, Wisconsin.
wishouse@mhtc.net http://www.wisconsinhouse.com

HUDSON

Jefferson Day House
1109 3rd St 54016
715-386-7111
Tom & Sue Tyler
All year

99-189-BB
4 rooms, 4 pb
Rated
C-yes/H-yes

Full breakfast
Snacks
Special diets avail., parlor, courtyard gazebo, dining room

1857 Italianate mansion 1 with antique furnishings 1 block from St. Croix River. All rooms have double whirlpools, fireplace, queen beds and A/C. Your romantic getaway destination! jeffersn@pressenter.com http://www.jeffersondayhouse.com

---

Phipps Inn
1005 3rd St 54016
715-386-0800 Fax: 715-386-9002
888-865-9388
Mary Ellen & Rich Cox
All year

129-209-BB
6 rooms, 6 pb
Visa, MC, AmEx
C-ltd/S-no/P-no/H-no

Full breakfast
Complimentary wine at check-in
Billiards room, tandem bikes

Described as the "Grande Dame" of Queen Anne houses in the St. Croix Valley, the Phipps Inn is a luxurious 1884 Victorian mansion nestled in the charming setting of Hudson's historic Third Street. mrcox@pressenter.com http://www.phippsinn.com

IRON RIVER

Iron River Trout Haus
PO Box 662
7420 Drummond Rd 54847
715-372-4219 Fax: 715-372-5511
888-262-1453
Ron & Cindy Johnson
All year

60-75-BB
4 rooms, 2 pb
Visa, MC, *Rated*, •
C-ltd/S-ltd/P-no/H-ltd

Full breakfast

Located on 40 acres of forest with the Iron River running through it. Centrally located in northern Wisconsin. Trout farm with fee fishing, smoked trout and fly fishing lessons available. info@trouthaus.com http://www.trouthaus.com

KENDALL

Cabin at Trails End
23009 Knollwood Rd 54638
608-427-3877
Bev & Ray Jurgens
All year

195-225-BB
1 rooms, 1 pb
Visa, MC, *Rated*
C-ltd/S-no/P-no/H-no

Full breakfast
Jacuzzi, Fireplace, Cable TV, Sauna, C/A

Secluded cabin furnished with a comfortable blend of antiques; gourmet breakfast served on private screen porch; abundant wildlife, wildflowers and nature trails.
cabin@mwt.net http://www.mwt.net/~cabin

KEWAUNEE

Historic Karsten Inn
122 Ellis St 54216
920-388-3800 Fax: 920-388-3808
800-277-2132
Roswitha Heuer
All year

59-149-BB
23 rooms, 23 pb
Most CC, •
C-yes/S-yes/P-yes/H-ltd
German

Continental plus breakfast
Cookies in the afternoon from 4-7:00 PM
Game room with pool table, great lobby with sitting area

The Historic Karsten Inn offers twenty-three guestrooms that recreate the intimacy of another era. Each room has an atmosphere with a personal feeling.
karsten@itol.com http://karsteninn.com

LA CROSSE

Chateau La Crosse
410 Cass 54601
608-796-1090 Fax: 608-796-0700
800-442-7969
Joan Lambert Smith
All year

125-200-BB
7 rooms, 6 pb
Most CC, *Rated*, •
S-no/P-no/H-yes
some German & Spanish

Full breakfast
Restaurant, aft. tea, snacks, lunch & dinner avail
Sitting room, library, Jacuzzis, suites, fireplaces, accom. bus. travelers.

Gothic stone castle of Mons Anderson, "Merchant Prince." Restored for $1,200,000. One of the most historic mansions in Wisconsin.
chateaulax@aol.com http://www.visitor-guide.com/chateaulacrosse

LAKE GENEVA

Case's Turn of the Century
1599 N Hillside Rd 53147
262-248-4989
Brenda & Bob Case
All year

95-175-BB
4 rooms, 3 pb
Most CC, *Rated*, •
C-ltd/S-ltd/P-no/H-no

Full country breakfast
Wonderful cheese & cracker tray, fresh fruit, wine
Sitting room, parlor, picture gallery, library, TV/VCR

A gracious 19th Century country estate. English flower garden with roses and trees galore. A delicious breakfast served. A warm welcome! Chamber of Commerce of Lake Geneva, Historical Registry, AARP. casebnb@genevaonline.com http://www.casesbnb.com

---

Eleven Gables Inn on Lake Geneva
493 Wrigley Dr 53147
262-248-8393
A. F. Milliette
All year

109-330-BB
12 rooms, 12 pb
Most CC, *Rated*, •
C-ltd/S-ltd/P-no/H-ltd

Continental Plus breakfast
Continental plus-midweek
Private pier, swim, fish, hiking, bike rental, courtesy phone, fax

Lakeside historic inn. Romantic bedrooms, bridal chamber, and now with country cottage and family coach house. Fireplaces, down quilts, wet bars, TVs, balconies.
egi@lkgeneva.com http://www.lkgeneva.com

The Geneva Inn
N-2009 State Rd 120 53147
262-248-5680 Fax: 262-248-5685
800-441-5881
Richard B. Treptow
All year

155-375-BB
37 rooms, 37 pb
Most CC
C-yes/S-yes/P-no/H-yes
German, French, Spanish

Continental plus breakfast
Restaurant, lunch/dinner
Turndown cognac & choc., whirlpools, fitness room, atrium, lake swimming

A relaxing retreat on the shores of Lake Geneva. Deluxe accommodations touched with English charm. Restaurant & lounge.
luxury@genevainn.com http://www.genevainn.com

Golden Oaks Mansion
421 Baker St 53147
262-248-9711 Fax: 262-249-8529
Nancy Golden Waspi & Family
All year

175-295-BB
6 rooms, 6 pb
Visa, MC, *Rated*, •
C-no/S-ltd/P-no/H-no

Full breakfast

No other B&B in Lake Geneva dedicates so much public space to the exclusive use of guests. goldenoaksmansion@aol.com http://www.goldenoaksmansion.com

---

Lazy Cloud Lodge
W4033 Highway 50 53147
262-275-3322 Fax: 262-275-8340
Carol & Keith Tiffany
All year

120-235-BB
13 rooms, 13 pb
Most CC, •
C-no/S-no/P-no/H-yes

Continental plus breakfast
Picnic basket dinner, complimentary wine & snacks
Double whirlpools & fireplaces, fridge & micro, private entrance, candles

Romantic hideaway with luxury suites & rooms. All accommodations include a double whirlpool tub & a fireplace with individual themes.
love@lazycloud.com http://www.lazycloud.com

LANCASTER

Martha's B&B & Hot Mustard
7867 University Farm Rd 53813
608-723-4711
Maury & Martha McLean
All year

60-BB
3 rooms
Visa, MC
C-yes/S-no/P-ltd/H-no

Full breakfast
Snacks
Library

Three generation farm house nestled among the beautiful hills and valleys of Wisconsin's unglaciated area. mcleanmm@mhtc.net http://www.allmustard.com

LODI

Victorian Treasure Inn
115 Prairie St 53555
608-592-5199 Fax: 608-592-7147
800-859-5199
Todd & Kimberly Seidl
All year

119-209-BB
8 rooms, 8 pb
Visa, MC, *Rated*, •
C-yes/S-no/P-no/H-no

Full breakfast
Afternoon tea, snacks, wine
Whirlpools, fireplaces, canopy beds, library, porches, parlors

Gracious hospitality & casual elegance in two historic 1890's Queen Anne Victorians featuring 7 individually decorated guestrooms. Meticulous, thoughtful amenities, antique furnishings. innkeeper@victoriantreasure.com http://www.victoriantreasure.com

MADISON

Annie's Garden
2117 Sheridan Drive 53704
608-244-2224 Fax: 608-244-2224
Annie & Larry Stuart
All year

97-189-BB
2 rooms, 2 pb
Most CC, *Rated*
C-ltd/S-no/P-no/H-no

Full breakfast
Snacks
Library, tennis court, Jacuzzi, beach, bicycle storage, fireplaces, suites

Beautiful views all seasons, on 300 acre park. Walk the lakeshore, meadows, or woods. Six minutes to downtown and campus.
larrystuart1@wmconnect.com http://www.bbinternet.com/annies

Arbor House, An Environmental Inn
3402 Monroe St 53711
608-238-2981 Fax: 608-238-1175
John & Cathie Imes
All year

110-220-BB
8 rooms, 8 pb
Visa, MC, AmEx, *Rated*
C-yes/S-no/P-no/H-yes

Full breakfast on weekends
Continental breakfast weekdays
Cable, massage available, cross-country skiing, 5 fireplaces.

Historic landmark across from UW Arboretum has an environmental emphasis. Minutes from the Capitol & UW campus. Corporate rates. http://www.arbor-house.com

---

Canterbury Inn
315 W. Gorham St 53703
608-258-8899 Fax: 608-283-2541
800-838-3850
Harvey & Trudy Barash
All year

130-275-BB
6 rooms, 6 pb
S-no/H-yes

A literary Bed and Breakfast atop a bookstore and cafe in the heart of Madison, Wisconsin. inn@madisoncanterbury.com http://www.madisoncanterbury.com

---

The Collins House
704 E Gorham St 53703
608-255-4230 Fax: 608-255-0830
Barb Pratzel
All year

105-180-BB
5 rooms, 5 pb
Visa, MC, Disc, *Rated*
C-yes/S-no/P-yes/H-no

Full breakfast
Evening pastries
Sitting room w/fireplace, library, movie videos, whirlpools, fireplace, deck

Restored Prairie School home. On Lake Mendota, near university and State Capitol. Elegant rooms, wonderful gourmet breakfasts and pastries. Welcoming, down-to-earth ambience. inncollins@aol.com http://www.collinshouse.com

---

University Heights
1812 Van Hise Ave
1812 Van Hise Ave 53705
608-233-3340 Fax: 608-233-3255
Betty Humphries
All year

90-180-BB
4 rooms, 4 pb
Visa, MC, Disc
C-ltd/S-no/P-no

Full breakfast

This American foursquare has large comfortable rooms. Glowing woodwork abounds throughout, with thoughtful Arts and Crafts detail work.
simplybet@aol.com http://www.madison-lodging.com

MADISON (REGION)

Cameo Rose Victorian Country Inn
1090 Severson Rd, *Belleville* 53508
608-424-6340

115-169-BB
5 rooms, 5 pb
Visa, MC, *Rated*
C-no/S-no/P-no/H-ltd
Dawn & Gary Bahr
All year

Full breakfast
Snacks during check-in 4-6 PM.
Sitting room, suites, fireplace, porch, hiking trails

Rated one of the prettiest Victorian-style B&B in the country on 120 acres of hills, woods, views and private hiking trails between vibrant Madison and New Glarus–America's Little Switzerland. innkeeper@cameorose.com http://www.cameorose.com

MILWAUKEE

The Brumder Mansion LLC
3046 W Wisconsin Ave 53208
414-342-9767 Fax: 414-342-4772
866-793-3676
Carol & Bob Hirschi
All year

79-225-BB
5 rooms, 5 pb
Visa, MC, AmEx, *Rated*, •
C-ltd/S-no/P-no/H-no

Full breakfast
Snacks, complimentary wine
Sitting room, library, Jacuzzi, suites, fireplace, cable TV, accom. bus. travelers

Historic Victorian mansion w/professional theatre on site. Exquisite antiques, fabulous romantic whirlpool suites w/fireplaces, full delicious breakfast served in dining room or in room. brumder@execpc.com http://www.brumdermansion.com

Lakeside Inn Cafe
801 N Cass St
801-805 N Cass St 53202
414-276-1577 Fax: 414-276-9869
Diane Benjamin
All year

85-150-BB
4 rooms, 4 pb
Visa, MC, AmEx, *Rated*, •
C-ltd/S-no/P-no/H-no

Full breakfast
Restaurant, bar service, lunch & dinner available
Sitting room, suites, cable TV, steam water shower, accom. bus. travelers

Very private second floor, view of city and urban life.
diane@lakesideinncafe.com http://www.lakesideinncafe.com

MINERAL POINT

Brewery Creek
23 Commerce St 53565
608-987-3298 Fax: 608-987-4388
Deborah & Jeff Donaghue
All year

119-189-BB
7 rooms, 7 pb
Most CC, *Rated*, •
C-ltd/S-no/P-no/H-no

Continental Plus breakfast
Restaurant, lunch & dinner available
Sitting room, library, Jacuzzis, fireplaces, cable TV, accom. bus. travelers

Award winning restoration of 1854 limestone warehouse. Restaurant on first floor. Inn rooms above. Beautifully decorated and appointed rooms. Private suites in historic stone cottage minutes away. brewpub@mhtc.net http://www.brewerycreek.com

NEWBURG

Welcome HOME
PO Box 333
4260 W Hawthorne Dr (Hwy Y) 53060
262-675-2525 Fax: 262-675-0817
Diane Miller All year

50-BB
2 rooms
C-yes/S-no/P-no/H-yes

Continental plus breakfast
Fruit, coffee, tea, cocoa, popcorn
Kitchenette, fireplace, porch, whirlpool, trail, TV/VCR, wheelchair friendly

Cheery, peaceful, inviting country home on a singing hill surrounded by acres of woodland & prairie. Watch wildlife from a screened porch, have a bonfire, soak in whirlpool tub. Wheelchair friendly! welcomehome@hnet.net http://www.hnet.net/~welcomehome

OSCEOLA

Croixwood
421 Ridge Rd 54020
715-294-2894 Fax: 715-294-2425
866-670-3838
Tom Huffman & Rhonda Hammerquist All year

195-228-BB
Most CC

Croixwood on the St. Croix is the St. Croix River Valley's newest Bed and Breakfast. If you are looking for a private couples only romantic retreat Croixwood is the perfect Inn for that special day. email@croixwood.com http://www.croixwood.net

Welcome Home, Newburg, WI

OSCEOLA

Pleasant Lake 2238 60th Ave 54020 715-294-2545 Fax: 715-755-3163 800-294-2545 Richard & Charlene Berg All year	99-159-BB 7 rooms, 7 pb Visa, MC, Disc, *Rated* C-ltd/S-no/P-no/H-ltd	Full breakfast Snacks Jacuzzis, fireplaces, use of canoe & paddleboat

Country home set on 32 wooded acres. Take a leisurely walk, canoe, sit by the crackling bonfire, relax in fireside whirlpools.
pllakebb@centurytel.net http://www.pleasantlake.com

PHILLIPS

Hidden Valley Inn & Resort W7724 Cty West 54555 715-339-2757 Fax: 715-339-1602 Kevin & Barbara Chapman All year	50-125-EP 10 rooms, 10 pb Visa, MC, *Rated* C-yes/S-ltd/P-ltd/H-ltd	Sitting room, fireplaces, accommodate business travelers

All our lodging is lakeside on a private wooded point.
http://www.win.bright.net/~hvrchap/

PORT WASHINGTON

Port Washington Inn 308 W Washington St 53074 262-284-5583 877-794-1903 Rita, Dave & Aaron Nelson All year	95-150-BB 4 rooms, 4 pb Visa, MC, AmEx C-ltd/S-ltd/P-no	Full breakfast

Autumn's magic, winter's wonder, spring's freshness, summer's shade ... no matter the season, the Port Washington Inn offers you a world apart.
info@port-washington-inn.com http://www.port-washington-inn.com

POYNETTE

Jamieson House PO Box 237 407 N. Franklin St 53955 608-635-4100 Fax: 608-635-3392 608-635-2277 Heidi Hutchison All year	80-165-BB 12 rooms, 12 pb Most CC, *Rated*, • C-ltd/S-no/P-ltd/H-no German	Full breakfast included in rm. rate Dinner at Emily's Fri and Sat evenings Bathrobes, Coffee Makers, TV/VCRs, Stereo/CD Players

Relax in European luxury and stay in one of three historic buildings on a two acre estate with a park-like setting and brick walkways. Enjoy a candlelit dinner at Emily's.
jamhouse@execpc.com http://www.jamiesonhouse.com

REEDSBURG

Parkview
211 N Park St 53959
608-524-4333 Fax: 608-524-1172
Tom & Donna Hofmann
All year

75-90-BB
4 rooms, 2 pb
Visa, MC, AmEx,
Rated, •
C-ltd/S-no/P-no/H-no

Full breakfast
Snacks, wake-up coffee
Sitting room, playhouse on property, park across the street

1895 Victorian home with comfortable antiques, across from City Park. Wisconsin Dells, Baraboo, Spring Green, bike trails. parkview@jvlnet.com http://www.parkviewbb.com

RICHLAND CENTER

Lamb's Inn, Cottage & Log Cabin
23761 Misslich Rd
23761 Misslich Dr 53581
608-585-4301 Fax: 608-585-2242
Dick & Donna Messerschmidt
All year

90-300-BB
8 rooms, 8 pb
Visa, MC, Disc, *Rated*
C-ltd/S-no/P-no/H-ltd

Full breakfast
Continental plus breakfast-cottage
Library, suites, fireplaces, gazebo with swing, trout in backyard spring

180 acre farm located in a beautiful valley. Cottage and log cabin also available. Gas fireplace, deck with grill, full kitchen, spectacular views and wrap-around decks.
lambsinn@mwt.net http://www.lambs-inn.com

SHEBOYGAN

English Manor
632 Michigan Ave 53081
920-208-1952 Fax: 920-208-3792
800-557-5277
Susan Hundley
All year

79-179-BB
5 rooms, 5 pb
Most CC, *Rated*, •
C-ltd/S-no/P-ltd/H-ltd

Full breakfast
Afternoon tea, snacks, complimentary wine
Sitting room, library, Jacuzzis, suites, fireplaces, TV, accom. bus. traveler

Lose yourself to romance, tranquility, and total pampering at this European-style inn; gourmet breakfast, afternoon tea, evening wine and cheese.
info@english-manor.com http://www.english-manor.com

SISTER BAY

Hillside Hotel of Ephraim
10957 Hillcrest Rd 54234
920-854-2417 Fax: 920-854-4240
800-423-7023
David & Karen McNeil
May–Oct., Jan–Feb

95-99-BB
12 rooms
Visa, MC, Disc, *Rated*
C-ltd/S-no/P-no/H-no

Full specialty breakfast
6-course gourmet dinner
Full rest., aftn. tea, featherbeds, ceiling fan, private beach, mooring

Country-Victorian hotel in resort with harbor view, original furnishings, spectacular views; near galleries, shops. Deluxe cottages with whirlpool baths.

STEVENS POINT

Dreams of Yesteryear
1100 Brawley St 54481
715-341-4525 Fax: 715-341-4248
Bonnie & Bill Maher
All year

62-149-BB
6 rooms, 4 pb
Visa, MC, *Rated*, •
C-ltd/S-no/P-no/H-no

Full breakfast
Afternoon tea, snacks
Sitting room, library, tennis court, hot tub, bike, pool, 2 3-room suites

Victorian restoration featured in Victorian Homes Magazine. It's truly the kind of place Victorian Dreams are made of.
bonnie@dreamsofyesteryear.com http://www.dreamsofyesteryear.com

---

A Victorian Swan on Water
1716 Water St 54481
715-345-0595 Fax: 713-345-0569
800-454-9886
Joan Ouellette
All year

70-140-BB
4 rooms, 4 pb
Most CC, *Rated*, •
C-ltd/S-no/P-no/H-no

Full breakfast
Snacks, complimentary wine
Sitting room, library, log cabin available

Enjoy award winning breakfast, beautiful gardens, a secret room and whirlpool in this 1889 Victorian home. Central Wisconsin location.
victorian@g2a.net http://www.bbinternet.com/victorian-swan

STURGEON BAY

Chanticleer Guest House
4072 Cherry Rd 54235
920-746-0334 Fax: 920-746-1368
Bryon Groeschl & Darrin Day
All year

120-210-BB
10 rooms, 10 pb
Visa, MC, Disc
S-ltd/P-no/H-ltd

Continental plus breakfast
Snacks
Jacuzzis, swimming pool, suites, fireplaces

Beautiful country inn nestled on 70 private acres in picturesque Door County, WI. Each romantic suite includes double whirlpool, fireplace, private bathroom.
chanticleer@itol.com http://www.chanticleerguesthouse.com

Cherry Hills Lodge
5905 Dunn Rd 54235
920-743-4222 800-545-2307
Diane & Peter Trenchard
All year

BB

Imagine a bed and breakfast for golfers. . . fine dining and comfort.

Cherry Hills Lodge and Golf Course, Door County's premier golf resort, combines a natural rural setting with the atmosphere of your favorite country club.
cherryhl@itol.com http://www.golfdoorcounty.com/

Colonial Gardens
344 N Third Ave 54235
920-746-9192 Fax: 920-746-9193
Joesph & Debra Hertel
All year

100-175-BB
5 rooms, 5 pb
Visa, MC, Disc, *Rated*
C-no/S-no/P-no/H-no

Full Breakfast delivered to room
Afternoon tea, snacks, complimentary wine
Sitting room, Jacuzzis, suites, fireplaces, cable TV, in-room fridge, stereo

Colonial Gardens is located on historic Third Ave. in downtown Sturgeon Bay, Door County, WI. relax@colgardensbb.com http://www.colgardensbb.com

---

Inn at Cedar Crossing
336 Louisiana St 54235
920-743-4200 Fax: 920-743-4422
Terry Smith
All year

119-189-BB
9 rooms, 9 pb
Most CC, *Rated*
C-ltd/S-no/P-no/H-no

Continental plus breakfast
Complimentary beverages, cookies
Restaurant, bar, sitting room, whirlpool in some rooms, fireplaces in rooms

Elegant 1884 inn situated in historic district near shops, restaurants, museum, beaches. Elegant romantic antique decor, fireplaces, whirlpools.
innkeeper@innatcedarcrossing.com http://www.innatcedarcrossing.com

---

Reynolds House
111 S 7th Ave 54235
920-746-9771 Fax: 920-746-9441
877-269-7401
Janet & Stan Sekula All year

65-155-BB
4 rooms, 4 pb
Visa, MC, *Rated*, •
S-no/P-no/H-no

Full breakfast
Afternoon tea, snacks
Sitting room, library, Jacuzzis, suites, fireplaces, cable TV

This architecturally significant Queen Anne Home built in 1900 is located within walking distance of downtown Sturgeon Bay. Romantic setting, luxurious accommodations.
jsekula@reynoldshousebandb.com http://www.reynoldshousebandb.com

---

The Sawyer House
101 S Lansing Ave 54235
920-746-1640 Fax: 920-746-1642
888-746-1614
Ruth Norton
All year

90-150-BB
4 rooms, 4 pb
Visa, MC
C-no/S-no/P-no/H-no

Full breakfast
Afternoon snacks (pie, cookies, cheesecake)
2 sitting rooms, large deck. Most rooms: gas fireplaces, whirlpool, A/C.

There is a place not too far away from here inviting you to relax and get away from it all. Among the beautiful countryside of Door County, nestled peacefully in a quiet neighborhood. sawyerhouse@itol.com http://www.bbonline.com/wi/sawyer

Reynolds House, Sturgeon Bay, WI

STURGEON BAY

Scofield House
PO Box 761
908 Michigan St 54235
920-743-7727 Fax: 920-743-7727
888-463-0204
Carolyn & Mike Pietreh

112-220-BB
6 rooms, 6 pb
Visa, MC, *Rated*
C-no/S-no/P-no
All year

Full gourmet breakfast
Complimentary snacks in the p.m.
A guest phone, refrigerator, and library of compl. video movies

Luxury and comfort are yours to enjoy, when you surround yourself in the ambience of the Scofield House. scofldhs@doorpi.net http://www.scofieldhouse.com

---

White Lace Inn
16 N 5th Ave 54235
920-743-1105 Fax: 920-743-8180
877-948-5223
Dennis & Bonnie Statz
All year

69-249-BB
18 rooms, 18 pb
Most CC, *Rated*
C-ltd/S-no/P-no/H-ltd

Full breakfast
Complimentary cookies, beverages
Sitting room, gazebo, gardens, fireplaces, whirlpools, TV/VCRs

The White Lace Inn's four historic homes are nestled in a friendly old neighborhood, bordered by a white picket fence, surrounded by gardens.
romance@whitelaceinn.com http://www.whitelaceinn.com

Whitefish Bay Farm
3831 Clark Lake Rd 54235
920-743-1560
Dick & Gretchen Regnery
All year

70-95-BB
4 rooms, 4 pb
Visa, MC, Disc, *Rated*
S-no/P-no/H-no
Danish

Full breakfast
Sitting room, ceiling fans, abundant homemade breakfast, bed turndown serv.

Quiet country B&B on 80 acre farm raising sheep. Comfortable rooms, private baths. Abundant homemade breakfast. wbfarm@itol.com http://www.whitefishbayfarm.com

WASHBURN

Pilgrim's Rest
27705 S Maple Hill Rd 54891
715-373-2964
Kent & Mary Beth Seldal
Closed Nov 22–Dec 29

60-110-BB
2 rooms, 2 pb
Rated
C-ltd/S-no/P-no/H-no

Full breakfast
Snacks
Sitting room, suites, hot springs spa, movies & popcorn

Country retreat with view of oldest mountains in North America. Furnished with antiques & lodge decor. Four course breakfast, trails & wildlife all around.
pilgrimrest@ncis.net http://www.ncis.net/pilgrimr/

WISCONSIN DELLS

The White Rose Inn
910 River Rd 53965
608-254-4724 Fax: 608-254-4585
800-482-4725
Marty Stuehler
All year

80-165-BB
13 rooms, 13 pb
Most CC, •
C-ltd/S-no/P-no/H-ltd
Russian, Dutch, German

Full scrumptious breakfast
The Secret Garden Cafe is our on-site restaurant.
Living room, Jacuzzis, outdoor pool, suites, fireplace,verandah, cable TV.

The White Rose Bed & Breakfast offers a romantic, private Victorian mansion, with unique, comfortable rooms with private baths, cable TV, 7 with whirlpool tubs, fireplaces, lavish gardens and pool. whiterose@jvlnet.com http://www.thewhiterose.com

Wyoming

BIG HORN

Spahn's Big Horn Mountain
PO Box 579
70 Upper Hideaway Ln 82833
307-674-8150
Ron & Bobbie Spahn
All year

100-165-BB
5 rooms, 5 pb
Rated, •
C-yes/S-ltd/P-no/H-no

Full breakfast
Dinner by reservation

Towering log home and rustic cabins adjacent to the Bighorn National Forest with a 100 mile view. Gracious mountain breakfasts served with binoculars.
spahn@bighorn-wyoming.com http://bighorn-wyoming.com

CASPER

Ivy House Inn
815 S Ash St 82601
307.265-0974 Fax: 307.268-8356
Tom and Kathy Johnson
All year

55-110-BB
5 rooms, 2 pb
Most CC
C-ltd/S-no/P-no/H-ltd

Full breakfast
Complimentary beverages
Sitting rooms, fireplaces, deck, spa, parking, internet access , TVs, VCRs

Historic Cape Cod style home with two guest suites, and three unique bedrooms. All rooms have access to deck and hot tub, internet, guest kitchens, TVs, VCRs, off-street parking.
ivyinn@yahoo.com http://www.ivyhouseinn.com

CHEYENNE

Nagle Warren Mansion
222 E 17th St 82001
307-637-3333 Fax: 307-638-6879
800-811-2610
Jim Osterfoss
All year

108-287-BB
12 rooms, 12 pb
Visa, MC, AmEx,
Rated, •
C-ltd/S-no/P-ltd/H-yes
Spanish, German

Full breakfast
Afternoon tea, restaurant
Jacuzzis, suites, fireplaces, cable TV, conference facilities

1888 Victorian with all of today's amenities. Comfortable and elegant. Let us spoil you while you explore the original West.
jim@nwmbb.com http://www.naglewarrenmansion.com

CODY

Angels' Keep
1241 Wyoming Ave 82414
307-587-6205 877-320-2800
Barbara Kelley
All year

85-105-BB
2 rooms, 2 pb
Visa, MC, •
C-ltd/S-ltd/P-no/H-no

Generous country breakfast
Beverages, cookies baked daily, other snacks
Gift shop on premises, queen beds, jetted tub, common area, TV/VCR in rooms

Our renovated 1930s mission style church in downtown Cody, WY features delightful accommodations & spectacular service.
angelskeep@cowboystate.net http://www.bbgetaways.com/angelskeep

CODY

Lockhart Inn
109 W Yellowstone Ave 82414
307-587-6074 Fax: 307-587-8644
800-377-7255
Cindy Baldwin
May 15-November 15

95-115-BB
7 rooms, 7 pb
Visa, MC, *Rated*, •
C-yes/S-ltd/P-no/H-no

All-you-can-eat breakfast
Complimentary beverages (hot & cold) & snacks
Property overlooks river, large veranda, sitting room, phones, cable TV

Historic home of famous author, Caroline Lockhart. Furnished with antiques, piano, parlor, overlooks Shoshone River, all non-smoking. All rooms–queen beds, private baths, full breakfast. lockhart@cowboystate.net http://www.codyvacationproperties.com

---

Mayor's Inn
1413 Rumsey 82414
307-587-0887 Fax: 307-587-0890
888-217-3001
Dale Delph
All year

70-205-BB
4 rooms, 4 pb
Visa, MC
C-ltd/S-ltd/P-no/H-no

Full breakfast
Coffee, tea, snacks
Back Porch Bar

Whether you are in town for a vacation adventure or getaway weekend, we invite you to enjoy the nostalgic experience of The Mayor's Inn.
info@mayorsinn.com http://www.mayorsinn.com

Parson's Pillow
1202 14th St 82414
307-587-2382 Fax: 307-527-8908
800-377-2348
Dorothy & Paul Olson
All year

65-95-BB
5 rooms, 5 pb
Most CC, *Rated*, •
C-ltd/S-no/P-ltd/H-no

Full breakfast
Sitting room, computer port

One of Cody's first churches, built in 1902. Comfortable, cozy rooms with feeling of home. Each room has its own theme. Hearty breakfast served at group table.
ppbb@trib.com http://www.cruising-america.com/parsonspillow

The Victorian House
927 14th St
1519 Beck Ave 82414
307-587-6000 Fax: 307-587-8048
800-587-6560
Wendy & Robert Evarts

88-185-BB
3 rooms, 3 pb
Most CC, •
C-ltd/S-no/P-no/H-no
All year

Full breakfast
Restricted, vegetarian
Fresh-water spa, cable TV, stereo, VCR, CD player

For Western luxury and timeless elegance, The Victorian House B&B is a historic three bedroom home built in 1906, tastefully restored and decorated exclusively with antiques and art of the old West. cghouses@wtp.net http://www.codyguesthouses.com

JACKSON

The Alpine House
PO Box 1126
285 N Glenwood St 83001
307-739-1570 Fax: 307-734-2850
800-753-1421
Hans & Nancy Johnstone
Summer, Winter

95-265-BB
22 rooms, 22 pb
Visa, MC, *Rated*, •
C-yes/S-no/P-no/H-yes

Full breakfast
Complimentary afternoon snacks and wine/beer list
PURE bath amenities, robes, outdoor hot tub, Finnish sauna, massage room

Century old timber beams frame this twenty-two room lodge. Located just 2 blocks from the famous Town Square, The Alpine House is a casually elegant Scandinavian retreat in the heart of it all! info@alpinehouse.com http://www.alpinehouse.com

---

The Huff House Inn
PO Box 1189
240 E Deloney 83001
307-733-4164 Fax: 307-739-9091
Jackie & Weldon Richardson

139-225-BB
9 rooms, 9 pb
Most CC, *Rated*, •
C-yes/S-no/P-no/H-no
All year

Full breakfast
Family friendly facility, sitting room, library, hot tubs, fireplaces

Historic house one and one-half blocks east of the town square, on the quiet side of town. Furnished with antiques and original art.
huffhousebnb@blissnet.com http://www.jacksonwyomingbnb.com

A Teton Tree House, Wilson, WY

JACKSON

The Parkway Inn
PO Box 494
125 Jackson St 83001
307-733-3143 Fax: 307-733-0955
800-247-8390
Carmen & Tom Robbins

119-215-BB
49 rooms, 49 pb
Most CC, *Rated*, •
C-ltd/S-ltd/P-no
Spanish, German
Closed November

Continental breakfast
Afternoon tea
Sitting room, Jacuzzis, pool, suites, cable TV, exercise gym with saunas

The style of the inn is reminiscent of turn-of-the-century architecture with white spindle rails and a cupola.

info@parkwayinn.com http://www.parkwayinn.com

The Wildflower Inn
PO Box 11000
3725 N Teton Village Rd 83002
307-733-4710
Fax: 307-739-0914
Ken & Sherrie Jern
All year

200-350-BB
5 rooms, 5 pb
Visa, MC, *Rated*, •
C-yes/S-no/P-no/H-no

Full breakfast
Complimentary wine, tea, coffee
Sitting room, deck, library, hot tubs, pond, solarium, wild ducks

Lovely log home on 3 acres of aspens, cottonwoods and, of course, wildflowers. Five sunny guestrooms, some with private decks. Two-room suite with fireplace, Jacuzzi, deck.

jhwildflowerinn@cs.com http://www.jacksonholewildflower.com

JACKSON (REGION)

A Teton Tree House
PO Box 550
6175 Heck of a Hill Rd, *Wilson* 83014
307-733-3233 Fax: 307-733-0714
Denny & Sally Becker
All year

145-365-BB
6 rooms, 6 pb
Visa, MC, Disc, *Rated*, •
C-ltd/S-no/P-no/H-no
Spanish

Healthy Heart—no eggs or meat
Juices, coffee, teas, beer and wine are available
A Grand Room with games and books galore; an outdoor hot tub

Tucked away, and yet close to two national parks and the town of Jackson, this B&B offers a quiet retreat amidst the trees with unique, comfortable rooms and a warm, friendly atmosphere.

atetontreehouse@aol.com http://www.cruising-america.com/tetontreehouse

LARAMIE (REGION)

A. Drummond's Ranch
399 Happy Jack Rd, *Cheyenne* 82007
307-634-6042 Fax: 307-634-6042
Taydie Drummond All year

70-175-BB
4 rooms, 2 pb
Visa, MC, *Rated*, •
C-ltd/S-no/P-yes/H-ltd
French

Full breakfast
Afternoon tea, snacks
Lunch, dinner (fee), sitting room, library, bikes, hot tub, sauna

Quiet, gracious retreat on 120 acres. Pristine mountain views, glorious night sky, private outdoor Jacuzzis, sauna, fine dining.

adrummond@juno.com http://www.cruising-america.com/drummond.html

NEWCASTLE

Flying V Cambria Inn
23726 Hwy 85 82701
307-746-2096 Fax: 307-746-1569
Larry & Twylla Napolitano
June-November

69-109-BB
10 rooms, 6 pb
Visa, MC, Disc
C-yes/S-ltd/P-ltd/H-ltd

Full breakfast
Restaurant, dinner, afternoon tea, bar service
Sitting room, fireplaces, satellite TV, game boards

Comfortable accommodations in a castle-like atmosphere; great food. Like taking a step back in time; located in the beautiful Black Hills of Wyoming.

flyingv@trib.com http://www.flyingvcambriainn.com

PINEDALE

Pole Creek Ranch
PO Box 278
244 Pole Creek Rd 82941
307-367-4433
Dexter & Carole Smith
All year

55-BB
3 rooms, 1 pb
C-yes/S-no/P-yes/H-no

Full breakfast
Dinner, snacks
sitting room, library, hot tub

You'll stay in a rustic log home with a breathtaking view of the Wind River Mountains, which are still unchanged from when the Indians and mountain men trapped and hunted on them. polecreekrancch@wyoming.com http://www.bbonline.com/wy/polecreek/

Puerto Rico

CEIBA

Ceiba Country Inn
PO Box 1067
Carr 977 KM 1.2 00735
787-885-0471 Fax: 787-885-0471
888-560-2816
Sue Newbauer & Dick Bray
All year

69-BB
9 rooms, 9 pb
Most CC, *Rated*, •
C-yes/S-yes/P-no/H-yes

Continental plus breakfast
Bar service, library, family friendly facility

Pastoral setting with a view of the sea. Centrally located for trips to the rain forest, beaches, outer islands, and San Juan.

prinn@juno.com http://www.geocities.com/countryinn00735

ISABELA

Villa Montana Resort
PO Box 530
Carr. 4466 Interior Bo. Bajuras 00662
787-872-9554 Fax: 787-872-9553
888-780-9195
Melody Daino All year

220-345-EP
Most CC, *Rated*, •
C-yes/S-yes/P-no/H-yes
Spanish, English, French

Lunch & Dinner available
Snacks, Restaurant, Bar, Sitting Rm, Bikes, Tennis, Jacuzzis, Pool, Cable TV

For those who want to get away from it all and relax in the endless tropical evenings. A place the family will enjoy, or for those who want to heighten their senses through sports and adventure. http://www.villamontana.com

PATILLAS

Caribe Playa Beach Resort
HC 764 Box 8490
Road #3, KM 112.1 00723
787-839-6339 Fax: 787-839-1817
George Engel
All year

90-104-EP
32 rooms, 32 pb
Visa, MC, AmEx, •
C-yes/S-yes/P-yes/H-yes
Spanish, Hungarian, Hebrew

Full breakfast
Sandwiches, salads, lunch, snacks, cocktails, dinner
Restaurant, lounge bar, sitting room, library, beach & pool, snorkel, massages

Modern studios on private picturesque Coconut Beach on the Caribbean Sea; swimming, snorkeling, fishing, scuba, pool, sundeck, beach barbecues and hammocks, TV & music room, open air terrace & bar. engel@caribeplaya.com http://www.caribeplaya.com

SAN JUAN

El Canario by the Sea Hotel
4 Condado Ave 00907
787-722-8640 Fax: 787-725-4921
800-533-2649
Mathilda Jean Baptiste
All year

85-119-BB
25 rooms, 25 pb
Most CC, *Rated*, •
C-yes/S-yes/P-no/H-no
Spanish

Tropical breakfast
A/C, private bath, Cable TV, telephone, in-room safe.
Inner garden courtyard

Simple, yet affordable, the friendly staff, informal atmosphere and terrific location makes this hotel a favorite with business and holiday travelers alike.
canariopr@aol.com http://www.canariohotels.com

El Canario Inn
1317 Ashford Ave 00907
787-722-3861 Fax: 787-722-0391
800-533-2649
Marcos Santana All year

85-119-BB
25 rooms, 25 pb
Most CC, *Rated*, •
C-yes/S-yes/P-no/H-no
Spanish

Continental plus breakfast
Patios, A/C rooms, color TV, phone, private bathroom, Bermuda ceiling fans

El Canario Inn is San Juan's most historic and unique B&B. Near beach, casinos, boutiques and restaurants. Relaxing patios are filled with tropical foliage and the melody of coquis.
canariopr@aol.com http://www.canariohotels.com

Embassy Guesthouse-Condado
PO Box 16876
1126 Calle Seaview 00907
787-725-8284 Fax: 787-725-2400
800-468-0615

45-145-BB
20 rooms, 20 pb
Most CC, *Rated*, •
C-yes/S-yes/P-no/H-ltd
Spanish, French
Jacques & Thierry
All year

Continental breakfast
Jacuzzi, fresh water swimming pool, cable TV

Located in the center of Condado, only steps to the beaches in San Juan. New fresh water swimming pool and Jacuzzi.
embassyguesthouse@worldnet.att.net http://home.att.net/~embassyguesthouse/

Hosteria Del Mar Beach Inn
#1 Tapia St Ocean Park 00911
787-727-3302
Fax: 787-268-0772
877-727-3302
Elsie Herger, Mercedes Mulet
All year

75-240-EP
8 rooms, 8 pb
Rated, •
C-yes/S-ltd/P-yes/H-yes
Spanish

Lunch, dinner, restaurant
Cable TV

Cozy beach Inn by the sea. Rooms with wonderful view of the Atlantic. One or two bedroom apartment, offering breakfast, lunch and dinner in a tropical gazebo on the beach. hosteria@caribe.net

---

Tres Palmas Inn
2212 Park Blvd 00913
787-727-4617 Fax: 787-727-5434
888-290-2076
Manuael & Eileen Peredo
All year

75-180-BB
15 rooms, 15 pb
Visa, MC, AmEx, *Rated*, •
C-yes/S-ltd/P-no/H-yes
Spanish

Continental breakfast
Sitting room, Jacuzzis, swimming pool, suites, cable TV, phone with dataport

This quaint 15 room beachfront Inn, recently renovated, is a refreshing alternative to traditional high priced and crowded hotels.
trespalm@coqui.net http://www.trespalmasinn.com

SAN JUAN (REGION)

El Prado Inn on the Park
1350 Luchetti St, *Condado*
00907
787-728-5925 Fax: 787-725-6978
800-468-4521
Monique & Gerardo Latimer

75-139-BB
22 rooms, 22 pb
Visa, MC, AmEx, •
C-yes/S-ltd/P-no/H-ltd
Spanish, French, Italian
All year

Continental plus breakfast
Library, pool, suites, cable TV, accommodate business travelers

This unique Spanish inn features Andalusian-Moorish decor and striking coffered ceilings in the suites of the original restored 1930's mansion, comfortable modern decor in 16 newly renovated rooms. elprado@santanderchannel.com

---

Hotel La Playa
Calle Amapola #6, *Isla Verde*
00979
787-791-1115 Fax: 787-791-4650
800-791-9626
David Yourch & Manual Godinez All year

85-115-BB
15 rooms, 15 pb
Most CC, *Rated*, •
C-yes/S-yes/P-no/H-yes
Spanish

Continental breakfast
Lunch & dinner available (fee)
Restaurant, bar service, open air deck located on beach

Small family oriented hotel w/ relaxing casual atmosphere, located on beach. Family owned business for over 35 years, in a residential area.
manager@hotellaplaya.com http://www.hotellaplaya.com

The Gallery Inn at Galeria San Juan
204 Norzagaray, *Old San Juan*
00901
787-722-1808 Fax: 787-977-3429
Manuco Gandia & Jan D'Esopo All year

145-350-BB
22 rooms, 22 pb
Visa, MC, AmEx, •
C-yes/S-ltd/P-yes/H-no
Sapnish, German

Continental plus breakfast
Bar service
Sitting room, conference room, music room

Enter a fascinating world of art and history. This wonderful 300 year-old rambling building overlooks the sea atop the north wall of 500-year old San Juan.
reservations@thegalleryinn.com http://www.thegalleryinn.com

VIEQUES

Hacienda Tamarindo
PO Box 1569
4.5 Km, Rt 996 00765
787-741-8525 Fax: 787-741-3215
Burr & Linda Vail
All year

125-180-BB
15 rooms, 15 pb
Visa, MC, AmEx, *Rated*, •
C-ltd/S-yes/P-no/H-yes
Spanish

Full breakfast
Bar service
Sitting room, library, tennis court, swimming pool

Perched on windswept hilltop overlooking the turquoise Caribbean. Uniquely designed and decorated with an accumulation of art and antiques.
hactam@aol.com http://www.enchanted-isle.com/tamarindo

Virgin Islands

ST. CROIX

Carringtons Inn St. Croix
4001 Estate Herman Hill
56 Herman Hill 00820
340-713-0508 Fax: 340-719-0841
877-658-0508
Claudia & Roger Carrington
All year

100-150-BB
5 rooms, 5 pb
Visa, MC, AmEx, *Rated*, •
S-ltd/P-no/H-no

Full breakfast
Snacks
Sitting room, swimming pool, cable TV, accommodate business travelers

Welcome to Carrington's Inn—your home in the Caribbean. Five spacious and beautifully decorated rooms surround the pool and patio. Personalized service is our trademark.
info@carringtonsinn.com http://www.carringtonsinn.com

ST. THOMAS

Bellavista B&B
2713 Murphy Gade 12-14 00802
340-714-5706
Fax: 340-777-6939
888-333-3063
Wendy and Frank Sarver
All year

110-185-BB
4 rooms, 4 pb
Most CC
C-ltd/S-ltd/P-no/H-no

Full breakfast
Evening cocktail hour
Concierge, turndown service, flowers in room, swimming pool, tropical garden

A delightfully inviting bed and breakfast overlooking the harbor at Charlotte Amalie. Experience the personalized service and quality amenities of a traditional B&B with distinctive Caribbean style.

mail@bellavistabnb.com http://www.bellavista-bnb.com

The Crystal Palace
PO Box 12200
12 Crystal Gade 00801
340-777-2277
Fax: 340-776-2797
Ronnie Lockhart
All year

65-115-BB
5 rooms, 2 pb
Most CC, •
C-yes/S-ltd/P-no/H-ltd
Spanish

Continental breakfast
Lunch and dinners by request
Cable TV, A/C, Honor bar

In historic district, on hill overlooking the harbor. Enjoy breakfast on porch, as the cruise ships come. Evenings, watch the ships leave, as the sun sets, sipping a drink from our honor bar! Enjoy!

CrystalPalace@St-Thomas.com http://www.crystalpalaceusvi.com/

Danish Chalet Inn
PO Box 4319
9E Gamble Nordsidevej 00803
340-774-5764
Fax: 340-777-4886
800-635-1531
Frank & Mary Davis
All year

68-125-BB
15 rooms, 6 pb
Visa, MC, *Rated*, •
S-yes/P-ltd/H-yes
English

Continental breakfast
Bar service ($1 drinks)
Sitting room, spa, Jacuzzi, sun deck, beach towels, games

Family inn overlooking Charlotte Amalie harbor, 5 min. to town, duty-free shops, restaurants. Cool breezes, honor bar, sun deck, Jacuzzi. Beach-15 min. Lovely 3 room apartment added.

fhd4319@aol.com http://www.danishchaletinn.com

Galleon House
PO Box 6577
4 C Commandant Gade 00804
340-774-6952
Fax: 340-774-6952
800-524-2052
Michel Deschenes
Dec-April

79-129-BB
14 rooms, 13 pb
Rated, •
C-yes/S-yes/P-no/H-no

Full breakfast
A/C in rooms, pool, snorkel gear, veranda, beach towels

Visit historical Danish town. Superb view of harbor with city charm; close to everything. Duty-free shopping, beach activities in 85-degree weather.

galhou@viaccess.vi http://www.galleonhouse.com

Island View Guest House
PO Box 1903
11-1C Contant 00803
340-774-4270
Fax: 340-774-6167
800-524-2023
Barbara Cooper
All year

65-100-BB
15 rooms, 13 pb
Rated, •
C-ltd/S-yes/P-no/H-no

Continental breakfast
Full breakfast available
Hors d'oeuvres (Friday), sandwiches, bar, gallery, swimming pool

Overlooking St. Thomas Harbor; honor bar and freshwater pool. Spectacular harbor view from all rooms. Convenient to town and airport.

islandview@attglobal.net http://www.st-thomas.com/islandviewguesthouse/

Alberta

BANFF (REGION)

Enjoy Living
149 Cougar Point Rd, *Canmore*
T1W 1A1
403-678-3026 Fax: 403-678-3042
800-922-8274
Garry & Nancy Thoen
All year

65-70-BB
2 rooms, 2 pb
Rated
C-yes/S-no/P-no/H-no

Full breakfast
Snacks
Sitting room, library, Jacuzzis, cable TV, accommodate business travelers

Modern B&B with mountain views in all directions, within walking distance to cafes, specialty shops, art galleries & fine dining.
enjoy@telusplanet.net http://canadianrockies.net/enjoyliving

BRAGG CREEK

The Leonard-Anderson
PO Box 671
Hwy 672 T0L 0K0
403-949-3499
Fax: 403-949-3499
LA Edwards
All year

75-100-BB
2 rooms, 1 pb
Visa
C-yes/S-no/P-no/H-no

Full breakfast
Romantic, Children welcome

Beautiful setting minutes from the Bragg Creek Hamlet. Enjoy the scenery, a Swedish sauna or your favorite recreational activities.
loriann@telusplanet.net

Morningside Inn
PO Box 974
43 White Ave T0L 0K0
403-949-3244
Fax: 403-949-3244
D. Vanderveer
All year

65-95-BB
3 rooms, 1 pb
Visa, •
C-yes/S-no/P-no/H-ltd

Full breakfast
Afternoon tea
Sitting room, library, fireplace, conference facilities

Valley setting close to mountains. Within walking distance to restaurants, shopping and the hamlet center. Close to golf, skiing, hiking, mountain climbing and caving.
deadonv@aol.com http://www.bbalberta.com/bbpages.asp?inn=418

CALGARY

Along River Ridge
1919 52nd St NW T3B 1C3
403-247-1330 Fax: 403-247-1328
888-434-9555
Dianne Haskell
All year

50-75-BB
3 rooms, 3 pb
Visa, MC, AmEx, *Rated*
C-ltd/S-no/P-no/H-ltd

Full breakfast
Afternoon tea, snacks, lunch & dinner avail
Sitting room, library, bikes, Jacuzzis, fireplaces, cable TV

A restful "all seasons" retreat on the Bow River less than 15 minutes to downtown Calgary.
haskell@riverridgebb.com http://www.riverridgebb.com

B&B at Harrison's
6016 Thornburn Dr NW T2K 3P7
403-274-7281 Fax: 403-531-0069
Susan & Ken Harrison
All year

70-85-BB
2 rooms, 2 pb
Rated, •
C-ltd/S-ltd/P-no/H-ltd

Full breakfast
Snacks
Sitting room, cable TV

Cozy, comfortable bungalow in quiet residential area. Enjoy our full & delicious breakfast overlooking our front garden.
bbharrison@shaw.ca http://www.bbcanada.com/1098

Big Springs Estate, Airdrie, AB

CALGARY

Calgary Westways Guesthouse 216 25th Ave SW T2S 0L1 403-229-1758 Fax: 403-229-1758 866-750-3341 Jonathon Lloyd All year	60-130-BB CAN$ 5 rooms, 5 pb Visa, MC, AmEx, *Rated*, • C-ltd/S-no/P-yes/H-no French	Full breakfast Romantic dinner for two Sitting room, Jacuzzis, fireplaces, cable TV, computer station work station

1912 Central Heritage Home within walking distance to downtown, Telus Convention Center and Stampede Park. All Guestrooms have en-suite/private bathroom, digital cable TV/VCR & phone with data port. calgary@westways.ab.ca http://www.westways.ab.ca

CALGARY (REGION)

Big Springs Estate RR 1, *Airdrie* T4B 2A3 403-948-5264 Fax: 403-948-5851 888-948-5851 Carol & Earle Whittaker All year	82-115-BB 5 rooms, 5 pb Visa, MC, AmEx, *Rated*, • C-yes/S-no/P-no/H-no	Full scrumptious breakfast Beverages & evening homemade snacks available Nature trail, hot tub, lounge

Gracious Inn set in foothills of Canadian Rockies in Alberta's Wild West. 25 min. to Calgary Airport, 1 hr to Rocky Mountains. 5 distinctive rooms, private baths.
bigsprings@bigsprings-bb.com http://www.bigsprings-bb.com

M&M Ranch PO Box 707 Hwy 762, *Bragg Creek* T0L 0K0 403-949-3272 Fax: 403-949-2846 Rebecca Horne & Bonnie MacLaine All year	BB 2 rooms Visa, MC, • C-ltd/S-ltd/P-ltd	Continental breakfast Complimentary wine or beer Library, bikes, tennis court, fireplaces

A small, family run business with Western riding available; close to the Rocky Mountains and the metropolitan city of Calgary.

CANMORE

A Log Cabin 605 5th St T1W 2E9 403-678-4849 Fax: 403-609-2626 Gaelle & Didier All year	65-80-BB 2 rooms, 2 pb Visa, MC, AmEx, *Rated*, • C-yes/S-no/P-no/H-no French, Spanish	French gourmet Full Breakfast Sitting room with fireplace

Welcome to a Traditional Canadian LOG HOME. French gourmet Full Breakfast. Two Suites rated ★★★ Canada-Select, private entrance, en-suite baths, queen bed, cable-TV-VCR, fridge & bar-sink. info@alogcabin.com http://www.alogcabin.com

CANMORE

Ambleside Lodge
123A Rundle Dr T1W 2L6
403-678-3976
Maureen & Len Crawford
11 months/year

75-90-BB
2 rooms, 2 pb
Visa, MC, AmEx, •
C-ltd/S-no/P-no/H-no

Full breakfast/cooked & continental
Complimentary tea, coffee plus cold drinks
36 ft guest lounge with log burning fireplace

Your hosts, Maureen and Len Crawford, would like to invite you to come and enjoy their home and hospitality in the heart of the majestic and awe inspiring Rocky Mountains of Alberta, Canada. lenmo@amblesidelodge.com http://www.amblesidelodge.com

---

Emerald Lakes Inn
233 Benchlands Terrace T1W 1G1
403-609-2707 Fax: 403-609-2707
877-363-7525
Mary
All year

70-200-BB
5 rooms, 2 pb
Visa, MC, AmEx, *Rated*, •
C-ltd/S-ltd/P-ltd/H-no
Japanese, German

Full plus early/late continental
Bottomless cookie jar, evening dessert, tea/coffee
Hot tub, jetted 2 person tub, library, video library, gym, piano, karaoke

Fine Oriental art, striking architecture, spectacular views of the Canadian Rockies, extensive amenities, warm hospitality, memorable fare, and pampering service. . .a world-class experience. emerlake@telusplanet.net http://www.emeraldlakesbbinn.com

DRUMHELLER

The Heartwood Haven
356 Fourth St W T0J 0Y3
403-823-4956 Fax: 403-823-4935
Norah & Bob Hamilton
All year

110-250-EP CAN$
5 rooms, 5 pb
Visa, MC, AmEx, *Rated*, •
C-yes/S-no/P-no/H-yes

Breakfast available (fee), afternoon tea
Sitting room, Jacuzzi, suites, fireplaces, cable TV, full service spa

The Heartwood Haven is known for its Old-World atmosphere coupled with modern day amenities . . . jet tubs, gas fireplaces, carriage beds, and antiques.
heartinn@telusplanet.net http://www.bbcanada.com/437.html

HINTON

Black Cat Guest Ranch
PO Box 6267
T7V 1X6
780-865-3084 Fax: 780-865-1924
800-859-6840
Amber & Perry Hayward

120-AP
16 rooms, 16 pb
Visa, MC, *Rated*, •
C-yes/S-no/P-no/H-no
All year

Full breakfast
All meals included in rate
Sitting room, piano, adult oriented, trails, patio, outdoor hot tub

A year-round lodge facing the front range of the Rockies, featuring trail rides and hiking in summer, cross-country skiing in winter.
bcranch@telusplanet.net http://www.blackcatranch.ab.ca

McCracken Country Inn
146 Brookhart St T7V 1Y8
1-780-865-5662 Fax: 1-780-865-5664 888-865-5662
Kyle & Fay McCracken

75-140-AP CAN$
9 rooms, 9 pb
Most CC, *Rated*
C-yes/S-no/P-ltd/H-yes
All year

Full breakfast
We offer home style cooking and fresh baking daily
Beautiful and relaxing parlor for our guests to enjoy

McCracken Country Inn offers the comfort and privacy of a luxury hotel with the ambience of an old Country Inn.
mccrackencountryinn@shaw.ca http://www.mccrackencountryinn.com

ICEFIELD PARKWAY (REGION)

Aurum Lodge
PO Box 76
Highway 11 at Cline River, *Nordegg* T0M 2H0
403-721-2117 Fax: 403-721-2118
Madeleine & Alan Ernst
All year

85-195-BB CAN$
6 rooms, 6 pb
Visa, MC
C-ltd/S-no/P-no/H-yes
German, French

Full breakfast
Set evening menu available by prior arrangement
Sitting room, deck, library, bicycles, snow shoes

Award winning Eco-tourism country inn in the Canadian Rockies. Secluded location, pristine wilderness, comfort, tranquillity and many attractions/activities close to Banff and Jasper National Parks. info@aurumlodge.com http://www.aurumlodge.com

JASPER (REGION)

Old Entrance B&B (& Bale)
PO Box 6054
Old Entrance, Highway 40
North, *Hinton* T7V 1X4
780-865-4760 Fax: 780-865-3665
Mary Luger & Carol Wray
All year

57-BB
2 rooms, 2 pb
MC, *Rated*, •
C-yes/S-ltd/P-ltd/H-yes

Full breakfast
Bicycles, fireplace, movies, trail rides, VCR/TV

A peaceful, relaxed guest ranch-like setting along the Athabasca River near Jasper National Park.
oldentrance@yahoo.com http://www.oldentrance.ab.ca

Overlander Mountain Lodge
PO Box 6118
Hwy 16, *Hinton* T7V 1X5
780-866-2330
Fax: 780-866-2332
Garth & Kathy Griffiths
All year

75-132-BB CAN$
Rated, •
C-yes/S-ltd/P-no/H-ltd
French, Spanish

Continental breakfast
Dinner, afternoon tea, restaurant
Bar service, sitting room, library, fireplaces, conference facilities

Beautiful lodge and rustic cabins overlooking Jasper National Park.
overland@telusplanet.net http://www.overlandermountainlodge.com

RED DEER

Dutchess Manor
4813 54 St T4N 2G5
403-346-7776
Susan Uiterwijk
All year

55-75-BB
3 rooms
Visa, *Rated*
C-no/S-no/P-no

Full breakfast

Cozy 1905 home, decorated European style. Full service aesthetic salon on premises.
dmanor@telusplanet.net http://www.bbcanada.com/143.html

RED DEER (REGION)

Alberta's Inn On The Lake
RR 1, Site 2, Box 32
91 Lakeview Ave, Gull Lake, Alberta, *Lacombe* T0C 1S0
403-748-3237
Corinne Johns-Sawyer
All year

115-BB
2 rooms, 2 pb
Rated, •
C-ltd/S-no/P-no/H-no

Scrumptious decadent breakfast
Complimentary wine & appetizer tray upon arrival
Games room, coffee/juice/snack/pop, bikes, cable TV, library

A Canada Select 4 1/2 Star B&B Accommodation (One of only two in Alberta!). Relax and enjoy a lakefront property close to many of Alberta's tourist spots.
info@onthelakebb.com http://www.onthelakebb.com

British Columbia

CHEMAINUS

Olde Mill House
PO Box 1046
9712 Chemainus Rd V0R 1K0
250-416-0049 877-770-6060
Marion Hawkins
All year

BB
3 rooms, 3 pb
Visa, MC
C-yes/S-ltd

Full breakfast
Refreshments upon arrival, host's fruit wine
Jacuzzi tub, air conditioning

Old world charm, comfort, elegance are words that describe this turn-of-the-century home. stay@oldemillhouse.ca http://www.oldemillhouse.ca

COQUITLAM (REGION)

Tall Cedars
720 Robinson St, *Vancouver*
V3J 4G1
604-936-6016 Fax: 604-936-6016
Dwyla & Edward
All year

55-75-BB
3 rooms
Rated, •
C-ltd/S-ltd/P-no/H-no

Full breakfast
Restaurants nearby, sitting room, garden, TV, videos

Comfortable "home away from home" inspected and approved by B.C. Ministry of Tourism. Comfy beds, smoking on garden balcony. Stanley Park, lakes, mountains and parks. Minutes to city center. tallcedars@shaw.ca http://www.tallcedarsvancouver.com

CRESTON (REGION)

Destiny Bay Resort
Site 12, Box 6
11935 Highway 3A, *Boswell*
V0B 1A0
250-223-8234 Fax: 250-223-8515
800-818-6633
Ron & Lynn Mondor

125-150-MAP
8 rooms, 8 pb
Visa, MC
C-ltd/S-ltd/P-no/H-ltd
May–October

Full breakfast
Dinner, restaurant, bar service
Fireplaces, sauna, beach

Lakeside resort featuring cozy sod-roofed lakefront cottages, delicious gourmet dinners and breakfast buffets. Adult oriented with no phones or TV.
destinyb@kootenay.com http://www.destinybay.com

GARIBALDI HIGHLANDS (REGION)

Nusalya Chalet
PO Box 927
2014 Glacier Heights Pl,
Whistler V0N 1T0
604-898-3039 Fax: 604-898-3039
877-604-9005
Bill & Sue McComish
All year

145-215-BB CAN$
3 rooms, 3 pb
Visa, MC, *Rated*, •
C-ltd/S-no/P-no/H-no

Full breakfast
Great Room and fireplace, hot tub spa, patio, guest computer & Internet

Escape from the crowds to dream adventures at Nu-Salya, A Five Star B&B just 35 minutes south of Whistler Creek-side Gondola, offering quiet serenity and spectacular Fjord & Towering Mountain views. stay@nusalya.com http://www.nusalya.com

GIBSONS

Bonniebrook Lodge
RR 5, 1532 Oceanbeach Esplanade
1532 Oceanbeach Esplanade
V0N 1V0
604-886-2887 Fax: 604-886-8853
877-290-9916
Karen & Philippe Lacoste

92-125-BB
7 rooms, 4 pb
Most CC, *Rated*, •
C-yes/S-no/P-no/H-ltd
French
February–Dec.

Full Canada Select breakfast
Dinner, restaurant
Jacuzzis, suites, fireplaces, cable TV, tennis courts

A romantic oceanside Inn. Anne Garber of the Vancouver Province sums up Bonniebrook, "Beyond a doubt the best accommodation and restaurant on the Sunshine Coast. Perfect for an intimate getaway." info@bonniebrook.com http://www.bonniebrook.com

GOLD BRIDGE

Tyax Mountain Lake Resort
Tyaughton Lake Rd V0K 1P0
250-238-2221 Fax: 250-238-2528
Robin
All year

80-98-EP
33 rooms, 33 pb
Visa, MC, AmEx, *Rated*, •
C-yes/S-ltd/P-ltd/H-yes
French, German

Full breakfast
Afternoon tea, snacks, restaurant, bar service
Sitting room, mountain bikes, tennis & volleyball courts, horseback riding,

Tucked away in the sunny Chilcotin Mountains lies Canada's second largest modern log structure. Nestled on glacier-fed Tyaughton Lake overlooking snowcapped mountains to 9,000 feet. fun@tyax.com http://www.tyax.com

GOLDEN

Sisters & Beans
PO Box 4082
1122 10th Ave South V0A 1H0
250-344-2443 Fax: 250-344-7992
Vreni or Nelli Tobler
All year

55-120-BB
4 rooms
Visa, MC
C-yes/S-no/P-no/H-ltd
German

Full breakfast
Dinner, restaurant
Sauna

Newly renovated period home with unique, licensed restaurant, in a small town located in the Columbia Valley. sistersandbeans@bc.ca http://www.bbcanada.com/2365.html

KAMLOOPS

Father's Country Inn
PO Box 152
3240 Tod Mountain Rd V0E 1Z0
250-578-7308 Fax: 250-578-7334
800-578-7322

75-125-BB CAN$
5 rooms, 5 pb
Visa, MC, •
C-ltd/S-no/P-no/H-no
David Brenda All year

Full breakfast
Dinners, afternoon tea, snacks
Sitting room, indoor pool, fireside lounge, Jacuzzi

Quiet, spacious, unique 6000 sq. ft Country Inn situated on a hillside overlooking ranches and meadows below. mmfathers@telus.net http://www.dconover.com

---

MacQueen's Manor
1049 Laurel Pl V1S 1R1
250-372-9383 Fax: 250-372-9384
800-677-5338
Jack and Pat Macqueen
All year

55-BB
3 rooms, 3 pb
Visa, AmEx, *Rated*, •
C-yes/S-no/P-ltd/H-no

Full gourmet breakfast
Snacks, complimentary sherry
Sitting room, cable TV, accommodate business travelers

Quiet modern home with country Victorian decor. All rooms feature private baths, TV/VCR, fruit baskets, chocolates, and fresh flowers.
macqueensmanor@telus.net http://www.bbcanada.com/3809.html

Place Royale
534 Robson Dr V2E 2B6
250-374-7224 Fax: 250-374-6474
866-851-1311/U
Frank Martens All year

53-75-BB
3 rooms, 3 pb
Visa, MC, *Rated*
C-ltd/S-no/P-no/H-no
German

Full gourmet, nutritious, delicious
Complimentary tea, coffee, dessert at night
Sitting room, hot tub, exercise room

Due to unexpected events Place Royale will be closed for the rest of 2002 but is still taking reservations for January 1, 2003 and beyond.
placeroyale@telus.net http://www.placeroyale.info

KELOWNA

An English Rose Garden
305 Stellar Dr V1W 4K5
250-764-5231 877-604-6259
Mina Muench
All year

BB
2 rooms, 2 pb
Visa, MC, AmEx, Most CC
C-ltd/S-ltd/P-no/H-no

Full breakfast
Tea Coffee juice wine cookies etc.
Sitting room, fireplaces, satellite TV, garden patio

Elegance inside and out. En-suites are tiled with marble countertops and gold faucets. Personalized breakfast served in a garden featuring waterfalls, streams, fishponds and over 100 rose bushes. arosegarden@telus.net http://www.anenglishrosegarden.com

KIMBERLEY (REGION)

Wasa Lakeside Resort
PO Box 122
4704 Spruce Rd, *Wasa Lake* V0B 2K0
250-422-3688 Fax: 250-422-3551
888-422-3636
James & Mary Swansburg
April 1–October 31

150-200-BB
3 rooms, 3 pb
Visa, MC, *Rated*, •
C-yes/S-no/P-no/H-ltd

Full breakfast
Sitting/game room, bikes, tennis, steamshower/Jacuzzi, suites, watersports

Your lake oasis hidden in the Rocky Mountains, south of Banff and Lake Louise near Kimberley. info@wasalakeresort.com http://www.wasalakeresort.com

LAC LA HACHE

Cariboo Log Guest House
3701 Hwy 97 V0K 1T0
250-396-4747 Fax: 250-396-7400
Hermann & Brigitte Ernst
All year

50-57-BB
6 rooms, 6 pb
Visa, MC, AmEx, *Rated*
C-yes/S-no/P-ltd/H-ltd
German, French

Full breakfast
Afternoon tea, lunch & dinner
Dining & sitting room, accm. bus. trav., family dining adv. reservation required

Stately, cozy, new log home nestled in rolling hills of Cariboo Plateau at Lake Lac LaHache. Family dining (European style). Reservations for dining required.
ernst@cariboogueshouse.com http://www.cariboogueshouse.com

MAYNE ISLAND

Oceanwood Country Inn
630 Dinner Bay Rd V0N 2J0
250-539-5074 Fax: 250-539-3002
Jonathan Chilvers
March 1–Nov 30

79-219-BB
12 rooms, 12 pb
Visa, MC, *Rated*, •
C-ltd/S-ltd/P-no/H-ltd
French

Full breakfast
Gourmet dinner at extra cost; comp. tea
Bar service, library, sitting room, bikes, hot tubs, sauna, tennis

Beautiful waterfront country inn in Canada's west coast Gulf Islands, a perfect romantic getaway. Twelve rooms, many with fireplace, double whirlpool or soaking tub, oceanview deck. Gourmet dining.
oceanwood@gulfislands.com http://www.oceanwood.com

MILL BAY

Shirley's Cozy Nest
2502 Fawn Rd V0R 2P0
250-743-8286 877-743-8286
Shirley & Paul Chmielewski
All year

BB
Visa, MC, *Rated*
C-yes/S-no

Hot tub, swings, patio

A warm welcome awaits you at Shirley's Cozy Nest. We provide a traditional bed and breakfast, emphasizing warmth, charm, and comfort. relax@shirlyscozynest.com

NEW AIYANSH

Miles Inn on T'Seax
PO Box 230
Nass Road V0J 1A0
604-633-2636 800-553-1199
Robert Miles
All year

80-BB
S-no

Country Inn, Bed and Breakfast situated in the Beautiful Nass Valley, overlooking the Nisga'a Memorial Lava Bed Provincial Park, 100 kilometers north of Terrace, B.C.
milesinn@kermode.net http://www.kermode.net/milesinn/

PARKSVILLE (REGION)

Creekside
1961 Harlequin Crescent, *Nanoose Bay* V9P 9J2
250-468-9310 Fax: 250-468-7343
Kathy McMaster & Rolf Meier
All year

55-65-BB
3 rooms, 3 pb
Visa, MC, *Rated*
C-ltd/S-no/P-no/H-no
German, Swiss-German

Full breakfast
Choice of tea or wine on arrival & late afternoon
Sitting room, spacious deck, piano, guitar

Nestled beside towering cedars on a hillside overlooking Dolphin Bay, our unique designer home is affordable elegance near Parksville. Enjoy gourmet breakfasts on the deck; walk to beach & trails. kathy@creeksidebb.com http://www.creeksidebb.com

---

Madrona Point Waterfront
1344 Madrona Dr, *Nanoose Bay* V9P 9C9
250-468-5972 Fax: 250-468-5976
Lise & Reg Johanson
All year

70-BB
2 rooms, 2 pb
Visa, MC
C-yes/S-no/P-yes/H-no
French

Full breakfast
Library, bicycles, Jacuzzis, suites, fireplaces, cable TV

Oceanfront rooms furnished with antiques and feather beds.
madronapoint@shaw.ca http://www.madronapoint.com

PENDER ISLAND

Oceanside Inn
PO Box 50
4230 Armadale Rd V0N 2M0
250-629-6691
Geoff Clydesdale
All year

100-200-BB
4 rooms, 4 pb
Visa, *Rated*, •
C-no/S-no/P-no/H-no

Full breakfast
Dinner in the Oceanfront dining room
Sitting room, library, private hot tubs/deck, suites, fireplaces, restaurant

Oceanside Inn, nestled on 3 acres of oceanfront tranquility, where our guests can retreat from the rapid pace of city life. Privacy is characteristic of life at Oceanside. All private outdoor hot tubs. oceanside@penderisland.com http://www.penderisland.com

PENTICTON (REGION)

Bear's Den
PO Box 172
189 Linden Ave, *Kaleden* V0H 1K0
250-497-6721 Fax: 250-497-6453
866-232-7722
Ross Arnot & Ed Schneider
All year

65-115-BB
4 rooms, 4 pb
Most CC, *Rated*
C-ltd/S-no/P-ltd/H-ltd

Full breakfast
Snacks, complimentary wine
Sitting room, Library, fireplaces, cable TV, hot tub, sundeck, gardens

Canada select four star home overlooking lakes, orchards, cities and mountains.
stay@bearsdenbb.com http://www.bearsdenbb.com

PORT MCNEILL

Hidden Cove Lodge
PO Box 258
Lewis Point V0N 2R0
250-956-3916 Fax: 250-956-3916
Dan & Sandra Kirby All year

99-299-BB CAN$
8 rooms, 8 pb
Visa, MC, *Rated*, •
C-ltd/S-ltd/P-no/H-ltd

Continental plus breakfast
Lunch & dinner, afternoon tea, snacks
Licensed dining, cottages with fireplaces, free moorage

Secluded cedar lodge and cottages on oceanfront bay, surrounded by forest and nature. Grizzly bear and killer whale tours. Licensed dining room.
hidcl@island.net http://www.pixsell.bc.ca/bcbbd/1/1000263.htm

PRINCE RUPERT

Eagle Bluff
200/201 Cow Bay Rd
100 Cow Bay Rd V8J 1A2
250-627-4955 Fax: 250-627-7945
800-833-1550
Bryan & Mary Allen Cox
All year

55-90-BB CAN$
6 rooms, 5 pb
Visa, MC
C-yes/S-ltd/P-no/H-ltd

Guest's choice of
Tea, coffee and kitchen facilities, common area
Full decks and sitting room, phone/fax and Internet

Experience Prince Rupert's waterfront. Fully renovated heritage home in historic Cow Bay. Shuttle service to airport & summer ferry/train schedule.
eaglebed@citytel.net http://www.citytel.net/eaglebluff

Pineridge
1714 Sloan Ave V8J 3Z9
250-627-4419 Fax: 250-624-2366
888-733-6733
Hans & Irmgard Buchholz
All year

70-90-BB
3 rooms, 3 pb
Visa, MC, *Rated*, •
C-ltd/S-no/P-no/H-no
German

Full breakfast
Sitting room, library, cable TV

Large comfortable rooms decorated with fine art and crafts, in a quiet residential neighborhood. Gourmet breakfasts. Private entrance to guest wing.
info@pineridge.bc.ca http://www.pineridge.bc.ca

Tall Trees
412 8th Ave E V8J 2M8
250-627-8578 877-627-8578 C
Kathy & Frank Butterfield
May to Sept.30th -High

80-100-BB CAN$
3 rooms, 3 pb
Visa, MC
C-yes/S-ltd/P-no/H-no

Full breakfast
Beverages
Courtesy pick-up/delivery, TV, guest entrances, off-street parking

Join us at Tall Trees for a relaxed, friendly, informal stay. Our rooms are designed and decorated with your comfort and privacy in mind. All rooms overlook the amazing rainforest behind our home. talltree@citytel.net http://www.talltreesbnb.com

QUALICUM BEACH

A Hollyford 106 Hoylake Rd V9K 1L7 250-752-8101 Fax: 205-752-8102 877-224-6559 Marjorie & Jim Ford All year	130-185-BB CAN$ 3 rooms, 3 pb Visa, MC, *Rated*, • C-ltd/S-ltd/P-no/H-ltd English	Continentals for early departures Wake-up and tuck-in trays Sitting room, library

Come for the food and all the rest! You'll feel right at home the minute you arrive. Casual elegance, haute cuisine breakfasts. A blend of Irish-Canadian fare served up by our host chef, Marjorie. mail@hollyford.ca http://www.hollyford.ca

---

Bahari 5101 Island Hwy W V9K 1Z1 250-752-9278 Fax: 250-752-9038 877-752-9278 Yvonne & Len Hooper Mar 1–Nov 30	125-210-BB CAN$ 3 rooms, 3 pb Visa, MC, AmEx, *Rated*, • C-ltd/S-no/P-ltd/H-no	Full breakfast Complimentary wine, snacks Sitting room, library, hot tubs, families welcome in apt.

Tranquil and elegant waterfront with panoramic views from decks & "Rotenburo" (outdoor hot tub). Spacious rooms and fireplaces.
stay@baharibandb.com http://www.baharibandb.com

QUALICUM BEACH (REGION)

Thyme Away PO Box 148 2280 Matterson Rd, *Coombs* V0R 1M0 250-248-9502 Barbara & Marcel Laplante	37-124-BB 3 rooms, 2 pb Visa, MC, • C-ltd/S-ltd/P-ltd/H-no All year	Fruit dish, omlettes, bennies, Delicious farm-style breakfasts Swimming pool, bikes, horseshoes, badminton, camp fires

A quiet country retreat with a backdrop of pines and a breathtaking mountain view. Close to the Coombs Country Market, famous for it's "Goats on the Roof", unique shops, artisans, and potters. countrycomfort@thymeaway.com http://www.thymeaway.com

REVELSTOKE

MacPherson Lodge PO Box 2615 2135 Clough Rd V0E 2S0 250-837-7041 Fax: 250-837-7077 888-875-4924 Lisa All year	45-90-BB 3 rooms, 1 pb Visa, MC, *Rated*, • C-yes/S-ltd/P-yes/H-no French	Full breakfast Wine Sitting room, library, suites, fireplace, cable TV, conference facilities

7 km from Revelstoke on Hwy 23 S, rustic log home furnished in antiques on 20-acres of natural wilderness, view rooms, balcony(s), king beds, loft sitting room.
bookrev@revelstoke.net http://www.macphersonlodge.com

Mt. MacKenzie Log Chalet 1800 Westerburg Rd V0E 2S1 250-837-2986 Fax: 250-837-2964 877-311-1313 Melanie & Colin Horel	75-95-BB 3 rooms, 3 pb Visa, MC C-ltd/S-ltd/P-no/H-no All year	Full breakfast Living room, library, in room TV/VCR, hot tub, firepit

Experience Country log living surrounded with panoramic views 5km South of Revelstoke. Antique decor, queen beds, private baths, loft library and great room with rock fireplace.
info@logchalet.com http://www.logchalet.com

Mulvehill Creek Wilderness Inn PO Box 1220 4200 Highway 23 South V0E 2S0 250-837-8649 Fax: 250-837-8649 877-837-8649 Cornelia & Rene J. Hueppi	95-195-BB 8 rooms, 8 pb Visa, MC, AmEx, *Rated*, • C-ltd/S-ltd/P-no/H-no German, Italian, Spanish, French All year	Full breakfast Dinner, tea, snacks, wine Lounge, fireplace, library, seminar facilities, billiards, darts, sundeck

Quiet country setting on 100 acres, wooded peninsula on Arrow Lake, wedding chapel, waterfall. All summer and winter sports on property or nearby. Hot tub, heated outdoor pool, trails, free canoes. lanier@mulvehillcreek.com http://www.mulvehillcreek.com

SALT SPRING ISLAND

Anchor Point
150 Beddis Rd V8K 2J2
250-538-0110 Fax: 250-538-0120
800-648-2560
Lynn & Ralph Bischoff
All year

75-95-BB
3 rooms, 3 pb
Visa, MC, *Rated*, •
C-ltd/S-no/P-no/H-no
German, French

Gourmet 3 course breakfast
Tea, snacks, appetizers
Suites with stove fireplace & private bath, Fireplace lounge, library, Jacuz

Be pampered! Relax in a traditional Cape residence. Ocean views & gourmet breakfasts. Designer guestrooms. Cozy robes & slippers. Hot tub spa, Library, Fireplace Lounge. Canada Select 4 Star. info@anchorpointbb.com http://www.anchorpointbb.com

---

Anne's Oceanfront Hideaway
168 Simson Rd V8K 1E2
250-537-0851 Fax: 250-537-0861
888-474-2663
Rick & Ruth-Anne Broad
All year

110-160-BB
4 rooms, 4 pb
Visa, MC, AmEx, *Rated*, •
S-no/P-no/H-yes

Full breakfast
Snacks
Sitting room, library, bikes, hot tubs, adult oriented, in-house massage avl

Come share the beauty & tranquility... luxurious 1995 home, 7000 square feet, verandahs, private entrance, some balconies, fireplaces, fridges, individual heat & air. annes@saltspring.com http://www.annesoceanfront.com

---

Cloud 9 Oceanview
238 Sun Eagle Dr V8K 1E5
250-537-2776 Fax: 250-537-2776
877-722-8233
John & Patricia Macpherson
All year

135-195-BB CAN$
3 rooms, 3 pb
Visa, MC, AmEx, *Rated*, •
C-ltd/S-ltd/P-ltd/H-ltd

Gourmet 4 1/2-Star full breakfast
Hot beverages, snacks, wine & bottled water
Outdoor hot tub, mountain bikes, guest lounges, stereo/CDs

New (2000) 4,000 sq.ft., 4½-Star luxury retreat, 5 tranquil acres, panoramic ocean views. Hot tub, heated floors, private entries/patios/bathrooms (Jacuzzi/soaker tubs), fireplaces, TV/VCRs.... space@cloud9oceanview.com http://www.cloud9oceanview.com

SIDNEY

Beacon Inn at Sidney
9724 Third St V8L 3A2
250-655-3288 877-420-5499
Graham Bell
All year

109-239-BB CAN$
9 rooms, 9 pb
Most CC, *Rated*, •
C-ltd/S-no/P-no/H-no

Coffee or tea delivered to room before breakfast
Comfortable parlor with fireplace, books, chess board, cards

Near Victoria, Butchart Gardens. Canada Select 5-Star, 1900s-inspired modern inn: luxurious rooms, en-suites with soaker or jetted bathtubs, cable TV, a/c, fireplaces. Virtual tours on website. info@beaconinns.com http://www.beaconinns.com

---

Orchard House
9646 6th St V8L 2W2
250-656-9194 888-656-9194
Gerry Martin
All year

60-70-BB
3 rooms, 2 pb

Full breakfast

Close to shops, beach and park. http://www.sidneybc.com/orchardhousebb/

SOOKE

Cape Cod
5782 Anderson Cove Rd V0S 1N0
250-642-3253 Fax: 250-642-3253
888-814-7773
Gwendolyn Utitz & Peter Ginman
Closed December-January

75-95-BB
1 rooms, 1 pb
Rated, •
C-yes/S-ltd/P-no/H-ltd
French, German

Full breakfast
Snacks, complimentary wine
Sitting room, library, tennis court, suites, cable TV, accom. bus. travelers

Modern Cape Cod-style home, on two wooded acres with ocean and forest views—totally private and peaceful. capecodbb@shaw.ca http://www.members.shaw.ca/capecodbb

SOOKE

Eliza Point B&B by the Sea 6514 Thornett Rd V0S 1N0 250-642-2705 Fax: 250-642-2704 Cheryl & Doug Read All year	175-200-BB CAN$ 2 rooms, 2 pb Visa, MC, *Rated*, • C-ltd/S-ltd/P-no/H-no	4 course gourmet/organic Coffee, tea, aperitif's, snacks Bicycles

Walk-on beach, private entrance & decks, Queen beds, feather beds, down duvets, modems, satellite TV, Jacuzzi, fireplace. In the heart of Eco-tourism yet close to Victoria for day trips. eliza@tnet.net http://vvv.com/~eliza

Ocean Wilderness Inn & Spa 109 West Coast Rd V0S 1N0 250-646-2116 Fax: 250-646-2317 800-323-2116 Marion Rolston All year	75-110-BB 9 rooms, 9 pb Visa, MC, *Rated*, • C-yes/S-no/P-yes/H-yes	Full breakfast Will make dinner reservations Snacks, refrigerator, sitting room, hot tubs

5 wooded acres with beach, whales, seals and hot tubs in romantic rooms with canopied beds. ocean@sookenet.com http://www.sookenet.com/ocean/

Seascape Inn 6435 Sooke Rd V0S 1N0 250-642-7677 Fax: 250-642-7677 888-516-8811 Sandy Bohn All year	65-135-BB 3 rooms, 3 pb Most CC, • C-ltd/S-ltd/P-ltd/H-no German	Full breakfast Suites, fireplaces, cable TV, hot tubs, large stone fireplace

Waterfront property overlooking Sooke Harbour. Unique "cabin," cottage and in house suite. Exceptional views. seascape@islandnet.com http://www.sookenet.com/seascape

Sooke Harbour House 1528 Whiffen Spit Rd RR #4 V0S 1N0 250-642-3421 Fax: 250-642-6988 800-889-9688 Sinclair & Frederique Philip All year	190-450-BB 28 rooms, 26 pb Most CC, *Rated*, • C-yes/S-no/P-ltd/H-yes French, English	Full or continental breakfast Set lunch included, dinner, restaurant Wet bar, entertainment, sitting room, piano, Jacuzzi, bikes, hot tubs

Romantic little Inn right on the water, located 45 minutes southwest of Victoria on Vancouver Island, BC. Wonderful attention to detail in every area of the Inn.
info@sookeharbourhouse.com http://www.sookeharbourhouse.com

SPENCESBRIDGE

The Garuda Inn Box 100 3642 Merritt-Spences Br V0K LA0 1-250-458-2311 Fax: 1-250-458-2318 1-866-849-3940 Laurianne Mac Millan All year	35-65-BB 12 rooms, 7 pb Visa, MC, *Rated*, • C-yes/S-ltd/P-ltd/H-yes French, Italian, Scottish	Full breakfast Restaurant open from 7.30am till 9pm. Lounge; riverside dining; giftshop; bakery; library; hiking; trail rides

The Garuda Inn is a beautiful Historic Inn on the bank of the Thompson river We offer time honored B&B, & first class dining in the nat. foods restaurant. The Garuda-Inn, where the past is present garudainn@hotmail.com http://www.garudainn.com

SURREY

B&B on the Ridge 5741 146th St V3S 2Z5 604-591-6065 Fax: 604-591-6059 888-697-4111 Dale & Mary Fennell All year	50-90-BB 3 rooms, 3 pb *Rated*, • C-ltd/S-ltd/P-no/H-ltd Hungarian	Full breakfast Snacks, refreshments upon arrival Sitting room, cable TV, accommodate business travelers

Escape from the city to a delightful, tastefully decorated B&B situated on 1/2 acre with its quiet country atmosphere. stay@bbridgesurrey.com http://www.bbridgesurrey.com

THETIS ISLAND

Cufra Cliffs
PO Box 6-15
410 Pilkey Point Rd V0R 2Y0
250-246-1509
Veronica & Graeme Shelford
All year

90-BB CAN$
C-ltd/S-ltd/P-no

Full breakfast

Cufra Cliffs sits 300 feet up Mooore Hill, above the Cufra Inlet and looking across Thetis Island at the mountains of Vancouver Island. You'll feel like you're "on top of the world."
veronica@cufracliffs.com http://www.cufracliffs.com

TOFINO

Cable Cove Inn
PO Box 339
201 Main St V0R 2Z0
250-725-4236 Fax: 250-725-2857
800-663-6449
All year

75-150-BB
6 rooms, 6 pb
Visa, MC, AmEx, *Rated*
S-no/P-no/H-ltd
Phil & Jennifer van Bourgondien

Continental plus breakfast
Sitting room, hot tubs, adult oriented, bicycles, airport trans

Cable Cove Inn offers you 6 lovely waterfront rooms. Each room has a fireplace, private waterfront deck, 4 poster queen bed & either a private hot tub outside or marble Jacuzzi inside. cablecin@island.net http://www.cablecoveinn.com

---

The Tide's Inn
PO Box 325
160 Arnet Rd V0R 2Z0
250-725-3765 Fax: 250-725-3325
Valerie Sloman
Closed Christmas

115-135-BB CAN$
3 rooms, 3 pb
Rated
C-ltd/S-no/P-no/H-no

Full breakfast
Coffee bar with teas, hot chocolate
Sitting room, hot tub, mini refrigerators, bicycles, airport trans

Enjoy spacious waterfront rooms with jetted tub or steam bath and fireplace all with ensuite baths and private entrances.
tidesinn@island.net http://www.tidesinntofino.com

UCLUELET

A Snug Harbour Inn
PO Box 318
460 Marine Dr V0R 3A0
250-726-2686 Fax: 250-726-2685
888-936-5222
Susan Brown and Drew Fesar
All year

130-190-BB
6 rooms, 6 pb
Visa, MC, *Rated*, •
C-no/S-no/P-yes/H-yes

Full breakfast
Snacks
Sitting room, hot tubs, fireplaces, private beach & decks, incredible views

One of Canada's finest Inns. Exceptional privacy, romance & incredible cliffside ocean-front setting. Private decks, fireplaces, luxury robes and heated floors. Handicapped + pet friendly rooms. asnughbr@island.net http://www.awesomeview.com

VANCOUVER

A TreeHouse B&B
2490 W 49th Ave V6M 2V3
604-266-2962 Fax: 604-266-2960
Barb & Bob Selvage
All year

77-123-BB
3 rooms, 3 pb
Visa, MC, AmEx, *Rated*, •
C-ltd/S-ltd/P-no/H-no

Full gourmet breakfast
Snacks
Sitting room, adult oriented, TV, videos, on-street parking, private decks

Sophisticated metropolitan home featuring contemporary art, on bus line and near most major attractions, prestigious Kerrisdale residential neighborhood, gourmet breakfasts.
bb@treehousebb.com http://www.treehousebb.com/

Barclay House in the West End
1351 Barclay St V6E 1H6
604-605-1351 Fax: 604-605-1382
800-971-1351
Patrik Burr All year

90-155-BB
5 rooms, 5 pb
Visa, MC, *Rated*, •
C-ltd/S-no/H-no

Full 3-course breakfast
Snacks, evening sherry
Sitting room, suites, cable TV

Downtown Vancouver! AAA Three Diamond rating. Frommer's favorite. Seattle Time's "perfect getaway" for two- February 3, 2002. A fully restored 1904 jewel nestled amid skyscrapers awaits! info@barclayhouse.com http://www.barclayhouse.com

VANCOUVER

Beautiful B&B
428 W 40 Ave V5Y 2R4
604-327-1102 Fax: 604-327-2299
The Sandersons
All year

70-150-BB
Rated, •
C-ltd/S-no/P-no/H-no

A warm welcome awaits you at Beautiful Bed and Breakfast, a gorgeous colonial home furnished with antiques located in one of Vancouver's finest neighborhoods.
sandbbb@portal.ca http://www.beautifulbandb.bc.ca

Graeme's House
2735 Waterloo St V6R 3J1
604-732-1488 888-732-6660
Ms. Graeme Webster
All year

67-84-BB
5 rooms, 3 pb
Rated
C-ltd/S-no/P-no/H-no

Continental plus breakfast
Afternoon tea, snacks
Sitting room, sundeck, roof garden, near English Bay

Charmingly decorated, renovated 1920's cottage on a quiet street very close to shops, restaurants, and buses. Lovely garden. Beach 1 km. away.
graeweb@telus.net http://www.GraemeWebster.com

The Inn at False Creek
1335 Howe St V6Z 1R7
604-682-0229 Fax: 604-662-7566
800-663-8474
James Yeo
All year

59-129-BB
157 rooms, 157 pb
Visa, MC, AmEx,
Rated, •
C-yes/S-yes/P-yes/H-yes
Most languages

Continental breakfast
Afternoon tea, snacks, lunch & dinner available
Swimming pool, suites, cable TV, accommodate business travelers

Small boutique hotel featuring Mediterranean style decor, fresh flowers in lobby and restaurant. quality@qualityhotel.ca http://www.qualityhotel.ca

---

Kenya Court Ocean Front Guest House
2230 Cornwall Ave V6K 1B5
604-738-7085
Dr. & Mrs. H.R. Williams
All year

95-110-BB
5 rooms, 5 pb
Rated
C-ltd/S-no/P-no/H-no
Italian, French, German

Full buffet breakfast
Complimentary tea/coffee
Sitting room, library, tennis courts, solarium, salt water swimming pool

Ocean-front heritage guesthouse overlooking Kitsilano Beach, mountains, English Bay. Gourmet breakfast served in rooftop solarium with stunning views of the ocean and city. In operation since 1986. h&dwilliams@telus.net

---

Manor Guest House
345 West 13th Ave V5Y 1W2
604-876-8494 Fax: 604-876-5763
Brenda Yablon
All year

50-130-BB
10 rooms, 6 pb
Visa, MC, *Rated*
C-ltd/S-no/P-no/H-no
French, German

Full gourmet vegetarian breakfast
Galley kitchen use
Conference facilities for up to 25, parlor/music room, English garden, decks

The Manor Guest House is an Edwardian mansion on the southeastern edge of downtown in a safe & elegant neighborhood, close to great shopping, restaurants & public transit.
info@manorguesthouse.com http://www.manorguesthouse.com/

Nelson House
977 Broughton St V6G 2A4
604-684-9793 866-684-9793
David Ritchie
Closed 12/24,25,31 & 1/1

52-125-BB
6 rooms, 4 pb
Visa, MC
C-ltd/S-ltd/P-no/H-no
French

Full breakfast
Jacuzzi ensuite, fireplaces, library, cable TV/VCR, 3 decks, bar fridges

Our 1907 Edwardian is set in a lovely garden only minutes walk from all of downtown's attractions. Adult-oriented, we offer a relaxing escape in six, spacious guestrooms, decorated with flair. info@downtownbedandbreakfast.com
http://www.downtownbedandbreakfast.com

VANCOUVER

Pacific Spirit Guest House 4080 W 35th Ave V6N 2P3 604-261-6837 Bernadette & Peter All year	45-50-BB 2 rooms Visa, MC, AmEx C-yes/S-ltd/P-yes/H-ltd	Full breakfast Welcome! fruits, cheese and drinks upon arrival. Guest area has stereo, wood burning fireplace, telephone and piano.

A walk in the forest is just steps away. This gem of a B&B is one of the best values in the city. Great convenient west-side location. Family friendly, romantic and private.
pspirit@quik.com http://www.vancouver.quik.com/pspirit

Palms Guest House 3042 Marine Dr V7V 1M4 604-926-1159 Fax: 604-9261451 800-691-4455 Heidi Schmidt All year	89-162-BB 4 rooms, 4 pb Visa, MC, AmEx, *Rated*, • C-ltd/S-ltd/P-no/H-no Spanish, German, Italian	Full breakfast Complimentary coffee & pastries Sitting room, terraces, gardens, library

The finest accommodation located in beautiful, privileged area.
info@palmsguesthouse.com http://www.palmsguesthouse.com

Shaughnessy Village 1125 West 12th Ave V6H 3Z3 604-736-5511 Fax: 604-737-1321 Jan Floody All year	50-109-BB 15 rooms, 15 pb Visa, MC, • C-ltd/S-yes/P-no/H-yes French, German, Japanese, Chinese	Full breakfast Lunch/dinner available, bar service Gym, billiards, library, crazy putt golf, sauna, swimming, tennis nearby

Our resort-style residence accommodates "B&B" visitors in a friendly & beautiful nautical atmosphere in theme rooms "like cruise ship cabins."
info@shaughnessyvillage.com http://www.shaughnessyvillage.com

The West End Guest House 1362 Haro St V6E 1G2 604-681-2889 Fax: 604-688-8812 888-546-3327 Evan Penner All year	99-160-BB 7 rooms, 7 pb Visa, MC, *Rated*, • C-ltd/S-no/P-no/H-no English, French	Full breakfast Bedside sherry (5-7pm) Sitting room w/TV, valet parking, library, piano, room phones, bicycles

Walk to Stanley Park, beaches; enjoy quiet ambiance of comfortable historic inn. Popular with romantic couples. Frplc., antiques, robes. Suite with fireplace, queen brass bed, steam shower. wegh@trilli.com http://www.westendguesthouse.com

VANCOUVER (REGION)

Murrayville 22054 Old Yale Rd, *Langley* V2Z 1B3 604-534-5004 Fax: 604-534-5004 888-534-8225 John & Susan Howard All year	33-45-BB 4 rooms, 1 pb • C-ltd/S-no/P-ltd/H-no	Full or continental plus breakfast Snacks, afternoon tea, guests' choice of breakfast Cable TV, free coffee on arrival, hot tub, sauna, tennis

Elegant new home furnished with antiques & original artwork. Gourmet, five course breakfast. Bridge nights on short notice. Advise on local fishing-antique sources. Convenient for Vancouver PGA.
murrayvillebb@shaw.ca http://www.bbcanada.com/1442.html

The Counting Sheep Inn 8715 Eagle Rd, *Mission* V2V 4J1 604-820-5148 Fax: 604-820-5149 Virginia Edwards All year	75-110-BB 3 rooms, 3 pb Visa, MC, *Rated*, • C-yes/S-no/P-ltd/H-no	Full breakfast Coffee, tea, picnic baskets Jacuzzi, robes, toiletries, sitting area, bicycles, library, TV/VCR, etc.

Romantic Accommodations at country inn and sheep farm, between Vancouver and Harrison Hot Springs, British Columbia. Full breakfast. All suites with private baths, Jacuzzi, fireplaces, and gardens. info@countingsheep.com http://www.countingsheep.com

VANCOUVER

Henley House
1025 8th Ave, *New Westminster* V3M 2R5
604-526-3919 Fax: 604-526-3913
866-526-3919
Annie O'Shaughnessy & Ross Hood All year

48-60-BB
3 rooms, 1 pb
Visa, MC, •
C-ltd/S-ltd/P-no/H-no

Full breakfast
Complimentary beverages, bedside chocolates
Guest lounges, library, Jacuzzi, robes, fireplace, cable TV, A/C, deck

Antique furnishings, lovely garden setting, and a warm welcome! Well known for our scrumptious breakfasts. Close to Vancouver center with easy access to airport, ferries, and Fraser Valley. home@henleyhouse.com http://www.henleyhouse.com

---

A Gazebo in the Garden
310 St James Rd East, *North Vancouver* V7N 1L2
604-983-3331 Fax: 604-980-3215
Monika & Jack Rogers
All year

90-140-BB
4 rooms, 4 pb
Visa, MC, *Rated*, •
C-ltd/S-no/P-no/H-no
Swedish

Delicious breakfasts
TV/VCR, gazebo, private gardens

Canada Select 4 Star Rating. Located on Vancouver's Scenic North Shore, minutes to Downtown Vancouver, Horseshoe Bay Ferries, BC Rail and Stanley Park. 1910 Frank Lloyd Wright "Prairie" style. mrogers@direct.ca http://www.agazebointhegarden.com

---

Capilano
1374 Plateau Dr, *North Vancouver* V7P 2J6
604-990-8889 Fax: 604-990-5177
877-990-8889
Soledad Lu & Doug Harvey

85-145-BB CAN$
3 rooms, 2 pb
Visa, MC, *Rated*
C-yes/S-no/P-no/H-no
Chinese
All year

Full breakfast
Coffee and tea in the room
Sitting room, fireplace, cable TV, microwave, coffee maker, telephone

New executive modern house ranging from a queen room to 1 or 2 bedroom suite with kitchenette, own entrance. 10 min. downtown Vancouver, Amtrack station, 15 min. from Horseshoe Bay Ferry. info@capilanobb.com http://www.capilanobb.com

---

Mountainside Manor
5909 Nancy Greene Way, *North Vancouver* V7R 4W6
604-990-9772 Fax: 604-985-8470
800-967-1319
Anne & Mike Murphy

70-95-BB
4 rooms, 4 pb
Visa, MC, *Rated*, •
C-yes/S-no/P-no/H-no
French
All year

Full breakfast
Coffee service
Sitting room, patio, hot tub

Among Vancouver North Shore's finest bed & breakfast accommodations, Mountainside Manor is a spectacular contemporary home overlooking downtown Vancouver from the wooded majesty of Grouse Mountain.
mtnside@attglobal.net http://www.mtnsideaccom.com

Norgate Park House
1226 Silverwood Crescent, *North Vancouver* V7P 1J3
604-986-5069 Fax: 604-986-8810
Vicki Tyndall All year

85-125-BB CAN$
3 rooms, 1 pb
Visa, MC, *Rated*, •
C-ltd/S-no/P-no/H-no

Full breakfast
Tea is offered in the evening.
Sitting room, TV, fireplace, in-room phones

A small lush green oasis in the big city awaits you. Delicious breakfasts, congenial surroundings, and have a quiet sleep.
norgate@bandbinn.com http://www.bandbinn.com/homes/9/

ThistleDown House
3910 Capilano Rd, *North Vancouver* V7R 4J2
604-986-7173 Fax: 604-980-2939
888-633-7173
Ruth Crameri and Rex Davidson All year

135-250-BB CAN$
5 rooms, 5 pb
Visa, MC, *Rated*, •
C-ltd/S-no/P-no/H-no
German

Full breakfast
Afternoon tea, sherry & port

ThistleDown is a 1920 Craftsman-style, heritage-listed home lovingly restored with great care and filled with antiques, hand-crafted furnishings and works of art from around the world. info@thistle-down.com http://www.thistle-down.com

VANCOUVER

Creekside 1515 Palmerston Ave, *West Vancouver* V7V 4S9 604-926-2599 Fax: 604-926-7545 John Boden & Donna Hawrelko All year	80-110-BB 2 rooms, 2 pb Visa, MC, • C-ltd/S-no/P-no/H-no Ukrainian	Full gourmet ranch breakfast Complimentary wine/snack Color TV, fireplace, 2 person Jacuzzi tubs, stocked refrigerator in rooms

Private, contemporary, woodsy, creek-side hideaway. Close to parks, skiing, beaches & ocean. 2 day minimum. donnajohnboden@telus.net

Lighthouse Park 4875 Water Lane, *West Vancouver* V7W 1K4 604-926-5959 Fax: 604-926-5755 800-245-9568 Hanna & Ron Pankow All year	85-110-BB 2 rooms, 2 pb *Rated*, • S-no/P-no/H-no	Full breakfast Private sitting room in each suite with cable TV/VCR, fridge, phone

Private romantic suites in the most spectacular part of Vancouver. Both suites have a private entrance, living room, bedroom, and bathroom. It's an easy walk to view the lighthouse in Lighthouse Park. stay@lighthousepark.com http://lighthousepark.com

VERNON

Castle on the Mountain 8227 Silver Star Rd V1B 8M8 250-542-4593 Fax: 250-542-2206 800-667-2229 Eskil & Sharon Larson All year	60-165-BB 5 rooms, 5 pb Visa, MC, AmEx, *Rated*, • C-ltd/S-ltd/P-no/H-ltd	Full breakfast Snacks Sitting room, bikes, library, Jacuzzis, suites, fireplaces.

Luxury Tudor mountainside estate. Panoramic views, romantic retreat suites, ensuite rooms, apartment for longer stays, outdoor spa, "all Canadian spoiler breakfast."
castle.eskila@telus.net

VICTORIA

A B&B at Amore by the Sea 246 Delgada Rd V9C 3W2 250-474-5505 Fax: 250-474-5957 888-82-VIEWS D. Spence All year	85-125-BB 3 rooms, 3 pb Visa, MC, *Rated*, • C-no/S-ltd/P-no/H-no French	Complementry Lavish Breakfast Hot tub & indoor pool overlooking West Coast Beach, Seaside Spa Services.

A World of luxury, relaxation and romance; Romantic Oceanfront Getaway & Spa. Step away from the everyday to Amore by the Sea & Seaside Spa. Rated–"One of North America's Most Romantic Hideaway"
visit@victoria-accommodation.com http://www.victoria-accommodation.com

A B&B at Swallow Hill Farm 4910 William Head Rd V9C 3Y8 250-474-4042 Fax: 250-474-4042 Gini & Peter Walsh All year	60-90-BB 2 rooms, 2 pb Visa, MC, *Rated*, • C-ltd/S-no/P-no/H-no	Full or continental breakfast Tea, coffee, cocoa, homebaked cookies Each suite has a private bathroom, a small fridge, and complimentary treats

Rediscover nature on beautiful Vancouver Island. Our country hideaway, near the picturesque city of Victoria, has 2 suites, an inspiring ocean & mountain view, antiques, & furniture built by owner. info@swallowhillfarm.com http://www.swallowhillfarm.com

A Haterleigh Heritage Inn 243 Kingston St V8V 1V5 250-384-9995 Fax: 250-384-1935 Paul & Elizabeth Kelly All year	140-215-BB 7 rooms, 7 pb Visa, MC, *Rated*, • S-no/P-no/H-no	Full breakfast Private Jacuzzis, sitting room, library, hot tubs

5 star rated by Tourism BC six years running. Frommer's Guide "Best B & B Inn, Victoria for 2002." 1901 heritage mansion lovingly restored. Full of stained glass & antiques. Only 2 blocks to centre. paulk@haterleigh.com http://www.haterleigh.com

Abigail's Hotel, Victoria, BC

VICTORIA

Abigail's Hotel 906 McClure St V8V 3E7 250-388-5363 Fax: 250-388-7787 800-561-6565 Dan & Frauke Behune All year	122-389-BB CAN$ 23 rooms, 23 pb Visa, MC, AmEx, *Rated*, • C-ltd/S-no/P-no/H-no	Full gourmet breakfast Afternoon refreshments Social hour, library, sitting room, Jacuzzi in some rooms

Luxuriously updated 1930 classic Tudor building. Private Jacuzzi tubs, fireplaces, goose-down comforters. innkeeper@abigailshotel.com http://www.abigailshotel.com/

Across the Harbour 485 Head St V9A 5S1 250-474-7497 Fax: 250-474-7397 866-474-7497 Barbara McDougall All year	125-150-BB 4 rooms, 4 pb Visa, MC, AmEx, *Rated*, • C-ltd/S-ltd/P-no/H-ltd	Full breakfast Guest lounge overlooking ocean; free parking; internet access in rooms

Oceanfront B TV/VCR, internet, hot breakfast served on veranda overlooking ocean, boardwalk to downtown, water taxi service, $125–150 US/night.
relax@acrosstheharbour.com http://www.acrosstheharbour.com

Amadeus Mozart House Inn 1524 Shasta Pl V8S 1X9 250-370-1524 Fax: 250-370-1624 877-601-1524 Astrid & Ralph Gottfried All year	86-196-BB 4 rooms, 4 pb Visa, MC, *Rated*, • C-ltd/S-no/P-no/H-ltd German	Four course gourmet breakfast Early morning coffee, tea hot chocolate, cookies Library, Drawing room, In house Spa treatments

5 Star Italianate Heritage Mansion in the heart of Victoria. Ocean & Mountain views, Fireplaces, Jacuzzis for 2, Antiques, 4-course gourmet breakfast, estate garden.
enquire@mozarthouse.com http://www.mozarthouse.com

Amethyst Inn at Regents Park 1501 Fort Street V8S 1Z6 250-595-2053 Fax: 250-595-2054 888-265-6499 Grace & Karl Sands All year	78-245-BB 16 rooms, 16 pb Visa, MC, *Rated*, • C-ltd/S-no/P-no/H-no English	Full Hot Gourmet Breakfast Sherry in the evenings Sitting room, fireplaces, spa

Built in 1885, Amethyst Inn authentically reflects the Victorian era. Amethyst Inn at Regents Park is Victoria's Exceptionally Romantic Inn.
innkeeper@amethyst-inn.com http://www.amethyst-inn.com

VICTORIA

An Ocean View
715 Suffolk St V9A 3J5
250-386-7330 Fax: 250-389-0280
800-342-9986
Yvette Craig
All year

85-120-BB
6 rooms, 6 pb
Visa, MC, *Rated*
C-ltd/S-no/P-no/H-no
French

Full buffet breakfast
Garden patios, TV, hot tub, king/queen beds, frplcs., refrigerators

Romantic accommodations, Mediterranean styled ocean and mountain view home a few blocks from downtown and Harbour. Private rooms.
anoceanview@sprint.ca http://anoceanview.com

Birds of a Feather Oceanfront B&B
206 Portsmouth Dr V9C 1R9
250-391-8889 Fax: 250-391-8883
1-800-730-4790
Annette Moen
All year

57-80-BB
3 rooms, 3 pb
Visa, MC, *Rated*, •
C-ltd/S-no/P-no/H-no
German

Full breakfast
Afternoon tea, snacks
Sitting room, library, bicycles, hot tubs, courtesy canoes, fireplace

Stay at Birds of a Feather Ocean-front B&B; an intimate, adult oriented West coast B&B in Victoria nestled on the shores of wildlife bird sanctuary on the Pacific Ocean just 15 mins from downtown. frontdesk@victorialodging.com http://www.victorialodging.com

---

Dashwood Manor
One Cook St V8V 3W6
250-385-5517 Fax: 250-383-1760
800-667-5517
Derek Dashwood, fam. & staff
All year

60-250-BB
14 rooms
Rated, •

Buffet
Wine and cheese in the evenings

Victoria's Heritage Inn by the Sea. Located next to fabled Beacon Hill Park.
frontdesk@dashwoodmanor.com http://www.dashwoodmanor.com

Evergreen Hideaway
619 Lomax Rd V9C 4A4
250-391-9909 Fax: 250-391-9909
800-769-8177
Susan & Terry Barker
All year

60-70-BB
3 rooms, 3 pb
Visa, MC, AmEx, *Rated*, •
C-ltd/S-ltd/P-no/H-yes
French, German, Dutch

Delicious home-cooked breakfast
Complimentary tea, coffee & home baking in rooms
Peaceful location, outdoor seating, guest sitting room, books, games

Country Hospitality ... Close to the City! Enjoy beautiful Victoria from our secluded home on 2 acres of tranquility. Wake up to a scrumptious breakfast prepared with the freshest ingredients. welcome@evergreenhideaway.com http://www.evergreenhideaway.com

---

The Gatsby Mansion @ Belleville Park
330 Quebec St
309 Belleville St V8V 1X2
250-388-9191 Fax: 250-920-5651
800-563-9656
Rita Roy
All year

129-319-BB CAN$
20 rooms, 19 pb
Visa, MC, AmEx, *Rated*, •
C-yes/S-no/P-no/H-no

Full breakfast from menu
2 restaurants open all day.
Afternoon tea, Sunday
Massage & Hair Studio,Internet Cafe, Jacuzzi, Sauna, Bicycle/Scooter rental

In an 1897 Queen-Anne Mansion, these unique accommodations overlook the Inner Harbour. 5-minute walk to City Center. Old-World charm, modern service.
information@bellevillepark.com http://www.bellevillepark.com

Humboldt House
867 Humboldt St V8V 2Z6
250-383-0152 Fax: 250-383-6402
888-383-0327
David & Vlasta Booth
All year

88-210-BB
6 rooms, 6 pb
Visa, MC, *Rated*, •
C-ltd/S-no/P-no/H-no
Czech, German, French

Full breakfast
Afternoon tea, complimentary champagne
Sitting room, library, Jacuzzis, suites, fireplaces, cable TV

Victoria's most romantic and private B feast on a gourmet breakfast in the privacy of your room. rooms@humboldthouse.com http://www.humboldthouse.com

VICTORIA

Iris Garden Country Manor 5360 W. Saanich Rd V9E 1J8 250-744-2253 Fax: 250-744-5690 877-744-2253 Sharon & Dave Layzell All year	75-115-BB 4 rooms, 4 pb Visa, MC, *Rated*, • C-ltd/S-no/P-no/H-no	Full breakfast Sitting room, library, pool, fireplaces, conference facilities, Jacuzzi

Providing a romantic, country getaway eight minutes from world-famous Butchart Gardens since 1986. "A delightful retreat! Warm, friendly hosts, scrumptious food. Truly a gem." Catherine W. stay@irisgardenvictoria.com http://www.irisgardenvictoria.com

Markham House 1853 Connie Rd V9C 4C2 250-642-7542 Fax: 250-642-7538 888-256-6888 Lyall & Sally Markham All year	60-137-BB 4 rooms, 4 pb Most CC, *Rated*, • C-ltd/S-no/P-ltd/H-no French	Full breakfast Afternoon tea, snacks V.C.R.s ,stereos in all rooms,guest lounge, turndown service, guest pantry

10 acre country hideaway, antiques- 30 minutes to Victoria, near beaches and hiking trails. Peace and quiet, suite with luxurious amenities, private cottage with wood stove and hot tub. mail@markhamhouse.com http://www.markhamhouse.com

Oak Bay Beach Hotel/Marine Resort 1175 Beach Dr V8S 2N2 250-598-4556 Fax: 250-598-6180 800-668-7758 Kevin & Shawna Walker All year	76-302-BB 50 rooms, 50 pb Visa, MC, AmEx, *Rated*, • C-yes/S-no/P-ltd/H-ltd	Continental breakfast Evening hot chocolate and cookies Shuttle service to downtown, use of mountain bikes, passes to Rec. Center

Perched at the ocean's edge, surrounded by pristine off-shore islands and overlooking the magnificent snow capped Mount Baker, lies a country inn that is the epitome of elegance and charm. info@oakbaybeachhotel.bc.ca http://www.oakbaybeachhotel.com

Scholefield House 731 Vancouver St V8V 3V4 250-385-2025 Fax: 250-383-3036 800-661-1623 Tana Dineen All year	79-225-BB CAN$ 3 rooms, 3 pb Visa, MC, *Rated*, • C-ltd/S-no/P-no/H-no	5 course champagne breakfast Complimentary sherry, tea & coffee in the Library Private guest library, English flower garden, 3 blocks to The Empress

Centrally located in downtown Victoria, 3 blocks from the Empress. 3 bedrooms with en suite bathrooms. 5-course breakfast. Tea & sherry in the Library. Easy walk to attractions, shopping, restaurants. mail@scholefieldhouse.com http://www.scholefieldhouse.com

Selkirk Guest House 934 Selkirk Ave V9A 2V1 250-389-1213 Fax: 250-389-1213 800-974-6638 Lyn & Norman Jackson	40-90-EP 5 rooms, 1 pb Visa, MC, *Rated* C-yes/S-ltd/P-yes/H-no All year	Full breakfast (optional) Library, Jacuzzi, suite, fireplace, cable TV, accom. bus. travelers

Historic waterfront Guest House bed and breakfast accommodation plus hostel, ideal for families. Unique setting on the Gorge Waterway.
selkirkvictoria@hotmail.com http://www.SelkirkGuestHouse.com

Spinnakers Brewpub & Guest House 308 Catherine St V9A 3S8 250-384-2739 Fax: 250-384-3246 877-838-2739 Paul Hadfield All year	90-165-BB 10 rooms, 10 pb Visa, MC, AmEx, *Rated*, • C-ltd/S-no/P-no/H-ltd	Full breakfast Lunch & dinner avail., snacks, afternoon tea Restaurant, bar service, Jacuzzis, suites, fireplaces, cable TV

Canada's first in-house Brewpub, offers heritage and contemporary accommodations in luxurious rooms with queen beds, deluxe bedding, Jacuzzi tubs, wood or gas fireplaces, original art & breakfast. spinnakers@spinnakers.com http://www.spinnakers.com

VICTORIA

The Wayward Navigator 337 Damon Dr V9B 5G5 250-478-6836 Fax: 250-478-6850 884-478-6808 Nancy Fry All year	65-130-BB 2 rooms, 2 pb Visa, MC, • C-ltd/S-ltd/P-ltd/H-no	Full breakfast Dinner, snacks, wine Sitting room, library, Jacuzzis, fireplace, cable TV, conferences

Classic passenger ship opulence with modern conveniences. Our 1st class state rooms & guest lounges are spacious and well appointed with elegant Victorian furnishings. Cedar decks, gazebos & hot tub. nancy@wayward.com http://www.wayward.com

VICTORIA (REGION)

Shady Shores Beach Resort PO Box 18 Site 118 6695 West Island Hwy, *Bowser* V0R 1G0 250-757-8595 Fax: 250-757-9507 888-863-4455	55-EP 7 rooms, 7 pb Visa, MC, *Rated*, • C-yes/S-ltd/P-no/H-ltd Carolyn Graeme All year	Jacuzzis, suites, fireplaces, cable TV, gazebo hot tub.

Centrally located on secluded beachfront. Enjoy beachcombing, bonfires, clam/oyster picking and salmon fishing. View an abundance of marine life from one of our seven fully-equipped suites.
info@shadyshoresbeachresort.com http://www.shadyshoresbeachresort.com

---

Anchors Guesthouse PO Box 7 1793 Cowichan Bay Rd, *Cowichan Bay* V0R 1N0 250-748-7206 877-991-1199 Gerry & Bill McGuinness	80-175-EP 2 rooms, 2 pb Most CC, *Rated*, • C-ltd/S-ltd/P-ltd/H-ltd Afrikans, French, Ger. All year	Cable TV, suites

Luxury oceanfront self-contained units, tastefully furnished for comfort in quaint fishing village. Private decks, dock and BBQs, sweeping views of marinas and mountains.
info@anchorsguesthouse.com http://www.anchorsguesthouse.com

Prancing Horse Estate PO Box 11 573 Ebedora Ln, *Malahat* V0R 2L0 250-743-9378 Fax: 250-743-9372 877-887-8834 Elaine & Allan Dillabaugh	106-227-BB 7 rooms, 7 pb Visa, MC, AmEx, *Rated*, • C-ltd/S-no/P-no/H-ltd All year	Full breakfast Restaurant Tennis, Jacuzzis, pool, suites, fireplace, cable TV, accom. bus. trvl.

Our Victorian Villa is located just 20 minutes north of Victoria overlooking the ocean and snow-capped Olympic mountain range. Our luxury suites offer double tubs and fireplaces. stay@prancinghorse.com http://www.prancinghorse.com

---

Ocean Breeze 2585 Sea View Rd. RR#1, *Mill Bay* V0R 2P0 250-743-0608 Fax: 250-743-0603 877-743-0654 Bev. & Alan Birchard	55-65-BB 3 rooms, 3 pb Visa, MC, *Rated* C-ltd/S-no/P-no/H-yes All year	Full breakfast Coffee and Tea served

Discover a relaxing getaway in this charming character home. Magnificent ocean views. Tastefully decorated with private bathrooms.
stay@oceanbreeze.bc.ca http://www.oceanbreeze.bc.ca

Beddis House 131 Miles Ave, *Salt Spring Island* V8K 2E1 250-537-1028 866-537-1028 Terry & Bev Bolton Feb 1-Nov 30	160-190-BB CAN$ 3 rooms, 3 pb Visa, MC, *Rated* C-ltd/S-no/P-no/H-no	Full breakfast Afternoon tea, home baking, early coffee to room Sitting room, library, fireplaces, private oceanfront decks

Canada Select 4.5 Star oceanfront property offering luxury bed & breakfast accommodation, in a magical setting. beddis@saltspring.com http://www.beddishousebandb.com

VICTORIA (REGION)

Mandeville Tudor Cottage By the Sea
1064 Landsend Rd, *Sidney* V8L 5L3
250-655-1587
Averil & Maurice Clegg
All year

85-BB
2 rooms, 2 pb
Rated, •
C-yes/S-ltd/P-ltd/H-no
French

Full breakfast
Sitting room, suites, fireplaces, cable TV, accommodate business travelers

Mandeville, at the northend of the Saanich Peninsula on Vancouver Island, is a picturesque Tudor Cottage set in one acre of forest, with lawns and gardens leading to the beach. mandeville@shaw.ca http://www.pixsell.bc.ca/bb/164.htm

---

Blinkbonny Gardens
7954 West Coast Rd, *Sooke* V0S 1N0
250-642-7954 Fax: 250-642-7954
Margaret & Peter Jones
All year

60-80-BB
2 rooms, 2 pb
C-ltd/S-no/P-ltd/H-ltd
Italian, French, Scottish

Continental plus breakfast
Afternoon tea
Sitting room, Jacuzzis, fireplaces, and cable TV

Overlooking the ocean, spectacular views, nature trails, afternoon tea served in ....., private Jacuzzis. peterwjones@shaw.ca

WHISTLER

Belle Neige
8597 Drifter Way V0N 1B8
604-938-9225 Fax: 604-938-9384
800-611-4869
Myrna & Todd
All year

65-115-BB
3 rooms, 2 pb
Visa, MC, *Rated*, •
C-ltd/S-no/P-no/H-no
French, Italian

Full breakfast can be Optional
Apres-ski winter hot tub
Jacuzzi on deck w/Mt vw, back country ski guiding

Tranquil Mt setting. Private suite w/kitchen or standard room. Après ski Jacuzzi on deck w/magnificent Mt view! Delicious full breakfast. Discounted ski passes. Door-to-door transfer—Vancouver Airport. myrna@direct.ca http://www.triple1.net/B/belle/

Durlacher Hof
7055 Nesters Road V0N 1B7
604-932-1924 Fax: 604-938-1980
1-877-932 1924
Peter & Erika Durlacher
All year

100-170-BB
8 rooms, 8 pb
Visa, MC, *Rated*, •
C-ltd/S-no/P-no/H-yes
German

Full breakfast
Afternoon tea
Lounge, sauna, hot tub, wheelchair accessible, packages, gift certificate

An enchanting mountain hideaway in Whistler. Painstaking attention to detail is evident in the cozy guest lounge and the immaculate pretty rooms-all with mountain views, down duvets and en-suite baths. info@durlacherhof.com http://www.durlacherhof.com

---

Golden Dreams
6412 Easy St V0N 1B6
604-932-2667 Fax: 604-932-7055
800-668-7055
Ann & Terry Spence
All year

65-95-BB
3 rooms, 1 pb
Visa, MC, *Rated*, •
C-yes/S-ltd/P-no/H-no
German, Ffrench

Full breakfast
Full guest kitchen, complimentary wine & snacks
Private fireside lounge, Outdoor hot tub, large BBQ deck, daily maid service

An established B&B offering all the secrets of great B&B stays! Be surrounded by nature's beauty, choose one of our unique "theme rooms" and be pampered with a wholesome breakfast. ann@goldendreamswhistler.com http://www.goldendreamswhistler.com

---

Inn at Clifftop Lane
2828 Clifftop Ln V0N 1B2
604-938-1229 Fax: 604-938-9880
888-281-2929
Sulee & Alan Sailer
All year

90-140-BB
5 rooms, 5 pb
Visa, MC, *Rated*, •
C-ltd/S-no/P-no/H-no
French, Thai

Full gourmet breakfast
Afternoon tea, snacks, dinner avail. sometimes
Sitting room, library, hot tub, Jacuzzis, fireplaces, free parking

Rated 4 1/2 stars, this warm and elegant B&B Inn offers a decor of antiques, fine fabrics, original artworks and gourmet breakfasts. Each guestroom has a Jacuzzi tub, fluffy bathrobes, cable TV/VCR. info@innatclifftop.com http://www.innatclifftop.com

WHISTLER

Renoir's Winter Garden 3137 Tyrol Crescent V0N 1B3 604-938-0546 Fax: 604-938-0547 Paul & Helga Ruiterman All year	85-125-BB 5 rooms, 4 pb Visa, MC, *Rated*, • C-yes/S-no/P-no/H-no German, Dutch	Full breakfast Jacuzzis, suite, cable TV, Internet access, accom. business travelers

Private guest entrance. Coffee & tea makings in each room, free Internet access, in-house art gallery. Nutritious, wholesome and tasty breakfast.
Renoir@dualmountain.com http://www.dualmountain.com/renoir

Manitoba

DAUPHIN

Touch of Africa–Guest Cottage & Ostrich Ranch PO Box 851 Highway 10 R7N 2T3 204-638-0085 Fax: 204-638-8174 Pieter & Dawn Willemse All year	60-BB 3 rooms, 2 pb Visa C-yes/S-ltd/P-ltd/H-yes Dutch	Continental plus breakfast Snacks Sitting room, bikes, fireplaces, cable TV, accom. bus. travelers

Private country cottage on Ostrich Ranch. Close to Riding Mountain National Park, across from Airport. Groups of up to 8 people welcome. Beautiful summer sunsets.
dwillemse@escape.ca http://www.bbcanada.com/2815.html

WINNIPEG

Twin Pillars 235 Oakwood Ave R3L 1E5 204-284-7590 Fax: 204-284-1913 Betty-Lou & Sonya All year	35-42-BB 4 rooms *Rated* C-yes/S-no/P-ltd/H-no French	Continental plus breakfast Library, bikes, suites, cable, acc. bus. trav., free laundry, guest kitchen

Beautiful antique rooms with modern conveniences; located across from park in quiet residential area near downtown Winnipeg.
twinpillars@shaw.ca http://www.escape.ca/~tls/twin.htm

New Brunswick

CHANCE HARBOUR

Mariner's Inn 32 Mawhinney Cove Rd 32 Mawhinney Cove Road E5J 2B8 506-659-2619 Fax: 506-659-1890 888-783-2455 Susan & Bill Postma All year	65-90-AP 11 rooms, 11 pb Visa, MC, *Rated*, • C-ltd/S-no/P-no/H-ltd French, German, Dutch	Continental breakfast plus Lunch, dinner, restaurant Bar service, sitting room, library, suites, fireplaces

Enjoy awe-inspiring ocean scenery of the world's highest tides, in a secluded romantic setting on the Bay of Fundy. postma@nbnet.nb.ca http://bayoffundy.com/mariner

MONCTON (REGION)

Auberge Wild Rose Inn
17 Baseline Rd., *Lakeville* E1H 1N5
506-383-9751 Fax: 506-860-7547
888-389-7673
Fred & Dianne Logan

54-129-BB
16 rooms, 16 pb
Most CC, *Rated*, •
C-ltd/S-no/P-no/H-no
French
All year

Full breakfast
Dinner; bar service
Sitting room, Jacuzzis, suites, fireplaces, Cable TV, business travelers

Cozy, comfortable inn exudes romance from the warm fireplaces to the quaint antiques. This, coupled with a gourmet breakfast, make for a memorable stay.
wildroseinn@hotmail.com http://www.wildroseinn.com

SAINT JOHN

Red Rose Mansion
112 Mount Pleasant Ave E2K 3V1
506-649-0913 Fax: 506-693-3233
888-711-5151
Denise Schonmann All year

88-186-BB
7 rooms, 7 pb
Most CC, *Rated*, •
C-ltd/H-ltd
French, German

Full or continental plus
Dinner, afternoon tea, snacks, bar service
Sitting room, library, Jacuzzis, suites, fireplaces, cable TV, bus. trav.

One of the most historic B&B Inns in New Brunswick. Magnificent mansion built for the founder of Red Rose Tea. redrose@nbnet.nb.ca http://www.redrosemansion.com

SAINT JOHN (REGION)

Shamper's Bluff Inn
59 Shamper's Bluff Rd, *Kingston Peninsula* E5N 1B9
506-763-2894 Fax: 506-763-2894
877-763-2894
Cathy & Gerald Buckley

65-90-BB
5 rooms, 5 pb
Visa, MC, *Rated*, •
C-ltd/S-ltd/P-no/H-no
French
All year

Full breakfast
Dinner, afternoon tea
Sitting room, bikes, Jacuzzis, fireplaces, hot tub, kayaks

Our waterside country inn is perfect for romance, fireplaces, Jacuzzis, candlelight dinners and walks through our beautiful grounds. It's all waiting just for you.
bluffin@nbnet.nb.ca http://www.shampersbluffinn.com

SAINT LOUIS DE KENT

Le gite de l'Oasis Acadienne
10617 rue Principale St E4X 1G1
506-876-1199 Fax: 506-876-1918
866-876-1199
Nicole Daigle & Victor Savoie
May-October

35-55-BB
6 rooms, 4 pb
Visa, MC, *Rated*, •
C-yes/S-no/P-no/H-no
French, Spanish, Portuguese

Full breakfast
Sitting room, library, cable TV, accomm. business travelers

Beautiful country B&B along the Kouchibouguacis River. Nature interpreter hosts. Great homemade preserves. Sea kayak tours offered by hosts.
kayak@nbnet.nb.ca http://www.kayakouch.com

SHEDIAC

Auberge Belcourt Inn
310 Main St E4P 2E3
506-532-6098 Fax: 506-533-9398
Pauline & Chris Pike
February-Novemeber

65-85-BB
7 rooms, 7 pb
Visa, MC, AmEx, *Rated*, •
C-ltd/S-ltd/P-no/H-no
French, Cantonese

Full breakfast
Dinner (off season)
Sitting room, library, fireplaces, cable TV

A spacious and elegantly restored Victorian home handsomely furnished with antiques. Breakfast is served in an oval dining room on fine antique china.
belcourt@nbnet.nb.ca http://www.sn2000.nb.ca/comp/auberge-belcourt

---

Auberge Maison Vienneau Inn
426 Main St
866-532-5412
Marie & Norbert Vienneau
All year

BB
4 rooms, 4 pb
French

Welcome to Maison Vienneau, a charming B&B that offers a taste of good wholesome maritime hospitality. infi@maisonvienneau.com http://www.maisonvienneau.com/

ST. ANDREWS

Windsor House of St Andrews
132 Water St E5B 1A8
506-529-3330 Fax: 506-529-4063
888-890-9463
Jay Remer & Greg Cohane
All year

150-225-BB
6 rooms, 6 pb
Visa, MC, AmEx, *Rated*, •
C-no/S-ltd/P-no/H-ltd
French

Lunch, dinner, restaurant, bar
Fireplace, cable TV, conferences, pool table, garden courtyard

Historic restoration of a 1798 Georgian sea captain's house with the most comfortable rooms filled with period antiques & the finest dining available in Eastern Canada.
windsorhouse@townsearch.com http://www.townsearch.com/windsorhouse

ST. ANDREWS BY THE SEA (REGION)

Pansy Patch Inn
59 Carleton St, *St. Andrews* E5B 1M8
506-529-3834 Fax: 506-529-9042
888-726-7972
Jeannie Foster
May to October

110-170-BB
9 rooms, 9 pb
Visa, MC, *Rated*, •
C-yes/S-no/P-no/H-no

Full gourmet breakfast
Fine dining aft. ., eve.
Tennis court, hot tubs, sauna, pool, library, kites, bikes, antiques

Most photographed home in New Brunswick, St. Croix Courier; featured in NY Times, Brides Canadian Homes & Gardens.
pansypatch@nb.aibn.com http://www.pansypatch.com

Newfoundland

CORNER BROOK

Adams House
PO Box 283
Roberts Drive A2H 6C9
709-634-0064 Fax: 709-634-0065
888-279-0064
Carla & Nelson Adams
All year

50-100-BB
4 rooms, 4 pb
Visa, MC, AmEx, *Rated*, •
C-yes/S-no/P-no/H-no

Full breakfast
All meals, with sufficient notice
Fresh flowers, beverage/snack, picnic snack for guests staying multiple days

Newfoundland's FIRST 4-star B&B, nestled in the beautiful Humber Valley. We feature elegant guestrooms with en-suite bathrooms. An abundance of antiques and local artwork is displayed throughout. nelsonadams01@hotmail.com http://adamsbandb.com

PORT BLANDFORD

Terra Nova Hospitality Home & Cottages
PO Box 111
A0C 2G0
709-543-2260
Fax: 709-543-2241
888-267-2373
Rhoda Parsons
All year

45-125-BB
11 rooms, 9 pb
Visa, MC, AmEx, *Rated*, •
C-ltd/S-ltd/P-no/H-yes

Full breakfast
Lunch, dinner, afternoon tea, snacks, restaurant
Bar service, sitting room, library, Jacuzzis, suites, fireplaces, cable

Full breakfast, all homemade jams and bread. Property overlooks the ocean.
terranova@nf.aibn.com http://www.terranova.nfld.net

ST. JOHN'S

ABBA Inn Downtown
36 Queen's Rd A1C 2A5
709-754-0047
800-563-3959
Michael & Irene
All year

60-200-BB
6 rooms, 6 pb
Visa, MC, AmEx,
Rated, •
S-no/H-no

Full breakfast
Pretty much anything can be arranged
24 High Speed Internet, VCR, stereo, computer, fax machine, iron, whirlpool

Nestled safely on elegant Queen's Road, well lit area, amongst cathedrals, theaters, fine restaurants. Everything touristy is w/in a 5 minute walk. Spacious rooms: cordless phones; desks; fireplaces.

info@abbainn.com http://www.abbainn.com

Nova Scotia

BRIDGEWATER

Fairview Inn Bridgewater
25 Queen St V4V 1P1
902-423-1102
Fax: 902-423-8329
800-725-8732
Helena & Stephen
All year

48-105-BB
25 rooms, 25 pb
Visa, MC, AmEx,
Rated, •
C-yes/S-no/P-no/H-no

Full breakfast
Fully licensed restaurant and quiet martini bar
Pool, hot tub, activity packages, original art work, business services

This fully restored plantation style inn boasts historically themed suites featuring private baths, hardwood floors throughout, antique furnishings, and original Nova Scotia Artwork.

info@nsinns.com http://www.nsinns.com

CHESTER

Haddon Hall
PO Box 640
67 Haddon Hill Rd B0J 1J0
902-275-3577
Fax: 902-275-5159
Cynthia O'Connell
April 1–Oct. 31

105-300-BB
10 rooms, 10 pb
Visa, MC, *Rated*, •
C-ltd/S-ltd/P-no/H-ltd

Continental breakfast
Dinner, restaurant
Sitting room, bar service, bicycles, fireplaces, cable TV, swimming pool

Hadden Hall is Nova Scotia's only four diamond AAA resort inn. Built in 1905 this 120 acre estate offers a spectacular panoramic ocean view.

haddon@tallships.ca http://www.haddonhallinn.com

HALIFAX

Halliburton House Inn
5184 Morris St B3J 1B3
902-420-0658 Fax: 902-423-2324
Robert Pretty
All year

100-200-BB CAN$
29 rooms, 29 pb
Most CC, *Rated*, •
C-yes/S-no/P-no/H-no

Continental plus breakfast
Dinner nightly, cocktails in library or courtyard
Restaurant, bar, suites, fireplace, cable, TV, garden courtyard

Fine dining and gracious lodging. Halliburton House Inn offers inn-style accommodations and Maritime hospitality in a trio of heritage townhouses. 29 guestrooms and suites with private bath.

innkeeper@halliburton.ns.ca http://www.halliburton.ns.ca

HALIFAX

Welcome In
1984 Connaught Ave B3H 4E1
902-423-1102 Fax: 902-423-8329
800-725-8732
H. Prsala & S. O'Leary
All year

95-165-BB CAN$
3 rooms, 3 pb
Visa, MC, AmEx,
Rated, •
C-yes/S-no/P-no/H-no
Czech, German, French

Full breakfast
Sitting room, kitchen, photocopying & fax services

All rooms have private en-suite baths, queen bed and cable TV. Some rooms with fireplaces, Jacuzzi tubs and private balconies.

info@NSinns.com http://www.NSinns.com

HALIFAX (REGION)

Anchors Gate
4281 Prospect Rd
Route 333, *Bayside* B3Z 1L4
902-852-3906 Fax: 902-852-4018
George & Nancy Pike
All year

69-89-BB
4 rooms, 4 pb
Visa, MC, *Rated*, •
C-yes/S-no/P-no/H-no

Full breakfast
Sitting room, 1 suite, cable TV, private entrances, balconies

"Nautical Theme" on Shad Bay, ocean access, hearty breakfasts, cable TV, fans, private bathrooms, private entrances & balconies, patios around the house, gardens, 3 rooms and 1 self-contained unit.

salr@accglobal.net http://www.anchorsgatebb.com

Blandford Inn
RR 1, *Blandford* B0J 1T0
902-228-2016 Fax: 902-228-2016
888-228-2016
Maureen Zinck

49-BB
4 rooms, 4 pb
Visa, MC
C-yes/S-ltd/P-no/H-yes
All year

Full breakfast
Evening meals order in advance
Ocean ambiance

A charming century old house with a new addition can accommodate small groups. Breakfast is served overlooking the harbor.

blandford.inn@ns.sympatico.ca http://www3.ns.sympatico.ca/blandford.inn.com

MARGAREE HARBOUR

Chimney Corner
PO Box 6
2581 Shore Road B0E 2B0
902-235-2104 Fax: 902-235-2104
888-211-9061
Jan & Bob Wheeler

54-62-BB
2 rooms, 2 pb
Visa, AmEx, *Rated*, •
C-ltd/S-no/P-no/H-no
July 1–October 15

Gourmet breakfast
Evening dessert
Sitting room, bicycles, satellite TV, kayak

Ocean front property with private beach. Gourmet breakfast, evening dessert, living room, queen beds, private baths, bicycles and kayak available.

chimney.corner@ns.sympatico.ca http://www3.ns.sympatico.ca/chimney.corner

PARRSBORO

The Maple Inn
PO Box 457
2358 Western Avenue B0M 1S0
902-254-3735 Fax: 902-254-3735
877-MAPLEIN

52-90-BB
9 rooms, 9 pb
Visa, MC, AmEx, *Rated*
C-yes/S-no/P-no/H-no
Trevor & Anne McNelly
All year

Full breakfast
Sitting room, cable TV, ceiling fans in rooms, lighted parking area

Lovingly restored 1893 property in Parrsboro on Bay of Fundy. 3 diamond rated by AAA, we provide the warmth and personal attention of a B&B, but with the privacy of a large inn. mapleinn@ns.sympatico.ca http://www3.ns.sympatico.ca/mapleinn

---

The Parrsboro Mansion
PO Box 579
15 Eastern Avenue B0M 1S0
902-254-2585 Fax: 902-254-2585
Sabine & Christian Schoene
June 1–October 15

58-75-BB
3 rooms, 3 pb
Visa, *Rated*, •
C-ltd/S-no/P-no/H-ltd
German

Full gourmet breakfast buffet
Afternoon tea
Sitting room, library, cable TV, sauna, exercise room, laundry facilities

Restored Italian-style mansion (c 1880) set on a 4 acre park in central and quiet location of Parrsboro. Full gourmet breakfast buffet.

parrsboro.m.bb@ns.sympatico.ca http://www3.ns.sympatico.ca/parrsboro.m.bb

PEGGY'S COVE

Peggy's Cove 19 Church Rd B0J 2N0 902-823-2265 Fax: 902-423-8329 800-725-8732 Helena Prsala & Stephen O'Leary All year	61-95-BB 5 rooms, 5 pb Visa, MC, AmEx, *Rated*, • C-ltd/S-no/P-no/H-no	Full breakfast Sitting room, outdoor hot tub, satellite TV-VCR in lounge

Overlooking beautiful Peggy's Cove, an artist's and photographer's paradise.
info@nsinns.com http://www.NSinns.com

PROSPECT VILLAGE (REGION)

Prospect 1758 Prospect Bay Rd, *Prospect* B3T 2B3 902-852-3401 Fax: 902-423-8329 800-SALT-SEA H. Prsala & S. O'Leary All year	61-95-BB 5 rooms, 5 pb Visa, MC, AmEx, *Rated*, • C-yes/S-no/P-no/H-no Czech, German, French	Full breakfast Sitting room, library, family friendly facility, kitchen, kayak, small beach

Restored oceanfront Convent located in quaint fishing village near Peggy's Cove, offering coastal hiking, Eco adventure packages.
info@nsinns.com http://www.NSinns.com

QUEENSLAND

Surfside Inn RR 2 Hubbards 9609 Highway #3 B0J 1T0 902-857-2417 Fax: 902-857-2107 800-373-2417 Michelle & Bill Batcules All year	80-179-BB CAN$ 7 rooms, 7 pb Most CC, *Rated*, • C-yes/S-no/P-no/H-yes	Continental plus breakfast Dining by candle light or on the ocean view deck. Sitting room, ocean view deck, beach, whirlpools

Originally built by a sea captain in the late 1800's, the Inn has been restored keeping the Victorian elegance while providing all of the modern amenities.
info@thesurfsideinn.com http://www.thesurfsideinn.com

TRURO

Elizabeth House 401 Robie St B2N 1L9 902-893-2346 Fax: 866-893-2346 Betty & Ray Bates All year	75-125-BB CAN$ 2 rooms, 2 pb Visa, MC, *Rated* C-yes/S-no/P-no/H-no English	Evening tea and homemade sweets Sitting room

Elizabeth House is the quaint home of a decorative painter. Relax in our guest lounge or on our upstairs deck.
elizabethhouse@ns.sympatico.ca http://www.bbcanada.com/elizabethhouse

WOLFVILLE (REGION)

The Farmhouse Inn PO Box 38 9757 Main St, *Canning* B0P 1H0 902-582-7900 Fax: 902-582-7480 800-928-4346 Doug & Ellen Bray All year	45-90-BB 5 rooms, 5 pb Visa, MC, AmEx, *Rated*, • C-yes/S-no/P-no/H-ltd	Full breakfast Afternoon tea A/C, guest parlour, 2-person whirlpool tubs, fireplaces, cable TV, VCR

Cozy 1840 renovated farmhouse in center of a quaint village. All rooms have queen, king or 2 twin beds, phone, A/C, TV, VCR, en-suite bathroom. All suites have 2-person whirlpool tub and/or fireplace.
farmhous@ns.sympatico.ca http://www.farmhouseinn.ns.ca

Ontario

ALGONQUIN PARK (REGION)

The Nordic Inn
PO Box 155
Hwy 35, *Dorset* P0A 1E0
705-766-2343 888-392-7777
Jane & Andre Tieman
All year

45-68-BB
5 rooms, 3 pb
Visa, MC, AmEx, *Rated*
C-yes/S-no/P-yes/H-no
Dutch, French

Full breakfast
Lunch/dinner available, snacks
Sitting room, bicycles, swimming pool, suites, fireplace.

Country fruit farm offering canoeing on our backyard river. Walk our llamas, visit 20 wineries, golf, hike, swim, see Niagara Falls.
info@thenordicinn.com http://www.thenordicinn.com

BARRIE

Cozy Corner
2 Morton Crescent L4N 7T3
705-739-0157 Fax: 705-739-1946
Charita & Harry Kirby
All year

55-75-BB
4 rooms, 3 pb
Visa, •
C-ltd/S-no/P-no/H-no
German, Spanish

Chef prepared Specialities
Authentic English Afternoon Tea, delightful welco
Sitting room, Jacuzzi, A/C, TVs, glorious breakfasts, chef in residence

B&B Award Winner. Find comfort and cleanliness. En-suite bathrooms, queen beds, firm mattresses, A/C, Jacuzzi, TVs, fireplace. Electronic air cleaning. European trained chef (owner) in residence.
cozyc@bconnex.net http://www.bconnex.net/~cozyc

BOWMANVILLE

Willow Pond Country
2460 Concession Rd #7
L1C 3K2
905-263-2405 Fax: 905-263-8623
Cell: 905-442-0992
Lynn & Randy Morrison

65-99-BB
2 rooms, 2 pb
Visa, MC
C-yes/S-no/P-ltd/H-ltd

Full breakfast
Coffee, tea, milk, cream, bottled water, fresh fruit
Heated in-ground pool, private gardens, pine suite, natural pond, coldwater creek

Peace, tranquility and a touch of luxury await you. Spot the Great Blue Heron and Canada Geese around our natural pond and creek. Relax in your private apt/suite or stay in the Main House with us. willowpond@attcanada.ca

BRIGHTON

Butler Creek Country Inn
RR#7, Country Rd #30-202
K0K 1H0
613-475-1248 Fax: 613-475-5267
877-477-5827
Burke & Ken All year

50-70-BB
5 rooms, 2 pb
Visa, MC, AmEx, *Rated*, •
C-yes/S-no/P-no/H-no
German, French

Full breakfast
Sitting room, fireplaces, large country property with meadows and stream.

Enjoy the rare combination of Victorian elegance, convenient location and peaceful setting. Central Air . Coffee/Tea making equipment in each room. Excellent base for exploring the area on day trips. butlerbb@reach.net http://www.butlercreekcountryinn.com

BURLINGTON

Wilkie House
1211 Sable Drive L7S 2J7
905-637-5553 Fax: 905-637-7294
866-233-2632
Nancy & Peter Wilkie
All year

60-BB
2 rooms, 2 pb
Most CC, •
C-ltd/S-no/P-no/H-no

Full breakfast
Vegetarian/organic on request
Sitting room, cable TV/VCR, laundry service, accommodate business travelers

We have pampered business & leisure travelers since 1994. Comfortable beds, private baths, and gourmet breakfasts in a relaxing quiet environment. Flexible check-in and breakfast times. nancy.wilkie@sympatico.ca http://www.canvisit.com/wilkiehouse

CAMBRIDGE

Spruceview Century Farm
1697 Cedar Creek Rd, RR4
N1R 5S5
519-621-2769 Fax: 519-621-2769
Debra & Alex Barrie
All year

60-85-BB CAN$
3 rooms, 1 pb
Visa, *Rated*
C-yes/S-no/P-no/H-no

Full breakfast
Dinner available, afternoon tea
Sitting room

A warm welcome awaits in spacious fieldstone house of 5th generation working farm. Enjoy a country breakfast. Relax on veranda take a walk through farm and maple bush or a back country lane. debra-barrie@sympatico.ca http://www.bbcanada.com/373.html

COLLINGWOOD

Cedar Chest
216 Cedar St L9Y 3A8
705-444-0484 Fax: 705-790-2507
Diane Chesterman
All year

75-85-BB
4 rooms
Most CC
C-ltd/S-no/P-ltd/H-no

Full breakfast
Snacks
Sitting room, Cable TV, accommodate business travelers

Victorian 1890 home furnished with antiques and stained glass.
dianechesterman@sympatico.ca http://www.bbcanada.com/cedarchest

COLLINGWOOD (REGION)

Pretty River Valley Country Inn
529742 SR 30/31
Off Hwy 124, *Nottawa* L0M 1P0
705-445-7598 Fax: 705-445-7598
Noel & Debbie Street All year

75-100-BB
8 rooms, 8 pb
Visa, MC, *Rated*, •
C-ltd/S-no/P-no/H-ltd

Full breakfast
Jacuzzis, suites, fireplaces, accommodate business travelers

Country Inn nestled in Blue Mountains. Studios and Suites, Whirlpools, private baths, WOODBURNING FIREPLACES, Central spa. Near hiking, golf, beaches, skiing, antiquing, shopping and restaurants. inn@cois.on.ca http://www.prettyriverinn.com

ELORA

Drew House
120 Mill St E N0B 1S0
519-846-2226 Fax: 519-846-2245
Kathlen Stanley & Roger Dufau All year

BB

Full breakfast

Nestled in the Village of Elora, Drew House offers a magical retreat from the pressures of everyday life. rduf@drewhouse.com http://www.drewhouse.com

FORESTERS FALLS

Whitewater
PO Box 23
1900 Foresters Falls Rd K0J 1V0
613-646-7638 Fax: 613-646-7368
877-352-9464
Jennifer Vallance
All year

45-95-BB
6 rooms, 3 pb
Visa, MC, •
C-yes/S-ltd/P-ltd/H-no

Full breakfast
Afternoon tea, complimentary wine
Sitting room, accommodate business travelers, campfire

Beautiful rural setting and peaceful 1903 home. Minutes from whitewater rafting, golfing, waterslide and theme parks, and an easy drive to Ottawa.
jenvictoriabb@yahoo.com http://www.bbcanada.com/2761.html

GANANOQUE

Manse Lane
465 Stone St South K7G 2A7
613-382-8642 888-565-6379
Jocelyn & George Bounds
All year

55-140-BB
4 rooms, 2 pb
Visa, MC, AmEx, *Rated*, •
C-ltd/S-no/P-no/H-no
French

Full breakfast
Afternoon tea
Sitting room, swimming pool, A/C, indoor bike storage

Casual elegance and warm, friendly hospitality in a century brick home.
http://www.bbcanada.com/942.html/

Maples of Grimsby, Grimsby, ON

GANANOQUE

The Victoria Rose Inn
279 King St West K7G 2G7
613-382-3368 Fax: 613-382-8803
888-246-2893
Liz & Ric Austin
All year

85-195-BB CAN$
11 rooms, 11 pb
Visa, MC, AmEx, *Rated*
C-ltd/S-no/P-no/H-no

Full breakfast
AC, Jacuzzis, fireplaces, award winning gardens, parlor, bike storage

Stately Victorian mansion built in 1872 elegantly appointed with Canadian antiques. Veranda overlooks 2 acres of estate grounds. Charming restaurant featuring casual fine dining.
vr@victoriaroseinn.com http://www.victoriaroseinn.com

GRIMSBY

Maples of Grimsby
3 Nelles Blvd L3M 3P9
905-945-5719
Georgina & Barry Staz
All year

65-95-BB
3 rooms, 2 pb
•
C-ltd/S-ltd/P-no/H-no

Full breakfast
Sitting room, swimming pool, library, fireplaces, cable TV, acc. bus. trav.

Tastefully decorated (1924) home. Enjoy hiking, antiquing, award-winning wineries or a peaceful retreat in our garden by the pool.
maples@sympatico.ca http://www.bbcanada.com/maples

GUELPH

Elm Park
646 Paisley Rd N1K 1A4
519-821-8734
Shirley McColeman
All year

40-50-BB
3 rooms
Visa, MC, AmEx
C-ltd/S-no/P-no/H-no

Full breakfast
Tea and coffee
Sitting room with TV and videos, deck, patio, free e-mail

Historic 1850s farmhouse, furnished with antiques and brass beds. All rooms have bar fridges, hairdryers, housecoats, tea and coffee. Free local telephone and e-mail access. One hour from Toronto. elmpark@elmparkbb.com http://www.elmparkbb.com

HAMILTON

Rutherford House
293 Park St South L8P 3G5
905-525-2422 Fax: 905-525-5236
David and Janis Topp
All year

60-BB
2 rooms, 2 pb
Visa, MC, *Rated*
C-ltd/S-no/P-no/H-no

Full breakfast
Sitting room, central A/C, parking, TV/VCR, fridges, coffee-makers

Late Victorian home in lovely Heritage District. Luxury and comfort—ensuite baths, down duvets, gourmet breakfasts, dining/sitting room with fireplace, two "host" tabby cats to greet you. david.janis.topp@sympatico.ca http://www.bbcanada.com/5198.htm

HAWKESTONE

The Verandahs RR 2 4 Palm Beach Rd L0L 1T0 705-487-1910 800-841-1019 Henry & Jean Kanty All year	60-68-BB 3 rooms, 3 pb Visa, MC, *Rated* C-ltd/S-no/P-no/H-no Polish	Full breakfast Tea, Coffee, Juice, Fruit, Cookies, Popcorn, etc. Sitting room, Library, Piano, Bicycles

Beautiful Victorian style home. Relax, let lake breezes cool you on the wide verandahs in summer. Indoors the cozy fireplace or A/C will keep you comfy. Gourmet full breakfasts (home baking). jeankanty@sympatico.ca http://www.verandahs.com

KINGSTON (REGION)

Denaut Mansion Country Inn 5 Matthew St, *Delta* K0E 1G0 613-928-2588 877-788-0388 David & Deborah Peets All year	85-115-BB 6 rooms, 6 pb Visa, MC, • C-ltd/S-no/P-no/H-no	Continental plus breakfast Dinner, bar service Sitting room, library, swimming pool, suites, accom. bus. travelers

A 153 year-old restored sandstone mansion. All rooms with en-suite, pool, private nature trail, complimentary canoes, loop cycle routes, nearby golf courses.
goodtimes@denautmansion.com http://www.denautmansion.com

KINGSVILLE

The Wedding House 98 Main St E N9Y 1A4 519-733-3928 Fax: 519-733-9987 877-733-3928 Linda & Tom Gelinas All year	50-70-BB 4 rooms, 4 pb Visa, MC, *Rated* C-yes/S-no/P-no/H-no	Full served breakfast or specials In-ground pool, in-home theater, walk to fine dining, many local attractions

Beautiful Victorian home lovingly restored, furnished with antiques and collectibles. Walk to fine dining. Inground pool, central air.
weddinghouse@sympatico.ca http://www.theweddinghousebb.com

KITCHENER

Aram's Roots and Wings 11 Sunbridge Crescent N2K 1T4 519-743-4557 Fax: 519-743-4166 877-743-4557 Carolyn Steele All year	50-100-BB CAN$ 4 rooms, 3 pb Visa, MC, AmEx, *Rated* C-yes/S-ltd/P-yes/H-ltd	Full breakfast Sitting room, Jacuzzis, swimming pool, suites, fireplaces, cable TV, trails

Country living in the city. Warm hospitality and a hearty breakfast awaits you. Heated pool, Jacuzzi and large rooms with king/queen beds.
rootsandwings@sgci.com http://www.bbcanada.com/1039.html

KITCHENER (REGION)

Willow Springs Suites 24 Brewery St, *Baden* N0B 1G0 519-634-8652 Fax: 519-634-8652 877-467-2083 Bruce & Dale Weber	39-52-BB 3 rooms, 3 pb Visa, *Rated* C-yes/S-no/P-no/H-yes All year	Full breakfast Snacks Jacuzzis, suites, fireplaces, cable TV, accommodate business travelers

Private suites in adjoining guesthouse beside the Baden waterway. Family friendly home, fenced yard, firepit, shaded sitting area and fish pond. All Units are special, and you will feel right at home!
willowspringsbandb@sentex.net http://www.bbcanada.com/2212.html

LA SALLE

L. & M. R. Nantais B&B
2240 Front Rd N9J 2C2
519-734-8916 Fax: 519-978-1048
888-524-0000
Larry & Marie-Rose Nantais
All year

35-100-BB
5 rooms, 2 pb
Rated, •
C-yes/S-ltd/P-yes/H-no
French

Brunch
Tea/coffee anytime; extra meals available
Public allowed anywhere door not closed

Peaceful, tranquil setting on the shores of International Detroit River, Windsor suburb. Ideal setting for romance, families, travelers passing through, salespersons. Retreat close to nature and God. LMRNantais@yahoo.com

LEAMINGTON (REGION)

B&B's
PO Box 98
216 Erie Street South, *Wheatley*
N0P 2P0
519-825-8008 Fax: 519-825-7737
800-851-3406
Bea & Bruce Patterson

75-100-BB
4 rooms, 4 pb
Visa, MC
C-ltd/S-ltd/P-no/H-no
German, French, Spanish
All year

Country style full breakfast
TV Room Pool Table Fooze Ball Table, Inground Pool Sundecks

1905 Victorian home. Large rooms with private en-suite bathrooms, private entrance, entertainment room, country style breakfasts. Close to Point Pelee National Park, birders' paradise. Central air. brucep@mnsi.net http://mnsi.net/~brucep

LIVELY

Fenton's
79 Field St P3Y 1B4
705-692-5510 Fax: 705-692-5223
Stan & Janet Fenton
All year

35-40-BB
2 rooms, 1 pb
Rated
C-yes/S-no/P-no

Full breakfast
Complimentary coffee, tea & soft drinks
Bathrobes, hair dryers, free parking

A warm & friendly welcome awaits you! We will do our best to make your visit to our town comfortable & enjoyable. Arrive as a stranger & leave as a friend!
fentonsbnb@sympatico.ca

MIDLAND

Little Lake Inn
669 Yonge St L4R 2E1
705-526-2750 Fax: 705-526-9005
888-297-6130
Jennifer Hart & Milton Haynes
All year

65-92-BB
4 rooms, 4 pb
Most CC, *Rated*
C-yes/S-no/P-no/H-ltd

Continental plus breakfast
Afternoon tea, complimentary wine
Sitting room, Jacuzzis, suites, fireplaces, cable TV, bus. travelers

AAA approved–rated 3 diamonds. Unique renovated century home overlooking Little Lake in the heart of Midland. info@littlelakeinn.com http://www.littlelakeinn.com

---

A Place For All Seasons
RR 1
168 Hummingbird Hill Rd
L4R 4K3
705-835-9948 Fax: 705-835-2724
877-915-9948
Eileen & Ron Bellamy

75-95-BB
4 rooms, 3 pb
Visa, MC, •
C-yes/S-ltd/P-no/H-no
All year

Full breakfast
Afternoon tea, snacks, dinner pkgs-book in advance
Guest lounge, swimming pool, cedar oasis spa, in room movies n/c

Chamber of Commerce "President's Award" Bi-weekly rates and packages available.
info@aplaceforallseasons.com http://www.aplaceforallseasons.com

NIAGARA (REGION)

Denwycke House at Grimsby
203 Main St E, *Grimsby*
L3M 1P5
905-945-2149 Fax: 905-945-6272
Patricia & John Hunter
All year

85-100-BB
2 rooms, 2 pb
Visa, MC, AmEx, *Rated*
C-ltd/S-no/P-no/H-no
French

Full breakfast
Fridge, coffee maker
Sitting room, suites, fireplaces, cable TV, data ports

Luxurious suites in a gracious 1846 heritage home on the Niagara Wine Route.
johnpathunter@cs.com http://www.denwycke.com

NIAGARA (REGION)

Inn on the Twenty
3836 Main St, *Jordan* L0R 1B1
905-562-5336 Fax: 905-562-3232
800-701-8074
Helen Young
All year

219-325-BB
31 rooms, 31 pb
Visa, MC, AmEx,
Rated, •
C-ltd/S-no/P-no/H-ltd

Continental breakfast
Winery on site, bicycles, boutiques & art galleries

Inn on the Twenty is comprised of our charming, 26 rooms and historic Vintage House in the village of Jordan. Cave Spring Cellars on site. Our well-known restaurant features regional cuisine and wine. heleny@vaxxine.com http://www.innonthetwenty.com

NIAGARA FALLS

Andrea's
4286 Simcoe St L2E 1T6
905-374-4776 Fax: 905-356-3563
Andrea Armstrong
All year

55-158-BB
3 rooms, 4 pb
Most CC
C-yes/S-no/P-no/H-no

Continental plus breakfast
Buffet
Dinner is included when you stay 2 nights.
Sitting room, private deck, sun porch, fireplaces, suite, fridge, cable

Enjoy a 20 minute breathtaking walk along the Niagara Gorge to the Falls and Casino. We are able to accommodate up to 8 people in our 2 bedroom, 2 bathroom suite plus 2 rooms with private bath. andrea.bed@sympatico.ca http://www.andreasbedandbreakfast.com

NIAGARA FALLS (REGION)

Blain-Lansing Post House Country Inn
PO Box 1037
95 Johnson Street, *Niagara on the Lake* L0S 1J0
905-468-9991 Fax: 905-468-9584
877-349-POST
Barbara & Dr. Charles Ganim
All year

75-250-BB
3 rooms, 3 pb
Visa, MC, AmEx, •
C-ltd/S-ltd/P-no/H-no

Full varied breakfast
Special ""health table""
Library, bikes, 2-person Jacuzzi, heated pool, suites, fireplace, Cable TV

Historic, 1835 property within a short stroll to Shaw theaters. Our home has been completely restored with en-suites. We offer a lavish breakfast in the conservatory. Tennis available. post@posthouseinn.com http://www.posthouseinn.com

NIAGARA ON THE LAKE

Burke House Inn, Circa 1826
PO Box 1037
94 Prideaux St L0S 1J0
905-468-9991
Fax: 905-468-9584
877-349-POST(7
Barbara Ganim
All year

89-150-BB
3 rooms

Special health table
Solarium, guest parlor

Burke House Inn circa 1826, located on one of Niagara On The Lake's most prestigious streets. This historic home was the original Thomas Burke House in the 1850s.
post@posthouseinn.com http://www.burkehouseinn.com

Centre House
PO Box 306
125 Centre St L9H 6K9
905-468-0726
Lorrie Anne Wannamaker
All year

75-85-BB
3 rooms, 3 pb
Visa, •
S-no/P-no/H-no

Full breakfast
Sitting room, cable TV, accommodate business travelers

A smoke-free, adult environment offers a guest parlour with fireplace, central air and a spacious front porch. Full breakfast is served at individual tables.
lawannamaker@sympathico.ca

Simcoe Manor, Niagara on the Lake, ON

NIAGARA ON THE LAKE

Linden House PO Box 1586 389 Simcoe Street L0S 1J0 905-468-3923 Fax: 905-468-8946 Elaine Landray & Donna Pearce All year	68-75-BB 3 rooms, 3 pb *Rated*, • C-ltd/S-no/P-no/H-no French, Spanish	Full breakfast Sitting room, cable TV, gazebo, garden

Cape Cod style home, circa 1990. Private guest entrance, lounge and central A/C, gourmet breakfast featured in Rise n' Dine Canada Cookbook.
linden@niagara.com http://www.niagarabb.com/linden

The Regent House 278 Regent St L0S 1J0 905-468-4361 Fax: 905-468-4813 John Hudson and Linda Smith All year	95-BB 3 rooms, 3 pb Visa, MC, AmEx C-ltd/S-no/P-no/H-no	Full breakfast Sitting room, cable TV, accommodate business travelers

An elegant historic home steps to the shops, restaurants and the Shaw Festival Theatres. Exquisitely appointed king, queen and twin air-conditioned rooms.
regenthouse@sympatico.ca http://www.historicbb.com

Simcoe Manor Box 623 242 Simcoe St L0S 1J0 905-468-4886 Fax: 905-468-5369 1-866-468-4886 John & Vera Gartner	100-200-BB 5 rooms, 5 pb Visa, MC C-ltd/S-ltd/P-no/H-ltd All year	Full gourmet breakfast Complimentary tea, coffee and soft drinks Guest parlour with fireplace ;reading materials; heated swim pool, cable TV

Stately "Old Town" home graciously harmonizes tradition, ambience & friendliness w/modern comfort. Park setting, steps from attractions, theatre, dining, shopping, golf. Air, fireplaces, porch. simcoemanor@cogeco.ca http://www.bbcanada.com/1100.html

Wishing Well Cottage PO Box 1656 156 Mary St L0S 1J0 905-468-4658 Maria Rekrut All year	100-BB C-ltd/S-no/P-no/H-no English, Italian, Spanish, French	Continental breakfast A/C, slippers provided

Circa 1871 historic summer cottage of the Canadian Soprano Maria Rekrut. This "Museum within a cottage" is filled with a private art collection, antiques and collectables.
wishingwellcottage1@hotmail.com http://www.wishingwellcottage.com

OAKVILLE

Brass Lantern
300 Lakeshore Rd W L6K 1G1
905-337-0201 1-866-399-2399
Johanna & Wayne Kendall
All year

50-62-BB
2 rooms, 2 pb
Visa
C-ltd/S-ltd/P-no/H-ltd
Dutch, French

Refreshments on arrival, cookies on the table
Sitting room, library, deck, parking at the door, A/C

Private guestrooms, queen size beds, private bathrooms, huge deck and air conditioning. Hearty breakfast menu with daily specials. Great hospitality...your home away from home while you are with us. brasslantern300@cogeco.ca http://bbcanada.com/brasslantern

ORANGEVILLE

Country Host Network
RR 5 Mono 5th Line
Hockley Valley L9W 2Z1
519-942-0686 Fax: 519-942-0686
Lesley Burns All year

49-BB
2 rooms, 1 pb
C-yes/S-no/P-no/H-yes

Full breakfast
Lunch, dinner, snacks
Sitting room, fireplaces, cable TV, central air, sauna

Country hideaway in Caledon/Headwaters festival country.
info@countryhost.com http://www.countryhost.com

OTTAWA

Albert House Inn
478 Albert St K1R 5B5
613-236-4479 Fax: 613-237-9079
800-267-1982
Cathy & John Delroy
All year

98-158-BB CAN$
17 rooms, 17 pb
Visa, MC, AmEx, *Rated*
C-ltd/S-ltd/P-no/H-no
French, English

Full breakfast
Complimentary beverages/modest room service menu.
Parlour, internet desk/ wireless internet, bicycle storage, fax/photocopier

Charming 1875 Victorian inn just a short walk to Parliament, shopping, dining, and entertainment. All rooms en-suite; fabulous full hot breakfasts and free Internet access. Parking available. contact@albertinn.com http://www.albertinn.com

---

Ambiance
330 Nepean St K1R 5G6
613-563-0421 1-888-366-8772
Maria or Michele
All year

85-110-BB CAN$
4 rooms, 2 pb
Visa, MC, AmEx
C-yes/S-no/P-no/H-no
French, Greek

Full gourmet breakfast daily
Complimentary coffee, teas, hot coco & soft drinks
Lounge, parking,A/C,iron & board, hair dryers, front deck, fridge, microwave

"A Downtown Home with Small Town Warmth" An elegantly appointed Victorian home built in 1904 and located in a quiet area of downtown Ottawa where you can park your car and walk everywhere. ambiancebandb@on.aibn.com http://www.ambiancebandb.com

---

Gasthaus Switzerland Inn
89 Daly Ave K1N 6E6
613-237-0335 Fax: 613-594-3327
888-663-0000
Sabina & Josef Sauter
All year

88-228-BB CAN$
22 rooms, 22 pb
Most CC, *Rated*
C-ltd/S-no/P-no/H-no
French, Swiss-German, German, Serbocroatian

Full Swiss breakfast
Air-conditioning, barbecue, garden, cable TV, fax

Warm Swiss atmosphere in Canada's beautiful capital. Distinctive European hospitality. Ideal for a romantic getaway. Clean, comfortable rooms. Close to tourist attractions. Limited free parking.
switzinn@gasthausswitzerlandinn.com http://www.gasthausswitzerlandinn.com

OWEN SOUND

Highland Manor Grand Victorian
867 4th Ave A West N4K 6L5
519-372-2699
Linda Bradford, Paul Neville
All year

BB
S-no

Fireplaces, antique elevator

Experience one of Canada's largest and oldest privately owned Victorian Mansions, open to the public year-round as an elegant B&B. Seated majestically atop the west hill of Owen Sound, Ontario. info@highlandmanor.ca http://www.highlandmanor.ca

PETERBOROUGH

Liftlock B&B
810 Canal Road K9L 1A1
705-742-0110 866-717-7707
Doreen Davies All year

55-85-BB
3 rooms, 3 pb
Visa, MC
C-ltd/S-ltd/P-ltd/H-yes

Full breakfast
Wheelchair accessible, online reservations, romantic

Located on Trent Canal, walking distance to downtown Peterborough, or the liftlocks. Golfing, tennis, fishing, gambling, museums, art galleries, free entertainment.
liftlock-bb@cogeco.ca http://liftlock-bed-and-breakfast.com

PETERBOROUGH (REGION)

Selwyn Shores Waterfront
2073 Selwyn Shores, RR3, *Lakefield* K0L 2H0
705-652-0277 Fax: 705-652-3389
877-735-9967
Dan & Martha Crawford
All year

50-65-BB
5 rooms, 2 pb
MC, *Rated*
C-ltd/S-no/P-no/H-ltd

Full breakfast
Afternoon tea, snacks
Sitting room, library, fireplaces, cable TV, canoe, waterfront, biz traveler

Waterfront–fishing and sunsets. Large common rooms with fireplaces. Full gourmet breakfast. Extensive decking and landscaping. Upscale decor. Dockage and Launch. Excellent local dining. sleep@selwynshores.com http://www.selwynshores.com

PORT HOPE

Butternut Inn
36 North St L1A 1T8
905-885-4318 Fax: 905-885-5464
800-218-6670
Bob & Bonnie Harrison
All year

109-129-BB CAN$
4 rooms, 4 pb
Visa, MC, AmEx, *Rated*, •
C-ltd/S-no/P-no/H-no

Full gourmet breakfast
Afternoon tea, soft drinks
Sitting room, solarium, large private garden, landscaped grounds

Luxuriously appointed 1850s home in the heart of antiquing, cycling golfing & fishing country. Gourmet cooking packages our specialty.
info@butternutinn.com http://www.butternutinn.com

PORT PERRY (REGION)

Landfall Farm
3120 Hwy 7A, RR 1, *Blackstock* L0B 1B0
905-986-5588
Merle Heintzman All year

41-BB
3 rooms, 1 pb
Rated
C-yes/S-ltd/P-ltd/H-no
French

Full breakfast
Sitting room, swimming pool, fireplace, TV, antique shop, natural pond

1868 Victorian stone farmhouse with original gingerbread trim, pine floors, etc. Extensive grounds, lighted and heated pool with cabana, antique shop, natural pond.
http://www.bbcanada.com/2648.html

PORT ROWAN

Bayview
PO Box 9
45 Wolven St N0E 1M0
519-586-3413 800-646-0668
Laura-Jane Charlton
All year

50-BB
3 rooms, 1 pb
Rated
C-ltd/S-ltd/P-no/H-no

Full breakfast
Sitting room, suites, cable TV, accommodate business travelers

Welcoming home catering to your needs. Victorian-style, modern facilities, sundecks, very comfortable. Guests quotes–"great food, peaceful, excellent visit, right at home.
bayview@execulink.com http://www.bbcanada.com/bayviewbb

SAULT STE. MARIE

Brockwell Chambers
183 Brock St P6A 3B8
705-949-1076 Fax: 705-949-1076
Mrs. Maria Sutton
All year

75-95-BB
4 rooms, 4 pb
C-ltd/S-no/P-no/H-no
Dutch, German

Full breakfast
Complimentary wine, snacks
Sitting room, Jacuzzis, fireplaces, cable TV

Elegant, modernized 1905 residence, all bedrooms en-suite with phone, TV, VCR; large dining and sitting rooms. bbed@soonet.ca http://www.bbcanada.com/1218.html

At Daybreak, Mitchell, ON

SAULT STE. MARIE

Eastbourne Manor	60-66-BB	Full breakfast
1048 Queen St E P6A 2C7	3 rooms, 3 pb	Afternoon tea
705-942-3648 888-431-5469	S-no/P-no/H-no	Fireplaces, cable TV
Linda & Richard Smith		
All year		

A beautifully restored 1903 Edwardian Heritage Home will welcome you to reside in a little piece of Ontario's history.

eastbournemanor@yahoo.com http://www3.sympatico.ca/eastbourne

STRATFORD

Avon & John	60-66-BB	Full English breakfast
72 Avon St N5A 5N4	3 rooms, 3 pb	Sitting room, library,
519-275-2954 Fax: 519-275-2956	Visa, MC, •	Jacuzzis, fireplaces, cable
877-275-2954	C-ltd/S-no/P-no/H-no	TV, accom. bus. travelers
Lenora & Ray Hopkins	Dutch, French, German	
All year		

A warm welcome awaits you at our beautiful Edwardian home and gorgeous garden. All rooms have central air, fridges, coffee makers and robes.

avonjohn@cyg.net http://www.cyg.net/~avonjohn

Woods Villa	110-160-BB	Full breakfast
62 John St N N5A 6K7	6 rooms, 6 pb	Sitting room, library,
519-271-4576	Visa, MC, *Rated*	swimming pool, fireplaces,
Ken Vinen	S-no/P-no/H-no	cable TV
All year		

Stratford's finest example of Victorian elegance, surrounded by an acre of private grounds. Memorable breakfasts. kvinen@orc.ca http://www.woodsvilla.orc.ca

STRATFORD (REGION)

At Daybreak	60-BB	Full breakfast
PO Box 1176	3 rooms, 3 pb	Dinner, afternoon tea, snacks
168 Ontario Road, *Mitchell*	Visa, MC, AmEx	Sitting room, bicycles,
N0K 1N0	C-ltd/S-ltd/P-ltd/H-no	swimming pool, fireplaces,
519-348-4884		indoor hot tub, cable TV
Dawn & Dale Lawrance-Turton		
All year		

A stately 1884 Victorian retreat with private baths, hot tub, pool, fireplace. Great breakfast, evening snacks, guest beverage area.

atdaybreak@ezlink.on.ca http://www.ezlink.on.ca/~atdaybreak

STRATFORD (REGION)

Waterlot Restaurant & Inn
PO Box 1077
17 Huron St, *New Hamburg*
N0B 2G0
519-662-2020 Fax: 519-662-2114
Gordon & Leslie Elkeer
All year

80-120-BB
3 rooms, 1 pb
Visa, MC, AmEx
S-no/P-no/H-no

Continental breakfast
Lunch & dinner available, bar
Gourmet shop sitting room

Just the place for a romantic gourmet. Quiet riverside escape. One of Ontario's finest dining establishments. waterlot@waterlot.com http://www.waterlot.com

TORONTO

213 Carlton, The Toronto Townhouse
213 Carlton St M5A 2K9
416-323-8898 877-500-0466
Frank & Tan
All year

63-109-BB
8 rooms, 3 pb
Visa, MC, AmEx
C-ltd/S-no/P-no/H-no

Continental plus breakfast
Central Air. Phones,fridges,& TV in some rooms. FREE parking.

1999 AND 2000 Toronto Tourism Award Winners sponsored by Diner's Club Int'l! Luxury suites and large rooms at affordable prices in the heart of downtown Toronto!
houseboy@toronto-townhouse.com http://www.toronto-townhouse.com

---

Alcina's
16 Alcina Ave M6G 2E8
416-656-6400
Jennie Coxe
All year

85-120-BB
3 rooms, 3 pb
C-ltd/S-ltd/P-no/H-no

Continental plus breakfast
Sitting room, quiet English garden, parking

Central, gracious, old Victorian house with "good bones." Enjoy the casual elegance of old oak stained glass, soft furnishings, and a quiet, English garden.
alcinas@idirect.com http://www.alcinasbb.com

Annex Guest House
241 Lippincott St M5S 2P4
416-588-0560
Karyn Hoffmitz
All year

160-BB
4 rooms, 1 pb
Visa, MC
C-ltd/S-no/P-no/H-no

Continental breakfast
Afternoon tea
Sitting room, library, suites, fireplaces

A comfortable Victorian home located in the heart of Downtown Toronto. A wonderful old neighborhood, the Annex is within walking distance of all major attractions in the city.
annexguesthouse@canada.com http://www.annexguesthouse.com

B&B My Guest
17 Gledhill Ave M4C 5K7
416-422-3663 Fax: 416-422-0465
Teri McIver
All year

60-BB
3 rooms, 1 pb
Visa, MC, AmEx, •
C-yes/S-no/P-ltd/H-no

Continental breakfast
And continental plus breakfasts
Sitting room, fireplaces, cable TV, accommodate business travelers

Your Toronto home away from home. Cozy Victorian house located next to Toronto's beaches. Greektown. Easy access to downtown by public transit system.
bmyguest@interlog.com http://www.bbmyguest.com

Lowtherhouse
72 Lowther Ave M5R 1C8
416-323-1589 800-265-4158
Linda & Jay Lilge
All year

55-110-BB
8 rooms, 8 pb
Visa, MC, AmEx, •
C-ltd/S-no/P-no/H-no
French

Full breakfast
Sitting area, cable TV, central air, accommodate business travelers, suites

Elegantly restored Victorian mansion in the quiet Annex neighborhood. We are within walking distance to the heart of Toronto's cultural, restaurant, shopping and entertainment districts. linda@lowtherhouse.ca http://www.lowtherhouse.ca

B&B My Guest, Toronto, ON

TORONTO

Marlay House 305 Saint George St M5R 2R2 416-921-1899 Melaine Smith All year	65-75-BB 4 rooms, 2 pb • C-ltd/S-no/P-no/H-no French	Continental plus breakfast Accommodate business travelers

Downtown retreat, close to everything. Walk to university, museums, fine restaurants, shopping and Yorkville galleries. 5 miles to subway.

saint.george@sympatico.ca http://www.bbcanada.com/1157.html

The Red Door 301 Indian Rd M6R 2X7 416-604-0544 Jean & Paul Pedersen All year	115-135-BB CAN$ 3 rooms, 3 pb Visa, MC, *Rated* C-ltd/S-no/P-no/H-no	Full breakfast Sitting room, library, suites, fireplaces, TV, AC

Spacious luxury accommodation on a quiet, tree-lined residential street close to High Park and minutes from downtown Toronto by Subway.

reddoor@idirect.com http://webhome.idirect.com/~reddoor/

Robin's Nest 13 Binscarth Rd M4W 1Y2 416-926-9464 Fax: 416-926-3730 877-441-4443 Robin Wilson All year	65-150-BB 3 rooms, 3 pb Visa, MC, *Rated*, • C-no/S-no/P-no/H-no	Full breakfast

An 1892 heritage home at a downtown location. Combine the elegance of a five-star hotel with the ambience of a English country home, and you have the Robin's Nest, one of Canada's finest B&Bs.

info@robinsnestbandbtoronto.com http://www.robinsnestbandbtoronto.com

The Red Door, Toronto, ON

ZEPHYR

High Fields Country Inn
11570 Concession 3 RR#1 L0E 1T0
905-473-6132 Fax: 905-473-1044
1-888-809-9992
Norma Daniel All year

170-370-BB CAN$
8 rooms, 8 pb
Visa, MC, AmEx, *Rated*, •
C-no/S-no/P-ltd/H-no
French, German

Continental plus breakfast
Full meal plans available
Outdoor pool, tennis court, 225 acres trails, sauna, gym

A unique blend of spa therapies, nature trails and warm hospitality make High Fields one of the most inviting retreats in Ontario.

highfields@ca.inter.net http://www.highfields.com

Prince Edward Island

CHARLOTTETOWN

Heritage Harbour House Inn
9 Grafton St C1A 1K3
902-892-6633 Fax: 902-892-8420
1-800-405-0066
Arie & Jinny van der Gaag
All year

55-120-BB
16 rooms, 16 pb
Visa, MC, AmEx, *Rated*, •
C-yes/S-no/P-no/H-yes
Spanish, Japanese

Full breakfast with all home baking

The elegance and character of a stately old family dwelling, with new rooms added.

hhhouse@attglobal.net http://www.peisland.com/heritagehouse

GEORGETOWN

The Georgetown Inn
PO Box 192
62 Richmond St C0A 1L0
902-652-2511 Fax: 902-652-2544
877-641-2414
Joan & Ken Taylor

53-79-BB
8 rooms, 8 pb
Visa, MC, AmEx, *Rated*, •
C-ltd/S-no/P-no/H-ltd
May through Oct.

Full breakfast
Dinner by request, complimentary wine.
Sitting room, cable TV, accommodate business travelers. Internet and email

1840's heritage home, totally remodeled, one block from historic Georgetown Harbour. Warm hospitality, excellent breakfasts.

gtowninn@isn.net http://www.georgetowninn.org

RUSTICO

Barachois Inn
Hunter River RR#3
2193 Church Rd C0A 1N0
902-963-2194 Fax: 902-963-2906
Judy & Gary MacDonald
All year

145-250-BB CAN$
8 rooms, 8 pb
Visa, MC, AmEx,
Rated, •
C-yes/S-no/P-no/H-yes
English, French

Full breakfast
Complimentary tea or coffee
Sitting rooms, grand piano, library, exercise room, sauna, meeting room

1880 Victorian house with verandah offering views of Rustico Bay, Victorian gardens and countryside. Antiques and art with extensive amenities. Walk to seashore.
sleep@barachoisinn.com http://www.barachoisinn.com

Quebec

AUCUNE (REGION)

Auberge Les Sources
8 Rue des Pins, *Pointe-au-Pic*
G0T 1M0
418-665-6952 Fax: 418-665-3802
Evelyne & Andre Litzelmann
All year

54-80-MAP
20 rooms, 20 pb
Visa, MC, *Rated*
C-yes/S-ltd/P-ltd/H-ltd
French, German, Italian, Spanish

Full breakfast
Lunch & dinner avail., restaurant
Sitting room, library, tennis court, fireplaces

Turn-of-the-century Canadian cedar-shingled residence. Close to St. Laurant River surrounded by an immense park bordered by hundred year old cedars.
info@aubergelessources.com http://www.aubergelessources.com

AYER'S CLIFF

Auberge Ripplecove
PO Box 246
700 Ripplecove Rd J0B 1C0
819-838-4296 Fax: 819-838-5541
800-668-4296
Jeffrey & Debra Stafford

160-350-BB
25 rooms, 25 pb
Rated, •
All year

Full breakfast
Dinner, breakfast and service included

On a peninsula overlooking the sparkling waters of Lake Massawippi in Quebec's Eastern Townships, the Ripplecove Inn shines like the rarest of gems.
info@ripplecove.com http://www.ripplecove.com

GEORGEVILLE

Auberge Georgeville 1889
71 Chemin Channel J0B 1T0
819-843-8683 Fax: 819-843-5045
888-843-8686
S. Beyrouty & M. Seline
All year

145-220-MAP
13 rooms, 8 pb
Visa, MC, AmEx,
Rated, •
C-ltd/S-ltd/P-no/H-no
French

Full gourmet breakfast
Dinner, afternoon tea
Restaurant, bar service, sitting room, library, bikes, walk to lake

Quebec's oldest historic inn with Laura Ashley & Waverly elegance on Lake Memphremagog. Multiple award-winning dining, wine cellar, bikes, golf, skiing & more. 20 min. north of I-91. Luxurious suite. aubgeorg@abacom.com http://www.aubergegeorgeville.com

LAURENTIANS (REGION)

Le Provincialat
2292 Rue Sacre-Coeur, *Lac Nominingue* J0W 1R0
819-278-4928 Fax: 819-278-4928
877-278-4928
Pierre Seers & Guillaume Petit
All year

50-60-BB
5 rooms, 2 pb
Visa, MC, *Rated*, •
C-ltd/S-no/P-no/H-no
French

Full breakfast
Dinner available on reservation
Sitting room, fireplace

Historical B smoke free, home cooking with the vegetables from our garden to your table; peace and quiet guaranteed. provincialat@qc.aira.com http://www.provincialat.com

Auberge Georgeville, 1889, Georgeville, QC

MONT TREMBLANT

Crystal-Inn
CP 4424
101 Joseph Thibault J8E 1A1
(819) 681-7775
Mario & Andrea
All year

70-90-BB
3 rooms, 2 pb
•
C-ltd/S-no/P-no/H-no
French, Italian, Spanish

Vegeterian or Vegan on demand
Tea; snacks
Sitting room, library, music corner, spa, hot tub

Mont-Tremblant is waiting for you! Come and discover all the various winter and summer activities! "YOUR STAY IS OUR GEM STONE!"
crystalinn@sympatico.ca http://www.crystal-inn.com

MONTREAL

Alacoque B&B Revolution
2091 St Urban St H2X 2N1
514-842-0938
Fax: 514-842-7585
Christian Alacoque
All year

40-100-BB
6 rooms, 2 pb
Visa, MC, AmEx, •
C-yes/S-yes/P-ltd/H-no
French

Full breakfast
Sitting room, library

An authentic 1830 townhouse finely furnished.
info@bbrevolution.com http://www.bbrevolution.com

Angelica Blue
1213 Sainte Elisabeth H2X 3C3
514-844-5048
Fax: 450-448-2114
800-878-5048
Linda Michelle Hornby
All year

53-93-BB
7 rooms, 5 pb
Visa, MC, *Rated*
C-yes/S-no/P-no/H-no
French

Full breakfast
Sitting room, bicycles, Jacuzzis, suites, cable TV

Splendid Victorian row house, late 1800s, wonderful charm.
info@angelicablue.com http://www.angelicablue.com

MONTREAL

Armor Manoir Sherbrooke 157 Sherbrooke E St H2X 1C7 514-285-0895 Fax: 514-284-1126 800-203-5485 Annick Legall All year	89-119-BB 15 rooms, 7 pb • C-yes/S-yes/P-no/H-no French	Continental breakfast Complimentary coffee 3 rooms with whirlpool, Jacuzzis, lake swimming, bicycles

Once a fine Victorian townhouse in downtown Montreal. Fine woodwork in foyer and some guest rooms. manoirsherbrooke@videotron.ca http://armormanoir.com

Auberge De La Fontaine 1301 Rachel East St H2J 2K1 514-597-0166 Fax: 514-597-0496 800-597-0597 Jean Lamothe All year	84-180-BB 21 rooms, 21 pb Visa, MC, AmEx, *Rated*, • C-yes/S-yes/P-no/H-yes French	Continental plus buffet Afternoon tea Some whirlpools; suite with view of park; private, terrace with whirlpool

Facing a magnificent park and ideally located in the heart of the Plateau Mont-Royal district. Our delightful, well-appointed rooms and suites will charm you.
info@aubergedelafontaine.com http://www.aubergedelafontaine.com

Auberge de la Place Royale 115 de la Commune West H2Y 2C7 514-287-0522 Fax: 514-287-1209 J. Aravantinos & F. Tsatoumas All year	99-225-BB 12 rooms, 12 pb Visa, MC, AmEx, *Rated* C-ltd/S-no/P-no/H-no English, French, Greek	Full breakfast Babysitting, fax & photocopy, laundry service, concierge

L'Auberge de la Place Royale is a charming small hotel, located in the heart of the picturesque Old Port of Montreal.
info@aubergeplaceroyale.com http://www.aubergeplaceroyale.com

Auberge Le Pomerol 819 rue de Maisonneuve E H2L 1Y7 514-526-5511 Fax: 514-523-0143 800-361-6896 Mario Landry All year	120-160-BB CAN$ 28 rooms, 28 pb Visa, MC, AmEx, *Rated*, • C-no/S-yes/P-no/H-no French, Spanish	Continental breakfast Wine Parking, elevator, fitness center, computer, Internet, meeting rooms

Century-old house with ultra-contemporary style located in the heart of the city.
info@aubergelepomerol.com http://www.aubergelepomerol.com

Aux Chambres au Village 850 de la Gauchetiere E H2L 2N2 514-844-6941 Bruno-Serge Boucher All year	45-55-BB 2 rooms *Rated*, • C-no/S-no/P-ltd/H-no French	Continental breakfast Air Cond, Fireplace, Kitchen, Internet access, parking

Looking for a quiet, homey and small B&B a block away from Montreal's action? Well, you've just found it! Bruno, your host, and the two cutest cats in town, Voltaire and Bouboulle, welcome you!
info@chambresauvillage.com http://www.chambresauvillage.com

MONTREAL (REGION)

La Maison Ducharme 10 de Richelieu, *Chambly* J3L 2B9 450-447-1220 Fax: 450-447-1018 888-387-1220 Danielle Deland & Edovard Bonaldo	78-100-BB 4 rooms, 4 pb Visa, MC, *Rated*, • C-ltd/S-ltd/P-no/H-no French May–November	Full breakfast Sitting room, bikes, tennis, pool, fireplaces, cable, accom. bus. trvl.

This old Fort Chambly officer's residence, transformed into a luxurious manor, offers exceptional comfort and a panoramic view on the Richelieu River rapids and the Chambly Basin. Precious antiques.
maisonducharme@videotron.ca http://www.maisonducharme.ca

MONTREAL (REGION)

Bagnell Hall Manor
1965 Grimshaw Rd, *Franklin*
J0S 1E0
450-827-2415
Fax: 450-827-2415
All year

45-BB
13 rooms, 1 pb
C-ltd/S-no/P-no/H-ltd
French
Mary Ann Ferko

Full breakfast
Dinner available, snacks
Sitting room, bicyles, Jacuzzis, swimming pool, accom. bus. travelers

Large, spacious country manor, beautifully decorated, located in picturesque, rural setting in southwest Quebec. Perfect getaway for peace and quiet!
bagnell-hall.manor@sympatico.ca

Gite Maison Jacques
4444 Paiement St, *Pierrefonds*
H9H 2S7
514-696-2450
Fax: 514-696-2564
Micheline & Fernand Jacques
March 1st to Dec. 1st

69-78-BB CAN$
3 rooms, 3 pb
Visa, MC, AmEx, *Rated*, •
C-yes/S-no/P-no/H-no
French

Full breakfast, home prepared
Compl. tea, coffee, juice
Sitting room, piano, fireplace, public transit nearby, parking on grounds

Perfect location for your arrival in Canada; near Dorval Airport, just minutes from attractions and historical sites. Stay with a Canadian couple, in a quiet suburb, with all the comforts of home. gite.maison.jacques@qc.aira.com http://www.maisonjacques.qc.ca

---

Auberge Des Gallant
1171 Chemin St-Henri, *Ste. Marthe Rigaud* J0P 1W0
450-459-4241 Fax: 450-459-4667
800-641-4241
Linda & Gerry Gallant
All year

175-250-MAP
25 rooms, 25 pb
Visa, MC, AmEx, Most CC, *Rated*, •
C-yes/S-ltd/P-ltd/H-yes
French

Full breakfast
Lunch, dinner, tea, snacks, restaurant, bar
Sitting room, library, bicycles, Jacuzzis, swimming pool, fireplace

In the heart of a deer and bird sanctuary, enjoy warm hospitality, luxurious rooms, fine dining and great wines! gallant@rocler.qc.ca http://www.gallant.qc.ca

NEW CARLISLE

Bay View Manor
PO Box 21
395-337 Rte 132 Bonaventure E
G0C 1Z0
418-752-2725 418-752-6718
Helen Sawyer

40-BB
5 rooms, 2 pb
Rated
C-yes/S-no/P-no
French
May–November

Full farm-fresh breakfast

Comfortable seaside country home, yet on the main highway of the ruggedly beautiful Gaspe Peninsula of Eastern Coastal Quebec.

NORTH BAY (REGION)

Hotel Miwapanee Lodge
1100 Miwapanee Rd, *Kipawa*
J0Z 2H0
819-627-3773
Fax: 819-627-1838
800-461-9076
Suzanne & James Mullin

75-110-BB
6 rooms, 6 pb
MC, AmEx, *Rated*
C-yes/S-ltd/P-no/H-no
All year

Breakfast available (fee)
Lunch and dinner available (fee)
Restaurant, bar service, sitting room, suites, fireplaces, hot tub, lake

Hotel Miwapanee Lodge awaits you on the shores of beautiful Lake Kipawa, Quebec.
james@miwapanee.com http://www.efni.com/~miw

OTTAWA (REGION)

Spruceholme Inn
204 Rue Principale, *Fort Coulonge* J0X 1R0
819-683-5635 Fax: 519-683-2139
888-263-1575
Marlene & Glenn Scullion

62-84-BB
6 rooms, 6 pb
Visa, MC, AmEx
C-ltd/S-ltd/P-no/H-no
French
All year

Continental plus breakfast
Dinner, restaurant, bar service
Sitting room, library, suites, cable TV, accom. bus. travelers

Historic Victorian inn, built in 1875, furnished with all the home's original antiques. The inn offers luxurious accommodations, personalized service and comfortable, but elegant atmosphere. spruceholme@renc.igs.net http://www.renc.igs.net/~spruceholme/

OTTAWA (REGION)

Pension Wunderbar Hotel PO Box 272 911 Chenin Riverside Rd, *Wakefield* J0X 3G0 819-459-2471 Margaret Kuen All year	35-52-EP 6 rooms, 6 pb Visa, MC, AmEx, *Rated*, • C-yes/S-yes/P-no/H-no French, Dutch, German	Bar, Fully equipped kitchens Suites, fireplaces, VCR & TV

Authentic Austrian inn nestled in Gatineau Hills, near skiing and other sports, 32 km from Ottawa. Romantic apartments with kitchens, wood-burning fireplaces.
http://www.bbcanada.com/491.html

PIKE RIVER

Auberge–Inn La Suisse 119, Route 133 J0J 1P0 450-244-5870 Fax: 450-244-5181 Roger Baertschi Closed 2 weeks in Jan.	75-85-BB 4 rooms, 4 pb Visa, MC, AmEx, *Rated* C-ltd/S-no/P-no/H-no French, Swiss, German	Continental Plus Lunch & dinner available Sitting room, A/C, nature path, TV, hair dryers

Small country inn, 45 minutes south of Montreal. We are a Swiss family who have been here over 30 years.
reservations@aubergelasuisse.com http://www.aubergelasuisse.com

POINTE-AU-PIC

Auberge La Chatelaine 830 chemin des Falaises G0T 1M0 418-665-4064 Fax: 418-665-4623 888-540-4064 Tom & Louise All year	79-130 Visa, MC, *Rated* S-ltd French	Generous buffet style breakfast Free bike use, parking

Located on a hillside, away from the road, surrounded by two and one half acres of land, this summer villa, filled with antiques, dates back to 1892.
lachatelaine@cite.net http://www.quebecweb.com/lachatelaine

QUEBEC CITY

Au Petit Chateau 664 St Joseph St G6V 1J4 418-833-2798 Fax: 418-833-5439 Helene & Richard Daignault All year	60-120-BB 4 rooms, 2 pb Visa, MC, AmEx, • C-yes/S-no/P-no/H-no French, Spanish, Portuguese	Continental plus breakfast Au Petit Chateau offers a full gourmet breakfast Air conditioning, hair dryer, radio-alarm clock, toiletries, and more

Au Petit Chateau is a 1914 Victorian, mansion-like, three-story Scottish-brick house located on a 25,000 square foot property overlooking the St-Lawrence River!
AUCHA55070@aol.com http://www.travelguides.com/home/Au_Petit_Chateau/

Battlefield 820 Eymard Ave G1S 4A1 418-681-6804 Fax: 418-681-7093 Dolores Dumais All year	60-BB 3 rooms *Rated* C-yes/S-no/P-no/H-ltd French, Spanish	Full breakfast Restaurant, lunch, dinner, snacks Sitting room, pool, bikes, tennis courts, Internet facilities

Inn is located in a residential area between Laval University and historic Quebec City.
dodoy@videotron.ca http://www.travelguides.com/home/battlefield

Au Gre du Vent 2 Fraser St, *Levis* G6V 3R5 418-838-9020 Fax: 418-838-9074 866-838-9070 Michelle & John All year	95-110-BB 5 rooms, 5 pb Visa, MC, *Rated* C-yes/S-no/P-ltd/H-no French	Breakfast prepared w/local products Full breakfast, healthy breakfast, fresh products Sitting room, pool & patio, bicycles storage facilities

Highest Quebec Province classification "5 Suns." Only 5 minutes from Hwy 20 and within walking distance to the ferry leading to the heart of Old Quebec City (crossing time: 10 minutes). augreduvent@msn.com http://www.bbcanada.com/augreduventbb

QUEBEC CITY (REGION)

La Dauphinelle
216 Ch. du Bout de l'Ile, *St. Petronille* G0A 4C0
418-828-1487 Fax: 418-828-1488
Denise Drapeau All year

110-BB CAN$
3 rooms, 3 pb
Visa, *Rated*
C-ltd/S-no/P-no/H-no
French

Full breakfast
Living room with marble fireplace Sunroom

15 minutes from Old Quebec. Nestled on Ile d'Orleans, in the heart of the historical district, La Dauphinelle invites you to come and enjoy quietness and rest in this enchanting Victorian villa. dauphine@ca.inter.net http://www.quebecweb.com/ladauphinelle

SAINT-JEAN-PORT-JOLI

La Maison aux Lilas
315 de GaspT ouest G0R 3G0
418-598-6844
Normand Brisebois All year

BB

St-Jean-Port-Joli est situé à une heure de Québec, au coeur de la Côte-du-sud, à la porte du Bas-St-Laurent sur la route de la Gaspésie . . . avec une vue splendide sur Charlevoix
bblilas@globetrotter.net http://www.cam.org/~bblilas/

ST. DONAT

Archambault Inn
221 Aubin St J0T 2C0
819-424-3542 Fax: 819-424-3542
888-745-0606
F. Vailhen and M. Bleuze
All year

30-70-BB
12 rooms, 6 pb
Visa, MC, *Rated*
C-yes/S-ltd/P-ltd/H-no
French

Full breakfast
Lunch, dinner, afternoon tea, snacks, restaurant
Sitting rm, library, bikes, Jacuzzis, swimming pool, suites, fireplaces, TV

Charming inn, lovely decorating, located in the wonderful Laurentians, in center of the village. Bike, snowmobile, and quad trails, only minutes from the gorgeous Lake Archambault. info@auberge-archambault.com http://www.auberge-archambault.com

ST. JEAN ILE D'ORLEANS

B&B au Giron de l'Isle
120 Chemin des Lieges G0A 3W0
418-829-0985 Fax: 418-829-1059
888-280-6636
Lucie & Gerard Lambert
All year

55-75-BB
4 rooms, 4 pb
Visa, MC, AmEx, *Rated*, •
C-ltd/S-no/P-no/H-no
French

Full breakfast
Afternoon tea
Bikes, suites, fireplaces, cable TV

B&B rated 5 "STARS" by Tourisme Quebec and Laureate of Quebec Tourism Grand Prize for 2001 and 2002.Located 25 minutes from the Old Quebec, you will appreciate the calm and beauty of our island. giron@total.net http://www.total.net/~giron

ST. PETRONILLE

Auberge La Goeliche
22 Chemin du Quai G0A 4C0
418-828-2248
Fax: 418-828-2745
888-511-2248
Andree Marchand All year

120-BB
18 rooms, 16 pb
Visa, MC, AmEx, *Rated*
C-yes/S-yes/P-no/H-yes
French, Spanish

Full breakfast
French cuisine
Sitting room, art shop, outdoor swimming pool, bar service

Overhanging the St. Lawrence River, this castle-like inn offers a breathtaking view of Quebec City, a 15-minute drive away.
infos@goeliche.ca http://www.goeliche.ca

STE. ADELE

Auberge Beaux Reves & Spa
2310 Blvd. Ste. Adele J8B 2N5
450-229-9226
Fax: 450-229-2999
800-279-7679
Hannes Lamothe All year

59-66-BB
7 rooms, 7 pb
Visa, MC, *Rated*, •
C-ltd/S-no/P-no/H-no
french

Full breakfast
lunches, diners, fondue
hot tub, sauna, massages, body care

Country Inn offering a unique outdoor Spa concept open year round. Hot tub, sauna, massages, body care and multi-activity packages.
welcome@beauxreves.com http://www.beauxreves.com

Saskatchewan

SASKATOON

Sunshine Inn 711 5th Avenue North S7K 2R1 306-651-1283 Fax: 306-651-1283 Joy Rousay All year	55-75-BB CAN$ 2 rooms, 2 pb Visa, MC, AmEx, *Rated*, • C-ltd/S-no/P-ltd/H-no	Full heart-healthy breakfast Desks, mini-fridges, private baths; close to downtown and major attractions

Revel in the convenient location of the Sunshine Inn—close to downtown and major attractions. Our serene, non-smoking, adult environment will prove to be a refreshing and memorable experience.

sunshineinn711@yahoo.ca http://www.sunshineinnbb.info

Yukon Territory

WHITEHORSE

Hawkins House 303 Hawkins St Y1A 1X5 867-668-7638 Fax: 867-668-7632 Carla Pitzel All year	70-120-BB 5 rooms, 5 pb Most CC, *Rated* C-ltd/S-no/P-no/H-no French, German	Full breakfast Complimentary fruit baskets, juice/coffee/tea Sitting room, free laundry facilities, private phone lines, fax, fridges

Lavish, spacious and bright best describe our new Victorian home in downtown Whitehorse. Experience one of our five Yukon theme rooms in our 5-star B&B.

cpitzel@internorth.com http://www.hawkinshouse.yk.ca

Midnight Sun 6188 6th Avenue Y1A 1N8 867-667-2255 Fax: 867-668-4376 866-284-4448 Fashid & Del All year	60-80-BB 4 rooms, 4 pb Visa, MC, AmEx, Most CC, *Rated*, • C-yes/S-no/P-no/H-no Persian, Hindi	Deluxe breakfast Fresh fruits, Snack, tea, Coffee, Juice, Ice-cream BBQ facilities, laundry facilies, free email/internet access, guest lounge

Yukon's largest and newest Bed & Breakfast in downtown Whitehorse. We are within walking distance to Main Street shopping, restaurants, a mall, visitor information center and most major attractions.

midnightsunyukon@netscape.net http://www.midnightsunbandbyukon.com

Africa

Mali

BAMAKO

Le Diplomat
On the River Niger
223-23-38-53 Fax: 223-23-70-31
Micheline Mescher All year

BB
English, French

A reminder of Mali's exotic side, Le Diplomate's sculpted ceilings, Oriental furniture and rugs take you to the land of the thousand and one nights.
ledip@le-mali.com http://www.le-mali.com/Ledip

South Africa

BLOUBERGSTRAND

Cape Gull Guest House
39 Gull Rd 7441
27-21-554-2262
Fax: 27-21-554-2262
Peter C Chodacki
All year

400 Rands¤-BB
3 rooms, 3 pb
C-ltd/S-ltd/P-no/H-no
English, Afrikaans

Continental breakfast
Tea/coffee

Luxurious sea side guest house in one of the safest finest parts of Cape Town—panoramic ocean and mountain views, safe area, easy access to all attractions, large new rooms, short walk to the beach. gull@netactive.co.za http://www.capetownvacation.com

SOMERSET

Villa Louise
43 Firmount Rd 7130
021-852-1630 Fax: 021-852-1648
Christian-Edmee Voarick
Open all year

500-700 SA ¤-BB
5 rooms, 4 pb
Visa
C-yes/S-yes/P-yes/H-yes
Eng, Ger, It, Fr, Dut, Afrikaan

Full breakfast
Dinner, afternoon tea, snacks, lunc

Very personal and delightfully civilized guesthouse, charming and individual with a mixture of Mediterranean and African style. Full amenities, delicious breakfast, full assistance and airport pick-up villalou@iafrica.com http://www.villalouise.com

Asia

Indonesia

BALI

Nirwana Cottages
Candidasa Beach 80871
62-0363-41136
Fax: 62-0363-41543
Mrs. Handayani W. Flemming
Open all year

35-60 US$-BB
12 rooms, 12 pb
Most CC
C-yes/S-yes/P-no/H-no
Malay, Eng, Germ, Danish

Restaurant
Afternoon tea

Peaceful bungalows A/C and hot water. Right on the ocean, large garden, swimming pool, restaurant serving home cooking style food. nirwanacot@denpasar.wasantara.net.id

Thailand

CHALONG

Hostel at Phuket Island
73/11 W. Chowfah Rd 83130
6676-281-325
Fax: 662-7111986 661-8396857
Nithi
All year

3.50-10.00 US$-BB
32 rooms, 15 pb
•
Visa, MC
C-yes/S-yes/P-no/H-no
Thai, English

Combintion Thai & European breakfast
Coffee, tea, pure drinking water

Member of TYHA, and license by TAT, new building, combination with single, double air-con, fan, and family room. hostthai@ksc.th.com http://www.phukethostel.com

Australia-S. Pacific

Australia

New South Wales

ADELONG

Beaufort Guesthouse
77 Tumut St 2729
+61-02-6946-2273
Fax: +61-02-6946-2553
Mike Matthews
All year

BB
14 rooms, 14 pb
English

Situated in the Heritage listed old gold mining town of Adelong half way between Sydney and Melbourne Beaufort Guesthouse is an ideal place to explore the magnificent Snowy Mountains. beaufort@dragnet.com.au http://www.beaufort-guesthouse.com.au

ARMIDALE

Shannon's End
212 Shannon Rd 2350
61-2-6775-1177
Fax: 61-2-6775-1176
Margaret & Rob Hadfield
All year

99 Australia ¤-BB
2 rooms, 2 pb
C-yes/S-ltd/P-ltd/H-ltd
English

Full breakfast with wide range of option
Fruit, juice, tea, coffee, cookies, choc. fudge

Set on a hilltop only 10 minutes from Armidale, Shannon's End offers peace and tranquility. Stunning views of Mt. Duval and the surrounding countryside are drawn into two tastefully decorated suites.
shannonsend @bluepin.net.au http://home.bluepin.net.au/shannonsend

BALMAIN

Claremont
12 Claremont St 2041
02-9810-8358
Fax: 02-9810-8358
Pauline & Steve
All year

165 Australia ¤-BB
2 rooms, 2 pb
Visa, MC, *Rated*
C-no/S-ltd/P-no/H-no
English

Continental breakfast
Tea and coffee making facilities

Claremont, in the harbourside suburb of Balmain, is a quaint, restored 19th century timber home, located on the peninsular about 3km from the heart of Sydney by bus or ferry.
pauline@insley.bu.aust.com http://www.bu.aust.com/insley/claremont

BERRY

Woodbyne Private Hotel
4 O'Keeffes Ln 2535
61-2-4448-6200
Fax: 61-2-4448-6211
Annette & Jeff Moore
All year

From 253 Australia ¤-BB
7 rooms, 7 pb
•
Visa, MC, AmEx, *Rated*
C-ltd/S-ltd/P-no/H-yes
English

Gourmet breakfast
Tea and coffee, snacks, Cheese plates, wines etc.

Woodbyne is a luxurious small hotel in the heart of the green rolling hills of South Coast NSW.

info@woodbyne.com.au http://www.woodbyne.com.au

BROKE

Green Gables Lodge
558 Milbrodale Rd 2330
02-6579-1258
Fax: 02-6579-1258
Geoff & Helen Sharrock
All year

110-205 Australia ¤-BB
3 rooms, 3 pb
Visa, MC, *Rated*
C-no/S-ltd/P-yes/H-no
English

Full breakfast
Tea, coffee, snacks, fresh fruit, chocolates

Intimate five star bed and breakfast on 43 acres. Large luxurious rooms, ensuites, private balconies overlooking vineyards & olive groves.

greengableslodge@bigpond.com http://www.greengableslodge.com.au

CENTRAL TILBA

Wirrina
Blacksmiths Ln 2546
02-4473-7279 Fax: 02-4473-7279
Jon & Kay Esman-Ewin
All year

105.00 Australia ¤-BB
3 rooms, 2 pb
Most CC, •
C-ltd/S-ltd/P-ltd/H-ltd
English

Full breakfast
Tea, herbteas, coffee, biscuits at all times.

In historic village; high standard comfort, excellent breakfast. Scenic, friendly locals; beaches, close golf course, open garden, bushwalking. Good stop on Sydney/Melbourne route.

goodnite@acr.net.au http://www.naturecoast-tourism.com.au/goodnite

DRUMMOYNE

Eboracum
18A Drummoyne Ave 2047
02-9181-3541
Jeannette & Michael York
All year

120.00 Australia ¤-BB
2 rooms, 1 pb
C-ltd/S-no/P-no/H-no
English

Tea, coffee etc.

Charming waterfrontage home, centrally located for business or pleasure, 5km. from City CBD, handy to transport.

mjyork@bigpond.com http://bedandbreakfastbook.com.au/hosts/eboracum.html

DUNBOGAN

Dunbogan
64 Camden Head Rd 2443
61-2- 6559 6222
Fax: 61-2- 6559 6222
Ann & Nigel Raymond
All year

90 Australia ¤-BB
4 rooms, 4 pb
Most CC, *Rated*
C-ltd/S-ltd/P-no/H-no
English

We aim to make your stay a happy one. You can have adventure or do nothing, just rest.

dunboganbb@tsn.cc http://bedandbreakfastbook.com.au/hosts/dunbogan.html

HUSKISSON

Jervis Bay Guesthouse
1 Beach St 2540
+61-2-4441-7658
Fax: +61-2-4441-7659
B. Rogers All year

130-220 Australia ¤-BB
4 rooms, 4 pb
Most CC, *Rated*, •
C-ltd/S-ltd/P-no/H-no
English, Jap, Fren

Full breakfast
Tea/coffee making facilities

Experience the drama and beauty of world-renowned Jervis Bay from our charming 4½ star luxury guesthouse. Walk on the lovely white-sand beach opposite, and admire the fantastic views from your room.

info@jervisbayguesthouse.com.au http://www.jervisbayguesthouse.com.au/

JASPERS BRUSH

Jaspers Brush
465 Strongs Rd 2368
02-4448-619402-4448-6254
Leonie & Ian Winlaw
All year

BB
2 rooms
English

Jaspers Brush is a non-smoking environment and there are no facilities for young children.

iwinlaw@oz http://www.jaspersbrushbandb.com.au

KEMPSEY

Netherby House
5 Little Rudder St 2440
61-065-631777
Fax: 61-065-631778
Mark Whitehead
Open all year

130 Australia ¤-BB
4 rooms, 4 pb
Most CC, •
C-yes/S-no/P-no/H-no
English

Full breakfast
Dinner available

Half-way Sydney to Brisbane. Restored country mansion, gourmet breakfast, antiques, fascinating collections.

netherby@midcoast.com.au http://www.midcoast.com.au/users/netherby

SCONE

Belltrees Country House
Gundy Road 2337
61-2-6546-1123
Fax: 61-2-6546-1193
Peter & Tina White All year

140-500 Australia ¤-MAP
16 rooms, 12 pb
Visa, MC, AmEx, •
C-yes/S-ltd/P-no/H-yes
English, French

Continental and full breakfast
Lunch, dinner, afternoon tea

Once a family home, now an exclusive rural retreat in Upper Hunter Valley

bookings@belltrees.com http://www.belltrees.com

SYDNEY

Australia Street
146 Australia St 2042
02-9557-0702
Fax: 02-9557-0702
Ian Collie &
Anne Zahalka All year

110 Australian ¤-BB
2 rooms
•
Visa, MC, *Rated*
C-yes/S-ltd/P-ltd/H-no
English

Continental breakfast
Coffee tea and biscuits provided

This large older style two story house in inner city Newtown (Sydney) is very close to shops, cafes, Sydney CBD and airport.

contact@australiastreetbnb.com.au http://www.australiastreetbnb.com.au

---

Bondi Beach Homestay
10 Forest Knoll Ave 2026
+61-2-9300-0800
Fax: +61-2-9300-9991
Barbara and Michael
Fredericks All year

110-140 Australia ¤-BB
3 rooms, 1 pb
•
Visa, MC
C-yes/S-no/P-no/H-ltd
English, German

Full breakfast
Tea, coffee, fruit juice

Stay at Barbara and Michael's Bondi Beach Homestay Bed and Breakfast for comfortable beachside accommodation and friendly hospitality in Sydney. Your home away from home in Sydney.

bondibnb@bigpond.net.au http://www.bondibeachhomestay.com.au

Hotel 59
59 Bayswater Rd 2011
61-2-9360-5900
Fax: 61-2-9360-1828
George Saras All year

88-135 Australia ¤-BB
9 rooms, 9 pb
Visa, MC, *Rated*, •
C-yes/S-ltd/P-no/H-no
English

Full breakfast

A small family owned European style B&B in a quiet tree lined street. Bayswater road is only a short stroll to the harbour, park and yachts of Rushcutters Bay.

hotel59@office.net.au http://www.interspace.net.au/inns/hotel59.html

SYDNEY

Simpsons of Potts Point
8 Challis Ave, Potts Point 2011
61-02-356-2199
Fax: 61-02-356-4476
Keith Wherry All year

165-265 Australia ¤-BB
14 rooms, 14 pb
Visa, MC, *Rated*, •
C-yes/S-ltd/P-ltd/H-yes
English

Continental plus breakfast
Coffee,tea,etc.

SIMPSONS is an intimate 14-room Hotel within 1892 historic mansion, in leafy, tree-lined Potts Point, yet only a 15-minute stroll along the water to Sydney city, the Opera House and other attractions.

hotel@simpsonspottspoint.com.au http://babs.com.au/simpsons/

Victoria Court Sydney
122 Victoria Street 2011
61-2-9357-3200
Fax: 61-2-9357-7606
Barbara & Syd Miller
All year

45-150 US$-BB
20 rooms, 20 pb
Visa, MC, AmEx, •
P-no/H-yes
English

Buffet breakfast

Small Historic Boutique Hotel in charming Victorian terrace house. Quiet location within minutes of the Opera House, Central Business District, Harbour and Beaches. All rooms have bathrooms & A/C.

info@VictoriaCourt.com.au http://www.VictoriaCourt.com.au

TERRIGAL

Terrigal Lagoon
58A Willoughby Rd 2260
02-4384-7393
Fax: 02-4385-9763
Bruce & Roz Fuller
All year

100-160 Australia ¤-BB
3 rooms, 1 pb
Visa, MC, *Rated*, •
C-ltd/S-no/P-no/H-no
English

Full breakfast

Modern, comfortable, private, facilities. Leafy gardens, large pool. Warm, friendly hospitality. Delicious breakfasts. Close to Terrigal beach. An hour from Sydney or the Hunter Valley.

enquiries@terrigalbnb.com.au http://www.terrigalbnb.com.au

WALLENDBEEN VILLAGE

Colleen & Old Sil's Farmhouse
Corang 2588
02-6943-2546
Fax: 02-6943-2573
Greg & Colleen Hines

150 Australia ¤-AP
4 rooms, 4 pb
Visa, MC, •
C-ltd/S-ltd/P-yes/H-yes
English
All year

Full Special Country Breakfast
Your choice of food

Let us show you Country Australia as our personal guests. Easily accessed. We will show you a great time and a good taste of Australia. All aspects of farming & grazing on our doorstep.

colleenhines@bigpond.com http://www.aussiefarmstay.com

Northern Territory

ALICE SPRINGS

Orangewood Alice Springs
PO Box 8871
9 McMinn Street 0871
61-8-89-524-114
Fax: 61-8-89-524-664
Lynne & Ross Peterkin
All year

From 165-220
Australia ¤-BB
4 rooms, 4 pb
•
Visa, MC
C-no/S-no/P-no/H-no
English

Full breakfast
Tea & Coffee. Homemade cake and/or biscuits. Fruit

Orangewood B&B promises quality accommodation and superior service in a comfortable home maintained exclusively for our guests. 4 bedrooms ensuite, guest lounge swimming pool. Quiet, central.

oranges@orangewood-bnb.au.com http://www.orangewood-bnb.au.com

Fern Cottage, Paddington, Queensland

Queensland

CAIRNS

Cairns Luxury
3 Vine Close 4870
+61-7-4033-6747
Fax: +61-7-4033-7232
Margaret Morgan
All year

125-135 Australia ¤-BB
3 rooms, 3 pb
•
C-ltd/S-ltd/P-no/H-no
English

Extensive Breakfast Menu
Tea, Coffee, Cookies, Wine, Snacks

Spacious A/C ensuite rooms with King, Queen and Single beds. Complimentary wine and snacks. Outside patio overlooking pool. Bus service and tour operators pick up close by. Tea and coffee.
margaret@cairnsluxurybandb.com.au http://www.cairnsluxurybandb.com.au

---

Galvin's Edge Hill
61 Walsh St 4870
+61-7-4032-1308
Jesse & Julie Low
All year

100 Australia ¤-BB
2 rooms
English

One of Cairns' finest examples of Queensland style architecture, this grand old Queenslander, built in the 1930s and renovated with tender loving care offers our guests luxury with a difference
jessup@ozemail.com.au http://www.cairns.aust.com/galvins

PADDINGTON

Fern Cottage
89 Fernberg Rd 4064
61-7-3511-6685
Fax: 61-7-3511-6685
Heather Humphrey
All year

90-100 Australia ¤-BB
3 rooms, 3 pb
•
Visa, MC, *Rated*
C-yes/S-no/P-no/H-ltd
English

Continental breakfast
Coffees and Teas

Fern Cottage, a charmingly 1930's Queenslander home in the trendy village of Paddington....A garden oasis in the Mecca of alfresco dining, boutiques, antique shops and art galleries. Indulge! heather@ferncottage.net http://www.ferncottage.net

TOWNSVILLE

The Rocks Guesthouse
20 Cleveland Terrace 4810
617-4771-5700
Fax: 617-4771-5711
Joe Sproats & Jennie Ginger
All Year

99-119 Australia ¤-BB
8 rooms, 4 pb
Visa, MC, AmEx, •
C-yes/S-ltd/P-no/H-yes
English

Tea, coffee, sherries, fully licensed premises

One of Townsville's earliest residences, The Rocks is a well known and loved property in the area which has witnessed the development of Townsville from the beginning.
therocks@therocksguesthouse.com http://therocksguesthouse.com

South Australia

ADELAIDE

Adelaide Old Terraces
26 Blackburn St.
62 High St, Burnside 5000
08-8364-543708-8364-6961
Ann Schioldann

140-160 Australia ¤-BB
MC, Am, Visa, •
C-ltd/S-no/P-no/H-no
Engl, Dani, Ger, Fr
All year

Fresh fruit, cereal, bread/yoghurt/juice
Tea and coffee

Relax in the privacy of an historic cottage for your exclusive use, ideally located in the inner city of Adelaide. stay@adela http://www.adelaideoldterraces.com.au

Tasmania

HOBART

Orana House
20 Lowelly Rd,
Lindisfarne 7015
61-3-6243-0404
Fax: 61-3-6243-9017
Claire & Brian Marshall
All year

95-150 Australia ¤-BB
10 rooms, 10 pb
•
Visa, MC, AmEx, *Rated*
C-ltd/S-no/P-no/H-ltd
English

Full breakfast
Homemade goodies for Afternoon Tea

Superior bed & breakfast accommodation in a beautifully restored Australian home. Close to centre of Hobart, just 6 minutes, yet only 12 minutes from airport. Explore southern Tasmania from Orana. oranahouse@optusnet.com.au http://www.oranahouse.com

LAUNCESTON

Edenholme Grange
14 St. Andrews St 7250
61-3-6334-6666
Fax: 61-3-6334-3106
Paul & Rosemary Harding

140-180 Australia ¤-BB
6 rooms, 6 pb
C-ltd/H-no
English
All year

Full breakfast

Experience past times in this grand, private Victorian mansion. There are uniquely themed rooms, furnished with antiques & some with spa baths. In grounds is a cottage, modern amenities, two bathrooms
edenholme@microtech.com.au http://www.vision.net.au/~webspace/edenholme/

York Mansions
9-11 York St 7250
03-6334-2933
Fax: 03-6334-2870
Ann & John Mitchell
All year

From 190 Australia ¤-BB
5 rooms, 5 pb, •
Visa, MC, AmEx, *Rated*
C-ltd/S-no/P-no/H-ltd
English

A gracious Georgian Mansion offering spacious self contained apartments, each with open fireplace and the luxurious elegance of yesteryear.
mail@yorkmansions.com.au http://www.yorkmansions.com.au

RANELAGH

Matilda's of Ranelagh
44 Louisa St 7109
03-6264-3493
Fax: 03-6264-3491
Pamela & Don Turnbull
All year

130-160 Australia ¤-BB
4 rooms, 4 pb
•
Most CC, *Rated*
C-no/S-no/P-no/H-yes
English

Full breakfast
A/noon tea, or glass of wine with cheese platter.

The house (c.1850), gardens & adjoining hoasts house are National Trust listed. A warm welcome is assured by your hosts and their 5 golden retrievers. This is a country house in the grand style. matilda@trump.net.au http://www.matildasofranelagh.com.au

SORELL

Blue Bell Inn
26 Somerville St 7172
613-6265-2804
Fax: 613-6265-3880
Barry & Marlene Gooding
All year

100-130 Australia ¤-BB
5 rooms, 5 pb
•
Visa, MC, AmEx
C-yes/S-no/P-no/H-ltd
English, Polish

Full breakfast
Dinner, Lunch, wine, tea/coffee

Heritage Inn (est. 1829) 8 min from Hobart Airport. Colonial style ensuite rooms. Restaurant, open fireplaces, local produce presented with Polish influence and featuring local wines. bluebell@trump.net.au http://www.rcat.asn.au/bluebell

Victoria

APOLLO BAY

Claerwen Retreat
480 Tuxion Rd. 3233
61-3-5237-7064
Fax: 61-3-5237-7054
Cornelia Elbrecht & Bill Whittakers
All year

132-297 Australia ¤-BB
8 rooms, 8 pb
•
Most CC, *Rated*
C-yes/S-no/P-no/H-yes
English, German, French

Full breakfast
Afternoon tea

Exclusively situated on top of the highest hill overlooking the Great Ocean Road coastline with panoramic views it provides an elegant retreat within easy reach to the surrounding national parks. cornelia_elbrecht@claerwen.com.au http://www.claerwen.com.au

BALLARAT

Aroma & Tranquility Cottages
115 Winter St 3350
03-5336-1343
Jenny Philippiadis
All year

145.00 Australia ¤-BB
6 rooms, 4 pb
Visa, MC, *Rated*
C-yes
English

Tranquil and luxurious 4-star accommodation awaits your sole private occupancy!!!! Pamper health packages, Gourmet meal options. Heated floors. Log fires. Spa baths. Cable TV. Hot breadmakers. philip@giant.net.au http://www.ballarat.com/aroma.htm

BELLELLEN NEAR HALLS GAP

Bellellen Homestead
PO Box 563
Stawell-Jallukar Road 3380
03-5358-4800
Fax: 03-5358-4800
Phil & Joanne Thomson
All year

150-180 Australia ¤-BB
4 rooms, 4 pb
•
Most CC, *Rated*
C-ltd/S-ltd/P-ltd/H-ltd
English

Full breakfast
Bar, tea & coffee supplied, all meals avail

Multi-award winning 4+ Star Grampians Bed & Breakfast offers luxurious accommodation for a discerning getaway. Captivating views, close to Halls Gap and vineyards. Ensuites, gardens and fine dining.
enquiries@bellellenhomestead.com.au http://www.bellellenhomestead.com.au

HEALESVILLE

The Retreat
PO Box 251, 3777
61-3-5962-4502
Fax: 61-3-5962-6304
Patricia Hill All Year

115 Australia ¤-BB
3 rooms, 2 pb
Visa, MC, *Rated*
S-no/P-ltd/H-ltd
English

Continental plus breakfast

Surrounded by natural bushland and State forest with beautiful 360 degree views, abundant birdlife, wallabies and wombats.
retreat@foxall.com.au http://www.healesvilleretreat.com.au

KALORAMA

Grey Gables
Grange Rd 3766
+61-3-9761-8609
Fax: +61-3-9728-8033
Lorna Boquest All year

195-275 Australia ¤-BB
3 rooms, 3 pb
Most CC, *Rated*
C-no/S-no/P-no/H-no
English

Menu selected, four course breakfast
Afernoon Tea/coffee, cookies, cake on arrival.

An award winning Bed & Breakfast set amid 2 acres of gardens in the beautiful Dandenong Ranges just east of Melbourne. Luxurious facilities are combined with warm, old fashioned hospitality. greygab@corplink.com.au http://www.greygables.com.au

MELBOURNE

Fountain Terrace
28 Mary St, St. Kilda 3182
03-9593-8123 Fax: 03-9593-8696
Heikki & Penny Minkkinen
All year

165-235 Australia ¤-BB
5 rooms, 5 pb
Most CC, *Rated*, •
C-ltd/S-no/P-no/H-ltd
English, Finnish, Germ

Full breakfast
Tea and coffee, glass of wine

The grandeur of New Orleans or elegant small private hotel in Europe Fountain Terrace provides excellent accommodation. Close to all facilities, a perfect place to stay whilst in Melbourne, Australia info@fountainterrace.com.au http://www.fountainterrace.com.au

MOUNT MARTHA

Marlin Cottage
PO Box 160
Wattle Ave 3934
+61-3-5974-4900
Fax: +61-3-5974-1959
Nancy & Richard Hawkins

125-145 Australia ¤
4 rooms
Visa, MC, *Rated*, •
C-yes/S-no/P-no/H-no
English
All year

Continental breakfast
tea/coffee/juice/jams,honey/etc.

One drive from Melbourne Marlin Cottage on the beautiful Mornington Peninsula, a seaside village with safe golden beaches. The guest wing is self contained, a luxury 4 star AAA rating apartment. nancyhawkins@ozemail.com.au http://babs.com.au/marlin/index.html

MURCHISON

Brecon House
55 Stevenson St 3610
61-3-5826-2003
Andrew & Gale Wainwright
All year

90-130 Australia ¤-BB
2 rooms, 2 pb
Visa, MC, *Rated*, •
C-ltd/S-no/P-no/H-no
English

Full breakfast
Tea, coffee, biscuits. Dinner by arrangement.

Undisturbed sleep; Luxurious bedrooms; En-suite bathrooms; Cosy sitting room with log fire; Relaxing armchairs; Abundant breakfast; Colonial era charm. Experience your dreams at Brecon House. brecon@origin.net.au http://www.bedandbrecon.com

PORT FAIRY

Myndarra Shepherds Cottage
RMB 6435 3284
03-5568-9201 Fax: 03-5568-9201
Lyn & Traff Morgan-Payler
All year

110-140 Australia ¤-BB
3 rooms, •
Visa, MC, AmEx, *Rated*
C-yes/S-ltd/P-no/H-ltd
English

Tempt yourself to exclusive enjoyment at our restful shepherd's cottage. Myndarra Shepherd's Cottage is nestled beside a grand historic driveway surrounded by rolling countryside and blue gums myndarra@bigpond.com.au

RICHMOND

Villa Donati
377 Church St
+61-3-9428-8104
Gayle Lamb & Trevor Finlayson All year

140-160 Australia ¤-BB
3 rooms, 3 pb
Most CC, *Rated*, •
C-ltd/S-no/P-no/H-ltd
English

Continental plus breakfast
Tea, coffee, wine.

Villa Donati is an historic Italianate villa, luxuriously appointed with fine bed linen, antiques and fine arts, located minutes from Melbourne's CBD, entertainment, sporting and shopping precincts.
email@villadonati.com http://www.villadonati.com

WILLIAMSTOWN

Heathville House
171 Aitken St 3016
61-03-9397-5959
Fax: 61-03-9397-0030
Stuart Absalom & Philip Mawer All year

120-140 Australia ¤-BB
4 rooms, 3 pb, •
Visa, MC, AmEx, *Rated*
C-yes/S-no/P-no/H-ltd
English

Full breakfast
Tea/coffee, biscuits, other refreshments

Heathville House, circa 1894, where the welcome is warm and friendly, offers the best in the tradition of bed and breakfast accommodation with all the comforts of home.
heath@jeack.com.au http://www.melbournebest.com.au/heathville.html

Western Australia

BUSSELTON

Martin Fields Country Retreat
Lot 25 Lockville Rd. 6280
61-8-9754-2001
Fax: 61-8-9754-2034
Jim & Jane Cummins

100-110 Australia ¤-BB
9 rooms, 7 pb
Visa, •
C-yes/S-yes/P-ltd/H-ltd
English, Chinese
All year

Full breakfast
Dinner (fee)

Well appointed guesthouse with ensuites facilities in all rooms. Enjoy a break at Martin Fields, a comfortable four-star country retreat set on 10 lovely acres overlooking tranquil Geographe Bay. jcummins@iinet.net.au http://www.iinet.net.au/~jcummins

PERTH

Possum Creek Lodge
6 Lenori Rd 6076
61-8-9257-1927
Fax: 61-8-9257-1927
Helen & Leon English
All year

From 125 Australia ¤-BB
3 rooms, 3 pb
Visa, MC
S-ltd/P-no/H-no
English

Generous continental breakfast

High quality fully self-contained suites set in a large garden.
possum@git.com.au http://www.holiday-wa.net/possum.htm

YALLINGUP

Laughing Clown Lodge
Corner Caves & Hemsley Roads 6282
61-8-9755-2341
Fax: 61-8-9755-2339
David & Shameen McPherson
All year

170-265 Australia ¤-BB
13 rooms, 13 pb
•
Most CC, *Rated*
C-no/S-no/P-no/H-no
English

Full brea…
Even…

5 star country retreat, on 10 landscaped … River wine region in Western Austr… A/C. hotel@clownlodge.com…

New Zealand

AKAROA

Kahikatea Country Retreat
Wainui Valley Rd, RD 2
88 Donovans Road, Wainui
03-304-7400
Fax: 03-304-7430
Jane & Joe Yates
All year

325 NZ¤-BB
2 rooms, 2 pb
•
Visa, MC, *Rated*
C-ltd/S-no/P-no/H-yes
Italian, English

Breakfast provisions supplied
Mini bar, free port, chocolates, tea, coffee

Luxurious country retreat overlooking Akaroa Harbour, 1 hour from Christchurch, New Zealand.
unwind@kahikatea.com http://www.kahikatea.com

AUCKLAND

Auckland Omahu House
35 Omahu Rd 1005
64-09-524-9697
Fax: 64-09-524-9997
Shirley & Keith Mossman
All year

165-185 NZ¤-BB
4 rooms, 4 pb
•
Visa, MC
C-ltd/S-ltd/P-no/H-ltd
English

Healthy—Hearty—Gourmet
Tea—coffee—snacks—fruit—wine

Spacious home built in 1928,renovated 1997."Omahu" is Maori for "quiet retreat" referring to the quiet residential setting of this home, with gardens surrounding the pool.
omahu.house@xtra.co.nz http://www.AucklandOmahuHouse.com

Bavaria Hotel
83 Valley Rd, Mt. Eden
0064-9-638-9641
Fax: 0064-9-638-966
Rudi Schmidt & Ulrike Stephan
Open all year

90-135 NZ¤-BB
11 rooms, 11 pb
•
Visa, MC, AmEx
C-yes/S-no/P-no/H-no
English, German, French

Delightful breakfast buffet
Afternoon tea, cookies and coffee

Generous, airy rooms all with private facilities in immaculately restored villa.
bavaria@xtra.co.nz http://www.bavariabandbhotel.co.nz/

Devereux Boutique Hotel
267 Remuera Rd
+64-9-524-5044
Fax: +64-9-524-5080
Peter and Jenni Mony
All year

155-265 NZ¤-BB
12 rooms, 10 pb
•
Visa, MC, AmEx, *Rated*
C-yes/S-no/P-no/H-ltd
Eng, French, Span, Ital, Dut

Full breakfast
Snacks drinks room service dinner by arrangement

Auckland's boutique hotel experience! Immerse yourself in an atmosphere that is delightfully different. A stunning 1890's grand historic villa set in a magical garden in middle earth, New Zealand.
info@devereux.co.nz http://www.devereux.co.nz/

Devonport Sea Cottage
3a Cambridge Terr
09-445-7117
Fax: 09-445-7117
John & Michele

100-150 NZ¤-EP
1 rooms, 1 pb
C-ltd/S-ltd/P-no/H-yes
English

Breakfast optional extra
The cottage has extensive food provisions.

...ivate, beautifully appointed, fully self-contained cottage in Devonport. ...land. Meters from the sea and park. Ask for our various rates,
...staysnz.co.nz/listings/46

AUCKLAND

Discover Superior Inns
PO Box 32130
Fax: 64-9-445-4131
All year

Rates: Inquire-BB
23 rooms, 23 pb
C-ltd/S-no/P-ltd/H-ltd
English

Discover 42 luxury B&B Inns throughout New Zealand all specially selected with attention to detail. admin@superiorinns.co.nz http://www.superiorinns.co.nz

---

Earnscliff
44 Williamson Ave 10
09-445-7557
Fax: 07-445-7602
Jenny & Graeme Dickey
All year

230-265 NZ¤-BB
2 rooms, 2 pb
•
Visa, MC, AmEx, *Rated*
C-ltd/S-no/P-no/H-ltd
English

Full breakfast
Tea coffee biscuits port chocolates wine

Bask in the glory of a bygone era at Earnscliff luxury bed and breakfast Auckland, where the past is brought into the present for your enjoyment.
earnscliff@xtra.co.nz http://www.earnscliff.co.nz

Heerdegen Hillcrest Homestay
89 Stanaway St 1310
09-419-0731
Fax: 09-419-0731
Pat & John Heerdegen
All year

From 100 NZ¤-MAP
2 rooms, 2 pb
•
Visa, MC
C-no/S-ltd/P-no/H-no
English

Continental plus breakfast
Pre-dinner drinks. Wine with dinner

New Zealand is great to visit. Beautiful country, friendly people, John provides airport greeting. Comfortable accommodation, quality cuisine.
pat-john@paradise.net.nz http://www.nzisgreat.co.nz

Mountain View
PO Box 59083
85A Wallace Rd 1730
+64-9-636-6535
Fax: +64-9-636-6126
Jenny & Ian Davis
All year

75-120 NZ¤-BB
6 rooms, 4 pb
•
Visa, MC
C-yes/S-no/P-no/H-ltd
English

Cooked or continental breakfast
Complimentary tea/coffee/hotchocolate

8mins Auckland Airport, quiet locality. NZ born hosts very hospitable. Helpful Auckland & NZ Information and directions available. Less than 25mins to most of Auckland's top tourist venues. mtviewbb@xtra.co.nz

---

Peace & Plenty Inn
6 Flagstaff Terrace
064-944-52925
Fax: 064-944-52901
Judith & Peter Machin
Open all year

200-230 NZ¤
5 rooms, 5 pb
•
Most CC
C-ltd/S-ltd/P-no/H-no
English

Full breakfast
Complimentary wine

Romantic luxury; historic waterfront home. Restaurants, shopping, ferry to city, steps away. Antiques, flowers, elegance, comfort, gourmet breakfasts; personal service.
peaceandplenty@xtra.co.nz http://www.peaceandplenty.co.nz

Sedgwick-Kent Lodge
65 Lucerne Rd
64-9-524-5219
Fax: 64-9-524 5218
Wout & Helma van der Lans
Open all year

190.00 NS¤-BB
5 rooms, 5 pb
•
Visa, MC, AmEx
C-ltd/S-ltd/P-no/H-no
English, French, German, Dutch

Breakfast included
Complimentary wine with dinner

Sited in the premium suburb of Remuera, Sedgwick Kent Lodge is a restored 1910 farmstead. accommodation@sedgwick.co.nz http://sedgwick.co.nz

AUCKLAND

Stafford Villa
PO Box 34361
2 Awanui St 1310
09-418-3022 Fax: 09-419-8197
Chris & Mark Windram
All year

245 NZ¤-BB
3 rooms, 3 pb
Most CC, *Rated*, •
C-yes/S-ltd/P-no/H-no
English

Sumptious Breakfast
Summer Barbecue on request

Stafford Villa is a heritage listed villa, recently restored in elegant classical style the house is set in a quiet street of tropical trees and shrubs, Nine minutes to Auckland city by car or ferry. rest@staffordvilla.co.nz http://www.staffordvilla.co.nz

BLENHEIM

Chardonnay Lodge
1048 Rapaura Rd, RD3
0064-3-570-5194
Fax: 0064-3-570-5196
George & Ellenor Mayo
Open all year

100-130 NZ¤-BB
3 rooms, 3 pb
Visa, MC, •
C-ltd/S-no/P-no/H-ltd
English

Silver and crystal to enhance
Ttea/coffee/snack

Centered in the heart of the Marlborough wine area. Friendly relaxed atmosphere. Self contained villas or homestay. chardonnaylodge@xtra.co.nz

---

Uno Piu
75 Murphys Rd
+64-03-578-2235
Fax: +64-03-578-2235
Gino & Heather Rocco
All year

170-250 NZ¤-BB
5 rooms, 5 pb
Visa, MC, *Rated*, •
C-ltd/S-ltd/P-ltd/H-no
It, Sp, Fren, Serbo-Croat

Pancakes with Maple syrup

Uno Piu offers Luxury Accommodation and dining by arrangement (Italian Cuisine)in an elegant 1917 Homestead. A separate charming Mudblock Cottage is beautifully furnished and set in its own garden. unopiu@xtra.co.nz http://www.geocities.com/unopiu

CHRISTCHURCH

Bangor Country Estate
Bangor Rd
64-03-318-7588
Fax: 64-03-318-8485
Cliff & Biba Baker
All year

800 NZ¤-MAP
6 rooms, 6 pb
Visa, MC, AmEx, •
C-ltd/S-no/P-no/H-yes
English

Full breakfast
Afternoon teas,
coffee/tea/softdrinks comp

Imagine a special place, a quiet & private retreat, discreetly hidden away from the hustle and bustle of the busy world, preserved by nostalgia & reminiscent of an era when style & elegance prevailed sales@bangor.co.nz http://www.bangor.co.nz

---

Windsor Hotel
52 Armagh St 8001
64-3-366-1503 Fax: 64-3-3669796
Carol Healy & Don Evans
All year

75-150 NZ¤-BB
40 rooms, 40 pb
Most CC, •
C-yes/S-no
English

Full breakfast
Complementary tea and coffee

Family owned and operated an inner city residence of "traditional style", providing comfortable and friendly accommodation, ample shared bathroom facilities, bathrobes available on request. reservations@windsorhotel.co.nz http://www.windsorhotel.co.nz

DUNEDIN

Sahara Guest House
619 George St
03-477-6662 Fax: 03-479-2551
Lynette & Bryan Ryder
Open all year

67-95 NZ¤-BB
10 rooms, 2 pb
Most CC, •
C-yes/S-no/P-no/H-yes
English

Full breakfast
Fruit basket

Gabled brick guesthouse was built as a substantial family home in 1906, centrally located; just a short walk to city centre, botanical gardens and museum.
b_ryder@xtra.co.nz http://www.dunedin-accommodation.co.nz

EASTBOURNE

Frinton by the Sea
55 Rona St 6008
04-562-7540
Fax: 04-562-7860
Wendy & Doug Stephenson
All year

100-120 NZ¤-BB
3 rooms, 2 pb
•
Visa, MC, *Rated*
C-ltd/S-no/P-no/H-no
English

Full breakfast
All day—Tea, Fresh Coffee, or Juice

Our warm and comfortable home is nestled into native bush overlooking our glorious Wellingon harbour.

frinton@xtra.co.nz http://www.frintonbythesea.co.nz

GISBORNE

Rangimarie Anaura Bay Beach
930 Anaura Bay Rd
64-21-63-3372
06-868-9940
Judy & David Newell
All year

BB
English

A peaceful haven we are happy to share with others. Our property covers 3½ acres, sweeps down to a beautiful white sand beach and is bordered on one side by a native bush reserve.

anaurastay http://www.bnb.co.nz/rangimarie.html

HOUHORA

Houhora Homestay
Far North Rd
0064-9-409-7884
Fax: 0064-9-4097884
Bruce & Jacqui Malcolm
All year

105.00-125.00 NZ¤-BB
3 rooms, 3 pb
•
Visa, MC
C-yes/S-ltd/P-no/H-ltd
English

Full or continental breakfast
Dinner by arrangement

Welcome to N Z's northernmost luxurious accommodation which is ideally situated to cater for those travelers visiting the Far North of our country.

houhora.homestay@xtra.co.nz http://www.topstay.co.nz

INVERCARGILL

Tudor Park
Ryal Bush, RD 6
03-221-7150
Fax: 03-221-7150
Joyce & John Robins
All year

120-150 NZ¤-BB
3 rooms, 3 pb
•
Visa, MC
C-yes/S-ltd/P-no/H-ltd
English

Continental breakfast
Tea, Coffee, comp. pre dinner drink if dining

Tudor Park is quality accommodation for the discerning traveler. We offer peace, comfort, and privacy wit all rooms having garden views, fresh flowers, cotton sheets and private facilities.

tudorparksouth@hotmail.com http://www.homestays.net.nz/tudorpark.htm

KATIKATI

Cotswold Lodge
183 Ongare Point Rd, RD 1
07-549-2110
Fax: 07-549-2109
Alison and Des Belsham
All year

115-125 NZ¤-BB
3 rooms, 3 pb
Visa, MC
S-no/P-no/H-yes
English

Full breakfast
Afternoon tea on arrival
Dinner by arrangement

A warm kiwi welcome awaits you in our rural home away from home, which looks out over orchards to the Kaimai Ranges. Rooms have ensuite bathrooms and own access to deck or verandah. cotswold@ihug.co.nz http://www.cotswold.co.nz

LAKE TAUPO

Paratiho by the Lake
RD 1, Turangi
Kowhai Dr, Upper Pukawa Bay
2751
64-7-386-6318
Fax: 64-7-386-6418
John & Valda Milner
All year

160-230 NZ¤-BB
•
Visa, MC
C-yes/S-no/P-ltd/H-yes
English

NZ cuisine, home grown vegetables and fruit

Paratiho-by-the-Lake Estate, built 1997, includes a two bedroom self-contained Cottage and a luxury large homestay suite with private panoramic views of lake and mountains surrounded by native bush john_milner@xtra.co.nz http://www.paratihonz.com

OAMARU

Clydehouse Homestay
32 Clyde St
03-437-2774
Fax: 03-437-2774 0800 259 334
Wenda & John Eason
All year

95-120 NZ¤-BB
3 rooms, 2 pb
•
Visa, MC, AmEx
C-yes/S-no/P-no/H-no
English

Fresh Fruit—Homemade Jams/Preserves
Tea & Coffee trays in rooms, Home made biscuits.

Unique private family home, built early 1900s, solid Oamaru limestone walls and a return verandah 5 Min from town and Little Blue Penguin Colony. Quiet area off main Rd. Look for Forth St. eason.clydehouse@xtra.co.nz http://www.clydehouse.co.nz

OTOROHANGA

Kamahi Cottage
229 Barber Rd, RD 5
0064-7-873-0849
Fax: 0064-7-873-0849
Evan & Elisabeth Cowan
All year

200.00 NZ¤-BB
1 rooms, 1 pb
•
Most CC
C-yes/S-no/P-no/H-no
English, Swiss-German

Continental plus breakfast
Tea/coffee & home baking.

Kamahi is a luxury country cottage near the world famous Waitomo caves. Set on the edge of a beautifully landscaped garden it has superb panoramic views and is an ideal private retreat for a couple. kamahi@wave.co.nz http://www.kamahi.co.nz

QUEENSTOWN

The Historic Stone House Inn
47 Hallenstein St
03-442-9812
Fax: 03-441-8293
Jo & Steve Weir
All year

250 NZ¤-BB
4 rooms, 4 pb
•
Visa, MC
C-ltd/S-no/P-no/H-ltd
English

Full breakfast
Tea, coffee, fruit & cookies, port, wine & cheese.

The Stone House provides historic charm with modern comforts. Lake views, fire-side drinks, Baz the cat, and a spa are provided for guests, and central Queenstown is just a few steps away. stone.house@xtra.co.nz http://www.stonehouse.co.nz

---

Trelawn Place
PO Box 117
George Rd, Arthurs Point 9197
64-3-442-9160
Fax: 64-3-442-9160
Nery Howard & Michael Clark
Closed June

180-250 NZ¤-BB
4 rooms, 4 pb
•
Visa, MC
C-yes/S-no/P-no/H-no
English

Full breakfast
Afternoon tea

Beautiful garden setting on river's edge. Spectacular mountain views. King-sized beds and cozy fireplaces. Separate self-contained honeymoon cottage.
trelawn@ihug.co.nz http://www.trelawnb-b.co.nz/

REMUERA

Aachen House Boutique Hotel
39 Market Rd 5
64-9-520-2329
Fax: 64-9-524-2898 0800-222-436
Joan & Greg McKirdy
Open all year

220-420 NZ¤-BB
9 rooms, 9 pb
•
Visa, MC, AmEx
C-no/S-no/P-no/H-yes
English

Full breakfast prepared by in-house chef
Coffee, tea, fruit juice, wineand port.

Acknowledged as Auckland's finest boutique hotel and the favorite of leading travel guides, this splendid Edwardian residence offers superior bed and breakfast accommodation in elegant surroundings.

info@aachenhouse.co.nz http://www.aachenhouse.co.nz

Cotter House Luxury City Stay
4 St. Vincent Ave
64-09-529-5156
Fax: 64-09-529-5186
Gloria Poupard-Walbridge
All year

500-300 NZ¤-BB
4 rooms, 3 pb
•
Visa, MC, AmEx
C-ltd/S-no/P-no/H-no
Eng, Fren, Sp, It, Portu

Gourmet 4-course breakfast/brunch
High Tea & Canapes with drinks from our Wine List

1847 Historic mansion combines luxury with exceptional hospitality. It features richly appointed high-tech guestrooms, a stroll from shops and restaurants in Auckland's most exclusive suburb.

info@cotterhouse.com http://www.cotterhouse.com

RICHMOND

Althorpe
13 Dorset St
03-544-8117
Fax: 03-544-8117
Jenny & Bob Worley
All year

120-140 NZ¤-BB
2 rooms, 2 pb
•
Visa, MC
C-ltd/S-no/P-no/H-no
English

Special gourmet breakfast
Tea/coffee, fruit/biscuits available at all times

Althorpe, built in 1887 has been fully restored for your comfort. Our guest rooms open onto verandahs overlooking our gardens, swimming and spa pool.

stay@althorpe.co.nz http://www.althorpe.co.nz

ROTORUA

Glenloch Fold
857 Poutakataka Rd 3221
64-7-333-1662
Fax: 64-7-333-1662
Kel & Gail McKirdy
All year

95-195 NZ¤-BB
3 rooms, 1 pb
•
C-yes/S-no/H-ltd
English

Continental plus breakfast
Hearty Country Dinner by arrangment.

Bed and Breakfast in the tranquil comfort of a Rotorua Country Home. Rooms have a country outlook onto gardens, rural fields and scenic lake views New Zealand is famous for. Scottish Highland Cattle.

info@glenloch-fold.co.nz http://www.glenloch-fold.co.nz

TAUPO

Beside the Lake
8 Chad St
07-378-5847
Fax: 07-378-5847
Irene & Roger Foote
All year

180.00 NZ¤-BB
2 rooms, 2 pb
•
Visa, MC
C-no/S-no/P-no/H-ltd
English

Breakfast of your choice.
Tea, coffee,snacks.

Our modern home, on the shore of beautiful Lake Taupo, offers two smoke free, luxurious bedrooms with lake views, balcony or terrace, TV,& air con/heating. An elevator serves the upstairs area.

foote.tpo@xtra.co.nz http://www.friars.co.nz/hosts/besidethelake.html

Hurunui Homestead Lodge, Wellington, New Zealand

TIMARU

Tighnafeile House	225-275 NZ¤-BB	Full breakfast
62 Wai-iti Rd	4 rooms, 4 pb	Tea, coffee, snacks, wine etc.
+64-3-684-3333	•	
Fax: +64-3-684-3328	Most CC, *Rated*	
Robin Jenkins	C-ltd/S-no/P-no/H-no	
All year	English	

Tighnafeile (pronounced Tyne-a-faylee) is Gaelic for "House Of Welcome." This 1911 Colonial Home has been restored to create a top class Boutique Lodging.

tighnafeile-house@timaru.co.nz http://www.tighnafeile.com

WELLINGTON

Hurunui Homestead Lodge	130-160 NZ¤-BB	Continental plus breakfast
PO Box 81	3 rooms, 2 pb	Snacks, teas, coffee, hot
15 Hurunui St 6010	•	chocolate, beer, soda
+64-4-902-8571	Visa, MC, *Rated*	
Fax: +64-4-902-8572	C-no/S-ltd/P-no/H-no	
Erica & Geoff Lineham	English	
All year		

Experience luxurious relaxation at this romantic country garden retreat, just 50mins from Wellington city. Secluded gardens with gazebo, heated pool, private spa, tennis and boule. Indulge & Enjoy!

hurunui@lineham.co.nz http://www.hurunui.lineham.co.nz

Killara Homestay	100-120 NZ¤-BB	Continental breakfast
PO Box 48	2 rooms, 2 pb	Tea, coffee, biscuits,
70 Ames St	•	chocolates
00-664-04-905-5544	Visa, MC, AmEx, *Rated*	
Fax: 00-664-04-905-5533	C-no/S-no/P-no/H-no	
Carole & Don Boddie	English	
All year		

Asolute beachfront home. Spacious, well appointed accommodation upstairs. Outstanding seaviews from bedrooms and guest lounge. Walk to local restaurants. Close to transport. 30 minutes to Wellington.

killara@paradise.net.nz http://www.killarahomestay.co.nz

WELLINGTON

Penryn Cove
32 Penryn Drive
04-233-8265
Fax: 04-233-8265
Eleanor & John Clark
All year

120-140 NZ¤-BB
2 rooms, 1 pb
Visa, MC, *Rated*
C-yes/S-no/P-no/H-no
English

Full breakfast
Complimentary wine, tea & coffee & snacks

We extend a warm welcome to our guests. Enjoy the tranquil, peaceful setting of Penryn Cove, surrounded by native bush reserve, set on the edge of a peninsula.

JWClark@xtra.co.nz http://www.travelwise.co.nz/listings/Penryn_Cove.html

---

Tinakori Lodge
182 Tinakori Rd
64-4-9393478
Fax: 64-4-9393475
Mel & John Ainsworth
Open all year

95 NZ¤
9 rooms, 5 pb
•
Most CC
C-ltd/S-no/P-no/H-no
English

Full breakfast
complimentary tea and coffee

Situated in historic Thorndon. Comfortable furnished 1870s house. Short walk to the Government Center and city which features a selection of fine restaurants. TV and phone in rooms.

b&b@tinakorilodge.co.nz http://www.tinakorilodge.co.nz

Caribbean

Antigua / Barbuda

ST JOHNS

Long Bay Resort Inn
PO Box 442
Long Bay #442
268-463-2005
Fax: 268-463-2439
800-291-2005
Christian J. Lafaurie
October 12– June 1

375-460 US$-MAP
26 rooms, 26 pb
•
Visa, MC, AmEx
C-yes/S-yes/P-no/H-no
English

Full breakfast
Lunch, dinner, restaurant, bar service

Small Caribbean resort/inn catering to the individual not the herd. We do not offer A/C, TV, radio, crab races.

longbay@candw.ag http://www.longbayhotel.com

Bahamas

ELEUTHERA

Romora Bay Club
Harbour Island
Colebrooke St
242-333-2325
Fax: 242-333-2500 800-688-0425
Lionel Rotcajg All year

185-320 US$-BB
22 rooms, 22 pb
•
Visa, MC, AmEx
C-yes/S-yes/P-no/H-yes
English, French, Ital, Sp

Continental plus breakfast
Restaurant under world class chef

4-star, 22 rooms resort on 6 acres of lush gardens, located on trendy bay side of Harbour Island Bahamas. Perfect holiday spot for family and couples.

info@romorabay.com http://www.romorabay.com

Belize

SAN PEDRO

Sundiver Beach Resort
4.5 miles North San Pedro
501-226-4265
Fax: 501-226-4293 877-297-8904
Tazmara Gowans & Kathryn Scott All year

85-350 US$-BB
12 rooms, 12 pb
•
Visa, MC
C-yes/S-yes/P-yes/H-no
English

Continental breakfast
Full Lunch Menu and Dinner Menu

Discover a resort on the Island of Ambergris Caye with crystal waters and white sand beaches to your doorstep. Relax by the pool or in one of our 12 air-conditioned rooms, or rent a beach house. sundiver@btl.net http://www.sundiverbeachresort.com

Cuba

HAVANA

Casa Grande
Ave 26 #1002 esq 32
Nuevo Vedado / Plaza
53-7-810101
Gisela Martinez All year

45-55 US$-BB
1 rooms, 1 pb
C-ltd/S-yes/P-no/H-ltd
Spanish, English, Italian

Full breakfast

Welcome to Casa Grande! Our spacious and elegant home is located in a choice residential neighborhood just 15 minutes by car from the main tourist attractions and nightspots in Havana. gisela@foxhiker.cjb.net http://home.sprintmail.com/~mariasanchez

Jamaica

FALMOUTH

FDR Pebbles
PO Box 1933
Main Street
876-617-2500
Fax: 816-617-2512 888-654-1337

217-360 US$-AP
96 rooms, 96 pb, •
C-yes/S-no/P-no/H-no
English
Tina Yap All year

Full breakfast
Restaurant, lunch, dinner, snacks, comp. wine

The all-inclusive FDR Pebbles offers families an exciting soft adventure holiday.
fdr@fdrholidays.com http://fdrfamily.com

LITTLE BAY

Coconuts
Little Bay
John Eugster All year

BB
English

Considered by many to be the nicest small resort rental in the whole of the Caribbean. 10 oceanside cottages/villas of 1-3 bedrooms. These stone and cedar wood cottages are right up on the ocean. coconuts@centurytel.net http://jamaica-cottages.com

NEGRIL

Charela Inn
PO Box 3033
Norman Manley Blvd
876-957-4648 Fax: 876-957-4414
Daniel Grizzle & Charmaine Bowen Open all year

108-210 US$-BB
49 rooms, 49 pb
•
Visa, MC, AmEx
C-yes/S-yes/P-no/H-yes
French, German, English

Full breakfast
Lunch, dinner, restaurant open all day.

A quiet, intimate hideaway on Negril beach, for singles, couples, and families. Set amidst lush tropical gardens, gourmet Jamaican/French cuisine is served.
chareca@cwjamaica.com http://www.charela.com

NEGRIL

Native Son Villas
Manley Blvd, Seaward Side
908-598-1158
Fax: 908-598-1151
Sarah Burton
Open all year

130-305 US$-BB
11 rooms, 10 pb
•
Visa, MC, AmEx
C-yes/S-yes/P-no/H-ltd
English, Jamaican Patois

Full breakfast
Welcome Beverage: Rum, Beer or Soda

Exclusive beachfront complex of four elegant houses in lush tropical gardens on private beach. Spacious rooms. Personal housekeeper/cook.
sarahburt@aol.com http://www.travelguides.com/bb/native_son/

PORT ANTONIO

Hotel Mocking Bird Hill
PO Box 254
809-993-7267
Fax: 809-993-7133
809-993-7134
Barbara Walker, Shireen Aga
Open all year

125-230 US$-EP
10 rooms, 10 pb
•
Most CC
C-ltd/S-yes/P-ltd/H-ltd
German, English, French

Restaurant (fee)
All meals available

Split-level, airy villa surrounded by rich tropical vegetation. A magnificent view of the mountains & coast. mockbrd@cwjamaica.com http://www.hotelmockingbirdhill.com

ROBINS BAY

Sonrise Beach Retreat
876-776-7676
Fax: 876-999-7169
Bob & Kim Chase
All year

BB
English

Unique & affordable Eco-Tourism experience awaits visitors to our secluded 18 acre Tropical Nature Reserve Resort/Sanctuary surrounded by thousands of acres of undeveloped coastal paradise to explore
sonrise@cwjamaica.com http://www.in-site.com/sonrise

RUNAWAY BAY

Franklyn D. Resort
PO Box 201
809-973-4591
Fax: 809-973-3071
800-654-1FDR
Tina Yap
All year

280-400 US$-AP
76 rooms, 76 pb
•
Visa, MC, AmEx
C-yes/S-ltd/P-no/H-no
English

Full breakfast
Restaurant, lunch, dinner, snacks, comp. wine

All suite, all-inclusive b/front resort with a Nanny for each family. Spacious suites, all meals, drinks, watersports, children's program, entertainment, tennis, and children under 16 stay free.
fdr@fdrholidays.com http://www.fdrholidays.com

ST. ANNS BAY

High Hope Estate
PO Box 11
876-972-2277
Fax: 876 972-1607
Ludovica & Dennis
All year

85-155 US$-AP
5 rooms, 5 pb
•
Visa, MC
C-ltd/S-ltd/P-no/H-no
English, Italian, German

Continental Breakfast included in rate.
Complimentary High Tea, lunch, and dinner.

Five (5) beautifully furnished guest rooms and located on 40 acres of botanical gardens High Hope offers guests the peace, tranquility, and natural beauty.
reservations@highhopeestate.com http://www.highhopeestate.com

Netherland Antilles

SABA

Captain'S Quarters
Windwardside
599-4-62201
Fax: 599-4-62377
Calvin Holm
Open all year

135-170 US$-BB
12 rooms, 12 pb
•
Most CC
C-yes/S-yes/P-yes/H-no
English, Dutch, Spanish

Full American breakfast
Restaurant (fee)

Charming cliffside Victorian Inn featuring antique 4-poster beds and sweeping ocean/mountain views-only minutes from rainforest, scuba, hiking and "gingerbread" villages.

sabacq@aol.com http://saba-online.com

St. Kitts / Nevis

BASSETERRE

Ocean Terrace Inn
PO Box 65
Wigley Avenue
869-465-2754
Fax: 869-465-1057
Michael W. James
All year

135-240 US$-EP
80 rooms, 80 pb
•
Most CC
C-yes/S-yes/P-no/H-no
English

Continental plus breakfast
Lunch, dinner, aft. tea, snacks, 3 Restaurants

The hotel is located 1/4 mile from the capital city of Basseterre, 2 miles from the Airport and 1/4 mile from the cruise port.

otistkitts@caribsurf.com http://www.oceanterraceinn.com

Trinidad / Tobago

MARAVAL

Monique's Guest House
114/116 Saddle Road
868-628-3334
Fax: 869-622-3232
Monica Charbonne
Open all year

60-70 US$-EP
20 rooms, 20 pb
•
Most CC
C-yes/S-yes/P-no/H-yes
English

Lunch, dinner, restaurant, snacks

Though small, our product compares with multinational hotels. Combined with personalized attention, and a homey atmosphere, we are "a unique mix."

moniques@carib-link.net http://www.moniquestrinidad.com/

Virgin Gorda

THE VALLEY

Olde Yard Inn
PO Box 26
284-495-5544
Fax: 284-495-5986 800-653-9273
Carol Kaufman
Open all year

100 US$-MAP
14 rooms, 14 pb
•
Visa
C-yes/S-yes/P-no/H-yes
English, French, Spanish

Full breakfast (fee)
Lunch, dinner, restaurant

14 charming rooms on hillside amidst tropical gardens, facing sea w/gourmet restaurant, acclaimed library. Romance & serenity abound. Concierge service. Comp. bottle of wine.
oldeyard@surfbvi.com http://www.oldeyardinn.com

Central-S. America

Belize

BELIZE CITY

Hill Bank Field Station
1 Eyre Street
02-75616 02-75635
Herbert Haylock
All year

150.00 US$-BB
6 rooms
English

pfbel@btl. http://www.pfbelize.org

Riverbend Guest House
Ladyville
PO Box 48
011-501-225-2297
Fax: 228-255-555 011-501-225-2297
Alan D. Deeks
All year

65 US $-BB
5 rooms, 3 pb
•
Visa
C-yes/S-no/P-no/H-no
English, Spanish

Continental breakfast

Situated along the scenic Belize River, Riverbend should be your first stay in scenic Belize. Just a short drive from the international airport, Riverbend provides a serene outpost for any traveler. riverbend@btl.net

SAN PEDRO TOWN

Corona Del Mar Hotel
PO Box 37
Ambergris Caye
501-226-2055
Fax: 501-226-2461
"Woody"/Helen Canaday
Low Season–High Season

75-160 US $-BB
16 rooms, 16 pb
•
Visa, MC, AmEx
C-yes/S-yes/P-no/H-yes
English, Spanish

Full breakfast
Coffee, fruit punch & rum punch "Free" all day

Corona del Mar Hotel/Apts is a small, friendly family style hotel a short 10 minute walk down the beach to the center of San Pedro Town on the Island of Ambergris Caye in the western Caribbean Sea. corona@btl.net http://www.ambergriscaye.com/coronadelmar

Bolivia

LA PAZ

Hotel Rosario
Casilla Central 12446
Avenida Illampu 704
591-2-245-1658
Fax: 591-2-245-1991
Eduardo Zeballos
Open all year

37-41 US$-BB
42 rooms, 42 pb
•
Visa, MC
C-yes/S-ltd/P-no/H-no
Spanish, English

Buffet breakfast
Restaurant serves dinner, afternoon tea, bar

Beautiful Colonial building with sunny courtyard. Centrally located, near the handicrafts markets. Bar "Jiwhaki" with a nice view of the city.
reservas@hotelrosario.com http://www.hotelrosario.com

Colombia

BOGOTA

La Casona del Patio Amarillo
Carrera 8 #69-24
571-212-8805
Fax: 571-212-8805
Maria Ortega
All year

35 US$-BB
14 rooms, 7 pb
•
Visa, MC, AmEx
C-yes/S-ltd/P-ltd/H-no
Spanish, English

Colombian coffee all day long, snacks, soda

La Casona del Patio Amarillo is located in a beautiful and safe neighborhood. The house was remodeled a few years ago to give the guests a sense of feeling at home.
casona@col1.telecom.com.co http://www.lacasonadelpatio.com

Costa Rica

CARATE

Lookout Inn
Apartado 12
Osa Peninsula
506-735-5431 815-941-4803
Terry Conroy
All year

178 US$-AP
3 rooms, 3 pb
C-yes/S-yes/P-no/H-no
English, Spanish

Mixed drinks, wine, beer additional.

Beautiful ocean/mountain side Inn with spectacular views, spacious rooms with private bath/fans, swimming pool, tropical garden, close to Corcovado National Park.
reservations@lookout-inn.com http://www.lookout-inn.com

LIMON

Pangea
Puerto Viejo de Talamanca
506-759-00604
Fax: 506-750-0191
All year

35.00 US$-BB
2 rooms, 2 pb
S-ltd/P-no/H-no
Italian, Eng, Fren, Germ, Sp

Fruits, crêpes, homemade jam, coffee,tea

Pangea B&B is in a village on the Caribbean coast in a Wild Life Refuge. We offer you exclusives wooden room equipped with mosquito net and fan and porch overlooking a tropical garden.
pangeacr@yahoo.es http://www.puertoviejo.net/pangea.htm

MANUEL ANTONIO

Makanda-By-The-Sea
PO Box 29
506-777-0442
Fax: 506-777-1032
Kimberly Barron
All Year

150-350 US$-BB
11 rooms, 11 pb
•
Visa, MC, AmEx, *Rated*
C-no/S-yes/P-ltd/H-no
English, Spanish

Full Breakfast delivered to room daily
Lunch and Dinner. Wedding receptions.

6 luxury villas, 5 luxury studios. Adults only property offering guest the best in personal service, romance & tranquility. Sunspot Poolside Bar & Grill offers up the Central Pacific's finest dining.
makanda@racsa.co.cr http://www.makanda.com

PLAYA OCOTAL

Hotel Villa Casa Blanca
PO Box 25216
Mi 33102-5216 SJO 992
506-670-0518
Fax: 506-670-0448
Modesta & Richard Berg
All Year

59-95 US$-BB
15 rooms, 15 pb
•
Most CC
C-ltd/S-ltd/P-no/H-ltd
Spanish, English, French

Breakfast buffet
Snacks, Soft Drinks, Wine, Beer

Poised on a hill, a short walk to the beach, overlooking the ocean is a Spanish villa with a blend of culture and elegance. This peaceful, garden ambiance is unforgettable.
vcblanca@racsa.co.cr http://www.costa-rica-hotels-travel.com

QUEPOS

Villas Nicolas
PO Box 236
6350
506-777-0481
Fax: 506-777-0451
Sheryl Livingstone
All Year

50-180 US$-EP
19 rooms, 19 pb
Most CC
C-yes
English, Spanish

Meals: Inquire

Villas Nicolas is an intimate series of 12 condos set in a terraced jungle overlooking the Pacific. sales@villasnicolas.com http://www.villasnicolas.com

---

Villas El Parque
Apartado 111
Manuel Antonio
506-777-0096
Fax: 506-777-0538
Viviana
Open all year

75-150 US $-BB
26 rooms, 26 pb
•
Visa, MC, AmEx
C-yes/S-yes/P-no/H-ltd
English, Spanish, French

Continental breakfast
Snack bar

The Hotel is perched high overlooking the pacific coast and small islands of Manuel Antonio bay. vparque@racsa.co.cr http://www.hotelvillaselparque.com

ROSARIO DE NARANJO

Vista del Valle Plantation Inn
Calle Indio
506-451-1165 506-450-0900
Elisa
All Year

120-160 US$-BB
12 rooms, 12 pb
•
MC, Visa
C-ltd/S-ltd/P-no/H-yes
English, Spanish

Full breakfast
full service restaurnant

A special place awaits the traveler in search of the perfect destination to experience the beauty of Costa Rica. At Vista del Valle, we create a worry-free haven of quiet & natural beauty for guests. mibrejo@so http://www.vistadelvalle.com

SAN JOSE

Hotel Hemingway
Ave. 9, Calle 9
506-221-1804
Fax: 506-221-1804
Eric Robinson
All year

46-56 US$-BB
17 rooms, 17 pb
•
Visa, MC, AmEx, *Rated*
C-yes/S-ltd/P-ltd/H-no
English, Spanish

Tropical buffet breakfast
Elegant open-air restaurant and bar on site

Steps to nightlife, museums, dining and shopping. Warm ambiance and jungle surroundings are accented with Mayan statues and Costa Rican art, setting your mood to venture out and discover Costa Rica. ernest@racsa.co.cr http://www.hemingwayinn.com

TAMARINDO

Sueño del Mar
Playa Langosta
506-653-0284 Fax: 506-653-0284
Nancy Money & Paul Thabault
All year

115-170 US$-BB
5 rooms, 5 pb
•
Visa
C-ltd/S-ltd/P-no/H-no
English, Spanish, French

Full breakfast
Dinners and lunches served upon request

Located directly on the beach, our B&B is intimate & tranquil with uniquely decorated rooms. Guests love the private outdoor Bali style showers. Gourmet breakfast, pool, and magnificent sunsets!
suenodem@racsa.co.cr http://www.sueno-del-mar.com

Ecuador

SAN PABLO

Hacienda Cusin
PO Box 123
Calle Chiriboga
593-6-918013
Fax: 593-6-918003 800-683-8148
Nicholas Millhouse
All year

75-200 US $-BB
45 rooms, 45 pb
•
Visa, MC, AmEx
C-yes/S-yes/P-no/H-no
Spanish, English, French

Full breakfast
Restaurant, snacks, afternoon tea

Restored 17th century Andean estate, antique and craft furnished. 400 years of welcome. Garden cottages, family suites. 12 acres of year-round blooming gardens.
hacienda@cusin.com.ec http://www.haciendacusin.com

Guatemala

ANTIGUA

La Casa de los Sueños.
1 Avenida Sur #1
502-832-0802
Alejandro Rayo All year

85-165 US$-BB
8 rooms, 8 pb
Spanish

La Casa de los Sueños is a wonderful colonial mansion recently renovated and turned into a delightful Bed and Breakfast.
information@lacasadelossuenos.com http://www.lacasadelossuenos.com

Honduras

TEGUCIGALPA

Confort Guest House
Colonia Palmira #528
Segunda Calle
504-239-1254
Fax: 504-239-8864
Antonio Ortiz Cover
All year around

65 US $-BB
12 rooms, 12 pb
•
Visa, MC, AmEx
C-yes/S-ltd/P-no/H-no
Spanish, English

Full breakfast free
Tea, snacks. Lunch and dinner (Fee).

Spanish style house, breakfast served in spacious room with city view. Access to Internet.
reservaciones@confortguest.com http://www.confortguest.com

Mexico

AJIJIC

Los Artistas
PO Box 19
Constitucion 105 45920
011-52-376-766-1027
Fax: 011-52-376-766-1762
Kent & Linda
All year

45-75 US$-BB
7 rooms, 7 pb
•
Rated
C-ltd/S-ltd/P-ltd/H-no
Spanish, English

Gourmet, full breakfast
Beverages

Frommer's 2002 Mexico describes Los Artistas as "one of Ajijic's loveliest homes . . . one of the best, most relaxing lodging values in Mexico." Easy walk to local shops, restaurants and lakeshore. artistas@laguna.com.mx http://www.losartistas.com

CANCUN

Cancun B&B
011-52-998-870963
Karl & Dee Cooper
All year

50 US$-BB
5 rooms, 4 pb
C-yes/S-ltd/P-no/H-ltd
Spanish

Private home located in a safe, middle class Mexican neighborhood. Three story house with lush tropical garden entry. Breakfast is served in a screened patio area surrounded by tropical plants. cancunbandb@hotmail.com
http://www.bedandbreakfast.com/bbc/p608436.asp

Maria De Lourdes Hotel
Ave. Yaxchilan #80 77500
98-844744
Fax: 98-841242
Patricio Millet
Open all year

35-50 US$-BB
57 rooms, 57 pb
•
Visa
C-yes/S-yes/P-no/H-no
Spanish, English

Continental breakfast
Restaurant, bar, dinner, afternoon

Maria de Lourdes Hotel is a budget hotel. Located in the downtown area.
hotelmariadelourdes@hotelmariadelourdes.com http://www.hotelmariadelourdes.com

CUERNAVACA

Las Ma[??]anitas
Ricardo Linares 107 62000
73-14-1466
Fax: 73-18-3672
Margot U. de Krause
Open all year

93-382 US$-EP
21 rooms, 21 pb
•
Visa, MC, AmEx
C-yes/S-yes/P-no/H-yes
Spanish, English, French

Full breakfast (fee)
Restaurant, lunch, dinner

Although located downtown, this inn is set amid a lush tropical garden. Member of the prestigious Relais & Chateaux and one of the finest places to stay and dine in all Mexico.
mkrause@lasmananitas.com.mx http://www.lasmananitas.com.mx/

GUADALAJARA

Casa de las Flores
Santos Degollado 175 45500
011-52-3659-3189
Stan Singleton
All Year

65 US $-BB
7 rooms, 7 pb
Visa, MC, *Rated*
C-yes/S-no/P-no/H-ltd
Spanish, English

Meals: Inquire

Casa de las Flores bed and breakfast is just 15 minutes away from the center of Guadalajara and just three blocks from the famous historic center of Tlaquepaque.
stanleys@prodigy.net.mx http://www.casadelasflores.com

Quinta Don Jose
Reforma #139 45500
52-333-635-7522
Fax: 52-333-659-9315
800-537-9567
Arturo Magana & Estela Cortez
All year

60-90 US$-BB
11 rooms, 11 pb
•
Visa, MC, *Rated*
C-yes/S-ltd/P-ltd/H-yes
Spanish, English

Full breakfast
24 Hour Fresh Brewed Coffee & Snacks in bar

An Oasis of Tranquility in the Heart of Tlaquepaque... Whether on business or vacation, "Quinta Don Jose B&B Hotel" offers you reasonable rates, a beautiful setting, and unique personal service!
info@quintadonjose.com http://www.quintadonjose.com

HUATULCO

Agua Azul la Villa
AP 25, lote 18, manzana 6
AP 25 70989
011-52-958-58-10265
Richard Gazer
All year

79-99 US$-BB
6 rooms, 6 pb
Visa, MC
C-no/S-no/P-no/H-no
English, Spanish

Continental breakfast
Honor bar

With stunningly beautiful ocean views and spacious private terraces off of every guestroom, Agua Azul la Villa offers a tranquil vacation destination in a tropical non-smoking environment for adults.
gaurei@hotmail.com http://www.aguaazullavilla.com

ISLA MUJERES

La Casa de los Sueños
Lotes 8/9—Fraccionamiento Sureste
Carretera Al Garrafon 77400
9987-70651 Fax: 9987-70708
Danielle Michon
All year

215-335 US$-BB
8 rooms, 8 pb
•
Visa, MC
C-no/S-no/P-no/H-no
Spanish, English, French

Full breakfast
Coffee and juice serve in your room

Located on the southern tip of Isla Mujeres facing Cancun, this luxury non-smoking Bed and Breakfast was built and designed to be the owner's residence in 1996.
info@lossuenos.com http://www.lossuenos.com

LA PAZ

Ventana Bay Resorts
2730 Topete 23060
011-52-612-12-60226
Fax: 011-52-612-12-51470
800-533-8452
William Edsell
All year

120 US$-BB
7 rooms, 7 pb
•
Visa, MC
C-yes/S-ltd/P-ltd/H-ltd
English, Spanish

Full breakfast

Bed and breakfast on the sea of Cortez in Baja, Mexico. All rooms include full breakfast, private baths and spectacular ocean views.
MRBILLBAJA@aol.com http://www.ventanabay.com

LORETO

Las Trojes Hotel
Calle Davis Norte S/N 23880
52-113-502-77
Fax: 52-113-511-13
Agustin & Adriana
All year

49 US$-BB
8 rooms, 8 pb
•
Visa
C-yes/S-yes/P-no/H-ltd
Spanish, English

Continental plus breakfast
Lunch, dinner, restaurant

Old Grainaries beautifully restored on the beach.
lastrojes@prodigy.net.mx http://www.costaloreto.com

PLAYA DEL CARMEN

Villa Amanecer
Calle 26 Norte 286, Centro
77710
984-873-2716
Fax: 984-873-2717
Eduardo Gil Villafa[??]a
All year

70-130 US$-BB
49 rooms, 49 pb
•
Visa, MC, AmEx
C-yes/S-yes/P-no/H-no
English, Sp, It, Fr

Various options of breakfast
Snacks, drinks, etc.

It is located in one of the most romantic spots of Playa del Carmen, reflecting a Mediterranean flair with all the grace and comfort you can expect. Also offering spacious furnished condos for rent. amanecer@playa.com.mx http://www.villa-amanecer.com

SAN CARLOS

San Carlos
55 La Costa 85506
907-279-7808
Fax: 907-258-3657
Terry & Yuya Stimson
Open all year

75 US$
2 rooms, 2 pb
•
Most CC
C-yes/S-no/P-no/H-no
English, Spanish

Continental breakfast
Arrange for Mexican breakfast

Ideal for strolls on a sandy beach, easy access to scuba diving, fishing for magnificent Marlin, and exploring Mexican art culture. Residential area
tstimson@compuserve.com http://www.travelguides.com/bb/sancarlos/

SAN CRISTOBAL DE LAS CASAS

El Jacarandal
Calle Comitan No. 7 29220
011-52-967-81065
Fax: 011-52-967-81065
Percy and Nancy Wood
November-August

120 US$-BB
4 rooms, 4 pb
C-ltd/S-no/P-no/H-no
Spanish, English

Full breakfast
Lunch, dinner, arranged the day before (fee)

Beauty and comfort in this colonial-style guest house, decorated with local art and handiwork, it flows gracefully from loggias to patios to terraced gardens full of English and exotic flowers. carolinewfallon@yahoo.com http://www.mexonline.com/jacarandal.htm

SAN MIGUEL DE ALLENDE

17th Century Casa
PO Box 496
Canal No. 58 37700
011-52-4-152-2492
Carmen McDaniel
All year

70-100 US$-BB
4 rooms, 4 pb
C-yes/S-ltd/P-yes/H-no
Spanish, English

Fresh juice, fruite plate, main dish, co
Morning coffee sent to room in the a.m., bar serv.

This beautiful renovated 17th Century house with its garden—like ambiance, new and uniquely decorated rooms, full Mexican breakfasts is the place to stay in Old Historic San Miguel de Allende. mcdaniel@unisono.net.mx
http://www.portalsanmiguel.com/17thcenturycasabandb/index.html

SAN MIGUEL DE ALLENDE

Arcos del Atascadero
Callejon Atascadero #5 37700
011-52-415-152-5299
Patty & David
All year

50-75 US$-BB
5 rooms, 3 pb
C-ltd/S-no/P-ltd/H-ltd
English, Spanish

Continental plus breakfast
Room Delivery
Fresh fruit, breads, coffee, many Mexican teas.

5 bedrooms decorated in Mexican flower themes by a Bellas Artes Painting Instructor. Lavish Continental breakfast delivered to your bedroom door. San Miguel Born Hostess speaks Perfect English.
congusto@cybermatsa.com.mx http://www.bedandbreakfastinmexico.com

---

Casa de las Limas
Ancha de San Antonio 14
011-52-4-152-0853
Cynthia B Huntington
All year

BB
Spanish

This elegant Spanish Colonial home, now converted into a bed and breakfast, was once part of the 17th century Palace owned by the Counts of the Canal family.
limetree@unisono.net.mx http://www.casalimas.com

Garden House
Animas #32 37700
415-446-7076
Fax: 415-446-7076
Craig Caffall
All year, except July

450-week, 1550-month
US$-EP
2 rooms, 2 pb
C-yes/S-no/P-ltd/H-ltd
English, Spanish

Beautifully built in 1970 by VW guru John Muir (How To Keep Your Volkswagen Alive, cir.1968), house has a large spacious living area (40'x30'=1200 Sq. Ft. approximately). Garden House with Hot Tub.
smahouse@aol.com http://www.vrbo.com/vrbo/1417.htm

Hacienda De Las Flores
Hospicio 16 37700
415-152-1808
Fax: 415-152-8383
A. Franyutti, C. Finkelstein
Open all year

76.00-153.00 US$-BB
16 rooms, 16 pb
•
Visa, MC
C-yes/S-no/P-yes/H-no
English, French

Full breakfast
Catering on request

Located only 2 blocks from downtown. Colonial style with TV, electric blankets, beautiful gardens a pool and a bar. hhflores@unisono.net.mx
http://www.unisono.net.mx/hhflores

Hotel Villa Jacaranda
Aldama 53 37700
011-52-415-210
Fax: 011-52-415-208 1800-310-9688
Don & Gloria Fenton
Open all year

130-190 US$-EP
16 rooms, 16 pb
•
Visa, MC, AmEx, *Rated*
C-yes/S-yes/P-yes/H-ltd
Spanish, English

Breakfast by arrangement
Restaurant, bar

Two cobblestone streets from Mexico's loveliest colonial square.
reservations@villajacaranda.com http://www.villajacaranda.com

TRONCONES

La Posada de los Raqueros
Apdo. Postal #90 40880
847-255-0635
Fax: 847-253-0863
Hans Brouwers
All year

55-125 US$-EP
4 rooms, 4 pb
•
Visa, MC, AmEx
C-ltd/S-yes/P-no/H-ltd
English, Dutch, Ger, Sp

Soft drinks, wine and beer avialable

La Posada de Los Raqueros (which translates to "Beachcomber's Inn") has a rich ambiance combining Asian, European and American elegance with a Mexican flavor.
raqueros@raqueros.com http://www.raqueros.com

ZIHUATANEJO

Casa Cuitlateca	340 US$-BB	Full breakfast
Calle Playa La Ropa, Apt. 124	4 rooms, 4 pb	Lunch, dinner (prix fix)
40880	•	
011-52-755-554-2448	Most CC, *Rated*	
Fax: 011-52-755-554-7394	C-ltd/S-yes/P-no/H-no	
877-541-1234	English, Spanish	
John Cahill		
All year		

This beautiful, private, luxury hotel has to be experienced! It is truly the jewel of Zihuatanejo, Mexico.
casa@altahotelgroup.com http://www.casacuitlateca.com/

Panama

BOCAS ISLAND

Hotel Las Brisas	20-40 US$-BB	Full breakfast
PO Box 1	40 rooms, 40 pb	Lunch, Dinner (fee)
507-757-9248	•	
Fax: 507-757-9247	Visa, MC, AmEx	
Harry Bendiburg	C-yes/S-yes/P-no/H-yes	
Open all year	Sp, Eng, Native Indian, Germ	

Boats come to our hotel to pick-up our guests and take them for tours to surrounding islands and indian villages.
bendi69@yahoo.com

VOLCAN

Hostal Cielito Sur	60-70 US$-BB	Full breakfast
PO Box 327	4 rooms, 4 pb	
Nueva Suiza	•	
507-771-2038	Visa, MC	
Fax: 507-771-2038	C-ltd/S-no/P-no/H-ltd	
Janet & Glenn Lee	English, Spanish	
All year, closed October		

The Hostal Cielito Sur Bed & Breakfast is a quiet, private, family-run country estate inn on 2½ hectares at an altitude of 1,600 meters above sea level in the Chiriqui highlands.
glee@cielitosur.com http://www.cielitosur.com

Peru

CUZCO

Picoaga Hotel	120-140 US$-EP	Buffet breakfast (fee)
Santa Teresa #344	70 rooms, 70 pb	2 Restaurants, International and Peruvian cuisine
084-22-7691	•	
Fax: 084-22-1246	Visa, MC, AmEx	
Alfredo Petrozzi	C-yes/S-ltd/P-no/H-no	
Open all year	Spanish, English, French	

Picoaga a first class hotel, originally the old mansion of Spanish Noble Marquis of Picoaga, now converted into a comfortable lodging. A few steps away from the "Plaza de Armas" the main square. picoaga@terra.com.pe http://www.picoagahotel.com

LIMA

Hostal Jose Luis
F. Paula Ugarriza 727 18
444-1015 Fax: 446-7177
Renso Coppo Open all year

24 US$-BB
24 rooms, 20 pb
C-yes/S-yes/P-yes/H-no
Spanish, English

Ask about breakfast availablity
Continental breakfast

The pension is located in the residential district of Miraflores, nice, quiet and safe. Family atmosphere with cooking and laundry facilities. 10 minutes to Central Park

hsjluis@terra.com.pe http://www.hoteljoseluis.com

Europe

Austria

DURNSTEIN

Hotel Scholss Durnstein
3601 Dürnstein A-3601
+43-2711-212
Fax: +43-2711-212-3
Hans & Rosemarie Thiery
April–October

218-335 Euro¤-BB
40 rooms, 40 pb
Most CC
C-yes/S-yes/P-ltd/H-yes
English, Fr, Ital

Full breakfast
Restaurant (fee)

Built in 1630, Renaissance castle converted into a hotel of great style.

hotel@schloss.at http://www.schloss.at

SALZBURG

Hotel Walkner
Eisenharting 4
A-5164 Seeham am
Obertrumer See A-5164
0043-6217-5550
Fax: 06217-5550-22
Walkner-Haberl Family

67.74-105.74 US$-BB
22 rooms, 22 pb
•
Most CC
C-yes/S-yes/P-yes/H-ltd
English, French, Ger
Open all year

Full breakfast
Lunch, afternoon tea

Breakfast & meals with views of the lake, on the sun terrace, cheese & butter from our own dairy. Solarium, keep-fit room, children's playground, heated pool.

hotel.walkner@eunet.at http://www.hotel-walkner.at

Schloss Haunsperg
Hammerstr. 32 A-5411
6245-80-662 Fax: 6245-85680
Fam. Von Gernerth
Open all year

160 US$-BB
8 rooms, 8 pb
Most CC, •
C-yes/S-yes/P-yes/H-no
Enlgish, Italian, Ger

Full breakfast
Snacks, complimentary wine

Our gracious 14 century country manor house offers 8 superbly appointed double rooms and suites with period furniture for 2-5 people.

info@schlosshaunsperg.com http://www.schlosshaunsperg.com

Steakhaus Im Landgasthof Fieg
Ellmaustraßse 2
Fuschl Nr. 60, 5330 Fuschi Am See A-5330
0043-6226-8231
Fax: 0043-6226-8231
Günter & Maria Fieg

18-25 Euro¤-BB
5 rooms, 5 pb
Visa, MC
C-yes/S-yes/P-yes/H-ltd
German, English
Open all year

Continental plus breakfast
Restaurant (fee), specialities: Crocodil, Ostrich

Only 20 kilometers to Salzburg. 6 lakes around 20 kilometers. Trekking paradise. Near the places from "Sound of Music." Welcome drink

office@steakhouse-fuschl.at http://www.steakhouse-fuschl.at

VIENNA

Hotel Kugel
Siebensterngasse 43 A-1070
+43-1-523-33-55
Fax: +43-1-523-33-55-5
Johannes Roller
February 8—January 7

60-86 US$-BB
34 rooms, 34 pb
•
C-yes/S-yes/P-yes/H-yes
German, Engl, Pol, Fren

Continental plus breakfast

Typical old-Viennese hotel in historic building, centrally located, with excellent access to all parts of Vienna. Moderately priced and with a very friendly, helpful staff.
office@hotelkugel.at http://www.hotelkugel.at

Hotel Pension Shermin
Rilkeplatz 7 A-1040
+43-1-5866-1830
Fax: +43-1-58661-8310
Ms. Sofie Abolahrar
Open all year

72-108 Euro¤-BB
11 rooms, 11 pb
Visa, MC, AmEx
C-yes/S-ltd/P-yes/H-no
English, Ger, Fren, Farsi

Full breakfast
Tee or coffee on request

A family run hotel-pension for accommodation in the city of Vienna. Within walking distance to major sights, cultural & entertainment centers and main subway (underground) station "Karlsplatz" pension.shermin@nextra.at http://www.hotel-pension-shermin.com

Belgium

BRUGES

Rubens House
Rubenslaan 23 B-8310
+32-50-674-889
An Tanghe
All year

60-65 US$-BB
1 rooms
C-ltd/S-no/P-no/H-no
Dutch, Engl, Fren, Ger

Continental plus breakfast
On request

Quiet residential area. Free parking. Only 10 min. walk to city centre. Central-heated guestroom bathroom next door. Small children's' bed available free (under 3 yrs). Generous breakfast. Warm welcome an.tanghe@pandora.be http://www.rubenshouse.com

---

Villa des Raisins
Torhoutse Steenweg 22 B-8200
32-50-67-5899
Fax: 32-50-67-5899
Carine & Dirk
All year

95-110 EURO¤-BB
3 rooms, 3 pb
Visa, MC, AmEx
C-yes/S-yes/P-no/H-no
Engl, Fren, Dutch, Germ, Ital

Full buffet breakfast with champagne
Dinner (not included in room rate)

Situated within short walking distance of the historical heart of Bruges, the carefully restored "Villa des Raisins" offers a unique and affordable luxury formula of bed and breakfast. info@villadesraisins.be http://www.villadesraisins.com

BRUGGE

Alegria
St.Jakobsstraat 34b B-8000
+32-50-330937
Fax: +32-50-347686
Veronique De Muynck
All year

62-124 US$-BB
3 rooms, 3 pb
•
Visa
C-yes/S-yes/P-yes/H-no
Italian, French, Dutch, Ger

Full breakfast

Alegria B&B is situated 100 meters from the market square of old Brugge.
alegriabb@skynet.be http://users.skynet.be/alegriabb/

BRUGGE

Anselmus Hotel
Ridderstraat 15 B-8000
+32-50-34-1374
Fax: +32-50-34-1916
Magda Maenhoudt
All year

88-98 US$-BB
10 rooms, 10 pb
•
Visa, MC, AmEx
C-yes/S-yes/P-no/H-no
French, Dutch, Eng, Germ, Sp

Continental plus breakfast
Afternoon tea, bar service

One of the most beautiful family run hotels in Bruges. Built in an old mansion house where Anselmus Boetius de Boodt once lived (16th century). Located in the town center.
info@anselmus.be http://www.anselmus.be

Hansa Hotel
Niklaas Desparsstraat 11 B-8000
+32-0-50-444-444
Fax: +32-0-50-444-440
Mr & Mrs Johan Creytens
All year

125-205 Euro¤-BB
24 rooms, 24 pb
•
Visa, MC, AmEx
C-ltd/S-ltd/P-no/H-no
Eng, Fren, Germ, Dutch

Full breakfast

A 19th century mansion house, renovated into a small luxurious family run hotel with modern facilities and personal service, in the old historic centre.
information@hansa.be http://www.hansa.be

BRUSSELS

Hotel Mozart S.A.
Rue Marche aux Fromages 23 B-1000
00-32-2-502-6661
Fax: 00-32-2-502-7758
Mr. Ben
All year

3,500-5,500 Belgiun¤-BB
47 rooms, 47 pb
Most CC
C-yes
Flemish, French, English

Continental breakfast
Breakfast room, refrigerator

Spend a night at the heart of Brussels, at Hotel Mozart, where a unique atmosphere prevails. A memorable stay that you'll never forget! The new Hotel is just 20 meters from the Market Square. hotel.mozart@skynet.be http://www.hotel-mozart.be

NAMUR

Best Western New Hotel De Lives
Ch De Liege 1178 B-5101
32-81-58-0513
Fax: 32-81-58-1577
Sir Francis Van der Elst
All year

50-120 US$-BB
20 rooms, 20 pb
•
Most CC, *Rated*
C-yes/S-yes/P-yes/H-yes
Eng, Fr, Dutch, Ger, Jap, Span, Ital

Full breakfast (fee)
Lunch, dinner, tea, snacks, restaurant

An ancient but stylish hotel, dating from the 19th. Century completely renovated. Pleasant and homey atmosphere. info@newhoteldelives.com http://www.newhoteldelives.com

SPA

Hotel La Heid Des Pairs
Ave. Prof. Henrijean 143 B-4900
+32-87-774346
Fax: +32-87-770644
Christian Depreter
All year

99-139 US$-BB
8 rooms, 8 pb
•
Visa, MC
C-ltd/S-ltd/P-no/H-no
French, English, Germ, Dutch

Inquire for restaurants nearby

Quietness and rest in a agreeable setting. You will be welcomed and served by the owner!
info@heiddespairs.be http://www.heiddespairs.be

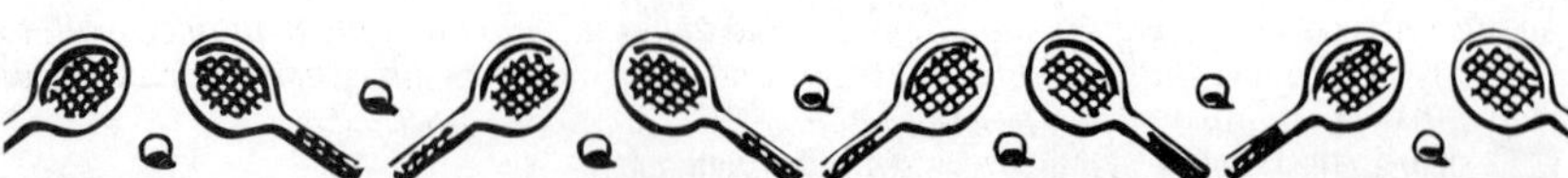

England, U.K.

BATH

Ashley Villa Hotel
26 Newbridge Rd BA1 3JZ
01224-421683
Sandra Hobson
All year

59-130 GB¤-BB
18 rooms, 17 pb
•
Visa, MC, AmEx, *Rated*
C-yes/S-ltd/P-no/H-ltd
English

Full breakfast
Full menu available for Evening Meals

Family run hotel, 1 mile city centre, car park, bar, restaurant, gardens, patio, outdoor pool. Family rooms, beautiful Premier rooms. Awards for hospitality and high standards of hygiene. ashleyvilla@clearface.co.uk http://www.ashleyvilla.co.uk

---

Dorian House
One Upper Oldfield Park BA2 3JX
0-1225-426-336
Fax: 0-1225-444-699
Mr. Robert & Mrs. Sue Castleton
All year

55-140 GB¤-BB
11 rooms, 11 pb
•
Most CC, *Rated*
C-yes/S-no/P-no/H-no
English

Full English & buffet breakfast

Enter an atmosphere of period charm in Dorian House. Panoramic views overlooking Bath. Five diamond rating by AA/RAC/ETC. Licensed. Off-street parking. Ten minutes walk to Roman Baths/City centre.
info@dorianhouse.co.uk http://www.dorianhouse.co.uk

Highways House
143 Wells Rd BA2 3AL
+44-0-1225-421238
Fax: +44-0-1225-481169 0800-074-9250
Andy & Ros Morley
Open All Year

65 GB ¤-BB
6 rooms, 6 pb
Visa, MC, AmEx, *Rated*
C-ltd/S-no/P-no/H-ltd
English, French

Full English breakfast

Built in 1874 Highways House is typical of Bath's Victorian architecture. We are a short walk from the rail station, and just off the A367 at the south of the city.
stay@highwayshouse.co.uk http://www.bandbbath.co.uk/

Marlborough House
1 Marlborough Lane BA1 2NQ
011-44-1225-318-175
Fax: 011-44-1225-466-127
Laura Dunlap
All year

60-85 GB¤-BB
7 rooms, 7 pb
•
Most CC
C-yes/S-no/P-yes/H-no
English

Abundant Vegetarian Breakfast
Lunch, Dinner, bagguettes, snacks

Elegant Vegetarian B&B in the heart of Georgian Bath. Furnished in lovely antiques, with four-poster beds and complementary sherry. Renowned for our relaxed atmosphere and easy conversation.
mars@manque.dircon.co.uk http://www.marlborough-house.net

Oldfields Hotel
102 Wells Rd BA2 3AL
01225-317984
Rod & Alex Kitcher
All year

85-130 US$-BB
14 rooms, 14 pb
•
Most CC, *Rated*
C-ltd/S-no/P-no/H-no
English

Full breakfast

An elegant and Traditional B&B with panoramic views of Bath and only 8 minutes walk to Bath city centre. Magnificent drawing room and dining room with spectacular views of Bath.
info@oldfields.co.uk http://www.oldfields.co.uk

BATH

Paradise House Hotel
86-88 Holloway BA2 4PX
01225-317734
Fax: 01225-482005
David & Annie Lanz
Open all year except Christmas

75.00 GB¤-BB
11 rooms, 11 pb
Most CC
C-yes/S-no/P-no/H-ltd
English, French

Full breakfast

Which 2001 Hotel of the Year "Brilliant" Award for Bed and Breakfast Accommodation. An elegant Georgian House in a unique setting overlooking City, 7 minutes walk from Roman Baths and Abbey.

info@paradise-house.co.uk http://www.paradise-house.co.uk

DERBYSHIRE

Biggin Hall
Biggin-by Hartington SK17 0DH
44-1298-84451
Fax: 44-1298-84681
James Moffett
Open all year

60-104 GB¤-BB
19 rooms, 19 pb
•
Visa, MC, AmEx, *Rated*
C-ltd/S-ltd/P-ltd/H-ltd
English

Continental breakfast
Dinner (fee), bar service

Set at 1000 feet in the Peak District, 17th-century Grade II listed Biggin Hall has been sympathetically restored, keeping its fine old character while giving house room to contemporary comforts.*

enquiries@bigginhall.co.uk http://www.bigginhall.co.uk

EXETER

Woodhayes Country House
Whimple EX5 2TD
01-404-82-2237
Fax: 01-404-82-2337
Eddie & Lynda Katz
All year

60-90 GB¤-BB
8 rooms, 8 pb
•
Most CC
C-ltd/S-ltd/P-no/H-no
English

Full breakfast
Afternoon tea, light meals, bar service

A small and friendly Georgian country house in four acres of beautiful Devon. Six spacious bedrooms individually decorated, delightful public rooms and a pretty cottage for self-catering.

info@woodhayes-hotel.co.uk http://www.woodhayes-hotel.co.uk

GLOUCESTERSHIRE

Calcot Manor
Gloucestershire GL8 8YJ
+44-0-1666-890391
Fax: +44-0-1666-890394
Richard Ball
All year

130-180 GB¤-BB
28 rooms, 28 pb
•
Most CC
C-yes/S-ltd/P-no/H-yes
English

Full breakfast
Two restaurants

Set in peaceful gardens, in the corner of the Cotswolds, this Country House Hotel offers 28 beautifully furnished bedrooms and suites.

reception@calcotmanor.co.uk http://www.calcotmanor.co.uk

HORLEY

The Lawn Guest House
30 Massetts Rd RH6 7DE
+44-0-1293-775751
Fax: +44-0-1293-821803
Adrian & Carole Grinsted
Open all year

50-75 GB¤-BB
12 rooms, 12 pb
•
Most CC, *Rated*
C-yes/S-no/P-yes/H-no
English, French

Full breakfast

Victorian house, NON smoking, 5 minutes Gatwick airport, 2 minutes centre of Horley, Rail station-300 yards; All rooms en suite, CTV hairdryers, tea/coffee/chocolate trays, d/d phones. Parking.

info@lawnguesthouse.co.uk http://www.lawnguesthouse.co.uk

LONDON

22 Jermyn Street 22 Jermyn St SW1Y 6HL 44-20-7734-2353 Fax: 44-20-7734-0750 800-682-7808 Henry Togna, Laurie Smith Open all year	205 GB¤-EP 18 rooms, 18 pb • Most CC C-yes/S-yes/P-yes/H-yes Eng, Fren, Ital, Sp, Arabic	Continental or full breakfast (fee) Lunch, dinner (fee)

Luxurious award winning townhouse in the heart of London, ideal for theatre. Let Henry and Laurie take care of you! Complimentary wine and snacks. 13 of the rooms are suites.
office@22jermyn.com http://www.22jermyn.com/

Luxury in London 3 Bradbourne St SW6 3TF 020-7736-7284 Amanda Turner All year	55/single, 70/double GB¤-BB 3 rooms, 3 pb C-ltd/S-no/P-no/H-no English	Continental plus breakfast

Luxury in London at affordable prices an interior decorators private home available for friendly bed and breakfast near all the sites and situated in a safe family area.
info@luxuryinlondon.clara.co.uk http://www.luxuryinlondon.co.uk

OXFORD

Nanford Guest House 137 Iffley Road 0X4 1EJ 01865-244743 Fax: 01865-249596 Bartholomew Cronin All year	58 US$-BB 10 rooms, 10 pb • Visa C-yes/S-yes/P-yes/H-yes French, Spanish	Full English breakfast

Period guest house located 5 minutes on foot from the university of Oxford. All rooms ensuite.
b.cronin@btinternet.com http://www.allworld-vacation.com/uk/eng10.htm

THAMES SURREY

Chase Lodge Hotel 10 Park Rd, Hampton Wick KT1 4AS 0208-943-1862 Fax: 0208-194-39363 D. & N. Stafford/Haworth Open all year	Rates: Inquire-BB 10 rooms, 10 pb • Visa, Most CC C-yes/S-yes/P-yes/H-no French, Spanish, German	Full breakfast Lunch, dinner, restaurant

Chase Lodge is situated in a quiet conservation area close to Hampton Court Palace. River Thames an area of great historical value.
info@chaselodgehotel.com http://www.chaselodgehotel.com

WINDERMERE

Linthwaite House Hotel Crook Rd LA23 3JA +44-15394-88600 Fax: +44-15394-88601 Mike Bevans Open all year	75-189 GB¤-BB 26 rooms, 26 pb • Visa C-no/S-yes/P-no/H-yes English, French	Full breakfast Lunch, dinner, restaurant, tea

Unstuffy country house in 14 acres of hilltop gardens with stunning views of Lake Windermere.
admin@linthwaite.com http://www.linthwaite.com

France

BAYEUX

La Caillerie
14240 Cahagnes F-14240
0033-231-25-2731
Samantha Acres
All year

380-700 French¤-BB
5 rooms, 5 pb
•
C-yes/S-no/P-ltd/H-no
English, French

Cooked breakfast available (fee)

Bed & Breakfast in an 18th Century 'Manoir' close to the D-day beaches, Mont St Michel, Bayeux and Honfleur. Delightful grounds and large well-furnished rooms. All ensuite.
lacaillerieacres@aol.com http://www.lacaillerie.77th.com

BEAULIEU-SUR-DORDOGNE

Chateau de Chauvac
19430 Bassignac-la-Bas F-19430
+33-5-55-91-5058
Fax: +33-5-55-91-5058
Dane & Terry Earnheart
All Year

115-145 US $-BB
6 rooms, 6 pb
•
C-ltd/S-ltd/P-yes/H-no
English, French

Continental breakfast
Champagne brunch and four course dinners available

Enjoy the best of French historic charm and warm American Hospitality in romantically restored 13th century chateau. Spectacular views and magical sunsets over the Dordgone River Valley!
info@chateauchauvac.com http://www.chateauchauvac.com

CAUNES

L'Ancienne Boulangerie
Rue St. Genes F-11160
33-468-780-132
Terry & Lois Link
February to December

25-60 US$-BB
5 rooms, 3 pb
C-yes/S-yes/P-yes/H-no
French, English

Continental breakfast

Comfortable, renovated bakery with pleasant terrace more than three centuries old in the heart of a medieval village with a 1,200-year-old abbey; surrounded by vineyards and communal forest.
ancienneboulangerie@compuserve.com http://www.caunes-minervois.com

CREPON

Manoir de Crepon
Route de Caen F-14480
332-31-22-2127
Fax: 332-31-22-8880
Anne Marie Poisson
All year

70 and up US$-BB
4 rooms, 4 pb
•
Visa, MC
C-yes/S-yes/P-yes/H-no
French, English

Continental breakfast

18th century manor house in tiny village of Crepon.

MAUSSANE LES ALPILLES

Castillon des Baux
Quartier du Touret F-13520
00-33-4-90-54-3193
Fax: 00-33-4-90-54-5131
Frederic Laloy
March through October

70-90 US$-EP
15 rooms, 15 pb
•
Visa, MC, AmEx, *Rated*
C-yes/S-yes/P-yes/H-no
French, Eng, Ital, Sp

Breakfast is served on a buffet

Situated in one of the most famous and nicer village of the Alpilles, in the heart of Provence: 5 minutes drive from les Baux and Saint Remy. Very quiet with spectacular views on the countryside.
castillondesbaux@aol.com http://www.castillondesbaux.com

PARIS

Hotel Britannique
20 Ave Victoria F-75001
33-1-42-33-7459
Fax: 33-1-42-33-8265
J.F. Danjou Open all year

124-171 Euro¤-EP
39 rooms, 39 pb
Visa, MC, AmEx, •
C-yes/S-yes/P-no/H-no
English, Spanish, French

Breakfast buffet 11 Euro
Afternoon tea

A charming "boutique" hotel in the historic heart of Paris. Quiet and romantic.
mailbox@hotel-britannique.fr http://www.hotel-britannic.com

Hotel De Banville
166 Boulevard Berthier F-75017
0331-42-67-7016
Fax: 0331—44-40-4277
Marianne Moreau All year

110-244 US$-EP
38 rooms, 38 pb
Visa, •
C-yes/S-yes/P-yes/H-no
English, Dutch, Spanish

Full breakfast
Afternoon tea, snacks

Warm French atmosphere near Etoile and Champs Elysees. Individuality and seduction in each of the 40 rooms. A tasteful selection of fabrics and paintings.
hotelbanville@wanadoo.fr http://www.hotelbanville.fr

Hotel Le Clos Medicis
56 Rue Monsieur le Prince
F-75006
01-43-29-1080
Fax: 01-43-54-2690
Olivier Meallet

150-250 Euros¤-EP
38 rooms, 38 pb
Visa, MC, AmEx, •
C-yes/S-yes/P-no/H-yes
English, Ital, Sp, Fren
Open all year

Buffet breakfast
Afternoon tea

Formerly private residence dating to 1860. Magnificent style house. Attractive garden & lounge with open fire.
message@closmedicis.com http://www.closmedicis.com

La Vie En Rose
Face au 11, Quai St. Bernard
F-75005
888-866-4730
Fax: 888-866-4730
David & Laura Ann Novick
All year

600-700 US$-BB
1 rooms, 1 pb
•
C-no/S-no/P-no/H-no
English, French, Spanish

Full breakfast
Wines beverages coffee/teas snacks all included.

American host offer oasis of tranquility in heart of Paris! One fortunate couple at a time enjoys this luxury vessel's splendid Captain's suite for a 5 star hotel room's cost, but get so much more!
bargeinn@aol.com http://www.la-vie-en-rose.com

PROVENCE

Le Mas D'Aigret
Les Baux de Provence F-13520
33-90-54-33-54
Fax: 33-9054-3354
Pip Phillips, Frederic Laloy
February 25—January 5

500-950 French-BB
16 rooms, 16 pb
Most CC
C-yes/S-yes/P-yes/H-no
English, French

Continental plus breakfast
Restaurant (fee)

This charming 350 year old farmhouse offers magnificent views of the Camargne and Mediterranean. A family run business with a wonderfully relaxed and friendly atmosphere. contact@nasdaigret.com http://www.nasdaigret.com

SAINT-LOUP LAMAIRÉ

Chateau de Saint-Loup
Saint-Loup Lamairé F-79600
33-05-49-64-8173
Fax: 33-05-49-64-8206
Charles-Henri Debartillat
All year

135-190 US$-EP
22 rooms, 18 pb
•
Visa, MC
C-yes/S-yes/P-yes/H-ltd
English, German

Eggs & bacon on request
Drinks with the Owner.
Dinner(55 $ per head)

15 guest rooms in the XVIIth Chateau and the Medieval tower, most with a canopied bed and a private bathroom, will treat you to centuries of history. Enjoy the marvelous XVIIIth gardens. CHdB@compuserve.com http://www.chateaudesaint-loup.com

SARLAT

Le Jardin
12-14 Jardin de Madame
F-24200
0033-05-53-28-96-07
Ann & Nick Dooley
March–November

47 US$-BB
3 rooms, 3 pb
C-yes/S-no/P-no/H-no
English, French

Continental breakfast
Evening Meals and Packed Lunches by arrangement

Situated 500m from the medieval town centre of Sarlat, "Le Jardin" is set in a large/quiet garden. Ideal for relaxing and letting you soak up the atmosphere of France.
nick@la-jardin.com http://www.la-jardin.com

ST-MARTIN-VALMEROUX

Hostellerie De La Maronne
Le Theil F-15140
04-71-69-2033
Fax: 04-71-69-2822
Alain and Lalasoa DeCock
April–November

81-138 US$-BB
21 rooms, 21 pb
•
Most CC
C-yes/S-yes/P-yes/H-yes
English, Spanish, French

Continental breakfast (fee)
Lunch, dinner, restaurant

Those that dreamed of nature will understand straightaway that this is the place. A peaceful life narrated through the gardens, morning at the poolside, end-of-day mists setting over the valley. hotelmaronne@cfi15.fr http://www.cfi15.fr/hotelmaronne

Germany

MURNAU AM STAFFELSEE

Alpenhof Murnau
Ramsachstrasse 8 D-82418
0049-8841-4910
Fax: 0049-8841-491100
Didier Morand
All year

148-260 US$-BB
77 rooms, 77 pb
•
Visa, MC, AmEx
C-yes/S-yes/P-yes/H-yes
German, Eng, Fren, Ital

Full breakfast
Restaurant, lunch, dinner, afternoon tea, snacks

The luxurious rooms all offer balconies with wonderful country and mountain views. The dining room is lovely and the food matches.
info@alpenhof-murnau.com http://www.alpenhof-murnau.com

OFFENBURG

Hotel Sonne
Hauptstrasse 94 D-77652
07-81-9-3216
Fax: 07-81-9-3216-40
Gabriele Schimpf-Schoeppner
Open all year

63-118 Euro¤-BB
34 rooms, 27 pb
Visa, MC
C-yes/S-yes/P-yes/H-no
English, French, German

Full breakfast
Restaurant (fee)

One of the oldest hotels in Germany. Rooms are furnished with antique furniture of the 19th century. info@hotel-sonne-offenburg.de

PFRONTEN

Berghotel Schlossanger Alp
Am Schlossanger 1 D-87459
083-631-381-91
Fax: 083-631-914555
Schlachter & Ebert Family
All year

56-89 Euro¤-BB
30 rooms, 30 pb
•
Visa
C-yes/S-yes/P-ltd/H-no
English, French, German

Full breakfast
Restaurant (fee), lunch

The chalet is built amid open fields, full of wooden beams & local folk ornaments.
ebert@schlossanger.de http://www.schlossanger.de

POTSDAM

Relexa Schlosshotel Cecilienhof
Neuer Garten D-14469
49-0-331-37050
Fax: 49-0-331-292498
Christina Ane
All year

151-243 US$-BB
42 rooms, 42 pb
•
Most CC
C-yes/S-yes/P-yes/H-ltd
German, English

Full breakfast
Restaurant open daily
7am–11pm, snacks

The Cecilienhof is the last castle of the Hohenzollern and was built 1914-1917 according to the precise wishes of Crownprince Wilhelm and his wife Cecilie as their residence.
potsdam.cecilienhof@relexa-hotel.de http://www.relexa-hotel.de

Greece

ATHENS

Philippos Hotel
3 Mitseon St G-11742
+30-10-922-3611
Fax: +30-10-922-3615
Philippos S.A.
All year

90-189 US$-BB
Greek

Mini bar

Hotel is located below the Acropolis within a few minutes walk from the historical sites and Plaka the old quarter of Athens
philippos@herodion.gr http://www.philipposhotel.gr

Hungary

BUDAPEST

Hotel Victoria
11 Bem RKP H-1011
36-1-457-8080
Fax: 36-1-457-8088
Zoltan Palmai Jr
Open all year

144-199 German¤-BB
27 rooms, 27 pb
•
Most CC
C-yes/S-yes/P-yes/H-no
Hungarian, German, English

Full breakfast
Snacks, bar service

Small 4-star hotel with familiar atmosphere. Each room has a splendid roundview of the city. Central location with reasonable prices.
victoria@victoria.hu http://www.victoria.hu/

KÖVESKÀL (REGION)

Kali Art Inn
Köveskàl, Fü. 8., *Budapest*
H-8274
+36-87-70-6090
Fax: +36-87-46-8412
Gergely Téglásy
March 15th–November 4th

78 US$-BB
14 rooms, 12 pb
Visa, MC, •
C-yes/S-ltd/P-yes/H-ltd
English, Germ, Hung, Russ

Continental plus breakfast
Tea, coffee, snacks, wines, bar, 4-course dinner

Settled in the natural reserve of the Köl basin near Lake Balaton, we pamper you with comfort, excellent food and wines, and the surrounding countryside.
mail@kali-art.com http://kali-art.com/adlanier/

Ireland

BANTRY BAY

Ballylickey Manor House
Ballylickey
00-353-27-50071
Fax: 00-353-27-50124
Mr. & Mrs. Graves
March–November

100 Irish¤-BB
12 rooms, 12 pb
•
Most CC
C-yes/S-yes/P-ltd/H-no
French, Spanish, German

Full breakfast
Lunch, dinner, afternoon tea

Ballylickey overlooks beautiful Bantry Bay, in the midst of magnificent scenery and within easy reach of Killarney. ballymh@eircom.net http://www.ballylickeymanorhouse.com

CARLOW TOWN

Barrowville Town House
Kilkenny Road
0503-43324
Fax: 0503-41953
Randal & Marie Dempsey
All year

35-40 Euro¤-BB
7 rooms, 7 pb
•
Visa, MC, AmEx
S-no/P-no/H-no
English, German, French

Full breakfast

A Premier Guesthouse of Quality. 3 star Georgian listed house. Antique furnishings, traditional or buffet breakfast in conservatory overlooking gardens.
http://www.barrowvillehouse.com

CONNEMARA

Ballynahinch Castle
Recess
+353-095-31006
Fax: +353-095-31085
Patrick O'Flaherty
Closed Christmas week & February

80-191 US$-BB
40 rooms, 40 pb
•
Most CC
C-yes/S-yes/P-no/H-no
Engl, Sp, Germ, Fren, Russ

Restaurant, lunch, dinner, afternoo

18th.C. manor castle, now a 4 star hotel in 350 acre private estate overlooking own wild salmon fishery. bhinch@iol.ie http://www.ballynahinch-castle.com

COUNTY GALWAY

Delphi Lodge
Leenane
353-954-2222
Peter Mantle
Closed Christmas, New Year

60-120 Euro¤-BB
12 rooms, 12 pb
•
Visa
C-no/S-yes/P-no/H-yes
French, English

Full breakfast
Lunch, dinner, afternoon tea

If you want to stay in a beautiful country house in one of the most spectacular settings in Ireland, come to Delphi Lodge in Connemara.
delfish@iol.ie http://www.delphilodge.ie

ENNISCORTHY

Ballinkeele House
Ballymurn
353-53-38105
Fax: 353-53-38468
John & Margaret Maher
March 1–November 6

65-75 ?-BB
5 rooms, 5 pb
•
Most CC
C-ltd/S-ltd/P-no/H-no
English, French

Full breakfast
Dinner available (fee) 38 $

Work off hostess home-cooked breakfasts (and dinners-by arrangement). Wellingtons for walking. Large drawing room. The atmosphere is deliciously early Victorian.
info@ballinkeele.com http://www.Ballinkeele.com

KILDARE

Hazel Hotel
Monasterevin
Dublin Road
353-45-525373
Fax: 353-45-525810
John Kelly
All year except Dec 24 & 25

50 US$-BB
23 rooms, 5 pb
•
Most CC
C-yes/S-yes/P-no/H-yes
English

Full breakfast
Lunches, After noon Tea, Evening Dinner,

Situated in the town of Monasterevin an area renowned for its Bloodstock Industry, and is on the Main Dublin, Cork Road N7. Japanese Gardens, Irish National Stud, and Curragh Race Course are nearby. sales@hazelhotel.com http://www.hazelhotel.com

LEENANE

Killary Lodge
Galway
353-0-95-42276
Fax: 353-0-95-42314
Kathy Evans
March–October

41-50 US$-BB
21 rooms, 21 pb
•
Visa, MC
C-yes/S-yes/P-no/H-no
English, German

Full breakfast
Restaurant, all meals (fee)

Relaxed informal hideaway on 30 acres by the sea in Connemara. Honesty bar and highly personal service.. lodge@killary.com http://www.killary.com

OUGHTERARD

River Run Lodge
Glann Road
353-91-552697
Fax: 353-91-552669
Anne & Tom Little
All year

60-78 Irish¤-BB
8 rooms, 5 pb
•
Visa, MC, AmEx
C-ltd/S-ltd/P-ltd/H-yes
English, French

A la carte and table d'hotel

River Run sits on the Owenriff which flows into Lough Corrib, the world-famous for angling. Just a short walk from the heart of the village, you'll find landscaped gardens, patios and walks. rivrun@indigo.ie
http://www.connemara.net/RiverRunLodge/index.html

TRALEE

Ballyseede Castle Hotel
Tralee
Ballyseede
353-66-712-5799
Fax: 353-66-712-5287
Bart W. O'Connor
Open all year

140-210 US$-BB
12 rooms, 12 pb
•
Most CC
C-no/S-yes/P-no/H-no
English

Full breakfast
Lunch, dinner, afternoon tea and snacks

A cosy, casual 15th century castle on 35 acres of parkland.
ballyseede@eircom.net http://www.ballyseedecastle.com

Italy

ANCONA

La Biancarda
Viale della Vittoria 44B
+39-071-280-0503
Fax: +39-071-2800503
Giovanna Caucci
Summer, May–October

BB
6 rooms, 4 pb
•
C-yes/S-yes/P-yes/H-ltd
English, Ital, Germ, Sp

La Biancarda is an ancient and elegant country house completely restored in 1988 that overlooks a lawn, the hills and the golf court and an orchard and the Conero Natural Park at the back. biancarda@libero.it http://www.inconero.it

ASSISI

Hotel 3 Esse Country House
Via di Valecchie 41 I-06081
075-816-363
Fax: 075-816-155
Maria Silvana Ciammaruchi
Open all year

80 US$-BB
20 rooms, 19 pb
•
Visa
C-yes/S-yes/P-yes/H-ltd
English, French, Italian

Continental breakfast
Afternoon tea, complimentary wine

The house is surrounded by extensive grounds where guests can relax in the shade of century old oak trees. info@countryhousetreesse.com
http://www.countryhouse3esse.com

Malvarina
Assisi
V. Sant' Appolinare 32 I-06081
075-806-4280 075-806-4280

BB
Italian
Claudio Fabrizi Family
All year

The delightful Malvarina farm with its charming, country-style accommodations, excellent local cuisine, warm and congenial host family, and ideal location.
info@malva http://www.malvarina.it

BARBERINO VAL D'ELSA

La Spinosa
Via Le Masse 8
055-807-5413
Fax: 055-806-6214
Ossola & Videsott
March–November

150.00-180.00 US$-BB
9 rooms, 9 pb
Visa, MC
C-yes/S-ltd/P-ltd/H-ltd
English, German, French

Continental plus breakfast
Bar service, cold lunch, organic wine, snacks

The love of nature, peace and total relaxation are the main reasons for staying at La Spinosa. info@laspinosa.it http://www.laspinosa.it

CANNOBIO

Hotel Pironi
Via Marconi, #35 I-28822
011-39-0323-70624
Fax: 011-39-0323-72184
Mr. Massimo Albertella
End March-Begin November

80-126 US$-BB
12 rooms, 12 pb
Most CC
C-yes/S-yes/P-no/H-no
Italian, Eng, Germ, Fren

Full breakfast

You may find this charming hotel in Cannobio on the Lago Maggiore set in a fascinating location between the lake and the medieval village.
info@pironihotel.it http://www.pironihotel.it

CAPRI

Hotel Villa Brunella
Via Tragara, 24 I-80073
081-837-0122
Fax: 081-837-0430
Ruggiero Vincenzo
March 19–November 6

260-340 US$-BB
20 rooms, 20 pb
•
Most CC
C-yes/S-yes/P-no/H-no
Italian, Engl, Fren, Ger

Continental breakfast
Restaurant, bar service

Nestled in the heart of luxuriant flowery garden framing the Faraglioni.
villabrunella@capri.it http://www.villabrunella.it

CASTELFRANCO EMILIA

Villa Gaidello
Via Gaidello 18/22 I-41013
059-92-6806
Fax: 059-92-6620
Paola Giovanna Bini
Closed August

120 US$-BB
8 rooms, 8 pb
Visa, MC, Disc
C-yes/S-ltd/P-no/H-no
Italian, French, English

Continental plus breakfast
Restaurant, lunch & dinner on request

250 year-old farmhouse located in the beautiful Po Valley. A vast agricultural estate, once the summer retreat of the Bini family. 8 apartments.
gaidello@tin.it http://members.aol.com/gaidello

CASTIGLIONE CHIAVARESE

Monte Pu
16030 Castiglione Chiavarese
Localita Monte Pu
+39-0185-408027
Fax: +39-0185-408027
Aurora Giani
Spring, Summer, Autumn

2x(35-43) Euro¤-BB
10 rooms, 10 pb
•
Most CC
C-yes/S-ltd/P-ltd/H-yes
Italian, English

Genoa breakfast
Regional dishes for Dinner
(Lunch on weekends)

Monte Pu is located in an optimal position for visiting outstanding of Liguria, such as Cinque Terre, Camogli, etc. Astonishing landscape at 700 meters above the sea, away from noise and paved roads.

info@montepu.it http://www.montepu.it/

CETONA

La Frateria Di Padre Eligio
Convento San Francesco I-53040
0578-238015
Fax: 0578-239220
Maria Grazia Daolio
Open all year

320.000 Italian-EP
6 rooms, 6 pb
Most CC
C-yes/S-yes/P-no/H-no
Italian, Engl, Fren

Full breakfast (fee)
Lunch, Dinner, Restaurant (fee)

After 12 years of painstaking restoration, carried out by volunteers and drug addicts, the Convent has returned to its beauty and its vocation.

frateria@ftbcc.it http://www.mondox.com

CORTINA D\XD5 AMPEZZO

Hotel Menardi
Via Majon No. 110 I-32043
0436-2400
Fax: 0436-862183
The Menardi Family
Summer and Winter

100-180 US$-BB
55 rooms, 55 pb
•
Most CC
C-yes/S-yes/P-no/H-no
English, Germ, Fren, Ital

Continental plus breakfast
Lunch, Dinner (fee)

At the turn of century: an ancient house, a family. An inn, with a stable and a bar, a post-house on the route connecting the Habsburg Empire to the Kingdom of Italy.

info@hotelmenardi.it http://www.hotelmenardi.it

CORTONA

Hotel Restaurant Corys
Torreone 6
0575-605141
Fax: 0575-631443
Rosalinda Crivelli & Silvia Pescatori
All year

83-124 US$-BB
7 rooms, 7 pb
•
Most CC
C-yes/S-yes/P-yes/H-yes
Italian, English

Continental breakfast

Hotel Corys it is a little charming, refined and elegant hotel, with every comfort, which overlooks the Tuscan Valdichiana and Lake Trasimeno, from its 600 meters' altitude.

info@corys.it http://www.corys.it

Relais Corte dei Papi
011-39-0575614109
Fax: 011-39-0575614963
David Papi
All year

180 US$-BB
8 rooms, 8 pb
•
Visa, MC, AmEx
C-yes/S-yes/P-yes/H-yes
Italian, Eng, Sp, Arabic

Full breakfast
Full restaurant, homemade wine, in-room dining

A peaceful and elegant Tuscan hideaway near all areas of interest. We offer beautiful rooms & suites with private bathrooms & air conditioning, swimming pool, restaurant, gardens, parking & more.

lacorte@technet.it http://www.iacortedeipapi.com

DIVIGNANO

Cascina Motto
Via Marzabotto 7 I-28010
0321-995-350
Fax: 0321-995-350
Roberta Plevani
March to November

62.00-72.30 US$-BB
2 rooms, 2 pb
C-yes/S-ltd/P-ltd/H-no
English, German

Continental breakfast

Two hectares of lawn and garden, fruit trees, boccecourt, swings and a charming outbuilding converted for the use of guests. The property was lately enhanced by the addition of a beautiful swimming pool.

david_robi@katamail.com http://www.casepiemontesi-novara.vze.com/motto.htm

FLORENCE

Albergo Torre Di Bellosguardo
Via Roti Michelozzi, 2 I-50124
055-229-8145
Fax: 055-229-008
Giovanni Amerigo Franchetti
Open all year

160-330 US$-EP
16 rooms, 16 pb
Most CC
C-yes/S-yes/P-yes/H-no
It, Eng, Fre, Ger, Span, Port.

Breakfast (fee)
Afternoon tea, bar service

13th century tower with 15th century villa. Sport center; Sauna, Jacuzzi, indoor swimming pool and gym.

info@torrebellosguardo.com http://www.torrebellosguardo.com

B&B For Women Only
Borgo Pinti 31 I-50121
+39-055-24-80056
Fax: +39-055-238-12-60
Paola Fazzini All year

150,000 Italian¤-BB
4 rooms
Visa, MC
C-ltd/S-no/P-ltd/H-no
Italian, English

Continental plus breakfast
Tea, coffee, snacks

B&B is an exclusive bed and breakfast for women only located at the top floor (no lift—68 steps) of a historical palace in the center of Florence, Italy.

beb@mail.cosmos.it http://www.bnb.it/beb

B&B Villa La Sosta
via Bolognese #83 I-50139
++39-0-55-495073
Fax: ++39-0-55-495073 ++39-0-335-8349992
Antonio & Giuseppina Fantoni

85-100 US$-BB
5 rooms, 5 pb, •
C-yes/S-no/P-no/H-ltd
Italian, English, Spanish
All year

Continental breakfast

Charming bed and breakfast, which dates back to the end of the 19th. Century.

info@villalasosta.com http://www.villalasosta.com

Caffellatte
via Pratese,34 I-50145
39-055-34-24-625
Fax: 39-055-34-32-393 +39-328-71-33-789
Alessio Vincenti All year

75 EUR¤-BB
7 rooms, 2 pb
•
Visa, MC, Most CC
C-yes/S-ltd/P-yes/H-ltd
English, French, Italian

Continental plus breakfast
Wine,snacks

Perfectly placed for visitors wanting to spend a short holiday in Florence, this friendly B&B is only 500m from the Cascine park notable for its scenic walks and sports facilities.

infocaffellatte@interfree.it
http://www.knowital.com/properties/florence/html3/caffellatte1.html

---

Casa Pucci
Via Santa Monica, 8 I-50124
055-21-6560
Fax: 055-21-6560
Tamara Pucci All year

88-95 US$-BB
3 rooms, 3 pb
Visa, MC
C-yes/S-no/P-ltd/H-no
English, Italian

Continenental breakfast

In a location near Ponte Vecchio (the Old Bridge) and the Palazzo Pitti (the Pitti Palace) there is Casa Pucci, a wonderful bed and breakfast in Florence Italy.

tapucci@tin.it http://casapucci.artwork-inform.com/

FLORENCE

Cimatori Guest House
Via Dante Alighieri 14 I-50122
+39-055-239-9145
Fax: +39-055-265-5000
Domenico Cuiuli
All year

115-155 US$-BB
5 rooms, 5 pb
Visa, MC, AmEx
C-ltd/S-no/P-no/H-no
English, Italian, French

Italian breakfast (coffee, tea & pastry)

Welcome to one of Florence's newest guest house located in the heart of all artistic and ethnic activity. info@cimatori.it http://www.cimatori.it

---

Florence Old Bridge
Via Guicciardini, 22
055-265-4262
Fax: 055-264-6693
Andrea, Paolo, Fabrizio, Barbara
All year

75-100 US$-EP
6 rooms, 6 pb
•
Visa, MC, AmEx
C-yes/S-ltd/P-no/H-no
English, Spanish, Italian

5 $ per person, in the tea room

Recently restored, the FOB is equipped with comfortable rooms furnished in old style and provided with A/C and private bathrooms, 100 meters from the Old Bridge.
florenceoldbridge@tin.it http://www.florenceoldbridge.com

Hotel Casci
Via Cavour 13
+39-055 211 686
Fax: +39-055 239 6461
The Lombardi Family
All year

BB
85 rooms, 85 pb
Italian

A small and welcoming family managed hotel in an ancient palace right in the center of Florence. info@hotelcasci.com http://www.allworld-vacation.com/italy/it26.htm

---

Hotel Morandi Alla Crocetta
Via Laura 50 I-50121
055-234-4747
Fax: 055-248-0954
Antuono Family
Open all year

70-100 US$-EP
10 rooms, 10 pb
•
Most CC, *Rated*
C-yes/S-yes/P-yes/H-no
Engl, French, Ital, Germ

Continental breakfast
Afternoon tea

A restored old Italian home that once was the monastery of the Crocetta.
welcome@hotelmorandi.it http://www.hotelmorandi.it

Il Ghiro
Via Faenza 63
+39-5528-2086
Fax: +39-5528-2086
Federico Bianchini
All year

60-75 US$-BB
5 rooms, 3 pb
Italian, English

Il Ghiro – una piccola pensione situata nel centro storico di Firenze a due passi dalla stazione centrale di S.M.N, dal mercato di S. Lorenzo e dal Duomo.
info@ilghiro.it http://www.ilghiro.it

Proconsolo Rooms
Via del Proconsolo 5 I-50122
05-521-7160 05-521-7160
Damjanovski Vladimir, MD
All year

BB
Italian

Find yourself relaxing after a Renaissance adventure deep in the heart of Florence at Proconsolo rooms.
proconsolo http://www.proconsolorooms.com

FLORENCE

Relais Cavalcanti
via Pellicceria 2 I-50123
39-055-210962
Fax: 39-055-2675211
Anna & Francesca
All year

95-115 US$-EP
4 rooms, 4 pb
Visa, MC
C-yes/S-yes/P-no/H-no
English

Tea, coffee and other drinks

A charming Relais in a XIIIth century palace of the centre of Florence next to the Ponte Vecchio and Uffizi. Relais Cavalcanti provides to its guests an unique panoramic view of the heart of Florence.

relaiscavalcanti@relaiscavalcanti.com http://www.relaiscavalcanti.com

---

Residenza La Torricella
Via Vecchia de Pozzolatico 25 I-50125
055-232-1808
Fax: 055-204-7402
Marialisa Manetti
01/04–31/10, 20/12–10/01

130 US$-BB
8 rooms, 8 pb
•
Visa, MC
C-yes/S-ltd/P-yes/H-no
English

Buffet breakfast
Coffee, tea

La Torricella is a Renaissance dwelling located in the hills surrounding the city of Florence. La Torricella is the ideal place for anyone who wishes to enjoy the quietude of the countryside. latorricella@tiscalinet.it http://www.karenbrown.com/italy/torricella.html

---

Tourist House Liberty
Via Ventisette Aprile #9 I-50129
0039-05547-1759
Fax: 0039-05548-3330
Alessandro Fiore
All year

70-110 Euro¤-EP
12 rooms, 9 pb
Visa, MC, AmEx
C-yes/S-no/P-ltd/H-no
Italian Engl French Port

Coffe

The Tourist House Liberty opened in May 1999, after it was completely remodeled. It's warm and cozy, perfect for who loves an elegant and environment in an economic category. libertyhouse@iol.it http://www.touristhouseliberty.it

GIGLIO PORTO

Pardini's Hermitage Hotel
Cala degli Alberi I-58013
+39-0564-80-9034
Fax: +39-0564-80-9177
Federigo Pardini
Open all year

90-135 US$-AP
13 rooms, 13 pb
•
Visa
C-yes/S-yes/P-yes/H-no
Ita, Germ, Engl, Fren

Full breakfast
Lunch and Dinner included in rate

Right on the sea-front, far away from any built-up area. Reachable from Giglio Porto only by boat or on foot.

hermit@ats.it http://www.finalserv.it/hermitage/

INVERNO PAVIA

Circolo Sibilla
Via C.na S. Giuseppe 18 I-27010
+39-382-73184
Fax: +39-2-7000555103
Penny Brucculeri
All year

70 US$-BB
3 rooms, 3 pb
C-yes/S-yes/P-yes/H-yes
English, French, Italian

Continental breakfast
Lunch/dinner are available on demand at 20 Euros.

Bed & Breakfast in the Lombard countryside far only 30 Km. from Milan, 15 from Pavia and 15 from Lodi. A quiet stop before or after a travel in Italy.

bpenny@libero.it http://utenti.lycos.it/circolosibilla

LAKE ORTA

Hotel Giardinetto
Via Provinciale 1 I-28028
0323-89118
Fax: 0323-89219
Caterina Primatesta
April 1–October 29

95-120 Euro¤-BB
59 rooms, 59 pb
•
Visa, MC, AmEx
C-yes/S-yes/P-yes/H-yes
Italian, Engl, Germ, Fren

Continental breakfast
Lunch, dinner, afternoon tea, restaurant

Beautifuly located directly on the lakefront, the Terrace Restaurant offers excellent meals inside or outside by candlelight.
hotelgiardinetto@tin.it http://www.lagodortahotels.com/giardinettoing.htm

MARATEA

Romantik Hotel Villa Cheta Elite
Via Timpone 46
Acquafredda I-85046
0973-878134
Fax: 0973-878135
Lamberto Aquadro & Stefania Aquadro
Open all year

110-160 US$-BB
20 rooms, 20 pb
•
Most CC
C-yes/S-yes/P-yes/H-no
German, English, Italian

Full breakfast
Restaurant, bar service

Splendid Liberty-style villa views the sea, beach close. Refined, efficient hospitality. Restaurant features local products.
villacheta@tin.it http://www.villacheta.it

MERANO

Castle Fragsburg
Via Fragsburg 3 I-39012
++39-0473-244071
Fax: ++39-0473-244493
Alexander Ortner Family
April–November

221-224 US$-BB
18 rooms, 18 pb
•
Visa, MC
C-yes/S-no/P-no/H-yes
Ital, Germ, Eng, Sp, Fren

Full breakfast
Restaurant, lunch, dinner

Old small hunting-Castle built by the Count of Memmingen. Superb position with splendid views to the valley below. Exclusive ambiente, completely renewed in the winter 2001.
info@fragsburg.com http://www.fragsburg.com

MONOPOLI

Il Melograno
Contrada Torricella 345 I-70043
080-690-9030
Fax: 080-74-7908
Roberta Guerra
Closed Nov. 10–March 18

280-430 US$-BB
37 rooms, 37 pb
•
Most CC
C-yes/S-yes/P-no/H-yes
Ital, Fren, Eng, Germ

Full breakfast
Lunch & dinner (fee)

16th. Century fortified farmhouse, now a 5 star Relais & Chateaux hotel. Located in the countryside in Southern Italy -private beach, 33 rooms and 4 suites furnished with antiques.
melograno@melograno.com http://www.melograno.com

MONTECARLO

Casa Satti
via Roma 31 I-55015
0039-0583-22347
Fax: 0039-0583-22007
Bianca Satti Tori
April to Nov 15.

120-230 US$-BB
4 rooms, 4 pb
C-yes/S-no/P-no/H-no
English, Italian

Continental breakfast
Many restaurants in Montecarlo!

Casa Satti is a unique Tuscan bed and breakfast, located in Montecarlo, a picturesque hilltop town midway between Florence, Lucca and Pisa, only 60 km from Siena.
info@casasatti.com http://www.casasatti.com

MONTEVETTOLINI

Villa Lucia
Via dei Bronzoli 144 I-51015
+39-0572-61-7790
Fax: +39-0572-62-8817
Lucia Ann Vallera
Closed winter

150 US$-BB
10 rooms, 10 pb
•
C-yes/S-yes/P-no/H-no
English, Ital, Fren, Sp

Continental plus breakfast
Other meals on request

Among 14 acres of olive groves. 500 year old farmhouse furnished in antiques teaches one the art of living today while exploring treasures of yesterday.
villalucia@yahoo.com http://www.bboftuscany.com

MONTICHIARI

Villa San Pietro
Via San Pietro, 25 I-25018
39-030-96-1232
Fax: 39-030-998-1098
Jacques & Annamaria Ducroz
All year

83 Euro¤-BB
3 rooms, 3 pb
•
Visa, MC
C-yes/S-no/P-no/H-no
Italian, Fren, Eng, Sp

Continental breakfast
5-course dinner upon request

Villa San Pietro is a 17th century house which has been recently restored retaining all its original character with massive oak beams, ancient brick floors, and beautiful antique furnishing.
annajacques@rocketmail.com http://www.art-with-attitude.com/villa/san_pietro.html

ORVIETO

Locanda Rosati Giampero
Buonviaggio 22 I-05018
0763 217314
Fax: 0763 217314
Rosati Family
March 1—January 7

93-118 US$-BB
10 rooms, 10 pb
•
Visa, MC
C-yes/S-no/P-yes/H-yes
English, Italian

Continental breakfast
Tea, coffee, wine, snacks and dinner

The Locanda Rosati lies in the hills barely 9 km from the Orvieto A1 toll highway exit.
info@locandarosati.orvieto.tr.it http://www.locandarosati.orvieto.tr.it

PERUGIA

Castello Dell' Oscano
Strada della Forcella 37 I-06134
++39075-584371
Fax: ++3975-690-666
Michele Ravano
Open all year

130-250 US$-BB
30 rooms, 30 pb
•
Most CC
C-yes/S-yes/P-yes/H-yes
Italian, English, French

Breakfast buffet (fee)
Dinner (fee), afternoon tea, snacks

Our castle and villa Ada (at 10 meters) are only 8 km. from the town center, but on a top of a hill with wonderful views in the middle of a luxury park of many species of trees.
info@oscano.com http://www.oscano.com

PISTOIA

Villa Vannini
Villa di Piteccio I-51030
0573-42031
Fax: 0573-42551
Marta Romiti
All year

85 US$-BB
11 rooms, 11 pb
Most CC
C-ltd/S-ltd/P-ltd/H-ltd
Italian, English, French

Full breakfast
Dinner

The Villa is surrounded by huge trees, it offers the comfort and quietness of an old country house, while having all the modern facilities. Food is of Toscan tradition.
v.vannini@dada.it http://villavannini.dadacasa.supereva.it

ROME

Caesar House Residenze Romane
Via Cavour, 310 I-00184
39-06-679-2674
Fax: 39-06-6978-1120
Julia
All year

165-225 US$-BB
6 rooms, 6 pb
•
Visa, MC, AmEx, *Rated*
C-yes/S-ltd/P-no/H-no
It, Eng, Fr, Filipino

Continental plus breakfast
Afternoon tea and coffee with pastries

Close to the Colosseum, the Trevi Fountain and the best known shops, a residence with the atmosphere of a private home offering a discreet and refined hospitality in syntony with the enchanted sites.
residenzeromane@libero.it http://www.caesarhouse.com

Roma Bed & Breakfast
via dei Gonzaga 159/E I-00164
+39-06-66155666
Fax: +39-06-6615-6021
Giancarlo & Myriam Negri
All year

90.00 US$-BB
7 rooms, 7 pb
•
Visa, MC, AmEx, *Rated*
C-yes/S-ltd/P-yes/H-no
Italian, English, French

Continental plus breakfast

Near Vatican (2 miles), in a very enchanting villa, we have rooms, suites and a nice Chalet, gardens and sun terraces all around. Well connected to the center. Free parking.
postmaster@roma-bandb.it http://www.roma-bandb.it/

Trastevere House
Vicolo del Buco, 7 I-00153
+39-06-588-3774
Fabrizio Gregori
All year

60-120 US$-BB
Italian

The old lodge, "Trastevere House", will welcome you in an ancient and distinctive palace of the 18th century, in the heart of the historical neighborhood.
trasteverehouse@hotmail.com http://www.travel.it/roma/trasteverehouse

ROSANO

Il Moro
Podere il moro, 6 I-50067
+39-055-830-3320
Fax: +39-055-830-3320
Paola Alberto Azzurra Bassi
April–October

73 Euro¤-BB
5 rooms, 5 pb
C-yes/S-no/P-no/H-yes
English, Italian

Wine

Il moro is an ancient country house surrounded by olive-tree and vines in Rosano s/Arno, only 11 km. from Florence.
info@countryroom-ilmoro.com http://www.countryroom-ilmoro.com

SAN QUIRICO D'ORCIA

Castello di Ripa d'Orcia
Via della Contea 1/16
0577-897376
Fax: 0577-898038
Aluffi Pentini Family
March–November

120 US$-BB
13 rooms, 13 pb
•
Visa, MC
C-ltd/S-ltd/P-no/H-no
English, French

Continental breakfast
Dinner—upon reservation

The castle of Ripa d'orcia is a mediaeval hamlet (XII cent.) turned to a comfortable country residence—bed & breakfast which offer hospitality along with the discovery of its fine wines production.
info@castelloripadorcia.com http://www.castelloripadorcia.com

SORRENTO

Hotel Il Nido Restaurant	70-80 US$-BB	Continental breakfast
Via Nastro Verde, 62 I-80067	26 rooms, 26 pb	A full Restaurant with a
+39-0818-782766	•	traditional cuisine.
Fax: +39-0818-073304	Visa, MC, AmEx	
Gianni	C-yes/S-ltd/P-ltd/H-ltd	
All year	Italian, English, French	

IL NIDO accoglie clienti con la sua cordiale atmosfera familiare dal lontano 1964.
info@ilnido.it http://www.ilnido.it

SPELLO

Hotel Palazzo Bocci	120-240 US$-EP	Half Board 30.00 $ per
via Cavour, 17 I-06038	23 rooms, 23 pb	person/day
074-230-1021	•	Outdoor Restaurant
Fax: 074-230-1464	Visa, MC, AmEx	Il Molino, Bar
Sig. Fabrizio Buono	C-yes/S-yes/P-no/H-yes	
Open all year	English, French, German	

The Palazzo Bocci, converted in 1992 from an 18th Century palazzo, retains the character of the historic building with frescoed ceilings and some walls.
bocci@bcsnet.it http://www.emmeti.it/Pbocci.it.html

SPOLETO

Convento di Agghielli	130 US$-MAP	Home-made cakes, biscuits
Frazione Pompagano I-06049	10 rooms, 10 pb	and jams
0743-225010	•	
Fax: 0743-225010	Visa, MC	
Marinella De Simone	C-yes/S-ltd/P-ltd/H-yes	
All year	Italian, English, German	

Ancient convent renewed and transformed into a splendid farm accommodation 2 miles from Spoleto, Umbria. Organic food at the restaurant and 8 suites and 2 double rooms for the rest. Wellness Center.
agghielli@virgilio.it http://www.agghielli.it

TAVERNELLE DI PANICALE

Montali	155 Euro¤-MAP	Continental plus breakfast
Via Montali 23	10 rooms, 10 pb	Wine and any drinks on
Tavernelle di Panicale I-06068	•	request
39-075-835-0680	Visa, MC	
Fax: 39-075-835-0144	C-ltd/S-no/P-no/H-ltd	
Luzia & Alberto Musacchio	English, Port, Sp, It	
End of March to end of October		

Very exclusive property, famous for unique gourmet vegetarian cuisine. AS seen on BBC "Summer holiday program." Breathtaking views of sunrise and sunset, absolutely "off the beaten tracks."
montali@montalionline.com http://www.montalionline.com

VENICE

Al Giardino	• 75 US$-BB	Coffee, capuccino, milk, tea,
Via Altinia 119/B I-30030	3 rooms, 3 pb	juice
+39-041-501-0556	Visa, MC	
Fax: +39-041-501-0556	C-yes/S-no/P-no/H-no	
Gianni Ferrarese	Ital, Eng, Ger, Fr, Sp	
All year		

A 15 minuti dal Centro Storico di Venezia, a 15 minuti dal centro di Mestre, a 10 minuti dall'Aeroporto e dal Casinò, a 20 minuti dalla Stazione FS.
algiardino@tiscali.it http://www.algiardinovenezia.it

VENICE

Albergo Quattro Fontane
Via Quattro Fontane, 16 I-30126
041-526-0227
Fax: 041-526-0726
Family Bevilacqua
April 1st. to Nov. 15th.

470-600,000 Italian¤-BB
59 rooms, 59 pb
•
Most CC
C-yes/S-yes/P-yes/H-no
Ital, Fren, Eng, Germ

Continental breakfast
Restaurant, afternoon tea, snacks

Historical residence in a garden, near the beach, 15 minutes from San Marco Square—all rooms and public spaces are furnished with antiques.

quafonve@tin.it http://www.quattrofontane.com

Hotel Concordia
Calle Larga San Marco 367 I-30124
041-520-6866
Fax: 041-520-6775
Mrs. Marina Caputo
Open all year

397 US$-BB
56 rooms, 56 pb
Most CC
C-yes/S-yes/P-yes/H-no
Ital, Eng, Ger, Sp, Fr

Generous buffet breakfast
Restaurant La Piazzeta, bar, tea, light meal

Unique hotel in Venice overlooking St. Mark's Square. Venetian atmosphere with every modern comfort, first class service.

info@hotelconcordia.com http://www.hotelconcordia.com

Locanda ai Bareteri
San March, 4966
+39-041-523-2233
Fax: +39-041-244-3450
Albert & Sergio
All year

75,00-155,00 US$-BB
9 rooms, 7 pb
Visa, MC
C-yes/S-ltd/P-yes/H-no
Italian, English, Spanish

Continental breakfast

Locanda ai Bareteri is a new guesthouse, centrally located, ready to accommodate small groups and solitary travelers alike. The estate offers spacious and relaxed accommodations, all newly refurbished.

info@bareteri.com http://www.bareteri.com

Netherlands

AMSTERDAM

Canal House Hotel
Keizersgracht 148 NL-1015 CX
020-622-5182
Fax: 020-624-1317
Brian & Mary Bennett
Open all year

140-190 US$-BB
26 rooms, 26 pb
•
Visa, MC
C-ltd/S-ltd/P-no/H-no
English, Dutch

Full Dutch breakfast

Charming 17th century house in the old city centre of Amsterdam. Ideal location for sightseeing or a canalside stroll.

info@canalhouse.nl http://www.canalhouse.nl

Maes
Herestraat 26hs NL-1015CB
31-20-427-5165
Fax: 31-20-427-5166
Ken and Vlad
All year

BB
Dutch

In the centre, only minutes away from the museums and within walking distance from all major sights and nightlife spots, yet in a quiet residential area:

maesbb94@xs4all.nl http://www.bedandbreakfastamsterdam.com

AMSTERDAM

The Townhouse
Akoleienstraat 2 NL-1016
+31-20-6129320
Fax: +31-20-6129328 +31-20-6129320
Robert & Ramon All year

89 US$-BB
2 rooms
Visa, MC, AmEx, *Rated*
C-yes/S-no/P-no/H-no
Eng, Ger, Spa, Ital, Fren, Dut

Continental breakfast
Fruits are available the whole day.

A Charming NEW B&B in the old city centre of Amsterdam. See our website: www.townhouse.nl info@townhouse.nl http://www.townhouse.nl

---

Truelove Guesthouse
Prinsenstraat 4 NL-1015DC
+20-320-2500
Sean Maguire
All year

BB
Dutch

The name Truelove found its origin in the U.K. where our family had a well-established ladies fashion house in Sheffield, England.
trueloveantiek@zonnet.nl http://www.truelove.be

EDAM

Hotel-Restaurant De Fortuna
Spuistraat 3 NL-1135 AV
0299-371671
Fax: 0299-371469
Family Dekker
Open all year

87.50-97.50 US$-BB
24 rooms, 24 pb
•
Visa, MC, AmEx, *Rated*
C-yes/S-yes/P-ltd/H-yes
English, German, Dutch

Full breakfast
Restaurant, bar service

This stylish and characteristic hotel consists of 5 beautifully restored houses dating back to the 17th century. The hotel is situated in the old centre of the picturesque Zuiderzee town of Edam. fortuna@fortuna-edam.nl http://www.fortuna-edam.nl

Poland

KRAKOW

Krakow B&B
Straszewskiego St
Fax: 516-883-0407
Ela
All year

60-70 US$-BB
1 rooms, 1 pb
Visa, MC, AmEx, •
C-yes/S-ltd/P-no/H-ltd
Polish, English

In room upfront provided on request

1st. bed and breakfast of this kind in Krakow. Most conveniently located in the city centre. mak42351@aol.com http://www.krakowbedandbreakfast.com

Portugal

AZORES

Aldeia da Fonte
Silveira
Lajes do Pico P-9930
+351-292-67-2777
Fax: +351-292-67-2700
Antonio Carrillo & Sonia Santos

60-125 US$-BB
32 rooms, 32 pb
Visa, MC, AmEx, •
C-ltd/S-ltd/P-yes/H-yes
Portuguese, English, German
All year

Continental breakfast
Portuguese, Chinese and International

There seldom have been a more dramatic setting for a hotel. Perched on cliffs high above the Atlantic Ocean, Aldeia da Fonte lays at the foot of the spectacular volcano, Mount Pico. info@aldeiafonte.com http://aldeiadafonte.com

LISBON

Quinta Da Capela
Estrada Velha de Monserate
P-2710
351-21-929-0170
Fax: 351-21-929-34-25
Arturo D. Pereira
Open all year

160 US$-BB
10 rooms, 10 pb
•
Most CC
C-yes/S-yes/P-yes/H-yes
English, German, French

Buffet breakfast
Dinner, tea, snacks, wine

30 minutes from Lisbon, surrounded by Sintra hills. Spectacular views, botanical gardens, lush vegetation, ancient castles, historical monuments. Beaches 10 minutes away.
quintadacapela@hotmail.com http://geocities.com/fazendeire2002/quintadacapela.html

VIANA DO CASTELO

Casa Santa Filomena
Estrada de Cabanas P-4900
02-617-4161 02-617-5936
Jose Street Kendall
All year

25-30 US$-BB
4 rooms, 4 pb
C-yes/S-yes/P-no/H-no
Portuguese

Continental breakfast
Beverages & snacks

soc.com.sm

Scotland, U.K.

ARGYLL

Taychreggan Hotel
Kilchrenan, by Taynuilt PA35 1HQ
+44-0-1866-833-211
Fax: +44-0-1866-833-244
Alastair Stevenson
All year

127-237 GB¤-BB
19 rooms, 19 pb
•
Most CC
C-no/S-yes/P-ltd/H-no
English, French

Full breakfast
five course table d'hote dinner/room service

Top Scottish country house hotel. Beautifully situated amid the mountains and forests of Argyll on the shores of Loch Awe. Fine dining and superb wine list, stylish and comfortable accommodation. info@taychregganhotel.co.uk http://www.taychregganhotel.co.uk

DUNOON

Enmore Country House
Marine Parade PA23 8HH
+44-369-70-2230
Fax: +44-369-70-2148
David & Angela Wilson
February–November

79-170 GB¤-BB
9 rooms, 9 pb
•
Visa, MC, AmEx
C-yes/S-yes/P-yes/H-no
French, English

Full breakfast
Lunch, dinner, afternoon tea, snacks, restaurant

Award winning hotel for both Cuisine, Hospitality & service. Just 1 hour from Glasgow airport via ferry. 3 golf courses within 10 minutes drive.
enmorehotel@btinternet.com http://enmorehotel.co.uk

ISLE OF SKYE

Kinloch Lodge
Sleat, Highland IV 43 8QY
0044-1471-833214
Fax: 0044-1471-833277
Lord & Lady MacDonald
March–November

90-190 GB¤
10 rooms, 10 pb
•
Most CC
C-yes/S-yes/P-yes/H-no
English

Full breakfast
Restaurant (fee), tea

Home of Lord and Lady MacDonald, Kinloch has achieved an enviable reputation for everything excellent over the past 25 years.
kinloch@dial.pipex.com http://www.kinloch-lodge.co.uk

NR. STIRLING

Cromlix House
Kinbuck, by Dunblane
FK15 9JT
+44-1786-822125
Fax: +44-1786-825450
David & Ailsa Assenti
Open all year

205-345 GB¤
14 rooms, 14 pb
•
Visa, MC, AmEx
C-yes/S-yes/P-no/H-no
English, German, French

Full breakfast
Restaurant-all meals (fee)

An idyllic 2,000 acre estate: one of the top ten hotels: antiques, history & welcome of an ancestral mansion. Outstanding cuisine. "Authentic excellence."
reservations@cromlixhouse.com http://www.cromlixhouse.com

ST. ANDREWS

Pinewood Country House
Tayport Road, St. Michaels
KY16 ODU
01334-839860
Fax: 01334-839868
Roger & Muriel Bedwell
All year

44-50 GB¤-BB
5 rooms, 5 pb
Visa, MC
C-ltd/S-ltd/P-ltd/H-no
English

Full breakfast

Four star guest house just 10 minutes from St. Andrews in Scotland UK. Set in the countryside on the edge of pine woods and close to Tentsmuir forest.
accommodation@pinewoodhouse.com http://www.pinewoodhouse.com

Spain

ARCOS DE LA FRONTERA

Hacienda El Santiscal
Avda. del Santiscal No. 129
E-11630
34-956-708313
Fax: 34-956-708268
Paqui Gallardo Carrasco
Open all year

12,000 Spanish¤
12 rooms, 12 pb
Most CC, •
C-ltd/S-yes/P-ltd/H-no
Eng, Fre, Arabic, Ger, Sp

Full Andalucian breakfast buffet
Restaurant (fee)

Splendid hotel and restaurant in a restored 15th century Andalusian manor house.
santiscal@gadesinfo.com http://www.santiscal.com

BARCELONA

BCN Rooms, S.L.
Valencia, 55 1/2/D E-08015
00-34-93-226-54-67
Fax: 00-34-93-226-22-69
Raimon Zamacois
All year

30-65 US$-BB
100 rooms, 60 pb
C-yes/S-yes/P-ltd/H-ltd
Sp, Fren, Eng, It

Habitaciones, desde 1 hasta 5 plazaa, en apartamentos privados en regimen de B&B. No es un hotel. Apartamentos desde 2 hasta 12 plazas, con o sin desayuno.
http://www.bcnrooms.com

BINISSALEM

Scott's Hotel
Plaza Iglesia, #12 E-07350
34-971-87-0100
Fax: 34-971-87-0267
George Scott
All year

175–330 US$-BB
17 rooms, 17 pb, •
Visa, MC, AmEx, *Rated*
C-ltd/S-ltd/P-no/H-ltd
Eng, Sp, Ger, Russ, Catalan, Czech

Continental plus breakfast
Dinner, well-stocked bar

Scott's has been reviewed as "Heaven! I've never stayed in any hotel more wholly satisfying." Located in the wine capital of Majorca, Spain, Europe's number one holiday destination. reserve@scottshotel.com http://www.scottshotel.com

CUENCA

Posada De San Jose
Julian Romero 4 E-16001
969-21-1300
Fax: 969-23-0365
Antonio & Jennifer Cortinas
Open all year

37.50-62.00 US$-BB
31 rooms, 22 pb
•
Most CC
C-yes/S-yes/P-yes/H-no
English, French, Spanish

Continental breakfast
Afternoon coffee,regional tapas, light suppers

The Posada de San Jose is situated in the heart of the old historic quarter of Cuenca, in a 17th century building. Its old portal invites you to admire the views.
info@posadasanjose.com http://www.posadasanjose.com

GRANADA

Hotel Reina Cristina
Calle Tablas 4 E-18002
34-958-25-3211
Fax: 34-958-25-5728
Federico Jimenez Gonzalez
Open all year

13-15,000 Spanish¤-BB
43 rooms, 43 pb
•
Most CC
C-yes/S-yes/P-ltd/H-yes
English, French, Spanish

Full breakfast
Lunch, dinner, restaurant

Mansion del s.XIX, que pertenecio a la familia Rosales y albergo en sus ultimos dias a Federico Garcia Lorca.
clientes@hotelreinacristina.com http://www.hotelreinacristina.com

JIMENA DE LA FRONTERA

Rancho Los Lobos
Jimena de la Frontera E-11339
34-956-64-0429
Fax: 34-956-64-1180
Wolf & Esther Zissler
All year

204-/week US$-BB
9 rooms, 3 pb
•
Visa, MC
C-ltd/S-yes/P-ltd/H-ltd
German, English, French, Span

Full breakfast
Dinner available, please ask.

Rancho Los Lobos is situated 30 km north of Gibraltar in a Natural Park with cork forests. Ideal for riding walking or biking tours. Apart we offer half-board service, a pool, tennis and relaxing. wolf@rancholoslobos.com http://www.rancholoslobos.com

LA PERA

Can Massa
Calle Vell E-17120
++34-972-48-8326
Fax: ++34-972-48-8326
Josep Massa Roura
All year

37-49 Euro¤-EP
4 rooms, 4 pb
Most CC
C-yes/S-ltd/P-no/H-no
Spanish, French, English, Port

Full breakfast 4 Euros (fee)

House in the village of La Pera, 20 km to the beach.–Refurbished cottage with 4 triple bedrooms (double bed+single bed)all with ensuite bathroom.–2 lounges, one of them with open fire and TV. jmassa@teleline.es http://www.toprural.com/canmassa

LOS MARINES

Finca Buenvino
Los Marines
Sierra Aracena E-21293
959-12-4034
Fax: 959-50-1029
Sam & Jeannie Chesterton
Closed 6 July–9 Sept & 15 Dec–7 Jan

210 Euros¤-MAP
4 rooms, 4 pb
Visa, MC
C-yes/S-ltd/P-no/H-no
Spanish, English, German, French

Three course dinner with wine Afternoon tea

Family-run B&B in the heart of the wooded Aracena Nature Reserve in Western Andalusia. buenvino@facilnet.es http://www.buenvino.com

PALMA DE MALLORCA

Hotel San Lorenzo
San Lorenzo 14 E-07012
971-72-8200
Fax: 971-71-1901
Rudolf Schmid
All year

115-210 US$-EP
6 rooms, 6 pb
•
Visa, MC, AmEx
C-ltd/S-yes/P-no/H-no
Spanish, English, German, French

Continental, breakfast card

17 century Manor House in the historical part of Palma converted into a lovely hotel with only 6 rooms and a colorful garden with swimming-pool.
info@hotelsanlorenzo.com http://www.hotelsanlorenzo.com

PENA MELLERA ALTA

Hotel La Tahona De Besnes
Besnes E-33578
98-541-5749
Fax: 98-541-5749
Lorenzo & Sarah Nilsson
Open all year

53-65 US$-BB
13 rooms, 13 pb
Most CC
C-yes/S-yes/P-no/H-ltd
Spanish, English

Restaurant (fee)
Lunch, dinner, snacks

Charmingly restored stone bakery offering rustic hideaway. Outdoor activities all year.
latahona@ctv.es http://www.latahonadebesnes.com

Switzerland

BLONAY/VEVEY

Hotel Restaurant Les Sapins
Lally CH-1807
+41-21-943-1395
Fax: +41-21-943-7119
Agnes & Roger Stutz
All year

150-180 Swiss¤-BB
12 rooms, 6 pb
•
Most CC
C-yes/S-yes/P-yes/H-yes
French, English, Germand Spanish

Lunch and dinner every day on request
Welcome drink at your arrival

High up in the Alpine meadowland above Lake Geneva, Les Sapins at Lally (altitude 4000 feet) offers wonderful views from its beautiful setting nestled in a Vaud mountainside.
info@les-sapins.ch http://www.les-sapins.ch

GENEVA

Hotel Des Tourelles
2 Boulevard James-Fazy CH-1201
+41-22-732-44-23
Fax: +41-22-732-76-20
Christine & Andre Meier
Closed Christmas to New Year

120-150 Swiss¤-BB
23 rooms, 20 pb
•
Visa, MC, AmEx
C-yes/S-yes/P-yes/H-no
French, English, Italian, German

Continental plus breakfast
Complimentary tea/coffee maker

In the heart of Geneva, next to the Rhone River, savor the Charm of the past with modern comfort and family atmosphere. destourelles@compuserve.com
http://www.smpage.ch/tourelles

LUGANO

Villa Principe Leopoldo
Via Montalbano 5 CH-6900
+41-91-985-8855
Fax: +41-91-985-8825
Maurie R.L. Urech
All year

470-780 Swiss¤-BB
70 rooms, 70 pb
•
Visa, MC, AmEx
C-yes/S-yes/P-yes/H-yes
Eng, Dl, Fr, Sp, Port, Ital

Buffet breakfast
Restaurant, lunch, dinner, afternoon

Superb hideaway mansion dominating Lugano and the arch which starts in Paradiso to reach Castagnola and shape one of the most inland-lake golf's in Europe.
info@leopoldohotel.com http://www.leopoldohotel.com

MONTREUX

Hotel Masson
Rue Bonivard 5 CH-1820
021-966-00-44
Fax: 021-966-00-36
Mrs. Anne-Marie Sevegrand
25th March–1st November

150-300 Swiss¤-EP
31 rooms, 31 pb
•
Most CC
C-yes/S-yes/P-yes/H-no
French, German, English

Full breakfast (fee)
Restaurant, Dinner, afternoon tea, bar service

Our hotel is situated in very quiet surroundings, with a restful garden.
sevegrand@hotelmasson.ch http://www.hotelmasson.ch

REGENSBERG

Rote Rose
8158 Regensberg CH-8158
011-41-1-853-0080
Fax: 011-41-1-853-1559
Christa Schaefer
March–December

250-300 Swiss¤-BB
9 rooms, 9 pb
•
C-ltd/S-no/P-no/H-yes
English, German, French, Italian

Continental plus breakfast
Afternoon tea, snacks

Elegant country inn. Spacious antique-filled suites. Unspoiled Medieval village.
info@rote-rose.com http://www.travelguides.com/home/roterose

SCHWANDEN OB SIGRISWIL

Gasthof Rothorn
Dorfstrasse, CH-3657
41-33-51-11-86 41+33 251 33 86
Trudi & Werner Amstutz
Ask about time of operation

Rates: Inquire-BB
13 rooms
C-ltd/S-ltd/P-ltd/H-ltd
German

Ask about breakfast

Komfortable Zimmer mit Dusche/WC, einige mit Balkon, die gemütliche, familiäre Atmosphäre und die ausgezeichnet Köche bieten das ganze Jahr Gewähr für schönste Ferienaufenthalte. rothorn@sw http://www.rothorn-schwanden.ch

ZURICH

Claridge Hotel Tiefenau
Steinwiesstrasse 8-10 CH-8032
41-1-267-8787
Fax: 41-1-251-2476
Mr. Beat R. Blumer
Open all year

330-580 Swiss¤-EP
30 rooms, 30 pb
•
Most CC
C-yes/S-yes/P-yes/H-no
Engl, Fren, Germ, Sp, Ital

Full champagne-Switz breakfast buffet
Local Zurich Specialities + Euro-Asian Specialties

Situated right in the City Center yet in a very quiet residential street just off the Theatre, the Museum of Fine Arts and the Conservatory. info@claridge.ch http://www.claridge.ch

Turkey

ISTANBUL

Hotel Saba
Sehit Mehmet Pasa Yokusu
No:8 34400
90-212-458-0262
Fax: 90-212-638-2002
Ramazan Soylemez
All year

55-130 US$-BB
26 rooms, 26 pb
Visa, MC, AmEx, *Rated*
C-yes/P-ltd
English, German

Continental breakfast

Charming Hotel quality Saba, you will enjoy Turkish hospitality, taste unique dishes and a sincere atmosphere. Get a clear view of Marmara Sea, the Hippodrome, St.Sophia and the Blue Mosque. hotelsaba@saba.com.tr http://www.saba.com.tr

Middle East

Egypt

CAIRO

Pharaoh Egypt Hotel
11 Ahmaed Orabi St 12411
202-347-4266
Fax: 202-302-3480
Sherif Soliman
All year

60-80 US$-BB
140 rooms, 140 pb
•
Most CC, *Rated*
C-yes/S-yes/P-yes/H-no
Eng, Fren, Ital, Egypsian

Continental breakfast
All kinds of food but upon request

Location: Down Town In The Heart Of Cairo Egypt. Located in the City center and near to train station. Near to the residential and diplomatic sector of Cairo on Giza, Mohandesseen. soliman@internetegypt.com http://www.pharaohegypt.com

Reservation Service Organizations

These are businesses through which you can reserve a room in thousands of private homes. In many cases, rooms in homes are available where there may not be an inn. Also, guest houses are quite inexpensive. RSOs operate in different ways. Some represent a single city or state. Others cover the entire country. Some require a small membership fee. Others sell a list of their host homes. Many will attempt to match you with just the type of accommodations you're seeking and you may pay the RSO directly for your lodging.

USA

ALASKA

Ketchikan Reservation Service
412 D-1 Loop Rd
Ketchikan 99901

Wanda Vandergriff

info@ketchikan-lodging.com http://www.ketchikan-lodging.com

ARIZONA

Mi Casa Su Casa
PO Box 950
Tempe 85280
480-990-0682 800-456-0682
Fax: 480-990-3390

$45–$350
•
Deposit 50%,
Events –100%
Most CC

Area served: NV, AZ, NM, UT
Mexico, Spain
9am–5pm, M–F,
9am–noon, Sat
Ruth T. Young
300 houses

One of the oldest B&B reservation services in the U.S. offers over 300 quality accommodations in selected B&B host homes, inns, guest cottages,apartments, ranches AZ, NM, UT, NV, Spain and Mexico. Our web page provides you with descriptions and pictures.

micasa@azres.com http://www.azres.com

DISTRICT OF COLUMBIA

B&B Accommodations, Ltd.
PO Box 12011
Washington 20005
413-582-9888
877-893-3233
Fax: 413-582-9669

$70–$200
•
Deposit $25,
Balance due 2 wks
Most CC
French, Spanish
Free brochure

Area served: Washington, D.C., MD, VA
10am–5pm M–F
Steve Lucas
85 houses

B&B Accommodations, Ltd. office is open Mon-Fri. 10:00 AM to 5:00 PM (EST), to assist you in the selection and booking of your B&B. You can also visit us 24 hours a day on the Web, find the locations that interest you most, even initiate reservations

bnbaccom@aol.com http://www.bedandbreakfastdc.com

ILLINOIS

Bed & Breakfast Chicago, Inc.
PO Box 14088
Chicago 60614
773-394-2000
800-375-7084
Fax: 773-394-2002

$95–$225
Most CC
Free brochure

Area served: City of Chicago
9am–5pm, M–F
Elizabeth Keeley
70 houses

Chicago's oldest and largest reservation service - offering a choice of 70 different accommodations including rooms in private homes, guest houses and inns or self-contained apartments.

stays@chicago-bed-breakfast.com http://www.chicago-bed-breakfast.com

LOUISIANA

Reserve New Orleans
PO Box 56576
New Orleans 70156
504-561-9080
866-867-6309
Fax: 504-523-2110

$65–$250, Deposit 20%,
Varies with season
Most CC
Spanish, French, German

Area served: Metro New Orleans
9am–5pm CST, Answering Service
Liz Dwyer
35 houses

Reserve New Orleans specializes in making arrangements for lodging, ground transportation, restaurants and tours for business and leisure travelers to New Orleans. Let us take you beyond the guidebooks to savor all that "The Big Easy" has to offer.

info@reserveneworleans.com http://www.reserveneworleans.com

MASSACHUSETTS

A B&B Agency Of Boston
47 Commercial Wharf
Boston 02110
617-720-3540
800-248-9262
Fax: 617-523-5761

$100-$170
•
Deposit 30%–50%
Visa, MC, AmEx
French, Spanish, German, Arab, Italian
Free brochure

Area served: Massachusetts
7am–9pm 7 days,
Also ans. machine
Ferne Mintz
160 houses

bosbnb@aol.com http://www.boston-bnbagency.com

Bed and Breakfast Cape Cod
PO Box 1312
Orleans 02653
508-255-3824
800-541-6226
Fax: 508-240-0599

$75–$185, Deposit 25%
Most CC
Free brochure

Area served: MA, Cape Cod
8–8 M–Sat. summer,
9am–5pm M–F winter
Susanne Strone Thibault
110 houses

PLEASE NOTE: about "1 night reservation" Rates listed are for "double occupancy", per room, per night unless indicated otherwise. "In season" reservations are for a minimum of 2 nights.

info@bedandbreakfastcapecod.com http://www.bedandbreakfastcapecod.com

NEW YORK

Abode Ltd.
PO Box 20022
New York 10021
212-472-2000
800-835-8880

$135–$425, Deposit 25%,
2 nights minimun
AmEx
Free brochure

Area served: NY: Manhattan
9am–5pm Mon–Fri
Shelli Leifer
35 houses

Abode is the "smart alternative" for temporary lodging in New York City. By reserving an apartment through Abode you'll stay at private residences in some of Manhattan's most fashionable neighborhoods. http://www.abodenyc.com

---

At Home In New York
140 West 55th. St
New York 10019
212-956-3125
800-692-4262
Fax: 212-265-8539

$100–$150
•
Deposit 25%
Visa, MC, AmEx
French, Spanish, German
Free brochure

Area served: New York
Italy, France, England
9am-5pm Mon-Fri
Lois H. Rooks
100 houses

athomeny@erols.com http://www.athomeny.com

B&B Network Of New York
130 Barrow St, #508
New York 10014
212-645-8134
800-900-8134

$110–$150
•
Deposit 25%
Free brochure

Area served: New York
8am–6pm Mon–Fri
Leslie Goldberg
200 houses

FOR YOUR CHOICE OF
INN OF THE YEAR

Did you find your stay at a Bed & Breakfast, Inn or Guesthouse listed in this Guide particularly enjoyable? Use the form below, or just drop us a note, and we'll add your vote for the "Inn of the Year." The winning entry will be featured in the next edition of **The Complete Guide to Bed & Breakfasts, Inns and Guesthouses in the U.S., Canada, and Worldwide.**

Please base your decision on:

- Helpfulness of Innkeeper
- Quality of Service
- Cleanliness
- Amenities
- Decor
- Food

Look for the winning Inn in the next Updated & Revised edition of **The Complete Guide to Bed & Breakfasts, Inns and Guesthouses in the U.S., Canada, and Worldwide.**

To the editors of **The Complete Guide to Bed & Breakfasts**:

I cast my vote for "Inn of the Year" for:

Name of Inn ______________________________

Address ______________________________

____

Phone ______________________________

Reasons ______________________________

____

I would also like to (please check one)

___ Recommend a new inn ___ Comment ___ Critique ___ Suggest

Name of Inn ______________________________

Address ______________________________

____

Phone ______________________________

Comment ______________________________

____

E-mail: ______________________________

Please send your entries to:

The Complete Guide to Bed & Breakfast Inns
Drawer D
Petaluma, CA 94953
or E-mail: lanier@TravelGuideS.com

PENNSYLVANIA

A B&B Connection of Philadelphia
PO Box 21
Devon 19333
610-687-3565
800-448-3619
Fax: 610-995-9524

$45–$200
•
Visa, MC, AmEx
Languages: many
Free brochure

Area served: Southeastern Pennsylvania
9am–5pm
Mary Alice Hamilton
150 houses

Since 1986,the Philadelphia area's foremost B&B reservation service. Our staff personally inspects each accommodation and has the expertise to help you select a conveniently located B&B that provides the hospitality and amenities you desire.

bnb@bnbphiladelphia.com http://www.bnbphiladelphia.com

B&B—The National Network
PO Box 44
Devon 19333
860-236-6698
800-727-7592
Fax: 860-232-7680

Michelle Sausa

info@go-lodging.com http://www.go-lodging.com

VIRGINIA

Blue Ridge B&B RSO
2458 Castleman Rd
Berryville 22611
540-955-1246
800-296-1246
Fax: 540-955-4240

$65–$150
•
Full deposit
Visa, MC, AmEx
Spanish, English
Free broch. SASE

Area served: VA, WV, MD, PA
10:30am–3:30pm, 12pm–9pm
Rita Z. Duncan
50 houses

Beautitful farms, quaint inns, historic homes, Shenandoah Valley, hiking, antiquing, white water rafting, horse back riding, many historical sites, golfing, swimming, fishing, near Skyline Drive, Harpers Ferry, indoor heated pool with hot tub at one end.

blurdgbb@shentel.net http://www.blueridgebb.com

JAMAICA

WESTMORELAND

Native Son Villas
Norman Manley Blvd
Jamaica, Negril
908-598-1158
Fax: 908-598-1151

$130–$305
•
Deposit 25%, Pay in advance
Visa, MC, AmEx
English, Jamaican Patois
Free brochure

Area served: Caribbean Jamaica, West Indies
8am–8pm
Sarah Burton
4 houses

A personal housekeeper/cook presides over each villa. She prepares meals as requested and cleans the villa daily. Babysittiing can also be arranged directly with her.

sarahburt@aol.com